Master the NCERT

Line by Line MCQs from Latest NCERT Books

for NEET/JEE

PHYSICS XI

KESHAV MOHAN

Co-authored by
Dharmendra Singh
Sunny Kumar

arihant
SUCCESS AND NOTHING LESS

arihant

SUCCESS AND NOTHING LESS

Arihant Prakashan (Series), Meerut

Administrative & Production Offices

Regd. Office

'Ramchhaya' 4577/15, Agarwal Road, Darya Ganj, New Delhi -110002

Tele: 011- 47630600, 43518550

Head Office

Kalindi, TP Nagar, Meerut (UP) - 250002

Tel: 0121-7156203, 7156204

Sales & Support Offices

Agra, Ahmedabad, Bengaluru, Bareilly, Chennai, Delhi, Guwahati, Hyderabad, Jaipur, Jhansi, Kolkata, Lucknow, Nagpur & Pune.

PRICE ₹495.00

PO No : TXT-XX-XXXXXXX-X-XX

Published by Arihant Publications (India) Ltd.

For further information about the books published by Arihant, log on to www.arihantbooks.com or e-mail at info@arihantbooks.com

Follow us on

Key Features

3 Level Chapter Analysis

On the first page of each chapter, NEET Analysis of 5 years is given on following 3 basis -
(i) Topics
(ii) Special format Questions
(iii) Chapter weightage

Topicwise No. of Ques asked in 5 Years (NEET)

Topics	No. of Questions				
	2024	2023	2022	2021	2020
Aristotle's Fallacy	–	–	–	–	–
Newton's First Law of Motion	–	–	–	–	–
Newton's Second Law of Motion	–	–	–	–	1
Newton's Third Law of Motion	–	–	–	–	–
Conservation of Momentum	–	–	–	1	–
Equilibrium of a Particle	–	–	–	–	–
Common Forces in Mechanics	1	2	–	–	1
Circular Motion	1	–	–	–	–

Special Type of Ques Asked in 5 Years (NEET)

Types	Years				
	2024	2023	2022	2021	2020
A-R	–	–	–	–	–
Statement Based	–	–	–	–	–
Matching	–	–	–	–	–

Last 5 Years Weigtage (NEET)

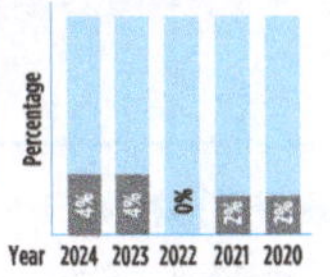

Marks Maximiser

Pseudo Force

- When the motion of a body is observed from a non-inertial frame, then to apply Newton's second law, we have to apply an imaginary force opposite to the direction of acceleration of non-inertial frame known as pseudo force.
- A body of mass m is placed in a lift (non-inertial frame) moving upward with acceleration a, the pseudo force on the body is shown in the figure here.

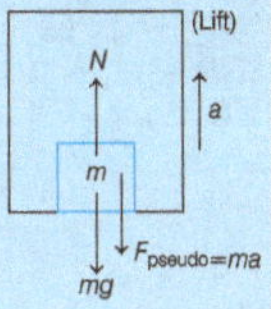

The normal reaction on the body is
$N = mg + F_{pseudo} = mg + ma = m(g + a)$

Marks Maximiser

Specialised box matter with NEET/JEE exclusive important information which may or may not be present in NCERT.

Physics Through Concept Master

Unique video support to explain difficult Topics/Concept of NCERT in simple and easy to understand language.

1. For a given pulley-block system as shown in figure alongside, the relation between accelerations a_1 and a_2 of blocks m_1 and m_2 is given by **[JEE Main 2022]**

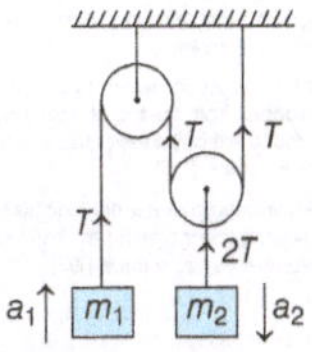

Constraint relation, $\Sigma \mathbf{T} \cdot \mathbf{a} = 0$

$\Rightarrow Ta_1 - 2Ta_2 = 0 \quad \therefore \quad a_1 = 2a_2$

2. For a pulley system, the acceleration of the masses in the system is given by

$$a = \frac{(m_2 - m_1)}{m_1 + m_2} g$$

and tension $T_1 = \left(\frac{2m_1 m_2}{m_1 + m_2}\right) g$

[NEET 2020]

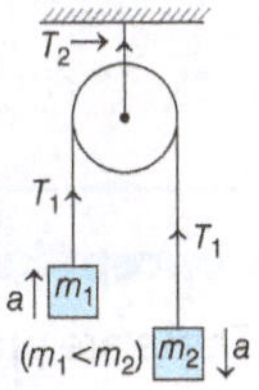

3. A body of mass m is placed on an inclined plane of inclination θ. A force F is acted on

PYQ Notes

3. A body of mass m is placed on an inclined plane of inclination θ. A force F is acted on the body at an angle α with the plane of inclination as shown in figure. If the coefficient of friction between body and plane of contact is μ, then the minimum value of force F_{min} required to pull the body is given by

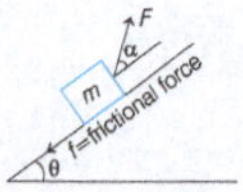

[NEET 2018]

$$F_{min} = \frac{mg(\sin\theta + \mu\cos\theta)}{\sqrt{1+\mu^2}}, \text{ where } \mu = \tan\alpha$$

For horizontal plane surface, $\theta = 0°$

$$\therefore \quad F_{min} = \frac{\mu mg}{\sqrt{1+\mu^2}}$$

1. For a given pulley-block system as shown in figure alongside, the relation between accelerations a_1 and a_2 of blocks m_1 and m_2 is given by [JEE Main 2022]

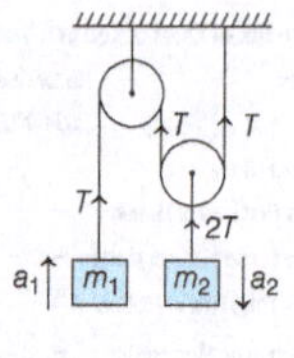

Constraint relation, $\Sigma \mathbf{T} \cdot \mathbf{a} = 0$

$\Rightarrow Ta_1 - 2Ta_2 = 0 \;\therefore\; a_1 = 2a_2$

PYQ Notes

NEET / JEE specific important points, which were asked in past years but not incorporated in present Rationalised NCERT .

Laws of Motion (Chapter at a Glance)

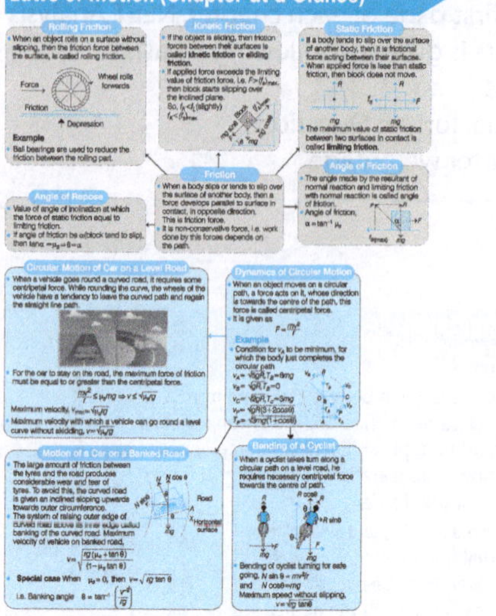

Chapter at a Glance

Completely Coloured Glorified Infographics to map all the key points of a chapter for quick review. These are present at the end of all Chapters.

Step by Step

Mastering NCERT

- Concept Builders
- Topical Questions
- Assertion and Reason Questions
- Statement Based
- Matching Type
- Numerical Type
- NCERT Exemplar
- Past Exams MCQs
- Skill Boosters

Concept Builders

1 Inertial frame of reference is also called unaccelerated frame of reference. [T/F]

2 Acceleration can be zero only, if there is a net external force on the body. [T/F]

3 An object in motion generally experience .... (gravitational/frictional) force, which is non-conservative.

4 If two stones of masses m_1 and m_2 ($m_1 > m_2$), are dropped from the top of a building, a person on the ground will find it easier to catch the light stone than heavy stone. [T/F]

5 A seasoned cricketer draws in his hands during a catch, allowing lesser time for the ball to stop and hence requires a smaller force. [T/F]

10 It is easier to push a lawn roller than pull it because effective weight of the lawn roller, while pushing is less than that while pulling. [T/F]

11 Kinetic friction is inversely proportional to the velocity of the body. [T/F]

12 What happens to coefficient of friction, when weight of body is doubled?

13 Two bodies are moving down on a slanted road, one by rolling and another by sliding. The friction on the rolling body will be less than the sliding body . [T/F]

14 When a body moves in a circular path, which thing experiences a centrifugal force?

15 If multiple forces are acting on a body, then all the forces will produce acceleration in the body. [T/F]

Step by Step Mastering NCERT

The scientifically designed practice exercise with all possible type of questions to be asked in competition like NEET/JEE.

Concept Builders

These are present as simple teasers like T/F, Fill ups and one word question. Thus, structured to build foundation stone of NCERT concepts.

Concept Builders

1 Inertial frame of reference is also called unaccelerated frame of reference. [T/F]

2 Acceleration can be zero only, if there is a net external force on the body. [T/F]

3 An object in motion generally experience .... (gravitational/frictional) force, which is non-conservative.

4 If two stones of masses m_1 and m_2 ($m_1 > m_2$), are dropped from the top of a building, a person on the ground will find it easier to catch the light stone than heavy stone. [T/F]

5 A seasoned cricketer draws in his hands during a catch, allowing lesser time for the ball to stop and hence requires a smaller force. [T/F]

Topical Questions

NEET/JEE like MCQs from line by line text of NCERT with complete tagging of pages. All these MCQs are arranged as per the Topic headings of NCERT.

Common Forces in Mechanics

57 Two masses $m_1 = 1$ kg and $m_2 = 2$ kg are connected by a light inextensible string and suspended by means of a weightless pulley as shown in figure. **NCERT Pg. 59**

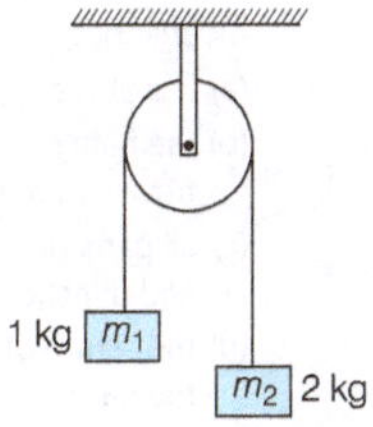

Assuming that both the masses start from rest, the distance the travelled by centre of mass of the system in 2 s is (given, $g = 10$ ms^{-2})

Assertion and Reason Questions

Direction (Q. Nos. 1-12) *In the following questions, a statement of Assertion is followed by a corresponding statement of Reason. Of the following statements, choose the correct one.*

(a) Both Assertion and Reason are correct and Reason is the correct explanation of Assertion.

(b) Both Assertion and Reason are correct but Reason is not the correct explanation of Assertion.

(c) Assertion is correct but Reason is incorrect.

(d) Assertion is incorrect but Reason is correct.

A-R Questions

Most Important special format MCQs category. All of these are also tagged with NCERT page numbers as well .

Statement Type Questions

In NEET Physics paper such types (Statement I & II) of statement based questions are asked.
Such Type of Questions are covered in step by step practice with NCERT page tagging.

Statement Based Questions

Direction (Q. Nos. 1-7) *In the following questions, two statements (I & II) are given. In the light of the given statements, choose the correct option given below.*

(a) Both Statement I and Statement II are false.

(b) Statement I is true but Statement II is false.

(c) Statement I is false but Statement II is true.

(d) Both Statement I and Statement II are true.

1 **Statement I** When we shake a mango tree, the mangoes fall down.

Statement II When a vehicle suddenly stopped, the passengers tend to fall forward. **NCERT Pg. 51**

2 **Statement I** A seasoned cricketer allows a longer time for his hands to stop the ball, while catching the ball his hand don't get hurted.

Statement II The novice (new player) keeps his hand fixed and tries to catch the ball almost instantly. He needs to provide a much greater force to stop the ball instantly and this hurts. **NCERT Pg. 53**

Matching Type Questions

1 A lift is going up. The total mass of the lift and the passengers is 2000 kg. The variation of speed of the lift is as shown in the diagram. **NCERT Pg. 55**

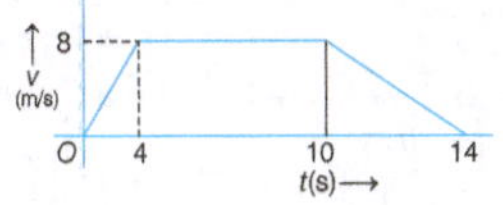

Match the quantity given in Column I with their magnitude in Column II. Choose the correct answer from the options given below.

Column I		Column II	
A.	Tension (in N) in the rope at time 1s	1.	20000

Matching Type Questions

Step by step practice includes the matching type MCQs. These are placed just after statement based MCQs and all are tagged with NCERT page numbers.

NCERT Exemplar Questions

1 A ball is travelling with uniform translatory motion. This means that
(a) it is at rest
(b) the path can be a straight line or circular and the ball travels with uniform speed
(c) all parts of the ball have the same velocity (magnitude and direction) and the velocity is constant
(d) the centre of the ball moves with constant velocity and the ball spins about its centre uniformly

2 A meter scale is moving with uniform velocity. This implies
(a) the force acting on the scale is zero, but a torque about the centre of mass can act on scale
(b) the force acting on the scale is zero and the torque acting about centre of mass of the scale is also zero

Past Exams' Questions

Selected PYQs with NCERT page tagging are present as the final check of preparation.

Skill Boosters

1 A bead of mass m is sliding on a parabolic path as shown in the figure. The equation of the parabola is $x^2 = 4ay$. If the bead is released from $y = 6a$, then its acceleration when it will reach at $y = a$ is (consider the motion is frictionless)

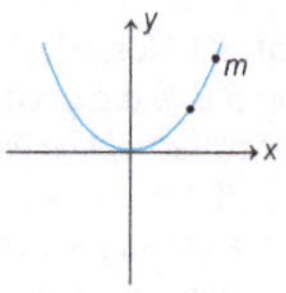

(a) $\frac{\sqrt{5}\,g}{2}$ (b) $\sqrt{2}\,g$ (c) g (d) $\frac{g}{\sqrt{2}}$

2 A light string ABC whose ends are fixed at points A and C. If a weight w attached to it at point B as shown in figure. If string is strong enough to withstand a maximum tension 100 N, then the largest value of w for the equilibrium of the system is [Take, $\cos 53° = \frac{3}{5}$]

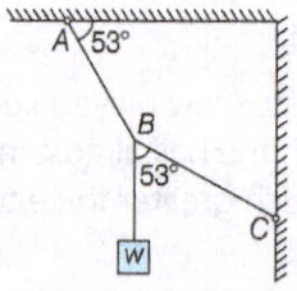

(a) 20 N (b) 35 N (c) 50 N (d) 44 N

Decoding the Questions

Answers and explanatory solutions of selected questions for better gripping of NCERT concepts.

NCERT Exemplar's Questions

NCERT Exemplar books are considered as one of the best problem books for competitive exams. Each chapter has selected exemplar problems to provide consolidation for preparations.

Past Exams Questions

NEET

1 A horizontal force 10 N is applied to a block A as shown in figure. The mass of blocks A and B are 2 kg and 3 kg, respectively. The blocks slide over a frictionless surface. The force exerted by block A on block B is

NCERT Pg. 65, NEET 2024

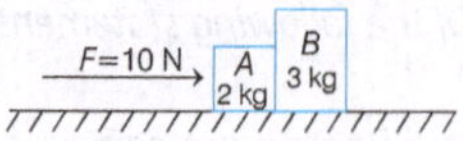

(a) zero (b) 4 N (c) 6 N (d) 10 N

JEE Main

13 In the given arrangement of a doubly inclined plane two blocks of masses M and m are placed. The blocks are connected by a light string passing over an ideal pulley as shown. The coefficient of friction between the surface of the plane and the blocks is 0.25. The value of m, for which $M = 10$ kg will move down with an

NCERT Pg. 61, JEE Main 2024

Skill Boosters

Brain Teasers present at the end of step by step practice to provide extra edge for preparation.

Step by Step

Decoding the Questions

Concept Builders

1 True (T) 2 False (F)
3 frictional 4 True (T)
5 False (F) 6 greater
7 False (F) 8 True (T)
9 zero 10 False (F)
11 False (F)
12 Remains unchanged
13 True (T)
14 Forcing agency
15 False (F) 16 infinite
17 False (F) 18 inward
19 No change 20 inward

Topical Questions

6 (c) When particle moves in a circle even with uniform or constant speed, it faces an external force towards its centre called centripetal force.

$F = ma = 1.0 \times 10^4 \times 50$
$= 5 \times 10^5$ N

16 (b) According to Newton's second law of motion, applied force,
$F = \frac{dp}{dt}$
or $dp = F \cdot dt$ or $dp = kt \cdot dt$
$\int_p^{3p} dp = k \int_0^T t\,dt$
or $[p]_p^{3p} = k\left[\frac{t^2}{2}\right]_0^T$
or $(3p - p) = \frac{1}{2}k[T^2 - 0]$
or $T = 2\sqrt{\frac{p}{k}}$

17 (b) Change in momentum,
$\Delta p = p_f - p_i$ ...(i)
Also, $\Delta p = F \cdot \Delta t$ ...(ii)
From Eqs. (i) and (ii), we get

20 (c) According to Newton's second law,
$F = \frac{dp}{dt} = \frac{mdv}{dt}$ $(\because p = mv)$
$\therefore (4t^2\,\hat{i} + 2t\,\hat{j}) = \frac{4dv}{dt}$
$\Rightarrow dv = \frac{1}{4}\int_0^3 (4t^2\,\hat{i} + 2t\,\hat{j})dt$
$\Rightarrow v = \frac{1}{4}\left[\frac{4t^3}{3}\hat{i} + \frac{2t^2}{2}\hat{j}\right]_0^3$
$\therefore v = 9\hat{i} + 2.25\hat{j}$

21 (c)

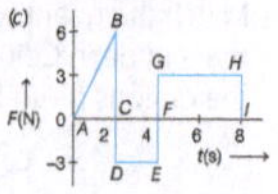

Contents

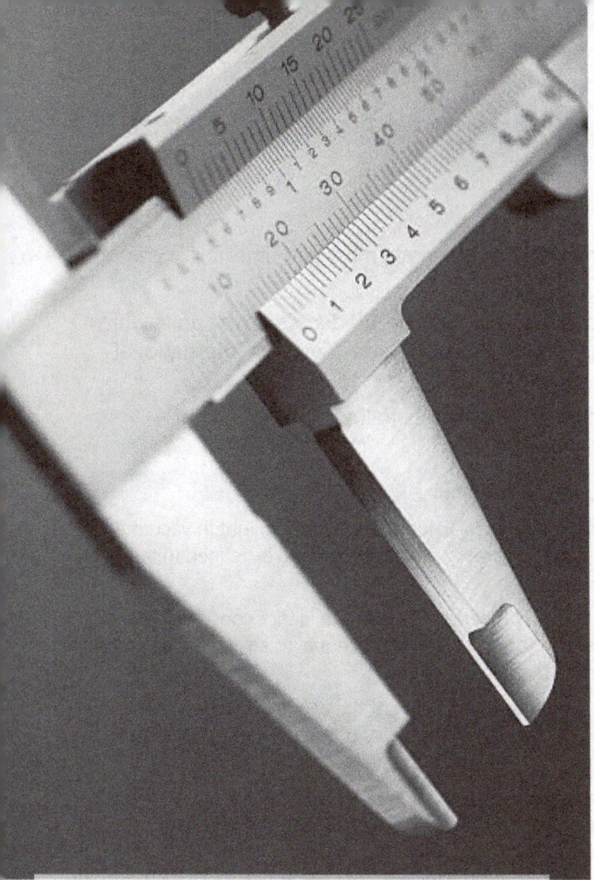

01 Units and Measurements

Topicwise No. of Ques asked in 5 Years (NEET)

Topics	No. of Questions				
	2024	2023	2022	2021	2020
International System of Units	–	–	1	–	1
Accuracy, Precision of Instruments and Errors in Measurement	1	2	1	1	1
Significant Figures	–	–	–	–	1
Dimensions of Physical Quantities	–	–	–	–	–
Dimensional Formulae and Dimensional Equations	1	–	–	–	–
Dimensional Analysis and Its Applications	1	–	1	2	1

Special Type of Ques Asked In 5 Years (NEET)

Types	Years				
	2024	2023	2022	2021	2020
A-R	–	–	–	–	–
Statement Based	–	–	–	–	–
Matching	–	1	–	–	–

Last 5 Years Weigtage (NEET)

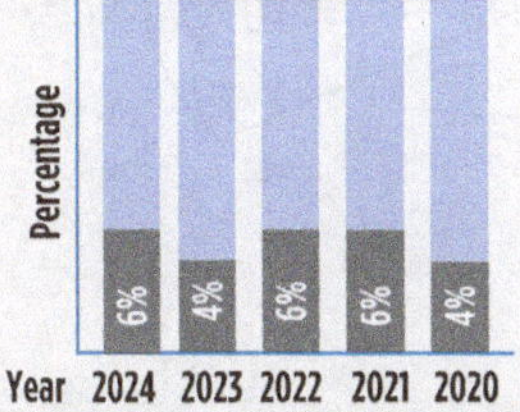

- All the quantities which are used to describe the laws of Physics are called **physical quantities**, e.g. length, mass, volume, etc.
- Physical quantities are of two types, **fundamental quantities** which are independent of other physical quantities and **derived quantities** which can be derived from the fundamental quantities.
- When a physical quantity is measured, the result is expressed as a **number** (or numerical measure) with a **unit**.
- The **unit** is an internationally accepted reference standard. In all cases, it is considered as, comparison of a physical quantity with a basic and arbitaily chosen standard.
- The units which are used to represent fundamental quantities are called **fundamental** or **base units**.

  The unit of derived quantities, which are represented in terms of fundamental units are called **derived units**.
- A complete set of these units, both the base units and derived units, is known as the **system of units**.

The International System of Units

- Some of the commonly used systems of units for measurement with the base units for length, mass and time are given as
  - (i) **CGS system** In this system, centimetre, gram and second are the fundamental units of length, mass and time. It is a Gaussian system of units and also known as **metric system of units**.
  - (ii) **FPS system** In this system, foot, pound and second are the fundamental units of length, mass and time. It is a British system of units but not a metric system of units.

(iii) **MKS system** In this system, metre, kilogram and second are the fundamental units of length, mass and time. It is known as metric system of units.

- In 1971, the **International Bureau of Weights and Measures (BIPM)** held its meeting and decided a system of units which is known as the **international system of units**. It is abbreviated as SI units from the french name 'Systeme International *d'* unites.
- This system contains 7 fundamental units and 2 supplementary units which are tabulated as follows.

Fundamental Quantities and Units

Fundamental quantity	Fundamental unit	Symbol	Definition
Length	metre	m	Metre is defined by taking the fixed numerical value of the speed of light in vacuum *c* to be 299792458 when expressed in the unit ms^{-1}, where the second is defined in terms of the caesium frequency Δv_{Cs}.
Mass	kilogram	kg	Kilogram is defined by taking the fixed numerical value of the Planck constant *h* to be $6.62607015 \times 10^{-34}$ when expressed in the unit J-s, which is equal to kg-m^2s^{-1}, where the metre and the second are defined in terms of *c* and Δv_{Cs}.
Time	second	s	Second is defined by taking the fixed numerical value of the caesium frequency Δv_{Cs}, the unperturbed ground state hyperfine transition frequency of the caesium-133 atom, to be 9192631770 when expressed in the unit Hz, which is equal to s^{-1}.
Electric current	ampere	A	Ampere is defined by taking the fixed numerical value of the elementary charge *e* to be $1.602176634 \times 10^{-19}$ when expressed in the unit C, which is equal to A s, where the second is defined in terms of Δv_{Cs}.
Temperature	kelvin	K	Kelvin is defined by taking the fixed numerical value of the Boltzmann constant *k* to be 1.380649×10^{-23} when expressed in the unit JK^{-1}, which is equal to kg-$m^2s^{-2}K^{-1}$, where the kilogram, metre and second are defined in terms of *h*, *c* and Δv_{Cs}.
Amount of substance	mole	mol	One mole contains exactly $6.02214076 \times 10^{23}$ elementary entities. This number is the fixed numerical value of the Avogadro constant. The amount of substance, of a system is a measure of the number of specified elementary entities. An elementary entity may be an atom, a molecule, an ion, an electron, any other particle or specified group of particles.
Luminous intensity	candela	cd	Candela is defined by taking the fixed numerical value of the luminous efficacy of monochromatic radiation of frequency 540×10^{12}, K_{cd} to be 683 when expressed in the unit lm W^{-1}, which is equal to cd sr W^{-1} or cd sr $kg^{-1}m^{-2}s^3$, where the kilogram, metre and second are defined in terms of *h*, *c* and Δv_{Cs}.

Supplementary Quantities and Units

Supplementary quantity	Supplementary unit	Symbol	Definition
Plane angle	radian	rad	The radian (rad) is the SI unit of angle and is defined as angle subtended at the centre of a circle by an arc of length equal to the radius of circle. Plane angle $(d\theta) = \dfrac{\text{Length of arc } (ds)}{\text{Radius } (r)}$ In figure, $d\theta$ is plane angle of arc of circle. 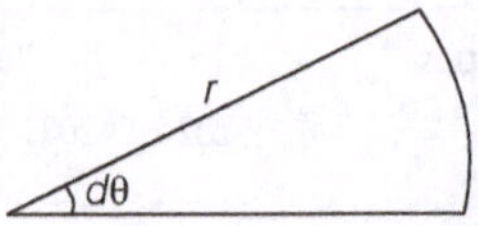 NEET 2022
Solid angle	steradian	sr	The steradian (sr) is the SI unit of solid angle and is defined as the solid angle subtended at the centre of a sphere by an area of the sphere equal to square of its radius. Solid angle $(d\Omega) = \dfrac{\text{Intercepted area of sphere } (dA)}{\text{Radius } (r)^2}$ In figure, $d\Omega$ is solid angle of spherical surface. 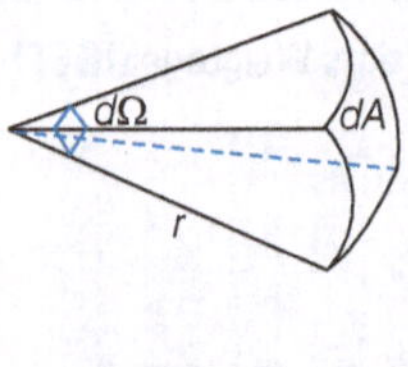

* Accuracy, Precision of Instruments and Errors in Measurement

- **Accuracy** refers to the closeness of observed values to the true value of any quantity. It is dependent on how many significant figures it carries. The accuracy increases with increasing significant digit size.
- **Precision** refers to the closeness between the different observed values of the same quantity. It defines the limitation of measuring instrument.
  It is dependent on least count, i.e. smallest value that can be measured by the measuring instrument.
  The smaller the least count, greater is the precision for a measuring instrument.
- **Error** difference in the true value and the measured value of a quantity is called **error of measurement**.
- The errors in measurement can be broadly classified as systematic and random errors
  (i) The **systematic errors** are those errors that tend to be in one direction, either positive or negative.
  Some sources of systematic errors are given as NEET 2023
  (a) **Instrumental Errors** These arise due to imperfect design or calibration of the measuring instrument.
  (b) **Imperfection in Experimental Technique or Procedure** It occurs due to external conditions such as change in temperature, humidity, wind velocity, pressure, etc., during experiment.
  (c) **Personal Errors** These arise due to an individuals bias, lack of proper setting of the apparatus or individuals carelessness in taking observations without observing proper precautions.
  (ii) The **random errors** are those errors which occur irregularly and hence are random with respect to sign and size. They arise due to random and unpredictable fluctuations in experimental conditions, personal errors by the observer taking readings etc.
- The **least count error** is the error associated with the resolution of the instrument. It occurs with both random and systematic errors.
- Some mathematical terms used for error calculations are given below
  (i) **Absolute Error** The magnitude of the difference between the individual measurement and the true value of the quantity is called the absolute error of the measurement. It is denoted by $|\Delta a|$.
  For n measurements, $a_1, a_2, a_3, a_4 \ldots\ldots a_n$

$$a_{\text{mean}} = \frac{a_1 + a_2 + a_3 + a_4 + \ldots\ldots + a_n}{n}$$

and $\Delta a_1 = a_1 - a_{\text{mean}}$,

$\Delta a_2 = a_2 - a_{\text{mean}}, \ldots$

$\Delta a_n = a_n - a_{\text{mean}}$

$$\therefore \quad a_{\text{mean}} = \sum_{i=1}^{n} a_i / n$$

  (ii) **Mean Absolute Error** The arithmetic mean of all the absolute errors is taken as the final or mean absolute error of the value of the physical quantity a and represented by Δa_{mean}.

$$\therefore \quad \Delta a_{\text{mean}} = \frac{|\Delta a_1| + |\Delta a_2| + \ldots + |\Delta a_n|}{n}$$

$$a_{\text{mean}} = \frac{1}{n}\sum_{i=1}^{n} |\Delta a_i|$$

  (iii) **Fractional or Relative Error** The relative error is the ratio of the mean absolute error Δa_{mean} to the mean value of a_{mean} of the quantity measured.

i.e. Relative error $= \dfrac{\Delta a_{\text{mean}}}{a_{\text{mean}}}$ NEET 2020

  (iv) **Percentage Error** When the relative error is expressed in percent, it is called percentage error.

$$\therefore \quad \delta a = \left(\frac{\Delta a_{\text{mean}}}{a_{\text{mean}}}\right) \times 100\%$$ NEET 2023

- **Least count** It is the smallest value of a physical quantity which can be measured accurately with an instrument.
- **Least count of vernier callipers** A vernier calliper consists of main scale along **with auxilary scale a sliding**, known as vernier scale.

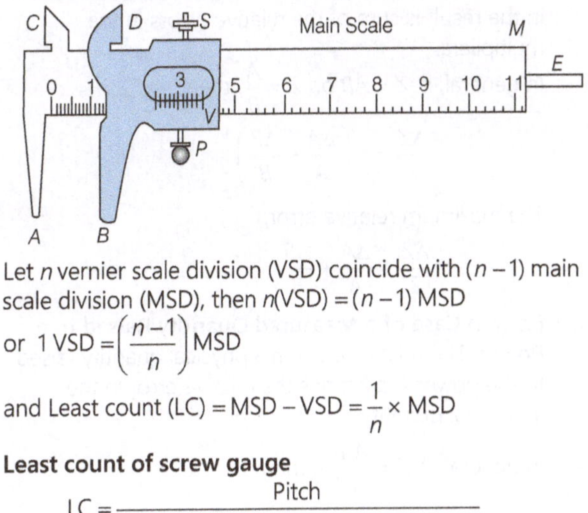

Let n vernier scale division (VSD) coincide with $(n-1)$ main scale division (MSD), then $n(\text{VSD}) = (n-1)$ MSD

or $1\text{ VSD} = \left(\dfrac{n-1}{n}\right)$ MSD

and Least count (LC) = MSD − VSD $= \dfrac{1}{n} \times$ MSD

- **Least count of screw gauge**

$$\text{LC} = \frac{\text{Pitch}}{\text{Number of divisions on circular scale}}$$

NEET 2021, 20

This topic is not included in latest rationalised NCERT, but it is given in latest NEET syllabus.

where, pitch is the distance moved by the screw head when the circular scale is given one complete rotation, i.e.

$$\text{Pitch} = \frac{\text{Distance moved by the screw on the linear scale}}{\text{Number of full rotations given}}$$

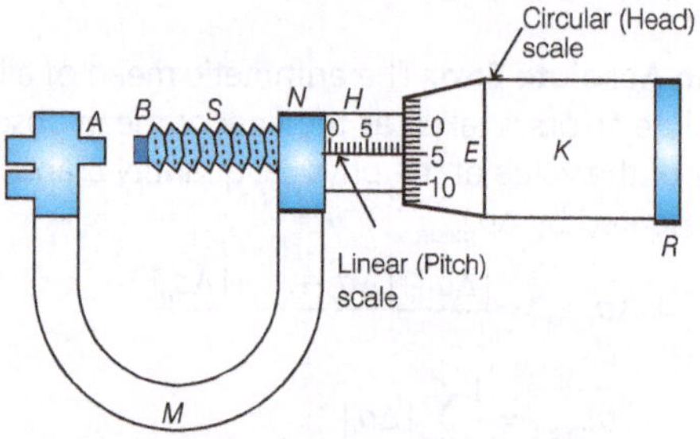

*Combination of Errors

Combination of the errors in various mathematical operations are as follows

(i) **Error of a Sum or a Difference** When two quantities are added or subtracted, the absolute error in the final result is the sum of the absolute error in the individual quantities.

If $Z = A + B$ or $Z = A - B$, then error ΔZ is given by

$$\pm \Delta Z = \pm \Delta A \pm \Delta B$$

However, the maximum value of the error ΔZ is given as

$$\Delta Z = \Delta A + \Delta B$$

(ii) **Error of a Product or a Quotient** When two quantities are multiplied or divided, the relative error in the result is sum of the relative errors in the multipliers.

In general, if $Z = AB$ or $Z = \frac{A}{B}$, then

$$\frac{\Delta Z}{Z} = \pm\left(\frac{\Delta A}{A} + \frac{\Delta B}{B}\right)$$

The maximum relative error,

$$\frac{\Delta Z}{Z} = \frac{\Delta A}{A} + \frac{\Delta B}{B}$$

(iii) **Error in Case of a Measured Quantity Raised to a Power** The relative error in a physical quantity raised to the power k is k times the relative error in the individual quantity.

In general, if $Z = \frac{A^p B^q}{C^r}$, then

$$\frac{\Delta Z}{Z} = p\left(\frac{\Delta A}{A}\right) + q\left(\frac{\Delta B}{B}\right) + r\left(\frac{\Delta C}{C}\right)$$

Significant Figures

- For a number which is the result of a measurement, the digits that are known reliable plus the first uncertain digits are known as **significant digits** or **significant figures.**
  e.g. In 1.62, the digits 1 and 6 are reliable and certain, while the digit 2 is uncertain. Thus, the measured value has three significant figures.
- A choice of change of different units does not change the number of significant digits or figures in a measurement.
- Larger the number of significant figures, greater will be the accuracy in measurement.
- **Rules for determining significant figures**
  (i) All the non-zero digits are significant. NEET 2022
  (ii) All the zeros between two non-zero(s) digits are significant, no matter where the decimal point is, if at all.
  (iii) If a number is less than 1, the zero(s) on the right of decimal point but to the left of the first non-zero digit are not significant.
  e.g. In <u>0.00</u>2308, the underlined zeros are not significant. The zero between 3 and 8 is significant.
  So, the number of significant figures are 4.
  (iv) The terminal or trailing zeros in a number without a decimal point are not significant.
  Thus, 123 m = 12300 cm = 123000 mm has three significant figures.
  (v) The trailing zeros in a number with a decimal point are significant.
  The numbers 3.500 or 0.06900 have four significant figures each.
  (vi) For a number greater than 1, without any decimal, the trailing zeros are not significant.
  (vii) If zero is taken on the left of a decimal, when number is less than one (such as 0.2340) is never significant but zeros at the end of such number are significant.
  (viii) In multiplicating or dividing factor, neither rounded numbers nor measured values are represented exactly but have infinite number of significant digits.
- **To remove the ambiguities in determining the number of significant figures**, every number is expressed as $a \times 10^b$, where a is number between 1 and 10 and b (known as to be **order of magnitude**) is any positive or negative exponent (or power) of 10.
  Such type of notation is called **scientific notation.**
- **Rules for arithmetic operations with significant figures** are as follows
  (i) In **addition** or **subtraction**, the final result should retain as many decimal places as are there in the number with the least decimal places.

This topic is not included in latest rationalised NCERT, but it is given in latest NEET syllabus.

e.g. $734.53 \text{ g} + 342.4 \text{ g} + 0.402 \text{ g} = 1077.322 \text{ g} \simeq 1077.3 \text{ g}$

There are five significant figures.

(ii) In **multiplication** or **division**, the final result should retain as many significant figures as are there in the original number with the least significant figures.

e.g. Density $= \frac{4.237}{2.5} = 1.69 \text{ gcm}^{-3} \simeq 1.7 \text{ gcm}^{-3}$

There are two significant figures.

Rounding Off

- The process of omitting the non-significant digits and retaining only the desired number of significant digits, in corporating the required modifications to the last significant digit is called **rounding off** the number.
- **Rules for rounding off a measurement**
  (i) If the number lying to the right of cut-off digit is less than 5, then the cut-off digit is retained as such. However, if it is more than 5, then the cut-off digits is increased by 1.
  e.g. $x = 5.34$ is rounded off to 5.3 to two significant digits and $x = 5.328$ is rounded off to 5.33 to three significant digits.
  (ii) If the insignificant digit to be dropped is 5, then the rule is
  (a) If the preceding digit is **even**, the insignificant digit is simply dropped, e.g. $x = 6.265$ is rounded off to $x = 6.26$ to three significant digits.
  (b) If the preceding digit is **odd**, the preceding digit is raised by 1. e.g. $x = 6.275$ is rounded off to $x = 6.28$ to three significant digits.
- **Rules for determining the uncertainty in the results of arithmetic calculations**
  (i) If a set of experimental data is specified to n-significant figures, a result obtained by combining the data will also be valid to n-significant figures.
  (ii) The relative error of a value of number specified to significant figures depend not only on number of significant figures but also on the number itself.
  (iii) Intermediate results in a multi-step computation should be calculated to one and more significant figures in every measurement than the number of digits in the least precise measurement.

Dimensions of Physical Quantities

- **Dimensions** of any physical quantity are those powers (exponents) which are raised on fundamental units to express the unit of that physical quantity.
  Dimensions are denoted with square brackets [ ].
- Dimensional symbols of seven fundamental quantities are given as Length → [L], Mass → [M], Time → [T], Electric current → [A], Temperature → [K], Luminous intensity → [cd], Amount of substance → [mol].
- For example, dimension formula of 'pressure' can be calculated as

NEET 2021

$$\text{Pressure} = \frac{\text{Force}}{\text{Area}} = \frac{\text{Mass} \times \text{Acceleration}}{\text{Length} \times \text{Breadth}}$$

$$= \frac{[\text{MLT}^{-2}]}{[\text{L}^2]} = [\text{ML}^{-1}\text{T}^{-2}]$$

So, dimension of pressure are $[\text{ML}^{-1}\text{T}^{-2}]$. Pressure has one dimension in mass, –1 dimension in length and –2 dimension in time.

Marks Maximiser

Some quantities do not possess dimensions, called **dimensionless quantities**. These are given below

- Trigonometic functions (e.g. $\cos x$, $\tan x$)
- Logarithmic functions (e.g. $\log x$),
- Exponential function (e.g. e^x),
- Pure numbers
- Ratio $\left(\text{e.g. strain} = \frac{\text{change in dimension}}{\text{original dimension}}, \text{ specific gravity}\right)$
- Angle
- Reynold number, Avogadro number and π

Dimensional Formulae and Dimensional Equations

- **Dimensional formula** of a physical quantity is an expression which shows how the given quantity is expressed in terms of the fundamental quantities.
  The dimensional formula is expressed in the form $[\text{M}^a\text{L}^b\text{T}^c]$, where a, b and c are dimensions of that quantity.
- An equation obtained by equating a physical quantity with its dimensional formula is called the **dimensional equation** of the physical quantity.
  Or the dimensional equations are the equations, which represent the dimensions of a physical quantity in terms of the base quantities. For example, the dimensional equations of volume [V] expressed as $[V] = [\text{M}^0\text{L}^3\text{T}^0]$.

Dimensional Analysis and Its Applications

- Dimensional analysis help us in deducing certain relations among different physical quantities, accuracy and dimensional consistency or homogeneity of different mathematical expressions.

- **Principle of Homogeneity of Dimensions** Only those physical quantities can be added or subtracted which have same dimensions.

Applications of Dimensions

(i) **To check dimensional correctness of any physical quantity**

As we know, $s = ut + \frac{1}{2}at^2$

Dimensionally, $[s] = [ut] = [at^2]$ or $[L]$
$= [LT^{-1}] [T] = [LT^{-2}] [T^2]$

So, $[L] = [L] = [L]$

As each term has the same dimension, so this equation is dimensionally correct.

(ii) **To convert any physical quantity from one system of units to another system of units**, we use $n_1u_1 = n_2u_2$ where, n_1 & n_2 are the magnitudes and u_1 & u_2 are the units of any physical quantity in two systems of units.

(iii) **To find a relation between interdependent physical quantities**

Let Q is a physical quantity which depends on x, y and z, then $Q = f(x, y, z)$

Let $Q \propto x^a$, $Q \propto y^b$

and $Q \propto z^c$.

Thus, $Q \propto x^a y^b z^c$.

where, Q is a physical quantity.

Note *A dimensionally correct equation need not be actually an exact (correct) equation, but a dimensionally wrong (incorrect) or inconsistent equation must be wrong.*

Limitations of Dimensional Analysis

Limitations of dimensional analysis are

- We cannot determine the value of dimensionless constant.
- This analysis fails under following circumstances
  (i) When a physical quantity is the sum or difference (e.g. $v^2 + 2as$) of two or more quantities.
  (ii) When a physical quantity depends upon more than three physical quantities.
  (iii) To derive a physical expression involving trigonometric, logarithmic and exponential functions.

PYQ Notes

1. The angle of 1′ (minute in arc) nearly equal to 2.91×10^{-4} rad. **[NEET 2023]**
2. The errors in the measurement which arises due to unpredictable fluctuations in temperature and voltage supply are random errors. **[NEET 2022]**
3. If a physical quantity (say y) depends on another physical quantity (say A, B, C), then the dimensional formula of y is given by

$$y = A^aB^bC^c$$ **[JEE Main 2019]**

where, a, b, c are the powers of physical quantity.

Step by Step

Mastering NCERT

- Concept Builders
- Topical Questions
- Assertion and Reason Questions
- Statement Based
- Matching Type
- Numerical Type
- NCERT Exemplar
- Past Exams MCQs
- Skill Boosters

Concept Builders

1 In .... (CGS/ SI) system of units , all the units can be obtained by multiplying and dividing the basic and supplementary units.

2 .... angle is the ratio of the intercepted area dA to the square of radius spherical surface.

3 The ...... (accuracy/ precision) of a measurement is a measure of how close the measured value to the true value of the quantity.

4 The systematic errors are those errors that tend to be in one direction, either positive or negative. [T/F]

5 Which error arises due to the imperfect design or calibration of measuring instrument ?

6 The smallest value that can be measured by a measuring instrument is called pitch. [T/F]

7 The magnitude of the difference between the individual measurement and the true value of the quantity is called the absolute error of the measurement. [T/F]

8 Which error is associated with the resolution of the instrument ?

9 When the......... (relative/absolute) error is expressed in percent, then it is called the percentage error.

10 When two quantities are multiplied or divided, then the relative error in the result is the sum of the relative errors in the multipliers. [T/F]

11 The relative error in a physical quantity raised to the power k is k times the relative error in the individual quantity. [T/F]

12 Which error indicates the true accuracy of the measurement?

13 The number of significant figure in 0.050 is .... (two / four)

14 If the insignificant digit to be dropped is more than 5, then the preceding digit will remain unchanged. [T / F]

15 If the insignificant digit to be dropped is 5, then if preceding digit is .... (even / odd), then the insignificant digit is simply dropped and if it is .... (even / odd). Then, the preceding digit is raised by 1.

16 Round off 31.325×10^{-5} upto 4 digits.

17 A physical quantity which has no dimension and no unit is ....

18 The dimensional formula of surface tension is ....

19 Write the dimension of the ratio of magnetic flux (ϕ) and permeability (μ).

20 If units of length, mass and force are chosen as fundamental units, then what will be the dimension of time?

Topical Questions

International System of Units

1 Which of the following system of units is not based on units of mass, length and time alone? NCERT Pg. 1
(a) SI (b) MKS (c) FPS (d) CGS

2 Which one of the following units is not that of mutual inductance? NCERT Pg. 2
(a) Henry (b) Weber
(c) Ohm-second (d) Volt second $(\text{ampere})^{-1}$

3 Which is different from others by units? NCERT Pg. 2
(a) Phase difference
(b) Mechanical equivalent of heat
(c) Loudness of sound
(d) Poisson's ratio

4 The acceleration due to gravity is 9.8 m/s^2, then its value in FPS system is NCERT Pg. 2
(a) 32 ft/s^2 (b) 42 ft/s^2 (c) 52 ft/s^2 (d) 62 ft/s^2

5 The solid angle subtended by the periphery of an area $1\ cm^2$ at a point situated symmetrically at a distance of 5 cm from the area is NCERT Pg. 2
(a) 2×10^{-2} sr (b) 4×10^{-2} sr
(c) 6×10^{-2} sr (d) 8×10^{-2} sr

6 Which of the following pairs of physical quantities may be represented in the same unit? NCERT Pg. 2
(a) Heat and temperature
(b) Temperature and mole
(c) Heat and work
(d) Specific heat and heat

7 The unit of Stefan's constant (σ) and heat capacity (C) is NCERT Pg. 2
(a) watt $m^{-2}K^{-4}$ and JK^{-1} (b) calorie m^{-2} and K^{-4}
(c) joule K^{-1} and mol^{-1} (d) erg K^{-1} and mol^{-1}

8 One barn is equal to NCERT Pg. 3
(a) $10^{-30}\ cm^2$ (b) $10^{30}\ m^2$
(c) $10^{28}\ m^2$ (d) $10^{-28}\ m^2$

9 The unit of $\frac{L}{R}$ is (where, L = inductance and R = resistance) NCERT Pg. 3
(a) second (b) $second^{-1}$
(c) volt (d) ampere

10 The damping force on an oscillator is directly proportional to the velocity. The unit of the constant of proportionality is NCERT Pg. 2
(a) $kg\text{-}ms^{-1}$ (b) $kg\text{-}ms^{-2}$
(c) kgs^{-1} (d) kg-s

11 What will be the unit of a in the following equation?
$$\left(p+\frac{a}{V^2}\right)\cdot(V-b)=\text{constant}$$
NCERT Pg. 2
(a) dyne $\times\ cm^2$ (b) dyne $\times\ cm^3$
(c) dyne $\times\ cm^4$ (d) dyne $\times\ cm^5$

12 Young's modulus of a wire can be determined by $Y=\frac{F}{A}\cdot\frac{l}{\Delta l}$, where L = length, A = area of cross-section, Δl = change in length of the wire when stretched with a force F. Find the factor of conversion to change it from CGS to MKS system. NCERT Pg. 2
(a) 10 (b) 1 (c) 0.1 (d) 0.01

Accuracy, Precision of Instruments and Errors in Measurement

13 The errors in the measurement of the radius of a sphere is 2% and that in its mass is 3%, then the error in the measuring the density of the sphere is Old NCERT Pg. 24
(a) 9% (b) 7% (c) 11% (d) 5%

14 The error in measuring the mass and radius of a solid sphere are ± 1% and ± 0.5%, respectively. The error in calculation of the moment of inertia of the solid sphere will be about Old NCERT Pg. 24
(a) ± 1.5% (b) ± 2.5% (c) ± 3% (d) ± 2%

15 Which of the following instruments has minimum least count? Old NCERT Pg. 24
(a) A vernier callipers with 20 divisions on the vernier scale coinciding with 19 main scale divisions.
(b) A screw gauge of pitch 1 mm and 100 divisions on the circular scale.
(c) A spherometer of pitch 0.1 mm and 100 divisions on the circular scale.
(d) An optical instrument that can measure length to within a wavelength of light.

16 The period of oscillation of a simple pendulum is $T=2\pi\sqrt{\frac{L}{g}}$. Measured value of L is 1.0 m from metre scale having a minimum division of 1 mm and time of one complete oscillation is 1.95 s measured from stopwatch of 0.01 s resolution. The percentage error in the determination of g will be Old NCERT Pg. 24
(a) 1.13% (b) 1.03%
(c) 1.33% (d) 1.30%

17 Choose the correct statement. Old NCERT Pg. 24
(a) Error in a measurement is equal to the sum of true value and measured value of the quantity.
(b) Systematic errors occur in both directions, positive and negative.
(c) Random errors occur irregularly and at random, in magnitude and direction.
(d) In constant errors, errors affect each observation by the different amount.

18 Which of the following statements is incorrect?
(a) Every measurement by measuring instrument has some error. Old NCERT Pg. 24
(b) A measurement can have more accuracy but less precision and *vice-versa*.
(c) Every calculated quantity that is based on measured values has some error.
(d) The magnitude of the difference between the true value of the quantity and the individual measurement value is called the relative error of the measurement.

19 While performing some experiments, five readings are observed as : 80.0, 80.5, 81.0, 81.5 and 82. Calculate the mean percentage error in these observations. Old NCERT Pg. 24
(a) 0.74% (b) 1.74% (c) 0.38% (d) 1.36%

20 The following observations were taken for determining surface tension T of water by capillary method. Diameter of capillary, $d = 1.25 \times 10^{-2}$ m, rise of water $h = 1.45 \times 10^{-2}$m. Using $g = 9.80\,m/s^2$ and the simplified relation $T = \frac{rhg}{2} \times 10^3$N/ m, the possible error in surface tension is closest to **Old NCERT Pg. 24**

(a) 1.5 % (b) 2.4 %
(c) 10 % (d) 5 %

21 One main scale division of a vernier callipers is a cm and nth division of the vernier scale coincide with $(n-1)$ th division of the main scale. The least count of the callipers (in mm) is **Old NCERT Pg. 24**

(a) $\frac{10na}{(n-1)}$ (b) $\frac{10a}{(n-1)}$
(c) $\left(\frac{n-1}{10n}\right)a$ (d) $\frac{10a}{n}$

22 A student measured the diameter of a small steel ball using a screw gauge of least count 0.001 cm. The main scale reading is 5 mm and zero of circular scale division coincides with 25 divisions above the reference level. If screw gauge has a zero error of –0.004 cm, the correct diameter of the ball is **Old NCERT Pg. 24**

(a) 0.053 cm (b) 0.525 cm
(c) 0.521 cm (d) 0.529 cm

23 In an experiment, the percentage of error occurred in the measurement of physical quantities A, B, C and D are 1%, 2%, 3% and 4%, respectively. Then, the maximum percentage error in the measurement of X and Y where $X = \frac{A^2B^{1/2}}{C^{1/3}D^3}$ and $Y = \frac{A^3B^2}{CD}$ **Old NCERT Pg. 24**

(a) 16%, 14% (b) –10%, – 20%
(c) 10%, 12% (d) $\left(\frac{3}{13}\right)$%, $\left(\frac{4}{17}\right)$%

24 In successive experiments while measuring the period of oscillation of a simple pendulum. The readings turn out to be 2.63 s, 2.56 s, 2.42 s, 2.71s and 2.80 s. Calculate the mean absolute error. **Old NCERT Pg. 25**

(a) 0.11 s (b) 0.42 s (c) 0.92 s (d) 0.10 s

25 For a conducting wire, its resistance, $R = 65 \pm 1\Omega$, length, $l = 5 \pm 0.1$ mm and diameter, $d = 10 \pm 0.5$ mm. Find error in calculation of its resistivity. **Old NCERT Pg. 26**

(a) 21% (b) 13% (c) 16% (d) 41%

26 Calculate the relative errors in measurement of two masses 1.02 g ± 0.01g and 9.89g ± 0.01g . **Old NCERT Pg. 26**

(a) ± 1% and ± 0.2% (b) ± 1% and ± 0.1%
(c) ± 2% and ± 0.3% (d) ± 3% and ± 0.4%

27 An object uniformly travels a distance of (13.8 ± 0.2) m in time (4 ± 0.3) s. Calculate the velocity with error limits. **Old NCERT Pg. 26**

(a) (6.10± 0.6) ms^{-1} (b) (6.10± 0.3) ms^{-1}
(c) (3.45± 0.6) ms^{-1} (d) (3.45± 0.3) ms^{-1}

28 Two resistors of resistances $R_1 = 100 \pm 3\Omega$ and $R_2 = 200 \pm 4\Omega$ are connected in parallel. The equivalent resistance of the parallel combination is **Old NCERT Pg. 26**

(a) $(66 \pm 1)\Omega$ (b) $(66.7 \pm 1.8)\Omega$
(c) $(66.3 \pm 2)\Omega$ (d) $(67 \pm 3)\Omega$

29 The diameter and height of a cylinder are measured by a meter scale to be 12.6± 0.1 cm and (34.2± 0.1) cm, respectively. What will be the error in its volume? **Old NCERT Pg. 26**

(a) 180 cm^3 (b) 80 cm^3
(c) 82 cm^3 (d) 84 cm^3

Significant Figures

30 The number of significant figures in the numbers 4.8000×10^4 and 48000.50 are respectively **NCERT Pg. 4**

(a) 5 and 6 (b) 5 and 7
(c) 2 and 7 (d) 2 and 6

31 The numbers 5.355 and 5.345 on rounding off to 3 significant figures will give **NCERT Pg. 4**

(a) 5.35 and 5.34 (b) 5.36 and 5.35
(c) 5.35 and 5.35 (d) 5.36 and 5.34

32 5.74 g of a substance occupies 1.2 cm^3. Express its density by keeping the significant figures in view. **NCERT Pg. 5**

(a) 4.9 g cm^{-3} (b) 5.2 g cm^{-3}
(c) 4.8 g cm^{-3} (d) 4.4 g cm^{-3}

33 If 3.8×10^{-6} is added to 4.2×10^{-5}, then the result in significant figures will be **NCERT Pg. 5**

(a) 4.58×10^{-5} (b) 4.6×10^{-5}
(c) 45×10^{-5} (d) None of these

34 Each side of a cube is measured to be 7.203 m. What are the total surface area and the volume of the cube to appropriate significant figures? **NCERT Pg. 5**

(a) 373.7 m^2, 311.3 m^3
(b) 311.3 m^2, 373.7 m^3
(c) 273.4 m^2, 342.4 m^3
(d) 423.4 m^2, 437.4 m^3

35 If $A = (1.0 \pm 0.2)$m and $B = (2.0 \pm 0.2)$m, then what will be the value of $\sqrt{AB}$? **NCERT Pg. 6**

(a) (1.4 ± 0.2) m (b) (1.4 ± 0.3) m
(c) (1.4 ± 0.4) m (d) (1.4 ± 0.5) m

Dimensions of Physical Quantities

36 Which of the following physical quantities has neither units nor dimensions? **NCERT Pg. 7**

(a) Relative velocity (b) Relative density
(c) Angle (d) Energy

37 If P, Q, R are physical quantities, having different dimensions, which of the following combinations can never be a meaningful quantity? **NCERT Pg. 7**

(a) $\frac{P-Q}{R}$ (b) $PQ - R$
(c) $\frac{PQ}{R}$ (d) $\frac{PR-Q^2}{R}$

38 Which of the following set have different dimension? **NCERT Pg. 7**

(a) Dipole moment, electric flux, electric field
(b) Heat, work done, energy
(c) Torque, work done, energy
(d) Pressure, Young's modulus, stress

39 $\frac{h}{2\pi}$ is the dimensions of **NCERT Pg. 7**

(a) velocity (b) momentum
(c) energy (d) angular momentum

Dimensional Formulae and Dimensional Equations

40 If L, C, R denotes, the inductance, capacitance and resistance respectively, then dimensional formula of C^2LR is **NCERT Pg. 7**

(a) $[M^1L^2T^{-1}]$ (b) $[M^0L^0T^{-3}]$
(c) $[M^0L^0T^3]$ (d) $[M^0L^0T^0]$

41 If E and g respectively denote energy density and acceleration due to gravity, then $\frac{E}{g}$ has the dimensions of **NCERT Pg. 7**

(a) $[M^1][L^{-2}][T^0]$ (b) $[M^1][L^{-2}][T^1]$
(c) $[M^{-1}][L^{-2}][T^0]$ (d) $[M^{-1}][L^2][T^{-1}]$

42 A quantity f is given by $f = \sqrt{\frac{hc^5}{G}}$, where c is speed of light, G universal gravitational constant and h is the Planck's constant. Dimension of f is that of **NCERT Pg. 7**

(a) area (b) volume
(c) momentum (d) energy

43 Obtain the dimensional formula for universal gas constant. **NCERT Pg. 7**

(a) $[ML^2T^{-2}\,mol^{-1}\,K^{-1}]$ (b) $[ML^3T^{-1}\,mol^{-2}\,K^{-2}]$
(c) $[M^2LT^{-1}\,mol^{-1}\,K^{-1}]$ (d) $[M^3LT^{-2}\,mol^{-1}\,K^{-2}]$

44 In the formula, $X = 3YZ^2$, X and Z have dimensions of capacitance and magnetic induction. The dimensions of Y in MKSQ system is **NCERT Pg. 7**

(a) $[M^{-3}L^{-2}T^4Q^4]$ (b) $[ML^2T^8Q^4]$
(c) $[M^{-2}L^{-3}T^2Q^4]$ (d) $[M^{-2}L^{-2}TQ^2]$

45 In a typical combustion engine, the work done by a gas molecule is given $W = \alpha^2\beta e^{\frac{-\beta x^2}{kT}}$, where x is the displacement, k is the Boltzmann constant and T is the temperature. If α and β are constants, dimensions of α will be **NCERT Pg. 7**

(a) $[MLT^{-2}]$ (b) $[M^0LT^0]$ (c) $[M^2LT^{-2}]$ (d) $[MLT^{-1}]$

46 The entropy of any system is given by

$$S = \alpha^2\beta \ln\left[\frac{\mu kR}{J\beta^2} + 3\right]$$

where, α and β are constants, μ, J, k and R are number of moles, mechanical equivalent of heat, Boltzmann constant and gas constant, respectively. $\left[\text{Take, } S = \frac{dQ}{T}\right]$ **NCERT Pg. 7**

Choose the incorrect option.

(a) α and J have the same dimensions
(b) S, β, k and μR have the same dimensions
(c) S and α have different dimensions
(d) α and k have the same dimensions

Dimensional Analysis and Its Applications

47 If speed V, acceleration A and force F are considered as fundamental units, the dimension of Young's modulus will be **NCERT Pg. 8**

(a) $[V^{-4}A^{-2}F]$ (b) $[V^{-2}A^2F^2]$
(c) $[V^{-2}A^2F^{-2}]$ (d) $[V^{-4}A^2F]$

48 The dimension of stopping potential V_0 in photoelectric effect in units of Planck's constant h, speed of light c and gravitational constant G and ampere A is **NCERT Pg. 8**

(a) $h^{-2/3}c^{-1/3}G^{4/3}A^{-1}$
(b) $h^{1/3}G^{2/3}c^{1/3}A^{-1}$
(c) $h^2G^{3/2}c^{1/3}A^{-1}$
(d) $h^0c^5G^{-1}A^{-1}$

49 If surface tension (S), moment of inertia (I) and Planck's constant (h), were to be taken as the fundamental units, the dimensional formula for linear momentum would be **NCERT Pg. 8**

(a) $S^{1/2}I^{1/2}h^{-1}$ (b) $S^{3/2}I^{1/2}h^0$
(c) $S^{1/2}I^{1/2}h^0$ (d) $S^{1/2}I^{3/2}h^{-1}$

50 Using the principle of homogeneity of dimensions, find out which of the following is correct. **NCERT Pg. 8**

(a) $T^2 = \frac{4\pi^2 r^3}{GM}$ (b) $T^2 = \frac{4\pi^2 r^3}{G}$

(c) $T^2 = \frac{4\pi^2 r^3}{G}$ (d) $T^2 = 4\pi^2 r^2$

51 If p represents radiation pressure, c is speed of light and s represents radiation energy striking unit per area second. The non-zero integers x, y, z, such that $p^x s^y c^z$ is dimensionless are **NCERT Pg. 8**

(a) $x = 1, y = 1, z = 1$ (b) $x = -1, y = 1, z = 1$

(c) $x = 1, y = -1, z = 1$ (d) $x = 1, y = 1, z = -1$

52 A new system of units is proposed in which , the unit of mass is α kg, unit of length is β m, and unit of time is γ s. What will be the value of 5 J in the new system? **NCERT Pg. 8**

(a) $5\alpha^{-2}\beta^{-1}\gamma^{-2}$ (b) $5\alpha^{-1}\beta^{-2}\gamma^{2}$

(c) $5\alpha^{-1}\beta^{2}\gamma^{2}$ (d) $5\alpha\beta^{2}\gamma^{-2}$

53 The potential energy of a particle varies with distance x from a fixed origin as $U = \frac{A\sqrt{x}}{x + B}$, where A and B are constants. The dimensions of AB are **NCERT Pg. 8**

(a) $[ML^{5/2} T^{-2}]$ (b) $[ML^2 T^{-2}]$

(c) $[M^{3/2}L^3 T^{-2}]$ (d) $[ML^{7/2} T^{-2}]$

54 If time t, velocity v and angular momentum l are taken as the fundamental units, then the dimensions of mass m in terms of t, v and l is **NCERT Pg. 8**

(a) $[t^{-1}v^{1}l^{-2}]$ (b) $[t^{1}v^{2}l^{-1}]$

(c) $[t^{-2}v^{-1}l^{1}]$ (d) $[t^{-1}v^{-2}l^{1}]$

55 The density of a material in CGS system is 10 g cm^{-3}. If unit of length becomes 10 cm and unit of mass becomes 100 g, the new value of density will be **NCERT Pg. 8**

(a) 10 units (b) 100 units

(c) 1000 units (d) 1 unit

56 Find the value of power of 60 J per min on a system that has 100 g, 100 cm and 1 min as the base units. **NCERT Pg. 8**

(a) 2.16×10^4 units (b) 2.16×10^6 units

(c) 3×10^4 units (d) 4×10^7 units

57 When 1 m, 1 kg and 1 min are taken as the fundamental units, the magnitude of the force is 36 units. What will be the value of this force in CGS system? **NCERT Pg. 8**

(a) 10^5 dyne (b) 10^3 dyne

(c) 10^8 dyne (d) 10^4 dyne

58 In a new system of units, unit of mass is α kg, unit of length is β m and unit of time is γ s. In this system, 10 J will be represented as **NCERT Pg. 8**

(a) $10\,\alpha^{-1}\beta^{2}\gamma^{2}$

(b) $10\,\alpha^{-2}\beta^{-1}\gamma^{-2}$

(c) $10\,\alpha^{-1}\beta^{-2}\gamma^{2}$

(d) $10\,\alpha\beta^{2}\gamma^{-2}$

59 The force of interaction between two atoms is given by $F = \alpha\beta \exp\left(-\frac{x^2}{\alpha kT}\right)$; where x is the distance, k is the Boltzmann constant and T is temperature and α and β are two constants. The dimensions of β is **NCERT Pg. 8**

(a) $[MLT^{-2}]$ (b) $[M^0L^2T^{-4}]$

(c) $[M^2L T^{-4}]$ (d) $[M^2L^2T^{-2}]$

60 A physical quantity of the dimensions of length that can be formed out of c, G and $\frac{e^2}{4\pi\varepsilon_0}$ is

[c is velocity of light, G is universal constant of gravitation and e is charge] **NCERT Pg. 8**

(a) $\frac{1}{c^2}\left[G\frac{e^2}{4\pi\varepsilon_0}\right]^{1/2}$ (b) $c^2\left[G\frac{e^2}{4\pi\varepsilon_0}\right]^{1/2}$

(c) $\frac{1}{c^2}\left[\frac{e^2}{G\,4\pi\varepsilon_0}\right]^{1/2}$ (d) $\frac{1}{c}G\frac{e^2}{4\pi\varepsilon_0}$

61 Planck's constant h, speed of light in vacuum c and Newton's gravitational constant G are three fundamental constant. Which of the following combinations of these has the dimension of length? **NCERT Pg. 8**

(a) $\frac{\sqrt{hG}}{c^{3/2}}$ (b) $\frac{\sqrt{hG}}{c^{5/2}}$

(c) $\sqrt{\frac{hc}{G}}$ (d) $\sqrt{\frac{Gc}{h^{3/2}}}$

62 If energy E, velocity v and time T are chosen as the fundamental quantities, the dimensional formula of surface tension will be **NCERT Pg. 8**

(a) $[Ev^{-2}T^{-1}]$ (b) $[Ev^{-1}T^{-2}]$

(c) $[Ev^{-2}T^{-2}]$ (d) $[E^2v^{-1}T^{-3}]$

63 The expression for viscous force F acting on a tiny steel ball of radius r moving in a viscous liquid of viscosity η with a constant speed v with the help of the method of dimensional analysis is **NCERT Pg. 8**

(a) $kr\eta v$ (b) $kr^2\eta v$

(c) $kr\eta v^{3/2}$ (d) $kr\eta^2 v$

64 Given that the amplitude of the scattered light is directly proportional to amplitude of incident light, volume of scattering dust particle, wavelength of the light and inversely proportional to distance from the scattering particle. Then, the relation of intensity of scattered light with the wavelength is NCERT Pg. 8

(a) $\frac{1}{\lambda^2}$ (b) $\frac{1}{\lambda^4}$

(c) $\frac{1}{\lambda^6}$ (d) $\frac{1}{\lambda^7}$

65 If $y = A \sin\left[\left(\frac{2\pi}{\lambda}(ct - x)\right)\right]$, where x and y are in metre, then NCERT Pg. 8

(a) the unit of λ will be same as that of x and A

(b) the unit of $(ct + x)$ will be same as that of $\frac{2\pi}{\lambda}$

(c) the unit of λ will be same as that of x but not of A

(d) the unit of c is same as that of $\frac{2\pi}{\lambda}$

Assertion and Reason Questions

Direction (Q. Nos. 1-10) *In the following questions, a statement of Assertion is followed by a corresponding statement of Reason. Of the following statements, choose the correct one.*

(a) Both Assertion and Reason are correct and Reason is the correct explanation of Assertion.

(b) Both Assertion and Reason are correct but Reason is not the correct explanation of Assertion.

(c) Assertion is correct but Reason is incorrect.

(d) Assertion is incorrect but Reason is correct.

1 Assertion Number of significant figure in 0.0003 is one and that in 0.3000 is four.

Reason Trailling zeros (the zero placed to the left of the number) are never significant. NCERT Pg. 4

2 Assertion Random errors arise due to random and unpredictable fluctuations in experimental conditions.

Reason Random errors occurred due to irregularity with respect to sign and size. Old NCERT Pg. 23

3 Assertion If the percentage errors in the measurement of mass and speed are 3% and 5% respectively, then percentage error in the estimation of kinetic energy will be 13%.

Reason The relative error in kinetic energy is given by

$$\frac{\Delta E}{E} = \frac{\Delta m}{m} + \frac{2\Delta v}{v}$$

Old NCERT Pg. 23

4 Assertion When a quantity appears with a power n greater than one in an expression, its error contribution to the final result decreases n times.

Reason In all mathematical operations, the errors are of additive in nature. Old NCERT Pg. 27

5 Assertion The method of dimensions analysis cannot validate the exact relationship between physical quantities in any equation.

Reason It does not distinguish between the physical quantities having same dimensions. NCERT Pg. 8

6 Assertion Special functions such as trigonometric, logarithmic and exponential functions are dimensionless.

Reason A pure number, ratio of similar physical quantities, such as angle and refractive index, has no dimensions. NCERT Pg. 8

7 Assertion The coefficient of linear expansion α given by

$$\alpha = \frac{\Delta L}{L\Delta Q}$$

$$[\alpha] = [Q^{-1}]$$

So, its unit is $(°C)^{-1}$ or K^{-1}.

Reason Coefficient of linear expansion is independent on temperature, whereas specific heat capacity is dependent on temperature. NCERT Pg. 8

8 Assertion When a small sphere moves at low speed through a fluid, the viscous force, opposing the motion is found experimentally to depend on the radius, velocity of the sphere and viscosity.

Reason If it is know that when mass is converted into energy $E = km^x c^y$ and Stokes' law becomes $F = k\eta rv$. NCERT Pg. 8

9 Assertion The force acting on a body can be divided by time, for which it acts, although force and time have different dimensions.

Reason Any vector quantity can be divided by a scalar irrespective of their dimensions. NCERT Pg. 8

10 Assertion Surface energy of a liquid is numerically equal to its surface tension.

Reason The dimensional formula of both surface energy and surface tension is $[ML^0T^{-2}]$. NCERT Pg. 8

Statement Based Questions

Direction (Q. Nos. 1-8) *In the following questions, two statements (I & II) are given. In the light of the given statements, choose the correct option given below.*

(a) Both Statement I and Statement II are false.
(b) Statement I is true but Statement II is false.
(c) Statement I is false but Statement II is true.
(d) Both Statement I and Statement II are true.

1 **Statement I** The errors while tend to occur in one direction, either positive or negative are called systematic errors.

Statement II The errors which occur regularly and at random, in magnitude and direction called random errors. Old NCERT Pg. 23

2 **Statement I** The accuracy of a measurement is that how close the measured value is to the true value of the quantity.

Statement II Random errors are those errors, which occurs at regular. Old NCERT Pg. 23

3 **Statement I** In a number without decimal, if zero appears as the last digit on the right side of non-zero, then this zero is counted in the significant figure only when the measurement is actually recorded by the experiment, hence this zero should not be counted.

Statement II If some physical measurement is $l = 50\,\text{m}$, it has two significant figures on the other side we have the measurement $l = 1460$, it has only 3 significant figures. NCERT Pg. 4

4 **Statement I** The number of significant figures in 0.06900 m is 4.

Statement II A choice of change of different unit does not change the number of significant figures. NCERT Pg. 3

5 **Statement I** If $x = a^n$, then fractional error $\Delta x/x$, is equal to $\left(\frac{\Delta a}{a}\right)$.

Statement II The relative error and percentage error truly indicates the accuracy of a measurement. Old NCERT Pg. 26

6 **Statement I** A physical quantity that does not have any unit must be dimensionless.

Statement II The physical relation involving logarithm, exponential, trigonometric ratio, etc., cannot be derived by method of dimensional analysis. NCERT Pg. 7

7 **Statement I** If dimensions are given, physical quantity may not be unique as many physical quantities have same dimensions.

Statement II Numerical constant k having no dimensions such as $\left(\frac{1}{2}\right)$, 1 or 2π, etc., can be deduced by methods of dimensions. NCERT Pg. 8

8 **Statement I** The equation $x = x_0 + u_0 t + \frac{1}{2}at^2$ is dimensionally incorrect.

Statement II Dimensional analysis can be used for checking the dimensional consistency of homogeneity of the equation. NCERT Pg. 8

Matching Type Questions

1 Match the Column I (physical quantity) with Column II (unit) and choose the correct answer from the option given below.

Column I	Column II
A. Capacitance	1. Am^2
B. Inductance	2. Wb
C. Magnetic flux	3. Coulomb (volt)$^{-1}$
D. Magnetic moment	4. Ohm-second

NCERT Pg. 3

Codes

	A	B	C	D		A	B	C	D
(a)	3	4	2	1	(b)	1	4	2	3
(c)	3	2	1	4	(d)	4	1	3	2

2 Match the Column I with Column II and choose the correct answer from the options given below. Old NCERT Pg. 23

Column I	Column II
A. Instrumental errors	1. External conditions such as change in temperature, humidity, etc.
B. Imperfection in experimental technique	2. Person's carelessness
C. Personal errors	3. Either positive or negative in one direction.
D. Systematic errors	4. Imperfect design or calibration of the measuring instruments.

Codes

	A	B	C	D
(a)	4	1	2	3
(b)	2	4	3	1
(c)	2	1	4	3
(d)	4	1	3	2

3 Match the physical quantities given in Column I with dimensions expressed in terms of mass [M], length [L], time [T] and charge [A] in Column II and choose the correct answer from the option given below. **NCERT Pg. 7**

Column I	Column II
A. Angular momentum	1. $[ML^2T^{-2}]$
B. Torque	2. $[ML^2T^{-1}]$
C. Inductance	3. $[L^2T^{-2}]$
D. Latent heat	4. $[ML^2A^{-2}T^{-2}]$

Codes

	A	B	C	D		A	B	C	D
(a)	2	1	4	3	(b)	1	3	2	4
(c)	1	2	3	4	(d)	2	4	1	3

4 Match the Column I (number) with Column II (number of significant figures) and choose the correct answer from the option given below. **NCERT Pg. 4**

Column I	Column II
A. 0.004608	1. 3
B. 8.9000	2. 5
C. 186	3. 6
D. 2.00891	4. 4

Codes

	A	B	C	D		A	B	C	D
(a)	1	4	2	3	(b)	4	2	1	3
(c)	3	4	1	2	(d)	4	2	3	1

5 Match the Column I (physical quantity) with Column II (dimension) and choose the correct answer from the option given below. **NCERT Pg. 7**

Column I	Column II
A. Boltzmann constant (k)	1. $[ML^2\ T^{-1}]$
B. Coefficient of viscosity (η)	2. $[ML^{-1}\ T^{-1}]$
C. Planck's constant (h)	3. $[MLT^{-3}\ K^{-1}]$
D. Thermal conductivity (K)	4. $[ML^2\ T^{-2}\ K^{-1}]$

Codes

	A	B	C	D		A	B	C	D
(a)	3	2	1	4	(b)	4	2	1	3
(c)	4	1	3	2	(d)	1	4	2	4

Numerical Type Questions

1 The pitch of a screw gauge is 1 mm and there are 100 divisions on the circular scale. While measuring the diameter of a wire, the linear scale reads 1 mm and 35th division on circular scale coincides with the reference line. The length of wire is 7.5 cm. The curved surface area (in cm^2) of the wire in appropriate number of significant figures .... **Old NCERT Pg. 24**

2 A vernier callipers has 1 mm marks on the main scale. It has 20 equal divisions on the vernier scale which match with 18 main scale divisions. For this vernier callipers, the least count is .... mm. **Old NCERT Pg. 24**

3 For $l = a^2 m^3 n^{\frac{1}{2}}$, where a is a constant. If percentage error in measurement of l and m are 18% and 4% respectively, then the percentage error for n will be ....%. **Old NCERT Pg. 25**

4 A student in the laboratory measure thickness of a wire using screw gauge. The readings are 1.19 mm, 1.20 mm, 1.23 mm and 1.22 mm. The percentage error is $\frac{x}{121}$%. The value of x is .... **Old NCERT Pg. 25**

5 The radius of sphere is measured to be (5 ± 0.75) cm. Suppose, the percentage error in its volume is x. The value of x is .... **Old NCERT Pg. 25**

6 The density of material in SI unit is 120 kg m^{-3}. In certain units in which the unit of length is 20 cm and the unit of mass is 40 g. The numerical value of density of the material is .... **NCERT Pg. 7**

7 The speed of a wave produced in water is given by $v = \lambda^{\alpha} g^{\beta} \rho^{\gamma}$, where λ, g and ρ are wavelength of wave, acceleration due to gravity and density of water, respectively. The value of $\alpha + \beta + \gamma$ is .... **NCERT Pg. 8**

8 The force is given in terms of time t and displacement x by the equation $F = A \sin Bt + C \cos Dt$.
If dimensional formula of AD is $[MLT^{-a}]$, then the value of a is .... **NCERT Pg. 8**

9 The time period of oscillation of simple pendulum is $T = 2\pi\sqrt{\frac{L}{g}}$. Measured value of L is 25 cm known to 1 mm accuracy and time for 50 oscillations of the pendulum is find to be 40s using a wrist watch of Ist revolution. The percentage error in the determination of g is ....% . **NCERT Pg. 9**

10 A capacitor having charge q is bring near to an uncharged capacitor, the formula $x = 3yz^2$, x and z have dimensions of capacitance and magnetic induction, respectively. Then, the dimensions of y in MKSQ system is $[M^{-3}L^{-2}T^{x}Q^{4}]$. Find x. **NCERT Pg. 9**

NCERT Exemplar Questions

1 The number of significant figures in 0.06900 is
(a) 5 (b) 4
(c) 2 (d) 3

2 The sum of the numbers 436.32, 227.2 and 0.301 in appropriate significant figures is
(a) 663.821 (b) 664
(c) 663.8 (d) 663.82

3 The numbers 2.745 and 2.735 on rounding off to 3 significant figures will give
(a) 2.75 and 2.74 (b) 2.74 and 2.73
(c) 2.75 and 2.73 (d) 2.74 and 2.74

4 The mass and volume of a body are 4.237 g and 2.5 cm^3, respectively. The density of the material of the body in correct significant figures is
(a) 1.6048 g cm^{-3} (b) 1.69 g cm^{-3}
(c) 1.7 g cm^{-3} (d) 1.695 g cm^{-3}

5 The length and breadth of a rectangular sheet are (16.2 ± 0.1) cm and (10.1 ± 0.1) cm, respectively. The area of the sheet in appropriate significant figures and error is
(a) (164 ± 3) cm^2 (b) (163.62 ± 2.6) cm^2
(c) (163.6 ± 2.6) cm^2 (d) (163.62 ± 3) cm^2

6 Which of the following pairs of physical quantities does not have same dimensional formula?
(a) Work and torque
(b) Angular momentum and Planck's constant
(c) Tension and surface tension
(d) Impulse and linear momentum

7 Measure of two quantities along with the precision of respective measuring instrument is $A = 2.5$ $ms^{-1} \pm 0.5$ ms^{-1} and $B = 0.10$ s $\pm$ 0.01 s. The value of AB will be
(a) (0.25 ± 0.08) m (b) (0.25 ± 0.5) m
(c) (0.25 ± 0.05) m (d) (0.25 ± 0.135) m

8 Young's modulus of steel is 1.9×10^{11} Nm^{-2}. When it is expressed in CGS units of dyne cm^{-2}, it will be equal to ($1N = 10^5$ dyne and $1\ m^2 = 10^4 cm^2$)
(a) 1.9×10^{10} (b) 1.9×10^{11}
(c) 1.9×10^{12} (d) 1.9×10^{13}

9 If momentum p, area A and time T are taken to be fundamental quantities, then energy has the dimensional formula
(a) $[pA^{-1}T^{1}]$ (b) $[p^2AT]$
(c) $[pA^{-1/2}T]$ (d) $[pA^{1/2}T^{-1}]$

10 In the expression $P = EL^2 m^{-5} G^{-2}$, where E, m, l and G denote energy, mass, angular momentum and gravitational constant, respectively. The dimensions of P are
(a) $[MLT^0]$ (b) $[M^2LT^{-1}]$
(c) $[M^0L^0T^0]$ (d) $[M^0LT^{-2}]$

Past Exams Questions

NEET

1 A force defined by $F = \alpha t^2 + \beta t$ acts on a particle at a given time t. The factor which is dimensionless, if α and β are constants, is **NCERT Pg. 7, NEET 2024**
(a) $\frac{\beta t}{\alpha}$ (b) $\frac{\alpha t}{\beta}$
(c) $\alpha\beta t$ (d) $\frac{\alpha\beta}{t}$

2 The quantities which have the same dimensions as those of solid angle are **NCERT Pg. 7, NEET 2024**
(a) strain and angle
(b) stress and angle
(c) strain and arc
(d) angular speed and stress

3 In a vernier callipers, $(N + 1)$ divisions of vernier scale coincide with N divisions of main scale. If 1 MSD represents 0.1 mm, the vernier constant (in cm) is **NCERT Pg. 11, NEET 2024**

(a) $\frac{1}{10N}$ (b) $\frac{1}{100(N+1)}$
(c) $100N$ (d) $10(N + 1)$

4 Plane angle and solid angle have **NCERT Pg. 2, NEET 2022**

(a) dimensions but no units
(b) no units and no dimensions
(c) both units and dimensions
(d) units but no dimensions

5 The area of a rectangular field (in m^2) of length 55.3 m and breadth 25 m after rounding off the value for correct significant digits is **NCERT Pg. 4, NEET 2022**

(a) 1382 (b) 1382.5 (c) 14×10^2 (d) 138×10^1

6 The dimension formula $[MLT^{-2}A^{-2}]$ belong to the **NCERT Pg. 7, NEET 2022**

(a) magnetic flux (b) self-inductance
(c) magnetic permeability (d) electric permittivity

7 If force $[F]$, acceleration $[a]$ and time $[T]$ are chosen as the fundamental physical quantities, find the dimensions of energy. **NCERT Pg. 7, NEET 2021**

(a) $[F]\,[a]\,[T]$ (b) $[F]\,[a]\,[T^2]$
(c) $[F]\,[a]\,[T^{-1}]$ (d) $[F]\,[a^{-1}]\,[T]$

8 Dimensions of stress are **NCERT Pg. 7, NEET 2020**

(a) $[ML^2T^{-2}]$ (b) $[ML^0T^{-2}]$
(c) $[ML^{-1}T^{-2}]$ (d) $[MLT^{-2}]$

9 The unit of thermal conductivity is **NCERT Pg. 2, NEET 2019**

(a) $J\,m^{-1}\,K^{-1}$ (b) $W\,m\,K^{-1}$
(c) $W\,m^{-1}\,K^{-1}$ (d) $J\,m\,K^{-1}$

JEE Main

10 Given below are two statements

Statement I Dimension formula of specific heat is $[L^2T^{-2}K^{-1}]$.

Statement II Dimension formula of gas constant is $[ML^2T^{-1}K^{-1}]$.

In the light of the above statements, choose the most appropriate answer from the options given below. **NCERT Pg. 7, JEE Main 2024**

(a) Both Statement I and Statement II are incorrect.
(b) Statement I is correct but Statement II is incorrect.
(c) Both Statement I and Statement II are correct.
(d) Statement I is incorrect but Statement II is correct.

11 The equation of stationary wave is

$$y = 2a\sin\left(\frac{2\pi nt}{\lambda}\right)\cos\left(\frac{2\pi x}{\lambda}\right).$$

NCERT Pg. 7, JEE Main 2024

Which of the following is not correct?

(a) The dimension of nt is [L]
(b) The dimension of x is [L]
(c) The dimension of $\frac{n}{\lambda}$ is [T]
(d) The dimension of n is $[LT^{-1}]$

12 In the equation $\left[x + \frac{a}{y^2}\right][y - b] = RT$, x is pressure, y is volume, R is universal gas constant and T is temperature. The physical quantity equivalent to the ratio a/b is **NCERT Pg. 8, JEE Main 2023**

(a) coefficient of viscosity (b) impulse
(c) energy (d) pressure gradient

13 Velocity v and acceleration a in two systems of units 1 and 2 are related as $v_2 = \frac{n}{m^2}v_1$ and $a_2 = \frac{a_1}{mn}$, respectively. Here, m and n are constants. The relations for distance and time in two systems respectively are **NCERT Pg. 8, JEE Main 2022**

(a) $\frac{n^3}{m^3}L_1 = L_2$ and $\frac{n^2}{m}T_1 = T_2$

(b) $L_1 = \frac{n^4}{m^2}L_2$ and $T_1 = \frac{n^2}{m}T_2$

(c) $L_1 = \frac{n^2}{m}L_2$ and $T_1 = \frac{n^4}{m^2}T_2$

(d) $\frac{n^2}{m}L_1 = L_2$ and $\frac{n^4}{m^2}T_1 = T_2$

14 The force is given in terms of time t and displacement x by the equation $F = A\cos Bx + C\sin Dt$

The dimensional formula of AD/B is **NCERT Pg. 8, JEE Main 2021**

(a) $[M^0LT^{-1}]$ (b) $[ML^2T^{-3}]$
(c) $[M^1L^1T^{-2}]$ (d) $[M^2L^2T^{-3}]$

Skill Boosters

1 Two full turns of the circular scale of a screw gauge cover a distance of 1 mm on its main scale. The total number of divisions on the circular scale is 50. Further, it is found that the screw gauge has a zero error of – 0.03 mm. While measuring the diameter of a thin wire, a student notes the main scale reading of 3 mm and the number of circular scale divisions in line with the main scale as 35. The diameter of the wire is

(a) 3.32 mm (b) 3.73 mm
(c) 3.67 mm (d) 3.38 mm

2 The sun is a hot plasma (ionised matter) with its inner core at a temperature exceeding 10^7 K and its outer surface at a temperature of about 6000 K. At these high temperatures, no substance remains in a solid or liquid phase. In what range do you expect the mass density of the sun to be ? (Take, mass of the sun $= 2.0 \times 10^{30}$ kg and radius of the sun $= 7.0 \times 10^8$ m)

(a) 1.4×10^3 kg m^{-3} (b) 1.6×10^3 kg m^{-3}
(c) 2×10^3 kg m^{-3} (d) 4×10^3 kg m^{-3}

3 A student measured the diameter of a small steel ball using a screw gauge of least count 0.001 cm. The main scale reading is 5 mm and zero of circular scale division coincides with 25 divisions above the reference level., If screw gauge has a zero error of -0.004 cm, the correct diameter of the ball is

(a) 0.053 cm (b) 0.525 cm
(c) 0.521 cm (d) 0.529 cm

4 In a simple pendulum, experiment for determination of acceleration due to gravity *g*, time taken for 20 oscillations is measured by using a watch of 1s least count. The mean value of time taken comes out to be 30s. The length of pendulum is measured by using a meter scale of least count 1 mm and the value obtained 55.0 cm. The percentage error in the determination of *g* is close to

(a) 0.7% (b) 6.8%
(c) 3.5% (d) 0.2%

5 In an experiment, the diameter of a wire is measured by a screw gauge of least count 0.001 cm is 0.050 cm. The length measured by a scale of least count, 0.1 cm is 110.0 cm. When a weight of 50N is suspended from the wire , the extension is measured to be 0.125 cm by a micrometer of least count 0.001 cm. The maximum error in the measurement of Young's modulus of the wire is

(a) 0.130×10^{11} N/m^2 (b) 0.109×10^{11} N/m^2
(c) 0.2×10^{12} N/m^2 (d) 1.0×10^{10} N/m^2

6 The current-voltage relation of diode is given by $I = (e^{1000\,V/T} - 1)$ mA, where the applied voltage *V* is in volt and the temperature *T* is in kelvin. If a student makes an error measuring ± 0.01 V while measuring the current of 5 mA at 300 K, what will be the error in the value of current (in mA) ?

(a) 0 (b) 1 (c) 0.2 (d) 0.5

7 The mass of a box measured by a grocer's balance is 2.3 kg . Two gold pieces of masses 20.15 g and 20.17 g are added to the box. What is (i) the total mass of the box (ii) and the difference in the mass of the pieces to correct significant figures ?

(a) 2.8 kg, 0.08 g (b) 2.9 kg, 0.02 g
(c) 2.3 kg, 0.02 g (d) 3.0 kg, 0.02 g

8 To find the distance *d* over which a signal can be seen clearly in foggy conditions, a railways engineer uses dimensional analysis and assumes that the distance depends on the mass density ρ of the fog, intensity *S* (power / area) of the light from the signal and its frequency *f*. The engineer finds that *d* is proportional to $S^{1/n}$. The value of *n* is

(a) 4 (b) 6
(c) 3 (d) 2

9 A gas bubble arise, from an explosion underwater and oscillates with a time period *T* which is proportional to $p^a d^b E^c$, where *p* is the static pressure, *d* is the density of the water and *E* is the total energy of explosion. The values of *A*, *B* and *C* will be

(a) $a = \frac{-5}{6}, b = \frac{1}{2}, c = \frac{1}{3}$ (b) $a - \frac{1}{2}, b = \frac{1}{3}, c = \frac{5}{6}$
(c) $a = -\frac{1}{4}, b = \frac{1}{3}, c = \frac{1}{2}$ (d) $a = \frac{1}{3}, b = -\frac{1}{4}, c = \frac{1}{2}$

Correct Codes

Topical Questions

1 (a)	2 (b)	3 (d)	4 (a)	5 (b)	6 (c)	7 (a)	8 (d)	9 (a)	10 (c)
11 (c)	12 (c)	13 (a)	14 (d)	15 (d)	16 (a)	17 (c)	18 (d)	19 (a)	20 (a)
21 (d)	22 (d)	23 (a)	24 (a)	25 (b)	26 (b)	27 (d)	28 (b)	29 (b)	30 (b)
31 (d)	32 (c)	33 (b)	34 (b)	35 (a)	36 (b)	37 (a)	38 (a)	39 (d)	40 (c)
41 (a)	42 (d)	43 (a)	44 (a)	45 (b)	46 (d)	47 (d)	48 (d)	49 (c)	50 (a)
51 (c)	52 (b)	53 (d)	54 (d)	55 (b)	56 (b)	57 (b)	58 (c)	59 (c)	60 (a)
61 (a)	62 (c)	63 (a)	64 (b)	65 (a)					

Assertion and Reason Questions

1 (b)	2 (b)	3 (a)	4 (d)	5 (a)	6 (b)	7 (c)	8 (c)	9 (a)	10 (b)

Statement Based Questions

1 (d)	2 (d)	3 (d)	4 (d)	5 (c)	6 (b)	7 (b)	8 (c)

Matching Type Questions

1 (a)	2 (a)	3 (a)	4 (b)	5 (b)

Numerical Type Questions

1 (3.18)	2 (0.1)	3 (12)	4 (150)	5 (45)	6 (24)	7 (1)	8 (3)	9 (5.4)	10 (4)

NCERT Exemplar Questions

1 (b)	2 (c)	3 (d)	4 (c)	5 (a)	6 (c)	7 (a)	8 (c)	9. (d)	10. (c)

Past Exams Questions

1 (b)	2 (a)	3 (b)	4 (d)	5 (c)	6 (c)	7 (b)	8 (c)	9 (c)	10 (b)
11 (c)	12 (c)	13 (a)	14 (b)						

Skill Boosters

1 (d)	2 (a)	3 (d)	4 (b)	5 (b)	6 (c)	7 (c)	8 (c)	9 (a)

Step by Step

Decoding the Questions

Concept Builders

1 SI
2 Solid
3 accuracy
4 True
5 Instrumental error
6 False
7 True
8 Least count error
9 relative
10 True
11 True
12 Relative error
13 two
14 False
15 even, odd
16 31.32×10^{-5}
17 Strain
18 $[MT^{-2}]$
19 $[M^0L^1 T^0A^1]$
20 $[M^{1/2}L^{1/2} F^{-1/2}]$

Topical Questions

2 (*b*) Weber is the unit of magnetic flux.

4 (*a*) As, 1 m = 3.2 ft

So, $9.8 \text{ m/s}^2 = 9.8\left(\frac{3.2\text{ft}}{s^2}\right)$

$\cong 32 \text{ ft/s}^2$

5 (*b*) Given, $dA = 1 \text{ cm}^2$ and $r = 5$ cm

$\therefore$ Solid angle, $d\Omega = \frac{dA}{r^2} = \frac{1}{(5)^2}$

$= 0.04 \text{ sr} = 4 \times 10^{-2}$ sr

7 (*a*) The unit of Stefan's constant σ is $Wm^{-2}K^{-4}$.

and heat capacity is expressed in units of thermal energy per degree temperature.

$$Q = C\Delta t \Rightarrow C = \frac{Q}{\Delta t}$$

So, the SI unit of heat capacity is JK^{-1}

9 (*a*) The unit of L/R is second because $\frac{L}{R}$ is a time constant.

10 (*c*) Given, damping force $\propto$ velocity

$$F \propto v \Rightarrow F = kv$$

$$\Rightarrow \quad k = \frac{F}{v}$$

$\therefore$ Unit of $k = \frac{\text{Unit of } F}{\text{Unit of } v}$

$= \frac{\text{kg-ms}^{-2}}{\text{ms}^{-1}} = \text{kgs}^{-1}$

11 (*c*) $\left(p + \frac{a}{V^2}\right) \cdot (V - b) = \text{constant}$

$p = \frac{F}{A} = \frac{\text{dyne}}{\text{cm}^2}$

Unit of p = unit of $\frac{a}{V^2}$

$\Rightarrow$ Unit of a = unit of $\frac{F}{A}V^2$

$= \frac{\text{dyne}}{\text{cm}^2} \times (\text{cm}^3)^2$

$= \text{dyne} \times \text{cm}^4$

12 (*c*) Y in CGS is dyne/cm^2.

Y in MKS is N/m^2.

$$1 \text{ dyne/cm}^2 = \frac{10^{-5}\text{N}}{\left(\frac{1}{100}\right)^2 \text{m}^2}$$

$(\because 1 \text{ N} = 10^5 \text{ dyne})$

$= 0.1 \text{ N/m}^2$

13 (*a*) $\rho = \frac{m}{V} = \frac{m}{\frac{4}{3}\pi r^3} = \frac{3m}{4\pi r^3}$

$\frac{\Delta\rho}{\rho} \times 100 = \left(\frac{\Delta m}{m} + 3\frac{\Delta r}{r}\right) \times 100$

$= [3\% + 3 \times (2\%)] = 9\%$

14 (*d*) Here, $I = \frac{2}{5}MR^2$

$\frac{\Delta I}{I} \times 100$

$= \pm\left(\frac{\Delta M}{M} \times 100 + \frac{2\Delta R}{R} \times 100\right)$

$= \pm\ (1 + 2 \times 0.5) = \pm\ 2\%$

15 (*d*) Wavelength of light,

$\lambda = 10^{-5}\text{cm} = 0.00001$ cm

Clearly, the optical instrument is the most precise.

16 (*a*) Error in length,

$\Delta L = 1$ mm

$= 1 \times 10^{-3}$m

$\because \quad T = 2\pi\sqrt{\frac{L}{g}}$

$\Rightarrow \quad \frac{\Delta g}{g} = \frac{\Delta L}{L} + \frac{2\Delta T}{T}$

$= \frac{10^{-3}}{1} + \frac{2 \times 10^{-2}}{1.95}$

$= 11.25 \times 10^{-3} \simeq 1.13 \times 10^{-2}$

$\because \Delta g / g \times 100 \simeq 1.13\%$

17 (*c*) Statement given in option (c) is correct but rest are incorrect and these can be corrected as

Error in a measurement is equal to the difference of true value and measured value of the quantity.

Systematic errors occur only in one direction, either positive or negative.

Constant errors affect each observation by the same amount.

19 (*a*) $O_{\text{mean}} = \mu = \frac{80.0 + 80.5 + 81.0 + 81.5 + 82}{5}$

$= \frac{405.0}{5} = 81$

Absolute errors in the observations are

$\Delta O_1 = |80.0 - \mu| = 1$

$\Delta O_2 = |80.5 - \mu| = 0.5$

$\Delta O_3 = |81.0 - \mu| = 0$

$\Delta O_4 = |81.5 - \mu| = 0.5$

$\Delta O_5 = |82 - \mu| = 1$

$\Delta O_{\text{mean}} = \sum_{i=1}^{5} \frac{|\Delta O_i|}{n}$

$= \frac{1 + 0.5 + 0 + 0.5 + 1}{5}$

$= \frac{3}{5} = 0.6$

$\frac{\Delta O_{\text{mean}}}{O_{\text{mean}}} \times 100\% = \frac{0.6}{81} \times 100\%$

$= 0.74\%$

20 (*a*) By ascent formula, we have surface tension

$T = \frac{rhg}{2} \times 10^3 \frac{N}{m} = \frac{dhg}{4} \times 10^3 \frac{N}{m}$ $\left(\because r = \frac{d}{2}\right)$

$\Rightarrow \frac{\Delta T}{T} = \frac{\Delta d}{d} + \frac{\Delta h}{h}$ [given, g is constant]

$\Rightarrow \frac{\Delta T}{T} \times 100$

$= \left(\frac{0.01 \times 10^{-2}}{1.25 \times 10^{-2}} + \frac{0.01 \times 10^{-2}}{1.45 \times 10^{-2}}\right) \times 100$

$= 1.5\%$

21 (*d*) $na' = (n-1)a$

$\Rightarrow a' = \left(\frac{n-1}{n}\right)a$

$\therefore$ Least Count (LC) = 1 MSD − 1 VSD

$= a - a'$

$= a - \left(\frac{n-1}{n}\right)a = \frac{a}{n}\text{cm} = \frac{10a}{n}\text{mm}$

22 (*d*) Vernier scale reading, VSR = 25

Zero error = −0.004 cm

Final reading

= MSR + VSR × LC − zero error

= 0.5 + 25 × 0.001 − (−0.004)

= 0.5 + 0.029 = 0.529 cm

23 (*a*) Given, $X = \frac{A^2 B^{1/2}}{C^{1/3} D^3}$

$\frac{\Delta X}{X} \times 100\% = 2\left(\frac{\Delta A}{A}\right) \times 100\% + \frac{1}{2}\left(\frac{\Delta B}{B}\right) \times 100\% + \frac{1}{3}\left(\frac{\Delta C}{C}\right) \times 100\% + 3\left(\frac{\Delta D}{D}\right) \times 100\%$ ...(i)

$= 2(1\%) + \frac{1}{2}(2\%) + \frac{1}{3}(3\%) + 3(4\%)$

$= 16\%$

$\frac{\Delta Y}{Y} \times 100 = 3 \times \left(\frac{\Delta A}{A}\right) \times 100 + 2\left(\frac{\Delta B}{B}\right) \times 100 + \left(\frac{\Delta C}{C}\right) \times 100 + \left(\frac{\Delta D}{D}\right) \times 100$

$= 3(1\%) + 2(2\%) + (3\%) + (4\%)$

$= 14\%$

24 (*a*)

$T_{mean} = \frac{2.63 + 2.56 + 2.42 + 2.71 + 2.80}{5}$

= 2.62 s

$\Delta T_1 = |2.63\text{ s} - 2.62\text{ s}| = 0.01\text{ s}$

$\Delta T_2 = |2.56\text{ s} - 2.62\text{ s}| = 0.06\text{ s}$

$\Delta T_3 = |2.42\text{ s} - 2.62\text{ s}| = 0.20\text{ s}$

$\Delta T_4 = |2.71\text{ s} - 2.62\text{ s}| = 0.09\text{ s}$

$\Delta T_5 = |2.80\text{ s} - 2.62\text{ s}| = 0.18\text{ s}$

$\Delta T_{mean} = [(0.01 + 0.06 + 0.20 + 0.09 + 0.18)]/5$

≈ 0.11 s

25 (*b*) Resistivity, $\rho = \frac{RA}{l}$

$\Rightarrow \rho = \frac{R\pi(d/2)^2}{l} = \frac{\pi R d^2}{4l}$

$\therefore \frac{\Delta\rho}{\rho} = \frac{\Delta R}{R} + 2\frac{\Delta d}{d} + \frac{\Delta l}{l}$

$\frac{\Delta\rho}{\rho} \times 100$

$= \left[\frac{1}{65} + 2\left(\frac{0.5 \times 10^{-3}}{10 \times 10^{-3}}\right) + \frac{0.1 \times 10^{-3}}{5 \times 10^{-3}}\right] \times 100$

$= 13.5\% \approx 13\%$

26 (*b*) The relative error in 1.02 g

= [± 0.01 / 1.02] × 100%

= ± 0.98% ≅ ± 1%

The relative error in 9.89 g

= (± 0.01 / 9.89) × 100%

= ± 0.1%

The relative errors in measurement of two masses are ± 1% and ± 0.1%.

27 (*d*) Velocity is given by

$v = \frac{\text{Distance}}{\text{Time}} = \frac{13.8}{4.0} = 3.45$

$\frac{\Delta v}{v} = \frac{\Delta d}{d} + \frac{\Delta t}{t}$

$\frac{\Delta v}{3.45} = \frac{0.2}{13.8} + \frac{0.3}{4.0}$

$\Rightarrow \Delta v = 0.089 \times 3.45 = 0.30$

$\therefore$ Velocity, $v = (3.45 \pm 0.3)\text{ ms}^{-1}$

28 (*b*) $\frac{1}{R'} = \frac{1}{R_1} + \frac{1}{R_2}$ ...(i)

$\Rightarrow R' = \frac{100 \times 200}{100 + 200}$

$= 66.7\,\Omega$

Then, from Eq. (i), we get

$\frac{\Delta R'}{R'^2} = \frac{\Delta R_1}{R_1^2} + \frac{\Delta R_2}{R_2^2}$

$\Rightarrow \Delta R' = (R'^2)\frac{\Delta R_1}{R_1^2} + (R'^2)\frac{\Delta R_2}{R_2^2}$

$= \left(\frac{66.7}{100}\right)^2 \times 3 + \left(\frac{66.7}{200}\right)^2 \times 4$

$= 1.78 \cong 1.8$

$\Rightarrow R' = (66.7 \pm 1.8)\,\Omega$

29 (*b*) $V = \pi r^2 h = \frac{\pi D^2 h}{4}$

$= \frac{\pi}{4} \times (12.6)^2 \times (34.2)$

$= 4262.22\text{ cm}^3$

$\frac{\Delta V}{V} = 2\left(\frac{\Delta D}{D}\right) + \frac{\Delta h}{h}$

$= \frac{2 \times 0.1}{12.6} + \frac{0.1}{34.2}$

$\Rightarrow \Delta V = 80.12 \simeq 80\text{ cm}^3$

32 (*c*) The density should be expressed to only 2 significant figures.

Density $= \frac{\text{Mass}}{\text{Volume}} = \frac{5.74}{1.2}$

$= 4.783 = 4.8\text{ g cm}^{-3}$

33 (*b*) $3.8 \times 10^{-6} + 4.2 \times 10^{-5}$

$= 4.58 \times 10^{-5}$

Thus, the addition of the given numbers is 4.6×10^{-5}.

34 (*b*) As the number of significant figures in the measured length is 4. So, the calculated area and the volume should be rounded off to 4 significant figures.

Surface area of the cube

$= 6l^2 = 6\,(7.203)^2$

$= 311.299254 = 311.3\text{ m}^2$

Volume of the cube $= l^3 = (7.203)^3$

$= 373.7\text{ m}^3$

35 (*a*) $AB = (1.0\text{ m})(2.0\text{ m}) = 2.0\text{ m}^2$

$x = \sqrt{AB} = \sqrt{2.0\text{ m}^2} = 1.414\text{ m}$

$x = \sqrt{AB} = 1.4\text{ m}$

$$\frac{\Delta x}{x}=\frac{1}{2}\left(\frac{\Delta A}{A}+\frac{\Delta B}{B}\right)$$
$$=\frac{1}{2}\left(\frac{0.2}{1.0}+\frac{0.2}{2.0}\right)$$
$$\Delta x = 0.21\,\text{m}$$

Rounding off to one significant figure, $x = 0.2$ m

$\therefore \sqrt{AB} = (1.4 \pm 0.2)$ m

40 (c) $C^2LR=(RC)\left(\frac{L}{R}\right)(RC)$

Dimensional formula = $[M^0L^0T^3]$

41 (a) E = energy density,

$$E=[M^1L^{-1}T^{-2}]$$
$$g=[L^1T^{-2}]$$

So, $\frac{E}{g}=\frac{[E]}{[g]}=\frac{[M^1L^{-1}T^{-2}]}{[L^1T^{-2}]}=[M^1L^{-2}T^0]$

42 (d) Dimensions of quantity f are

$$[f]=\frac{[h]^{\frac{1}{2}}[c]^{\frac{5}{2}}}{[G]^{\frac{1}{2}}} \quad ...(i)$$

As, $h=\frac{E}{\nu}$

$$[h]=[ML^2T^{-2}][T]=[ML^2T^{-1}]$$

$$c=[LT^{-1}] \text{ and } G=\frac{F\cdot r^2}{m^2}$$

$$\Rightarrow [G]=\frac{[MLT^{-2}][L^2]}{[M^2]}$$
$$=[M^{-1}L^3T^{-2}]$$

So, dimensions of f using Eq. (i),

$$[f]=\frac{[ML^2T^{-1}]^{\frac{1}{2}}[LT^{-1}]^{\frac{5}{2}}}{[M^{-1}L^3T^{-2}]^{\frac{1}{2}}}$$
$$=[ML^2T^{-2}]$$

Thus, it is the dimensions of energy.

43 (a) $R=\frac{(p)(V)}{(n)(T)}$

$$[R]=\frac{[ML^{-1}T^{-2}][L^3]}{[\text{mol}][K]}$$
$$=[ML^2T^{-2}\text{mol}^{-1}K^{-1}]$$

44 (a) $[X]=[M^{-1}L^{-2}T^2Q^2]$

and $[Z]$ = Dimensions of magnetic induction

$$=[MT^{-1}Q^{-1}]$$

$$[Y]=\frac{[X]}{[Z^2]}$$
$$\Rightarrow [Y]=\frac{[M^{-1}L^{-2}T^2Q^2]}{[M^2T^{-2}Q^{-2}]}$$
$$=[M^{-3}L^{-2}T^4Q^4]$$

45 (b) $W=\alpha^2\beta e^{-\beta x^2/kT}$

$$[W]=[ML^2T^{-2}]$$

$\therefore$ Dimensions of $[\alpha^2\beta]=[ML^2T^{-2}]$

$$\Rightarrow \alpha=\left[\frac{ML^2T^{-2}}{\beta}\right]^{1/2} \quad ...(i)$$

$$\Rightarrow \left[\frac{\beta x^2}{kT}\right]=[M^0L^0T^0]$$

$$\Rightarrow [\beta]=\frac{[k][T]}{[x^2]} \quad ...(ii)$$

Energy of gaseous molecule,

$$E=\frac{3}{2}kT$$

$$\Rightarrow [k]=[E]/[T]=[ML^2T^{-2}K^{-1}]$$

Substituting the value of k in Eq. (ii), we get

$$[\beta]=\frac{[ML^2T^{-2}K^{-1}][K]}{[L^2]}=[MT^{-2}]$$

Substituting the value of β in Eq. (i), we get

$$[\alpha]=\left\{\frac{[ML^2T^{-2}]}{[MT^{-2}]}\right\}^{1/2}=[M^0LT^0]$$

46 (d) $S=\alpha^2\beta\ln\left[\frac{\mu kR}{J\beta^2}+3\right] \quad ...(i)$

As, $S=\frac{dQ}{T}$ [given]

$$\Rightarrow [S]=\frac{[ML^2T^{-2}]}{[K]} \quad ...(ii)$$

Boltzmann constant, $k=\frac{\text{Energy}}{T}$

$$\Rightarrow [k]=\frac{[ML^2T^{-2}]}{[K]} \quad ...(iii)$$

From Eqs. (ii) and (iii), we can write

$$[S]=[k]=\frac{[ML^2T^{-2}]}{[K]} \quad ...(iv)$$

$\because$ Gas constant,

$$[R]=\frac{[\text{Energy}]}{[nT]}=\frac{[ML^2T^{-2}]}{[\text{mol K}]} \quad ...(v)$$

and mechanical equivalent of heat

$$[J]=[M^0L^0T^0] \quad ...(vi)$$

As, $[\mu kR]=[J\beta]^2$

Using Eqs. (iii), (v) and (vi), we get

$$\Rightarrow [\text{mol}]\times\frac{[ML^2T^{-2}]}{[K]}\times\frac{[ML^2T^{-2}]}{[\text{mol K}]}$$
$$=[\beta^2]$$
$$\Rightarrow [\beta]=[ML^2T^{-2}K^{-1}] \quad ...(vii)$$

Using Eq. (i), we can write

$$[\alpha^2]=\frac{[S]}{[\beta]}=\frac{[ML^2T^{-2}K^{-1}]}{[ML^2T^{-2}K^{-1}]}$$
$$\Rightarrow \alpha=[M^0L^0T^0] \quad ...(viii)$$

So, from Eqs. (iii) and (viii), we can say that α and k have different dimensions.

47 (d) $[V]=[LT^{-1}]$

$$[A]=[LT^{-2}]$$
$$[F]=[MLT^{-2}]$$
$$[Y]=[ML^{-1}T^{-2}]$$
$$[Y]=[V]^\alpha[A]^\beta[F]^\gamma \quad ...(i)$$
$$[ML^{-1}T^{-2}]=[LT^{-1}]^\alpha[LT^{-2}]^\beta[MLT^{-2}]^\gamma$$
$$=[M^\gamma L^{\alpha+\beta+\gamma}T^{-\alpha-2\beta-2\gamma}]$$

Now, comparing powers of basic quantities on both sides, we get

$$\gamma=1$$
$$\alpha+\beta+\gamma=-1$$

and $-\alpha-2\beta-2\gamma=-2$

Solving these equations, we get

$$\alpha=-4,\ \beta=2,\ \gamma=1$$

Substituting α,β and γ in Eq. (i), we get

$$[Y]=[V^{-4}A^2F]$$

48 (d) Let $V_0=(h)^a\cdot(c)^b\cdot(G)^c\cdot(A)^d \quad ...(i)$

Then, $[V_0]=\frac{[ML^2T^{-2}]}{[AT]}=[ML^2T^{-3}A^{-1}]$

$$[h]=\left[\frac{\text{Energy}}{\text{Frequency}}\right]=\frac{[ML^2T^{-2}]}{[T^{-1}]}$$
$$=[ML^2T^{-1}]$$

$$[c]=[\text{Speed}]=[LT^{-1}]$$

$$[G]=\frac{[MLT^{-2}][L^2]}{[M^2]}=[M^{-1}L^3T^{-2}]$$

Substituting the dimensions of V_0, h, C, G and A in Eq. (i) and equating dimension on both sides, we get

$$[ML^2T^{-3}A^{-1}]=[ML^2T^{-1}]^a\times[LT^{-1}]^b\times[M^{-1}L^3T^{-2}]^c\times[A]^d$$

$\Rightarrow \quad a - c = 1 \quad$ ...(ii)

$2a + b + 3c = 2 \quad$ ...(iii)

$-a - b - 2c = -3 \quad$ ...(iv)

$d = -1 \quad$ ...(v)

On solving above equations, we get

$a = 0, b = 5,$

$c = -1, d = -1$

Substituting these values in Eq. (i), we get

$V_0 = h^0 \cdot c^5 \cdot G^{-1} \cdot A^{-1}$

49 (c) Let, $p \propto (h)^a (S)^b (l)^c$

or $p = kh^a S^b l^c$

Thus, $[p] = [h]^a [S]^b [l]^c \quad$ ...(i)

Then, the respective dimensions of the given physical quantities, i.e.

$[p]$ = [mass × velocity] = $[MLT^{-1}]$

$[l]$ = [mass × distance^2]

$= [ML^2T^0]$

$[S]$ = [force/length]

$= [ML^0T^{-2}]$

$[h] = [ML^2T^{-1}]$

Then, substituting these dimensions in Eq. (i), we get

$[MLT^{-1}] = [ML^2T^{-1}]^a [MT^{-2}]^b [ML^2]^c$

Equating the dimensions, we have

$a + b + c = 1$

$2(a + c) = 1 \quad \text{or} \quad a + c = \frac{1}{2}$

$-a - 2b = -1$

or $a + 2b = 1$

Solving these three equations, we get

$a = 0, b = \frac{1}{2}, c = \frac{1}{2}$

$\therefore \quad p = h^0 S^{\frac{1}{2}} l^{\frac{1}{2}}$

or $p = S^{\frac{1}{2}} l^{\frac{1}{2}} h^0$

50 (a) $T^2 = \frac{4\pi^2 r^3}{GM}$

$[T^2] = \frac{[L]^3}{[M^{-1}L^3T^{-2}][M^1]} = [M^0L^0T^2]$

$[T^2] = [T^2]$

Therefore, this equation satisfies the principle of homogeneity of dimensions.

51 (c) Let, $\alpha = p^x s^y c^z \quad$ ...(i)

$\alpha = [M^0L^0T^0]$

Dimensions of radiation pressure,

$[P] = \left[\frac{F}{A}\right] = \frac{[MLT^{-2}]}{[L]^2} = [ML^{-1}T^{-2}]$

Dimensions of radiation energy per unit area per unit time

$[S] = \frac{[E]}{[A \times T]} = \frac{[ML^2T^{-2}]}{[L^2][T]} = [MT^{-3}]$

Dimensions of speed of light

$[c] = [LT^{-1}]$

From Eq. (i),

$[\alpha] = [ML^{-1}T^{-2}]^x [MT^{-3}]^y [LT^{-1}]^z$

$\Rightarrow [\alpha] = [M^{x+y} L^{-x+z} T^{-2x-3y-z}]$

From the principle of homogeneity of dimension,

$x + y = 0, -x + z = 0,$

$-2x - 3y - z = 0$

After solving, we get

$x = 1, y = -1, z = 1$

52 (b) We know that, joule is the unit of energy and the dimension formula of energy is $[ML^2T^{-2}]$.

Comparing with $[M^aL^bT^c]$, we get

$a = 1, b = 2, c = -2$

As, $n_2 = n_1 \left[\frac{M_1}{M_2}\right]^a \left[\frac{L_1}{L_2}\right]^b \left[\frac{T_1}{T_2}\right]^c$

$= 5\left[\frac{1\text{ kg}}{\alpha\text{ kg}}\right]^1 \left[\frac{1\text{ m}}{\beta\text{m}}\right]^2 \left[\frac{1\text{s}}{\gamma\text{s}}\right]^{-2}$

$= \frac{5\gamma^2}{\alpha\beta^2}$

$n_2 = 5\alpha^{-1}\beta^{-2}\gamma^2$

53 (d) Given, $U = \frac{A\sqrt{x}}{x + B}$

Dimensions of $U = [ML^2T^{-2}]$

According to the principle of homogeneity,

Dimensions of B = Dimensions of $x = [M^0LT^0]$

$\therefore$ Dimensions of A

$= \frac{\text{Dimensions of } U \times \text{Dimensions of } (x+B)}{\text{Dimensions of } \sqrt{x}}$

$= \frac{[ML^2T^{-2}][M^0LT^0]}{[M^0L^{1/2}T^0]} = [ML^{5/2}T^{-2}]$

Hence, dimensions of AB

$= [ML^{5/2}T^{-2}][M^0LT^0]$

$= [ML^{7/2}T^{-2}]$

54 (d) As per question, $m \propto t^a v^b l^c$

or $m = kt^a v^b l^c \quad$ ...(i)

Substituting all these dimensions in Eq. (i), we get

$[M^1L^0T^0] = [M^0L^0T^1]^a [M^0L^1T^{-1}]^b [M^1L^2T^{-1}]^c$

$[M^1L^0T^0] = [M^cL^{b+2c}T^{a-b-c}]$

On comparing powers, we get

$c = 1,$

$b + 2c = 0 = b + 2 = 0 \Rightarrow b = -2$

$a - b - c = 0$

$\Rightarrow \quad a = -1$

$\therefore$ We can write $[m] = [t^{-1}v^{-2}l^1]$

55 (b) Dimensions of density

$= \frac{[M]}{[L]^3} = [ML^{-3}]$

Given, $n_1 = 10$, $M_1 = 1\text{g}$, $L_1 = 1\text{ cm}$

In new system, $n_2 = ?$, $M_2 = 100\text{ g}$, $L_2 = 10\text{ cm}$

So, conversion of 10 g cm^{-3} (n_1) into new system

$n_2 = n_1 \times \left[\frac{M_1}{M_2}\right]\left[\frac{L_1}{L_2}\right]^{-3}$

$= 10 \times \left(\frac{1}{100}\right)\left(\frac{1}{10}\right)^{-3}$

$= 10 \times \frac{1}{100} \times 10 \times 10 \times 10$

= 100 units

56 (b) Given, power

$P_1 = \frac{\text{Work done}}{\text{Time taken}} = \frac{60\text{ J}}{1\text{min}} = \frac{60\text{ J}}{60\text{ s}}$

$= 1\text{ W or kg-m}^2\text{s}^{-3}$

Given, $P_1 = 1\text{ W}, M_1 = 1\text{ kg} = 1000\text{ g},$
$L_1 = 1\text{ m} = 100\text{ cm}, T_1 = 1\text{s}$

In new system,

$P_2 = ?, M_2 = 100\text{ g}, L_2 = 100\text{ cm},$
$T_2 = 1\text{ min} = 60\text{ s}$

$\therefore$ Conversion of 60 J per min or 1 W in a new system, i.e.

$$P_2 = P_1\left[\frac{M_1}{M_2}\right]^a\left[\frac{L_1}{L_2}\right]^b\left[\frac{T_1}{T_2}\right]^c$$

Now, [power] $=[ML^2T^{-3}]$

So, $a=1, b=2$ and $c=-3$.

$$\Rightarrow \quad P_2 = 1\left[\frac{1000}{100}\right]^1\left[\frac{100}{100}\right]^2\left[\frac{1}{60}\right]^{-3}$$

$= 2.16\times 10^6$ units

$\therefore 60\ \text{J min}^{-1} = 2.16\times 10^6$ new units of power

57 (*b*) As, dimensional formula of force $=[MLT^{-2}]$

$n_1 = 36, M_1 = 1$ kg, $L_1 = 1$m, $T_1 = 1\ \text{min} = 60$ s

$n_2 = ?, M_2 = 1$g, $L_2 = 1$ cm, $T_2 = 1$ s

So, conversion of 36 units into CGS system, i.e.

$$n_2 = n_1\left[\frac{M_1}{M_2}\right]^a\left[\frac{L_1}{L_2}\right]^b\left[\frac{T_1}{T_2}\right]^c$$

$$\Rightarrow n_2 = n_1 \left[\frac{1\ \text{kg}}{1\text{g}}\right]^1\left[\frac{1\ \text{m}}{1\ \text{cm}}\right]^1\left[\frac{1\ \text{min}}{1\ \text{s}}\right]^{-2}$$

$$= 36\left[\frac{1000\ \text{g}}{1\ \text{g}}\right]\left[\frac{100\ \text{cm}}{1\ \text{cm}}\right]^1\left[\frac{60\ \text{s}}{1\ \text{s}}\right]^{-2}$$

$= 10^3$ dyne

58 (*c*) Given, $10\ \text{J} = 10\ \text{kg m}^2\text{s}^{-2}$

$\therefore$ SI system	New system
value, $n_1 = 10$	value, $n_2 = ?$
mass, $M_1 = 1$ kg	mass, $M_2 = \alpha$ kg
length, $L_1 = 1$ m	length, $L_2 = \beta$ m
time, $T_1 = 1$s	time, $T_2 = \gamma$ second

Energy, $[E] = [ML^2T^{-2}]$

$\because \quad a=1, b=2, c=-2$

$$\therefore \quad n_2 = n_1\left[\frac{M_1}{M_2}\right]^a\left[\frac{L_1}{L_2}\right]^b\left[\frac{T_1}{T_2}\right]^c$$

$$n_2 = 10\times\left(\frac{1}{\alpha}\right)\left(\frac{1}{\beta}\right)^2\left(\frac{1}{\gamma}\right)^{-2}$$

$$\therefore \quad n_2 = 10\,\alpha^{-1}\beta^{-2}\gamma^2$$

59 (*c*) Given, $F = \alpha\beta\exp(-x^2/\alpha kT)$

$$\left(\frac{-x^2}{\alpha kT}\right) = [M^0L^0T^0]$$

$\Rightarrow$ Dimensions of α = Dimensions of (x^2/kT)

$$[\alpha] = \frac{[M^0L^2T^0]}{[M^1L^2T^{-2}]}$$

$$[\alpha] = [M^{-1}L^0T^2] \quad \text{...(i)}$$

Now, from given equation, we have dimensions of

$[F] = [\alpha][\beta]$

$$[\beta] = \frac{[F]}{[\alpha]}$$

$$= \frac{[M^1L^1T^{-2}]}{[M^{-1}L^0T^2]} \quad [\because \text{using Eq. (i)}]$$

$$= [M^2LT^{-4}]$$

60 (*a*) As force between two charges,

$$F = \frac{e^2}{4\pi\varepsilon_0 r^2}$$

$$\Rightarrow \quad \frac{e^2}{4\pi\varepsilon_0} = r^2\cdot F$$

Putting dimensions of *r* and *F*, we get

$$\left[\frac{e^2}{4\pi\varepsilon_0}\right] = [L^2][MLT^{-2}] \quad \text{...(i)}$$

Also, force between two masses,

$$F = \frac{Gm^2}{r^2} \Rightarrow G = \frac{Fr^2}{m^2}$$

$$\Rightarrow [G] = \frac{[MLT^{-2}][L^2]}{[M^2]}$$

$$\Rightarrow [G] = [M^{-1}L^3T^{-2}] \quad \text{...(ii)}$$

and $$\left[\frac{1}{c^2}\right] = \frac{1}{[L^2T^{-2}]} = [L^{-2}T^2] \quad \text{...(iii)}$$

Now, checking for option (a)

$$= \frac{1}{c^2}\left(\frac{Ge^2}{4\pi\varepsilon_0}\right)^{1/2}$$

$$= [L^{-2}T^2]\{[M^{-1}L^3T^{-2}][L^2][MLT^{-2}]\}^{1/2}$$

$$= [L^{-2}T^2][L^6T^{-4}]^{1/2} = [L]$$

61 (*a*) According to question, the length can be written as

$$l \propto h^a c^b G^c$$

or $l = k\,h^ac^bG^c$

$$[M^0L^1T^0] = [M\,L^2T^{-1}]^a\,[LT^{-1}]^b\,[M^{-1}L^3T^{-2}]^c$$

Applying the principle of homogeneity, we get

$$a - c = 0 \quad \text{... (i)}$$

$$2a + b + 3c = 1 \quad \text{... (ii)}$$

$$-a - b - 2c = 0 \quad \text{... (iii)}$$

Solving the Eq. (i), (ii) and (iii), we get

$$a = c = \frac{1}{2}, \ b = \frac{-3}{2}$$

Thus, we get, $l = k\dfrac{\sqrt{hG}}{c^{3/2}}$

62 (*c*) We know that, surface tension,

$$S = \frac{\text{Force } [F]}{\text{Length } [L]}$$

So, $$[S] = \frac{[MLT^{-2}]}{[L]} = [ML^0T^{-2}]$$

Energy, *E* = Force × Displacement

$\Rightarrow [E] = [MLT^{-2}][L] = [ML^2T^{-2}]$

$[v] = [LT^{-1}]$

As, $S \propto E^a v^b T^c$, where, *a*, *b* and *c* are constants.

From the principle of homogeneity,

$$[ML^0T^{-2}] = [ML^2T^{-2}]^a [LT^{-1}]^b [T]^c$$

$$\Rightarrow [ML^0T^{-2}] = [M^aL^{2a+b}T^{-2a-b+c}]$$

Equating the powers on both sides, we get

$a = 1, 2a + b = 0 \Rightarrow b = -2$

and $-2a - b + c = -2$

$\Rightarrow \quad c = (2a+b) - 2 = 0 - 2 = -2$

So, $[S] = [Ev^{-2}T^{-2}]$

63 (*a*) Let, $F = kr^a\eta^bv^c$

where, *k* is a dimensionless constant.

$F = [M\,L\,T^{-2}]$

Radius, $r = [L]$,

$\eta = [M^1\,L^{-1}\,T^{-1}]$

$v = [L\,T^{-1}]$, here, we get

$$[M\,L\,T^{-2}] = [L]^a [M\,L^{-1}\,T^{-1}]^b\,[L\,T^{-1}]^c = [M^bL^{a-b+c}T^{-b-c}]$$

Comparing the powers, we get

$$b = 1 \quad \text{...(i)}$$

$$a - b + c = 1 \quad \text{...(ii)}$$

and $$-b - c = -2 \quad \text{...(iii)}$$

On solving these three equations, we get

$a = 1, b = 1$ and $c = 1$

Hence, the relation becomes

$$F = k\,r\,\eta\,v$$

64 (b) Given, $A_s = kA^1 V^1 x^{-1} \lambda^d$
where, k is the constant of proportionality.
$\therefore \quad [L] = [L]\,[L^3]\,[L^{-1}]\,[L^d]$
$= [L^{3+d}]$
Comparing the powers, we get
or $1 = 3 + d$
or $d = -2$
i.e. $A_s \propto \dfrac{1}{\lambda^2}$
But intensity $(I_s) \propto$ amplitude $(A_s)^2$
$\therefore \quad I_s \propto \dfrac{1}{\lambda^4}$

65 (a) As, $y = A\sin\left[\left(\dfrac{2\pi}{\lambda}\right)\right][ct - x]$
Since, angle has $[M^0L^0T^0]$ dimensions
$\therefore \quad \dfrac{c}{\lambda}t = [M^0L^0T^0]$
$\lambda = ct = [M^0L^1T^0]$
$x = \lambda = [M^0L^1T^0]$
$A = [M^0L^1T^0]$
$\therefore$ The, unit of λ is same as that of x and A.

Assertion and Reason Questions

3 (a) Since, $K = \dfrac{1}{2}mv^2$, hence relative error in KE is given by
$\dfrac{\Delta E}{E} = \dfrac{\Delta m}{m} + \dfrac{2\Delta v}{v}$
$\dfrac{\Delta E}{E} \times 100 = \dfrac{\Delta m}{m} \times 100 + \dfrac{2\Delta v}{v} \times 100$
$= 3\% + 2 \times 5\%$
$= 13\%$
Thus, both Assertion and Reason are correct.

4 (d) When a quantity appears with a power n greater than one in an expression, its error contribution to the final result increases n times. So, quantities with higher power in the expression should be measured with maximum accuracy.

7 (c) Specific heat, $C = \dfrac{Q}{m\Delta T}$
i.e. $[C] = \dfrac{[ML^2T^{-2}]}{[M]\,[Q]}$
i.e. $[C] = [L^2T^{-2}Q^{-1}]$
So, its depend on temperature but coefficient of linear expansion also depend on temperature.

8 (c) Here, $F = k\eta^x r^y v^z$
$[MLT^{-2}] = [ML^{-1}T^{-1}]^x\,[L]^y\,[LT^{-1}]^z$
or $[MLT^{-2}] = [M^xL^{-x+y+z}T^{-x-z}]$
$x = 1;\ -x + y + z = 1$
and $-x - z = -2$
Solving these for x, y and z, we get
$x = y = z = 1$
So, Eq. (i) becomes
$F = k\eta rv$
On experimental ground $k = 6\pi$.
So, $F = 6\pi\eta rv$.

9 (a) Any vector quantity can be divided by a scalar quantity irrespective of their dimensions, hence both are correct.

10 (b) Potential energy per unit area of surface film is called surface energy and it turns out that
Surface tension = Surface energy
Now, surface tension
$= \dfrac{F}{L} = \dfrac{[MLT^{-2}]}{[L]} = [ML^0T^{-2}]$
Surface energy
$= \dfrac{E}{A} = \dfrac{[ML^2T^{-2}]}{[L^2]} = [ML^0T^{-2}]$
So, both Assertion and Reason are correct but Reason is not the correct explanation of Assertion.

Statement Based Questions

2 (d) Random errors occur irregularly and hence are random in to sign and size.

5 (c) For $x = a^n$, the fractional error $\dfrac{\Delta x}{x}$ is equal to $n\left(\dfrac{\Delta a}{a}\right)$.

6 (b) The physical quantity like exponential, logarithm, trigonometric ratio, etc., do not have dimensions, therefore they cannot be derived using dimensional analysis.

Matching Type Questions

4 (b) A $\rightarrow$ 4, B $\rightarrow$ 2, C $\rightarrow$ 1 and D $\rightarrow$ 3.

5 (b) A. As, internal energy,
$U = \dfrac{1}{2}kT$
$\Rightarrow [ML^2T^{-2}] = [k]\,[K]$
$\Rightarrow [k] = [ML^2T^{-2}K^{-1}]$
B. Viscous force, $F = \eta A\dfrac{dv}{dx}$
$\Rightarrow [\eta] = \dfrac{[MLT^{-2}]}{[L^2]][LT^{-1}][L^{-1}]}$
$= [ML^{-1}T^{-1}]$
C. Energy, $E = h\nu$
$\Rightarrow [ML^2T^2] = [h]\,[T^{-1}]$
$\Rightarrow [h] = [ML^2T^{-1}]$
D. $\dfrac{dQ}{dt} = \dfrac{kA\Delta\theta}{l}$
$\Rightarrow [k] = \dfrac{[ML^2T^{-3}L]}{[L^2K]}$
$= [MLT^{-3}K^{-1}]$
Hence, A $\rightarrow$ 4, B $\rightarrow$ 2, C $\rightarrow$ 1 and D $\rightarrow$ 3.

Numerical Type Questions

1 (3.18) Least count of screw gauge
$= \dfrac{1\text{ mm}}{100} = 0.01$ mm
Diameter of wire
$= (1 + 35 \times 0.01)$ mm
$= 1.35$ mm
Curved surface area (in cm^2),
$S = 2\pi\left(\dfrac{d}{2}\right)(L)$
$= \pi dL = \pi(1.35 \times 10^{-1})(7.5)$
$\Rightarrow \quad S = 3.1808\text{ cm}^2$
Rounding off to two significant digits, $S = 3.18\text{ cm}^2$

2 (0.1) Least count of vernier calliper

$LC = 1\ MSD - 1\ VSD$ ... (i)

$\Rightarrow$ 20 divisions of vernier scale = 18 division of main scale

$\therefore 1\ VSD = \frac{18}{20}\ MSD = 0.9\ mm$ [From Eq. (i)]

$\Rightarrow LC = 1\ MSD - 1\ VSD$
$= 1\ mm - 0.9\ mm = 0.1\ mm$

3 (12) $l = a^2 m^3 n^{\frac{1}{2}}$

So, $\frac{\Delta l}{l} = \frac{2\Delta a}{a} + \frac{3\Delta m}{m} + \frac{1}{2}\frac{\Delta n}{n}$

Here, a is constant.

So, $\frac{\Delta l}{l} \times 100 = \frac{3\Delta m}{m} \times 100 + \frac{1}{2}\frac{\Delta n}{n} \times 100$

$\Rightarrow 18 = 3 \times 4 + \frac{1}{2}\left(\frac{\Delta n}{n} \times 100\right)$

$\Rightarrow \frac{\Delta n}{n} \times 100 = 12\%$

4 (150) We have,

$\bar{x} = \frac{1.19 + 1.20 + 1.23 + 1.22}{4}$

$\Rightarrow \bar{x} = 1.21$

So, $|\bar{x} - x_1| = 0.02$
$|\bar{x} - x_2| = 0.01$
$|\bar{x} - x_3| = 0.02$
$|\bar{x} - x_4| = 0.01$

Then, $\Delta x = \frac{0.02 + 0.01 + 0.02 + 0.01}{4}$
$= 0.015$

So, percentage error $= \frac{0.015}{1.21} \times 100$
$= \frac{150}{121}\%$

$\therefore x = 150$

5 (45) Volume of sphere, $V = \frac{4}{3}\pi R^3$

Percentage error in volume,

$\frac{\Delta V}{V} \times 100 = 3 \times \frac{\Delta R}{R} \times 100$
$= 3 \times \frac{0.75}{5} \times 100 = 45\%$

Hence, $x = 45$

6 (24) For the two system of units

$N_1 u_1 = N_2 u_2$

$\Rightarrow 120 \frac{kg}{m^3} = N_2 \frac{40\ g}{(20\ cm)^3}$

$\Rightarrow N_2 = \frac{120 \times 10^3 \times (20)^3}{10^6 \times 40} = 24$

7 (1) Speed of wave produced in water, $v = \lambda^\alpha g^\beta \rho^\gamma$ ...(i)

$[LT^{-1}] = [L]^\alpha [LT^{-2}]^\beta [ML^{-3}]^\gamma$
$= [M^\gamma L^{\alpha + \beta - 3\gamma} T^{-2\beta}]$

Comparing the powers, we get

$\gamma = 0, -2\beta = -1 \Rightarrow \beta = \frac{1}{2}$

$\alpha + \beta - 3\gamma = 1$

$\Rightarrow \alpha + \frac{1}{2} - 3(0) = 1 \Rightarrow \alpha = \frac{1}{2}$

So, $\alpha + \beta + \gamma = \frac{1}{2} + \frac{1}{2} + 0 = 1$

8 (3) Dimensions of $A = [MLT^{-2}]$, $D = [T^{-1}]$

Dimensions of $AD = [MLT^{-2}][T^{-1}]$
$= [MLT^{-3}]$

Hence, the value of a is 3.

9 (5.4) Time period is given by, $T = \frac{t}{n}$

Further, $T = 2\pi\sqrt{\frac{L}{g}}$

$\Rightarrow g = \frac{4\pi^2 L}{T^2} = \frac{4\pi^2 L}{\left(\frac{t}{n}\right)^2} = \frac{4\pi^2 n^2 L}{t^2}$

$\Rightarrow g \propto \frac{L}{t^2}$

Percentage error in the value of g is

$\frac{\Delta g}{g} \times 100 = \frac{\Delta L}{L} \times 100 + 2\frac{\Delta t}{t} \times 100$
$= \frac{0.1}{25} \times 100 + 2 \times \frac{1}{40} \times 100$
$= 0.4 + 5 = 5.4\%$

10 (4) Here, $q = cV$, $c = \frac{q}{V} = \frac{q^2}{W}$ $\left[\text{as } V = \frac{W}{q}\right]$

So, $[x] \to [c] = \left[\frac{Q^2}{ML^2T^{-2}}\right]$
$= [M^{-1}L^{-2}T^2Q^2]$

and $F = Bil\sin\theta$, $[B] = \left[\frac{F}{il}\right]$

So, $[z] \to [B] = \left[\frac{MLT^{-2}}{QT^{-1}L}\right] = [MT^{-1}Q^{-1}]$

But as it, $x = 3yz^2$

i.e. $y = \frac{x}{(3z^2)}$

So, $[y] = \frac{[M^{-1}L^{-2}T^2Q^2]}{[MT^{-1}Q^{-1}]^2}$

or $[y] = [M^{-3}L^{-2}T^4Q^4]$

$[M^{-3}T^{-2}T^X Q^4] = [M^{-3}T^{-2}T^4Q^4]$

Thus, $x = 4$

NCERT Exemplar Questions

1 (*b*) In 0.06900, the underlined zeros are not significant. Hence, number of significant figures are four (6900).

2 (*c*) Sum of the given numbers
$= 436.22 + 227.2 + 0.301 = 663.821$

Amongst the given numbers, the least decimal places is in the number 227.2, i.e. 1. So, the final sum should be rounded off up to one decimal point, i.e. 663.8

4 (*c*) Density of the material

$= \frac{\text{Mass}}{\text{Volume}} = \frac{4.237g}{2.5\ cm^3}$

$= 1.6948\ gcm^{-3}$

$\therefore$ Density $= 1.7\ g\ cm^{-3}$

5 (*a*) Given, length, $l = (16.2 \pm 0.1)$ cm

Breadth, $b = (10.1 \pm 0.1)$ cm

Area, $A = l \times b$
$= (16.2\ cm) \times (10.1\ cm)$

$\therefore = 163.62\ cm^2$

Rounding off up to three significant digits, area

$A = 164\ cm^2$

$\therefore \frac{\Delta A}{A} = \frac{\Delta l}{l} + \frac{\Delta b}{b} = \frac{0.1}{16.2} + \frac{0.1}{10.1}$

$\Rightarrow \Delta A = A \times \frac{2.63}{163.62}$

$= 163.62 \times \frac{2.63}{163.62} = 2.63\ cm^2$

or $\Delta A = 3\ cm^2$

(by rounding off to one significant figure)

$\therefore$ Area, $A = A \pm \Delta A = (164 \pm 3)\ cm^2$

6 (c) Tension = Force

$\therefore$ Dimensional formula of tension $= [MLT^{-2}]$

Surface tension $= \dfrac{\text{Force}}{\text{Length}}$

$\therefore$ Dimensional formula of surface tension is

$$= \frac{[MLT^{-2}]}{[L]} = [ML^0T^{-2}]$$

7 (a) Given, $A = 2.5\ ms^{-1} \pm 0.5\ ms^{-1}$, $B = 0.10\ s \pm 0.01 s$

Let $x = AB = (2.5)(0.10) = 0.25$ m

$$\because \frac{\Delta x}{x} = \frac{\Delta A}{A} + \frac{\Delta B}{B} = \frac{0.5}{2.5} + \frac{0.01}{0.10}$$

$$= \frac{0.05 + 0.025}{0.25} = \frac{0.075}{0.25}$$

$\Rightarrow \Delta x = 0.075 = 0.08$ m, (rounding off up to two significant figures.)

$\therefore \quad AB = x + \Delta x = (0.25 \pm 0.08)$ m

8 (c) Given, Young's modulus, $Y = 1.9 \times 10^{11}\ N\,m^{-2}$

$1 N = 10^5$ dyne and $1\ m^2 = 10^4\ cm^2$

$\therefore Y = 1.9 \times 10^{11} \times 10^5 / (100)^2$

$\Rightarrow Y = 1.9 \times 10^{12}$ dyne cm^{-2}

9 (d) Given,

We can write energy E as

$$E \propto p^a A^b T^c$$

$$\Rightarrow \quad E = kp^a A^b T^c$$

where, k is dimensionless constant of proportionality.

Dimensions of $[E] = [ML^2T^{-2}]$

and $[p] = [MLT^{-1}]$

$[A] = [L^2]$

$[T] = [T]$

$[E] = [k][p]^a[A]^b[T]^c$

Putting all the dimensions, we get

$$[ML^2T^{-2}] = [MLT^{-1}]^a[L^2]^b[T]^c$$

$$= [M^aL^{2b+a}T^{-a+c}]$$

By principle of homogeneity of dimensions,

$$a = 1, 2b + a = 2$$

$\Rightarrow \quad 2b + 1 = 2 \Rightarrow b = 1/2$,

$-a + c = -2$

$\Rightarrow \quad c = -2 + a = -2 + 1 = -1$

Hence, $\quad E = [pA^{1/2}T^{-1}]$

10 (c) The given expression is

$$P = EL^2m^{-5}G^{-2}$$

Dimensions of energy,

$$E = [ML^2T^{-2}]$$

Angular momentum,

$$L = [ML^2T^{-1}]$$

Mass, $m = [M]$

Gravitational constant,

$$G = [M^{-1}L^3T^{-2}]$$

Substituting dimensions of each term in the given expression,

$$P = [ML^2T^{-2}] \times [ML^2T^{-1}]^2 \times [M]^{-5} \times [M^{-1}L^3T^{-2}]^{-2}$$

$$= [M^{1+2-5+2}L^{2+4-6}T^{-2-2+4}]$$

$$= [M^0L^0T^0]$$

Therefore, P is a dimensionless quantity.

Past Exams Questions

1 (b) Given, $F = \alpha t^2 + \beta t$

We know that, dimensions on the both sides will be the same, i.e.,

$$[F] = [\alpha t^2] = [\beta t]$$

$\Rightarrow [\alpha][T^2] = [ML^1T^{-2}]$

$\Rightarrow \quad \alpha = [M^1L^1T^{-4}]$

and $[\beta][T] = [M^1LT^{-2}]$

$\Rightarrow \quad \beta = [M^1L^1T^{-3}]$

(a) $\dfrac{[\beta t]}{[\alpha]} = \dfrac{[M^1L^1T^{-2}]}{[M^1L^1T^{-4}]} = [T^{+2}]$

(b) $\dfrac{[\alpha t]}{[\beta]} = \dfrac{[M^1L^1T^{-4}][T]}{[M^1L^1T^{-3}]} = [M^0L^0T^0]$

Hence, option (b) is correct.

2 (a) Strain and angle are dimensionless quantities as solid angle.

Arc has dimension of length.

Stress has dimension of pressure.

3 (b) Given, 1 MSD = 0.1 mm

$(N + 1)$ VSD = N MSD

$$\therefore \quad 1\text{ VSD} = \left(\frac{N}{N+1}\right)\text{MSD}$$

Least count or vernier constant,

$$1\text{ MSD} - 1\text{ VSD} = \left[1 - \frac{N}{N+1}\right]\text{MSD}$$

$$= \left(\frac{1}{N+1}\right)\text{MSD} = \left(\frac{0.1}{N+1}\right)\text{mm}$$

$$= \frac{1}{100(N+1)}\text{ cm}$$

5 (c) Area = Length × Breadth

$= 55.3 \times 25 = 1382.5$

$= 13.825 \times 10^2 = 13.83 \times 10^2$

$= 13.8 \times 10^2 = 14 \times 10^2$

6 (c) As we know that, magnetic flux

$$\phi_B = BA$$

$$[\phi] = [ML^2T^{-2}A^{-1}]$$

Dimensions of self induction,

$$[L] = [ML^2T^{-2}A^{-2}]$$

Dimensions of magnetic permeability, $\mu_0 = [MLT^{-2}A^{-2}]$

Dimensions of electrical permittivity

$$\varepsilon = [M^{-1}L^{-1}T^4A^2]$$

So, the correct option is (c).

7 (b) Energy depends on force, acceleration and time as,

$$[E] = [F]^a[a]^b[T]^c$$

$$\Rightarrow [ML^2T^{-2}] = [MLT^{-2}]^a[LT^{-2}]^b[T]^c$$

$$\Rightarrow [ML^2T^{-2}] = [M]^a[L]^{a+b}[T]^{-2a-2b+c}$$

Comparing the powers of M, L and T on both sides, we get

$$a = 1, a + b = 2$$

and $\quad -2a - 2b + c = -2$

$\Rightarrow 1 + b = 2 \Rightarrow b = 1$

$\Rightarrow -2(1) - 2(1) + c = -2 \Rightarrow c = 2$

The dimensions of the energy are $[F]^1[a]^1[T]^2$.

9 (c) The rate of heat flow through a conductor of length L and area of cross-section A is given by

$$\frac{dQ}{dt} = KA\frac{\Delta T}{L}\ \text{J/s or watt}$$

where, K = coefficient of thermal conductivity and

ΔT = change in temperature

$$\Rightarrow \quad K = \frac{L}{A\Delta T}\frac{dQ}{dt}$$

$$\therefore \text{Unit of } K = \frac{\text{metre}}{(\text{metre})^2 \times \text{kelvin}} \times \text{watt}$$

$$= Wm^{-1}K^{-1}$$

10 (*b*) We know that,

$$\Delta Q = ms\Delta T$$

$$\Rightarrow \quad s = \frac{\Delta Q}{m\Delta T}$$

$$\Rightarrow \quad [s] = \frac{[Q]}{[m][\Delta T]}$$

$$= \frac{[ML^2T^{-2}]}{[M]\ [K]} = [L^2T^{-2}K^{-1}]$$

Thus, Statement I is correct.

Again, using ideal gas equation

$$pV = nRT \Rightarrow R = \frac{pV}{nT}$$

$$\Rightarrow \quad [R] = \frac{[p][V]}{[n]\ [T]} = \frac{[ML^{-1}T^{-2}]\ [L^3]}{[mol]\ [K]}$$

$$= [ML^2T^{-2}\ mol^{-1}\ K^{-1}]$$

Thus, Statement II is incorrect.

11 (*c*) Compare the given equation with standard equation of standing wave.

$y = A \sin \omega t \cos kx$

Thus, $\omega = \frac{2\pi n}{\lambda}, k = \frac{2\pi}{\lambda}$

2π is dimensionless

$$[\omega] = T^{-1} = \left[\frac{n}{\lambda}\right]$$

$$[nT] = [\lambda] = [L]$$

$$[n] = \left[\frac{\lambda}{T}\right] = [\lambda\omega]$$

$$[n] = [LT^{-1}]$$

$$\Rightarrow \left[\frac{n}{\lambda}\right] = [T^{-1}]$$

Hence, $\frac{n}{\lambda}$ has dimension of T^{-1} not T.

12 (*c*) Given, $\left[x + \frac{a}{y^2}\right][y - b] = RT$

Compare with above equation,

$$\left(p + \frac{a}{V^2}\right)(V - b) = RT$$

$$[a] = [p][V^2] \Rightarrow [b] = [V]$$

$$\frac{[a]}{[b]} = \frac{[p][V^2]}{[V]} = [p][V]$$

$$p = \frac{[F]}{[A]} = \frac{[MLT^{-2}]}{[L^2]}$$

$$= [ML^{-1}T^{-2}]$$

$$V = [L^3]$$

So $\frac{[a]}{[b]} = [ML^{-1}T^{-2}][L^3]$

$$= [ML^2T^{-2}] = \text{Energy}$$

13 (*a*) Given, $v_2 = \frac{n}{m^2} v_1$

$\because$ Velocity, $v = \frac{\text{Displacement}}{\text{Time}}$

$$\therefore \quad \frac{L_2}{T_2} = \frac{n}{m^2} \cdot \frac{L_1}{T_1} \quad \text{...(i)}$$

and $\quad a_2 = \frac{a_1}{mn}$

$$\therefore \quad \frac{L_2}{T_2^2} = \frac{L_1}{T_1^2} \cdot \frac{1}{mn} \quad \text{...(ii)}$$

On dividing Eq. (ii) by Eq. (i), we get

$$\frac{L_2 / T_2^2}{L_2 / T_2} = \frac{L_1 / T_1^2 \cdot 1 / mn}{n / m^2 \cdot L_1 / T_1}$$

$$\Rightarrow \quad T_2 = \frac{n^2}{m} T_1$$

As, $\quad L_2 = \frac{T_2}{T_1} \cdot L_1 \frac{n}{m^2}$

$$= \frac{n^2}{m} L_1 \frac{n}{m^2}$$

$$= \frac{n^3}{m^3} L_1$$

14 (*b*) Given,

Equation of force,

$$F = A \cos Bx + C \sin Dt$$

Now, trigonometric ratios are dimensionless.

$\therefore [Bx] = [M^0L^0T^0]$

$\Rightarrow [B]\ [L^1] = [M^0L^0T^0]$

$\Rightarrow [B] = [M^0\ L^{-1}T^0]$ ...(i)

Similarly, $[Dt] = [M^0L^0T^0]$

$$\Rightarrow [D] = \frac{[M^0\ L^0T^0]}{[t]}$$

$$= [M^0\ L^0T^{-1}] \quad \text{...(ii)}$$

and $\quad [A] = [F] = [MLT^{-2}]$ ...(iii)

From Eqs. (i), (ii) and (iii), we get

$$\frac{[AD]}{[B]} = \frac{[MLT^{-2}][M^0L^0T^{-1}]}{[M^0L^{-1}T^0]}$$

$$= \frac{[MLT^{-3}]}{[L^{-1}]} = [ML^2T^{-3}]$$

Skill Boosters

1 (*d*) The diameter = Main scale reading + Circular scale reading × LC − Zero error

$$= 3 + 35 \times \frac{1}{2 \times 50} - (-0.03)$$

$$= 3.38 \text{ mm}$$

2 (*a*) Given, mass of the sun,

$M = 2.0 \times 10^{30}$ kg

and radius of the sun,

$R = 7.0 \times 10^8$ m

$\therefore$ Volume of the sun,

$$V = \frac{4}{3}\pi R^3 = \frac{4}{3} \times 3.14 \times (7.0 \times 10^8)^3$$

$$= 1.437 \times 10^{27} m^3$$

$\therefore$ Density of the sun,

$$\rho = \frac{M}{V} = \frac{2.0 \times 10^{30}}{1.437 \times 10^{27}}$$

$$= 1391.8 \text{ kgm}^{-3}$$

$$\cong 1.4 \times 10^3 \text{ kgm}^{-3}$$

3 (*d*) Given, LC = 0.001 cm

MSR = 5 mm = 0.5 cm

Number coinciding division on the circular scale reading VSR = 25

Zero error = − 0.004 cm

Reading obtained from the screw gauge is given as

= MSR + VSR × LC − Zero error

$= 0.5 + (25 \times -0.001) - (-0.004)$

$= 0.529$ cm

Thus, the diameter of the ball is 0.529 cm.

4 (*b*) Relation used for finding acceleration due to gravity by using a pendulum is given by

$$g = \frac{4\pi^2 l}{T^2}$$

So, percentage error in value of g will be

$$100 \times \frac{\Delta g}{g} = \left[\frac{\Delta l}{l} + \frac{2\Delta T}{T}\right] \times 100 \quad ...(i)$$

Given, $\Delta l = 0.1$ cm, $l = 55$ cm,

$\Delta T = 1$ s and T for 20 oscillations $= 30$ s

$$100 \times \frac{\Delta g}{g} = \left[\frac{0.1}{55} + 2 \times \frac{1}{30}\right] \times 100$$

Hence, percentage error in g will be

$$= \frac{10}{55} + \frac{20}{3} = 6.8\%$$

5 (b) $Y = \dfrac{F/A}{\dfrac{\Delta L}{L}}$

As, $A = \dfrac{\pi d^2}{4}$

$$\Rightarrow \quad Y = \frac{4FL}{(\pi d^2)(\Delta L)}$$

$$\frac{\Delta Y}{Y} = 2\frac{\Delta d}{d} + \frac{\Delta(\Delta L)}{\Delta L} + \frac{\Delta L}{L}$$

$$= 2 \times \frac{0.001}{0.05} + \frac{0.001}{0.125} + \frac{0.1}{110}$$

$$= 0.0489$$

$$Y = \frac{4FL}{\pi d^2(\Delta L)}$$

$$= \frac{4 \times 50 \times 1.1}{\pi(0.05 \times 10^{-2})^2 \times 0.125 \times 10^{-2}}$$

$$= 2.24 \times 10^{11} \text{ N/m}^2$$

$$\Delta Y = 0.0489 \times 2.24 \times 10^{11}$$

$$= 0.109 \times 10^{11} \text{ N/m}^2$$

6 (c) Given, $I = (e^{1000V/T} - 1)$ mA

$dV = \pm 0.01$ V, $T = 300$ K,

$$I = 5 \text{ mA}$$

$$\Rightarrow I = e^{1000V/T} - 1$$

$$I + 1 = e^{1000V/T}$$

Taking log on both sides, we get

$$\log(I+1) = \frac{1000V}{T}$$

$$\Rightarrow \frac{d(I+1)}{I+1} = \frac{1000}{T} dV$$

$$\frac{dI}{I+1} = \frac{1000}{T} dV$$

$$\Rightarrow \quad dI = \frac{1000}{T} \times (I+1) dV$$

$$\Rightarrow \quad dI = \frac{1000}{300} \times (5+1) \times 0.01$$

$$= 0.2 \text{ mA}$$

So, error in the value of current is 0.2 mA.

7 (c) Given, mass of the box,

$m = 2.3$ kg

Mass of first gold piece,

$$m_1 = 20.15 \text{ g} = 0.02015 \text{ kg}$$

Mass of second gold piece,

$$m_2 = 20.17 \text{ g} = 0.02017 \text{ kg}$$

Total mass of the box,

$$M = m + m_1 + m_2$$

$$= 2.3 + 0.02015 + 0.02017$$

$$= 2.34032 \text{ kg}$$

Rounding off the total mass of the box upto 1 decimal place, we get

Total mass of the box, $M = 2.3$ kg

Similarly, difference in masses of gold pieces,

$$\Delta m = m_2 - m_1$$

$$= 20.17 - 20.15$$

$$= 0.02 \text{ g}$$

Since, the masses of two gold pieces have two decimal places.

Therefore, the final result is corrected upto two decimal places.

8 (c) Let x, y and z be the dimensions of ρ, S and f.

So, $\quad d = K\rho^x S^y f^z \quad$ ... (i)

When K is the proportionality constant which has no dimensions.

Putting the dimensions in Eq. (i) we get

$$M^0L^1T^0 = [ML^{-3}]^x [MT^{-3}]^y [T^{-1}]^z$$

$$= M^{x+y}L^{-3x}T^{-3y-z}$$

Equating the powers of M, L and T, we get

$$x + y = 0 \Rightarrow x = -y$$

$$-3x = 1 \Rightarrow x = -\frac{1}{3}$$

or $\quad y = \dfrac{1}{3}$

From Eq. (i),

$$d \propto S^y$$

$$d \propto S^{1/3}$$

Hence, $\quad n = 3$

9 (a) Given, $T \propto p^a d^b E^c$

$$T = Kp^a d^b E^c$$

$K =$ Constant and dimensionless quantity.

$$\therefore [T] = [ML^{-1}T^{-2}]^a [ML^{-3}]^b [ML^2T^{-2}]^c$$

$$[T] = [M^{a+b+c} L^{-a-3b+2c} T^{-2a-2c}]$$

Equating the powers of M, L, T on both sides, we get,

$0 = a + b + c \quad$ ... (i)

$0 = -a - 3b + 2c \quad$ ... (ii)

$1 = -2a - 2c \quad$ ... (iii)

From Eqs. (i), (ii) and (iii), we get

$$a = -\frac{5}{6}, \; b = \frac{1}{2}, \; c = \frac{1}{3}$$

02

Scan for **Physics Through Concept Master** *Videos*

Motion in a Straight Line

Topicwise No. of Ques asked in 5 Years (NEET)

Topics	No. of Questions				
	2024	2023	2022	2021	2020
Average Velocity and Average Speed	–	1	–	–	–
Instantaneous Velocity and Speed	–	–	–	–	–
Acceleration	–	–	–	–	–
Kinematic Equations for Uniformly Accelerated Motion	1	2	2	2	2

Special Type of Ques Asked In 5 Years (NEET)

Types	Years				
	2024	2023	2022	2021	2020
A-R	–	–	–	–	–
Statement Based	–	–	–	–	–
Matching	–	–	–	–	–

Last 5 Years Weigtage (NEET)

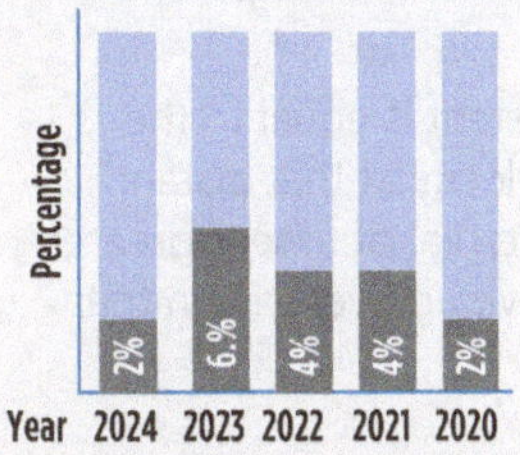

- **Motion** is the change in position of an object with respect to time.
- The study of motion without consideration of its cause is called **kinematics**.
- The study of motion of objects along a straight line is known as **rectilinear motion**.
- An object in motion can be considered as point object when the distance travelled by it, is very large (in a reasonable duration of time) compared to the size of object.

*Position, Path Length and Displacement

- The set of axes and a reference point, both are required to specify **the position of an object**. The position of an object is described by a coordinate system consisting of three mutually perpendicular axes (x, y and z-axes).
- The point of intersection of three axes (i.e. x, y and z-axes) is called origin O and serves as **reference point**.
- A **frame of reference** is a set of coordinates that can be used to determine positions and velocities of object in that frame.
- If one or more coordinates of an object change with time, we can say that **object is in motion**. Otherwise, the **object is said to be at rest** with respect to the frame of reference.
- **Path length** Total length of the path traversed by an object during motion is called **distance** or **total path length**.

** This topic is not included in latest rationalised NCERT. But it is given in latest NEET syllabus.*

As shown in figure, suppose a body moves from position A to B through C, then distance covered $= AC + CB$

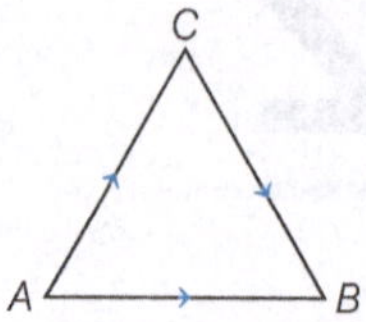

- It is a scalar quantity which has magnitude only and no direction.
- It cannot be negative or zero.

- **Displacement** The shortest distance between the initial and final positions of any object is called its displacement.

  In above figure, displacement = **AB**.

  It is denoted by Δx and is given by $\Delta x = x_2 - x_1$

  where, x_1 and x_2 are the positions of the object at time t_1 and t_2.
  - Displacement is a vector quantity because it has magnitude and direction both.
  - It may be positive, negative or zero.
  - Displacement does not depend on the choice of the origin of coordinate system.
  - The magnitude of displacement may or may not be equal to the path length traversed by an object.
  - The magnitude of displacement travelled by an object in a given interval of time is less than or equal to the distance travelled in that time interval.

*Average Velocity and Average Speed

- **Average velocity** is defined as the change in position or displacement Δx divided by the time interval Δt, in which the displacement occurs. NEET 2019

$$\bar{v} = \frac{x_2 - x_1}{t_2 - t_1} = \frac{\Delta x}{\Delta t}$$

  where, x_2 and x_1 are the positions of the object at time t_2 and t_1, respectively.
  - It can be positive or negative depending upon the sign of the displacement. It is zero, if the displacement is zero.
  - The SI unit of average velocity is ms^{-1}.

- **Average speed** is defined as the total path length divided by the total time interval during which the motion has taken place.

$$\text{Average speed} = \frac{\text{Total path length}}{\text{Total time interval}}$$ NEET 2023

  - It is always positive and its SI unit is m/s.

- If the motion of an object is along a straight line and in the same direction, the magnitude of displacement is equal to the total path length. In that case, the magnitude of average velocity is equal to the average speed.
- Average speed can be greater than or equal to magnitude of average velocity.

Marks Maximiser

Different Cases of Average Velocity

- When particle moves with speed v_1 upto half time of its total motion and for rest ot the time it is moving with speed v_2, then average velocity $v_{av} = \frac{v_1 + v_2}{2}$

  Clearly, average speed is the arithmetic mean of the individual speed.
- When particle moves the first half of a distance at a speed of v_1 and second half of the distance at speed v_2, then average velocity $v_{av} = \frac{2v_1v_2}{v_1 + v_2}$

  Clearly, the average speed is the harmonic mean of the individual speeds.
- When particle covers one third distance at speed v_1, next one third at speed v_2 and last one third at speed v_3, then average velocity, $v_{av} = \frac{3v_1v_2v_3}{v_1v_2 + v_2v_3 + v_1v_3}$.

Instantaneous Velocity and Speed

- **Instantaneous velocity** The velocity of moving object at particular instant of time is called instantaneous velocity.

  It is equal to limiting value of the average velocity in small time interval taken around that instant, when the time interval approaches zero. In other words, $v = \lim_{\Delta t \to 0} \frac{\Delta x}{\Delta t} = \frac{dx}{dt}$

  Also, $\frac{dx}{dt}$ is the rate of change of position with respect to time at that instant.

- **Instantaneous speed** The speed of moving object at particular instant of time is called instantaneous speed.

  If object moves a distance of Δx in time interval Δt, then its average speed $= \frac{\Delta x}{\Delta t}$

  $\therefore$ Instantaneous speed $= \lim_{t \to 0} \frac{\Delta x}{\Delta t}$

- If an object moving along a straight line covers equal distances in equal intervals of time, it is said to be in **uniform motion along a straight line**.

  For uniform motion, instantaneous velocity is same as the average velocity at all instants.
- Instantaneous speed or simply speed is the magnitude of instantaneous velocity.
- If the instantaneous speed at an instant is equal to the magnitude of the instantaneous velocity at that instant, then average speed over a finite interval of time is greater or equal to the magnitude of the average velocity in that interval of time.

** This topic is not included in latest rationalised NCERT. But it is given in latest NEET and JEE syllabus.*

Acceleration

- The rate of change in velocity of a moving object is called **acceleration**.

  $$\text{Acceleration} = \frac{\text{Change in velocity}}{\text{Time}}$$

  - It can be positive, negative or zero.
  - It is a vector quantity and its SI unit is m/s^2.

  The types of acceleration are given below

- **Average acceleration** The ratio of net change in velocity of a moving object to the time taken for change is called average acceleration.

  Average acceleration $\bar{a}$ over a time interval is given as the change of velocity divided by the time interval.

  $$\bar{a} = \frac{v_2 - v_1}{t_2 - t_1} = \frac{\Delta v}{\Delta t}$$

  where, v_2 and v_1 are the instantaneous velocities at time t_2 and t_1, respectively.

- **Instantaneous acceleration** It is the rate of change in velocity of moving object at particular instant of time.

  It is equal to the limiting value of the average acceleration of the object in small time interval around that instant, when time interval approaches to zero.

  For Concept Master Video

  $$a = \lim_{\Delta t \to 0} \frac{\Delta v}{\Delta t} = \frac{dv}{dt} = \frac{d^2x}{dt^2}$$

- **Uniform acceleration** A moving object is said to have uniform acceleration, if magnitude and direction of acceleration remain constant.
- **Non-uniform acceleration** A moving object is said to have non-uniform acceleration, if magnitude and direction of acceleration or any of them changes with time.

Kinematic Equations for Uniformly Accelerated Motion

For uniformly accelerated motion, kinematic equations are simple relations that relate displacement x, initial velocity u, final velocity v and acceleration a.

(i) $v = u + at$

(ii) $x = ut + \frac{1}{2}at^2$ NEET 2022

(iii) $v^2 = u^2 + 2ax$ NEET 2023, 20

Note The displacement travelled in nth second is given by

$$x_n = u + \frac{a}{2}(2n - 1)$$ NEET 2021

- For constant acceleration, we can write average velocity as $\bar{v} = \frac{v + u}{2}$.
- **Free Fall** When an object is dropped from a height above the surface of earth, then it falls under the influence (if air resistance is considered negligible) of earth gravity, this motion is called free fall.

  The acceleration of object falling freely is equal to the acceleration due to gravity g.

  - For a freely falling body, the equations of motion are

    (i) $v = u + gt$

    (ii) $s = ut + \frac{1}{2}gt^2$ NEET 2019

    (iii) $v^2 - u^2 = 2gh$

  - For a body falling freely under the action of gravity, g is taken as positive.
  - For a body thrown vertically upward, g is taken as negative.
  - When a body is just dropped, initial velocity $u = 0$.

- For a body thrown vertically up with initial velocity u,
  - Maximum height reached, $h = \frac{u^2}{2g}$ NEET 2023
  - Time of ascent = Time of descent $= \frac{u}{g}$
  - Total time of flight $= \frac{2u}{g}$
  - Velocity of fall at the point of projection $= u$
  - Velocity attained by a body dropped from height h,

    $$v = \sqrt{2gh}$$

- **Galileo's law of odd number** According to this law, "the distances traversed during equal intervals of time, by a body falling from rest, stand to one another in the same ratio as the odd numbers beginning with unity. i.e. 1 : 3 : 5 : 7......... .
- When brakes are applied to a moving vehicle, the distance travelled by it before stopping is called **stopping distance**.

  $$\text{Stopping distance, } d_s = \frac{-v_0^2}{2a}$$

  where, v_0 = initial velocity and a = deceleration.

- For one-dimensional motion, basic equations of velocity and acceleration can be written as

  (i) $v = \frac{dx}{dt}$

  (ii) $a = \frac{dv}{dt}$

  (iii) $ds = v dt$

  (iv) $dv = a dt$ or $v dv = a dx$

Marks Maximiser

Different Cases of Uniform Acceleration Motion

- If a body starts from rest and moves with uniform acceleration, then distance covered by the body in t second is proportional to t^2 (i.e. $s \propto t^2$).
  The ratio of distance covered in 1s, 2s and 3s is 1 : 4 : 9.
- If a body starts from rest and moves with uniform acceleration, distance covered by the body in nth second is proportional to $(2n-1)$ [i.e., $s_n \propto (2n-1)$]
  The ratio of distance covered in 1s, 2s and 3s is 1 : 3 : 5.
- A body moving with a velocity u is stopped by the application of brakes after covering a distance s. If the same body moves with velocity nu and same braking force is applied on it, then it will come to rest after covering a distance of $n^2 s$. We can say that if u becomes n times, then s becomes n^2 times.

Graphs Related to Motion of an Object in a Straight Line

Some important graphs related to the motion of an object in a straight line are shown in the table given below

Position-Time Graphs

Different Conditions	Graphs
(i) Stationary object (Body at rest)	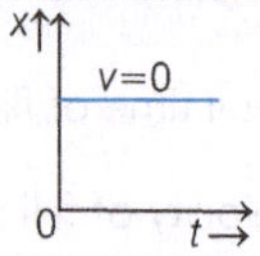
(ii) An object is in uniform motion with positive velocity	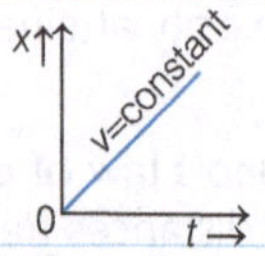
(iii) An object is in uniform motion with negative velocity	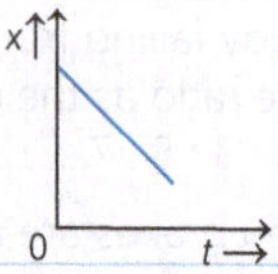
(iv) Motion of an object with positive acceleration	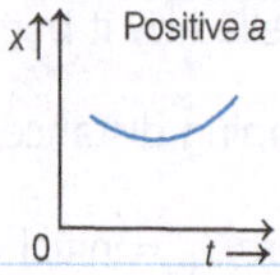
(v) Motion of an object with negative acceleration	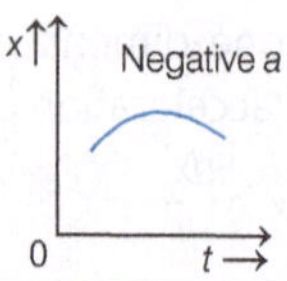
(vi) Motion of an object with zero acceleration For Concept Master Video	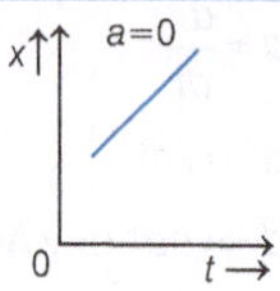

Important Points related to Position-Time Graphs, for Motion of an Object in a Straight Line

- Position-time graph gives instantaneous value of displacement at any instant.
- Slope of position-time graph gives velocity.

Velocity-Time Graphs

Different Conditions	Graphs
(i) Motion in positive direction with positive acceleration	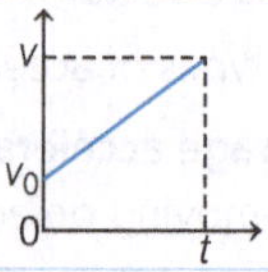
(ii) Motion in positive direction with negative acceleration	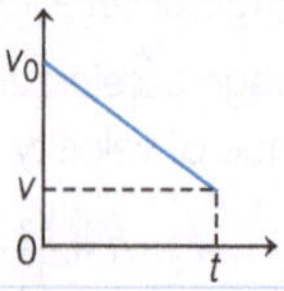
(iii) Motion in negative direction with negative acceleration	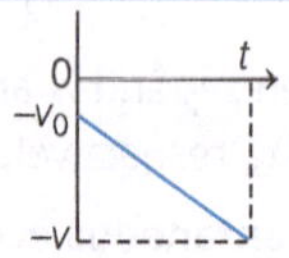
(iv) Motion of an object with negative acceleration that changes direction at time t_1 (Between 0 to t_1, it moves in the + ve x-direction and between t_1 and t_2 it moves in opposite direction.)	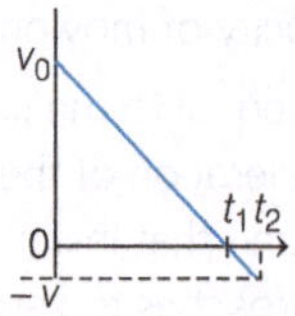

Important Points related to Velocity-Time Graphs, for Motion of an Object in a Straight Line

- In velocity-time graph, acceleration at an instant is the slope of the tangent to the velocity-time curve at that instant.
- In velocity-time graph, area under the velocity-time curve represents the displacement over a given time interval.

Acceleration-Time Graphs

Different Conditions	Graphs
(i) When the object is at rest or moving with uniform velocity	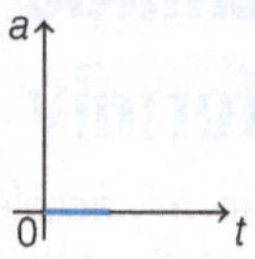
(ii) When the object is moving with uniform acceleration	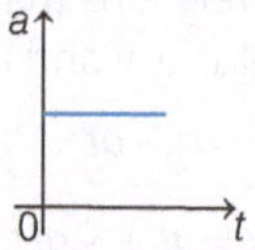
(iii) When the object is moving with non-uniform acceleration	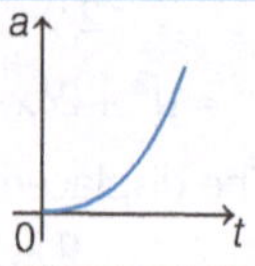

*Relative Velocity

- The relative velocity of object A with respect to object B is defined as the time rate of change of relative position of object A with respect to object B.
- If two objects A and B are moving with velocities v_A and v_B in one-dimension, then relative velocity of object A with respect to object B is as follows
  - If both objects are moving in the **same direction**, then
    $$v_{AB} = v_A - v_B$$
  - If both objects are moving in **opposite direction**, then
    $$v_{AB} = v_A - (-v_B), \quad v_{AB} = v_A + v_B$$
- Position-time graphs of two objects with equal velocities are shown here. They are straight lines parallel to each other. If $v_A = v_B$, then relative velocity, $v_{AB} = v_A - v_B = 0$

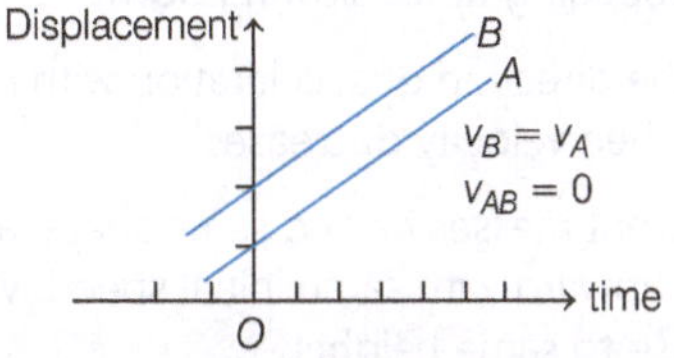

Marks Maximiser

Different Cases in Relative Velocity

- Position-time graph of two objects with unequal velocities and $v_A > v_B$, are shown below,

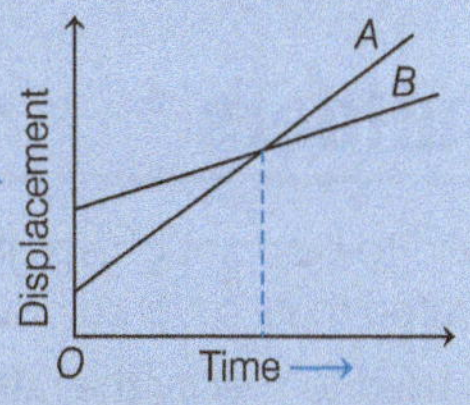

- Position-time graph of two objects with velocities in opposite directions are shown below.
  Here, $v_{BA} = -v_{AB}$

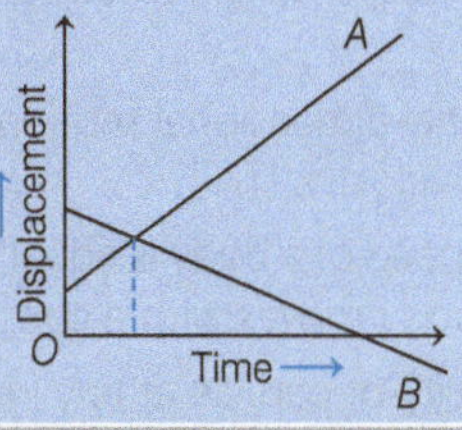

Caution Points

- The change in speed of a particle depends on the directions of velocity and acceleration and is independent of the choice of origin and axis.
- A particle is speeding up or speeding down is not decided by the sign of acceleration. A particle with increasing speed may have negative acceleration.
- A particle has zero velocity does not mean its zero acceleration. The particle is momentarily at rest, but may have non-zero acceleration.

PYQ Notes

1. If a body covers different distances $d_1, d_2, d_3, \ldots$ with different speeds $v_1, v_2, v_3, \ldots$ respectively, then average speed of the body is given by **[JEE Main 2023]**
   $$\Rightarrow \quad v_{av} = \frac{d_1 + d_2 + d_3 \ldots}{\frac{d_1}{v_1} + \frac{d_2}{v_2} + \frac{d_3}{v_3} + \ldots}$$
2. If the displacement-time graphs of two moving objects A and B are given as

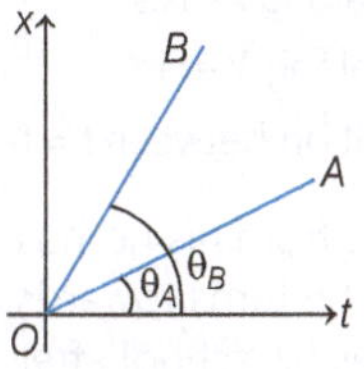

   Then, $\theta_B > \theta_A$
   $\Rightarrow \tan\theta_B > \tan\theta_A$
   $\therefore$ (Slope of B) > (Slope of A)
   $\Rightarrow$ Velocity of B > Velocity of A
   Also, $\dfrac{v_B}{v_A} = \dfrac{\tan\theta_B}{\tan\theta_A}$ **[NEET 2022]**
3. The slope of v^2 *versus* x graph gives two times of acceleration.

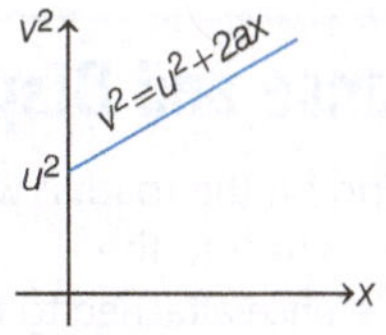

   $\therefore$ Slope $= 2a$ **[JEE Main 2021]**
4. If a body travels a certain distance with different speeds $v_1, v_2, v_3 \ldots$ in different time intervals, t_1, t_2, t_3 .... respectively, then average speed is given by
   $$v_{av} = \frac{v_1 t_1 + v_2 t_2 + v_3 t_3 + \ldots}{t_1 + t_2 + t_3 + \ldots}$$ **[NEET 2019]**

* *This topic is not included in latest rationalised NCERT, but it is given in latest NEET syllabus.*

Step by Step

Mastering NCERT

- Concept Builders
- Topical Questions
- Assertion and Reason Questions
- Statement Based
- Matching Type
- Numerical Type
- NCERT Exemplar
- Past Exams MCQs
- Skill Boosters

Concept Builders

1 An object is said to be point object, if its size is very small as compared to its covered distance. [T/F]

2 Which term is used to specify the reference to describe the position of an object in kinematics?

3 The displacement of an object can be either equal or .... (greater/less) than the distance travelled by the object.

4 A particle in one-dimensional motion have zero speed and non-zero velocity. [T/F]

5 The average speed of a body is equal to its instantaneous speed, if the body moves with a constant speed. [T/F]

6 The zero velocity of particle at any instant implies zero acceleration at that instant. [T/F]

7 Speedometer measures the .... of a vehicle. (instantaneous speed/average speed)

8 When a body moves with constant velocity, its average velocity over any time interval is same as is instantaneous velocity. [T/F]

9 A body is always at rest in a frame that is fixed to the body itself. [T/F]

10 The displacement of a body is zero, then the distance covered by it is necessarily zero. [T/F]

11 For which situation, the average velocity over an interval of time becomes equal to instantaneous velocity?

12 The limit of the average acceleration as the time interval Δt goes to zero is called .... (instantaneous speed/instantaneous acceleration).

13 The direction in which an object moves, can be determined by the direction of acceleration. [T/F]

14 In which type of motion, a body is said to be accelerate without speeding up or slowing down.

15 What is the direction of acceleration with respect to velocity when velocity decreases.

16 Two different masses having same shape are thrown vertically upward with same initial speed. Will both masses rise to same heights.

17 If an object thrown upward, then acceleration due to gravity is in .... direction of the motion of the object till its highest point. (same/opposite)

18 The maximum height obtained by a particle which is thrown upward, is .... $\left[gt^2 / \frac{1}{2}gt^2\right]$

19 When brakes are applied on a moving body, the distance travelled by it before stopping is .... $\left[\frac{v_0}{2a} / \frac{v_0^2}{2a}\right]$

20 Distance travelled by freely falling body in 4th second is .... m.

Topical Questions

Position, Distance and Displacement

1 For a car moving on the road, it will be considered to be at rest with respect to the **Old NCERT Pg. 40**

(a) frame of reference attached to the ground
(b) frame of reference attached to a person sitting inside the car
(c) frame of reference attached to a person outside the car
(d) None of the above

2 The coordinates of object with respect to a frame of reference at $t = 0$ s are $(-1, 0, 3)$. If at $t = 5$ s, its coordinates are $(-1, 0, 4)$, then the object is in **Old NCERT Pg. 40**

(a) motion along Z-axis
(b) motion along X-axis
(c) motion along Y-axis
(d) rest position between $t = 0$ s and $t = 5$ s

3. Snehit starts from his home and walks 50 m towards north, then he turns towards east and walks 40 m and then reaches his school after moving 20 m towards south. Then his displacement from his home to school is **Old NCERT Pg. 40**

(a) 50 m (b) 110 m
(c) 80 m (d) 40 m

4. A particle covers half of the circular path of radius R.The displacement and the path length of the particle are **Old NCERT Pg. 40**

(a) $2R, \pi R$ (b) $2\pi R, 0$ (c) $\frac{\pi R}{2}, 2R$ (d) $\pi R, R$

5. A particle is moving without changing its direction along X-axis, then **Old NCERT Pg. 40**

(a) the displacement is greater than the path length
(b) the path length is greater than the displacement
(c) the displacement is equal to the path length
(d) the displacement is along X-axis and path length is along Y-axis

6. A man is walking along the boundary of a square park of side a metre. The ratio of distance to displacement covered by the man after completing one and half revolution along its boundaries is **Old NCERT Pg. 40**

(a) $\sqrt{3}:2$ (b) $1:2\sqrt{3}$
(c) $1:3\sqrt{2}$ (d) $3\sqrt{2}:1$

Average Velocity and Average Speed

7. A person travels along a straight road for the first half-time with speed 4 m/s and the next half-time with speed 8 m/s. The average velocity of the man is **Old NCERT Pg. 42**

(a) 4 m/s (b) 6 m/s (c) 8m/s (d) 12 m/s

8. A particle moving with uniform acceleration has average velocities x, y and z over the successive intervals of time p, q and r respectively, then the value of $\frac{x-y}{y-z}$ is **Old NCERT Pg. 42**

(a) $\frac{p-q}{q-r}$ (b) $\frac{p-q}{p+r}$ (c) $\frac{p+q}{q-r}$ (d) $\frac{p+q}{q+r}$

9. A cyclist moving on a circular track of radius 40 m completes half a revolution in 40 s. Its average velocity is **Old NCERT Pg. 42**

(a) zero (b) 2 ms^{-1} (c) 4π ms^{-1} (d) 8π ms^{-1}

10. A runner starts from O and comes back to O following path $OQRO$ in 1h. What is net displacement and average speed? **Old NCERT Pg. 42**

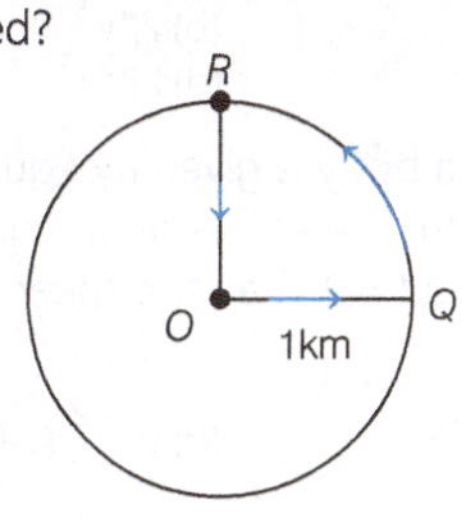

(a) 0,3.57 km/h (b) 0,0 km/h
(c) 0,2.57 km/h (d) 0,1 km/h

11. A car is moving on a straight road from A to B for first one-fourth distance with speed 40 m/s and the next half with speed 80 m/s and the last one-fourth with speed 120 m/s. Then, the average speed of the car will be **Old NCERT Pg. 42**

(a) 49.26 m/s (b) 90.46 m/s
(c) 68.57 m/s (d) 54.26 m/s

12 Study the following statements. **Old NCERT Pg. 42**

I. The unit of average speed is same as that of velocity.
II. If one or more coordinates of an object changes with time, we say that the object is at rest with respect to the given reference frame.

Which of the following option is correct?

(a) Only I (b) Only II
(c) Both I and II (d) Neither I nor II

Instantaneous Velocity and Speed

13 If the velocity of a particle is $v = 2t + 3t^2$, then the distance travelled by it between 1s and 2s is **NCERT Pg. 14**

(a) 5m (b) 10 m
(c) 12 m (d) 15 m

14 Velocity is given by $v = 4t(1-2t)$, then find time at which velocity is maximum. **NCERT Pg. 14**

(a) 0.25 s (b) 1 s
(c) 0.45 s (d) 4 s

15 The displacement x of a particle varies with time t, $x = ae^{-pt} + be^{qt}$, where a, b, p and q are positive constants. The velocity of the particle will **NCERT Pg. 14**

(a) go on increasing with time
(b) be independent of p and q
(c) drop to zero when $p = q$
(d) go on decreasing with time

16 The motion of an object is described by $s = s_0(1-e^{-pt})$; $t \geq 0$, $s_0 > 0$, $p > 0$. With what velocity does the object start? **NCERT Pg. 14**

(a) $\sqrt{ps_0}$ (b) $\frac{s_0}{p}$ (c) $2s_0p$ (d) s_0p

17 The motion of an object is given by the equation $\frac{dv}{dt} = 4 - 2v$, where v is the speed in ms^{-1} and t is time in s. The object is at rest at $t = 0$. The speed varies with time as **NCERT Pg. 14**

(a) $2(1-e^{-2t})$ (b) $2(1+e^{-2t})$ (c) $1-e^{-2t}$ (d) $1+e^{-2t}$

18 The distance x of a particle moving in one-dimension, is related to time t by the equation $t = \sqrt{x} + 4$, where x is in metres and t in second. The displacement of the particle when its velocity is zero, will be **NCERT Pg. 14**

(a) 16 m (b) 32 m (c) 0 (d) 8 m

19 The x-t graph for motion of a car is given below. **NCERT Pg. 14**

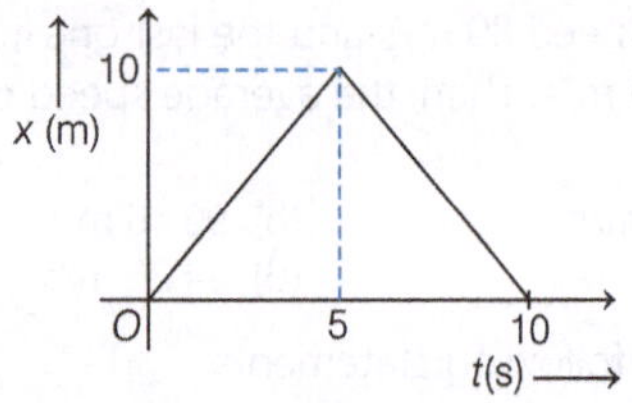

With reference to the graph, which of the given option(s) is/are incorrect?

(a) The instantaneous speed during the interval $t = 5$ s to $t = 10$ s is negative at all time instants during the interval.

(b) The velocity and the average velocity for the interval $t = 0$ s to $t = 5$ s are equal and positive.

(c) The car changes its direction of motion at $t = 5$ s.

(d) The instantaneous speed and the instantaneous velocity are positive at all time instants during the interval $t = 0$ s to $t = 5$ s.

Acceleration

20 A body starts from rest with acceleration $2\ m/s^2$ till it attains the maximum velocity, then retards to rest with $3\ m/s^2$. If total time taken is 10 s, then the maximum attained speed is **NCERT Pg. 15**

(a) 8 m/s (b) 12m/s
(c) 10 m/s (d) 4 m/s

21 A car starts from rest, attains a velocity of $18\ kmh^{-1}$ with an acceleration of $0.5\ ms^{-2}$, travels 4 km with this uniform velocity and then comes to halt with a uniform deceleration of $0.2\ ms^{-2}$. The total time of travel of the car is **NCERT Pg. 15**

(a) 853 s (b) 800 s
(c) 855 s (d) 835 s

22 Speeds of a particle at 3rd and 8th seconds are 20 m/s and 0 m/s respectively, then average acceleration between 3rd and 8th seconds will be **NCERT Pg. 15**

(a) $3\ m/s^2$ (b) $4\ m/s^2$
(c) $5 m/s^2$ (d) $6\ m/s^2$

23 The velocity of a particle is given by the expression **NCERT Pg. 15**

$$v(x) = 3x^2 - 4x$$

where, x is distance covered by the particle. The expression for acceleration is

(a) $(3x^2 - 4x)(6x - 4)$
(b) $6(3x^2 - 4x)$
(c) $(6x - 4)^2$
(d) $(3x^2 - 4x)6x$

24 A vehicle starts from rest and moves with uniform acceleration α on a straight road from time $t = 0$ to x. After that it moves with constant deceleration and stops. The average speed of the car during this process is **NCERT Pg. 16**

(a) $\frac{\alpha x}{4}$ (b) $\frac{3\alpha x}{2}$
(c) $\frac{\alpha x}{2}$ (d) αx

25 An object is moving along the path $OABO$ with constant speed, then **NCERT Pg. 16**

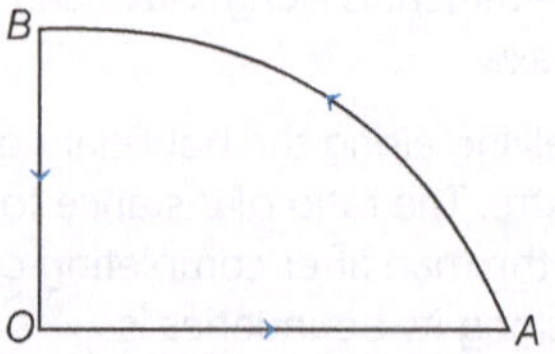

(a) the acceleration of the object while moving along to path $OABO$ is zero

(b) the acceleration of the object along the path OA and BO is zero

(c) there must be some acceleration along the path AB

(d) Both (b) and (c)

26 The motion of a particle along a straight line is described by equation $x = 8 + 12t - t^3$, where x is in metre and t in second. The retardation of the particle when its velocity becomes zero, is **NCERT Pg. 16**

(a) $24\ ms^{-2}$ (b) zero
(c) $6\ ms^{-2}$ (d) $12\ ms^{-2}$

27 A particle of unit mass undergoes one-dimensional motion such that its velocity varies according to $v(x) = 3x^{-2n}$, where x is the position of the particle. The acceleration of the particle as a function of x is given by **NCERT Pg. 16**

(a) $15nx^{-2n-1}$ (b) $-18nx^{-4n-1}$
(c) $-15nx^{-2n+1}$ (d) $-18ne^{-4n+1}$

28 The relation between time and distance is $t = \alpha x^2 + \beta x$, where α and β are constants. The retardation is **NCERT Pg. 16**

(a) $2\alpha v^3$ (b) $2\beta v^3$
(c) $2\alpha\beta v^3$ (d) $2\beta^2 v^3$

29 The motion of a body is given by equation $a = 5 - 2v$, where a and v are the acceleration and velocity. The body is at rest at $t = 0$, then the speed in terms of time is given by **NCERT Pg. 16**

(a) $v = \frac{2}{5}(1 - e^{-2t})$ (b) $v = \frac{2}{5}(1 + e^{-2t})$
(c) $v = \frac{1}{2}(5 - e^{-2t})$ (d) $v = \frac{5}{2}(1 - e^{-2t})$

30 A particle moves in a straight line having displacement as $x^2 = 3t^2 + 4$, then its acceleration is proportional to **NCERT Pg. 16**

(a) $\frac{1}{x} - \frac{1}{x^2}$ (b) $\frac{1}{x^3}$

(c) $-\frac{t}{x^2}$ (d) $\frac{1}{x} - \frac{t^2}{x^3}$

31 The displacement of a moving object in a straight line at any instant of time t is given by $x = 10t + 15t^3$, where x is in metre and t in second. The difference of average acceleration in the interval $t = 0$ to $t = 2$s and instantaneous acceleration at $t = 2$s is **NCERT Pg. 16**

(a) 90 m/s^2 (b) 180 m/s^2

(c) 135 m/s^2 (d) 9.8 m/s^2

32 The position of a particle as a function of time t, is given by $x(t) = pt + qt^2 - rt^3$, where p, q and r are constants. When the particle attains zero acceleration, then its velocity will be **NCERT Pg. 16**

(a) $r + \frac{q^2}{2p}$ (b) $p + \frac{r^2}{4q}$

(c) $p + \frac{q^2}{3r}$ (d) $q + \frac{r^2}{p}$

33 For motion of the car between $t = 18$ s and $t = 20$ s, which of the given statement is correct? **NCERT Pg. 16**

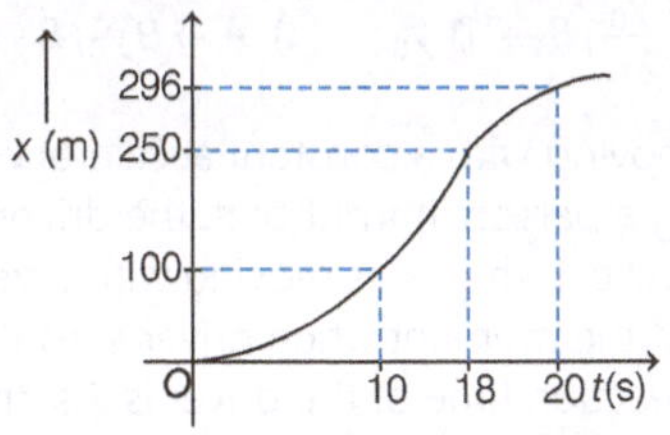

(a) The car is moving in a positive direction with a positive acceleration.

(b) The car is moving in a negative direction with a positive acceleration.

(c) The car is moving in positive direction with a negative acceleration.

(d) The car is moving in negative direction with a negative acceleration.

Kinematic Equations for Uniformly Accelerated Motion

34 A car is moving with a velocity of 30 ms^{-1}. On applying the brakes, the velocity decreases to 15 ms ^{1} in 2 s. The acceleration of the car is **NCERT Pg. 17**

(a) + 7.5 ms^{-2} (b) − 7.7 ms^{-2}

(c) − 7.5 ms^{-2} (d) + 15 ms^{-2}

35 Given below is a velocity-time graph. With reference to the graph, which of the following statement is correct? **NCERT Pg. 17**

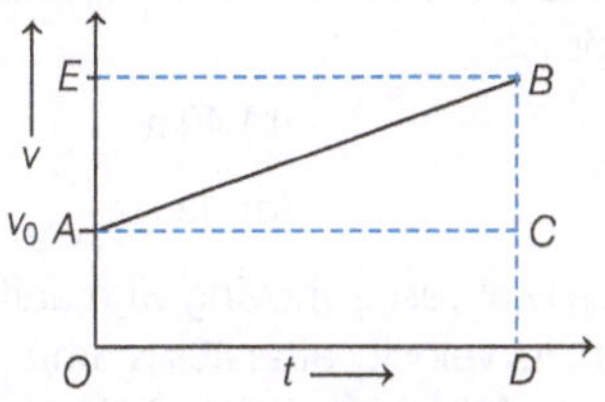

(a) The area under the given curve is $\frac{1}{2}(v + v_0)t - v_0 t$.

(b) The area under the given curve is $\frac{1}{2}(v + v_0)t + v_0 t$.

(c) The displacement of the object in terms of v_0 and a is $x = v_0 t + \frac{1}{2}at^2$.

(d) The relation $x = v_0 t + \frac{1}{2}at^2$ is same as $x = \left(\frac{v - v_0}{2}\right)t$.

36 An object starts from rest and moves with uniform acceleration a. The final velocity of the particle in terms of the distance x covered by it is given as **NCERT Pg. 18**

(a) $\sqrt{2ax}$ (b) $2ax$ (c) $\sqrt{\frac{ax}{2}}$ (d) $\sqrt{ax}$

37 A particle is situated at $x = 3$ m at $t = 0$. It starts moving from rest with a constant acceleration of 4 ms^{-2}. The position of the particle at $t = 3$ s is **NCERT Pg. 18**

(a) $x = +21$ m (b) $x = +18$ m

(c) $x = -21$ m (d) None of these

38 A body sliding on a smooth inclined plane requires 6 s to reach the bottom, starting from rest at the top. How much time does it take to cover one-ninth (1/9) the distance starting from rest at the top? **NCERT Pg. 18**

(a) (1/54) s (b) 2 s

(c) (9/6) s (d) 4 s

39 The velocity of a particle at an instant is 15 ms^{-1}. After 5s, its velocity will become 25 ms^{-1}. The velocity at 4s, before the given instant will be **NCERT Pg. 18**

(a) 23 ms^{-1} (b) 7 ms^{-1}

(c) 25 ms^{-1} (d) 15 ms^{-1}

40 A body covers a distance of 6 m in 3rd second and 12 m in 6th second, if the motion is uniformly accelerated. How far will it travel in the next 3 s? **NCERT Pg. 18**

(a) 46 cm (b) 48 cm

(c) 84 cm (d) 132 cm

41 A car moving with velocity 10 m/s is stopped by the application of certain force at a distance of 20 m. If the velocity of the car is 30 m/s, then the distance at which the car stops is **NCERT Pg. 18**

(a) $\frac{40}{3}$ m (b) 40m
(c) 60 m (d) 180 m

42 A body initially at rest is moving with uniform acceleration. Its velocity after 10s is 5m/s. The displacement of the body in last 2s is **NCERT Pg. 18**

(a) 8 m (b) 9 m
(c) 10 m (d) 12 m

43 Two bodies of different masses m_a and m_b are dropped from the different heights x and y. The ratio of the time taken by the two bodies to cover these distances is **NCERT Pg. 19**

(a) $x:y$ (b) $y:x$
(c) $\sqrt{x}:\sqrt{y}$ (d) $x^2:y^2$

44 The object is released from rest under gravity at height y. The equation of motion which incorrectly expresses the above situation is **NCERT Pg. 19**

(a) $v = 9.8\,t\ \text{ms}^{-1}$ (b) $y = 4.9\,t^2$ m
(c) $v^2 = 19.6\,y\ \text{m}^2\text{s}^{-2}$ (d) $y = 9.8t^2\text{ms}^{-1}$

45 A ball is thrown vertically upwards with a velocity of 10 ms^{-1} from a building of height 100 m. The maximum height attained by the ball above the ground is (use $g = 10\ \text{ms}^{-2}$) **NCERT Pg. 19**

(a) 105 m (b) 110 m
(c) 10 m (d) 5 m

46 From a tower of height H, a particle is thrown vertically upwards with a speed u. The time taken by the particle to hit the ground is n times the time taken by it to reach the highest point of its path. The relation between H, u and n is **NCERT Pg. 19**

(a) $2gH = n^2u^2$ (b) $gH = (n-2)^2u^2$
(c) $2gH = nu^2(n-2)$ (d) $gH = (n-2)^2u^2$

47 A man is standing on the top of a building 100 m high. He throws two stones vertically upward, one at $t = 0$ and other after a time interval (less than 2 s). The later stone is thrown at a velocity of half the first. The vertical gap between first and second stone is 15 m at $t = 2$ s. The gap is found to remain constant. The velocities with which the stones were thrown are (take $g = 10\,\text{ms}^{-2}$) **NCERT Pg. 19**

(a) 20 ms^{-1}, 10 ms^{-1}
(b) 10 ms^{-1}, 5 ms^{-1}
(c) 16 ms^{-1}, 8 ms^{-1}
(d) 30 ms^{-1}, 15 ms^{-1}

48 A stone falls freely under gravity. It covers distance h_1, h_2 and h_3 in the first 5 s, the next 5 s and the next 5 s, respectively. The relation between h_1, h_2 and h_3 is **NCERT Pg. 20**

(a) $h_1 = 2h_2 = 3h_3$ (b) $h_1 = \frac{h_2}{3} = \frac{h_3}{5}$
(c) $h_2 = 3h_1$ and $h_3 = 3h_2$ (d) $h_1 = h_2 = h_3$

49 The table below shows the motion of an object under free fall. The position of the object after different time intervals of 0, τ, 2τ and 3τ, are given in the second column. With the reference to this table, the missing entries A and B are **NCERT Pg. 20**

t	y	y in terms of y_0 [$= (-1/2)\,g\tau^2$]	Distance traversed in successive intervals	Ratio of distances traversed
0	0	0		
τ	$-(1/2)\,g\tau^2$	y_0	y_0	1
2τ	$-4\,(1/2)\,g\tau^2$	$4y_0$	$3y_0$	3
3τ	$-9\,(1/2)\,g\tau^2$	A	$5y_0$	5
4τ	$-16(1/2)\,g\tau^2$	$16y_0$	$7y_0$	7
5τ	$-25\,(1/2)\,g\tau^2$	$25y_0$	$9y_0$	9
6τ	$-36\,(1/2)\,g\tau^2$	$36y_0$	B	11

(a) $A \to 9y_0; B \to 11y_0$ (b) $A \to 11y_0; B \to 9y_0$
(c) $A \to \frac{9y_0}{2}; B \to 11y_0$ (d) $A \to 9y_0; B \to \frac{11y_0}{2}$

50 A car is moving with a constant acceleration of $4\ \text{m s}^{-2}$. On seeing a person in front of it, the driver suddenly applies brake. If the car is moving with a velocity of 20 ms^{-1} at the moment when driver sees the person and the reaction time of the driver is 2 s, then the distance it travels after the moment he sees the person and just before applying the brake is **NCERT Pg. 20**

(a) 48 m (b) 40 m
(c) 8 m (d) 45 m

51 A car moving with speed of 54 km/h can be stopped by applying brakes after moving at least 10m. If the car is moving with speed 108 km/h, then the minimum stopping distance is **NCERT Pg. 20**

(a) 30 m (b) 35 m (c) 40 m (d) 45 m

52 Two persons A and B conduct an experiment to measure reaction time of A. B drops a ruler vertically through the gap between A's thumb and forefinger. After A catches it, the distance d travelled by the ruler is $d = 21.0$ cm. The reaction time for this particular case is **NCERT Pg. 21**

(a) 0.2 s (b) 0.3 s
(c) 0.4 s (d) 0.1 s

Graphs Related to Motion of an Object in Straight Line

53 A car starts from rest at time $t = 0$ s from the origin O and picks up speed till $t = 10$ s and thereafter moves with uniform speed till $t = 18$ s. The brakes are applied and the car stops at $t = 20$ s and $x = 296$ m. The position-time graph which best represents the above situation is **NCERT Pg. 16**

(a)
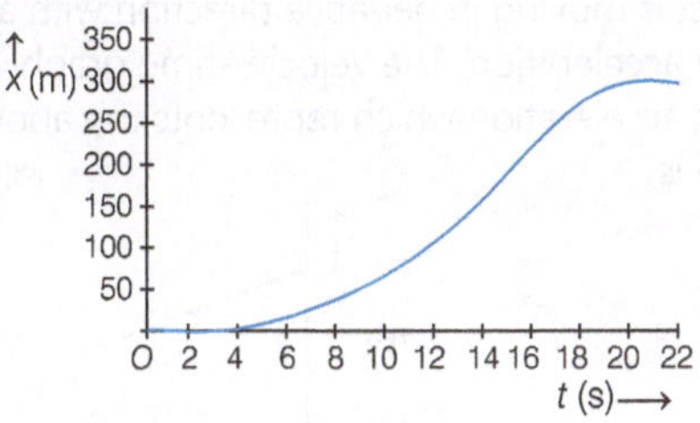

(b)
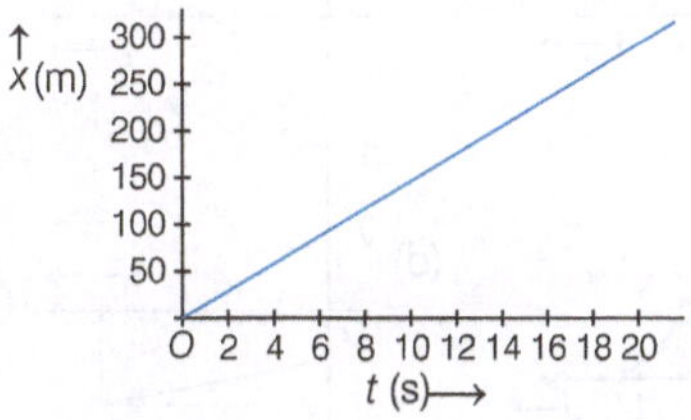

(c)
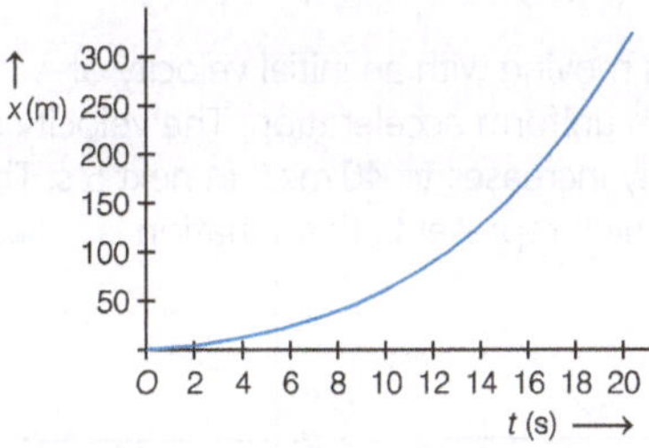

(d) None of the above

54 A particle starts from the origin at time $t = 0$ and moves along the positive X-axis. The graph of velocity with respect to time is shown in figure. What is the position of the particle at time $t = 5$ s? **NCERT Pg. 16**

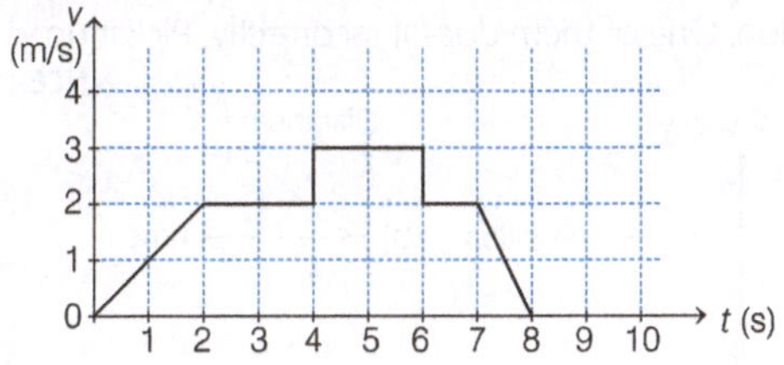

(a) 6 m
(b) 3 m
(c) 10 m
(d) 9 m

55 Figure shows the time-displacement curve of the particles P and Q. Which of the following statement is correct? **NCERT Pg. 16**

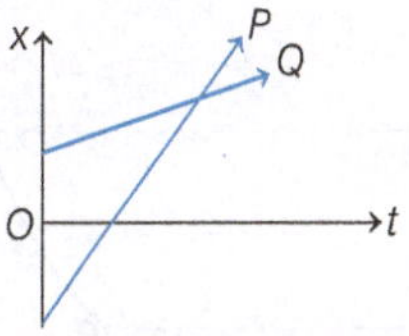

(a) Both P and Q move with uniform equal speed.
(b) P is accelerated and Q moves with uniform speed, but the speed of P is more than the speed of Q.
(c) Both P and Q move with uniform speeds but the speed of P is more than the speed of Q.
(d) Both P and Q move with uniform speeds but the speed of Q is more than the speed of P.

56 The displacement-time graph of a moving particle with constant acceleration is shown in figure. The velocity-time graph is given by **NCERT Pg. 16**

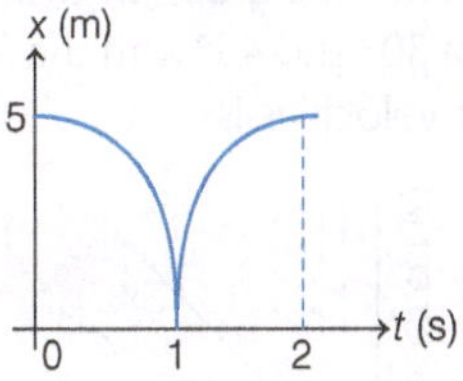

(a)
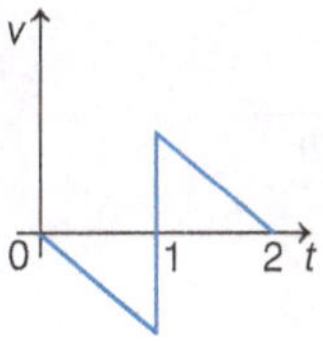

(b)
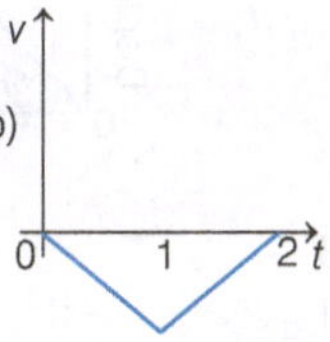

(c)
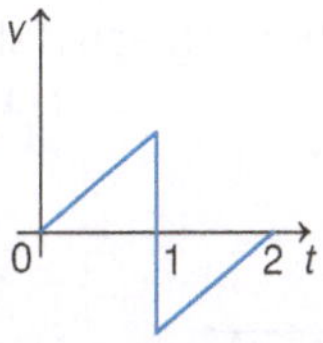

(d)
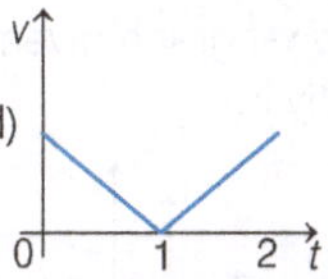

57 In the following graph, average velocity is geometrically represented by **Old NCERT Pg. 42**

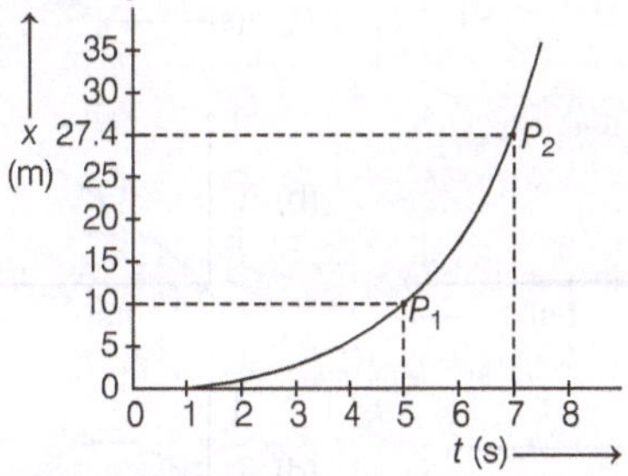

(a) length of the line $P_1 P_2$
(b) slope of the straight line $P_1 P_2$
(c) slope of the tangent to the curve at P_1
(d) slope of the tangent to the curve at P_2

58 In figure, displacement-time (x - t) graph given below, **Old NCERT Pg. 42**

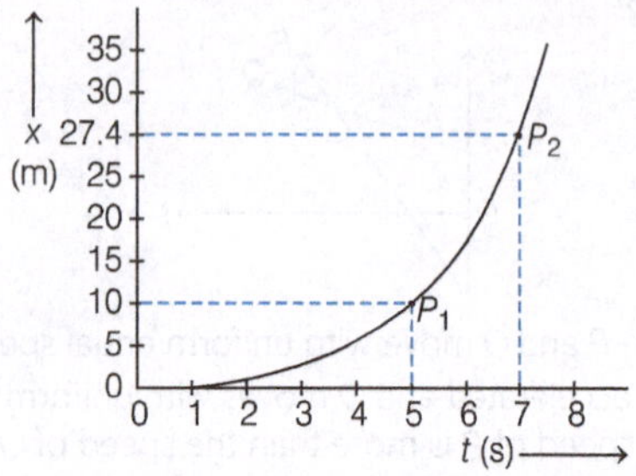

the average velocity between time $t = 5$ s and $t = 7$s is

(a) 8 ms^{-1}
(b) 8.7 ms^{-1}
(c) 7.8 ms^{-1}
(d) 13.7 ms^{-1}

59 The displacement-time graph of two moving particles make angles of 30° and 45° with the X-axis. The ratio of square of their velocities is **Old NCERT Pg. 42**

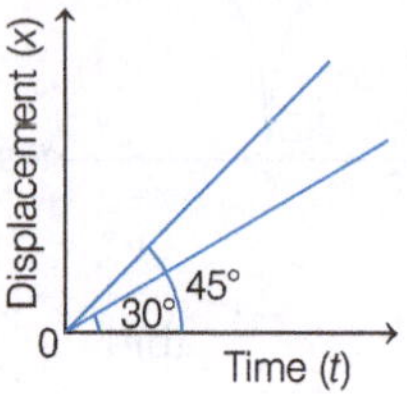

(a) 1 : 3 (b) 1 : 2
(c) 1 : 1 (d) 3 : 2

60 For the x-t graph given below, the v -t graph is shown correctly in **Old NCERT Pg. 42**

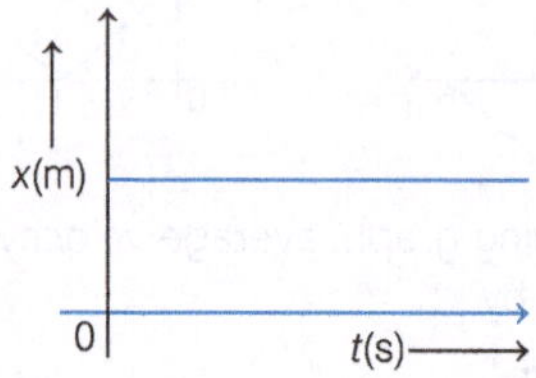

(a)
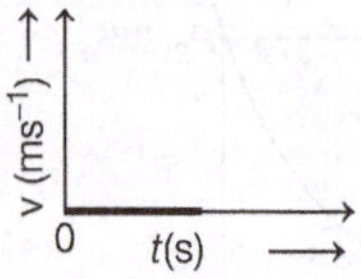

(b)
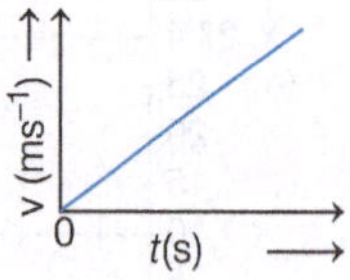

(c)
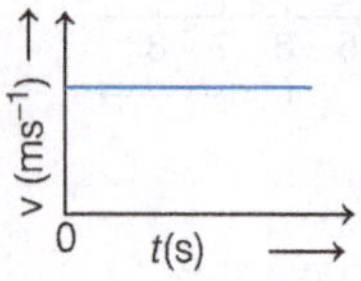

(d)
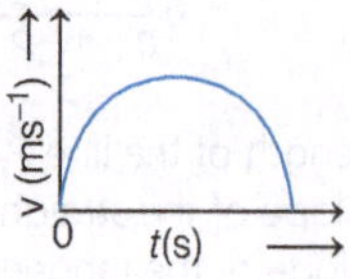

61 A car moves along a straight line according to the x-t graph given alongside. The instantaneous velocity of the car at $t = t_1$ is **NCERT Pg. 16**

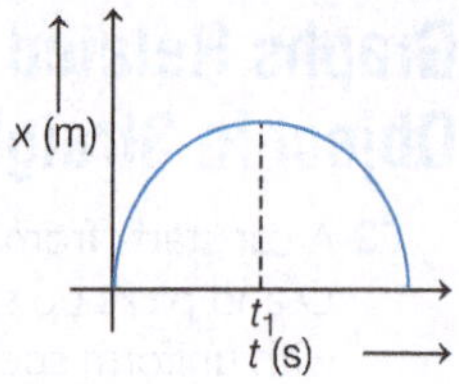

(a) zero
(b) positive
(c) Data insufficient
(d) Cannot be determined

62 An object is moving in negative direction with a negative acceleration. The velocity-time graph with constant acceleration which represents the above situation is **NCERT Pg. 16**

(a)
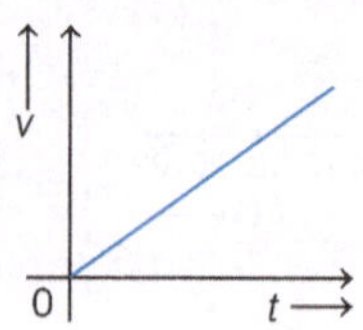

(b)
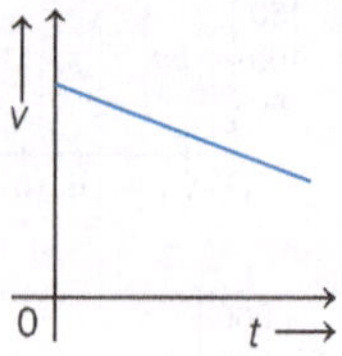

(c)
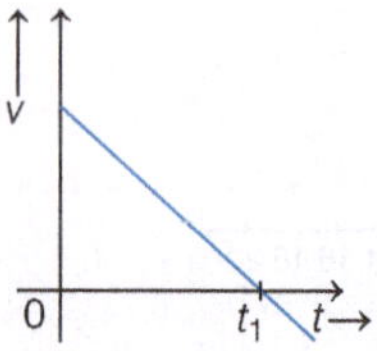

(d)
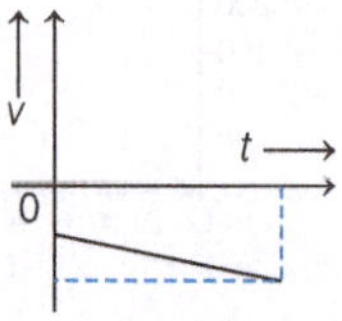

63 An object is moving with an initial velocity of 30 ms^{-1} with uniform acceleration. The velocity of object continuously increases to 40 ms^{-1} in next 5 s. The v-t graph which represents this situation is **NCERT Pg. 16**

(a)
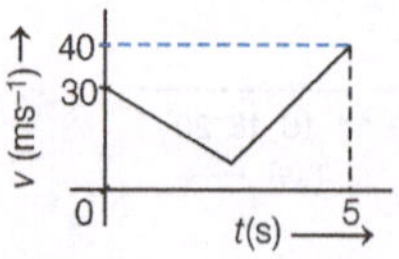

(b)
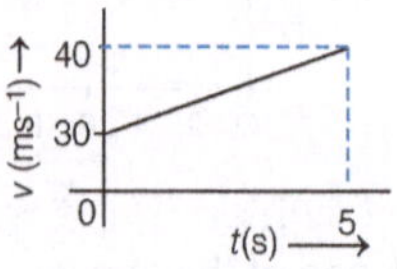

(c)
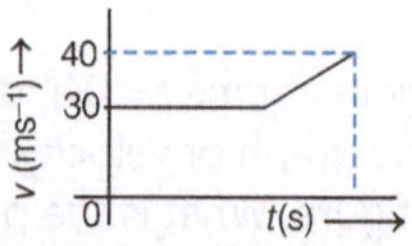

(d) None of these

64 All the graphs below are intended to represent the same motion. One of them does it incorrectly. Pick it up. **NCERT Pg. 16**

(a)
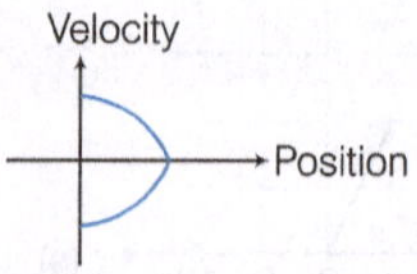

(b)
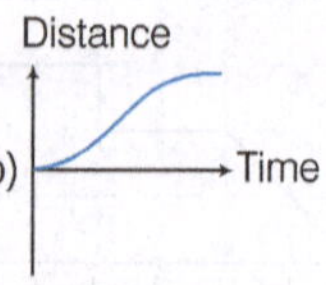

(c)
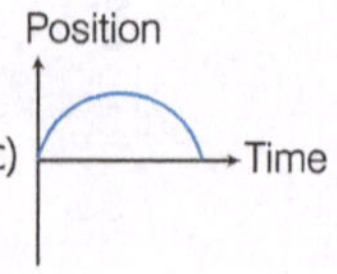

(d)
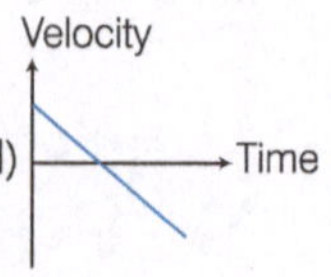

65 A particle is thrown upwards, then correct v-t graph will be **NCERT Pg. 16**

(a) 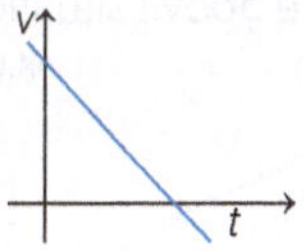

(b) 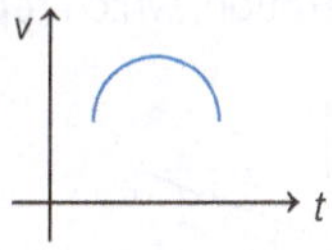

(c) 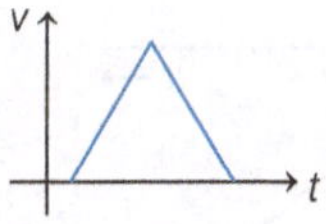

(d) 

66. Which of the following graph represents motion with uniformly decelerated? **NCERT Pg. 16**

(a) 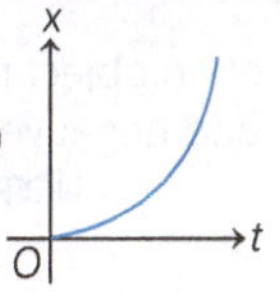

(b) 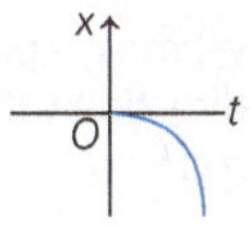

(c) 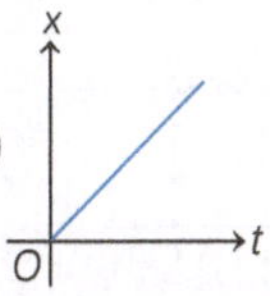

(d) 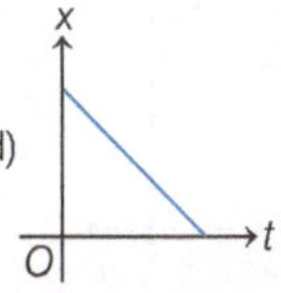

67. From given velocity-time graph, which of the following is acceleration-time graph? **NCERT Pg. 16**

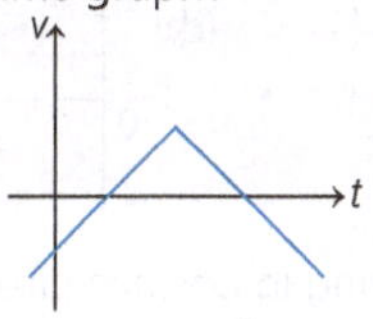

(a) 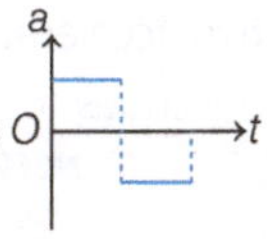

(b) 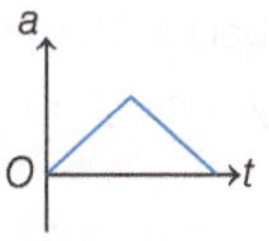

(c) 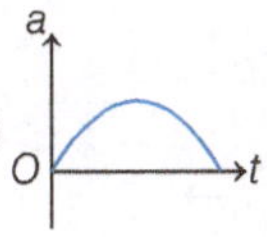

(d) 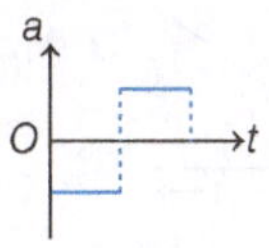

68. A particle starts from rest. The acceleration-time graph is shown in the figure. The maximum speed of the particle is **NCERT Pg. 16**

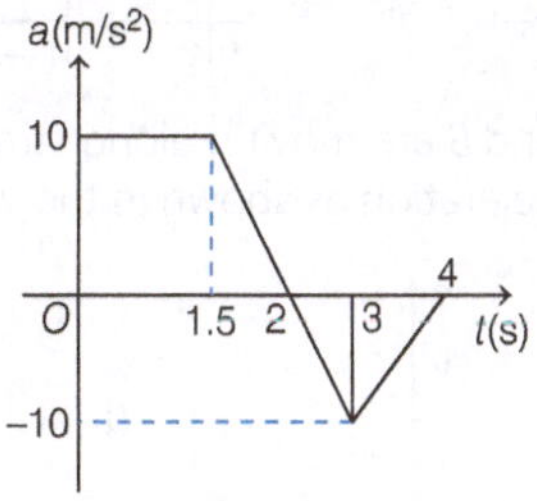

(a) 17.5 m/s (b) 27.5m/s (c) 7.5m/s (d) 12.5m/s

69. The displacement-time graph of a moving particle is shown below. The particle is moving with a constant acceleration during the region of **NCERT Pg. 16**

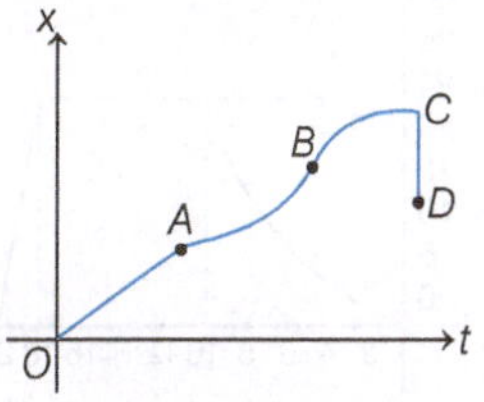

(a) OA (b) AB
(c) BC (d) CD

70. The velocity (v) of a particle moving along X-axis varies with its position x as shown in figure. The acceleration (a) of particle varies with position (x) as **NCERT Pg. 16**

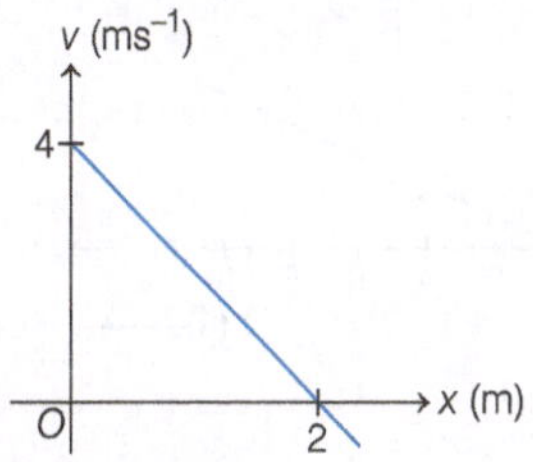

(a) $a^2 = x + 3$
(b) $a = 2x^2 + 4$
(c) $2a = 3x + 5$
(d) $a = 4x - 8$

71 A particle starts from origin O from rest and moves with a uniform acceleration along the positive X-axis. Identify all figures that correctly represent the motion qualitatively.
(a = acceleration, v = velocity, x = displacement, t = time) **NCERT Pg. 16**

(A) 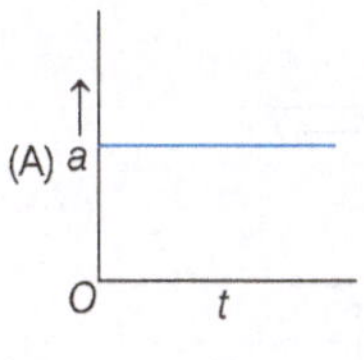

(B) 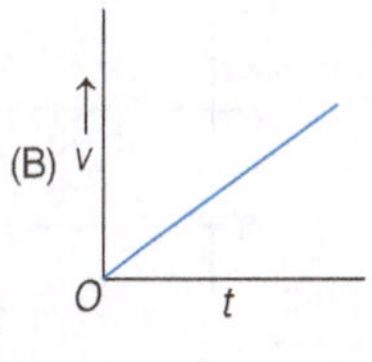

(C) 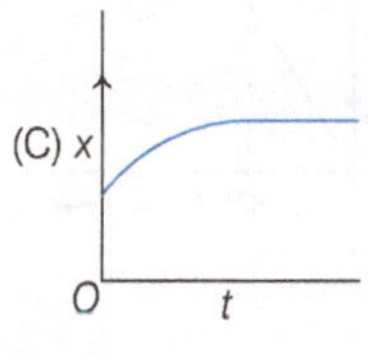

(D) 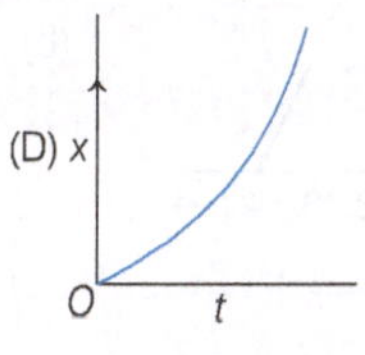

(a) (A) (b) (A), (B), (C)
(c) (B), (C) (d) (A), (B), (D)

72 The resulting *a*-*t* graph for the given *v*-*t* graph is correctly represented in **Old NCERT Pg. 45**

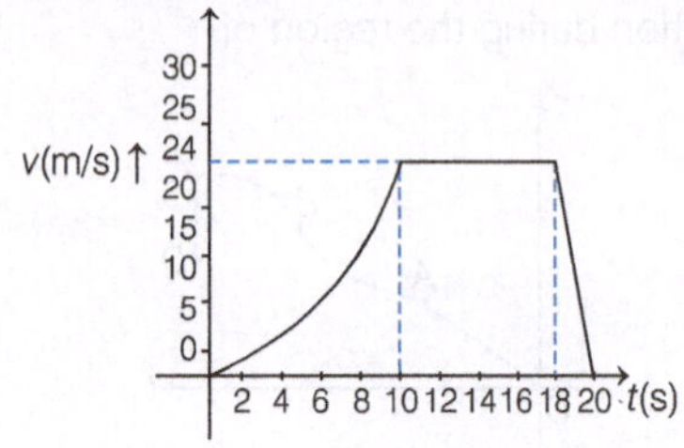

(a) 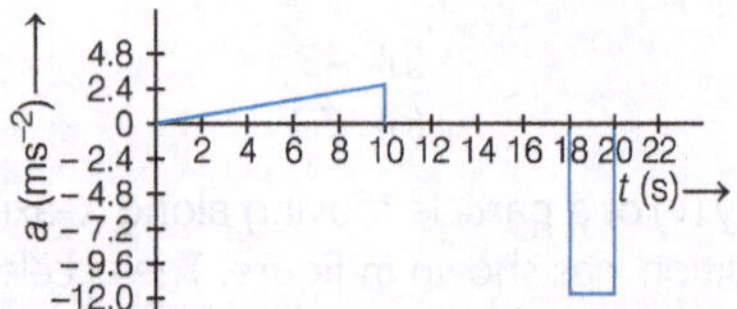

(b) 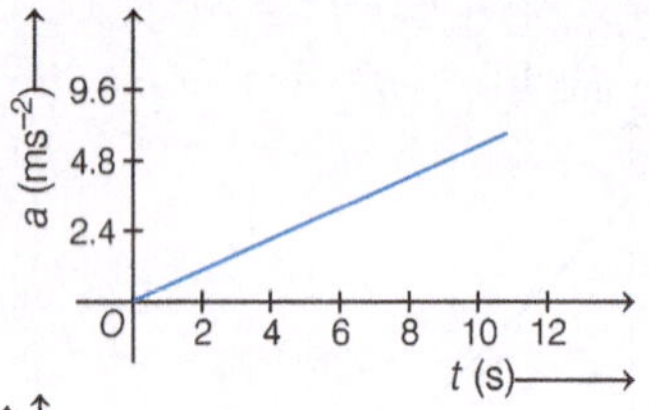

(c) 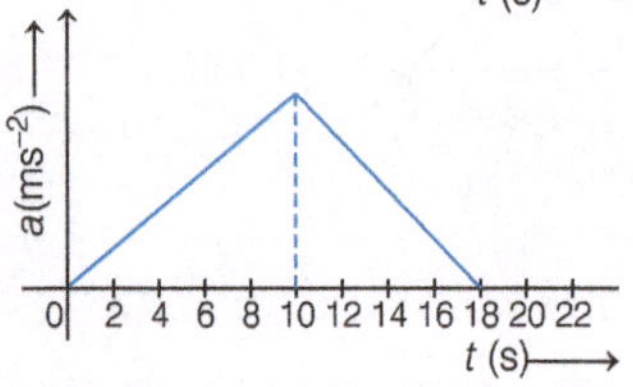

(d) None of the above

73 A particle starts from rest at $t = 0$ s and undergoes an acceleration a in ms^{-2} with time t in seconds which is shown in figure. Which one of the following plot represents velocity v (in ms^{-1}) *versus* time t in second? **NCERT Pg. 16**

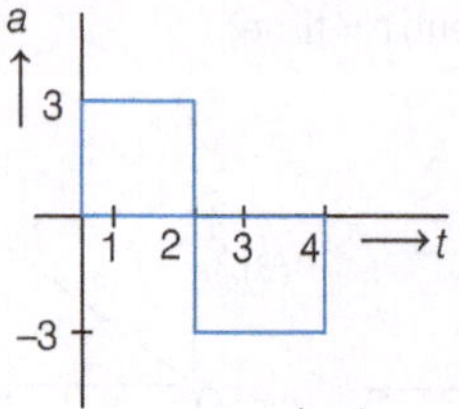

(a) 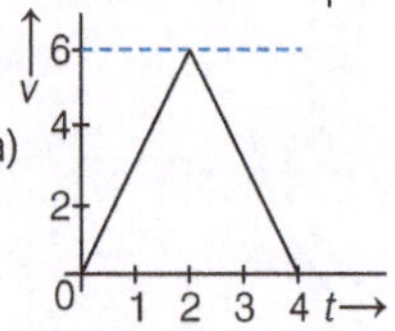

(b) 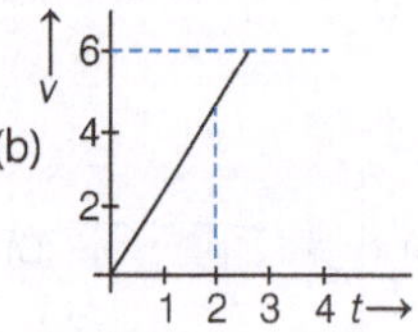

(c) 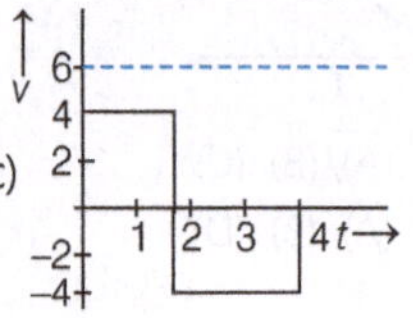

(d) 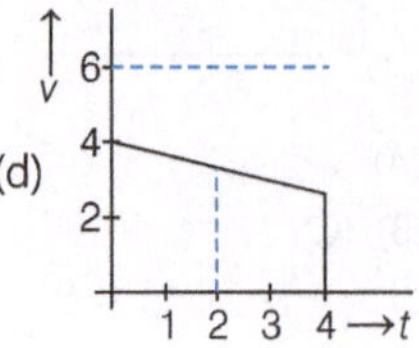

74 An object is moving in a positive direction with a positive acceleration. The velocity-time graph with constant acceleration, which represents the above situation is **NCERT Pg. 16**

(a) 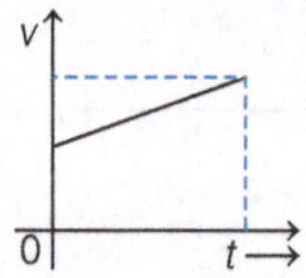

(b) 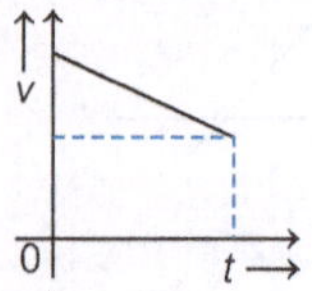

(c) 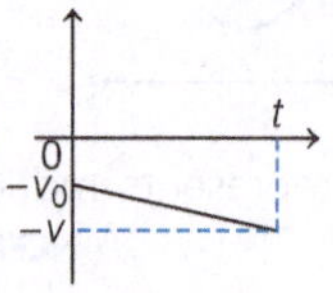

(d) 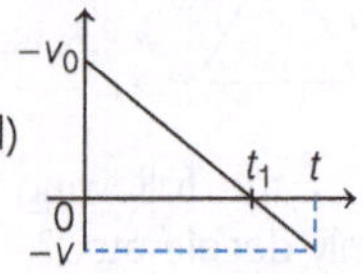

75 The velocity-time graph for motion of an object moving in positive direction with a constant and negative acceleration is **NCERT Pg. 16**

(a) 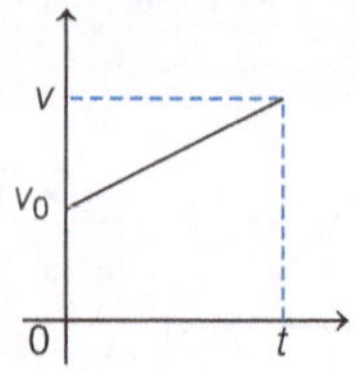

(b) 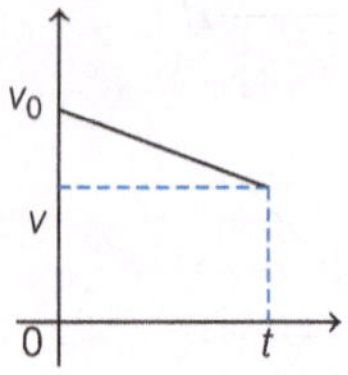

(c) 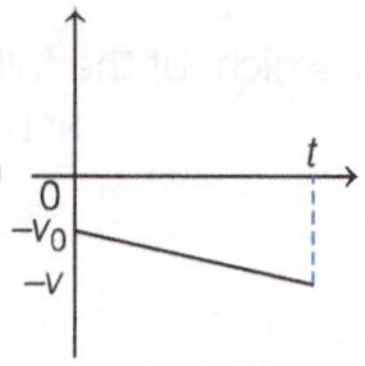

(d) 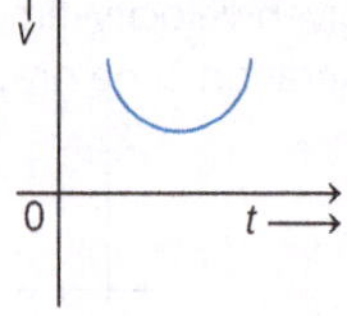

76 An object is moving in positive direction till time t_1 and then turns back with the same negative acceleration. The velocity-time graph which best describes the situation is **NCERT Pg. 16**

(a) 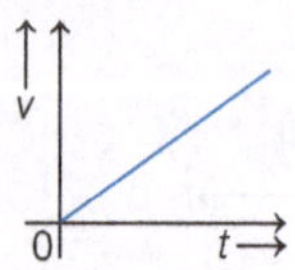

(b) 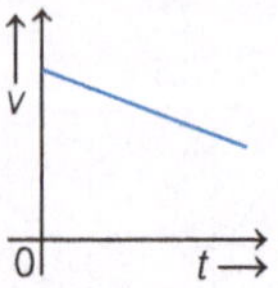

(c) 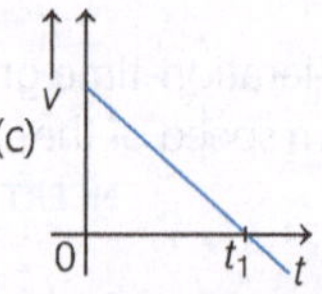

(d) 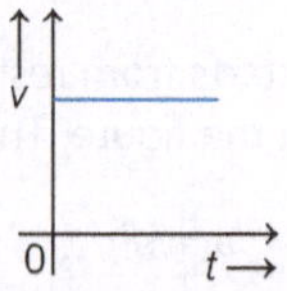

77 Two cars *A* and *B* are moving along straight line with constant acceleration as shown in the velocity-time graph. **NCERT Pg. 16**

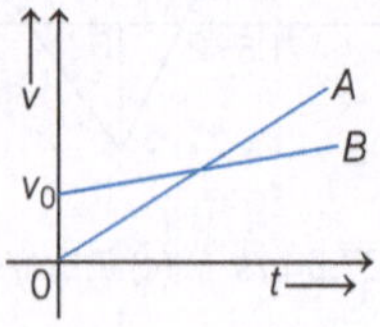

The correct relation between their accelerations is

(a) $a_A > a_B$ (b) $a_A < a_B$
(c) $a_A = a_B$ (d) $a_A = a_B/2$

Relative Velocity in One-dimension

78 Consider two objects A and B moving uniformly with average velocities v_A and v_B in one-dimension, along X-axis. If $x_A(0)$ and $x_B(0)$ are positions of objects A and B, respectively at time $t = 0$, the displacement from object A to object B is given by Old NCERT Pg. 51

(a) $x_{BA}(t) = x_B(t) - x_A(t)$
(b) $x_{AB}(t) = x_B(t) - x_A(t)$
(c) $x_{BA}(t) = [x_B(0) - x_A(0)] + (v_B - v_A)t$
(d) Both (a) and (c)

79 The relative velocity v_{BA} or v_{AB} is zero for two particles moving along X-axis uniformly. The position-time graph for this situation will be Old NCERT Pg. 51

(a) straight lines parallel but inclined to time axis
(b) straight lines parallel and also parallel to time axis
(c) straight lines intersecting each other at some point
(d) curves and not straight lines

80 Two particles A and B are moving in a straight line with the same speed. Which of the following option correct for the relative motion of the two particles? Old NCERT Pg. 51

(a) The relative velocity v_{AB} or v_{BA} is zero, only if they are moving in the same direction.
(b) If the particles are moving in opposite direction, the magnitude of v_{BA} or v_{AB} is twice than the magnitude of velocity of A or that of B.
(c) The relative velocity v_{AB} or v_{BA} is always zero.
(d) Both (a) and (b)

81 The average velocities of the objects A and B are v_A and v_B, respectively. The velocities are related such that $v_A > v_B$.. Which of the following option is true for this situation? Old NCERT Pg. 52

(a) v_{AB} is positive and object A overtakes object B after some time
(b) v_{BA} is positive and object A overtakes object B after some time
(c) The x-t graph for the situation is such that one graph is steeper than the other and they meet at a common point
(d) Both (a) and (c)

82 A passenger train of length 60 m travels at a speed of 80 km/h. Another freight train of length 120 m travels at a speed of 30 km/h. The ratio of times taken by the passenger train to completely cross the freight train when : (i) they are moving in the same direction and (ii) in the opposite direction is Old NCERT Pg. 52

(a) $\frac{3}{2}$ (b) $\frac{25}{11}$ (c) $\frac{11}{5}$ (d) $\frac{5}{2}$

83 A person is moving with a velocity of 10 ms^{-1} towards north. A car moving with a velocity of 20 ms^{-1} towards south crosses the person. The velocity of car relative to the person is Old NCERT Pg. 52

(a) $-30\ ms^{-1}$ (b) $+20\ ms^{-1}$
(c) $10\ ms^{-1}$ (d) $-10\ ms^{-1}$

84 A ball A is thrown vertically upwards with speed v_1. At the same instant another ball B is released from rest at height h. At time t, the velocity of A relative to B is Old NCERT Pg. 52

(a) v_1 (b) $v_1 - 2gt$ (c) $\sqrt{v_1^2 - 2gh}$ (d) $v_1 - gt$

85 A bus is moving with speed 12 m/s on a straight road. A scooterist wishes to overtake the bus in 120s. If the bus is at a distance of 1 km from the scooterist. The speed with which the scooter should chase the bus is Old NCERT Pg. 52

(a) 18 m /s (b) 20.33 m/s (c) 25.66 m/s (d) 17. 28 m/s

Assertion and Reason Questions

Direction (Q. No. 1-10) *In the following questions, a statement of Assertion is followed by a corresponding statement of Reason. Of the following statements, choose the correct one.*

(a) Both Assertion and Reason are correct and Reason is the correct explanation of Assertion.
(b) Both Assertion and Reason are correct but Reason is not the correct explanation of Assertion.
(c) Assertion is correct but Reason is incorrect.
(d) Assertion is incorrect but Reason is correct.

1 **Assertion** In real-life, in a number of situations, the object is treated as a point object.
Reason An object is treated as point object as far as its size is much smaller than the distance it moves in a reasonable duration of time. NCERT Pg. 13

2 **Assertion** For motion along a straight line and in the same direction, the magnitude of average velocity is equal to the average speed.

Reason For motion along a straight line and in the same direction, the magnitude of displacement is equal to the path length. Old NCERT Pg. 42

3 **Assertion** For uniform motion, velocity is the same as the average velocity at all instants.

Reason In uniform motion along a straight line, the object covers equal distances in equal intervals of time. Old NCERT Pg. 42

4 **Assertion** A body cannot be accelerated when it is moving uniformly.

Reason When direction of motion of the body changes, then body may have acceleration. NCERT Pg. 16

5 **Assertion** In realistic situation, the *x-t*, *v-t* and *a-t* graphs will be smooth.

Reason Physically acceleration and velocity cannot change values abruptly at an instant. NCERT Pg. 17

6 **Assertion** A body is momentarily at rest at the instant, if it reverse the direction.

Reason A body cannot have acceleration, if its velocity is zero at a given instant of time. NCERT Pg. 19

7 **Assertion** For a body falling freely under the action of gravity, g is taken as negative.

Reason For a body thrown vertically upward, g is taken as negative. NCERT Pg. 19

8 **Assertion** From the top of the roof of a house, two balls of different masses are thrown vertically upward with the same speed. They attain the same height and during their return journey, they came to the thrower with the same speed.

Reason The maximum height to which a ball rises and the speed it attains on returning back do not depend on the mass of the ball. NCERT Pg. 19

9 **Assertion** A negative acceleration of a body can be associated with speeding up of the body.

Reason Increase in speed of a moving body is independent of its direction of motion. NCERT Pg. 19

10 **Assertion** When the objects *A* and *B* move in the same direction, then relative velocity of object *A* w.r.t. object *B* is $v_{AB} = v_A - v_B$.

Reason When the objects *A* and *B* move in opposite direction, then relative velocity of object *B* w.r.t. object *A* is $v_{BA} = v_B - v_A$. Old NCERT Pg. 52

Statement Based Questions

Direction (Q.Nos 1-8) *In the following question, Statement I and Statement II are given. Read these statements and choose the most appropriate answer from the options given below*

(a) Both Statement I and Statement II are incorrect.
(b) Statement I is correct but Statement II is incorrect.
(c) Statement I is incorrect but Statement II is correct.
(d) Both Statement I and Statement II are correct.

1 **Statement I** The average and instantaneous velocities have same value in a uniform motion.
Statement II In uniform motion, the velocity of an object increases uniformly. NCERT Pg. 14

2 **Statement I** The accelerated motion of an object may be due to change in magnitude of velocity or direction of velocity or both.

Statement II Acceleration can be produced only by change in the magnitude of the velocity. NCERT Pg. 15

3 **Statement I** The position-time graph of a body moving uniformly in straight line is parallel to position axis.
Statement II The position-time graph in a non-uniform motion gives constant velocity at all instant of time. NCERT Pg. 16

4 **Statement I** The displacement is the longest distance between initial and final position.

Statement II Displacement of a body may be zero when distance travelled by an object is not zero. NCERT Pg. 16

5 **Statement I** A body is said to be free falling, if acceleration of body is equal to acceleration due to gravity.
Statement II A body falling freely may do so with constant acceleration. NCERT Pg. 19

6 **Statement I** For a given time interval, velocity is single valued while average speed may have many values.
Statement II Velocity is a vector quantity and speed is scalar quantity. NCERT Pg. 20

7. **Statement I** The slope of *x-t* graph at any point gives the instantaneous velocity of the object at the instant corresponding to that point.

Statement II The *x-t* graph for an object having uniformly accelerated motion is parabolic in nature. NCERT Pg. 18

8. **Statement I** Higher the value of the reaction time means high precision in road safety.
Statement II The area of the acceleration-displacement curve of a body gives change in kinetic energy per unit mass. NCERT Pg. 17

Matching Type Questions

1 In the given figure, let P, Q and R represent the position of a car at different instants of time. **Old NCERT Pg. 40**

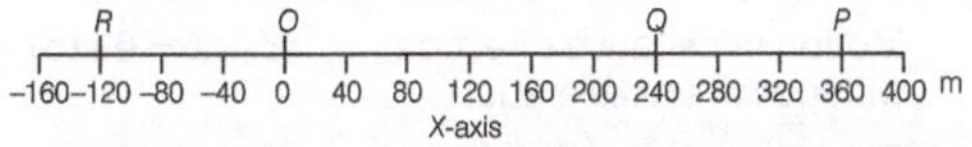

With reference to the above given figure, match the Column I (displacement/path length) with Column II (value) and select the correct answer from the options given below.

	Column I		Column II
A.	Displacement of car in moving from O to P	1.	480 m
B.	Path length of car from O to R	2.	360 m
C.	Path length of car for its motion from O to P and back to Q	3.	240 m
D.	Displacement of car for its motion from O to P and back to Q	4.	120 m

Codes

	A	B	C	D
(a)	2	4	1	3
(b)	4	3	2	1
(c)	3	4	1	2
(d)	1	2	4	3

2 Given x-t graph represent the motion of an object. Match the Column I (parts of graph) with Column II (representation) and select the correct answer from the options given below. **Old NCERT Pg. 42**

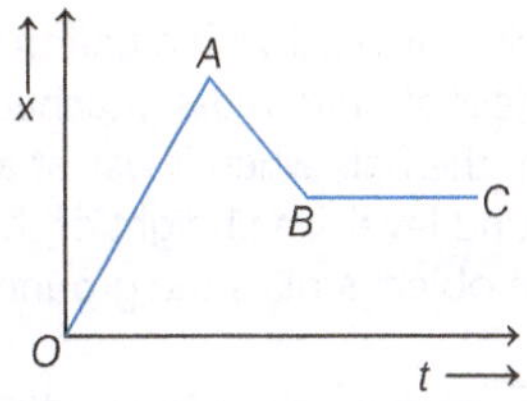

	Column I		Column II
A.	Part OA of graph	1.	Positive velocity
B.	Part AB of graph	2.	Object at rest
C.	Part BC of graph	3.	Negative velocity
D.	Point A in the graph	4.	Change in direction of motion

Codes

	A	B	C	D		A	B	C	D
(a)	1	2	3	4	(b)	1	3	2	4
(c)	2	1	3	4	(d)	4	3	2	1

3 The position of an object moving along X-axis is given by $x(t) = a - bt^2$, where $a = 8.5$ m, $b = 2.5$ ms^{-2} and t is measured in seconds.

For the above situation, match the Column I (speed/velocity) with Column II (value) and select the correct answer from the options given below. **NCERT Pg. 15**

	Column I		Column II
A.	Velocity of object at $t = 2.0$ s	1.	-15 ms^{-1}
B.	Velocity of object at $t = 0$ s	2.	-10 ms^{-1}
C.	Instantaneous speed of an object at $t = 2.0$ s	3.	0 ms^{-1}
D.	Average velocity between $t = 2.0$ s and $t = 4.0$ s	4.	10 ms^{-1}

Codes

	A	B	C	D
(a)	1	2	3	4
(b)	2	3	4	1
(c)	4	3	4	1
(d)	3	2	1	4

4 Given below is a velocity-time graph for an object in motion along a straight line. **NCERT Pg. 16**

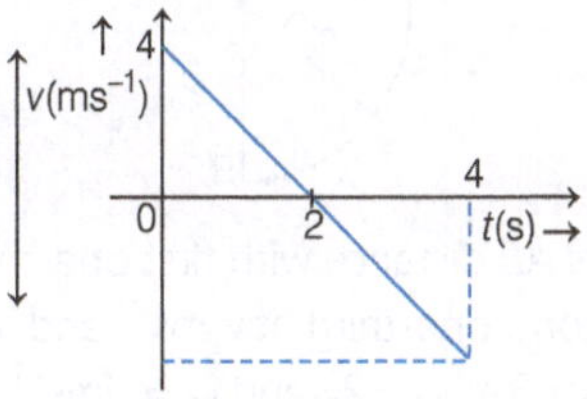

With reference to the above given figure, match the Column I (displacement/distance) with Column II (magnitude) and select the correct answer from the options given below.

	Column I		Column II
A.	The distance covered by the object in time $t = 0$ s to $t = 2$ s.	1.	8 m
B.	The acceleration of the object in time $t = 0$ s to $t = 2$ s.	2.	-2 ms^{-2}
C.	The displacement of the object in time $t = 0$ s to $t = 4$ s.	3.	4 m
D.	The distance of object in time $t = 0$ s to $t = 4$ s.	4.	0

Codes

	A	B	C	D		A	B	C	D
(a)	3	2	1	4	(b)	1	2	3	4
(c)	3	2	4	1	(d)	4	2	1	3

5 Based on the below velocity-time graph for an object in motion along a straight line with constant acceleration, match the Column I (description of motion) with Column II (time interval) and select the correct answer from the options given below. **NCERT Pg. 16**

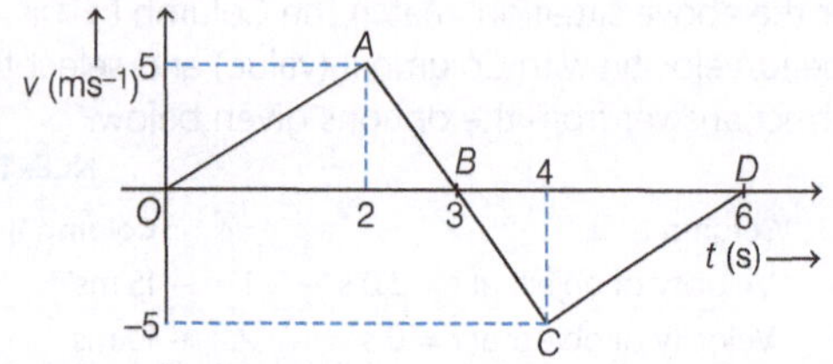

	Column I		Column II
A.	Motion in positive direction with positive acceleration.	1.	$t = 2s$ to $t = 4s$
B.	Motion in positive direction till time t and then turns back with same negative acceleration.	2.	$t = 4s$ to $t = 6s$
C.	Motion in negative direction with positive acceleration.	3.	$t = 0s$ to $t = 6s$
D.	Displacement is zero.	4.	$t = 0s$ to $t = 2s$

Codes

	A	B	C	D		A	B	C	D
(a)	4	1	3	2	(b)	3	2	4	1
(c)	3	1	4	2	(d)	4	1	2	3

Numerical Type Questions

1 In 1.0s, a particle goes from point A to point B, moving in a semicircle (see figure). The magnitude of the average velocity is x m/s. The value of x is .... **Old NCERT Pg. 42**

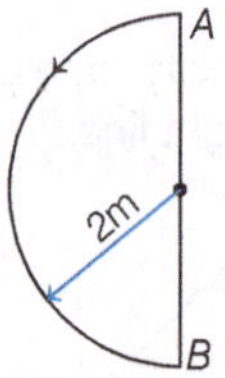

2 A car covers AB distance with first one-third at velocity v_1 ms^{-1}, second one-third at $v_2 ms^{-1}$ and last one-third at v_3 ms^{-1}. If $v_3 = 3v_1$, $v_2 = 2v_1$ and $v_1 = 11 ms^{-1}$, then the average velocity of the car is ...... ms^{-1}. **Old NCERT Pg. 42**

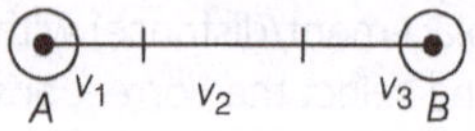

3 The distance travelled by an object in time t is given by $3.5t^2 + t$. The instantaneous speed (in ms^{-1}) of the object at $t = 4s$ is .... **NCERT Pg. 14**

4 A car is moving with speed of 100 km /h and after applying the brake, it will move 16m before it stop. If the same car is moving with a speed of half the reported speed, then it will stop after travelling...... m distance. **NCERT Pg. 18**

5 The velocity of the bullet become one-third after it penetrate 8 cm in a wooden block. Assume that the bullet is facing constant resistance during its motion in the block. The bullet stops completely after travelling at $(6 + x)$ cm inside the block. The value of x is .... **NCERT Pg. 18**

6 A Juggler throws balls vertically upward with some initial velocity in air. When the first ball reaches its highest position, he throws the next ball. Assuming the Juggler throws 3 balls per second, the maximum height the balls can reach is H metre. The value of $9H$ is ...m. (Take, $g = 10\ ms^{-2}$) **NCERT Pg. 19**

7 A stone of mass 1 kg is dropped from a height of 20 m. The height at which the magnitude of velocity become equal to the magnitude of acceleration due to gravity is......m. (Take, $g = 10\ m/s^2$) **NCERT Pg. 19**

8 A ball is moving upward with a uniform velocity of $5ms^{-1}$. An object of finite mass attached to ball is dropped from the ball, when it was at a height of 60m from the ground level. The height of the ball from the ground, when object strikes the ground is...... m. **NCERT Pg. 19**

9 A ball is dropped from the top of a 100 m high tower on a planet. In the last $\frac{1}{2}$ s before hitting the ground, it cover a distance of 19m. Acceleration due to gravity near the surface on the planet is .... ms^{-2}. **NCERT Pg. 19**

10 A truck A is moving with a speed of 40 kmh^{-1} and truck B is moving with a speed of 70 kmh^{-1}, along parallel straight paths. If both the trucks starts from the same point, then the position of truck A with respect to truck B after 20 min is ...... km behind. **Old NCERT Pg. 51**

NCERT Exemplar Questions

1 Among the four graphs shown in the figure, there is only one graph for which average velocity over the time interval $(0, T)$ can vanish for a suitably chosen T. Which one is it?

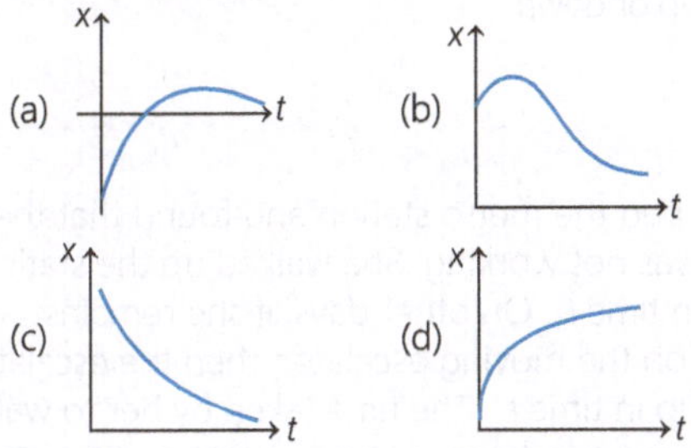

2 A lift is coming from 8th floor and is just about to reach 4th floor. Taking ground floor as origin and positive direction upwards for all quantities, which one of the following is correct?
(a) $x < 0, v < 0, a > 0$
(b) $x > 0, v < 0, a < 0$
(c) $x > 0, v < 0, a > 0$
(d) $x > 0, v > 0, a < 0$

3 In one-dimensional motion, instantaneous speed v satisfies $0 \le v < v_0$.
(a) The displacement in time T must always take non-negative values
(b) The displacement x in time T satisfies, $-v_0 T < x < v_0 T$
(c) The acceleration is always a non-negative number
(d) The motion has no turning points

4 A vehicle travels half the distance l with speed v_1 and the other half with speed v_2, then its average speed is
(a) $\frac{v_1 + v_2}{2}$ (b) $\frac{2v_1 + v_2}{v_1 + v_2}$ (c) $\frac{2v_1 v_2}{v_1 + v_2}$ (d) $\frac{l(v_1 + v_2)}{v_1 v_2}$

5 The displacement of a particle is given by $x = (t-2)^2$, where x is in metre and t in second. The distance covered by the particle in first 4 s is
(a) 4 m (b) 8 m (c) 12 m (d) 16 m

6 At a metro station, a girl walks up a stationary escalator in time t_1. If she remains stationary on the escalator, then the escalator takes her up in time t_2. The time taken by her to walk upon the moving escalator will be
(a) $(t_1 + t_2)/2$ (b) $t_1 t_2 / (t_2 - t_1)$
(c) $t_1 t_2 / (t_2 + t_1)$ (d) $t_1 - t_2$

7 The variation of quantity A with respect to quantity B, plotted in figure describes the motion of a particle in a straight line.

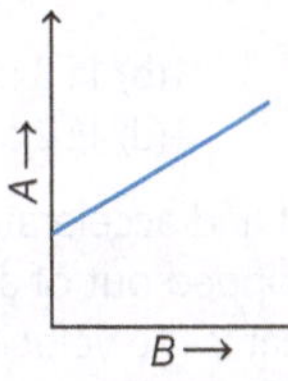

(a) Quantity B may represent time
(b) Quantity A is velocity, if motion is uniform
(c) Quantity A is distance, if motion is non-uniform
(d) Quantity B is velocity, if motion is uniformly accelerated

8 For one-dimensional motion, described by
$$x = t - \sin t$$
(a) $x(t) = 0$ for all $t > 0$ (b) $v(t) > 0$ for all $t > 0$
(c) $a(t) < 0$ for all $t > 0$ (d) $v(t)$ lies between 0 and 2

Past Exams Questions

NEET

1 The velocity (v)-time (t) plot of the motion of a body is shown below

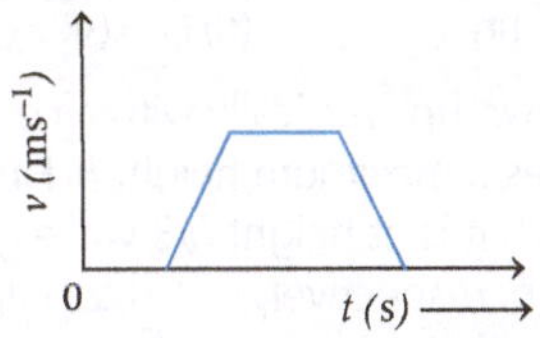

NCERT Pg. 16, NEET 2024

The acceleration (a)- time (t) graph that best suits this motion is

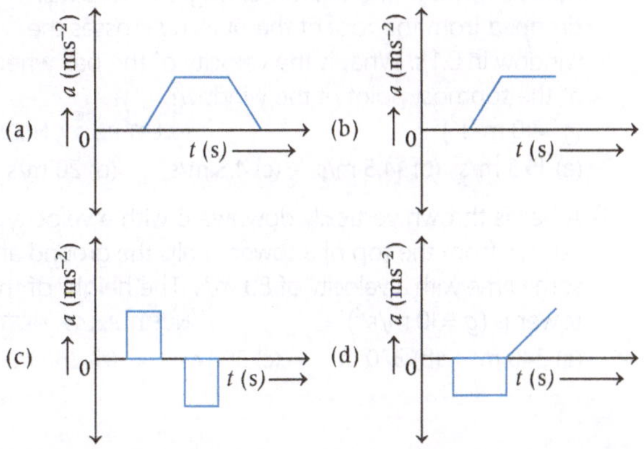

2 A bullet from a gun is fired on a rectangular wooden block with velocity u. When bullet travels 24 cm through the block along its length horizontally, velocity of bullet becomes $u / 3$. Then it further penetrates into the block in the same direction before coming to rest exactly at the other end of the block. The total length of the block is **NCERT Pg. 18, NEET 2023**

(a) 24 cm (b) 28 cm
(c) 30 cm (d) 27 cm

3 A horizontal bridge is built across a river. A student standing on the bridge throws a small ball vertically upwards with a velocity 4 m s^{-1}. The ball strikes the water surface after 4 s. The height of bridge above water surface is (Take, $g = 10$ m s^{-2}) **NCERT Pg. 19, NEET 2023**

(a) 60 m (b) 64 m (c) 68 m (d) 56 m

4 The ratio of the distances travelled by a freely falling body in the 1st, 2nd, 3rd and 4th second **NCERT Pg. 20, NEET 2021**

(a) 1 : 4 : 9 : 16 (b) 1 : 3 : 5 : 7
(c) 1 : 1 : 1 : 1 (d) 1 : 2 : 3 : 4

5 A car starts from rest and accelerates at 5 m/s^2. At $t = 4$ s, a ball is dropped out of a window by a person sitting in the car. What is the velocity and acceleration of the ball at $t = 6$ s? (Take, $g = 10$ m/s^2) **NCERT Pg. 17, NEET 2021**

(a) 20 m/s, 5 m/s^2 (b) 20 m/s, 0
(c) $20\sqrt{2}$ m/s, 0 (d) $20\sqrt{2}$ m/s, 10 m/s^2

6 A small block slides down on a smooth inclined plane, starting from rest at time $t = 0$. Let s_n be the distance travelled by the block in the interval $t = n - 1$ to $t = n$. Then, the ratio $\frac{s_n}{s_{n+1}}$ is **NCERT Pg. 20, NEET 2021**

(a) $\frac{2n-1}{2n}$ (b) $\frac{2n-1}{2n+1}$ (c) $\frac{2n+1}{2n-1}$ (d) $\frac{2n}{2n-1}$

7 A person sitting in the ground floor of a building notices through the window of height 1.5 m, a ball dropped from the roof of the building crosses the window in 0.1 s. What is the velocity of the ball when it is at the topmost point of the window? ($g = 10$ m/s^2) **NCERT Pg. 19, NEET 2020**

(a) 15.5 m/s (b) 14.5 m/s (c) 4.5 m/s (d) 20 m/s

8 A ball is thrown vertically downward with a velocity of 20 m/s from the top of a tower. It hits the ground after some time with a velocity of 80 m/s. The height of the tower is ($g = 10$ m/s^2) **NCERT Pg. 19, NEET 2020**

(a) 340 m (b) 320 m (c) 300 m (d) 360 m

9 A person standing on the floor of an elevator drops a coin. The coin reaches the floor in time t_1, if the elevator is at rest and in time t_2, if the elevator is moving uniformly. Then, which of the following option is correct? **NCERT Pg. 19, NEET 2019**

(a) $t_1 < t_2$ or $t_1 > t_2$ depending upon whether the lift is going up or down
(b) $t_1 < t_2$
(c) $t_1 > t_2$
(d) $t_1 = t_2$

10 Preeti reached the metro station and found that the escalator was not working. She walked up the stationary escalator in time t_1. On other days, if she remains stationary on the moving escalator, then the escalator takes her up in time t_2. The time taken by her to walk up on the moving escalator will be **NCERT Pg. 18, NEET 2017**

(a) $\frac{t_1 + t_2}{2}$ (b) $\frac{t_1 t_2}{t_2 - t_1}$ (c) $\frac{t_1 t_2}{t_2 + t_1}$ (d) $t_1 - t_2$

11 If the velocity of a particle is $v = At + Bt^2$, where A and B are constants, then the distance travelled by it between 1 s and 2 s is **NCERT Pg. 14, NEET 2016**

(a) $3A + 7B$ (b) $\frac{3}{2}A + \frac{7}{3}B$ (c) $\frac{A}{2} + \frac{B}{3}$ (d) $\frac{3}{2}A + 4B$

JEE Main

12 A particle initially at rest starts moving from reference point $x = 0$ along X-axis, with velocity v that varies as, $v = 4\sqrt{x}$ m/s. The acceleration of the particle is .... ms^{-2}. **NCERT Pg. 15, JEE Main 2024**

13 Two trains A and B of length l and $4l$ are travelling into a tunnel of length L in parallel tracks from opposite directions with velocities 108 km/h and 72 km/h, respectively. If train A takes 35 s less time than train B to cross the tunnel, then length L of tunnel is (Given, $L = 60l$) **NCERT Pg. 15, JEE Main 2023**

(a) 1200 m (b) 1800 m (c) 2700 m (d) 900 m

14 A ball is released from a height h. If t_1 and t_2 be the time required to complete first half and second half of the distance, respectively. Then, choose the correct relation between t_1 and t_2. **NCERT Pg. 19, JEE Main 2022**

(a) $t_1 = (\sqrt{2})t_2$ (b) $t_1 = (\sqrt{2} - 1)t_2$
(c) $t_2 = (\sqrt{2} + 1)t_1$ (d) $t_2 = (\sqrt{2} - 1)t_1$

15 A ball is thrown up vertically with a certain velocity, so that it reaches a maximum height h. Find the ratio of the times in which it is at height $h/3$ while going up and coming down, respectively. **NCERT Pg. 19, JEE Main 2022**

(a) $\frac{\sqrt{2}-1}{\sqrt{2}+1}$ (b) $\frac{\sqrt{3}-\sqrt{2}}{\sqrt{3}+\sqrt{2}}$ (c) $\frac{\sqrt{3}-1}{\sqrt{3}+1}$ (d) $\frac{1}{3}$

Skill Boosters

1 A drunkard is walking along a straight road. He takes 7 steps forward and 5 steps backward and so on. Each step is 1 m long and takes 1 s. There is a pit on the road 13 m away from the starting point. The drunkard will fall into the pit after

(a) 36 s (b) 30 s (c) 43 s (d) 39 s

2 The velocity-time graphs of a bike and a truck are shown in the figure. (i) the difference between the distance travelled by the bike and the truck in 15 s and (ii) the time at which the bike will catch up with the truck are, respectively.

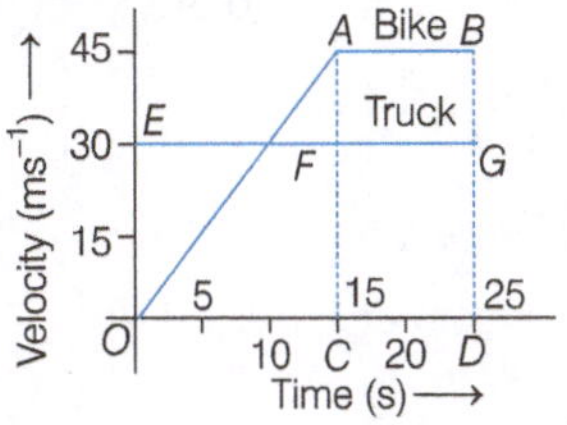

(a) 112.5 m and 15 s (b) 337.5 m and 25 s
(c) 225.5 m and 10 s (d) 112.5 m and 22.5 s

3 Two cars A and B simultaneously start a race. The velocity of car A varies with time as $v = \frac{50}{\sqrt{95}}\sqrt{t}$ ms^{-1} for $0 \le t \le 95$ s and $v = 50$ m/s for $v > 95$ s. The car B moves together with car A to a place, where both have velocity of 20 m/s, after this place car B move with constant velocity for one second and then follows. Velocity-time relation identical to car A. In this way, car B acquires the constant velocity in one second after car A acquires it. How much more distance car A covers in the first 100 s?

(a) Less than 25 m (b) Less than 30 m
(c) Equal to 30 m (d) Equal to 20 m

4 A length of path ACB is 1500 m and the length of the path ADB is 2100 m. Two particles start from point A simultaneously around the track $ACBDA$. One of them travels the track in clockwise sense and other in anti-clockwise sense with their respective constant speeds. After 12 s from the start, the first time they meet at the point B. After minimum time (in s) in which they meet first at point B, will they again meet at the point B is time $t_{min} = (12)^x$ s. Find the value of x.

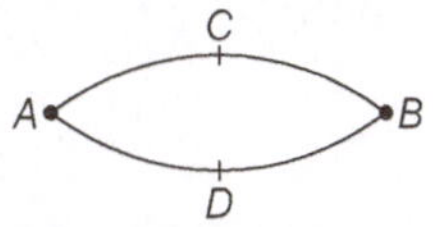

(a) 5 (b) 4 (c) 3 (d) 2

5 A student used to go to his coaching institute every evening and he takes 20 min. Once on his way, he realised that he had forgotten his book at home. He knew that if he continued walking to the coaching at the same speed, he would be there 8 min before the bell, so he went back home for the book and arrived the coaching 10 min late. If he had walked all the way with his usual speed, the fraction of the way to coaching institute had he covered at that moment when he turned back is

(a) $\frac{20}{3}$ (b) $\frac{9}{20}$ (c) $\frac{9}{10}$ (d) $\frac{3}{2}$

6 A stone is dropped from the top of a tall cliff and n seconds later another stone is thrown vertically downward with a velocity u. Then, the second stone overtakes the first, below the top of the cliff at a distance given by

(a) $\frac{g}{2}\left[\frac{n\left(u - \frac{gn}{2}\right)}{(u - gn)}\right]^2$ (b) $\frac{g}{2}\left[\frac{n\left(\frac{u}{2} - gn\right)}{(u - gn)}\right]^2$

(c) $\frac{g}{2}\left[\frac{n\left(\frac{u}{2} - gn\right)}{\left(\frac{u}{2} - gn\right)}\right]^2$ (d) $\frac{g}{2}\left[\frac{(u - gn)}{\left(\frac{u}{2} - gn\right)}\right]^2$

7 On a highway, two buses A and B are running at the same velocity of magnitude 30 ms^{-1}. The brakes cause a deceleration of $\frac{30}{7}$ ms^{-2} in bus A and that of bus B is 3 ms^{-2}. In an emergency when driver of the front bus applies brakes, immediately its rear light turns red and braking begins. In response, driver of the rear bus also applies brakes to avoid a collision with the front bus. Every driver takes 1 s to apply the brakes after he saw a need for it. If bus A ahead of bus B, then the minimum separation between the buses before driver of bus A applies the brake is x_1. If bus B is running ahead of bus A, then the minimum separation between the buses before the driver of bus B applies brake is x_2. The ratio of x_1 and x_2 is

(a) 7 : 8 (b) 15 : 1 (c) 1 : 8 (d) 3 : 5

8 A passenger train passes a certain station at $\frac{100}{9}$ ms^{-1} and covers a distance of 8 km with this speed and then stops at the next station, 10 km from the first with uniform deceleration. A local train starting from the first station covers the same distance in double this time and stops at the next station. The maximum speed of local train is v_0 and it covers a part of the distance with uniform acceleration and the rest with uniform deceleration. The value of v_0 (in km/h) is

(a) 50.8 (b) 48.6
(c) 33.3 (d) 42.6

9 On a long horizontally moving belt, a child runs to and fro with a speed 9 km/h (with respect to the belt) between his father and mother located 50 m apart on the moving belt. The belt moves with a speed of 4 km/h. For an observer on the stationary platform, the speed of the child running in the direction of motion of the belt is

(a) 4 km/h (b) 5 km/h
(c) 9 km/h (d) 13 km/h

10 A rocket is moving in a gravity free space with a constant acceleration of 2 ms^{-2} along + x-direction (see figure). The length of a chamber inside rocket is 4 m. A ball is thrown from the left end of the chamber in + x-direction with a speed of 0.3 ms^{-1} relative to the rocket. At the same time, another ball is thrown in x-direction with a speed of 0.2 ms^{-1} from its right end relative to the rocket. The time in seconds when the two balls hit each other is

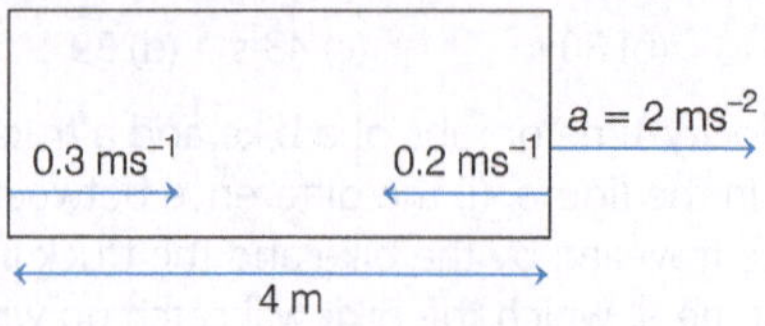

(a) 6 s (b) 7 s
(c) 2 s (d) 9 s

Correct Codes

Topical Questions

1 (b)	2 (a)	3 (a)	4 (a)	5 (c)	6 (d)	7 (b)	8 (d)	9 (b)	10 (a)
11 (c)	12 (a)	13 (b)	14 (a)	15 (a)	16 (d)	17 (a)	18 (c)	19 (a)	20 (b)
21 (d)	22 (b)	23 (a)	24 (c)	25 (d)	26 (d)	27 (b)	28 (a)	29 (d)	30 (b)
31 (a)	32 (c)	33 (c)	34 (c)	35 (c)	36 (a)	37 (a)	38 (b)	39 (b)	40 (b)
41 (d)	42 (b)	43 (c)	44 (d)	45 (a)	46 (c)	47 (a)	48 (b)	49 (a)	50 (a)
51 (c)	52 (a)	53 (a)	54 (d)	55 (c)	56 (a)	57 (b)	58 (b)	59 (a)	60 (a)
61 (a)	62 (d)	63 (b)	64 (a)	65 (a)	66 (b)	67 (a)	68 (a)	69 (b)	70 (d)
71 (d)	72 (a)	73 (a)	74 (a)	75 (b)	76 (c)	77 (a)	78 (d)	79 (a)	80 (d)
81 (d)	82 (c)	83 (a)	84 (a)	85 (b)					

Assertion and Reason Questions

1 (a)	2 (a)	3 (b)	4 (d)	5 (a)	6 (c)	7 (b)	8 (a)	9 (b)	10 (c)

Statement Based Questions

1 (b)	2 (b)	3 (a)	4 (c)	5 (c)	6 (d)	7 (d)	8 (c)

Matching Type Questions

1 (a)	2 (b)	3 (b)	4 (c)	5 (d)

Numerical Type Questions

1 (4)	2 (18)	3 (29)	4 (4)	5 (3)	6 (5)	7 (10)	8 (80)	9 (8)	10 (10)

NCERT Exemplar Questions

1 (b)	2 (a)	3 (b)	4 (c)	5 (b)	6 (c)	7 (a)	8 (d)

Past Exams Questions

1 (c)	2 (d)	3 (b)	4 (b)	5 (d)	6 (b)	7 (b)	8 (c)	9 (d)	10 (c)
11 (b)	12 (8)	13 (b)	14 (d)	15 (b)					

Skill Boosters

1 (c)	2 (d)	3 (c)	4 (d)	5 (b)	6 (a)	7 (b)	8 (c)	9 (d)	10 (c)

Step by Step

Decoding the Questions

Concept Builders

1 True (T)

2 Frame of reference

3 less

4 False (F)

5 True (T)

6 False (F)

7 instantaneous speed

8 True (T)

9 True (T)

10 False (F)

11 For constant velocity

12 instantaneous acceleration

13 False (F)

14 Uniform circular motion

15 Opposite to the velocity

16 Yes

17 opposite

18 $\frac{1}{2}gt^2$

19 $\frac{v_0^2}{2a}$

20 35

Topical Questions

3 (*a*)

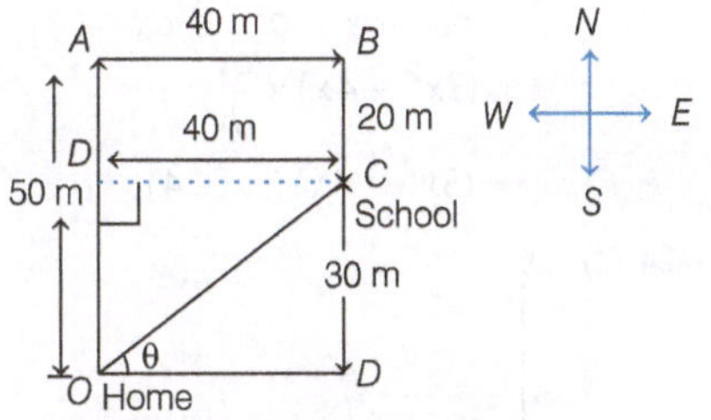

Displacement of Snehit is *OC*.

$$\therefore\ OC = \sqrt{OD^2 + CD^2}$$
$$= \sqrt{(30)^2 + (40)^2}$$
$$= 50 \text{ m}$$

6 (*d*)

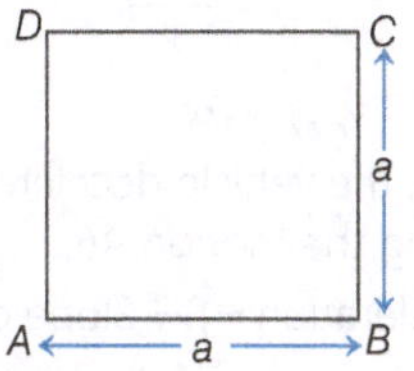

Distance covered,

$$d_1 = AB + BC + CD + DA + AB + BC$$
$$= a + a + a + a + a + a = 6a$$

and displacement covered,

$$d_2 = AC$$
$$= \sqrt{a^2 + a^2} = \sqrt{2}a$$
$$\therefore\ \frac{d_1}{d_2} = \frac{6a}{\sqrt{2}a} = 3\sqrt{2} : 1$$

7 (*b*) $v_{av} = \frac{v_1 t_1 + v_2 t_2}{t_1 + t_2}$

$$= \frac{4 \times \frac{t}{2} + 8 \times \frac{t}{2}}{\frac{t}{2} + \frac{t}{2}}$$
$$= 6 \text{ m/s}$$

8 (*d*) Let initial velocity $= 0$

and acceleration $= a$

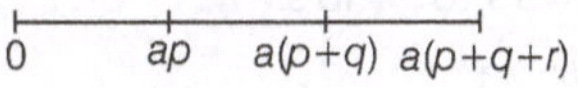

$$\therefore\ x = \frac{0 + ap}{2} = \frac{1}{2}ap$$
$$y = \frac{ap + a(p+q)}{2} = ap + \frac{1}{2}aq$$
$$z = \frac{a(p+q) + a(p+q+r)}{2}$$
$$= ap + aq + \frac{1}{2}ar$$
$$\therefore\ \frac{x-y}{y-z} = \frac{-\frac{1}{2}ap - \frac{1}{2}aq}{-\frac{1}{2}aq - \frac{1}{2}ar} = \frac{p+q}{q+r}$$

9 (*b*) Average velocity

$$= \frac{\text{Displacement}}{\text{Time taken}}$$
$$= \frac{2R}{t} = \frac{2 \times 40}{40}$$
$$= 2 \text{ ms}^{-1}$$

10 (*a*) As runner starts from *O* and comes back to *O*, so net displacement is zero.

$$\text{Average speed} = \frac{\text{Total distance}}{\text{Total time}}$$
$$= \frac{OQ + QR + RO}{\text{Total time}}$$
$$= \frac{1 \text{ km} + (2\pi r)\left(\frac{90°}{360°}\right)\text{km} + 1 \text{ km}}{1\text{h}}$$

($\because$ angle of sector *OQR* is 90°)

$$= \frac{1 + 2\pi \times 1\left(\frac{1}{4}\right) + 1}{1}$$
$$= 2 + \frac{\pi}{2} = 3.57 \text{ km/h}$$

11 (*c*) According to the question, the situation is as shown

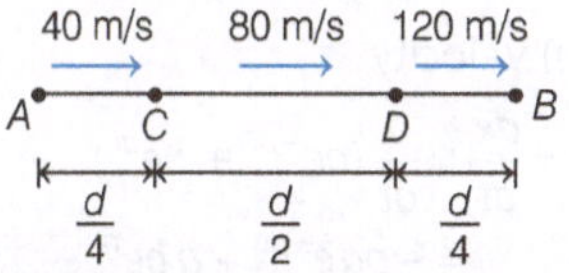

From *A* to *C*,

$$\text{Time taken, } t_1 = \frac{d/4}{40} = \frac{d}{160}$$

From *C* to *D*,

$$\text{Time taken, } t_2 = \frac{d/2}{80} = \frac{d}{160}$$

From *D* to *B*,

$$\text{Time taken, } t_3 = \frac{d/4}{120} = \frac{d}{480}$$

$$\text{Total time} = t_1 + t_2 + t_3$$
$$= \frac{d}{160} + \frac{d}{160} + \frac{d}{480}$$
$$= \frac{3d + 3d + d}{480} = \frac{7d}{480}$$
$$\text{Average speed} = \frac{\text{Total distance}}{\text{Total time}}$$
$$= \frac{d}{7d/480}$$
$$= 68.57 \text{ m/s}$$

13 (*b*) Velocity of a particle,

$$v = \frac{dx}{dt} = 2t + 3t^2 \qquad \left(\because v = \frac{dx}{dt}\right)$$
$$\Rightarrow\ dx = (2t + 3t^2)dt$$
$$\int_{x_1}^{x_2} dx = \int_1^2 (2t + 3t^2)\,dt$$

$$=2\left(\frac{t^2}{2}\right)_1^2+3\left(\frac{t^3}{3}\right)_1^2$$

$$x_2-x_1=(2^2-1^2)+(2^3-1^3)$$

$$\Delta x=(3)+(7)\ =10\text{ m}$$

14 (*a*) For maximum velocity,

$$\frac{dv}{dt}=0$$

Given, $v=4t(1-2t)$

$$\Rightarrow\quad v=4t-8t^2$$

$$\Rightarrow\quad \frac{d}{dt}(4t-8t^2)=0$$

$$\Rightarrow\quad 4-16t=0$$

$$\Rightarrow\quad t=\frac{1}{4}\text{ s}=0.25\text{ s}$$

Again taking differentiation, we get

$$\frac{d^2v}{dt^2}=-16<0$$

So, at $t=0.25$ s, velocity is maximum.

15 (*a*) Velocity,

$$v=\frac{dx}{dt}=\frac{d}{dt}(ae^{-pt}+be^{qt})$$

$$=-pae^{-pt}+q\,be^{qt}$$

Acceleration,

$$a=\frac{dv}{dt}=\frac{d}{dt}(-pae^{-pt}+q\,be^{qt})$$

$$=p^2ae^{-pt}+q^2be^{qt}$$

Acceleration is positive, so velocity goes on increasing with time.

16 (*d*) Velocity, $v=\dfrac{dx}{dt}$

$$=\frac{d}{dt}s_0(1-e^{-pt})$$

$$=s_0\,pe^{-pt}$$

At $t=0,\quad v=s_0p$

17 (*a*) $\quad dt=\dfrac{dv}{4-2v}$

$$\Rightarrow\quad \int dt=\int\frac{dv}{4-2v}$$

$$\Rightarrow\quad t=-\frac{1}{2}\ln(4-2v)+C\quad \text{...(i)}$$

Since, at $t=0, v=0$.

From Eq. (i), we get

$$0=-\frac{1}{2}\ln(4-0)+C$$

$$\Rightarrow\quad C=\frac{1}{2}\ln 4$$

Again, from Eq. (i), we get

$$t=-\frac{1}{2}\ln(4-2v)+\frac{1}{2}\ln 4$$

$$=-\frac{1}{2}\ln\left(\frac{4-2v}{4}\right)$$

$$t=-\frac{1}{2}\ln\left(1-\frac{v}{2}\right)$$

$$\Rightarrow\quad 1-\frac{v}{2}=e^{-2t}\Rightarrow v=2(1-e^{-2t})$$

18 (*c*) Given, $t=\sqrt{x}+4$

$$\Rightarrow\quad \sqrt{x}=t-4$$

$$\Rightarrow\quad x=(t-4)^2$$

$$\Rightarrow\quad x=t^2+16-8t$$

$\therefore$ Velocity, $v=\dfrac{dx}{dt}=2t-8$

When $\quad v=0$, then

$$2t-8=0$$

$$t=4\text{ s}$$

$$\therefore\ x=4^2+16-8\times 4=0$$

19 (*a*) The instantaneous speed is always positive as it is the magnitude of the velocity at an instant. So, it is positive during $t=5$ s to $t=10$ s.

20 (*b*)

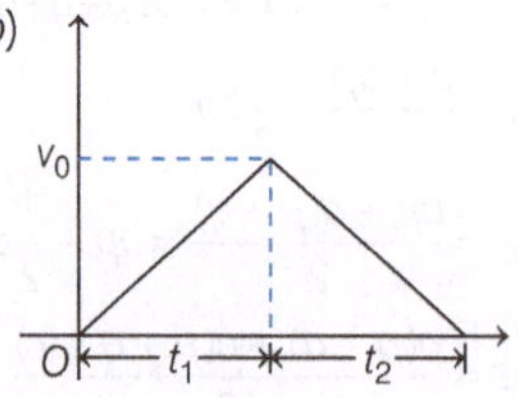

Let acceleration, $\alpha=2\text{m/s}^2$

and deceleration, $\beta=3\text{ m/s}^2$

Total time, $\quad t_1+t_2=10\text{s}\quad$ ...(i)

$$\therefore\quad \alpha=\frac{v_0}{t_1}$$

$$\Rightarrow\quad v_0=\alpha t_1=2t_1$$

and $\quad \beta=\dfrac{v_0}{t_2}$

$$\Rightarrow\quad v_0=\beta t_2=3t_2$$

Now, $\quad v_0=2t_1=3t_2$

$$\Rightarrow\quad t_2=\frac{2t_1}{3}\quad \text{... (ii)}$$

From Eqs. (i) and (ii), we get

$$t_1=6\text{s}$$

$\therefore$Maximum velocity,

$$v_0=2t_1=2\times 6=12\text{ m/s}$$

21 (*d*) The given situation is shown below.

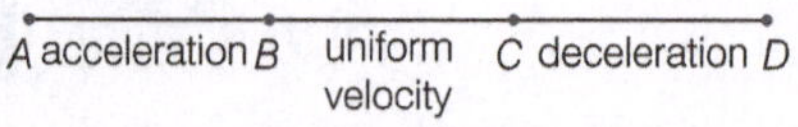

For motion of car from *A* to *B*,

$$a=0.5\text{ ms}^{-2}$$

$$v=18\times\frac{5}{18}\text{ ms}^{-1}=5\text{ ms}^{-1}$$

Time, $\quad t_1=\dfrac{v-u}{a}$

$$\Rightarrow\quad t_1=\frac{5-0}{0.5}=10\text{ s}$$

For motion of car from *B* to *C*,

$s=4$ km $=4000$ m and $v=5\text{ ms}^{-1}$

$$t_2=\frac{\text{distance}}{\text{velocity}}=\frac{4000}{5}=800\text{ s}$$

For motion of car from *C* to *D*,

$v=0, u=5\text{ ms}^{-1}$

and $a=-0.2\text{ ms}^{-2}$ (negative sign shows deceleration)

Time taken, $t_3=\dfrac{v-u}{a}$

$$=\frac{0-5}{-0.2}=25\text{ s}$$

Total time taken, $T=t_1+t_2+t_3$

$$\Rightarrow\quad T=(10+800+25)\text{ s}=835\text{ s}$$

22 (*b*) Average acceleration

$$=\frac{\Delta v}{\Delta t}=\frac{20-0}{8-3}=\frac{20}{5}=4\text{ m/s}^2$$

23 (*a*) Given, $v(x)=3x^2-4x$

$$\therefore\quad a=\frac{dv}{dt}=\frac{dv}{dx}\times\frac{dx}{dt}=v\frac{dv}{dx}$$

$$=(3x^2-4x)\times\frac{dv}{dx}$$

$$=(3x^2-4x)(6x-4)$$

24 (*c*)

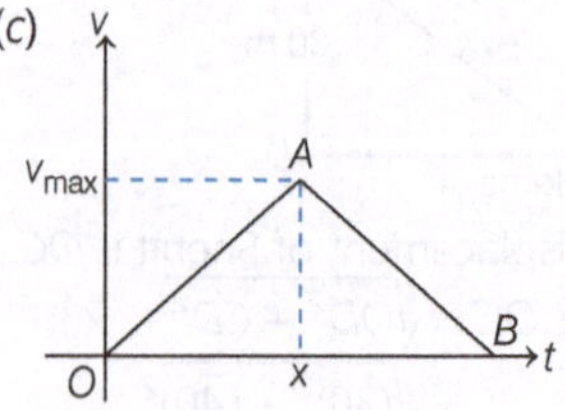

Acceleration $=\alpha=$ Slope of *OA*

$$=\frac{v_{max}}{x}$$

$$\therefore\quad v_{max}=\alpha x$$

Now, the vehicle decelerates during the motion *AB*.

Deceleration $=\beta=$ Slope of *AB*

$$= \frac{v_{max}}{t}$$

$\therefore$ Time, $t = \frac{v_{max}}{\beta}$

Distance travelled during AB,

$$s = \frac{v_{max}^2}{2\beta}$$

$\therefore$ Average speed, $v_{av} = \frac{s}{t}$

$$= \frac{\frac{v_{max}^2}{2\beta}}{\frac{v_{max}}{\beta}} = \frac{v_{max}}{2} = \frac{\alpha x}{2}$$

26 (*d*) Given, $x = 8 + 12t - t^3$

So, $v = 12 - 3t^2$ and $a = -6t$

When $v = 0$, then $t = \sqrt{\frac{12}{3}} = 2$ s

and $a = -6 \times 2 = -12 \text{ ms}^{-2}$

27 (*b*) Given, $v(x) = 3x^{-2n}$

$$a = \frac{dv(x)}{dt} = \frac{dx}{dt} \cdot \frac{dv}{dx}$$

$$\Rightarrow a = v\frac{dv}{dx} = (3x^{-2n})(-2n \times 3x^{-2n-1})$$

$$\Rightarrow a = -18\, nx^{-4n-1}$$

28 (*a*) Given, $t = \alpha x^2 + \beta x$

$$\frac{dt}{dx} = 2\alpha x + \beta$$

$$\Rightarrow \frac{dx}{dt} = v = \frac{1}{2\alpha x + \beta}$$

As acceleration, $a = \frac{dv}{dt} = \frac{dv}{dx}\frac{dx}{dt}$

$$\Rightarrow a = v \cdot \frac{dv}{dx} = v\left(\frac{-2\alpha}{(2\alpha x + \beta)^2}\right)$$

$$= -2\alpha v \cdot v^2 = -2\alpha v^3$$

29 (*d*) The acceleration is given as,

$$a = 5 - 2v$$

$$\Rightarrow \frac{dv}{dt} = 5 - 2v$$

$$\Rightarrow \frac{dv}{5 - 2v} = dt$$

At $t = 0, v = 0$

$$\therefore \int_0^v \frac{dv}{5 - 2v} = \int_0^t dt$$

$$\Rightarrow -\frac{1}{2}\ln\left(\frac{5 - 2v}{5}\right) = t$$

$$\Rightarrow v = \frac{5}{2}(1 - e^{-2t})$$

30 (*b*) The displacement of the particle is

$$x^2 = 3t^2 + 4$$

$$\Rightarrow 2x \cdot \frac{dx}{dt} = 6t$$

$$\Rightarrow x \cdot v = 3t$$

$$\Rightarrow x \cdot \frac{dv}{dt} + v \cdot \frac{dx}{dt} = 3$$

$$\Rightarrow x \cdot a + v^2 = 3$$

$$\Rightarrow x.a + \left(\frac{3t}{x}\right)^2 = 3$$

$$\Rightarrow x \cdot a + \frac{9t^2}{x^2} = 3$$

$$\Rightarrow a = \frac{3(x^2 - 3t^2)}{x^3}$$

$$= \frac{3 \times 4}{x^3}$$

$$\therefore a \propto \frac{1}{x^3}$$

31 (*a*) Given, $x = 10t + 15t^3$

$$v = \frac{d}{dt}(10t + 15t^3)$$

$$= 10 + 45t^2$$

$\therefore$ At $t = 0$, $v_0 = 10 + 0 = 10$ m/s

At $t = 2$ s, $v' = 10 + 45 \times 2^2$

$$= 190 \text{ m/s}$$

$$\Delta v = v' - v_0 = 190 - 10 = 180 \text{ m/s}$$

$$\Delta t = (2 - 0)\text{ s} = 2\text{s}$$

$\therefore$ Average acceleration,

$$a_{av} = \frac{\Delta v}{\Delta t} = \frac{180}{2} = 90 \text{ m/s}^2$$

Instantaneous acceleration,

$$a_{ins} = \frac{dv}{dt} = \frac{d}{dt}(10 + 45t^2) = 90t$$

At $t = 2$s, $a_{ins} = 90 \times 2 = 180 \text{ m/s}^2$

$\therefore a_{ins} - a_{av} = 180 - 90 = 90 \text{ m/s}^2$

32 (*c*) Position of particle is,

$$x(t) = pt + qt^2 - rt^3$$

So, its velocity is,

$$v = \frac{dx}{dt} = p + 2qt - 3rt^2$$

and acceleration is,

$$a = \frac{dv}{dt} = 2q - 6rt$$

Acceleration is zero, then

$$2q - 6rt = 0$$

$$\Rightarrow t = \frac{2q}{6r} = \frac{q}{3r}$$

Substituting t in expression of velocity, we get

$$v = p + 2q\left(\frac{q}{3r}\right) - 3r\left(\frac{q}{3r}\right)^2$$

$$= p + \frac{2q^2}{3r} - \frac{q^2}{3r} = p + \frac{q^2}{3r}$$

33 (*c*) For negative acceleration, the x - t graph moves downward. But the car is moving in positive direction as the position coordinate is increasing in the positive direction.

34 (*c*) Acceleration of the car,

$$a = \frac{v - v_0}{t} = \frac{(15 - 30)}{2}$$

$$= -\frac{15}{2} = -7.5 \text{ ms}^{-2}$$

35 (*c*) Displacement of the object = Area under v -t curve

$$x = \frac{1}{2}(v - v_0)t + v_0 t \quad \text{... (i)}$$

Also, $v = v_0 + at$

$$\Rightarrow v - v_0 = at \quad \text{...(ii)}$$

Putting the value of $(v - v_0)$ from Eq. (ii) in Eq. (i), we get

$$x = \frac{1}{2}at \times t + v_0 t$$

$$\Rightarrow x = \frac{1}{2}at^2 + v_0 t$$

36 (*a*) Using relation, $v^2 = v_0^2 + 2ax$

or $v^2 = 2ax$ $[\because v_0 = 0]$

$\therefore v = \sqrt{2ax}$

37 (*a*) Using relation,

$$x = x_0 + v_0 t + \frac{1}{2}at^2$$

$$= 3 + \frac{1}{2} \times 4 \times (3)^2$$

$$= +21 \text{ m}$$

38 (*b*) Body is initially at rest, $u = 0$

The displacement of particle is given as

$$s = ut + \frac{1}{2}at^2 \quad \text{...(i)}$$

Substituting $u = 0$ in Eq. (i), we get

$$s = \frac{1}{2}at^2$$

$$s \propto t^2 \Rightarrow \frac{t_1}{t_2} = \sqrt{\frac{s_1}{s_2}} \quad \text{...(ii)}$$

Given, $t_2 = 6\text{ s}$

$$s_1 = \frac{s}{9}, s_2 = s$$

where, s is the total distance covered by body, so from Eq. (ii), we get

$$t_1 = \sqrt{\frac{\frac{s}{9}}{s}} \times t_2 = \frac{1}{3} \times 6 = 2\text{ s}$$

39 (*b*) As, $v = u + at$ ...(i)

From Eq. (i), $a = \frac{v-u}{t}$

$$\Rightarrow \quad a = \frac{25-15}{5} = \frac{10}{5} = 2\text{ ms}^{-2}$$

Now, velocity at 4s, before the given instant is given as

$$v = u + at$$

$$\Rightarrow \quad 15 = u + (2)(4)$$

$$\Rightarrow \quad u = 7\text{ ms}^{-1}$$

40 (*b*) The distance covered in nth second is given by

$$s_n = u + \frac{a}{2}(2n-1)$$

For $n = 3$s, $s_3 = 6$ m, we get

$$6 = u + \frac{a}{2}(2\times 3 - 1) = u + \frac{5a}{2}$$

$$\Rightarrow \quad 6 = u + \frac{5a}{2} \quad \text{...(i)}$$

Similarly for distance of 12 m in 6th second,

$$12 = u + \frac{a}{2}(12-1)$$

$$\Rightarrow \quad 12 = u + \frac{11}{2}a \quad \text{...(ii)}$$

From Eqs. (i) and (ii), we get

$$6 - \frac{5a}{2} = 12 - \frac{11a}{2}$$

$$\Rightarrow \quad a = \frac{6}{6} \times 2 = 2\text{ ms}^{-2}$$

and $u = 6 - \frac{5a}{2} = 6 - \frac{10}{2} = 1\text{ ms}^{-1}$

Distance travelled in next 3s,

$$s = s_9 - s_6$$

$$= \left(ut + \frac{1}{2}at^2\right)_{t = 9\text{ s}} - \left(ut + \frac{1}{2}at^2\right)_{t = 6\text{ s}}$$

$$\Rightarrow \quad s = \left(1\times 9 + \frac{1}{2}\times 2\times 81\right) - \left(1\times 6 + \frac{1}{2}\times 2 \times 36\right)$$

$$\Rightarrow \quad s = 90 - 42 = 48\text{ cm}$$

41 (*d*) In first situation,

$$v^2 = u^2 - 2as$$

$$\Rightarrow \quad 0 = (10)^2 - 2\times a\times 20$$

$$\therefore \quad a = \frac{5}{2}\text{ m/s}^2$$

In second situation,

$$v^2 = u^2 - 2as$$

$$\Rightarrow \quad 0 = (30)^2 - 2\times\frac{5}{2}\times s$$

$$\therefore \quad s = \frac{30\times 30}{5} = 180\text{ m}$$

42 (*b*) $a = \frac{v-u}{t} = \frac{5-0}{10} = \frac{1}{2}\text{ m/s}^2$

Now, displacement of the body in last 2s,

$$s = s_{10} - s_8$$

$$= \frac{1}{2}\times a\times(10)^2 - \frac{1}{2}\times a\times(8)^2$$

$$= \frac{1}{2}\times\frac{1}{2}\times(10)^2 - \frac{1}{2}\times\frac{1}{2}\times(8)^2$$

$$= 25 - 16 = 9\text{ m}$$

43 (*c*) For first body,

$$u = 0, s = x, t = t_1$$

$$\therefore \quad s = ut_1 + \frac{1}{2}gt_1^2$$

$$\Rightarrow \quad x = 0 + \frac{1}{2}gt_1^2$$

$$\therefore \quad t_1 = \sqrt{\frac{2x}{g}}$$

For second body,

$$u = 0, s = y, t = t_2$$

$$\therefore \quad s = ut_2 + \frac{1}{2}gt_2^2$$

$$\Rightarrow \quad y = 0 + \frac{1}{2}gt_2^2$$

$$\Rightarrow \quad t_2 = \sqrt{\frac{2y}{g}}$$

$$\because \quad \frac{t_1}{t_2} = \sqrt{\frac{2x}{g}\times\frac{g}{2y}} = \sqrt{x} : \sqrt{y}$$

44 (*d*) The equations of motion are

$$v = 9.8\,t\text{ ms}^{-1} \quad (\text{using } v = v_0 + at)$$

$$y = \frac{1}{2}\times(9.8)\times t^2\text{ m} = 4.9\,t^2\text{ m} \quad (\text{using } y = v_0t + 1/2\,at^2)$$

$$v^2 = 2\times(9.8)\times y \quad (\text{using } v^2 = v_0^2 + 2ay)$$

$$= 19.6y\text{ m}^2\text{s}^{-2}$$

45 (*a*) The given situation can be shown below as

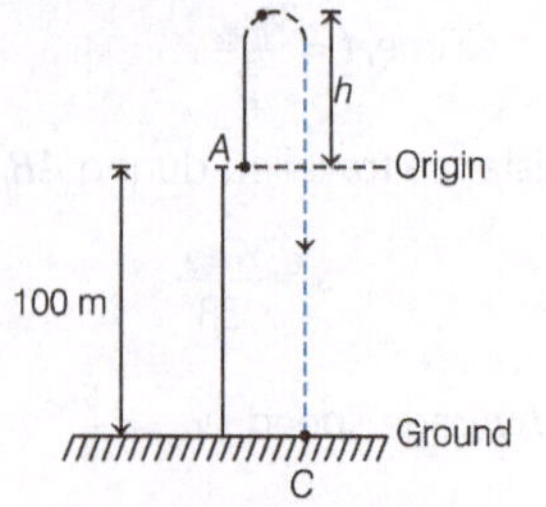

At maximum height, v = final velocity = 0 ms^{-1}

v_0 = initial velocity = 10 ms^{-1},

$a = -g = -10\text{ ms}^{-2}$

Using the relation,

$$v^2 = v_0^2 + 2gh$$

or $(0)^2 = (10)^2 + 2\times(-10)\times h$

or $h = \frac{-100}{-20} = 5\text{ m}$

$\therefore$ Maximum height above ground $= (100+5)\text{ m} = 105\text{ m}$

46 (*c*) Time taken to reach the maximum height,

$$t_1 = \frac{u}{g}$$

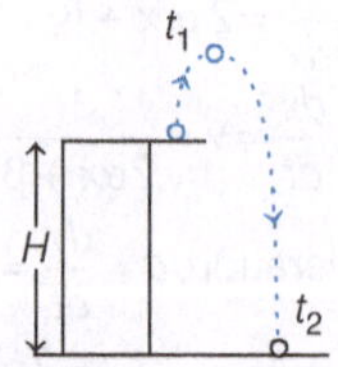

If t_2 is the time taken to hit the ground, then

$$-H = ut_2 - \frac{1}{2}gt_2^2$$

But $t_2 = nt_1$ (Given)

So, $-H = u\frac{nu}{g} - \frac{1}{2}g\frac{n^2u^2}{g^2}$

$$\Rightarrow \quad -H = \frac{nu^2}{g} - \frac{1}{2}\frac{n^2u^2}{g}$$

$$\Rightarrow \quad 2gH = nu^2(n-2)$$

47 (*a*) For first stone,

Taking the vertical upward motion of the stone upto highest point.

$$\therefore \quad (0)^2 - u_1^2 = 2(-g)h_1$$

or $\quad h_1 = \dfrac{u_1^2}{2g}$ ...(i)

For second stone,

Taking the vertical upward motion of the second stone upto highest point.

$\therefore \quad (0)^2 - u_2^2 = 2(-g)h_2$

or $\quad h_2 = \dfrac{u_2^2}{2g}$ ...(ii)

Subtracting Eq. (ii) from Eq. (i), we get

$$h_1 - h_2 = \frac{u_1^2}{2g} - \frac{u_2^2}{2g}$$

$\because \quad u_2 = \dfrac{u_1}{2}$

$\therefore \quad 15 = \dfrac{u_1^2}{2g} - \dfrac{u_1^2}{8g} = \dfrac{3u_1^2}{8g}$

or $u_1^2 = \dfrac{15 \times 8g}{3} = \dfrac{15 \times 8 \times 10}{3} = 400$

or $\quad u_1 = 20 \text{ ms}^{-1}$

and $u_2 = \dfrac{u_1}{2} = 10 \text{ ms}^{-1}$

48 (*b*) Distance covered in first 5s,

$$h_1 = ut + \frac{1}{2}at^2 = 0 + \frac{1}{2}a(5)^2 \qquad [\because u = 0]$$

$\Rightarrow \quad h_1 = \dfrac{25a}{2}$ ...(i)

Distance covered in first 10 s,

$$s_2 = 0 + \frac{1}{2}a(10)^2 = \frac{100a}{2}$$

So, distance covered in second 5 s,

$h_2 = s_2 - h_1 = \dfrac{75a}{2}$ ...(ii)

Distance covered in first 15 s,

$$s_3 = 0 + \frac{1}{2}a(15)^2 = \frac{225a}{2}$$

So, distance covered in last 5 s,

$h_3 = s_3 - s_2 = \dfrac{125a}{2}$ ...(iii)

Using Eqs. (i), (ii) and (iii), we get

$$\frac{h_1}{\frac{25a}{2}} = \frac{h_2}{\frac{75a}{2}} = \frac{h_3}{\frac{125a}{2}}$$

$\Rightarrow \quad h_1 = \dfrac{h_2}{3} = \dfrac{h_3}{5}$

49 (*a*) Since, initial velocity is zero ($v_0 = 0$).

We have, $\quad y = -(1/2)\, g\tau^2$ ...(i)

For missing term *A*,

Time interval $= 3\tau$

$$y = -\frac{1}{2} \times g \times (3\tau)^2 = -9\left(\frac{1}{2}g\tau^2\right)$$

$$A = y = +9\, y_0 \qquad \left[\because y = -\frac{1}{2}g\tau^2\right]$$

For $t = 5\tau$, using Eq. (i),

$$y_1 = -\frac{1}{2} \times g \times (5\tau)^2 = 25y_0$$

For $\quad t = 6\tau$,

$$y_2 = -\frac{1}{2} \times g \times (6\tau)^2 = 36y_0$$

$$\therefore B = y_2 - y_1 = 36y_0 - 25y_0 = 11y_0$$

50 (*a*) $\quad s = v_0 t_r + (1/2)at_r^2$

$$= 20 \times 2 + (1/2)\, 4 \times (2)^2 = 40 + (2)(2)^2 = 48 \text{ m}$$

51 (*c*) The stopping distance is given by

$$d_s = -\frac{u^2}{2a}$$

$\Rightarrow \quad d_s \propto u^2$

$$\therefore \quad \frac{d_{s_1}}{d_{s_2}} = \left(\frac{u_1}{u_2}\right)^2 = \left(\frac{54}{108}\right)^2 = \left(\frac{1}{2}\right)^2$$

$$\therefore \quad d_{s_2} = 4d_{s_1} = 4 \times 10 = 40 \text{ m}$$

52 (*a*) The distance travelled *d* and the reaction time t_r are related by

$$d = \frac{1}{2}gt_r^2 \quad \text{or} \quad t_r = \sqrt{\frac{2d}{g}}$$

or $\quad t_r = \sqrt{\dfrac{2 \times 0.21}{9.8}} \approx 0.2 \text{ s}$

53 (*a*) According to given situation, we observe that the car is speeding up from origin to $t = 10$ s, so *x*-*t* graph has a curve with increasing slope. It is in uniform motion only between $t = 10$ s and $t = 18$ s. So, for $t = 10$ s and $t = 18$ s, the graph must be a straight line inclined to time axis as shown below

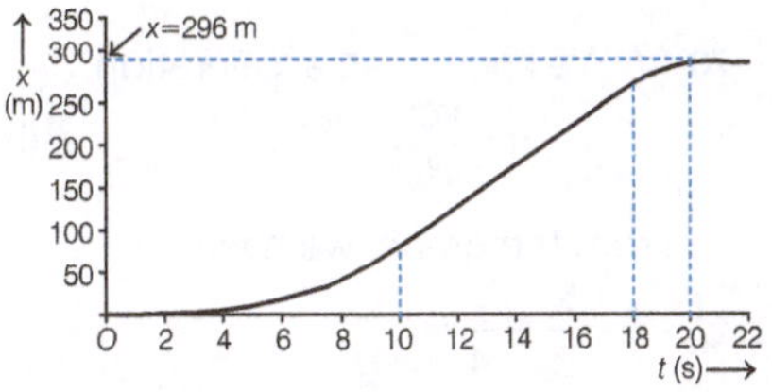

At $t = 20$ s, the car stops at position $x = 296$ m and hence the *x*-*t* graph from $t = 20$ s onwards must be a straight line parallel to time axis.

From $t = 18$ s to $t = 20$ s, the car slows down by applying brakes. So, the curve has decreasing slope between this interval.

54 (*d*)

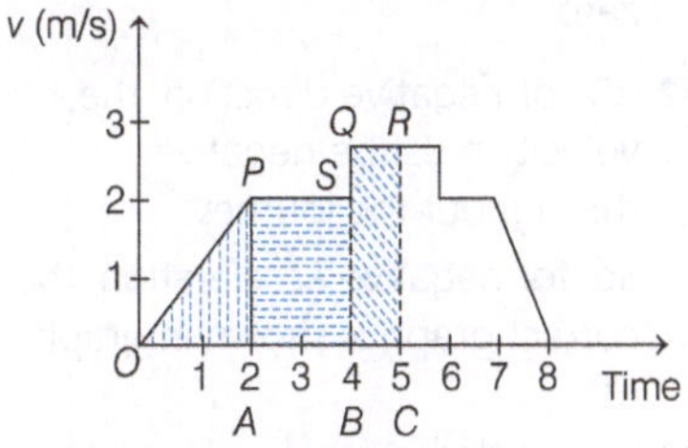

$\therefore$ Displacement of particle

= Area of triangle *OPA* + Area of rectangle *PSBA* + Area of rectangle *QBCR*

$$= \left(\frac{1}{2} \times 2 \times 2\right) + (2 \times 2) + 3 \times 1 = 2 + 4 + 3 = 9 \text{ m}$$

56 (*a*) For time 0 to 1 s s – slope is negative

Hence, velocity will be negative.

For time 0 to 2 s – slope is positive.

Hence, velocity will be positive.

58 (*b*) Given, $x_2 = 27.4$ m, $x_1 = 10$ m, $t_2 = 7$s and $t_1 = 5$ s

Average velocity between 5 s and 7s is

$$\bar{v} = \frac{x_2 - x_1}{t_2 - t_1} = \frac{27.4 - 10}{7 - 5} = \frac{17.4}{2} = 8.7 \text{ ms}^{-1}$$

59 (*a*) As slope = $\tan\theta$

The ratio of square of velocities,

$$v_A^2 : v_B^2 = \tan^2\theta_A : \tan^2\theta_B = \tan^2 30° : \tan^2 45° = \frac{1}{3} : 1 = 1 : 3$$

61 (*a*)

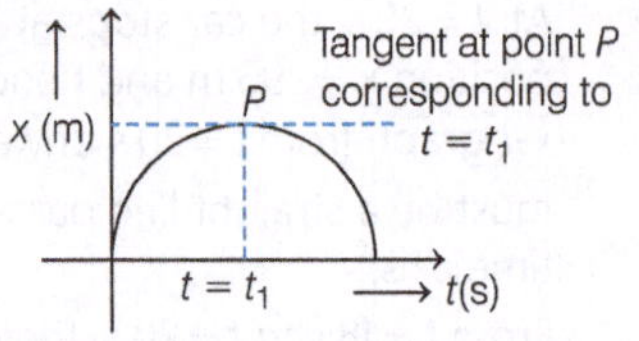

At $t = t_1$, the tangent is parallel to time axis as shown above and hence, its slope is zero. Thus, instantaneous velocity at $t = t_1$ is zero.

62 (*d*) For negative direction, the velocity must be negative throughout the journey.

So, for negative acceleration, the correct graph is shown in graph (d).

64 (*a*)

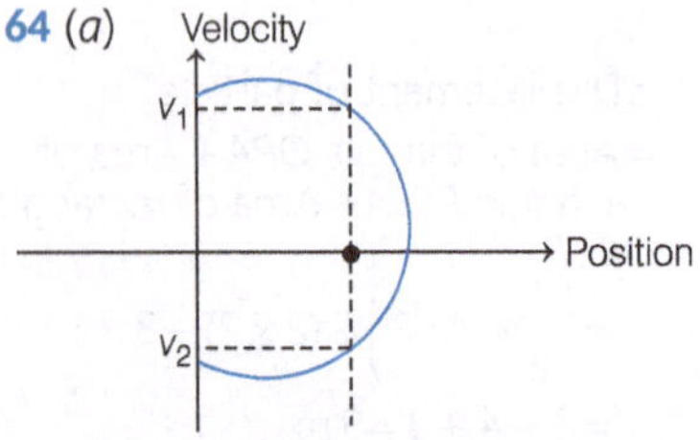

A particle can not have two instantaneous velocities at same position.

65 (*a*) A particle thrown upward is an example of motion under gravity. Throughout, the motion of the particle, acceleration due to gravity acts downward, i.e. in y-direction, so $a = -g =$ constant.

Since, acceleration is negative, slope of v- t graph must be negative.

At highest point, the velocity becomes zero. After that, the particle moves downward with negative velocity as shown below.

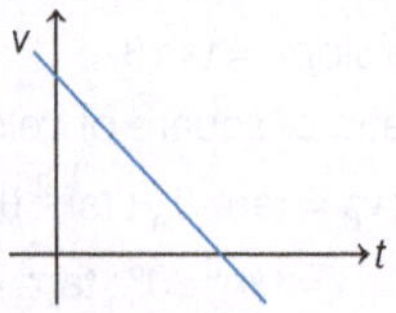

66 (*b*) For uniformly decelerated motion,

$$a = -k$$

$$\Rightarrow \quad \frac{dv}{dt} = -k$$

$$\Rightarrow \quad \int dv = -\int k dt$$

$$\Rightarrow \quad v = -kt$$

$$\Rightarrow \quad \frac{dx}{dt} = -kt$$

$$\Rightarrow \quad \int dx = -\int ktdt$$

$$\therefore \quad x = -\frac{1}{2}kt^2$$

$\therefore$ x-t graph is a parabola opening in downward direction.

67 (*a*) The given v-t graph is

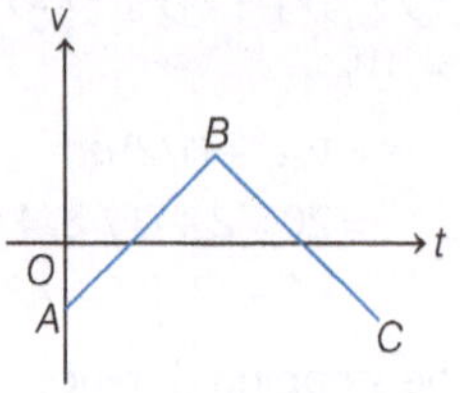

For the region AB, $a =$ Slope of $AB = +\text{ve}$

For the region BC, $a =$ Slope of $BC = -\text{ve}$

$\therefore$ Option (a) is the correct answer.

68 (*a*) The maximum speed of the particle is upto 2s due to its positive acceleration.

$\therefore v_{max} =$ Area of a-t graph upto 2s

$$= 10 \times 1.5 + \frac{1}{2}(2 - 1.5) \times 10$$

$$= 17.5 \text{ m/s}$$

69 (*b*) For the region AB, the graph is parabola.

$$\therefore \quad x = kt^2$$

$$\because \quad v = \frac{dx}{dt} = 2kt$$

$\therefore$ Acceleration,

$$a = \frac{dv}{dt} = 2k = \text{Constant.}$$

Hence, the particle is moving with constant acceleration in the region of AB.

70 (*d*) We know that, acceleration,

$$a = \frac{vdv}{dx} \quad \text{...(i)}$$

From the graph, we have

$$\frac{x}{2} + \frac{v}{4} = 1$$

$$\Rightarrow \quad 2x + v = 4 \quad \text{...(ii)}$$

$$\Rightarrow \quad \frac{dv}{dx} = -2 \quad \text{...(iii)}$$

From Eqs. (i), (ii) and (iii), we get

$$a = (4 - 2x)(-2)$$

$$= -8 + 4x$$

$$\Rightarrow \quad a = 4x - 8$$

71 (*d*) Since, the particle starts from rest, this means, initial velocity, $u = 0$.

Also, it moves with uniform acceleration along positive X-axis. This means, its acceleration (a) is constant.

$\therefore$ Given, a - t graph in (A) is correct.

As we know, for velocity-time graph,

slope = acceleration.

Since, the given v-t graph in (B) represents that its slope is constant and non-zero.

$\therefore$ Graph in (B) is also correct.

Also, the displacement of such a particle with respect to time is given by

$$x = ut + \frac{1}{2}at^2$$

$$= 0 + \frac{1}{2}at^2$$

$$\Rightarrow x \propto t^2$$

So, x *versus* t graph would be a parabola with starting from origin. This is correctly represented in displacement-time graph given in (D).

72 (*a*) Average acceleration for different time intervals is the slope of v-t graph, which is as follows

For 0 -10 s,

$$\bar{a} = \frac{(24 - 0) \text{ ms}^{-1}}{(10 - 0) \text{ s}} = 2.4 \text{ ms}^{-2}$$

For 10 s -18 s,

$$\bar{a} = \frac{(24 - 24) \text{ ms}^{-1}}{(18 - 10) \text{ s}} = 0 \text{ ms}^{-2}$$

For 18 s-20 s,

$$\bar{a} = \frac{(0 - 24) \text{ ms}^{-1}}{(20 - 18) \text{ s}} = - 12 \text{ ms}^{-2}$$

So, the corresponding a-t graph for the given v-t graph is as follows

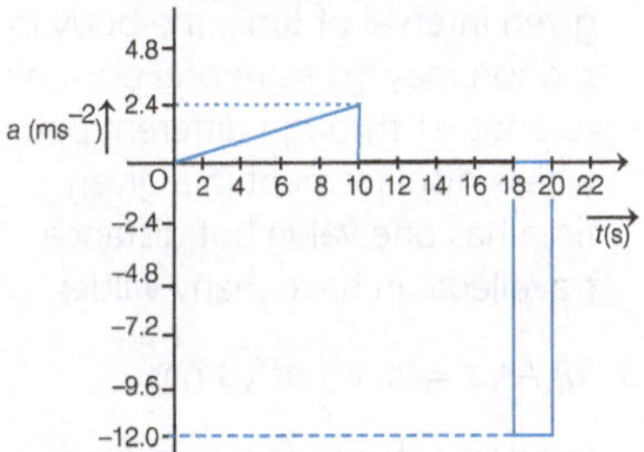

73 (*a*) For $t = 0$ s to $t = 2$ s; a is positive, i.e. $a > 0$.

So, v - t graph will be a straight line with positive slope.

For $t = 2$ s to $t = 4$ s, a is negative, i.e. ($a < 0$). So, v-t graph will be a straight line with negative slope. Complete v-t graph will be as below.

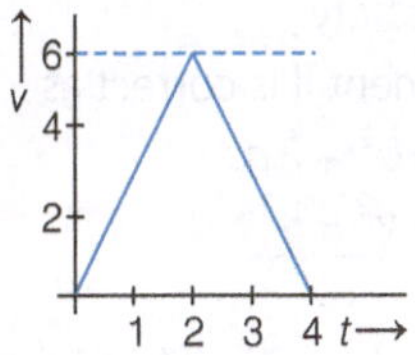

Also, v = Area under a-t graph for $t = 0$ s to $t = 2$ s

$$= 3 \times 2$$

$\Rightarrow \quad v = 6\ ms^{-1}$, which is the maximum velocity attained.

75 (*b*) For negative acceleration, the slope of the graph must be negative.

For positive direction, velocity must be positive, so graph (b) is correct.

76 (*c*) The object is moving in positive direction till time $t = 0$ to $t = t_1$ and at $t = t_1$, we find that the velocity becomes negative, i.e. the object changes its direction at $t = t_1$ and continues to move in negative direction.

77 (*a*) Slope of the v - t graph gives the value of constant acceleration.

So, in the given graph as shown below

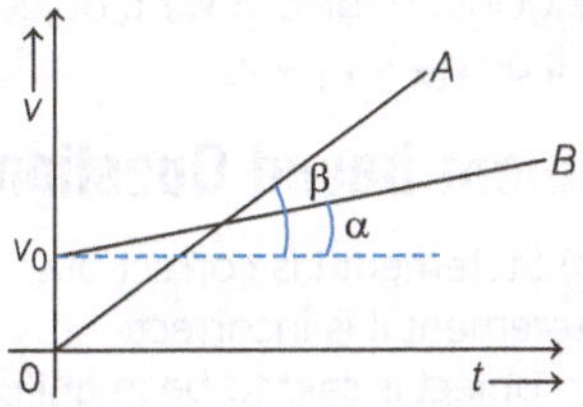

$$\beta > \alpha \Rightarrow \tan\beta > \tan\alpha$$

Hence, $a_A > a_B$

78 (*d*) For uniform velocity,

$$x_A(t) = x_A(0) + v_A t$$

and $x_B(t) = x_B(0) + v_B t$

$\therefore$ The displacement from object A to object B is given by

$$x_{BA}(t) = x_B(t) - x_A(t)$$
$$= [x_B(0) - x_A(0)] + (v_B - v_A)t$$

79 (*a*) If v_{BA} or v_{AB} is zero, then $v_A = v_B$ as $v_{AB} = v_{BA} = |v_A - v_B|$.

For uniform motion, the position-time graph will be straight lines parallel to each other and inclined to time axis as shown below for given situation.

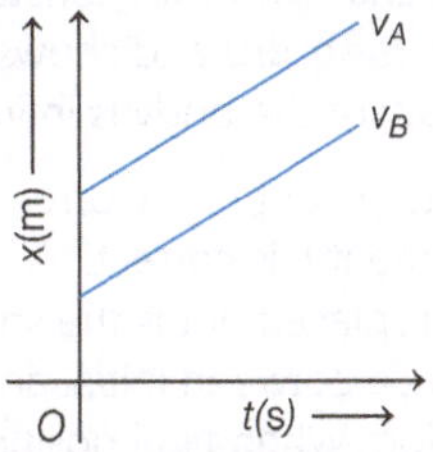

80 (*d*) **Case I** If particles are moving in same direction.

$$v_{AB} = v_A - v_B = 0$$

$\Rightarrow \quad v_A = v_B \quad$ ...(i)

Also, $\quad v_{BA} = v_B - v_A = 0$

$\Rightarrow \quad v_B = v_A \quad$ ...(ii)

From Eqs. (i) and (ii), we get

A and B must be moving in same direction as ($v_A = v_B$).

Case II If particles are moving in opposite direction,

i.e. $\quad v_A = -v_B$

$$v_{AB} = v_A - v_B = -v_B - v_B = -2v_B$$
$$|v_{AB}| = 2|v_B| = 2|v_A|$$

Also, $v_{BA} = v_B - v_A = v_B - (-v_B)$

$$= 2v_B$$
$$|v_{BA}| = 2|v_B| = 2|v_A|$$

Hence, for motion in opposite direction, the magnitude of v_{BA} or v_{AB} is twice than the magnitude of velocity of A or that of B.

81 (*d*) If $v_A > v_B$, then $v_{BA} = v_B - v_A$ will be negative and $v_{AB} = v_A - v_B$ will be positive.

The x-t graph thus plotted for A and B is as shown below in which object A overtakes object B at time $t = 3$ s.

From graph, it can be concluded that, one graph is steeper than the other and they meet at a common point.

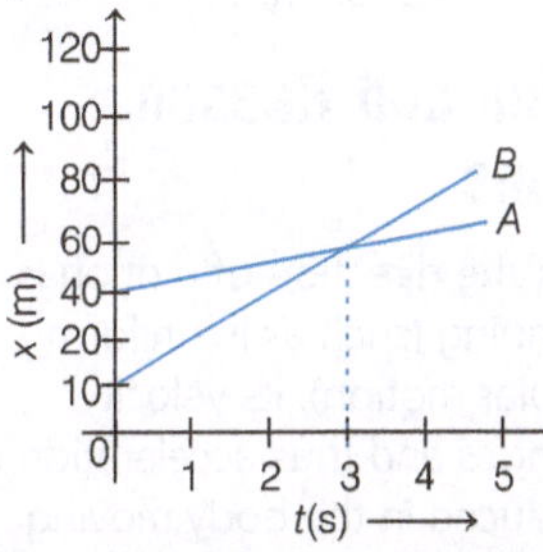

82 (*c*) Ratio of time when trains move in same direction with time when trains move in opposite direction is

$$\frac{t_1}{t_2} = \frac{\left(\frac{l_1 + l_2}{|v_1 - v_2|}\right)}{\left(\frac{l_1 + l_2}{|v_1 + v_2|}\right)} = \frac{|v_1 + v_2|}{|v_1 - v_2|}$$

where, $l_1 + l_2$ = sum of lengths of trains which is same as distance covered by trains to cross each other.

So, $\quad \dfrac{t_1}{t_2} = \dfrac{80 + 30}{80 - 30} = \dfrac{110}{50} = \dfrac{11}{5}$

83 (*a*) Let south to north direction be positive.

Velocity of car, $v_C = -20\ ms^{-1}$

Velocity of person, $v_P = +10\ ms^{-1}$

$\because \quad v_{CP} = v_C - v_P$

$$= (-20) - (10)$$
$$= -30\ ms^{-1}$$

84 (*a*) For the ball A, the final velocity at time t is

$$v_A = v_1 - gt$$

For the ball B, the final velocity at time t is

$$v_B = 0 + gt = gt$$

$\therefore$ The relative velocity of ball A with respect to ball B is

$$v_{AB} = v_A - (-v_B) = v_A + v_B$$
$$= v_1 - gt + gt = v_1$$

85 (b) The relative speed of scooter with respect to bus is

$$v_{sb} = v_s - v_b = v_s - 12$$

Now, $d = v_{sb} \cdot t$

$\Rightarrow 1000 = (v_s - 12) \times 120$

$\therefore \quad v_s = \frac{1000}{120} + 12$

$= 20.33$ m/s

Assertion and Reason Questions

4 (d) If the direction of motion is changing (such as in uniform circular motion), its velocity changes and thus acceleration is produced in the body moving uniformly.

5 (a) The x - t, v - t and a - t graphs will be smooth, which means that physically, the values of acceleration and velocity cannot change abruptly as changes are always continuous.

6 (c) When a particle is released from rest position under gravity, then $v = 0$ at initial point but $a = g$, i.e. $a \neq 0$.

8 (a) Both Assertion and Reason are correct and Reason is the correct explanation of Assertion. As both the balls of different masses falls under the effect of gravity, which is independent of mass.

9 (b) A body having negative acceleration can be associated with a speeding up, if object moves along negative x-direction with speed.

10 (c) When objects A and B move in opposite direction, then relative velocity of object B w.r.t. object A will be $v_{BA} = v_B + v_A$.

Statement Based Questions

1 (b) Statement I is correct but Statement II is incorrect.
An object is said to be in uniform motion if it undergoes equal displacement in equal interval of time.

2 (b) Statement I is correct but Statement II is incorrect.
Change in the direction of the velocity also produces acceleration as in the case of circular motion. The change in magnitude or direction of the velocity or both can produce acceleration.

3 (a) Both Statement I and Statement II are incorrect.
If the position-time graph of a body moving uniformly in a straight line is parallel to position axis, it means that the position of body changing with constant time, which is absurd and shows that the velocity of the body is infinite.

4 (c) Statement I is incorrect but Statement II is correct.
The displacement is the shortest distance between initial and final position. When final position of a body coincides with its initial position, displacement is zero, but distance travelled is not zero.

5 (c) Statement I is incorrect but Statement II is correct.

If acceleration of a car is equal to g that does not mean car is falling freely. When a body falling freely only gravitational force acts on it in vertically downward direction. Due to this downward acceleration, the velocity of a body increases and will be maximum when the body touches the ground.

6 (d) Both Statement I and Statement II are correct. For a given interval of time, the body in motion may go from one position to another through different paths, where displacement in a given time has one value but distance travelled can have many values.

7 (d) As, $s = ut + \frac{1}{2}at^2$, s has quadratic dependence on time, when object moves with constant acceleration, the x-t graph is parabolic in nature.

8 (c) Statement I is incorrect as reaction time is the time a person takes to observe, think and act. For example, a person is driving vehicle, suddenly a child appears on the road, then the time elapsed before he applies the brakes, is called reaction time. So, lower the reaction time, more will be the road safety.

Statement II is correct as

$$v^2 = u^2 + 2as,$$
$$as = \frac{v^2 - u^2}{2}$$
$$\Delta K = \frac{1}{2}m(v^2 - u^2)$$
$$\therefore \Delta K = mas,$$

So, Area of acceleration-displacement graph, $\Delta K / m$

Matching Type Questions

1 (a) A. Displacement of the car in moving from O to P is
$\Delta x = x_2 - x_1 = (+360 \text{ m}) - 0 \text{ m}$
$= +360$ m

B. Path length of the car in moving from O to R is 120 m, as path length is the total distance traversed by the car from O to R.

C. For the motion of the car from O to P and back to Q.
Path length
$= (+360 \text{ m}) + (+120 \text{ m})$
$= +480$ m

D. In the above case, displacement $= (+240 \text{ m}) - (0 \text{ m}) = +240$ m

2 (*b*) In x-t graph,

$OA \rightarrow$ Positive slope $\rightarrow$ Positive velocity

$AB \rightarrow$ Negative slope $\rightarrow$ Negative velocity

$BC \rightarrow$ Zero slope $\rightarrow$ Object at rest

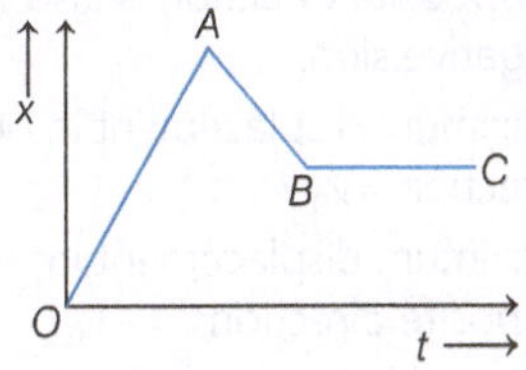

At point A, there is a change in sign of velocity, hence the direction of motion must have changed at A.

3 (*b*) Given, $x(t) = a - bt^2$, $a = 8.5$ m and $b = 2.5\ \text{ms}^{-2}$

$\therefore\ x(t) = 8.5 - 2.5t^2$

Velocity of object $= \frac{dx}{dt} = -2bt$

A. Velocity at

$t = 2.0\ \text{s} = \left.\frac{dx}{dt}\right|_{t=2} = -4b$

$= -4 \times 2.5 = -10\ \text{ms}^{-1}$

B. Velocity at

$t = 0\text{s} = \left.\frac{dx}{dt}\right|_{t=0} = 0\ \text{ms}^{-1}$

C. Instantaneous speed at

$t = 2$ s $=$ Magnitude of velocity

$= |-10\ \text{ms}^{-1}| = 10\ \text{ms}^{-1}$

D. Average velocity

$= \frac{x(t_2) - x(t_1)}{t_2 - t_1} = \frac{x(4) - x(2)}{4 - 2}$

$= \frac{[a - b(4)^2] - [a - b(2)^2]}{2}$

$= -6b = -15\ \text{ms}^{-1}$

4 (*c*) A. Distance of the object between $t = 0$ s to $t = 2$ s.

$=$ Area under v-t graph

$= \frac{1}{2} \times 2 \times 4 = 4$ m

B. $a =$ slope of graph

$= \frac{0 - 4}{2 - 0} = -2\ \text{m/s}^2$

C. For $t = 0$ s to $t = 4$ s,

Displacement $=$ Area under v-t curve $t = 0$ s to $t = 2$ s $+$ Area under v-t curve ($t = 2$s to $t = 4$ s)

$= \frac{1}{2} \times 2 \times 4 + \frac{1}{2} \times 2 \times (-4)$

$= 4\ \text{m} + (-4\ \text{m}) = 0$

D. For $t = 0$ s to $t = 4$ s,

Distance covered $=$ Area under v-t curve considering all areas as positive.

$=$ Area under v-t curve ($t = 0$ s to $t = 2$ s) $+$ Area under v-t curve ($t = 2$ s to $t = 4$ s)

$= 4\ \text{m} + 4\ \text{m} = 8$ m

5 (*d*)

A. For $t = 0$ s to $t = 2$ s, the motion is in positive direction as the velocity is positive and the acceleration is positive, since the slope of the straight line is positive.

B. For $t = 2$ s to $t = 4$ s, the object is moving in positive direction, till time $t_1 = 2$ s, and then turns back with the same negative acceleration till $t = 4$ s.

C. For $t = 4$ s to $t = 6$ s, the object is moving in negative direction, since the velocity is negative. The acceleration is positive, since the slope of the straight line is positive.

D. Displacement for overall journey ($t = 0$s to $t = 6$ s) $=$ Total area under v-t graph considering the area below time axis as negative $=$ [Area under v-t curve for $t = 0$ to $t = 3$ s] $+$ [Area under v-t curve for $t = 3$ s to $t = 6$ s] $=$ Area of triangle (OAB) $+$ Area of triangle (BCD)

$= \frac{1}{2} \times 3 \times 5 + \frac{1}{2} \times 3 \times (-5) = 0$

Numerical Type Questions

2 (18) Let total distance AB is l.

$$v_{av} = \frac{l}{\left(\frac{l}{v_3} + \frac{l}{v_2} + \frac{l}{v_1}\right)\frac{1}{3}}$$

$$= \frac{3}{\left(\frac{1}{v_1} + \frac{1}{v_2} + \frac{1}{v_3}\right)}$$

$$= \frac{3}{\frac{1}{11} + \frac{1}{22} + \frac{1}{33}} = 18\ \text{m/s}$$

3 (29) Given, $s = 3.5t^2 + t$

$v = \frac{ds}{dt} = 7t + 1$

Speed at $t = 4$s,

$v = 7 \times 4 + 1 = 29\ \text{ms}^{-1}$

4 (4) For the first situation,

Speed of car, $u_1 = 100$ km/h

$= \frac{250}{9}$ m/s

After applying brake, distance travelled, $s_1 = 16$ m

For the second situation,

$u_2 = \frac{125}{9}$ m/s

We know that,

$s = \frac{u^2}{2a}$

$\Rightarrow\ s \propto u^2$

$\because\ \frac{s_2}{s_1} = \left(\frac{u_2}{u_1}\right)^2 = \left(\frac{125/9}{250/9}\right)^2$

$\Rightarrow\ s_2 = \frac{s_1}{4} = \frac{16}{4} = 4$ m

5 (3) Let initial velocity of bullet $= u$

Final velocity of bullet $= \frac{u}{3}$

Distance travelled by bullet, $s = 8$ cm

Using $v^2 = u^2 + 2as$

$\Rightarrow\ a = \frac{u^2}{18}$

By equation of motion,

$u^2 = 2\left[\frac{u^2}{18}\right](6 + x)$

$\left(\because v = 0, a = \frac{u^2}{18}, s = 6 + x\right)$

$\therefore\ x = 3$

6 (5) Let u be the initial velocity.

Time taken by ball to reach highest point,

$t = \frac{u}{g}$ (as final velocity at top = 0)

Frequency of throw, $n = \frac{1}{t}$

$\Rightarrow \quad 3 = \frac{g}{u} \quad (\because n = 3)$

$\Rightarrow \quad u = \frac{g}{3}$

The maximum height the balls can reach,

$$H_{max} = \frac{u^2}{2g} = \frac{\left(\frac{g}{3}\right)^2}{2g} = \frac{g}{18}$$

$$H_{max} = \frac{9 \times 10}{18} = 5\text{m}$$

7 (10) Using equation of motion,

$$v^2 = u^2 + 2gh$$

$\Rightarrow \quad h = \frac{g}{2} \quad [\because v = g, u = 0]$

So, required height

$$= 20 - h = 20 - \frac{g}{2} = 10\text{m}$$

8 (80) For object, using equation of motion,

$$h = ut + \frac{1}{2}gt^2$$

$\Rightarrow \quad 60 = -5t + \frac{1}{2} \times 10 \times t^2$

$\Rightarrow \quad t = 4\text{s}$

Height of ball,

$$H = ut + 60$$
$$= (5 \times 4) + 60 = 80\text{m}$$

9 (8) Using $s = ut + \frac{1}{2}at^2$

$\Rightarrow \quad s = 0 \times t + \frac{1}{2}gt^2 \quad [\because u = 0]$

$\Rightarrow \quad 200 = gt^2 \quad [\because s = 100\text{ m}]$

$\Rightarrow \quad t = \sqrt{\frac{200}{g}} \quad$ ...(i)

In last $\frac{1}{2}$ s body travel a distance of 19 m.

So in $\left(t - \frac{1}{2}\right)$ s, distance travelled is 81 m.

Now, $\quad \frac{1}{2}g\left(t - \frac{1}{2}\right)^2 = 81$

$\Rightarrow \quad \left(t - \frac{1}{2}\right) = \sqrt{\frac{81 \times 2}{g}}$

Using Eq. (i), we get

$$\frac{1}{2} = \frac{1}{\sqrt{g}}\left(\sqrt{200} - \sqrt{81 \times 2}\right)$$

$\Rightarrow \quad g = 8\text{ m/s}^2$

10 (10) $s_{BA} = u_{BA} \times t = (u_B - u_A)t$

$$= (70 - 40)\frac{20}{60} = 10\text{ km}$$

$s_{BA} = -s_{BA} = -10\text{ km} = 10\text{ km}$ behind

NCERT Exemplar Questions

1 (*b*) In graph (b), for one value of displacement, there are two different points of time. Hence, for one time, the average velocity is positive and for other time, it is negative.

As there are opposite velocities in the interval 0 to *T*, hence average velocity can vanish in (b). This can be seen in the figure below.

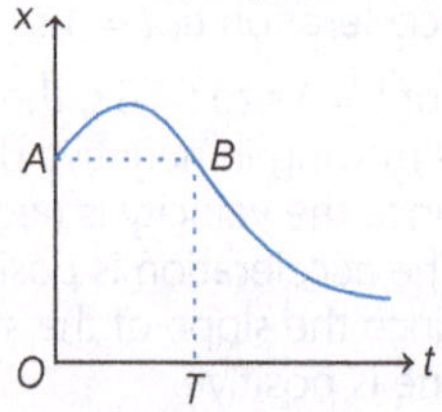

2 (*a*) As the lift is coming in downward direction, displacement will be negative, i.e. $x < 0$. When the lift reaches 4th floor, it is about to stop and hence, motion is retarding in nature, hence $a > 0$.

As displacement is in negative direction, so velocity will also be negative, i.e. $v < 0$. This can be shown in the graph below.

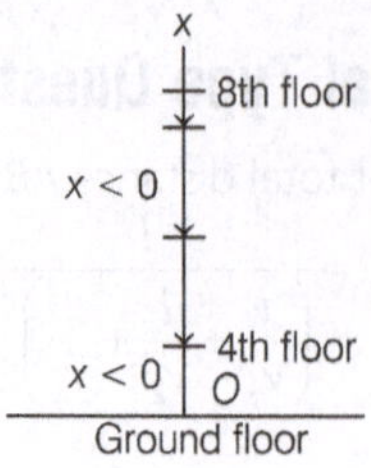

3 (*b*) For maximum and minimum displacement, we have to keep in mind the magnitude and direction of maximum velocity.

As maximum velocity in positive direction is v_0, maximum velocity in opposite direction is also v_0 with negative sign.

Maximum displacement in one direction $= v_0 T$

Maximum displacement in opposite directions $= -v_0 T$

Hence, $-v_0 T < x < v_0 T$.

4 (*c*) Time taken to travel first half distance, $t_1 = \frac{l/2}{v_1} = \frac{l}{2v_1}$

Time taken to travel second half distance, $t_2 = \frac{l}{2v_2}$

Total time $= t_1 + t_2$

$$= \frac{l}{2}\left[\frac{1}{v_1} + \frac{1}{v_2}\right]$$

We know that,

$$v_{av} = \frac{\text{Total distance}}{\text{Total time}}$$
$$= \frac{l}{\frac{l}{2}\left[\frac{1}{v_1} + \frac{1}{v_2}\right]} = \frac{2v_1v_2}{v_1 + v_2}$$

5 (*b*) Given, $x = (t - 2)^2$

$$v = \frac{dx}{dt} = \frac{d}{dt}(t-2)^2 = 2(t-2)\text{ ms}^{-1}$$

$$a = \frac{dv}{dt} = \frac{d}{dt}[2(t-2)]$$
$$= 2[1 - 0] = 2\text{ ms}^{-2}$$

When $\quad t = 0\text{ s}; \quad v = -4\text{ ms}^{-1}$

$\quad t = 2\text{ s}; \quad v = 0\text{ ms}^{-1}$

$\quad t = 4\text{ s}; \quad v = 4\text{ ms}^{-1}$

v-t graph for these values is shown below.

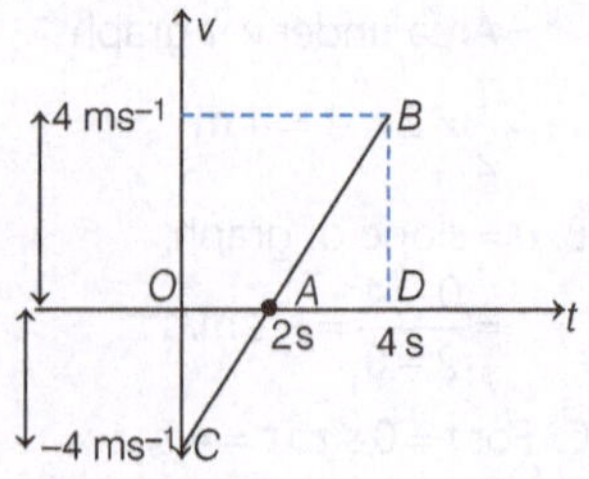

Distance travelled = Area of the graph

$= \text{Area } CAO + \text{Area } ABD$

$= \frac{1}{2} \times 4 \times 2 + \frac{1}{2} \times 2 \times 4 = 8 \text{ m}$

6 (*c*) Let displacement is L, then

Velocity of girl, $v_g = \frac{L}{t_1}$

Velocity of escalator, $v_e = \frac{L}{t_2}$

Net velocity of the girl

$= v_g + v_e$

If t is total time taken in covering distance L, then

$$\frac{L}{t} = \frac{L}{t_1} + \frac{L}{t_2} \Rightarrow t = \frac{t_1 t_2}{t_1 + t_2}$$

8 (*d*) Given, $x = t - \sin t$

Velocity, $v = \frac{dx}{dt} = \frac{d}{dt}[t - \sin t]$

$= 1 - \cos t$

Acceleration,

$$a = \frac{dv}{dt} = \frac{d}{dt}[1 - \cos t] = \sin t$$

As acceleration $a > 0$ for all $t > 0$

Hence, $x(t) > 0$ for all $t > 0$

Velocity, $v = 1 - \cos t$

$v_{max} = 1 - (\cos t)_{min} = 1 - (-1) = 2$

$v_{min} = 1 - (\cos t)_{max} = 1 - 1 = 0$

Hence, v lies between 0 and 2.

Past Exams Questions

1 (*c*) We know that

$$a = \frac{dv}{dt}$$

For v = constant, $a = 0$

Thus, for v - t graph when v is positive and linearly increasing, a will be positive constant and if v is decreasing linearly, a will be negative constant.

Hence, option (c) is correct.

2 (*d*) The given situation is shown below

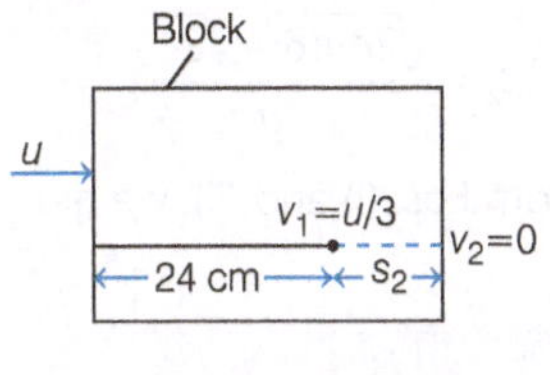

$s_1 = 24 \text{ cm}$

$v_1^2 = u^2 - 2as_1$

$\Rightarrow \left(\frac{u}{3}\right)^2 = u^2 - 2a \times 0.24$

$\Rightarrow 0.48a = \frac{8}{9}u^2$

$\Rightarrow a = \frac{8u^2}{9 \times 0.48} = \frac{u^2}{0.54}$

According to second condition,

$0 = v_1^2 - 2as_2$

$\Rightarrow 0 = \left(\frac{u}{3}\right)^2 - 2 \times \frac{u^2}{0.54} \times s_2$

$\Rightarrow \frac{u^2}{9} = \frac{2u^2}{0.54} s_2$

$\Rightarrow s_2 = \frac{0.54}{9 \times 2} = 0.03 \text{ m} = 3 \text{ cm}$

$\therefore$ Total length of the block

$= s_1 + s_2$

$= 24 + 3 = 27 \text{ cm}$

3 (*b*) Maximum height attain by the ball,

$$h' = \frac{v^2}{2g} = \frac{4^2}{2 \times 10} = 0.8 \text{ m}$$

Time of flight from bridge to bridge,

$$t_1 = \frac{2v}{g} = \frac{2 \times 4}{10} = 0.8 \text{ s}$$

Total time of flight is given as 4 s.

Time taken by the ball to reach at the surface of water from highest point,

$$t_2 = 4 - \frac{t_1}{2} = 4 - \frac{0.8}{2} = 3.6 \text{ s}$$

$\therefore \quad h = 0 \times t_2 + \frac{1}{2} g t_2^2$

$h = \frac{1}{2} \times 10 \times (3.6)^2 = 64.8 \text{ m}$

$\therefore$ Now, height of bridge above water surface,

$H = h - h' = 64.8 - 0.8 = 64 \text{ m}$

4 (*b*) Distance travelled by freely falling body in nth second,

$s_n = u + \frac{1}{2} g(2n - 1)$

$s_1 = \frac{1}{2} g(2 \times 1 - 1) = \frac{g}{2}$

$s_2 = \frac{1}{2} g(2 \times 2 - 1) = \frac{3g}{2}$

$s_3 = \frac{1}{2} g(2 \times 3 - 1) = \frac{5g}{2}$

$s_4 = \frac{1}{2} g(2 \times 4 - 1) = \frac{7g}{2}$

$\therefore s_1 : s_2 : s_3 : s_4 = 1 : 3 : 5 : 7$

5 (*d*) $a = 5 \text{ m/s}^2$

At $t = 4$ s, $v = u + at$

$\Rightarrow v = 0 + (5)4 \Rightarrow v = 20 \text{ m/s}$

At $t = 4$ s,

$v_x = 20 \text{ m/s}$ (due to the car)

$a_y = g = 10 \text{ m/s}^2$

$\therefore \quad v_y = u + a_y t$

$\Rightarrow \quad v_y = 0 + 10 \times 2$

$\Rightarrow \quad v_y = 20 \text{ m/s}$

The net velocity at $t = 6$s,

$v = \sqrt{v_x^2 + v_y^2}$

$\Rightarrow \quad v = 20\sqrt{2} \text{ m/s}$

Thus, the velocity of the ball at $t = 6$ s is $20\sqrt{2}$ m/s.

and $a_x = 0 \text{ ms}^{-2}$

$a_y = 10 \text{ ms}^{-2}$

Now, the net acceleration at $t = 6$ s,

$a = \sqrt{a_x^2 + a_y^2} \Rightarrow a = 10 \text{ ms}^{-2}$

6 (*b*) Distance covered in nth seconds, $s_n = 0 + \frac{a}{2}(2n - 1)$

Distance cover in $(n+1)$th seconds,

$s_{n+1} = 0 + \frac{a}{2}(2n + 2 - 1)$

$\Rightarrow \frac{s_n}{s_{n+1}} = \frac{(2n-1)}{(2n+1)}$

7 (*b*) If u be the velocity at the top most point of the window,

$h = ut + \frac{1}{2} gt^2$

$\Rightarrow \quad 1.5 = u \times 0.1 + \frac{1}{2} \times 10 \times (0.1)^2$

$\Rightarrow \quad u = 14.5 \text{ m/s}$

8 (*c*) $h = \frac{v^2 - u^2}{2g} = \frac{(80)^2 - (20)^2}{2 \times 10}$

($\because$ given, $g = 10 \text{ m/s}^2$)

$= 300 \text{ m}$

9 (*d*) Let h be the height through which the coin is dropped. Then, according to the equation of motion, $h = ut + \frac{1}{2}gt^2$

$\Rightarrow \quad t = \sqrt{\frac{2h}{g}} \quad [\because u = 0]$

$\Rightarrow \quad t \propto \frac{1}{\sqrt{g}}$

As the elevator is moving uniformly acceleration is zero.

$\therefore$ Relative acceleration of the lift when it is either moving upward or downward is given as, $g' = g \pm a$

$= g \pm 0 = g$

Hence, the time for the coin to reach the floor will remain same, i.e. $t_1 = t_2$.

10 (*c*) Speed of walking

$= \frac{h}{t_1} = v_1$

Speed of escalator $= \frac{h}{t_2} = v_2$

Time taken when she walks over running escalator,

$t = \frac{h}{v_1 + v_2} \Rightarrow t = \frac{t_1 t_2}{t_1 + t_2}$

11 (*b*) $v = At + Bt^2$

$\Rightarrow \frac{dx}{dt} = At + Bt^2 \quad \left[\because v = \frac{dx}{dt}\right]$

$\int_{x_1}^{x_2} dx = \int_1^2 (At + Bt^2)\, dt$

$\Rightarrow \quad \Delta x = x_2 - x_1$

$= A\left[\frac{t^2}{2}\right]_1^2 + B\left[\frac{t^3}{3}\right]_1^2$

$= \frac{3A}{2} + \frac{7B}{3}$

12 (8) Velocity of particle is given,

$v = 4\sqrt{x}$ m/s

$\Rightarrow \quad v = \frac{dx}{dt} = 4\sqrt{x}$

$\Rightarrow \quad \frac{dx}{\sqrt{x}} = 4dt$

Integrating we have,

$\int_0^x \frac{dx}{\sqrt{x}} = 4\int_0^t dt$

$2\sqrt{x} = 4t \Rightarrow 4x = 16t^2$

So, position of the particle is

$\Rightarrow \quad x = 4t^2$

$\Rightarrow$ Velocity, $v = \frac{dx}{dt} = 4 \times 2t$

Acceleration, $a = \frac{dv}{dt} = 8 \text{ m/s}^2$

13 (*b*) $v_A = 108$ km/h $= 30$ m/s

$v_B = 72$ km/h $= 20$ m/s

Time taken to cross the tunnel by train B – Time taken to cross the tunnel by train $A = 35$ s

$\Rightarrow \quad \frac{L + 4l}{20} - \frac{L + l}{30} = 35$

$\Rightarrow \quad \frac{60l + 4l}{20} - \frac{60l + l}{30} = 35$

$(\because L = 60l)$

$\Rightarrow \quad l = 30$ m

$\therefore$ Length of the tunnel,

$L = 60l = 60 \times 30 = 1800$ m

14 (*d*) Distance travelled by the ball in first half.

$h_1 = \frac{1}{2}gt_1^2$

$\Rightarrow \quad \frac{h}{2} = \frac{1}{2}gt_1^2$

$\Rightarrow \quad h = gt_1^2 \quad$ ...(i)

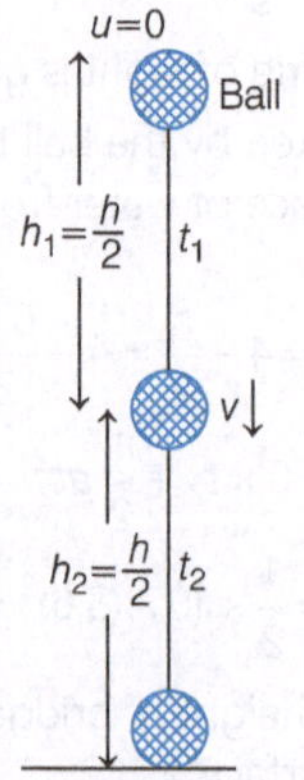

If v be the velocity of ball after travelling distance h_1, then

$v = gt_1 \quad$ ...(ii)

Distance travelled by the ball in second half,

$h_2 = vt_2 + \frac{1}{2}gt_2^2$

$\Rightarrow \quad \frac{h}{2} = gt_1t_2 + \frac{1}{2}gt_2^2$

[From Eq. (ii)]

$\Rightarrow \quad \frac{gt_1^2}{2} = gt_1t_2 + \frac{1}{2}gt_2^2$

[From Eq. (i)]

$\Rightarrow \quad t_1^2 = 2t_1t_2 + t_2^2$

$\Rightarrow t_2^2 + 2t_1t_2 - t_1^2 = 0$

$\Rightarrow \quad t_2 = \frac{-2t_1 \pm \sqrt{4t_1^2 + 4t_1^2}}{2}$

$\Rightarrow \quad t_2 = -t_1 \pm t_1\sqrt{2}$

Taking + ve sign only.

$t_2 = -t_1 + t_1\sqrt{2} = t_1(-1 + \sqrt{2})$

$\Rightarrow t_2 = t_1(\sqrt{2} - 1)$

15 (*b*) According to the question,

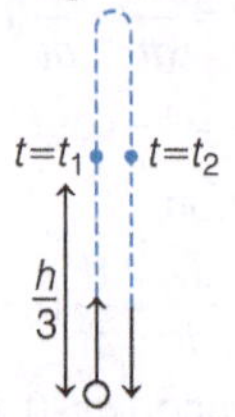

Let the two times be t_1 and t_2 respectively, while going up and coming down when they are at $h/3$ height above ground.

Now, as given

$H_{max} = h = \frac{u^2}{2g}$

(using $v^2 = u^2 - 2gh$ and $v = 0$ at topmost point)

$\Rightarrow \quad u = \sqrt{2gh}$

$\therefore \quad \frac{h}{3} = \sqrt{2gh}\,t - \frac{1}{2}gt^2$

$\Rightarrow 3gt^2 - 6\sqrt{2gh}\,t + 2h = 0$

Now, using quadratic formula,

$t_1 = \frac{6\sqrt{2gh} - \sqrt{72gh - 24gh}}{6g}$

$= \frac{\sqrt{2gh}(6 - \sqrt{24})}{6g} \quad$ ...(i)

Similarly,

$t_2 = \frac{\sqrt{2gh}(6 + \sqrt{24})}{6g} \quad$ ...(ii)

From Eqs. (i) and (ii), we get

$$\frac{t_1}{t_2} = \frac{6-\sqrt{24}}{6+\sqrt{24}}$$

$$\Rightarrow \frac{t_1}{t_2} = \frac{\sqrt{3}-\sqrt{2}}{\sqrt{3}+\sqrt{2}}$$

Skill Boosters

1 (c) Displacement of the drunkard in first twelve steps $= 7 - 5 = 2$ m

Time taken for first 12 steps $= 12$ s

Time taken by the drunkard to cover first 6 m of journey,

$$t_1 = \frac{12}{2} \times 6 = 36 \text{ s}$$

If the drunkard takes 7 steps more, he will fall into the pit.

So, time taken by the drunkard to cover last 7 steps $= 7$ s

$\therefore$ Total time taken $= 36 + 7 = 43$ s

Thus, the drunkard will fall into the pit after 43 s.

2 (d) Distance travelled by bike in 15 s

$$= \frac{1}{2} \times AC \times OC$$

$$= \frac{1}{2} \times 45 \times 15 = \frac{675}{2} \text{ m}$$

Distance travelled by truck in 15 s

$$= v \times t = 30 \times 15 = 450 \text{ m}$$

Required difference in distance,

$$= 450 - \frac{675}{2}$$

$$= \frac{225}{2} = 112.5 \text{ m}$$

Let bike catches truck in time t, then distance travelled by both of them will be equal

$$\frac{675}{2} + 45(t-15) = 30t$$

$$\Rightarrow \quad t = 22.5 \text{ s}$$

3 (c) It is clear that car A gains constant velocity at $t = 95$ s but car B gains constant velocity at $t = 96$ s

Thus, extra distance travelled by car A

$$= (100 - 95)50 = 250 \text{ m}$$

and extra distance travelled by car B

$$= (100 - 96)\, 50 + 20 \times 1 = 220 \text{ m}$$

$$\therefore \Delta s = 250 - 220 = 30 \text{ m}$$

4 (d) The velocity of first particle is $v_1 = \frac{1500}{12}$ ms^{-1} and the velocity of second particle is $v_2 = \frac{2100}{12}$ ms^{-1}.

Let after completing n_1 and n_2 trips, they will again meet at the point B.

$$\therefore \frac{3600 n_1}{v_1} = \frac{3600 n_2}{v_2} = t$$

$$\text{or} \quad \frac{n_1}{n_2} = \frac{v_1}{v_2} = \frac{\frac{1500}{12}}{\frac{2100}{12}}$$

$$= \frac{1500}{2100} = \frac{5}{7}$$

$$\therefore \quad t_{min} = \frac{3600 \times 5}{v_1}$$

$$= \frac{3600 \times 5}{1500} \times 12$$

$$= 144 \text{ s} = (12)^x$$

$$\therefore \quad x = 2$$

5 (b) Let the distance between home and turning point C is l. The distance between the coaching and home is $L = 20\,v$.

According to the problem,

$$\frac{l}{v} + \frac{l}{v} + \frac{l}{v} + \frac{L-l}{v}$$

$$= 20 \text{ min} + 8 \text{ min} + 10 \text{ min}$$

$$\text{or} \quad \frac{2l}{v} + \frac{L}{v} = 38 \text{ min}$$

$$\text{or} \quad \frac{2l}{v} + \frac{20v}{v} = 38 \text{ min}$$

$$\text{or} \quad \frac{2l}{v} = 18 \text{ min}$$

$$\text{or} \quad \frac{l}{v} = 9 \text{ min}$$

The fraction is $\frac{l}{L} = \frac{9v}{20v} = \frac{9}{20}$

6 (a) Let the two stones meet at time t.

For the first stone,

$$s_1 = \frac{1}{2} g t^2 \; (\because u = 0) \quad \text{...(i)}$$

For the second stone,

$$s_2 = u(t-n) + \frac{1}{2} g (t-n)^2 \quad \text{...(ii)}$$

Since, displacement is same.

$$\therefore \frac{1}{2} g t^2 = u(t-n) + \frac{1}{2} g (t-n)^2$$

[using Eqs. (i) and (ii)]

$$\Rightarrow \frac{1}{2} g t^2 = ut - un + \frac{1}{2} g t^2 - gtn + \frac{1}{2} g n^2$$

$$\Rightarrow ut - gtn = un - \frac{1}{2} g n^2$$

$$\Rightarrow t = \frac{un - \frac{1}{2} g n^2}{u - gn} = \frac{n\left(u - \frac{gn}{2}\right)}{u - gn}$$

Substituting this value of t in Eq. (i), we get

$$s_1 = \frac{1}{2} g \left[\frac{n\left(u - \frac{gn}{2}\right)}{u - gn}\right]^2$$

7 (b) If collision does not take place. The final velocities of both should be same.

$$\therefore \quad v_f = 30 - \frac{30}{7} t = 30 - 3(t-1)$$

$$\Rightarrow \quad t = -\frac{21}{9}$$

The negative of t indicates that both comes in rest before collision.

The distance moved by bus B before coming in rest is

$$s_1 = 30 \times 1 + \frac{30^2}{2 \times 3}$$

$$= 180 \text{ m}$$

The distance moved by bus A before coming in rest is

$$s_2 = \frac{30^2}{2 \times \frac{30}{7}} = \frac{30 \times 7}{2} = 105 \text{ m}$$

$$\therefore \quad x_1 = s_1 - s_2 = 180 - 105 = 75 \text{ m}$$

For $x_2, v_f = 30 - \frac{30}{7}(t-1) = 30 - 3t$

$$\text{or} \quad \frac{30}{7} t - \frac{30}{7} = 3t \text{ or } \frac{9}{7} t = \frac{30}{7}$$

$$\therefore \quad t = \frac{10}{3} \text{ s}$$

The positive value of t indicates that before collision, velocities of both buses are non-zero but same.

So, the distance moved by A before collision is

$$s_1 = 30\times 1 + 30\times\left(\frac{10}{3}-1\right) - \frac{1}{2}\times\frac{30}{7}\left(\frac{10}{3}-1\right)^2$$

$$s_1 = \frac{265}{3}\text{ m}$$

$$s_2 = 30\times\frac{10}{3} - \frac{1}{2}\times 3\times\left(\frac{10}{3}\right)^2$$

$$= 100 - \frac{50}{3} = \frac{250}{3}$$

$$x_2 = s_1 - s_2 = \frac{265}{3} - \frac{250}{3}$$

$$= 5\text{ m}$$

$$\because\ \frac{x_1}{x_2} = \frac{75}{5} = 15$$

8 (c) ABC is the velocity-time graph for the passenger train and ODE that of the local train.

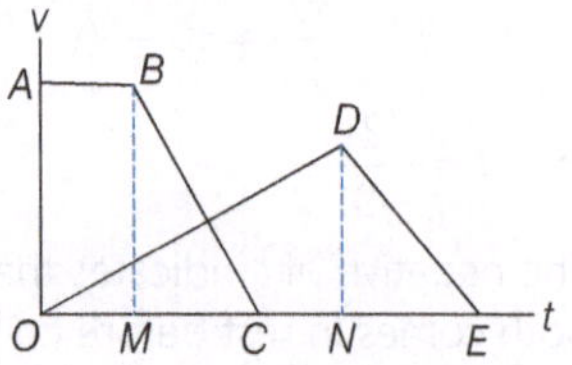

Area $OMBA = 8$ km

and area $MCB = 2$ km

$$\therefore \text{Area } OMBA = \left(\frac{100}{9}\times\frac{18}{5}\right)\times OM$$

$$= 8\text{ km}$$

$$\therefore\quad OM = \frac{1}{5}\text{ h}$$

and area $MCB = \frac{1}{2}MC \times MB$

$$= 2\text{ km}$$

$$\text{or } \frac{1}{2}MC\times\left(\frac{100}{9}\times\frac{18}{5}\right) = 2\text{ km}$$

$$\therefore\ MC = \frac{1}{10}\text{ h}$$

$$\therefore\ OC = OM + MC$$

$$= \frac{1}{5} + \frac{1}{10} = \frac{3}{10}$$

$$\therefore\ OE = 2\times\frac{3}{10} = \frac{3}{5}$$

$$\text{Area } ODE = \frac{1}{2}\times DN\times OE$$

$$\text{or } 10\text{ km} = \frac{1}{2}v_0\times\frac{3}{5}$$

$$\therefore\quad v_0 = \frac{100}{3}\text{ km/h}$$

$$\therefore\quad = 33.3\text{ km/h}$$

9 (d) Speed of belt w.r.t. ground

$$\therefore\quad v_{BG} = 4\text{ km/h}$$

Speed of child w.r.t. belt

$$\therefore\quad v_{CB} = 9\text{ km/h}$$

For an observer on a stationary platform, a speed of child running in the direction of motion of the belt is

$$v_{CG} = v_{CB} + v_{BG}$$

$$= 9\text{ km/h} + 4\text{ km/h}$$

$$= 13\text{ km/h}$$

10 (c) The situation is depicted as given below

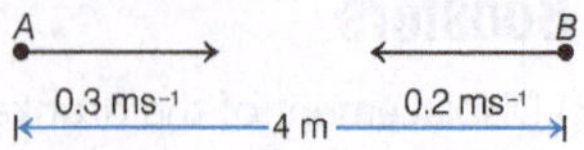

For motion of ball A relative to rocket.

Consider motion of two balls with respect to rocket.

Maximum distance of ball A from left wall,

$$s = \frac{u^2}{2a} = \frac{0.3\times 0.3}{2\times 2}$$

$$= \frac{0.09}{4} \approx 0.02\text{ m}$$

$$(\text{as, } 0 = u^2 - 2as)$$

So, collision of two balls will take place very near to left wall.

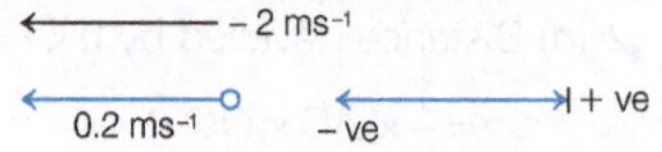

Motion of ball B relative to rocket,

For ball B, $s = ut + \frac{1}{2}at^2$

$$\Rightarrow\ -4 = 0.2t - \left(\frac{1}{2}\right)2t^2$$

$$\Rightarrow\quad t^2 - 0.2t - 4 = 0$$

$$t = \frac{0.2 \pm \sqrt{0.04 + 16}}{2}$$

$$\Rightarrow\quad t \simeq 2\text{ s}$$

Topicwise No. of Ques asked in 5 Years (NEET)

Topics	No. of Questions				
	2024	2023	2022	2021	2020
Scalars and Vectors	–	–	–	–	–
Multiplication of Vectors by Real Numbers	–	–	–	–	–
Addition and Subtraction of Vectors-Graphical Method	–	–	–	–	–
Resolution of Vectors	–	–	–	–	–
Vector Addition-Analytical Method	–	–	–	–	–
Motion in a Plane	–	–	–	–	–
Relative Velocity in Two-dimensions	–	–	–	–	–
Projectile Motion	–	1	–	1	–
Uniform Circular Motion	1	1	–	1	–

Special Type of Ques Asked In 5 Years (NEET)

Types	Years				
	2024	2023	2022	2021	2020
A-R	–	–	–	–	–
Statement Based	–	–	–	–	–
Matching	–	–	–	–	–

Last 5 Years Weigtage (NEET)

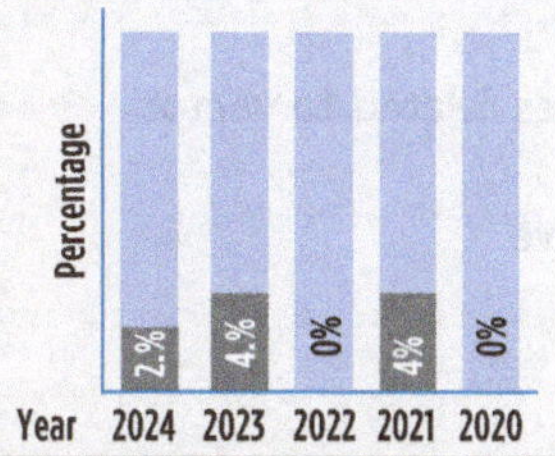

03

Scan for **Physics Through Concept Master** *Videos*

Motion in a Plane

The concept of position, displacement, velocity and acceleration in two dimensional motion or motion in a plane (projectile motion, uniform circular motion) are described by vectors.

Scalars and Vectors

- A **scalar** quantity is a quantity that has magnitude only. It is specified completely by a number, along with the proper unit.
  e.g. distance, mass of an object, etc.
  - The rules for combining scalars are the rules of ordinary algebra.
  - Scalars can be added, subtracted, multiplied and divided just as ordinary numbers. But addition and subtraction of scalars are done only for quantities with same units.
  - However, multiplication and division of scalars can be done for the quantities with different units.
- A **vector** quantity is a quantity that has both a magnitude and a direction. e.g. Displacement, velocity, acceleration, etc.
  - A vector is represented by bold face or an arrow placed over a letter, e.g. **A**, **a**, **p**, **q**, **r** or $\vec{A}$, $\vec{a}$, $\vec{p}$, $\vec{q}$, $\vec{r}$ etc.
    The magnitude of the respective vectors are denoted by light face or a vector placed in mod sign, e.g. A, a, p, q, r or $|\mathbf{A}|, |\mathbf{a}|, |\mathbf{p}|, |\mathbf{q}|, |\mathbf{r}|$, etc.
  - A vector quantity obeys the **triangular law** or **parallelogram law** of vector addition.

Position and Displacement Vectors

- A vector which gives the position of an object with respect to origin of a co-ordinate system is called position vector. It is represented by **r**.
- If P and P' be the positions of the object at time t and t', respectively as shown, then

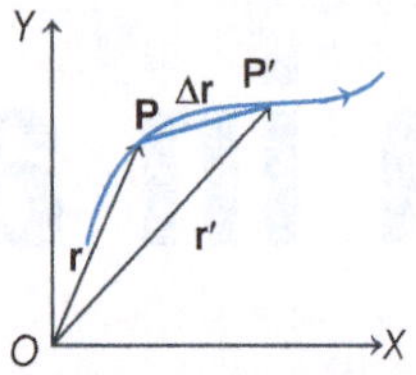

OP and **OP′** are the **position vectors** of the object at time t & t'.

- A vector which gives the change in position of an object in a particular direction is called **displacement vector**. It is represented by Δ**r**.
- If the object moves from P to P' (see above figure), the vector **PP′** is called the **displacement vector** corresponding to motion from point P to point P'.
- The magnitude of displacement is either less or equal to the path length of an object between two points.
- The displacement vector **PQ** for different courses of motion is shown in figure below.

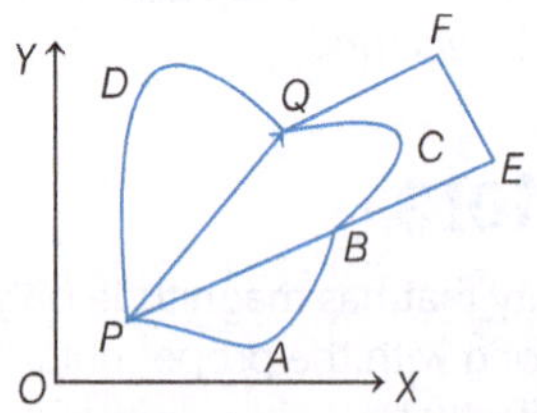

In above figure, displacement vector **PQ** is same for different paths of journey say *PABCQ*, *PDQ* and *PBEFQ*. So magnitude of displacement is either less or equal to the path length of an object between two points.

Equality of Vectors

- Two vectors **A** and **B** are said to be equal, if and only, if they have the same magnitude and the same direction.

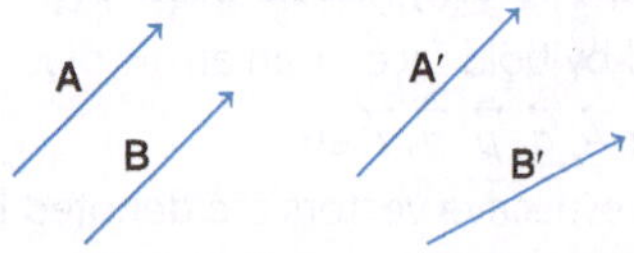

(a) (b)

- In Fig (a), two vectors **A** and **B** are equal vectors as they have same lengths and same directions.
- In Fig (b), two vectors **A′** and **B′** are unequal vectors as they have same lengths but different directions.

Multiplication of Vectors by Real Numbers

- Multiplying a vector **A** with a positive number λ gives a vector whose magnitude is changed by the factor λ but the direction is the same as that of **A**, as shown in Fig. (a) i.e. $|\lambda \mathbf{A}| = \lambda |\mathbf{A}|$, if $\lambda > 0$
- Multiplying a vector **A** by a negative number $-\lambda$ gives another vector whose direction is opposite to the direction of **A** and whose magnitude is λ times $|\mathbf{A}|$, as shown in Fig (b).

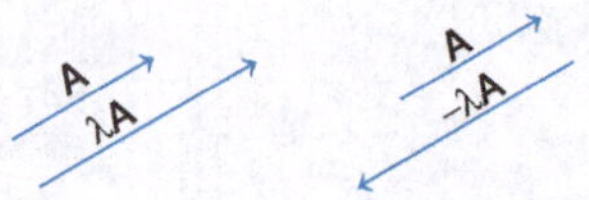

(a) (b)

- If a factor λ by which a vector **A** is multiplied having its own physical dimension, then the dimension of λ**A** is the product of dimensions of λ and **A**.

Addition and Subtraction of Vectors —Graphical Method

- **General rule for addition of vectors** It states that the vectors to be added are arranged in such a way so that the head of first vector coincides with the tail of second vector, whose head coincides with the tail of third vector and so on, then the single vector drawn from the tail of the first vector to the head of the last vector represents their resultant vector.
- Sum of two vectors **A** and **B** can be found, if we place vector **B**, so that its tail is at the head of the vector **A**, then join the tail of **A** to the head of **B**.
- This line OQ represents a vector **R**, that is sum of vectors **A** and **B**. The resultant **R** of vectors **A** and **B** is represented as shown in the figure below.

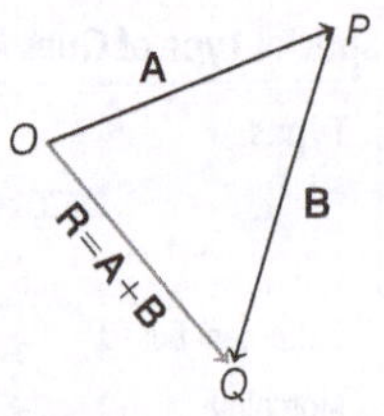

Since, in this procedure of vector addition, vectors are arranged head-to-tail, this graphical method is known as **head-to-tail method**. This is also known as **triangle method of vector addition**.

- Following are **important properties related to vector addition**
  (i) Vectors addition is **commutative**, i.e. $\mathbf{A} + \mathbf{B} = \mathbf{B} + \mathbf{A}$
  (ii) Vector addition is **associative**, i.e. $(\mathbf{A} + \mathbf{B}) + \mathbf{C} = \mathbf{A} + (\mathbf{B} + \mathbf{C})$

- When two equal and opposite vectors are added (says **A** and −**A**). Then, the resultant vector will have zero magnitude as, their magnitudes are same but directions are opposite. It is represented by **0** called a **null vector** or a **zero vector**, i.e.

$$\mathbf{A}-\mathbf{A}=\mathbf{0} \text{ and } |\mathbf{0}|=0$$

- Since, the magnitude of a null vector is zero, its direction cannot be specified. The main properties of **0** are

  (i) $\mathbf{A}+\mathbf{0}=\mathbf{A}$ (ii) $\lambda\mathbf{0}=\mathbf{0}$ (iii) $0\mathbf{A}=\mathbf{0}$

- **Parallelogram method of vector addition** is equivalent to the triangle method. In this vectors addition, says **A** and **B**, have their tail at common origin *O* and represented by the two adjacent sides of a parallelogram. The sum of (**A** + **B**) is represented by the diagonal (*OS*) of the parallelogram directed from *O* as shown in the figure below.

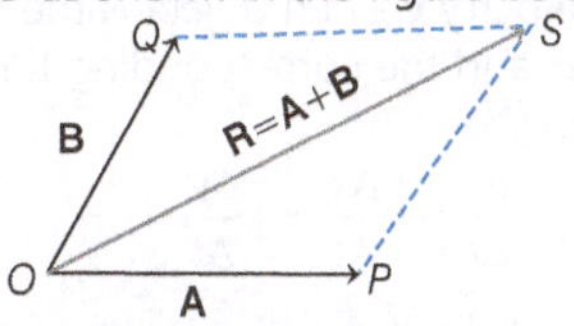

- **Subtraction of vectors** can be defined in terms of addition of vectors. We define the difference of two vectors **A** and **B** as the sum of two vectors **A** and −**B**, as shown in figure below, i.e.

$$\mathbf{A}-\mathbf{B}=\mathbf{A}+(-\mathbf{B})$$

- The vector −**B** is added to vector **A** to get difference of vectors **A** and **B**. The sum of vectors **A** and **B** is also shown in the same figure below for comparison.

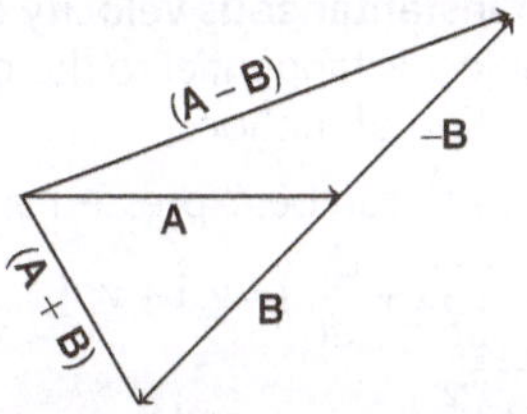

- Following are **important properties related to vector subtraction.**

  (i) It does not follow **commutative law**, $\mathbf{A}-\mathbf{B}\neq\mathbf{B}-\mathbf{A}$

  (ii) It does not follow **associative law**,

  $(\mathbf{A}-\mathbf{B})-\mathbf{C}$ does not to be equal to $\mathbf{A}-(\mathbf{B}-\mathbf{C})$

Resolution of Vectors

- The process of splitting a vector into two or more than two vectors is called **resolution of a vector**. The splitted vector is known as the **components of the vector**.
- The components of a vector along two or three mutually perpendicular axes are called **rectangular components of the vector**.
- Vector **A** can be resolved along two coplanar vectors **a** and **b** as shown in figure below as $\mathbf{A}=\lambda\mathbf{a}+\mu\mathbf{b}$, **where** λ **and** μ **are real numbers.**

Here, all the three vectors **A**, **a** and **b** lie in the same plane.

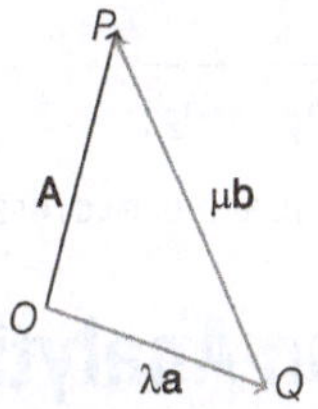

- A **unit vector** is a vector of unit magnitude and points in a particular direction. It has no dimension and unit. It is used to specify a direction only.
- A unit vector is represented by bold face with a cap(^).

  A unit vector associated with a vector **A** is $\hat{\mathbf{n}}=\dfrac{\mathbf{A}}{|\mathbf{A}|}$

  where, $\hat{\mathbf{n}}$ is along **A**.

- Unit vectors along the *X*, *Y* and *Z*-axes of a rectangular coordinate systems are denoted by $\hat{\mathbf{i}}$, $\hat{\mathbf{j}}$ and $\hat{\mathbf{k}}$, respectively. Since, these are unit vectors, we have $|\hat{\mathbf{i}}|=|\hat{\mathbf{j}}|=|\hat{\mathbf{k}}|=1$

  These unit vectors are perpendicular to each other.

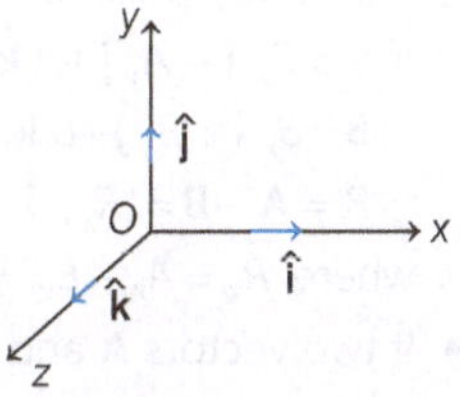

- If we multiply a unit vector, say $\hat{\mathbf{n}}$ by a scalar λ, the result is a vector $\lambda=\lambda\hat{\mathbf{n}}$.
- **If a vector A lies in *XY*-plane** such that it is inclined at an angle θ with *X*-axis as shown in the figure, then

  (i) $\mathbf{A}=\mathbf{A}_x\hat{\mathbf{i}}+\mathbf{A}_y\hat{\mathbf{j}}$

  (ii) Component of vector **A** along *X*-axis is $A_x=A\cos\theta$.

  (iii) Component of vector **A** along *Y*-axis is $A_y=A\sin\theta$.

  (iv) $A=\sqrt{A_x^2+A_y^2}$ and $\tan\theta=\dfrac{A_y}{A_x}$.

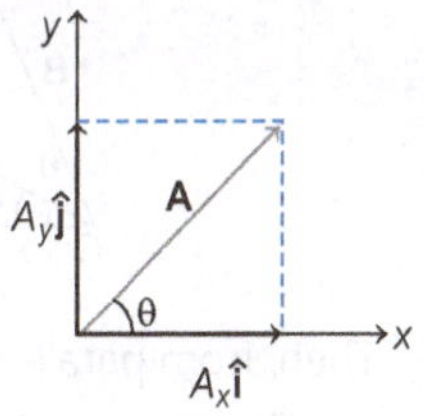

- **If a vector A lies in space**, such that α, β & γ are the angles between **A** and *X*, *Y* & *Z*-axes, respectively, as shown in the figure, then we have

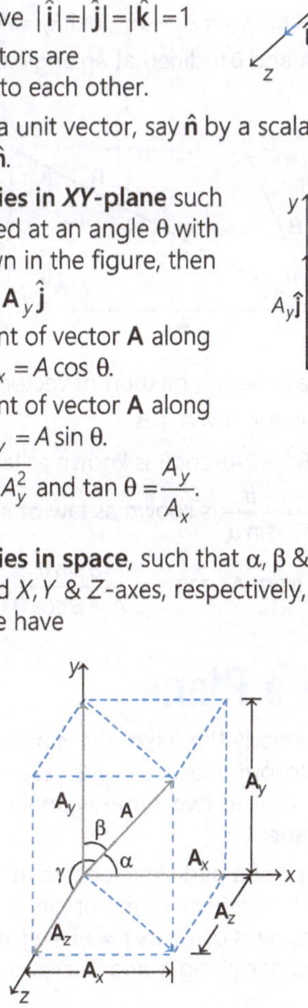

(i) $A_x = A\cos\alpha$; $A_y = A\cos\beta$; $A_z = A\cos\gamma$

(ii) $\mathbf{A} = A_x\hat{\mathbf{i}} + A_y\hat{\mathbf{j}} + A_z\hat{\mathbf{k}}$

(iii) $|\mathbf{A}| = A = \sqrt{A_x^2 + A_y^2 + A_z^2}$

- A position vector **r** in space is expressed as $\mathbf{r} = x\hat{\mathbf{i}} + y\hat{\mathbf{j}} + z\hat{\mathbf{k}}$.

Vector Additon-Analytical Method

- Vectors can be added by analytical method, i.e. adding the vectors by combining their respective components along the coordinate axis.

  If two vectors are $\mathbf{A} = A_x\hat{\mathbf{i}} + A_y\hat{\mathbf{j}} + A_z\hat{\mathbf{k}}$

  and $\mathbf{B} = B_x\hat{\mathbf{i}} + B_y\hat{\mathbf{j}} + B_z\hat{\mathbf{k}}$

  Then, resultant, $\mathbf{R} = \mathbf{A} + \mathbf{B} = R_x\hat{\mathbf{i}} + R_y\hat{\mathbf{j}} + R_z\hat{\mathbf{k}}$

  where, $R_x = A_x + B_x$, $R_y = A_y + B_y$ and $R_z = A_z + B_z$.

- This method can be extended to subtraction of vectors.

  If $\mathbf{A} = A_x\hat{\mathbf{i}} + A_y\hat{\mathbf{j}} + A_z\hat{\mathbf{k}}$

  $\mathbf{B} = B_x\hat{\mathbf{i}} + B_y\hat{\mathbf{j}} + B_z\hat{\mathbf{k}}$, then

  $\mathbf{R} = \mathbf{A} - \mathbf{B} = (R_x)\hat{\mathbf{i}} + (R_y)\hat{\mathbf{j}} + (R_z)\hat{\mathbf{k}}$

  where, $R_x = A_x - B_x$, $R_y = A_y - B_y$ and $R_z = A_z - B_z$

- If two vectors **A** and **B** inclined at an angle θ, as shown below

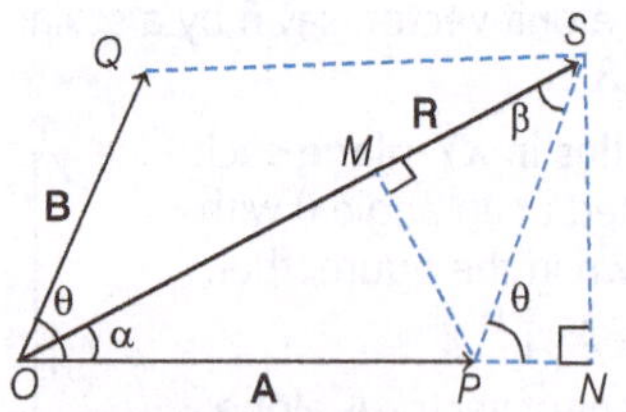

Then, from parallelogram method of vector addition,

(i) Resultant vector, $\mathbf{R} = \mathbf{A} + \mathbf{B}$.

(ii) $R = \sqrt{A^2 + B^2 + 2AB\cos\theta}$ is known as **law of cosines.**

(iii) $\dfrac{R}{\sin\theta} = \dfrac{A}{\sin\beta} = \dfrac{B}{\sin\alpha}$ is known as **law of sines.**

(iv) Angle of **R** from **A**, $\tan\alpha = \dfrac{B\sin\theta}{A + B\cos\theta}$.

Motion in a Plane

- The motion of a body that takes place along two different directions (or co-ordinate axes) with respect to origin at the same time is called **two-dimensional motion** or **motion in a plane.**
- **Position vector r** of a particle P located in a plane (two dimensions) with reference to the origin of an XY-reference frame is given by $\mathbf{r} = x\hat{\mathbf{i}} + y\hat{\mathbf{j}}$, where x and y are components of **r** along X and Y-axes.
- If the positions of a particle are P and P' at time t and t', respectively as shown below, then its **displacement vector**,

  $\Delta\mathbf{r} = \mathbf{r}' - \mathbf{r} = (x'\hat{\mathbf{i}} + y'\hat{\mathbf{j}}) - (x\hat{\mathbf{i}} + y\hat{\mathbf{j}}) = \hat{\mathbf{i}}\Delta x + \hat{\mathbf{j}}\Delta y$

  where, $\Delta x = x' - x$, $\Delta y = y' - y$.

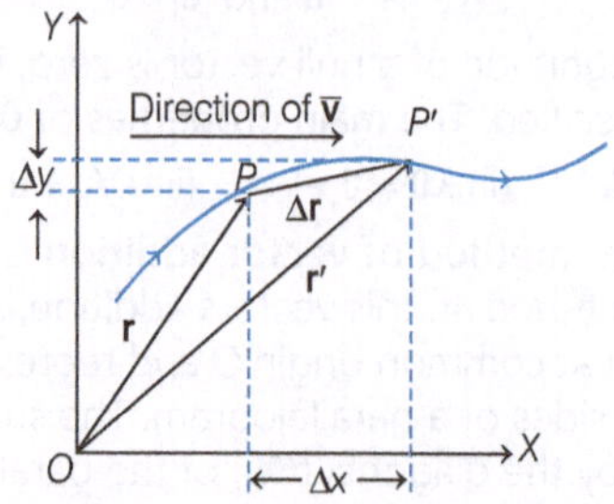

- The **average velocity** $\bar{\mathbf{v}}$ of an object is the ratio of the displacement $\Delta\mathbf{r}$ and the corresponding time-interval Δt. Mathematically,

$$\bar{\mathbf{v}} = \frac{\Delta\mathbf{r}}{\Delta t} = \hat{\mathbf{i}}\frac{\Delta x}{\Delta t} + \hat{\mathbf{j}}\frac{\Delta y}{\Delta t}$$

  or $$\bar{\mathbf{v}} = \bar{v}_x\hat{\mathbf{i}} + \bar{v}_y\hat{\mathbf{j}}$$

  The **direction of the average velocity** is same **as that of Δr.**

- The **instantaneous velocity** is given by the limiting value of the average velocity as the time-interval approaches zero, i.e.

$$\mathbf{v} = \lim_{\Delta t\to 0}\bar{\mathbf{v}} = \lim_{\Delta t\to 0}\frac{\Delta\mathbf{r}}{\Delta t} = \frac{d\mathbf{r}}{dt}$$

- The **direction of instantaneous velocity** at any point on the path of an object is tangential to the path at that point and is in the direction of motion.
- **v** in component form can be expressed as

$$\mathbf{v} = \frac{d\mathbf{r}}{dt} = \frac{dx}{dt}\hat{\mathbf{i}} + \frac{dy}{dt}\hat{\mathbf{j}} = v_x\hat{\mathbf{i}} + v_y\hat{\mathbf{j}}$$

$$\Rightarrow \quad |\mathbf{v}| = \sqrt{v_x^2 + v_y^2}$$

  where, $v_x = \dfrac{dx}{dt}$, $v_y = \dfrac{dy}{dt}$

  and direction of **v** is given by

$$\tan\theta = \frac{v_y}{v_x} \text{ or } \theta = \tan^{-1}\left(\frac{v_y}{v_x}\right)$$

- The components v_x, v_y and the direction θ of velocity **v** are shown in figure below.

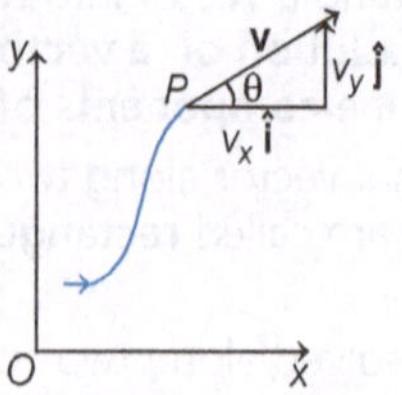

- As the time interval Δt approaches to zero, the average velocity $\bar{v}$ approaches to instantaneous velocity v shown in figures below.

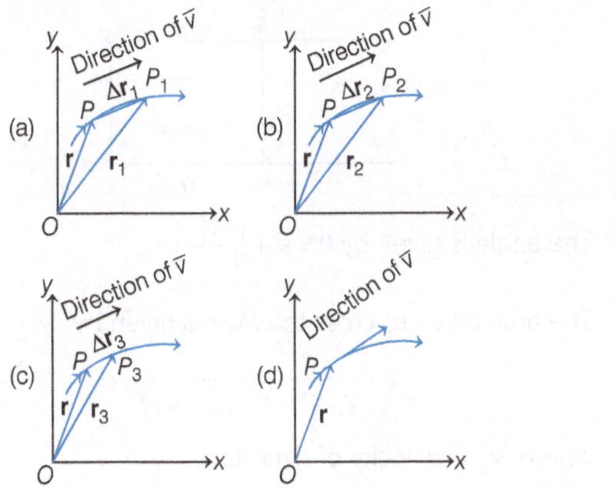

- **Average acceleration** a of an object for a time-interval Δt moving in XY-plane is the change in velocity divided by the time interval, i.e. $\bar{\mathbf{a}} = \dfrac{\Delta \mathbf{v}}{\Delta t} = \dfrac{\Delta v_x}{\Delta t}\hat{\mathbf{i}} + \dfrac{\Delta v_y}{\Delta t}\hat{\mathbf{j}} = a_x\hat{\mathbf{i}} + a_y\hat{\mathbf{j}}$
- **Instantaneous acceleration** is the limiting value of the average acceleration as the time-interval approaches zero i.e.,

$$\mathbf{a} = \lim_{\Delta t \to 0} \frac{\Delta \mathbf{v}}{\Delta t} = \frac{d\mathbf{v}}{dt} = a_x\hat{\mathbf{i}} + a_y\hat{\mathbf{j}}$$

where, $a_x = \dfrac{dv_x}{dt}, a_y = \dfrac{dv_y}{dt}$

- The average acceleration for three time intervals $\Delta t_1, \Delta t_2$ and Δt_3 are shown in Figs. (a), (b) and (c) and in the limiting condition $\Delta t \to 0$, the average acceleration becomes instantaneous acceleration is shown in Fig. (d).

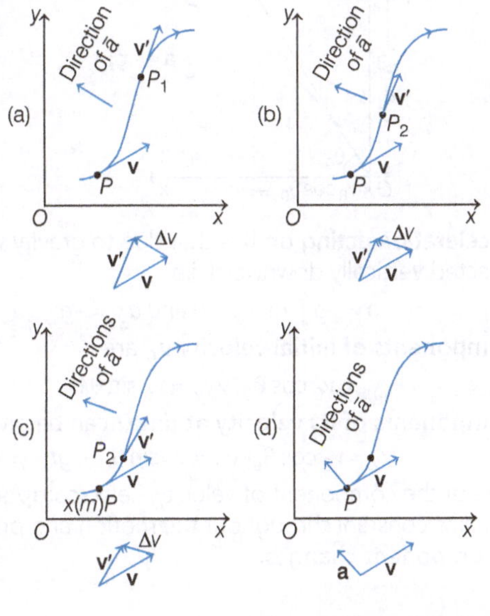

- In one-dimension, the velocity and acceleration of an object are always along the same straight line (either in the same direction or in the opposite direction). However, for motion in two or three dimensions, velocity and acceleration vectors may have any angle between 0° and 180° between them.

Motion in a Plane with Constant Acceleration

- Suppose an object is moving in XY-plane with constant acceleration **a**. Let the position and velocity of the object be $\mathbf{r}_0$ and $\mathbf{v}_0$ at time $t = 0$ and **r** and **v** at any time t. Then,
  (i) $\mathbf{v} = \mathbf{v}_0 + \mathbf{a}t$

  In terms of components, $v_x = u_{0x} + a_x t, v_y = u_{0y} + a_y t$

  (ii) $\bar{\mathbf{v}} = \dfrac{\mathbf{v}_0 + \mathbf{v}}{2}$

  (iii) $\mathbf{r} = \mathbf{r}_0 + \mathbf{v}_0 t + \dfrac{1}{2}\mathbf{a}t^2$.

  In component form, $x = x_0 + v_{0x}t + \dfrac{1}{2}a_x t^2$

  $$y = y_0 + v_{0y}t + \frac{1}{2}a_y t^2$$

- The motion in a plane (two-dimensions) can also be treated as two separate simultaneous one dimensional motions with constant acceleration along two perpendicular directions.

*Relative Velocity in Two-dimensions

- If two objects A and B are moving with velocities $\mathbf{v}_A$ and $\mathbf{v}_B$ respectively (each with respect to some common frame of reference, say ground), then velocity of object A relative to that of B is $\mathbf{v}_{AB} = -\mathbf{v}_{BA}$

  If θ be the angle between $\mathbf{v}_A$ and $\mathbf{v}_B$, then

  $\mathbf{v}_{AB} = \sqrt{v_A^2 + v_B^2 - 2v_A v_B \cos\theta}$

- If the relative velocity v_{AB} makes an angle β with v_B, then

$$\beta = \tan^{-1}\left(\frac{v_B \sin\theta}{v_A - v_B \cos\theta}\right)$$

*Rain-man problems

If rain falls with velocity $\mathbf{v}_r$ relative to ground at an angle θ with vertical, the velocity of man relative to ground is $\mathbf{v}_m$, then the man should hold his umbrella in the direction of velocity of rain relative to man $\mathbf{v}_{rm}$, so that he may not get wet as shown in figure.

This topic is not included in latest rationalised NCERT, but it is given in latest NEET syllabus.

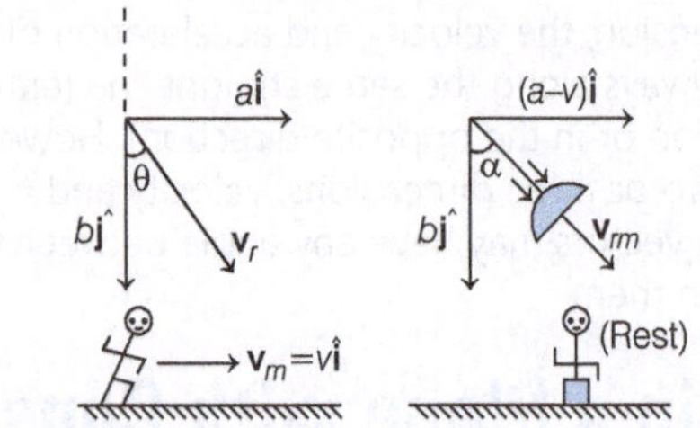

The velocity of rain with respect to man, $\mathbf{v}_{rm} = (a-v)\hat{\mathbf{i}} - b\hat{\mathbf{j}}$

$\Rightarrow \quad v_{rm} = \sqrt{(a-v)^2 + b^2}$

The direction of umbrella is α given in the following table

$a > v$	$a = v$	$a < v$
$\tan\alpha = \frac{a-v}{b}$ 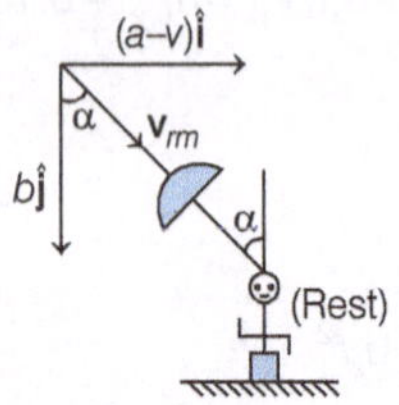	$\tan\alpha = 0$ $\Rightarrow \alpha = 0°$ ∴ Rain appears to fall vertically 	$\tan\alpha = \frac{v-a}{b}$ 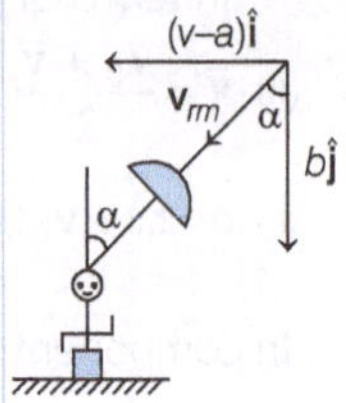

*Swimmer-River Problems

- If a swimmer swims in a river with velocity relative to river flow $\mathbf{v}_{sr}$ and the velocity of river is $\mathbf{v}_r$, then the velocity of swimmer with respect to ground,

$$\mathbf{v}_s = \mathbf{v}_{sr} + \mathbf{v}_r$$

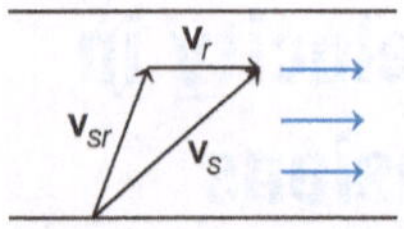

- If a swimmer wants to cross a river with minimum possible time, then he should swim perpendicular to the direction of river flow such that the swimmer reaches at point C along the path AC shown in figure below.

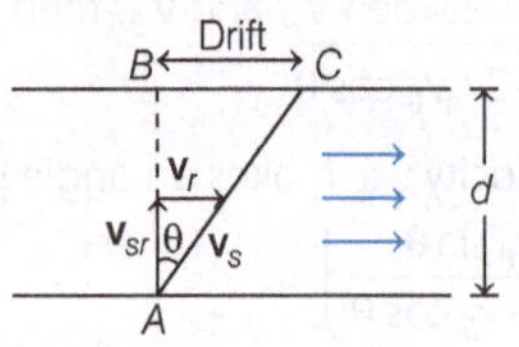

The minimum time required to cross the river, $t_{\min} = \frac{d}{v_{sr}}$

The drift BC is given by

Drift $= BC = v_r \cdot t_{\min} = \left(\frac{v_r}{v_{sr}}\right) d$

- If a swimmer wants to cross a river along shortest possible path AB as shown in figure below, then he should swim at an angle (90°+θ) with the direction of river flow.

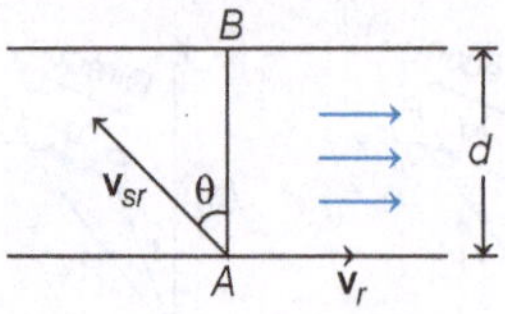

The angle is given by $\theta = \sin^{-1}\left(\frac{v_r}{v_{sr}}\right)$

The time taken to cross the river is given by

$$t = \frac{d}{v_{sr}\cos\theta} = \frac{d}{\sqrt{v_{sr}^2 - v_r^2}}$$

where, $\mathbf{v}_r$ = velocity of river flow,

$\mathbf{v}_{sr}$ = velocity of swimmer with respect to river or velocity of swimmer in still water

and d = width of the river.

Projectile Motion

- When a body is projected obliquely near the Earth's surface, then body moves along a curved path under constant acceleration (g). This type of motion of body is called **projectile motion** and projected body is called **projectile**. Such a projectile might be a football, a cricket ball, a baseball, etc.
- For an object, after being projected with initial velocity $\mathbf{v}_0$ that makes an angle θ_0 with X-axis as shown below.

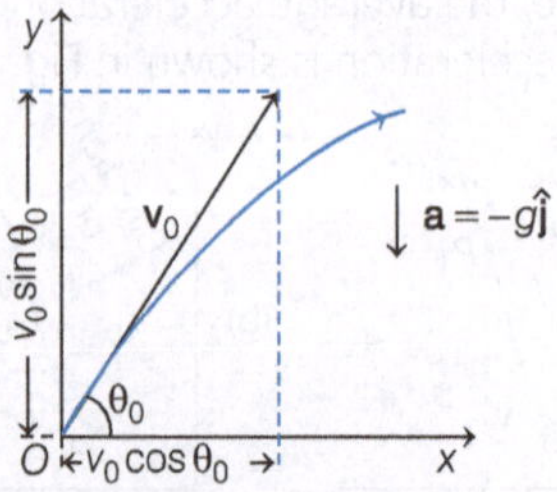

(i) **Acceleration acting on it** is that due to gravity which is directed vertically downward, i.e.

$$\mathbf{a} = -g\,\hat{\mathbf{j}} \text{ or } a_x = 0 \text{ and } a_y = -g$$

(ii) **Components of initial velocity $\mathbf{v}_0$** are

$$v_{0x} = v_0\cos\theta_0, v_{0y} = v_0\sin\theta_0$$

(iii) **Components of its velocity at time** t can be given by

$$v_x = v_0\cos\theta_0, v_y = v_0\sin\theta_0 - gt$$

(iv) One of the component of velocity, i.e. **x-component** remains constant throughout the motion and only the **y-component changes.**

This topic is not included in latest rationalised NCERT, but it is given in latest NEET syllabus.

(v) **At maximum height**, $v_y = 0$ and therefore $\tan^{-1}\frac{v_y}{v_x} = 0$.

(vi) The initial positions of the projectile in x and y directions are $x_0 = 0$, $y_0 = 0$.

(vii) The **position of the projectile after time t in x and y directions** are

$$x = v_{0x}t = (v_0 \cos\theta_0)t$$

$$y = v_{0y}t + \frac{1}{2}a_y t^2 = (v_0 \sin\theta_0)t - \frac{1}{2}gt^2$$

- The equation of **path of a projectile** is given by

$$y = x\tan\theta_0 - \frac{1}{2}\frac{gx^2}{(v_0\cos\theta_0)^2}$$

Since, g, θ_0 and v_0 are constants, the above equation is of the form of $y = ax + bx^2$, in which a and b are constants. This is the equation of a parabola, i.e. the path of the projectile is a **parabola** shown in figure below.

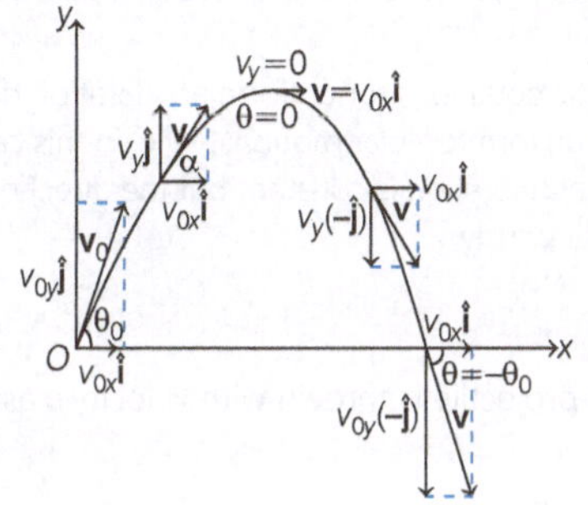

- **Velocity of projectile after time t;**

$$v = \sqrt{v_{0x}^2 + v_y^2}$$

and $$\alpha = \tan^{-1}\frac{v_y}{v_{0x}}$$ **NEET 2021**

- **Time of maximum height** is the time taken by the projectile to reach the maximum height. It is given as

$$t_m = \frac{v_0\sin\theta_0}{g}$$

- **Time of flight** is the total time T_f during which the projectile is in flight. It is given as $T_f = \frac{2v_0\sin\theta_0}{g}$.

Note $T_f = 2t_m$, which is expected because of the symmetry of the parabolic path.

- **Maximum height of a projectile** is the maximum height h_m reached by the projectile. It is given as

$$h_m = \frac{(v_0\sin\theta_0)^2}{2g}$$ **NEET 2023, 21**

- The horizontal distance travelled by a projectile during the time of flight is called **horizontal range** R of projectile. It is the distance travelled during the time of flight T_f. It is given as

$$R = \frac{v_0^2\sin 2\theta_0}{g}.$$

R is maximum when $\sin 2\theta_0$ is maximum, i.e. when $\theta_0 = 45°$, then its maximum value is $R_{max} = \frac{v_0^2}{g}$.

For **Concept Master** *Video*

- Two particles thrown with same initial speed cover same horizontal range, when their angle of projection is complementary i.e. θ and $90° - \theta$.

Marks Maximiser

Horizontal projectile motion under different cases

Projectile thrown up from top	Projectile thrown down from top
(a) $y = (-u\sin\theta)t + \frac{1}{2}gt^2$	(a) $y = (u\sin\theta)t + \frac{1}{2}gt^2$
(b) $x = (u\cos\theta)t$	(b) $x = u\cos\theta \cdot t$
(c) $v_y = \sqrt{(u\sin\theta)^2 + 2gy}$	(c) $v_y = \sqrt{(u\sin\theta)^2 + 2gy}$
(d) $\alpha = \tan^{-1}\left[\frac{-u\sin\theta + gt}{u\cos\theta}\right] = \tan^{-1}\left[\frac{\sqrt{u^2\sin^2\theta + 2gy}}{u\cos\theta}\right]$	(d) $\alpha = \tan^{-1}\left[\frac{\sqrt{u^2\sin^2\theta + 2gy}}{u\cos\theta}\right]$

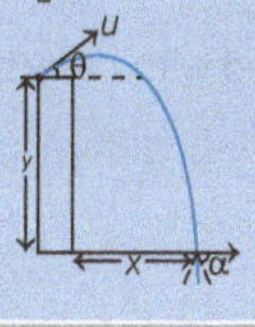

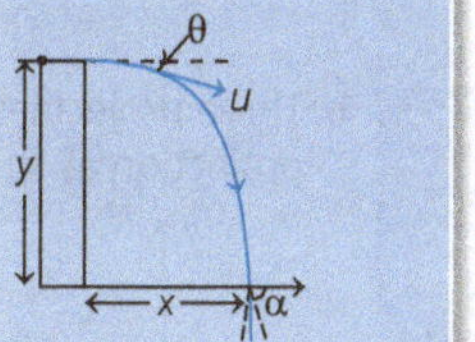

Uniform Circular Motion

- When an object follows a circular path at a constant speed, the motion of the object is called **uniform circular motion**.
- **Angular position** is the angle **made by radius vector with a given reference line.**
- **Angular displacement (θ)** is the angle through which the radius vector turns for a given time interval on the circle.

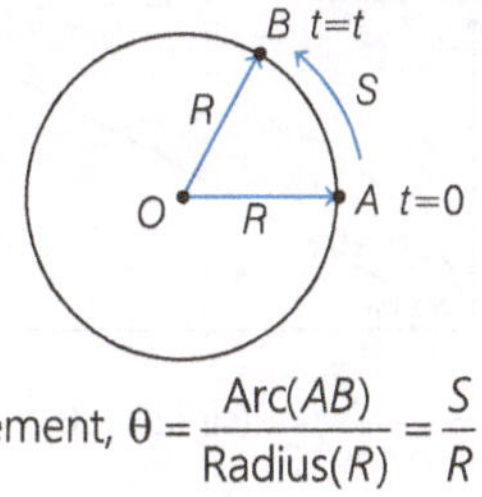

Angular displacement, $\theta = \frac{\text{Arc}(AB)}{\text{Radius}(R)} = \frac{S}{R}$

$\therefore$ $S = R\theta$

- **Average angular Velocity** is defined as the ratio of change in angular position ($\Delta\theta$) to a given time interval (Δt).

It is given as $\omega = \frac{\Delta\theta}{\Delta t} = \frac{\theta_2 - \theta_1}{t_2 - t_1}$

- **Instantaneous angular velocity** (ω) is defined as the rate at which the radius vector of an object with respect to the centre on the circle rotates.

$$\omega = \lim_{\Delta t \to 0} \frac{\Delta\theta}{\Delta t} = \frac{d\theta}{dt}$$

- **Relation between linear speed and angular speed** is given as $v = R\omega$
- If T be the **time period** and ν be the **frequency** of particle performing uniform circular motion, then

$$\omega = \frac{2\pi}{T} = 2\pi\nu$$ **NEET 2019**

- A body undergoing uniform circular motion is acted upon by an acceleration directed towards centre. This acceleration is called **centripetal acceleration.**

For Concept Master Video

Centripetal acceleration, $a_c = \frac{v^2}{R} = \omega^2 R$

Where, R is the radius of the circular path.

- Thus, a **particle in uniform circular motion has**
  - A **tangential velocity** with constant magnitude and continuously changing direction.
  - Only radial or **centripetal acceleration** directed towards centre of the circle.
  - A **constant angular velocity** about the centre of circle.
  - A **constant period of revolution** and hence constant frequency of revolution.

Caution Points

- Vector equation $\mathbf{v} = \mathbf{v}_0 + \mathbf{a}t$ and $\mathbf{r} = \mathbf{r}_0 + \mathbf{v}_0 t + \frac{1}{2}\mathbf{a}t^2$ do not involve any axis but we can resolve them as x-component and y-component.
- The shape of trajectory of the motion of particle does not depend only acceleration but also depends on initial condition of motion (initial position and initial velocity).
- The kinematic equations for uniform acceleration do not apply to the case of uniform circular motion. Since, in this case, the magnitude of acceleration is constant but the direction is changing continuously.

PYQ Notes

1. Three projectiles are projected with different angle of projection as shown in figure. **[NEET 2020]**

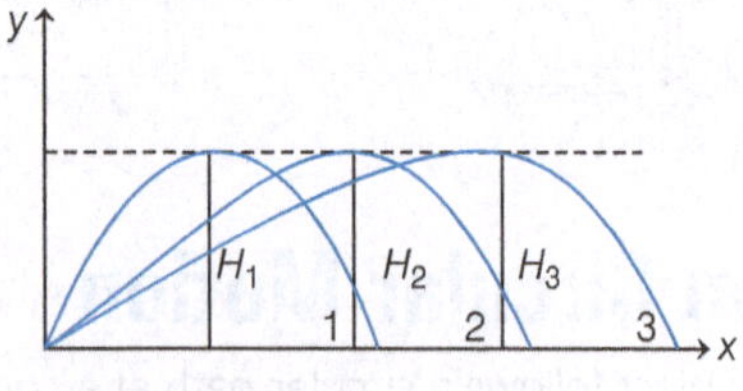

From the figure, $H_1 = H_2 = H_3 = H$

As, $H = u_y^2 / 2g$

$\therefore$ $T_1 = T_2 = T_3$

But $R_3 > R_2 > R_1$

2. When a projectile is thrown as shown in figure on a inclined plane, then **[JEE Main 2020]**

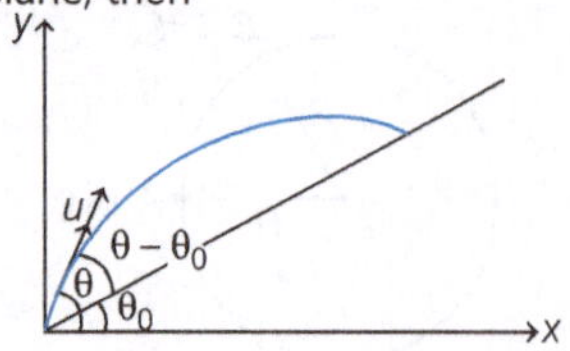

$$R = \frac{u^2}{g\cos^2\theta_0}(\sin(2\theta - \theta_0) - \sin\theta_0)$$

$$R_{mas} = \frac{u^2}{g(1 + \sin\theta_0)}$$

Time of flight, $T = \frac{2u\sin(\theta - \theta°)}{g\cos\theta°}$

3. When a projectile is thrown with velocity u as shown in figure. **[NEET 2019]**

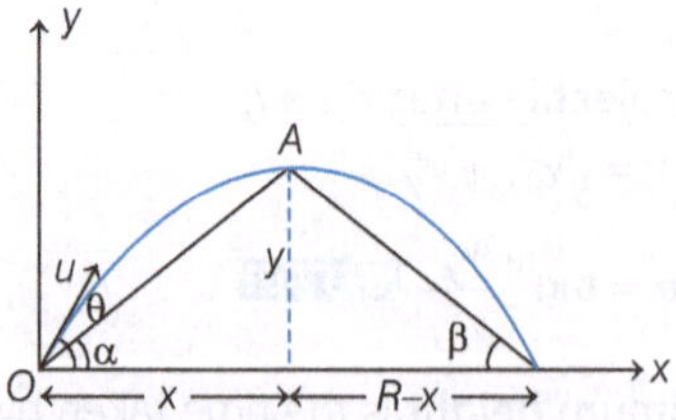

We have, $\tan\theta = \tan\alpha + \tan\beta$

4. If two particles A and B move with velocity $\mathbf{v}_1$ and $\mathbf{v}_2$ having position vectors $\mathbf{r}_1$ and $\mathbf{r}_2$, respectively, then

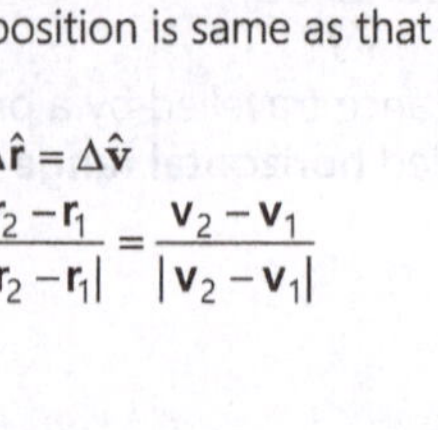

the particles A and B collide, when the direction of their relative position is same as that of relative velocity.

i.e. $\Delta\hat{\mathbf{r}} = \Delta\hat{\mathbf{v}}$

$\Rightarrow$ $\frac{\mathbf{r}_2 - \mathbf{r}_1}{|\mathbf{r}_2 - \mathbf{r}_1|} = \frac{\mathbf{v}_2 - \mathbf{v}_1}{|\mathbf{v}_2 - \mathbf{v}_1|}$ **[NEET 2017]**

Step by Step

Mastering NCERT

- Concept Builders
- Topical Questions
- Assertion and Reason Questions
- Statement Based
- Matching Type
- Numerical Type
- NCERT Exemplar
- Past Exams MCQs
- Skill Boosters

Concept Builders

1 Does a scalar quantity depend on the frame of reference chosen?

2 Name a quantity which have both magnitude and direction but still not considered as a vector quantity.

3 The magnitude of $|\mathbf{A}+\mathbf{B}|$ is same as that of $|\mathbf{B}+\mathbf{A}|$. [T/F]

4 If a ball is thrown up and received back by the thrower, what will be the magnitude of displacement vector of ball?

5 If **A**, **B** and **C** are mutually perpendicular vectors then what is the value of $\mathbf{A}\cdot(\mathbf{B}+\mathbf{C})$?

6 The angle between $(\hat{\mathbf{i}}+\hat{\mathbf{j}})$ and $(\hat{\mathbf{i}}-\hat{\mathbf{j}})$ is .... [0°/90°].

7 If the magnitude of resultant of two vectors of equal magnitudes is equal to the magnitude of either vectors, then what will be the angle between two vectors?

8 The direction of velocity at any point on the path of an object is tangential to the path at that point and is in the direction of motion. [T/F]

9 The average acceleration of an object for a time interval Δt moving in x - y plane is given by $a=\frac{dV}{dt}$. [T/F]

10 A projectile motion only possesses horizontal velocities. [T/F]

11 .... (Horizontal/Vertical) component of velocity remains unchanged during the flight of an oblique projectile.

12 A football is thrown in a parabolic path. At what point the acceleration will be perpendicular to the velocity?

13 A projectile fired from the ground follows a parabolic path. The speed of the projectile is maximum at the top of its path. [T/F]

14 The instantaneous velocity of a projectile is tangential to its parabolic path. [T/F]

15 What is the maximum height at which a body can reach during a flight?

16 The centripetal acceleration is .... (a/not a) constant vector.

17 A body executing uniform circular motion has its position vector and acceleration vector in .... (same/opposite) direction.

18 The kinematic equations for uniform acceleration can be applied in case of a uniform circular motion. [T/F]

19 What is the angle between velocity vector and acceleration vector in uniform circular motion?

20 The direction of centripetal acceleration does not depend on the direction of rotation of the body. It always acts along the radius towards the centre of the circle. [T/F]

Topical Questions

Scalars and Vectors

1 Which of the following is necessary condition of vector? NCERT Pg. 27

(a) It has only magnitude.
(b) It has only direction.
(c) It has both magnitude and direction.
(d) It has both magnitude and direction and also obeys the law of vector addition.

2 If the position vectors of a body are $\mathbf{r}_1$ and $\mathbf{r}_2$, then the displacement vector of the body is NCERT Pg. 28

(a) $(\mathbf{r}_1+\mathbf{r}_2)$
(b) $(\mathbf{r}_1-\mathbf{r}_2)$
(c) $(\mathbf{r}_2-\mathbf{r}_1)$
(d) $\frac{\mathbf{r}_1}{|\mathbf{r}_2|}$

3 Set of vectors **A** and **B**, **P** and **Q** are as shown below

NCERT Pg. 28

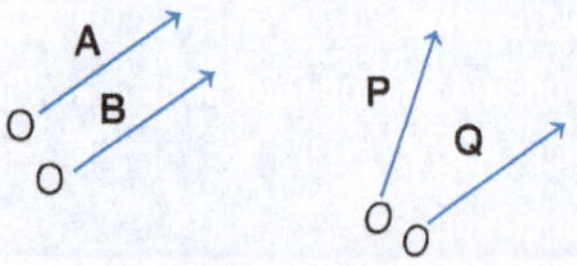

Length of **A** and **B** is equal, similarly length of **P** and **Q** is equal. Then, the vectors which are equal, are

(a) **A** and **P**
(b) **P** and **Q**
(c) **A** and **B**
(d) **B** and **Q**

Multiplication of Vectors by Real Numbers

4 If **A** is a vector of magnitude 7 units due north. What is the magnitude and direction of a vector -3**A**?

NCERT Pg. 29

(a) 7 units due east
(b) 21 units due west
(c) 7 unit due south
(d) 21 units due south

5 Choose the correct option regarding the given figure.

NCERT Pg. 29

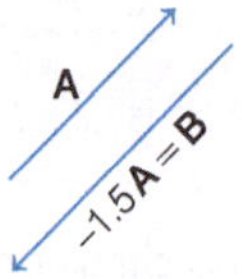

(a) **B** = **A**
(b) **B** = – **A**
(c) |**B**| = | **A** |
(d) |**B**| ≠ | **A** |

Addition and Subtraction of Vectors-Graphical Method

6 **A** and **B** are two inclined vectors and **R** is their sum. Choose the correct figure for the given description.

NCERT Pg. 29

(a) 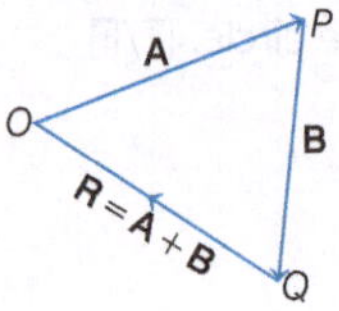

(b) 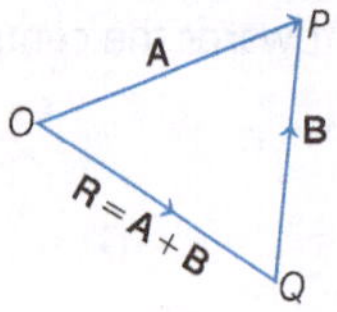

(c) 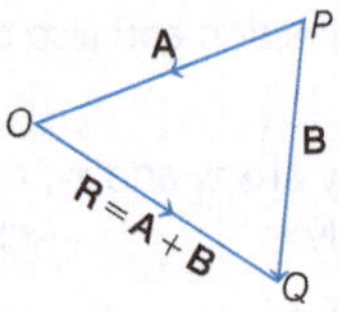

(d) 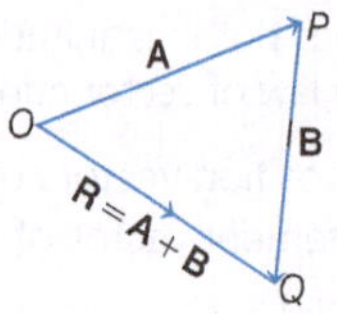

7 **A**, **B** and **C** are inclined vector such that **B** – **A** = **C**, choose the correct figure for the given relation.

NCERT Pg. 30

(a) 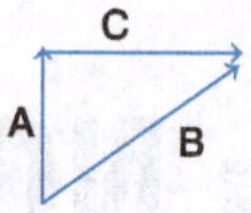

(b) 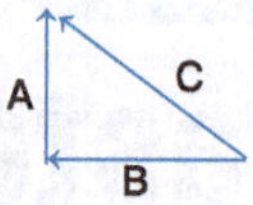

(c) 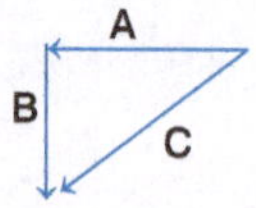

(d) 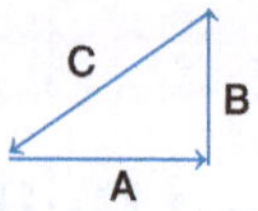

8 If **A** + **B** + **C** = **0** then,

NCERT Pg. 30

(a) Vectors **A**, **B** and **C** are parallel.
(b) Vector **A** is parallel to vector (**B** + **C**).
(c) Vector **A** is anti-parallel to vector (**B** + **C**)
(d) Vector **A** is parallel to vector (**B** – **C**)

9 Given, **a** + **b** + **c** + **d** = **0**, which of the following statement are incorrect?

NCERT Pg. 30

(a) **a**, **b**, **c** and **d** must each be a null vector.
(b) The magnitude of (**a** + **c**) equals the magnitude of (**b** + **d**).
(c) The magnitude of **a** can never be greater than the sum of the magnitudes of **b**, **c** and **d**.
(d) **b** + **c** must lie in the plane of **a** and **d**, if **a** and **d** are not collinear and in the line of **a** and **d**, if they are collinear.

Resolution of Vectors

10 Magnitude of a vector Q is 5 and magnitude of its y-component is 4. So, the magnitude of the x-component of this vector is

NCERT Pg. 32

(a) 8 (b) 3 (c) 6 (d) 8

11 A vector is inclined at an angle 60° to the horizontal. If its rectangular component in the horizontal direction is 50 N, then its rectangular component in the vertical direction is

NCERT Pg. 32

(a) 25 N (b) 75 N (c) 87 N (d) 100 N

12 Three vectors are given as $\mathbf{P} = 3\hat{i} - 4\hat{j}, \mathbf{Q} = 6\hat{i} - 8\hat{j}$ and $\mathbf{R} = (3/4)\,\hat{i} - \hat{j}$, then which of the following is correct?

NCERT Pg. 32

(a) **P**, **Q** and **R** are equal vectors
(b) **P** and **Q** are parallel but **R** is not parallel
(c) **P**, **Q** and **R** are parallel
(d) **P**, **Q** and **R** are null vectors

13 Consider vectors **a**, **b** and **c** as

NCERT Pg. 32

$\mathbf{a} = a_x\hat{i} + a_y\hat{j} + a_z\hat{k}, \mathbf{b} = b_x\hat{i} + b_y\hat{j} + b_z\hat{k}$
$\mathbf{c} = c_x\hat{i} + c_y\hat{j} + c_z\hat{k}$

Then, for a vector $\mathbf{T} = \mathbf{a} + \mathbf{b} - \mathbf{c}$ has its y-component in the form of

(a) $a_y + b_y + c_y$
(b) $-a_y + b_y - c_y$
(c) $a_y + b_y - c_y$
(d) $a_y - b_y + c_y$

14 Unit vector in the direction of the resultant of vectors $\mathbf{A} = -3\hat{i} - 2\hat{j} - 3\hat{k}$ and $\mathbf{B} = 2\hat{i} + 4\hat{j} + 6\hat{k}$ is **NCERT Pg. 32**

(a) $\frac{-3\hat{i} + 2\hat{j} - 3\hat{k}}{\sqrt{14}}$ (b) $-\hat{i} + 2\hat{j} + 3\hat{k}$

(c) $\frac{-\hat{i} + 2\hat{j} + 3\hat{k}}{\sqrt{14}}$ (d) $-2\hat{i} - 4\hat{j} + 8\hat{k}$

15 If a vector **A** makes an angle α, β and γ with the X, Y and Z-axes, respectively. Then, $\sin^2 \alpha + 2\cos^2 \alpha + \cos^2 \beta + \cos^2 \gamma$ is equal to **NCERT Pg. 33**

(a) 0 (b) 1 (c) 2 (d) 3

Vector Addition-Analytical Method

16 Which of the following statement is correct? **NCERT Pg. 33**

(a) Displacing a vector parallel to itself leaves the vector unchanged.
(b) Three equal vectors cannot add upto zero.
(c) If $|\mathbf{A}+\mathbf{B}| \neq |\mathbf{A}-\mathbf{B}|$, they are perpendicular vectors.
(d) Both (b) and (c)

17 The resultant of two vectors of equal magnitude is twice of magnitude of either of the vectors. The angle between them is **NCERT Pg. 33**

(a) 60° (b) 120° (c) 0° (d) 180°

18 Two vectors **P** and **Q** are inclined at an angle θ and **R** is their resultant as shown in the figure. **NCERT Pg. 33**

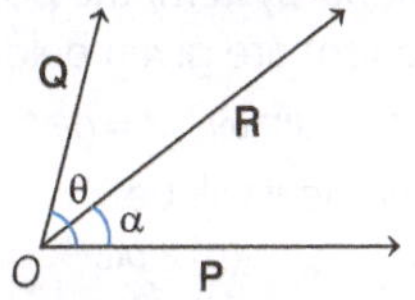

Keeping the magnitude and the angle of the vectors same, if the directions of **P** and **Q** are interchanged, then there is a change in which of the following with regard to **R**?

(a) Magnitude
(b) Direction
(c) Both magnitude and direction
(d) None of the above

19 For two vectors **A** and **B** which lie in a plane. Which of the following statement is correct? **NCERT Pg. 34**

(a) If magnitude of **A** and **B** vector is 3 and 4 and they add upto give vector having magnitude of 5, then they must be perpendicular vector.
(b) If they add up to give more than 5, then they must be inclined at obtuse angle.
(c) If they add upto give less than 5, then they must be inclined at acute angle.
(d) None of the above

20 Vectors **A** and **B** include an angle α between them. If $(\mathbf{A}+\mathbf{B})$ and $(\mathbf{A}-\mathbf{B})$, respectively subtend angles θ_1 and θ_2 with **A**, then $(\tan\theta_1 + \tan\theta_2)$ is **NCERT Pg. 34**

(a) $\frac{B^2 \cos 2\alpha}{A^2 - B^2 \cos^2 \alpha}$

(b) $\frac{-B^2 \cos 2\alpha}{A^2 - B^2 \cos^2 \alpha}$

(c) $\frac{-B^2 \sin 2\alpha}{A^2 - B^2 \cos^2 \alpha}$

(d) $\frac{B^2 \sin 2\alpha}{A^2 - B^2 \cos^2 \alpha}$

21 Two forces **P** and **Q** of magnitude $2F$ and $3F$, respectively,are at an angle θ with each other. If the force **Q** is doubled, then their resultant also gets doubled. Then, the angle θ is **NCERT Pg. 34**

(a) 60° (b) 120°
(c) 30° (d) 90°

22 It is found that $|\mathbf{A}+\mathbf{B}| = |\mathbf{A}|$. This implies **NCERT Pg. 34**

(a) $|\mathbf{B}| = 1$ (b) **A**, **B** are anti-parallel
(c) **A**, **B** are perpendicular (d) **A**; $\mathbf{B} \leq 0$

23 Find the value of difference of unit vectors **A** and **B** whose angle of inclination is θ. **NCERT Pg. 34**

(a) $2\sin(\theta/2)$ (b) $2\cos(\theta/2)$
(c) $\sin(\theta/2)$ (d) $\cos(\theta/2)$

24 Given, $|\mathbf{A}+\mathbf{B}| = P, |\mathbf{A}-\mathbf{B}| = Q$. The value of $P^2 + Q^2$ is **NCERT Pg. 34**

(a) $2(A^2 + B^2)$ (b) $A^2 - B^2$
(c) $A^2 + B^2$ (d) $2(A^2 - B^2)$

25 For two vectors **A** and **B**, $|\mathbf{A}+\mathbf{B}| = |\mathbf{A}-\mathbf{B}|$ is always true, when **NCERT Pg. 34**

(a) $|\mathbf{A}| = |\mathbf{B}| \neq 0$
(b) $|\mathbf{A}| = |\mathbf{B}| \neq 0$ and **A** and **B** are parallel or anti-parallel
(c) when either $|\mathbf{A}|$ or $|\mathbf{B}|$ is zero or **A** and **B** are perpendicular to each other
(d) $|\mathbf{A}| = 1$ and $|\mathbf{B}| = 0$

26 Two vectors **A** and **B** have equal magnitudes. The magnitude of $(\mathbf{A}+\mathbf{B})$ is n times the magnitude of $(\mathbf{A}-\mathbf{B})$. The angle between **A** and **B** is **NCERT Pg. 34**

(a) $\sin^{-1}\left(\frac{n^2-1}{n^2+1}\right)$

(b) $\sin^{-1}\left(\frac{n-1}{n+1}\right)$

(c) $\cos^{-1}\left(\frac{n^2-1}{n^2+1}\right)$

(d) $\cos^{-1}\left(\frac{n-1}{n+1}\right)$

Motion in a Plane

27 Suppose a particle moves along a curve shown by the thick line and the positions of particle are represented by P at t and P' at t'. **NCERT Pg. 35**

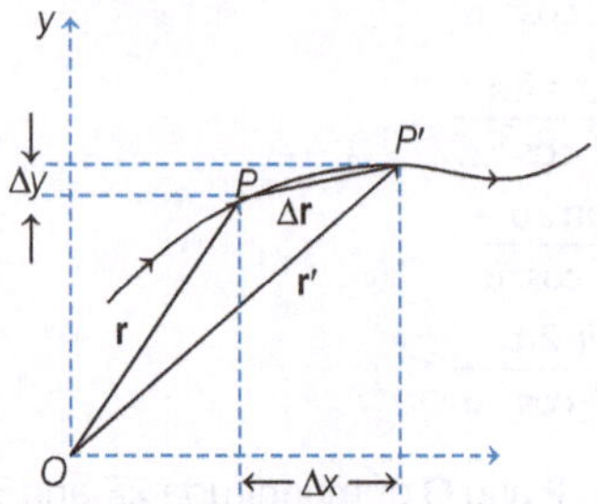

where, coordinates of P is (2, 3) and P' is (5, 6). Net displacement of the particle will be

(a) zero (b) $7\hat{i} + 9\hat{j}$
(c) $10\hat{i} + 18\hat{j}$ (d) $3\hat{i} + 3\hat{j}$

28 A particle starts moving from point (2, 3, 5). Displacement for the particle is $4\hat{i} - 2\hat{j} + \hat{k}$. The final coordinates of the particle is **NCERT Pg. 35**

(a) (6, 1, 0) (b) (8, 10, 2)
(c) (6, – 1, 6) (d) (8, 2,10)

29 A particle starting from the origin (0, 0) moves in a straight line in the (X, Y) plane. Its coordinates at a later time are $(\sqrt{3}, 1)$. The path of the particle makes with the X-axis an angle of **NCERT Pg. 35**

(a) 30° (b) 45° (c) 60° (d) 15°

30 A person moves 15m north, then 20 m east, then $30\sqrt{2}$ m south-west. His displacement from the original position is **NCERT Pg. 35**

(a) zero
(b) 18 m towards west
(c) 10 m towards west
(d) 15 m towards east

31 A bird flies from (–2 m, 4 m, –3 m) to (5 m, –2 m, –3 m) in the xyz-coordinates. The bird's displacement vector and magnitude are **NCERT Pg. 35**

(a) $(4\hat{i} + 2\hat{j} - 6\hat{k})$, 6.2 m (b) $(10\hat{i} - 6\hat{j})$, 9.2 m
(c) $(7\hat{i} - 6\hat{j})$, 9.2 m (d) $(10\hat{i} + 6\hat{j} - 6\hat{k})$, 6.2 m

32 A particle is moving such that its position coordinates (x, y) are $(2m, 3m)$ at $t = 0$ s, $(6m, 7m)$ at time 2 s and $(13m, 14m)$ at time $t = 5$ s. Average velocity vector $(\mathbf{v}_{av})$ from $t = 0$s to $t = 5$ s is **NCERT Pg. 35**

(a) $\frac{1}{5}(13\hat{i} + 14\hat{j})$ (b) $\frac{11}{5}(\hat{i} + \hat{j})$
(c) $2(\hat{i} + \hat{j})$ (d) $\frac{7}{3}(\hat{i} + \hat{j})$

33 The direction of instantaneous velocity is shown by **NCERT Pg. 35**

(a)
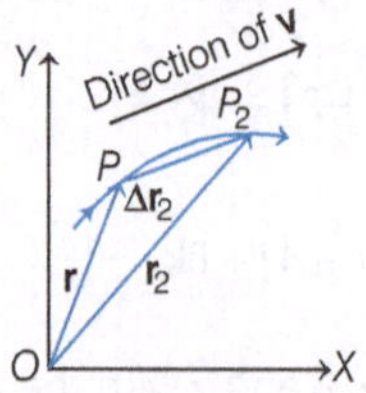

(b)
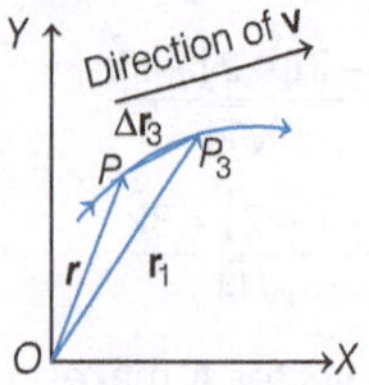

(c)
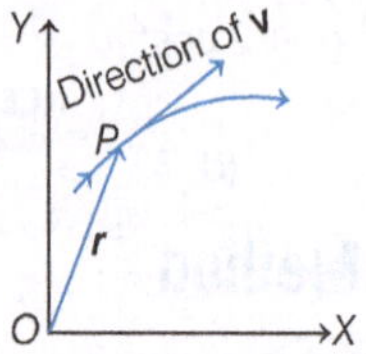

(d)
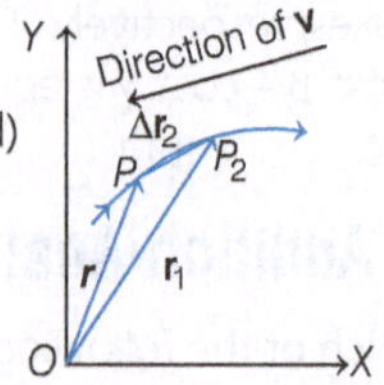

34 A body is moving with velocity $\mathbf{v} = k(y\hat{i} + x\hat{j})$, where k is a constant. The general equation for its path is **NCERT Pg. 35**

(a) $y + x^2 =$ constant
(b) $x + y^2 = 0$
(c) $xy =$ constant
(d) $y^2 - x^2 =$ constant

35 The position of a particle is given by $\mathbf{r} = 3t\hat{i} + 2t^2\hat{j} + 5\hat{k}$, then the direction of $\mathbf{v}$ (t) at $t = 1$ s in **NCERT Pg. 35**

(a) 45° with X-axis (b) 63° with Y-axis
(c) 30° with Y-axis (d) 53° with X-axis

36 In three dimensional system, the position coordinates of a particle (in motion) are given below **NCERT Pg. 35**

$$x = a\cos\omega t,\ \ y = a\sin\omega t,\ \ z = a\omega t$$

The velocity of particle will be

(a) $\sqrt{2}\, a\omega$ (b) $2\, a\omega$
(c) $a\omega$ (d) $\sqrt{3}\, a\omega$

37 A particle moves in a plane such that its coordinate changes with time as $x = at^2 + bt$ and $y = ct$, where a, b and c are constants. Then, which of the following statement is correct? **NCERT Pg. 36**

(a) Acceleration of particle is constant.
(b) Velocity of particle is constant.
(c) Acceleration depends only on its x-component.
(d) Acceleration depends only on its y-component.

38 A particle is moving eastwards with a velocity of 5 ms^{-1}. In 10s, the velocity changes to 5 ms^{-1} northwards. The average acceleration in this time is **NCERT Pg. 36**

(a) $2\sqrt{2}$ ms^{-2} towards north-east
(b) $1/\sqrt{2}$ ms^{-2} towards north
(c) 2 ms^{-2} towards north
(d) $1/\sqrt{2}$ ms^{-2} towards north-west

39 The x and y-coordinates of the particle at any time are $x = 5t - 2t^2$ and $y = 10t$, respectively, where x and y are in metres and t in seconds. The acceleration of the particle at $t = 2$ s is **NCERT Pg. 36**

(a) 0 (b) 5 ms^{-2}
(c) $-4\ ms^{-2}$ (d) $-8\ ms^{-2}$

40 The position vector of particle changes with time according to the relation $\mathbf{r}(t) = 15t^2\hat{\mathbf{i}} + (4 - 20t^2)\hat{\mathbf{j}}$. What is the magnitude of the acceleration (in ms^{-2}) at $t = 1$ s? **NCERT Pg. 36**

(a) 50 (b) 100
(c) 25 (d) 40

41 A particle starts from origin at $t = 0$ with a velocity $5.0\,\hat{\mathbf{i}}\ ms^{-1}$ and moves in XY-plane under action of force which produces a constant acceleration of $(3.0\,\hat{\mathbf{i}} + 2.0\,\hat{\mathbf{j}})\ ms^{-2}$. What is the y-coordinate of the particle at the instant, if x-coordinate is 84 m? **NCERT Pg. 37**

(a) 36 m (b) 24 m
(c) 39 m (d) 18 m

Relative Velocity in Two-dimensions

42 Buses A and B are moving in the same direction with velocities $20\hat{\mathbf{i}}\ ms^{-1}$ and $15\hat{\mathbf{i}}\ ms^{-1}$, respectively. Then, relative velocity of A with respect to B is **Old NCERT Pg. 76**

(a) $35\,\hat{\mathbf{i}}\ ms^{-1}$ (b) $5\,\hat{\mathbf{i}}\ ms^{-1}$
(c) $5\,\hat{\mathbf{j}}\ ms^{-1}$ (d) $35\,\hat{\mathbf{j}}\ ms^{-1}$

43 Rain is falling vertically with a speed of 35 ms^{-1}. A woman rides a bicycle with a speed of 12 ms^{-1} in east to west direction. The direction in which she should hold her umbrella is **Old NCERT Pg. 76**

(a) at $\cos^{-1}$ (0.343) with vertical towards east
(b) at $\tan^{-1}$ (0.343) with vertical towards west
(c) at $\cos^{-1}$ (0.343) with vertical towards west
(d) at $\tan^{-1}$ (0.343) with vertical towards east

44 A car driver is moving towards a rocket launching pad with a velocity of $8\hat{\mathbf{i}}\ ms^{-1}$. He observed the rocket to be moving with a speed of 10 ms^{-1}. A stationary observer will see the rocket to be moving with a speed of **Old NCERT Pg. 76**

(a) 5 ms^{-1} (b) 6 ms^{-1}
(c) 7 ms^{-1} (d) 8 ms^{-1}

45 The stream of a river is flowing with a speed of 2 km/h. A swimmer can swim at a speed of 4 km/h. What should be the direction of the swimmer with respect to the flow of the river to cross the river straight? **Old NCERT Pg. 76**

(a) 60° (b) 120°
(c) 90° (d) 150°

46 A man standing on a road has to hold his umbrella at 30° with the vertical to keep the rain away. He throws the umbrella and starts running at 10 kmh^{-1}. He finds that raindrops are hitting his head vertically. The actual speed of raindrops is **Old NCERT Pg. 76**

(a) 20 kmh^{-1} (b) $10\sqrt{3}\ kmh^{-1}$
(c) $20\sqrt{3}\ kmh^{-1}$ (d) 10 kmh^{-1}

47 A girl can swim with speed 5kmh^{-1} in still water. She crosses a river 2 km wide, where the river flows steadily at 2 kmh^{-1} and she makes strokes normal to the river current. Find how far down the river she go when she reaches the other bank. **Old NCERT Pg. 76**

(a) 1 km (b) 2 km (c) 800 m (d) 750 m

48 A girl riding a bicycle with a speed of 5 ms^{-1} towards east direction sees raindrops falling vertically downwards. On increasing the speed to 15 ms^{-1}, rain appears to fall making an angle of 45° of the vertical. Find the magnitude of velocity of rain. **Old NCERT Pg. 76**

(a) 5 ms^{-1} (b) $5\sqrt{5}\ ms^{-1}$
(c) 25 ms^{-1} (d) 10 ms^{-1}

49 A particle is moving along the X-axis with its coordinate given by $x(t) = 10 + 8t - 3t^2$. Another particle is moving along the Y-axis with its coordinate as a function of time given by $y(t) = 5 - 8t^3$. At $t = 1$ s, the speed of the second particle as measured in the frame of the first particle is given as $\sqrt{v}$. Then, v (in m/s) is **Old NCERT Pg. 76**

(a) 430 ms^{-1} (b) 580 ms^{-1}
(c) 450 ms^{-1} (d) 380 ms^{-1}

50 A swimmer swims in a river aiming to reach exactly opposite point on the bank of a river. His speed of swimming is 1 m/s at an angle 120° with the direction of flow of water. The speed of water in stream is **Old NCERT Pg. 76**

(a) 1.0 m/s (b) 0.5 m/s (c) 0.25 m/s (d) 0.43 m/s

51 The width of a river is 1.5 km. The velocity of a boat is $\sqrt{41}$ km/h. The boat covered the width of river in shortest time 18 min, then the velocity of river stream is **Old NCERT Pg. 76**

(a) $\sqrt{41}$ km/h (b) $\sqrt{29}$ km/h
(c) 4 km/h (d) 3 km/h

52 A river is flowing from east to west with a speed 7 ms^{-1}. A swimmer can swim in still water at a speed of 14 ms^{-1}. If he wants to start from point A on south bank and reach opposite point B on north bank, in what direction should be swim? **Old NCERT Pg. 76**

(a) 30° east of north
(b) 60° east of north
(c) 30° west of north
(d) 60° west of north

53 A boy riding a bicycle with a speed of 5 ms^{-1} towards east direction, observes rain falling vertically down. If he increases his speed to 17 ms^{-1}, rain appears to meet him at 45° to the vertical. What is the speed of the rain? **Old NCERT Pg. 76**

(a) $5\sqrt{2}$ ms^{-1} (b) 13 ms^{-1} (c) $10\sqrt{2}$ ms^{-1} (d) 10 ms^{-1}

Projectile Motion

54 When the projectile is projected obliquely from the ground level with initial velocity v_0 and if the air resistance is not neglected, then choose the correct statement. **NCERT Pg. 39**

(a) The projectile traverses a perfect parabolic path.
(b) It will hit the ground with the same speed with which it was projected from it.
(c) Range of the projectile $< \frac{v_0^2}{g}$.
(d) Maximum height of the projectile $> \left(\frac{v_0 \sin \theta_0}{2g}\right)$.

55 A biker stands on the edge of a cliff 490 m above the ground and throws a stone horizontally with an initial speed of 15 ms^{-1}. Which one of the following statement is correct? **NCERT Pg. 39**

(a) The time taken by the stone to reach the ground is 30 s.
(b) The time taken by the stone to reach the ground is 20 s.
(c) The speed with which it hits the ground is 99 ms^{-1}.
(d) None of the above

56 A ball is thrown horizontally from the top of a tower of height H with velocity 20 m/s. A man is standing at the foot of tower starts running at the same instant when ball is thrown. What should be the velocity of man to catch the ball before striking to the ground. (Consider height of man negligible). **NCERT Pg. 39**

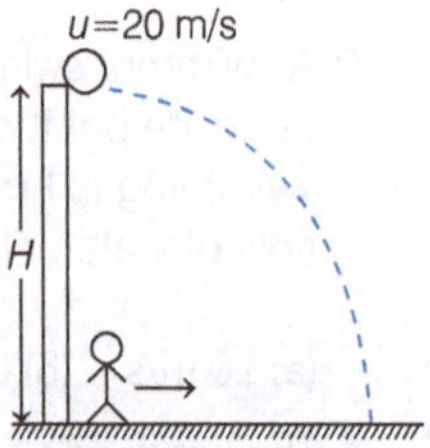

(a) 10m/s (b) $\sqrt{2gH}$ (c) 20 m/s (d) 30 m/s

57 At the top most point of the trajectory for an object that has been projected at an angle θ with the horizontal, has acceleration **NCERT Pg. 39**

(a) $> g$ (b) $< g$ (c) zero (d) $= g$

58 A ball is projected with velocity 10 ms^{-1} in a direction making an angle 30° with the horizontal, what is the position coordinate (in metres) of the ball after 1s? **NCERT Pg. 39**

(a) (8.66, 0.1) (b) (9.8, 1.0)
(c) (4.26, 5.29) (d) (0.4, 8.66)

59 If the initial velocity in horizontal direction of a projectile is unit vector $\hat{\mathbf{i}}$ and the equation of trajectory is $y = 5x(1-x)$. Then, y components of initial velocity is [Take, $g = 10$ m/s^2] **NCERT Pg. 39**

(a) $2\hat{\mathbf{j}}$ (b) $3\hat{\mathbf{j}}$ (c) $4\hat{\mathbf{j}}$ (d) $5\hat{\mathbf{j}}$

60 A projectile is thrown at an angle θ to the horizontal from O and it hits the ground at O'. During the entire motion, (select the wrong statement). **NCERT Pg. 39**

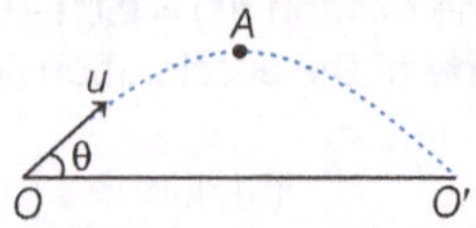

(a) Power delivered by gravity at O is negative.
(b) Power delivered by gravity at O' is negative.
(c) Power delivered by gravity at O' is positive.
(d) Power delivered by gravity at A is zero.

61 The equations of motion of a projectile are given by $x = 18t$ and $2y = 54t - 9.8t^2$. The angle θ of projection is **NCERT Pg. 39**

(a) $\tan^{-1}(3)$ (b) $\tan^{-1}(1.5)$
(c) $\sin^{-1}\frac{2}{3}$ (d) $\cos^{-1}\frac{2}{3}$

62 A projectile is fired from the surface of the earth with a velocity of 5 ms^{-1} at an angle θ with the horizontal. Another projectile fired from another planet with a velocity of 3 ms^{-1} at the same angle, follows a trajectory of the projectile fired from the earth. The value of the acceleration due to gravity on the planet is (in ms^{-2}) is (given, $g = 9.8$ ms^{-2}) **NCERT Pg. 39**

(a) 3.5 (b) 5.9 (c) 16.3 (d) 110.8

63 A projectile is given an initial velocity of $(\hat{\mathbf{i}} + 2\hat{\mathbf{j}})$ ms^{-1}, where $\hat{\mathbf{i}}$ is along the ground and $\hat{\mathbf{j}}$ is along vertical. If $g = 10$ ms^{-2}, the equation of its trajectory is **NCERT Pg. 39**

(a) $y = x - 5x^2$ (b) $y = 2x - 5x^2$
(c) $4y = 2x - 5x^2$ (d) $4y = 2x - 25x^2$

64 Amongst the following graphs, which graph represents the correct relation between the height of projectile (h) and time (t), when a particle (projectile) is thrown from the ground obliquely? **NCERT Pg. 39**

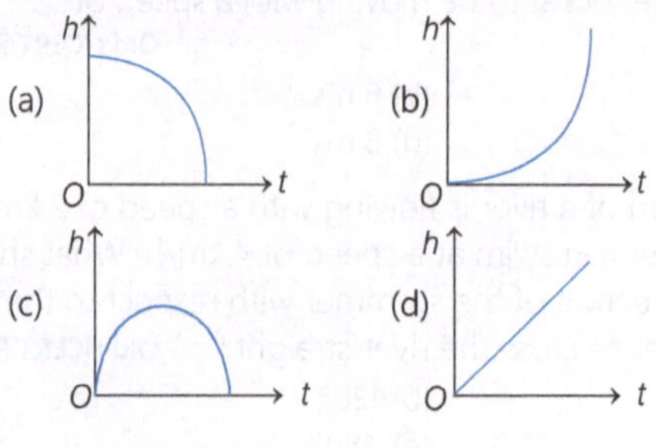

65 Two stones were projected simultaneously in the same vertical plane from same point obliquely, with different speeds and angles with the horizontal. The trajectory of path followed by one, as seen by the other, is **NCERT Pg. 39**

(a) parabola (b) straight line
(c) circle (d) hyperbola

66 Time taken by a stone to reach the maximum height is 5.8 s, then total time taken by the stone during which it was in flight is **NCERT Pg. 39**

(a) 5.8 s (b) 11.6 s
(c) 2.9 s (d) 4.2 s

67 An aircraft flying horizontally with the speed 480 kmh^{-1} releases a bomb at a height of 980 m from the ground. It will strike the ground at (use, $g = 10\ ms^{-2}$) **NCERT Pg. 39**

(a) 1 km (b) 2 km
(c) 2.8 km (d) 1.867 km

68 A fighter plane flying horizontally at an altitude of 1.0 km with speed 720 km h^{-1}' passes directly overhead an anti -aircraft gun. At what angle from the vertical should the gun be fired for the shell will muzzle speed 400 ms^{-1} to hit the plane. (Take $g = 10\ ms^{-2}$) **NCERT Pg. 39**

(a) 60° (b) 45°
(c) 38° (d) 30°

69 A boy stands on the edge of a cliff 980 m above the ground and throws a stone horizontally with a speed of 19.8 ms^{-1}. The velocity of the stone at ground is **NCERT Pg. 39**

(a) 99 m/s (b) 49 m/s
(c) 140 m/s (d) 180 m/s

70 A boy playing on the roof of a 10 m high building throws a ball with a speed of 10 m/s at an angle of 30° with the horizontal. How far from the throwing point will the ball become at the height of 10 m from the ground? [$g = 10\ m/s^2$, $\sin 30° = 1/2$, $\cos 30° = \sqrt{3}/2$] **NCERT Pg. 39**

(a) 6.66 m (b) 18.66 m
(c) 2.88 m (d) 8.66 m

71 The ceiling of a hall is 30 m high. A ball is thrown with 60 ms^{-1} at an angle θ, so that it could reach the ceiling of the hall and come back to the ground. The angle of projection θ that the ball was projected is given by **NCERT Pg. 39**

(a) $\sin\theta = \frac{1}{\sqrt{8}}$ (b) $\sin\theta = \frac{1}{\sqrt{6}}$
(c) $\sin\theta = \frac{1}{\sqrt{3}}$ (d) $\sin\theta = \frac{1}{\sqrt{5}}$

72 Two projectiles having different masses m_1 and m_2 are projected at an angle α and (90° – α) with the same speed from same point. The ratio of their maximum heights is **NCERT Pg. 39**

(a) $\cot\alpha : \sin\alpha$ (b) 1 : 1
(c) $\tan^2\alpha : 1$ (d) $1 : \tan\alpha$

73 Two projectiles A and B thrown with speeds in the ratio $1 : \sqrt{2}$ acquired the same height. If A is thrown at an angle of 45° with the horizontal, then angle of projection of B will be **NCERT Pg. 39**

(a) 0° (b) 60°
(c) 30° (d) 45°

74 Given below figure show three paths of a rock with different initial velocities. The correct increasing order for the respective initial horizontal velocity component (ignoring the effect of air resistance) is **NCERT Pg. 39**

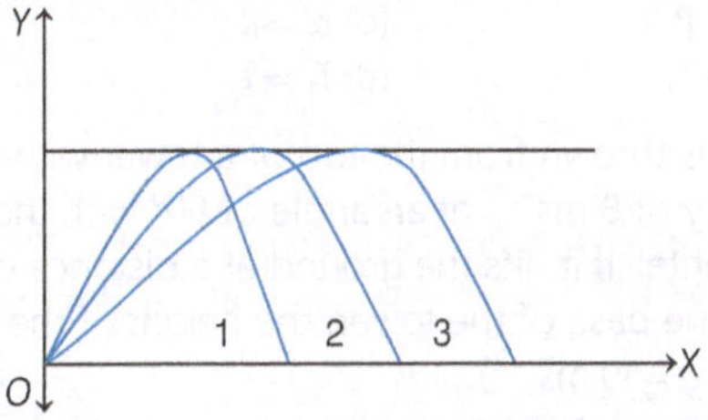

(a) 1 < 2 < 3 (b) 3 < 2 < 1
(c) 2 < 1 < 3 (d) 3 < 1 < 2

75 A man can throw a stone to a maximum distance of 80 m. The maximum height to which it will rise, is **NCERT Pg. 39**

(a) 30 m (b) 20 m
(c) 10 m (d) 40 m

76 A player kicks a ball at a speed of 15 ms^{-1}, so that its horizontal range is maximum. Another player 13.5 m away in the direction of kick starts running in the same direction at the same instant of hit. If he has to catch the ball just before it reaches the ground, he should run with a velocity equal to (Take $g = 10\ ms^{-2}$) **NCERT Pg. 39**

(a) $2\sqrt{2}\ ms^{-1}$ (b) $5\sqrt{2}\ ms^{-1}$
(c) $3\sqrt{2}\ ms^{-1}$ (d) $10\sqrt{2}\ ms^{-1}$

77 Three particles A, B and C are projected from the same point with the same initial speeds making angle 30°, 45° and 60°, respectively with the horizontal. Which of the following statement is correct? **NCERT Pg. 40**

(a) A, B and C have unequal ranges.
(b) Ranges of A and C are less than that of B.
(c) Ranges of A and C are equal and greater than that of B.
(d) A, B and C have equal ranges.

78 For angles of projection of a projectile at angles $(45° - \theta)$ and $(45° + \theta)$, the horizontal ranges described by the projectile are in the ratio of **NCERT Pg. 40**

(a) 1 : 3 (b) 2 : 3
(c) 3 : 2 (d) 1 : 1

79 A shell is fired from a fixed artillery gun with an initial speed u such that it hits the target on the ground at a distance 49 m from it. If t_1 and t_2 are the values of the time taken by it to hit the target in two possible ways, the product $t_1 t_2$ is **NCERT Pg. 40**

(a) 12 s^2 (b) 18 s^2
(c) 10 s^2 (d) 8 s^2

80 Two particles are projected with speed u at angles α and β (both acute) to the horizontal, respectively. If the height reached by the first particle is greater than that of the second, then which one of the following is correct? (T_1 and T_2 are the time of flights). **NCERT Pg. 40**

(a) $\alpha < \beta$ (b) $\alpha = \beta$
(c) $T_1 > T_2$ (d) $T_1 = T_2$

81 A ball is thrown from the top of a tower with an initial velocity of 8 ms^{-1}, at an angle of 60° with the horizontal. If it hits the ground at a distance of 16 m from the base of the tower, the height of the tower is (Take, $g = 10\ ms^{-2}$) **NCERT Pg. 40**

(a) 42 m (b) 28.5 m (c) 52.2 m (d) 98.6 m

82 If a person can throw a stone to maximum height of h metre vertically, then the maximum distance through which it can be thrown horizontally at an angle θ by the same person is **NCERT Pg. 40**

(a) $\frac{h}{2}$ (b) h
(c) $2h$ (d) $3h$

83 Find angle of projection with the horizontal in terms of maximum height attained and horizontal range. **NCERT Pg. 40**

(a) $\tan^{-1}\frac{2H}{R}$ (b) $\tan^{-1}\frac{4R}{H}$
(c) $\tan^{-1}\frac{4H}{R}$ (d) $\tan^{-1}\frac{H}{R}$

84 The speed of a projectile at the maximum height is (1/2) of its initial speed. Find the ratio of range of projectile to the maximum height attained. **NCERT Pg. 40**

(a) $4\sqrt{3}$ (b) $\frac{4}{\sqrt{3}}$
(c) $\frac{\sqrt{3}}{4}$ (d) 6

85 A body is projected at $t = 0$ with a velocity 10 ms^{-1} at an angle of 60° with the horizontal. The radius of curvature of its trajectory at $t = 1$ s is R. Neglecting air resistance and taking acceleration due to gravity $g = 10\ ms^{-2}$, the value of R is **NCERT Pg. 40**

(a) 10.3 m (b) 2.8 m
(c) 5.1 m (d) 2.5 m

Uniform Circular Motion

86 An insect trapped in a circular groove of radius 12 cm moves along the groove steadily and completes 7 revolutions in 100 s. Which one of the following statement is correct? **NCERT Pg. 40**

(a) The angular speed of insect is 1.68 rad/s.
(b) The linear speed of the motion is 5.3 cm/s.
(c) The magnitude of acceleration is 6.78 cm/s^2.
(d) The acceleration vector is a constant vector.

87 For a particle performing uniform circular motion, choose the incorrect statement from the following. **NCERT Pg. 40**

(a) Magnitude of particle velocity (speed) remains constant.
(b) Particle velocity remains directed parallel to radius vector.
(c) Direction of acceleration keeps changing as particle moves.
(d) None of the above

88 If a car is executing a uniform circular motion, then its centripetal acceleration represents

(a) a scalar quantity **NCERT Pg. 40**
(b) constant vector
(c) not a constant vector
(d) constant direction and changing magnitude

89 A particle is moving with a uniform speed v in a circular path of radius r with the centre at O. When the particle moves from a point P to Q on the circle such that $\angle POQ = \theta$, then the magnitude of the change in velocity is **NCERT Pg. 41**

(a) $2v\cos(2\theta)$ (b) zero
(c) $2v\sin\left(\frac{\theta}{2}\right)$ (d) $\frac{v\sin\theta}{2}$

90 A particle is moving on a circular path with uniform angular speed ω. The radius of the circular path is r. The acceleration of the particle along the direction perpendicular to the radius of the circular path is **NCERT Pg. 41**

(a) $\omega^2 r$ (b) 0
(c) ωr^2 (d) $\frac{r^2}{\omega}$

91 A particle is moving with 10 ms^{-1} in a circle of radius 5m, find out the magnitude of average velocity if particle is moved by 60° in 1 s. **NCERT Pg. 41**

(a) 5 ms^{-1} (b) 10 ms^{-1}
(c) $5\sqrt{3}$ ms^{-1} (d) 20 ms^{-1}

92 Two particles A and B are moving in uniform circular motion in concentric circles of radii r_A and r_B with speed v_A and v_B, respectively. Their time period of rotation is the same. The ratio of angular speed of A to that of B will be NCERT Pg. 41

(a) $v_A : v_B$ (b) $r_B : r_A$ (c) 1 : 1 (d) $r_A : r_B$

93 Two cars A and B move along a concentric circular path of radius r_A and r_B with velocities v_A and v_B maintaining constant distance, then $\frac{v_A}{v_B}$ is equal to NCERT Pg. 41

(a) $\frac{r_B}{r_A}$ (b) $\frac{r_A}{r_B}$ (c) $\frac{r_A^2}{r_B^2}$ (d) $\frac{r_B^2}{r_A^2}$

94 A cyclist starts from centre O of a circular park of radius 500 m and moves along the path $OPRQO$ as shown in figure. If he maintains constant speed of 5 ms^{-1}, what is his acceleration at point R? NCERT Pg. 42

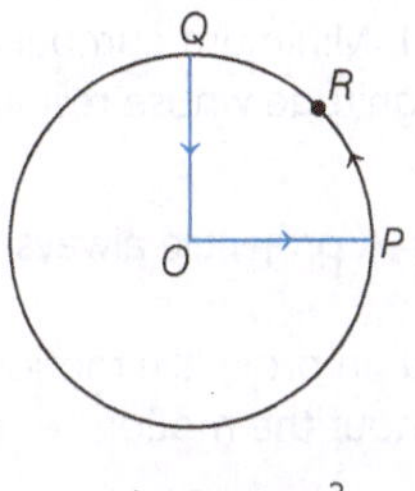

(a) 0.05 ms^{-2} (b) 0.1 ms^{-2}
(c) 0.01 ms^{-2} (d) 1 ms^{-2}

95 If the length of the second's hand in a stop clock is 3 cm, then linear velocity of its tip is NCERT Pg. 42

(a) 4.28 ms^{-1} (b) 0.1047 ms^{-1}
(c) 0.00314 ms^{-1} (d) 1.424 ms^{-1}

96 What is the centripetal acceleration of a point mass which is moving on a circular path of radius 5m with speed 23 ms^{-1}? NCERT Pg. 42

(a) 106 ms^{-2} (b) 90 ms^{-2}
(c) 60 ms^{-2} (d) None of these

97 Two bodies of masses m_1 and m_2, respectively are moving in circles of radii r_1 and r_2, respectively. Their speeds are such that they make complete circles in the same time t. The ratio of their centripetal accelerations is NCERT Pg. 42

(a) $m_1 r_1 : m_2 r_2$ (b) $m_1 : m_2$
(c) $r_1 : r_2$ (d) 1 : 1

98 A car revolves uniformly in a circle of diameter 0.80 m and completes 100 rev min^{-1}. Its angular velocity is NCERT Pg. 42

(a) 10.467 $rads^{-1}$ (b) 0.6 $rads^{-1}$
(c) 46.26 $rads^{-1}$ (d) 8 $rads^{-1}$

99 A car is revolving at the rate of 72 revolutions per minute in a uniformly circular path. Find the velocity of the car which is 25 cm away from its centre. NCERT Pg. 42

(a) 1 ms^{-1} (b) 1.5 ms^{-1} (c) 2 ms^{-1} (d) 2.5 ms^{-1}

100 A particle is moving on a circular path of radius 35 cm. If its speed is 1200 revolution per minutes, then the time taken by the particle to complete the circular path is NCERT Pg. 42

(a) 0.05s (b) 0.004s (c) 0.12s (d) 0.15s

Assertion and Reason Questions

Direction (Q. Nos. 1-10) *In the following questions, a statement of Assertion is followed by a corresponding statement of Reason. Of the following statements, choose the correct one.*

(a) Both Assertion and Reason are correct and Reason is the correct explanation of Assertion.
(b) Both Assertion and Reason are correct but Reason is not the correct explanation of Assertion.
(c) Assertion is correct but Reason is incorrect.
(d) Assertion is incorrect but Reason is correct.

1 **Assertion** Magnitude of resultant of two vectors may be less than the magnitude of either vector.

Reason Addition and subtraction of scalars can be done only for quantities with same units. NCERT Pg. 29

2 **Assertion** Vector addition of two vectors is always greater than their vector subtraction.

Reason At $\theta = 90°$, addition and subtraction of vectors are equal. NCERT Pg. 30

3 **Assertion** Vector subtraction is commutative.
Reason Subtraction of vectors can be defined in terms of addition of vectors. NCERT Pg. 30

4 **Assertion** Sum of maximum height for angles α and $90° - \alpha$ is independent of the angle of projection.

Reason For angles α and $90° - \alpha$, the horizontal range R is same. NCERT Pg. 39

5 **Assertion** At highest point of the projectile path, acceleration due to gravity makes an angle of 90° with the velocity of the projectile.

Reason At maximum height, the vertical component of velocity is zero. NCERT Pg. 39

6 Assertion Two particles of different mass, projected with same velocity at same angles, then the maximum height attained by both the particles will be same.
Reason The maximum height of projectile is independent of particle mass. NCERT Pg. 39

7 Assertion The maximum height of projectile is always 25% of the range.
Reason For maximum range, projectile should be projected at 35°. NCERT Pg. 40

8 Assertion The range of a projectile is maximum at 45°.
Reason The maximum height depends only on vertical component of velocity of projection. NCERT Pg. 40

9 Assertion Kinematics equations for uniform accelerated motion cannot be applied to in case of uniform circular motion.
Reason In uniform circular motion, magnitude of acceleration is constant but its direction is changing. NCERT Pg. 40

10 Assertion Uniform circular motion is uniformly accelerated motion.
Reason In uniform circular motion, velocity of the object is changing continuously in direction and the object undergoes acceleration. NCERT Pg 40

Statement Based Questions

Direction (Q. Nos. 1-8) *In the following questions, two statements (I & II) are given. In the light of the given statements, choose the correct option given below.*

(a) Both Statement I and Statement II are false.
(b) Statement I is true but Statement II is false.
(c) Statement I is false but Statement II is true.
(d) Both Statement I and Statement II are true.

1 Statement I The difference of two vectors can be treated as sum of two vectors.
Statement II Vectors obey triangle law of addition. NCERT Pg. 29

2 Statement I The direction of vector $\lambda \mathbf{A}$, $(\lambda < 0)$ is same as the direction of vector **A**.
Statement II If a vector is multiplied by zero, then the resultant is a scalar. NCERT Pg. 29

3 Statement I Vectors can be added and subtracted geometrically.
Statement II Vectors cannot be divided as directions cannot be divided. NCERT Pg. 29

4 Statement I Minimum number of co-planar vectors of unequal magnitude whose resultant can be zero is three.
Statement II Minimum number of collinear vectors of unequal magnitude whose resultant can be zero is two. NCERT Pg. 29

5 Statement I A projectile always follows a parabolic path.
Statement II In projectile motion, momentum is never zero throughout the motion. NCERT Pg. 38

6 Statement I At highest point of projectile, possesses velocity only along the vertical direction.
Statement II At highest point of projectile, the velocity and acceleration are parallel to each other. NCERT Pg. 39

7 Statement I The motion of a projectile can be treated as the result of two separate, simultaneously occurring components of motions.
Statement II At the maximum height for a projectile, the *x*-component of the velocity is zero. NCERT Pg. 39

8 Statement I When an object follows a circular path at a constant speed, the motion of the object is called uniform circular motion.
Statement II The acceleration of an object in uniform circular motion is always directed away the centre of the circle. NCERT Pg. 40

Matching Type Questions

1 Match the Column I (magnitude of vectors **A** and **B**) with Column II (relationship between **A** and **B**).
NCERT Pg. 29

	Column I		Column II
A.	$\xrightarrow{|\mathbf{A}| = l}$ $\xrightarrow{|\mathbf{B}| = 2l}$	1.	$\mathbf{A} = -\mathbf{B}$
B.	$\xrightarrow{|\mathbf{A}| = l}$ $\xleftarrow{|\mathbf{B}| = l}$	2.	$\mathbf{A} = \mathbf{B}$
C.	$\xrightarrow{|\mathbf{A}| = 2l}$ $\xleftarrow{\mathbf{B} = l}$	3.	$2\mathbf{A} = \mathbf{B}$
D.	$\xrightarrow{|\mathbf{A}| = l}$ $\xrightarrow{|\mathbf{B}| = l}$	4.	$\mathbf{A} = -2\mathbf{B}$

Choose the correct answer from the options given below.

Codes

	A	B	C	D		A	B	C	D
(a)	2	4	1	2	(b)	3	1	4	2
(c)	3	1	2	4	(d)	2	3	4	1

2 A football player kicks a ball at an angle of 37° to the horizontal with an initial speed of 15 ms^{-1}. Assuming that the ball travels in a vertical plane, match Column I (distance/time) with Column II (values).
(Given, $\sin 37° = 0.601$; $\sin 74° = 0.961$) **NCERT Pg. 38**

	Column I		Column II
A.	Time at which ball reaches the highest point (in s)	1.	4.16
B.	Maximum height reached (in m)	2.	1.84
C.	Horizontal range of the projectile (in m)	3.	0.92
D.	Time for which ball is in air (in s)	4.	22.02

Choose the correct answer from the options given below.

Codes

	A	B	C	D		A	B	C	D
(a)	3	1	4	2	(b)	2	4	3	1
(c)	3	4	1	2	(d)	4	1	2	3

3 Trajectory of a particle motion is given as $y = x - \frac{x^2}{80}$, when x and y are in meters. For this projectile motion match column I with column II (respective values). (Take, $g = 10\ m/s^2$) **NCERT Pg. 38**

	Column I		Column II
A.	Angle of projection	1.	20 m
B.	Angle of velocity with horizontal after us	2.	45°
C.	Maximum height	3.	80 m
D.	Horizontal range	4.	$\tan^{-1}\frac{1}{2}$

Choose the correct answer from the options given below.

Codes

	A	B	C	D		A	B	C	D
(a)	2	4	3	1	(b)	1	2	3	4
(c)	3	1	2	4	(d)	2	2	1	3

4 The equation of motion of a projectile is $y = mx - nx^2$, where m and n are constants. Match Column I (quantities) with Column II (relations). **NCERT Pg. 38**

	Column I		Column II
A.	Time of flight	1.	$\frac{m^2}{4n}$
B.	Initial velocity of projection	2.	$\frac{m}{n}$
C.	Maximum height	3.	$m\sqrt{\frac{2}{ng}}$
D.	Horizontal range	4.	$\sqrt{\frac{g(1+m^2)}{2n}}$

Choose the correct answer from the options given below.

Codes

	A	B	C	D		A	B	C	D
(a)	4	3	2	1	(b)	1	3	4	2
(c)	3	4	2	1	(d)	3	4	1	2

Numerical Type Questions

1 A train is moving along a straight line with a constant acceleration a. A boy standing in the train throws a ball forward with speed of 10 ms^{-1}, at an angle of 60° to the horizontal. The boy has to move forward by 1.15 m inside the train to catch the ball back at the initial height. The acceleration a of the train is .... m/s^2. **NCERT Pg. 37**

2 A particle starts from the origin at $t = 0$ s with a velocity of $10.0\hat{j}$ m/s and moves in X-Y plane with a constant acceleration of $(8.0\hat{i} + 2.0\hat{j})\ m/s^2$. The velocity of the particle after 5 s is .... m/s. [Here, $\sqrt{5} = 2.23$] **NCERT Pg. 37**

3 A ball is thrown from a point with a speed v_0 at an angle of projection θ. From the same point and at the same instant, a person starts running with a constant speed $\frac{v_0}{2}$ to catch the ball. The angle of projection (in degree) of this ball is .... °. NCERT Pg. 38

4 A particle is in projectile motion and the maximum range of this particle is 18 km. This particle explodes into two equal masses, when it was at highest point of its motion. One mass drops vertically downwards, then horizontal distance covered by second mass from time of explosion is ...... km. NCERT Pg. 38

5 Six particles situated at the corners of a regular hexagonal of side d move at a constant speed v. If each particle maintains a direction such that it is always directed towards the particle situated at the next consecutive corner. The time after which the particles will meet each other is $\frac{xd}{v}$. Then, value of x is .... Old NCERT Pg. 76

6 The distance between two moving particles A and B at any time is d. If v_{AB} be relative velocity and v_x and v_y are the components of v_{AB}, then the time when they are closest to each other is $\frac{dv_y}{v_{AB}^{\alpha}}$. The value of α is .... Old NCERT Pg. 76

7 A boy is riding on a flat train moving with velocity 20 ms^{-1}. The boy throws a ball which according to him makes angle 30° with the horizontal and in line with track. Another boy on the ground observes the ball to rise vertically. He sees the ball to rise by .... m. Old NCERT Pg. 76

8 A boy wants to cross a river from point P to point Q. Line PQ makes an angle of 45° with the flow of river. Magnitude of velocity of the swimmer is same as that of the river. The angle θ with the line PQ should be ......°, so that the boy reaches point Q. Old NCERT Pg. 76

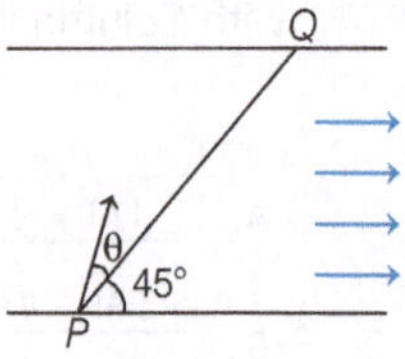

9 A particle P moves in counter-clockwise direction on a circular path as shown in the figure. The movement of particle is such that it sweeps out a length $s = t^3 + 5$, where s is in metre and t is in second. The radius of the path is 16 m. The acceleration of P when $t = 2$ s is nearly .... ms^{-2}. NCERT Pg. 40

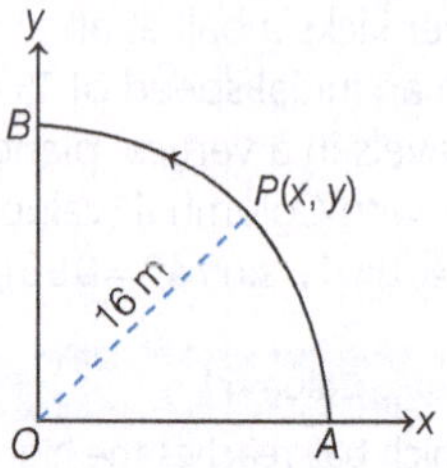

NCERT Exemplar Questions

1 Which one of the following statement is correct?
(a) A scalar quantity is the one that is conserved in a process.
(b) A scalar quantity is the one that can never take negative values.
(c) A scalar quantity is the one that does not vary from one point to another in space.
(d) A scalar quantity has the same value for observers with different orientation of the axes.

2 Figure shows the orientation of two vectors **u** and **v** in the XY-plane. If $\mathbf{u} = a\hat{\mathbf{i}} + b\hat{\mathbf{j}}$ and $\mathbf{v} = p\hat{\mathbf{i}} + q\hat{\mathbf{j}}$, then which of the following option is correct?

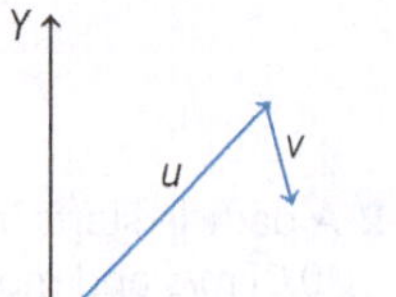

(a) a and p are positive, while b and q are negative
(b) a, p and b are positive, while q is negative
(c) a, q and b are positive, while p is negative
(d) a, b, p and q are all positive

3 The component of a vector **r** along X-axis will have maximum value, if
(a) **r** is along positive Y-axis
(b) **r** is along positive X-axis
(c) **r** makes an angle of 45° with the X-axis
(d) **r** is along negative Y-axis

4 The horizontal range of a projectile fired at an angle of 15° is 50 m. If it is fired with the same speed at an angle of 45°, its range will be
(a) 60 m (b) 71 m (c) 100 m (d) 141 m

5 In a two-dimensional motion, instantaneous speed v_0 is a positive constant, then which of the following are necessarily correct?
(a) The average velocity is not zero at any time
(b) Average acceleration must always vanish
(c) Displacements in equal time intervals are equal
(d) Equal path lengths are traversed in equal intervals

Past Exams Questions

NEET

1 A particle moving with uniform speed in a circular path maintains NCERT Pg. 41, NEET 2024

(a) constant velocity
(b) constant acceleration
(c) constant velocity but varying acceleration
(d) varying velocity and varying acceleration

2 The angular acceleration of a body, moving along the circumference of a circle, is NCERT Pg. 40, NEET 2023

(a) along the radius towards the centre
(b) along the tangent to its position
(c) along the axis of rotation
(d) along the radius, away from centre

3 A bullet is fired from a gun at the speed of $280\ ms^{-1}$ in the direction 30° above the horizontal. The maximum height attained by the bullet is ($g = 9.8\ ms^{-2}$, $\sin 30° = 0.5$) NCERT Pg. 38, NEET 2023

(a) 2000 m (b) 1000 m
(c) 3000 m (d) 2800 m

4 A particle moving in a circle of radius R with a uniform speed takes a time T to complete one revolution. If this particle were projected with the same speed at an angle θ to the horizontal, the maximum height attained by it equals $4R$. The angle of projection θ is then given by NCERT Pg. 40, NEET 2021

(a) $\theta = \cos^{-1}\left(\frac{gT^2}{\pi^2 R}\right)^{1/2}$ (b) $\theta = \cos^{-1}\left(\frac{\pi^2 R}{gT^2}\right)^{1/2}$

(c) $\theta = \sin^{-1}\left(\frac{\pi^2 R}{gT^2}\right)^{1/2}$ (d) $\theta = \sin^{-1}\left(\frac{2gT^2}{\pi^2 R}\right)^{1/2}$

5 A car starts from rest and accelerates at $5\ m/s^2$. At $t = 4$ s, a ball is dropped out of a window by a person sitting in the car. What is the velocity and acceleration of the ball at $t = 6$ s? (Take $g = 10\ m/s^2$) NCERT Pg. 37, NEET 2021

(a) $20\sqrt{2}$ m/s, 10 m/s^2 (b) 20 m/s, 5 m/s^2
(c) 20 m/s, 0 (d) $20\sqrt{2}$ m/s, 0

6 When an object is shot from the bottom of a long smooth inclined plane kept at an angle 60° with horizontal, it can travel a distance x_1 along the plane. But when the inclination is decreased to 30° and the same object is shot with the same velocity, it can travel x_2 distance. Then, $x_1 : x_2$ will be NCERT Pg. 38, NEET 2019

(a) $\sqrt{2}:1$ (b) $1:\sqrt{3}$
(c) $1:2\sqrt{3}$ (d) $1:\sqrt{2}$

7 A particle moves so that its position vector is given by $\mathbf{r} = \cos \omega t\hat{x} + \sin \omega t\hat{y}$, where, ω is a constant. Which of the following is true? NCERT Pg. 36, NEET 2016

(a) Velocity and acceleration both are perpendicular to **r**.
(b) Velocity and acceleration both are parallel to **r**.
(c) Velocity is perpendicular to **r** and acceleration is directed towards the origin.
(d) Velocity is perpendicular to **r** and acceleration is directed away from the origin.

8 In the given figure, $a = 15\ m/s^2$ represents the total acceleration of a particle moving in the clockwise direction in a circle of radius $R = 2.5$ m at a given instant of time. The speed of the particle is NCERT Pg. 40, NEET 2016

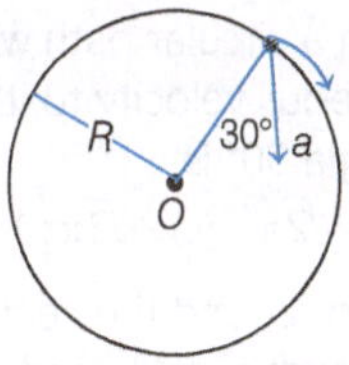

(a) 4.5 m/s (b) 5.0 m/s
(c) 5.7 m/s (d) 6.2 m/s

9 If the magnitude of sum of two vectors is equal to the magnitude of difference of the two vectors, the angle between these vectors is NCERT Pg. 33, NEET 2016

(a) 90° (b) 45°
(c) 180° (d) 0°

JEE Main

10 If two vectors **A** and **B** having equal magnitude R are inclined at an angle θ, then NCERT Pg. 34, JEE 2024

(a) $|\mathbf{A}+\mathbf{B}| = 2R\sin\left(\frac{\theta}{2}\right)$ (b) $|\mathbf{A}-\mathbf{B}| = 2R\cos\left(\frac{\theta}{2}\right)$

(c) $|\mathbf{A}-\mathbf{B}| = \sqrt{2}R\sin\left(\frac{\theta}{2}\right)$ (d) $|\mathbf{A}+\mathbf{B}| = 2R\cos\left(\frac{\theta}{2}\right)$

11 The angle of projection for a projectile to have same horizontal range and maximum height is NCERT Pg. 39, JEE 2024

(a) $\tan^{-1}\left(\frac{1}{2}\right)$ (b) $\tan^{-1}\left(\frac{1}{4}\right)$

(c) $\tan^{-1}(2)$ (d) $\tan^{-1}(4)$

12 The initial speed of a projectile fired from ground is u. At the highest point during its motion, the speed of projectile is $\sqrt{3}/2u$. The time of flight of the projectile is

NCERT Pg. 38, JEE Main 2023

(a) $\frac{2u}{g}$ (b) $\frac{u}{2g}$ (c) $\frac{u}{g}$ (d) $\frac{\sqrt{3}u}{g}$

13 A body is moving with constant speed, in a circle of radius 10 m. The body completes one revolution in 4 s. At the end of 3rd second, the displacement of body (in m) from its starting point is **NCERT Pg. 40, JEE Main 2023**

(a) 30 (b) $10\sqrt{2}$ (c) 5π (d) 15π

14 The angle between vectors **A** and (**A** − **B**) is

NCERT Pg. 33, JEE Main 2021

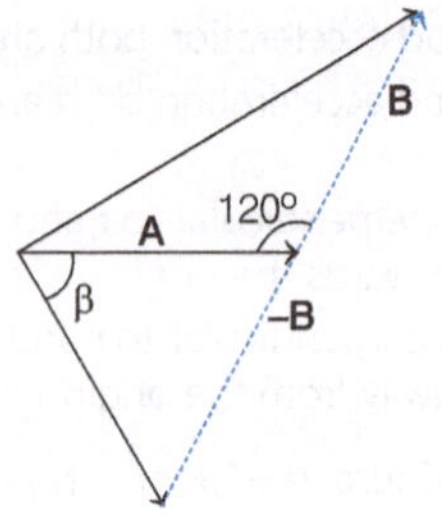

(a) $\tan^{-1}\left(\frac{A}{0.7B}\right)$

(b) $\tan^{-1}\left(\frac{-\frac{B}{2}}{A-B\frac{\sqrt{3}}{2}}\right)$

(c) $\tan^{-1}\left(\frac{\sqrt{3}B}{2A-B}\right)$

(d) $\tan^{-1}\left(\frac{B\cos\theta}{A-B\sin\theta}\right)$

15 Two guns A and B can fire bullets at speeds 1 km/s and 2 km/s, respectively. From a point on a horizontal ground, they are fired in all possible directions. The ratio of maximum areas covered by the bullets on the ground fired by the two guns is **NCERT Pg. 38, JEE Main 2019**

(a) 1 : 4
(b) 1 : 16
(c) 1 : 8
(d) 1 : 2

Skill Boosters

1 A cyclist riding on a circular path with constant velocity. The ratio of instantaneous velocity to its average velocity when he turn by an angle 90° is

(a) $\pi : 2\sqrt{2}$ (b) $1 : \sqrt{2}\pi$ (c) $2\sqrt{2}\pi : 1$ (d) $\sqrt{2}\,\pi : 1$

2 A star is revolving around the centre of galaxy, subtends an angle 4s. It arc length is 4.4 ly and speed of the star is 8AU per second, then how much time it with take to complete 4 rev. ($1\text{ly} = 9.46 \times 10^{15}$ m, $1\text{AU} = 1.5 \times 10^{11}$ m)

(a) 4.1×10^{8} s (b) 4.5×10^{10} s
(c) 3.5×10^{6} s (d) 7.2×10^{8} s

3 Two comets A and B, move with constant velocities $\mathbf{v}_1$ and $\mathbf{v}_2$. At the initial moment, their position vectors are $\mathbf{r}_1$ and $\mathbf{r}_2$, respectively. The condition for comets A and B for their collision is

(a) $\frac{\mathbf{r}_1 - \mathbf{r}_2}{|\mathbf{r}_1 - \mathbf{r}_2|} = \frac{\mathbf{v}_2 - \mathbf{v}_1}{|\mathbf{v}_2 - \mathbf{v}_1|}$

(b) $\mathbf{r}_1 \cdot \mathbf{v}_1 = \mathbf{r}_2 \cdot \mathbf{v}_2$

(c) $\mathbf{r}_1 \times \mathbf{v}_1 = \mathbf{r}_2 \times \mathbf{v}_2$

(d) $\mathbf{r}_1 - \mathbf{r}_2 = \mathbf{v}_1 - \mathbf{v}_2$

4 A ship A is moving westwards with a speed of 10 km h^{-1} and a ship B 100 km south of A, is moving northwards with a speed of 10 km h^{-1}. The time after which the distance between them becomes shortest is

(a) 0 h (b) 5 h (c) $5\sqrt{2}$ h (d) $10\sqrt{2}$ h

5 Velocity of a flying enemy drone is 500 m/s. It is flying at a constant height of 250 m. The drone passes over an anti-drone gun that can fire at any time and in any direction with speed 100 m/s. The time interval during which the drone is in danger of being hit by the gun bullets is

(a) $2\sqrt{2}$ s (b) 3 s
(c) 2 s (d) $3\sqrt{2}$ s

6 Two balls are thrown with same speed at the same instant from the same point at angle of projection α and β with horizontal. If they are simultaneously hit the top and bottom of vertical pole. The value of $\frac{\cos\alpha}{\cos\beta}$ is

(a) 1 (b) 2 (c) 3 (d) $\frac{1}{2}$

7 A small ball is to be thrown, so as to just pass through three equal rings of diameter 2 m and placed in parallel vertical planes at distance 8 m apart with their highest points at height 32 m above the point of projection as shown in the figure. If the angle of projection with horizontal is α. The value of $\tan\alpha$ is

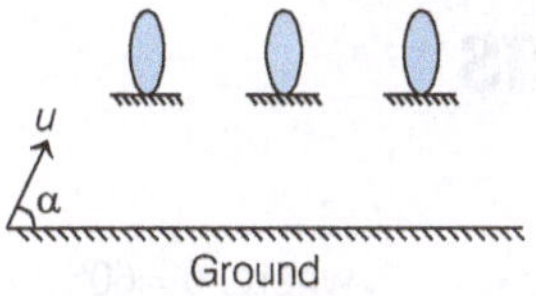

(a) 1 (b) 5 (c) 0.5 (d) 10

8 Several particles are thrown from a point in various directions but with the same initial speed v_0. At any subsequent time t before they reach the ground, they lie on the surface of

(a) paraboloid (b) sphere
(c) ellipsoid (d) straight line

9 A stone is projected with initial velocity of 30 ms^{-1}. If the maximum height reached by stone on a wall at distance 45 m from the point of projection is (3375×10^{-n}) m. Find the value of n.

(a) 3 (b) 2 (c) 1 (d) 4

10 Two particles A and B are moving on two concentric circle of radii R_1 and R_2 with equal angular speed ω. At $t = 0$, their positions and direction of motion are shown in the figure. The relative velocity $\mathbf{v}_A - \mathbf{v}_B$ at $t = \pi / 2\omega$ is given by

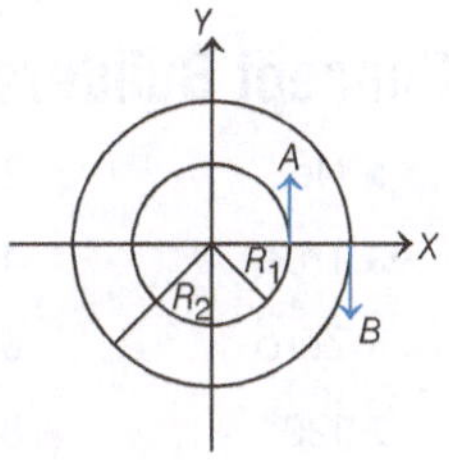

(a) $\frac{\omega}{2}(R_1 + R_2)\hat{\mathbf{i}}$ (b) $\frac{-\omega}{2}(R_1 - R_2)\hat{\mathbf{i}}$

(c) $\omega(R_1 - R_2)\hat{\mathbf{i}}$ (d) $\omega(R_2 - R_1)\hat{\mathbf{i}}$

Correct Codes

Topical Questions

1 (d)	2 (c)	3 (c)	4 (d)	5 (d)	6 (d)	7 (a)	8 (c)	9 (a)	10 (b)
11 (c)	12 (c)	13 (c)	14 (c)	15 (c)	16 (a)	17 (c)	18 (b)	19 (a)	20 (c)
21 (b)	22 (b)	23 (a)	24 (a)	25 (c)	26 (c)	27 (d)	28 (c)	29 (a)	30 (b)
31 (c)	32 (b)	33 (c)	34 (d)	35 (d)	36 (a)	37 (a)	38 (d)	39 (c)	40 (a)
41 (a)	42 (b)	43 (b)	44 (b)	45 (b)	46 (a)	47 (c)	48 (b)	49 (b)	50 (b)
51 (c)	52 (a)	53 (b)	54 (c)	55 (c)	56 (c)	57 (d)	58 (a)	59 (d)	60 (b)
61 (b)	62 (a)	63 (b)	64 (c)	65 (b)	66 (b)	67 (d)	68 (d)	69 (c)	70 (d)
71 (b)	72 (c)	73 (c)	74 (a)	75 (b)	76 (c)	77 (b)	78 (d)	79 (c)	80 (c)
81 (c)	82 (c)	83 (c)	84 (b)	85 (b)	86 (b)	87 (b)	88 (c)	89 (c)	90 (b)
91 (a)	92 (c)	93 (b)	94 (a)	95 (c)	96 (a)	97 (c)	98 (a)	99 (c)	100 (a)

Assertion and Reason Questions

1 (b)	2 (d)	3 (d)	4 (b)	5 (a)	6 (a)	7 (c)	8 (c)	9 (a)	10 (b)

Statement Based Questions

1 (d)	2 (a)	3 (b)	4 (b)	5 (d)	6 (a)	7 (b)	8 (a)

Matching Type Questions

1 (b)	2 (a)	3 (d)	4 (d)

Numerical Type Questions

1 (5)	2 (44.6)	3 (60)	4 (18)	5 (2)	6 (2)	7 (7)	8 (45)	9 (15)

NCERT Exemplar Questions

1 (d)	2 (b)	3 (b)	4 (c)	5 (d)

Past Exams Questions

1 (d)	2 (c)	3 (b)	4 (d)	5 (a)	6 (b)	7 (c)	8 (c)	9 (a)	10 (d)
11 (d)	12 (c)	13 (b)	14 (c)	15 (b)					

Skill Boosters

1 (a)	2 (b)	3 (a)	4 (b)	5 (a)	6 (a)	7 (a)	8 (b)	9 (b)	10 (d)

Step by Step

Decoding the Questions

Concept Builders

1 No
2 Current
3 True
4 Zero
5 Zero
6 90°
7 120°
8 True (T)
9 False (F)
10 False (F)
11 Horizontal
12 At highest point
13 False (F)
14 True (T)
15 $H_{max} = \frac{R}{2}$
16 not a
17 opposite
18 False (F)
19 90°
20 True (T)

Topical Questions

2 (c) Let the positions of the body are at A and B, then

$$\mathbf{OA} = \mathbf{r}_1, \ \mathbf{OB} = \mathbf{r}_2$$

∴ The displacement vector is

$$\mathbf{AB} = \mathbf{OB} - \mathbf{OA} = (\mathbf{r}_2 - \mathbf{r}_1)$$

3 (c) Among the given vectors, **A** and **B** are equal vectors as they have same magnitude (length) and direction.

4 (d) Given, $\mathbf{A} = 7$ units (North)

∴ $-3\mathbf{A} = -3 \times 7$ units (North) $= 21$ units (South)

5 (d) $|\mathbf{B}| = -1.5\,|\mathbf{A}|$. So when **A** is multiplied by -1.5, then its direction gets reversed and magnitude would be 1.5 times $|\mathbf{A}|$.

Thus, $|\mathbf{B}| \neq |\mathbf{A}|$.

8 (c) Given, $\mathbf{A} + \mathbf{B} + \mathbf{C} = 0$

$\Rightarrow \quad \mathbf{A} = -(\mathbf{B} + \mathbf{C})$

As the vector $(\mathbf{B} + \mathbf{C})$ is multiplied by a negative number, so vector **A** is anti-parallel to vector $(\mathbf{B} + \mathbf{C})$.

9 (a)

(a) $\mathbf{a} + \mathbf{b} + \mathbf{c} + \mathbf{d}$ can be zero in many ways other than **a, b, c** and **d** must each be a null vector, e.g. if the vectors are in different directions, then their resultant will be zero.

(b) Since $\mathbf{a} + \mathbf{b} + \mathbf{c} + \mathbf{d} = 0$

∴ $\mathbf{a} + \mathbf{c} = -(\mathbf{b} + \mathbf{d})$

or $|\mathbf{a} + \mathbf{c}| = |\mathbf{b} + \mathbf{d}|$

(c) Since $\mathbf{a} + \mathbf{b} + \mathbf{c} + \mathbf{d} = 0$

∴ $\mathbf{a} = -(\mathbf{b} + \mathbf{c} + \mathbf{d})$

or $|\mathbf{a}| = |\mathbf{b} + \mathbf{c} + \mathbf{d}|$

As magnitude of $(\mathbf{b} + \mathbf{c} + \mathbf{d})$ can be equal or less than the sum of magnitudes of **b, c** and **d** but can never be greater.

Therefore, **a** also can never be greater than the sum of the magnitudes of **b, c** and **d**.

(d) Since $\mathbf{a} + \mathbf{b} + \mathbf{c} + \mathbf{d} = 0$

or $\mathbf{a} + (\mathbf{b} + \mathbf{c}) + \mathbf{d} = 0$

The resultant of three vectors **a**, $(\mathbf{b} + \mathbf{c})$ and **d** can be zero only when they lie in a plane and can be represented by the three sides of triangle taken in one order.

If **a** and **d** are collinear, then $(\mathbf{b} + \mathbf{c})$ must be in the line of **a** and **d**, only then the vector sum of all the vectors will be zero.

Thus, the statement given in option (a) is incorrect, rest are correct.

10 (b) $|\mathbf{Q}|^2 = Q_x^2 + Q_y^2$

Substituting the given values, we get

$$(5)^2 = Q_x^2 + 4^2 \Rightarrow Q_x = \sqrt{9} = 3$$

11 (c) Given, vector can be shown below as

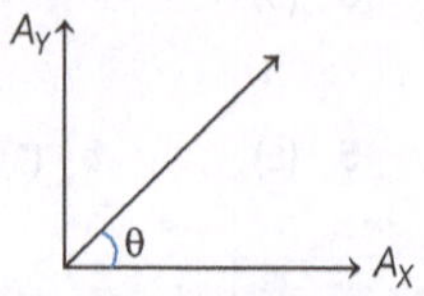

where, $\theta = 60°$

Then, $\tan\theta = \frac{A_y}{A_x}$ or $A_y = A_x \tan\theta$

$\Rightarrow \quad A_y = 50 \tan 60° = 50 \times \sqrt{3}$ $(\because \sqrt{3} = 1.732)$

$= 86.6 \simeq 87$ N

12 (c) Given, $\mathbf{P} = 3\hat{\mathbf{i}} - 4\hat{\mathbf{j}}$

$\mathbf{Q} = 6\hat{\mathbf{i}} - 8\hat{\mathbf{j}} = 2(3\hat{\mathbf{i}} - 4\hat{\mathbf{j}}) = 2\mathbf{P}$

and Also,

$$\mathbf{R} = \frac{3}{4}\hat{\mathbf{i}} - \hat{\mathbf{j}} = \frac{1}{4}(3\hat{\mathbf{i}} - 4\hat{\mathbf{j}}) = \frac{\mathbf{P}}{4}$$

So, **P**, **Q** and **R** are parallel with unequal magnitude.

14 (c) Resultant vector of **A** and **B** is

$$\mathbf{R} = \mathbf{A} + \mathbf{B} = -\hat{\mathbf{i}} + 2\hat{\mathbf{j}} + 3\hat{\mathbf{k}}$$

Unit vector in the direction of **R** is

$$\hat{\mathbf{R}} = \frac{\mathbf{R}}{|\mathbf{R}|} = \frac{-\hat{\mathbf{i}} + 2\hat{\mathbf{j}} + 3\hat{\mathbf{k}}}{\sqrt{14}}$$

15 (c) If $\cos\alpha$, $\cos\beta$ and $\cos\gamma$ be the direction cosines of a vector, then

$$\cos^2\alpha + \cos^2\beta + \cos^2\gamma = 1 \quad \text{...(i)}$$

and we know,

$$\sin^2\alpha + \cos^2\alpha = 1 \quad \text{...(ii)}$$

From Eqs. (i) and (ii), we get

$$\cos^2\alpha + \cos^2\beta + \cos^2\gamma + \sin^2\alpha + \cos^2\alpha = 1 + 1$$

$$\sin^2\alpha + 2\cos^2\alpha + \cos^2\beta + \cos^2\gamma = 2$$

16 (a) Three equal vectors can add upto zero when each of them is inclined at 120° with the other.

If $|\mathbf{A} + \mathbf{B}| = |\mathbf{A} - \mathbf{B}|$, they are inclined at 90° as shown below.

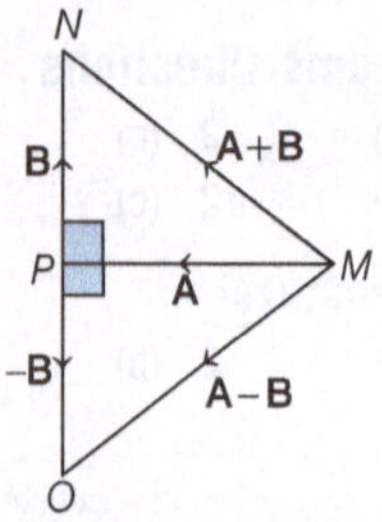

In this figure, length of MN is equal to length of MO.
So, $|\mathbf{A}+\mathbf{B}| = |\mathbf{A}-\mathbf{B}|$.
Thus, the statement given in option (a) is correct, rest are incorrect.

17 (c) Given, $|\mathbf{A}| = |\mathbf{B}|$ and $|\mathbf{R}| = 2|\mathbf{A}|$

$\therefore \quad R^2 = A^2 + B^2 + 2AB\cos\theta$

$\Rightarrow \quad (2A)^2 = A^2 + A^2 + 2A^2\cos\theta$

$\therefore \quad \theta = 0°$

18 (b) Since, the magnitude and angle between the vectors are unchanged, so the magnitude of the resultant **R** will be same. However, the direction of **R** will get changed.

19 (a) Since, $(5)^2 = (3)^2 + (4)^2$ which is in accordance to pythagoras theorem. So, the vectors can be shown in the figure as

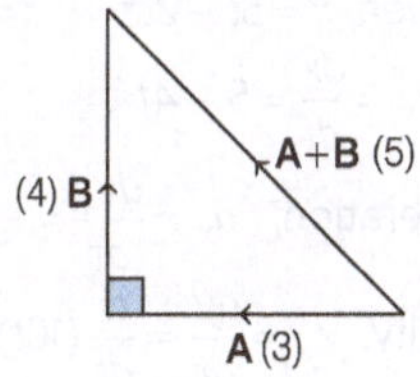

$\therefore$ **A** and **B** are perpendicular.
However, if the length of **A** + **B** vector is more than or less than 5, then they should be inclined at acute and obtuse angle, respectively.
Thus, the statement given in option (a) is correct, rest are incorrect.

20. (c) Here, the angle between **A** and **B** is α.

$\because$ (**A** + **B**) makes an angle θ_1 with **A**

$$\therefore \tan\theta_1 = \frac{B\sin\alpha}{A + B\cos\alpha}$$

Similarly, $\tan\theta_2 = \dfrac{B\sin\alpha}{A - B\cos\alpha}$

Now,

$$\tan\theta_1 - \tan\theta_2 = \frac{-2B^2\sin\alpha\cos\alpha}{A^2 - B^2\cos^2\alpha}$$

$$= \frac{-B^2\sin 2\alpha}{A^2 - B^2\cos^2\alpha}$$

21 (b) Resultant force $\mathbf{F}_r$ of any two forces $\mathbf{F}_1$ (i.e. **P**) and $\mathbf{F}_2$ (i.e. **Q**) with an angle θ between them can be given by vector addition as

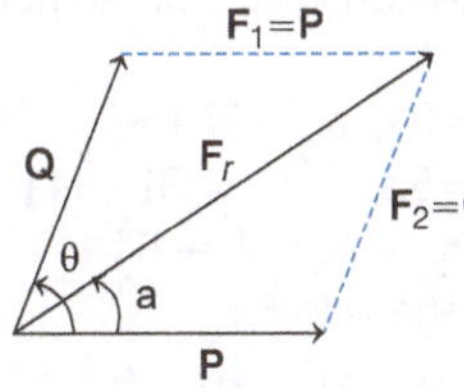

In first case

$F_r^2 = 13F^2 + 12F^2\cos\theta \quad$ ... (i)

In second case $F_1 = 2F$

and $\quad F_2 = 6F$

$4F_r^2 = 40F^2 + 24F^2\cos\theta \quad$ ... (ii)

From Eq. (i) and Eq. (ii), we get;

$$52F^2 + 48F^2\cos\theta = 40F^2 + 24F^2\cos\theta$$

or $\cos\theta = -1/2$

or $\theta = 120° \quad (\because \cos 120° = -1/2)$

22 (b) $|\mathbf{A}+\mathbf{B}|^2 = |\mathbf{A}|^2$

$\Rightarrow |\mathbf{A}|^2 + |\mathbf{B}|^2 + 2|\mathbf{A}||\mathbf{B}|\cos\theta = |\mathbf{A}|^2$

$\Rightarrow \quad |\mathbf{B}|[|\mathbf{B}| + 2|\mathbf{A}|\cos\theta] = 0$

$\Rightarrow \quad |\mathbf{B}| = 0$

or $|\mathbf{B}| + 2|\mathbf{A}|\cos\theta = 0$

$\Rightarrow \quad \cos\theta = -\dfrac{|\mathbf{B}|}{2|\mathbf{A}|} \quad$ ...(i)

If **A** and **B** are parallel, then $\theta = 0°$.
Hence, from Eq. (i),

$\cos 0° = 1 = -\dfrac{|\mathbf{B}|}{2A}$

$\Rightarrow \quad |\mathbf{B}| = -2|\mathbf{A}|$

Hence, the given condition can only be implied of either $|\mathbf{B}| = 0$ or **A** and **B** are parallel provided $|\mathbf{B}| = -2|\mathbf{A}|$.

23 (a) Difference of vectors **A** and **B** can be given as

$|(\mathbf{A}-\mathbf{B})|^2 = A^2 + B^2 - 2AB\cos\theta$

$= 1 + 1 - 2\cos\theta$

[$\because$ **A** and **B** are unit vectors]

$= 2 - 2\cos\theta = 2(1-\cos\theta)$

$= 2 \times 2\sin^2(\theta/2)$

$= 4\sin^2\left(\dfrac{\theta}{2}\right)$

$|\mathbf{A}-\mathbf{B}| = 2\sin(\theta/2)$

24 (a) According to the question, representation of vectors **A** and **B** can be shown as follows

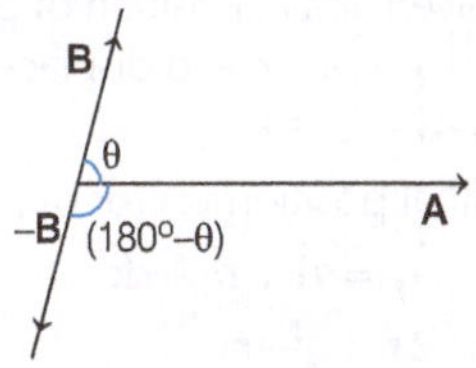

Given, $\quad |\mathbf{A}+\mathbf{B}| = P$

$\Rightarrow \quad |\mathbf{A}+\mathbf{B}|^2 = P^2$

$P^2 = A^2 + B^2 + 2AB\cos\theta \quad$ ...(i)

Also, $\quad |\mathbf{A}-\mathbf{B}| = Q$

$\Rightarrow \quad |\mathbf{A}-\mathbf{B}|^2 = Q^2$

$\Rightarrow A^2 + B^2 + 2AB\cos(180°-\theta) = Q^2$

$\Rightarrow A^2 + B^2 - 2AB\cos\theta = Q^2 \quad$ ...(ii)

Adding Eqs. (i) and (ii), we get

$$P^2 + Q^2 = 2(A^2 + B^2)$$

25 (c) Given, $|\mathbf{A}+\mathbf{B}| = |\mathbf{A}-\mathbf{B}|$

$\Rightarrow \quad \sqrt{|\mathbf{A}|^2 + |\mathbf{B}|^2 + 2|\mathbf{A}||\mathbf{B}|\cos\theta}$

$= \sqrt{|\mathbf{A}|^2 + |\mathbf{B}|^2 - 2|\mathbf{A}||\mathbf{B}|\cos\theta}$

$\Rightarrow \quad |\mathbf{A}||\mathbf{B}|\cos\theta = 0$

$\Rightarrow \quad |\mathbf{A}| = 0$ or $|\mathbf{B}| = 0$

or $\cos\theta = 0 \Rightarrow \theta = 90°$

Thus, $|\mathbf{A}+\mathbf{B}| = |\mathbf{A}-\mathbf{B}|$ is always true, when either $|\mathbf{A}|$ or $|\mathbf{B}|$ is zero or **A** and **B** are perpendicular to each other.

26 (c) Given, $|\mathbf{A}| = |\mathbf{B}|$ or $A = B \quad$ ...(i)

Now, $\quad \mathbf{R} = \mathbf{A} + \mathbf{B}$

$R^2 = 2A^2 + 2A^2\cos\theta \quad$ ...(ii)

[$\because$ using Eq. (i)]

Again, $\mathbf{R}' = \mathbf{A} - \mathbf{B}$

$\Rightarrow \quad R'^2 = A^2 + B^2 - 2AB\cos\theta$

$R'^2 = 2A^2 - 2A^2\cos\theta \quad$ ...(iii)

Given, $R = nR'$ or $\left(\dfrac{R}{R'}\right)^2 = n^2$

Dividing Eq. (ii) with Eq. (iii), we get

$$\frac{n^2}{1} = \frac{1+\cos\theta}{1-\cos\theta}$$

or $\quad \dfrac{n^2-1}{n^2+1} = \dfrac{(1+\cos\theta)-(1-\cos\theta)}{(1+\cos\theta)+(1-\cos\theta)}$

$\Rightarrow \quad \dfrac{n^2-1}{n^2+1} = \dfrac{2\cos\theta}{2} = \cos\theta$

or $\quad \theta = \cos^{-1}\left(\dfrac{n^2-1}{n^2+1}\right)$

27 (*d*) $\Delta \mathbf{r} = (5\hat{\mathbf{i}} + 6\hat{\mathbf{j}}) - (2\hat{\mathbf{i}} + 3\hat{\mathbf{j}})$
$= 3\hat{\mathbf{i}} + 3\hat{\mathbf{j}}$

28 (*c*) Given, initial position of particle, $\mathbf{r}_i = 2\hat{\mathbf{i}} + 3\hat{\mathbf{j}} + 5\hat{\mathbf{k}}$ and displacement, $\Delta \mathbf{r} = 4\hat{\mathbf{i}} - 2\hat{\mathbf{j}} + \hat{\mathbf{k}}$

Let final position vector of particle,
$$\mathbf{r}_f = a\hat{\mathbf{i}} + b\hat{\mathbf{j}} + c\hat{\mathbf{k}}$$
Now, $\Delta \mathbf{r} = \mathbf{r}_f - \mathbf{r}_i$
or $\mathbf{r}_f = \Delta \mathbf{r} + \mathbf{r}_i$
$= 4\hat{\mathbf{i}} - 2\hat{\mathbf{j}} + \hat{\mathbf{k}} + 2\hat{\mathbf{i}} + 3\hat{\mathbf{j}} + 5\hat{\mathbf{k}}$
$= 6\hat{\mathbf{i}} - \hat{\mathbf{j}} + 6\hat{\mathbf{k}}$

Hence, final coordinates of the particles are (6, −1, 6).

29 (*a*) The given situation is shown below

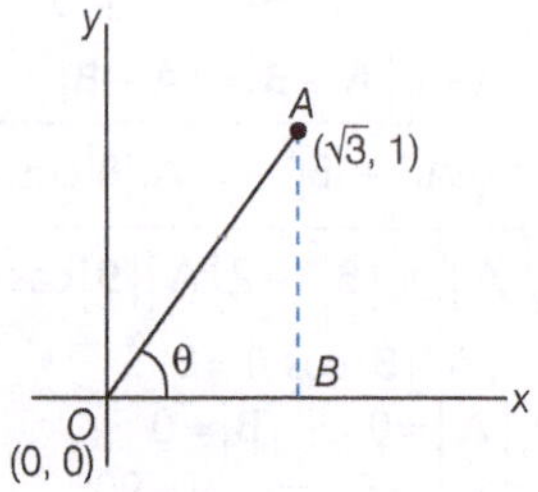

$$\tan\theta = \frac{1-0}{\sqrt{3}-0} = \frac{1}{\sqrt{3}}$$
$$\theta = 30°$$

30 (*b*)

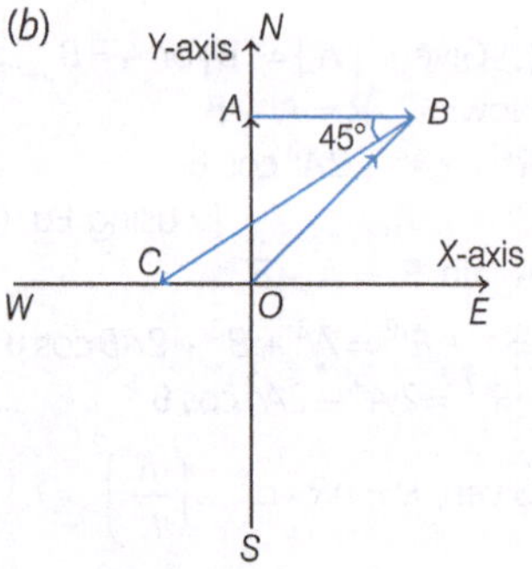

$$\mathbf{OA} = 15\hat{\mathbf{j}}$$
$$\mathbf{AB} = 20\hat{\mathbf{i}}$$
The movement along south-west direction,
$$\mathbf{BC} = -30\sqrt{2}(\cos 45°\,\hat{\mathbf{i}} + \sin 45°\,\hat{\mathbf{j}})$$
$$= -30\hat{\mathbf{i}} - 30\hat{\mathbf{j}}$$
Using triangle vector law,
$$\mathbf{OB} = \mathbf{OA} + \mathbf{AB}$$
$$= 15\hat{\mathbf{j}} + 20\hat{\mathbf{i}} = 20\,\hat{\mathbf{i}} + 15\,\hat{\mathbf{j}}$$
Now, triangle *BCO*
$$\mathbf{OC} = \mathbf{OB} + \mathbf{BC} = -10\hat{\mathbf{i}} - 15\hat{\mathbf{j}}$$
$\therefore |\mathbf{OC}| \simeq 18$ m towards west

32 (*b*) Position vector of the particle at
$$t = 0\text{ s},\quad \mathbf{r}_{0\text{s}} = 2\hat{\mathbf{i}} + 3\hat{\mathbf{j}}$$
$$t = 5\text{ s},\quad \mathbf{r}_{5\text{s}} = 13\hat{\mathbf{i}} + 14\hat{\mathbf{j}}$$
$$\Delta \mathbf{r} = \mathbf{r}_{5\text{s}} - \mathbf{r}_{0\text{s}} = 11\hat{\mathbf{i}} + 11\hat{\mathbf{j}}$$
Average velocity,
$$\bar{\mathbf{v}} = \frac{\Delta \mathbf{r}}{\Delta t} = \frac{11\hat{\mathbf{i}} + 11\hat{\mathbf{j}}}{5} = \frac{11}{5}(\hat{\mathbf{i}} + \hat{\mathbf{j}})$$

34 (*d*) Given, $\mathbf{v} = ky\hat{\mathbf{i}} + kx\hat{\mathbf{j}}$
$$\Rightarrow \frac{dx}{dt} = ky, \frac{dy}{dt} = kx$$
$$\frac{dy}{dx} = \frac{dy}{dt} \times \frac{dt}{dx} = \frac{kx}{ky}$$
$$\Rightarrow y\,dy = x\,dx$$
On Integrating, $y^2 - x^2 =$ constant
Hence, option (d) is correct.

35 (*d*) $\mathbf{v}(t) = \dfrac{d\mathbf{r}}{dt} = 3\hat{\mathbf{i}} + 4t\hat{\mathbf{j}}$
At $t = 1$ s,
$$\mathbf{v} = 3\hat{\mathbf{i}} + 4\hat{\mathbf{j}}$$
Thus, its direction is $\theta = \tan^{-1}\left[\dfrac{4}{3}\right]$
$\cong 53°$ with *X*-axis

36 (*a*) $\mathbf{r} = a[\cos\omega t\,\hat{\mathbf{i}} + \sin\omega t\,\hat{\mathbf{j}} + \omega t\,\hat{\mathbf{k}}]$
$$\because \mathbf{v} = \frac{d\mathbf{r}}{dt}$$
$$\Rightarrow \quad \mathbf{v} = -a\omega\sin\omega t\,\hat{\mathbf{i}} + a\omega\cos\omega t\,\hat{\mathbf{j}} + a\omega\hat{\mathbf{k}})$$
$$|\mathbf{v}| = \sqrt{(-a\,\omega\sin\omega t)^2 + (a\omega\cos\omega t)^2 + (a\omega)^2}$$
$$= \sqrt{2}\,\omega a$$

37 (*a*) Position vector of the particle,
$\mathbf{r} = x\hat{\mathbf{i}} + y\hat{\mathbf{j}} = (at^2 + bt)\hat{\mathbf{i}} + (ct)\hat{\mathbf{j}}$
Velocity, $\mathbf{v} = \dfrac{d\mathbf{r}}{dt} = (2at + b)\hat{\mathbf{i}} + c\hat{\mathbf{j}}$
It means, velocity is not constant as it varies with time.
Acceleration, $\mathbf{a} = \dfrac{d\mathbf{v}}{dt} = (2a)\hat{\mathbf{i}}$
This means, acceleration of the particle is constant throughout the motion.
Thus, the statement given in option (a) is correct, rest are incorrect.

38 (*d*) $\mathbf{v}_1 = +5\hat{\mathbf{i}}$

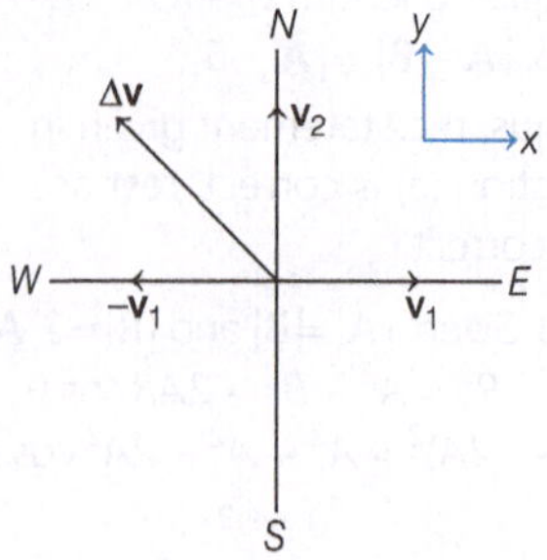

$$\mathbf{v}_2 = +5\hat{\mathbf{j}}$$
$$\Delta \mathbf{v} = \mathbf{v}_2 - \mathbf{v}_1 = 5\hat{\mathbf{j}} - 5\hat{\mathbf{i}}$$
$$\therefore \quad a = \frac{|\Delta \mathbf{v}|}{t} = \frac{5\sqrt{2}}{10} = \frac{1}{\sqrt{2}}\text{ ms}^{-2}$$
For direction, $\tan\alpha = \dfrac{-5}{5} = -1$
Average acceleration is $\dfrac{1}{\sqrt{2}}\text{ms}^{-2}$ towards north-west.

39 (*c*) Given, $x = 5t - 2t^2$
$$v_x = \frac{dx}{dt} = 5 - 4t$$
Acceleration, $a_x = \dfrac{dv_x}{dt} = -4\text{ ms}^{-2}$
Velocity, $v_y = \dfrac{dy}{dt} = \dfrac{d}{dt}(10t) = 10$
$\therefore$ Acceleration, $a_y = \dfrac{dv_y}{dt} = 0$
$\therefore$ Net acceleration of the particle,
$$\mathbf{a}_{\text{net}} = -4\,\hat{\mathbf{i}}\text{ ms}^{-2}$$
or $a_{\text{net}} = -4\text{ ms}^{-2}$

40 (*a*) Position vector of particle is given as
$$\mathbf{r} = 15t^2\hat{\mathbf{i}} + (4 - 20t^2)\hat{\mathbf{j}}$$
Acceleration of particle is
$$\mathbf{a} = \frac{d^2\mathbf{r}}{dt^2} = \frac{d}{dt}(30t\hat{\mathbf{i}} - 40t\hat{\mathbf{j}})$$
$$= 30\hat{\mathbf{i}} - 40\hat{\mathbf{j}}$$
$$|\mathbf{a}|_{t=1\text{s}} = 50\text{ ms}^{-2}$$

41 (*a*) $\mathbf{r}(t) = \mathbf{v}_0 t + \dfrac{1}{2}\mathbf{a}t^2$
$= (5.0t + 1.5t^2)\hat{\mathbf{i}} + 1.0t^2\hat{\mathbf{j}}$ ...(i)
As, $\mathbf{r}(t) = x(t)\hat{\mathbf{i}} + y(t)\hat{\mathbf{j}}$ ...(ii)
Comparing Eqs. (i) and (ii), we get
$$x(t) = 5.0t + 1.5t^2$$
and $y(t) = 1.0t^2$
Given, $x(t) = 84$m
$$\Rightarrow \quad 5.0t + 1.50t^2 = 84$$

or $\quad 1.50\,t^2 + 5.0t - 84 = 0$

Solving the above quadratic equation, the value of t is given as,

$$= \frac{-5 \pm \sqrt{5^2 - 4(1.50)(-84)}}{2(1.50)}$$

$\Rightarrow \quad t = 6\text{ s}$

At $\; t = 6\text{s}, \quad y = 1.0(6)^2 = 36\text{ m}$

42 (*b*) $\mathbf{v}_{AB} = \mathbf{v}_A - \mathbf{v}_B$

$= 20\hat{\mathbf{i}} - 15\hat{\mathbf{i}} = 5\hat{\mathbf{i}}\text{ ms}^{-1}$

43 (*b*) In figure below $\mathbf{v}_r$ represents the velocity of rain and $\mathbf{v}_b$ is the velocity of the bicycle.

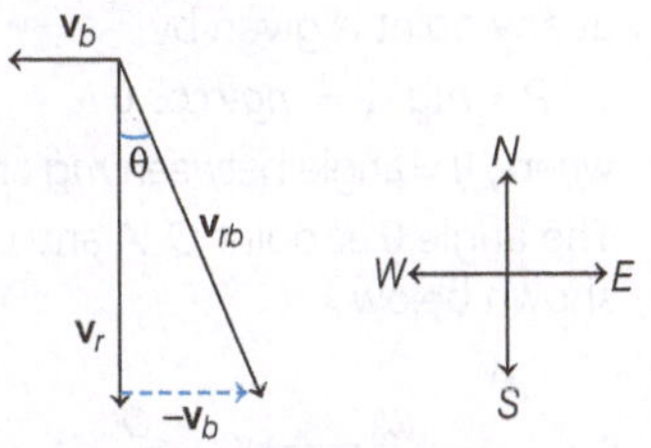

Then, angle θ is given by

$$\tan\theta = \frac{v_b}{v_r} = \frac{12}{35} = 0.343$$

or $\quad \theta = \tan^{-1}(0.343)$

So, the cyclist should hold the umbrella to the vertical in the west.

44 (*b*) The velocity of car driver

$= 8\,\hat{\mathbf{i}}\text{ ms}^{-1}$

Velocity of rocket $= v_y\hat{\mathbf{j}}\text{ ms}^{-1}$

Relative velocity of rocket w.r.t. car

$= 8\hat{\mathbf{i}} - v_y\,\hat{\mathbf{j}}$

Since, the speed of the rocket observed by the car driver is 10 ms^{-1}.

$\therefore\; (v_y)^2 + (8)^2 = (10)^2$

$\Rightarrow \quad v_y = 6\text{ ms}^{-1}$

Velocity of rocket $= v_y\,\hat{\mathbf{j}} = (6\hat{\mathbf{j}})\text{ ms}^{-1}$

$\therefore$ Relative speed of rocket w.r.t. a stationary observer

$= 6 - 0 = 6\text{ ms}^{-1}$

45 (*b*) Let the velocity of the swimmer is v_s and velocity of river is v_r

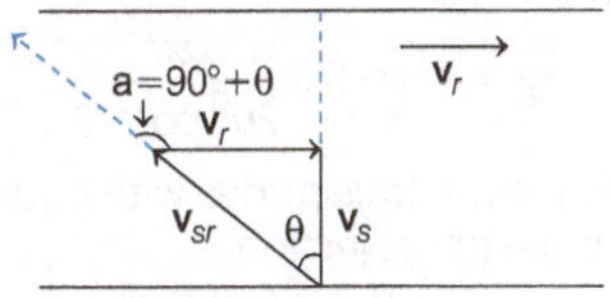

From diagram, angle θ is

$$\sin\theta = \frac{v_r}{v_{sr}} = \frac{2\text{ km/h}}{4\text{ km/h}} = \frac{1}{2}$$

$\Rightarrow \quad \theta = 30°$

Clearly, $\;\alpha = 90° + 30° = 120°$

46 (*a*)

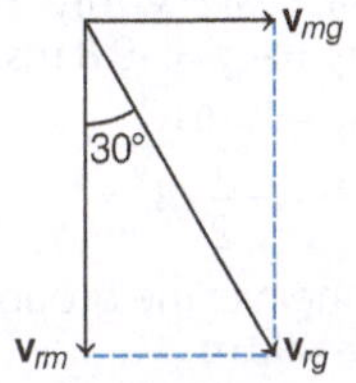

Here, $\mathbf{v}_{rg}$ = velocity of the rain with respect to the ground,

$\mathbf{v}_{mg}$ = velocity of the man with respect to the ground

and $\;\mathbf{v}_{rm}$ = velocity of the rain with respect to the man.

Here, when the man throws the umbrella and starts running, then $|\mathbf{v}_{mg}| = 10\text{ kmh}^{-1}$

$v_{rg}\sin 30° = v_{mg}$

or $\quad v_{rg} = \frac{10}{\sin 30°} = 20\text{ kmh}^{-1}$

47 (*c*) Given, speed of girl, v_g

Speed of river, v_r

Width of river, d

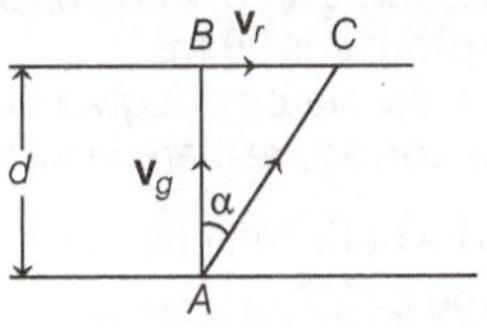

Since, the girl dive the river normal to the flow of the river, time taken by the girl to cross the river,

$$t = \frac{d}{v_g} = \frac{2\text{ km}}{5\text{ kmh}^{-1}} = \frac{2}{5}\text{ h}$$

In this time, the girl will go down the river by the distance *AC* due to river current.

$\therefore$ Distance travelled along the river

$$= v_r \times t = 2 \times \frac{2}{5}$$

$$= \frac{4}{5}\text{ km} = 800\text{ m}$$

48 (*b*) Given, velocity of girl,

$\mathbf{v}_g = 5\hat{\mathbf{i}}\text{ ms}^{-1}$

Let velocity of rain,

$\mathbf{v}_r = v_x\hat{\mathbf{i}} + v_y\hat{\mathbf{j}}\text{ms}^{-1}$

Relative velocity of rain, $\mathbf{v}_{rg}$

$= (v_x - 5)\hat{\mathbf{i}} + v_y\hat{\mathbf{j}}$

Now, it is vertical, so

$$\tan\theta = \frac{v_x - 5}{v_y} = 0$$

$\Rightarrow\; v_x = 5 \qquad$ ...(i)

On increasing the speed of the girl, relative velocity becomes $(v_x - 15)\hat{\mathbf{i}} + v_y\hat{\mathbf{j}}$

$$\tan\theta = \tan 45° = \frac{v_x - 15}{v_y} = 1$$

$\Rightarrow\; v_x - 15 = v_y \Rightarrow v_y = -10$

[using Eq. (i)]

$\Rightarrow$ Magnitude of velocity of rain

$= \sqrt{(5)^2 + (10)^2} = 5\sqrt{5}\text{ ms}^{-1}$

49 (*b*) $v_A = v_x = \frac{dx}{dt} = 8 - 6t$

or v_A at $t = 1\text{ s}$,

$\Rightarrow \quad \mathbf{v}_A = +2\hat{\mathbf{i}}\text{ ms}^{-1}$

Velocity of particle *B*,

$v_B = v_y$

$= -8 \times 3t^2$

At $\quad t = 1\text{ s}$,

$\Rightarrow\; \mathbf{v}_B = -24\hat{\mathbf{j}}\text{ ms}^{-1}$

Speed of particle *B* w.r.t. particle *A*,

$\mathbf{v}_{BA} = -2\hat{\mathbf{i}} - 24\hat{\mathbf{j}}$

$\Rightarrow$ Magnitude of velocity,

$|\mathbf{v}_{BA}| = \sqrt{(2)^2 + (24)^2}$

But given $|\mathbf{v}_{BA}| = \sqrt{v}$

$\Rightarrow \qquad v = 580\text{ ms}^{-1}$

50 (*b*) Let u be the speed of stream and v be the speed of swimmer started from *A*.

He wants to reach at point *B* directed opposite to *A*.

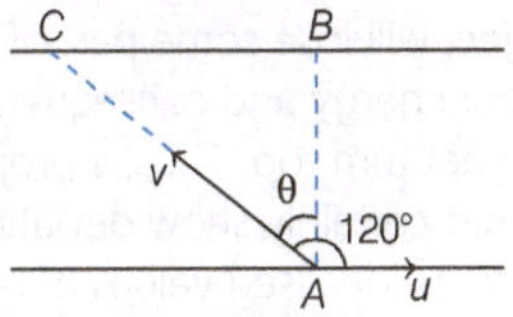

From figure

$u = v\sin\theta = v\sin 30°$

$= 0.5\text{ m/s}$

51 (*c*) Now, speed in the direction of shortest path

$$= \frac{\text{Path}}{\text{Time}}$$

$$\therefore \sqrt{(v_b)^2 - u^2} = \frac{d}{t}$$

$$\sqrt{41 - u^2} = \frac{1.5}{\frac{3}{10}}$$

$$\Rightarrow u = 4 \text{ km/h}$$

52 (*a*)

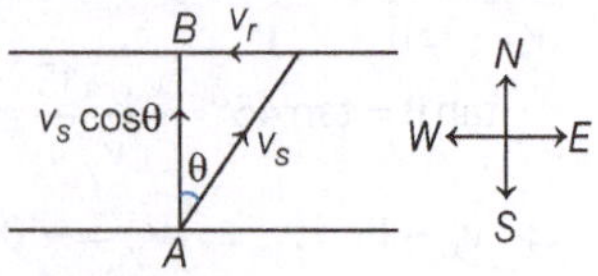

From the figure,

$v_s \sin\theta = v_r$

$14 \sin\theta = 7$

$\theta = 30°$, in east-north direction.

53 (*b*) Let east is in $\hat{\mathbf{i}}$ direction and vertical downwards is $\hat{\mathbf{j}}$ direction.

The velocity of rain, $\mathbf{v}_r = a\hat{\mathbf{i}} + b\hat{\mathbf{j}}$

Case I Given, velocity of boy,

$\mathbf{v}_b = 5\hat{\mathbf{i}}$

Now, velocity of rain with respect to boy,

$$\mathbf{v}_{rb} = \mathbf{v}_r - \mathbf{v}_b = (a-5)\hat{\mathbf{i}} + b\hat{\mathbf{j}}$$

∵ Rain appears to fall downwards,

$\therefore \; a - 5 = 0 \Rightarrow a = 5$

Case II $\mathbf{v}_b = 17\hat{\mathbf{i}}$

$\therefore \mathbf{v}_{rb} = \mathbf{v}_r - \mathbf{v}_b = (a-17)\hat{\mathbf{i}} + b\hat{\mathbf{j}}$

∵ Rain appears to fall at 45°

$\therefore \; b = a - 17 \Rightarrow b = -12$

So, velocity of rain, $\mathbf{v}_r = 5\hat{\mathbf{i}} - 12\hat{\mathbf{j}}$

$$|\mathbf{v}_r| = \sqrt{5^2 + (-12)^2} = 13 \text{ m/s}$$

54 (*c*) Here, air resistance is a form of dissipative force. In the presence of such an opposing force, any object will lose some part of its initial energy and consequently, momentum too. Thus, a projectile would certainly show deviation from its idealised values of range, maximum height and trajectory. Hence, the statement given in option (c) is correct, rest are incorrect.

55 (*c*) The equation of motion

$$x(t) = x_0 + v_{0x}t$$

$$y(t) = y_0 + v_{0y}t + \left(\frac{1}{2}\right)a_y t^2$$

Here, $x_0 = y_0 = 0$, $v_{0y} = 0$

$a_y = -g = -9.8 \text{ ms}^{-2}$

$v_{0x} = 15 \text{ ms}^{-1}$

$$y(t) = -\frac{1}{2}gt^2 \quad \text{...(i)}$$

The stone hits the ground when $y(t) = -490$ m

Substituting the given values in Eq. (i), we get

$$-490 = -\left(\frac{1}{2}\right)(9.8)t^2$$

$$t = 10 \text{ s}$$

∴ The time taken by the stone to reach the ground is 10 s.

The velocity component for the stone are $v_x = v_{0x}$ and $v_y = v_{0y} - gt$.

So, when the stone hits the ground

$v_x = v_{0x} = 15 \text{ ms}^{-1}$

$v_y = 0 - 9.8 \times 10 = -98 \text{ ms}^{-1}$

Therefore, the speed of the stone,

$$= \sqrt{(15)^2 + (-98)^2}$$

$$\cong 99 \text{ ms}^{-1}$$

Thus, the speed with which it hits the ground is 99 ms^{-1}.

Thus, the statement given in option (c) is correct, rest are incorrect.

56 (*c*) The horizontal distance covered by the ball,

$$R = u \cdot T = 20T$$

∴ The speed of the man to catch the ball,

$$v = \frac{R}{T} = \frac{20 \cdot T}{T} = 20 \text{ m/s}$$

58 (*a*) $x = (u\cos\theta)t = 10\cos 30° \times 1$

$= 8.66$ m

Similarly,

$$y = u\sin\theta t - \frac{1}{2}gt^2$$

$$= 10\sin 30° \times 1 - \frac{1}{2} \times 9.8 \times 1^2$$

$= 0.1$ m

So, the position coordinate of the ball after 1s is (8.66 m, 0.1 m).

59 (*d*) $y = 5x - 5x^2$ ...(i)

But we know that, equation of projectile motion is given as

$$y = x\tan\theta - \frac{1}{2}\frac{gx^2}{u^2\cos^2\theta} \quad \text{...(ii)}$$

Comparing Eqs. (i) and (ii), we get

$\tan\theta = 5$

$$\Rightarrow \frac{u_y}{u_x} = 5 \Rightarrow u_y = 5u_x$$

Since, $\mathbf{u}_x = \hat{\mathbf{i}}$

$u_x = |\mathbf{u}_x| = 1 \text{ m/s}^2$

$u_y = 5 \times 1 = 5 \text{ m/s}^2$

$\therefore \; \mathbf{u}_y = u_y\hat{\mathbf{j}} = 5\hat{\mathbf{j}}$

60 (*b*) The power delivered by gravity at any point is given by

$$P = m\mathbf{g} \cdot \mathbf{v} = mgv\cos\theta$$

where, θ = angle between $m\mathbf{g}$ and $\mathbf{v}$.

The angle θ at point O, A and O′ is shown below

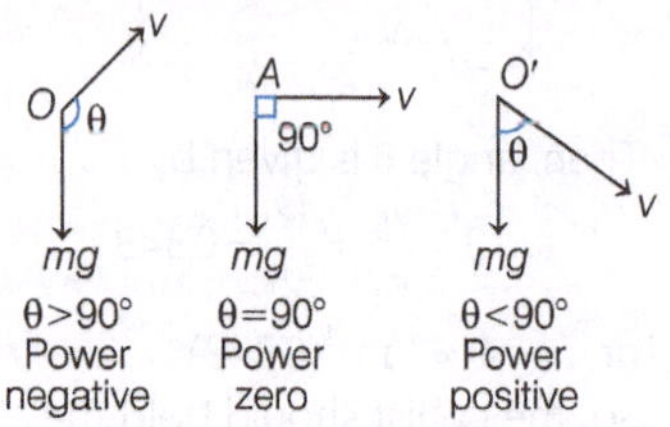

61 (*b*) Given, equations of motion are

$$x = 18t,\; 2y = 54t - 9.8t^2$$

General equations of projectile are

$$x = u\cos\theta \cdot t$$

and $\; y = u\sin\theta \cdot t - \frac{1}{2}gt^2$

Comparing it with given equation,

$u\cos\theta = 18$

and $\; u\sin\theta = \frac{54}{2}$

$$\Rightarrow \frac{u\sin\theta}{u\cos\theta} = \frac{54/2}{18}$$

$$\Rightarrow \theta = \tan^{-1}(1.5)$$

62 (*a*) The trajectory of a projectile projected at an angle θ with the horizontal direction from ground is given by

$$y = x\tan\theta - \frac{gx^2}{2u^2\cos^2\theta}$$

For same trajectories with equal angle of projection,

$$\frac{g}{u^2} = \text{constant}$$

$$\Rightarrow \frac{g_{\text{earth}}}{u^2_{\text{earth}}} = \frac{g_{\text{planet}}}{u^2_{\text{planet}}}$$

$$\frac{9.8}{5^2} = \frac{g_{\text{planet}}}{3^2}$$

$$\Rightarrow g_{\text{planet}} = \frac{9.8 \times 9}{25} = 3.5 \text{ ms}^{-2}$$

63 (*b*) Magnitude of initial velocity,

$$u = \sqrt{5} \text{ ms}^{-1}$$

Equation of trajectory of projectile,

$$y = x \tan\theta - \frac{gx^2}{2u^2 \cos^2\theta}$$

$$= x\tan\theta - \frac{gx^2 \sec^2\theta}{2u^2}$$

$$= x\tan\theta - \frac{gx^2}{2u^2}(1 + \tan^2\theta)$$

$$[\because \sec^2\theta = 1 + \tan^2\theta]$$

Substituting the given values, we get

$$\therefore y = x \times 2 - \frac{10(x)^2}{2(\sqrt{5})^2}[1 + (2)^2]$$

$$\left[\because \tan\theta = \frac{u_y}{u_x} = \frac{2}{1} = 2\right]$$

$$y = 2x - 5x^2$$

64 (*c*) When a particle is thrown from the ground obliquely, then initially it ascends, reaching maximum height before gradually decending to the ground level as depicted in option (c).

65 (*b*) Velocities of the stones at some instant t can be given as

$$\mathbf{v}_1 = u_1 \cos\theta_1 \hat{\mathbf{i}} + (u_1 \sin\theta_1 - gt)\hat{\mathbf{j}}$$

and $$\mathbf{v}_2 = u_2 \cos\theta_2 \hat{\mathbf{i}} + (u_2 \sin\theta_2 - gt)\hat{\mathbf{j}}$$

$\Rightarrow$ Relative velocity,

$$\mathbf{v}_1 - \mathbf{v}_2 = (u_1 \cos\theta_1 - u_2\cos\theta_2)\hat{\mathbf{i}} + (u_1 \sin\theta_1 - u_2 \cos\theta_2)\hat{\mathbf{j}}$$

$$= \text{constant}$$

Relative acceleration,

$$\mathbf{a}_1 - \mathbf{a}_2 = -g\hat{\mathbf{j}} - (-g\hat{\mathbf{j}}) = 0$$

So, the trajectory of path followed by one as seen by other will be straight line, making a constant angle with horizontal.

66 (*b*) By using, $2t_m = T_f$

where, t_m is the time-taken by the stone to reach the maximum height and T_f is the total flight of the stone.

Given, $t_m = 5.8\text{s}$

$$\Rightarrow T_f = 2 \times 5.8 = 11.6 \text{ s}$$

67 (*d*) Time taken by the bomb to fall through a height h of 980 m

$$t = \sqrt{\frac{2h}{g}} = \sqrt{\frac{2 \times 980}{10}} = 14 \text{ s}$$

Distance at which the bomb strikes the ground

$$= \text{Horizontal velocity} \times t$$

$$= 480 \times 14 \times \frac{1}{3600}$$

$$= \frac{6720}{3600} = 1.867 \text{ km}$$

68 (*d*) Let after time t shell hits the plane, then $u_x t = vt$

[Here, u_x is horizontal component]

$$u \sin\theta t = vt$$

$$\sin\theta = \frac{v}{u} = \frac{200}{400}$$

$$\theta = 30°$$

69 (*c*) Here, vertical height,

$$h = 980 \text{ m}$$

Initial velocity is only in x-direction,

$$u_x = v_x = 19.8 \text{ m/s}$$

Use the formula along Y-axis,

$$v_y^2 + u_y^2 = 2gh \quad [\because u_y = 0]$$

$$v_y^2 = 19208$$

Hence, final velocity

$$= \sqrt{v_x^2 + v_y^2}$$

$$= \sqrt{392 + 19208}$$

$$= 140 \text{ m/s}$$

70 (*d*) The given situation is shown below

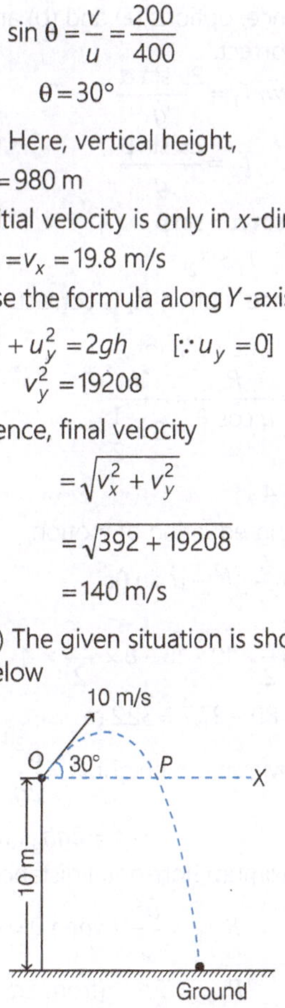

$$OP = R = \frac{u^2 \sin 2\theta}{g}$$

$$= \frac{10^2 \times \sin(2 \times 30°)}{10}$$

$$= \frac{10\sqrt{3}}{2} = 5\sqrt{3} = 8.66 \text{ m}$$

71 (*b*) $H = \dfrac{u^2 \sin^2\theta}{2g}$

$$\Rightarrow 30 = \frac{(60)^2 \sin^2\theta}{2g}$$

$$\Rightarrow \sin\theta = \frac{1}{\sqrt{6}}$$

72 (*c*) Maximum height,

$$H = \frac{u^2 \sin^2\alpha}{2g}$$

For same speed of projection,

$$H \propto \sin^2\alpha$$

$$\therefore \frac{H_1}{H_2} = \frac{\sin^2\alpha}{\sin^2(90° - \alpha)}$$

$$= \frac{\sin^2\alpha}{\cos^2\alpha} = \tan^2\alpha$$

73 (*c*) Given condition, $h_1 = h_2$

For projectile maximum height attained, $h = \dfrac{u^2 \sin^2\theta}{2g}$

$$\Rightarrow u_1^2 \sin^2 45° = u_2^2 \sin^2\theta$$

$$\Rightarrow \sin^2\theta = \frac{u_1^2}{u_2^2}\sin^2 45° = \frac{1}{2}\cdot\frac{1}{2} = \frac{1}{4}$$

$$\left[\because \text{given, } \frac{u_1}{u_2} = \frac{1}{\sqrt{2}}\right]$$

$$\Rightarrow \theta = 30°$$

74 (*a*) Range of a projectile,

$$R = \frac{u^2 \sin 2\theta}{g} = \frac{2u^2 \sin\theta\cos\theta}{g}$$

$$= \frac{2(u\sin\theta)(u\cos\theta)}{g} = \frac{2u_x u_y}{g}$$

$\Rightarrow R \propto$ horizontal initial velocity component (u_x)

Thus, the correct order will be $1 < 2 < 3$.

75 (*b*) As, range of a projectile,

$$R = \frac{u^2 \sin 2\theta}{g}$$

and it is maximum $\theta = 45°$

$$\therefore \frac{u^2}{g} = 80 \text{ m}$$

Maximum height, $h=\dfrac{u^2\sin^2\theta}{2g}$

$=\dfrac{80}{2}(\sin^2 45^\circ)=40\times\dfrac{1}{2}=20$ m

76 (c) $R_{max}=\dfrac{u^2}{g}=\dfrac{15^2}{10}=22.5$ m

Time of flight,

$$T=\frac{2u\sin 45^\circ}{g}$$

$$=\frac{2\times 15\times\frac{1}{\sqrt{2}}}{10}$$

$$=\frac{3}{\sqrt{2}}\text{ s}$$

The player can catch the ball, if he covers d distance in T time.

Here, $d=22.5-13.5=9$ m

∴Velocity of that player

$$=\frac{d}{T}=\frac{9}{\frac{3}{\sqrt{2}}}=3\sqrt{2}\text{ m/s}$$

77 (b) Horizontal range R of projectile is $\dfrac{u^2\sin 2\theta}{g}$.

Clearly, for maximum horizontal range, $\sin 2\theta=1$

or $2\theta=90^\circ$ or $\theta=45^\circ$.

Hence, ranges of A and C are less than that of B.

78 (d) Horizontal range of projectile,

For $\alpha=(45^\circ-\theta)$,

$$R_1=\frac{u^2\sin 2(45^\circ-\theta)}{g}$$

$$=\frac{u^2\cos 2\theta}{g}$$

For $\alpha=(45^\circ+\theta)$,

$$R_2=\frac{u^2\cos 2\theta}{g}$$

Hence, $\dfrac{R_1}{R_2}=\dfrac{1}{1}$ or $R_1:R_2=1:1$

79 (c) Given, range will be same for time t_1 and t_2, so angle of projection will be θ and $(90^\circ-\theta)$.

$\therefore t_1=\dfrac{2u\sin\theta}{g}$, $t_2=\dfrac{2u\sin(90^\circ-\theta)}{g}$

Now, $t_1\cdot t_2$

$$=\frac{2}{g}\left[\frac{2u^2\cos\theta\sin\theta}{g}\right]$$

but $R=\dfrac{2u^2\cos\theta\sin\theta}{g}=49$ m

$\therefore t_1t_2=\dfrac{2}{g}\times 49=\dfrac{2\times 49}{9.8}=10\text{ s}^2$

80 (c) Given, $H_1>H_2$

$H_1=\dfrac{u^2\sin^2\alpha}{2g}$ and $H_2=\dfrac{u^2\sin^2\beta}{2g}$

$\therefore \dfrac{u^2\sin^2\alpha}{2g}>\dfrac{u^2\sin^2\beta}{2g}$

$\sin^2\alpha-\sin^2\beta>0$

$(\sin\alpha+\sin\beta)(\sin\alpha-\sin\beta)>0$

$\therefore \sin\alpha-\sin\beta>0$

$\sin\alpha>\sin\beta$

$\alpha>\beta$

Hence, options (a) and (b) are incorrect.

Now, $T_1=\dfrac{2u\sin\alpha}{g}$

$T_2=\dfrac{2u\sin\beta}{g}$

$\because \sin\alpha>\sin\beta$

$\therefore \quad T_1>T_2$

Hence, option (c) is correct.

81. (c) Time of flight,

$$T=\frac{R}{u\cos\theta}=\frac{16}{8\times\frac{1}{2}}$$

$T=4$ s

Using equation of motion,

$$h=\frac{1}{2}gt^2-u\sin\theta t$$

$$=\frac{1}{2}\times 10\times 16-8\times\frac{\sqrt{3}}{2}\times 4$$

$=80-27.7=52.2$ m

82 (c) Maximum height, $h=\dfrac{u^2}{2g}$

$\Rightarrow \quad u^2=2gh$ ...(i)

Maximum horizontal distance

$R_{max}=\dfrac{u^2}{g}$ (when $\theta=45^\circ$),

$\Rightarrow \quad R_{max}=2h$ [from Eq. (i)]

83 (c) Maximum height,

$$H=\frac{u^2\sin^2\theta}{2g} \quad \text{... (i)}$$

Horizontal range,

$$R=\frac{u^2\sin 2\theta}{g} \quad \text{... (ii)}$$

Dividing Eq. (i) by Eq. (ii), we get

$$\frac{H}{R}=\frac{\tan\theta}{4}\Rightarrow\theta=\tan^{-1}\frac{4H}{R}$$

84 (b) Let u be the initial speed, so speed at hightest point

$$u\cos\theta=\frac{u}{2}\Rightarrow\theta=60^\circ$$

$\because$ Horizontal range, $R=\dfrac{u^2\sin 2\theta}{g}$

and maximum height, $H=\dfrac{u^2\sin^2\theta}{2g}$

$\Rightarrow \dfrac{R}{H}=\dfrac{4}{\tan\theta}=\dfrac{4}{\tan 60^\circ}=\dfrac{4}{\sqrt{3}}$

85 (b) Components of velocity

$v_x=u\cos\theta+a_xt$ and

$v_y=u\sin\theta+g_yt$

Here, components of velocity at $t=1$ s, is

$v_x=5$ m/s [as $a_x=0$]

$=5$ m/s

and $v_y=10\times\dfrac{\sqrt{3}}{2}+(-10)\times(1)$

$=5\sqrt{3}-10$

$\Rightarrow |v_y|=|10-5\sqrt{3}|$ m/s

Now, angle made by the velocity vector at time of $t=1$ s

$$|\tan\alpha|=\left|\frac{v_y}{v_x}\right|=\frac{|10-5\sqrt{3}|}{5}$$

$\Rightarrow \tan\alpha=|2-\sqrt{3}|$ or $\alpha=15^\circ$

∴ Radius of curvature of the trajectory of the projected body

$R=v^2/g\cos\alpha$

$$=\frac{(5)^2+(10-5\sqrt{3})^2}{10\times 0.97}$$

$[\because v^2=v_x^2+v_y^2$ and $\cos 15^\circ=0.97]$

$\Rightarrow \quad R=2.77\text{ m}\approx 2.8$ m

86 (b) Given, $R=12$ cm and $T=100$ s

Angular speed, $\omega=\dfrac{2\pi}{T}=\dfrac{2\pi\times 7}{100}$

$=0.44$ rad/s

Linear speed, $v = \omega R = 0.44 \times 12$
$= 5.3$ cm/s

The direction of velocity v is along the tangent to the circle at every point. The acceleration is directed towards the centre of the circle. Since, this direction changes continuously, hence acceleration here is not constant vector.

The magnitude of acceleration,
$a = \omega^2 R = (0.44)^2 \times 12 = 2.3 \text{ cm/s}^2$

Thus, the statement given in option (b) is correct, rest are incorrect.

87 (*b*) Statement given in option (b) is incorrect and it can be corrected as
For a particle performing uniform circular motion, velocity will be tangential in the direction of motion at a particular point.
Rest statements are correct.

88 (*c*) For a uniform circular motion,
centripetal acceleration, $a_c = \dfrac{v^2}{R}$

Since, v and R are constants, the magnitude of the centripetal acceleration of the car is also constant.
However, the direction changes pointing towards the centre. Therefore, a centripetal acceleration is not a constant vector.

89 (*c*)

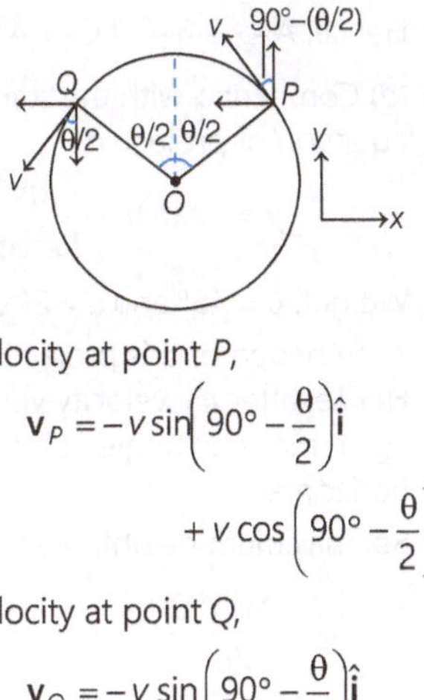

Velocity at point P,

$$\mathbf{v}_P = -v \sin\left(90° - \frac{\theta}{2}\right)\hat{\mathbf{i}} + v\cos\left(90° - \frac{\theta}{2}\right)\hat{\mathbf{j}}$$

Velocity at point Q,

$$\mathbf{v}_Q = -v \sin\left(90° - \frac{\theta}{2}\right)\hat{\mathbf{i}} - v\cos\left(90° - \frac{\theta}{2}\right)\hat{\mathbf{j}}$$

Thus, change in velocity,

$$\Delta\mathbf{v} = \mathbf{v}_Q - \mathbf{v}_P$$
$$\Rightarrow |\Delta\mathbf{v}| = 2v\sin\frac{\theta}{2}$$

90 (*b*) The velocity of the particle perpendicular to the radius of the circular path,

$$v = \omega r$$

For uniform circular motion,

$$\omega = \text{constant}$$
$$\therefore \quad v = \omega r = \text{constant}$$
$$a = \frac{dv}{dt} = 0$$

91 (*a*) When particle moved by an angle of 60°, i.e. from A to B on the circular path, then according to figure, displacement AB is equal to radius r because it forms an equilateral triangle.
So, displacement $(AB) = 5$ m
Given, $t = 1$ s

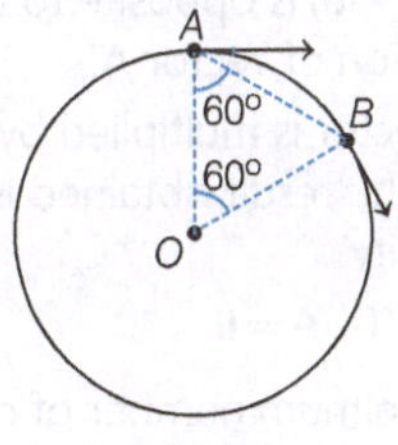

$\therefore$ Average velocity

$$= \frac{\text{Displacement } (AB)}{\text{Time}}$$
$$= \frac{r}{1} = 5 \text{ ms}^{-1}$$

92 (*c*) $\dfrac{\omega_A}{\omega_B} = \dfrac{2\pi}{T_A} \times \dfrac{T_B}{2\pi} = \dfrac{T_B}{T_A}$

$$= \frac{1}{1} \text{ or } 1:1 \; [\because T_A = T_B \text{ (given)}]$$

93 (*b*) We know that, linear speed $v = \omega r$, where angular velocity ω is constant.

$$\therefore \quad v \propto r \text{ or } \frac{v_A}{v_B} = \frac{r_A}{r_B}$$

94 (*a*) Given, $v = 5$ m/s
Radius of the circle, $r = 500$ m
Now, acceleration at point R,

$$a_R = \frac{v^2}{r} = \frac{5^2}{500} = \frac{25}{500} = 0.05 \text{ m/s}^2$$

95 (*c*) Linear velocity, $v = \omega r = \dfrac{2\pi}{T} r$

$$= \frac{2\pi}{60} \times 3 \times 10^{-2}$$
$$= 0.00314 \text{ ms}^{-1}$$

96 (*a*) Given, speed, $v = 23 \text{ ms}^{-1}$
and radius, $r = 5$ m
Centripetal acceleration,

$$a_c = \frac{v^2}{r} = \frac{23 \times 23}{5}$$
$$= 105.8 \approx 106 \text{ ms}^{-2}$$

97 (*c*) $T_1 = T_2$

$$\Rightarrow \quad \frac{2\pi r_1}{v_1} = \frac{2\pi r_2}{v_2}$$
$$\Rightarrow \quad \frac{v_1}{v_2} = \frac{r_1}{r_2} \quad \text{...(i)}$$

Ratio of centripetal acceleration,

$$a_{c_1} : a_{c_2} = \frac{v_1^2}{r_1} \times \frac{r_2}{v_2^2}$$
$$= \frac{r_1^2}{r_2^2} \times \frac{r_2}{r_1} = \frac{r_1}{r_2} = r_1 : r_2 \text{ [from Eq. (i)]}$$

98 (*a*) $r = \dfrac{\text{Diameter}}{2} = \dfrac{0.80 \text{ m}}{2} = 0.40$ m

Frequency, $\nu = \dfrac{100}{60} \text{ revs}^{-1}$

Time period, $T = \dfrac{1}{\nu} = \dfrac{60}{100} = 0.60$

$\therefore$ Angular velocity, $\omega = \dfrac{2\pi}{T}$

$$= \frac{2 \times 3.14}{0.60} = 10.467 \text{ rad s}^{-1}$$

99 (*c*) Given, frequency,

$$\nu = 72 \text{ rev min}^{-1} = \frac{72}{60} \text{ rev s}^{-1},$$

radius $r = 25 \text{ cm} = 25 \times 10^{-2}$ m,
Linear velocity, $v = \omega r = (2\pi\nu)r$

$$= \frac{66}{35} \text{ ms}^{-1}$$
$$= 2 \text{ ms}^{-1} \text{ (approx)}$$

100 (*a*) $\omega = 40\pi$ rad/s
The time to complete the circular path,

$$T = \frac{2\pi R}{v} = \frac{2\pi R}{\omega R} = \frac{2\pi}{\omega}$$
$$= \frac{2\pi}{40\pi} = 0.05 \text{ s}$$

Assertion and Reason Questions

1 (b) Let, $|\mathbf{A}| = 4, |\mathbf{B}| = 3$ and $\theta = 120°$, then

Resultant of two vectors **A** and **B** is

$$|\mathbf{R}| = \sqrt{4^2 + 3^2 + 2 \times 4 \times 3 \cos(120°)}$$

$$= \sqrt{25 - 12} = \sqrt{13} \quad \left(\because \cos 120° = -\frac{1}{2}\right)$$

$$\therefore \quad |\mathbf{R}| < |\mathbf{A}|$$

2 (d) $|\mathbf{A} + \mathbf{B}| = \sqrt{A^2 + B^2 + 2AB\cos\theta}$

$$|\mathbf{A} - \mathbf{B}| = \sqrt{A^2 + B^2 - 2AB\cos\theta}$$

$$|\mathbf{A} + \mathbf{B}| = |\mathbf{A} - \mathbf{B}| = \sqrt{A^2 + B^2} \quad [\text{At } \theta = 90°]$$

Therefore, Assertion is incorrect but Reason is correct.

3 (d) Vector subtraction is not commutative, i.e. $\mathbf{A} - \mathbf{B} \neq \mathbf{B} - \mathbf{A}$

4 (b) Maximum height, $H_1 = \dfrac{u^2 \sin^2\alpha}{2g}$

and $\quad H_2 = \dfrac{u^2 \sin^2(90° - \alpha)}{2g}$

$$\Rightarrow \quad H_1 + H_2 = \frac{u^2}{2g}$$

Thus, $H_1 + H_1$ is independent of angle of projection.

As, horizontal range, $R = \dfrac{u^2 \sin 2\theta}{g}$

So, for same value of initial velocity, horizontal range of projectile is same for complementary angles.

Therefore, Assertion and Reason are correct but Reason is not the correct explanation of Assertion.

7 (c) $R_{max} = \dfrac{u^2 \sin(2 \times 45°)}{g}$

$$= \frac{u^2 \sin 90°}{g} = \frac{u^2}{g} \quad \text{...(i)}$$

$$\therefore \quad H = \frac{u^2 \sin^2 45°}{2g}$$

$$= \frac{u^2}{4g} = \frac{R_{max}}{4} \quad \text{[from Eq. (i)]}$$

So, H is 25% of R_{max}.

Therefore, Assertion is correct but Reason is incorrect.

8 (c) Horizontal range,

$$R = \frac{u^2 \sin 2\theta}{g}$$

At, $\quad \theta = 45°$

$\sin 2\theta = 1$

$$\therefore \quad R_{max} = \frac{u^2}{g} = \text{maximum range}$$

The maximum height,

$$H_{max} = \frac{u_y^2}{2g}$$

Therefore, H_{max} also depends on g.

Statement Based Questions

2 (a) The direction of vector $\lambda\mathbf{A}, (\lambda < 0)$ is opposite to the direction of vector **A**.

If a vector is multiplied by zero, then the result obtained is a vector quantity.

$$0 \cdot \mathbf{A} = \mathbf{0}$$

4 (b) Minimum number of collinear vectors of equal magnitude whose resultant can be zero is two.

6 (a) At highest point of projectile, possesses velocity only along the horizontal direction and is perpendicular to acceleration.

7 (b) Statement I is correct but II is incorrect and it can be corrected as

For a projectile motion, the x-component of velocity remains constant throughout the motion.

8 (a) Statement I is correct but II is incorrect and it can be corrected as

The acceleration of an object in uniform circular motion is always directed towards the centre of the circle.

Matching Type Questions

1 (b)

A. As, $|\mathbf{B}| = 2|\mathbf{A}|$ and they both are in the same direction, so $2\mathbf{A} = \mathbf{B}$.

B. As, $|\mathbf{A}| = |\mathbf{B}|$ and but both are in opposite direction, so $\mathbf{A} = -\mathbf{B}$

C. As, $|\mathbf{A}| = 2|\mathbf{B}|$ but both are in opposite direction, so $\mathbf{A} = -2\mathbf{B}$.

D. $|\mathbf{A}| = |\mathbf{B}|$ and both are in same direction, so $\mathbf{A} = \mathbf{B}$.

Hence, A $\rightarrow$ 3, B $\rightarrow$ 1, C $\rightarrow$ 4 and D $\rightarrow$ 2.

2 (a) Time of ascent

$$= \frac{u \sin\theta}{g} = \frac{15 \times \sin 37°}{9.8} = 0.92 \text{ s}$$

$$H = \frac{u^2 \sin^2\theta}{2g} = \frac{(15)^2 \sin^2 37°}{9.8}$$

$$= 4.16 \text{ m}$$

$$R = \frac{u^2 \sin 2\theta}{g} = \frac{(15)^2 \sin 74°}{9.8}$$

$$= 22.02 \text{ m}$$

$$T = \frac{2u \sin\theta}{g}$$

$$= \frac{2 \times 15 \sin 37°}{9.8} = 1.84 \text{ s}$$

Hence, A $\rightarrow$ 3 B $\rightarrow$ 1 C $\rightarrow$ 4, D $\rightarrow$ 2

3 (d) Comparing with the standard equation of projectile,

$$y = x\tan\theta - \frac{gx^2}{2u^2\cos\theta}$$

We get, $\theta = 45°$ and $u = 20\sqrt{2}$ ms^{-1}

Time period of this projectile is 4s. Hence, after 4s, velocity vector will again make an angle 45° with horizontal.

So, maximum height,

$$h = \frac{u^2 \sin^2\theta}{2g}$$

$$= \frac{(20\sqrt{2})^2 \sin^2(45°)}{2 \times 10}$$

$$H = \frac{400 \times 2 \times \frac{1}{2}}{20} = \frac{400}{20} = 20 \text{ m}$$

and horizontal range,

$$R = \frac{u^2 \sin 2\theta}{g} = \frac{(20\sqrt{2})^2 \sin 2(45°)}{10}$$

$$= \frac{400 \times 2 \times 1}{10} \qquad (\because \sin 90° = 1)$$

$$\Rightarrow \qquad R = 80 \text{ m}$$

Hence, A → 2, B → 2, C → 1, D → 3

4 (*d*) The given equation of projectile is

$$y = mx - nx^2$$

Comparing with equation of trajectory of the projectile,

$$y = x\tan\theta - \frac{gx^2}{2u^2\cos^2\theta}$$

$$\therefore \quad \tan\theta = m$$

$$\frac{g}{2u^2\cos^2\theta} = n$$

$$\Rightarrow \quad u^2 = \frac{g(1+\tan^2\theta)}{2n}$$

$$\Rightarrow \quad u = \sqrt{\frac{g(1+m^2)}{2n}}$$

Time of flight,

$$T = \frac{2u\sin\theta}{g} = \frac{2u\cos\theta}{g} \times \tan\theta$$

$$= \frac{2}{g} \times \sqrt{\frac{g}{2n}} \times m$$

$$= m\sqrt{\frac{2}{ng}}$$

Horizontal range,

$$R = \frac{u^2 \sin 2\theta}{g}$$

$$= \frac{2u^2 \sin\theta \cdot \cos\theta}{g}$$

$$= \frac{2u^2\cos^2\theta}{g} \times \tan\theta = \frac{m}{n}$$

Maximum height,

$$H = \frac{u^2 \sin^2\theta}{2g}$$

$$= \frac{u^2\cos^2\theta}{2g} \times \tan^2\theta = \frac{m^2}{4n}$$

Hence, A → 3, B → 4, C → 1 and D → 2.

Numerical Type Questions

1 (5) The projectile motion of the ball with respect to boy is given below

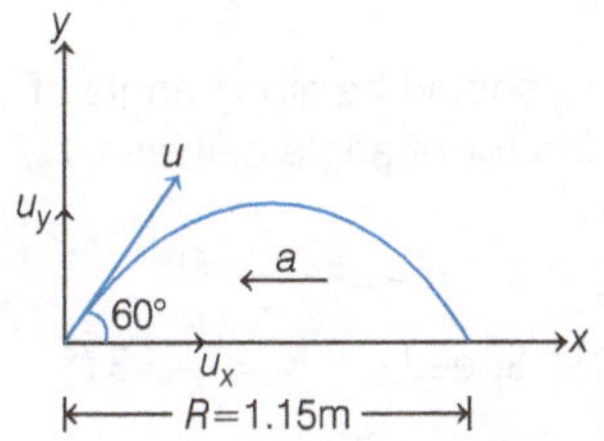

$$u = 10 \text{ m/s},$$

$$u_x = u\cos\theta = 10\cos 60° = 5 \text{ m/s}$$

$$u_y = u\sin\theta = 10\sin 60° = 5\sqrt{3} \text{ m/s}$$

$$T = \frac{2u_y}{g} = \frac{2 \times 5\sqrt{3}}{10} = \sqrt{3} \text{ s}$$

Apply equation of motion along *x*-direction,

$$R = u_x T - \frac{1}{2} a T^2$$

$$\Rightarrow 1.15 = 5 \times \sqrt{3} - \frac{1}{2} a \times (\sqrt{3})^2$$

$$\therefore \quad a = 5 \text{ m/s}^2$$

2 (44.6) Given, $\mathbf{u} = 10.0\hat{\mathbf{j}}$ at $t = 0$ s

$$d\mathbf{v} = (8.0\hat{\mathbf{i}} + 2.0\hat{\mathbf{j}})dt$$

$$\text{So,} \quad \int_u^v d\mathbf{v} = (8.0\hat{\mathbf{i}} + 2.0\hat{\mathbf{j}}) \int_{t=0}^{t=5} dt$$

$$\mathbf{v} - \mathbf{u} = 40.0\hat{\mathbf{i}} + 10.0\hat{\mathbf{j}}$$

$$\mathbf{v} = 40.0\hat{\mathbf{i}} + 20.0\hat{\mathbf{j}}$$

$$|\mathbf{v}| = \sqrt{40^2 + 20^2}$$

$$= 44.6 \text{ m/s}$$

3 (60) The man will catch the ball, if the horizontal component of velocity should be equal to the constant speed of man.

$$\therefore \quad v_0 \cos\theta = \frac{v_0}{2}, \ \theta = 60°$$

4 (18) As we know that, range is maximum, when $\theta = 45°$

$$\therefore R_{max} = \frac{u^2 \sin 2\theta}{g} = \frac{u^2}{g} = 18 \text{ km}$$

And at highest point,

$$v = u_x = u\cos 45°$$

The velocity of another mass,

$$v = 2u\cos 45°$$

Now, horizontal distance covered by other mass after explosion is

$$= v \times \frac{T}{2} = 2u\cos 45° \times \frac{u\sin 45°}{g}$$

$$= \frac{2u^2}{g} \sin 45° \times \cos 45°$$

$$= \frac{u^2}{g} = 18 \text{ km}$$

5 (2)

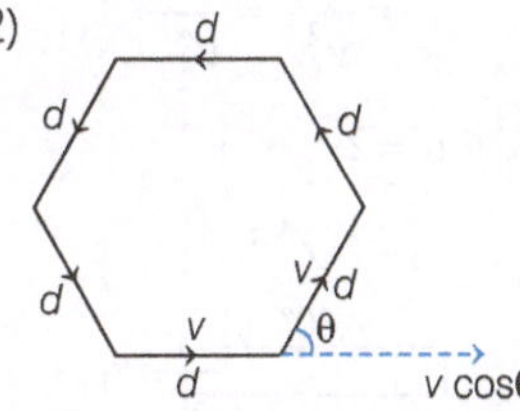

Here, we can say that all particles will meet at the centre of the hexagon and the separation between any two consecutive particles decreases at the rate of approach velocity.

$$v_{app} = v - v\cos\theta \qquad [\because \theta = 60°]$$

$$= v - \frac{v}{2} = \frac{v}{2}$$

The initial separation is *d* and it decreases to zero as velocity approach to $\frac{v}{2}$.

$$\therefore \qquad t = \frac{d}{v_{app}} = \frac{d}{\frac{v}{2}} = \frac{2d}{v} = \frac{xd}{v}$$

Hence, $x = 2$

6 (2) Here, $v_{AB}^2 = v_x^2 + v_y^2$

and $\quad \tan\theta = \dfrac{v_y}{v_x}$

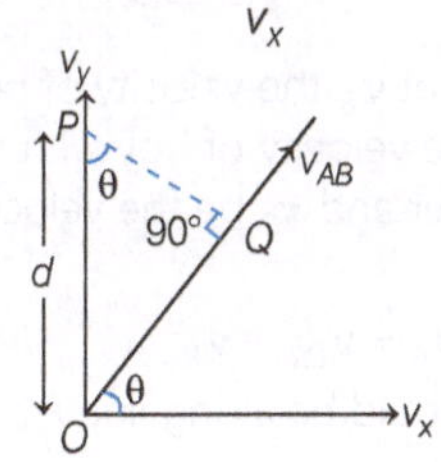

$$\therefore \quad \cos\theta = \frac{v_x}{\sqrt{v_x^2 + v_y^2}} = \frac{v_x}{v_{AB}}$$

$$\text{and } \sin\theta = \frac{v_y}{v_{AB}}$$

The minimum distance between these two particles is

$$PQ = OP\cos\theta = \frac{dv_x}{v_{AB}}$$

and time $= \dfrac{OQ}{v_{AB}} = \dfrac{OP\sin\theta}{v_{AB}}$

$$= \frac{d\sin\theta}{v_{AB}}$$

$$= \frac{dv_y}{v_{AB}^2} = \frac{dv_y}{v_{AB}^{\alpha}}$$

$\therefore \quad \alpha = 2$

7 (7)

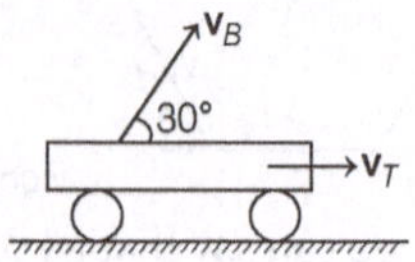

$\because \mathbf{v}_{ball/train} = \mathbf{v}_{ball} - \mathbf{v}_{train}$

$\therefore \mathbf{v}_{ball} = \mathbf{v}_{ball/train} + \mathbf{v}_{train}$

and $v_x = v\cos\theta - v_T$

$\Rightarrow \quad v_x = v\cos 30° - v_T$

Here, x-component must be zero.

$\therefore 0 = v\cos 30° - v_T$

$$v = \frac{v_T}{\cos 30°} = \frac{20}{\frac{\sqrt{3}}{2}} = \frac{40}{\sqrt{3}} \text{ m/s}$$

Now, $v_y = \dfrac{40}{\sqrt{3}} \times \sin 30° = \dfrac{20}{\sqrt{3}}$ m/s

$\therefore$Maximum height reached by ball

$$= \frac{v_y^2}{2g} = \frac{\left(\frac{20}{\sqrt{3}}\right)^2}{2\times 9.8}$$

$$= \frac{400}{3\times 2\times 9.8} \simeq 7 \text{ m}$$

8 (45) Let $\mathbf{v}_B$ the velocity of boy, $\mathbf{v}_{BR}$ be the velocity of boy with respect to river and $\mathbf{v}_R$ be the velocity of river.

$\therefore \quad \mathbf{v}_B = \mathbf{v}_{BR} + \mathbf{v}_R$

$\mathbf{v}_B$ should be along line PQ.

As per question,

Magnitude of velocity of boy

= Magnitude of velocity of river

$\Rightarrow \quad |\mathbf{v}_B| = |\mathbf{v}_R|$

If we represent the given scenario as follows

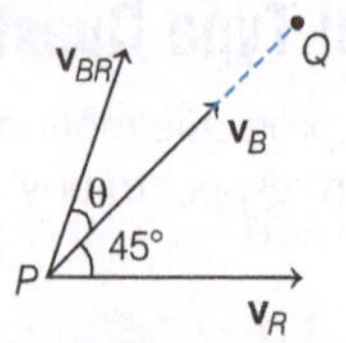

$\therefore v_B$ should be along angle of bisector of angle between $\mathbf{v}_{BR}$ and $\mathbf{v}_R$.

$\therefore \quad \theta = 45°$

9 (15) Speed, $\quad v = \dfrac{ds}{dt} = 3t^2$

$$a_t = \frac{dv}{dt} = 6t$$

$\therefore$Tangential acceleration at $t = 2$ s,

$$a_t = 6\times 2 = 12 \text{ ms}^{-2}$$

and at $t = 2$ s, $v = 3(2)^2$

$$= 12 \text{ ms}^{-1}$$

$\therefore$ Centripetal acceleration,

$$a_c = \frac{v^2}{R} = \frac{144}{16} \text{ ms}^{-2} = 9 \text{ ms}^{-2}$$

$\therefore$Net acceleration $= \sqrt{a_t^2 + a_c^2}$

$$\approx 15 \text{ ms}^{-2}$$

NCERT Exemplar Questions

1 (*d*) A scalar quantity is independent of direction and hence has the same value for observers with different orientations of the axes.

2 (*b*) Clearly from the diagram,

$\mathbf{u} = a\hat{\mathbf{i}} + b\hat{\mathbf{j}}$

As $\mathbf{u}$ is in the first quadrant, hence both components a and b will be positive.

For $\mathbf{v} = p\,\hat{\mathbf{i}} + q\hat{\mathbf{j}}$, as it is in positive x-direction and located downward hence x-component p will be positive but y-component q will be negative.

3 (*b*) Let $\mathbf{r}$ makes an angle θ with positive X-axis. Component of $\mathbf{r}$ along X-axis is

$$r_x = |\mathbf{r}|\cos\theta$$

$$(r_x)_{\max} = |\mathbf{r}|(\cos\theta)_{\max}$$

$$= |\mathbf{r}|\cos 0° = |\mathbf{r}|$$

($\because \cos\theta$ is maximum at $\theta = 0°$)

As $\theta = 0°$, $\mathbf{r}$ is along positive X-axis.

4 (*c*) Given, $\theta = 15°$ and $R = 50$ m

We know that, range,

$$R = \frac{u^2\sin 2\theta}{g} \quad \text{... (i)}$$

where, θ is angle of projection.

Putting all the given values in Eq. (i), we get

$$\Rightarrow R = 50 \text{ m} = \frac{u^2\sin(2\times 15°)}{g}$$

$$\Rightarrow \quad 50\times g = u^2\sin 30°$$

$$= u^2 \times \frac{1}{2}$$

$$= 7\times 2\times\sqrt{5} \text{ ms}^{-1}$$

$$= 14\sqrt{5} \text{ ms}^{-1}$$

For $\theta = 45°$,

$$R = \frac{u^2\sin(2\times 45°)}{g} = \frac{u^2}{g}$$

($\because \sin 90° = 1$)

$$\Rightarrow \quad R = \frac{(14\sqrt{5})^2}{g} = \frac{14\times 14\times 5}{9.8}$$

$$= 100 \text{ m}$$

5 (*d*) We know that, speed, v_0

$$= \frac{\text{total distance travelled}}{\text{time taken}}$$

Hence, total distance travelled

= path length = speed × time taken

If v_0 is positive, so equal path lengths are traversed in equal intervals.

As it is independent of displacement, so it will not give any information regarding average velocity and acceleration.

Past Exams Questions

1 (*d*) The direction of motion changes continuously in a circular motion, therefore circular motion is an accelerated motion.

So, uniform circular motion have varying velocity as well as varying acceleration.

2 (*c*) The direction of angular acceleration of a body moving along the circumference of the circular path is perpendicular to the plane in which rotation takes place i.e. along the axis of rotation.

3 (*b*) Maximum height attained by the bullet.

$$H_{max} = \frac{(280)^2 \sin^2 30°}{2 \times 9.8} = 1000 \text{ m}$$

4 (*d*) Maximum height attained by particle is given as

$$H_{max} = \frac{u^2 \sin^2 \theta}{2g} \quad \text{...(i)}$$

$$H_{max} = 4R \quad \text{(given)}$$

Also, we know that,

speed of the particle in circular path, $u = \frac{2\pi R}{T}$

Substituting the values in the Eq. (i), we get

$$4R = \frac{\left(\frac{2\pi R}{T}\right)^2 \sin^2 \theta}{2g}$$

$$\Rightarrow \theta = \sin^{-1}\left(\frac{2gT^2}{\pi^2 R}\right)^{1/2}$$

5 (*a*) Velocity at $t = 4$ s, $v = u + at$

$$v = 5 \times 4 = 20 \text{ m/s}$$

At this time a ball is dropped out of a window by a person sitting in the car. The velocity of ball after $t = 6$ s is given by

Vertical velocity of $v_y = u_{ball} + a(\Delta t)$

$$= 0 + 10 \times (6 - 4) = 20 \text{ ms}^{-1}$$

Horizontal velocity of ball,

$$v_x = 20 \text{ ms}^{-1}$$

$$v_{net} = \sqrt{v_x^2 + v_y^2}$$

$$= 20\sqrt{2} \text{ m/s}$$

Acceleration of the ball will be equal to gravitational acceleration g. i.e. 10 m/s^2

6 (*b*) The motion of object shot in two cases can be depicted as below

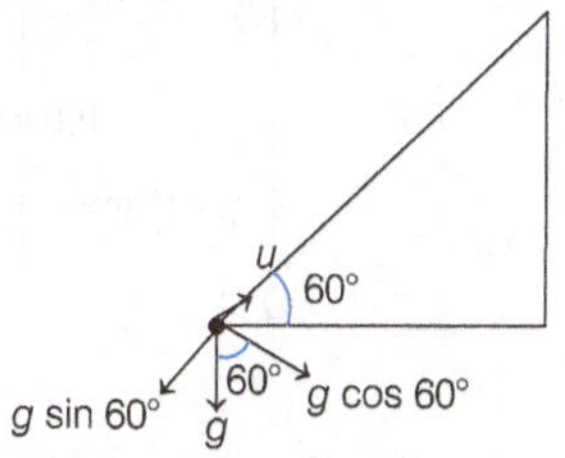

Case I

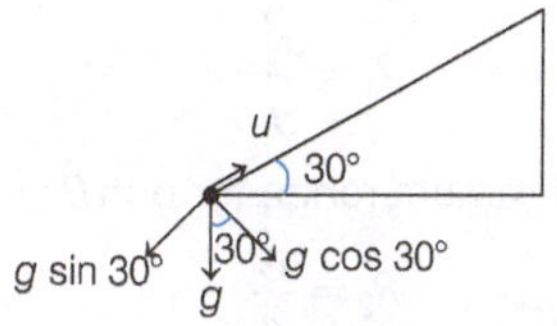

Case II

Using third equation of motion,

$$v^2 = u^2 - 2gh \quad \text{... (i)}$$

As the object stops finally, so

$$v = 0$$

For inclined motion,

$$g = g \sin\theta \text{ and } h = x$$

Substituting these values in Eq. (i), we get

$$\Rightarrow \quad u^2 = 2g \sin\theta \, x$$

$$\Rightarrow \quad x = \frac{u^2}{2g \sin\theta}$$

For case (I), $x_1 = \frac{u^2}{2g \sin 60°}$

For case (II), $x_2 = \frac{u^2}{2g \sin 30°}$

$$\Rightarrow \quad \frac{x_1}{x_2} = \frac{u^2}{2g \sin 60°} \times \frac{2g \sin 30°}{u^2}$$

$$= \frac{1}{2} \times \frac{2}{\sqrt{3}} = \frac{1}{\sqrt{3}} \text{ or } 1 : \sqrt{3}$$

7 (*c*) Given, position vector

$(\mathbf{r}) = (\cos \omega t\hat{\mathbf{x}} + \sin \omega t\hat{\mathbf{y}})$

Velocity is given by $\mathbf{v} = \frac{d\mathbf{r}}{dt}$

$$\Rightarrow \mathbf{v} = (-\omega \sin \omega t\hat{\mathbf{x}} + \omega \cos \omega t\hat{\mathbf{y}})$$

Acceleration is given by $\mathbf{a} = \frac{d\mathbf{v}}{dt}$

$$\Rightarrow \quad \mathbf{a} = (-\omega^2 \cos \omega t\hat{\mathbf{x}} - \omega^2 \sin \omega t\hat{\mathbf{y}})$$

If the dot product of two vectors is zero, that means the vectors are perpendicular to each other.

$$\mathbf{v} \cdot \mathbf{r} = -\omega \sin \omega t \cos \omega t + \omega \sin \omega t$$

$$\cos \omega t = 0$$

$\therefore$ $\mathbf{v}$ is perpendicular to $\mathbf{r}$.

$$\mathbf{a} \cdot \mathbf{r} = -\omega^2 \cos^2 \omega t - \omega^2 \sin^2 \omega t$$

$$= -\omega^2(\cos^2 \omega t + \sin^2 \omega t) = -\omega^2$$

$\therefore$ $\mathbf{v}$ is perpendicular to $\mathbf{r}$ and it indicates that acceleration is towards the origin.

8 (*c*) Centripetal acceleration of a particle moving on a circular path is given by

$$a_c = \frac{v^2}{R}$$

In the given figure,

$$a_c = a \cos 30° = 15 \cos 30° \text{ m/s}^2$$

$$\Rightarrow \frac{v^2}{R} = 15 \cos 30° \Rightarrow v = 5.7 \text{ m/s}$$

9 (*a*) $|\mathbf{P} + \mathbf{Q}| = |\mathbf{P} - \mathbf{Q}|$

Let angle between **P** and **Q** is ϕ.

$$\therefore \quad P^2 + Q^2 + 2PQ \cos \phi = P^2 + Q^2 - 2PQ \cos \phi$$

$$\Rightarrow \quad 4PQ \cos \phi = 0$$

$$\Rightarrow \quad \cos \phi = 0 \quad [\because P, Q \neq 0]$$

$$\Rightarrow \quad \phi = \frac{\pi}{2} = 90°$$

10 (*d*) We have,

$$|\mathbf{A} + \mathbf{B}|^2 = (\mathbf{A} + \mathbf{B}) \cdot (\mathbf{A} + \mathbf{B})$$

$$= |\mathbf{A}|^2 + |\mathbf{B}|^2 + 2|\mathbf{A}||\mathbf{B}| \cos \theta$$

Given, $|\mathbf{A}| = |\mathbf{B}| = R$

So, $|\mathbf{A} + \mathbf{B}|^2 = 2R^2(1 + \cos \theta)$

$$\Rightarrow |\mathbf{A} + \mathbf{B}|^2 = 2R^2 \cdot 2\cos^2\left(\frac{\theta}{2}\right)$$

or, $|\mathbf{A} + \mathbf{B}| = 2R \cos\left(\frac{\theta}{2}\right)$

11 (*d*) Given, projectile range = Maximum height

$$\Rightarrow \quad \frac{u^2 \sin 2\theta}{g} = \frac{u^2 \sin^2 \theta}{2g}$$

$$\Rightarrow \quad \tan \theta = 4$$

$$\Rightarrow \quad \theta = \tan^{-1}(4)$$

12 (*c*) During the projectile motion, horizontal component of velocity does not change.

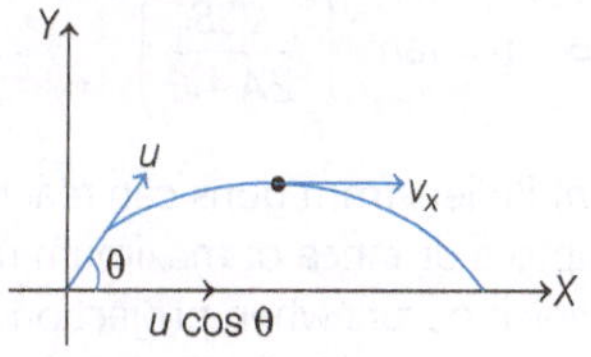

Given that, $v_x = \frac{\sqrt{3}}{2} u$

$$u \cos \theta = \frac{\sqrt{3}}{2} u$$

$\Rightarrow \quad \theta = 30°$

Time of flight,

$$T = \frac{2u \sin 30°}{g}$$

$$\Rightarrow \quad T = \frac{u}{g}$$

13 (*b*) Time period, $T = 4$ s

Body will cover $\frac{3}{4}$th part of circle in 3 s.

The given situation can be drawn as

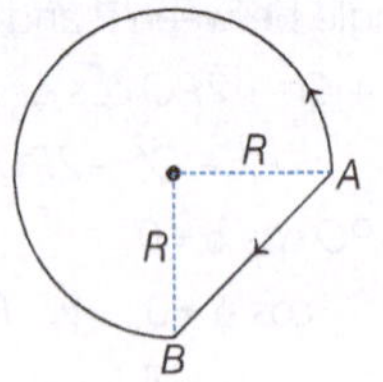

Displacement,

$$AB = \sqrt{R^2 + R^2} = \sqrt{2}R$$

$$= \sqrt{2} \times 10 = 10\sqrt{2} \text{ m}$$

14 (*c*) The angle between **A** and **B**,

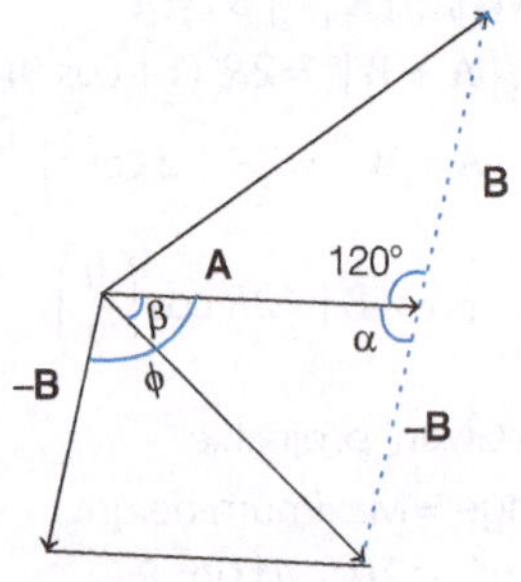

$$\alpha = 180° - 120° = 60°$$

From the figure, $\phi = 120°$

$$\tan\beta = \frac{|-\mathbf{B}| \sin\phi}{|\mathbf{A}| + |-\mathbf{B}| \cos\phi} = \frac{B \sin 120°}{A + B \cos 120°}$$

$$\Rightarrow \quad \beta = \tan^{-1}\left(\frac{\sqrt{3}B}{2A - B}\right)$$

15 (*b*) Bullets from guns can reach upto a distance of maximum range which occurs when projection is made at angle of 45°.

Maximum range for gun *A*,

$$R_1 = \frac{u_1^2}{g}$$

Maximum range for gun *B*,

$$R_2 = \frac{u_2^2}{g}$$

So, ratio of covered areas

$$= \frac{\pi(R_1)^2}{\pi(R_2)^2} = \frac{\pi \cdot u_1^4 / g^2}{\pi \cdot u_2^4 / g^2}$$

$$= \frac{u_1^4}{u_2^4} = 1 : 16$$

Skill Boosters

1 (*a*)

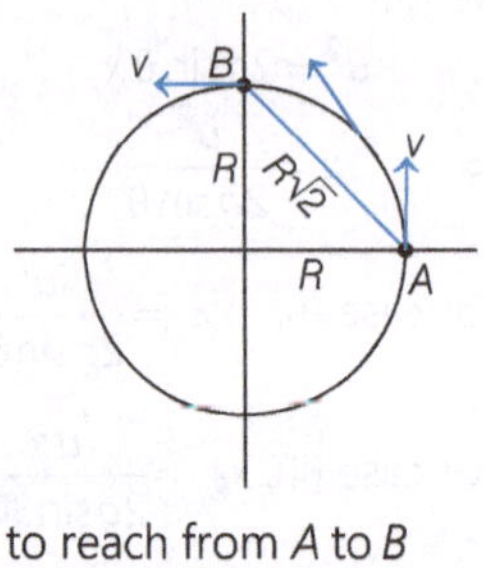

Time to reach from *A* to *B*

$$= \frac{2\pi R}{4} \times \frac{1}{v} = \frac{\pi R}{2v}$$

Displacement from *A* to *B* $= R\sqrt{2}$

Now, average velocity from *A* to *B*

$$= \frac{\text{displacement}}{\text{time}}$$

$$= \frac{R\sqrt{2}}{\frac{\pi R}{2v}} = \frac{R\sqrt{2} \times 2v}{\pi R}$$

$$= \frac{2\sqrt{2}v}{\pi}$$

Instantaneous velocity at *B* is $-v\hat{\mathbf{i}}$

$$\therefore \frac{\text{Instantaneous velocity}}{\text{average velocity}} = \pi : 2\sqrt{2}$$

2 (*b*) Length of arc,

$$= 4.4 \times 9.46 \times 10^{15} \text{ m}$$

$$= 4.1624 \times 10^{16} \text{ m}$$

Speed of body, $v = 8 \text{ AUs}^{-1}$

$$= 1.5 \times 10^{11} \times 8$$

$$= 12 \times 10^{12} \text{ ms}^{-1}$$

$[\because 1 \text{ AU} = 1.5 \times 10^{11}]$

We know that, length of arc subtended by an angle, $l = R\,\theta$

Here, R = radius of arc

Substituting the values in above expression, we get

$$4.1624 \times 10^{16} = R \times 4 \times \left(\frac{1°}{3600}\right) \times \left(\frac{\pi}{180°}\right)$$

$$R = 2.146 \times 10^{21} \text{ m}$$

We know that, time = distance/speed

$$t = \frac{n \times 2\pi R}{v}$$

($\because$ Distance $= n \times$ length of circular path)

Substituting the values in above expression, we get

$$t = \frac{4 \times 2\pi \times 2.146 \times 10^{21}}{1.2 \times 10^{12}}$$

$$= 4.5 \times 10^{10} \text{ s}$$

3 (*a*) The direction of the relative velocity of one with respect to other should be directed towards the relative position of the other particle.

i.e., $\dfrac{\mathbf{r}_1 - \mathbf{r}_2}{|\mathbf{r}_1 - \mathbf{r}_2|} \rightarrow$ direction of relative position of 1 w.r.t. 2.

Similarly, $\dfrac{\mathbf{v}_1 - \mathbf{v}_2}{|\mathbf{v}_1 - \mathbf{v}_2|} \rightarrow$ direction of velocity of 2 w.r.t. 1.

So, for collision of *A* and *B*, we get

$$\frac{\mathbf{r}_1 - \mathbf{r}_2}{|\mathbf{r}_1 - \mathbf{r}_2|} = \frac{\mathbf{v}_2 - \mathbf{v}_1}{|\mathbf{v}_2 - \mathbf{v}_1|}$$

4 (*b*) It is clear from the diagram that the shortest distance between the ships *A* and *B* is *PQ*.

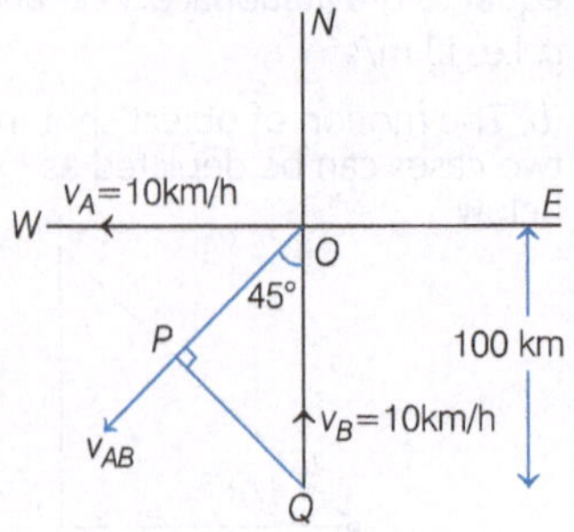

Here, $\sin 45° = \frac{PQ}{OQ}$

$\Rightarrow \quad PQ = 100 \times \frac{1}{\sqrt{2}}$

$= 50\sqrt{2}$ km

Also, $v_{AB} = \sqrt{v_A^2 + v_B^2}$

$= \sqrt{10^2 + 10^2}$

$= 10\sqrt{2}$ km/h

So, time taken for them to reach shortest path.

$$t = \frac{PQ}{v_{AB}} = \frac{50\sqrt{2}}{10\sqrt{2}} = 5 \text{ h}$$

5 (*a*) The equation of trajectory of bullets is

$$y = x\tan\theta - \frac{\frac{1}{2}gx^2}{u^2}(1+\tan^2\theta) \quad ...(i)$$

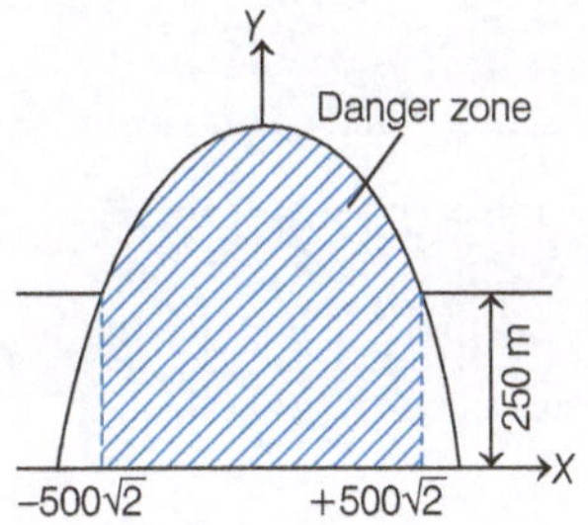

For a given value of x, maximum y can be determined from

$$\frac{dy}{d(\tan\theta)} = x - \frac{\frac{1}{2}gx^2}{u^2}(2\tan\theta) = 0$$

or $\tan\theta = \frac{u^2}{gx}$

On substituting the expression for $\tan\theta$ in eq. (i), we get

$$y_{\text{max.}} = x\frac{u^2}{gx} - \frac{\frac{1}{2}gx^2}{u^2}\left[1 + \frac{u^4}{g^2x^2}\right]$$

$$y_{\text{max.}} = \frac{u^2}{2g} - \frac{\frac{1}{2}gx^2}{u^2}$$

The shell can hit an area defined by

$$y \le \frac{u^2}{2g} = \frac{\frac{1}{2}gx^2}{u^2}$$

On substituting numerical values, $y = 250$ m, $u = 100$ m/s $g = 10$ m / s^2, we get

$$\frac{x^2}{2000} \le 250$$

or $-500\sqrt{2} \le x \le 500\sqrt{2}$

The drone can travel $1000\sqrt{2}$ m while it can be hit, so it is in danger for a period of

$$\frac{1000\sqrt{2}}{500} = 2\sqrt{2}\text{ s}$$

6 (*a*) For second ball, $T = \frac{2u\sin\beta}{g}$

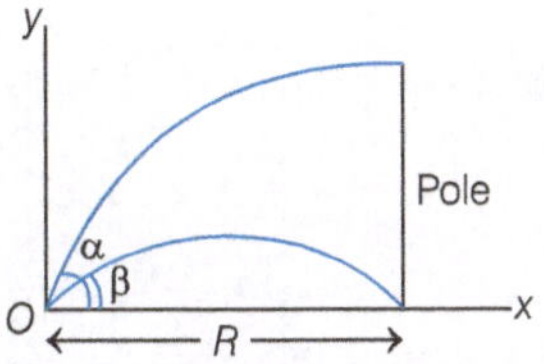

and $\quad R = \frac{u^2\sin 2\beta}{g}$

For first ball, $R = (u\cos\alpha)T$

Substituting the value of T, we have

$$\Rightarrow \frac{u^2\sin 2\beta}{g} = u\cos\alpha \times \frac{2u\sin\beta}{g}$$

$$\Rightarrow \frac{2u^2\sin\beta\cos\beta}{g} = \frac{u\cos\alpha \times 2u\sin\beta}{g}$$

$$\therefore \quad \frac{\cos\alpha}{\cos\beta} = 1$$

7 (*a*) In figure, points A, B and C are lying on the trajectory of the path of the ball. The equation of trajectory is

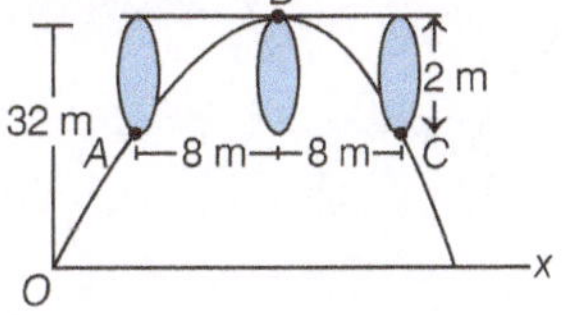

$$y = x\tan\alpha - \frac{gx^2}{2u^2\cos^2\alpha}$$

For point A,

$$32 - 2 = x\tan\alpha - \frac{5x^2}{u^2\cos^2\alpha}$$

$$\text{or } 30 = x\tan\alpha - \frac{5}{u^2}x^2(1+\tan^2\alpha) \quad ...(i)$$

For point B,

$$32 = (x+8)\tan\alpha - \frac{5}{u^2}(x+8)^2(1+\tan^2\alpha) \quad ...(ii)$$

For point C,

$$32 - 2 = (x+16)\tan\alpha - \frac{5(x+16)^2}{u^2}(1+\tan^2\alpha)$$

$$\Rightarrow 30 = (x+16)\tan\alpha - \frac{5(x+16)^2(1+\tan^2\alpha)}{u^2} \quad ...(iii)$$

Subtracting Eq. (i) from Eq. (ii),

$$2 = 8\tan\alpha - \frac{5}{u^2}(1+\tan^2\alpha)(x^2+16x+64-x^2)$$

$$\Rightarrow 2 = 8\tan\alpha - \frac{5}{u^2}(1+\tan^2\alpha)(16x+64) \quad ...(iv)$$

Subtracting Eq. (i), from Eq. (iii), we get

$$0 = 16\tan\alpha - \frac{5(1+\tan^2\alpha)}{u^2}(x^2+32x+256-x^2) \quad ...(v)$$

From Eqs. (iv) and (v), we get

$$\tan^2\alpha = \frac{32\times 2}{64} = 1$$

$\therefore \quad \tan\alpha = 1$

8 (*b*) Here, $x = (v_0\cos\alpha)t$

$$y = (v_0\sin\alpha)t - \frac{1}{2}gt^2$$

$$\therefore \quad y + \frac{1}{2}gt^2 = (v_0\sin\alpha)t$$

and $\quad x = (v_0\cos\alpha)t$

$$\Rightarrow v_0^2t^2 = \left(y + \frac{1}{2}gt^2\right)^2 + x^2$$

Thus, for a given values of t_1, the particles lie on circle (on sphere in three dimension).

9 (*b*) The equation of trajectory is

$$y = x\tan\alpha - \frac{gx^2}{2u^2\cos^2\alpha}$$

$\because$ y is maximum

$$\therefore \quad \frac{dy}{d\alpha} = 0$$

$$\therefore 0 = x\sec^2\alpha - \frac{gx^2}{2u^2}$$

2 sec α sec α, tan α

or $\frac{gx}{u^2}\tan\alpha = 1$ or

$$\tan\alpha = \frac{u^2}{gx} = \frac{900}{10\times 45} = 2$$

$$\therefore y = 45\times 2 - \frac{10\times 45\times 45}{2\times 900}(1+4)$$

$$= 33.75 \text{ m}$$

$$= 3375\times 10^{-2} \text{ m}$$

$$\therefore n = 2$$

10 (*d*) Angle covered by each particle in time duration 0 to $\frac{\pi}{2\omega}$ is

$$\theta = \omega\times t = \omega\times\frac{\pi}{2\omega} = \frac{\pi}{2} \text{ rad}$$

So, positions of particles at $t = \frac{\pi}{2\omega}$ is as shown below;

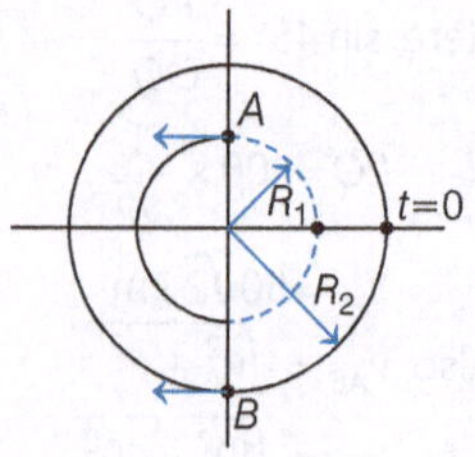

Velocities of particles at $t = \frac{\pi}{2\omega}$ are

$$\mathbf{v}_A = -\omega R_1\hat{\mathbf{i}}, \ \mathbf{v}_B = -\omega R_2\hat{\mathbf{i}}$$

$\therefore$ Velocity of A with respect to B,

$$\mathbf{v}_{AB} = \mathbf{v}_A - \mathbf{v}_B$$

$$= \omega R_1\hat{\mathbf{i}} - (-\omega R_2\hat{\mathbf{i}})$$

$$= \omega(R_2 - R_1)\hat{\mathbf{i}}$$

04

Scan for **Physics Through Concept Master** *Videos*

Laws of Motion

Topicwise No. of Ques asked in 5 Years (NEET)

Topics	2024	2023	2022	2021	2020
Aristotle's Fallacy	–	–	–	–	–
Newton's First Law of Motion	–	–	–	–	–
Newton's Second Law of Motion	–	–	–	–	1
Newton's Third Law of Motion	–	–	–	–	–
Conservation of Momentum	–	–	–	1	–
Equilibrium of a Particle	–	–	–	–	–
Common Forces in Mechanics	1	2	–	–	1
Circular Motion	1	–	–	–	–

(No. of Questions)

Special Type of Ques Asked In 5 Years (NEET)

Types	2024	2023	2022	2021	2020
A-R	–	–	–	–	–
Statement Based	–	–	–	–	–
Matching	–	–	–	–	–

(Years)

Last 5 Years Weigtage (NEET)

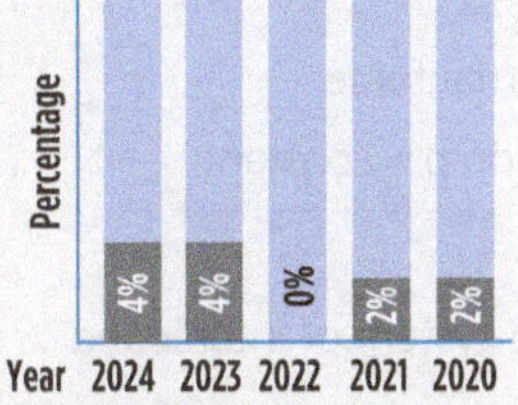

A force is required to put a stationary body in motion or to stop a moving body. An external agency is needed to provide this force. This agency may or may not be in contact with the body.

Aristotle's Fallacy

- Aristotelian law of motion is flawed, and it may be concluded as, An external force is required to keep a body in motion.
- The opposing forces such as friction (in solids) and viscous force (in fluids) are always present in the natural world, so external forces are required to keep bodies in uniform motion.

Law of Inertia

Inertia is the property of an object by virtue of which it cannot change its state of rest or motion or direction of motion in the absence of external force. Inertia means **resistance to change**.

Newton's First Law

- It states that, every body continues to be in its state of rest or of uniform motion in a straight line unless compelled by some external force to act otherwise. It is also known as **Galileo's law of inertia**.
- Inertia is directly proportional to the mass of the body. i.e. Heavier the body, greater is the force required to change its state and hence greater is inertia.
- It can be simply expressed as, if the net external force on a body is zero, its acceleration is zero and acceleration can be non-zero only, if there is a net external force on the body. NEET 2019

Newton's Second Law

- The second law of motion refers to the general situation when there is a net external force acting on the body.

Momentum

- Momentum of a body is defined as the product of its mass m and velocity $\mathbf{v}$ and is denoted by $\mathbf{p}$.

$$\mathbf{p} = m\mathbf{v}$$

It is a vector quantity.

- Greater is the change in momentum in a given time, the greater is the force that needs to be applied.
- The same force for the same time causes the same change in momentum for different bodies.
- **Newton's second law of motion** states that, the rate of change of momentum of a body is directly proportional to the applied force and takes place in the direction in which the force acts.

  Thus, $F = \frac{d\mathbf{p}}{dt} = ma$
- Some important points about second law are given below
  (i) In the second law, $\mathbf{F} = 0$ implies $\mathbf{a} = 0$. The second law is obviously consistent with the first law.
  (ii) The second law of motion is a vector law. It is equivalent to three equations, one for each component of the vectors.
  $$F_x = \frac{dp_x}{dt} = ma_x,\ F_y = \frac{dp_y}{dt} = ma_y,\ F_z = \frac{dp_z}{dt} = ma_z$$
  (iii) If a force is not parallel to the velocity of the body, but makes some angle with it, then force changes only the component of velocity along the direction of force. The component of velocity normal to the force remains unchanged.
  (iv) The acceleration of an object is proportional to the net force $\mathbf{F}_{net}$ on the object and inversely proportional to the mass m of the object.
  $$a \propto F_{net} \text{ and } a \propto \frac{1}{m}$$
  $$F_{net} = ma$$
  (v) More fundamental relationship,
  $$F_{net} = \frac{d(mv)}{dt} = m\frac{dv}{dt} + v\frac{dm}{dt}$$
  (vi) The second law of motion is a local relation which means acceleration at an instant does not depend on the history of motion.
- **Impulsive force** is a large force which acts on a body for a very short interval of time and produces a finite change in its linear momentum.
- **Impulse** of a force is equal to the product of average force and the time interval for which it acts.

  Impulse $= F_{av} \times t =$ change in linear momentum. NEET 2021
- Force acting for short time dt, then impulse $= \mathbf{F} \cdot dt$
- Impulse = Area under F versus t curve

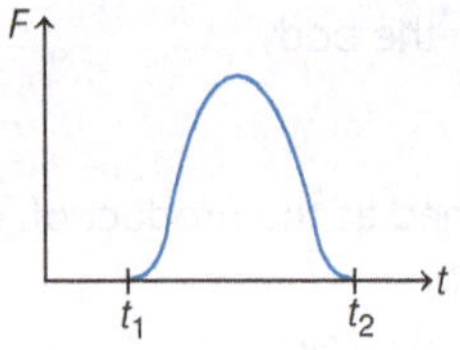

- If force acting for a finite interval of time, then impulse $= \int_{t_1}^{t_2} \mathbf{F} \cdot dt$
- If a constant force acts for an interval Δt, then impulse $= \mathbf{F}\Delta t$.
- **Impulse-momentum theorem** It states that impulse of a force is equal to the change in momentum.

Marks Maximiser

Pseudo Force

- When the motion of a body is observed from a non-inertial frame, then to apply Newton's second law, we have to apply an imaginary force opposite to the direction of acceleration of non-inertial frame known as pseudo force.
- A body of mass m is placed in a lift (non-inertial frame) moving upward with acceleration a, the pseudo force on the body is shown in the figure here.

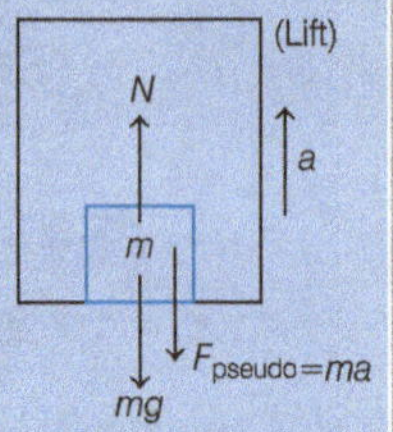

  The normal reaction on the body is
  $N = mg + F_{pseudo} = mg + ma = m(g + a)$

Newton's Third Law

- It states that, to every action, there is always an equal and opposite reaction.
- Forces always occur in pairs. Force on a body A by B is equal and opposite to the force on the body B by A.

  i.e. (Force on A by B) $\mathbf{F}_{AB} = -\mathbf{F}_{BA}$ (Force on B by A)

  If you are considering the system of two bodies as a whole, then $\mathbf{F}_{AB}$ and $\mathbf{F}_{BA}$ are internal forces of the system $(A + B)$.
- There is no cause-effect relation implied in the third law. The force on A by B and the force on B by A act at the same instant.
- Action and reaction forces act on different bodies not on the same body. This law is applicable whether the bodies are at rest or in motion.
- Single isolated force is not possible, force is always possible in action-reaction pair form.

Conservation of Momentum

- According to this law, **total linear momentum of a system of particles remains constant or conserved in the absence of any external force.**

  For an isolated system with no external force,

  i.e. $\mathbf{F} = 0$ or $\frac{d\mathbf{p}}{dt} = 0$ or $\mathbf{p} =$ constant

  or $\mathbf{p}_1 + \mathbf{p}_2 + \ldots + \mathbf{p}_n =$ constant
- The total momentum of an isolated system of interacting particles is conserved. NEET 2019

- If two bodies A and B have initial momenta $\mathbf{p}_A$ and $\mathbf{p}_B$, and after collision their final momenta are $\mathbf{p}'_A$ and $\mathbf{p}'_B$, then according to conservation law of linear momentum,

$$\mathbf{p}'_A + \mathbf{p}'_B = \mathbf{p}_A + \mathbf{p}_B$$

Note **Applications of conservation of linear momentum** If a machine gun fires N bullets each of mass m and velocity v in time interval t, the force needed to hold the gun steady,

$$F = \frac{Nmv}{t}$$

Equilibrium of a Particle

- Equilibrium of a particle in mechanics refers to the situation when the net external force on the particle is zero.
- Equilibrium condition can be attained, if the two forces acting on a particle are equal and opposite to each other.
  i.e. $\mathbf{F}_1 = -\mathbf{F}_2$

Concurrent Forces

- Forces acting together on a body at the same point are called concurrent forces.
- A number of concurrent forces acting on a body are said to be in equilibrium, if the resultant of these forces is zero or if the concurrent forces can be represented completely by the sides of a closed polygon taken in the same order. Mathematically,

$$\mathbf{F}_1 + \mathbf{F}_2 + \mathbf{F}_3 + \ldots + \mathbf{F}_n = 0$$ NEET 2019

- In other words, the resultant of any two forces says $\mathbf{F}_1$ and $\mathbf{F}_2$ obtained by parallelogram law of forces must be equal and opposite to the third force $\mathbf{F}_3$ as shown in figure below.

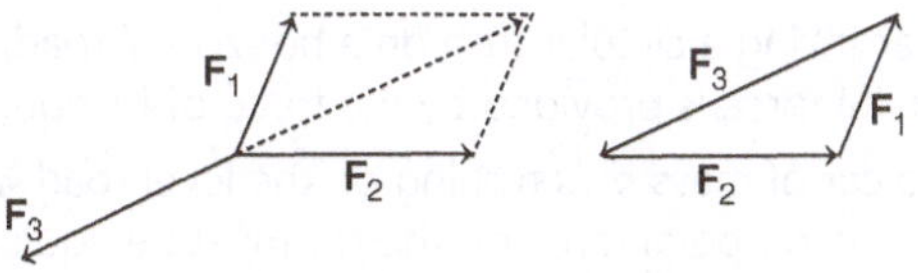

Equilibrium of concurrent forces

Lami's theorem

According to this theorem, when three concurrent forces $\mathbf{F}_1$, $\mathbf{F}_2$ and $\mathbf{F}_3$ acting on a body are in equilibrium as shown in figure alongside, then

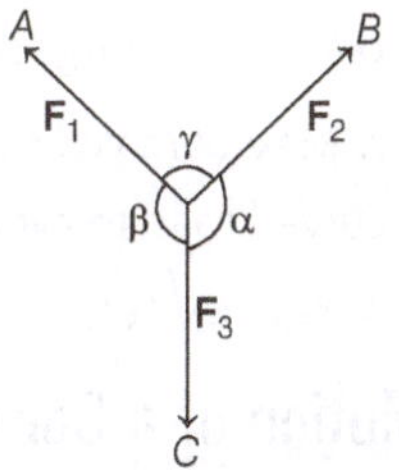

$$\frac{F_1}{\sin\alpha} = \frac{F_2}{\sin\beta} = \frac{F_3}{\sin\gamma}$$

where, α = angle between $\mathbf{F}_2$ and $\mathbf{F}_3$,

β = angle between $\mathbf{F}_3$ and $\mathbf{F}_1$

and γ = angle between $\mathbf{F}_1$ and $\mathbf{F}_2$.

Common Forces in Mechanics

- In mechanics, common forces except gravitational force are **contact forces**. Some of the common forces are **friction**, **normal reaction**, **buoyant force**, **spring force**, etc.
- When bodies are in contact (i.e. book resting on a table, a system of rigid bodies connected by rods, hinges and other type of supports), there are mutual contact forces (for each pair of bodies) satisfying the third law.
- Contact forces also arise, when solids are in contact with fluids.
- When a spring is compressed or extented by an external force, a restoring force is generated. The restoring force in the spring is called **tension**. Tension is usually proportional to compression or elongation (for small displacements).
- The **spring force** F is written as $F = -kx$, where x is the displacement and k is the force constant.

Marks Maximiser

Rules for tension in a string

- Direction of tension in a string always along the string and away from the object.
- In an ideal string, tension at all points of the string will be same.
- Tension can be extensional or compressional as shown.

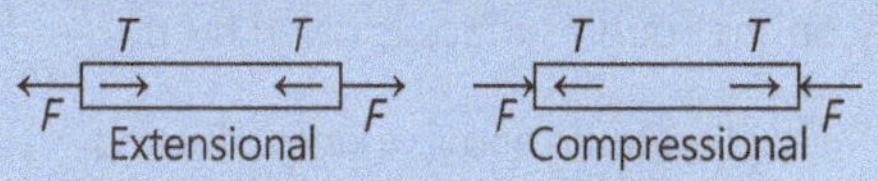

- Tension is extensional in string and chain.
- Tension can be extensional or compressional in a rod.

Friction

- It is opposing force that is set-up between the surface of contact when one body slides or rolls or tends to do so on the surface of another body. NEET 2023
- The component of contact force normal to the surfaces in contact is called **normal reaction**. The component parallel to the surfaces in contact is called **friction**.
- **Static Friction** Force of friction which comes into play between two bodies before one body has not actually starts moving over the other is called static friction and it is denoted by f_s.
- The limiting value of static friction $f_{s\,(\max)}$ is independent of the area of contact and varies with normal force N approximately as $f_{s\,(\max)} = \mu_s N$ NEET 2023
- Static friction opposes impending motion. Impending motion means the motion that would take place (but does not actually take place) under the applied force, if friction were absent.

- **Limiting Friction** The magnitude of the force of limiting friction (f) between any two bodies in contacts is directly proportional to the normal reaction (N) between them. i.e. $f \propto N$.
- Limiting friction between any two bodies in contact depends on the nature of material of the surfaces in contact and their roughness and smoothness.
- Limiting friction is independent of the apparent contact area, so long as normal reaction between two bodies in contact remains constant.
- **Kinetic Friction** Frictional force that opposes relative motion between surfaces in contact is called kinetic or sliding friction and is given by $f_k = \mu_k N$ where, μ_k = coefficient of kinetic friction.
- Coefficient of kinetic friction μ_s is always less than coefficient of static friction μ_k.
- **Variation of friction force with applied force** is shown in the graph below

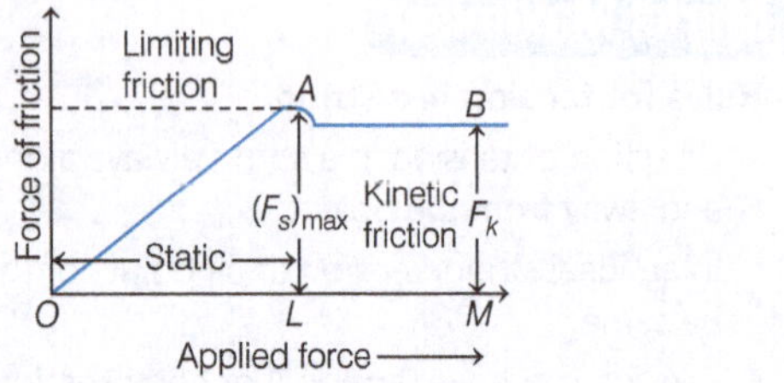

- When the relative motion has begun, the acceleration of the body on the rough surface is given by $a = \dfrac{F - f_k}{m}$

  where, F = applied force and f_k = kinetic friction.
- If a body is moving on a rough surface with constant velocity, then $F = f_k$ and if the applied force on the body is removed, then its acceleration is $\dfrac{-f_k}{m}$ and it eventually comes to stop.
- **Angle of Friction** The angle between the resultant of limiting friction f and normal reaction N with the direction of N is called angle of friction λ.

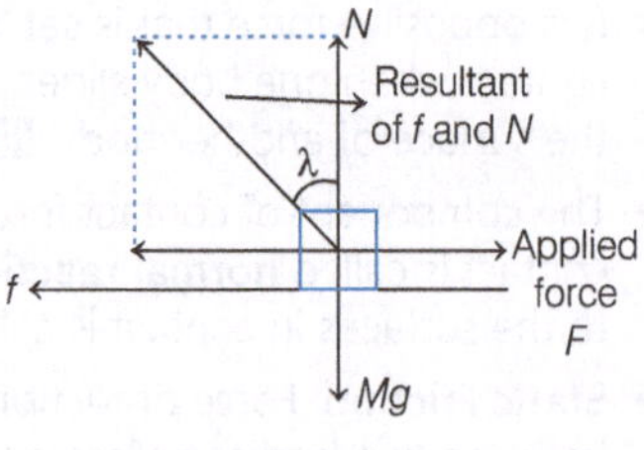

$$\therefore \quad \tan\lambda = \frac{f}{N} = \mu$$

or $\lambda = \tan^{-1}\mu$

- **Angle of Repose** The minimum angle of inclination of a plane with the horizontal, such that the body placed on the plane just starts to slide down is known as angle of repose θ.

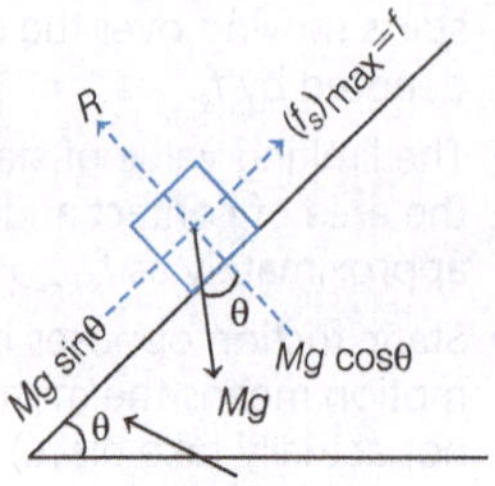

Angle of repose

$f = Mg\sin\theta$

and $N = Mg\cos\theta$

$$\mu = \frac{f}{N} = \tan\theta = \frac{Mg\sin\theta}{Mg\cos\theta} \Rightarrow \theta = \tan^{-1}\mu$$

- Angle of friction (λ) = Angle of repose (θ)
- In many situations, like in a machine with different moving parts, friction does have a negative role.
- **Rolling Friction** Friction which comes into play when a body like a ring or a sphere rolls without slipping over a horizontal surface is known as rolling friction.
- In rolling motion, the surfaces get momentarily deformed a little and this result in a finite area (not a point) of the body being in contact with the surface. The net effect is that the component of the contact force parallel to the surface opposes motion.
- The static and kinetic friction is much greater (even by 2 or 3 orders of magnitude) than the rolling friction.
- Ball bearings are used between two moving parts of a machine to reduce friction.

Circular Motion

- **Centripetal Force** When an object moves on a circular path, a force acts on it, whose direction is towards the centre of the path, this force is called centripetal force. Centripetal force acting on a particle of mass m on a circular path of radius r is given by $F = \dfrac{mv^2}{r}$ **NEET 2019**
- For a stone rotated in a circle by a string, the centripetal force is provided by the tension in the string.

Motion of a Car on Level Road

- For a car taking a circular turn on a horizontal road, the centripetal force is provided by the force of friction.
- When a car of mass m is turning on the level road without skidding, centripetal force on the car must be equal or less than static friction.

i.e. $\mu_s mg \geq \dfrac{mv_{max}^2}{r}$

[μ = coefficient of friction]

or $v_{max} \leq \sqrt{\mu_s \cdot rg}$

$\therefore$ Maximum velocity on a curved road to avoid skidding is $v_{max} = \sqrt{\mu_s rg}$.

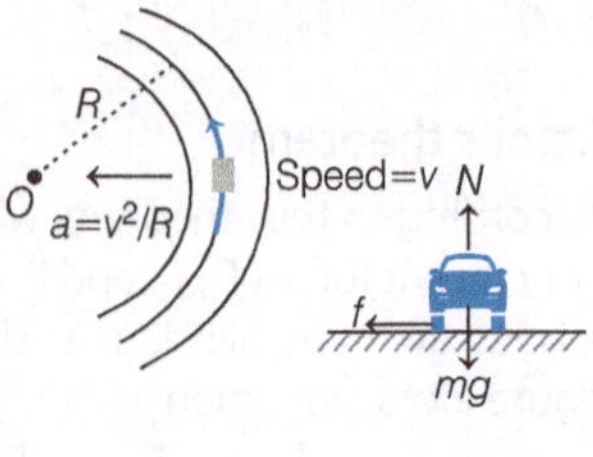

Motion of a Car on Banked Road

- The contribution of the friction to the circular motion of a car (while taking a turn) can be reduced, if road is banked.

- Component of friction force ($f \cos\theta$) and component of normal reaction ($N \sin\theta$) provide required centripetal force for safe turning.

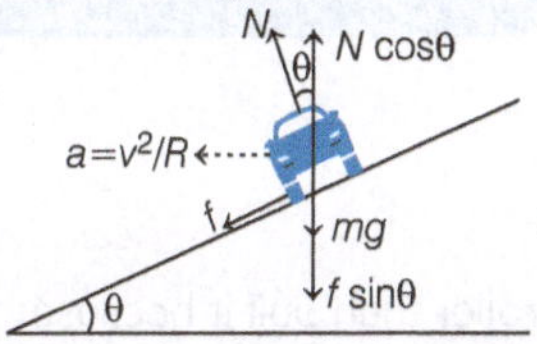

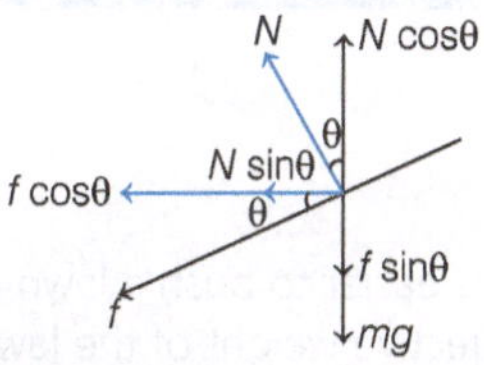

- Maximum velocity of a car on banked road is given by

$$v_{max} = \sqrt{rg\left[\frac{\mu_s + \tan\theta}{1-\mu_s \tan\theta}\right]}$$

where, θ = inclination of road and r = radius of turn.

If $\mu_s = 0$, then $v_{max} = \sqrt{rg \tan\theta}$.

Bending of Cyclist

- A cyclist obtain the necessary centripetal force while taking the turn by bending himself along the turn.
- Here, the component of normal reaction $N \sin\theta$ provide central force (centripetal force).

$$N \sin\theta = \frac{mv^2}{r}, \quad N \cos\theta = mg$$

Maximum speed of cyclist, $v = \sqrt{rg \tan\theta}$

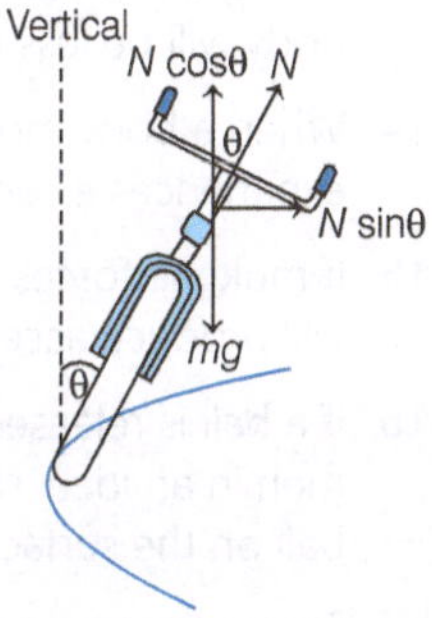

Solving Problems in Mechanics

To solve a typical problem in mechanics, we use the following steps

***Step* 1** Draw a diagram showing schematically the various parts of the assembly of bodies, the links, supports, etc.

***Step* 2** Choose a convenient part of the assembly as one system.

***Step* 3** Draw a separate diagram which shows this system and all the forces on the system by the remaining part of the assembly. Also, include the forces on the system by other agencies. A diagram of this type is known as **free body diagram.**

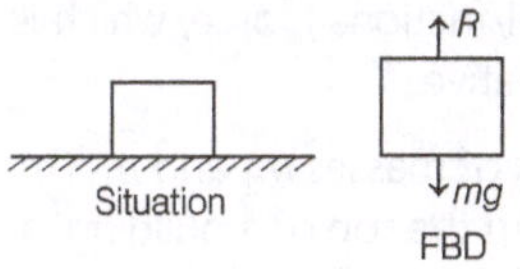

***Step* 4** In free body diagram, mark the magnitude and direction of the forces that are either given or you are sure of. The rest should be treated as unknowns. These will be determined using laws of motion.

***Step* 5** If necessary, we can follow the same procedure for any other part of the system. The equations of laws of motion obtain for different parts of the system can be solved to obtain the desired results.

Caution Points

- Force can have different directions relative to motion but is always parallel to acceleration.
- A body being momentarily at rest ($v = 0$) doesn't mean force or acceleration are necessarily zero.
- Force acting on a body depends on its current situation, not its past motion. Its not carried from earlier motion.
- The second law of motion applies equally to inanimate and animate objects, both require external forces for acceleration. For instance, walking depends on the frictional force.

PYQ Notes

1. For a given pulley-block system as shown in figure alongside, the relation between accelerations a_1 and a_2 of blocks m_1 and m_2 is given by **[JEE Main 2022]**

   Constraint relation, $\Sigma \mathbf{T} \cdot \mathbf{a} = 0$

   $\Rightarrow Ta_1 - 2Ta_2 = 0 \therefore a_1 = 2a_2$

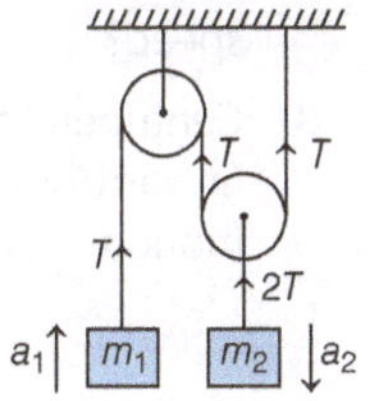

2. For a pulley system, the acceleration of the masses in the system is given by

$$a = \frac{(m_2 - m_1)}{m_1 + m_2} g$$

   and tension $T_1 = \left(\frac{2m_1m_2}{m_1+m_2}\right) g$ **[NEET 2020]**

   For Concept Master Video

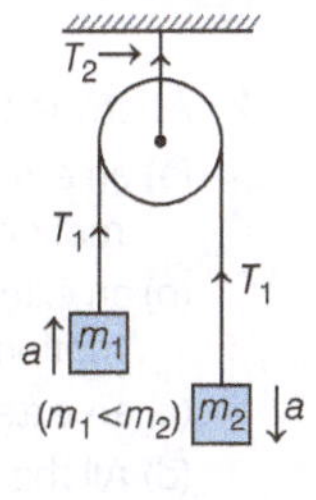

3. A body of mass m is placed on an inclined plane of inclination θ. A force F is acted on the body at an angle α with the plane of inclination as shown in figure. If the coefficient of friction between body and plane of contact is μ, then the minimum value of force F_{min} required to pull the body is given by **[NEET 2018]**

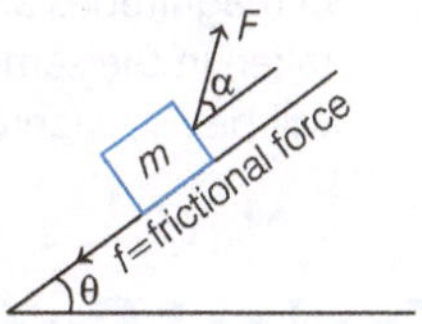

$$F_{min} = \frac{mg(\sin\theta + \mu\cos\theta)}{\sqrt{1+\mu^2}}, \text{ where } \mu = \tan\alpha$$

   For horizontal plane surface, $\theta = 0°$

$$\therefore \quad F_{min} = \frac{\mu mg}{\sqrt{1+\mu^2}}$$

4. Tension in the string moving in circular motion when a small mass is tied at one end is given by $T = m\omega^2 l$ where, ω = angular velocity and l = length of the string. **[NEET 2017]**

Step by Step

Mastering NCERT

- Concept Builders
- Topical Questions
- Assertion and Reason Questions
- Statement Based
- Matching Type
- Numerical Type
- NCERT Exemplar
- Past Exams MCQs
- Skill Boosters

Concept Builders

1 Inertial frame of reference is also called unaccelerated frame of reference. [T/F]

2 Acceleration can be zero only, if there is a net external force on the body. [T/F]

3 An object in motion generally experience .... (gravitational/frictional) force, which is non-conservative.

4 If two stones of masses m_1 and m_2 $(m_1 > m_2)$, are dropped from the top of a building, a person on the ground will find it easier to catch the light stone than heavy stone. [T/F]

5 A seasoned cricketer held out his hands during a catch, allowing lesser time for the ball to stop and hence requires a smaller force. [T/F]

6 The greater change in the momentum in a given time, the .... (lesser/greater) is the force needed to be applied.

7 Vehicle stops on applying brakes. This phenomenon violates the principle of conservation of momentum. [T/F]

8 Law of conservation of linear momentum is independent of frame of reference, though linear momentum depends on frame of reference. [T/F]

9 Three forces start acting simultaneously on a particle moving with a velocity **v**. These forces are represented in magnitudes and direction by three sides of triangle taken in the same order. The net force on the particle will be .... (zero/ $3F$).

10 It is easier to push a lawn roller than pull it because effective weight of the lawn roller, while pushing is less than that while pulling. [T/F]

11 Kinetic friction is inversely proportional to the velocity of the body. [T/F]

12 What happens to coefficient of friction, when weight of body is doubled?

13 Two bodies are moving down on a slanted road, one by rolling and another by sliding. The friction on the rolling body will be less than the sliding body . [T/F]

14 When a body moves in a circular path, which thing experiences a centrifugal force?

15 If multiple forces are acting on a body, then all the forces will produce acceleration in the body. [T/F]

16 If a ball is released from rest on smooth inclined plane, then in an ideal situation, the distance travelled by the ball on the surface will be .... (finite/infinite).

17 For uniform circular motion, the direction of centripetal force depends on the sense of rotation. [T/F]

18 In accordance with Newton's third law, the seat will press the child .... (inward/outward), providing necessary centripetal force.

19 If a force is acting on a moving body perpendicular to the direction of motion, then what will be the effect on the speed?

20 Centripetal force is a force that provides radial .... (inward/outward) acceleration to a body in circular motion.

Topical Questions

Aristotle's Fallacy

1 What was the flaw in Aristotle's law of motion? **NCERT Pg. 50**

(a) He assumed that energy is conserved
(b) He assumed that momentum is conserved
(c) He assumed that motion cannot be negative
(d) He did not take into account of friction

2 Aristotle's law of motion may be phrased as **NCERT Pg. 50**

(a) an external force is required to keep a body in uniform motion
(b) an external force is not required to keep a body in uniform motion
(c) an external force is a force which occur themselves
(d) All the above are not related to Aristotle's law of motion

3 An arrow shot from a bow keeps flying since the air behind the arrow keeps pushing it. This idea of framework is developed by NCERT Pg. 50

(a) Aristotle (b) Newton
(c) Galileo (d) Kepler

Newton's First Law of Motion

4 According to Galileo's experiment for a double inclined plane that are smooth, when a ball is released from rest on one of the planes rolls down and climb up the other of decreased slope, the final height of the ball is NCERT Pg. 50

(a) less than the initial height
(b) more than the initial height
(c) equal to the initial height
(d) more or less than the initial height

5 Inertia is that property of a body by virtue of which the body is NCERT Pg. 51

(a) unable to change by itself the state of rest
(b) unable to change by itself the state of uniform motion
(c) unable to change by itself the direction of motion
(d) unable to change by itself the state of rest or of uniform motion

6 If no external force acts on a particle, then which of the following statement is incorrect about particle? NCERT Pg. 51

(a) Particle may be at rest.
(b) Particle moves with uniform velocity on linear path.
(c) Particle moves with uniform speed on circle.
(d) None of the above

7 A passenger getting down from a moving bus, falls in the direction of the motion of bus. This is an example of NCERT Pg. 52

(a) second law of motion
(b) third law of motion
(c) inertia of rest
(d) inertia of motion

8 A portion of a meteor moving at a constant rate of 50 kmh^{-1} gets separated from its surface, when it enter earth's atmosphere. Find the velocity of the portion of meteor at the instant after it gets separated. NCERT Pg. 52

(a) 100 kmh^{-1} (b) 50 kmh^{-1}
(c) 0 kmh^{-1} (d) 200 kmh^{-1}

9 When a car is stationary, there is no net force acting on it. During pick-up, it accelerates. This happens due to NCERT Pg. 52

(a) net external force
(b) net internal force
(c) may be external or internal force
(d) None of the above

10 If a running bus stops suddenly, our feet stop due to friction, but the rest of the body continues to move forward due to NCERT Pg. 52

(a) momentum (b) force
(c) inertia (d) impulse

11 Neglect the effect of rotation of earth, suppose the earth suddenly stops attracting objects placed near surface. A person standing on the surface of the earth will NCERT Pg. 52

(a) remain standing (b) fly up
(c) sink into earth (d) Either (b) or (c)

12 An astronaut accidentally gets separated out of his small spaceship accelerating in interstellar space at a constant rate of 100 ms^{-2}. What is the acceleration of the astronaut, the instant after he is outside the spaceship? (Assume that there are no nearby stars to exert gravitational force on him) NCERT Pg. 52

(a) 0 (b) 1
(c) ∞ (d) Data insufficient

Newton's Second Law of Motion

13 A smaller and a bigger iron ball are dropped from a small height on a glass pane placed on a table. Only bigger ball breaks the glass pane, because NCERT Pg. 53

(a) bigger ball transfers greater momentum than smaller
(b) bigger ball transfers lesser momentum than smaller
(c) bigger ball transfer equal momentum as smaller
(d) None of the above

14 When a stone is rotated with uniform speed in horizontal plane by means of a string, the magnitude of the momentum is fixed but its direction changes. A force is needed to cause this change in momentum vector. This force is provided by NCERT Pg. 54

(a) gravity
(b) our hand through the string
(c) Both gravity and our hand through the string
(d) None of the above

15 A rocket is going upwards with accelerated motion. A man sitting in it feels his weight increased 5 times his own weight. If the mass of the rocket including that of the man is 1.0×10^4 kg, how much force is being applied by rocket engine? (Take, $g = 10 ms^{-2}$) NCERT Pg. 54

(a) $5 \times 10^4 N$ (b) $5 \times 10^5 N$
(c) $5 \times 10^8 N$ (d) $2 \times 10^4 N$

16 A particle of mass m is moving in a straight line with momentum p. Starting at time $t = 0$, a force $F = kt$ acts in the same direction on the moving particle during time interval T, so that its momentum changes from p to $3p$. Here, k is a constant. The value of T is **NCERT Pg. 54**

(a) $\sqrt{\frac{2p}{k}}$ (b) $2\sqrt{\frac{p}{k}}$ (c) $\sqrt{\frac{2k}{p}}$ (d) $2\sqrt{\frac{k}{p}}$

17 A force of 10 N acts on a body of mass 0.5 kg for 0.25s starting from rest. What is its momentum now? **NCERT Pg. 54**

(a) 0.25 N-s (b) 2.5 N-s
(c) 0.5 N-s (d) 0.75 N-s

18 A machine gun fires a bullet of mass 40 g with a velocity of 1200 ms^{-1}. The man holding it can exert a maximum force of 144 N on the gun. How many bullets can be fired per second at the most? **NCERT Pg. 54**

(a) Only one
(b) Three
(c) Can fire any number of bullets
(d) 144×48

19 When a ball of mass 0.1 kg hits the ground from the height of 20m and bounce back to the same height, then find out the force exerted on the ball, if the time of impact is 0.04 s. (Take, $g = 10$ m/s^2) **NCERT Pg. 54**

(a) 100 N (b) 200 N
(c) 300 N (c) 1000 N

20 A body of mass 4 kg is at rest. If a force $F = (4t^2\hat{i} + 2t\,\hat{j})$ N is applied on the object, then the velocity (in m/s) of the object at $t = 3$ s is **NCERT Pg. 54**

(a) $9\hat{i} + 4\hat{j}$ (b) $4\hat{i} + 9\hat{j}$
(c) $9\hat{i} + 2.25\hat{j}$ (d) $9\hat{i} + \hat{j}$

21 The force F acting on a particle of mass m is indicated by the force-time graph shown below. The change in momentum of the particle over the time interval from 0 to 8s is **NCERT Pg. 54**

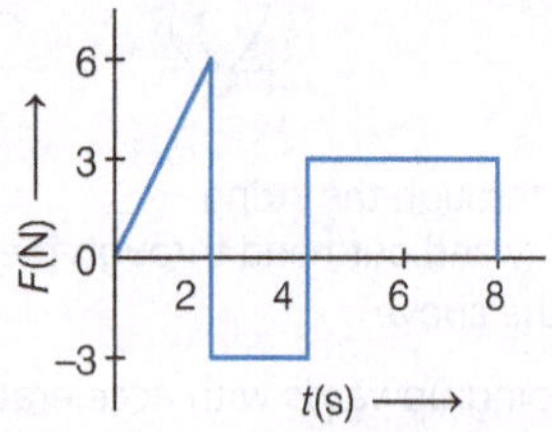

(a) 24 N-s (b) 20 N-s
(c) 12 N-s (d) 6 N-s

22 A rocket of initial mass 8000 kg ejects gases at a constant rate of 12 kg s^{-1} with constant relative speed of 11 km s^{-1}. What is the acceleration of the rocket, one minute after the blast ? **NCERT Pg. 54**

(a) 25 m s^{-2} (b) 50 m s^{-2}
(c) 18 m s^{-2} (d) 35 m s^{-2}

23 A body of mass 1 kg starting from origin with initial velocity of $(3\hat{i} + 4\hat{j})$ ms^{-1}. If a constant force of $(2\hat{i} - 3\hat{j})$ N acts on it, find the coordinate of point it reaches in 3 s. **NCERT Pg. 54**

(a) (18, −1.5) (b) (9, 1.5)
(c) (18, 1.5) (d) (9, −1.5)

24 Figure shows x-t and y-t diagrams of a particle moving in two-dimensions. **NCERT Pg. 54**

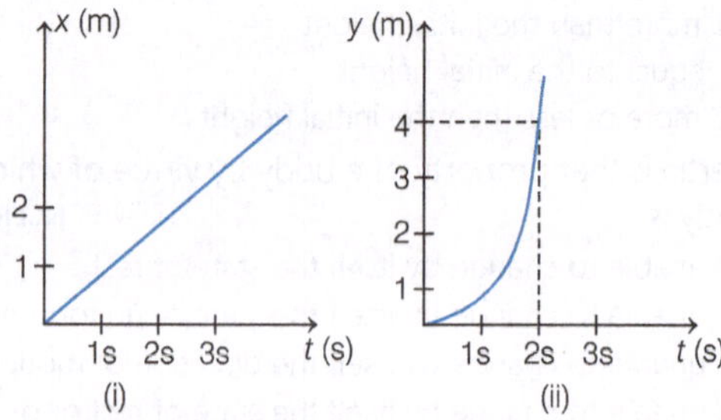

If the particle has a mass of 500 g, find the force (direction and magnitude) acting on the particle.

(a) 8 N along X-axis
(b) 12 N along X-axis
(c) 1 N along Y-axis
(d) 3 N along Y-axis

25 The motion of a particle of mass m is described by $y = ut + gt^2$. Find the force acting on the particle. **NCERT Pg. 54**

(a) Zero (b) mg
(c) $2\,mg$ (d) $3\,mg$

26 A bullet of mass 0.04 kg moving with a speed of 90 ms^{-1} enters a heavy wooden block and stopped after 3s. What is the average resistive force exerted by the block on the bullet? **NCERT Pg. 54**

(a) 1 N (b) 1.2 N
(c) 2 N (d) 3 N

27 While launching a satellite of mass 10^4 kg, a force of 5×10^5 N is applied for 20s. The velocity attained by the satellite at the end of 20s, is **NCERT Pg. 55**

(a) 4 km/s (b) 3 km/s
(c) 1 km/s (d) 2 km/s

28 A gun applied a force F on a bullet which is given by $F = (100 - 0.5 \times 10^5 t)$ N. The bullet emerges out with speed 400 m/s, then find out the impulse exerted till force on the bullet becomes zero. **NCERT Pg. 55**

(a) 0.2 N-s (b) 0.3 N-s
(c) 0.1 N-s (d) 0.4 N-s

29 The force-time (F-t) graph for linear motion of a body initially at rest is shown in figure. The segments shown are circular, the linear momentum gained in 4 s is **NCERT Pg. 55**

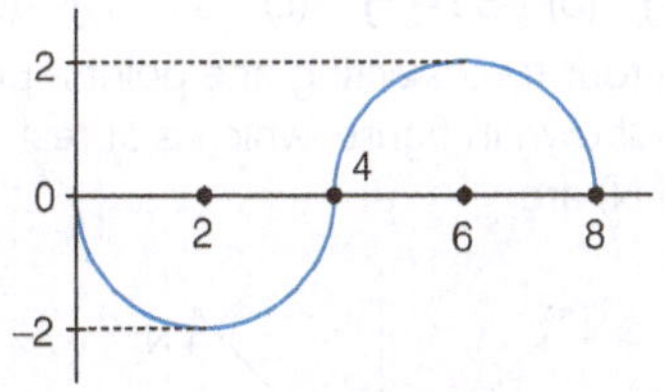

(a) 8 N-s (b) 4π N-s
(c) 2π N-s (d) 8π N-s

30 A batsman hits back at ball straight in the direction of the bowler without changing its initial speed of 12 ms^{-1}. If the mass of the ball is 0.15 kg, find the impulse imparted to the ball. (Assume linear motion of the ball) **NCERT Pg. 55**

(a) 1.8 N-s (b) 3.6 N-s
(c) 3.6 N-m (d) 1.8 N-m

Newton's Third Law of Motion

31 Which of the following statement is incorrect regarding Newton's third law of motion?
(a) To every action, there is always an equal and opposite reaction. **NCERT Pg. 56**
(b) Action and reaction act on the same body.
(c) There is no cause-effect relation between action and reaction.
(d) Action and reaction forces are simultaneous.

32 Every action has an equal and opposite reaction, which suggests that **NCERT Pg. 56**
(a) action and reaction always act on different bodies
(b) the forces of action and reaction cancel to each other
(c) the forces of action and reaction cannot cancel to each other
(d) Both (a) and (c)

33 A book is lying on the table. What is the angle between the action of the book on the table and reaction of the table on the book? **NCERT Pg. 56**
(a) 0° (b) 30° (c) 45° (d) 180°

34 Twelve one-rupee coins are put on top of each other on a table, where mass of each coin is 20g. The reaction of the 7th coin (counted from bottom) on the 8th coin is (take, $g = 10\ m/s^2$) **NCERT Pg. 56**
(a) 2N (b) 1N
(c) 3 N (d) 4N

35 A motor boat of mass 100 kg is running on the surface of a river with the acceleration of 5 m/s^2 and suddenly due to high waves in the water it decrease it's acceleration to 2.5 m/s^2. The force applied by the motor on the boat to do this is **NCERT Pg. 56**
(a) 200 N (b) 800 N (c) 400 N (d) 250 N

36 A man is standing at a spring platform. Reading of spring balance is 70 kg-wt. If man jumps outside platform, then reading of spring balance is **NCERT Pg. 56**
(a) increase
(b) decrease
(c) first increase then decrease to zero
(d) remains same

37 If a lift is moving with constant acceleration a in the upward direction, then the force applied by mass m on the floor of the lift will be **NCERT Pg. 56**
(a) mg (b) $m(g+a)$ (c) $2\,ma$ (d) $m(g-a)$

38 A 6000 kg rocket is set for vertical firing. The exhaust speed is 900 ms^{-1}. To give an initial upward acceleration of 20 ms^{-2}, the amount of gas ejected per second to supply the needed thrust will be ($g = 10\,ms^{-2}$) **NCERT Pg. 56**
(a) 185 kg s^{-1} (b) 200 kg s^{-1}
(c) 240 kg s^{-1} (d) 150 kg s^{-1}

39 A steam of water flowing horizontally with a speed of 50 ms^{-1} gushes out of a tube of cross-sectional area $10^{-3} m^2$, and hits at a vertical wall nearby. What is the force exerted on the wall by the impact of water? **NCERT Pg. 56**
(a) 2500 N (b) 625 N (c) 650 N (d) 2250 N

40 A rocket with a lift off mass 3×10^3 kg is blasted upwards with an initial acceleration of 10 ms^{-2}. The initial thrust of the blast is (Take $g = 10\ ms^{-2}$) **NCERT Pg. 56**
(a) 2×10^5 N (b) 3×10^5 N
(c) 6×10^4 N (d) 5×10^4 N

41 A stone of mass 2 kg is lying on the floor of a train which is accelerating with 4 ms^{-2}. The net force acting on the stone is **NCERT Pg. 56**
(a) 2 N (b) 4 N (c) 6 N (d) 8 N

42 A helicopter of mass 1500 kg rises with a vertical acceleration of 12 ms^{-2}. The total mass of the crew and passengers is 500 kg. Choose the correct statements from the following. (Take, $g = 10\,ms^{-2}$) **NCERT Pg. 56**
(i) The force on the floor of the helicopter by the crew and passengers is 1.25×10^4 N vertically downwards.
(ii) The action of the rotor of the helicopter on the surrounding air is 44×10^3 N vertically downwards.
(iii) The force on the helicopter due to the surrounding air is 44×10^3 N vertically upwards.
(a) (i) and (ii) (b) (ii) and (iii)
(c) (i) and (iii) (d) All of these

Conservation of Momentum

43 A rigid ball of mass $2M$ strikes a rigid wall at 30° and gets reflected without loss of speed as shown in the figure.
The value of impulse imparted by the wall on the ball will be NCERT Pg. 57

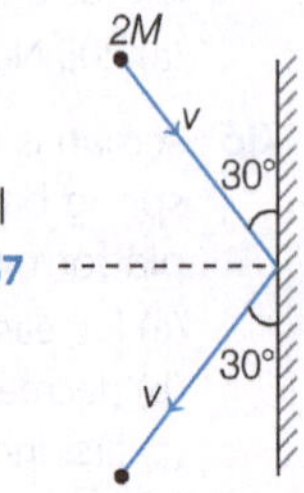

(a) Mv (b) $2Mv$
(c) $\frac{Mv}{2}$ (d) $\frac{Mv}{3}$

44 In an isolated system (i.e. a system with no external force), total momentum of interacting particles is conserved. It follows NCERT Pg. 57
(a) Newton's first law (b) Newton's second law
(c) Newton's third law (d) Both (b) and (c)

45 A 100 kg gun fires a ball of 1 kg horizontally from a cliff of height 500 m. It falls on the ground at a distance of 400 m from the bottom of the cliff. The recoil velocity of the gun is (take, $g = 10\,ms^{-2}$) NCERT Pg. 57
(a) $0.2\ ms^{-1}$ (b) $0.4\ ms^{-1}$
(c) $0.6\ ms^{-1}$ (d) $0.8\ ms^{-1}$

46 An explosion breaks a rock into three parts in a horizontal plane. Two of them go off at right angles to each other. The first part of mass 1 kg moves with a speed of $12\ ms^{-1}$ and the second part of mass 2 kg moves with $8\ ms^{-1}$speed. If the third part flies off with $4ms^{-1}$ speed, then its mass is NCERT Pg. 57
(a) 3 kg (b) 5 kg
(c) 7 kg (d) 17 kg

47 A trolley of mass 200 kg moves with a uniform speed of $36\ kmh^{-1}$ on a frictionless track. A child of mass 20 kg runs on the trolley from one end to the other (10 m away) with a speed of $4\ ms^{-1}$ relative to the trolley in a direction opposite to its motion and ultimately jumps out of the trolley. With how much velocity has the trolley moved from the time, the child begins to run? NCERT Pg. 57
(a) 10.36 m/s (b) 11.36 m/s
(c) 12.36 m/s (d) 14.40 m/s

Equilibrium of a Particle

48 Three concurrent coplanar forces 1 N, 2 N and 3 N are acting along different directions on a body can keep the body in equilibrium, if NCERT Pg. 58
(a) 2 N and 3 N act at right angle
(b) 1 N and 2 N act at acute angle
(c) 1 N and 2 N act at right angle
(d) Cannot be possible

49 Two forces $\mathbf{F}_1 = 3\hat{i} - 4\hat{j}$ and $\mathbf{F}_2 = 2\hat{i} - 3\hat{j}$ are acting upon a body of mass 2 kg. Find the force $\mathbf{F}_3$, which acts on the body will make it stable. NCERT Pg. 58
(a) $5\hat{i} + 7\hat{j}$ (b) $-5\hat{i} - 7\hat{j}$ (c) $-5\hat{i} + 7\hat{j}$ (d) $5\hat{i} - 7\hat{j}$

50 There are four forces acting at a point P produced by strings as shown in figure, which is at rest. The forces F_1 and F_2 (in N) are NCERT Pg. 58

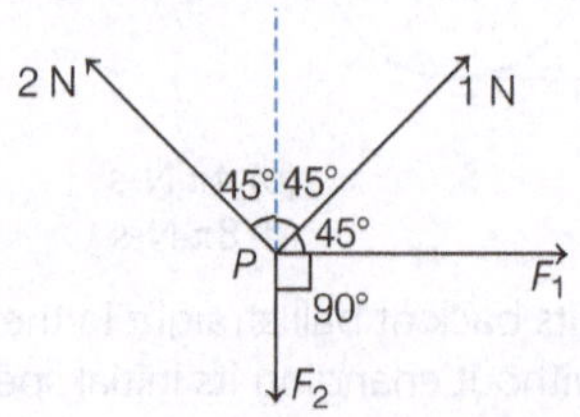

(a) 0.7, 2.1 (b) 4.1, 2.1
(c) 2.31, 1.0 (d) 3.0, 1.4

51 Given figure is the part of a horizontally stretched structure. Section AB is stretched with a force of 10 N. The tensions in the sections BC and BF, are NCERT Pg. 58

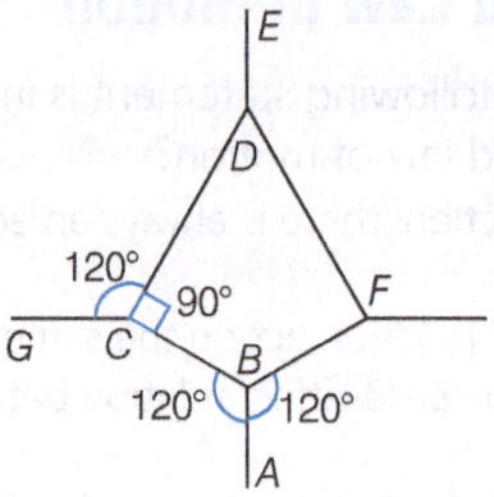

(a) 10 N, 11 N
(b) 10 N, 6 N
(c) 10 N, 10 N
(d) Cannot be calculated due to insufficient data

52 A block is kept on a frictionless inclined surface with angle of inclination α. The incline is given an acceleration a to keep the block stationary, then a is equal to NCERT Pg. 58

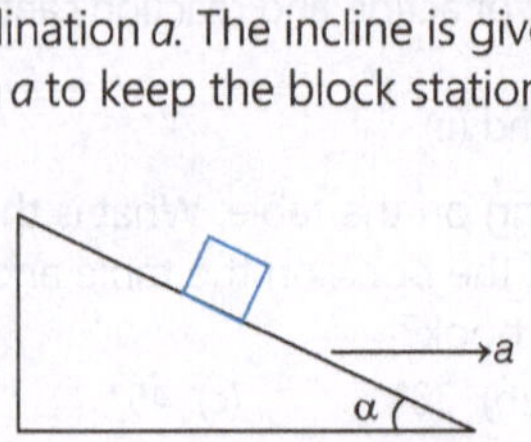

(a) g (b) $g \tan \alpha$
(c) $g/\tan \alpha$ (d) $g \operatorname{cosec} \alpha$

53 Which of the following groups of forces could be in equilibrium? NCERT Pg. 58
(a) 3N, 4N, 5N (b) 4N, 5N, 10N
(c) 30N, 40N, 80N (d) 1N, 3N, 5N

54 A block of mass 5 kg is suspended with two strings, as shown in figure. Find the tension in each sting, if the system is in equilibrium. (Take, $g = 10 \text{ m/s}^2$) **NCERT Pg. 58**

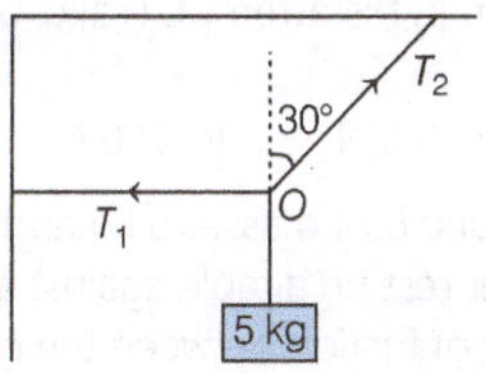

(a) $\left(\frac{50}{\sqrt{3}}, \frac{100}{\sqrt{3}}\right)$ N (b) $\left(\frac{100}{\sqrt{3}}, \frac{50}{\sqrt{3}}\right)$ N

(c) $\left(\frac{150}{\sqrt{5}}, \frac{200}{\sqrt{5}}\right)$ N (d) $(50\sqrt{3}, 100\sqrt{3})$ N

55 A mass M is hung with a light inextensible string as shown in the figure. Find the tension of the horizontal string. **NCERT Pg. 58**

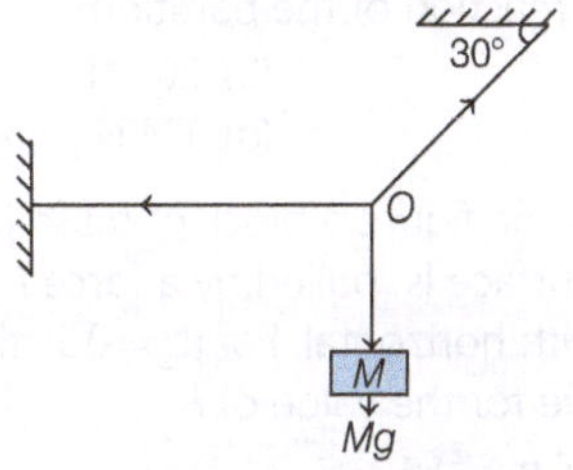

(a) $\sqrt{2}\, Mg$ (b) $\sqrt{3}\, Mg$

(c) $2\, Mg$ (d) $3\, Mg$

56 A block of mass 4 kg is suspended by a massless rope of length 2 m from the ceiling. A force of 70 N is applied in the horizontal direction at the horizontal direction at the midpoint P of the rope, as shown in the figure. The angle made by the rope with the vertical in equilibrium is (take $g = 10 \text{ ms}^{-2}$) **NCERT Pg. 58**

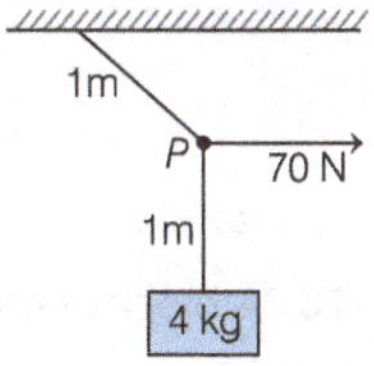

(a) 30° (b) 40°

(c) 60° (d) 45°

Common Forces in Mechanics

57 Two masses $m_1 = 1$ kg and $m_2 = 2$ kg are connected by a light inextensible string and suspended by means of a weightless pulley as shown in figure. **NCERT Pg. 59**

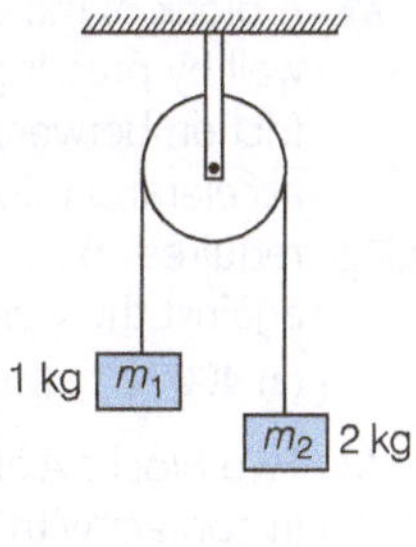

Assuming that both the masses start from rest, the distance the travelled by centre of mass of the system in 2 s is (given, $g = 10 \text{ ms}^{-2}$)

(a) $\frac{20}{9}$ m (b) $\frac{40}{9}$ m

(c) $\frac{20}{3}$ m (d) $\frac{1}{3}$ m

58 Three equal weights A, B and C of mass 2 kg each are hanging on a string over a fixed frictionless pulley as shown in the figure. The tension in the string connecting weight B and C is (given, $g = 9.8 \text{ ms}^{-2}$) **NCERT Pg. 59**

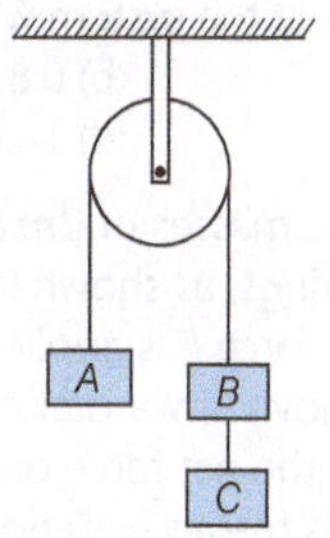

(a) zero (b) 9.8 N

(c) 13.3 N (d) 19.6 N

59 A pendulum of mass m hangs from a support fixed to a trolley. The direction of the string (i.e. angle θ) when the trolley roll down on a plane of inclination α with acceleration a is **NCERT Pg. 59**

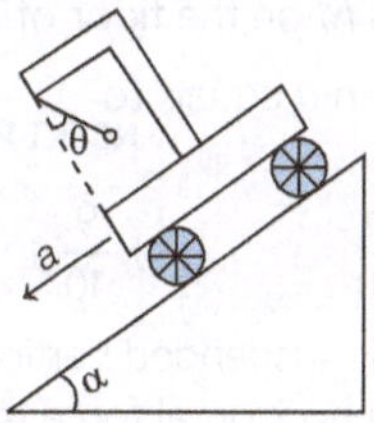

(a) $\tan^{-1}\left(\frac{a - g\sin\alpha}{g\cos\alpha}\right)$ (b) $g\tan\alpha$

(c) $\tan^{-1}\left(\frac{a\sin\alpha}{g}\right)$ (d) $\tan^{-1}\left(\frac{a + g\sin\alpha}{g\cos\alpha}\right)$

60 Block A of weight 50 N rests on a frictionless inclined plane of slope angle 30° as shown in the figure. A flexible cord attached to A passes over a frictionless pulley and is connected to block B of weight w. Find the weight w for which the system is in equilibrium. **NCERT Pg. 59**

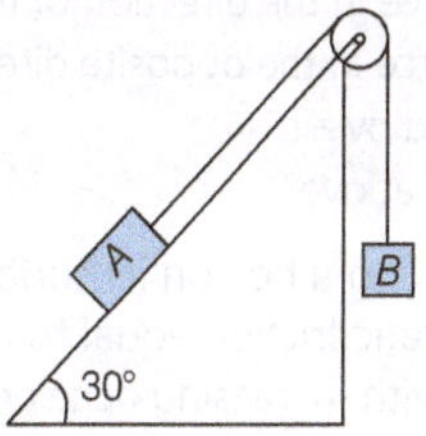

(a) 25 N (b) 50 N

(c) 75 N (d) 100 N

61 Two blocks of masses 40 kg and 20 kg are connected by a weightless string passing over a frictionless pulley as shown in the figure . **NCERT Pg. 59**

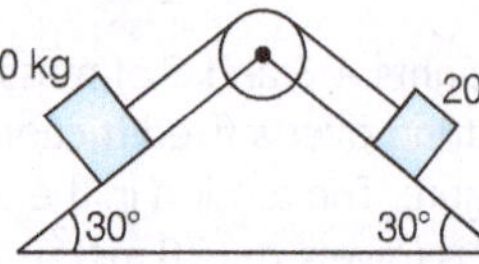

The acceleration of the system would be
(a) $0.7\ ms^{-2}$ (b) $0.8\ ms^{-2}$
(c) $1.6\ ms^{-2}$ (d) $1.4\ ms^{-2}$

62 Three blocks with masses $m, 2m$ and $3m$ are connected by strings, as shown in the figure. After an upward force F is applied on block m, the masses move upward at constant speed v. What is the net force on the block of mass $2m$? (g is the acceleration due to gravity) **NCERT Pg. 59**

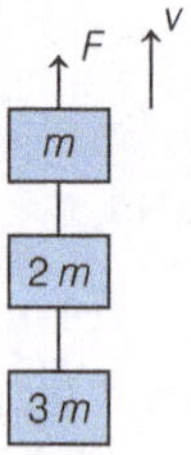

(a) Zero (b) $2\ mg$
(c) $3\ mg$ (d) $6\ mg$

63 If cabin is descending in vertical direction with acceleration a and reaction by mass M on the floor of cabin is $\frac{9\ Mg}{10}$, then a equals to **NCERT Pg. 59**

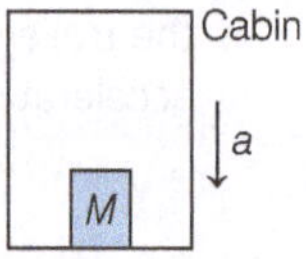

(a) g (b) $\frac{g}{10}$ (c) $\frac{9}{10}g$ (d) $\frac{10}{9}g$

64 A mass of 10 kg is suspended vertically by a rope from the roof. When a horizontal force is applied on the mass, the rope deviated at an angle of 45° at the roof point. If the suspended mass is at equilibrium, the magnitude of the force applied is (Take, $g = 10\ ms^{-2}$) **NCERT Pg. 59**
(a) 70 N (b) 200 N
(c) 100 N (d) 140 N

65 If a box is lying in the compartment of an accelerating train and box is stationary relative to the train. What force cause the acceleration of the box? **NCERT Pg. 60**
(a) Frictional force in the direction of train
(b) Frictional force in the opposite direction of train
(c) Force applied by air
(d) None of the above

66 A trolley is carrying a box on its surface having coefficient of static friction equal to 0.3. Now the trolley starts moving with increasing acceleration. Find the maximum acceleration of the trolley, so that the box does not slide back on the trolley. **NCERT Pg. 60**
(a) $2\ ms^{-2}$ (b) $3\ ms^{-2}$
(c) $4\ ms^{-2}$ (d) $5\ ms^{-2}$

67 A boy prevents fall of his book on the ground by pressing it against a vertical wall. If weight of his book is 10 kg and μ_s of the wall is 0.2. Find the minimum force needed by him in his attempt. (Take, $g = 10\ ms^{-2}$) **NCERT Pg. 60**
(a) 300 N (b) 400 N (c) 500 N (d) 600 N

68 Two bodies A and B of masses 5 kg and 10 kg in contact with each other rest on a table against a rigid partition. The coefficient of friction between the bodies and the table is 0.15. A force of 200 N is applied horizontally at A. **NCERT Pg. 60**

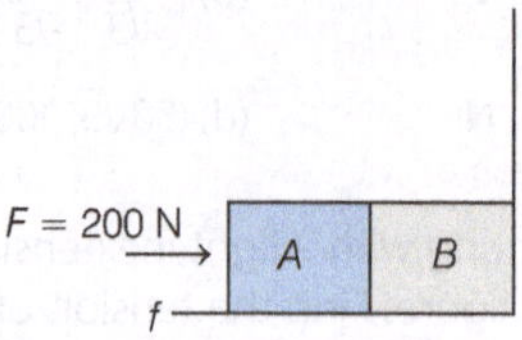

What is the reaction of the partition?
(a) 170 N (b) 204 N
(c) 177.5 N (d) 174 N

69 As shown in the figure a block of mass 15 kg lying on a horizontal surface is pulled by a force F acting at an angle 30° with horizontal. For $\mu_s = 0.5$, the block will just start to move for the value of F. **NCERT Pg. 60**
(Given, $g = 10\ ms^{-2}$)

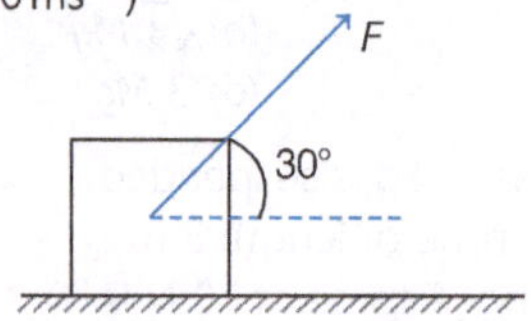

(a) 50 N (b) 30 N (c) 67 N (d) 60 N

70 A block of mass m is placed on a surface with a vertical cross-section given by $y = \frac{x^2}{3}$, here x and y are in SI units. If the coefficient of friction is 0.5, the maximum height above the ground at which the block can be placed without slipping is **NCERT Pg. 60**
(a) $\frac{1}{2}$ m (b) $\frac{3}{8}$ m (c) $\frac{13}{3}$ m (d) $\frac{3}{16}$ m

71 A block of mass 10 kg is held against a rough vertical wall by pressing it with a finger. If the coefficient of friction between the block and the wall is 0.2 and the acceleration due to gravity is g. The minimum force required to be applied by the finger to hold the block against the wall will be (take $g = 10\ ms^{-2}$) **NCERT Pg. 60**
(a) 400 N (b) 200 N (c) 600 N (d) 500 N

72 Two blocks A and B of masses 5 kg and 10 kg are placed in contact with each other rest on a rough horizontal surface as shown in the figure. The coefficient of friction between the blocks and surface is 0.2. A horizontal force of 200 N is applied to block *A*. The acceleration of the system is (Take $g = 10\ ms^{-2}$) **NCERT Pg. 60**

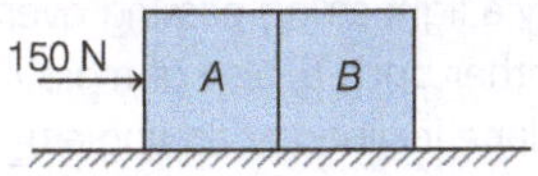

(a) $15\ ms^{-2}$ (b) $6\ ms^{-2}$ (c) $8\ ms^{-2}$ (d) $10\ ms^{-2}$

73 Which one of the following statement is correct? **NCERT Pg. 60**

(a) Frictional force is in the direction of relative motion.
(b) Limiting value of static friciton is directly proportional to normal reaction.
(c) Rolling friction is larger than sliding friction.
(d) Coefficient of sliding friction has dimensions of length.

74 A block of mass *m* slides on the wooden wedge, which in turn slides backward on the horizontal surface. The ratio of the acceleration of the block with respect to that of the wedge is [Given, $m = 8$ kg, $M = 16$ kg] Assume all the surface shown in the figure to be frictionless. **NCERT Pg. 60**

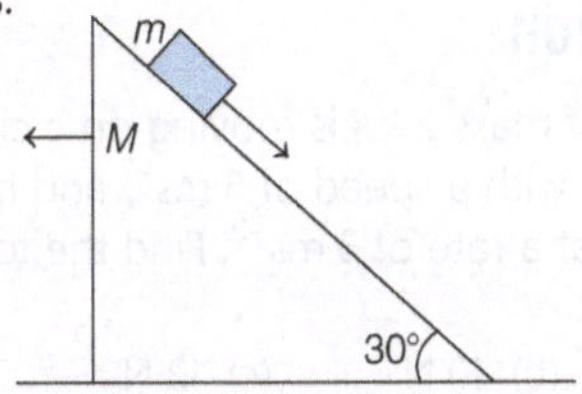

(a) $\sqrt{3}$ (b) $2\sqrt{3}$ (c) $\frac{1}{\sqrt{3}}$ (d) $4\sqrt{3}$

75 A monkey of mass 30 kg climbs on a massless rope which can stand a maximum tension of 320 N. In which of the following cases will the rope break ? (Take, $g = 10\ ms^{-2}$) **NCERT Pg. 60**

(a) The monkey climbs up with an acceleration of $2\ ms^{-2}$.
(b) The monkey climbs up with an acceleration of $0.5\ ms^{-2}$.
(c) The monkey climbs up with a uniform speed of $5\ ms^{-1}$.
(d) The monkey falls down the rope freely under gravity.

76 A system consists of three masses m_1, m_2 and m_3 connected by a string passing over a pulley *P*. The mass m_1 hangs freely and m_2 and m_3 are on a rough horizontal table (the coefficient of friction $= \mu$).

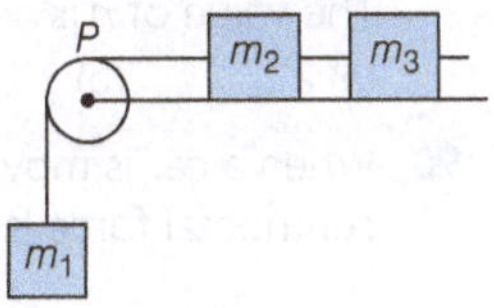

The pulley is frictionless and of negligible mass. The downward acceleration of mass m_1 is (assume, $m_1 = m_2 = m_3 = m$) **NCERT Pg. 60**

(a) $\frac{g(1-g\mu)}{9}$ (b) $\frac{2g\mu}{3}$
(c) $\frac{g(1-2\mu)}{3}$ (d) $\frac{g(1-2\mu)}{2}$

77 What is the acceleration of the block and the trolley system as shown in figure, if the coefficient of kinetic friction between the trolley and the surface is 0.04? What is the tension *T* in the string? Neglect the mass of the string. (Take, $g = 10\ ms^{-2}$) **NCERT Pg. 60**

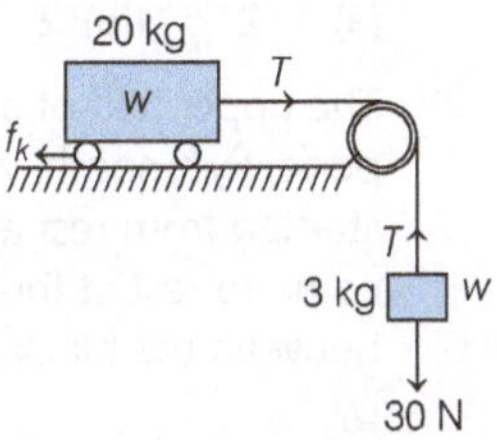

(a) $a = 0.96\ ms^{-2}$, $T = 50$ N
(b) $a = 0.42\ ms^{-2}$, $T = 27.1$ N
(c) $a = 0.96\ ms^{-2}$, $T = 27.1$ N
(d) $a = 0.42\ ms^{-2}$, $T = 42.6$ N

78 A block of mass 10 kg is kept on a rough inclined plane as shown in the figure. A force of 3 N is applied on the block. The coefficient of static friction between the plane and the block is 0.6. What should be the minimum value of force *F*, such that the block does not move downward? (Take, $g = 10 ms^{-2}$) **NCERT Pg. 60**

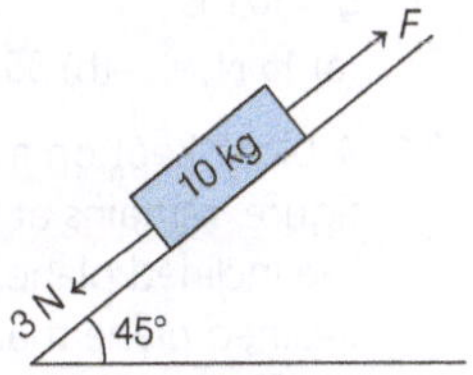

(a) 32 N (b) 25 N (c) 23 N (d) 18 N

79 A box of mass 8 kg is placed on a rough inclined plane of inclination 30°. Its downward motion can be prevented by applying a horizontal force *F*, then find the value of *F* for which friction between the block and the inclined surface is minimum. (Take, $g = 10\ ms^{-2}$) **NCERT Pg. 60**

(a) $\frac{80}{\sqrt{3}}$ (b) $40\sqrt{3}$ (c) $\frac{40}{\sqrt{3}}$ (d) $80\sqrt{3}$

80 A plank with a box on it at one end is gradually raised about the other end. As the angle of inclination with the horizontal reaches 30°, the box starts to slip and slides 4.0 m down the plank in 4.0 s.
The coefficients of static and kinetic friction between the box and the plank will be, respectively (take, $g = 10\ ms^{-2}$) **NCERT Pg. 60**

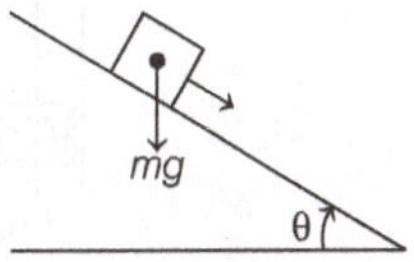

(a) 0.6 and 0.6 (b) 0.6 and 0.5
(c) 0.5 and 0.6 (d) 0.4 and 0.3

81 F_1 and F_2 are the minimum and maximum forces needed to keep a body on a rough inclined plane stationary. If θ be the angle of inclination of the surface, so that $\tan\theta = 2\mu$. Find the ratio of F_1 and F_2. **NCERT Pg. 60**

(a) 1 : 2 (b) 2 : 1 (c) 1 : 3 (d) 3 : 1

82 The upper half of an inclined plane of inclination θ is perfectly smooth, while lower half is rough. A block starting from rest at the top of the plane will again come to rest at the bottom, if the coefficient of friction between the block and lower half of the plane is given by **NCERT Pg. 60**

(a) $\mu = \dfrac{1}{\tan\theta}$ (b) $\mu = \dfrac{2}{\tan\theta}$

(c) $\mu = 2\tan\theta$ (d) $\mu = \tan\theta$

83 A block of mass 4 kg kept at rest on a rough inclined plane making an angle of 60° with the horizontal. The coefficient of static friction between the block and the plane is 0.8. The friction force on the block is (Take, $g = 10\ \text{ms}^{-2}$) **NCERT Pg. 60**

(a) 16 N (b) 35 N (c) 51 N (d) 19 N

84 A block kept on a rough inclined plane, as shown in the figure, remains at rest upto a maximum force 2 N down the inclined plane. The maximum external force up the inclined plane that does not move the block is 10 N. The coefficient of static friction between the block and the plane is (Take, $g = 10\ \text{m/s}^2$) **NCERT Pg. 60**

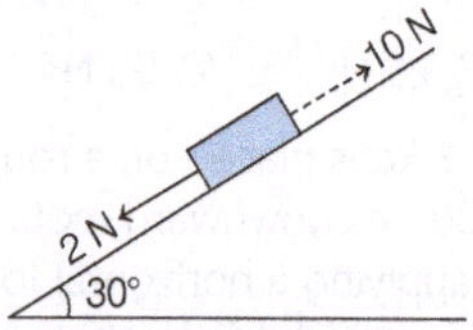

(a) $\dfrac{2}{3}$ (b) $\dfrac{\sqrt{3}}{2}$ (c) $\dfrac{\sqrt{3}}{4}$ (d) $\dfrac{1}{2}$

85 Two masses $m_1 = 5$ kg and $m_2 = 10$ kg connected by an inextensible string over a frictionless pulley, are moving as shown in the figure. The coefficient of friction of horizontal surface is 0.15. The minimum weight m that should be put on top of m_2 to stop the motion is **NCERT Pg. 60**

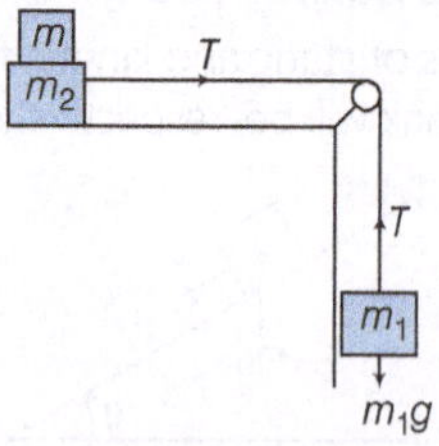

(a) 18.3 kg (b) 23.3 kg (c) 43.3 kg (d) 10.3 kg

86 In the given figure, a body A of mass m slides on plane inclined at angle θ_1 to the horizontal and μ is the coefficient of friction between A and the plane. A is connected by a light string passing over a frictionless pulley to another body B, also of mass m, sliding on a frictionless plane inclined at an angle θ_2 to the horizontal. Which of the following statement(s) is/are correct? **NCERT Pg. 60**

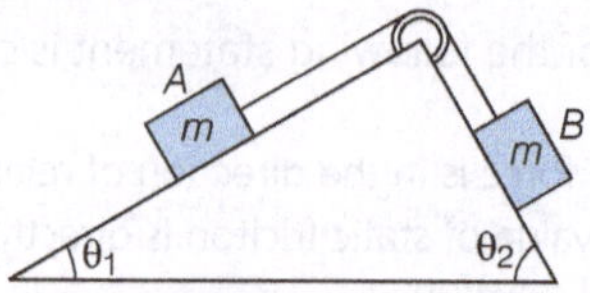

(a) A will never move up the plane.

(b) A will just start moving up the plane, when $\mu = \dfrac{\sin\theta_2 + \sin\theta_1}{\cos\theta_1}$

(c) For A to move up the plane, θ_2 must always be greater than θ_1.

(d) B will always slide down with constant speed.

Circular Motion

87 A particle of mass 2 kg is moving on a circular path of radius 10 m with a speed of 5 ms^{-1} and its speed is increasing at a rate of 3 ms^{-2}. Find the force acting on the particle. **NCERT Pg. 63**

(a) 5 N (b) 10 N (c) 12 N (d) 14 N

88 A particle is moving on a circular path of 10 m radius. At any instant of time, its speed is 5 ms^{-1} and the speed is increasing at a rate of 2 ms^{-2}. The magnitude of net acceleration at this instant is **NCERT Pg. 63**

(a) 5 ms^{-2} (b) 2 ms^{-2}

(c) 3.2 ms^{-2} (d) 4.3 ms^{-2}

89 Two stones of masses m and $2m$ are whirled in horizontal circles. The heavier one in a radius of $\dfrac{r}{2}$ and the lighter one in radius of r. The tangential speed of lighter stone is n times that of the value of heavier stone, when they experience same centripetal forces. The value of n is **NCERT Pg. 63**

(a) 2 (b) 3 (c) 4 (d) 1

90 When a car is moving along a circle on a level road, the centripetal force is provided by f, where f denotes as **NCERT Pg. 63**

(a) $f < \mu_s N = \dfrac{mv^2}{r}$ (b) $\dfrac{mv^2}{r} = f \le \mu_s N$

(c) $f = \mu_s N = \dfrac{mv^2}{r}$ (d) $f = \mu_k N = \dfrac{mv^2}{r}$

91 If a car is moving in uniform circular motion, then what should be the value of velocity of a car ,so that car will not move away from the circle? **NCERT Pg. 63**

(a) $v < \sqrt{\mu_s Rg}$ (b) $v \leq \sqrt{\mu_s Rg}$
(c) $v < \sqrt{\mu_k Rg}$ (d) None of these

92 A car is negotiating a curved road of radius R. The road is banked at an angle θ. The coefficient of friction between the tyres of the car and the road is μ_s. The maximum safe velocity on this road is **NCERT Pg. 63**

(a) $\sqrt{gR\left(\frac{\mu_s + \tan\theta}{1-\mu_s\tan\theta}\right)}$ (b) $\sqrt{\frac{g}{R}\left(\frac{\mu_s + \tan\theta}{1-\mu_s\tan\theta}\right)}$

(c) $\sqrt{\frac{g}{R^2}\left(\frac{\mu_s + \tan\theta}{1-\mu_s\tan\theta}\right)}$ (d) $\sqrt{gR^2\left(\frac{\mu_s + \tan\theta}{1-\mu_s\tan\theta}\right)}$

93 The mass of a bicycle rider along with the bicycle is 50 kg. He wants to cross over a circular turn of radius 20 m with a speed of 10 ms^{-1}. If the coefficient of friction between the tyres and the road is 0.6, the frictional force required by the rider to cross the turn, is **NCERT Pg. 63**

(a) 300 N (b) 600 N
(c) 500 N (d) 150 N

94 A stone of mass 2 kg is tied to a string of length 25m and is whirled round in a horizontal circle. What is the maximum speed with which the stone can be whirled around, if the string can withstand a maximum tension of 200 N ? **NCERT Pg. 63**

(a) 10 ms^{-1} (b) 50 ms^{-1}
(c) 20 ms^{-1} (d) 25 ms^{-1}

95 A disc revolves with a speed $26\frac{1}{2}$ rev/ min, and has a radius of 30 cm. Two coins A and B are placed at 4 cm and 28 cm away from the centre of the disc. If the coefficient of friction between the coins and the disc is 0.2 which of the coins will revolve with the disc? **NCERT Pg. 63**

(a) A (b) B
(c) Both A and B (d) Neither A nor B

96 A car is moving on a circular path of radius 300 m such that the magnitudes of the tangential acceleration and centripetal acceleration are equal. The time taken by the car to complete first quarter of revolution, if it is moving with an initial speed of 54 km/h is $t(1-e^{-\pi/2})$s. The value of t is **NCERT Pg. 63**

(a) 40 (b) 50 (c) 20 (d) 30

97 A car of mass 580 kg negotiates a banked curve of radius 40 m on a frictionless road. If the banking angle is 45°, then the speed of the car is **NCERT Pg. 63**

(a) 20 ms^{-1} (b) 30 ms^{-1} (c) 5 ms^{-1} (d) 10 ms^{-1}

98 A particle of mass m is suspended from a ceiling through a string of length L. The particle moves in a horizontal circle of radius r such that $r = \frac{L}{2}$. The speed of particle will be **NCERT Pg. 63**

(a) $\sqrt{\sqrt{3}rg}$ (b) $\sqrt{\frac{rg}{\sqrt{3}}}$

(c) $2\sqrt{rg}$ (d) $\sqrt{\frac{rg}{2}}$

99 A circular racetrack of radius 300 m is banked at an angle of 15°. If the coefficient of friction between the wheels of the race car and the road is 0.2. Find optimum speed of the race car to avoid wear and tear on its tyres and maximum permissible speed to avoid slipping. (Take $g = 9.8\ ms^{-2}$ and $\tan 15° = 0.27$) **NCERT Pg. 64**

(a) $v_o = 48\ ms^{-1}$, $v_{max} = 60\ ms^{-1}$
(b) $v_o = 28.1\ ms^{-1}$, $v_{max} = 38.1\ ms^{-1}$
(c) $v_o = 62.2\ ms^{-1}$, $v_{max} = 73.4\ ms^{-1}$
(d) None of the above

Assertion and Reason Questions

Direction (Q. Nos. 1-12) *In the following questions, a statement of Assertion is followed by a corresponding statement of Reason. Of the following statements, choose the correct one.*

(a) Both Assertion and Reason are correct and Reason is the correct explanation of Assertion.
(b) Both Assertion and Reason are correct but Reason is not the correct explanation of Assertion.
(c) Assertion is correct but Reason is incorrect.
(d) Assertion is incorrect but Reason is correct.

1 **Assertion** It is always necessary that external agency of force is in contact with the object while applying force on object.

Reason A stone released from top of a building accelerates downward due to gravitational pull of the earth. **NCERT Pg. 49**

2 **Assertion** Aristotle stated that an external force is required to keep a body in motion.

Reason Opposing forces are always present in the natural world. **NCERT Pg. 50**

3 **Assertion** A body is momentarily at rest but still some force is acting on it at that time.

Reason When a force acts on a body, it may not have some acceleration. **NCERT Pg. 51**

4 **Assertion** Product of mass and velocity (i.e. momentum) is basic to the effect of force on motion.

Reason Same force for same time causes the same change in momentum for different bodies. **NCERT Pg. 53**

5 **Assertion** The second law of motion can be applied on both animate and inanimate objects.

Reason An animate object requires an external force to accelerate. **NCERT Pg. 53**

6 **Assertion** If the momentum of a body is zero, it means that force or acceleration are necessarily zero at that instant.

Reason Force on a body at a given time is determined by the direction of motion only. **NCERT Pg. 54**

7 **Assertion** There is no appreciable change in the position of the body during the action of the impulsive force.

Reason In case of impulsive force, the time of action of the force should be very short. **NCERT Pg. 55**

8 **Assertion** If we consider system of two bodies A and B as a whole, $\mathbf{F}_{AB}$ and $\mathbf{F}_{BA}$ are internal forces of the system $(A+B)$. They add to give a null force.

Reason Internal forces in a body or a system of particles cancel away in pairs. **NCERT Pg. 56**

9 **Assertion** Newton's third law of motion is applicable only when bodies are in motion.

Reason Newton's third law applies to all types of forces, e.g. gravitational, electric or magnetic forces, etc. **NCERT Pg. 56**

10 **Assertion** At the microscopic level, all bodies are made up of charged constituents (like nuclei and electrons) and various contact forces exist between them.

Reason These forces are due to elasticity of bodies, molecular collisions and impacts, etc. **NCERT Pg. 59**

11 **Assertion** If force is not parallel to the velocity of the body, but makes some angle with it, it changes the component of velocity along the direction of force.

Reason The component of velocity normal to the force remains unchanged. **NCERT Pg. 59**

12 **Assertion** On a merry-go-around, our body are subjected to an inward force.

Reason We have a feeling of being pushed outward in the direction of impending motion. **NCERT Pg. 63**

Statement Based Questions

Direction (Q. Nos. 1-7) *In the following questions, two statements (I & II) are given. In the light of the given statements, choose the correct option given below.*

(a) Both Statement I and Statement II are false.
(b) Statement I is true but Statement II is false.
(c) Statement I is false but Statement II is true.
(d) Both Statement I and Statement II are true.

1 **Statement I** When we shake a mango tree, the mangoes fall down.

Statement II When a vehicle suddenly stopped, the passengers tend to fall forward. **NCERT Pg. 51**

2 **Statement I** A seasoned cricketer allows a longer time for his hands to stop the ball, while catching the ball his hand don't get hurted.

Statement II The novice (new player) keeps his hand fixed and tries to catch the ball almost instantly. He needs to provide a much greater force to stop the ball instantly and this hurts. **NCERT Pg. 53**

3 **Statement I** Forces in nature always occur between pair of bodies.

Statement II Action and reaction forces are not simultaneous forces. **NCERT Pg. 56**

4 **Statement I** The familiar equation $mg = R$ for a body on a table is true only if the body is in equilibrium.

Statement II The equality of mg and R is based on the third law of motion. **NCERT Pg. 58**

5 To solve a problem in mechanics, we need to consider an assembly of different bodies.

Statement I Different bodies exert force on each other.

Statement II Few selected body experiences force of gravity. **NCERT Pg. 59**

6 **Statement I** Friction is always an undesirable force.

Statement II Static friction is a self-adjusting force upto its limit $\mu_s N$, where μ_s is the coefficient of static friction. **NCERT Pg. 60**

7 **Statement I** When stone is rotated at greater speed in circular path, greater force is required.

Statement II When stone is rotated in a circle of smaller radius, greater force is required. **NCERT Pg. 63**

Matching Type Questions

1 A lift is going up. The total mass of the lift and the passengers is 2000 kg. The variation of speed of the lift is as shown in the diagram. **NCERT Pg. 55**

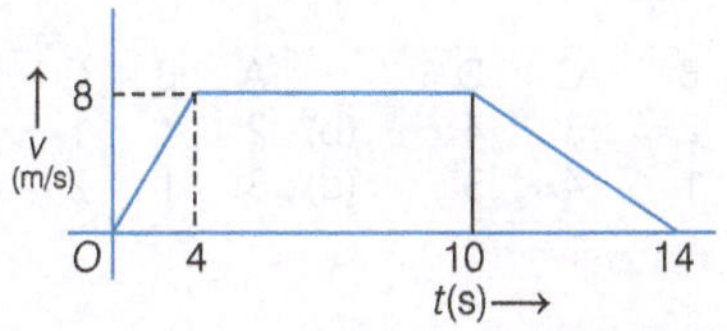

Match the quantity given in Column I with their magnitude in Column II. Choose the correct answer from the options given below.

Column I	Column II
A. Tension (in N) in the rope at time 1s	1. 20000
B. Tension (in N) in the rope at time 6s.	2. $\frac{40}{7}$
C. Tension (in N) in the rope at time 12 s.	3. 24000
D. Average velocity (in m/s) during motion.	4. 16000

Codes

	A	B	C	D		A	B	C	D
(a)	3	4	2	1	(b)	2	3	4	1
(c)	3	1	4	2	(d)	4	2	3	1

2 A man of mass 60 kg stands in a weighing scale in a moving lift. Now, match the Column I with Column II. Choose the correct answer from the options given below. (Take, $g = 10$ m/s^2) **NCERT Pg. 59**

Column I (Situation of the lift)	Column II (Reading of weighing scale in newton)
A. When lift is moving upward with uniform speed of 4 m/s	1. 240
B. When lift is moving downward with uniform acceleration of 6 m/s^2	2. 600
C. When lift is moving upward with uniform acceleration of 6 m/s^2	3. 0
D. When lift's mechanism fails	4. 960

Codes

	A	B	C	D		A	B	C	D
(a)	2	1	3	4	(b)	2	1	4	3
(c)	1	3	4	2	(d)	3	1	4	2

3 a_1, a_2, a_3 and a_4 are common accelerations in different conditions of the block system, then match the Column I with Column II. Choose the correct answer from the options given below. **NCERT Pg. 59**

Column I	Column II
A. 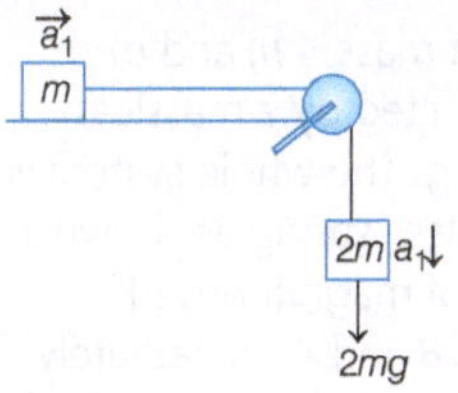 Then, a_1 = ?	1. $\frac{g}{5}$
B. 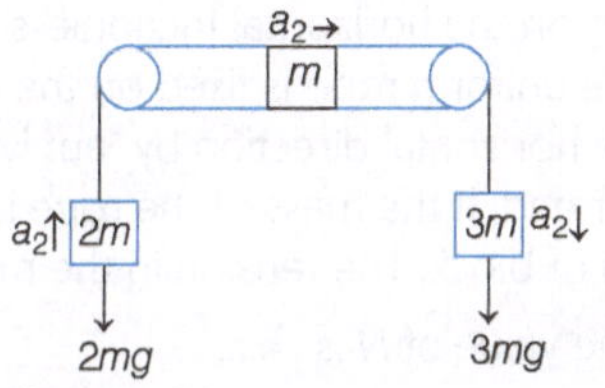 Then, a_2 = ?	2. $\frac{g}{3}$
C. 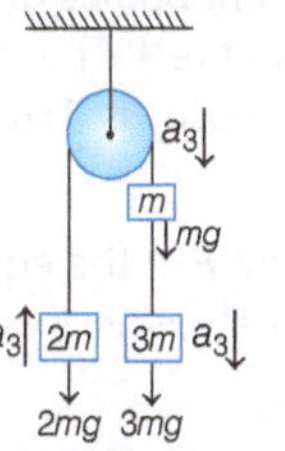 Then, a_3 = ?	3. $\frac{g}{6}$
D. 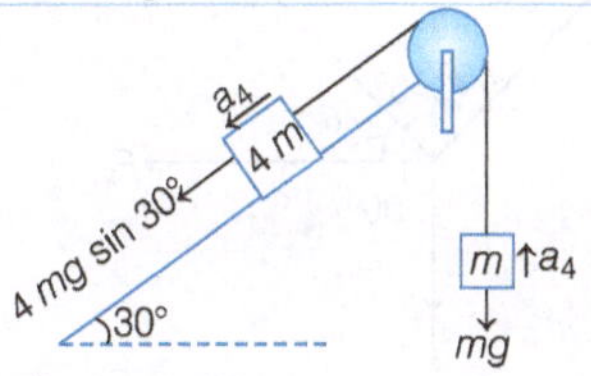 Then, a_4 = ?	4. $\frac{2g}{3}$

Codes

	A	B	C	D
(a)	4	2	3	1
(b)	3	2	4	3
(c)	4	3	2	1
(d)	3	4	2	1

4 A body starting from rest moves along a smooth inclined plane of length l, height h and inclination angle θ. Match the Column I with Column II. Choose the correct answer from the options given below. **NCERT Pg. 59**

Column I	Column II
A. Acceleration of body along the inclined plane.	1. $\sqrt{2l/g\sin\theta}$
B. Velocity of body when it reaches at the bottom	2. $g\sin\theta$
C. Time taken by the body to reach the bottom	3. $\sqrt{l/g\sin\theta}$
D. Time taken to reach half distance along the inclined plane	4. $\sqrt{2gl\sin\theta}$

Codes

	A	B	C	D		A	B	C	D
(a)	1	2	3	4	(b)	2	4	1	3
(c)	2	1	4	3	(d)	3	1	2	4

Numerical Type Questions

1 Two blocks A and B of mass $4\,m$ and m respectively are connected by a massless and in extensible string. The whole system is suspended by a massless spring as shown in the figure. The ratio of magnitudes of acceleration of blocks B and A immediately after the string is cut, is .... **NCERT Pg. 53**

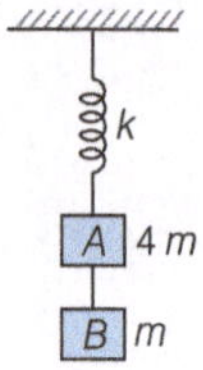

2 A block is lying on the horizontal frictionless surface. One end of the uniform rope is fixed on the block which is pulled in the horizontal direction by applying a force $2F$ at the other end. If the mass of the rope is one-third the mass of block. The tension in the middle of the rope is $\frac{NF}{4}$. The value of N is .... **NCERT Pg. 53**

3 If same force act on two different bodies of different masses 4 kg and 12 kg initially at rest. The ratio of time required to attain same final velocity is $1 : \alpha$. The value of α is .... **NCERT Pg. 53**

4 Four forces are acting at a point P in the equilibrium as shown in figure. The ratio of force F_2 to F_1 is $1 : 3x$, where x is .... **NCERT Pg. 57**

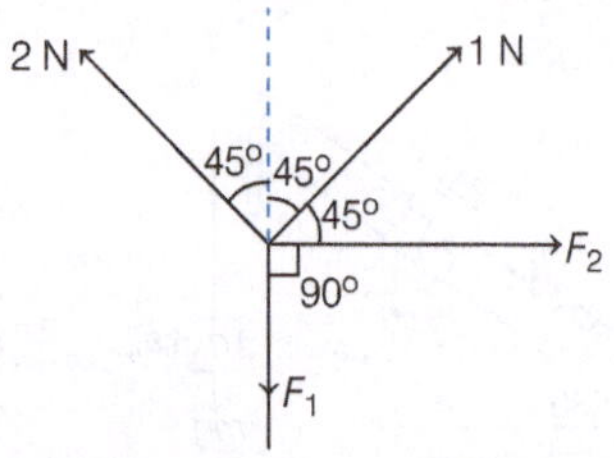

5 The coefficient of static friction between two blocks is 0.4 and the table is smooth. The maximum horizontal force that can be applied to move the blocks together is ...... N. (Take, $g = 10\,\text{ms}^{-2}$) **NCERT Pg. 60**

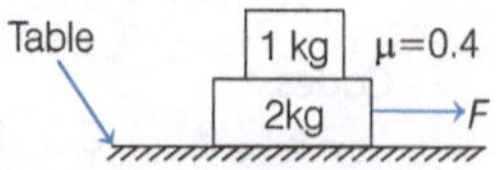

6 Starting from rest, a body slides down a 30° inclined plane in four times the time it takes to slide the same distance in the absence of friction. The coefficient of friction between the body and the inclined plane is $\frac{15}{x\sqrt{3}}$, the value of x is .... **NCERT Pg. 60**

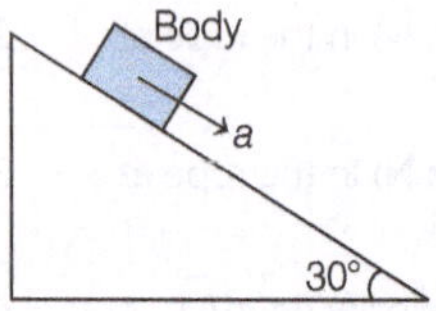

7 A car is moving on a plane inclined at 30° to the horizontal with an acceleration of $10\,\text{ms}^{-2}$ parallel to the plane upward. A bob is suspended by a string from the roof of the car. The angle in degrees which the string makes with the vertical is $15x$. The value of x is .... (Take, $g = 10\,\text{ms}^{-2}$) **NCERT Pg. 63**

8 A particle is moving on a circular path of 15 m radius. At an instant of time, its speed is $5\,\text{ms}^{-1}$ and the speed is increasing at the rate of $3\,\text{ms}^{-2}$. The magnitude of net acceleration at this instant is .... **NCERT Pg. 63**

9 A block starts moving up an inclined plane of inclination 30° with an initial velocity of v_0. It comes back to its initial position with velocity $v_0 / 2$. The value of the coefficient of kinetic friction between the block and the inclined plane is close to $I/500$, the nearest integer to I is .... **NCERT Pg. 63**

10 A small bob tied at one end of a thin string of length 10 m is describing a vertical circle so that the maximum and minimum tension in the string are in the ratio 3 : 1. The velocity of the bob at the highest position is ...... m/s. (Take $g = 10\,\text{m/s}^2$) **NCERT Pg. 63**

NCERT Exemplar Questions

1 A ball is travelling with uniform translatory motion. This means that

(a) it is at rest

(b) the path can be a straight line or circular and the ball travels with uniform speed

(c) all parts of the ball have the same velocity (magnitude and direction) and the velocity is constant

(d) the centre of the ball moves with constant velocity and the ball spins about its centre uniformly

2 A meter scale is moving with uniform velocity. This implies

(a) the force acting on the scale is zero, but a torque about the centre of mass can act on scale

(b) the force acting on the scale is zero and the torque acting about centre of mass of the scale is also zero

(c) the total force acting on it need not be zero but the torque on it is zero

(d) Neither the force nor the torque need to be zero

3 A cricket ball of mass 150 g has an initial velocity $\mathbf{u} = (3\hat{\mathbf{i}} + 4\hat{\mathbf{j}})\ \text{ms}^{-1}$ and a final velocity $\mathbf{v} = -(3\hat{\mathbf{i}} + 4\hat{\mathbf{j}})\ \text{ms}^{-1}$, after being hit.

The change in momentum (final momentum – initial momentum) is (in kg-ms^{-1})

(a) zero (b) $-(0.45\hat{\mathbf{i}} + 0.6\hat{\mathbf{j}})$

(c) $-(0.9\hat{\mathbf{i}} + 1.2\hat{\mathbf{j}})$ (d) $-5(\hat{\mathbf{i}} + \hat{\mathbf{j}})$

4 Conservation of momentum in a collision between particles can be understood from

(a) conservation of energy

(b) Newton's first law only

(c) Newton's second law only

(d) Both Newton's second and third laws

5 A hockey player is moving northward and suddenly turns westward with the same speed to avoid an opponent. The force that acts on the player is

(a) frictional force along westward

(b) muscle force along southward

(c) frictional force along south-west

(d) muscle force along south-west

6 A body of mass 2 kg travels according to the law $x(t) = pt + qt^2 + rt^3$, where $q = 4\ \text{ms}^{-2}$, $p = 3\ \text{ms}^{-1}$ and $r = 5\ \text{ms}^{-3}$. The force acting on the body at $t = 2$ s is

(a) 136 N (b) 134 N

(c) 158 N (d) 68 N

7 A body with mass 5 kg is acted upon by a force $\mathbf{F} = (-3\hat{\mathbf{i}} + 4\hat{\mathbf{j}})$ N. If its initial velocity at $t = 0$ is $\mathbf{u} = (6\hat{\mathbf{i}} - 12\hat{\mathbf{j}})\ \text{ms}^{-1}$, the time at which it will just have a velocity along the Y-axis is

(a) never (b) 10 s

(c) 2 s (d) 15 s

8 A car of mass m starts from rest and acquires a velocity along east, $\mathbf{v} = v\hat{\mathbf{i}}\ (v > 0)$ in 2 s. Assuming the car moves with uniform acceleration, the force exerted on the car is

(a) $\frac{mv}{2}$ eastward and is exerted by the car engine

(b) $\frac{mv}{2}$ eastward and is due to the friction on the tyres exerted by the road

(c) more than $\frac{mv}{2}$ eastward exerted due to the engine and overcomes the friction of the road

(d) $\frac{mv}{2}$ exerted by the engine

Past Exams Questions

NEET

1 A horizontal force 10 N is applied to a block A as shown in figure. The mass of blocks A and B are 2 kg and 3 kg, respectively. The blocks slide over a frictionless surface. The force exerted by block A on block B is

NCERT Pg. 65, NEET 2024

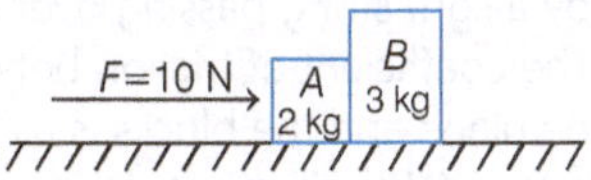

(a) zero (b) 4 N (c) 6 N (d) 10 N

2 A bob is whirled in a horizontal plane by means of a string with an initial speed of wrpm. The tension in the string is T. If the speed becomes 2ω while keeping the same radius, the tension in the string becomes

NCERT Pg. 79, NEET 2024

(a) T (b) $4T$ (c) $T/4$ (d) $\sqrt{2}T$

3 A bullet from a gun is fired on a rectangular wooden block with velocity u. When bullet travels 24 cm through the block along its length horizontally, velocity of bullet becomes $u/3$. Then, it further penetrates into the block in the same direction before coming to rest exactly at the other end of the block. The total length of the block is **NCERT Pg. 55, NEET 2023**

(a) 24 cm (b) 28 cm
(c) 30 cm (d) 27 cm

4 A football player is moving southward and suddenly turns eastward with the same speed to avoid an opponent. The force that acts on the player while turning is **NCERT Pg. 54, NEET 2023**

(a) along northward (b) along north-east
(c) along south-west (d) along eastward

5 Calculate the maximum acceleration of a moving car so that a body lying on the floor of the car remains stationary. The coefficient of static friction between the body and the floor is 0.15 ($g = 10\ \text{ms}^{-2}$). **NCERT Pg. 60, NEET 2023**

(a) $150\ \text{ms}^{-2}$ (b) $1.5\ \text{ms}^{-2}$
(c) $50\ \text{ms}^{-2}$ (d) $1.2\ \text{ms}^{-2}$

6 A ball of mass 0.15 kg is dropped from a height 10 m, strikes the ground and rebounds to the same height. The magnitude of impulse imparted to the ball is nearly ($g = 10\ \text{m/s}^2$) **NCERT Pg. 55, NEET 2021**

(a) 0 (b) 4.2 kg-m/s
(c) 2.1 kg-m/s (d) 1.4 kg-m/s

7 A small block slides down on a smooth inclined plane, starting from rest at time $t = 0$. Let S_n be the distance travelled by the block in the interval $t = n - 1$ to $t = n$. Then, the ratio $\dfrac{S_n}{S_{n+1}}$ is **NCERT Pg. 59, NEET 2021**

(a) $\dfrac{2n}{2n-1}$ (b) $\dfrac{2n-1}{2n}$ (c) $\dfrac{2n-1}{2n+1}$ (d) $\dfrac{2n+1}{2n-1}$

8 A truck is stationary and has a bob suspended by a light string, in a frame attached to the truck. The truck, suddenly moves to the right with an acceleration of a. The pendulum will tilt **NCERT Pg. 51, NEET 2020**

(a) to the left and the angle of inclination of the pendulum with the vertical is $\sin^{-1}\left(\dfrac{g}{a}\right)$

(b) to the left and angle of inclination of the pendulum with the vertical is $\tan^{-1}\left(\dfrac{a}{g}\right)$

(c) to the left and angle of inclination of the pendulum with the vertical is $\sin^{1-}\left(\dfrac{a}{g}\right)$

(d) to the left and angle of inclination of the pendulum with the vertical is $\tan^{-1}\left(\dfrac{g}{a}\right)$

9 Calculate the acceleration of the block and trolley system shown in the figure. The coefficient of kinetic friction between the trolley and the surface is 0.05. ($g = 10\ \text{m/s}^2$, mass of the string is negligible and no other friction exists) **NCERT Pg. 61, NEET 2020**

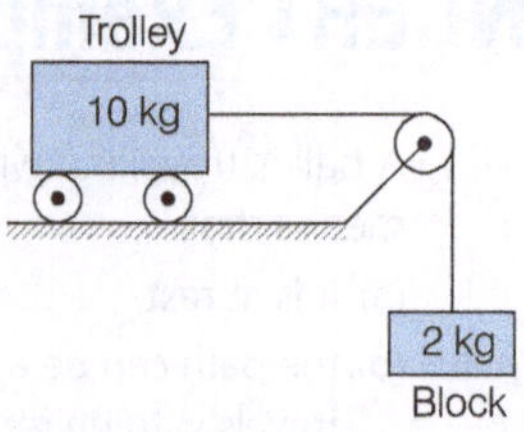

(a) $1.25\ \text{m/s}^2$ (b) $1.50\ \text{m/s}^2$
(c) $1.66\ \text{m/s}^2$ (d) $1.00\ \text{m/s}^2$

10 A particle moving with velocity **v** is acted by three forces shown by the vector triangle PQR.

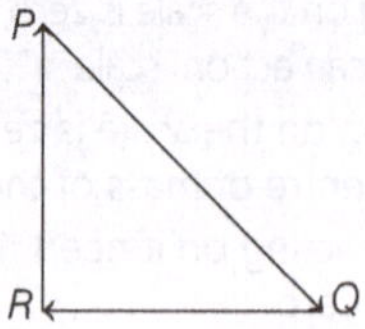

The velocity of the particle will **NCERT Pg. 58, NEET 2019**

(a) decrease
(b) remain constant
(c) change according to the smallest force QR
(d) increase

11 An object flying in air with velocity $(20\hat{\mathbf{i}} + 25\hat{\mathbf{j}} - 12\hat{\mathbf{k}})$ suddenly breaks in two pieces whose masses are in the ratio 1 : 5. The smaller mass flies off with a velocity $(100\hat{\mathbf{i}} + 35\hat{\mathbf{j}} + 8\hat{\mathbf{k}})$. The velocity of the larger piece will be **NCERT Pg. 58, NEET 2019**

(a) $4\hat{\mathbf{i}} + 23\hat{\mathbf{j}} - 16\hat{\mathbf{k}}$ (b) $-100\hat{\mathbf{i}} - 35\hat{\mathbf{j}} - 8\hat{\mathbf{k}}$
(c) $20\hat{\mathbf{i}} + 15\hat{\mathbf{j}} - 80\hat{\mathbf{k}}$ (d) $-20\hat{\mathbf{i}} - 15\hat{\mathbf{j}} - 80\hat{\mathbf{k}}$

12 A body of mass m is kept on a rough horizontal surface (coefficient of friction $= \mu$). Horizontal force is applied on the body but it does not move. The resultant of normal reaction and the frictional force acting on the object is given **F**, where **F** is **NCERT Pg. 61, NEET 2019**

(a) $|\mathbf{F}| = mg + \mu\, mg$ (b) $|\mathbf{F}| = \mu mg$
(c) $|\mathbf{F}| \le mg\sqrt{1+\mu^2}$ (d) $|\mathbf{F}| = mg$

JEE Main

13 In the given arrangement of a doubly inclined plane two blocks of masses M and m are placed. The blocks are connected by a light string passing over an ideal pulley as shown. The coefficient of friction between the surface of the plane and the blocks is 0.25. The value of m, for which $M = 10$ kg will move down with an accleration of 2 m/s^2 is (Take, $g = 10\ m/s^2$ and $\tan 37° = \frac{3}{4}$)

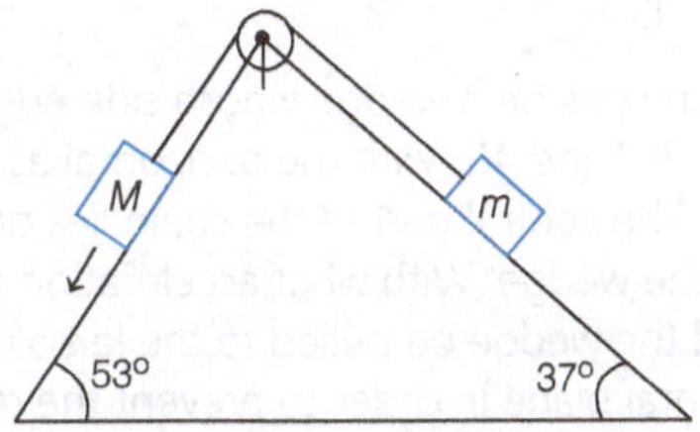

NCERT Pg. 61, JEE Main 2024

(a) 6.5 kg (b) 4.5 kg (c) 9 kg (d) 2.25 kg

14 Given below are two statements.

Statement I The limiting force of static friction depends on the area of contact and independent of materials.

Statement II The limiting force of kinetic friction is independent of the area of contact and depends on materials.

In the light of the above statements, choose the most appropriate answer from the options given below.

NCERT Pg. 60, JEE Main 2024

(a) Statement I is incorrect but Statement II is correct.
(b) Statement I is correct but Statement II is incorrect.
(c) Both Statement I and Statement II are incorrect.
(d) Both Statement I and Statement II are corrrect.

15 A body of mass 200 g is tied to a spring of spring constant 12.5 N/m, while the other end of spring is fixed at point O. If the body moves about O in a circular path on a smooth horizontal surface with constant angular speed 5 rad/s, then the ratio of extension in the spring to its natural length will be NCERT Pg. 63, JEE Main 2023

(a) 2 : 5 (b) 1 : 2
(c) 2 : 3 (d) 1 : 1

16 A bag is gently dropped on a conveyor belt moving at a speed of 2 m/s. The coefficient of friction between the conveyor belt and bag is 0.4. Initially, the bag slips on the belt before it stops due to friction. The distance travelled by the bag on the belt during slipping motion is [Take, $g = 10\ m/s^2$] NCERT Pg. 60, JEE Main 2023

(a) 2 m (b) 0.5 m
(c) 3.2 m (d) 0.8 m

17 A uniform metal chain of mass m and length L passes over a massless and frictionless pulley. It is released from rest with a part of its length l is hanging on one side and rest of its length $L - l$ is hanging on the other side of the pulley. At a certain point of time, when $l = \frac{L}{x}$, the acceleration of the chain is $\frac{g}{2}$. Find the value of x.

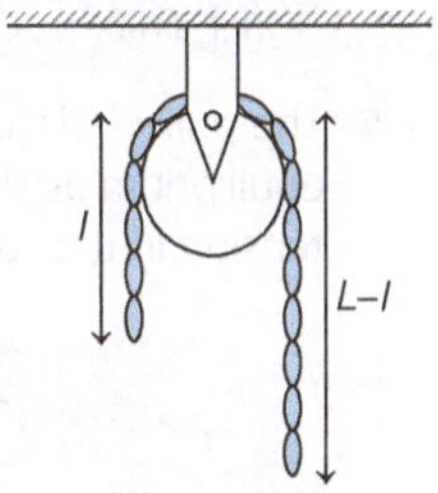

NCERT Pg. 54, JEE Main 2022

(a) 6 (b) 2 (c) 1.5 (d) 4

Skill Boosters

1 A bead of mass m is sliding on a parabolic path as shown in the figure. The equation of the parabola is $x^2 = 4ay$. If the bead is released from $y = 6a$, then its acceleration when it will reach at $y = a$ is (consider the motion is frictionless)

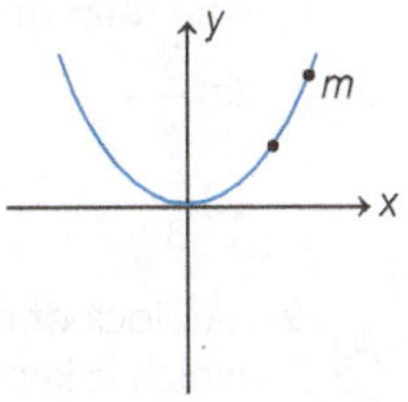

(a) $\frac{\sqrt{5}\,g}{2}$ (b) $\sqrt{2}\,g$ (c) g (d) $\frac{g}{\sqrt{2}}$

2 A light string ABC whose ends are fixed at points A and C. If a weight w attached to it at point B as shown in figure. If string is strong enough to withstand a maximum tension 100 N, then the largest value of w for the equilibrium of the system is [Take, $\cos 53° = \frac{3}{5}$]

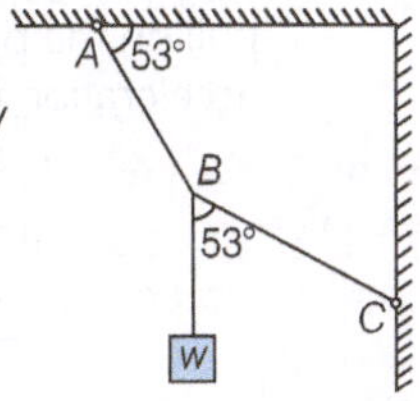

(a) 20 N (b) 35 N
(c) 50 N (d) 44 N

3 A time varying force $F = 20\sqrt{2}\,t$ starts acting on the 3 kg block kept on a rough horizontal surface ($\mu = 0.2$) at $t = 0$. The ratio of moment of time when the block leaves the surface to the moment of time when the horizontal motion begins, will be

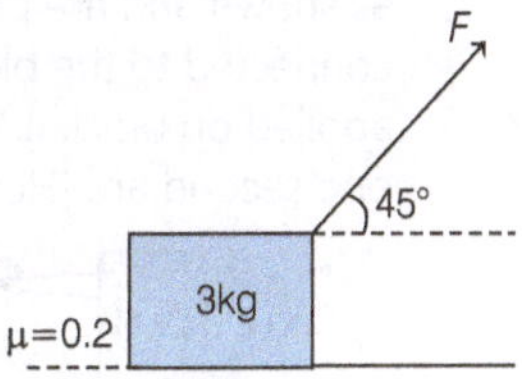

(a) 2 : 3 (b) 3 : 4
(c) 6 : 1 (d) 4 : 1

4 If a block of mass m is placed over a wedge of same mass m. Both the block and the wedge are placed on a fixed inclined plane, then the displacement of block with respect to ground in one second is [Assuming all surfaces to be smooth]

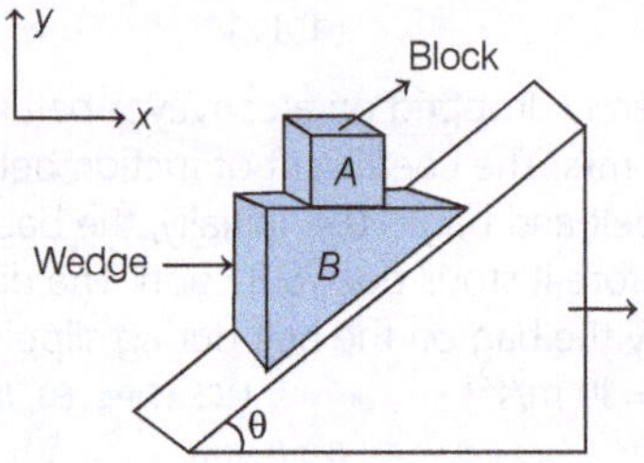

(a) $\frac{g \sin \theta}{1+\sin \theta}$ (b) $\frac{g \sin^2 \theta}{1+\sin^2 \theta}$

(c) $\frac{2g \sin^2 \theta}{1+\sin \theta}$ (d) $\frac{2g \sin \theta}{1+\sin^2 \theta}$

5 The pulley P is just sufficient to keep the 21 N block in equilibrium as shown in figure. Pulleys are ideal. The tension in the cable connected with ceiling is

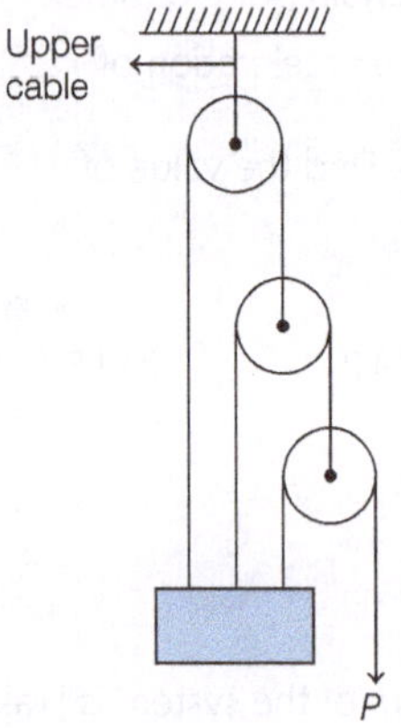

(a) 2 N (b) 5 N (c) 3 N (d) 8 N

6 Two identical blocks I and II each having a mass of 20 kg are connected to each other by a light inextensible string as shown and are placed over a rough surface. Pulleys are connected to the blocks. If a time varying force of $40t$ N applied on block II, then acceleration of the blocks after one second are [Here, t is in second]

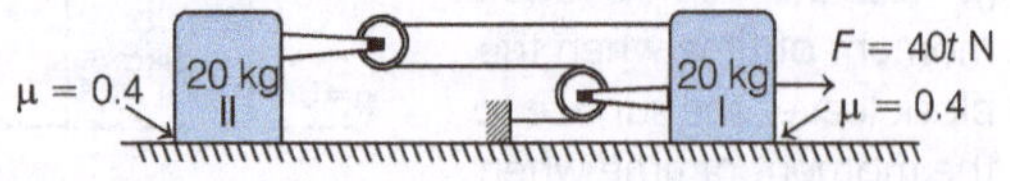

(a) $a_1 = \frac{3}{2}$ m/s^2, $a_2 = \frac{6}{13}$ m/s^2

(b) $a_1 = \frac{4}{13}$ m/s^2, $a_2 = \frac{6}{13}$ m/s^2

(c) $a_1 = \frac{6}{13}$ m/s^2, $a_2 = \frac{8}{13}$ m/s^2

(d) $a_1 = \frac{4}{13}$ m/s^2, $a_2 = \frac{8}{13}$ m/s^2

7 A chain rests on a wedge whose side edges make angles 30° and 45° with the horizontal as shown in figure. The central part of the chain lies on the upper tip of the wedge. With what acceleration (in m/s^2) should the wedge be pulled to the left along the horizontal plane in order to prevent the displacement of the chain with respect to the wedge?

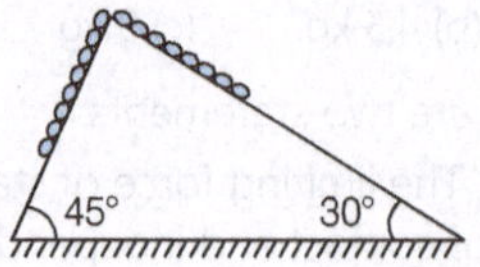

(a) $\frac{5(\sqrt{2}+1)}{\sqrt{3}+\sqrt{2}}$ (b) $\frac{5(\sqrt{2}-1)}{\sqrt{3}-\sqrt{2}}$

(c) $\frac{10(\sqrt{2}+\sqrt{3})}{\sqrt{2}-1}$ (d) $\frac{10(\sqrt{2}-1)}{\sqrt{3}+\sqrt{2}}$

8 A bead C can move freely on a horizontal rod. The bead is connected by blocks B and D by a string as shown in the figure. [Take, $\cos 37° = \frac{4}{5}$]

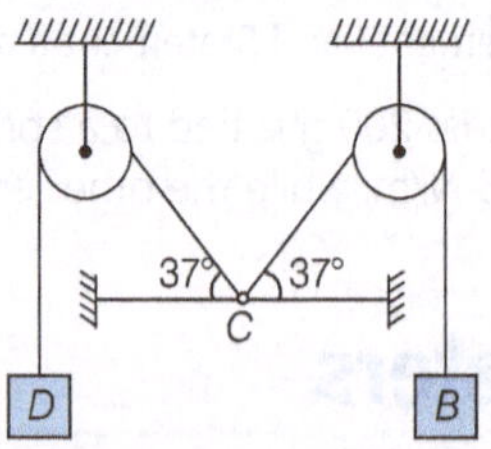

The ratio of velocities of block B to block D is

(a) $\frac{3}{4}$ (b) $\frac{4}{3}$

(c) $\frac{2}{3}$ (d) $\frac{3}{2}$

9 A block of mass m rests on top of a block of mass $2m$ which is kept on a table. The coefficient of kinetic friction between all surfaces is $\mu = 1$. A massless string is connected to each mass and wraps half-way around a massless pulley as shown in figure. Assume that you pull on the pulley with a force of 6 mg. What is the acceleration of your hand?

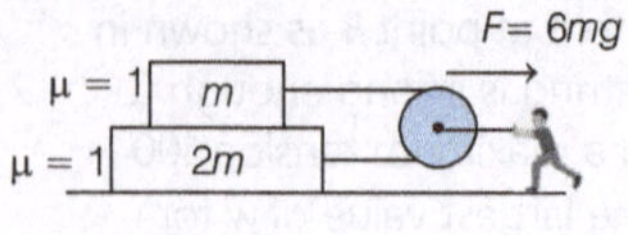

(a) $\frac{5g}{4}$ (b) $\frac{3g}{4}$

(c) $\frac{2g}{3}$ (d) $\frac{5g}{2}$

10 In a picnic park, there is a device called rotor, where people stand on a platform inside a large cylinder that rotates about a vertical axis.
When the rotor reaches a certain angular velocity, the platform drops away. The minimum coefficient of friction for the people not to slide down is [Take the radius to be 2m and the period to be 2s]

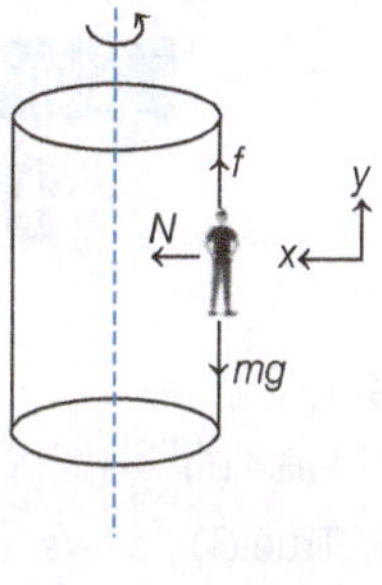

(a) 0.25 (b) 0.5 (c) 0.75 (d) 0.4

Correct Codes

Topical Questions

1 (d)	2 (a)	3 (a)	4 (c)	5 (d)	6 (c)	7 (d)	8 (b)	9 (a)	10 (c)
11 (a)	12 (a)	13 (a)	14 (b)	15 (b)	16 (b)	17 (b)	18 (b)	19 (a)	20 (c)
21 (c)	22 (c)	23 (a)	24 (c)	25 (c)	26 (b)	27 (c)	28 (c)	29 (c)	30 (b)
31 (b)	32 (d)	33 (d)	34 (b)	35 (d)	36 (c)	37 (b)	38 (b)	39 (a)	40 (c)
41 (d)	42 (b)	43 (a)	44 (d)	45 (b)	46 (b)	47 (a)	48 (d)	49 (c)	50 (a)
51 (c)	52 (b)	53 (a)	54 (a)	55 (b)	56 (c)	57 (a)	58 (c)	59 (a)	60 (a)
61 (c)	62 (a)	63 (b)	64 (c)	65 (a)	66 (b)	67 (c)	68 (c)	69 (c)	70 (d)
71 (d)	72 (c)	73 (b)	74 (b)	75 (a)	76 (c)	77 (c)	78 (a)	79 (a)	80 (b)
81 (c)	82 (c)	83 (a)	84 (b)	85 (b)	86 (c)	87 (a)	88 (c)	89 (a)	90 (b)
91 (b)	92 (a)	93 (a)	94 (b)	95 (a)	96 (c)	97 (a)	98 (b)	99 (b)	

Assertion and Reason Questions

1 (d)	2 (a)	3 (c)	4 (c)	5 (b)	6 (d)	7 (a)	8 (a)	9 (d)	10 (a)
11 (b)	12 (b)								

Statement Based Questions

1 (d)	2 (d)	3 (c)	4 (b)	5 (b)	6 (c)	7 (d)

Matching Type Questions

1 (c)	2 (b)	3 (c)	4 (b)

Numerical Type Questions

1 (4)	2 (7)	3 (3)	4 (1)	5 (12)	6 (16)	7 (2)	8 (3.4)	9 (173)	10 (20)

NCERT Exemplar Questions

1 (c)	2 (b)	3 (c)	4 (d)	5 (c)	6 (a)	7 (b)	8 (b)

Past Exams Questions

1 (c)	2 (b)	3 (d)	4 (b)	5 (b)	6 (b)	7 (c)	8 (b)	9 (a)	10 (b)
11 (a)	12 (c)	13 (b)	14 (a)	15 (c)	16 (b)	17 (d)			

Skill Boosters

1 (d)	2 (b)	3 (c)	4 (b)	5 (c)	6 (b)	7 (d)	8 (a)	9 (a)	10 (b)

Step by Step

Decoding the Questions

Concept Builders

1 True (T)	2 False (F)
3 frictional	4 True (T)
5 False (F)	6 greater
7 False (F)	8 True (T)
9 zero	10 False (F)
11 False (F)	
12 Remains unchanged	
13 True (T)	
14 Forcing agency	
15 False (F)	16 infinite
17 False (F)	18 inward
19 No change	20 inward

Topical Questions

6 (*c*) When particle moves in a circle even with uniform or constant speed, it faces an external force towards its centre called centripetal force.
This means, in the absence of external force, a particle cannot move with uniform speed in a circle.

11 (*a*) If downward attractive force on the earth stops, the upward self-adjusting force also stops. Due to inertia, the person resists any change to its state of rest. So, the person will remain standing.

12 (*a*) Once the astronaut is out of spaceship, the net force acting on the astronaut is zero.
Therefore, net acceleration of the astronaut will be zero.

13 (*a*) Since, momentum is directly proportional to mass of the body. Hence, bigger ball can transfer greater momentum to the glass pane and so it breaks.

15 (*b*) Force applied by rocket engine is

$$F = ma = 1.0 \times 10^4 \times 50$$
$$= 5 \times 10^5 \text{ N}$$

16 (*b*) According to Newton's second law of motion, applied force,

$$F = \frac{dp}{dt}$$

or $dp = F \cdot dt$ or $dp = kt \cdot dt$

$$\int_p^{3p} dp = k\int_0^T t\,dt$$

or $[p]_p^{3p} = k\left[\frac{t^2}{2}\right]_0^T$

or $(3p - p) = \frac{1}{2}k[T^2 - 0]$

or $T = 2\sqrt{\frac{p}{k}}$

17 (*b*) Change in momentum,

$\Delta p = p_f - p_i$ ...(i)

Also, $\Delta p = F \cdot \Delta t$ ...(ii)

From Eqs. (i) and (ii), we get

$$F \cdot \Delta t = p_f - p_i$$

or $10 \times 0.25 = p_f - mv_i$

$= p_f - 0.5 \times 0$

or $p_f = 2.5$ N-s

18 (*b*) From Newton's second law,

$$F = n \cdot \left(\frac{\Delta p}{\Delta t}\right)$$

$\Rightarrow F = n\left(\frac{mv - 0}{\Delta t}\right)$

$\therefore 144 = n \times \frac{40 \times 10^{-3} \times 1200}{1}$

$\Rightarrow n = 3$

19 (*a*) The velocity of the ball before hitting the ground, $v_1^2 = u^2 + 2gh$

$\Rightarrow v_1 = \sqrt{2gh}$

$= \sqrt{2 \times 10 \times 20} = 20$ m/s

$$\text{Force} = \frac{|\Delta p|}{\Delta t} = \frac{|mv_2 - mv_1|}{\Delta t}$$

$$= \frac{|m(v_2 - v_1)|}{\Delta t} = \frac{0.1 \times 40}{0.04}$$

$= 100$ N

20 (*c*) According to Newton's second law,

$$F = \frac{dp}{dt} = \frac{mdv}{dt} \quad (\because p = mv)$$

$\therefore (4t^2\,\hat{\mathbf{i}} + 2t\,\hat{\mathbf{j}}) = \frac{4dv}{dt}$

$\Rightarrow \int_0^v dv = \frac{1}{4}\int_0^3 (4t^2\,\hat{\mathbf{i}} + 2t\,\hat{\mathbf{j}})dt$

$\Rightarrow v = \frac{1}{4}\left[\frac{4t^3}{3}\hat{\mathbf{i}} + \frac{2t^2}{2}\hat{\mathbf{j}}\right]_0^3$

$\therefore v = 9\hat{\mathbf{i}} + 2.25\hat{\mathbf{j}}$

21 (*c*)

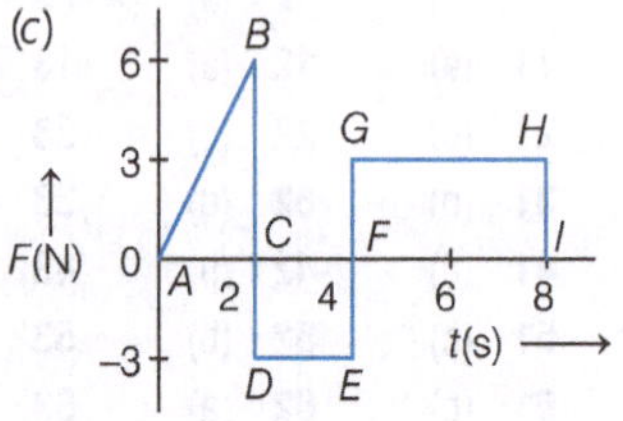

For 0 to 2s, Δp_1

$= \frac{1}{2} \times 2 \times 6 = 6$ kg-ms^{-1}

For 2 to 4s, $\Delta p_2 = 2 \times -3$

$= -6$ kg-ms^{-1}

For 4 to 8s, Δp_3 = Area under the rectangle

$= 4 \times 3 = 12$ kg-ms^{-1}

So, total change in momentum for 0 to 8s,

$$\Delta p_{net} = \Delta p_1 + \Delta p_2 + \Delta p_3$$
$$= 12 \text{ N-s}$$

22 (*c*) Acceleration of the rocket at any instant t is

$$a = \frac{v_r \frac{dm}{dt}}{M - t\frac{dm}{dt}}$$

$\therefore a = \frac{11000 \times 12}{8000 - 60 \times 12} \approx 18 \text{ ms}^{-2}$

23 (*a*) Given, initial velocity,

$u = 3\hat{\mathbf{i}} + 4\hat{\mathbf{j}}$

Force, $F = 2\hat{\mathbf{i}} - 3\hat{\mathbf{j}}$

$u_x = 3\ \text{ms}^{-1}$

$u_y = 4\ \text{ms}^{-1}$

$F_x = 2\ \text{N}, F_y = -3\ \text{N}$

$a_x = \frac{F_x}{m} = \frac{2}{1} = 2\ \text{m/s}^2 \quad [\because F = ma]$

$a_y = \frac{F_y}{m} = \frac{-3}{1} = -3\ \text{m/s}^2$

$s_x = u_x t + \frac{1}{2} a_x t^2 = 18\ \text{m}$

$s_y = u_y t + \frac{1}{2} a_y t^2 = -1.5\ \text{m}$

So, required x and y-coordinates of point $= (18, -1.5)$

24 (*c*) x-t graph of the particle is a straight line, i.e. its acceleration is zero and hence force acting along X-axis is zero.

y-t graph of the particle is a curved line.

Hence, $y = t^2$

$a_y = \frac{d^2y}{dt^2} = 2$

$\therefore$ Force along Y-axis

$= m \times a_y = 0.5 \times 2 = 1\ \text{N}$

25 (*c*) $y = ut + gt^2 = ut + \frac{1}{2} \cdot 2gt^2$

Acceleration, $a = 2g$

Force $= m \times a = m \cdot 2g$

$= 2mg$

26 (*b*) From first equation of motion,

$v = u - at$

$0 = 90 - a \times 3$

$\Rightarrow a = 30\ \text{m/s}^2$

$F = m \cdot a = 0.04 \times 30 = 1.2\ \text{N}$

27 (*c*) Impulse applied on the satellite is equal to the change in momentum.

i.e. $F \cdot t = m(v - u)$

$5 \times 10^5 \times 20 = 10^4 (v - 0)$

$\Rightarrow v = 1000\ \text{m/s} = 1\ \text{km/s}$

28 (*c*) When $F = 0$, then

$100 - 0.5 \times 10^5 t = 0$

$\Rightarrow t = 2 \times 10^{-3}\ \text{s}$

$\therefore$ Impulse, $I = \int F dt$

$= \int_0^{2 \times 10^{-3}} (100 - 0.5 \times 10^5 t) dt$

$= \left[100t - 0.5 \times 10^5 \frac{t^2}{2} \right]_0^{2 \times 10^{-3}}$

$= 0.1\ \text{N-s}$

29 (*c*) Impulse from 0 to 4 s

= Area enclosed by graph from 0 to 4 s

$= \frac{\pi r^2}{2} = \frac{\pi (2)^2}{2} = 2\pi\ \text{N-s}$

30 (*b*) The situation is as depicted below

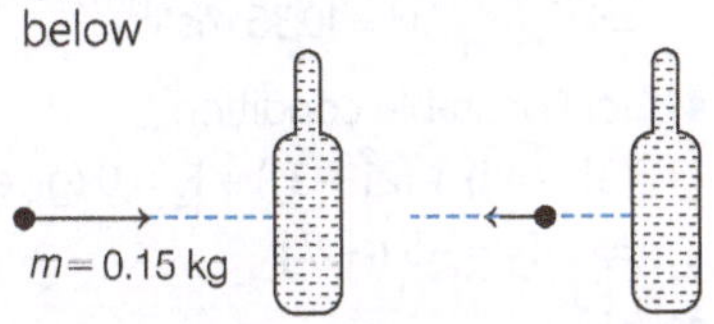

Initial momentum	Final momentum
$= mv = 0.15 \times 12$	$= mv = 0.15 \times 12$
$= 1.8$ N-s to right	$= 1.8$ N-s to left

Impulse = Final momentum − Initial momentum

= 3.6 N-s towards left

34 (*b*) According to question, 7th coin is under the weight of 5 coins above it.

Hence, reaction of the 7th coin on the 8th coin

= force on the 7th coin due to 8th coin

= weight of 5 coins

$= 5\,mg = 5 \times 20 \times 10^{-3} \times 10 = 1\ \text{N}$

$[\because m = 20\ \text{g} = 20 \times 10^{-3}\ \text{kg}]$

35 (*d*) Change in force

$= 100(5 - 2.5) = 250\ \text{N}$

37 (*b*) f_{applied} = Gravitational force + Force due to acceleration

$= mg + ma = m(g + a)$

38 (*b*) Thrust force on the rocket,

$f_t = v\left(\frac{-dm}{dt}\right)$ (upward)

Net force on the rocket,

$f_{\text{net}} = f_t - w$

$\Rightarrow ma = v\left(\frac{-dm}{dt}\right) - mg$

$\Rightarrow \left(\frac{-dm}{dt}\right) = \frac{m(g + a)}{v}$

$\therefore$ Rate of gas ejected per second

$= \frac{(6000)(10 + 20)}{900} = 200\ \text{kg s}^{-1}$

39 (*a*) Mass of water gushed out per second, m

= Area × velocity × density

$= 10^{-3} \times 50 \times 1000 = 50\ \text{kg}$

Force exerted on the wall by the impact of water,

$F = m\left(\frac{v - u}{t}\right)$

$= 50 \times \left(\frac{-50}{1}\right) = -2500$

$|F| = 2500\ \text{N}$

40 (*c*) $F = m(a + g)$

$= (3 \times 10^3)(10 + 10)$

$= 6 \times 10^4\ \text{N}$

41 (*d*) Force acting on the stone,

$F = ma \Rightarrow F = 2 \times 4 = 8\ \text{N}$

42 (*b*) (i) Force on the floor by the crew and passengers

$= m(g + a)$

$= 500(10 + 12)$

$= 11 \times 10^3\ \text{N}$

It acts vertically downwards.

(ii) Action of the rotor of the helicopter on the surrounding air

$= (M + m)(g + a)$

$= (1500 + 500)(10 + 12)$

$= 44 \times 10^3\ \text{N}$

It acts vertically downwards.

(iii) Force on the helicopter due to the surrounding air is equal and opposite to the action of the rotor of the helicopter on the surrounding air.

43 (*a*) Change in momentum of the ball $= \mathbf{p}_f - \mathbf{p}_i$

$= (-p_{fx}\hat{\mathbf{i}} - p_{fy}\hat{\mathbf{j}}) - (p_{ix}\hat{\mathbf{i}} - p_{iy}\hat{\mathbf{j}})$

$= -\hat{\mathbf{i}}(+p_{fx} + p_{ix}) - \hat{\mathbf{j}}(p_{fy} - p_{iy})$

$= -2p_{ix}\hat{\mathbf{i}} \quad [\because p_{fy} - p_{iy} = 0]$

Here, $p_{ix} = p_{fx} = p_i \cos 60° = \frac{Mv}{2}$

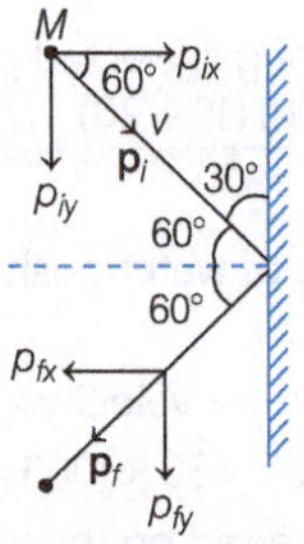

∵ Impulse imparted by the wall = Change in momentum of the ball = Mv

45 (b) Time taken by the ball to reach the ground,

$$t = \sqrt{\frac{2h}{g}} = \sqrt{\frac{2 \times 500 \text{ m}}{10 \text{ ms}^{-2}}} = 10 \text{ s}$$

Horizontal distance covered $= ut$

∴ $400 = u \times 10$

⇒ $u = 40 \text{ ms}^{-1}$

Initial momentum = Final momentum

$$0 = Mv + mu$$

$$v = -\frac{mu}{M} = -\frac{(1 \text{ kg})(40 \text{ ms}^{-1})}{100 \text{ kg}}$$

$$= -0.4 \text{ ms}^{-1}$$

46 (b) $m_1\mathbf{v}_1 + m_2\mathbf{v}_2 + \mathbf{p}_3 = 0$

From figure given below

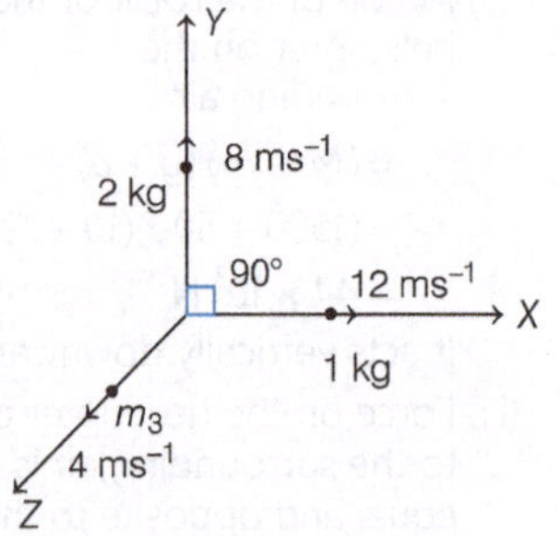

∴ $(1 \times 12\hat{\mathbf{i}}) + (2 \times 8\hat{\mathbf{j}}) + \mathbf{p}_3 = 0$

⇒ $\mathbf{p}_3 = -(12\hat{\mathbf{i}} + 16\hat{\mathbf{j}})$

∴ $p_3 = 20 \text{ kg-ms}^{-1}$

Now, $m_3 = \frac{p_3}{v_3} = \frac{20}{4} = 5 \text{ kg}$

47 (a) Speed of 200 kg trolley $= 10 \text{ ms}^{-1}$

Let v' be the absolute value of velocity of trolley and v_b be the absolute velocity of child after the beginning of journey.

So, $v_b = (v' - 4)$

Momentum before the child begins to run,

$$p = (200 + 20) \times 10$$
$$= 2200 \text{ kg ms}^{-1}$$

Momentum after the child starts running

$$= 200v' + 20(v' - 4)$$
$$= 220v' - 80$$

Apply conservation of linear momentum, $2200 = 220v' - 80$

⇒ $v' = 10.36 \text{ ms}^{-1}$

49 (c) For stable condition,

$(3\hat{\mathbf{i}} - 4\hat{\mathbf{j}}) + (2\hat{\mathbf{i}} - 3\hat{\mathbf{j}}) + \mathbf{F}_3 = 0$ (given)

⇒ $\mathbf{F}_3 = -5\hat{\mathbf{i}} + 7\hat{\mathbf{j}}$

50 (a)

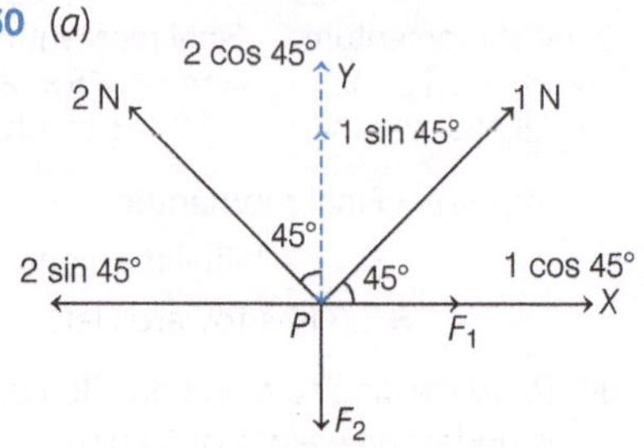

At equilibrium, $\Sigma F_x = 0$ and $\Sigma F_y = 0$

⇒ $2\cos 45° + \sin 45° = F_2$

and $2\sin 45° = F_1 + \cos 45°$

⇒ $F_1 \simeq 0.7 \text{ N}$ and $F_2 \simeq 2.1 \text{ N}$

51 (c)

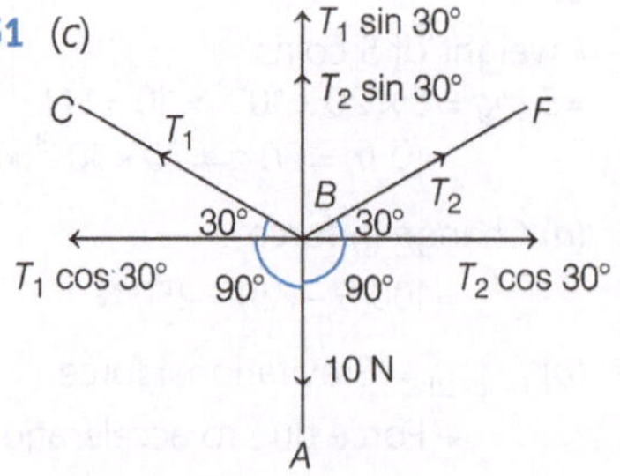

For equilibrium along horizontal direction,

$$T_1 \cos 30° = T_2 \cos 30°$$

Let, $T_1 = T_2 = T$

Again, for equilibrium along vertical direction,

$$T_1 \sin 30° + T_2 \sin 30° = 10$$

⇒ $T = 10 \text{ N}$

52 (b)

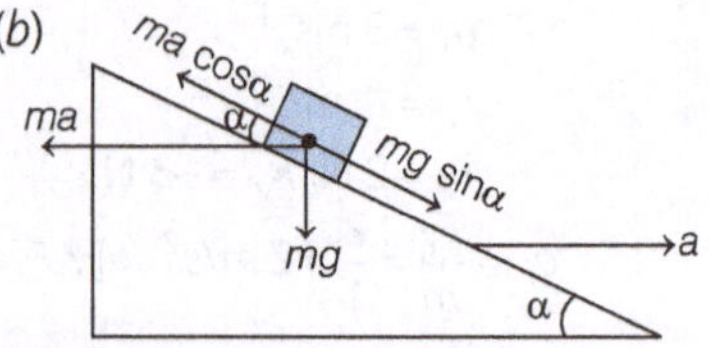

If forces acting on it are in equilibrium. i.e.

$$ma \cos \alpha = mg \sin \alpha$$

⇒ $a = g \tan \alpha$

54 (a) The free body diagram of the given system is drawn as

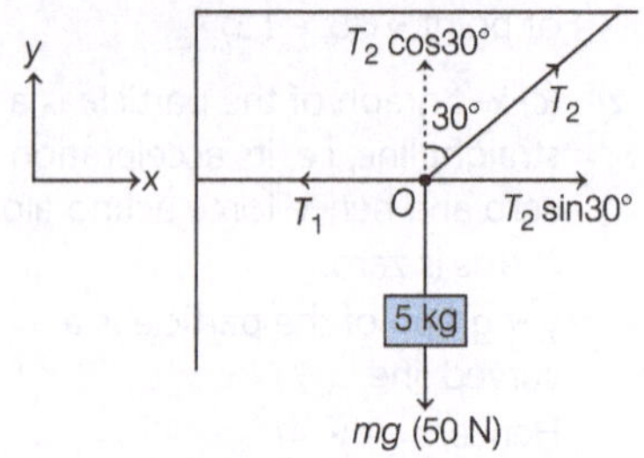

Applying equations for equilibrium,

$$\Sigma F_x \Rightarrow T_2 \sin 30° - T_1 = 0$$

So, $T_1 = \frac{T_2}{2}$ ...(i)

$$\Sigma F_y \Rightarrow T_2 \cos 30° - 50 = 0$$

So, $T_2 = \frac{100}{\sqrt{3}} \text{ N}$ ...(ii)

Put this in Eq. (i), we get

$$T_1 = \frac{50}{\sqrt{3}} \text{ N}$$

55 (b) For vertical equilibrium of P,

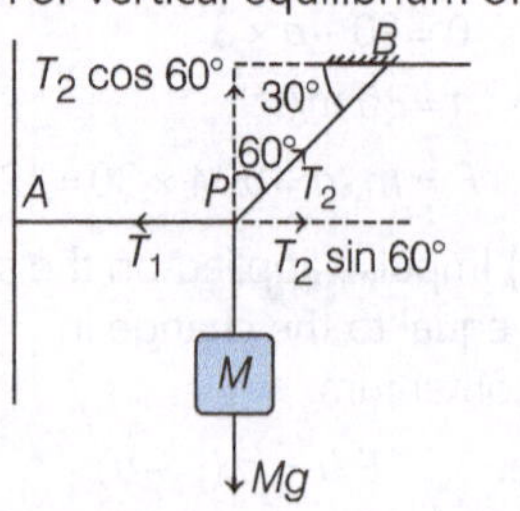

$$T_2 \cos 60° = Mg$$

i.e. $T_2 = 2Mg$ ...(i)

and for horizontal equilibrium of P,

$T_1 = T_2 \sin 60° = T_2(\sqrt{3}/2)$ ...(ii)

Substituting the value of T_2 from Eq. (i), we get

$$T_1 = (2Mg) \times (\sqrt{3}/2) = \sqrt{3}\, Mg$$

56 (c)

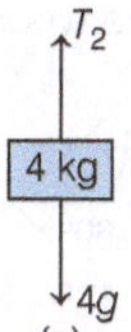

(a)

The free body diagram of 4 kg block is as shown in figure (a).

In equilibrium, $T_2 = 4g = 40$ N

The free body diagram of the point P is as shown in figure (b).

$$T_1 \sin\theta = 70 \text{ N} \quad \text{...... (i)}$$

$$T_1 \cos\theta = T_2 = 40 \text{ N} \quad \text{......(ii)}$$

Dividing Eq. (i) by Eq. (ii), we get

$$\theta \simeq 60°$$

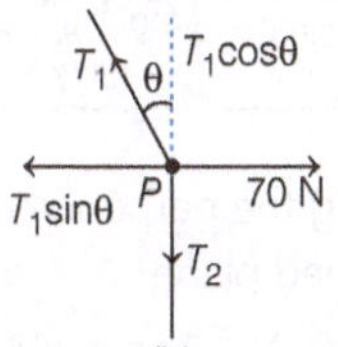

(b)

57 (a) $2g - T = 2a$ ...(i)

$$T - g = a \quad \text{...(ii)}$$

Adding Eqs. (i) and (ii), we get

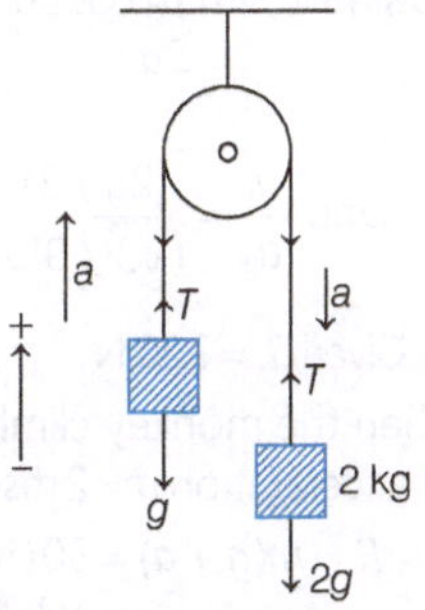

$$g = 3a \Rightarrow a = \frac{g}{3}$$

Acceleration of COM

$$= \frac{m_1a_1 + m_2a_2}{m_1 + m_2} = \frac{-g}{9}$$

$$s = ut + \frac{1}{2}a_{CM}t^2 = -\frac{20}{9} \text{ m}$$

58 (c) According to the figure shown,

$$(m_2 + m_3)g - T' = (m_2 + m_3)a \quad \text{...(i)}$$

and $T' - m_1g = m_1a$ ...(ii)

Adding Eqs. (i) and (ii), we get

$$a = \left(\frac{m_2 + m_3 - m_1}{m_2 + m_3 + m_1}\right)g \quad \text{...(iii)}$$

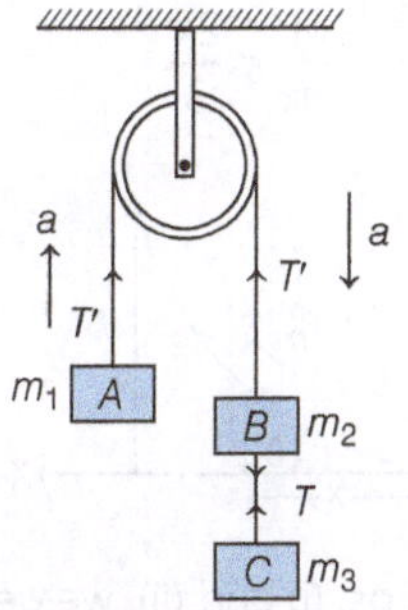

Between B and C,

$$m_3g - T = m_3a$$

$$\Rightarrow \quad T = m_3(g - a) \quad \text{...(iv)}$$

On substituting the value of a from Eqs. (iii) to (iv),

$$T = \frac{2m_1m_3}{m_1 + m_2 + m_3} \times g$$

$$\Rightarrow \quad T = \frac{2 \times 2 \times 2}{2 + 2 + 2} \times 9.8 = 13.3 \text{ N}$$

59 (a)

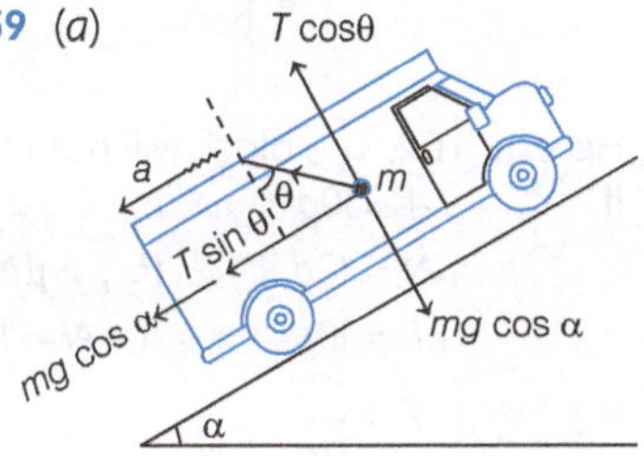

$$\Rightarrow \quad T\sin\theta = ma - mg\sin\alpha \quad \text{...(i)}$$

$$T\cos\theta = mg\cos\alpha \quad \text{...(ii)}$$

Using Eqs. (i) and (ii), we get

$$\tan\theta = \frac{a - g\sin\alpha}{g\cos\alpha}$$

$$\Rightarrow \quad \theta = \tan^{-1}\left(\frac{a - g\sin\alpha}{g\cos\alpha}\right)$$

60 (a) As the system is in equilibrium,

$$\therefore \quad T = w \quad \text{...(i)}$$

and $T = mg\sin 30°$ ...(ii)

From Eqs. (i) and (ii), we get

$$w = mg\sin 30° = (50\text{N}) \times \frac{1}{2} = 25\text{N}$$

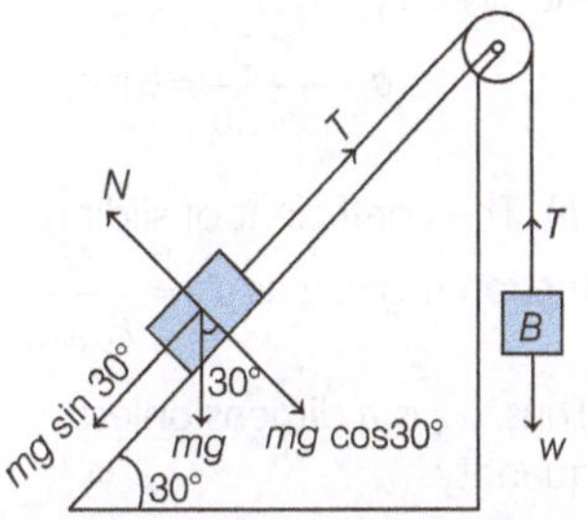

61 (c)

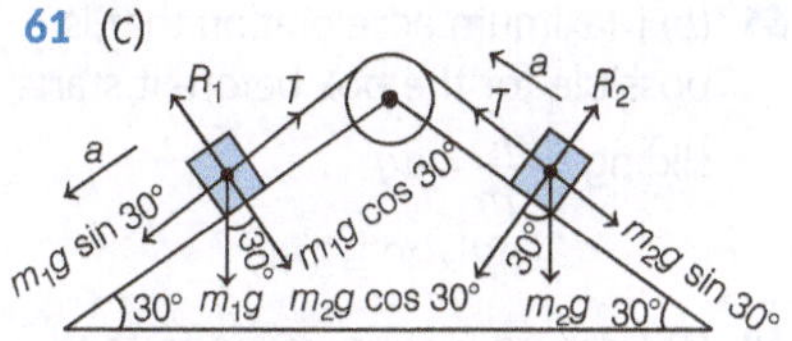

Equations of motion are

$$m_1g\sin 30° - T = m_1a \quad \text{...(i)}$$

$$T - m_2g\sin 30° = m_2a \quad \text{...(ii)}$$

Adding Eqs. (i) and (ii), we get

$$(m_1 + m_2)a = (m_1 - m_2)g\sin 30°$$

$$(40 + 20)a = (40 - 20)\,9.8 \times \frac{1}{2} = 98$$

$$\Rightarrow \quad a = \frac{98}{60} = 1.6 \text{ ms}^{-2}$$

63 (b) By Newton's third law of motion,

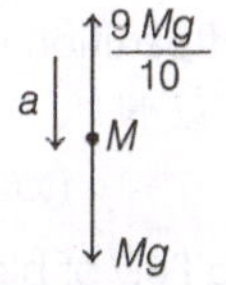

Reaction by floor on mass M

$$= \frac{9Mg}{10} \quad \text{(upward)}$$

From figure,

$\mathbf{F}_{net}$ on cabin of mass M

$$= Mg - \frac{9Mg}{10} = \frac{Mg}{10}$$

(downward)

By second law,

$$\frac{Mg}{10} = Ma \Rightarrow a = \frac{g}{10}$$

64 (c) FBD of the given system is as follow

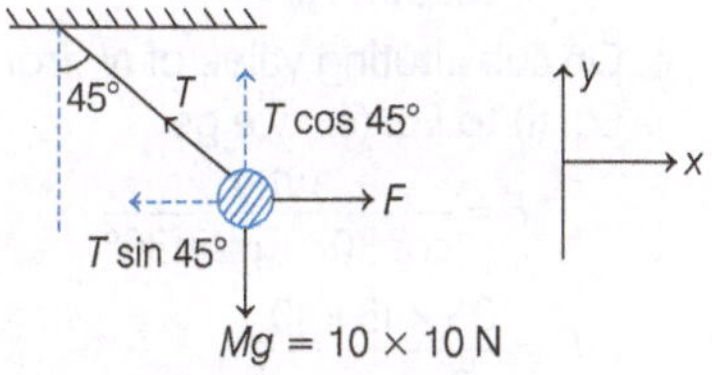

For equilibrium condition of the mass,

$$F = T\sin 45° \quad \text{...(i)}$$

$$Mg = T\cos 45° \quad \text{...(ii)}$$

Using Eqs. (i) and (ii), we get

$$\frac{F}{Mg} = 1$$

$$\Rightarrow F = Mg = 10 \times 10 = 100 \text{ N}$$

66 (*b*) Maximum acceleration that is possible for the box before it starts sliding $= \frac{f_s}{m} = \mu g$

$= 0.3 \times 10 = 3\,\text{ms}^{-2}$

68 (*c*) Limiting friction acting to the left as shown below is given by

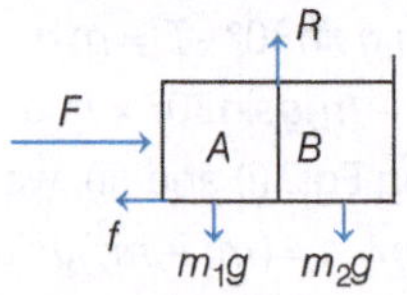

$f = \mu R = 22.5$ N

$[\because R = (m_1 + m_2)g]$

$\therefore$ Net force acting on the partition towards the right,

$F' = F - f = 177.5$ N

Reaction of partition

$= 177.5$ N

(towards the left)

69 (*c*) Drawing FBD of block,

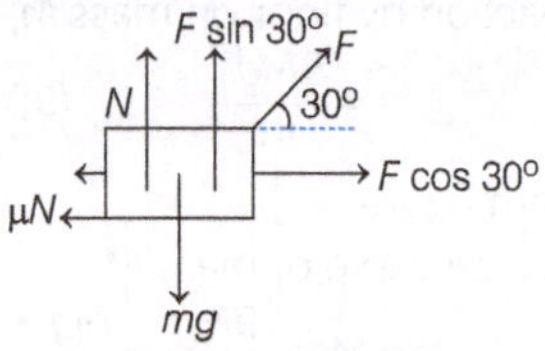

$N + F\sin 30° = mg$

or $N = mg - F\sin 30°$ ...(i)

$F\cos 30° - \mu N = ma_x$

As block is on the verge of slipping, then

$a_x = 0$

$F\cos 30° = \mu N$ ...(ii)

On substituting value of N from Eq. (i) to Eq. (ii), we get

$$F = \frac{\mu mg}{\cos 30° + \mu \sin 30°}$$

$$F = \frac{0.5 \times 15 \times 10}{\frac{\sqrt{3}}{2} + 0.5 \times \frac{1}{2}}$$

$F = 67$ N

70 (*d*) Block is under limiting friction, so

$\mu = \tan\theta$ ...(i)

Equation of the surface,

$$y = \frac{x^2}{3}$$

Slope, $\frac{dy}{dx} = \frac{2x}{3}$ ...(ii)

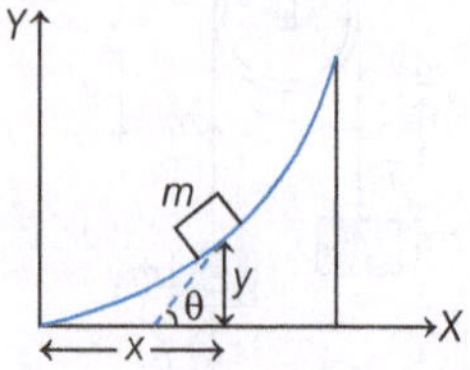

From Eqs. (i) and (ii), we get

$$\mu = \frac{2x}{3}$$

$\Rightarrow x = \frac{3}{4}$ so $y = \frac{3}{16}$ m

71 (*d*)

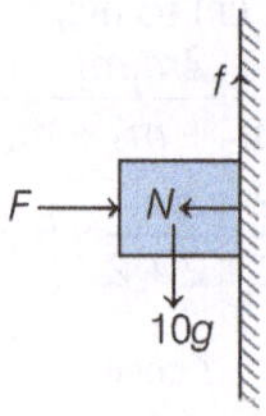

Here, $\mu = 0.2$. The block will not fall, if

$f = 10g$

$\mu N = 10g$ $(\because f = \mu N)$

$\mu F = 10g$ $(\because N = F)$

$$F = \frac{10g}{\mu}$$

$\Rightarrow F = \frac{10 \times 10}{0.2}$ $(\because \mu = 0.2)$

$\therefore F = 500$ N

72 (*c*) Force of friction on A

$= \mu m_A g = 10$ N

Force of friction on B

$= \mu m_B g = 20$ N

Taking two blocks forming one system, therefore net force acting on the blocks is

$F = 150 - 10 - 20 = 120$ N

Let a be common acceleration of the system.

$\therefore a = \frac{120}{5 + 10} = 8\,\text{ms}^{-2}$

73 (*b*) The coefficient of sliding friction is given as $\mu_S = \frac{N}{F_{\text{sliding}}}$

Thus, μ_S is a dimensionless quantity.

74 (*b*) FBD of the wedge

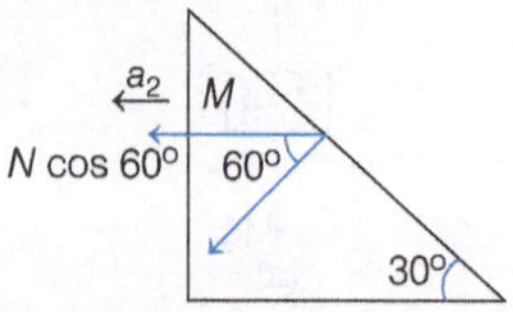

$N\cos 60° = Ma_2$

$\Rightarrow N = 32a_2$

Now, FBD of the block with respect to the wedge

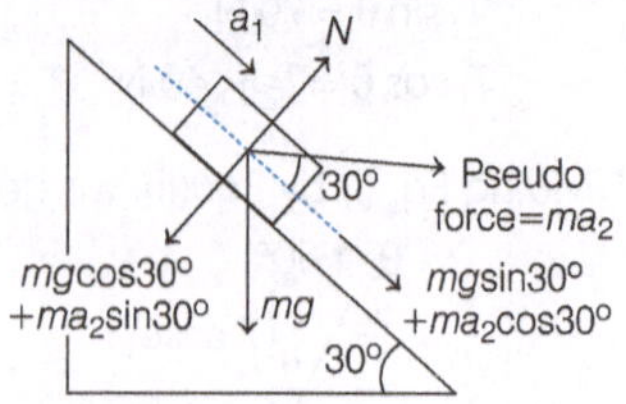

Along the perpendicular to the inclined plane,

$N = 8g\cos 30° - 8a_2 \sin 30°$

$\Rightarrow a_2 = \frac{\sqrt{3}}{9} g$

Along the inclined plane,

$mg\sin 30° + ma_2 \cos 30° = ma_1$

$\Rightarrow a_1 = \frac{2g}{3}$

$\because$ Ratio, $\frac{a_1}{a_2} = \frac{(2g/3)}{(\sqrt{3}/9)g} = 2\sqrt{3}$

75 (*a*) Given, $T = 320$ N

When the monkey climbs up with an acceleration $a = 2\,\text{ms}^{-2}$

$R = m(g + a) = 30(10 + 2)$

$= 360$ N

$\therefore R > T$

Hence, the rope will break.

76 (*c*) First of all consider the forces on the blocks as shown below

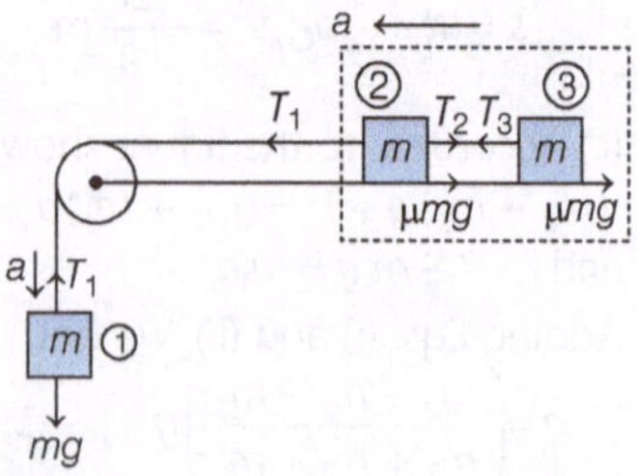

For the Ist block,

$$mg - T_1 = m \times a \quad \text{...(i)}$$

Let us consider 2nd and 3rd block as a system.

So, $T_1 - 2\mu mg = 2m \times a$ ...(ii)

Adding Eqs. (i) and (ii), we get

$$mg(1-2\mu) = 3m \times a$$

$$\Rightarrow \quad a = \frac{g}{3}(1-2\mu)$$

77 (c)

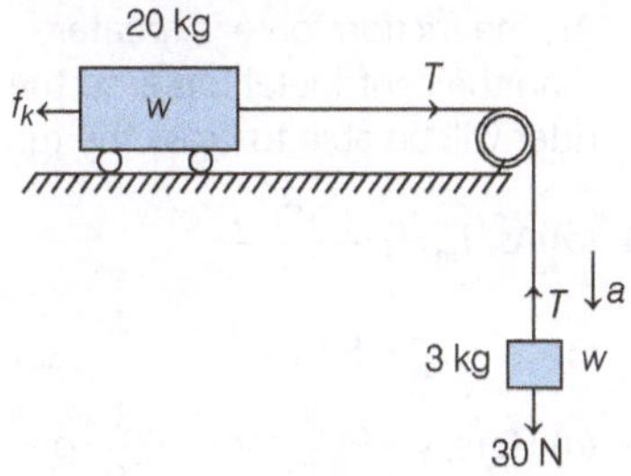

$$30 - T = 3a \quad \text{...(i)}$$

Apply the second law of motion to the trolley, $T - f_k = 20\,a$

Now, $f_k = \mu_k N = 0.04 \times 200$

Thus, the equation for the motion of the trolley is

$$T - 0.04 \times 200 = 20a$$

$$\Rightarrow \quad T - 8 = 20a \quad \text{...(ii)}$$

Adding Eqs. (i) and (ii), we get

$$a = \frac{22}{23}\ \text{ms}^{-2} = 0.96\ \text{ms}^{-2}$$

Putting the value of a in Eq. (i), we get

$$T = 30 - 3(0.96) = 27.1\ \text{N}$$

78 (a) Free body diagram, for the given figure is as follows

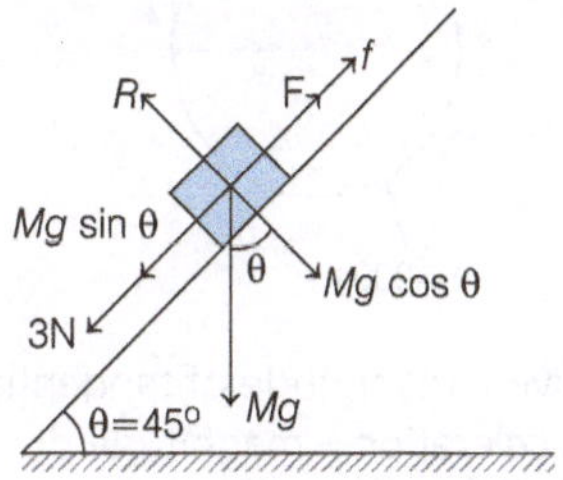

$$3 + Mg\sin\theta = F + f$$

$$\Rightarrow \quad 3 + Mg\sin\theta = F + \mu R \quad \text{...(i)}$$

Similarly,

$$Mg\cos\theta = R \quad \text{...(ii)}$$

Substituting the value of R from Eq. (ii) into Eq. (i), we get

$$3 + Mg\sin\theta = F + \mu(Mg\cos\theta) \quad \text{...(iii)}$$

$$3 + (10 \times 10\sin 45^\circ) - (0.6 \times 10 \times 10\cos 45^\circ) = F$$

or $F \simeq 32$ N

79 (a)

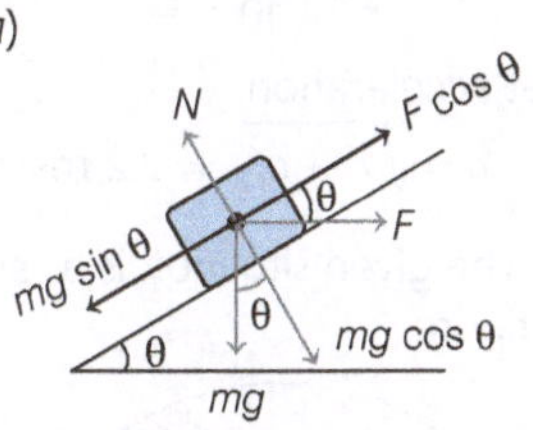

$$F\cos\theta = mg\sin\theta$$

$$\Rightarrow \quad F = \frac{80}{\sqrt{3}}$$

80 (b)

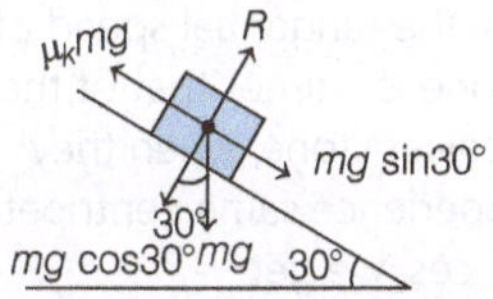

The coefficient of static friction,

$$\mu_s = \tan 30^\circ = \frac{1}{\sqrt{3}} = 0.6$$

$$\Rightarrow \quad a = \frac{4}{8} = 0.5\ \text{ms}^{-2}$$

From diagram, for motion of block, $ma = mg\sin 30^\circ - \mu_k mg$

$$\Rightarrow \quad a = g\sin 30^\circ - \mu_k g$$

$$0.5 = 10 \times \frac{1}{2} - \mu_k \times 10$$

$$\Rightarrow \quad \mu_k = \frac{5-0.5}{10} = 0.45 \simeq 0.5$$

81 (c)

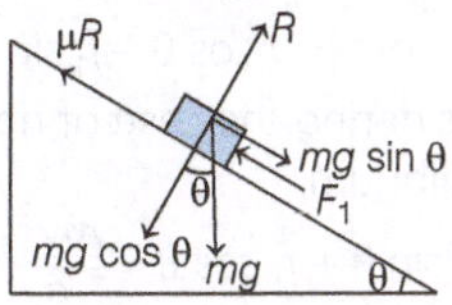

I

For equilibrium in case I,

$$\mu R + F_1 = mg\sin\theta$$

$$F_1 = mg\sin\theta - \mu R = mg\sin\theta - \mu mg\cos\theta \quad [\because R = mg\cos\theta]$$

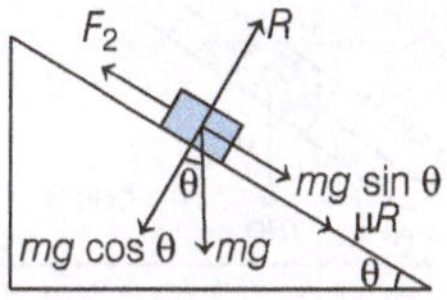

II

Similarly, for equilibrium in case II,

$$F_2 = \mu R + mg\sin\theta = \mu mg\cos\theta + mg\sin\theta \quad [\because R = mg\cos\theta]$$

$$\because \quad \frac{F_1}{F_2} = \frac{\sin\theta - \mu\cos\theta}{\sin\theta + \mu\cos\theta}$$

Putting $\mu = \frac{1}{2}\tan\theta$

$$F_1 : F_2 = 1 : 3$$

82 (c)

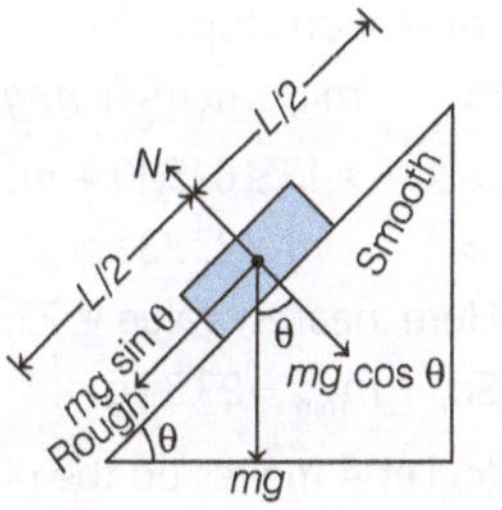

Since, initial and final speeds are zero, hence

work done by gravitational force = work done by friction force

$$f_g \cdot L = f_f \cdot \frac{L}{2} \quad \text{... (i)}$$

(as only lower half has friction)

Here, $f_g = mg\sin\theta$

and $f_f = \mu N = \mu mg\cos\theta$

On substituting values in Eq. (ii) and solving, we get

$$\Rightarrow \quad \mu = 2\tan\theta$$

84 (b)

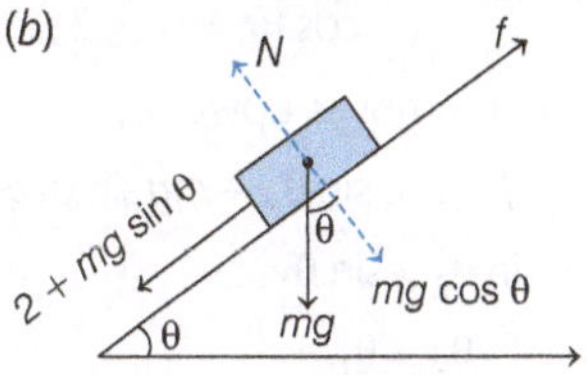

So, equating forces, we have;

$$2 + mg\sin\theta = f$$

or $2 + mg\sin\theta = \mu\, mg\cos\theta$ ...(i)

Similarly,

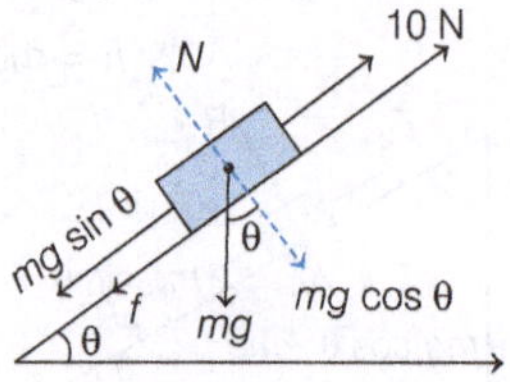

Now, equating forces, we have

$$mg\sin\theta + f = 10\text{ N}$$

or $mg\sin\theta + \mu mg\cos\theta = 10$ ...(ii)

Now, solving Eqs. (i) and (ii), we get

$$mg\sin\theta = 4 \quad \text{...(iii)}$$

and $\mu\, mg\cos\theta = 6$ ...(iv)

Dividing Eqs. (iii) and (iv), we get

$$\mu = \frac{\sqrt{3}}{2}$$

85 (*b*) Motion stops

$\Rightarrow \quad m_1 g \le \mu(m_2 + m)g$

$\Rightarrow \quad 5 \times 10 \le 0.15(10 + m) \times 10$

$\Rightarrow \quad m \ge 23.33$ kg

Here, nearest value is 23.3 kg

So, $m_{min} = 23.3$ kg

86 (*c*) Let *A* moves up the plane, then *B* will move downward as shown.

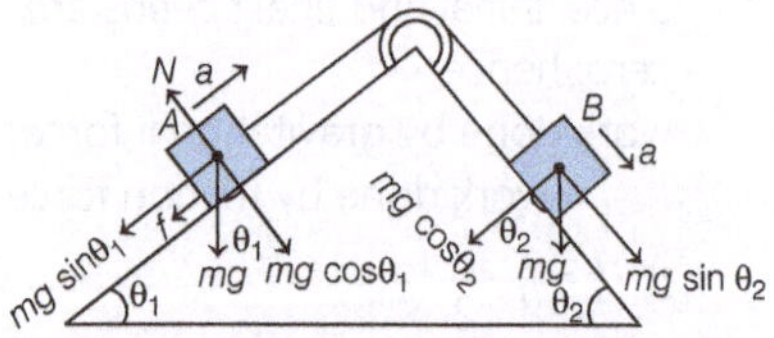

When *A* just starts moving up ,

$$mg\sin\theta_1 + f = mg\sin\theta_2$$

where, $f = \mu N = \mu\, mg\cos\theta_1$

$\Rightarrow mg\sin\theta_1 + \mu\, mg\cos\theta_1 = mg\sin\theta_2$

$$\Rightarrow \mu = \frac{\sin\theta_2 - \sin\theta_1}{\cos\theta_1}$$

When *A* moves upwards,

$$f = mg\sin\theta_2 - mg\sin\theta_1 > 0$$

$\Rightarrow \sin\theta_2 > \sin\theta_1$

$\Rightarrow \quad \theta_2 > \theta_1$

87 (*a*) Radial acceleration (centripetal acceleration)

$$= \frac{v^2}{r} = \frac{5 \times 5}{10} = 2.5\text{ ms}^{-2}$$

Force = Mass × Acceleration

= 2× 2.5 = 5N

88 (*c*) Tangential acceleration, $a_t = 2\text{ ms}^{-2}$

$\Rightarrow$ Radial acceleration,

$$a_r = \frac{v^2}{r} = \frac{(5)^2}{10} = 2.5\text{ ms}^{-2}$$

Net acceleration,

$$a = \sqrt{a_r^2 + a_t^2} = 3.2\text{ ms}^{-2}$$

89 (*a*) The given situation is as shown in figure.

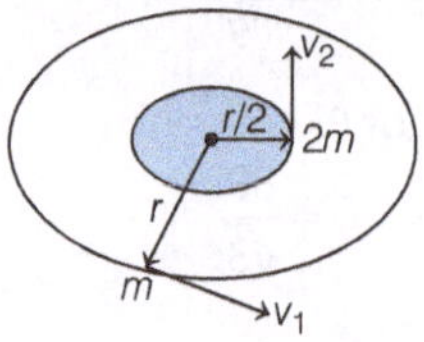

As, the tangential speed of lighter stone is *n* times that of the value of heavier stone, when they experience same centripetal forces, we get

$$(F_c)_{heavier} = (F_c)_{lighter}$$

$$\Rightarrow \quad \frac{2m(v)^2}{(r/2)} = \frac{m(nv)^2}{r}$$

$$\Rightarrow \quad n = 2$$

92 (*a*)

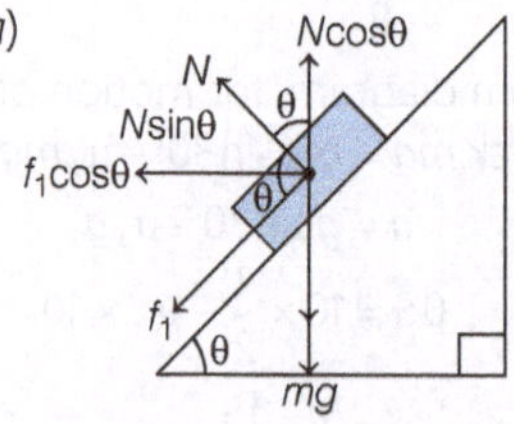

Considering the case of vertical equilibrium,

$$N\cos\theta = mg + f_1\sin\theta$$

$$\Rightarrow \quad mg = N\cos\theta - f_1\sin\theta \quad \text{...(i)}$$

Considering the case of horizontal equilibrium,

$$N\sin\theta + f_1\cos\theta = \frac{mv^2}{R} \quad \text{...(ii)}$$

Dividing Eq. (ii) by Eq. (i), we get

$$\frac{v^2}{gR} = \frac{\sin\theta + \mu_s\cos\theta}{\cos\theta - \mu_s\sin\theta} \quad (\because f_1 = \mu_s N)$$

$$\Rightarrow \quad v = \sqrt{gR\left(\frac{\tan\theta + \mu_s}{1 - \mu_s\tan\theta}\right)}$$

93 (*a*) Centripetal force

$$= \frac{mv^2}{r} = \frac{50 \times 10 \times 10}{20} = 250\text{ N}$$

Required frictional force to cross the turn

$$= \mu mg = 0.6 \times 50 \times 10$$

$$= 300\text{ N}$$

As, the friction force is greater than the centripetal force, so the rider will be able to cross the turn.

94 (*b*) As, $T_{max} = \frac{mv^2_{max}}{r}$

$\Rightarrow \quad v_{max} = 50\text{ ms}^{-1}$

95 (*a*) Here, $\nu = 26\frac{1}{2}$ rpm $= \frac{53}{120}$ rps

$$\omega = 2\pi\nu = 2.77\text{ rads}^{-1}$$

The coin will revolve with the disc, if $\frac{mv^2}{r} \le \mu mg$

$$m\omega^2 r \le \mu mg$$

For given μ and ω, the condition if $r \le \frac{\mu g}{\omega^2}$.

As, $\frac{\mu g}{\omega^2} = \frac{0.2 \times 10}{(2.77)^2} \approx 25.9$ cm

For coin *A*, *r* = 4 cm

The above condition is satisfied, therefore coin *A* will revolve with the disc.

For coin *B*, *r* = 28 cm, the above condition is not satisfied, therefore coin *B* will not revolves.

96 (*c*)

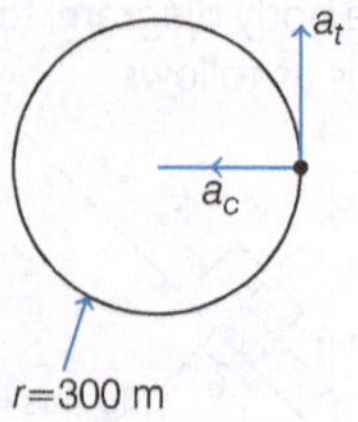

Given, magnitude of tangential acceleration = magnitude of centripetal acceleration

$$\Rightarrow \quad \frac{dv}{dt} = \frac{v^2}{r}$$

$$\Rightarrow \quad \frac{dv}{ds} . v = \frac{v^2}{r}$$

$$\Rightarrow \quad \int_{u=15}^{v} \frac{dv}{v} = \frac{1}{r} \int_0^s ds$$

$$\Rightarrow \quad [\ln v]_{15}^{v} = \frac{s}{r}$$

$$\Rightarrow \quad v = 15 e^{s/r}$$

$$\Rightarrow \quad \frac{ds}{dt} = 15 e^{s/r}$$

$$\Rightarrow \quad \int_0^{\pi r/2} e^{-s/r} ds = 15 \int_0^{t_0} dt$$

$$\Rightarrow t_0 = \frac{r}{15}(1 - e^{-\pi/2}) = \frac{300}{15}(1 - e^{-\pi/2})$$

$$\Rightarrow t_0 = 20(1 - e^{-\pi/2}) = t(1 - e^{-\pi/2}) \quad \text{(given)}$$

$\because \quad t = 20$ s

97. (*a*) The angle of banking

$$\tan\theta = \frac{v^2}{rg}$$

$$\tan 45° = \frac{v^2}{40 \times 10}$$

$$\Rightarrow \quad v = 20 \text{ m/s}$$

98 (*b*) According to the question,

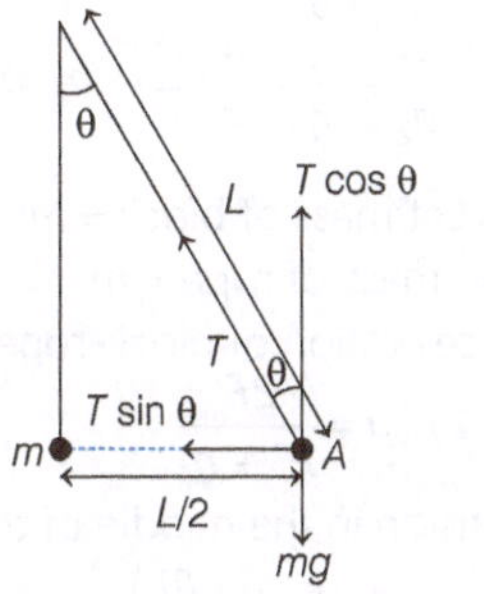

From the diagram,

$$\tan\theta = v^2 / rg$$

$$\Rightarrow \quad v = \sqrt{rg \tan\theta} \quad \text{...(i)}$$

Now, from figure,

$$\sin\theta = \frac{L/2}{L} = \frac{1}{2}$$

$$\Rightarrow \quad \theta = 30°$$

From Eq. (i),

$$v = \sqrt{rg \tan 30°} = \sqrt{\frac{rg}{\sqrt{3}}}$$

99 (*b*) Optimum speed,

$$v_o = \sqrt{gR \tan\theta} = 28.1 \text{ ms}^{-1}$$

and
$$v_{max} = \sqrt{\frac{gR(\mu_s + \tan 15°)}{1 - \mu_s \tan 15°}}$$

$$= \sqrt{\frac{9.8 \times 300\,(0.2 + 0.27)}{1 - 0.2\,(0.27)}}$$

$$= 38.1 \text{ ms}^{-1}$$

Assertion and Reason Questions

1 (*d*) It is not always necessary that external agency of force is in contact with the object, while applying force on object.

Force can be applied on a body/particle without contact or with contact, it depends on the agency, applying force. e.g. Earth pulls (exerts force) from distance.

3 (*c*) A stationary body ($v = 0$) may still have some acceleration, e.g. when a body is thrown in upward direction, it comes to rest at highest position, but at that time, it still have acceleration equal to acceleration due to gravity g.

4 (*c*) As we know, momentum,

$$\mathbf{p} = m\mathbf{v}$$

Change in momentum **p** can be brought by changing force **F**.

As, $\mathbf{F} = \dfrac{d\mathbf{p}}{dt}$ = rate of change of momentum with time.

$\Rightarrow d\mathbf{p} = \mathbf{F}dt \Rightarrow md\mathbf{v} = \mathbf{F}dt$

So, in order to keep, $\mathbf{F}dt$ constant, $md\mathbf{v}$ should be constant, here m and $d\mathbf{v}$ can change from one body to another body.

Thus, same force for same time can cause different change in momentum for different bodies.

5 (*b*) Second law of motion can be applied to both inanimate and animate objects. For example, without the external force of friction, we cannot walk on the ground.

6 (*d*) If momentum of a body is zero, i.e. velocity of it should be zero. It does not mean that force or acceleration are necessarily zero at that instant.

7 (*a*) The time of action of the force is very short, therefore one can assume that there is no appreciable change in the position of the body during the action of the impulsive force.

8 (*a*) Internal forces in a body cancel away as they form action & reaction pairs.

9 (*d*) According to Newton's third law of motion, it is impossible to have a single force out of mutual interaction between two bodies, whether they are moving or at rest. It means, third law of motion is applicable to all the bodies either at rest or in motion and this law is also applicable to all types of forces.

12 (*b*) The concept of force in physics should not be confused with the concept of the feeling of force.

Statement Based Questions

3 (*c*) Action and reaction forces are simultaneous forces.

4 (*b*) The equality of mg and R has no connection with the third law of motion because two forces mg and R can be different.

5 (*b*) The statement II is false and it can be corrected as,
Each body in the assembly experiences the force of gravity.

6 (*c*) Statement I is false, it corrected as,

Friction is an undesirable force sometimes, not always. In many situation, like in a machine with different moving parts, friction does have a negative role.

7 (*d*) When a stone is rotated in horizontal circle, then centripetal force is required which is given as

$$F = \frac{mv^2}{r}$$

$$\therefore \quad F \propto v^2, \; F \propto \frac{1}{r}$$

From above, it is clear that when stone is rotated with greater speed, then greater force (centripetal force) is required. Again, when stone is rotated in a circle of smaller radius, greater force is required.

Matching Type Questions

1 (*c*) At $t = 0$ to $t = 4$ s,

Acceleration = Slope of v-t graph

$$= \frac{8}{4} = 2 \text{ m/s}^2$$

At $t = 4$ s to $t = 10$ s,

Acceleration $= 0$

At $t = 10$ s to $t = 14$ s,

Acceleration $= -\frac{8}{4} = -2 \text{ m/s}^2$

For the lift

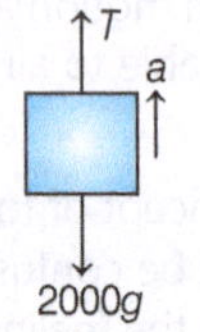

$$T - 2000g = 2000a$$
$$T = 2000(g + a)$$

A. At $t = 1$ s, $a = 2 \text{ m/s}^2$

$T = 2000(g + a)$

$= 2000(10 + 2) = 24000$ N

B. At $t = 6$ s, $a = 0$

$T = 2000(10 + 0) = 20000$ N

C. At $t = 12$ s, $a = -2 \text{ m/s}^2$

$T = 2000(10 - 2) = 16000$ N

D. At $t = 0$ to $t = 14$ s.

Displacement = Area of v-t graph

$$= \frac{1}{2}(6 + 14) \times 8 = 80 \text{ m}$$

Average velocity

$$= \frac{80}{14} = \frac{40}{7} \text{ m/s}$$

Hence, A → 3, B → 1, C → 4 D → 2.

2 (*b*)

A. For uniform speed, acceleration, $a = 0$

∴ Reading of weighing scale, $R = mg = 60 \times 10 = 600$ N.

B. When lift is moving downward with uniform acceleration, then

Reading of weighing scale

$= mg - ma = m(g - a)$

$= 60(10 - 6) = 240$ N

C. When lift is moving upward with uniform acceleration, then

Reading of weighing scale

$= mg + ma = m(g + a)$

$= 60(10 + 6) = 960$ N

D. When lift's mechanism fails, then it will start falling down freely.

Thus, reading of weighing scale $= 0$ N

Hence, A → 2, B → 1, C → 4 D → 3.

3 (*c*)

A. Pulling force $= 2mg$

Total mass $= 3m$

$$a_1 = \frac{2mg}{3m} = \frac{2g}{3}$$

B. Net pulling force

$= 3mg - 2mg = mg$

Total mass

$= 3m + m + 2m = 6m$

$$a_2 = \frac{mg}{6m} = \frac{g}{6}$$

C. Net pulling force

$= 3mg + mg - 2mg = 2mg$

Total mass

$= 3m + m + 2m = 6m$

$$a_3 = \frac{2mg}{6m} = \frac{g}{3}$$

D. Net pulling force

$= 4mg \sin 30° - mg = mg$

Total mass $= 4m + m = 5m$

$$a_4 = \frac{mg}{5m} = \frac{g}{5}$$

Hence, A → 4, B → 3, C → 2 D → 1.

4 (*b*)

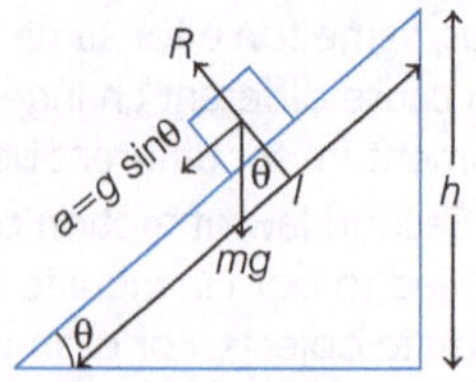

A. $ma = mg \sin\theta$

$\therefore a = g \sin\theta$

B. Velocity at bottom,

$v = \sqrt{2gh} = \sqrt{2gl \sin\theta}$

C. $v = u + at$

$\sqrt{(2gl \sin\theta)} = 0 + g \sin\theta t$

$$t = \frac{\sqrt{2gl \sin\theta}}{g \sin\theta}$$

$$= \sqrt{\frac{2gl \sin\theta}{g^2 \sin^2\theta}} = \sqrt{\frac{2l}{g \sin\theta}}$$

D. If $l' = \frac{l}{2}$, then $t = \sqrt{\frac{l}{g \sin\theta}}$

Hence, A → 2, B → 4, C → 1 D → 3.

Numerical Type Questions

1 (4) Before the string is cut

Spring force, $f = kx = 5\,mg$

For just after the string is cut

FBD

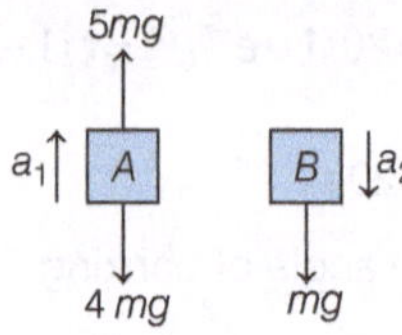

For block A, $5mg - 4mg = 4ma_1$

$$\Rightarrow \quad a_1 = \frac{g}{4}$$

For block B, $mg = ma_2$

$$\Rightarrow \quad a_2 = g$$

Ratio of acceleration of A and B,

$$\frac{a_1}{a_2} = \frac{\frac{g}{4}}{g} = \frac{1}{4} \Rightarrow a_2 : a_1 = 4 : 1$$

2 (7) Let mass of block $= M$ and mass of rope $= m$

Acceleration of block-rope system

$$a = \frac{2F}{M + m}$$

Tension in the middle of the rope,

$$T = \left(M + \frac{m}{2}\right)a$$

$$= \left(M + \frac{m}{2}\right)\left(\frac{2F}{M + m}\right)$$

Given, $m = \frac{M}{3}$

$$\because \quad T = \frac{7F}{4}$$

So, the value of N is 7.

3 (3) Force on mass 4 kg, $F = 4a_1$

$$\Rightarrow \quad a_1 = \frac{F}{4}$$

Force on mass 12 kg, $F_2 = 12a_2$

$$\Rightarrow \quad a_2 = \frac{F}{12}$$

Using equation, $v = u + at$

For 4 kg, $v_1 = 0 + \frac{F}{4} t_1$

For 12 kg,

$$v_2 = 0 + \frac{F}{12} t_2$$

Given, $(v_1 = v_2)$

$$\frac{F}{4} t_1 = \frac{F}{12} t_2 \Rightarrow \frac{t_1}{t_2} = \frac{4}{12} = \frac{1}{3}$$

So, the value of α is 3.

4 (1)

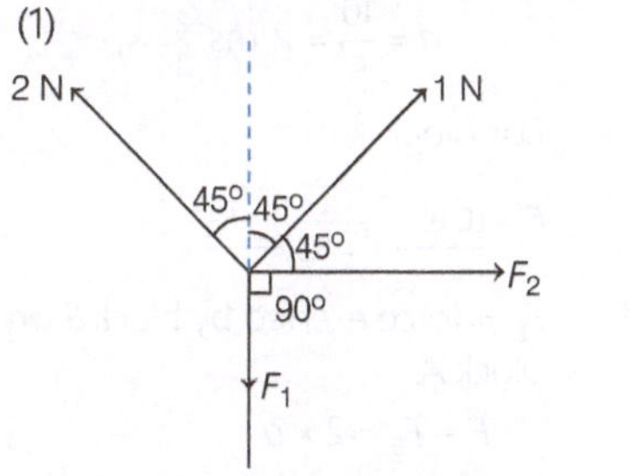

$F_x = F_2 + 1\cos 45° - 2\cos 45°$

$F_x = 0$ for equilibrium

$F_2 = -\cos 45°$ ...(i)

$F_y = 1\sin 45° + 2\sin 45° - F_1$

$F_y = 0$ for equilibrium

$F_1 = 3\sin 45°$ ...(ii)

From Eqs. (i) and (ii), we get

$$\frac{F_2}{F_1} = -\frac{\cos 45°}{3\sin 45°} = -\frac{1}{3}$$

So, $x = 1$ (ignore negative sign)

5 (12) Given, $\mu = 0.4$

$\because \quad F = ma$

$F = (1 + 2)a = 3a$ ...(i)

From free body diagram of 1 kg block,

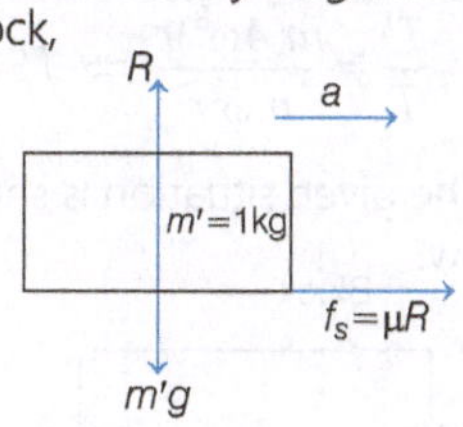

Force balance in x- direction,

$F_s = \mu R = m' a$ ...(ii)

Force balance in y- direction,

$$R = m' g$$

$$\mu m' g = m' a$$

$\Rightarrow 0.4 \times 1 \times 10 = 1 \times a \Rightarrow a = 4\, ms^{-2}$

Put the value of a in Eq. (i), we get

$$F = 3 \times 4 = 12\, N$$

6 (16) Given, initial velocity of block is zero for a frictionless surface.

$$a = g\sin\theta$$

Distance travel by block,

$$s = 0 \times t_1 + \frac{1}{2} \times g\sin\theta \times t_1^2$$

$\therefore \; s = \frac{1}{2} g\sin\theta\, t_1^2 = \frac{g}{4} t_1^2$ ...(i)

In presence of friction,

$$a = g\sin\theta - \mu\, g\cos\theta$$

$$= \frac{g}{2} - \frac{\mu\sqrt{3}}{2g} = \frac{g}{2}(1 - \sqrt{3}\,\mu)$$

Distance travel by block,

$s = \frac{1}{2}\left[\frac{g}{2}(1 - \sqrt{3}\mu)\right] t_2^2$ ...(ii)

Dividing Eq. (ii) by Eq. (i) and solving, we get

$$\mu = \frac{15}{16\sqrt{3}}$$

So, the value of x is 16.

7 (2)

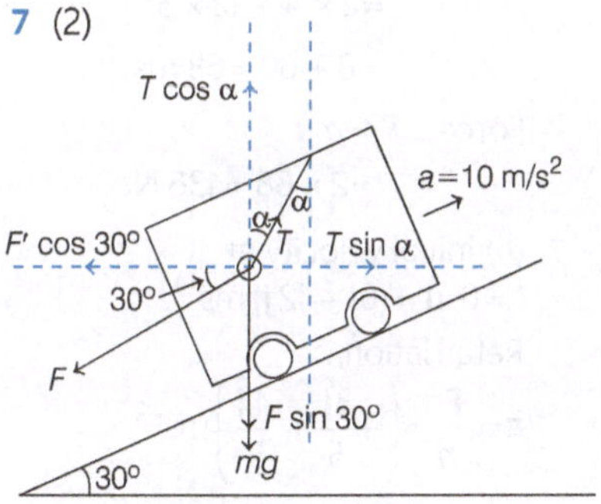

Here, F' is the pseudo force in the car's frame and T is the tension in the string.

In equilibrium, $\Sigma F_x = 0$ and $\Sigma F_y = 0$

$\Rightarrow \quad F\cos 30° = T\sin\alpha$

$\Rightarrow \quad \frac{ma\cos 30°}{\sin\alpha} = T$ ...(i)

$F\sin 30° + mg = T\cos\alpha$

$\Rightarrow ma\sin 30° + mg$

$$= \frac{ma\cos 30°}{\sin\alpha}(\cos\alpha)$$

[$\because$ Using Eq. (i)]

$$\Rightarrow a\sin 30° + g = \frac{a\cos 30°}{\sin\alpha}(\cos\alpha)$$

$$10 \times \frac{1}{2} + 10 = \frac{10 \times \sqrt{3}}{2}\cot\alpha$$

$\Rightarrow \alpha = 30° = 15x$ (given)

So, value of x is 2.

8 (3.4) Given, $r = 15\, m$, $v = 5\, ms^{-1}$, $a_t = 3\, ms^{-2}$

$$\therefore a_r = \frac{v^2}{r} = \frac{5 \times 5}{15} = 1.66\, ms^{-2}$$

The net acceleration, $a = \sqrt{a_r^2 + a_t^2}$

$\Rightarrow \; a = 3.4\, ms^{-2}$

9 (173) According to the question,

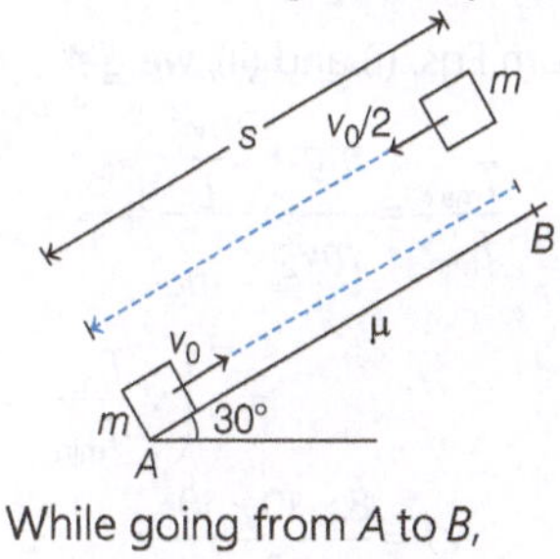

While going from A to B,

$$a_1 = g\sin 30° + \mu g\cos 30°$$

$\Rightarrow \; a_1 = 5 + 5\sqrt{3}\,\mu$ ...(i)

($\because g = 10\, ms^{-2}$)

$v_0^2 - 0 = 2a_1 s$

$\Rightarrow \; s = \frac{v_0^2}{2a_1} = \frac{v_0^2}{2(5 + 5\sqrt{3}\,\mu)}$ ...(ii)

[Using Eq. (i)]

The acceleration of the block while coming from B to A is

$a_2 = g\sin 30° - \mu g\cos 30°$

$\Rightarrow a_2 = 5 - 5\sqrt{3}\,\mu$ ...(iii)

Again, using third equation of motion, we get

$$\left(\frac{v_0}{2}\right)^2 - 0 = 2a_2 s \Rightarrow s = \frac{v_0^2}{8a_2}$$

$\Rightarrow \quad s = \frac{v_0^2}{8(5 - 5\sqrt{3}\,\mu)}$ ...(iv)

Using Eqs. (ii) and (iv), we get

$$\Rightarrow \frac{v_0^2}{2(5 + 5\sqrt{3}\,\mu)} = \frac{v_0^2}{8(5 - 5\sqrt{3}\,\mu)}$$

$$\Rightarrow \quad \mu = \frac{\sqrt{3}}{5}$$

So, $\frac{l}{500} = \frac{\sqrt{3}}{5} = 0.346$

$\Rightarrow \quad l = 0.346 \times 500 = 173$

10 (20) Now, $T_{max} - mg = \frac{mv_1^2}{L}$

$\Rightarrow \quad T_{max} = mg + \frac{mv_1^2}{L}$ ...(i)

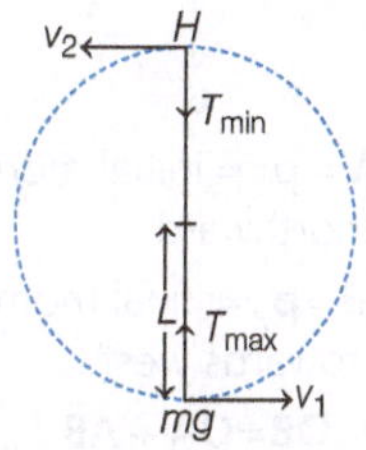

$$T_{min} + mg = \frac{mv_2^2}{L}$$

$$\Rightarrow \quad T_{min} = \frac{mv_2^2}{L} - mg \qquad \text{...(ii)}$$

From Eqs. (i) and (ii), we get

$$\frac{T_{max}}{T_{min}} = \frac{mg + \frac{mv_1^2}{L}}{\frac{mv_2^2}{L} - mg} = \frac{3}{1}$$

$$\left(\because \frac{T_{max}}{T_{min}} = \frac{3}{1}\right)$$

$$\Rightarrow \quad v_2^2 = \frac{8 \times 10 \times 10}{2}$$

$$(\because L = 10 \text{ m})$$

$$\Rightarrow \quad v_2 = 20 \text{ m/s}$$

NCERT Exemplar Questions

2 (b) We know that, $F = \frac{dp}{dt}$

Given that meter scale is moving with uniform velocity, hence $dp = 0$, then force, $F = 0$.

As all parts of the scale is moving with uniform velocity and total force is zero, hence torque will also be zero.

3 (c) Change in momentum

= Final momentum − Initial momentum

$= m\mathbf{v} - m\mathbf{u} = m(\mathbf{v} - \mathbf{u})$

$= (0.15)\,[-(3\hat{\mathbf{i}} + 4\hat{\mathbf{j}}) - (3\hat{\mathbf{i}} + 4\hat{\mathbf{j}})]$

$= -(0.9\hat{\mathbf{i}} + 1.20\hat{\mathbf{j}})$ kg-ms^{-1}

Hence,

$\Delta\mathbf{p} = -(0.9\hat{\mathbf{i}} + 1.2\hat{\mathbf{j}})$ kg-ms^{-1}

5 (c) Consider the adjacent diagram

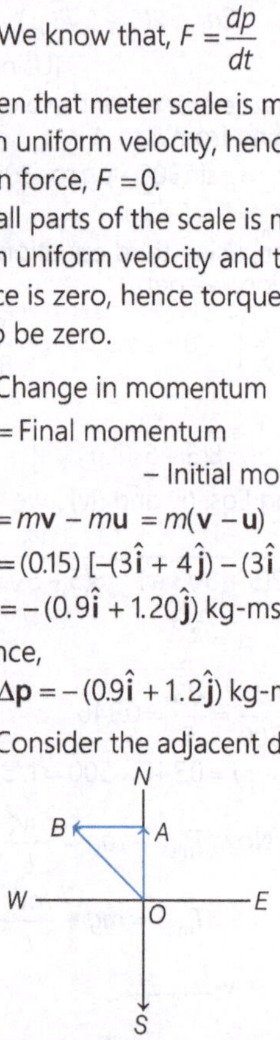

Let, $\mathbf{OA} = \mathbf{p}_1$ = initial momentum of player northward

and $\mathbf{AB} = \mathbf{p}_2$ = final momentum of player towards west.

Clearly, $\mathbf{OB} = \mathbf{OA} + \mathbf{AB}$

Change in momentum $= \mathbf{p}_2 - \mathbf{p}_1$

$= \mathbf{AB} - \mathbf{OA} = \mathbf{AB} + (-\mathbf{OA})$

= Clearly resultant AR will be along south-west.

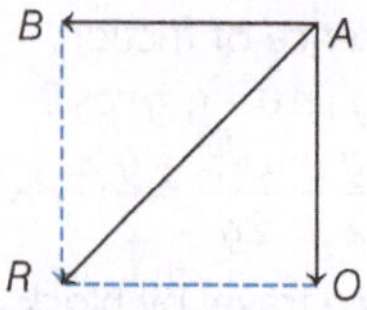

6 (a) $x(t) = pt + qt^2 + rt^3$

$$v = \frac{dx}{dt} = p + 2qt + 3rt^2$$

$$a = \frac{dv}{dt} = 0 + 2q + 6rt$$

At $t = 2$ s, $a = 2q + 6 \times 2 \times r$

$= 2 \times 4 + 12 \times 5$

$= 8 + 60 = 68$ ms^{-2}

Force, $F = ma$

$= 2 \times 68 = 136$ N

7 (b) Initial velocity at $t = 0$, $\mathbf{u} = (6\hat{\mathbf{i}} - 12\hat{\mathbf{j}})$ ms^{-1}

Retardation,

$$\mathbf{a} = \frac{\mathbf{F}}{m} = \left(-\frac{3\hat{\mathbf{i}}}{5} + \frac{4\hat{\mathbf{j}}}{5}\right) \text{ms}^{-2}$$

As final velocity is along Y-axis only, its x-component must be zero.

From $v = u + at$, for x-component only,

$$0 = 6\hat{\mathbf{i}} - \frac{3\hat{\mathbf{i}}}{5}t$$

$$t = \frac{5 \times 6}{3} = 10 \text{ s}$$

8 (b) We know that, $\mathbf{v} = \mathbf{u} + \mathbf{a}t$

$$\Rightarrow \quad v\hat{\mathbf{i}} = 0 + \mathbf{a} \times 2 \qquad (\because u = 0)$$

$$\Rightarrow \quad \mathbf{a} = \frac{v}{2}\hat{\mathbf{i}}$$

Force, $\mathbf{F} = m\mathbf{a} = \frac{mv}{2}\hat{\mathbf{i}}$

Therefore, force acting on the car is $\frac{mv}{2}$ towards east. As external force on the system is only friction, so the force $\frac{mv}{2}$ is by friction on the tyres exerted by the road.

Past Exams Questions

1 (c) Net force on blocks A and $B = 10$ N

Acceleration of both blocks A and $B = \frac{F}{m}$

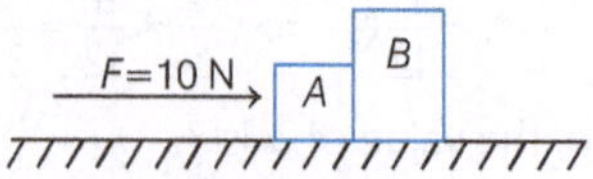

$$a = \frac{10}{5} = 2 \text{ ms}^{-2}$$

For block A,

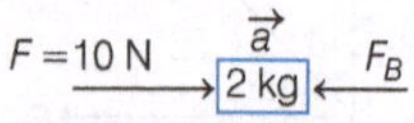

F_B = force exerted by block B on block A.

$$F - F_B = 2 \times a$$

$$\Rightarrow 10 - F_B = 2 \times 2 \Rightarrow F_B = 6 \text{ N}$$

For block B,

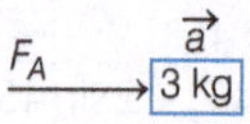

Force exerted by block A on block B,

$$F_A = 3a = 6 \text{ N}$$

2 (b) The tension in the string will be equal to centripetal force

$$F_c = \frac{mv^2}{r} = m\omega^2 r$$

According to question, $T = m\omega^2 r$

and $T' = m(2\omega)^2 r$

$$\frac{T'}{T} = \frac{m(4\omega^2)r}{m\omega^2 r} \Rightarrow T' = 4T$$

3 (d) The given situation is shown below.

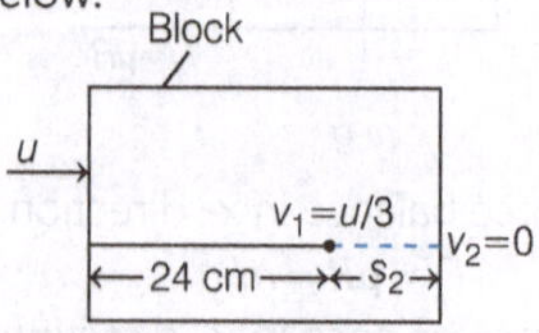

Using, $v^2 = u^2 - 2as$

$$\Rightarrow \quad v_1^2 = u^2 - 2as$$

$$\Rightarrow \quad \left(\frac{u}{3}\right)^2 = u^2 - 2a \times 0.24$$

$$\Rightarrow \quad 0.48a = \frac{8}{9}u^2$$

$$\Rightarrow \quad a = \frac{8u^2}{9 \times 0.48} = \frac{u^2}{0.54}$$

According to second condition,

$$0 = v_1^2 - 2as_2$$

$$\Rightarrow \quad 0 = \left(\frac{u}{3}\right)^2 - 2 \times \frac{u^2}{0.54} \times s_2$$

$$\Rightarrow \quad \frac{u^2}{9} = \frac{2u^2}{0.54} s_2$$

$$\Rightarrow \quad s_2 = \frac{0.54}{9 \times 2} = 0.03 \text{ m} = 3 \text{ cm}$$

$\therefore$ Total length of the block

$$= s_1 + s_2$$

$$= 24 + 3 = 27 \text{ cm}$$

5 (*b*) For the given situation,

$$F = ma = \mu mg$$

$$\Rightarrow \quad a = \mu g = 0.15 \times 10$$

$$= 1.5 \text{ ms}^{-2}$$

6 (*b*) For case (1), ball dropped from the 10 m height and strikes to the ground.

Now, the velocity of the ball just before striking to the ground is

$$v_1 = \sqrt{2gh}$$

$$\Rightarrow \quad v_1 = 10\sqrt{2} \text{ m/s}$$

For case (2), ball rebounds to the same height. The velocity with which the ball just reaches to the same height,

$$v_2 = -\sqrt{2gh}$$

$$\Rightarrow \quad v_2 = -10\sqrt{2} \text{ m/s}$$

Now, magnitude of the impulse imparted to the ball,

$$|\text{Impulse}| = m|\Delta \bar{v}|$$

$$= 0.15\,|-10\sqrt{2} - (10\sqrt{2})|$$

$$= 0.15\,|-2 \times 10\sqrt{2}|$$

$$= 4.2 \text{ kg-m/s}$$

7 (*c*) Distance travelled by object during *n* th second is given by

$$S_n = u + \frac{a}{2}(2n-1)$$

$$\Rightarrow \quad S_n = 0 + \frac{g\sin\theta}{2}(2n-1) \quad \text{... (i)}$$

Distance travelled during $(n+1)$th second,

$$S_{n+1} = 0 + \frac{g\sin\theta}{2}[2(n+1)-1] \quad \text{... (ii)}$$

Using Eqs. (i) and (ii), we get

$$\frac{S_n}{S_{n+1}} = \frac{2n-1}{2n+1}$$

9 (*a*) The given situation is shown in the following diagram.

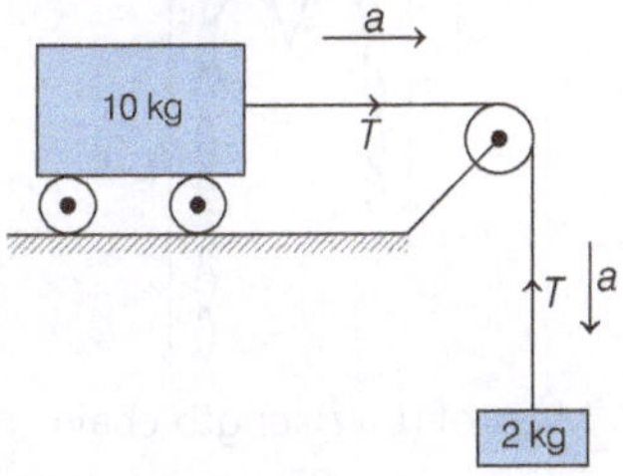

If *a* be the acceleration of the system then, equation of motion of 10 kg trolley, $T - \mu R = 10a$

$$\Rightarrow \quad T - 0.05 \times 10g = 10a$$

$$[\because \mu = 0.05,\ R = 10g]$$

$$\Rightarrow T - 0.05 \times 10 \times 10 = 10a$$

$$\Rightarrow \quad T - 5 = 10a \quad \text{...(i)}$$

Equation of motion of 2 kg block,

$$2g - T = 2a$$

$$20 - T = 2a \quad \text{...(ii)}$$

Adding Eqs. (i) and (ii), we have

$$20 - 5 = 12a$$

$$\Rightarrow \quad a = \frac{15}{12} = 1.25 \text{ ms}^{-2}$$

10 (*b*) As the three forces are represented by three sides of a triangle taken in order, then they will be in equilibrium.

$$\Rightarrow \mathbf{F}_{\text{net}} = \mathbf{F}_{PQ} + \mathbf{F}_{QR} + \mathbf{F}_{RP} = 0$$

$$\mathbf{F}_{\text{net}} = m \times \mathbf{a} = m\frac{d\mathbf{v}}{dt} = 0$$

$$\Rightarrow \quad \frac{d\mathbf{v}}{dt} = 0 \text{ or } \mathbf{v} = \text{constant}$$

So, the velocity of particle remain constant.

11 (*a*) The given question can be shown diagramatically here

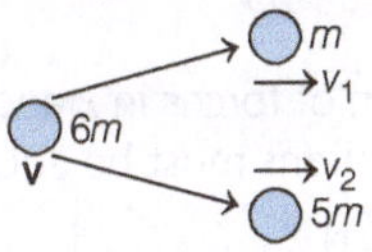

From the conservation of linear momentum, we have

$$6mv = mv_1 + 5mv_2$$

$$6(20\hat{\mathbf{i}} + 25\hat{\mathbf{j}} - 12\hat{\mathbf{k}})$$

$$= 100\hat{\mathbf{i}} + 35\hat{\mathbf{j}} + 8\hat{\mathbf{k}} + 5v_2$$

$$\Rightarrow \quad 5v_2 = 20\hat{\mathbf{i}} + 115\hat{\mathbf{j}} - 80\hat{\mathbf{k}}$$

$$\Rightarrow \quad v_2 = 4\hat{\mathbf{i}} + 23\hat{\mathbf{j}} - 16\hat{\mathbf{k}}$$

12 (*c*) The situation can be drawn as

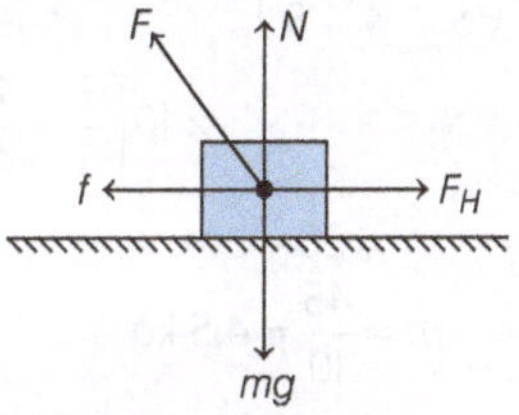

The frictional force,

$$f = \mu N = \mu\, mg \qquad [\because N = mg]$$

From free body diagram, the resultant force is

$$|\mathbf{F}| = \sqrt{N^2 + f^2}$$

$$= \sqrt{(mg)^2 + (\mu mg)^2}$$

$$= mg\sqrt{1 + \mu^2}$$

This is the minimum force required to move the object. But as the body is not moving.

$$\therefore \quad |\mathbf{F}| \le mg\sqrt{1 + \mu^2}$$

13 (*b*)

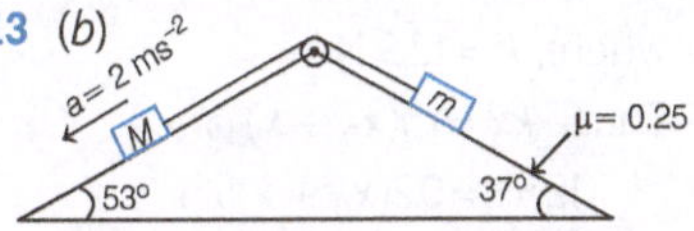

FBD for mass *M*,

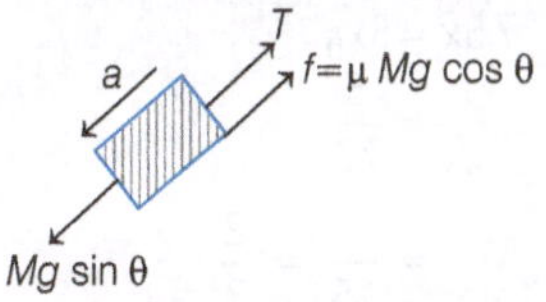

For mass *M*,

$$F_{\text{net}} = Ma$$

$$\Rightarrow Mg\sin 53° - \mu Mg\cos 53° - T = Ma$$

$$\text{or } Mg(\sin 53° - \mu\cos 53°) - T = 2M \quad \text{...(i)}$$

FBD for mass *m*,

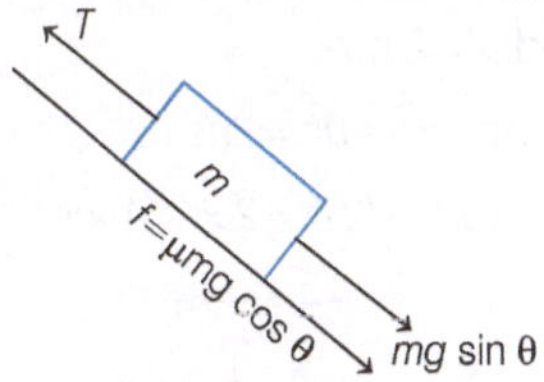

$$T - mg(\sin 37° + \mu\cos 37°) = 2m \quad \text{...(ii)}$$

Adding Eq. (i) and Eq. (ii) and substituting values, we get

$$100\left(\frac{4}{5}-\frac{1}{4}\times\frac{3}{5}\right)-m$$

$$\times 10\left(\frac{3}{5}+\frac{1}{4}\times\frac{4}{5}\right)$$

$$=20+2m$$

$$\Rightarrow \quad m=\frac{45}{10}=4.5 \text{ kg}$$

14 (*a*) Limiting force of static friction and kinetic friction does not depend on the area of contact but they depends on materials.

15 (*c*)

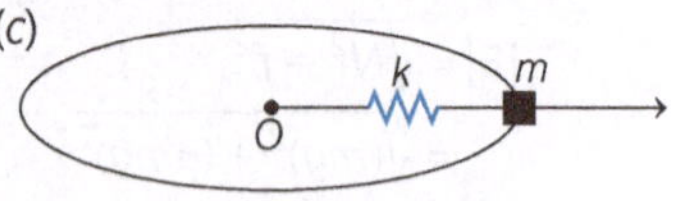

Extension in spring due to centripetal force, $F=\frac{mv^2}{r}=mr\omega^2$

$$r=x_0+x$$

$$= \text{natural length} + \text{extension}$$

$\because \quad F=kx$

where, $k=12.5$ N/m

Thus, $kx=m(x_0+x)\,\omega^2$

$$12.5x=0.2(x_0+x)5^2$$

$$12.5x=5x_0+5x$$

$$\Rightarrow \quad 7.5x=5x_0$$

$$\Rightarrow \quad \frac{x}{x_0}=\frac{5}{7.5}$$

$$=\frac{1}{1.5}=\frac{2}{3}$$

16 (*b*) Since, the bag is slipping on the conveyor belt, retardation due to friction will be

$$a=\frac{-\mu Mg}{M}=-\mu g$$

or $\quad a=-0.4\times 10=-4 \text{ ms}^{-2}$

In the frame of conveyor, $v=0$ and $u=2$ m/s

Using, $v^2-u^2=2as$

$\therefore \quad (0)^2-(2)^2=2\times -4\times s$

or $\quad -4=-8s$

or $\quad s=\frac{1}{2}=0.5$ m

17 (*d*) Mass of complete chain $=m$

Length of chain $=L$

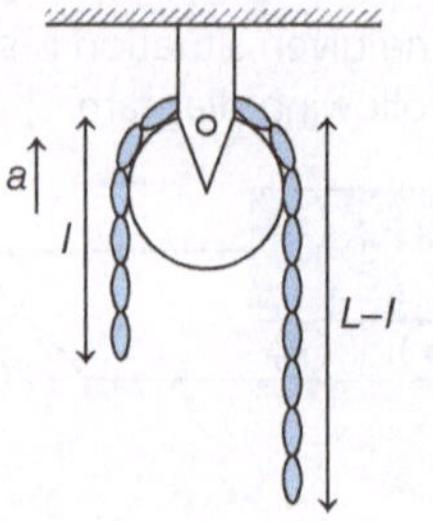

Mass of $(L-l)$ length chain

$$=\frac{m}{L}(L-l)$$

Force on $(L-l)$ length chain

$$=\frac{m}{L}(L-l)\,g$$

Mass of l length chain $=\frac{ml}{L}$

Force on l length chain $=\frac{ml}{L}g$

Now, $\frac{m(L-l)}{L}g-\frac{ml}{L}g=ma$

$$a=\frac{(L-2l)}{L}g \Rightarrow \frac{g}{2}=\frac{L-2l}{L}g$$

$$L=4l$$

$$\Rightarrow \quad l=\frac{L}{4}=\frac{1}{x}$$

$$x=4$$

Skill Boosters

1 (*d*) The value of coordinate x at $y=a$ is

$$x^2=4a(a) \Rightarrow \quad x=\pm 2a$$

The slope of curve at $(2a, a)$ is

$$m=\tan\theta=\frac{2x}{4a}=\frac{2(2a)}{4a}=1$$

$$\Rightarrow \quad \theta=45°$$

So, tangential acceleration

$$=g\sin\theta=\frac{g}{\sqrt{2}}$$

2 (*b*) Sum of forces in x and y-directions must be equal. $\Sigma F_x=0$

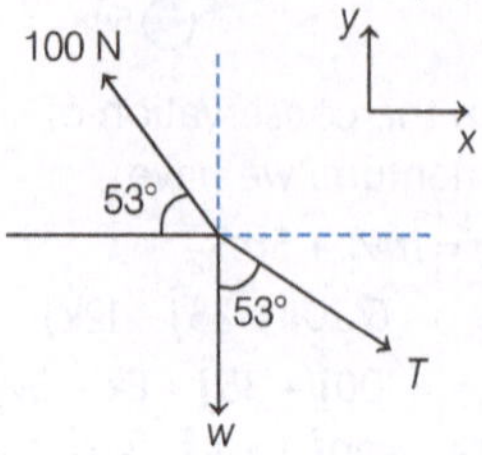

$$T\sin 53°-100\cos 53°=0$$

or $\quad T=100\cot 53°$

$$=\frac{300}{4}=75 \text{ N}$$

$$\Sigma F_y=0$$

$$100\sin 53°-w-T\cos 53°=0$$

$$w=100\sin 53°-T\cos 53°$$

$$=\frac{400}{5}-75\times\frac{3}{5}$$

$$=80-45=35 \text{ N}$$

3 (*c*) From FBD of block,

$$N=30-20t$$

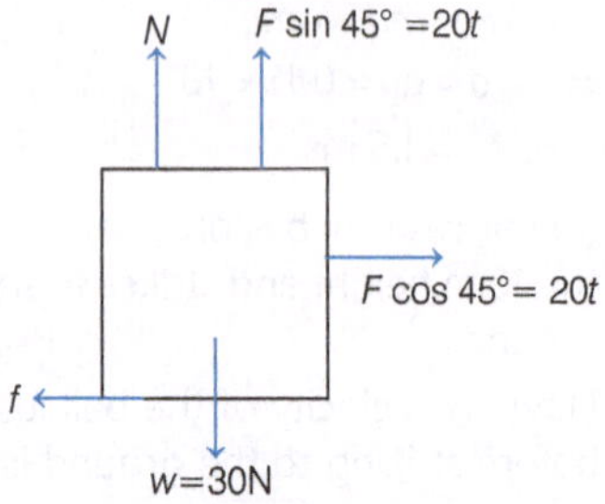

(a) The block leaves the contact with surface, when $N=0$, $t_1=1.5$ s

(b) The block begins horizontal motion, when $F\cos 45°=f_{max}$

$$\therefore \quad 20t_2=\mu(30-20t_2)$$

$$20t_2=0.2(30-20t_2)$$

$$24t_2=6$$

$$t_2=\frac{1}{4}\text{ s}=0.25 \text{ s}$$

$$\therefore \quad \frac{t_1}{t_2}=\frac{1.5}{0.25}=6:1$$

4 (*b*) The FBD of block *A* and wedge is

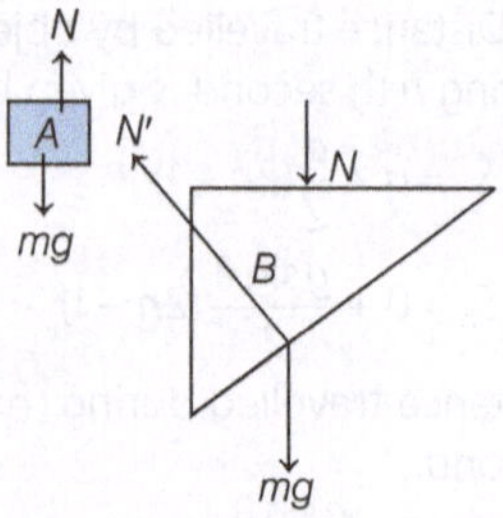

From FBD, it is clear that block cannot accelerate in x-direction, it can accelerate in y-direction only. This means for an observation on wedge block moves in $+x$-direction.

For block A,

$$mg - N = m(a \sin \theta) \quad ...(i)$$

For wedge B,

$$(N + mg) \sin \theta = ma \quad ...(ii)$$

On solving Eqs. (i) and (ii), we get

$$a = \left[\frac{2g \sin \theta}{1 + \sin^2 \theta}\right]$$

The acceleration of block A,

$$a_A = a \sin \theta$$

$$= \left[\frac{2g \sin \theta}{1 + \sin^2 \theta}\right] \sin \theta$$

$$= \left[\frac{2g \sin^2 \theta}{1 + \sin^2 \theta}\right]$$

Displacement of block A in 1 s is

$$s = 0 + \frac{1}{2} a_A t^2$$

$$= \frac{1}{2} \times \left[\frac{2g \sin^2 \theta}{1 + \sin^2 \theta}\right] \times (1)^2$$

$$= \left[\frac{g \sin^2 \theta}{1 + \sin^2 \theta}\right]$$

5 (c)

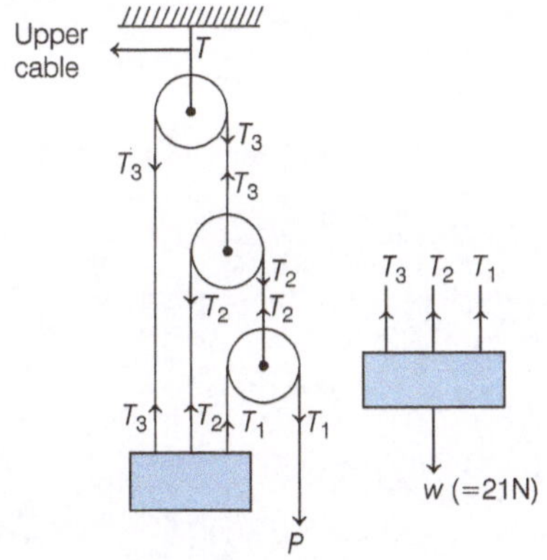

From the figure, $T_1 = P$

$$T_2 = 2T_1 = 2P$$

$$T_3 = 2T_2 = 4P$$

For the equilibrium of block,

$$T_1 + T_2 + T_3 = 21$$

$$\Rightarrow P + 2P + 4P = 21$$

$$\Rightarrow \quad 7P = 21 \Rightarrow P = 3 \text{ N}$$

$$\therefore \quad T = P = 3 \text{ N}$$

6 (b) The given system is represented as

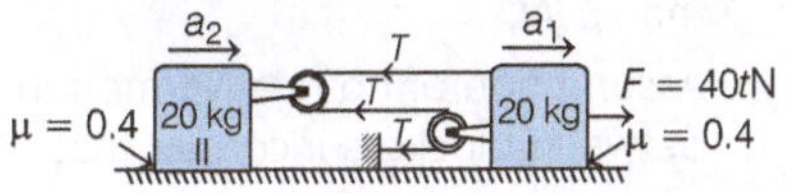

$$2a_2 = 3a_1$$

Considering block I

$$F - 3T - f = 20a_1 \quad ...(i)$$

Considering block II

$$2T - f = 20a_2 = 30a_1 \quad ...(ii)$$

Solving Eqs. (i) and (ii), we get

$$F - 3\left(\frac{f}{2} + 15a_1\right) - f = 20a_1$$

$$F = 65a_1 + \frac{5}{2}f \quad ...(iii)$$

When motion starts

$$t = \frac{\mu mg}{40} = 8 \text{ N and } a_1 > 0$$

Solving, we get

$$F = 20 \text{ N} \Rightarrow t = \frac{1}{2} \text{ s}$$

Motion of blocks will begin at

$$t = \frac{1}{2} \text{ s}$$

At $t = 1$ s, $F = 40$ N

From Eq. (iii), we get

$$40 = 65a_1 + 20$$

$$a_1 = \frac{20}{65} = \frac{4}{13} \text{ m/s}^2$$

$$a_2 = \frac{3}{2}a_1 = \frac{6}{13} \text{ m/s}^2$$

7 (d) Consider the parts of chain on either size of incline as two different elements.

Along the inclined plane,

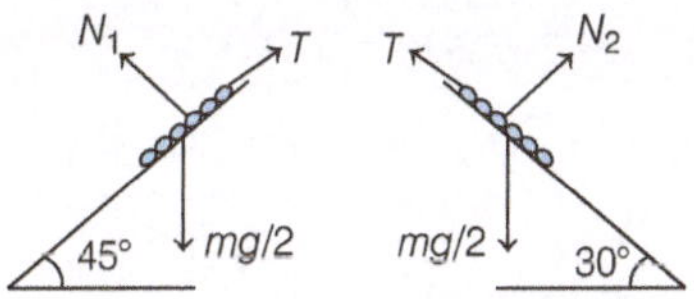

$$\frac{mg}{2} \sin 45° - T = \frac{m}{2} a \cos 45° \quad ... (i)$$

and $T - \frac{mg}{2} \sin 30°$

$$= \frac{m}{2} a \cos 30° ... (ii)$$

On solving Eqs. (i) and (ii), we get

$$a = \frac{g(\sin 45° - \sin 30°)}{\cos 30° + \cos 45°}$$

$$= \frac{10\left(\frac{1}{\sqrt{2}} - \frac{1}{2}\right)}{\frac{\sqrt{3}}{2} + \frac{1}{\sqrt{2}}} = \frac{10(\sqrt{2} - 1)}{\sqrt{3} + \sqrt{2}} \text{ m/s}^2$$

8 (a) Along the length of string, velocity component is same for all the points on string.

Thus,

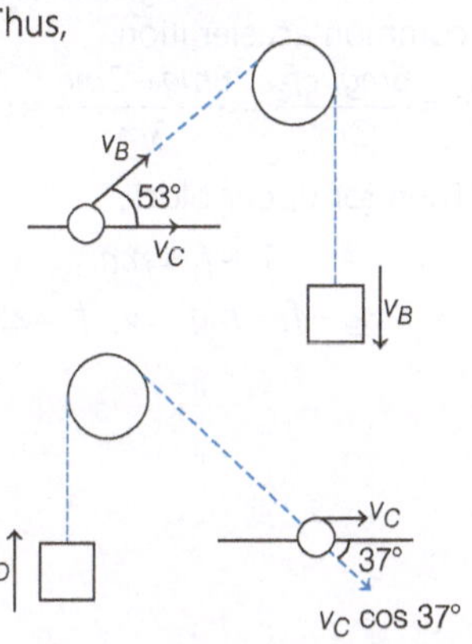

$$v_B = v_C \cos 53° \quad ...(i)$$

$$v_C \cos 37° = v_D \quad ...(ii)$$

From Eqs. (i) and (ii), we get

$$v_D = \frac{v_B \cos 37°}{\cos 53°} = \frac{v_B\left(\frac{4}{5}\right)}{\left(\frac{3}{5}\right)}$$

$$v_D = \frac{4}{3} v_B \Rightarrow \quad \frac{v_B}{v_D} = \frac{3}{4}$$

9 (a) The FBD both the blocks are

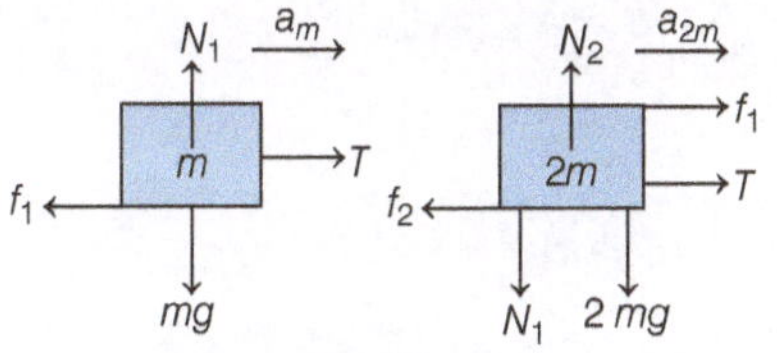

Fig. (a)

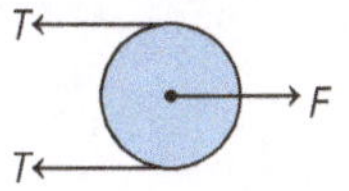

Fig. (b)

where, f_1 force of friction between blocks

and f_2 is force of friction between block and ground.

From FBD of pulley, we get

$$T = \frac{F}{2} = 3\,mg$$

Now, first decide whether there is slipping between blocks or not.

During accelerated motion of blocks, friction force between blocks must be less than $\mu_s N$.

Let blocks move together with common acceleration,

$$a = \frac{6mg - f_2}{3m} = \frac{6mg - 3mg}{3m} = g$$

Then for upper block,

$$T - f_1 = ma$$

$$\Rightarrow 3mg - f_1 = mg \Rightarrow f_1 = 2mg$$

$f_1 \le$ limiting static friction but here f_1 is coming out to be greater than $\mu_s N$.

Assumption of no relative motion between blocks is incorrect that means there is relative motion, therefore f_1 is kinetic friction.

$$a_m = \frac{3mg - \mu mg}{m} = 2g$$

(towards right)

$$a_{2m} = \frac{3mg + \mu mg - 3\mu mg}{2m} = g/2$$

(towards right)

Applying pulley constraint to get acceleration of hand,

$$a_p = \frac{a_1 + a_2}{2}$$

Acceleration of pulley = Acceleration of hand

$$a_p = \frac{a_m + a_{2m}}{2} = \frac{2g + g/2}{2}$$

$$= 5g/4 \text{ (towards right)}$$

10 (*b*) In this case, normal reaction of surface provides centripetal force and friction force prevents the man from sliding vertically.

From Newton's second law,

$$\Sigma F_x = N = \frac{mv^2}{r} \quad \text{...(i)}$$

$$\Sigma F_y = f - mg = 0 \quad \text{...(ii)}$$

where, $f = \mu N = \frac{\mu m v^2}{r}$ ...(iii)

From Eqs. (i), (ii) and (iii), we get

$$\mu = \frac{rg}{v^2} = \frac{rg}{\left(\frac{2\pi r}{T}\right)^2}$$

$$= \frac{gT^2}{4\pi^2 r} = \frac{10 \times 2^2}{4 \times (3.14)^2 \times 2}$$

$$\simeq 0.5$$

05

Scan for **Physics Through Concept Master** Videos

Work, Energy and Power

Topicwise No. of Ques asked in 5 Years (NEET)

Topics	No. of Questions				
	2024	2023	2022	2021	2020
Scalar Product	–		–	–	–
Notions of Work and KE : The Work-Energy Theorem	–	–	–	–	–
Work	–	–	–	–	1
Kinetic Energy	–	–	–	1	–
Work Done by a Variable Force	–	–	–	–	–
The Work-Energy Theorem for a Variable Force	–	1	–	–	–
Concept of Potential Energy	–	–	–	–	–
Conservation of Mechanical Energy	–	–	–	–	–
Potential Energy of a Spring	–	–	–	–	1
Power	1	–	1	1	–
Collision	1	–	–	–	–

Special Type of Ques Asked In 5 Years (NEET)

Types	Years				
	2024	2023	2022	2021	2020
A-R	–	–	–	–	–
Statement Based	–	–	–	–	–
Matching	–	–	–	–	–

Last 5 Years Weigtage (NEET)

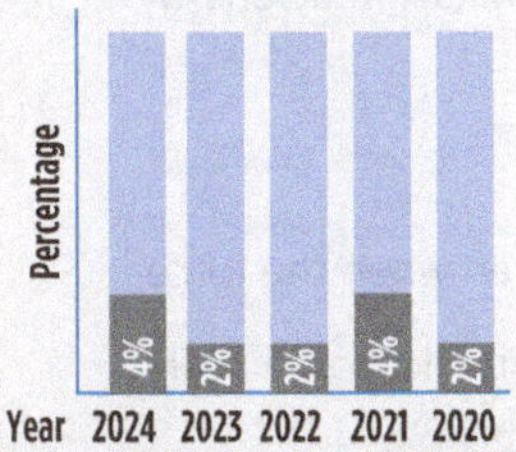

The terms work, energy and power are frequently used in our daily life. In this chapter, we will develop an understanding of these three physical quantities in details.

Scalar Product

- The scalar product or dot product of any two vectors **A** and **B** is denoted as $\mathbf{A} \cdot \mathbf{B} = AB \cos \theta$

  where, θ is the angle between the two vectors **A** and **B** as shown in figures.

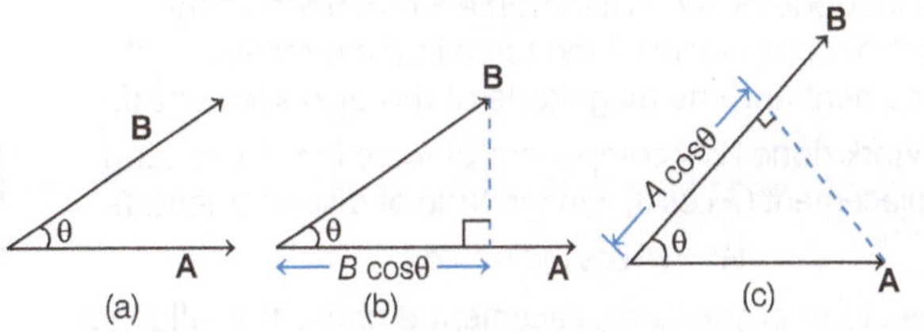

Geometrically, $\mathbf{A} \cdot \mathbf{B} = A(B \cos \theta) = A$ [Projection of **B** onto **A** as shown in Fig. (b)]

$= B\,(A \cos \theta) = B$ [Projection of **A** onto **B** as shown in Fig. (c)]

- Scalar product obeys following laws
  (i) Commutative law; $\mathbf{A} \cdot \mathbf{B} = \mathbf{B} \cdot \mathbf{A}$
  (ii) Distributive law; $\mathbf{A} \cdot (\mathbf{B} + \mathbf{C}) = \mathbf{A} \cdot \mathbf{B} + \mathbf{A} \cdot \mathbf{C}$
  Further, $\mathbf{A} \cdot (\lambda \mathbf{B}) = \lambda\, (\mathbf{A} \cdot \mathbf{B})$, where λ is a real number.

- For unit vectors $\hat{\mathbf{i}}, \hat{\mathbf{j}}, \hat{\mathbf{k}}$, we have
$\hat{\mathbf{i}} \cdot \hat{\mathbf{i}} = \hat{\mathbf{j}} \cdot \hat{\mathbf{j}} = \hat{\mathbf{k}} \cdot \hat{\mathbf{k}} = 1$ and $\hat{\mathbf{i}} \cdot \hat{\mathbf{j}} = \hat{\mathbf{j}} \cdot \hat{\mathbf{k}} = \hat{\mathbf{k}} \cdot \hat{\mathbf{i}} = 0$
- If two vectors are given as $\mathbf{A} = A_x\hat{\mathbf{i}} + A_y\hat{\mathbf{j}} + A_z\hat{\mathbf{k}}$ and $\mathbf{B} = B_x\hat{\mathbf{i}} + B_y\hat{\mathbf{j}} + B_z\hat{\mathbf{k}}$, then their scalar product will be
$$\mathbf{A} \cdot \mathbf{B} = (A_x\hat{\mathbf{i}} + A_y\hat{\mathbf{j}} + A_z\hat{\mathbf{k}}) \cdot (B_x\hat{\mathbf{i}} + B_y\hat{\mathbf{j}} + B_z\hat{\mathbf{k}})$$
$$= A_xB_x + A_yB_y + A_zB_z$$
- Angle between two vectors,
$$\cos\theta = \frac{\mathbf{A} \cdot \mathbf{B}}{|A||B|} = \frac{A_xB_x + A_yB_y + A_zB_z}{\sqrt{A_x^2 + A_y^2 + A_z^2}\sqrt{B_x^2 + B_y^2 + B_z^2}}$$
- Scalar product of a vector with itself gives the square of its magnitude.
i.e. $\mathbf{A} \cdot \mathbf{A} = A \cdot A\cos 0° = A^2$
In component form, $A = \sqrt{A_x^2 + A_y^2 + A_z^2}$ and $A \geq 0$.
$$\therefore \quad \mathbf{A} \cdot \mathbf{A} = A^2 = A_x^2 + A_y^2 + A_z^2$$
- From the definition of scalar product, if **A** and **B** are perpendicular to each other, then
$$\mathbf{A} \cdot \mathbf{B} = A_xB_x + A_yB_y + A_zB_z = 0$$

Notions of Work and Kinetic Energy : The Work-Energy Theorem

According to work-energy theorem, **the change in kinetic energy of a particle is equal to the work done on it by the net force.**

$$K_f - K_i = W$$

where, K_i and K_f are initial and final kinetic energies of the object and W is work done by a force **F** over a displacement **s**.

Work

- The work done by a constant force **F** is defined as the product of component of the force in the direction of the displacement and the magnitude of this displacement **d**.
Thus, work done W = component of force in the direction of displacement $(F\cos\theta) \times$ magnitude of displacement(d).
$$W = (F\cos\theta)d = \mathbf{F} \cdot \mathbf{d}$$
- An object undergoes a displacement **d** under the influence of force **F** is shown in figure below.

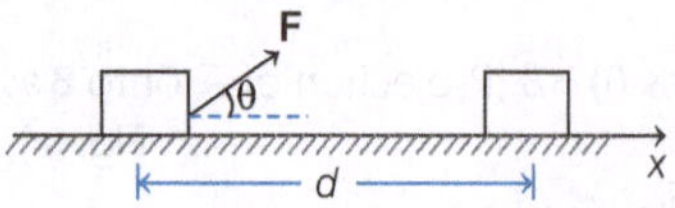

- **No work is done, if**
  (i) the displacement is zero.
  (ii) the force is zero.
  (iii) the force and displacement are mutually perpendicular as shown in figure below,
  i.e. for $\theta = \frac{\pi}{2}$ rad$(= 90°)$.

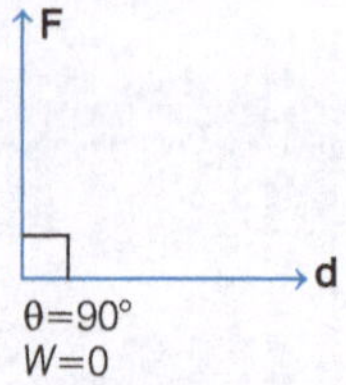

- Work done is a scalar quantity. It can be **positive** or **negative**.
  (i) If θ lies between 0° and 90°, then work is **positive**. In this situation, the velocity of the body increases.

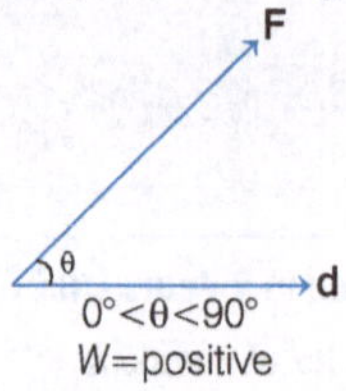

  (ii) If θ lies between 90° and 180°, then work is **negative.** In this situation, the velocity of the body decreases.

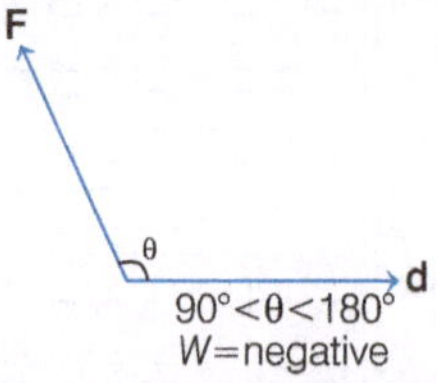

- The work and energy have same dimensions which is $[ML^2T^{-2}]$. Their SI unit is joule (J) but there are some alternating also, which are given below.

erg	10^{-7} J
electron volt (eV)	1.6×10^{-19} J
Calorie (cal)	4.18 J
Kilowatt hour (kWh)	3.6×10^{6} J

Kinetic Energy

- Energy is the capacity or ability of a body of doing work and kinetic energy is the amount of work done in stopping the moving body or the amount of work done in giving a velocity to the body from its rest position.
- If an object of mass m has velocity v, its kinetic energy
$$KE = \frac{1}{2}m\mathbf{v} \cdot \mathbf{v} = \frac{1}{2}mv^2$$
It is a scalar quantity.
- The expression $KE = \frac{1}{2}mv^2$ holds even when the force applied varies in magnitude or in direction or in both, magnitude and direction.

Work done by a Variable Force

- Suppose, a body is displaced from initial position x_i to final position x_f under the action of a variable force $F(x)$ as shown in the given figure.

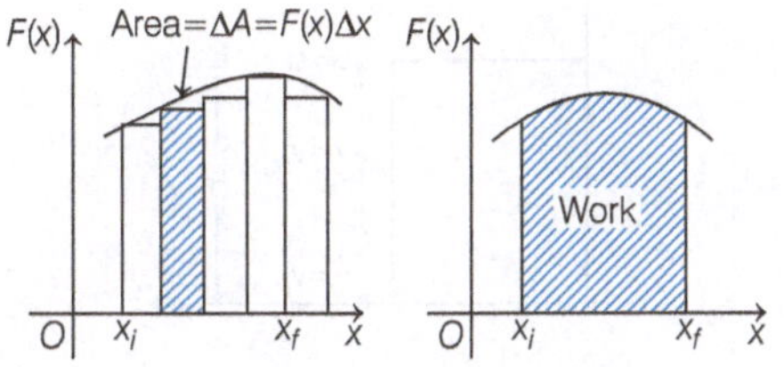

- If the displacement are allowed to approach zero, i.e. $\Delta x \to 0$, then the total work done, NEET 2019

$$W = \lim_{\Delta x \to 0} \sum_{x_i}^{x_f} F(x)\,\Delta x = \int_{x_i}^{x_f} F(x)dx$$

= Area under the force $F(x)$ *versus* displacement x curve.

Thus, for a varying force, the work done can be expressed as a definite integral of force over displacement.

Marks Maximiser

Geometrical Interpretation of Work Done

Work done = Area under force *versus* displacement curve.

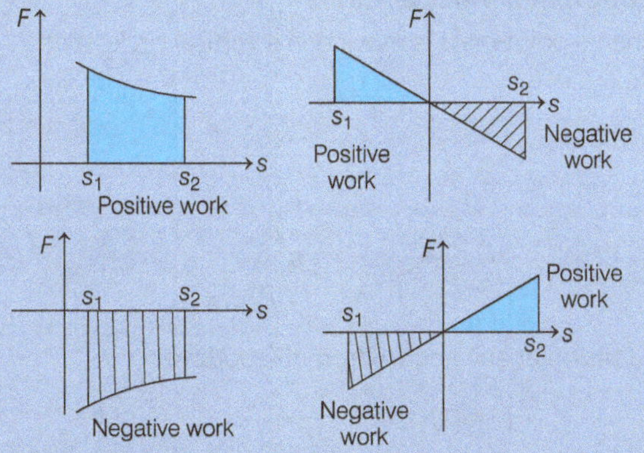

Motion of an Object on a Curved Surface

- When a car moves on a convex bridge of radius r,

  Centripetal force $= mg\sin\theta - N = \dfrac{mv^2}{r}$

  and reaction force, $N = mg\cos\theta - \dfrac{mv^2}{r}$

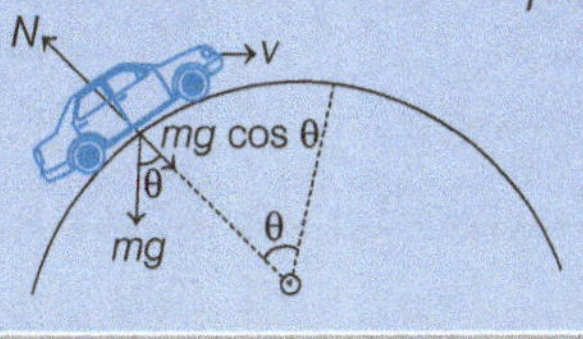

- When a car moves on a concave bridge of radius r,

  Centripetal force $= N - mg\cos\theta = \dfrac{mv^2}{r}$

  and reaction force, $N = mg\cos\theta + \dfrac{mv^2}{r}$

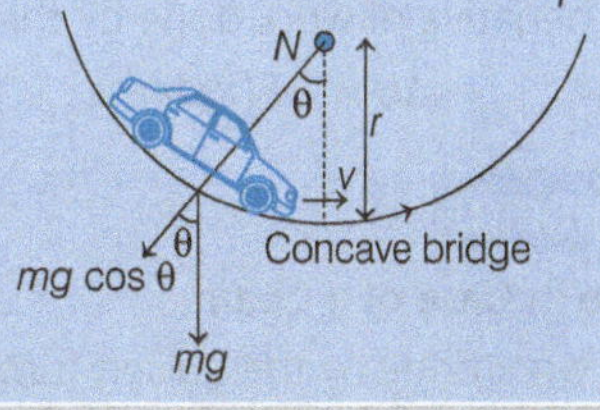

The Work-Energy Theorem for a Variable Force

The work done by a variable force is equal to change in kinetic energy. The work-energy theorem is an integral form of Newton's second law.

$$\therefore \quad K_f - K_i = W \qquad \left[\because W = \int_{x_i}^{x_f} F\,dx\right]$$

The Concept of Potential Energy

The potential energy is the stored energy by virtue of the position and configuration of a body.

- **Gravitational potential energy** of an object is the negative of work done by the gravitational force in raising the object to that height.

$$U(h) = mgh$$ NEET 2021

- If h is taken as a variable, the gravitational force F equals to the negative of the derivative of $U(h)$ with respect to h.

  Thus, $F = -\dfrac{d}{dh}U(h) = -mg$, negative sign indicates that the gravitational force is downward.

- Equation $\dfrac{1}{2}mv^2 = mgh$, shows that gravitational potential energy of the object at height h when the object is released, manifests itself as kinetic energy of the object on reaching the ground.

- Mathematically, the potential energy $U(x)$ is defined for the force $F(x)$ as $F(x) = -\dfrac{dU}{dx}$

$$\Rightarrow \quad \int_{x_i}^{x_f} F(x)dx = \int_{U_i}^{U_f} dU = U_i - U_f$$

- **Work done by conservative and non-conservative force**

  (i) The work done by a **conservative force** such as gravity depends upon initial and final positions only not upon the path taken.

(ii) If the work done or the kinetic energy depend on other factors such as the velocity or the particular path taken by the object, then the force is known as **non-conservative force.**

- The change in potential energy for a conservative force ΔU is equal to the negative of work done by the force,

$$\Delta U = -F(x)dx$$

Marks Maximiser

Work done in Case of a Chain

Case I The work done by the pulling force to bring the hanging part on to the table. Weight of hanging part $= \frac{m}{n} g$

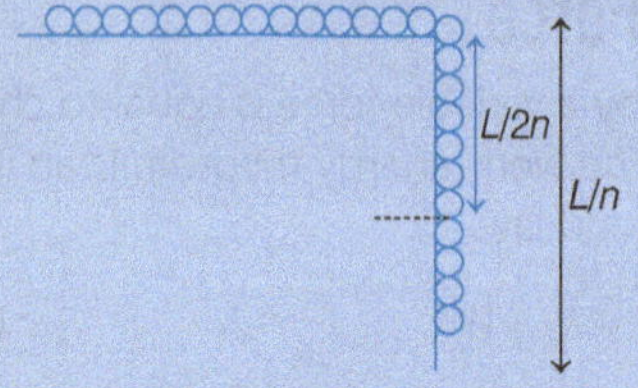

$$\text{Work} = \frac{mgh}{n} = \frac{mg}{n}\frac{L}{2n} = \frac{mgL}{2n^2}$$

Case II Work done in pulling the chain partially, such that $\frac{1}{n_2}$ part is hanging from the edge of the table is given by

$$W = \frac{mgL}{2}\left[\frac{1}{n_1^2} - \frac{1}{n_2^2}\right]$$

The Conservation of Mechanical Energy

- It states that, "the total mechanical energy of a system is conserved, if the forces doing work on it, are conservative."

i.e. $K_i + U(x_i) = K_f + U(x_f)$

The quantity $K + U(x)$ is called the **total mechanical energy** of the system. Individually, the kinetic energy and the potential energy may vary from point to point but the sum is always constant.

- **There are some other characteristics of conservative force**, which are given below

(a) A force $F(x)$ is conservative, if it can be derived from a scalar quantity $U(x)$ by the relation $F(x) = -\frac{\Delta U}{\Delta x}$.

(b) The work by the conservative force depends only on the ends point.

(c) The work done by conservative force in a closed path is zero.

- When a ball of mass m being dropped from a cliff of height H, then

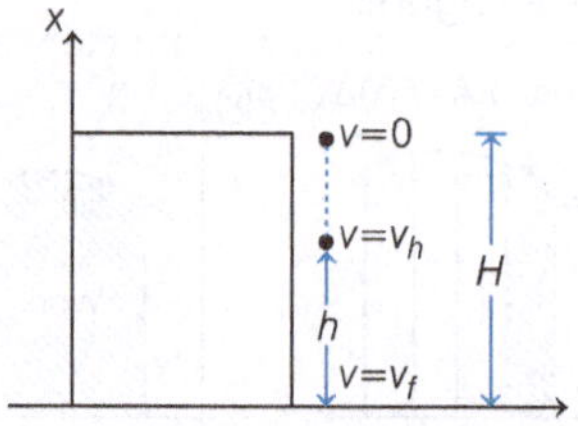

(a) The total mechanical energies E_0, E_h and E_H of the ball at the indicated heights zero (ground level), h and H are

$$E_H = mgH$$

NEET 2021

$$E_h = mgh + \frac{1}{2}mv_h^2$$

$$E_0 = \frac{1}{2}mv_f^2$$

(b) Applying conservation of mechanical energy at different levels, we get

$$v_f = \sqrt{2gH}$$

$$\therefore \quad v_h = \sqrt{2g(H-h)}$$

For Concept Master Video

Marks Maximiser

Motion in a Vertical Circle

When a point mass is moving in a vertical circle, then

NEET 2020, 19

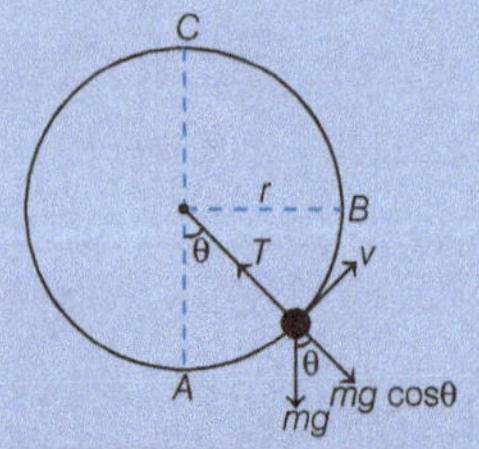

- Tension at any angle θ from the bottom,

$$T = mg\cos\theta + \frac{mv^2}{r}$$

- The conservation of mechanical energy is valid at any points like A, B, C on the vertical circle.

i.e. $E_A = E_B = E_C$

- To complete a circle by a point mass m, $T_C \geq 0$

$$\therefore \; T_C = mg\cos 180° + \frac{mv_C^2}{r} = \frac{mv_C^2}{r} - mg$$

$$\frac{mv_C^2}{r} - mg \geq 0$$

For Concept Master Video

$\Rightarrow \quad v_C \geq \sqrt{rg}$

Also, $\quad E_A = E_C$

$\Rightarrow \quad \frac{1}{2} m v_A^2 = mg(2r) + \frac{1}{2} m(\sqrt{rg})^2$

$\therefore \quad v_A = \sqrt{5rg}$

Hence, **minimum velocity at the bottom to complete vertical circle is** $\sqrt{5rg}$.

- When the string is horizontal, $\theta = 90°$, minimum velocity, $v_B = \sqrt{3gr}$.

The Potential Energy of a Spring

- When a block attached to a massless spring and resting on a smooth horizontal surface as shown in the figure below. The spring is light and may be treated as massless.

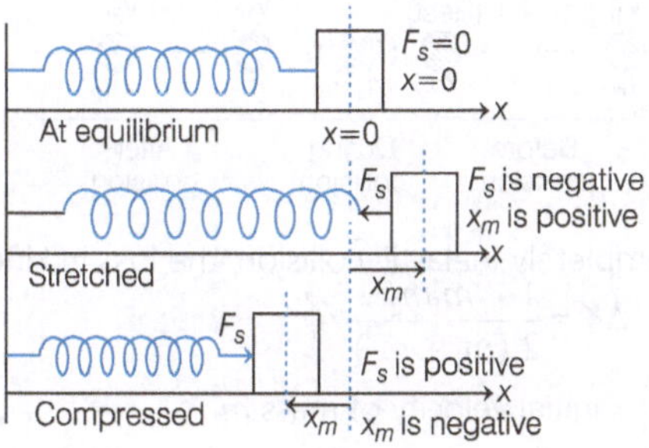

Then, work done in stretching or compressing by amount x_m of a spring by the spring force is called potential energy of spring and can be written as

$$W_s = \int_0^{x_m} F_s \, dx = -\int_0^{x_m} kx \, dx = -\frac{kx_m^2}{2}$$ **NEET 2023**

where, k is the spring constant.

- Potential energy of a spring can also be obtained by the magnitude of area of triangle as shown in figure below.

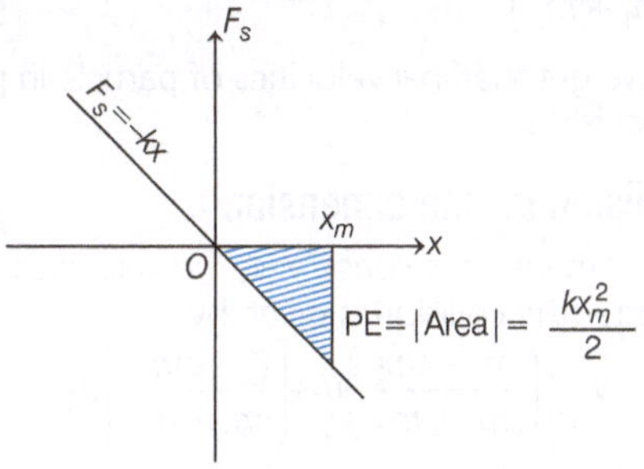

- For compression of spring, the potential energy is negative while for expansion of spring, the potential energy is positive.

- The work done by external pulling force is negative of work done by spring force.

$$\therefore \quad W_{ext} = -W_S = +\frac{kx_m^2}{2}$$

- If the spring is stretched (or compressed) from initial displacement x_i to a final displacement x_f, then the work done by the spring force is

$$W_S = \frac{1}{2} k(x_i^2 - x_f^2)$$ **NEET 2019**

- The work done by the spring force in a cyclic process is zero, as

$$W_S = -\int_{x_i}^{x_i} kx dx$$

$$= \frac{1}{2} k(x_i^2 - x_i^2) = 0$$

Thus, the work done by spring force depends only on the initial and final positions. So, the **spring force is a conservation force.**

- If the block of mass m is extended to x_m and released from rest, then its total mechanical energy at any arbitrary point x (where, $-x_m < x < x_m$) remains constant.

i.e. $\quad \frac{1}{2} kx_m^2 = \frac{1}{2} kx^2 + \frac{1}{2} mv^2$

However, in spring-block system, the kinetic energy gets converted to potential energy and *vice-versa*. Hence, the total sum of KE and PE is constant. This is graphically represented by

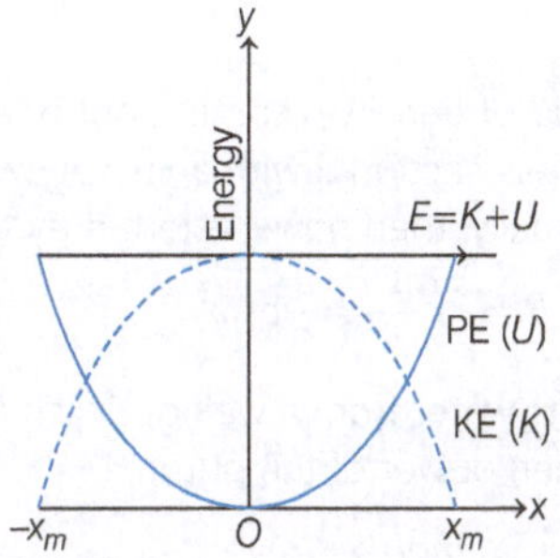

- For an extension or compression of x, the potential energy of spring,

$$U(x) = \frac{1}{2} kx^2$$

- The potential energy $U(x)$ of the spring is zero in the equilibrium position.
- The maximum speed of the spring is given by

$$v_m = \sqrt{\frac{k}{m}} x_m$$

Power

- It is defined as the time rate at which work is done or energy is transferred.
- The **average power** of a force is defined as the ratio of the work W, to the total time t taken, $P_{av} = \frac{W}{t}$.
- The **instantaneous power** is defined as the limiting value of the average power as time interval approaches zero.

$$P = \frac{dW}{dt} = \mathbf{F} \cdot \mathbf{v}$$

where, $\mathbf{v}$ is the instantaneous velocity when the force is $\mathbf{F}$.
- It is a **scalar quantity** and its dimensions are $[ML^2T^{-3}]$.
- In SI system, its unit is **watt (W) or Js^{-1}**.
  Another unit of power is **1 hp (horse power)** = 746 W
- The slope of work-time curve gives the instantaneous power, as $\tan\theta = P = \frac{dW}{dt}$

  The area under power-time graph gives the work done.

$$\therefore \quad W = \int P\,dt = \text{Area under } P\text{-}t \text{ curve}$$

Marks Maximiser

Calculation of Power Under Different Cases

- A crane lifts a body of mass m with a constant velocity v from the ground, it power is $P = Fv = mgv$.
- The power of a machine gun firing n bullets each of mass m with a velocity v in a time interval t is given by $P = \frac{nmv^2}{2t}$.
- When a liquid of density ρ coming out of a hose pipe of area of cross-section A with a velocity v and strikes the wall normally, then power exerted by the liquid,

$$P = \frac{1}{2}\frac{mv^2}{t} = \frac{1}{2}\rho A v^3$$

- If a motor lifts water from a well of depth h and with a velocity v, then power of the pump,

$$P = \frac{mgh + \frac{1}{2}mv^2}{t}$$

Collision

- It is an isolated event, in which two or more colliding bodies exert strong forces on each other for a short duration of time.
- In all types of collisions, the total linear momentum is conserved, i.e. the initial momentum of the system is equal to the final momentum of the system.

  This implies, $\Delta\mathbf{p}_1 + \Delta\mathbf{p}_2 = 0$, where $\mathbf{p} = m\mathbf{v}$
- Collision is of two types, elastic and inelastic collisions.
  - **Elastic Collision** The collision in which momentum and kinetic energy both are conserved.
  - **Inelastic collision** The collision in which linear momentum is conserved but kinetic energy is not conserved.

Collision in One-Dimension

- If the initial and final velocities of both the bodies are along the same straight line, then it is called a **one-dimensional collision** or **head-on collision**.

Inelastic Collision in One-Dimension

- The 1-D completely inelastic collision for two masses m_1 and m_2 is shown in figure below. The particle m_1 moves with velocity v_{1i} and the particle m_2 is at rest. After collision, the particles m_1 and m_2 move with velocities v_{1f} and v_{2f}

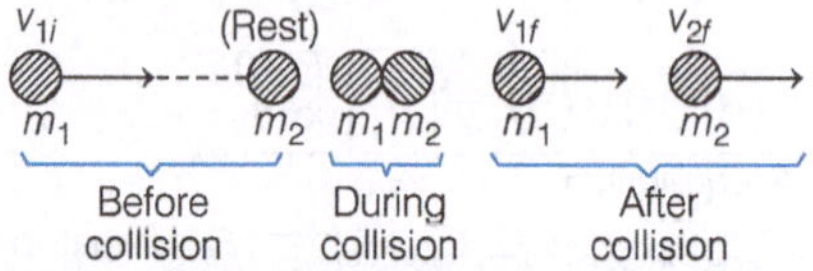

- In 1-D completely inelastic collision, the loss in kinetic energy, $\Delta K = \frac{1}{2}\frac{m_1 m_2}{(m_1 + m_2)} v_{1i}^2$

  where, v_{1i} = initial velocity of mass m_1.
- After collision, the velocity of two masses are

$$v_{1f} = \frac{(m_1 - m_2)}{(m_1 + m_2)} v_{1i}, \quad v_{2f} = \frac{2m_1 v_{1i}}{m_1 + m_2}$$

- There are two cases as given below

  ***Case* I** If the two masses are equal, $v_{1f} = 0$ and $v_{2f} = v_{1i}$.

  ***Case* II** If one mass dominates, i.e. $m_2 > m_1$
  $v_{1f} \cong -v_{1i}$ and $v_{2f} \cong 0$

For Concept Master Video

- Loss in kinetic energy is given by

$$\Delta K = \frac{1}{2}\left[\frac{m_1 m_2}{m_1 + m_2}\right](1 - e^2)(u_1 - u_2)^2$$

- For $e = 0$, we get the final velocities of particle in perfectly inelastic collision.

Elastic Collision in One-dimension

- As linear momentum is conserved, the velocities of particles after the collision is given by

$$v_1 = \left(\frac{m_1 - em_2}{m_1 + m_2}\right)u_1 + \left[\frac{(1+e)m_2}{m_1 + m_2}\right]u_2$$

and
$$v_2 = \left[\frac{(1+e)\,m_1}{m_1 + m_2}\right]u_1 + \left(\frac{m_2 - em_1}{m_1 + m_2}\right)u_2$$

For perfectly elastic collision, $e = 1$, i.e. maximum coefficient of restitution.

Collision in Two-Dimensions

- For collision in two-dimensions or a plane as shown in the figure below, the x and y-components equations are

$$m_1 v_{1f} = m_1 v_{1f} \cos\theta_1 + m_2 v_{2f} \cos\theta_2$$

$$0 = m_1 v_{1f} \sin\theta_1 - m_2 v_{2f} \sin\theta_2$$

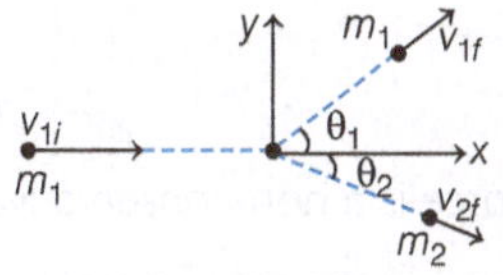

- If the **collision is elastic**, then

$$\frac{1}{2} m_1 v_{1i}^2 = \frac{1}{2} m_1 v_{1f}^2 + \frac{1}{2} m_2 v_{2f}^2$$

- In a **perfectly elastic collision**, total energy and total linear momentum of colliding particles remain conserved.
- **Rebounding of a ball on collision with the floor**
  (i) Speed of the ball after the nth rebound,
  $$v_n = e^n v_0 = e^n \sqrt{2gh_0}$$
  (ii) Height covered by the ball after the nth rebound,
  $$h_n = e^{2n} h_0$$

Caution Points

- For two bodies, $F_{12} + F_{21} = 0$, whereas $W_{12} + W_{21} \neq 0$, where F_{12} and F_{21} are action and reaction force between them, W_{12} and W_{21} are the work done by these forces.
  But, sometimes $W_{12} + W_{21} = 0$ is also true.
- By using work-energy theorem, work done by a force can be calculated without knowing the exact nature of the force.
- The work-energy theorem is a scalar form of Newton's second law. The principle of conservation of mechanical energy is another form of work-energy theorem for only conservative force.

i.e. $W_c = \Delta K$. As, $W_c = -\Delta U$

$\therefore \quad -\Delta U = \Delta K \quad \Rightarrow \quad \Delta(U + K) = 0$

$\therefore \quad U + K =$ Total mechanical energy = constant.

- The work-energy theorem is applicable for all type of inertial frames. It can also be applicable for non-inertial frames provided the pseudo force is considered in the calculation of net force acting on the body.

(a) Work-energy theorem for inertial frames, $W_c + W_{nc} = \Delta K$

(b) Work-energy theorem for non-inertial frames,

$$W_c + W_{nc} + W_{pseudo} = \Delta K$$

PYQ Notes

1. If the potential energy is given as $U = \frac{A}{r^m} + \frac{B}{r^n}$, where A, B are constants and m, n are positive constants, then the equilibrium position or mean position can be given by force, $F = -\frac{dU}{dr} = 0$ or $\frac{dU}{dr} = 0$

   The types of equilibrium can be identified by sign of $\frac{d^2U}{dr^2}$

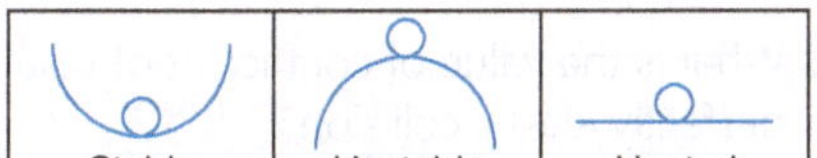

Stable equilibrium	Unstable equilibrium	Neutral equilibrium
$\frac{dU}{dr}=0, \frac{d^2U}{dr^2}>0$	$\frac{dU}{dr}=0, \frac{d^2U}{dr^2}<0$	$\frac{dU}{dr}=0, \frac{d^2U}{dr^2}=0$

   If a particle of potential energy U is moving on a circular path, then centripetal force, $F = -\frac{dU}{dr} = \frac{mv^2}{r}$

   Total energy, $E = \text{KE} + \text{PE} = -\frac{r}{2}\left(\frac{dU}{dr}\right) + U$

   [JEE Main 2022, 21, 18]

2. If the water falls from a height h with mass flow rate m to operate a turbine, then power generated by turbine is given by $P_{output} = P_{input} - P_{loss}$

   If $P_{loss} = x\%$ of P_{input}, then

$$P_{output} = P_{input}\left(1 - \frac{x}{100}\right) = mgh\left(1 - \frac{x}{100}\right)$$

   [NEET 2021]

3. If the conservative force as well as non-conservative force are acting on a system, then the work done by non-conservative force (frictional force, viscous force etc.) is given by

$$W_C + W_{NC} = \Delta K$$

   or $W_{NC} = E_f - E_i$

   where, E_i and E_f are initial and final mechanical energy of the system. **[NEET 2020, 19, 18, 17]**

4. **Coefficient of restitution** (e) is the ratio of the relative velocity of separation after the collision to the relative velocity of approach before collision,

   i.e. $$e = \frac{v_2 - v_1}{u_1 - u_2}$$

   For perfectly elastic collision, $e = 1$.

   For perfectly inelastic collision, $e = 0$

   For an inelastic collision, $e < 1$. **[NEET 2018]**

Step by Step

Mastering NCERT

- Concept Builders
- Topical Questions
- Assertion and Reason Questions
- Statement Based
- Matching Type
- Numerical Type
- NCERT Exemplar
- Past Exams MCQs
- Skill Boosters

Concept Builders

1 What is the angle between force $\mathbf{F} = 3\hat{\mathbf{i}} - 4\hat{\mathbf{j}} + 3\hat{\mathbf{k}}$ and displacement $\mathbf{s} = 3\hat{\mathbf{i}} + 3\hat{\mathbf{j}} + \hat{\mathbf{k}}$?

2 If a force acts perpendicular to the direction of motion of a body, then what is the amount of work done?

3 The change in .... (kinetic/potential) energy of a particle is equal to the work done on it by net force.

4 Work done by a man holding a weight at fixed position is zero. [T/F]

5 The earth moving around the sun in a circular orbit is acted upon by a force and hence work must be done on the earth by the force. [T/F]

6 Work done .... (can/cannot) be negative.

7 A light body and a heavy body have equal momentum. Which body has greater kinetic energy?

8 A body can have energy without momentum. [T/F]

9 When the momentum of a body is doubled, its kinetic energy becomes .... (two/four) times the initial kinetic energy.

10 Does the potential energy of a spring decreases or increases when it is compressed or stretched?

11 According to the principle of conservation of energy under the action of .... (conservative/frictional) force, the sum of potential energy and kinetic energy of a particle remains constant.

12 The spring force is a non-conservative force. [T/F]

13 What is defined as the time rate at which work done or energy is transferred?

14 If the speed of water flowing through a pipe is v, then power proportional to v^2. [T/F]

15 What is the power dissipated by an engine, if the rails run in a plane surface with zero friction?

16 The instantaneous power is defined as the limiting value of the average power as time interval approaches zero. [T/F]

17 The collision in which momentum and kinetic energy both are conserved before and after the collision is called .... (elastic/inelastic) collision.

18 Energy exchange will be .... (maximum/minimum) in perfectly elastic collision, if the colliding bodies have equal masses.

19 Two bodies moving towards each other collide and move away in direction opposite to each other. There is some rise in temperature of the body in the process. Which type of collision is it?

20 What is the value of coefficient of restitution for perfectly elastic collision?

Topical Questions

Scalar Product

1 Find the angle between force $\mathbf{F} = (3\hat{\mathbf{i}} + 4\hat{\mathbf{j}} - 5\hat{\mathbf{k}})$ unit and displacement $\mathbf{d} = (5\hat{\mathbf{i}} + 4\hat{\mathbf{j}} + 3\hat{\mathbf{k}})$ unit. **NCERT Pg. 71**

(a) $\cos^{-1}(0.49)$ (b) $\cos^{-1}(0.32)$
(c) $\cos^{-1}(0.60)$ (d) $\cos^{-1}(0.90)$

2 Find the scalar product of two vectors $\mathbf{A} = 3\hat{\mathbf{i}} - 4\hat{\mathbf{j}} + 5\hat{\mathbf{k}}$ and $\mathbf{B} = -\hat{\mathbf{i}} + 2\hat{\mathbf{j}} + 3\hat{\mathbf{k}}$. **NCERT Pg. 71**

(a) 9 (b) 4
(c) 10 (d) 3

3 For what value of λ, the vectors $\mathbf{a} = 2\hat{\mathbf{i}} + \lambda\hat{\mathbf{j}} + 3\hat{\mathbf{k}}$ and $\mathbf{b} = 2\hat{\mathbf{i}} + \hat{\mathbf{j}} - \hat{\mathbf{k}}$ are orthogonal? **NCERT Pg. 71**

(a) 2 (b) –1 (c) 0 (d) –2

4. A ray of light travelling in the direction $(\hat{\mathbf{i}} + \sqrt{3}\,\hat{\mathbf{j}})$ is incident on a plane mirror. After reflection, it travels along the direction $(\hat{\mathbf{i}} - \sqrt{3}\,\hat{\mathbf{j}})$. Mark the correct option. **NCERT Pg. 71**

(a) The angle of incidence is 30°.
(b) The angle of reflection is 60°.
(c) The angle of incidence is 45°.
(d) The angle of reflection is 45°.

5. Two vectors **A** and **B** are such that $|\mathbf{A}+\mathbf{B}|=|\mathbf{A}-\mathbf{B}|$, then the angle between **A** and **B** is **NCERT Pg. 71**
(a) 60° (b) 90°
(c) 30° (d) 0°

Notions of Work and KE : The Work-Energy Theorem

6 Two moving objects having same kinetic energy are stopped by application of equal retarding force. Which object will come to rest at short distance? **NCERT Pg. 73**
(a) Bigger
(b) Smaller
(c) Both at same distance
(d) Cannot say

7 A car weighing 1400 kg is moving at a speed of 54 kmh^{-1} up a hill. When the motor stops, it is just able to reach the destination which is at a height of 10 m above the point. Then, the work done against friction (negative of the work done by the friction) is (Take, $g=10\ ms^{-2}$) **NCERT Pg. 73**
(a) 10 kJ (b) 15 kJ (c) 17.5 kJ (d) 25 kJ

8 A bullet of mass 20 g is moving with a speed of 150 ms^{-1}. It strikes a target and is brought to rest after piercing 10 cm into it. Calculate the average force of resistance offered by the target. **NCERT Pg. 73**
(a) 2500 N (b) 2000 J
(c) 2250 N (d) 2100 J

9 Consider a drop of rain water having mass 1 g falling from a height of 1 km. It hits the ground with a speed of 50 m/s. The work done by the (i) gravitational force and the (ii) resistive force of air is (Take, $g=10\ m/s^2$) **NCERT Pg. 73**
(a) (i) –10 J and (ii) – 8.25 J
(b) (i) 1.25 J and (ii) – 8.25 J
(c) (i) 100 J and (ii) 8.75 J
(d) (i) 10 J and (ii) – 8.75 J

10 A body which is moving with 10 ms^{-1} is sliding up on a rough inclined plane having inclination of 30°. Find the height upto which it can go, if coefficient of friction of the inclined surface is 0.1. **NCERT Pg. 73**
(a) 4.26 m (b) 5.25 m
(c) 6.25 m (d) 7.25 m

11 A uniform cable of mass M and length L is placed on a horizontal surface such that its $\left(\frac{1}{n}\right)$ th part is hanging below the edge of the surface. To lift the hanging part of the cable upto the surface, the work done should be **NCERT Pg. 73**
(a) $\frac{2MgL}{n^2}$ (b) $nMgL$
(c) $\frac{MgL}{n^2}$ (d) $\frac{MgL}{2n^2}$

Work

12 A force $\mathbf{F}=(5\hat{i}+6\hat{j}-4\hat{k})$ acting on a body produces a displacement $\mathbf{d}=6\hat{i}+5\hat{k}$. The work done by the force is **NCERT Pg. 73**
(a) 18 units (b) 15 units
(c) 12 units (d) 10 units

13 A uniform force of $(3\hat{i}+\hat{j})$N acts on a particle of mass 2 kg. So, the particle is displaced from position $(2\hat{i}+\hat{k})$ m to position $(4\hat{i}+3\hat{j}-\hat{k})$ m. The work done by the force on the particle is **NCERT Pg. 73**
(a) 9 J (b) 6 J
(c) 13 J (d) 15 J

14 The earth is moving around the sun in a circular orbit, is acted upon by a force. So, work done on the earth by the force is **NCERT Pg. 73**
(a) zero (b) + ve
(c) – ve (d) None of these

15 Work done by gravitational force in one revolution of earth around the sun on its elliptical path is zero because **NCERT Pg. 73**
(a) force is always perpendicular to displacement
(b) displacement is zero
(c) displacement is non-zero
(d) Both (a) and (c)

16 In which case, work done will be zero **NCERT Pg. 73**
(a) a weight-lifter while holding a weight of 100 kg on his shoulders for 1 min
(b) a locomotive against gravity is running on a level plane with a speed of 60 kmh^{-1}
(c) a person holding a suitcase on his head and standing at a bus terminal
(d) All of the above

17 A ball is released from the top of a tower. The ratio of work done by force of gravity in 1st second, 2nd second and 3rd second of the motion of ball is **NCERT Pg. 73**
(a) 1 : 2 : 3 (b) 1 : 4 : 16
(c) 1 : 3 : 5 (d) 1 : 9 : 25

18 A force of 10 N is applied on an object of mass 2 kg placed on a rough surface having coefficient of friction equals to 0.2. Work done by applied force in 4 s is **NCERT Pg. 73**
(a) 120 J (b) 240 J
(c) 250 J (d) 100 J

19 A block of mass 1 kg is pushed up a surface inclined to horizontal at an angle of 30° by a force of 10 N parallel to the inclined surface as shown in the figure.

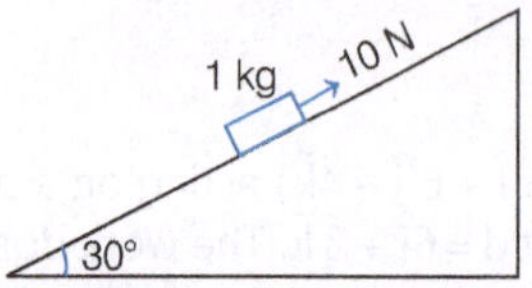

If the block is pushed up by 10 m along the incline, then the work against gravity is
(Take, $g = 10 \text{ m s}^{-2}$) **NCERT Pg. 73**
(a) 10 J (b) 50 J
(c) 100 J (d) 150 J

20 In the given curved road, if particle is released from *A*, then if friction is zero; which of the following statement is correct? **NCERT Pg. 73**

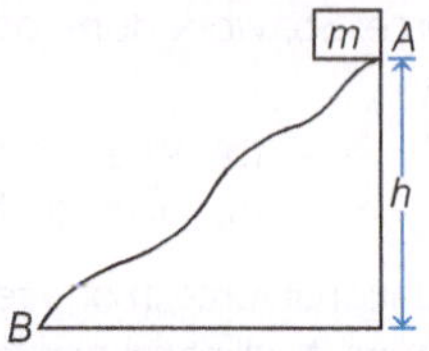

(a) Kinetic energy at *B* must be *mgh*.
(b) Kinetic energy at *B* must be zero.
(c) Kinetic energy at *B* must be less than *mgh*.
(d) Kinetic energy at *B* must not be equal to zero.

Kinetic Energy

21 An electron and a proton are detected in a cosmic ray experiment, the first with kinetic energy 12 keV, and the second with 120 keV. The ratio of their speeds is (where m_e and m_p are masses of electron and proton respectively) **NCERT Pg. 74**
(a) $\sqrt{\frac{1}{10}\frac{m_e}{m_p}}$ (b) $\sqrt{\frac{1}{10}\frac{m_p}{m_e}}$
(c) $\frac{1}{10}\frac{m_e}{m_p}$ (d) $\frac{1}{10}\frac{m_p}{m_e}$

22 The kinetic energy of an air molecule (10^{-21} J) in eV is **NCERT Pg. 74**
(a) 6.2 meV (b) 4.2 meV
(c) 10.4 meV (d) 9.7 meV

23 When a man increases his speed by 2 ms^{-1}, he finds that his kinetic energy is doubled, the original speed of the man is **NCERT Pg. 74**
(a) $2(\sqrt{2}-1) \text{ ms}^{-1}$ (b) $2(\sqrt{2}+1) \text{ ms}^{-1}$
(c) 4.5 ms^{-1} (d) None of these

24 A running man has half the kinetic energy to that a boy of half of his mass. The man speeds up by 1 ms^{-1}, so he has same kinetic energy as that of the boy. The original speed of the man is **NCERT Pg. 74**
(a) $\sqrt{2} \text{ ms}^{-1}$ (b) $\sqrt{2}-1 \text{ ms}^{-1}$
(c) $\frac{1}{\sqrt{2}-1} \text{ ms}^{-1}$ (d) $\frac{1}{\sqrt{2}} \text{ ms}^{-1}$

25 An object of mass 10 kg is moving with velocity of 10 ms^{-1}. A force of 50 N acted upon it for 2 s. The percentage increase in its kinetic energy is **NCERT Pg. 74**
(a) 25% (b) 50% (c) 75% (d) 300%

26 A particle of mass 10 g moves along a circle of radius 6.4 cm with a constant tangential acceleration. What is the magnitude of this acceleration, if the kinetic energy of the particle becomes equal to 8×10^{-4} J by the end of the second revolution after the beginning of the motion? **NCERT Pg. 74**
(a) 0.15 ms^{-2} (b) 0.18 ms^{-2} (c) 0.2 ms^{-2} (d) 0.1 ms^{-2}

27 A force which is inversely proportional to the speed, is acting on a body. The kinetic energy of the body starting from rest is **NCERT Pg. 74**
(a) a constant
(b) inversely proportional to time
(c) directly proportional to time
(d) directly proportional to square of time

28 Kinetic energy of a particle is increased by 4 times. What will be the relation between initial and final momentum? **NCERT Pg. 74**
(a) $p_2 = 2p_1$ (b) $p_2 = \frac{p_1}{2}$
(c) $p_2 = p_1$ (d) $p_2 = 4p_1$

29 Two masses of 1 g and 4 g are moving with equal kinetic energy. The ratio of the magnitudes of their momentum is **NCERT Pg. 74**
(a) 4 : 1 (b) $\sqrt{2}$: 1 (c) 1 : 2 (d) 1 : 16

30 If momentum of a moving body is increased to 50% of its initial value, then percentage increase in its kinetic energy will be **NCERT Pg. 74**
(a) 50% (b) 125% (c) 100% (d) 75%

Work Done by a Variable Force

31 A bullet of mass *m* fired at an angle 30° to the horizontal leaves the barrel of the gun with a velocity *v*. The bullet hits a soft target at a height *h* above the ground while it is moving downward and emerge out with half the kinetic energy, it had before hitting the target. Which of the following statement is correct in respect of bullet after it emerges out of the target? **NCERT Pg. 75**

(a) The velocity of the bullet will be reduced to half its initial value.
(b) The velocity of the bullet will be more than half of its earlier velocity.
(c) The bullet will continue to move along the same parabolic path.
(d) The bullet will move in a straight line.

32 Find the work done on a particle of mass m by a force $\mathbf{F} = C\left[\frac{x}{(x^2+y^2)^{3/2}}\hat{\mathbf{i}} + \frac{y}{(x^2+y^2)^{3/2}}\hat{\mathbf{j}}\right]$, where C is a constant of appropriate dimensions, when the particle is taken from the point (2, 0) m to the point (0, 2) m along a circular path of radius r about the origin in XY-plane. **NCERT Pg. 75**

(a) $r^2/2$ (b) $b^2/2$
(c) Zero (d) k/r^3

33 A force $F = 10 + 10y$ acts on a particle in y-direction, where F is in newton and y in metre. Work done by this force to move the particle from $y = 0$ to $y = 1$ m is **NCERT Pg. 75**

(a) 5 J (b) 15 J
(c) 20 J (d) 30 J

34 When a rubber band is stretched by a distance x, it exerts a restoring force of magnitude $F = ax + bx^2$, where a and b are constants. The work done in stretching the unstretched rubber band by L is **NCERT Pg. 75**

(a) $aL^2 + bL^3$ (b) $\frac{1}{2}(aL^2 + bL^3)$
(c) $\frac{aL^2}{2} + \frac{bL^3}{3}$ (d) $\frac{1}{2}\left(\frac{aL^2}{2} + \frac{bL^3}{3}\right)$

35 A body of mass 3 kg is under a force which causes a displacement in it given by $s = t^2/3$ (in metre). Work done by the force in 2 s is **NCERT Pg. 75**

(a) 2 J (b) 3.8 J (c) 5.2 J (d) 2.6 J

36 A 10 kg brick moves along X-axis. Its acceleration as a function of its position is shown in figure. What is the net work performed on the brick by the force causing the acceleration as the brick moves from $x = 0$ to $x = 8.0$ m? **NCERT Pg. 75**

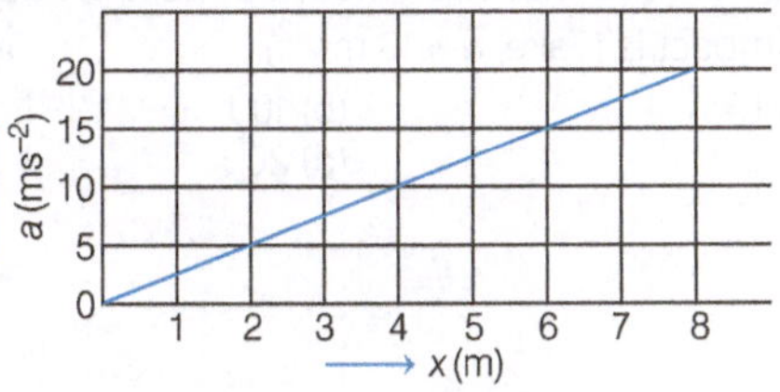

(a) 400 J (b) 800 J (c) 200 J (d) 100 J

37 A body moves from point A to B under the action of a force varying in magnitude as shown in figure, then the work done is (force is expressed in newton and displacement in metre) **NCERT Pg. 75**

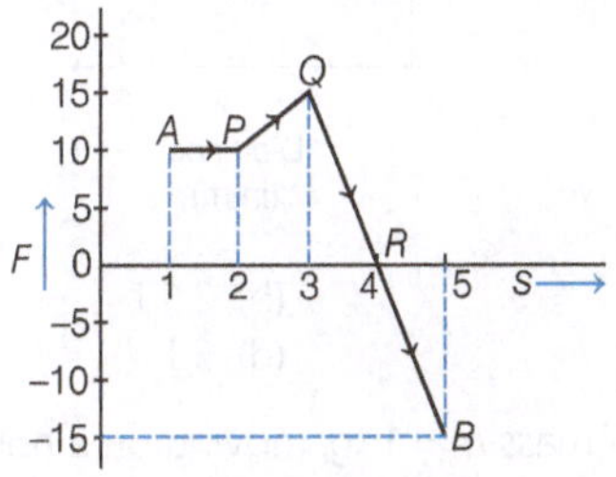

(a) 30 J (b) 22.5 J
(c) 25 J (d) 27 J

38 A woman pushes a trunk on a railway platform which has a rough surface. She applies a force of 100 N over a distance of 10 m. Thereafter, she gets progressively tired and her applied force reduces linearly with distance to 50 N. The total distance through which the trunk has been moved is 20 m. If the frictional force is 50 N, then total work done by the two forces over 20 m is **NCERT Pg. 75**

(a) −2000 J (b) 500 J
(c) 750 J (d) −200 J

39 A force of $\mathbf{F} = 2x\hat{\mathbf{i}} + 2\hat{\mathbf{j}} + 3z^2\hat{\mathbf{k}}$ N is acting on a particle. Find the work done by this force in displacing the body from (1, 2, 3) m to (3, 6, 2) m. **NCERT Pg. 75**

(a) −10 J (b) 100 J
(c) 10 J (d) −3 J

40 A force acts on a 2 kg object, so that its position is given as a function of time as $x = 3t^2 + 5$. What is the work done by this force in first 5 seconds? **NCERT Pg. 75**

(a) 850 J (b) 900 J
(c) 950 J (d) 875 J

The Work-Energy Theorem for a Variable Force

41 A block of mass 10 kg moving in x-direction with a constant speed of 10 ms^{-1} is subjected to a retarding force $F = 0.1x$ J/m during its travelling from $x = 20$ m to 30 m. Its final kinetic energy will be **NCERT Pg. 76**

(a) 475 J (b) 450 J
(c) 275 J (d) 250 J

42 A particle moves in one dimension from rest under the influence of a force that varies with the distance travelled by the particle as shown in the figure. The kinetic energy of the particle after it has travelled 3 m is **NCERT Pg. 76**

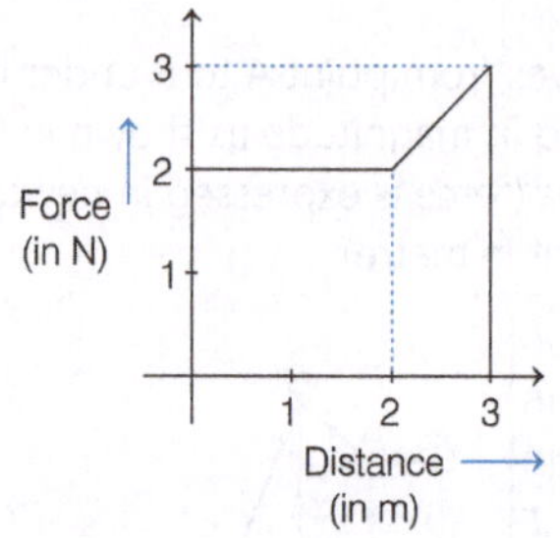

(a) 4 J (b) 2.5 J
(c) 6.5 J (d) 5 J

43 A block of mass $m = 1$ kg, moving on a horizontal surface with speed $v_i = 2\ \text{ms}^{-1}$ enters a rough patch ranging from $x = 0.10$ m to $x = 2.01$ m. The retarding force F_r on the block in this range is inversely proportional to x over this range,

$$F_r = \frac{-k}{x} \text{ for } 0.1 < x < 2.01\text{ m}$$

$$= 0 \text{ for } x < 0.1\text{m and } x > 2.01\text{ m, where } k = 0.5\text{ J.}$$

NCERT Pg. 76

What is the speed v_f of the block as it crosses this patch?

(a) $2\ \text{ms}^{-1}$ (b) $40\ \text{ms}^{-1}$
(c) $1\ \text{ms}^{-1}$ (d) $4\ \text{ms}^{-1}$

Concept of Potential Energy

44 Which of the following option is correct? **NCERT Pg. 77**

(a) Absolute value of potential energy cannot be determined.
(b) Absolute value of kinetic energy can be determined because velocity is not measured in relative terms.
(c) Absolute value of force cannot be determined because measurement of acceleration is not possible.
(d) None of the above

45 A metre stick weighing 500 g, is displaced through an angle of 60° in vertical plane as shown. The change in its potential energy is ($g = 10\ \text{ms}^{-2}$) **NCERT Pg. 77**

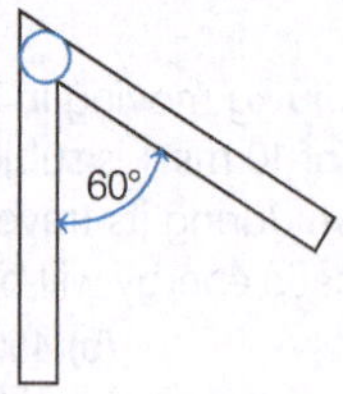

(a) 1.5 J (b) 2.5 J (c) 30 J (d) 45 J

46 A ball is projected vertically upwards with a certain initial speed. Another ball of the same mass is projected at an angle of 60° to the vertical with the same initial speed. At highest point of their journey, the ratio of their potential energies will be **NCERT Pg. 77**

(a) 1 : 1 (b) 2 : 1
(c) 3 : 2 (d) 4 : 1

47 A ball bounces to 75% of its original height. The percentage loss of potential energy in each bounce is **NCERT Pg. 77**

(a) 100% (b) 75%
(c) 50% (d) 25%

48 The potential energy $U(x)$ can be assumed zero when **NCERT Pg. 77**

(a) $x = 0$
(b) gravitational force is constant
(c) infinite distance from the gravitational source
(d) All of the above

49 The potential energy of a body is increased in which of the following cases? **NCERT Pg. 77**

(a) If work is done by conservative force
(b) If work is done against conservative force
(c) If work is done by non-conservative force
(d) If work is done against non-conservative force

50 A particle in a certain conservative force field has a potential energy given by $U = \frac{10xy}{z}$. The force exerted on it is **NCERT Pg. 77**

(a) $\left(\frac{10y}{z}\right)\hat{\mathbf{i}} + \left(\frac{10x}{z}\right)\hat{\mathbf{j}} + \left(\frac{10xy}{z^2}\right)\hat{\mathbf{k}}$

(b) $-\left(\frac{10y}{z}\right)\hat{\mathbf{i}} - \left(\frac{10x}{z}\right)\hat{\mathbf{j}} + \left(\frac{10xy}{z^2}\right)\hat{\mathbf{k}}$

(c) $-\left(\frac{10y}{z}\right)\hat{\mathbf{i}} - \left(\frac{10x}{z}\right)\hat{\mathbf{j}} - \left(\frac{10xy}{z^2}\right)\hat{\mathbf{k}}$

(d) $\left(\frac{10y}{z}\right)\hat{\mathbf{i}} + \left(\frac{10x}{z}\right)\hat{\mathbf{j}} - \left(\frac{10xy}{z^2}\right)\hat{\mathbf{k}}$

51 A bolt of mass 0.1 kg falls from the ceiling of an elevator moving down in a uniform speed of $5\ \text{ms}^{-1}$. It hits the floor of the elevator (length of the elevator = 10 m) and does not rebound. The amount of heat produced by the impact is (Take, $g = 10\ \text{ms}^{-2}$) **NCERT Pg. 77**

(a) 5 J (b) 10 J
(c) 15 J (d) 20 J

Conservation of Mechanical Energy

52 Which of the following option is correct? **NCERT Pg. 78**

(a) Conservation of mechanical energy does not consider only conservative force.
(b) Conservation of energy consider both conservative and non-conservative forces.
(c) Conservation of energy consider only conservative force.
(d) Mass converted into energy in nuclear reaction is called mass-defect.

53 When a body is falling from a certain height from the surface of the earth, then **NCERT Pg. 78**

(a) its kinetic energy decreases continuously
(b) its potential energy increases continuously
(c) its total mechanical energy remains constant at each point
(d) kinetic energy and potential energy are equal at each point

54 An artificial satellite orbiting the earth in very thin atmosphere loses its energy gradually due to the dissipation against atmospheric resistance, however small. As it comes closer to the earth, its speed **NCERT Pg. 78**

(a) increases (b) equal to
(c) decreases (d) less than equal to

55 A 2 kg block slides on a horizontal floor with a speed of 4 ms^{-1}. It strikes an uncompressed spring and compresses it, till the block is motionless. The force of kinetic friction is 15 N and spring constant is 10000 Nm^{-1}. The spring is compressed by **NCERT Pg. 78**

(a) 5.5 cm (b) 2.5 cm
(c) 11.0 cm (d) 8.5 cm

56 A ball bounces to 80% of its original height. What fraction of its mechanical energy is lost in each bounce? **NCERT Pg. 78**

(a) 20% (b) 25%
(c) 26% (d) 30%

57 A simple pendulum is released from A as shown in the figure. If m and l represent the mass of the bob and length of the pendulum respectively, the gain in kinetic energy at B is **NCERT Pg. 78**

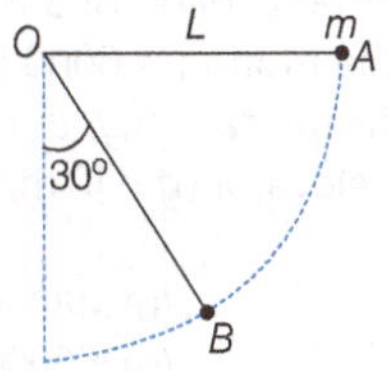

(a) $\frac{mgl}{2}$ (b) $\frac{\sqrt{3}}{2}mgl$
(c) $\frac{mgl}{\sqrt{2}}$ (d) $\frac{2}{\sqrt{3}}mgl$

58 A body of mass 5 kg is thrown vertically up with a kinetic energy of 490 J. The height at which the kinetic energy of the body becomes half of the original value is **NCERT Pg. 78**

(a) 12.5 m (b) 10 m
(c) 2.5 m (d) 5 m

59 What is the ratio of kinetic energy of a particle at the bottom to the kinetic energy at the top when it just loops a vertical loop of radius r? **NCERT Pg. 78**

(a) 5 : 1 (b) 2 : 3
(c) 5 : 2 (d) 7 : 2

60 k/r^2 represents the force under which a particle is moving in a circle of radius r. The total energy of the particle is **NCERT Pg. 78**

(a) $\frac{k}{2r}$ (b) $\frac{2k}{r}$
(c) $\frac{-k}{r}$ (d) $-\frac{k}{2r}$

61 A bob of mass m is suspended by a light string of length L. It is imparted a horizontal velocity v_0 at the lowest point A such that it completes a semi-circular trajectory in the vertical plane. The string becomes slack only on reaching the topmost point C as shown in figure. Then, the speed of bob (v_0) at point A is **NCERT Pg. 78**

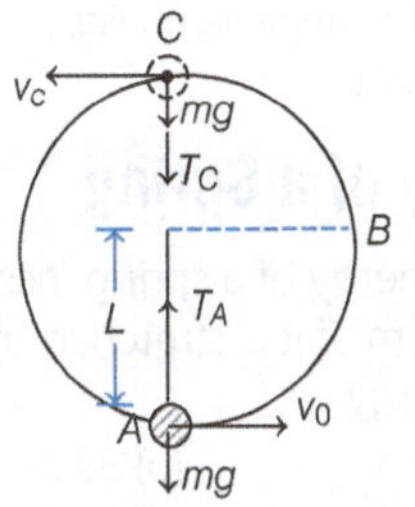

(a) $\sqrt{5gL}$ (b) $\sqrt{2gL}$
(c) $\sqrt{3gL}$ (d) $\sqrt{7gL}$

62 A bullet of mass 20 g moving horizontally with a velocity 5 m/s strikes a block of wood of mass 30 g and gets embedded in the block. The block is suspended from the ceiling by a massless string. The height to which block rises is **NCERT Pg. 78**

(a) 0.5 m (b) 0.2 m
(c) 0.6 m (d) 0.1 m

63 Which graph represents conservation of total mechanical energy? **NCERT Pg. 78**

(a)
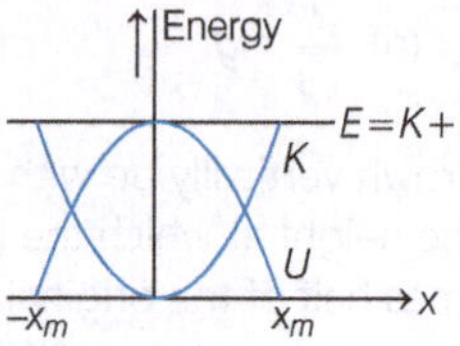

(b)
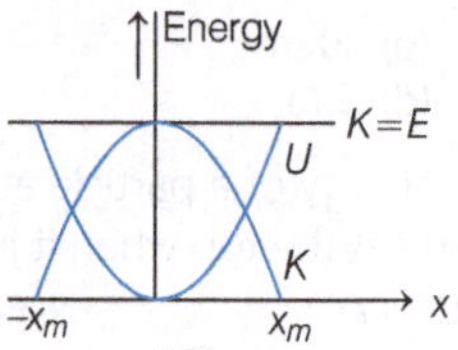

(c)
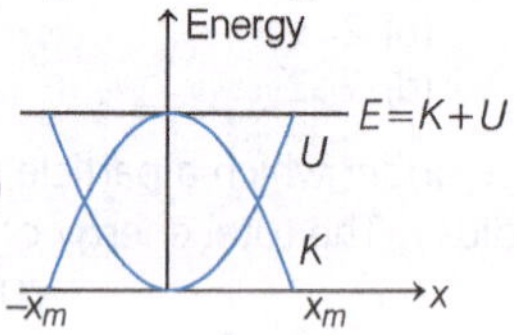

(d)
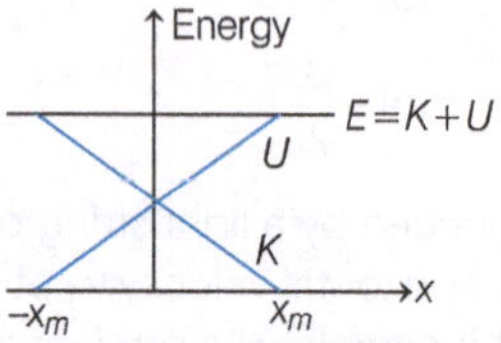

64 According to the equivalence of mass and energy, which of the following option is incorrect? **NCERT Pg. 78**

(a) The mass of an isolated system is conserved.
(b) Matter is neither created nor destroyed.
(c) Matter might change its phase.
(d) All of the above

Potential Energy of a Spring

65 The potential energy of a spring increases by 15 J when stretched by 3 cm. If it is stretched by 4 cm, the increase in potential energy is **NCERT Pg. 80**

(a) 27 J (b) 30 J
(c) 33 J (d) 36 J

66 The ratio of spring constants of two springs is 2 : 3. What is the ratio of their potential energy, if they are stretched by the same force? **NCERT Pg. 80**

(a) 2 : 3 (b) 3 : 2 (c) 4 : 9 (d) 9 : 4

67 A spring is compressed by 10 cm, if a block of mass is dropped on it from a height of 40 cm. If the force constant of the spring is 980 Nm^{-1}, then what is the mass of the block? **NCERT Pg. 80**

(a) 1 kg (b) 2 kg (c) 3kg (d) 4 kg

68 A car of mass 1000 kg moving with a speed 18 km/h on a smooth road, collide with a horizontally mounted spring of spring constant 6.25×10^3 Nm^{-1}. What is the maximum compression of the spring? **NCERT Pg. 80**

(a) 1 m (b) 2 m (c) 3 m (d) 5 m

69 A spring gun of spring constant 90 N/cm is compressed 12 cm by a ball of mass 16 g. If the trigger is pulled, the velocity of the ball is **NCERT Pg. 80**

(a) 50 ms^{-1} (b) 40 ms^{-1}
(c) 90 ms^{-1} (d) 60 ms^{-1}

70 Which of the following option is correct about non-conservative force? **NCERT Pg. 80**

(a) It depends on velocity of the object.
(b) It depends on the particular path taken by the object.
(c) It depend on the initial and final positions of the object.
(d) Both (a) and (b)

Power

71 A force $(4\hat{i} + \hat{j} - 2\hat{k})$ N acting on a body maintains its velocity at $(\hat{i} + 2\hat{j} + 3\hat{k})$ ms^{-1}. The power exerted is **NCERT Pg. 83**

(a) 4 W (b) 5W (c) zero (d)8 W

72 A one kilowatt motor is used to pump water from a well 10 m deep. The quantity of water pumped out per second is nearly **NCERT Pg. 83**

(a) 1kg (b) 10 kg (c) 100 kg (d) 1000 kg

73 In a hydroelectric power station, the water is flowing at 2 ms^{-1} in the river, which is 100 m wide and 5 m deep. The maximum power output from the river is **NCERT Pg. 83**

(a) 1.5 MW (b) 2 MW
(c) 2.5 MW (d) 3 MW

74 A machine gun fires 360 bullets per minute, with a velocity of 600 ms^{-1}. If the power of the gun is 5.4 kW, then mass of each bullet is **NCERT Pg. 83**

(a) 5 kg (b) 0.5 kg (c) 5 g (d) 0.5 g

75 An elevator in a building can carry a maximum of 10 persons, with the average mass of each person being 68 kg. The mass of the elevator itself is 920 kg and it moves with a constant speed of 3 m/s. The frictional force opposing the motion is 6000 N. If the elevator is moving up with its full capacity, the power delivered by the motor to the elevator ($g = 10$ m/s^2) must be at least **NCERT Pg. 83**

(a) 62360 W (b) 48000 W
(c) 56300 W (d) 66000 W

76 At time $t = 0$ s, particle starts moving along X-axis. If its kinetic energy increases uniformly with time t, the net force acting on it must be proportional to **NCERT Pg. 83**

(a) $\frac{1}{\sqrt{t}}$ (b) $t^{3/2}$

(c) $t^{1/3}$ (d) $t^{4/3}$

77 A body of mass 1 kg begins to move under the action of a time dependent force $\mathbf{F} = (2t\,\hat{\mathbf{i}} + 3t^2\hat{\mathbf{j}})$ N, where $\hat{\mathbf{i}}$ and $\hat{\mathbf{j}}$ are unit vectors along X and Y-axis. What power will be developed by the force at the time t? **NCERT Pg. 83**

(a) $(2t^2 + 4t^4)$ W (b) $(2t^3 + 3t^4)$ W
(c) $(2t^3 + 3t^5)$ W (d) $(2t + 3t^3)$ W

Collision

78 A ball of mass m moving with a speed $2v$ collides head-on with an identical ball at rest. If 0.2 is the coefficient of restitution, then what will be the ratio of velocity of two balls after collision? **NCERT Pg. 83**

(a) $\frac{2}{3}$ (b) $\frac{3}{2}$

(c) $\frac{1}{2}$ (d) $\frac{3}{4}$

79 A particle of mass 1 g moving with a velocity $\mathbf{v}_1 = (3\hat{\mathbf{i}} - 2\hat{\mathbf{j}})\ \text{ms}^{-1}$ experiences a perfectly inelastic collision with another particle of mass 2 g and velocity $\mathbf{v}_2 = (4\hat{\mathbf{j}} - 6\hat{\mathbf{k}})\ \text{ms}^{-1}$. The velocity of the particle is **NCERT Pg. 83**

(a) 2.3 ms^{-1} (b) 4.6 ms^{-1}
(c) 9.2 ms^{-1} (d) 6 ms^{-1}

80 A particle of mass m moving in the x-direction with speed $2v$ is hit by another particle of mass $2m$ moving in the y-direction with speed v. If the collision is perfectly inelastic, the percentage loss in the energy during the collision is close to **NCERT Pg. 83**

(a) 44% (b) 50% (c) 56% (d) 62%

81 In a collinear collision, a particle with an initial speed v_0 strikes a stationary particle of the same mass. If the final total kinetic energy is 50% greater than the original kinetic energy, the magnitude of the relative velocity between the two particles after collision, is **NCERT Pg. 83**

(a) $\frac{v_0}{4}$ (b) $\sqrt{2}\,v_0$

(c) $\frac{v_0}{2}$ (d) $\frac{v_0}{\sqrt{2}}$

82 Consider the collision depicted in figure to be between two billiard balls with equal masses $m_1 = m_2$. The first ball is called the cue while the second ball is called the target. The billiard player wants to sink the target ball in a corner pocket, which is at an angle $\theta_2 = 37°$.

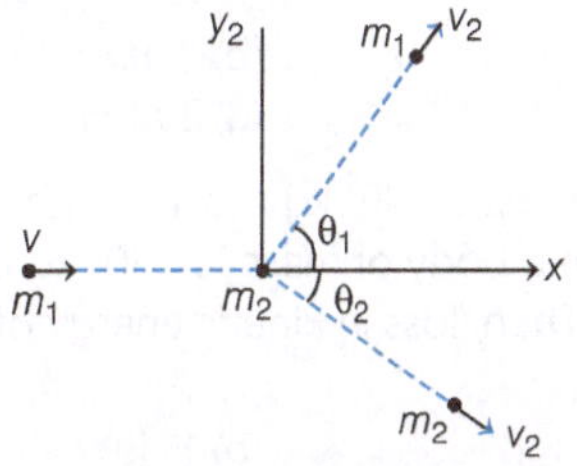

NCERT Pg. 83

Assume that the collision is elastic and that friction and rotational motion are not important. Obtain θ_1.

(a) 58° (b) 54°
(c) 53° (d) 90°

83 Body of mass M is much heavier than the other body of mass m. The heavier body with speed v collides elastically with the lighter body, which was at rest initially. The speed of lighter body after collision is **NCERT Pg. 83**

(a) $2v$ (b) $3v$ (c) v (d) $v/2$

84 A moving block having mass m collides with another stationary block having mass $4m$. The lighter block comes to rest after collision. When the initial velocity of the lighter block is v, then the value of coefficient of restitution (e) will be **NCERT Pg. 83**

(a) 0.8 (b) 0.25
(c) 0.5 (d) 0.4

85 A ball of 0.5 kg collided with wall at 30° and bounced back elastically. The speed of ball was 12m/s. The contact remained for 1s. What is the force applied by wall on the ball? **NCERT Pg. 83**

(a) $12\sqrt{3}$ N (b) $\sqrt{3}$ N
(c) $6\sqrt{3}$ N (d) $3\sqrt{3}$ N

86 Body A of mass $4m$ moving with speed u collides with another body B of mass $2m$ at rest. The collision is head-on and elastic in nature. After the collision, the fraction of energy lost by the colliding body A is **NCERT Pg. 83**

(a) $\frac{8}{9}$ (b) $\frac{4}{9}$ (c) $\frac{5}{9}$ (d) $\frac{1}{9}$

87 A toy truck of mass $2m$ elastically collides with a toy car of mass m, speed of truck is v and car is at rest. Find the velocity of car after collision. **NCERT Pg. 83**

(a) $\frac{4v}{3}$ (b) $\frac{v}{3}$

(c) v (d) $\frac{2v}{3}$

88 Two objects of mass m each moving with speed u m/s collide at 90°, then final momentum is (assume collision is inelastic) NCERT Pg. 83
(a) mu (b) $2\ mu$
(c) $\sqrt{2}\ mu$ (d) $2\sqrt{2}\ mu$

89 A body of mass 5×10^3 kg moving with speed 2 m/s collides with a body of mass 15×10^3 kg inelastically and sticks to it. Then, loss in kinetic energy of the system will be NCERT Pg. 83
(a) 7.5 kJ (b) 15 kJ
(c) 10 kJ (d) 5 kJ

90 The height attained by a ball after 3 rebounds on falling from a height of h on floor, having coefficient of restitution e is NCERT Pg. 83
(a) e^3h (b) e^4h (c) e^5h (d) e^6h

91 A spherical ball of mass m_1 collides head-on with another ball of mass m_2 at rest. The collision between the two balls is elastic. The fraction of kinetic energy lost by m_1 is NCERT Pg. 83
(a) $\frac{4m_1m_2}{(m_1+m_2)^2}$ (b) $\frac{m_1}{m_1+m_2}$
(c) $\frac{m_2}{m_1+m_2}$ (d) $\frac{m_1m_2}{(m_1+m_2)^2}$

92 A molecule in a gas container hits a horizontal wall with speed 200 ms^{-1} and angle 30° with the normal and rebounds with the same speed. Which of the following option is correct? NCERT Pg. 84
(a) Momentum is not conserved.
(b) Elastic collision occurs here.
(c) Inelastic collision occurs here.
(d) Both (a) and (b)

Assertion and Reason Questions

Direction (Q. Nos. 1-10) *In the following questions, a statement of Assertion is followed by a corresponding statement of Reason of the following statements, choose the correct one.*
(a) Both Assertion and Reason are correct and Reason is the correct explanation of Assertion.
(b) Both Assertion and Reason are correct but Reason is not the correct explanation of Assertion.
(c) Assertion is correct but Reason is incorrect.
(d) Assertion is incorrect but Reason is correct.

1 **Assertion** If momentum of a body increases by 50%, its kinetic energy will increase by 125%.
Reason Kinetic energy is proportional to square of velocity. NCERT Pg. 74

2 **Assertion** If only conservative force acts on the system, then total mechanical energy is conserved.
Reason Work done by a conservative force is equal to change in potential energy. NCERT Pg. 78

3 **Assertion** Decrease in mechanical energy is more in case of an object sliding up a relatively less inclined plane due to friction.
Reason The coefficient of friction between the block and the surface decreases with the increase in the angle of inclination. NCERT Pg. 78

4 **Assertion** Friction is a non-conservative force.
Reason This is because work done against friction, in moving a body over a closed path is never zero. NCERT Pg. 80

5 **Assertion** Two springs of force constants k_1 and k_2 are stretched by the same force. If $k_1 > k_2$, then work done in stretching the first (W_1) is less than work done in stretching the second (W_2).
Reason Spring force, $F = k_1x_1 = k_2x_2$ NCERT Pg. 80

6 **Assertion** Work done by spring force in a cyclic process is zero.
Reason The work by a conservative force depends only on initial and final positions. NCERT Pg. 80

7 **Assertion** Graph between potential energy of a spring *versus* the extension or compression of spring is a parabola.
Reason Potential energy of a stretched or compressed spring is proportional to the square of its extension or compression. NCERT Pg. 81

8 **Assertion** Force applied on a block moving in one-dimension is producing a constant power, then the motion should be uniformly accelerated.
Reason This constant power multiplied with time is equal to the change in kinetic energy. NCERT Pg. 83

9 **Assertion** Two particles are moving in the same direction do not lose all their energy in completely inelastic collision.
Reason Principle of conservation of momentum holds true for all kinds of collisions. NCERT Pg. 84

10 **Assertion** n small balls each of mass m colliding elastically each second on surface with velocity u. The force experienced by surface is mnu.
Reason After elastic collision, the ball rebound with same velocity. NCERT Pg.. 84

Statement Based Questions

Direction (Q.Nos 1-8) *In the following question, statement I and statement II are given. Read then statements and choose most appropriate answer from the options given below :*

(a) Both Statement I and Statement II are incorrect.
(b) Statement I is correct but Statement II is incorrect.
(c) Statement I is incorrect but Statement II is correct.
(d) Both Statement I and Statement II are correct.

1 **Statement I** Work done will be zero, if force and displacement are mutually perpendicular to each other.

Statement II Work done can only be zero or positive. **NCERT Pg. 73**

2 **Statement I** Work done by a conservative force in a closed path is zero.

Statement II A conservative force depends only on the end points. **NCERT Pg. 73**

3 **Statement I** When a stationary bomb exploded into two pieces, their speed are the inverse ratio of their masses.

Statement II Explosion violates the law of conservation of linear momentum. **NCERT Pg. 74**

4 **Statement I** Two bodies of masses m_1 and m_2 have equal kinetic energies, the ratio of their linear momentum is given by, $\frac{p_1}{p_2} = \sqrt{\frac{m_1}{m_2}}$

Statement II Kinetic energy of a moving body increased to four times when its speed is increased to double. **NCERT Pg. 74**

5 **Statement I** The work done on bringing a body down from the top to the base along a frictionless inclined plane is same as the work done in bringing it down the vertical side.

Statement II The gravitational force on the body along the inclined plane is different as that along the vertical side. **NCERT Pg. 78**

6 **Statement I** There is no loss of mechanical energy when a ball is sliding on a rough surface.

Statement II Potential energy of a body at height h and kinetic energy of the same body at surface is same when body drop from height h to the surface. **NCERT Pg. 80**

7 **Statement I** In elastic collision, initial kinetic energy is equal to the final kinetic energy.

Statement II When a ball m_1 collides with other ball m_2, then both ball move together after the collision in a perfect elastic collision. **NCERT Pg. 83**

8 **Statement I** A particle of mass m moving with speed u collides with stationary point particle of mass M. If the maximum energy loss possible is given as $f(1/2\, mv^2)$, then $f = (m / M + m)$.

Statement II Maximum energy loss occurs when the particle get stuck together as a result of the collision. **NCERT Pg. 83**

Matching Type Questions

1 Match the Column I (work done) with Column II (value). **NCERT Pg. 74**

Column I	Column II
A. Work done in pulling out a bucket from well by a person and by gravitational force	1. Positive and negative
B. Work done by friction on a body sliding down an inclined plane	2. Negative
C. Work done by a person in pulling a luggage on a rough surface	3. Positive
D. Work done by air in bringing a vibrating pendulum to rest and by gravitational force	4. Negative and positive

Choose the correct answer from the options given below

Codes

	A	B	C	D		A	B	C	D
(a)	4	1	2	3	(b)	3	2	1	4
(c)	4	2	1	3	(d)	1	2	3	4

2 A body of mass 0.3 kg is taken up an inclined plane to length 10 m and height 5m, and then allowed to slide down to bottom again, then match the items of Column I with the respective items in Column II. (Given, $\mu_k = 0.5$) **NCERT Pg. 75**

Column I	Column II
A. Work done by gravitational force over the round trip	1. 18.5 J
B. Work done by the applied force over upward journey	2. 10.9 J
C. Work done by frictional force over round trip	3. 0
D. Kinetic energy of the body at the end of trip	4. −7.6 J

Choose the correct answer from the options given below

Codes

	A	B	C	D		A	B	C	D
(a)	3	1	2	4	(b)	3	1	4	2
(c)	1	3	4	2	(d)	4	3	2	1

3 Acceleration *versus* x and potential *versus* x graph of a particle moving along X-axis as shown in figure. Mass of the particle is 1 kg and velocity at $x = 0$ is 4 m/s. Match the following Column I and Column II at $x = 8$ m. **NCERT Pg. 76**

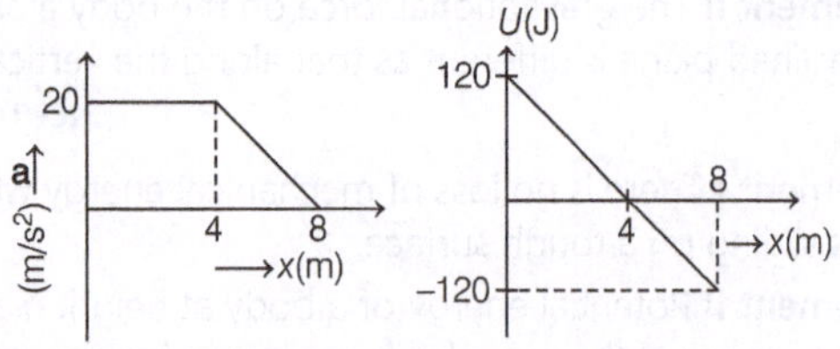

Column I		Column II	
A.	Final kinetic energy	1.	120 J
B.	Work done by conservative forces	2.	240 J
C.	Total work done	3.	128 J
D.	Work done by forces other than gravity	4.	– 120 J

Choose the correct answer from the options given below

Codes

	A	B	C	D
(a)	2	4	3	1
(b)	4	2	3	1
(c)	3	2	1	4
(d)	3	2	4	1

Numerical Type Questions

1 A force $\mathbf{F} = (1 + 3x)\,\hat{\mathbf{i}}$, acts on a particle in the x-direction, where F is in newton and x is in metre. The work done by this force during a displacement from $x = 0$ to $x = 4$ m, is ... ... J. **NCERT Pg. 74**

2 A block of mass m (as shown in figure) moving with kinetic energy K compresses a spring through a distance 25 cm when its speed is halved. The value of spring constant of used spring will be $n\,K$ Nm^{-1} for $n =$ ...... **NCERT Pg. 74**

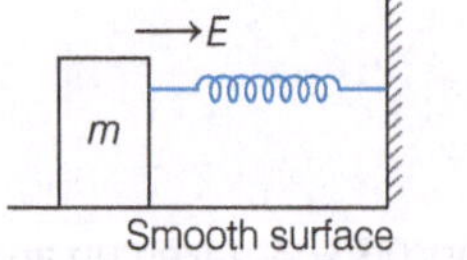

3 A small bob tied at one end of a thin string of length 4m is describing a vertical circle, so that the maximum and minimum tension in the string are in the ratio 5 : 1. The velocity of the bob at the highest position is .... m/s. (Take, $g = 10$ m/s^2) **NCERT Pg. 78**

4 A body of mass 4 kg is initially at rest. It starts moving unidirectionally under the influence of a source of constant power P. Its displacement in 4 s is $\frac{1}{3}\alpha^2\sqrt{\frac{P}{2}}$ m.

The value of α will be .... **NCERT Pg. 83**

5 A block moving horizontally on a smooth surface with a speed of 60 ms^{-1} splits into two equal parts. If one of the parts moves at 80 ms^{-1} in the same direction, then the fractional change in the kinetic energy will be $x : 9$, where x is .... **NCERT Pg. 84**

6 A body of mass 1 kg collides head-on elastically with a body at rest of mass 3 kg. After collision, the smaller body reverses its direction of motion and moves with a speed of 2 m/s. The initial speed of the smaller body before collision is .... ms^{-1}. **NCERT Pg. 84**

7 A ball with a speed of 8 m/s collides with another identical ball at rest. After the collision, the direction of each ball makes an angle of 30° with the original direction. The ratio of velocities of the balls after collision is $x : y$, where x is .... **NCERT Pg. 84**

8 A body of mass m is moving along the X-axis with initial velocity $u\hat{\mathbf{i}}$. It collides elastically with a particle of mass $10\,m$ at rest and then moves with half its initial kinetic energy (see figure). If $\sin\theta_1 = \sqrt{n}\sin\theta_2$, then value of n is .... **NCERT Pg. 84**

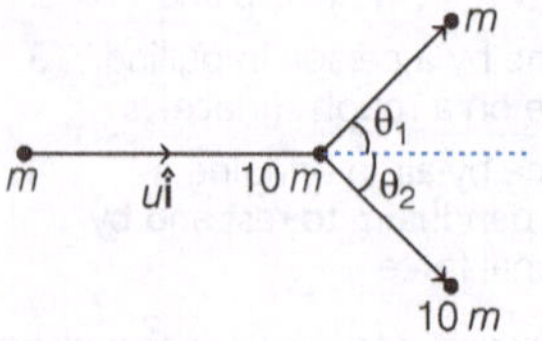

NCERT Exemplar Questions

1 Two inclined frictionless tracks, one gradual and the other steep meet at A from where two stones are allowed to slide down from rest, one on each track as shown in figure.

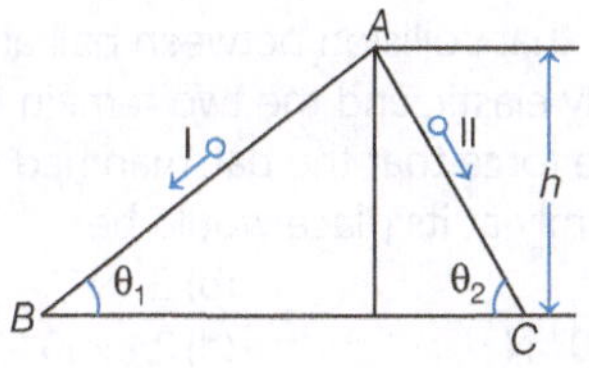

Which of the following statement is correct?

(a) Both the stones reach the bottom at the same time but not with the same speed.
(b) Both the stones reach the bottom with the same speed and stone I reaches the bottom earlier than stone II.
(c) Both the stones reach the bottom with the same speed and stone II reaches the bottom earlier than stone I.
(d) Both the stones reach the bottom at different times and with different speeds.

2 The potential energy function for a particle executing linear SHM is given by $U(x) = \frac{1}{2}kx^2$, where k is the force constant of the oscillator. For $k = 0.5\ \text{Nm}^{-1}$, the graph of $U(x)$ *versus* x is shown in the figure. A particle of total energy E turns back when it reaches $x = \pm x_m$. If U and K indicate the PE and KE, respectively of the particle at $x = + x_m$, then which of the following is correct?

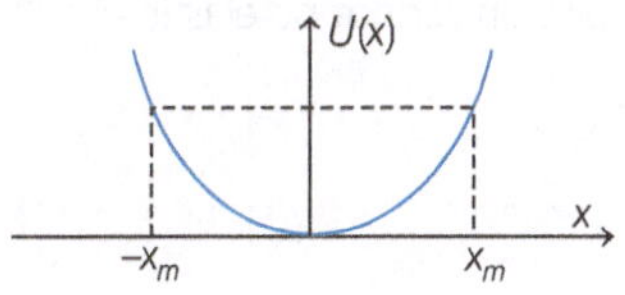

(a) $U = 0, K = E$ (b) $U = E, K = 0$
(c) $U < E, K = 0$ (d) $U = 0, K < E$

3 A body of mass 0.5 kg travels in a straight line with velocity $v = a\,x^{3/2}$, where $a = 5\ \text{m}^{-1/2}\text{s}^{-1}$. The work done by the net force during its displacement from $x = 0$ to $x = 2$ m is

(a) 1.5 J (b) 50 J
(c) 10 J (d) 100 J

4 A body is moving unidirectionally under the influence of a source of constant power supplying energy.
Which of the diagrams shown in figure correctly shows the displacement-time curve for its motion?

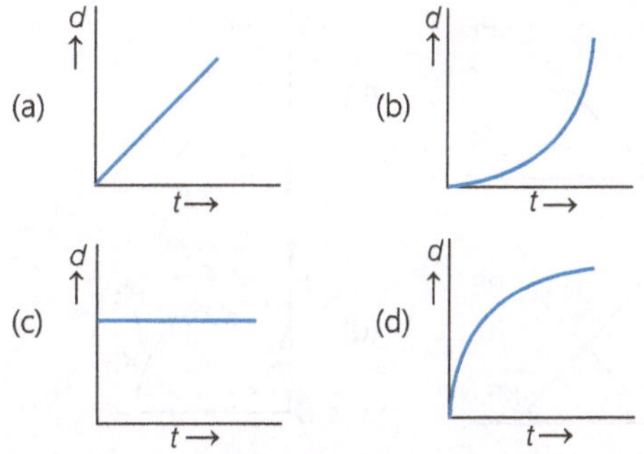

5 Which of the diagrams shown in figure most closely shows the variation in kinetic energy of the earth as it moves once around the sun in its elliptical orbit?

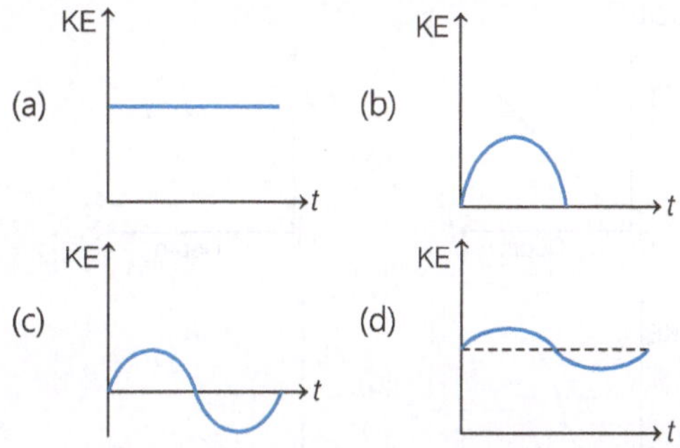

6 Which of the diagrams shown in figure represents variation of total mechanical energy of a pendulum oscillating in air as a function of time?

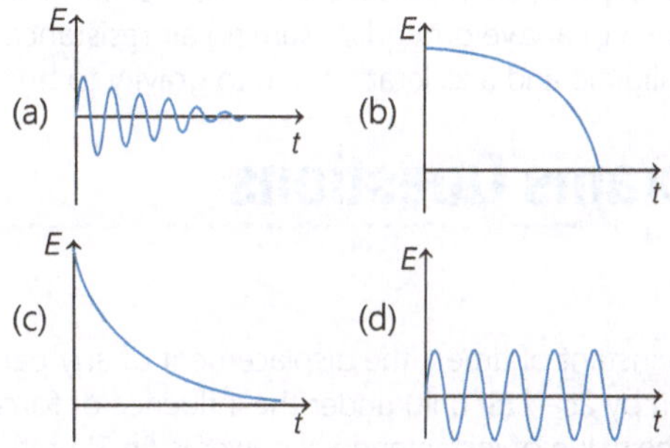

7 A mass of 5 kg is moving along a circular path of radius 1 m. If the mass moves with 300 rev min^{-1}, then its kinetic energy (in J) would be

(a) $250\pi^2$ (b) $100\pi^2$ (c) $5\pi^2$ (d) 0

8 A raindrop falling from a height h above ground, attains a near terminal velocity when it has fallen through a height $(3/4)h$. Which of the following diagrams shown in figure correctly shows the change in kinetic and potential energy of the drop during its fall on to the ground?

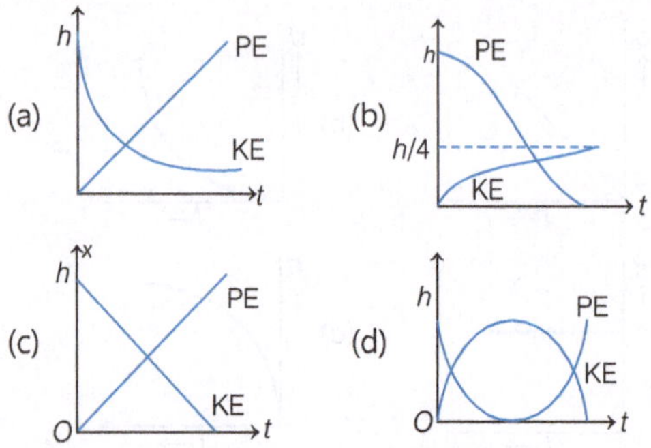

9 Which of the diagrams in figure correctly shows the change in kinetic energy of an iron sphere falling freely in a lake having sufficient depth to impart it a terminal velocity?

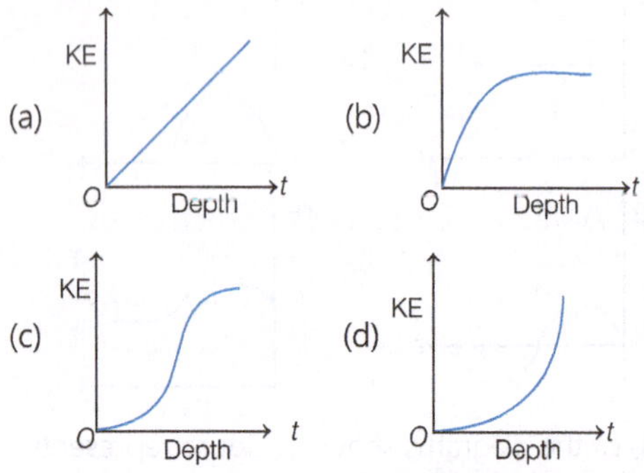

10 In a shotput event, an athlete throws the shotput of mass 10 kg with an initial speed of 1 ms^{-1} at 45° from a height 1.5 m above ground. Assuming air resistance to be negligible and acceleration due to gravity to be 10 ms^{-2}, the kinetic energy of the shotput when it just reaches the ground will be

(a) 2.5 J (b) 5.0 J (c) 52.5 J (d) 155.0 J

11 A cricket ball of mass 150 g moving with a speed of 126 kmh^{-1} hits at the middle of the bat, held firmly at its position by the batsman. The ball moves straight back to the bowler after hitting the bat.
Assuming that collision between ball and bat is completely elastic and the two remain in contact for 0.001s, the force that the batsman had to apply to hold the bat firmly at its place would be

(a) 10.5 N (b) 21 N
(c) 1.05×10^4 N (d) 2.1×10^4 N

12 Two blocks M_1 and M_2 having equal masses are free to move on a horizontal frictionless surface and M_2 is attached to a massless spring as shown in figure. Initially, M_2 is at rest and M_1 is moving towards M_2 with speed v and collides head-on with M_2.

Then, which of the following statement is correct?

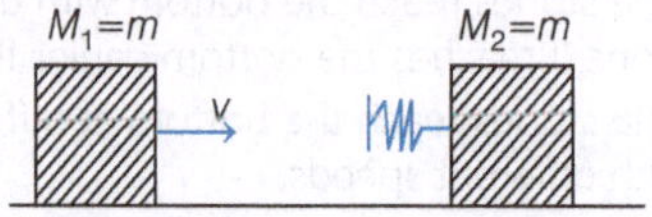

(a) While spring is fully compressed the system, all the KE of M_1 is stored as PE of spring.
(b) While spring is fully compressed the system, momentum is not conserved, though final momentum is equal to initial momentum.
(c) If spring is massless, the final state of the M_1 is state of rest.
(d) If the surface on which blocks are moving has friction, then collision cannot be elastic.

Past Exams Questions

NEET

1 At any instant of time t, the displacement of any particle is given by $2t-1$ (SI unit) under the influence of force of 5 N. The value of instantaneous power is (in SI unit) **NCERT Pg. 83, NEET 2024**

(a) 10 (b) 5 (c) 7 (d) 6

2 Two bodies A and B of same mass undergo completely inelastic one dimensional collision. The body A moves with velocity v_1 while body B is at rest before collision. The velocity of the system after collision is v_2. The ratio is **NCERT Pg. 84, NEET 2024**

(a) 1 : 2 (b) 2 : 1 (c) 4 : 1 (d) 1 : 4

3 The potential energy of a long spring when stretched by 2 cm is U. If the spring is stretched by 8 cm, potential energy stored in it will be **NCERT Pg. 80, NEET 2023**

(a) $4U$ (b) $8U$ (c) $16U$ (d) $2U$

4 An electric lift with a maximum load of 2000 kg (lift + passengers) is moving up with a constant speed of 1.5 m/s. The frictional force opposing the motion is 3000 N. The minimum power delivered by the motor to the lift in watts is ($g = 10$ m/s^2) **NCERT Pg. 83, NEET 2022**

(a) 23000 (b) 20000
(c) 34500 (d) 23500

5 A particle is released from height S from the surface of the earth. At a certain height its kinetic energy is three times its potential energy. The height from the surface of earth and the speed of the particle at that instant are, respectively **NCERT 78, NEET 2021**

(a) $\frac{S}{4}, \frac{3gS}{2}$ (b) $\frac{S}{4}, \frac{\sqrt{3gS}}{2}$ (c) $\frac{S}{2}, \frac{\sqrt{3gS}}{2}$ (d) $\frac{S}{4}, \sqrt{\frac{3gS}{2}}$

6 A point mass m is moved in a vertical circle of radius r with the help of a string. The velocity of the mass is $\sqrt{7gr}$ at the lowest point. The tension in the string at the lowest points is **NCERT 78, NEET 2020**

(a) 6 mg (b) 7 mg (c) 8 mg (d) 1 mg

7 A particle of mass 5 m at rest suddenly breaks on its own into three fragments. Two fragments of mass m each move along mutually perpendicular direction with each speed v. The energy released during the process is **NCERT Pg. 83, NEET 2019**

(a) $\frac{3}{5}mv^2$ (b) $\frac{5}{3}mv^2$ (c) $\frac{3}{2}mv^2$ (d) $\frac{4}{3}mv^2$

8 A particle moves from a point $(-2\hat{i}+5\hat{j})$ to $(4\hat{j}+3\hat{k})$ when a force of $(4\hat{i}+3\hat{j})$ N is applied. How much work has been done by the force? **NCERT Pg. 74, NEET 2016**

(a) 8 J (b) 11 J
(c) 5 J (d) 2 J

9 A bullet of mass 10 g moving horizontally with a velocity of 400 m/s strikes a wooden block of mass 2 kg which is suspended by light inextensible string of length 5 m. As a result, the centre of gravity of the block is found to rise a vertical distance of 10 cm. The speed of the bullet after it emerges out horizontally from the block will be **NCERT Pg. 129, AIPMT 2016**

(a) 100 ms^{-1} (b) 80 ms^{-1}
(c) 120 ms^{-1} (d) 160 ms^{-1}

10 A ball is thrown vertically downwards from a height of 20 m with an initial velocity v_0. It collides with the ground, loses 50 % of its energy in collision and rebounds to the same height. The initial velocity v_0 is (Take, $g = 10\ ms^{-2}$) **NCERT Pg. 78, AIPMT 2015**

(a) 14 ms^{-1} (b) 20 ms^{-1}
(c) 28 ms^{-1} (d) 10 ms^{-1}

11 A particle of mass m is driven by a machine that delivers a constant power k watts. If the particle starts from rest, the force on the particle at time t is **NCERT Pg. 83, AIPMT 2015**

(a) $\sqrt{\frac{mk}{2}}\,t^{-1/2}$ (b) $\sqrt{mk}\,t^{-1/2}$
(c) $\sqrt{2mk}\,t^{-1/2}$ (d) $\frac{1}{2}\sqrt{mk}\,t^{-1/2}$

JEE Main

12 Four particles A, B, C and D of masses $\frac{m}{2}, m, 2m, 4m$, have same momentum, respectively. The particle with maximum kinetic energy is **NCERT Pg. 74, JEE Main 2024**

(a) A (b) C (c) D (d) B

13 A stone is projected at angle 30° to the horizontal. The ratio of kinetic energy of the stone at point of projection to its kinetic energy at the highest point of flight will be **NCERT Pg. 74, JEE Main 2023**

(a) 1 : 2 (b) 4 : 1 (c) 1 : 4 (d) 4 : 3

14 A bullet of mass 0.1 kg moving horizontally with speed 400 ms^{-1} hits a wooden block of mass 3.9 kg kept on a horizontal rough surface. The bullet gets embedded into the block and moves 20 m before coming to rest. The coefficient of friction between the block and the surface is (Given, $g = 10\ m/s^2$) **NCERT Pg. 84, JEE Main 2023**

(a) 0.50 (b) 0.90 (c) 0.25 (d) 0.65

15 A bullet of mass 200 g having initial kinetic energy 90 J is shot inside a long swimming pool as shown in the figure. If it's kinetic energy reduces to 40 J within 1 s, the minimum length of the pool, the bullet has to travel, so that it completely comes to rest is **NCERT Pg. 74, JEE Main 2022**

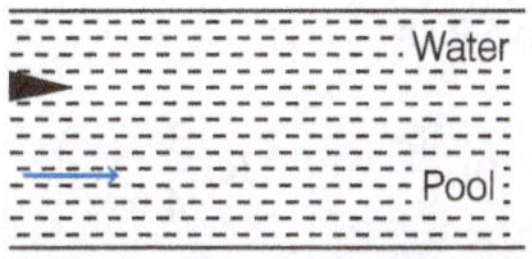

(a) 45 m (b) 90 m
(c) 125 m (d) 25 m

16 An automobile of mass m accelerates starting from origin and initially at rest, while the engine supplies constant power P. The position is given as a function of time by **NCERT Pg. 83, JEE Main 2021**

(a) $\left(\frac{9P}{8m}\right)^{1/2} \cdot t^{3/2}$ (b) $\left(\frac{8P}{9m}\right)^{1/2} \cdot t^{2/3}$
(c) $\left(\frac{9m}{8P}\right)^{1/2} \cdot t^{3/2}$ (d) $\left(\frac{8P}{9m}\right)^{1/2} \cdot t^{3/2}$

Skill Boosters

1 The potential energy of a 1 kg particle free to move along the X-axis is given by $U(x) = \left[\frac{x^4}{4} - \frac{x^2}{2}\right]$ J.

The total mechanical energy of the particle is 2 J. Then, maximum speed (in ms^{-1}) is

(a) $\frac{3}{\sqrt{2}}$ (b) $\sqrt{2}$
(c) $\frac{1}{\sqrt{2}}$ (d) 2

2 A small block slides down from the top of hemisphere of radius $R = 6$ m as shown in the figure. The height h at which the block will lose contact with the surface of the sphere is
(Assume there is no friction between the block and the hemisphere)

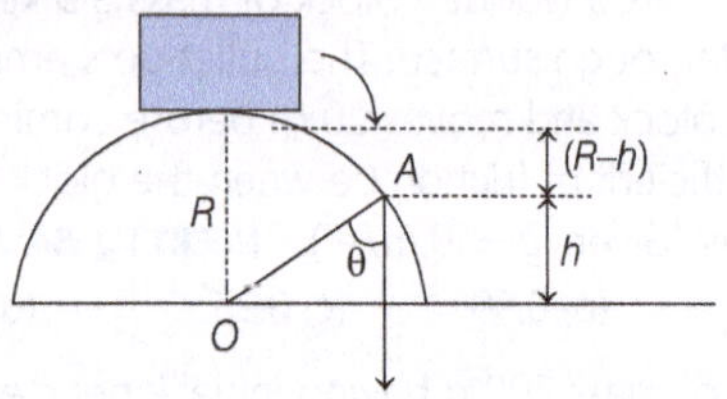

(a) 1 m (b) 2 m (c) 3 m (d) 4 m

3 A high speed moving car strikes to a spring, made up of combination of two springs (A and B) and compresses the spring by 8.75 cm. If spring constant of spring A is 300 N/m and spring B, is 400 N/m, then ratio of energy stored in A and B i.e., $\frac{E_A}{E_B}$ is

(a) $\frac{4}{3}$ (b) $\frac{16}{9}$ (c) $\frac{3}{4}$ (d) $\frac{9}{16}$

4 Four blocks of mass m, $2m$, $4m$ and $8m$ are placed on an ice surface as shown in the figure.
Another block of mass m moving with speed v collides with mass m in perfectly inelastic manner. All the subsequent collisions are also perfectly inelastic. By the time, the last block of mass m starts moving the total energy loss is P% of the original energy.
The value of P is close to

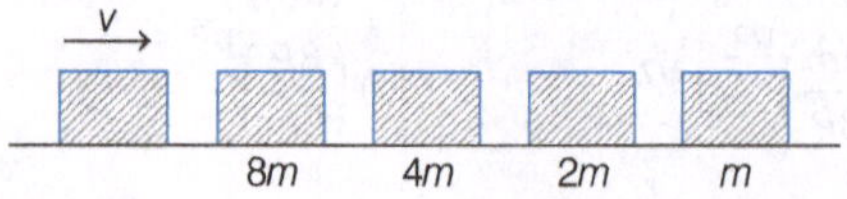

(a) 77 (b) 94
(c) 37 (d) 84

5 A machine can convert wind energy into electrical energy. But, it can convert only a fixed fraction of wind energy intercepted by its blades into electrical energy. If v is the speed of the wind, then power output will be most likely proportional to

(a) v^2 (b) v^3
(c) v^4 (d) $\sqrt{v}$

6 U is the potential energy, K is the kinetic energy and E is the mechanical energy. Which of the following is not possible for a stable system?

(a) $U > E$ (b) $U < E$
(c) $E > K$ (d) $K > E$

7 At time $t = 0$ s, particle starts moving along X-axis. If its kinetic energy increases uniformly with time t, the net force acting on it must be proportional to

(a) $\frac{1}{\sqrt{t}}$ (b) $t^{3/2}$
(c) $t^{1/3}$ (d) $t^{4/3}$

8 Two vehicles X and Y have masses 40 kg and 10 kg, respectively. Each vehicle is acted upon by a force of 80 N. If both vehicles acquire same kinetic energy in times t_x and t_y respectively, then $\frac{t_x}{t_y}$ is

(a) $\frac{1}{8}$ (b) $\frac{1}{2}$ (c) $\frac{2}{1}$ (d) $\frac{1}{4}$

9 A body of mass $4m$ is lying in XY-plane at rest. It suddenly explodes into three pieces. Two pieces each of mass m move perpendicular to each other with equal speeds v. The total kinetic energy generated due to explosion is

(a) mv^2 (b) $(3/2)\,mv^2$
(c) $2\,mv^2$ (d) $4\,mv^2$

10 Two identical balls A and B are released from the positions shown in the figure. They collide elastically on horizontal portion XY. The ratio of heights attained by A and B after collision will be (neglect friction)

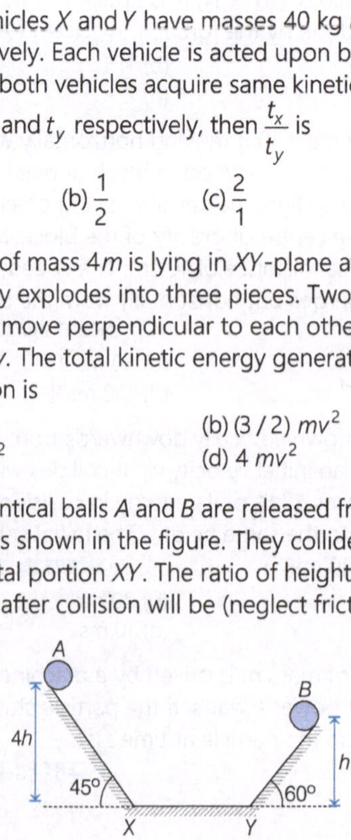

(a) 1 : 4 (b) 3 : 1 (c) 4 : 13 (d) 2 : 13

Correct Codes

Topical Questions

1 (b)	2 (b)	3 (b)	4 (a)	5 (b)	6 (c)	7 (c)	8 (c)	9 (d)	10 (a)
11 (d)	12 (d)	13 (a)	14 (b)	15 (b)	16 (d)	17 (c)	18 (b)	19 (b)	20 (a)
21 (b)	22 (a)	23 (b)	24 (c)	25 (d)	26 (d)	27 (c)	28 (a)	29 (c)	30 (b)
31 (b)	32 (c)	33 (b)	34 (c)	35 (d)	36 (b)	37 (b)	38 (c)	39 (d)	40 (b)
41 (a)	42 (c)	43 (c)	44 (a)	45 (b)	46 (d)	47 (d)	48 (d)	49 (b)	50 (b)
51 (b)	52 (b)	53 (c)	54 (a)	55 (a)	56 (a)	57 (b)	58 (d)	59 (a)	60 (d)
61 (a)	62 (b)	63 (c)	64 (b)	65 (a)	66 (b)	67 (a)	68 (b)	69 (c)	70 (d)
71 (c)	72 (b)	73 (b)	74 (c)	75 (d)	76 (a)	77 (c)	78 (a)	79 (b)	80 (c)
81 (b)	82 (c)	83 (a)	84 (b)	85 (c)	86 (a)	87 (a)	88 (c)	89 (a)	90 (d)
91 (a)	92 (b)								

Assertion and Reason Questions

1 (a)	2 (a)	3 (c)	4 (a)	5 (a)	6 (a)	7 (a)	8 (d)	9 (b)	10 (d)

Statement Based Questions

1 (b)	2 (d)	3 (b)	4 (d)	5 (d)	6 (c)	7 (b)	8 (c)

Matching Type Questions

1 (d)	2 (b)	3 (c)

Numerical Type Questions

1 (28)	2 (24)	3 (10)	4 (4)	5 (10)	6 (4)	7 (1)	8 (10)

NCERT Exemplar Questions

1 (c)	2 (b)	3 (b)	4 (b)	5 (d)	6 (c)	7 (a)	8 (b)	9 (b)	10 (d)
11 (c)	12 (c)								

Past Exams Questions

1 (a)	2 (b)	3 (c)	4 (c)	5 (d)	6 (c)	7 (d)	8 (c)	9 (c)	10 (b)
11 (a)	12 (a)	13 (d)	14 (c)	15 (a)	16 (d)				

Skill Boosters

1 (a)	2 (d)	3 (a)	4 (b)	5 (b)	6 (a)	7 (a)	8 (c)	9 (b)	10 (c)

Step by Step

Decoding the Questions

Concept Builders

1 90°	2 Zero
3 kinetic	4 True (T)
5 False	6 can
7 Light body	8 True (T)
9 four	10 Increases
11 conservative	12 False (F)
13 Power	14 False (F)
15 Zero	16 True (T)
17 elastic	18 maximum
19 Inelastic	20 Unity

Topical Questions

1 (*b*) Given, $\mathbf{F} = (3\hat{\mathbf{i}} + 4\hat{\mathbf{j}} - 5\hat{\mathbf{k}})$ unit

and $\mathbf{d} = (5\hat{\mathbf{i}} + 4\hat{\mathbf{j}} + 3\hat{\mathbf{k}})$ unit

$\therefore \quad \mathbf{F} \cdot \mathbf{d} = F_x d_x + F_y d_y + F_z d_z$

$= 3(5) + 4(4) + (-5)(3) = 16$ units

Now, $\mathbf{F} \cdot \mathbf{F} = F^2 = F_x^2 + F_y^2 + F_z^2$

$= 9 + 16 + 25 = 50$ units

$\Rightarrow \quad F = \sqrt{50}$ units

and $\mathbf{d} \cdot \mathbf{d} = d^2 = d_x^2 + d_y^2 + d_z^2$

$= 25 + 16 + 9 = 50$ units

$\Rightarrow \quad d = \sqrt{50}$ units

$\therefore \quad \cos\theta = \dfrac{16}{\sqrt{50}\,\sqrt{50}} = \dfrac{16}{50} = 0.32$

$\left(\because \cos\theta = \dfrac{\mathbf{F} \cdot \mathbf{d}}{Fd}\right)$

$\Rightarrow \quad \theta = \cos^{-1}(0.32)$

2 (*b*) Given, $\mathbf{A} = 3\hat{\mathbf{i}} - 4\hat{\mathbf{j}} + 5\hat{\mathbf{k}}$

$\mathbf{B} = -\hat{\mathbf{i}} + 2\hat{\mathbf{j}} + 3\hat{\mathbf{k}}$

$\mathbf{A} \cdot \mathbf{B} = (3\hat{\mathbf{i}} - 4\hat{\mathbf{j}} + 5\hat{\mathbf{k}}) \cdot (-\hat{\mathbf{i}} + 2\hat{\mathbf{j}} + 3\hat{\mathbf{k}})$

$\mathbf{A} \cdot \mathbf{B} = 4$

3 (*b*) If **a** and **b** are orthogonal, then

$\mathbf{a} \cdot \mathbf{b} = 0$

$(2\hat{\mathbf{i}} + \lambda\hat{\mathbf{j}} + 3\hat{\mathbf{k}}).(2\hat{\mathbf{i}} + \hat{\mathbf{j}} - \hat{\mathbf{k}}) = 0$

$4 + \lambda - 3 = 0$

$\lambda = -1$

4. (*a*) If θ = angle of incidence.

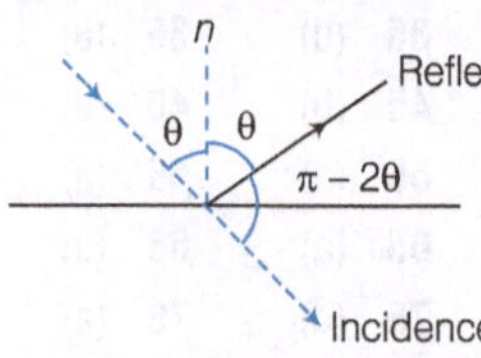

The angle between incidence ray and reflected ray is $\pi - 2\theta$.

$\therefore (\hat{\mathbf{i}} + \sqrt{3}\,\hat{\mathbf{j}}) \cdot (\hat{\mathbf{i}} - \sqrt{3}\,\hat{\mathbf{j}})$

$= |\hat{\mathbf{i}} + \sqrt{3}\,\hat{\mathbf{j}}|\,|\hat{\mathbf{i}} - \sqrt{3}\,\hat{\mathbf{j}}| \cos(\pi - 2\theta)$

or $1 - 3 = \sqrt{1+3}\,\sqrt{1+3}\,)(-\cos 2\theta$

or $\cos 2\theta = \dfrac{-2}{-4} = \dfrac{1}{2}$

or $\cos 2\theta = \cos 60°$

$\therefore \quad \theta = 30°$

5. (*b*) $|\mathbf{A} + \mathbf{B}| = |\mathbf{A} - \mathbf{B}|$

$\Rightarrow |\mathbf{A} + \mathbf{B}|^2 = |\mathbf{A} - \mathbf{B}|^2$

$(\mathbf{A} + \mathbf{B}) \cdot (\mathbf{A} + \mathbf{B}) = (\mathbf{A} - \mathbf{B}) \cdot (\mathbf{A} - \mathbf{B})$

$\Rightarrow A^2 + B^2 + 2AB\cos\theta$

$= A^2 + B^2 - 2AB\cos\theta$

$\Rightarrow 4AB\cos\theta = 0$

$\Rightarrow \quad \cos\theta = 0$

$\Rightarrow \quad \theta = 90°$

6 (*c*) Applying work-energy theorem on both moving objects,

$\dfrac{1}{2} m_1 v_1^2 = Fx_1$

and $\dfrac{1}{2} m_2 v_2^2 = Fx_2$

Since, both moving objects have same kinetic energy,

i.e. $\dfrac{1}{2} m_1 v_1^2 = \dfrac{1}{2} m_2 v_2^2$

$\Rightarrow \quad Fx_1 = Fx_2$

$\Rightarrow \quad x_1 = x_2$

Therefore, both the objects will come to rest at the same distance.

7 (*c*) Here, work done by a car,

i.e. $W_g = mgh = 1400 \times 10 \times 10$

According to work-energy theorem, we get

$W_g + W_f = \dfrac{1}{2} mv^2$

$1400 \times 10 \times 10 + W_f = \dfrac{1}{2} \times 1400 \times 15 \times 15$

$\Rightarrow \quad W_f = 17.5$ kJ

8 (*c*) According to work-energy theorem, we have

$K - K' = W = Fs$

$\therefore \quad \dfrac{1}{2} mu^2 - 0 = Fs$

$\Rightarrow \quad F = \dfrac{mu^2}{2s}$

$= \dfrac{0.02 \times (150)^2}{2 \times 0.1} = 2250$ N

9 (*d*) (i) Work done by gravitational force, $W_g = mgh$

$= 10^{-3} \times 10 \times 1 \times 10^3 = 10$ J

(ii) Now, from work-kinetic energy theorem, we have

$\Delta K = W_{\text{gravity}} + W_{\text{air resistance}}$

$\Rightarrow \dfrac{1}{2} mv^2 = mgh + W_{\text{air resistance}}$

$\Rightarrow W_{\text{air resistance}} = m\left(\dfrac{1}{2}v^2 - gh\right)$

$= 10^{-3}\left(\dfrac{1}{2} \times 50 \times 50 - 10 \times 10^3\right)$

$= -8.75$ J

10 (*a*) According to work-energy theorem,

Kinetic energy = Work against gravity + Work against friction

Thus, using the figure given below, we have

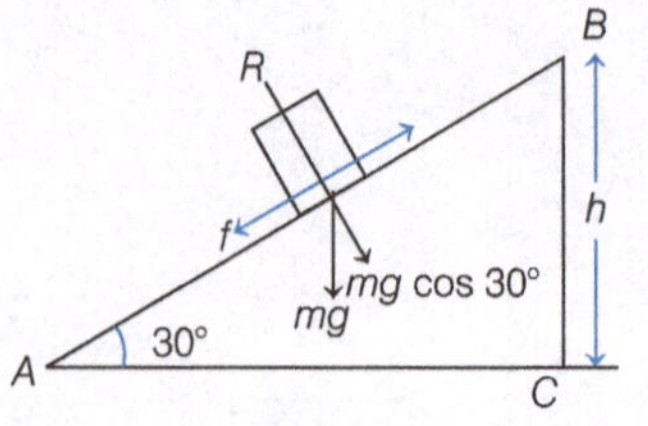

$$\frac{1}{2}mv^2 = mgh + \mu R \cdot AB$$

$$\Rightarrow \frac{1}{2}mv^2 = mgh + \mu\, mg\cos 30^\circ \cdot \frac{h}{\sin 30^\circ}$$

$$\left[\because AB = \frac{h}{\sin 30^\circ} \text{ and } R = mg\cos 30^\circ\right]$$

$$\Rightarrow \frac{1}{2}\times m \times (10)^2 = mgh + \mu mg \cot 30^\circ \times h$$

$$\Rightarrow h = \frac{50}{11.732} = 4.26 \text{ m}$$

11 (*d*)

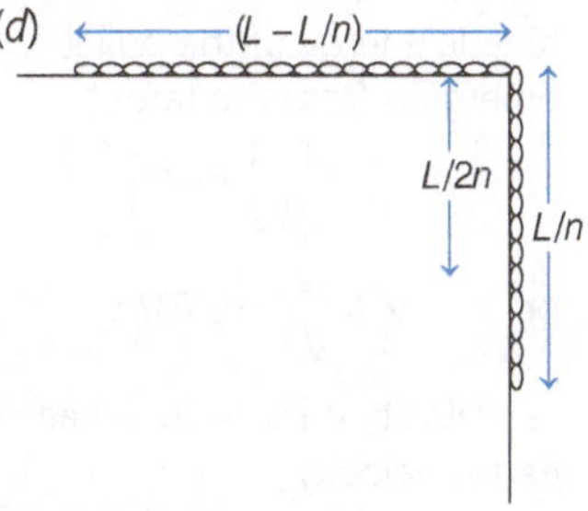

Given, mass of the cable is M.

So, mass of $\frac{1}{n}$th part of the cable, i.e. hanged part of the cable

$$= M/n \quad \text{...(i)}$$

Now, centre of mass of the hanged part will be its middle point.

So, its distance from the top of the table will be $L/2n$.

$\therefore$ Initial potential energy of the hanged part of cable,

$$U_i = \left(\frac{M}{n}\right)(-g)\left(\frac{L}{2n}\right)$$

$$\Rightarrow \quad U_i = -\frac{MgL}{2n^2} \quad \text{...(ii)}$$

When whole cable is on the table, its potential energy will be zero.

$$\therefore \quad U_f = 0 \quad \text{...(iii)}$$

Now, using work-energy theorem,

$$W_{\text{net}} = \Delta U = U_f - U_i$$

$$\Rightarrow \quad W_{\text{net}} = 0 - \left(-\frac{MgL}{2n^2}\right)$$

[using Eqs. (ii) and (iii)]

$$\Rightarrow \quad W_{\text{net}} = \frac{MgL}{2n^2}$$

12 (*d*) Work done, $W = \mathbf{F}\cdot\mathbf{d}$

$$= (5\hat{\mathbf{i}} + 6\hat{\mathbf{j}} - 4\hat{\mathbf{k}})\cdot(6\hat{\mathbf{i}} + 0\hat{\mathbf{j}} + 5\hat{\mathbf{k}})$$

$$= 30 + 0 - 20 = 10 \text{ units}$$

13 (*a*) Displacement,

$$\mathbf{s} = \mathbf{r}_2 - \mathbf{r}_1 = (4\hat{\mathbf{i}} + 3\hat{\mathbf{j}} - \hat{\mathbf{k}}) - (2\hat{\mathbf{i}} + \hat{\mathbf{k}})$$

$$= (2\hat{\mathbf{i}} + 3\hat{\mathbf{j}} - 2\hat{\mathbf{k}})\text{m}$$

$\therefore$ Work done,

$$\mathbf{W} = \mathbf{F}\cdot\mathbf{s} = (3\hat{\mathbf{i}} + \hat{\mathbf{j}})\cdot(2\hat{\mathbf{i}} + 3\hat{\mathbf{j}} - 2\hat{\mathbf{k}})$$

$$= 9 \text{ J}$$

15 (*b*) Gravitational force is conservative and hence, it is independent of path.
As, displacement is zero, work done by gravitational force in one revolution of earth around the sun on its elliptical path is zero.

16 (*d*) Work done by weight-lifter is zero because there is no displacement.

In a locomotive, work done is zero because force due to gravity and displacement are mutually perpendicular to each other.

In case of a person holding a suitcase on his head and standing at a bus terminal, work done is zero because there is no displacement.

17 (*c*) Displacement of ball in tth second,

$$s = gt - \frac{1}{2}g \quad \left[\because s_n = u + \frac{1}{2}g(2t-1)\right]$$

$$= g\left(t - \frac{1}{2}\right)$$

$$\Rightarrow \quad s \propto \left(t - \frac{1}{2}\right)$$

or $s_1 : s_2 : s_3$

$$= \left(1 - \frac{1}{2}\right) : \left(2 - \frac{1}{2}\right) : \left(3 - \frac{1}{2}\right) = 1:3:5$$

Now, $\quad W = mgs \quad (\because W = Fs)$

$$W \propto s$$

$$\therefore \quad W_1 : W_2 : W_3 = 1:3:5$$

18 (*b*) Force of friction acting in opposite direction $= \mu mg$

$$= 0.2 \times 2 \times 10 = 4 \text{ N}$$

Net force on the body,

$$F = 10 \text{ N} - 4 \text{ N} = 6 \text{ N}$$

$$\text{Acceleration, } a = \frac{F}{m} = \frac{6}{2} = 3 \text{ ms}^{-2}$$

$\therefore$ Distance travelled in 4 s,

$$s = \frac{1}{2}at^2$$

$$= \frac{1}{2}\times 3 \times 16 = 24 \text{ m}$$

Work done by applied force, i.e.

$$W = F\cdot s$$

$$= 10 \times 24 = 240 \text{ J}$$

19 (*b*) The various forces acting on the block are as shown in the figure.

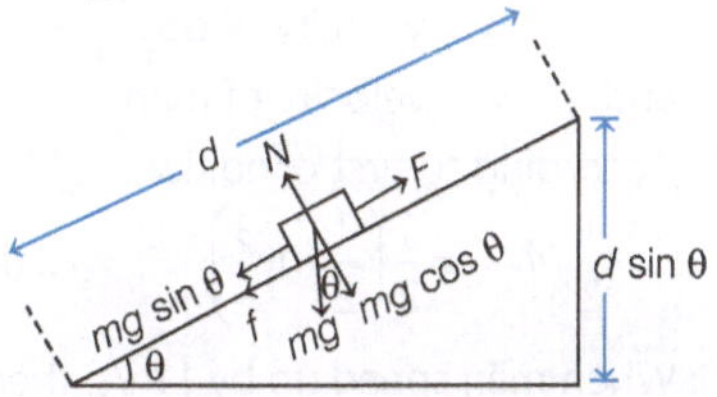

$\therefore$ Work done against gravity is

$$W_g = mgd\sin\theta = (1)\times(10)\times 10 \times \sin 30^\circ = 100 \times \frac{1}{2} = 50 \text{ J}$$

20 (*a*) In a conservative field, loss of PE or gain of KE depends only on the initial and final points and not on path covered. So, kinetic energy at point B will be equal to PE, i.e. mgh.

Thus, option (a) is correct, rest are incorrect.

21 (*b*) The kinetic energy of a body is

$$K = \frac{1}{2}mv^2 \Rightarrow K \propto mv^2$$

$$\therefore \quad \frac{K_e}{K_p} = \left(\frac{m_e}{m_p}\right)\left(\frac{v_e}{v_p}\right)^2$$

$$\Rightarrow \quad \frac{v_e}{v_p} = \sqrt{\left(\frac{K_e}{K_p}\right)\left(\frac{m_p}{m_e}\right)}$$

$$= \sqrt{\left(\frac{12}{120}\right)\left(\frac{m_p}{m_e}\right)} = \sqrt{\frac{1}{10}\cdot\frac{m_p}{m_e}}$$

22 (*a*) The kinetic energy of an air molecule is

$$K = \frac{10^{-21}\ \text{J}}{1.6 \times 10^{-19}\ \text{J/eV}}$$

$$\simeq 0.0062\ \text{eV} \simeq 6.2\ \text{meV}$$

23 (*b*) $\frac{K_1}{K_2} = \left(\frac{v_1}{v_2}\right)^2$

$$\Rightarrow \quad \frac{1}{2} = \frac{v_1^2}{(v_1+2)^2} \qquad (\because K_2 = 2K_1)$$

$$\Rightarrow \quad v_1^2 + 4v_1 + 4 = 2v_1^2$$

$$\Rightarrow \quad v_1^2 - 4v_1 - 4 = 0$$

$$v_1 = \frac{4 \pm \sqrt{16+16}}{2}$$

$$= 2(\sqrt{2}+1)\ \text{ms}^{-1} \text{ or } 2(1-\sqrt{2})\ \text{ms}^{-1}$$

24 (*c*) Let m = mass of boy, M = mass of man,

v = velocity of boy

and v' = velocity of man

According to first condition,

$$\frac{1}{2}Mv'^2 = \frac{1}{2}\left(\frac{1}{2}mv^2\right) \qquad \text{...(i)}$$

When man speed up by 1 m/s, then

$$\frac{1}{2}M(v'+1)^2 = 1\left(\frac{1}{2}mv^2\right) \qquad \text{...(ii)}$$

Dividing Eq. (ii) by Eq. (i), we get

$$\frac{\frac{1}{2}M(v'+1)^2}{\frac{1}{2}M(v')^2} = \frac{\frac{1}{2}mv^2}{\frac{1}{4}mv^2}$$

$$\Rightarrow \quad v' = \frac{1}{\sqrt{2}-1}\ \text{ms}^{-1}$$

25 (*d*) Acceleration of object,

$$a = \frac{F}{m} = \frac{50}{10} = 5\ \text{m/s}^2$$

If v be the final velocity, then

$$v = u + at = 10 + 5 \times 2 = 20\ \text{m/s}$$

$$\text{Initial kinetic energy} = \frac{1}{2}mu^2 = 5 \times 10^2\ \text{J}$$

$$\text{Final kinetic energy} = \frac{1}{2}mv^2 = 20 \times 10^2\ \text{J}$$

% increase in kinetic energy

$$= \frac{(20-5) \times 10^2}{5 \times 10^2} \times 100 = 300\%$$

26 (*d*) $\text{KE} = \frac{1}{2}mv^2 = 8 \times 10^{-4}\ \text{J}$

$$\Rightarrow \quad v^2 = \frac{8 \times 2 \times 10^{-4}}{m} = \frac{16 \times 10^{-4}}{0.01}$$

$$= 16 \times 10^{-2} \qquad \text{...(i)}$$

By third equation of motion,

$$v^2 = u^2 + 2a_t s$$

$$\Rightarrow \quad v^2 = 2a_t s \qquad [\because u = 0]$$

$$\text{or} \quad v^2 = 2a_t(4\pi r)$$

($\because$ particle covers 2 revolutions)

$$\Rightarrow \quad a_t = \frac{v^2}{8\pi r}$$

$$= \frac{16 \times 10^{-2}}{8 \times 3.14 \times 6.4 \times 10^{-2}} \qquad \text{[from Eq. (i)]}$$

$$\therefore \quad a_t = 0.1\ \text{ms}^{-2}$$

27 (*c*) $F \propto \frac{1}{v}$

$$\Rightarrow \quad F = \frac{k}{v} \Rightarrow ma = \frac{k}{v}$$

$$\Rightarrow \quad m\frac{dv}{dt} = \frac{k}{v}$$

$$\Rightarrow \quad \int mv\,dv = \int k\,dt$$

$$\Rightarrow \quad m\frac{v^2}{2} = kt \Rightarrow \text{KE} \propto t$$

$$\left(\because \text{KE} = \frac{1}{2}mv^2\right)$$

28 (*a*) $p_1 = \sqrt{2mK_1}$ ...(i)

$$K_2 = 4K_1$$

$$\text{Hence,} \quad p_2 = \sqrt{2mK_2}$$

$$= \sqrt{2m(4K_1)} = 2\sqrt{2mK_1}$$

$$\text{or} \quad p_2 = 2p_1 \qquad \text{[from Eq. (i)]}$$

29 (*c*) $p = \sqrt{2mK}$ $\qquad \left(\because K = \frac{p^2}{2m}\right)$

For same kinetic energy, $p \propto \sqrt{m}$

$$\Rightarrow \quad \frac{p_1}{p_2} = \sqrt{\frac{m_1}{m_2}} = \sqrt{\frac{1}{4}} = \frac{1}{2} = 1:2$$

30 (*b*) $p_f = p_i + \frac{50}{100} \times p_i$

$$p_f = \frac{3p_i}{2} \qquad \text{...(i)}$$

$$K_f = \frac{p_f^2}{2m} = \frac{\left(\frac{3p_i}{2}\right)^2}{2m} \qquad \text{[from Eq. (i)]}$$

$$= \frac{9p_i^2}{8m}$$

$\therefore$ % increase in kinetic energy

$$= \frac{\frac{9p_i^2}{8m} - \frac{p_i^2}{2m}}{\frac{p_i^2}{2m}} \times 100$$

$$= \frac{5}{4} \times 100 = 125\%$$

31 (*b*)

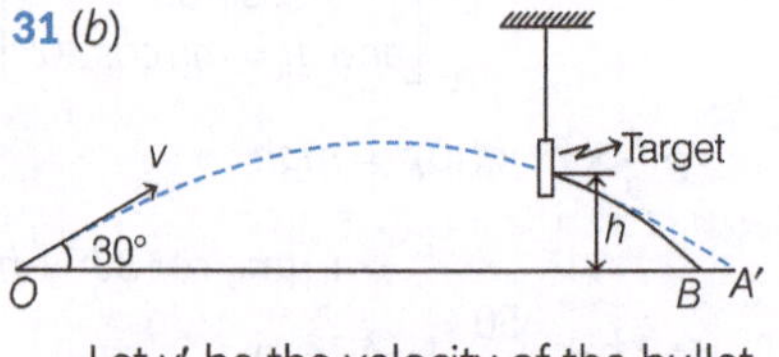

Let v' be the velocity of the bullet after emerging from the target.

Kinetic energy of the bullet emerging from the target

$$\frac{1}{2}mv'^2 = \frac{1}{2}\left(\frac{1}{2}mv^2\right)$$

$$\text{or} \quad v' = \frac{v}{\sqrt{2}} = 0.707\,v$$

i.e. velocity is more than half of its earlier velocity.

As the bullet loses some of its vertical component, therefore velocity on emerging from the target changes.

The bullet will move in a different parabolic path.

32 (*c*) Given, $\mathbf{F} = C\left[\frac{x}{(x^2+y^2)^{3/2}}\hat{\mathbf{i}} + \frac{y}{(x^2+y^2)^{3/2}}\hat{\mathbf{j}}\right]$

As, $\mathbf{r} = x\hat{\mathbf{i}} + y\hat{\mathbf{j}}$

$$\therefore r^2 = x^2 + y^2$$

$$\therefore \quad \mathbf{F} = C\left[\frac{x}{r^3}\hat{\mathbf{i}} + \frac{y}{r^3}\hat{\mathbf{j}}\right] = \frac{C}{r^3}[x\hat{\mathbf{i}} + y\hat{\mathbf{j}}]$$

The work done is given by

$$W = \int_{r_1}^{r_2} \mathbf{F} \cdot d\mathbf{r}$$

$$= \int_{(0,2)}^{(2,0)} \frac{C}{r^3}[x\hat{\mathbf{i}} + y\hat{\mathbf{j}}] \cdot [dx\hat{\mathbf{i}} + dy\hat{\mathbf{j}}]$$

$$= \frac{C}{r^3}\left[\int_0^2 x\,dx + \int_2^0 y\,dy\right] = 0$$

33 (*b*) The work done by the force in displacing the particle from $y_1 = 0$ to $y_2 = 1$ m will be

$$W = \int_{y_1}^{y_2} F dy = \int_0^{y_1} (10 + 10y) dy$$

$$= \left[10y + 10\frac{y^2}{2}\right]_0^1$$

$$W = 15 \text{ J}$$

34 (c) $|dW| = |F dx|$

$$|W| = \int_0^L (ax + bx^2)\, dx$$

$$= \left[\frac{ax^2}{2}\right]_0^L + \left[\frac{bx^3}{3}\right]_0^L$$

$$|W| = \frac{aL^2}{2} + \frac{bL^3}{3}$$

35 (d) $v = \frac{ds}{dt} = \frac{2t}{3}; a = \frac{d^2s}{dt^2} = \frac{2}{3}$

Force is constant, because acceleration is constant.

Work done,

$$W = \int_0^2 F ds = \int_0^2 m \frac{d^2s}{dt^2} ds$$

$$= \int_0^2 m \frac{d^2s}{dt^2} \frac{ds}{dt} \cdot dt$$

$$= \int_0^2 3 \times \frac{2}{3} \times \frac{2t}{3} dt$$

$$= \frac{4}{3}\left(\frac{t^2}{2}\right)_0^2 = 2.6 \text{ J}$$

36 (b) From the figure, $a = \alpha x$, where α is the slope of the graph.

$$\Rightarrow \quad \alpha = \frac{a}{x} = \frac{20}{8} = 2.5 \text{ s}^{-2}$$

The force on the brick is in positive x-direction and according to the Newton's second law, its magnitude is given by

$$F = ma = m\alpha x$$

If x_f is the final coordinate, the work done by the force is

$$W = \int_0^{x_f} F dx = m\,\alpha \times \int_0^{x_f} x dx$$

$$= m\alpha \times \left(\frac{x^2}{2}\right)_0^{x_f} = \frac{m\alpha \times x_f^2}{2}$$

$\{x_f = 8 \text{ m}\}$ (given, $m = 10$ kg)

$$= \frac{10 \times 2.5 \times 64}{2} = 800 \text{ J}$$

37. (b) According to given figure,

$$W_{AB} = W_{12} + W_{23} + W_{34} + W_{45}$$

$$= 10 \times 1 + \frac{1}{2}(10 + 15) \times 1 + \frac{1}{2} \times 1 \times 15 - \frac{1}{2} \times 1 \times 15$$

$$= 10 + 12.5 = 22.5 \text{ J}$$

38 (c) The plot of the applied force is shown in figure.

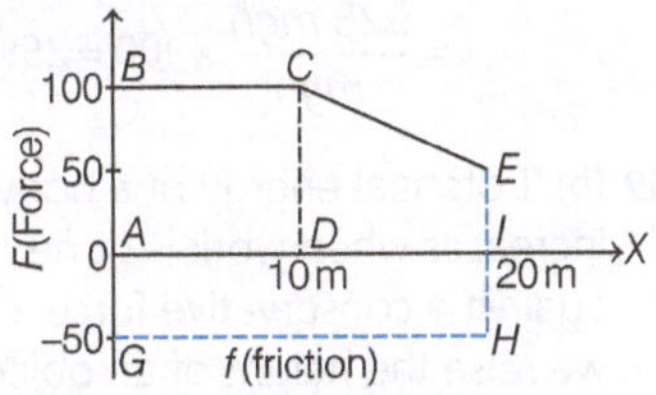

$$\therefore \quad W_F = 100 \times 10 + \frac{1}{2}(100 + 50) \times 10$$

$$= 1000 + 750$$

$$= 1750 \text{ J}$$

The work done by the frictional force is

W_f = area of the rectangle $AGHI$

$$W_f = (-50) \times 20 = -1000 \text{ J}$$

$$W = W_F + W_f$$

$$= 1750 - 1000$$

$$= 750 \text{ J}$$

39 (d) $W = \int_{r_1}^{r_2} \mathbf{F} \cdot d\mathbf{r}$

$$= \int_{(1,2,3)}^{(3,6,2)} (2x\hat{\mathbf{i}} + 2\hat{\mathbf{j}} + 3z^2\hat{\mathbf{k}}) \cdot (dx\hat{\mathbf{i}} + dy\hat{\mathbf{j}} + dz\,\hat{\mathbf{k}})$$

$$= \int_1^3 2x\,dx + \int_2^6 2dy + \int_3^2 3z^2\,dz$$

$$= 2\left[\frac{x^2}{2}\right]_1^3 + 2[y]_2^6 + 3\left[\frac{z^3}{3}\right]_3^2$$

$$= (9-1) + 2(6-2) + (8-27)$$

$$= -3 \text{J}$$

40 (b) Velocity, $v = \frac{dx}{dt} = \frac{d(3t^2 + 5)}{dt}$

or $\quad v = 6t$ m/s ...(i)

$$W = \int_{x_0}^{x_5} F \cdot dx \quad \text{...(ii)}$$

The force acting on this object is given by

$$F = ma = m \times \frac{dv}{dt}$$

$$= m \times \frac{d(6t)}{dt}$$

[∵ using Eq. (i)]

$$F = m \times 6$$

$$= 6m = 12 \text{ N}$$

Also, $x = 3t^2 + 5$

At $t = 0$,

$$x_0 = 3 \times (0)^2 + 5 = 5 \text{ m}$$

and at $t = 5$ s,

$$x_5 = 3 \times (5)^2 + 5 = 80 \text{ m}$$

Put the values in Eq. (ii),

$$W = 12 \times \int_5^{80} dx = 900 \text{ J}$$

41 (a) $W = K_f - K_i$

$$\Rightarrow K_f = W + K_i = \int_{x_1}^{x_2} Fxdx + \frac{1}{2}mv^2$$

$$= \int_{20}^{30} -0.1x dx + \frac{1}{2} \times 10 \times (10)^2$$

$$= -0.1\left[\frac{x^2}{2}\right]_{20}^{30} + 500$$

$$\Rightarrow \quad K_f = -25 + 500 = 475 \text{ J}$$

42 (c)

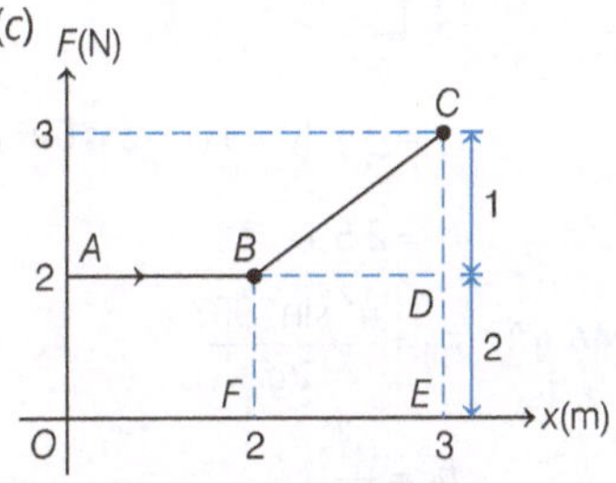

$$W = ABFO + \Delta BCD + BDEF$$

$$= 2 \times 2 + \frac{1}{2} \times 1 \times 1 + 2 \times 1 = 6.5 \text{ J}$$

Now, from work-energy theorem,

$$\Delta W = K_f - K_i$$

$$\Rightarrow \quad K_f = \Delta W = 6.5 \text{ J} \quad [\because K_i = 0]$$

43 (c) According to the work-energy theorem,

$$K_f = K_i + W = K_i + \int_{x_1}^{x_2} F dx$$

$$K_f = K_i + \int_{0.10}^{2.01} \frac{-k}{x} dx$$

$$= \frac{1}{2} mv_i^2 - |k \ln(x)|_{0.10}^{2.01}$$

$$= \frac{1}{2} \times 1 \times (2)^2 - k \ln (2.01 / 0.10)$$

$$\Rightarrow \quad K_f = 2 - 0.5 \times 3 \qquad [\because k = 0.5 \text{ J}]$$

$$= 2 - 1.5 = 0.5 \text{ J}$$

$$\Rightarrow \quad v_f = \sqrt{2K_f / m}$$

$$= \sqrt{2 \times 0.5 / (1)} = 1 \text{ ms}^{-1}$$

44. (*a*) The option (a) is correct but rest are incorrect and these can be corrected as,

Like velocity, potential energy is also measured only in relative terms. Their absolute value cannot be determined.

Difference of velocity and difference of potential energy can be measured. So, acceleration can also be measured.

45 (*b*) $\Delta U = mgh(1 - \cos\theta)$

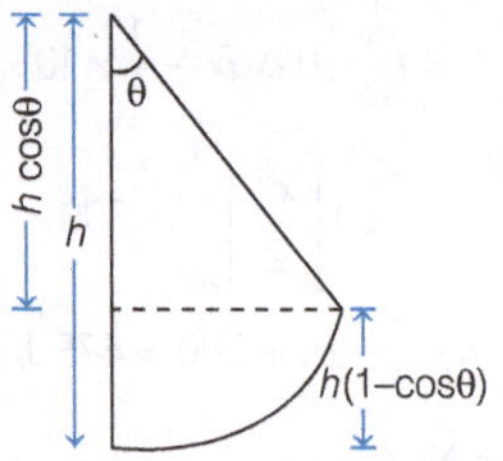

$$= \frac{1}{2} \times 10 \times 1 (1 - \cos 60°)$$

$$= 2.5 \text{ J}$$

46 (*d*) $h_1 = \dfrac{u^2 \sin^2 90°}{2g}$

$$h_1 = \frac{u^2}{2g} \qquad \text{...(i)}$$

$$h_2 = \frac{u^2 \sin^2 \theta}{2g}$$

$$\theta = (90° - 60°) = 30°$$

(Angle made with the horizontal)

$$h_2 = \frac{u^2 \sin^2 30°}{2g} = \frac{u^2}{8g} \qquad \text{...(ii)}$$

Divide Eq. (i) by Eq. (ii), we get

$$\frac{h_1}{h_2} = \frac{u^2 / 2g}{u^2 / 8g} = \frac{4}{1}$$

$$\frac{(\text{PE})_1}{(\text{PE})_2} = \frac{mgh_1}{mgh_2} = \frac{4}{1} = 4:1$$

47 (*d*) $U_i = mgh$

$$U_f = mg \times (75\% \text{ of } h)$$

$$= mg(0.75\, h)$$

$\therefore$ Percentage loss in potential energy in each bounce

$$= \frac{\Delta U}{U_i} \times 100$$

$$= \frac{mgh - 0.75\, mgh}{mgh} \times 100$$

$$= \frac{0.25\, mgh}{mgh} \times 100 = 25\%$$

49 (*b*) Potential energy of a body increases when work is done against a conservative force, e.g. if we raise the height of an object, its potential energy increases. It is because work is done against gravitational force which is a conservative force.

50 (*b*) $F_x = -\dfrac{\partial U}{\partial x} = -\dfrac{\partial}{\partial x}\left(\dfrac{10xy}{z}\right)$

$$= -\frac{10y}{z}$$

$$F_y = -\frac{\partial U}{\partial y} = -\frac{\partial}{\partial y}\left(\frac{10xy}{z}\right) = -\frac{10x}{z}$$

$$F_z = -\frac{\partial U}{\partial z} = -\frac{\partial}{\partial z}\left(\frac{10xy}{z}\right) = \frac{10xy}{z^2}$$

$$\therefore \mathbf{F} = F_x \hat{\mathbf{i}} + F_y \hat{\mathbf{j}} + F_z \hat{\mathbf{k}}$$

$$= -\left(\frac{10y}{z}\right)\hat{\mathbf{i}} - \left(\frac{10x}{z}\right)\hat{\mathbf{j}} + \left(\frac{10xy}{z^2}\right)\hat{\mathbf{k}}$$

51 (*b*) As a relative velocity of the bolt w.r.t. elevator is zero, therefore in the impact, only potential energy of the bolt is converted into heat energy.

Amount of heat produced $= mgh$

$$= (0.1) \times (10)(10) = 10 \text{ J}$$

52 (*b*) In elastic collision, the conservation of mechanical energy consider only conservative force while conservation of energy consider both conservative and non-conservative force.

Mass converted into energy in nuclear reaction is called nuclear energy.

54 (*a*) When an artificial satellite comes closer to the earth, its gravitational potential energy decreases, kinetic energy increases and hence, velocity of the satellite increases $\{\because \text{KE} = (1/2)\, mv^2\}$.

However, total energy of the satellite continuously decreases at a very small rate due to atmospheric resistance.

55 (*a*) Initial kinetic energy of the block = potential energy stored in the spring + work done against friction

$$\frac{1}{2} \times 2 \times 4^2 = \frac{1}{2} \times 10000 \times x^2 + 15x$$

or $\quad 5000x^2 + 15x - 16 = 0$

$$x = \frac{-15 \pm 565}{10000}$$

$$\Rightarrow \quad x = \frac{550}{10000} \text{ m}$$

$$\therefore \quad x = 0.055 \text{ m} = 5.5 \text{ cm}$$

56 (*a*) Let a ball falls from a height h, then $K = mgh$

$\therefore$ Loss of kinetic energy due to the rebounce,

$$K - K' = mg(h - h')$$

$$= mgh \times 0.2$$

$\therefore$ Fractional loss in kinetic energy of ball in each rebounce

$$= \frac{K - K'}{K}$$

$$= \frac{mgh \times 0.2}{mgh} = 0.2 \ \%$$

Fractional loss $= 0.2 \times 100\% = 20\%$

57 (*b*) Loss of potential energy

$$= mgh = mgl \cos 30°$$

$$= \frac{\sqrt{3}}{2}\, mgl$$

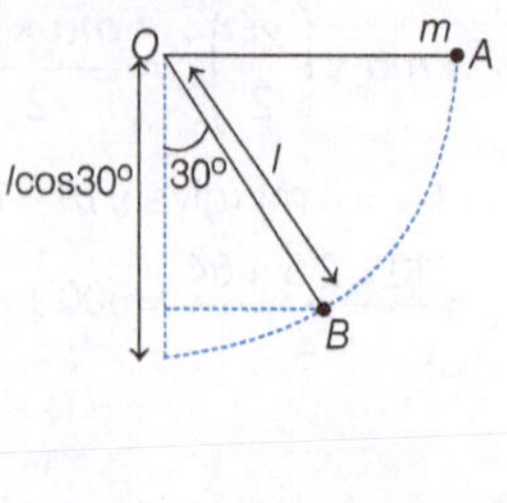

According to law of conservation of energy,

loss of potential energy = gain in kinetic energy

$\therefore$ Kinetic energy gained $= \dfrac{\sqrt{3}}{2} mgl$

58 (d) $\dfrac{1}{2} mu^2 = \dfrac{1}{2}\left(\dfrac{1}{2} mu^2\right) + mgh$

$\Rightarrow \quad 490 = 245 + 5 \times 9.8 \times h$

$$h = \frac{245}{49} = 5\,\text{m}$$

59 (a)

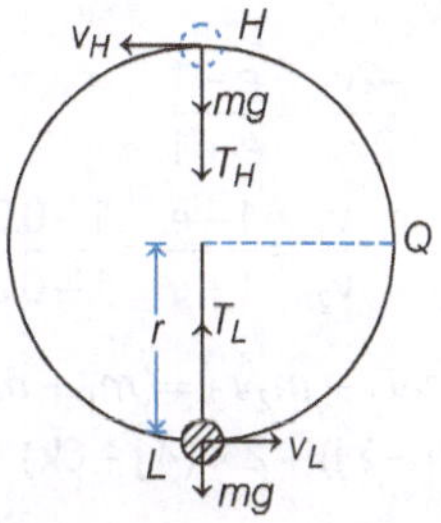

At bottom point,

i.e. $\quad E = \dfrac{1}{2} mv_L^2 \quad$ ...(i)

The tension on the string is

$$T_L = \frac{mv_L^2}{r} + mg$$

At top point, the tension (T_H) in string becomes zero, so

$$mg = \frac{mv_H^2}{r}$$

$\Rightarrow \quad v_H = \sqrt{gr}$

and total energy,

$$E_T = \frac{1}{2} mv_H^2 + 2mgr$$

$$= \frac{5}{2} mgr \quad \text{...(ii)}$$

Equating Eqs. (i) and (ii), we get

$$\frac{5}{2} mgr = \frac{1}{2} mv_L^2$$

$\Rightarrow \quad v_L = \sqrt{5gr}$

$$\frac{K_L}{K_H} = \frac{\frac{1}{2} mv_L^2}{\frac{1}{2} mv_H^2} = \left(\frac{v_L}{v_H}\right)^2$$

$$= \frac{5\,gr}{gr} = \frac{5}{1} = 5:1$$

60 (d) $\dfrac{mv^2}{r} = \dfrac{k}{r^2} \Rightarrow mv^2 = \dfrac{k}{r}$

$\therefore \quad \text{KE} = \dfrac{1}{2} mv^2 = \dfrac{k}{2r}$

$$U = \int_r^0 -F\,dr = \int_r^0 -\frac{k}{r^2}\,dr$$

$$U \text{ or PE} = \left[\frac{k}{r}\right]_r^0 = -\frac{k}{r}$$

Total energy

$$= \text{KE} + \text{PE} = \frac{k}{2r} + \left(\frac{-k}{r}\right) = \frac{-k}{2r}$$

61 (a) The total mechanical energy E of the system is conserved. We take the potential energy of the system to be zero at the lowest point A. Thus, at A,

$$E = \frac{1}{2} mv_0^2 \quad \text{... (i)}$$

The resultant force at A provides the necessary centripetal force.

i.e. $\quad T_A - mg = \dfrac{mv_0^2}{L}$

At the highest point C, the tension in the string (T_C) becomes zero.

Thus, at C, $mg = \dfrac{mv_C^2}{L}$

and total energy,

$$E = \frac{1}{2} mv_C^2 + 2mgL \quad \text{...(ii)}$$

$\Rightarrow \quad v_C^2 = gL \quad$ ...(iii)

From Eqs. (ii) and (iii), we get

$$E = \frac{1}{2} mgL + 2mgL$$

$$= \frac{5}{2} mgL \quad \text{...(iv)}$$

Equating Eqs. (i) and (iv), we get

$$\frac{5}{2} mgL = \frac{m}{2} v_0^2$$

or $\quad v_0 = \sqrt{5\,gL}$

62 (b)

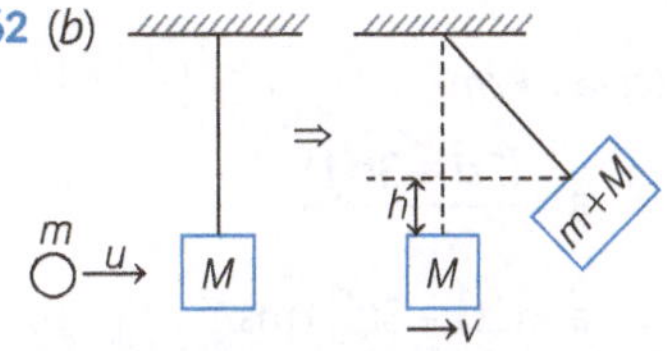

By conservation of linear momentum,

$$mu + 0 = (m + M)\,v$$

$\therefore \quad v = \left(\dfrac{m}{m + M}\right) u$

$$= \left(\frac{0.02}{0.02 + 0.03}\right) 5$$

$\therefore \quad v = 2\,\text{m/s}$

Applying conservation of mechanical energy,

$$\frac{1}{2} mv^2 = mgh$$

$\therefore \quad h = \dfrac{v^2}{2g} = \dfrac{2 \times 2}{2 \times 10} = 0.2\,\text{m}$

64 (b) Till the end of the nineteenth century, physicists believed that in every physical and chemical process, the mass of an isolated system is conserved.

Matter might change its phase, e.g. glacial ice could melt into a gushing stream, but matter is neither created nor destroyed.

But Einstein showed that matter can be destroyed into energy and *vice-versa*. Thus, option (b) is incorrect, rest are correct.

65 (a) PE $\propto x^2$

$\because \quad \dfrac{(\text{PE})_2}{(\text{PE})_1} = \left(\dfrac{x_2}{x_1}\right)^2$

$\Rightarrow (\text{PE})_2 = 15 \times \left(\dfrac{4}{3}\right)^2 = 27\,\text{J}$

66 (b) The spring forces are

$$F = k_1 x_1 \text{ and } F = k_2 x_2$$

$\therefore \quad k_1 x_1 = k_2 x_2$

$\Rightarrow \quad \dfrac{k_1}{k_2} = \dfrac{x_2}{x_1}$

$\Rightarrow \quad \dfrac{(\text{PE})_1}{(\text{PE})_2} = \dfrac{k_1 x_1^2}{k_2 x_2^2} = \dfrac{k_1}{k_2} \times \left(\dfrac{k_2}{k_1}\right)^2$

$$= \frac{k_2}{k_1} = \frac{3}{2} \quad \left[\because \frac{k_1}{k_2} = \frac{2}{3}\right]$$

67 (a) $\dfrac{1}{2} kx^2 = \dfrac{1}{2} \times 980 \times \dfrac{10 \times 10}{100 \times 100}$

$$= 4.9\,\text{J} \quad \text{... (i)}$$

Loss of potential energy of mass m

$$= mgh = m \times g \times \frac{(40+10)}{100}$$

$$= m \times 9.8 \times \frac{1}{2} = 4.9\, m \quad \text{... (ii)}$$

According to the law of conservation of energy,

From Eqs. (i) and (ii),

$$4.9\, m = 4.9 \Rightarrow m = \frac{4.9}{4.9} = 1\text{ kg}$$

68 (*b*) At maximum compression x_m,

$$\frac{1}{2}mv^2 = \frac{1}{2}kx_m^2$$

$$\Rightarrow 10^3 \times 5 \times 5 = 6.25 \times 10^3 \times x_m^2$$

$$\Rightarrow x_m^2 = \frac{25}{6.25} \Rightarrow x_m = 2\text{ m}$$

69 (*c*) Loss in potential energy of spring = Gain in kinetic energy of ball

$$\frac{1}{2}kx^2 = \frac{1}{2}mv^2$$

$$\Rightarrow 90 \times 10^2 \times (12 \times 10^{-2})^2 = 16 \times 10^{-3} \times v^2$$

$$\Rightarrow v = 90 \text{ ms}^{-1}$$

70 (*d*) If the work done or the kinetic energy depend on other factors such as the velocity or the particular path taken by the object, the force would be called non-conservative.

71 (*c*) The power exerted is, $P = \mathbf{F} \cdot \mathbf{v}$

$$= (4\hat{\mathbf{i}} + \hat{\mathbf{j}} - 2\hat{\mathbf{k}}) \cdot (\hat{\mathbf{i}} + 2\hat{\mathbf{j}} + 3\hat{\mathbf{k}})$$

$$= 4 \times 1 + 1 \times 2 - 2 \times 3 = 0$$

72 (*b*) $P = \frac{W}{t} = \frac{mgh}{t} \quad [\because W = mgh]$

$$\Rightarrow \frac{P}{gh} = \frac{m}{t}$$

$$\Rightarrow \frac{1000}{10 \times 10} = \frac{m}{t}$$

$$\Rightarrow \frac{1000}{100} \times 1 = m \quad (\because t = 1\text{ s})$$

$$\Rightarrow m = 10\text{ kg}$$

73 (*b*) Given, area of river, $A = 100\text{ m} \times 5\text{ m} = 500\text{ m}^2$

Density of water, $\rho = 10^3\text{ kg/m}^3$

and $v = 2\text{ ms}^{-1}$

$\therefore$ Mass of water flowing per second, $m = A\rho v$

$$= 500 \times 10^3 \times 2$$

$$= 10^6\text{ kg/s}$$

Power of power station, P = Kinetic energy of water flowing per second

$$= \frac{1}{2}mv^2 = \frac{1}{2} \times 10^6 \times 2^2$$

$$= 2 \times 10^6\text{ W} = 2\text{ MW}$$

74 (*c*) Here, $n = \frac{360}{60} = 6$ bullets s^{-1}

Power of gun = kinetic energy of bullets

$$5.4 \times 10^3 = \frac{1}{2}(nm)v^2$$

$$2 \times 5400 = 6 \times m(600)^2$$

$$\Rightarrow m = 5\text{ g}$$

75 (*d*) Total weight of elevator and passengers

$$= (M + 10\,m)g = (920 + 680) \times 10$$

$$= 16000\text{ N}$$

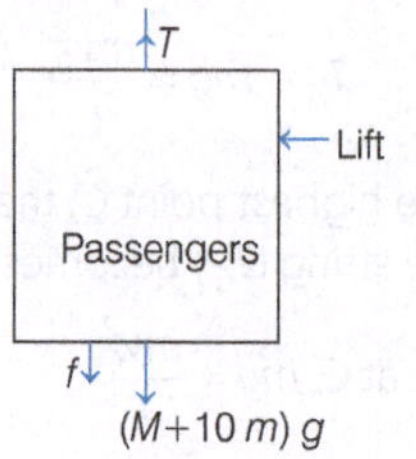

Force of friction = 6000 N

Total force (T) applied by the motor of elevator

$$= 16000 + 6000 = 22000\text{ N}$$

$$P = F \cdot v = 22000 \times 3 \quad [\because v = 3\text{ms}^{-1}]$$

$$= 66000\text{ W}$$

76 (*a*) It is given that, $\frac{dK}{dt}$ = constant

$$\Rightarrow K \propto t \Rightarrow v \propto \sqrt{t} \quad \left(\because K = \frac{1}{2}mv^2\right)$$

Acceleration, $a = \frac{dv}{dt} \Rightarrow a \propto \frac{1}{\sqrt{t}}$

So, $F \propto \frac{1}{\sqrt{t}}$.

77 (*c*) $\mathbf{a} = \mathbf{F}/m$

$$\Rightarrow \mathbf{a} = \frac{(2t\hat{\mathbf{i}} + 3t^2\hat{\mathbf{j}})}{1}$$

$$\Rightarrow \mathbf{a} = (2t\hat{\mathbf{i}} + 3t^2\hat{\mathbf{j}})\text{ ms}^{-2}$$

$$\int dv = \int a\,dt = \int (2t\hat{\mathbf{i}} + 3t^2\hat{\mathbf{j}})\,dt$$

$$\mathbf{v} = t^2\hat{\mathbf{i}} + t^3\hat{\mathbf{j}}$$

$$P = \mathbf{F} \cdot \mathbf{v} = (2t\hat{\mathbf{i}} + 3t^2\hat{\mathbf{j}}) \cdot (t^2\hat{\mathbf{i}} + t^3\hat{\mathbf{j}})$$

$$= (2t^3 + 3t^5)\text{ W}$$

78 (*a*) $m_1u_1 + m_2u_2 = m_1v_1 + m_2v_2$

$$\Rightarrow m \times 2v + m \times 0 = m(v_1 + v_2)$$

$$\Rightarrow v_1 + v_2 = 2v \quad \text{...(i)}$$

Also, coefficient of restitution,

$$e = \frac{v_2 - v_1}{u_1 - u_2} = \frac{v_2 - v_1}{2v - 0}$$

$$\therefore v_2 - v_1 = 2e \times v \quad \text{...(ii)}$$

Dividing Eq. (ii) by Eq. (i), we get

$$\frac{v_2 - v_1}{v_2 + v_1} = e$$

$$\Rightarrow \frac{-2v_1}{2v_2} = \frac{e-1}{e+1}$$

$$\Rightarrow \frac{v_1}{v_2} = \frac{1-e}{1+e} = \frac{1-0.2}{1+0.2} = \frac{2}{3}$$

79 (*b*) $m_1\mathbf{v}_1 + m_2\mathbf{v}_2 = (m_1 + m_2)\mathbf{v}$

$$1 \times (3\hat{\mathbf{i}} - 2\hat{\mathbf{j}}) + 2 \times (4\hat{\mathbf{j}} - 6\hat{\mathbf{k}}) = (1+2)\,\mathbf{v}$$

$$\Rightarrow 3\hat{\mathbf{i}} + 6\hat{\mathbf{j}} - 12\hat{\mathbf{k}} = 3\mathbf{v}$$

$$\Rightarrow \mathbf{v} = \hat{\mathbf{i}} + 2\hat{\mathbf{j}} - 4\hat{\mathbf{k}}$$

$$\therefore v = |\mathbf{v}| = \sqrt{1 + 4 + 16} = 4.6\text{ms}^{-1}$$

80 (*c*) Consider the movement of two particles as shown below

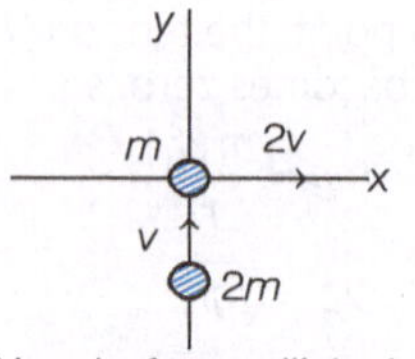

(Just before collision)

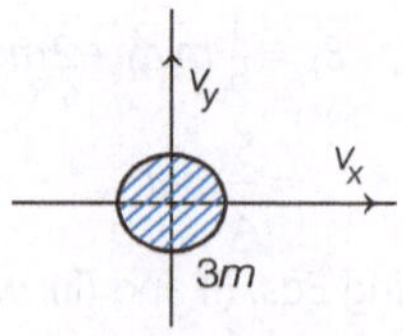

(Just after collision)

According to conservation of linear momentum in *x*-direction, we have

$$(p_i)_x = (p_f)_x$$

or $2mv = (2m + m)\,v_x$

or $v_x = \frac{2}{3}v$

By conserving linear momentum in *y*-direction, we get

$(p_i)_y = (p_f)_y$

or $2mv = (2m + m)\, v_y$

or $v_y = \frac{2}{3} v$

Initial kinetic energy of the two particles system is

$$E_i = \frac{1}{2} m (2v)^2 + \frac{1}{2} (2m)(v)^2$$

Final kinetic energy of the combined two particles system is

$$E_f = \frac{1}{2}(3m)\left(\frac{4v^2}{9} + \frac{4v^2}{9}\right)$$

$$= \frac{3m}{2}\left(\frac{8v^2}{9}\right) = \frac{4mv^2}{3}$$

$$\Delta E = E_i - E_f = \frac{5}{3} mv^2$$

Percentage loss in the energy during the collision,

$$\frac{\Delta E}{E_i} \times 100 \simeq 56\%$$

81 (b) $\frac{1}{2} mv_2^2 + \frac{1}{2} mv_1^2 = \frac{150}{100} \times \frac{1}{2} mv_0^2$

$$v_2^2 + v_1^2 = \frac{3}{2} v_0^2 \quad \text{...(i)}$$

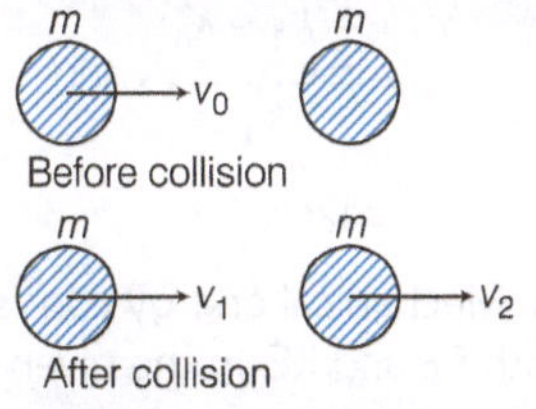

Conservation of momentum gives,

$$mv_0 = mv_1 + mv_2$$

$$v_0 = v_2 + v_1 \quad \text{...(ii)}$$

Squaring both sides,

$$v_0^2 = v_2^2 + v_1^2 + 2v_1v_2 \quad \text{...(iii)}$$

From Eqs. (i) and (iii), we have

$$2v_1v_2 = \frac{-v_0^2}{2}$$

$$\therefore (v_1 - v_2)^2 = (v_1 + v_2)^2 - 4v_1v_2 = 2v_0^2$$

or $v_{rel} = \sqrt{2}\, v_0$

82 (c) When two equal masses undergo a glancing elastic collision with one of them at rest, then after the collision, they will move at right angles to each other.

So, according to question, the first ball on hitting the second ball, makes an angle of 90° with the other one.

So, $\theta_1 = 90° - \theta_2 = 90° - 37° = 53°$.

83 (a) $Mv + m \times 0 = Mv_1 + mv_2$

$$\Rightarrow M(v - v_1) = mv_2 \quad \text{...(i)}$$

Again, from the conservation of kinetic energy (as collision is of elastic nature),

$$\frac{1}{2} Mv^2 + \frac{1}{2} m \times 0 = \frac{1}{2} Mv_1^2 + \frac{1}{2} mv_2^2$$

$$\Rightarrow M(v^2 - v_1^2) = mv_2^2 \quad \text{...(ii)}$$

Dividing Eq. (i) by Eq. (ii),

$$\frac{M(v - v_1)}{M(v + v_1)(v - v_1)} = \frac{mv_2}{mv_2^2}$$

$$v_2 = v + v_1 \quad \text{...(iii)}$$

From Eqs. (i) and (iii),

$$M(v - v_1) = m(v + v_1)$$

$$v_1 = \frac{(M - m)v}{(M + m)}$$

and $v_2 = \frac{2Mv}{(M + m)}$

As $M >> m$

So, $v_1 = v$

$\Rightarrow$ $v_2 = v + v = 2v$ {from Eq. (iii)}

84 (b) $m_1u_1 + m_2u_2 = m_1v_1 + m_2v_2$

$\Rightarrow mv + 4m \times 0 = 0 + 4mv_2$

or $v_2 = \frac{v}{4}$ ...(i)

$$e = \frac{v_2 - v_1}{u_1 - u_2} = \frac{\frac{v}{4} - 0}{v - 0} \quad \text{[from Eq. (i)]}$$

$$= \frac{1}{4} = 0.25$$

85 (c) $F = \frac{\Delta p}{\Delta t}$

or $F = \frac{(p_f)_H - (p_i)_H}{\Delta t}$

In this elastic collision, final and initial velocities will be same but direction will be changed.

$\therefore$ Horizontal component,

$$(p_f)_H = mv\cos 30°$$

and $(p_i)_H = -mv\cos 30°$

$$\therefore F = \frac{mv\cos 30° - (-mv\cos 30°)}{\Delta t}$$

$$= \frac{2\,mv\cos 30°}{\Delta t}$$

$$= \frac{2 \times 0.5 \times 12 \times \cos 30°}{1}$$

$$= 6\sqrt{3}\ \text{N}$$

86 (a)

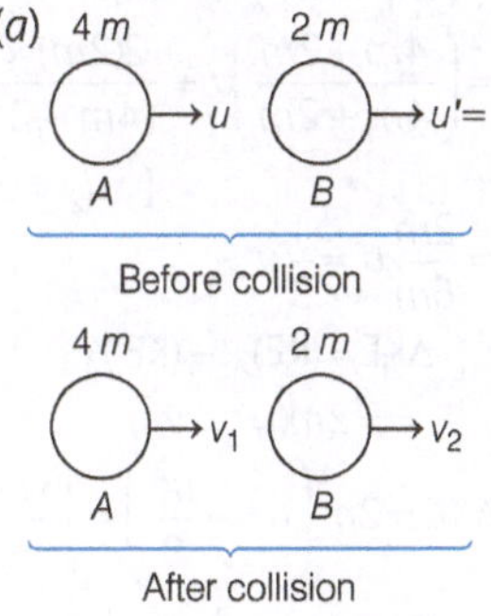

$$(4m)u + (2m)u' = (4m)v_1 + (2m)v_2$$

$$4mu = 4mv_1 + 2mv_2 \quad [\because u' = 0]$$

or $2u = 2v_1 + v_2$ ... (i)

The kinetic energy of A before collision is

$$(\text{KE})_A = \frac{1}{2}(4m)u^2 = 2\,mu^2$$

Kinetic energy of B before collision, $(\text{KE})_B = 0$

The kinetic energy of A after collision is

$$(\text{KE}')_A = \frac{1}{2}(4m)v_1^2 = 2\,mv_1^2$$

Kinetic energy of B after collision,

$$(\text{KE}')_B = \frac{1}{2}(2m)v_2^2 = mv_2^2$$

As, initial kinetic energy of the system = final kinetic energy of the system

$\Rightarrow (\text{KE})_A + (\text{KE})_B = (\text{KE}')_A + (\text{KE}')_B$

$$2\,mu^2 + 0 = 2mv_1^2 + mv_2^2$$

or $2u^2 = 2v_1^2 + v_2^2$ ... (ii)

From Eqs. (i) and (ii), we get

$$4u^2 = 4v_1^2 + v_2^2 + 4v_1v_2$$

$$\Rightarrow 4v_1^2 + 2v_2^2 = 4v_1^2 + v_2^2 + 4v_1v_2$$

$$\Rightarrow v_2 = 4v_1$$

From Eq. (i), we get

$$2u = 2v_1 + 4v_1$$

$$v_1 = \frac{1}{3}u \text{ and } v_2 = \frac{4}{3}u$$

or the final velocity of A can be directly calculated by using the formula.

The velocity after collision is given by

$$v_1 = \left(\frac{m_1 - m_2}{m_1 + m_2}\right)u_1 + \frac{2m_2u_2}{m_1 + m_2}$$

$$= \left(\frac{4m - 2m}{4m + 2m}\right)u + \frac{2(2m) \times 0}{(4m + 2m)}$$

$$[\because u_2 = u' = 0]$$

$$= \frac{2m}{6m}u = \frac{1}{3}u$$

$$\Delta KE = (KE)_A - (KE')_A$$

$$= 2m(u^2 - v_1^2)$$

$$\Delta KE = 2m\left(u^2 - \frac{u^2}{9}\right) = \frac{16\,mu^2}{9}$$

$$\frac{\Delta KE}{(KE)_A} = \frac{16\,mu^2}{9} \times \frac{1}{2\,mu^2} = \frac{8}{9}$$

87 (a) $m_tu_t + m_cu_c = m_tv_1 + m_cv_2$

$$2mv + 0 = 2mv_1 + mv_2$$

$$2v = 2v_1 + v_2 \quad \text{...(i)}$$

For elastic collision, coefficient of restitution, $e = 1$

i.e. $\frac{v_2 - v_1}{u_t - u_c} = 1$

$$\frac{v_2 - v_1}{v - 0} = 1$$

$$\Rightarrow \quad v = v_2 - v_1 \quad \text{... (ii)}$$

From Eqs. (i) and (ii), we have

$$2v_2 - 2v_1 = 2v_1 + v_2$$

$$v_2 = 4v_1$$

$$\Rightarrow \quad 2v = \frac{2v_2}{4} + v_2$$

[from Eq. (i)]

$$\Rightarrow \quad v_2 = \frac{4v}{3}$$

88 (c) $|mu\hat{\mathbf{i}} + mu\hat{\mathbf{j}}| = p_f$

$$\sqrt{m^2u^2 + m^2u^2} = p_f$$

$$\Rightarrow \quad p_f = \sqrt{2}\,mu$$

89 (a) For perfectly inelastic collision $(e = 0)$,

Loss in kinetic energy of system,

$$\Delta E_K = \frac{1}{2}\left(\frac{m_1m_2}{m_1 + m_2}\right) \times v_1^2$$

$$= \frac{1}{2} \times \left(\frac{5 \times 10^3 \times 15 \times 10^3}{5 \times 10^3 + 15 \times 10^3}\right) \times 2^2$$

$$= 7.5 \times 10^3 \text{ J} = 7.5 \text{ kJ}$$

90 (d) The velocity of ball before collision is

$$v_i = \sqrt{2gh_i}$$

$$[\text{using } v^2 = u^2 + 2gh]$$

and after collision, $v_f = ev_i$

$$\left[\because e = \frac{\text{velocity after collision}}{\text{velocity before collision}}\right]$$

$$= e\sqrt{2gh_i}$$

$\therefore$ Height attained after first rebound,

$$h_f = \frac{v_f^2}{2g} = e^2h_i$$

Similarly, after nth rebound, velocity is

$$v_n = e^nv_i = e^n\sqrt{2gh_i}$$

Height for third rebound, $n = 3$ and $h_i = h$

$$\therefore \quad h_3 = e^{2 \times 3}h = e^6h$$

91 (a) Given, $e = 1$ (elastic collision)

$$u_2 = 0$$

The velocities of the two balls after collision are

$$v_1 = \left(\frac{m_1 - m_2}{m_1 + m_2}\right)u_1 + \left(\frac{2m_2}{m_1 + m_2}\right)u_2$$

$$\therefore v_1 = \left(\frac{m_1 - m_2}{m_1 + m_2}\right) \cdot u_1$$

$\therefore$ Initial kinetic energy of mass m_1 is

$$K_1 = \frac{1}{2}m_1u_1^2$$

Final kinetic energy of mass m_1 is

$$K_2 = \frac{1}{2}m_1v_1^2 = \frac{1}{2}m_1\left(\frac{m_1 - m_2}{m_1 + m_2}\right)^2 \cdot u_1^2$$

$\therefore$ Fraction of kinetic energy lost is

$$\frac{\Delta K}{K_1} = \frac{4m_1m_2}{(m_1 + m_2)^2}$$

92 (b) Linear momentum remains conserved in elastic collision as well as in inelastic collision but kinetic energy remains conserved only in an elastic collision.

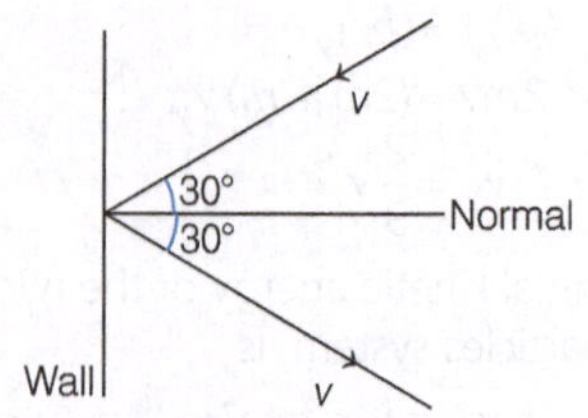

Given that the speed of the molecule of gas is same before and after the collision, therefore its kinetic energy is conserved. Hence, the collision is elastic.

Assertion and Reason Questions

1 (a) $p_2 = p_1 + 50\%$ of $p_2 = \frac{3}{2}p_1$

$$\therefore \quad v_2 = \frac{3}{2}v_1$$

As, $\quad K \propto v^2$;

so $K_2 = \frac{9}{4}K_1$

$$\text{Increase in KE} = \frac{K_2 - K_1}{K_1} \times 100$$

$$= \frac{\frac{9}{4}K_1 - K_1}{K_1} \times 100$$

$$= 125\%$$

3 (c) Mechanical energy consists of both PE and KE. In the given cases, some of the mechanical energy is converted into heat energy and it is more in the case when inclination is less due to increased (as θ decreases, value of $\cos\theta$ will increases) friction force on an inclined plane,

$$f_r = \mu mg\cos\theta$$

The coefficient of friction does not depend on the angle of inclination of the plane. It depends only on the nature of surfaces in contact.

4 (a) In case of friction, work done in moving a body over a closed path is never zero. It is because some work is converted into heat energy.

So, friction is a non-conservative force.

5 (*a*) As we know that, spring force, $F_s = kx$

Given, $F = k_1x_1 = k_2x_2$; $\frac{k_1}{k_2} = \frac{x_2}{x_1}$

The work done in stretching is equal to elastic potential energy,

i.e. $W = E = kx^2$

$$\Rightarrow \frac{W_1}{W_2} = \frac{E_1}{E_2} = \frac{k_1x_1^2}{k_2x_2^2}$$

$$= \frac{k_1}{k_2} \cdot \left(\frac{k_2}{k_1}\right)^2 = \frac{k_2}{k_1}$$

$$\left(\because \frac{x_1}{x_2} = \frac{k_2}{k_1}\right)$$

$\Rightarrow$ Since, $k_1 > k_2$, so $W_2 > W_1$.

6 (*a*) Work done by conservative force in a cycle process $= W_c = 0$

As, spring force is a conservative force.

$\therefore \quad W_{spring} = 0$

8 (*d*) From work-energy theorem,

$$W = \Delta KE = \frac{1}{2}mv^2 \quad \text{...(i)}$$

$$W = P \times t \quad \text{...(ii)}$$

From Eqs. (i) and (ii), we get

$$P \times t = \Delta KE = \frac{1}{2}mv^2 \quad \text{...(iii)}$$

$$v^2 \propto t \text{ or } v \propto t^{1/2}$$

$$\frac{dv}{dt} \propto t^{-1/2}$$

or $\quad a \propto t^{-1/2}$

Thus, the motion is not uniformly accelerating.

9 (*b*) In completely inelastic collision of two particles, they stick together and move as a single particle with a common velocity.

In perfectly inelastic collision of two particles maximum loss of kinetic energy occurs but they do not lose all their energy.

Principle of conservation of momentum holds true for all kinds of collisions.

10 (*d*) A is false but R is true.

In elastic collision, kinetic energy remains conserved, therefore the ball rebounds with same velocity.

$F \times t =$ change in momentum

$\therefore \quad F \times 1 = m \times n(u + u)$

$\Rightarrow \quad F = 2mnu.$

Statement Based Questions

1 (*b*) Statement I is correct but Statement II is incorrect.

The work done in displacing an object by applying force F is given by

$W = F \cdot s = Fs \cos\theta$

If $\theta = 0°$, then work done will be zero.

Work can be both positive and negative. If θ is between 0° and 90°, then work done will be positive. If θ is between 90° and 180°, then work done will be negative.

3 (*b*) Statement I is correct but Statement II is incorrect.

The explosion is due to the internal force hence the momentum is conserved.

Therefore, explosion does not violates the law of conservation of linear momentum.

4 (*d*) Both Statement I and Statement II are correct.

As we know that, $p = \sqrt{2mK}$

For same kinetic energy (K)

$$p \propto \sqrt{m}$$

$$\Rightarrow \quad \frac{p_1}{p_2} = \sqrt{\frac{m_1}{m_2}}$$

5 (*d*) Both Statement I and Statement II are correct.

Work done in moving an object against the gravitational force depends only on the initial and final position of the object, not upon the path taken.

The gravitational force on the body along the inclined plane varies with the angle of inclination.

6 (*c*) Statement I is incorrect but Statement II is correct.

In case of sliding on a rough surface, mechanical energy is not conserved and a fraction of it is converted into heat. Sliding cause displacement of point of contact.

7 (*b*) Statement I is correct but Statement II is incorrect.

If both bodies move together, then the collision is known as perfectly inelastic collision.

8 (*c*) Statement I is incorrect but Statement II is correct.

Energy, $E = \frac{p^2}{2m}$, where p is momentum and m is the mass of the moving particle.

Maximum energy loss occurs when the particle get stuck together as a result of the collision.

Maximum energy loss

$$(\Delta E) = \frac{p^2}{2m} - \frac{p^2}{2(m+M)}$$

where, $(m + M)$ is the resultant mass when the particles get stuck.

$$\Delta E = \frac{p^2}{2m}\left[1 - \frac{m}{m+M}\right]$$

$$= \frac{p^2}{2m}\left[\frac{M}{m+M}\right]$$

Also, $p = mv$

$$\therefore \quad \Delta E = \frac{m^2v^2}{2m}\left[\frac{M}{m+M}\right]$$

$$= \frac{mv^2}{2}\left[\frac{M}{m+M}\right]$$

Comparing the expression with

$$\Delta E = f\left(\frac{1}{2}mv^2\right)$$

$$f = \frac{M}{m+M}$$

Matching Type Questions

1 (*d*)

A. A person pulling out a bucket from well perform positive work done but gravitational force acts negative work done, i.e. gravitational force oppose motion of the bucket.

B. When a body slides down an inclined plane, friction acts in the opposite direction of motion, making the work done by friction negative.

C. Work done by a person in pulling a luggage is positive because force exerted by the person is in the direction of luggage's motion.

D. Air resistance does negative work, slow down the pendulum, while gravity does positive work, aiding its motion.

2 (*b*)

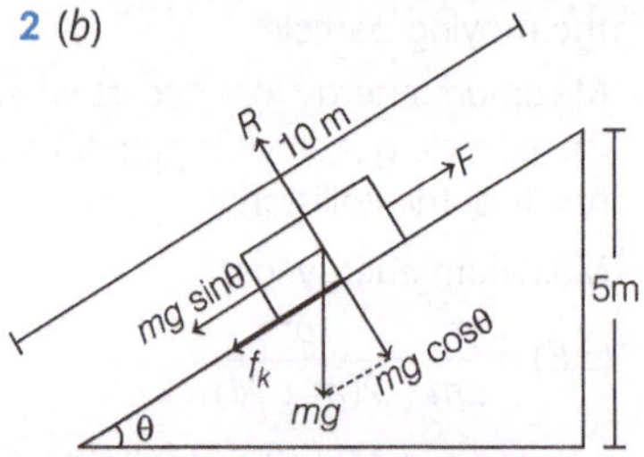

A. As we know gravitational force is conservative. So, work done by it in round trip is zero.

B. Force needed to move the body up,

$F = mg\sin\theta + f_k$

$= mg\sin\theta + \mu_k R$

Work done $= F \times l$

$= (mg\sin\theta + \mu_k R) \times l$

$= mg(\sin\theta + \mu_k \cos 30°) \times l$

$= 0.3 \times 9.8 \cdot (\sin 30° + 0.5 \times \cos 30°) \times 10$

$\therefore W = 18.5\text{ J}$

C. Work done by frictional force over round trip,

$W = -f_k(l + l)$

$= -2\mu_k mg\cos\theta \times l$

$= -7.6\text{ J}$

D. KE of the body at end of trip = Work done by the net force in moving down the plane

$= mg(\sin\theta - \mu_k\cos\theta)l$

$= 0.3 \times 9.8 \times (0.5 - 0.13) \times 10$

$\therefore \quad \text{KE} = 10.9\text{ J}$

3 (*c*) As we know, $v^2 - u^2 = 2ax$

$$\frac{v^2 - u^2}{2} = ax$$

So, area under *a-x* graph

$$= \frac{1}{2} \times (8 + 4) \times 20 = 120\,\text{m}^2/\text{s}^2$$

$$\frac{v^2 - u^2}{2} = 120\,\text{m}^2/\text{s}^2$$

So, $\Delta\text{KE} = \frac{1}{2}m(v^2 - u^2) = 120\text{ J}$

Work done by all the forces

$= \Delta\text{KE} = 120\text{ J}$

$K_f - K_i = 120$

$K_f = 120 + K_i \left\{ K_i = \frac{1}{2}mv^2 = 8\text{J} \right\}$

$K_f = 128\text{J}$

(K_f = final kinetic energy)

Work done by conservative forces (from *U versus x* graph)

$= U_i - U_f = 240\text{ J}$

Work done by external forces

= Total work done – Work done by conservative forces

$= 120 - 240 = -120\text{ J}$

Numerical Type Questions

1 (*28*) Given, $\mathbf{F} = (1 + 3x)\hat{\mathbf{i}}$

$$W = \int_0^4 F \cdot dx = \int_0^4 (1 + 3x)\,dx$$

$$W = \left[x + \frac{3x^2}{2}\right]_0^4 = 28\text{ J}$$

2 (*24*) Change in kinetic energy = Gain in potential energy

$$\Rightarrow \frac{1}{2}mv^2 - \frac{1}{2}m\left(\frac{v}{2}\right)^2 = \frac{1}{2}kx^2$$

$$\Rightarrow K - \frac{1}{4}K = \frac{1}{2}k(25 \times 10^{-2})^2$$

$\Rightarrow \quad k = 24K = nK$

$\therefore \quad n = 24$

3 (*10*)

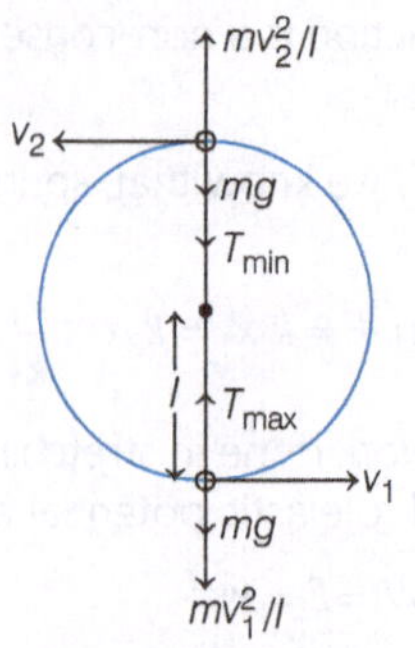

$$T_{max} = mg + mv_1^2/l$$

and $T_{min} = mv_2^2/l - mg$

$$\because \frac{T_{max}}{T_{min}} = \frac{mg + mv_1^2/l}{mv_2^2/l - mg} = \frac{5}{1} \text{ (given)}$$

$$\Rightarrow mg + mv_1^2/l = 5mv_2^2/l - 5mg$$

Here, $v_1 = \sqrt{v_2^2 + 4gl}$

$$\Rightarrow mg + \frac{m}{l}(v_2^2 + 4gl) = \frac{5mv_2^2}{l} - 5mg$$

$$\Rightarrow v_2 = \sqrt{\frac{10gl}{4}} = \sqrt{\frac{10 \times 10 \times 4}{4}}$$

$$= \sqrt{100} = 10\text{ m/s}$$

4 (*4*) $P = F \times v$

$P = m \times a \times v$

$$\Rightarrow P = m\frac{dv}{dt} \cdot v$$

$$\Rightarrow \int P\,dt = \int mv\,dv$$

$$\Rightarrow \quad Pt = \frac{mv^2}{2}$$

$$\Rightarrow \quad v = \sqrt{\frac{2Pt}{m}} \Rightarrow \frac{ds}{dt} = \sqrt{\frac{2Pt}{m}}$$

$$\Rightarrow \int ds = \int \sqrt{\frac{2Pt}{m}}\,dt$$

$$\Rightarrow \quad s = \sqrt{\frac{2P}{m}} \cdot \frac{t^{3/2}}{3/2} = \frac{2}{3}\sqrt{\frac{2P}{m}} \cdot t^{3/2}$$

($\because t = 4$ s and $m = 4$ kg)

$$= \frac{4^2}{3}\sqrt{\frac{P}{2}} = \frac{\alpha^2\sqrt{\frac{P}{2}}}{3} \quad \text{(given)}$$

$\therefore \quad \alpha = 4$

5 (*10*) $\text{KE}_i = \frac{1}{2}m(60)^2 = 1800\,m$

By using law of conservation of momentum,

$$mu = m_1v_1 + m_2v_2$$

$$\therefore \quad v_2 = \frac{m \times 60 - m/2 \times 80}{m/2}$$

$$= \frac{20m}{m/2} = 40\,\text{ms}^{-1}$$

$$KE_f = \frac{1}{2}m_1v_1^2 + \frac{1}{2}m_2v_2^2$$

$$= \frac{1}{2}\frac{m}{2}(v_1^2 + v_2^2) = 2000\,m$$

$$\frac{KE_f}{KE_i} = \frac{2000m}{1800m}$$

$$= \frac{10}{9} = \frac{x}{9} \quad \text{[given]}$$

So, $x = 10$

6 (4) Before collision,

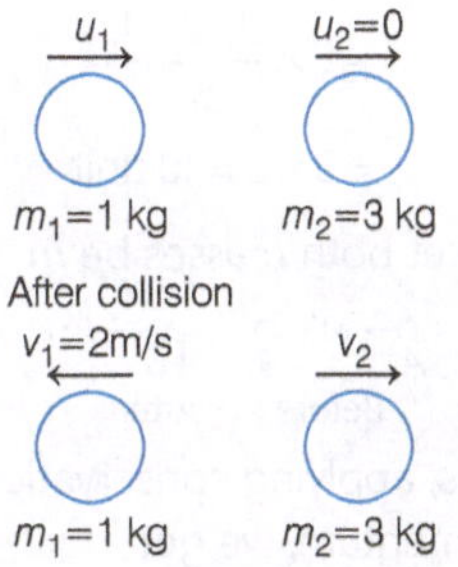

Applying conservation of momentum, $p_i = p_f$

$$\Rightarrow m_1u_1 + m_2u_2 = m_1v_1 + m_2v_2$$

$$\Rightarrow 1 \cdot u_1 + 3 \times 0 = 1 \times (-2) + 3v_2$$

$$\Rightarrow v_2 = \frac{u_1 + 2}{3} \quad \text{...(i)}$$

In elastic collision, kinetic energy is conserved, hence

$$\Rightarrow \frac{1}{2}m_1u_1^2 + \frac{1}{2}m_2u_2^2 = \frac{1}{2}m_1v_1^2 + \frac{1}{2}m_2v_2^2$$

$$\Rightarrow \frac{1}{2} \times 1 \times u_1^2 + \frac{1}{2} \times 3 \times 0$$

$$= \frac{1}{2} \times 1 \times (-2)^2 + \frac{1}{2} \times 3 \times v_2^2$$

$$\Rightarrow \frac{u_1^2}{2} + 2 + \frac{3}{2}v_2^2 = 2 + \frac{3}{2}\left(\frac{u_1+2}{3}\right)^2$$

$$\Rightarrow u_1^2 - 2u_1 - 8 = 0$$

$$\Rightarrow (u_1 - 4)(u_1 + 2) = 0$$

$$\Rightarrow u_1 = 4 \text{ m/s}$$

7 (1) The situation is shown below

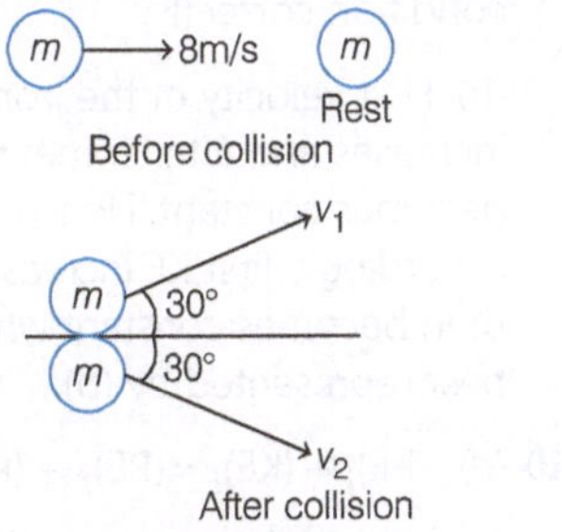

Using conservation of linear momentum in y-direction,

$$0 = mv_1 \sin 30° - mv_2 \sin 30°$$

$$\Rightarrow \quad v_1 = v_2 \quad \text{or} \quad v_1 : v_2 = 1:1$$

Since, $v_1 : v_2 = x : y$ (given)

$$\therefore \quad x = 1$$

8 (10) For particle 1,

$$K_f = \frac{1}{2}K_i$$

$$\Rightarrow \frac{1}{2}m_1v_1^2 = \left(\frac{1}{2}m_1u^2\right) \times \frac{1}{2}$$

$$\Rightarrow \quad v_1 = \frac{u}{\sqrt{2}}$$

Applying conservation of momentum in y-direction, i.e.

$$10mv_2 \sin\theta_2 = mv_1 \sin\theta_1$$

$$10mv_2 \sin\theta_2 = \frac{mu}{\sqrt{2}} \cdot \sqrt{n}\sin\theta_2$$

$$\Rightarrow \quad v_2 = \frac{u\sqrt{n}}{10\sqrt{2}} \quad \text{...(i)}$$

Also, collision is elastic, so KE is conserved.

$$\Rightarrow \frac{1}{2}mu^2 = \frac{1}{2}mv_1^2 + \frac{1}{2}(10m)v_2^2$$

On substituting values of v_1 and v_2, we get

$$u^2 = \left(\frac{u}{\sqrt{2}}\right)^2 + 10\left(\frac{u^2n}{100 \times 2}\right)$$

$$\Rightarrow \quad \frac{u^2}{2} = \frac{u^2n}{10 \times 2} \Rightarrow n = 10$$

NCERT Exemplar Questions

1 (c) From conservation of mechanical energy,

$$\frac{1}{2}mv^2 = mgh$$

(for both tracks I and II)

$$v = \sqrt{2gh}$$

Hence, speed is same for both stones.

For stone as shown below, a_1 = acceleration along inclined plane $= g\sin\theta_1$

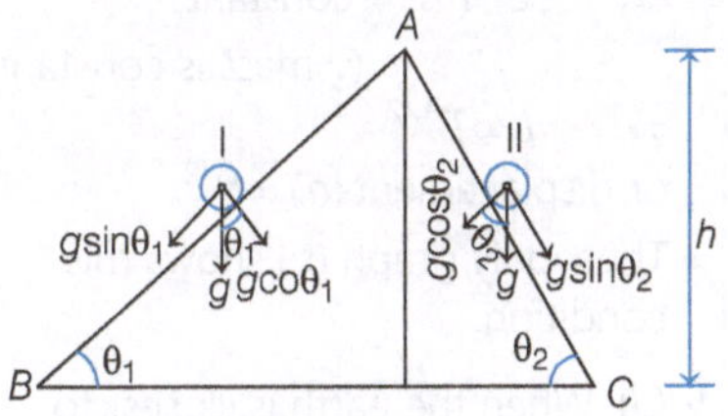

Similarly, for stone II, $a_2 = g\sin\theta_2$ as $\theta_2 > \theta_1$, hence $a_2 > a_1$.

Also, lengths for track II is also less, hence stone II reaches earlier than stone I.

2 (b) Total energy,

$$E = PE + KE \quad \text{...(i)}$$

At $x = x_m, v = 0$

$$\Rightarrow \quad KE = 0$$

From Eq. (i),

$$E = PE + 0 = PE$$

$$= U(x_m) = \frac{1}{2}kx_m^2$$

$$\Rightarrow \quad E = U$$

3 (b) Velocity of the body at $x = 0$,

$$v_1 = 5 \times 0 = 0$$

Velocity of the body at $x = 2$ m,

$$v_2 = 5 \times (2)^{3/2} \text{ m/s}$$

According to work-energy theorem,

$$W = \frac{1}{2}m(v_2^2 - v_1^2)$$

$$= \frac{1}{2}0.5\,[(5(2^{3/2}))^2 - (0)^2]$$

$$= 50 \text{ J}$$

4 (b) Given, power = constant

We know that, power,

$$P = \frac{dW}{dt} = \frac{\mathbf{F} \cdot d\mathbf{s}}{dt}$$

As, body is moving unidirectionally.

Hence, $\mathbf{F} \cdot d\mathbf{s} = Fds \cos 0°$

$$P = \frac{Fds}{dt} = Fv = \text{constant}$$

($\because P =$ constant by question)

Now, writing dimensions, [F] [v] = constant

$\Rightarrow$ $[MLT^{-2}]\,[LT^{-1}] = \text{constant}$

$\Rightarrow$ $L^2\, T^{-3} = \text{constant}$

($\because$ mass is constant)

$\Rightarrow$ $L \propto T^{3/2}$

or displacement $(d) \propto t^{3/2}$

Thus, only graph (b) shows this condition.

5 (*d*) When the earth is closest to the sun, speed of the earth is maximum, hence KE is maximum. When the earth is farthest from the sun, speed is minimum, hence KE is minimum but never zero and negative.

Therefore, option (d) is correct.

6 (*c*) When a pendulum oscillates in air, it loses energy continuously in overcoming resistance due to air.

Therefore, total mechanical energy of the pendulum decreases continuously with time which is shown in graph (c).

7 (*a*) $\omega = 300$ rev min^{-1}

$$= \frac{300 \times 2 \times \pi}{60} \text{ rads}^{-1}$$

$$= 10\,\pi \text{ rads}^{-1}$$

$$v = \omega R = (10\pi \times 1) = 10\pi \text{ ms}^{-1}$$

$$\text{KE} = \frac{1}{2} mv^2$$

$$= \frac{1}{2} \times 5 \times (10\pi)^2 = 250\,\pi^2 \text{ J}$$

8 (*b*) When raindrop falls first velocity increases, hence first KE also increases. After sometime speed (velocity) becomes constant, this is called terminal velocity, hence KE also becomes constant. PE decreases continuously as the drop is falling continuously.

Hence, only graph (b) shows this condition correctly.

9 (*b*) First velocity of the iron sphere increases and after sometime becomes constant. Hence, accordingly first KE increases and then becomes constant which is best represented by (b).

10 (*d*) $(\text{PE})_i + (\text{KE})_i = (\text{PE})_f + (\text{KE})_f$

$$\Rightarrow \quad mgh + \frac{1}{2} mv^2 = 0 + (\text{KE})_f$$

$$\Rightarrow \quad (\text{KE})_f = mgh + \frac{1}{2} mv^2$$

$$\Rightarrow (\text{KE})_f = 10 \times 10 \times 1.5 + \frac{1}{2} \times 10 \times (1)^2$$

$$= 150 + 5 = 155 \text{ J}$$

11 (*c*) Given, $m = \dfrac{3}{20}$ kg

$$\Delta t = \text{time of contact} = 0.001 \text{ s}$$

$$u = 35 \text{ ms}^{-1}$$

As collision is completely elastic, so

$$v = -35 \text{ ms}^{-1}$$

Change in momentum of the ball,

$$\Delta p = m(v - u)$$

$$= \frac{3}{20}(-35 - 35)$$

$$= -\frac{21}{2} \text{ kg-ms}^{-1}$$

$$F = \frac{\Delta p}{\Delta t} = \frac{-21/2}{0.001} \text{ N}$$

$$= -1.05 \times 10^4 \text{ N}$$

The direction of force will be negative as compared to the direction of the ball.

12 (*c*) $M_1 = m$ $\qquad$ $M_2 = m$

(a) The spring will continue to compress until the two blocks acquire common velocity.

(b) As surfaces are frictionless, so momentum of the system will be conserved.

(c) If spring is massless, whole energy of M_1 will be imparted to M_2 and M_1 will be at rest.

(d) Collision is inelastic, even if friction is not involved. This is because energy is stored as PE during collision.

Hence, only statement given in option (c) is correct.

Past Exams Questions

1 (*a*) Given, $x = 2t - 1$ unit

Force, $F = 5$ N

Instantaneous power, $P = F.v$

Thus, $P = F\dfrac{dx}{dt}$

$$= 5 \times \frac{d(2t - 1)}{dt}$$

$$= 5 \times 2 = 10 \text{ unit}$$

2 (*b*) Let both masses be m

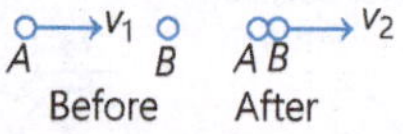

Thus, applying conservation of momentum, we get

$$m_1u_1 + m_2u_2 = m_1v_1 + m_2v_2$$

Both masses *A* and *B* stick together as a system.

So, $mv_1 = 2mv_2$ $\qquad [\because u_2 = 0]$

$$v_1 = 2v_2$$

$$\Rightarrow \quad \frac{v_1}{v_2} = \frac{2}{1}$$

Hence, option (b) is correct.

3 (*c*) $\dfrac{1}{2} kx_1^2 = U$

$$\Rightarrow \quad k = \frac{2U}{x_1^2} \quad \text{...(i)}$$

When $x_2 = 8$ cm, then

$$U = \frac{1}{2} kx_2^2$$

$$= \frac{1}{2} \times \frac{2U}{x_1^2} \times x_2^2$$

[From Eq. (i)]

$$= U \cdot \left(\frac{x_2}{x_1}\right)^2 = U\left(\frac{8}{2}\right)^2 = 16U$$

4 (c)

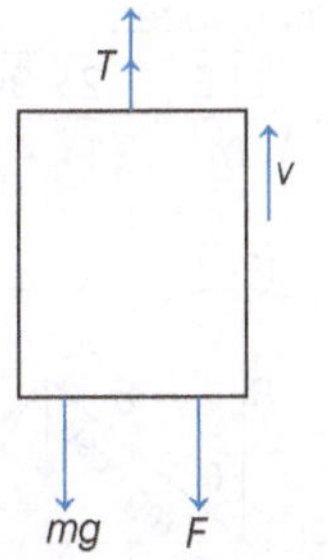

Tension, $T = mg + F$
$= 2000 \times 10 + 3000$
$= 23000$ N

Power, $P = T \cdot v = 23000 \times 1.5$
$= 34500$ W

5 (d)

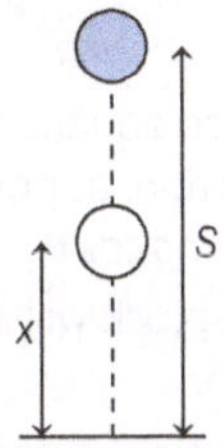

At height S, total energy,
$$\text{TE} = mgS + 0 = mgS$$
At height x, total energy,
$$\text{TE} = \text{PE} + \text{KE} = mgx + 3mgx$$
As, KE is 3 times of PE,
$$mgS = 4\,mgx \Rightarrow x = \frac{S}{4} \quad \text{...(i)}$$
Now, we shall determine the speed of the particle at this height.

As, $\text{KE} = 3 \times mgx$
$$\text{KE} = 3 \times mg\frac{S}{4} \quad \text{[from Eq. (i)]}$$
$$\frac{1}{2}mv^2 = \frac{3}{4}mgS$$
$$\Rightarrow v = \sqrt{\frac{3}{2}gS}$$

6 (c) Velocity of point mass in vertical circle at lowest point,
$$v_l = \sqrt{7gr}$$
$$\therefore \quad v_l = \sqrt{7gr} > \sqrt{5gr}$$
Hence, point mass will have completed the vertical circular path.

We know that,

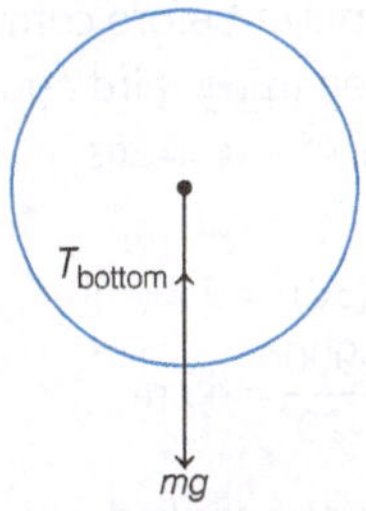

$$T_{\text{bottom}} - mg = \frac{mv^2}{r}$$
$$= \frac{m}{r}(\sqrt{7gr})^2$$
$$\Rightarrow T_{\text{bottom}} - mg = 7mg$$
$$\Rightarrow \quad T_{\text{bottom}} = 8\,mg$$

7 (d)

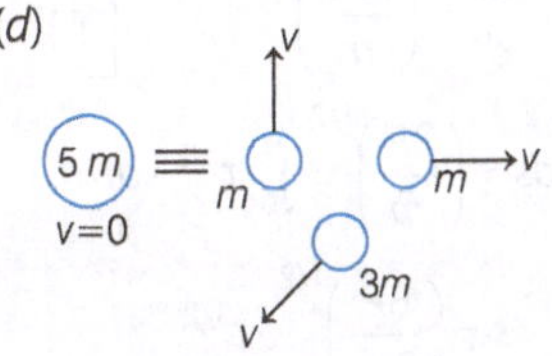

By law of conservation of momentum,
$$5m \times 0 = mv\hat{\mathbf{i}} + mv\hat{\mathbf{j}} + 3m\mathbf{v}'$$
$$\Rightarrow \mathbf{v}' = -\frac{v}{3}\hat{\mathbf{i}} - \frac{v}{3}\hat{\mathbf{j}}$$
$$\therefore |\mathbf{v}'| = \sqrt{\left(-\frac{v}{3}\right)^2 + \left(-\frac{v}{3}\right)^2} = \frac{v\sqrt{2}}{3}$$
$\therefore$ Energy released,
$$E = \frac{1}{2}mv^2 + \frac{1}{2}mv^2 + \frac{1}{2} \times 3m\left(\frac{v\sqrt{2}}{3}\right)^2$$
$$= mv^2 + \frac{mv^2}{3} = \frac{4}{3}mv^2$$

8 (c) $\Delta\mathbf{s} = \mathbf{r}_2 - \mathbf{r}_1 = 4\hat{\mathbf{j}} + 3\hat{\mathbf{k}} - (-2\hat{\mathbf{i}} + 5\hat{\mathbf{j}})$
$$= 2\hat{\mathbf{i}} - \hat{\mathbf{j}} + 3\hat{\mathbf{k}}$$
$$\mathbf{F} = (4\hat{\mathbf{i}} + 3\hat{\mathbf{j}}) \text{ N}$$
$\therefore$ Work done, $W = \mathbf{F} \cdot \Delta\mathbf{s}$
$$= (4\hat{\mathbf{i}} + 3\hat{\mathbf{j}}) \cdot (2\hat{\mathbf{i}} - \hat{\mathbf{j}} + 3\hat{\mathbf{k}})$$
$$= 8 - 3 = 5 \text{ J}$$

10 (b) When the ball hits the ground,
$$\text{TE} = \frac{1}{2}mv_0^2 + mgh$$
It loses 50% energy, it is left with 50% of energy, this left energy is converted into potential energy.
$$= \frac{50}{100}\left[\frac{1}{2}mv_0^2 + mgh\right] = mgh$$
or $v_0 = \sqrt{2gh}$
$$= \sqrt{2 \times 10 \times 20} = 20 \text{ m/s}$$

11 (a) As the machine delivers a constant power.

So $F \cdot v = \text{constant} = k$ (watts)
$$\Rightarrow m\frac{dv}{dt} \cdot v = k$$
$$\Rightarrow \int v\,dv = \frac{k}{m}\int dt$$
$$\Rightarrow \frac{v^2}{2} = \frac{k}{m}t \Rightarrow v = \sqrt{\frac{2kt}{m}}$$
Now, force on the particle is given by
$$F = m\frac{dv}{dt} = m\frac{d}{dt}\left(\frac{2kt}{m}\right)^{1/2}$$
$$= \sqrt{2km} \cdot \left(\frac{1}{2}t^{-1/2}\right)$$
$$= \sqrt{\frac{mk}{2}} \cdot t^{-1/2}$$

12 (a) Kinetic energy K and momentum p are related as
$$K = \frac{p^2}{2m}$$
For same momentum,
$$K \propto \frac{1}{m}$$
Particle A has least mass.
$\therefore$ Particle A has maximum kinetic energy.

13 (d)

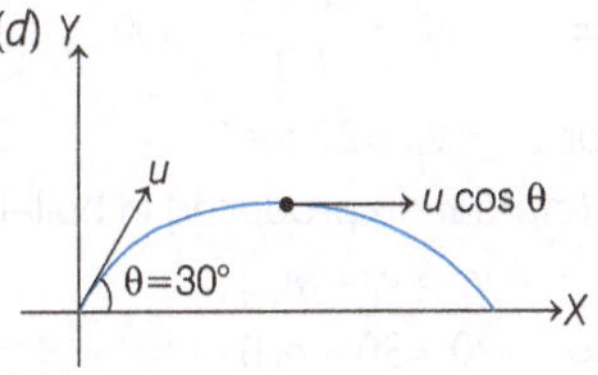

Kinetic energy of particle at point of projection, $K_1 = \frac{1}{2} mu^2$

Kinetic energy at highest point,

$$K_2 = \frac{1}{2} mu^2 \cos^2 \theta$$

$$= \left(\frac{1}{2} mu^2\right) \times \left(\frac{\sqrt{3}}{2}\right)^2 \quad [\because \theta = 30°]$$

$$= \frac{3}{4} K_1$$

$$\Rightarrow \frac{K_1}{K_2} = \frac{4}{3}$$

14 (c)

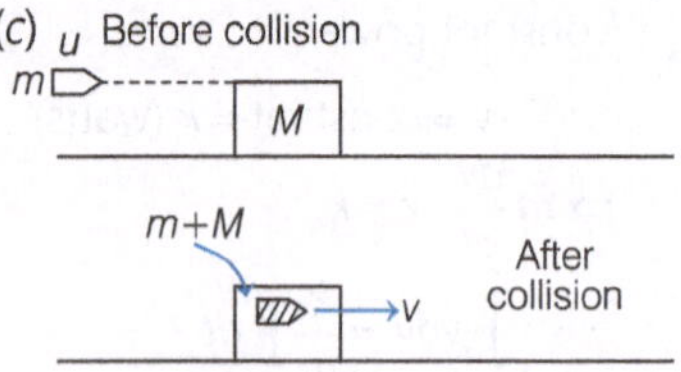

By conservation of momentum,

$$mu = (m + M) v$$

$$\Rightarrow 0.1 \times 400 = (0.1 + 3.9) v$$

$$\Rightarrow v = \frac{0.1 \times 400}{4} = 10 \text{ m/s}$$

KE of block and bullet system = work done against friction

$$\Rightarrow \frac{1}{2}(m + M) v^2 = \mu(m + M) g \times S$$

$$\Rightarrow \mu = \frac{v^2}{2gS} = \frac{10^2}{2 \times 10 \times 20}$$

$$= \frac{1}{4} = 0.25$$

15 (a) $KE_i = \frac{1}{2} mv_i^2$

$$\Rightarrow \quad 90 = \frac{1}{2} \times 0.2 \times v_i^2$$

or $v_i = 30 \text{ ms}^{-1}$

Since, KE reduces to 40 J in 1 s,

$$\frac{1}{2} mv_f^2 = 40$$

$$\Rightarrow \quad v_f^2 = \frac{40 \times 2}{0.2} = 400$$

or $\quad v_f = 20 \text{ ms}^{-1}$

Retardation produced in bullet,

$$v_f = v_i + at$$

$$\Rightarrow \quad 20 = 30 + a(1)$$

$$\Rightarrow \quad a = -10 \text{ ms}^{-2}$$

If l be the length of pool travelled by the bullet before coming to rest, then using third equation of motion, $v^2 - u^2 = 2as$

or $v_f^2 - v_i^2 = 2al$

$$\Rightarrow 0 - (30)^2 = 2 \times (-10) l \quad [\because v_f = 0]$$

$$\Rightarrow l = \frac{-900}{-20} = 45 \text{ m}$$

16 (d) Energy supplied = Kinetic energy

$$\Rightarrow \quad Pt = \frac{1}{2} mv^2$$

$$\Rightarrow \quad v = \left(\frac{2Pt}{m}\right)^{1/2}$$

or $$\frac{ds}{dt} = \left(\frac{2Pt}{m}\right)^{1/2} \quad \left[\because v = \frac{ds}{dt}\right]$$

$$\int_0^s ds = \left(\frac{2P}{m}\right)^{1/2} \int_0^t t^{1/2} \cdot dt$$

$$\Rightarrow \quad s = \left(\frac{8P}{9m}\right)^{1/2} \cdot t^{3/2}$$

Skill Boosters

1 (a) $U(x) = \left(\frac{x^4}{4} - \frac{x^2}{2}\right)$

For minimum value of

$$U, \frac{dU}{dx} = 0$$

$$\Rightarrow \quad \frac{4x^3}{4} - \frac{2x}{2} = 0$$

$$\Rightarrow \quad x^3 - x = 0$$

$$\Rightarrow \quad x(x^2 - 1) = 0$$

$$\Rightarrow \quad x = 0, x = \pm 1$$

Minimum potential energy

$$= \frac{1^4}{4} - \frac{1^2}{2} = \frac{1}{4} - \frac{1}{2} = \frac{-1}{4}$$

According to law of conservation of energy,

maximum kinetic energy = total mechanical energy − minimum potential energy

Maximum kinetic energy

$$= 2 - \left(-\frac{1}{4}\right) = \frac{9}{4}$$

$\therefore$ Maximum speed

$$= \sqrt{\frac{2KE}{m}} = \sqrt{\frac{2 \times 9}{1 \times 4}} = \frac{3}{\sqrt{2}}$$

2 (d)

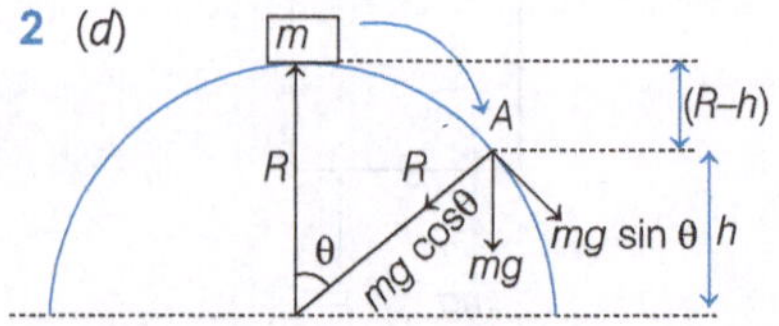

The block can be shown as

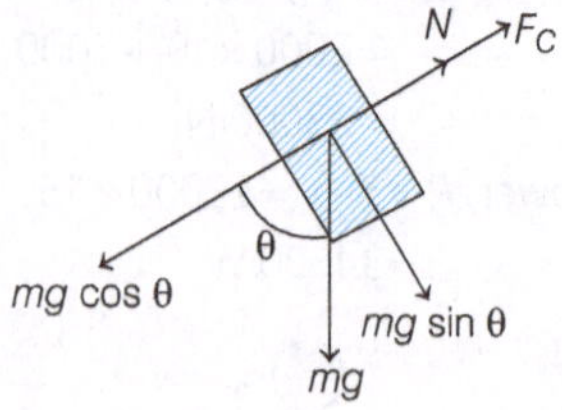

So, the force equation along the radial direction, at point A can be written as $mg \cos \theta = N + F_C$

At point A, block will lose contact, i.e. $N = 0$

$$\therefore \quad mg \cos \theta = F_C = \frac{mv^2}{R} \quad \text{...(i)}$$

where, v is the tangential velocity.

Also, $\quad \cos \theta = \frac{h}{R} \quad$ ...(ii)

Now, from energy conservation, we have

$$mg(R - h) = \frac{1}{2} mv^2 \quad \text{...(iii)}$$

From Eqs. (i), (ii) and (iii), we have

$$mg\left(\frac{h}{R}\right) = \frac{2mg(R - h)}{R}$$

$$h = \frac{2R}{3} = 4 \text{ m}$$

3 (a) Given,

$$k_A = 300 \text{ N/m}, k_B = 400 \text{ N/m}$$

Let when the combination of springs is compressed by force F. Spring A is compressed by x. Therefore, compression in spring B,

$$x_B = (8.75 - x) \text{ cm.}$$

In series force is same across both spring.

So, $F = 300 \times x = 400(8.75 - x)$

Solving we get, $x = 5$ cm

$$x_B = 8.75 - 5 = 3.75 \text{ cm}$$

$$\frac{E_A}{E_B} = \frac{\frac{1}{2}k_A(x_A)^2}{\frac{1}{2}k_B(x_B)^2}$$

$$= \frac{300 \times (5)^2}{400 \times (3.75)^2} = \frac{4}{3}$$

4 (*b*) According to the question, all collisions are perfectly inelastic, so after the final collision, all blocks are moving together.

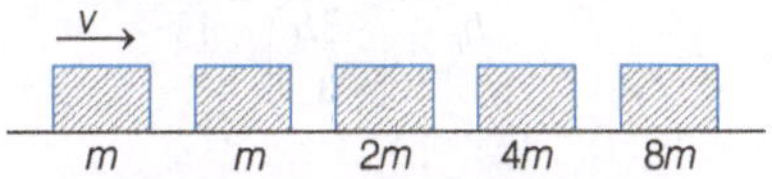

Let the final velocity be v', using momentum conservation,

$$mv = (m + m + 2m + 4m + 8m)v'$$

$$\Rightarrow \quad v' = \frac{v}{16}$$

Now, initial energy, $E_i = \frac{1}{2}mv^2$

Final energy,

$$E_f = \frac{1}{2} \times 16m \times \left(\frac{v}{16}\right)^2$$

$$= \frac{1}{2}\frac{mv^2}{16}$$

Energy loss,

$$E_i - E_f = \frac{1}{2}mv^2 - \frac{1}{2}m\frac{v^2}{16}$$

$$= \frac{1}{2}mv^2\left[1 - \frac{1}{16}\right]$$

$$= \frac{1}{2}mv^2\left[\frac{15}{16}\right]$$

The total energy loss is P% of the original energy.

$$\therefore \%P = \frac{\text{Energy loss}}{\text{Original energy}} \times 100$$

$$= \frac{\frac{1}{2}mv^2\left[\frac{15}{16}\right]}{\frac{1}{2}mv^2} \times 100 = 93.75\%$$

Hence, value of P is close to 94.

5. (*b*) Force exerted by wind,

$$F = m\frac{dv}{dt} + v\frac{dm}{dt}$$

As, v = constant

$$F = v\frac{dm}{dt} = v\frac{d}{dt}(V_0 \times \rho),$$

$$V_0 = \text{volume} = v\rho\frac{d}{dt}(Al)$$

$$= v\rho A\frac{dl}{dt} = v\rho Av = \rho Av^2$$

So, power $= Fv = \rho Av^3$

i.e. power $\propto v^3$

6 (*a*) According to the law of conservation of energy,

$$K + U = E$$

$$\Rightarrow \quad K = E - U \quad \text{...(i)}$$

$$\text{or} \quad U = E - K \quad \text{...(ii)}$$

Since, kinetic energy K is always positive, hence

$$E - U > 0 \quad \text{[from Eq. (i)]}$$

$$E > U$$

Since, potential energy may be negative, hence

$$E - K < 0 \quad \text{[from Eq. (ii)]}$$

$$E < K$$

If kinetic energy and potential energy both have some small positive value, then $U < E$ and $K < E$.

Hence, $U > E$ is not possible.

7 (*a*) It is given that, $\frac{dK}{dt}$ = constant

where, K = kinetic energy.

$$\Rightarrow \quad K \propto t$$

$$\Rightarrow \quad v \propto \sqrt{t} \quad \left(\because K = \frac{1}{2}mv^2\right) \quad \text{...(i)}$$

Also, power $(P) = Fv$

$$\Rightarrow \quad P = \frac{dK}{dt} = \text{constant}$$

$$\Rightarrow \quad F \propto \frac{1}{v}$$

$$\Rightarrow \quad F \propto \frac{1}{\sqrt{t}} \quad \text{[From Eq. (i)]}$$

8 (*c*) Acceleration,

$$a_x = \frac{F}{m_x} = \frac{80}{40} = 2 \text{m/s}^2$$

and $a_y = \frac{F}{m_y} = \frac{80}{10} = 8 \text{ m/s}^2$

As, $K_x = K_y$

$$\frac{1}{2}m_x v_x^2 = \frac{1}{2}m_y v_y^2$$

$$\Rightarrow \frac{1}{2}m_x(a_x t_x)^2 = \frac{1}{2}m_y(a_y t_y)^2$$

$$\Rightarrow \frac{1}{2}40(2 \cdot t_x)^2 = \frac{1}{2}10(8t_y)^2$$

$$\Rightarrow \quad \frac{t_x^2}{t_y^2} = 4$$

$$\Rightarrow \quad \frac{t_x}{t_y} = \frac{2}{1}$$

Hence, the ratio of $t_x : t_y$ is 2 : 1.

9 (*b*) Two pieces of mass m which are moving perpendicular to each other with equal speeds v. So, the third part of mass $2m$ will move as shown in the figure below.

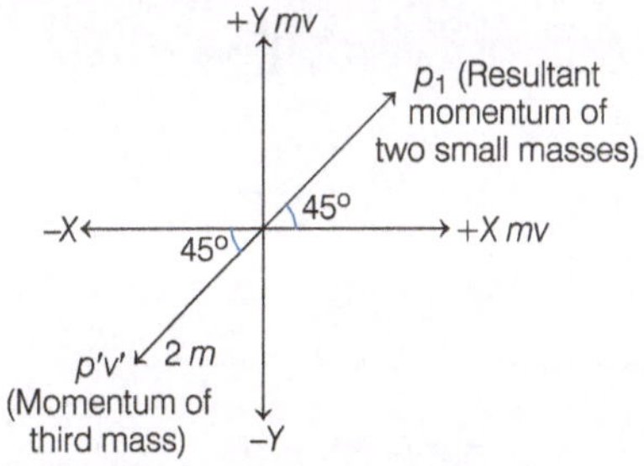

Let the velocity of third part be v'.

From the conservation of momentum,

$$p_1 = p'$$

$$\Rightarrow \sqrt{p^2 + p^2 + p' \cos 90°}$$

$$= 2mv'$$

where, $p = mv$ = momentum due to each small mass.

$$\Rightarrow \sqrt{2p^2 + p^2(0)} = 2mv'$$

$$\sqrt{2}(mv) = (2m)v'$$

$$\Rightarrow v' = \frac{v}{\sqrt{2}}$$

So, total kinetic energy generated by the explosion

$$= \frac{1}{2}mv^2 + \frac{1}{2}mv^2 + \frac{1}{2}(2m)v'^2$$

$$= mv^2 + m \times \left(\frac{v}{\sqrt{2}}\right)^2$$

$$= mv^2 + \frac{mv^2}{2} = \frac{3}{2}mv^2$$

10 (c) Given, $m_A = m_B = m$

For elastic collision with two identical balls, they exchange velocity after collision.

$$\therefore \quad v_A = \sqrt{2gh},$$

$$v_B = \sqrt{2g(4h)} = 2\sqrt{2gh}$$

∴ Height attained by ball A,

$$h_A = \frac{v_A^2}{2g} = h < 4h$$

Height attained by ball B, $h_B > h$.

So, ball B will follow the path as shown below

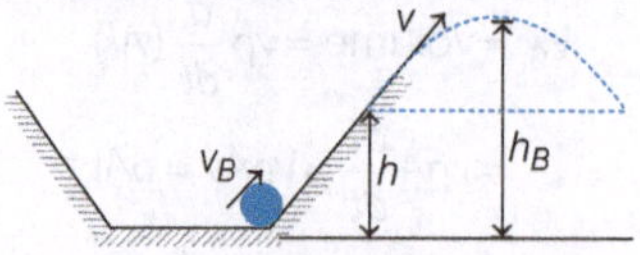

By conservation of mechanical energy,

$$\frac{1}{2}mv_B^2 = mgh + \frac{1}{2}mv^2$$

$$\Rightarrow \frac{1}{2}m(8gh) = mgh + \frac{1}{2}mv^2$$

$$\therefore \quad v = \sqrt{6gh}$$

∴ The height attained by the ball B is

$$h_B = h + (h_B)_{max}$$

$$= h + \frac{v^2 \sin^2 60°}{2g}$$

$$= h + \frac{(6gh)\left(\frac{\sqrt{3}}{2}\right)^2}{2g}$$

$$= h + \frac{9h}{4} = \frac{13h}{4}$$

∴ The ratio of heights attained by balls A and B is

$$\frac{h_A}{h_B} = \frac{h}{\left(\frac{13h}{4}\right)} = \frac{4}{13}$$

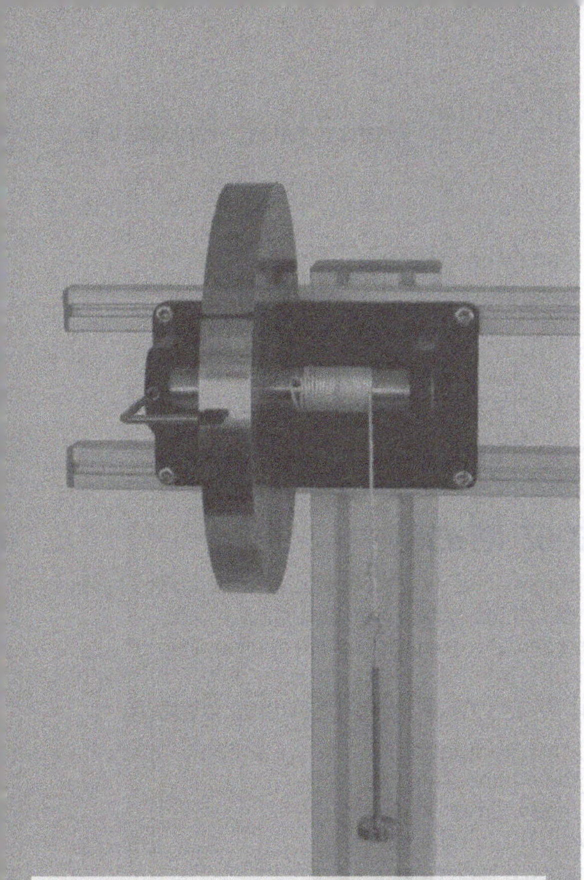

06

Scan for **Physics Through Concept Master** Videos

System of Particles and Rotational Motion

Topicwise No. of Ques asked in 5 Years (NEET)

Topics	No. of Questions				
	2024	2023	2022	2021	2020
Centre of Mass	–	–	1	–	2
Vector Product of Two Vectors	–	–	–	1	–
Angular Velocity and Its Relation with Linear Velocity	–	1	1	–	–
Torque and Angular Momentum	–	–	–	–	1
Equilibrium of a Rigid Body	–	–	–	1	–
Moment of Inertia	1	1	1	1	–
Kinematics of Rotational motion about a Fixed Axis	–	–	1	–	1
Dynamics of Rotational Motion About a Fixed Axis	–	–	–	–	–

Special Type of Ques Asked In 5 Years (NEET)

Types	Years				
	2024	2023	2022	2021	2020
A-R	–	–	–	–	–
Statement Based	–	–	–	–	–
Matching	–	–	–	–	–

Last 5 Years Weigtage (NEET)

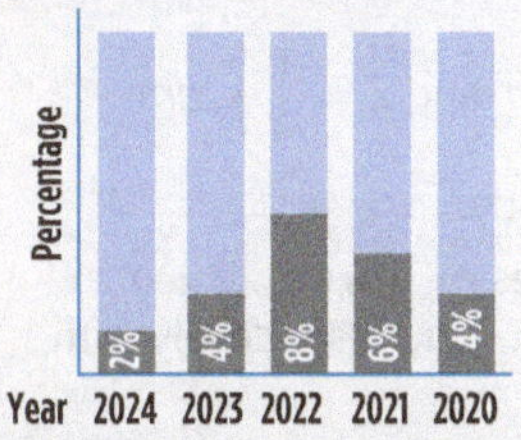

Introduction

- **Rigid body** Ideally a rigid body is a body having a perfectly definite and fixed shape. The distances between all pairs of particles of such a body do not change on the application of a force. e.g. A wheel can be considered as rigid body by ignoring a little change in its shape.
- A rigid body can possess pure translational motion, pure rotational motion or a combination of both of these motions.
- A type of motion in which every particle of the rigid body moves through same linear distance in a straight line for a given time interval is known as **pure translational motion**.
- In pure translational motion at any instant of time, all particles of the body have the same velocity.

  Translation (sliding) motion of a block down an inclined plane is shown in the figure. Here all the particles of the block are moving together, i.e. they have same velocity at any instant of time.

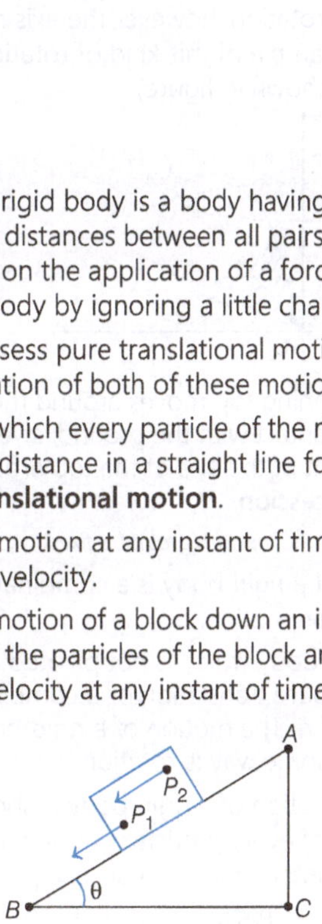

- If a rigid body is constrained, so that it cannot have translation motion, then only possible motion of such a rigid body is **rotation**. The line or fixed axis about which the body is rotating is its **axis of rotation**.
- In **pure rotation motion of a rigid body** about a fixed axis, every particle of the body moves in a circle with different radii which lies in a plane perpendicular to the axis and has its centre on the axis.

- The figure shows a rigid body rotation about Z-axis. Each point on the body such as P_1 or P_2 describes a circle with its centre (C_1 or C_2) on the axis of rotation.
  The radius of the circle (r_1 or r_2) is the perpendicular distance of the point (P_1 or P_2) from the axis. A point on the axis like P_3 remains stationary.

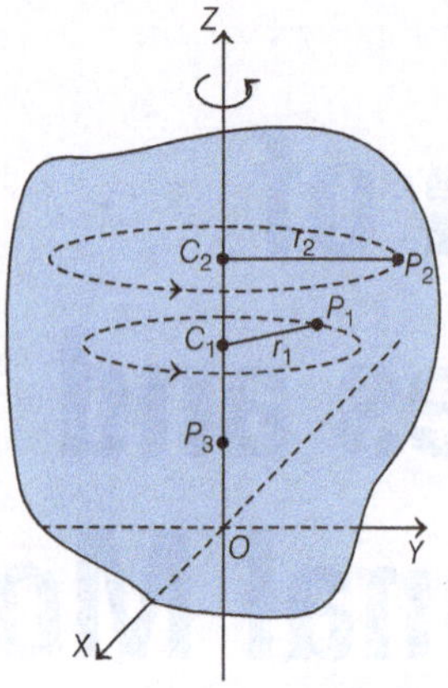

- In some examples of rotation, however the axis may not be fixed. A prominent example of this kind of rotation is a top spinning in place (as shown in figure).

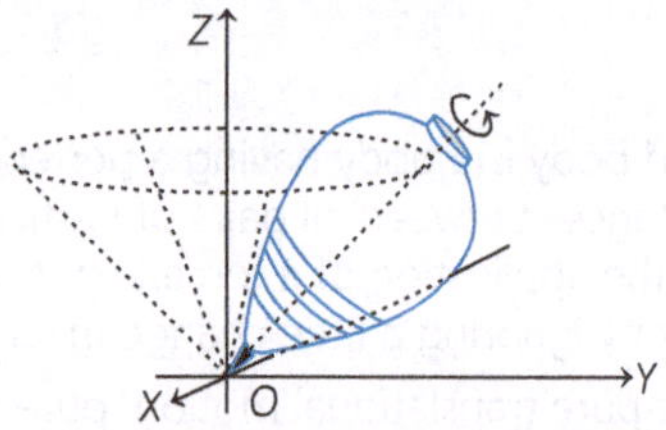

The axis of such a spinning top moves around the vertical through its point of contact with the ground, sweeping out a cone. This movement of the axis of the top around the vertical is termed **precession**.

Note *The point of contact of the top with ground is fixed.*

- The **rolling motion** of a rigid body is a combination of translation and rotation motion.
- The motion of a rigid body which is not pivoted or fixed in some way is either a pure translation or a combination of translation and rotation. The motion of a rigid body which is pivoted or fixed in some way is rotation.
- A pure translational motion of a rigid body is shown in figure. Here, velocity of every particle is same and angle OP makes with horizontal remain equal i.e. $\alpha_1 = \alpha_2 = \alpha_3$.

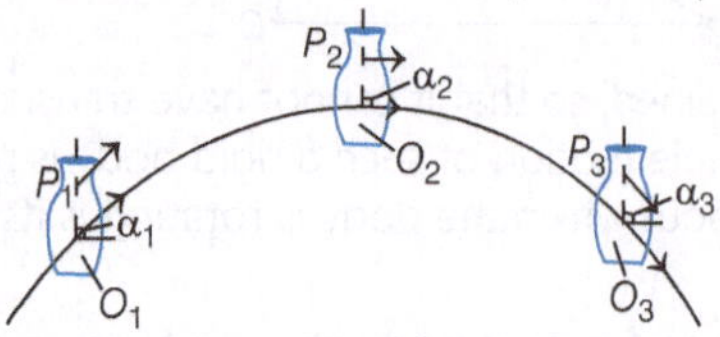

- A combination of translational and rotational motion of a rigid body is shown in figure. At any instants, the velocities of point O and P are different.
  Here, $\alpha_1 \neq \alpha_2 \neq \alpha_3$

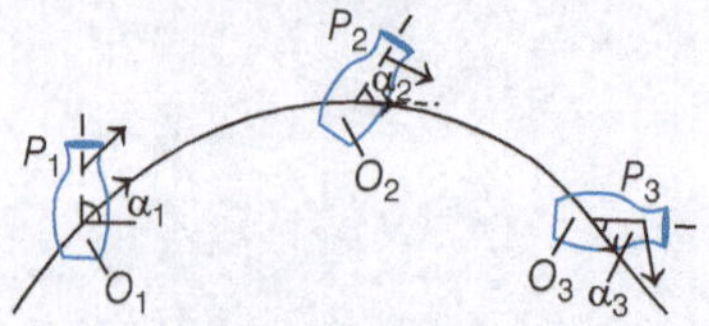

Centre of Mass

The centre of mass of a system of particles is the point where the entire mass of the system may be assumed to be concentrated and all external forces are applied on it.

Centre of Mass of a Two Particles System

Consider the two particles of masses m_1 and m_2 are placed at distances x_1 and x_2 from origin O, respectively. The position of centre of mass x_{CM} is given as

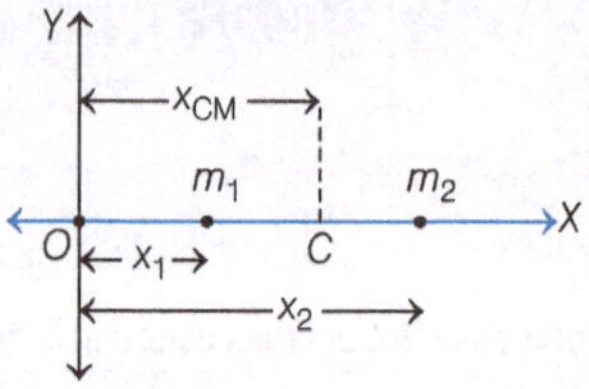

$$x_{CM} = \frac{m_1x_1 + m_2x_2}{m_1 + m_2}$$ NEET 2022, 20

Note *If* $m_1 = m_2 = m$, *then* $x_{CM} = \frac{x_1 + x_2}{2}$. *i.e. For two particles of equal mass, the centre of mass lies exactly mid-way between them.*

Centre of Mass of *n*-particles System

- **Centre of mass**
  (i) **of *n*-particles system is**

$$x_{CM} = \frac{m_1x_1 + m_2x_2 + \ldots + m_nx_n}{m_1 + m_2 + \ldots + m_n} = \frac{\sum_{i=1}^{n} m_ix_i}{\sum_{i=1}^{n} m_i}$$

$$y_{CM} = \frac{m_1y_1 + m_2y_2 + \ldots + m_ny_n}{m_1 + m_2 + \ldots + m_n} = \frac{\sum_{i=1}^{n} m_iy_i}{\sum_{i=1}^{n} m_i}$$

$$z_{CM} = \frac{m_1z_1 + m_2z_2 + \ldots + m_nz_n}{m_1 + m_2 + \ldots + m_n} = \frac{\sum_{i=1}^{n} m_iz_i}{\sum_{i=1}^{n} m_i}$$

  (ii) **of rigid bodies is**

$$X = \frac{1}{M}\int x\,dm,\ Y = \frac{1}{M}\int y\,dm \text{ and } Z = \frac{1}{M}\int z\,dm$$

where, M is the total mass of the body.

- For a system of n-particles of masses m_1, m_2, m_3 ....m_n having the position vectors $\mathbf{r}_1, \mathbf{r}_2, \mathbf{r}_3$ ....$\mathbf{r}_n$ respectively with respect to origin, then position vector of centre of mass of the system is given as

$$\mathbf{r}_{CM} = \frac{m_1\mathbf{r}_1 + m_2\mathbf{r}_2 + m_3\mathbf{r}_3 + \ldots\ldots + m_n\mathbf{r}_n}{m_1 + m_2 + m_3 + \ldots\ldots + m_n}$$

$$= \frac{\sum_{i=1}^{n} m_i\mathbf{r}_i}{\sum_{i=1}^{n} m_i} = \frac{\sum_{i=1}^{n} m_i\mathbf{r}_i}{M}$$

where, $M = \sum_{i=1}^{n} m_i$

Centre of Mass of a Rigid Body

- For rigid body, $\mathbf{r}_{CM} = \frac{1}{M}\int \mathbf{r}\,dm$
- If we choose the centre of mass at the origin of our coordinate system, then

$$\mathbf{r}_{CM} = 0$$

i.e. $\int \mathbf{r}\,dm = 0$

or $\int x\,dm = \int y\,dm = \int z\,dm = 0$

- Centre of mass of symmetrical bodies, e.g. for uniform rod, circular plate, etc., lies at their centre.

Motion of Centre of Mass

- The centre of mass of a system of particles is considered to be moving as if all the mass of the system was concentrated at the centre of mass and all the external forces were applied at that point.
- Velocity and acceleration of centre of mass respectively are as follows

$$\mathbf{v} = \frac{m_1\mathbf{v}_1 + m_2\mathbf{v}_2 + \ldots + m_n\mathbf{v}_n}{m_1 + m_2 + \ldots + m_n}$$

$$\mathbf{a} = \frac{m_1\mathbf{a}_1 + m_2\mathbf{a}_2 + \ldots + m_n\mathbf{a}_n}{m_1 + m_2 + \ldots + m_n}$$

Note *To determine the motion of the centre of mass, knowledge of internal forces of the system of particles is not required. For this purpose, we need to know only the external forces.*

$$M\mathbf{a}_{CM} = \mathbf{F}_{ext}$$

- When a projectile explodes into fragments mid-way in air, then centre of mass continues along the same parabolic trajectory because total external force (i.e., force of gravity) remains same.

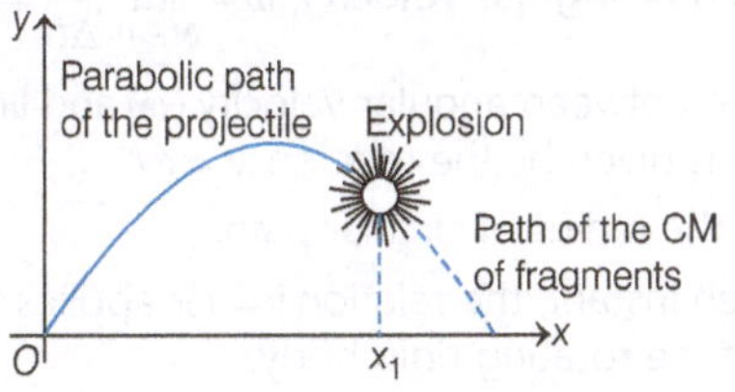

Marks Maximiser

Centre of mass of some symmetric bodies

Semi-circular ring

$y_{CM} = \frac{2R}{\pi}$, $x_{CM} = 0$

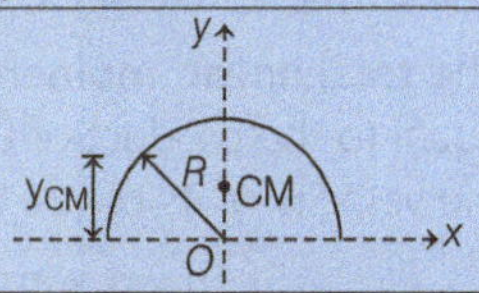

Semi-circular disc

$y_{CM} = \frac{4R}{3\pi}$, $x_{CM} = 0$

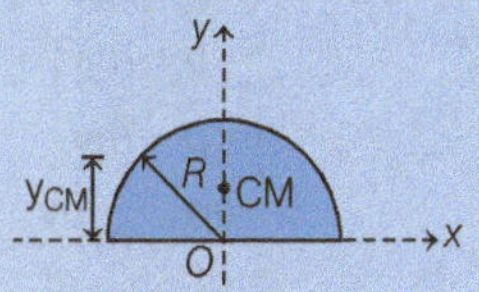

Rectangular plate (By symmetry)

$x_{CM} = \frac{b}{2}$

$y_{CM} = \frac{L}{2}$

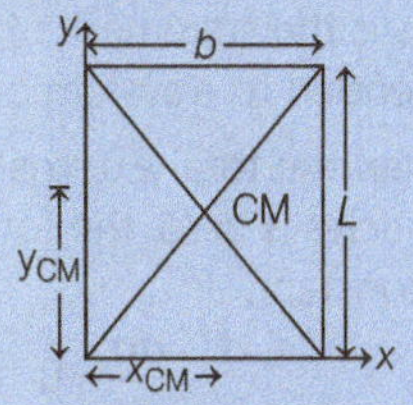

Triangular plate

At the centroid,

$y_{CM} = \frac{h}{3}$

$x_{CM} = 0$

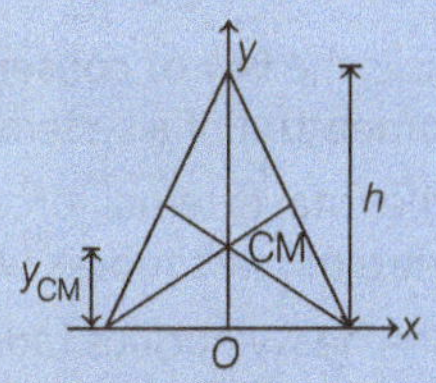

Circular cone (solid)

$y_{CM} = \frac{h}{4}$

$x_{CM} = 0$

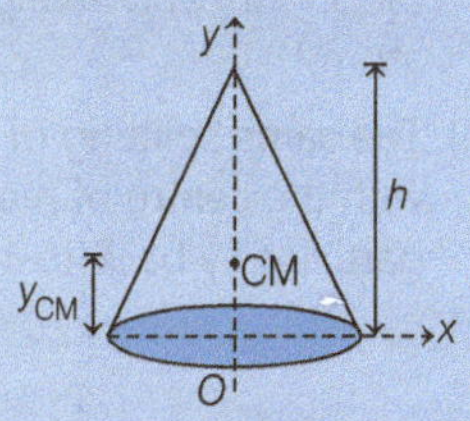

Circular cone (hollow)

$y_{CM} = \frac{h}{3}$

$x_{CM} = 0$

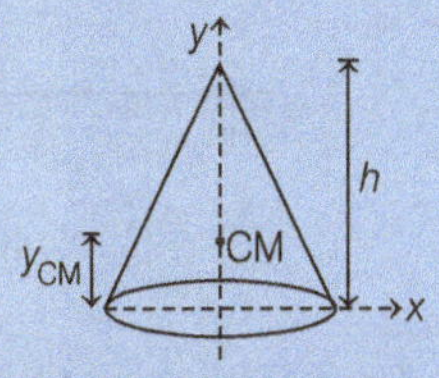

Hemispherical shell

$y_{CM} = \frac{R}{2}$

$x_{CM} = 0$

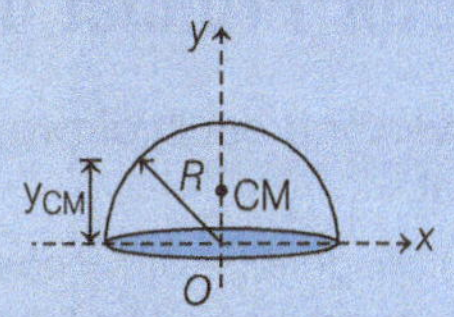

Solid hemisphere

$y_{CM} = \frac{3R}{8}$

$x_{CM} = 0$

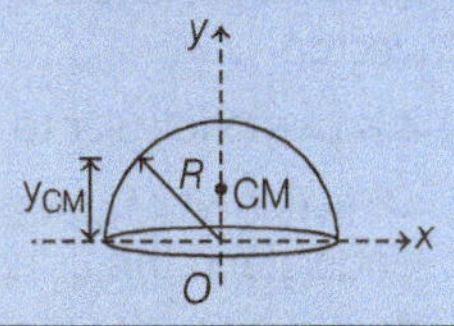

Linear Momentum of a System of Particles

- The **total linear momentum of a system of particles** is equal to the product of the total mass of the system and the velocity of its centre of mass.

$$p = p_1 + p_2 + \dots\dots$$
$$p = m_1 v_1 + m_2 v_2 + \dots\dots$$
$$\mathbf{p} = m\mathbf{v}$$
$$\frac{d\mathbf{p}}{dt} = m\frac{d\mathbf{v}}{dt} = m\mathbf{a} = \mathbf{F}_{ext}$$

This is the statement of **Newton's second law of motion** extended to a system of particles.

- When the total external force acting on a system of particles is zero, the total linear momentum of the system is constant.

i.e. $\frac{d\mathbf{p}}{dt} = 0$ or $\mathbf{p} = \text{constant}$

This is the **law of conservation of the total linear momentum** of a system of particles.

- If the total external force acting on the system is zero, the centre of mass moves with constant velocity e.g.
  - (i) A heavy nucleus radium (Ra) splits into a lighter nucleus radon (Rn) and an alpha particle (nucleus of helium atom).
  - (ii) The same splitting of the heavy nucleus radium (Ra) with the centre of mass at rest. The two product particles fly back-to-back.

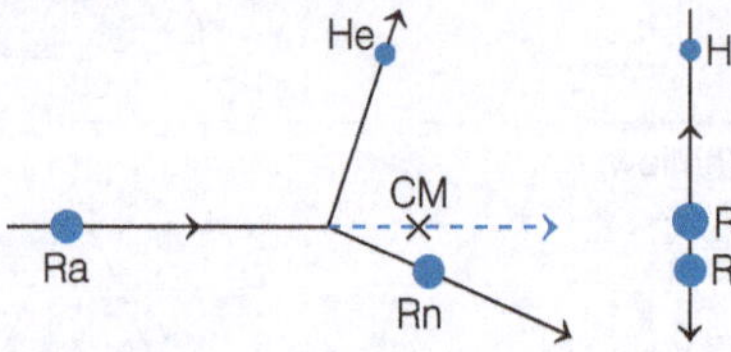

(i) (ii)

Vector Product of Two Vectors

- A vector product of two vectors **a** and **b** is a vector **c** such that **NEET 2021**
  - (i) magnitude of $\mathbf{c} = ab\sin\theta$, where a & b are the magnitudes of **a** & **b** and θ is the angle between the two vectors.
  - (ii) **c** is perpendicular to the plane containing **a** and **b**.
  - (iii) Direction of **c** is perpendicular to both **a** and **b**. We can understand this using right handed screw rule.

    This right handed screw rule is illustrated in Fig. (i).

Alternately, if one curls up the fingers of right hand around a line perpendicular to the plane of the vectors **a** and **b** and if the fingers are curled up in the direction from **a** to **b**, then the stretched thumb points in the direction of **c**, as shown in Fig (ii).

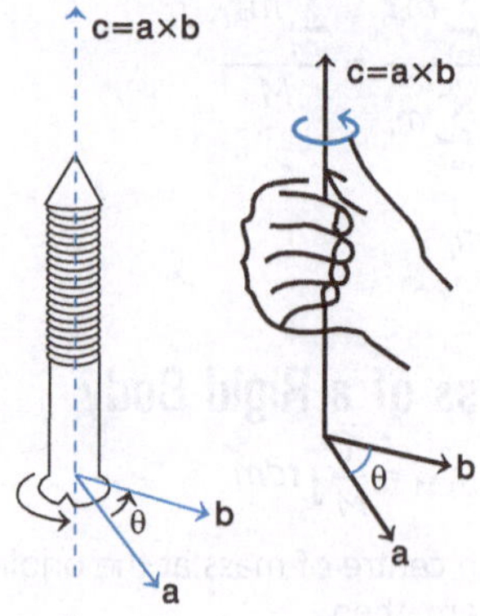

(i) (ii)

- Vector product of two vectors **a** and **b** is not commutative.

i.e. $\mathbf{a} \times \mathbf{b} = -(\mathbf{b} \times \mathbf{a})$

- Vector products are distributive with respect to vector addition, i.e. $\mathbf{a} \times (\mathbf{b} + \mathbf{c}) = \mathbf{a} \times \mathbf{b} + \mathbf{a} \times \mathbf{c}$
- The vector product among cartesian unit vectors $\hat{\mathbf{i}}, \hat{\mathbf{j}}$ and $\hat{\mathbf{k}}$ are given as

$$\hat{\mathbf{i}} \times \hat{\mathbf{i}} = \mathbf{0}, \quad \hat{\mathbf{j}} \times \hat{\mathbf{j}} = \mathbf{0}, \quad \hat{\mathbf{k}} \times \hat{\mathbf{k}} = \mathbf{0},$$
$$\hat{\mathbf{i}} \times \hat{\mathbf{j}} = \hat{\mathbf{k}}, \quad \hat{\mathbf{j}} \times \hat{\mathbf{k}} = \hat{\mathbf{i}}, \quad \hat{\mathbf{k}} \times \hat{\mathbf{i}} = \hat{\mathbf{j}}$$

Here, **0** is null vector

- If $\mathbf{a} = a_x\hat{\mathbf{i}} + a_y\hat{\mathbf{j}} + a_z\hat{\mathbf{k}}$

and $\mathbf{b} = b_x\hat{\mathbf{i}} + b_y\hat{\mathbf{j}} + b_z\hat{\mathbf{k}}$,

then $\mathbf{a} \times \mathbf{b} = \begin{vmatrix} \hat{\mathbf{i}} & \hat{\mathbf{j}} & \hat{\mathbf{k}} \\ a_x & a_y & a_z \\ b_x & b_y & b_z \end{vmatrix}$

Angular Velocity and its Relation with Linear Velocity

- The **average angular velocity** of the particle over the interval Δt is $\frac{\Delta\theta}{\Delta t}$, i.e. $\overline{\omega} = \frac{\Delta\theta}{\Delta t}$

where, $\Delta\theta$ is angular displacement.

- **Instantaneous angular velocity,** $\omega = \lim_{\Delta t \to 0} \frac{\Delta\theta}{\Delta t} = \frac{d\theta}{dt}$
- The relation between angular velocity (ω) and linear velocity (v) is given by the relation, $v = \omega r$

where, r is the radius of circular path.

- At any given instant, the relation $v = \omega r$ applies to all particles of the rotating rigid body.

Thus, for a particle at a perpendicular distance r_i from the fixed axis, the linear velocity v_i at a given instant is given by

$$v_i = \omega r_i$$

- As pure translational motion of a body is characterised by all parts of the body having the same velocity at any instant of time.

  Similarly, pure rotation can be characterised by all parts of the body having the same angular velocity at any instant of time.
- For rotation about a fixed axis, the angular velocity vector lies along the axis of rotation and points out in the direction in which a right handed screw would advance, if the head of the screw is rotated with the body as shown in figure below.

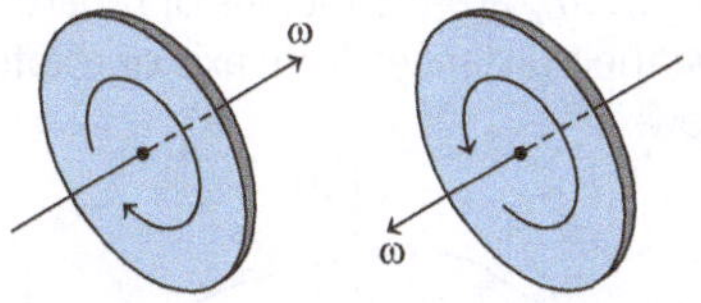

- For rotation about a fixed axis, the direction of the vector ω does not change with time.
  Its magnitude may, however change from instant to instant. For the more general rotation, both the magnitude and direction of ω may change from instant to instant.
- **Angular acceleration** α is defined as the rate of change of angular velocity, i.e. $\alpha = \frac{d\omega}{dt}$. If the axis of rotation is fixed, the direction of ω and α is also fixed. **NEET 2023, 22**

Torque and Angular Momentum

- The turning effect of the force about the axis of rotation is called **torque** or **moment of force**. It is also referred as couple.
- If a force **F** acts on a single particle at a point whose position vector with respect to the origin is given by vector **r** as shown in figure below, then moment of force is given by

$$\tau = \mathbf{r} \times \mathbf{F}$$ **NEET 2020**

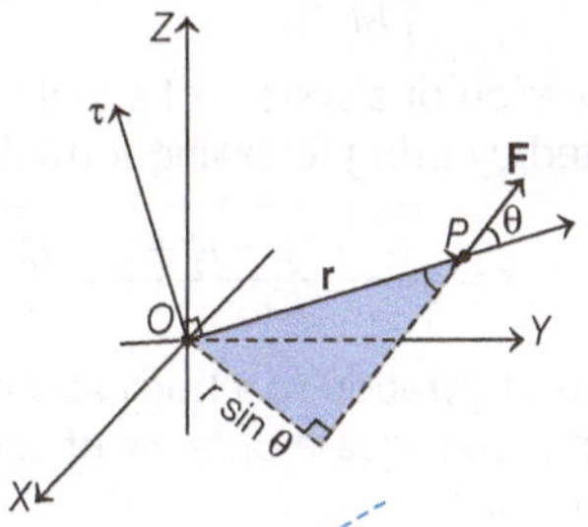

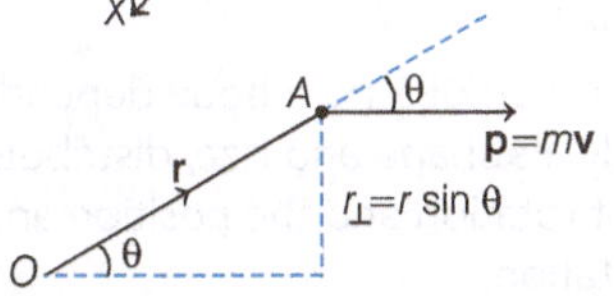

- The magnitude of τ is given as $\tau = \mathbf{rF}\sin\theta = r_\perp F = rF_\perp$
  where, $r_\perp = r\sin\theta$ is the perpendicular distance of the line of action of **F** from the origin and $F_\perp (= F\sin\theta)$ is the component of **F** in the the direction perpendicular to **r**.
  (a) When $\theta = 0°$ or $180°$, then $\tau = 0$ (minimum).
  (b) When $\theta = 90°$, then $\tau = rF$ (maximum).
- The moment of force is a vector quantity and its SI unit is **N-m**.
- The quantity **angular momentum** can be referred to as moment of (linear) momentum.

  Consider a particle of mass m and linear momentum **p** at a position **r** relative to origin.

  The angular momentum **L** is given as $\mathbf{L} = \mathbf{r} \times \mathbf{p}$.
- The magnitude of the angular momentum vector is $L = rp\sin\theta$.
- Angular momentum of a system of n particles,

$$\mathbf{L} = \mathbf{L}_1 + \mathbf{L}_2 + \mathbf{L}_3 + \ldots\ldots\ldots + \mathbf{L}_n = \sum_{i=1}^{i=n} \mathbf{L}_i = \sum_{i=1}^{i=n} \mathbf{r}_i \times \mathbf{p}_i$$

- The time rate of the total angular momentum of a system of particles about a point is equal to the sum of the external torques acting on the system taken about the same point.

  i.e. $$\tau = \tau_{ext} = \frac{d\mathbf{L}}{dt}$$
- If total external torque on a system of particle is zero, then the total angular momentum of the system is conserved.
  If $\tau_{ext} = 0$, then

$$\frac{d\mathbf{L}}{dt} = 0$$

  or $$\mathbf{L} = \text{constant}$$

Equilibrium of a Rigid Body **NEET 2021**

- A rigid body is said to be in **equilibrium**, if both of its linear momentum and angular momentum remain same with time.
- If total force or vector sum of all forces acting on the body is zero, then linear momentum of the body remains constant, so the body is in **translatory equilibrium.** i.e.

$$\mathbf{F}_1 + \mathbf{F}_2 + \ldots\ldots\ldots + \mathbf{F}_n = \sum_{i=1}^{n} \mathbf{F}_i = 0$$

  and linear momentum, $\mathbf{p} = \text{constant}$.
- If the total torque, i.e. the vector sum of the torques on the rigid body is zero, then angular momentum of the body remains constant, so the body is in **rotational equilibrium.**

  i.e. $$\tau_1 + \tau_2 \ldots\ldots\ldots + \tau_n = \sum_{i=1}^{n} \tau_i = 0$$

  and angular momentum $\mathbf{L} = \text{constant}$

- If all the forces acting on the body are coplanar, then we need only three conditions to be satisfied for mechanical equilibrium. Two of these conditions correspond to translational equilibrium, the sum of components of the forces along any two perpendicular axes in the plane must be zero. The third condition corresponds to rotational equilibrium. The sum of the components of the torques along any axis perpendicular to the plane of the forces must be zero.
- A body may be in partial equilibrium, i.e. it may be in translational equilibrium and not in rotational equilibrium or it may be in rotational equilibrium and not in translational equilibrium.
- A pair of equal and opposite forces with parallel lines of action is known as a **couple** or **torque**. A couple produces rotation without translation.
- For a couple with forces $-\mathbf{F}$ and $\mathbf{F}$ acting at A and B points with position vectors $\mathbf{r}_1$ and $\mathbf{r}_2$ with respect to some origin O as shown in figure.

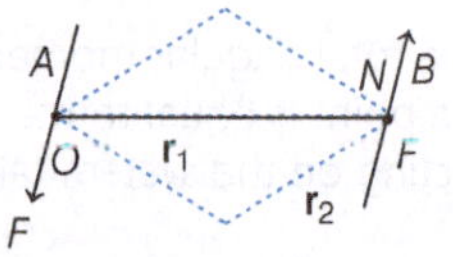

The moment of couple = total torque = $(\mathbf{r}_2 - \mathbf{r}_1) \times \mathbf{F}$

- According to **principle of moment**, when an object is in rotational equilibrium, then algebraic sum of all torques acting on it is zero. Clockwise torques are taken negative and anti-clockwise torques are taken positive.
- In case of the lever as shown in figure below,

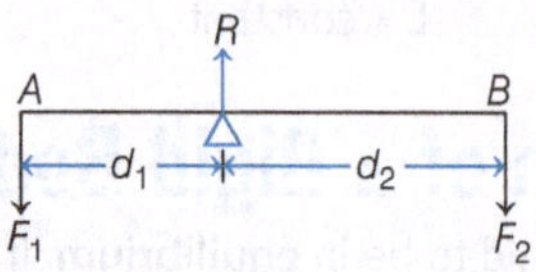

- Force F_1 is usually some weight to be lifted. It is called the **load** and its distance from fulcrum d_1 is called the **load arm.**
- Force F_2 is the effort applied to lift the load and distance d_2 of the effort from the fulcrum is the effort arm.

At equilibrium, load arm × load = effort × effort arm

$$\Rightarrow \quad F_1 d_1 = F_2 d_2$$

The above equation expresses the principle of moments for a lever.

- The ratio $\frac{F_1}{F_2}$ is called the **mechanical advantage** (MA).

$$MA = \frac{F_1}{F_2} = \frac{d_2}{d_1}$$

- A small effort is applied to lift a heavy load, if MA > 1, i.e. $d_2 > d_1$.

- **Centre of Gravity** If a body is supported on a point such that the total gravitational torque about this point is zero, then this point is called centre of gravity of the body.

$$\Sigma m_i r_i = 0$$

Moment of Inertia

- Moment of inertia is the analogue of mass in rotational motion.
- The moment of inertia (I) of a body about an axis is defined as the sum of the products of the mass of the particles of the body and the square of the respective distance of the particles from the axis of rotation.

$$I = m_1 r_1^2 + m_2 r_2^2 + \ldots + m_n r_n^2 = \sum_{i=1}^{n} m_i r_i^2$$

where, $m_1, m_2 \ldots, m_n$ are the masses of n-particles and $r_1, r_2, \ldots, r_n$ be their distances from axis of rotation as shown in figure below.

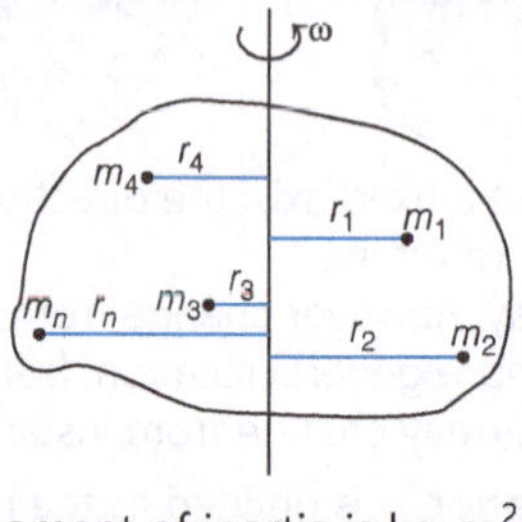

- The SI unit of moment of inertia is kg-m^2 and dimensional formula is $[ML^2]$.
- The kinetic energy of a rotating body,

$$k = \frac{1}{2} I\omega^2 \qquad (I = MR^2)$$

where, I = moment of inertia and

ω = angular velocity of rotating body.

- The **radius of gyration** of a body about an axis is defined as the distance from the axis of a mass point whose mass is equal to the mass of whole body and whose moment of inertia is equal to the moment of inertia of the body about the axis of rotation. It is denoted by K.

$$k = \sqrt{\frac{I}{M}}$$

NEET 2023, 22, 21

- Radius of gyration of a system of equal mass particles is also calculated by using following formula

$$k = \sqrt{\frac{r_1^2 + r_2^2 + r_3^2 + \ldots + r_n^2}{n}}$$

Hence, radius of gyration of a body about a given axis is equal to root mean square distance of constituent particles from the given axis.

- The radius of gyration of a rigid body depends on the mass of the body, its shape and size, distribution of mass about the axis of rotation and the position and orientation of the axis of rotation.

*Theorem of Parallel Axes

- It states that "the moment of inertia of a body about any axis is equal to the moment of inertia of the body about a parallel axis passing through the centre of mass plus the product of the mass of the body and the square of the distance between the two parallel axes."
- Two such axes are shown in figure for a body of mass M. If a is the distance between the axes and I_{CM} and I_0 are the respective moments of inertia about these axes, then

$$I_0 = I_{CM} + Ma^2$$

For Concept Master Video

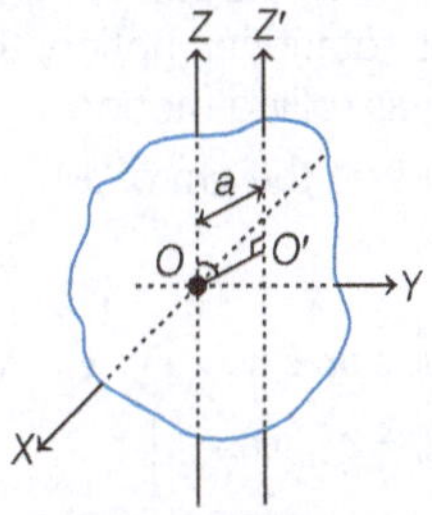

*Theorem of Perpendicular Axes

- It states that "the moment of inertia of a planar body (lamina) about an axis perpendicular to its plane, is equal to the sum of its moment of inertia about two perpendicular axes concurrent with perpendicular axis and lying in the plane of the body".

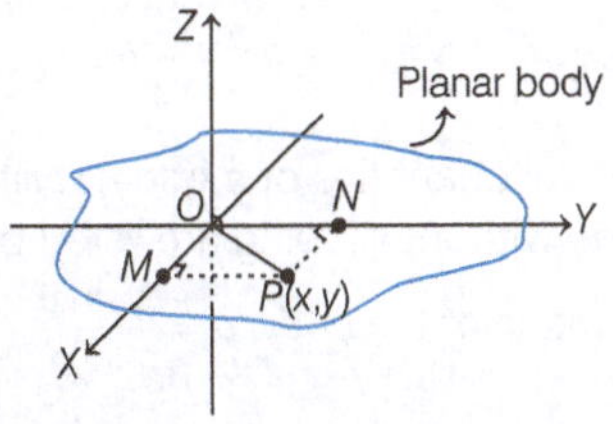

$\therefore \quad I_Z = I_X + I_Y$

where, I_X, I_Y and I_Z are the moments of inertia about the X, Y and Z-axes, respectively.

Moment of inertia of some regular bodies about specific axis

S.No.	Body	Axis of Rotation	Figure	Moment of Inertia
1.	Thin circular ring, radius R	(a) About an axis passing through CG and perpendicular to its plane	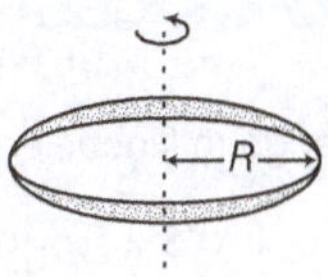	MR^2
		(b) About its diameter	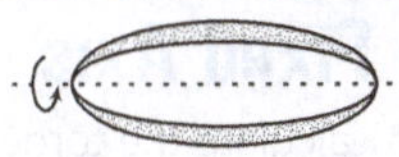	$\frac{1}{2}MR^2$
2.	Circular disc, radius R	(a) Perpendicular to disc at centre	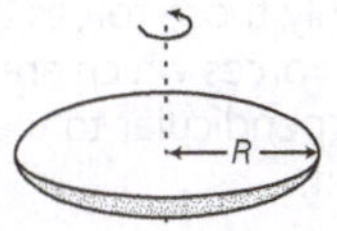	$\frac{1}{2}MR^2$
		(b) About its diameter	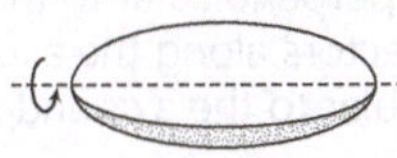	$\frac{1}{4}MR^2$
3.	Long uniform thin rod	About an axis passing through its centre of mass and perpendicular to the rod		$\frac{ML^2}{12}$
4.	Hollow cylinder, radius R	About its own axis	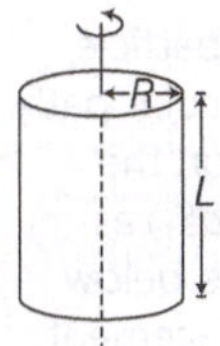	MR^2
5.	Solid cylinder, radius R	About its own axis	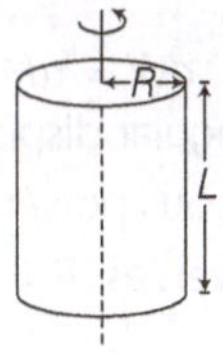	$\frac{1}{2}MR^2$
6.	Solid sphere, radius R	About its diametric axis		$\frac{2}{5}MR^2$

Kinematic Equations of Rotational Motion

NEET 2022, 20, 19

- The kinematic equations for rotational motion with uniform angular acceleration are given below

(i) $\omega = \omega_0 + \alpha t$ (ii) $\theta - \theta_0 = \omega_0 t + \frac{1}{2}\alpha t^2$

(iii) $\omega^2 - \omega_0^2 = 2\alpha(\theta - \theta_0)$

where, θ_0 & ω_0 are initial angular displacement and angular velocity, θ & ω are final angular displacement & angular velocity and α is angular acceleration.

* These topics are not included in latest rationalised NCERT, but it is given in latest NEET syllabus.

Dynamics of Rotational Motion About a Fixed Axis

NEET 2019

- In order to calculate the torque on a rigid body, Consider only those forces that lie in planes perpendicular to the axis. Forces which are parallel to the axis will give torques perpendicular to the axis and need not be taken into account.
- Consider only those components of the position vectors which are perpendicular to the axis. Components of position vectors along the axis will result in torques perpendicular to the axis and need not be taken into account.

Work done by a torque

- Work done by a force $\mathbf{F}_1$ acting on a particle of a body rotating about a fixed axis; the particle describes a circular path with centre C on the axis; arc P_1P_1' (dS_1) as shown in figure below gives the displacement of the particle.

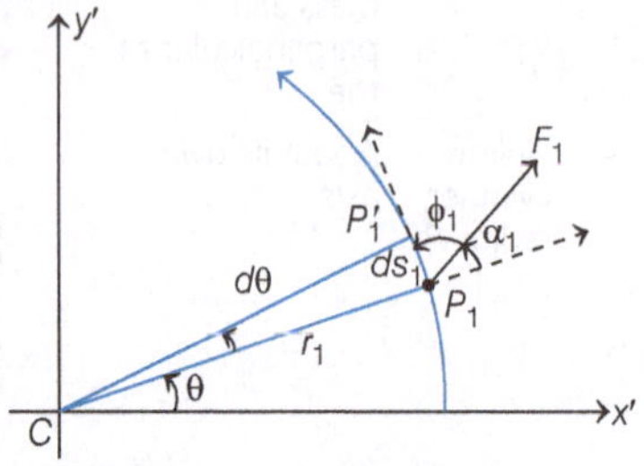

i.e. $dW = \tau d\theta$

where, $d\theta$ is angular displacement.

- The instantaneous power in rotational motion about a fixed axis is given as $P = \tau \dfrac{d\theta}{dt} = \tau\,\omega$
- **Comparison of translational and rotational Motions**

Linear Motion	Rotational Motion about a Fixed Axis
Displacement, x	Angular displacement, θ
Velocity, $v = dx/dt$	Angular velocity, $\omega = d\theta/dt$
Acceleration, $a = dv/dt$	Angular acceleration, $\alpha = d\omega/dt$
Mass, M	Moment of inertia, I
Force, $F = Ma$	Torque, $\tau = I\alpha$
Work, $dW = Fds$	Work, $dW = \tau d\theta$
Kinetic energy, $K = Mv^2/2$	Kinetic energy, $K = \dfrac{I\omega^2}{2}$
Power, $P = Fv$	Power, $P = \tau\omega$
Linear momentum, $p = Mv$	Angular momentum, $L = I\omega$

Angular Momentum in case of Rotations about of Fixed Axis

- The general expression for **angular momentum** in rotational motion about a fixed axis is given as

$$\mathbf{L} = \sum_{i=1}^{N} r_i \times p_i \quad \text{and torque } \tau = I\alpha$$

- If the external torque on the rotating body is zero, then angular momentum on the body is conserved. This is **law of conservation of angular momentum.**

As, $\dfrac{dL}{dt} = 0$

$L = \text{constant}$, $I\omega = \text{constant}$ or $I_1\omega_1 = I_2\omega_2$

For Concept Master Video

Marks Maximiser

- **Rolling Motion** When a body performs translation motion as well as rotational motion, then this type of motion is known as rolling motion.
- Velocity at a point on the rim of a rolling wheel,

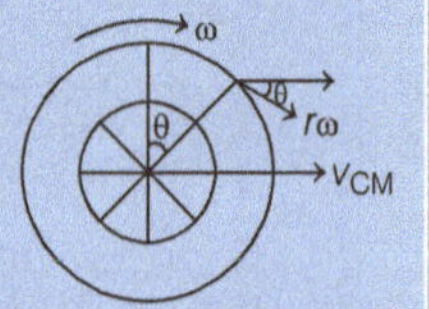

For pure rolling $v_{cm} = r\omega$

As, v_{net} is the vector sum of v_{cm} and ωr

$$\Rightarrow \quad v_{net} = 2v_{cm}\cos\left(\frac{\theta}{2}\right)$$

- Angular momentum of a rolling wheel about an axis passing through the point of contact P and perpendicular to the plane of wheel

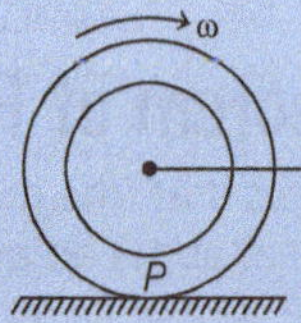

$$\mathbf{L} = \mathbf{L}_{translation} + \mathbf{L}_{rotation}$$
$$\mathbf{L} = (I_{CM} + mR^2)\omega = I_p\omega$$

- The kinetic energy of rolling is given as

$$KE_{rolling} = \frac{1}{2}Mv_{CM}^2 + \frac{1}{2}I\omega^2 = \frac{1}{2}Mv_{CM}^2\left(1 + \frac{k^2}{R^2}\right)$$

- Various physical quantities of a body, rolling on an inclined plane without slipping are listed below

(i) Acceleration of the body, $a = \dfrac{g\sin\theta}{1 + \dfrac{k^2}{R^2}}$

where, θ = angle of inclination.

(ii) Velocity of the body when it reaches the bottom,

$$v = \sqrt{\frac{2gh}{1 + \dfrac{k^2}{R^2}}}$$

(iii) Time taken by a rolling body to reach the bottom,

$$t = \frac{1}{\sin\theta}\sqrt{\frac{2h(1 + k^2/R^2)}{g}}$$

(iv) Change in kinetic energy due to rolling ($v_2 > v_1$)

$$\Delta KE = \frac{1}{2}m\left(1 + \frac{k^2}{R^2}\right)(v_2^2 - v_1^2)$$

Caution Points

- Newton's second law for a system of particles,
$$\mathbf{F}_{ext} = M\mathbf{a}_{CM}$$
It is based on Newton's second law and Newton third law of motion for a particle.
- The external torque acting on a system,
$$\tau_{ext} = \frac{d\mathbf{L}}{dt}$$
It is based on Newton's second law and Newton's third law for particles and also that the forces between two particles act along the line joining these particles.
- The conditions $\mathbf{F}_{ext} = 0$ and $\tau_{ext} = 0$ are independent from each other. For example, in a couple, $F_{ext} = 0$ but $\tau_{ext} \neq 0$.
- When a rigid body is in translational equilibrium condition i.e. $\sum_{i=1}^{n} F_i = 0$, then total torque, i.e. $\sum_{i=1}^{n} \tau_i$ is independent of the origin.
- The centre of gravity and centre of mass of bodies much smaller than earth are at same point.

PYQ Notes

1. From a body of mass M, a part of mass m is removed, then moment of inertia of remaining part is given as
I = Moment of inertia of whole body − Moment of inertia of removed part **[NEET 2021]**
2. A sphere of radius a and mass m rolls along a horizontal plane with constant speed v. It encounters an inclined plane at angle θ and climbs upward. If it rolls without slipping, the distance travelled by sphere on inclined plane is
$$l = \frac{7v^2}{10g\sin\theta}$$ **[JEE Main 2021]**
3. A cord is wound round a wheel of radius r. The axis of wheel is horizontal and MI about it is I. A weight mg is attached to the cord. The weight falls from the rest. After falling a distance h, the angular velocity of wheel is
$$\omega = \sqrt{\frac{2mgh}{I + mr^2}}$$ **[JEE Main 2020]**
4. When a solid sphere of mass M, radius R and radius of gyration K rolls on inclined plane, then distance covered by the cylinder on the inclined plane,
$$x = \frac{v^2}{2g\sin\theta}\left[1 + \frac{K^2}{R^2}\right]$$
where, θ is the angle of inclination **[NEET 2019]**
5. If two uniform circular discs of moment of inertia I_1 & I_2, are rotating independently in the same direction with angular speeds ω_1 and ω_2 around their common axis passing through their centres, at some instant, they get stuck together and start rotating as a single system about their common axis with angular speed ω, then
$$\omega = \frac{I_1\omega_1 + I_2\omega_2}{I_1 + I_2}$$ **[NEET 2017]**
6. Acceleration of an object rolling down on an inclined plane is given by
$$a = \frac{g\sin\theta}{1 + \frac{I}{mr^2}}$$
where, θ = angle of inclination of inclined plane,
m = mass of object
and I = moment of inertia about the axis through centre of mass. **[NEET 2016, 14]**
7. Total kinetic energy of a rolling body is given by
$$KE_{total} = KE_{translational} + KE_{rotational}$$
$$KE_{total} = \frac{1}{2}mv_{CM}^2\left[1 + \frac{k^2}{r^2}\right]$$
[v_{CM} is the velocity of centre of mass and k is radius of gyration]
(a) KE of a rolling body solid cylinder, $K = \frac{3}{4}mv_{CM}^2$
(b) KE of a rolling solid sphere, $K = \frac{7}{10}mv_{CM}^2$
(c) KE of a rolling hollow sphere, $K = \frac{5}{6}mv_{CM}^2$
[NEET 2015]

Step by Step

Mastering NCERT

- Concept Builders
- Topical Questions
- Assertion and Reason Questions
- Statement Based
- Matching Type
- Numerical Type
- NCERT Exemplar
- Past Exams MCQs
- Skill Boosters

Concept Builders

1 In rotation of a rigid body about a fixed axis, every particle of the body moves in a circle, which lies in a plane parallel to the axis. [T/F]

2 In an isolated system, if external force on the system is zero, then the centre of mass moves with uniform acceleration. [T/F].

3 To determine the motion of the centre of mass, knowledge of .... forces of system of particle is not required. [internal, external]

4 If there are no external forces, the centre of mass of a binary star moves in a .... path. [helical/straight]

5 Vector product does not follow distributive law with respect to vector addition. [T/F]

6 For rotation about a fixed axis, the direction of the vector is changed but not the magnitude. [T/F]

7 The time rate of the total angular momentum of a system of particles about a point is equal to sum of the .... torques. [internal/external]

8 A pair of forces of equal magnitude but acting in opposite directions with different lines of action can not produce any motion. [T/F]

9 Torque depends only on the .... (transverse/radial) component of force.

10 The total torque on a system is dependent of the origin if the total external force is zero. [T/F]

11 The centre of gravity of a body always coincides with its centre of mass. [T/F]

12 Moment of inertia of hollow bodies is more than that of solid bodies having same mass, same size and shape. [T/F]

13 Theorem of perpendicular axes cannot be applied on cubical bodies. [T/F]

14 The instantaneous speed of the point of contact during rolling on ground is .... (zero/non-zero)

15 For a cube, moment of inertia about an axis passing through centres of opposite faces is .... (maximum/minimum)

16 Theorem of parallel axes is applicable for three dimensional bodies only. [T/F]

17 Minimum number of propellers required in a helicopter is .... (two, three)

18 The bottom of a ship made heavy so that its .... remains low. (centre of gravity/centre of mass).

19 For pure rolling motion, work done against friction is .... (zero/non-zero)

20 A cat falls to ground from a height, it stretched its body along with the tail so that its moment of inertia becomes .... (high/low)

Topical Questions

Centre of Mass

1 For an ideal rigid body, **NCERT Pg. 92**

(a) shape is changable
(b) Deformation is too much
(c) the distance between all pairs of particles will change
(d) shape is perfectly definite.

2 A ball is rolling on a plane surface with constant velocity v. Sum of total external forces acting on the ball is **NCERT Pg. 93**

(a) variable
(b) constant
(c) cannot be determined
(d) zero

3 In a spinning top, axis moves around the vertical through its point of contact with the ground sweeping out a cone. This movement of the axis of the top around the vertical is known as **NCERT Pg. 94**

(a) precession (b) translation
(c) rotation (d) rolling

4 The centre of mass of a system of two particles divides, the distance between them **NCERT Pg. 95**

(a) in inverse ratio of square of masses of particles
(b) in direct ratio of square of masses of particles
(c) in inverse ratio of masses of particles
(d) in direct ratio of masses of particles

5 Three identical spheres of mass M each are placed at the corners of an equilateral triangle of side 2 m. Taking one of the corner as the origin, the position vector of the centre of mass is **NCERT Pg. 96**

(a) $\sqrt{3}(\hat{i}-\hat{j})$ (b) $\frac{\hat{i}}{\sqrt{3}}+\hat{j}$ (c) $\frac{\hat{i}+\hat{j}}{3}$ (d) $\hat{i}+\frac{\hat{j}}{\sqrt{3}}$

6 Centre of Mass (CM) of the given system of particles will be at **NCERT Pg. 97**

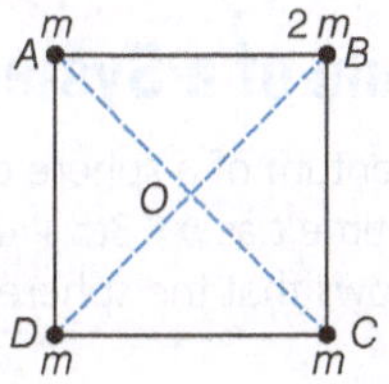

(a) OD (b) OC (c) OB (d) AO

7 The centre of mass of three particles of masses 1 kg, 2 kg and 3 kg is at (3, 3, 3) with reference to a fixed coordinate system. Where should a fourth particle of mass 4 kg be placed, so that the centre of mass of the system of all particles shifts to a point (1, 1, 1)? **NCERT Pg. 97**

(a) (−1, −1, −1) (b) (−2, −2, −2)
(c) (2, 2, 2) (d) (1, 1, 1)

8 Find the centre of mass of a uniform L-shaped lamina (a thin flat plate) with dimensions as shown in the figure alongside. The mass of the lamina is 3 kg. **NCERT Pg. 97**

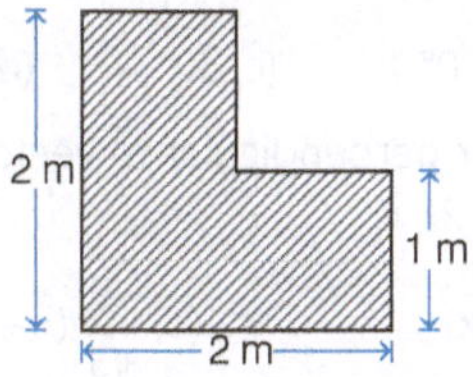

(a) (5/6) m, (5/6) m (b) (3/4) m, (3/4) m
(c) (5/8) m, (5/8) m (d) (3/5) m, (3/5) m

9 Distance of the centre of mass of a solid uniform cone from its vertex is z_0. If the radius of its base is R and its height is h, then z_0 is equal to **NCERT Pg. 97**

(a) $\frac{h^2}{4R}$ (b) $\frac{3h}{4}$ (c) $\frac{5h}{8}$ (d) $\frac{3h^2}{8R}$

10 Three point particles of masses 1.0 kg, 1.5 kg and 2.5 kg are placed at three corners of a right angle triangle of sides 4.0 cm, 3.0 cm and 5.0 cm as shown in the figure. The centre of mass of the system is at a point **NCERT Pg. 97**

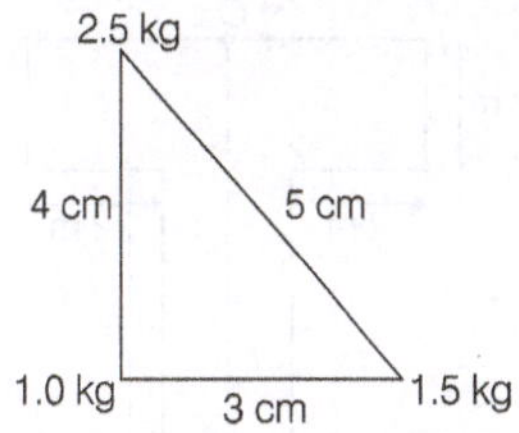

(a) 2.0 cm right and 0.9 cm above 1 kg mass
(b) 0.6 cm right and 2.0 cm above 1 kg mass
(c) 1.5 cm right and 1.2 cm above 1 kg mass
(d) 0.9 cm right and 2.0 cm above 1 kg mass

11 The position vector of the centre of mass $\mathbf{r}_{cm}$ of an asymmetric uniform bar of negligible area of cross-section as shown in figure is **NCERT Pg. 97**

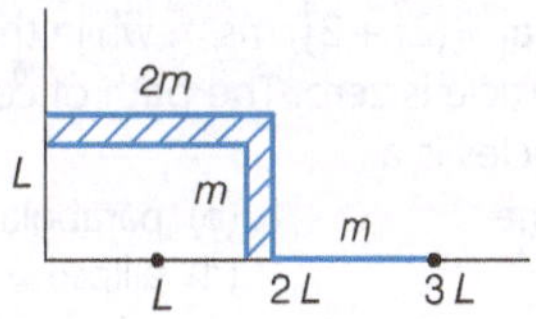

(a) $\mathbf{r}=\frac{13}{8}L\,\hat{x}+\frac{5}{8}L\,\hat{y}$ (b) $\mathbf{r}=\frac{11}{8}L\,\hat{x}+\frac{3}{8}L\,\hat{y}$

(c) $\mathbf{r}=\frac{3}{8}L\,\hat{x}+\frac{11}{8}L\,\hat{y}$ (d) $\mathbf{r}=\frac{5}{8}L\,\hat{x}+\frac{13}{8}L\,\hat{y}$

12 Particles of masses $m, 2m, 3m, \ldots, nm$ are placed on the same line at distance $L, 2L, 3L, \ldots, nL$ from O. The distance of centre of mass from O is **NCERT Pg. 97**

(a) $\frac{(2n+1)L}{4}$ (b) $\frac{L}{(2n+1)}$

(c) $\frac{n(n^2+1)L}{2}$ (d) $\frac{(2n+1)L}{3}$

13 If the density of material of cone and cylinder shown in figure is same, then which of the following is correct about the y-coordinate of COM (Y_{COM}) w.r.t. point O. **NCERT Pg. 97**

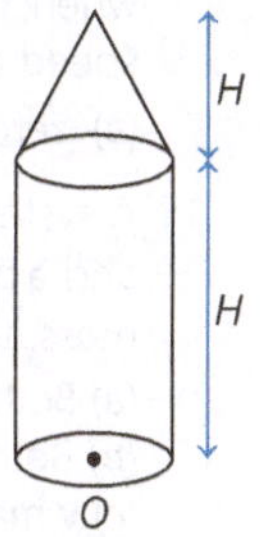

(a) $y_{COM} > H$
(b) $y_{COM} = H$
(c) $y_{COM} < H$
(d) None of the above

14 A solid cube of edge a is melted and moulded in eight identical small solid cubes and are placed on one other on a straight line with the edge of bottom cube on the same horizontal plane on which big cube was placed, then the vertical shift in centre of mass is **NCERT Pg. 97**

(a) $\frac{3a}{2}$ (b) $2a$ (c) $\frac{5a}{2}$ (d) $3a$

15 The distance of the centre of mass of the T-shaped plate from O is **NCERT Pg. 97**

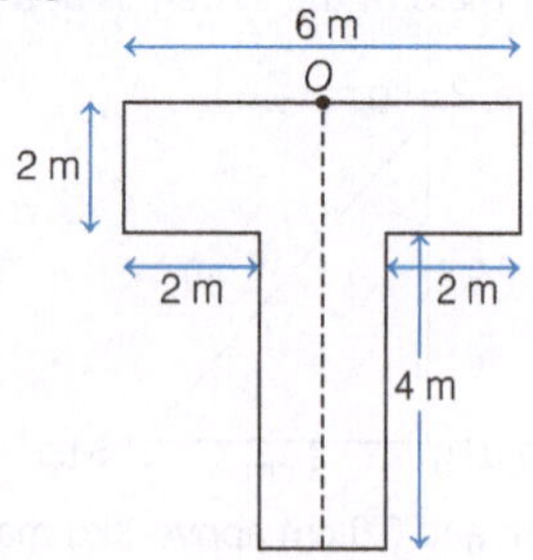

(a) 7 m (b) 2.7 m
(c) 4 m (d) 2.2 m

Motion of Centre of Mass

16 Two particles of equal masses have velocities $\mathbf{v}_1 = 4\,\hat{\mathbf{i}}\ \text{ms}^{-1}$ and $\mathbf{v}_2 = 4\,\hat{\mathbf{j}}\ \text{ms}^{-1}$. First particle has an acceleration $\mathbf{a}_1 = (2\hat{\mathbf{i}} + 2\hat{\mathbf{j}})\ \text{ms}^{-2}$, while the acceleration of the other particle is zero. The path of centre of mass of the two particles is a **NCERT Pg. 99**

(a) straight line (b) parabola
(c) circle (d) ellipse

17 Two persons of masses 55 kg and 65 kg respectively, are at the opposite ends of a boat. The length of the boat is 3 m and weighs 100 kg. The 55 kg man walks upto the 65 kg man and sits with him. If the boat is in still water, the centre of mass of the system shifts by **NCERT Pg. 99**

(a) 3 m (b) 2.3 m
(c) zero (d) 0.75 m

18 Two particles A and B initially at rest move towards each other under a mutual force of attraction. At the instant, when the speed of A is v and the speed of B is $2v$, the speed of centre of mass of the system is **NCERT Pg. 99**

(a) zero (b) v (c) $1.5v$ (d) $3v$

19 A system of particle is free from any external force, if **v** and **a** be the velocity and acceleration of the centre of mass, then choose the correct statement. **NCERT Pg. 99**

(a) Both **v** and **a** must be zero
(b) Both **v** and **a** must be non-zero
(c) **v** may be zero but **a** must be zero
(d) **v** must be zero but **a** may be zero

20 A particle of mass 1 kg has velocity $\mathbf{v}_1 = 2t\,\hat{\mathbf{i}}$ and another particle of mass 2 kg has velocity $\mathbf{v}_2 = t^2\hat{\mathbf{j}}$. Net force on centre of mass of system at $t = 2$ s is **NCERT Pg. 99**

(a) $\frac{20}{9}$ unit (b) $\sqrt{68}$ unit
(c) $\frac{\sqrt{80}}{3}$ unit (d) 10 unit

21 A projectile is fired at an angle and it was following a parabolic path. Suddenly, it explodes into fragments. Choose the correct statement regarding this situation. **NCERT Pg. 100**

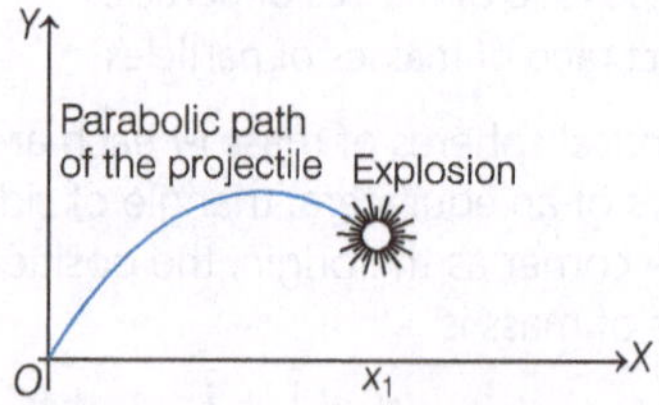

(a) Due to explosion CM shifts upwards.
(b) Due to explosion CM shifts downwards.
(c) Due to explosion CM traces its path back to origin.
(d) CM continues to move along same parabolic path.

Linear Momentum of a System of Particles

22 The linear momentum of a sphere of mass of 2 kg varies with time t as $p = 3t^2 + 4$, where p and t are in SI units. It follows that the sphere moving with a **NCERT Pg. 100**

(a) constant acceleration
(b) variable acceleration
(c) constant speed
(d) constant velocity

Vector Product of Two Vectors

23 The vector product of two vectors $\mathbf{A} = 2\hat{\mathbf{i}} + \hat{\mathbf{j}} - \hat{\mathbf{k}}$ and $\mathbf{B} = -\hat{\mathbf{i}} - \hat{\mathbf{j}} + 2\hat{\mathbf{k}}$ is **NCERT Pg. 103**

(a) $2\hat{\mathbf{i}} + 3\hat{\mathbf{j}} - \hat{\mathbf{k}}$ (b) $\hat{\mathbf{i}} + 3\hat{\mathbf{j}} + \hat{\mathbf{k}}$
(c) $-\hat{\mathbf{i}} + 3\hat{\mathbf{j}} + 2\hat{\mathbf{k}}$ (d) $\hat{\mathbf{i}} - 3\hat{\mathbf{j}} - \hat{\mathbf{k}}$

24 Two vectors **P** and **Q** are given in space as $\mathbf{P} = 2\hat{\mathbf{i}} - 3\hat{\mathbf{j}} + \hat{\mathbf{k}}$ and $\mathbf{Q} = -4\hat{\mathbf{i}} + 6\hat{\mathbf{j}} - 2\hat{\mathbf{k}}$. The angle between **P** and **Q** is **NCERT Pg. 103**

(a) 90° (b) 0° (c) 30° (d) 60°

25 The unit vector perpendicular to vectors $\mathbf{A} = 2\hat{\mathbf{i}} + \hat{\mathbf{j}} + \hat{\mathbf{k}}$ and $\mathbf{B} = \hat{\mathbf{i}} - \hat{\mathbf{j}} + 2\hat{\mathbf{k}}$ is **NCERT Pg. 103**

(a) $\frac{1}{\sqrt{3}}(\hat{\mathbf{i}} - \hat{\mathbf{j}} - \hat{\mathbf{k}})$ (b) $\frac{1}{\sqrt{3}}(\hat{\mathbf{i}} + \hat{\mathbf{j}} - \hat{\mathbf{k}})$
(c) $\frac{1}{3}(\hat{\mathbf{i}} - \hat{\mathbf{j}} - \hat{\mathbf{k}})$ (d) $\frac{1}{3}(\hat{\mathbf{i}} + \hat{\mathbf{j}} - \hat{\mathbf{k}})$

Angular Velocity and its Relation with Linear Velocity

26 A body is rotating with angular velocity $\omega = (3\hat{i} - 4\hat{j} - \hat{k})$. The linear velocity of a point having position vector $\mathbf{r} = (5\hat{i} - 6\hat{j} + 6\hat{k})$ is **NCERT Pg. 105**

(a) $6\hat{i} + 2\hat{j} - 3\hat{k}$ (b) $-18\hat{i} - 23\hat{j} + 2\hat{k}$
(c) $-30\hat{i} - 23\hat{j} + 2\hat{k}$ (d) $6\hat{i} - 2\hat{j} + 8\hat{k}$

27 A circular plate rotating about its axis with angular speed ω is placed lightly (without any translational push) on a perfectly frictionless table. The radius of the disc is R. Let v_A, v_B and v_C be the magnitudes of linear velocities of the points A, B and C on the disc as shown below. Then, **NCERT Pg. 105**

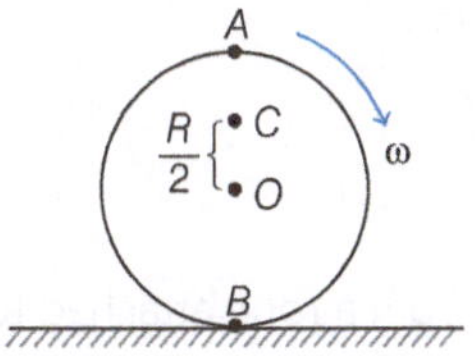

(a) $v_A > v_B > v_C$ (b) $v_A < v_B < v_C$
(c) $v_A = v_B > v_C$ (d) $v_A = v_B < v_C$

28 Point masses m_1 and m_2 are placed at the opposite ends of a rigid rod of length L and negligible mass. The rod is to be set rotating about an axis perpendicular to it. The position of point P on this rod through which the axis should pass, so that the work required to set the rod rotating with angular velocity ω_0 is minimum, is given by **NCERT Pg. 105**

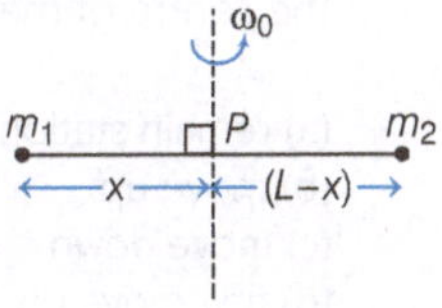

(a) $x = \dfrac{m_1 L}{m_1 + m_2}$ (b) $x = \dfrac{m_1}{m_2} L$
(c) $x = \dfrac{m_2}{m_1} L$ (d) $x = \dfrac{m_2 L}{m_1 + m_2}$

Torque and Angular Momentum

29 A point mass m is attached to a massless string whose other end is fixed at P as shown in figure. The mass is undergoing circular motion in XY-plane with centre O and constant angular speed ω. If the angular momentum of the system, about O and P be $\mathbf{L}_O$ and $\mathbf{L}_P$ respectively, then **NCERT Pg. 106**

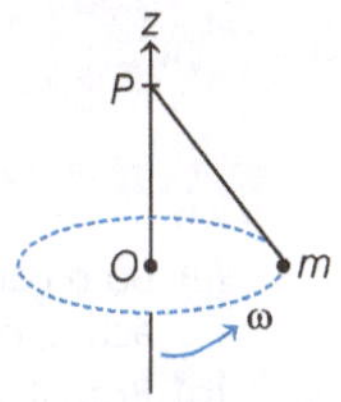

(a) $\mathbf{L}_O$ and $\mathbf{L}_P$ do not vary with time
(b) $\mathbf{L}_O$ varies with time while $\mathbf{L}_P$ remains constant
(c) $\mathbf{L}_O$ remains constant while $\mathbf{L}_P$ varies with time
(d) $\mathbf{L}_O$ and $\mathbf{L}_P$ both vary with time

30 Let $\mathbf{F}$ be the force acting on a particle having position vector $\mathbf{r}$ and τ be the torque of this force about the origin. Then, **NCERT Pg. 106**

(a) $\mathbf{r} \cdot \tau = 0$ and $\mathbf{F} \cdot \tau \neq 0$ (b) $\mathbf{r} \cdot \tau = 0$ and $\mathbf{F} \cdot \mathbf{r} = 0$
(c) $\mathbf{r} \cdot \tau \neq 0$ and $\mathbf{F} \cdot \tau \neq 0$ (d) $\mathbf{r} \cdot \tau = 0$ and $\mathbf{F} \cdot \tau = 0$

31 Torque of a force $\mathbf{F} = 2\hat{i} + 3\hat{j}$ N acting at a point (1m, 0, 3m) about an axis in XY-plane whose equation is $y = 3x$ is **NCERT Pg. 106**

(a) $\dfrac{9}{\sqrt{10}}$ Nm (b) $\dfrac{19}{\sqrt{10}}$ Nm (c) 6 Nm (d) 0

32 Figure shows a lamina in XY-plane. Two axes Z and Z' pass perpendicular to its plane. A force F acts in the plane of lamina at point P as shown. Which of the following statement is correct? (The point P is closer to Z'-axis than the Z-axis.) **NCERT Pg. 106**

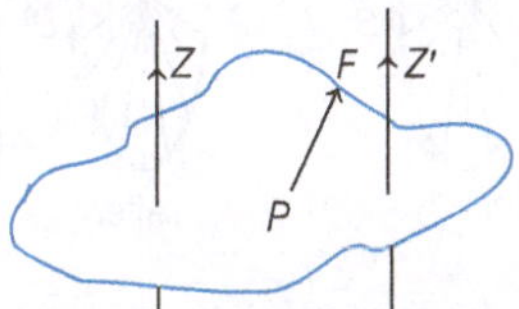

(a) Torque τ caused by $\mathbf{F}$ about Z-axis is along $-\hat{k}$.
(b) Torque τ' caused by $\mathbf{F}$ about Z'-axis is along $-\hat{k}$.
(c) Torque τ caused by $\mathbf{F}$ about Z-axis is less in magnitude than that about Z'-axis.
(d) Total torque is given by $\tau + \tau'$.

33 Figure shows two identical particles 1 and 2, each of mass m, moving in opposite directions with same speed $\mathbf{v}$ along parallel lines. At a particular instant, $\mathbf{r}_1$ and $\mathbf{r}_2$ are their respective position vectors drawn from point A which is in the plane of the parallel lines. Choose the correct option. **NCERT Pg. 107**

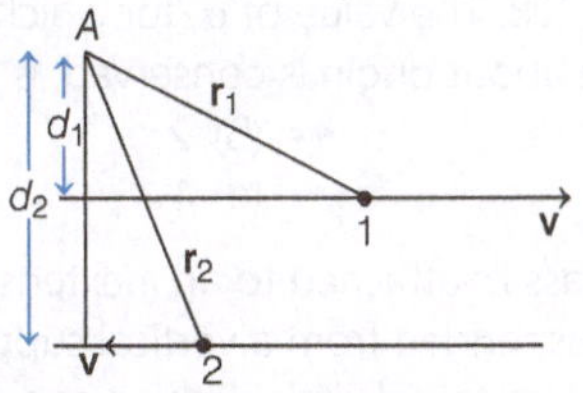

(a) Angular momentum L_1 of particle 1 about A is $m\mathbf{v}(d_1) \otimes$.
(b) Angular momentum L_2 of particle 2 about A is $m\mathbf{v}\mathbf{r}_2 \odot$.
(c) Total angular momentum of the system about A is $\mathbf{L} = m\mathbf{v}(\mathbf{r}_1 + \mathbf{r}_2) \odot$.
(d) Total angular momentum of the system about A is $\mathbf{L} = m\mathbf{v}(d_2 - d_1) \otimes$.

where, $\odot$ represents a unit vector coming out of the page and $\otimes$ represents a unit vector going into the page.

34 The net external torque on a system of particles about an axis is zero. Which of the following statement is incorrect? **NCERT Pg. 106**
(a) The forces may be acting radially from a point on the axis.
(b) The forces may be acting on the axis of rotation.
(c) The forces may be acting perpendicular to the axis of rotation.
(d) The torque caused by some forces may be equal and opposite to that caused by other forces.

35 A cycle rim is rotated over its axle in a vertical plane by holding ends of axle using 2-strings A and B.

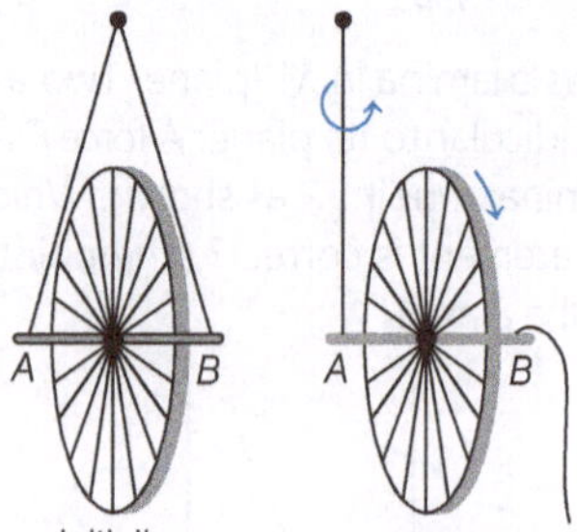

Such that the rim is vertical. If you leave one string, the rim will tilt. Now, keeping the rim in vertical position with both the strings in one hand, put the wheel in fast rotation around the axle with the other hand. Then, leave one string, say B, from your hand.
What will happen, if we leave string B? **NCERT Pg. 107**
(a) The rim will stop rotating
(b) The rim will rotate in a vertical plane and the plane of rotation will precesses about string A
(c) The rim will rotate in a horizontal plane
(d) String at A is twisted

36 A force $\mathbf{F} = \alpha\hat{\mathbf{i}} + 3\hat{\mathbf{j}} + 6\hat{\mathbf{k}}$ is acting at a point $\mathbf{r} = 2\hat{\mathbf{i}} - 6\hat{\mathbf{j}} - 12\hat{\mathbf{k}}$. The value of α, for which angular momentum about origin is conserved, is **NCERT Pg. 108**
(a) -1
(b) 2
(c) zero
(d) 1

37 A bob of mass m attached to an inextensible string of length l is suspended from a vertical support. The bob rotates in a horizontal circle with an angular speed ω rads^{-1} about the vertical support. About the point of suspension, **NCERT Pg. 108**
(a) angular momentum is conserved
(b) angular momentum changes in magnitude but not in direction
(c) angular momentum changes in direction but not in magnitude
(d) angular momentum changes both in direction and magnitude

Equilibrium of a Rigid Body

38 ABC is an equilateral triangle with O as its centre. $\mathbf{F}_1$, $\mathbf{F}_2$ and $\mathbf{F}_3$ represent three forces acting along the sides AB, BC and AC, respectively. If the total torque about O is zero, then the magnitude of $\mathbf{F}_3$ is **NCERT Pg. 109**

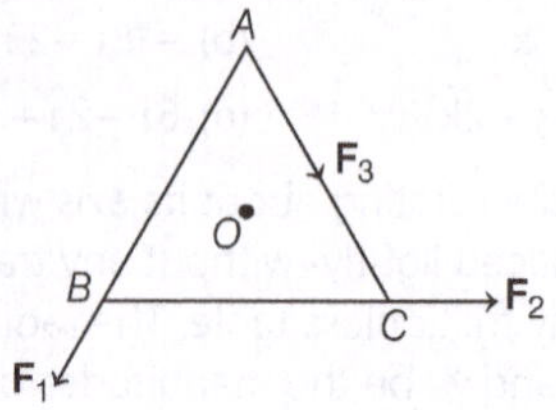

(a) $F_1 + F_2$
(b) $F_1 - F_2$
(c) $\frac{F_1 + F_2}{2}$
(d) $2(F_1 + F_2)$

39 A man hangs from a rope attached to a hot-air balloon. The mass of the man is greater than the mass of the balloon and its contents. The system is stationary in air. If the man now climbs up to the balloon using the rope, the centre of mass of the man plus balloon' system will **NCERT Pg. 109**
(a) remain stationary
(b) move up
(c) move down
(d) first move up and then return

40 A rigid rod of length L is acted upon by some forces. All forces labelled F have the same magnitude. **NCERT Pg. 110**
Which of the following statements is correct?

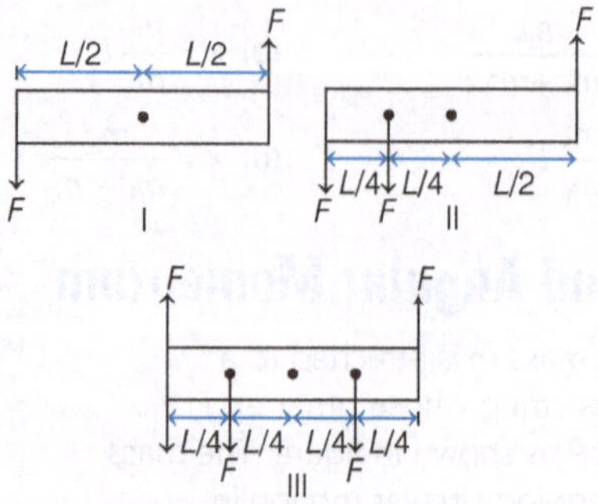

(a) Both I and II cases will have a non-zero net torque acting on the rod about its centre
(b) Both II and III cases will have a non-zero net torque acting on the rod about its centre
(c) Both I and III cases will have a non-zero net torque acting on the rod about its centre
(d) The net torque is zero in all cases

41 In the game of see-saw, what should be the displacement of boy B from right edge to keep the see-saw in equilibrium? ($M_1 = 40$ kg and $M_2 = 60$ kg) **NCERT Pg. 111**

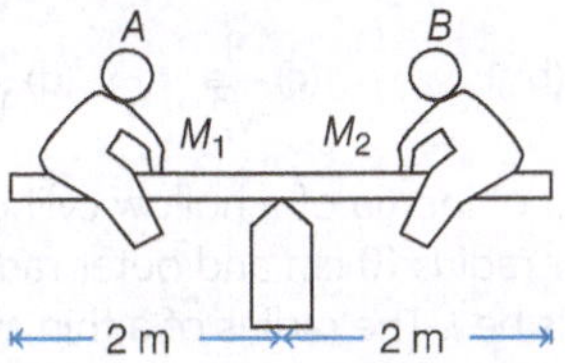

(a) $\frac{4}{3}$ m (b) 1 m (c) $\frac{2}{3}$ m (d) Zero

42 A rod of weight w is supported by two parallel knife edges A and B; and is in equilibrium in a horizontal position. The knives are at a distance d from each other. The centre of mass of the rod is at distance x from A. The normal reaction on A is **NCERT Pg. 111**

(a) $\frac{wx}{d}$ (b) $\frac{wd}{x}$ (c) $\frac{w(d-x)}{x}$ (d) $\frac{w(d-x)}{d}$

43 A uniform rod of length 1 m and mass 5.5 kg is supported on two knife-edges placed 10 cm from each end. A 45 N weight is suspended at 30 cm from one end. The reactions at the knife edges is **NCERT Pg. 111**

(a) 60 N, 40 N (b) 75 N, 25 N
(c) 61.2 N, 38.8 N (d) 55 N, 45 N

44 Two point objects of masses 1.5 g and 2.5 g respectively, are at a distance of 16 cm apart. The centre of gravity is at a distance x from the object of mass 1.5 g, where x is **NCERT Pg. 111**

(a) 10 cm (b) 6 cm (c) 13 cm (d) 3 cm

45 A metal bar 70 cm long and 4 kg in mass supported on two knife edges placed 10 cm from each end. A 6 kg weight is suspended at 30 cm from one end. What are the reactions at the knife edges? (Assume the bar to be of uniform cross-section and homogeneous) **NCERT Pg. 111**

(a) 45 N and 43 N (b) 50 N and 35 N
(c) 55 N and 43 N (d) 54 N and 30 N

46 Which of the following statements are correct? **NCERT Pg. 112**

A. Centre of mass of a body always coincides with the centre of gravity of the body.
B. Centre of mass of a body is the point at which the total gravitational torque on the body is zero.
C. A couple on a body produce both translational and rotational motion in a body.
D. Mechanical advantage greater than one means that small effort can be used to lift a large load.

(a) B and D (b) A and B (c) B and C (d) C and D

47 A 3 m long ladder weighing 20 kg leans on a frictionless wall. Its feet rest on the floor 1m from the wall as shown in figure. Find the reaction forces of the wall and the floor. **NCERT Pg. 113**

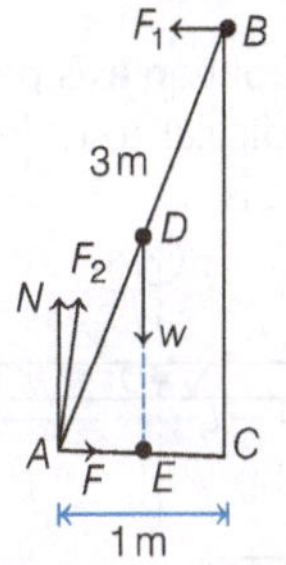

(a) 34.6 N and 199 N (b) 25 N and 175 N
(c) 30 N and 180 N (d) 35 N and 160 N

Moment of Inertia

48 Two masses are joined with a light rod and the system is rotating about the fixed axis as shown in the figure. The moment of inertia of the system about the axis is **NCERT Pg. 114**

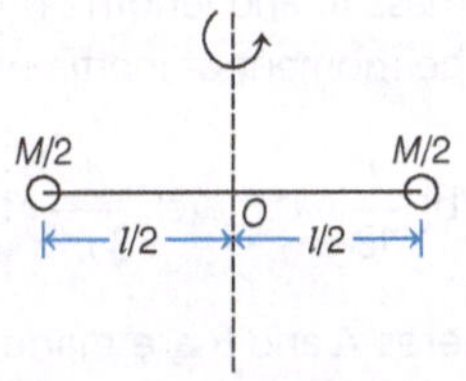

(a) $Ml^2/2$ (b) $Ml^2/4$ (c) Ml^2 (d) $Ml^2/6$

49 From a circular disc of radius R and mass $9M$, a small disc of mass M and radius $\frac{R}{3}$ is removed concentrically. The moment of inertia of the remaining disc about an axis perpendicular to the plane of the disc and passing through centre is **NCERT Pg. 114**

(a) $4MR^2$ (b) $\frac{40}{9}MR^2$ (c) $10MR^2$ (d) $\frac{37}{9}MR^2$

50 Two identical rods of mass M and length l are lying in a horizontal plane at an angle α. The moment of inertia of the system of two rods about an axis passing through O and perpendicular to the plane of the rods is **NCERT Pg. 114**

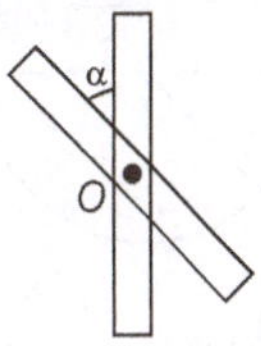

(a) $Ml^2/3$ (b) $Ml^2/12$
(c) $Ml^2/4$ (d) $Ml^2/6$

51 Find ratio of radius of gyration of a disc and ring of same radii at their tangential axis in plane. NCERT Pg. 115

(a) $\sqrt{\frac{5}{6}}$ (b) $\sqrt{\frac{5}{3}}$ (c) 1 (d) $\frac{2}{3}$

52 A rod is rotating about an axis passing through its centre and perpendicular to its length. The radius of gyration for the rod is NCERT Pg. 115

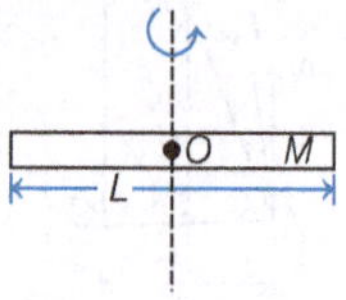

(a) $L/12$ (b) $L/\sqrt{12}$ (c) $L/6$ (d) $L/\sqrt{6}$

53 A disc of mass M and radius R is rotating about one of its diameter. The value of radius of gyration for the disc is NCERT Pg. 115

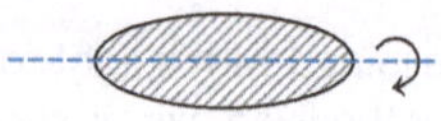

(a) $R/4$ (b) $R/2$ (c) $R/6$ (d) $2R/3$

54 A thin wire of mass M and length L is bent to form circular ring. The moment of inertia of this ring about its axis is NCERT Pg. 116

(a) $\frac{1}{4\pi^2}ML^2$ (b) $\frac{1}{12}ML^2$ (c) $\frac{1}{3\pi^2}ML^2$ (d) $\frac{1}{\pi^2}ML^2$

55 Two solid spheres A and B are made of metals of different densities ρ_A and ρ_B, respectively. If their masses are equal,then the ratio of their moments of inertia (I_B/I_A) about their respective diameters is NCERT Pg. 116

(a) $\left(\frac{\rho_B}{\rho_A}\right)^{2/3}$ (b) $\left(\frac{\rho_A}{\rho_B}\right)^{2/3}$ (c) $\frac{\rho_A}{\rho_B}$ (d) $\frac{\rho_B}{\rho_A}$

56 From a uniform circular disc of radius R and mass 9 M, a small disc of radius $\frac{R}{3}$ is removed as shown in the figure. The moment of inertia of the remaining disc about an axis perpendicular to the plane of the disc and passing through centre of disc is NCERT Pg. 116

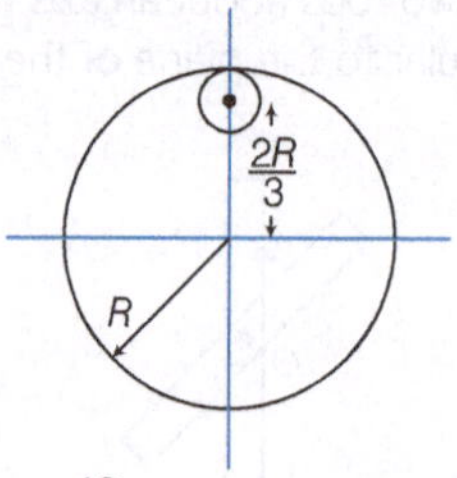

(a) $4MR^2$ (b) $\frac{40}{9}MR^2$ (c) $10MR^2$ (d) $\frac{37}{9}MR^2$

57 The moment of inertia of a uniform cylinder of length l and radius R about its perpendicular bisector is I. What is the ratio l/R such that the moment of inertia is minimum? NCERT Pg. 116

(a) $\frac{\sqrt{3}}{2}$ (b) 1 (c) $\frac{3}{\sqrt{2}}$ (d) $\sqrt{\frac{3}{2}}$

58 The moment of inertia of a hollow cylinder of length 30 cm (inner radius 10 cm and outer radius 20 cm) about its axis be I. The radius of a thin cylinder of the same mass such that its moment of inertia about its axis is also I, is NCERT Pg. 116

(a) 16 cm (b) 14 cm (c) 12 cm (d) 18 cm

59 Three identical spherical shells, each of mass m and radius r are placed as shown in figure. Consider an axis XX' which is touching two shells and passing through diameter of third shell. NCERT Pg. 116

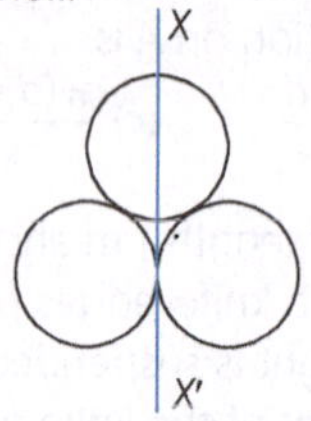

Moment of inertia of the system consisting of these three spherical shells about XX' axis is

(a) $4\,mr^2$ (b) $\frac{11}{5}mr^2$ (c) $3\,mr^2$ (d) $\frac{16}{5}mr^2$

60 A uniform rod kept vertically on the ground falls from rest. Its foot does not slip on the ground, then choose the incorrect statement. NCERT Pg. 116

(a) No part of the rod can have acceleration greater than g in any position.
(b) At any position of the rod, different points on it have different accelerations.
(c) Any particular point on the rod has different accelerations for different positions of the rod
(d) The maximum acceleration of any point on the rod, at any position, is 1.5 g.

Theorems of Perpendicular and Parallel Axes

61 The moment of inertia of a thin uniform rod of length L and mass M about an axis passing through a point at a distance of $L/3$ from one of its ends and perpendicular to the rod is Old NCERT Pg. 167

(a) $\frac{ML^2}{12}$ (b) $\frac{ML^2}{9}$
(c) $\frac{7ML^2}{48}$ (d) $\frac{ML^2}{48}$

62 Consider a uniform square plate of side a and mass m. The moment of inertia of this plate about an axis perpendicular to its plane and passing through one of its corner is **Old NCERT Pg. 167**

(a) $\frac{5}{6}ma^2$ (b) $\frac{1}{12}ma^2$ (c) $\frac{7}{12}ma^2$ (d) $\frac{2}{3}ma^2$

63 Seven identical circular planar discs, each of mass M and radius R are welded symmetrically as shown in the figure. The moment of inertia of the arrangement about the axis normal to the plane and passing through the point P is **Old NCERT Pg. 167**

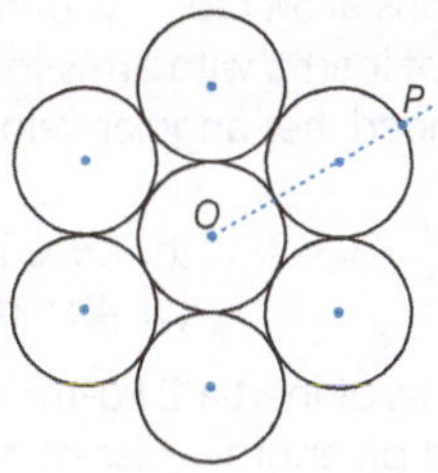

(a) $\frac{19}{2}MR^2$ (b) $\frac{55}{2}MR^2$ (c) $\frac{73}{2}MR^2$ (d) $\frac{181}{2}MR^2$

64 With reference to figure of a cube of edge a and mass m, choose the correct option. (O is the centre of the cube.) **Old NCERT Pg. 167**

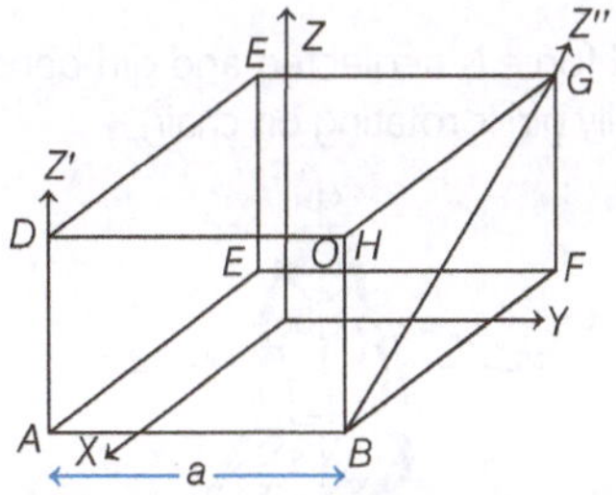

(a) The moment of inertia of cube about Z-axis is $I_Z = I_X + I_Y$

(b) The moment of inertia of cube about Z'-axis is $I_{Z'} = I_Z + \frac{ma^2}{2}$

(c) The moment of inertia of cube about Z''-axis is $= I_Z + \frac{ma^2}{2}$

(d) $I_X \neq I_Y$

Kinematics of Rotational Motion About a Fixed Axis

65 The wheel of a car is rotating at the rate of 1200 rpm. On pressing the accelerator for 10 s, it starts rotating at 4500 rpm. The angular acceleration of the wheel is **NCERT Pg. 117**

(a) 30 rads^{-2} (b) 1880 degs^{-2}
(c) 40 rads^{-2} (d) 1980 degs^{-2}

66 When a ceiling fan is switched OFF, its angular velocity falls to half while it makes 36 rotations. How many more rotations will it make before coming to rest? (Assume uniform angular retardation) **NCERT Pg. 117**

(a) 36 (b) 24
(c) 18 (d) 12

67 The angular speed of a motor wheel is increased from 1200 rpm to 3120 rpm in 16 s. (i) What is its angular acceleration, assuming the acceleration to be uniform? (ii) How many revolutions does the motor make during this time? **NCERT Pg. 117**

(a) 4π rads^{-2} and 200 (b) 2π rads^{-2} and 470
(c) 4π rads^{-2} and 576 (d) 3π rads^{-2} and 390

68 The angular velocity of a wheel increases from 100 rps to 300 rps in 10 s. The number of revolutions made during that time is **NCERT Pg. 117**

(a) 600 (b) 1500
(c) 1000 (d) 2000

Dynamics of Rotational Motion About a Fixed Axis

69 To maintain a rotor at a uniform angular speed of 100 rads^{-1}, an engine needs to transmit torque of 100 N-m. The power of the engine is **NCERT Pg. 119**

(a) 10 kW (b) 100 kW
(c) 10 MW (d) 100 MW

70 A cord of negligible mass is wound round the rim of a flywheel (disc) of mass 20 kg and radius 20 cm. A steady pull of 25 N is applied on the cord as shown in figure. The flywheel is mounted on a horizontal axle with frictionless bearings. **NCERT Pg. 119**

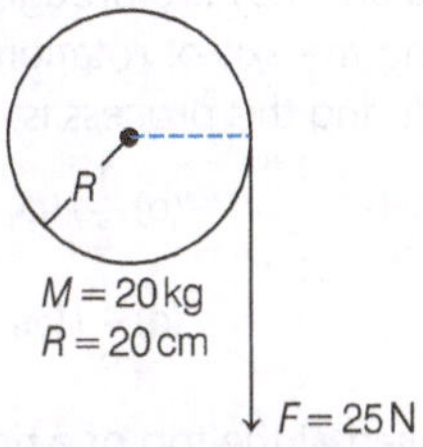

Compute the angular acceleration of the flywheel.

(a) 12.50 rad/s^2 (b) 6 rad/s^2
(c) 10 rad/s^2 (d) 8 rad/s^2

71 A flywheel of moment of inertia 0.4 kg-m^2 and radius 0.2 m is free to rotate about a central axis. If a string is wrapped around it and it is pulled with a force of 10N, then its angular velocity after 4 s will be **NCERT Pg. 119**

(a) 10 rads^{-1} (b) 5 rads^{-1}
(c) 20 rads^{-1} (d) 15 rads^{-1}

72 A hollow cylinder and solid sphere of mass M and radius r are rotating about an axis passing through its centre. If torques of equal magnitude are applied to them, then the ratio of angular accelerations produced is **NCERT Pg. 119**

(a) $\frac{2}{5}$ (b) $\frac{5}{2}$

(c) $\frac{5}{4}$ (d) $\frac{4}{5}$

73 A solid cylinder of mass 50 kg and radius 0.5 m is free to rotate about the horizontal axis. A massless string is wound round the cylinder with one end attached to it and other hanging freely. Tension in the string required to produce an angular acceleration of 2 revs^{-2} is **NCERT Pg. 119**

(a) 25 N (b) 50 N (c) 78.5 N (d) 157 N

74 A thin horizontal circular disc is rotating about a vertical axis passing through its centre. An insect is at rest at a point near the rim of disc. The insect now moves along a diameter of the disc to reach its other end. During the journey of the insect, the angular speed of the disc **NCERT Pg. 119**

(a) continuously decreases

(b) continuously increases

(c) first increases and then decreases

(d) remains unchanged

75 A flywheel of moment of inertia 10 kg m^2 is rotating with angular velocity 50 rad/s. It is brought to rest in 10 s. The required average power is **NCERT Pg. 119**

(a) 1250 W (b) 625 W (c) 2500 W (d) 500 W

76 Two discs of same moment of inertia rotating about their regular axis passing through centre and perpendicular to the plane of disc with angular velocities ω_1 and ω_2. They are brought into contact face to face coinciding the axis of rotation.The expression for loss of energy during this process is **NCERT Pg. 119**

(a) $\frac{1}{2}I(\omega_1+\omega_2)^2$ (b) $\frac{1}{4}I(\omega_1-\omega_2)^2$

(c) $I(\omega_1-\omega_2)^2$ (d) $\frac{1}{8}I(\omega_1-\omega_2)^2$

77 A force F is applied at the top of a ring of mass M and radius R placed on a rough horizontal surface as shown in figure. Friction is sufficient to prevent slipping. The frictional force acting on the ring is **NCERT Pg. 119**

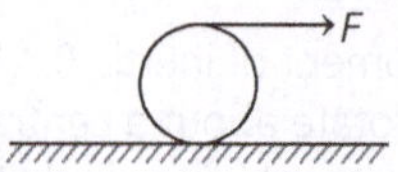

(a) $\frac{F}{2}$ towards right (b) $\frac{F}{3}$ towards left

(c) $\frac{2F}{3}$ towards right (d) zero

78 A wheel having moment of inertia 2 kg m^2 about its vertical axis. Rotates at the rate of 60 rpm about this axis. The torque which can stop the wheel's rotation in one minute would be **NCERT Pg. 119**

(a) $\frac{2\pi}{15}$ N-m (b) $\frac{\pi}{12}$ N-m

(c) $\frac{\pi}{15}$ N-m (d) $\frac{\pi}{18}$ N-m

Angular Momentum in case of Rotation about a Fixed Axis

79 An ice skater spins at 3π rads^{-1} with her arms extended. If her moment of inertia with arms folded is 75% of that with arms extended, her angular velocity when she folds her arms is **NCERT Pg. 122**

(a) π rad s^{-1} (b) 2π rad s^{-1}

(c) 3π rad s^{-1} (d) 4π rad s^{-1}

80 A disc of moment of inertia 2 kg-m^2 revolving with 8 rad/s is placed on another disc of moment of inertia 4 kg-m^2 revolving with 4 rad/s. What is the angular frequency of composite disc? **NCERT Pg. 122**

(a) 4 rad/s (b) $\frac{3}{16}$ rad/s

(c) $\frac{16}{3}$ rad/s (d) $\frac{16}{5}$ rad/s

81 If frictional force is neglected and girl bends her hand, then (initially girl is rotating on chair) **NCERT Pg. 122**

(a) I_{girl} will reduce (b) I_{girl} will increase

(c) ω_{girl} will reduce (d) ω_{girl} remains constant

82 When acrobat bends his body (assume no external torque) **NCERT Pg. 122**

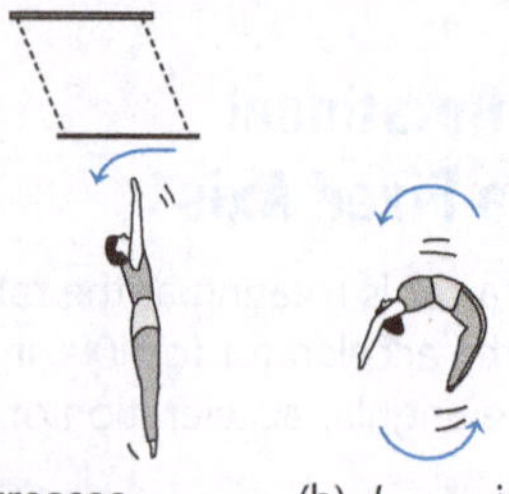

(a) $I_{acrobat}$ decreases (b) $I_{acrobat}$ increases

(c) $\omega_{acrobat}$ decrease (d) $\omega_{acrobat}$ remains constant

83 A dancer spins about himself with an angular speed ω With his arms extended. When he draws his hands in, his moment of inertia reduces by 40%, then his new angular velocity would be NCERT Pg. 122

(a) $\frac{3\omega}{5}$ (b) $\frac{4\omega}{5}$

(c) $\frac{5\omega}{4}$ (d) $\frac{5\omega}{3}$

84 A man standing on a platform holds weights in his outstretched arms. The system rotates freely about a central vertical axis. If he now draws the weights inwards close to his body, then choose the incorrect statement. NCERT Pg. 122

(a) The angular velocity of the system will increase.

(b) The angular momentum of the system will decrease.

(c) The kinetic energy of the system will increase.

(d) He will have to expand some energy to draw the weights.

Assertion and Reason Questions

Direction (Q. Nos. 1-10) *In the following questions, a statement of Assertion is followed by a corresponding statement of Reason. Of the following statements, choose the correct one.*

(a) Both Assertion and Reason are correct and Reason is the correct explanation of Assertion.

(b) Both Assertion and Reason are correct but Reason is not the correct explanation of Assertion.

(c) Assertion is correct but Reason is incorrect.

(d) Assertion is incorrect but Reason is correct.

1 Assertion The centre of mass of a system of particles at rest remains at rest.

Reason The external force acting on the system of particles is zero. NCERT Pg. 99

2 Assertion The motion of the centre of mass describes the translational part of the motion.

Reason Translational motion always means straight line motion. NCERT Pg. 99

3 Assertion The centre of mass of a system of particles under the influence of a conservative force moves along the same path as a single particle having the same mass and the same initial conditions.

Reason The total energy of an isolated system of particles remains constant. NCERT Pg. 100

4 Assertion The angular velocity of a rigid body in motion is defined for the whole body.

Reason All points on a rigid body performing pure rotational motion are having same angular velocity. NCERT Pg. 103

5 Assertion A ladder is more apt to slip. When you are high up on it than when you just begin to climb.

Reason At the high up on a ladder, the torque is large and on climbing up the torque is small. NCERT Pg. 105

6 Assertion For a system of particles under central force field, the total angular momentum is conserved.

Reason The torque acting on such a system is zero. NCERT Pg. 105

7 Assertion The total momentum of an isolated system of particles remains constant.

Reason There is no external force acting on the system of particles. NCERT Pg. 107

8 Assertion The torque acting on a rigid body is equal to the rate of change of its angular momentum.

Reason Torque is a measure of the rotational force acting on a body. NCERT Pg. 107

9 Assertion Due to global warming, duration of day is decreasing.

Reason Angular mometum of earth is a constant quantity. NCERT Pg. 108

10 Assertion The size and the shape of the rigid body remains unaffected under the effect of external force.

Reason The distance between two particles remains constant in a rigid body. NCERT Pg. 109

Statement Based Questions

Direction (Q. Nos. 1-8) *In the following questions, Statement I and Statement II are given. Read these statements and choose the most appropriate answer from the options given below.*

(a) Both Statement I and Statement II are incorrect.
(b) Statement I is correct but Statement II is incorrect.
(c) Statement I is incorrect but Statement II is correct.
(d) Both Statement I and Statement II are correct.

1 Statement I The speed of whirlwind in a tornado is alarmingly high.
Statement II If no external torque acts on a body, its angular velocity conserved. **NCERT Pg. 103**

2 Statement I In rolling, all points of a rigid body have same linear velocity.
Statement II The rotational motion does not affect the linear velocity. **NCERT Pg. 103**

3 Statement I For a general rotational motion, angular momentum **L** and angular velocity ω need not be parallel.
Statement II For a general translational motion, momentum **p** and velocity **v** are always perpendicular. **NCERT Pg. 107**

4 Statement I If the total force on the body is zero, then the total linear momentum of the body does not change with time.
Statement II If the total torque on the rigid body is zero, the total angular momentum of the body does not change with time. **NCERT Pg. 109**

5 Statement I During acceleration, volume of rigid body remain constant.
Statement II Under action of force, shape of rigid body can change easily. **NCERT Pg. 109**

6 Statement I For lever shown, the ratio of $\frac{F_1}{F_2}$ is equal to mechanical advantage, i.e. $MA = \frac{F_1}{F_2} = \frac{d_2}{d_1}$.

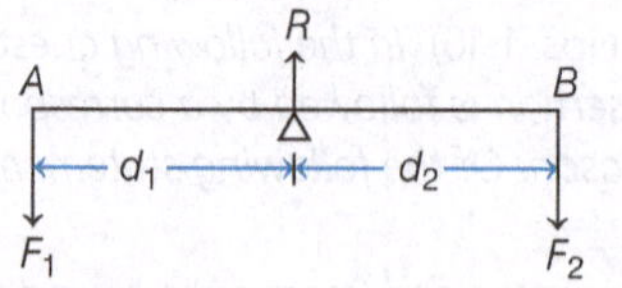

Statement II In a lever, at equilibrium, load arm × effort arm = load × effort. **NCERT Pg. 110**

7 Statement I Moment of force is a vector quantity.
Statement II Angular momentum may not be parallel to angular velocity. **NCERT Pg. 114**

8 Statement I Angular momentum of a particle moving in a straight line is always constant with respect to fixed point.
Statement II Moment of inertia of a body remains same irrespective of position of axis of rotation. **NCERT Pg. 114**

Matching Type Questions

1 Match the Column I (given example) with Column II (type of motion). Choose the correct answer from the options given below. **NCERT Pg. 92**

	Column I	Column II
A.	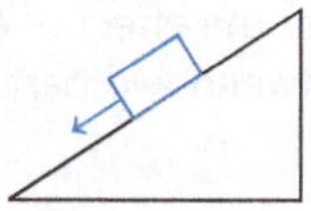 A block over an inclined plane	1. Rolling
B.	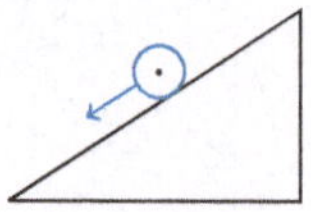 A cylinder over an inclined plane	2. Translation
C.	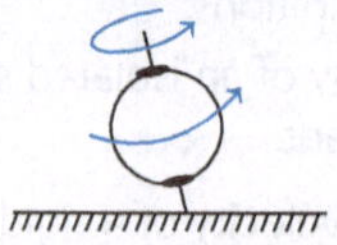 A spinning top	3. Rotation
D.	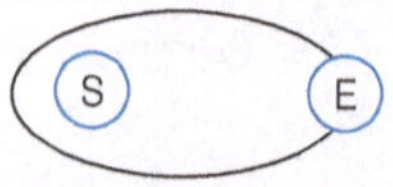 Earth-Sun system	4. Precession

Codes

	A	B	C	D
(a)	2	1	4	3
(b)	2	3	1	4
(c)	3	1	2	4
(d)	3	1	2	4

2 Match the Column I (rotation of different bodies) with Column II (their moment of inertia). Choose the correct answer from the options given below. **NCERT Pg. 114**

Column I	Column II
A. Thin circular ring of radius R having axis perpendicular to the plane and passing through centre	1. $MR^2/2$
B. Thin circular ring of radius R having axis passing through its diameter	2. $ML^2/12$
C. Thin rod of length L having axis perpendicular to the rod and passing through mid-point	3. MR^2
D. Circular disc of radius R having axis passing through its diameter	4. $MR^2/4$

Codes

	A	B	C	D		A	B	C	D
(a)	3	2	2	1	(b)	2	3	1	2
(c)	3	1	2	1	(d)	3	1	2	4

3 Match the Column I (rotation of different bodies) with Column II (their moment of inertia). Choose the correct answer from the options given below. **NCERT Pg. 114**

Column I	Column II
A. Circular disc of radius R about an axis passing through the diameter	1. $MR^2/4$
B. Hollow cylinder of radius R about an axis passing through the axis of cylinder	2. MR^2
C. Solid cylinder of radius R about an axis passing through the axis of cylinder.	3. $MR^2/2$
D. Solid sphere of radius R about an axis passing through its diameter.	4. $(2/5)\ MR^2$

Codes

	A	B	C	D
(a)	4	3	2	1
(b)	1	2	3	4
(c)	1	3	2	4
(d)	2	1	3	4

Numerical Type Questions

1 Three identical spheres each of mass M are placed at the corner of a right angle triangle with mutually perpendicular sides equal to 6 m each. Take point of intersection of position vector of mutually perpendicular sides as origin the magnitude of position vector of centre of mass of system will be $\sqrt{x}$. The value of x is .... **NCERT Pg. 92**

2 A particle of mass $m = 4$ kg is projected with initial speed of 10 m/s at angle of 45° with the horizontal. The torque of the weight of the particle about the point of projection when the particle is at the highest point is $-N\hat{k}$. The value of N is .... (Take, $g = 10\ m/s^2$) **NCERT Pg. 105**

3 A tube of length L is filled completely with an incompressible liquid of mass m and closed at both ends. When tube is rotated in a horizontal plane about one of its ends with angular velocity ω **NCERT Pg. 105**

The force exerted by the liquid at the other end is $\frac{mL\omega^2}{n}$, then the value of n is ....

4 A circular disc of radius R and thickness $\frac{R}{6}$ has moment of inertia I about an axis passing through its centre and perpendicular to its plane. It is melted and recasted into a solid sphere. The moment of inertia of the sphere about its diameter is $\frac{I}{n}$. The value of n is .... **NCERT Pg. 114**

5 Radius of gyration of a body about an axis at a distance 3 cm from its centre of mass is 5 cm. Its radius of gyration about a parallel axis passing through its centre of mass is x cm, then the value of x is .... **NCERT Pg. 114**

6 A rectangular box of length 0.03 m is held horizontally with one of its sides on the edge of a platform of height 20 m. When released, it slips off the table in time $t = 0.01$ s. The angle of rotation (in rad) when it hits the ground will be .... **NCERT Pg. 116**

7 A bullet of mass 6 g and speed 250 m/s is fired into a door and get embedded exactly at the centre of a door. The door is 120 cm wide and weight 15 kg. It is hinged at one end and rotate about a vertical axis, the angular speed of door just after the bullet embeds into it is 15×10^{-x} rad/s, then the value of x is .... **NCERT Pg. 121**

8 A child stands at the centre of a turn table with his two arms outstretched. The turn table is set rotating with an angular speed of 22 rev/min. If he folds his hands back and reduces his moment of inertia to 2/3 times the initial value, then angular speed of child is ...... rad/s. **NCERT Pg. 122**

NCERT Exemplar Questions

1 For which one of the following does the centre of mass lie outside the body?

(a) A pencil (b) A shot put
(c) A dice (d) A bangle

2 Which of the following points is the likely position of the centre of mass of the system shown in figure?

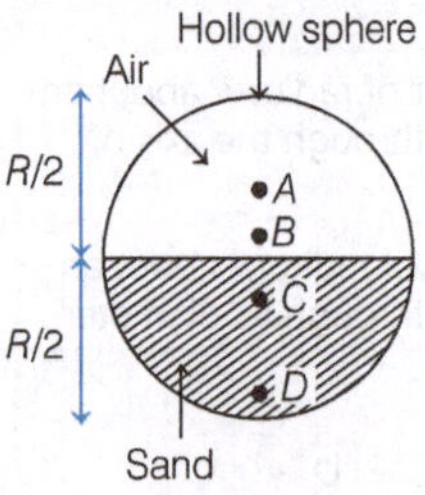

(a) A (b) B (c) C (d) D

3 A particle of mass m is moving in YZ-plane with a uniform velocity v with its trajectory running parallel to positive Y-axis and intersecting Z-axis at $z = a$ in figure. The change in its angular momentum about the origin as it bounces elastically from a wall at y constant is

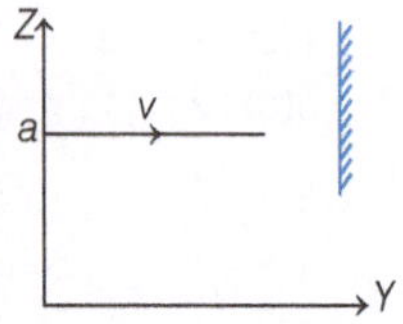

(a) $mva\,\hat{\mathbf{e}}_x$ (b) $2\,mva\,\hat{\mathbf{e}}_x$ (c) $ymv\,\hat{\mathbf{e}}_x$ (d) $2\,ymv\,\hat{\mathbf{e}}_x$

4 When a disc rotates with uniform angular velocity, which of the following statement is not correct?

(a) The sense of rotation remains same.
(b) The orientation of the axis of rotation remains same.
(c) The speed of rotation is non-zero and remains same.
(d) The angular acceleration is non-zero and remains same.

5 A uniform square plate has a small piece Q of an irregular shape removed and glued to the centre of the plate leaving a hole behind as shown in figure below. The moment of inertia about the Z-axis is

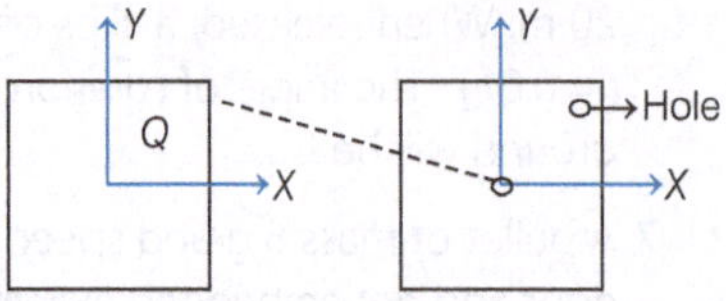

(a) increases (b) decreases
(c) the same
(d) changed in unpredicted manner

6 The density of a non-uniform rod of length 1m is given by $\rho(x) = a(1 + bx^2)$, where a and b are constants and $0 \le x \le 1$. The centre of mass of the rod will be at

(a) $\frac{3(2+b)}{4(3+b)}$ (b) $\frac{4(2+b)}{3(3+b)}$ (c) $\frac{3(3+b)}{4(2+b)}$ (d) $\frac{4(3+b)}{3(2+b)}$

7 A merry-go-round, made of a ring like platform of radius R and mass M, is revolving with angular speed ω. A person of mass M is standing on it. At one instant, the person jumps off the plat form, radially away from the centre of the platform (as seen from the platform). The speed of the platform afterwards is

(a) 2ω (b) ω (c) $\frac{\omega}{2}$ (d) 0

8 The variation of angular position θ of a point on a rotating rigid body with time t is shown in figure.

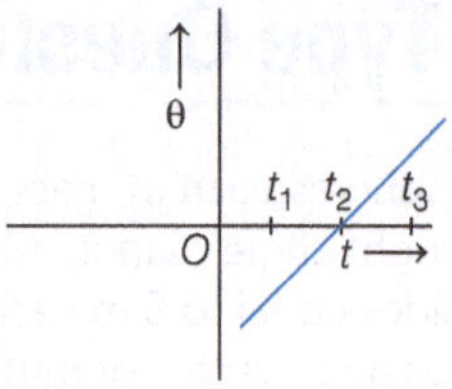

In which direction, the body is rotating?

(a) Clockwise
(b) Anti-clockwise
(c) May be clockwise or anti-clockwise
(d) None of the above

9 A disc of radius R is rotating with an angular speed ω_0 about a horizontal axis. It is placed on a horizontal table. The coefficient of kinetic friction is μ_k. What was the velocity of its centre of mass before being brought in contact with the table?

(a) $\omega_0 R$ (b) Zero (c) $\frac{\omega_0 R}{2}$ (d) $2\omega_0 R$

Past Exams Questions

NEET

1 The moment of inertia of a thin rod about an axis passing through its mid-point and perpendicular to the rod is 2400 g cm^2. The length of the 400 g rod is nearly

NCERT Pg. 114, NEET 2024

(a) 8.5 cm (b) 17.5 cm (c) 20.7 cm (d) 72.0 cm

2 Two objects of mass 10 kg and 20 kg, respectively are connected to the two ends of a rigid rod of length 10 m with negligible mass. The distance of the centre of mass of the system from the 10 kg mass is

NCERT Pg. 97, NEET 2022

(a) $\frac{20}{3}$ m (b) 10 m (c) 5 m (d) $\frac{10}{3}$ m

3 The ratio of the radius of gyration of a thin uniform disc about an axis passing through its centre and normal to its plane to the radius of gyration of the disc about its diameter is **NCERT Pg. 115, NEET 2022**

(a) $\sqrt{2}:1$ (b) $4:1$
(c) $1:\sqrt{2}$ (d) $2:1$

4 The angular speed of a fly wheel moving with uniform angular acceleration changes from 1200 rpm to 3120 rpm in 16 s. The angular acceleration in rad/s^2 is **NCERT Pg. 117, NEET 2022**

(a) 4π (b) 12π
(c) 104π (d) 2π

5 From a circular ring of mass M and radius R, an arc corresponding to a 90° sector is removed. The moment of inertia of the remaining part of the ring about an axis passing through the centre of the ring and perpendicular to the plane of the ring is K times MR^2. Then, the value of K is **NCERT Pg. 115, NEET 2021**

(a) $\frac{3}{4}$ (b) $\frac{7}{8}$
(c) $\frac{1}{4}$ (d) $\frac{1}{8}$

6 The angular speed of the wheel of a vehicle is increased from 360 rpm to 1200 rpm in 14 s. Its angular acceleration is **NCERT Pg. 117, NEET (Oct.)2020**

(a) 2π rad/s^2 (b) 28π rad/s^2
(c) 120π rad/s^2 (d) 1 rad/s^2

7 A particle starting from rest, moves in a circle of radius r. It attains a velocity of v_0 m/s in the nth round. Its angular acceleration will be **NCERT Pg. 117, NEET 2019**

(a) $\frac{v_0}{n}$ rad/s^2 (b) $\frac{v_0^2}{2\pi n r^2}$ rad/s^2
(c) $\frac{v_0^2}{4\pi n r^2}$ rad/s^2 (d) $\frac{v_0^2}{4\pi n r}$ rad/s^2

8 The moment of the force, $\mathbf{F} = (4\hat{\mathbf{i}} + 5\hat{\mathbf{j}} - 6\hat{\mathbf{k}})$ N at $(2, 0, -3)$, about the point $(2, -2, -2)$, is given by **NCERT Pg. 106, NEET 2018**

(a) $-7\hat{\mathbf{i}} - 8\hat{\mathbf{j}} - 4\hat{\mathbf{k}}$ (b) $-4\hat{\mathbf{i}} - \hat{\mathbf{j}} - 8\hat{\mathbf{k}}$
(c) $-8\hat{\mathbf{i}} - 4\hat{\mathbf{j}} - 7\hat{\mathbf{k}}$ (d) $-7\hat{\mathbf{i}} - 4\hat{\mathbf{j}} - 8\hat{\mathbf{k}}$

JEE Main

9 A thin circular disc of mas M and radius R is rotating in a horizontal plane about an axis passing through its centre and perpendicular to its plane with angular velocity ω. If another disc of same dimensions but of mass $\frac{M}{2}$ is placed gently on the first disc coaxially, then the new angular velocity of the system is **NCERT Pg. 105, JEE Main 2024**

(a) $\frac{4}{5}\omega$ (b) $\frac{3}{2}\omega$ (c) $\frac{2}{3}\omega$ (d) $\frac{5}{4}\omega$

10 Ratio of radius of gyration of a hollow sphere to that of a solid cylinder of equal mass, for moment of inertia about their diameter axis AB as shown in figure is $\sqrt{\frac{8}{x}}$.

The value of x is **NCERT Pg. 115, JEE Main 2024**

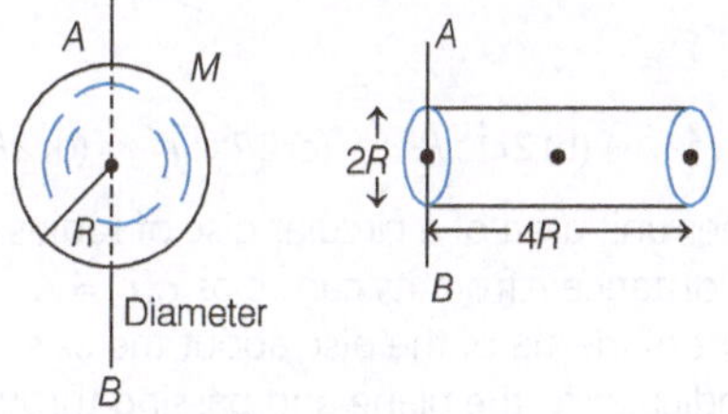

(a) 51 (b) 34 (c) 67 (d) 17

11 A disc of radius R and mass M is rolling horizontally without slipping with speed v. It then moves up an inclined smooth surface as shown in figure. The maximum height that the disc can go up the incline is

NCERT Pg. 93, JEE Main 2024

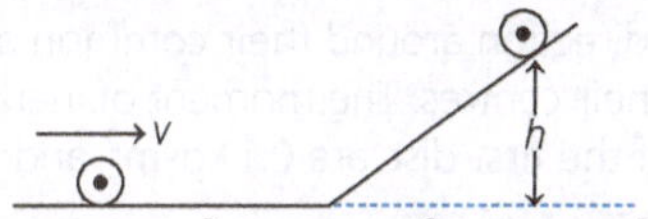

(a) $\frac{2}{3}\frac{v^2}{g}$ (b) $\frac{3}{4}\frac{v^2}{g}$ (c) $\frac{1}{2}\frac{v^2}{g}$ (d) $\frac{v^2}{g}$

12 A triangular plate is shown below. A force $\mathbf{F} = 4\hat{\mathbf{i}} - 3\hat{\mathbf{j}}$ is applied at point P. The torque at points O and Q with respect to point P are **NCERT Pg. 106, JEE Main 2021**

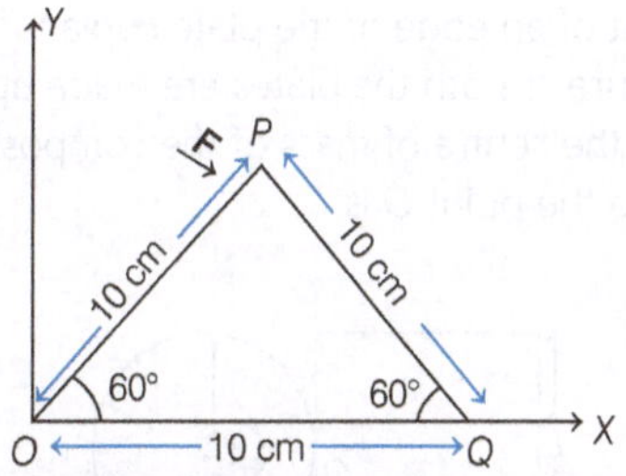

(a) $-15 - 20\sqrt{3}$, $15 - 20\sqrt{3}$
(b) $15 + 20\sqrt{3}$, $15 - 20\sqrt{3}$
(c) $15 - 20\sqrt{3}$, $15 + 20\sqrt{3}$
(d) $-15 + 20\sqrt{3}$, $15 + 20\sqrt{3}$

13 The figure shows two solid discs with radius R and r, respectively. If mass per unit area is same for both, what is the ratio of MI of bigger disc around axis AB (which is perpendicular to the plane of the disc and passing through its centre) of MI of smaller disc around one of its diameters lying on its plane?

Given, M is the mass of the larger disc. (MI stands for moment of inertia) **NCERT Pg. 115, JEE Main 2021**

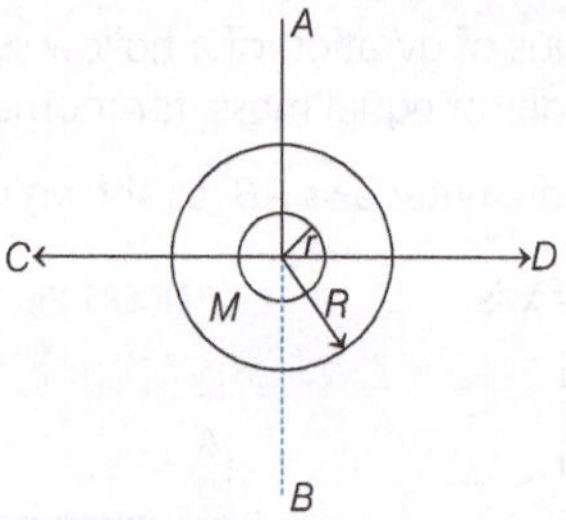

(a) $R^2 : r^2$ (b) $2r^4 : R^4$ (c) $2R^2 : r^2$ (d) $2R^4 : r^4$

14 Mass per unit area of a circular disc of radius a depends on the distance r from its centre as $\sigma(r) = A + Br$. The moment of inertia of the disc about the axis, perpendicular to the plane and passing through its centre is **NCERT Pg. 115, JEE Main 2020**

(a) $2\pi a^4 \left(\frac{A}{4} + \frac{B}{5}\right)$ (b) $2\pi a^4 \left(\frac{aA}{4} + \frac{B}{5}\right)$

(c) $\pi a^4 \left(\frac{A}{4} + \frac{aB}{5}\right)$ (d) $2\pi a^4 \left(\frac{A}{4} + \frac{aB}{5}\right)$

15 Two uniform circular discs are rotating independently in the same direction around their common axis passing through their centres. The moment of inertia and angular velocity of the first disc are 0.1 kg-m^2 and 10 rad s^{-1} respectively, while those for the second one are 0.2 kg-m^2 and 5 rad s^{-1}, respectively. At some instant they get stuck together and start rotating as a single system about their common axis with some angular speed. The kinetic energy of the combined system is **NCERT Pg. 122, JEE Main 2020**

(a) $\frac{10}{3}$ J (b) $\frac{20}{3}$ J

(c) $\frac{5}{3}$ J (d) $\frac{2}{3}$ J

16 Four particles A, B, C and D with masses $m_A = m$, $m_B = 2m$, $m_C = 3m$ and $m_D = 4m$ are at the corners of a square. They have accelerations of equal magnitude with directions as shown. The acceleration of the centre of mass of the particles (in ms^{-2}) is **NCERT Pg. 99, JEE Main 2019**

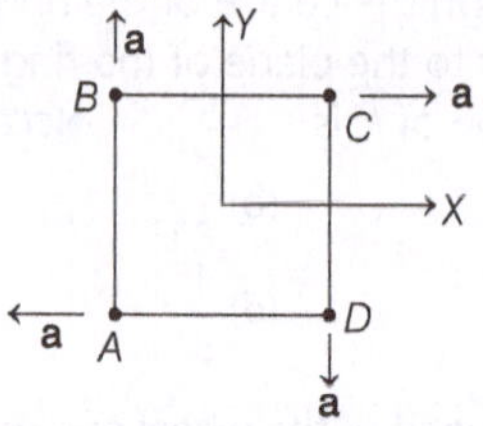

(a) $\frac{a}{5}(\hat{i} - \hat{j})$ (b) $a(\hat{i} - \hat{j})$ (c) zero (d) $\frac{a}{5}(\hat{i} + \hat{j})$

Skill Boosters

1 A square plate of edge length L and a circular disc of diameter L are placed touching each other at the mid-point of an edge of the plate coplanarly as shown in the figure. If both the plates are made up of same material, the centre of mass of the composite plate relative to the point O is

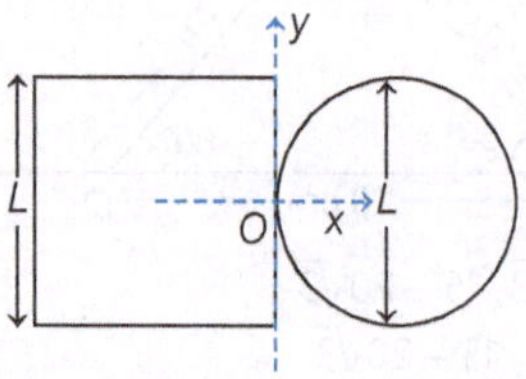

(a) $\left(\frac{3\pi + 4}{\pi - 4}\right) L$ along X-axis. (b) $\left(\frac{\pi - 4}{\pi + 4}\right) L$ along X-axis.

(c) $\left(\frac{3\pi + 4}{\pi - 4}\right) \frac{L}{2}$ along X-axis. (d) $\left(\frac{\pi - 4}{\pi + 4}\right) \frac{L}{2}$ along X-axis.

2 The length AB is cut in the form of an arc of a ring of mass m that makes an angle 45° at its centre of curvature O. If this arc is allowed to rotate in the XY-plane about Z-axis passing through the centre of curvature, then the moment of inertia of the circular arc AB about Z-axis is

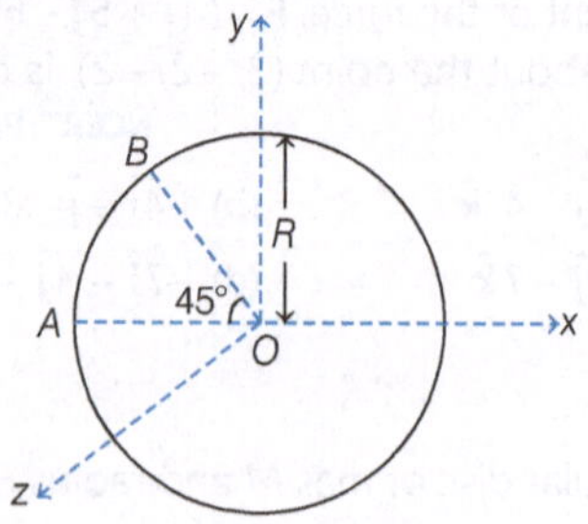

(a) $\frac{1}{2} mR^2$ (b) $\frac{2}{3} mR^2$

(c) $\frac{1}{8} mR^2$ (d) $\frac{1}{6} mR^2$

3 A tricycle weighing 50 kg has two large rear wheels separated by 1 m apart and a small front wheel symmetric to the two large wheels which are 1.5 m behind the front wheel. If the centre of gravity of the tricycle is at a horizontal distance of 30 cm behind the front wheel and the rider whose weight is 70 kg be 10 cm behind the front wheel as shown in the figure, where r is considered for rider and t is for the tricycle, the thrust on each rear wheel is

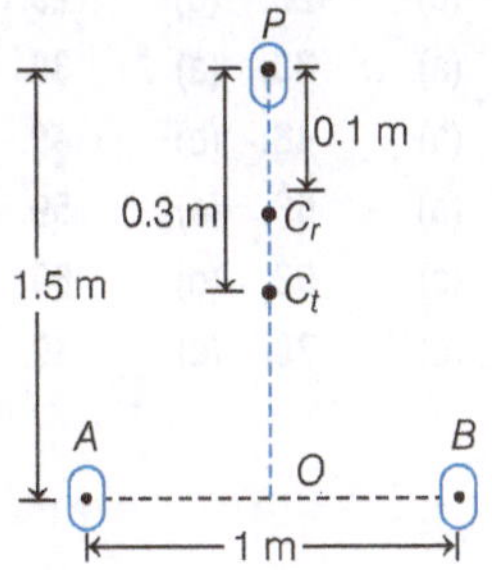

(a) 348 N (b) 526 N
(c) 214 N (d) 386 N

4 A circular platform is mounted on a vertical frictionless axle. Its radius is $r = 2$ m and its moment of inertia $I = 200$ kg-m^2. It is initially at rest. A 70 kg man stands on the edge of the platform and begins to walk along the edge at speed $v_0 = 1.0\text{ms}^{-1}$ relative to the ground. The angular velocity of the platform is 0.7 rad s^{-1}. When the man has walked once around the platform, so that he is at his original position on it, his angular displacement relative to ground is

(a) $\frac{6}{5}\pi$ (b) $\frac{5}{6}\pi$ (c) $\frac{4}{5}\pi$ (d) $\frac{5}{4}\pi$

5 A boy of mass $m = 50$ kg stands at the end A of a flat plank AB of wood of mass $M = 100$ kg and length $l = 10$ m floating in the still water. The end B of the plank is at a distance of 30 m from the seaboard as shown in the given figure. The boy walks a distance of 6 m on the plank towards the seaboard.

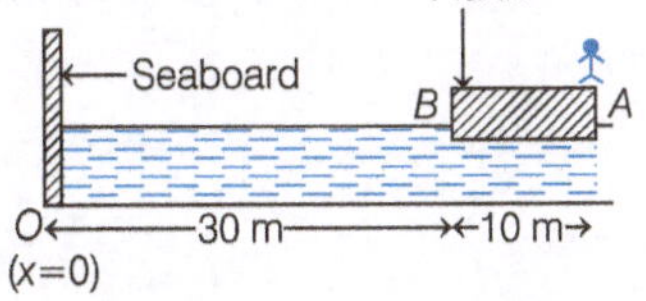

Distance between the boy and seaboard is (Neglect viscosity of water)

(a) 28 m (b) 32 m (c) 36 m (d) 30 m

6 A boy of mass $m = 50$ kg is standing on a stationary long plank of mass $M = 250$ kg floating on still water in a lake. He starts running with a velocity $v = 6\text{ms}^{-1}$ relative to the plank.

The velocity of the boy relative to a stationary observer on the bank of the lake is

(a) 3.5 m/s (b) 5.0 m/s (c) 8.5 m/s (d) 6.0 m/s

7 A body of mass m and length l is whirled in a horizontal circle with a uniform speed v. The tension in the string is T. The length of the string is gradually reduced such that the angular momentum of the body about the centre of the circle remains constant. At the instant of time when the length of the string is $\frac{l}{2}$, the tension in the string will be

(a) $3T$ (b) $\frac{T}{2}$ (c) $\frac{3}{2}T$ (d) $8T$

8 A uniform rod AB of mass $M = 0.4$ kg and length $L = 1$ m lies on a horizontal frictionless table with its end A pivoted to the table. A ball of mass $m = 0.2$ kg moving along the surface of the table with velocity $u = 5$m/s perpendicular to the rod collides with the free end B of the rod. If the collision is elastic, the angular velocity of the rod after collision is

(a) 4.0 rad /s (b) 4.5 rad / s
(c) 5.0 rad /s (d) 6.0 rad / s

9 A light weight boy holds two heavy dumb-bells of equal mass with outstretched arms while standing on a turn-table which is rotating at an angular frequency of 2 rad/s when the dumb-bells are at a distance 80 cm from the axis of rotation. The boy suddenly pulls the dumb-bells towards his chest until they are at a distance 40 cm from the axis of rotation. The new angular frequency of rotation ω_2 of the turn-table will be equal to

(a) 4 rad/s (b) 8 rad/s (c) 16 rad/s (d) 12 rad/s

10 A block of mass $m_1 = 2$ kg is attached to a block $m_2 = 4$ kg by means of a light string going over a pulley which is a solid disc of mass $M = 8$ kg and radius $R = 10$ cm. Initially the block of mass m_1 is on the floor and the block of mass m_2 is held at a height $h = 1$ m above the floor. The block of mass m_2 is now released. The speed of this block just before it hits the floor is

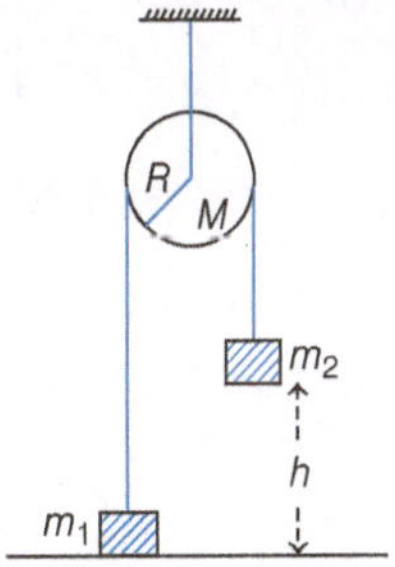

(a) 5 m/s (b) 2 m/s (c) 12 m /s (d) 8 m/s

Correct Codes

Topical Questions

1. (d)	2. (d)	3. (a)	4. (c)	5. (d)	6. (c)	7. (b)	8. (a)	9. (b)	10. (d)
11. (a)	12. (d)	13. (c)	14. (a)	15. (d)	16. (a)	17. (c)	18. (a)	19. (c)	20. (b)
21. (d)	22. (b)	23. (d)	24. (b)	25. (a)	26. (c)	27. (c)	28. (d)	29. (c)	30. (d)
31. (a)	32. (b)	33. (d)	34. (c)	35. (b)	36. (a)	37. (a)	38. (a)	39. (a)	40. (a)
41. (c)	42. (d)	43. (c)	44. (a)	45. (c)	46. (a)	47. (a)	48. (b)	49. (b)	50. (d)
51. (a)	52. (b)	53. (b)	54. (a)	55. (b)	56. (a)	57. (d)	58. (a)	59. (a)	60. (a)
61. (b)	62. (d)	63. (d)	64. (b)	65. (d)	66. (d)	67. (c)	68. (d)	69. (a)	70. (a)
71. (c)	72. (a)	73. (d)	74. (c)	75. (a)	76. (b)	77. (d)	78. (c)	79. (d)	80. (c)
81. (a)	82. (a)	83. (d)	84. (b)						

Assertion and Reason Questions

1 (a)	2 (c)	3 (a)	4 (b)	5 (a)	6 (a)	7 (a)	8 (a)	9 (d)	10 (a)

Statement Based Questions

1 (b)	2 (a)	3 (b)	4 (d)	5 (b)	6 (b)	7 (d)	8 (b)

Matching Type Questions

1 (a)	2 (d)	3 (b)

Numerical Type Questions

1 (8)	2 (200)	3 (2)	4 (5)	5 (4)	6 (10)	7 (2)	8 (33)

NCERT Exemplar Questions

1 (d)	2 (c)	3 (b)	4 (d)	5 (b)	6 (a)	7 (a)	8 (b)	9 (b)

Past Exams Questions

1 (a)	2 (a)	3 (a)	4 (a)	5 (a)	6 (a)	7 (c)	8 (d)	9 (c)	10 (c)
11 (b)	12 (b)	13 (d)	14 (d)	15 (b)	16 (a)				

Skill Boosters

1 (d)	2 (c)	3 (b)	4 (b)	5 (c)	6 (b)	7 (d)	8 (d)	9 (b)	10 (b)

Step by Step

Decoding the Questions

Concept Builders

1. False (F)
2. False(F)
3. Internal
4. Straight
5. False (F)
6. False (F)
7. External
8. False (F)
9. Transverse
10. False (F)
11. False (F)
12. True (T)
13. True (T)
14. Zero
15. Minimum
16. False (F)
17. Two
18. Centre of gravity
19. Zero
20. High

Topical Questions

2. (*d*) Since, centre of mass of ball is moving with constant velocity, hence total external force acting on the ball is zero.

4 (*c*) Let the centre of mass of the system lies at origin.

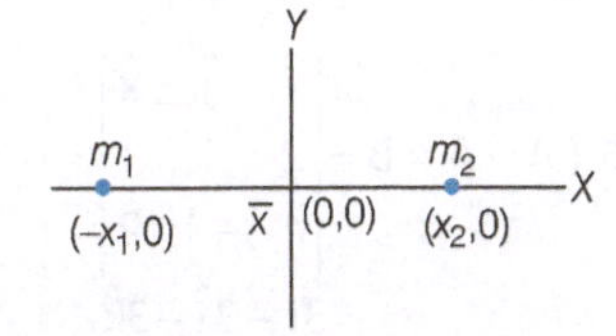

$$\therefore\ 0 = [m_1(-x_1) + m_2x_2]/(m_1 + m_2)$$

$$\Rightarrow \quad \frac{x_1}{x_2} = \frac{m_2}{m_1}$$

5 (*d*)

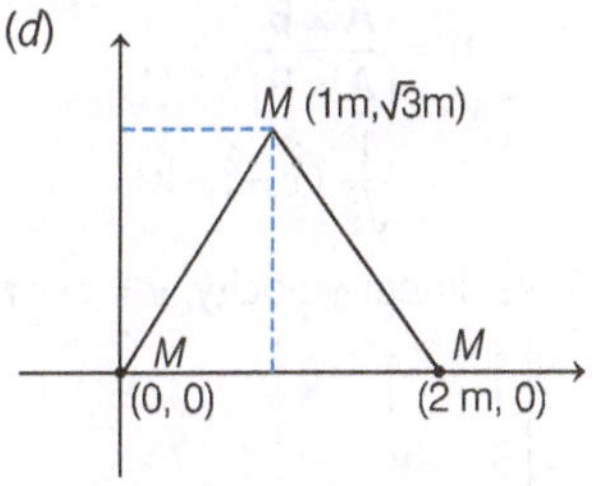

$$x = \frac{M \times 0 + M \times 1 + M \times 2}{M + M + M} = 1$$

$$y = \frac{M \times 0 + M(\sqrt{3}) + M \times 0}{M + M + M}$$

$$y = \frac{\sqrt{3}\,M}{3M} = \frac{1}{\sqrt{3}}$$

So, position vector of the centre of mass is $\left(\hat{\mathbf{i}} + \frac{\hat{\mathbf{j}}}{\sqrt{3}}\right)$.

6 (*c*) If all the masses were same, the CM was at *O*.
But as the mass at *B* is 2*m*, so the CM of the system will shift towards *B*. So, CM will be on line *OB*.

7 (*b*) Centre of mass of a system of particles is given by

$$x_{CM} = \frac{1 \times x_1 + 2 \times x_2 + 3 \times x_3}{1 + 2 + 3} = 3$$

$$[\because x_{CM} = y_{CM} = z_{CM} = 3]$$

$$\Rightarrow \quad x_1 + 2x_2 + 3x_3 = 18 \qquad \text{...(i)}$$

When fourth particle is placed, then

$$x_{CM} = y_{CM} = z_{CM} = 1 \qquad \text{(given)}$$

$$\Rightarrow x_{CM} = \frac{1 \times x_1 + 2 \times x_2 + 3 \times x_3 + 4 \times x_4}{(1 + 2 + 3 + 4)}$$

$$\Rightarrow x_1 + 2x_2 + 3x_3 + 4x_4 = 10 \quad \text{...(ii)}$$

On solving Eqs. (i) and (ii), we get

$$4x_4 = 10 - 18$$

$$\Rightarrow \quad x_4 = -2$$

Similarly, $y_4 = -2,\ z_4 = -2$

8 (*a*) We can think of the L-shape to consist of 3 squares each of length 1 m as shown in figure.
The centre of mass of the whole *L*-shape (X, Y) is the centre of mass of these mass points C_1, C_2 and C_3.

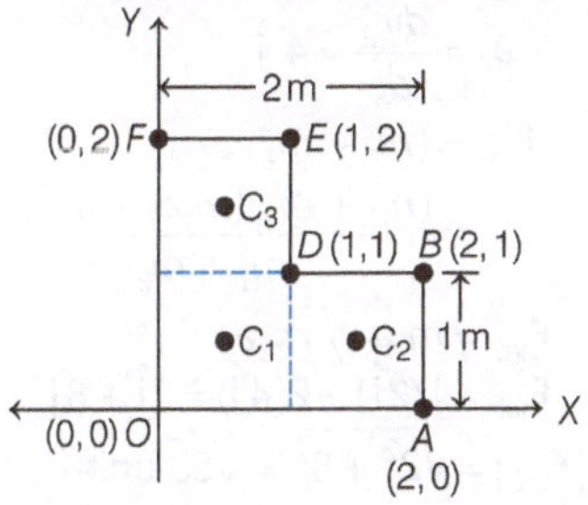

Hence,

$$X = \frac{[1(1/2) + 1(3/2) + 1\,(1/2)]\ \text{kg-m}}{(1 + 1 + 1)\ \text{kg}}$$

$$= \frac{5}{6}\ \text{m}$$

$$Y = \frac{[1(1/2) + 1(1/2) + 1(3/2)]\ \text{kg-m}}{(1 + 1 + 1)\ \text{kg}}$$

$$= \frac{5}{6}\ \text{m}$$

9 (*b*) As shown in figure, therefore

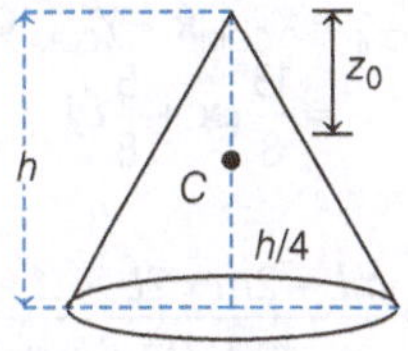

$$h - z_0 = \frac{h}{4}$$

$$\text{or } z_0 = h - \frac{h}{4} = \frac{3h}{4}$$

10 (*d*) We choose origin as shown in the figure.

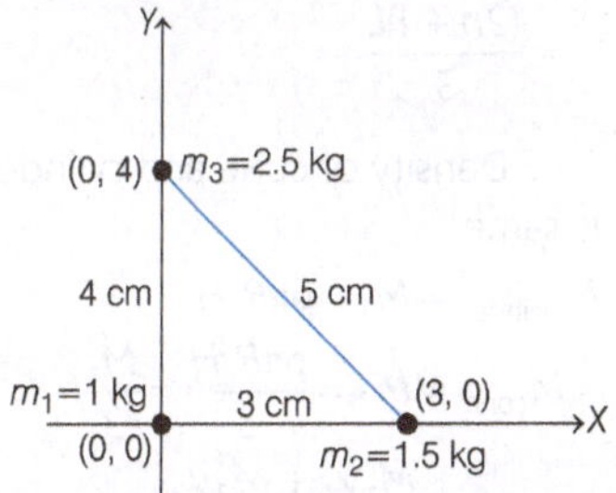

$$x_{CM} = \frac{1 \times 0 + 1.5 \times 3 + 2.5 \times 0}{1 + 1.5 + 2.5}$$

$$= 0.9\ \text{cm}$$

Similarly,

$$y_{CM} = \frac{1 \times 0 + 1.5 \times 0 + 2.5 \times 4}{1 + 1.5 + 2.5}$$

$$= 2.0\ \text{cm}$$

11 (*a*)

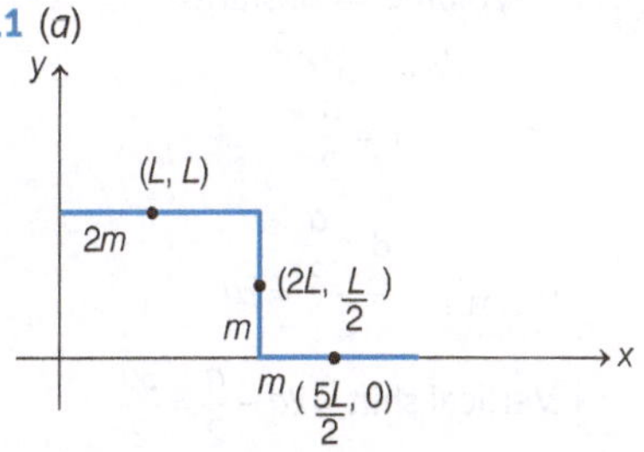

So, $X_{COM} = \left(\frac{2mL + m2L + m\frac{5L}{2}}{4\,m} \right)$

$= \frac{13}{8} L$

and $Y_{COM} = \frac{2mL + m \times \frac{L}{2} + m \times 0}{4\,m}$

$= \frac{5L}{8}$

So, position vector of COM is

$\mathbf{r}_{COM} = X_{COM}\hat{\mathbf{x}} + Y_{COM}\,\hat{\mathbf{y}}$

$= \frac{13}{8} L\hat{\mathbf{x}} + \frac{5}{8} L\hat{\mathbf{y}}$

12 (*d*) $\because$

$x_{CM} = \frac{mL + 2m \times 2L + \ldots + nm \cdot nL}{m + 2m + \ldots + nm}$

$= \frac{L(1^2 + 2^2 + \ldots + n^2)}{(1 + 2 + \ldots + n)}$

$= L \frac{\sum n^2}{\sum n} = L \frac{\frac{n(n+1)(2n+1)}{6}}{\frac{n(n+1)}{2}}$

$= \frac{(2n+1)L}{3}$

13 (*c*) $\because$ Density of cone and cylinder is same

$M_{cylinder} = M_1 = \rho \pi R^2 H$

$M_{cone} = M_2 = \frac{\rho \pi R^2 H}{3} = \frac{M_1}{3}$

$y_{COM} = \frac{M_1 y_1 + M_2 y_2}{M_1 + M_2}$

$= \frac{M_1 (H/2) + M_2 (H + H/4)}{M_1 + M_2}$

$y_{COM} = \frac{11H}{16} < H$

14 (*a*) $(Y_{COM})_i = \frac{a}{2}$

Volume = constant

$(a)^3 = 8(r)^3$

$\Rightarrow \quad r = \frac{a}{2}$

$(Y_{COM})_f = \frac{8 \times \frac{a}{2}}{2} = 2a$

Vertical shift $= 2a - \frac{a}{2} = \frac{3a}{2}$

15 (*d*) $y_{COM} = \frac{A_1 y_1 + A_2 y_2}{A_1 + A_2}$

$= \frac{12 \times 1 + 8 \times 4}{12 + 8} = 2.2\text{ m}$

16 (*a*) Velocity of centre of mass,

$\mathbf{v}_{CM} = \frac{m_1 \mathbf{v}_1 + m_2 \mathbf{v}_2}{m_1 + m_2}$

$= \frac{(\mathbf{v}_1 + \mathbf{v}_2)m}{2m} \quad [\because m_1 = m_2 = m]$

$= \frac{4\hat{\mathbf{i}} + 4\hat{\mathbf{j}}}{2} = 2(\hat{\mathbf{i}} + \hat{\mathbf{j}})\text{ ms}^{-1}$

Similarly, acceleration of centre of mass,

$\mathbf{a}_{CM} = \frac{\mathbf{a}_1 + \mathbf{a}_2}{2}$

$= \frac{2\hat{\mathbf{i}} + 2\hat{\mathbf{j}} + 0}{2} = (\hat{\mathbf{i}} + \hat{\mathbf{j}})\text{ ms}^{-2}$

Since, from above values, it can be seen that $\mathbf{v}_{CM}$ is parallel to $\mathbf{a}_{CM}$, so the path will be a straight line.

17 (*c*) Here on the entire system, net external force on the system is zero, hence the centre of mass remains unchanged.

18 (*a*) As no external force is applied on the system. Therefore, $F_{ext} = 0$

So, there is no acceleration of CM. This means velocity of the CM remain constant.

As, initial velocity of CM, $v_{i\,CM} = 0$

$\Rightarrow$ final velocity of CM, $v_{f\,CM} = 0$

19 (*c*) The velocity of COM remains constant if no external force act on the system.

$\mathbf{a}_{COM} = 0$

20 (*b*) At; $t = 2\text{ s}$

$\mathbf{a}_1 = \frac{d\mathbf{v}_1}{dt} = 2\hat{\mathbf{i}},$

$\mathbf{a}_2 = \frac{d\mathbf{v}_2}{dt} = 4\,\hat{\mathbf{j}}$

$\mathbf{F}_{net} = (m_1 + m_2)\,\mathbf{a}_{CM}$

$= \frac{(m_1 + m_2)(m_1 \mathbf{a}_1 + m_2 \mathbf{a}_2)}{m_1 + m_2}$

$\mathbf{F}_{net} = m_1 \mathbf{a}_1 + m_2 \mathbf{a}_2$

$\mathbf{F}_{net} = 1(2\hat{\mathbf{i}}) + 2(4\hat{\mathbf{j}}) = 2\hat{\mathbf{i}} + 8\hat{\mathbf{j}}$

$|\mathbf{F}_{net}| = \sqrt{2^2 + 8^2} = \sqrt{68}\text{ unit}$

21 (*d*) Since, the explosion is due to internal forces, so the motion of CM after explosion will follow the same parabolic path as it would have followed if there was no explosion.

22 (*b*) As, $F = \frac{dp}{dt}$

$\Rightarrow \quad F = \frac{d}{dt}(3t^2 + 4) = 6t$

$ma = 6t, \; 2a = 6t$

$\Rightarrow \quad a = (3t)\text{ m/s}^2$

So, $\quad a \propto t$

So, the sphere moving with a variable acceleration.

23 (*d*) Vector product,

$\mathbf{A} \times \mathbf{B} = \begin{vmatrix} \hat{\mathbf{i}} & \hat{\mathbf{j}} & \hat{\mathbf{k}} \\ 2 & 1 & -1 \\ 1 & -1 & 2 \end{vmatrix}$

$= \hat{\mathbf{i}} - 3\hat{\mathbf{j}} - \hat{\mathbf{k}}$

24 (*b*)

$\mathbf{P} \times \mathbf{Q} = \begin{vmatrix} \hat{\mathbf{i}} & \hat{\mathbf{j}} & \hat{\mathbf{k}} \\ 2 & -3 & 1 \\ -4 & 6 & -2 \end{vmatrix}$

$\therefore PQ \sin\theta = \hat{\mathbf{i}}(6 - 6) - \hat{\mathbf{j}}(-4 + 4) + \hat{\mathbf{k}}(12 - 12)$

$\Rightarrow \quad PQ \sin\theta = 0$

$\Rightarrow \quad \theta = 0°$

25 (*a*) $\mathbf{A} \times \mathbf{B} = \begin{vmatrix} \hat{\mathbf{i}} & \hat{\mathbf{j}} & \hat{\mathbf{k}} \\ 2 & 1 & 1 \\ 1 & -1 & 2 \end{vmatrix}$

$= 3\hat{\mathbf{i}} - 3\hat{\mathbf{j}} - 3\hat{\mathbf{k}}$

$\therefore |\mathbf{A} \times \mathbf{B}| = \sqrt{3^2 + (-3)^2 + (-3)^2}$

$= 3\sqrt{3}$

Unit vector perpendicular to vector **A** and **B** is given as

$\hat{\mathbf{n}} = \frac{\mathbf{A} \times \mathbf{B}}{|\mathbf{A} \times \mathbf{B}|}$

$= \frac{1}{\sqrt{3}}(\hat{\mathbf{i}} - \hat{\mathbf{j}} - \hat{\mathbf{k}})$

26 (*c*) As, linear velocity, $\mathbf{v} = \omega \times \mathbf{r}$

$= \begin{vmatrix} \hat{\mathbf{i}} & \hat{\mathbf{j}} & \hat{\mathbf{k}} \\ 3 & -4 & -1 \\ 5 & -6 & 6 \end{vmatrix}$

$= -30\hat{\mathbf{i}} - 23\hat{\mathbf{j}} + 2\hat{\mathbf{k}}$

27 (*c*) Velocity at a point on the circular plate (disc) $v = R\omega$, where r is the distance of point from O.

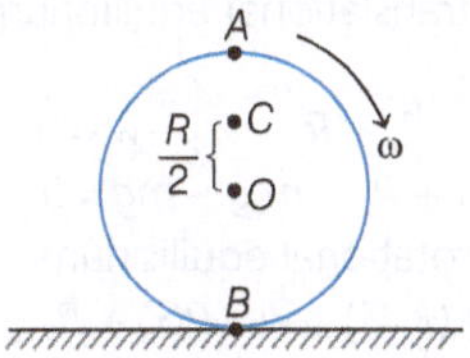

Since, $R_A = R_B$

$v_A = v_B$

Also, $R_C < R_A$ or R_B

$\Rightarrow v_A = v_B > v_C$

28 (*d*) The position of point P on this rod through which the axis should pass, so that the work required to set the rod rotating with minimum angular velocity ω_0, is their centre of mass, we have,

$$m_1 x = m_2(L - x)$$

$$\Rightarrow m_1 x = m_2 L - m_2 x$$

$$\Rightarrow x = \frac{m_2 L}{m_1 + m_2}$$

29 (*c*)

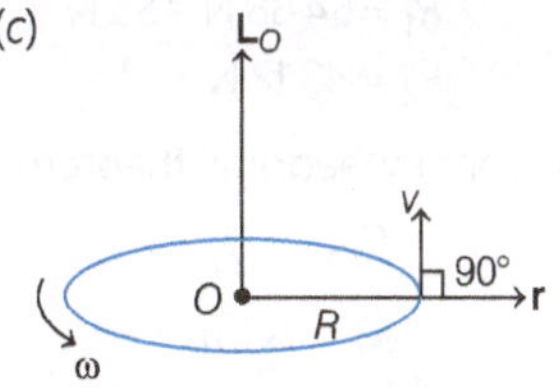

For $\mathbf{L}_O$,

$$|\mathbf{L}| = (mvr \sin\theta)$$
$$= m(R\omega)(R)\sin 90^\circ$$
$$= mR^2\omega$$
$$= \text{constant}$$

Direction of $\mathbf{L}_O$ is always upwards, therefore $\mathbf{L}_O$ is constant.

For $\mathbf{L}_P$,

$$|\mathbf{L}_P| = (mvr \sin\theta)$$
$$= (m)(R\omega)(l)\sin 90^\circ$$
$$= (mRl\omega).$$

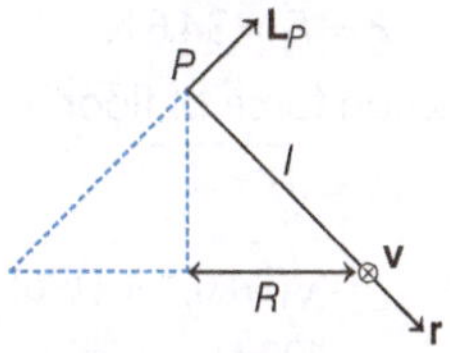

Magnitude of $\mathbf{L}_P$ will remains constant but direction of $\mathbf{L}_P$ keeps on changing, i.e. it varies with time.

30. (*d*) Torque, $\tau = \mathbf{r} \times \mathbf{F}$

τ is perpendicular to plane containing $\mathbf{r}$ and $\mathbf{F}$, then

$$\mathbf{r} \cdot \tau = 0$$
$$\mathbf{F} \cdot \tau = 0$$

31. (*a*) Torque about (1, 0, 3)

$$= \mathbf{r} \times \mathbf{F} = (\hat{\mathbf{i}} + 3\hat{\mathbf{k}}) \times (2\hat{\mathbf{i}} + 3\hat{\mathbf{j}})$$
$$= 3\hat{\mathbf{k}} + 6(+\hat{\mathbf{j}}) + 9(-\hat{\mathbf{i}})$$

A vector along the axis can be found by joining two points lying on the line such as (0, 0) and (1, 3). The vector can be $\mathbf{r} = \hat{\mathbf{i}} + 3\hat{\mathbf{j}}$

The components of torque along $\mathbf{r}$

$$= \frac{\tau \cdot \mathbf{r}}{|\mathbf{r}|}$$
$$= \frac{(-9\hat{\mathbf{i}} + 6\hat{\mathbf{j}} + 3\hat{\mathbf{k}}) \cdot (\hat{\mathbf{i}} + 3\hat{\mathbf{j}})}{\sqrt{1^2 + 3^2}}$$
$$= \frac{9}{\sqrt{10}} \text{ N-m}$$

32 (*b*) Torque τ about Z-axis,

$\tau = \mathbf{r} \times \mathbf{F}$, which is along $\hat{\mathbf{k}}$

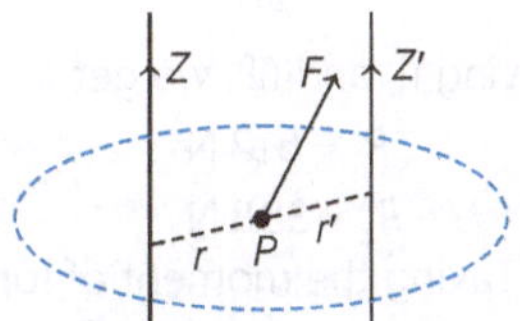

Torque about Z'- axis

$\tau' = \mathbf{r}' \times \mathbf{F}$, which is along$-\hat{\mathbf{k}}$

As $|\tau| = Fr$

Clearly, $r_\perp > r_\perp'$

$\Rightarrow |\tau|_Z > |\tau|_{Z'}$

We are always calculating resultant torque about a common axis. Hence, total torque is not given by $\tau + \tau'$ because τ and τ' are not about common axis.

33 (*d*) For particle 1, $\mathbf{L}_1 = \mathbf{r}_1 \times m\mathbf{v} \odot$ is out of plane of the paper and perpendicular to $\mathbf{r}_1$ and $(m\mathbf{v})$.

Similarly, $\mathbf{L}_2 = \mathbf{r}_2 \times m(-\mathbf{v}) \otimes$ is into the plane of the paper and perpendicular to $\mathbf{r}_2$ and $-m\mathbf{v}$.

Hence, total angular momentum about A

$$\mathbf{L} = \mathbf{L}_1 + \mathbf{L}_2$$
$$= \mathbf{r}_1 \times m\mathbf{v} + (-\mathbf{r}_2 \times m\mathbf{v})$$

$|\mathbf{L}| = mv\,d_1 - mvd_2$ as $d_2 > d_1$, total angular momentum will be inward.

Hence, $\mathbf{L} = m\mathbf{v}(d_2 - d_1) \otimes$

34 (*c*) We know that, torque on a system of particles,

$$\tau = \mathbf{r} \times \mathbf{F} = rF\sin\theta\,\hat{\mathbf{n}} \quad \text{...(i)}$$

When forces are acting perpendicular to the axis of rotation,

$\theta = 90^\circ, |\tau| = rF$ [from Eq. (i)]

35 (*b*) The rim keeps rotating in a vertical plane and the plane of rotation turns around the string A, i.e. the axis of rotation of the rim or its angular momentum precesses about the string A.

36 (*a*) As, angular momentum about origin is conserved.

i.e. $L = \text{constant}$

Torque, $\tau = 0$

$\Rightarrow \mathbf{r} \times \mathbf{F} = 0$

$$\Rightarrow \begin{vmatrix} \hat{\mathbf{i}} & \hat{\mathbf{j}} & \hat{\mathbf{k}} \\ 2 & -6 & -12 \\ \alpha & 3 & 6 \end{vmatrix} = 0$$

$$\Rightarrow (-36 + 36)\hat{\mathbf{i}} - (12 + 12\alpha)\hat{\mathbf{j}} + (6 + 6\alpha)\hat{\mathbf{k}} = 0$$

$\Rightarrow (1 + \alpha) = 0$

$\Rightarrow \alpha = -1$

38 (*a*) If we take clockwise torque negative, then magnitude of total torque is

$$\tau_{net} = \tau_{F_1} + \tau_{F_2} + \tau_{F_3}$$
$$0 = F_1 r + F_2 r - F_3 r$$
$$\Rightarrow F_3 = F_1 + F_2$$

39. (*a*) As the system is stationary in air, the net external vertical forces on it is zero. Therefore, the centre of mass of the system, which initially at rest, will always be at rest.

40 (*a*) In case I, net torque about its centre is

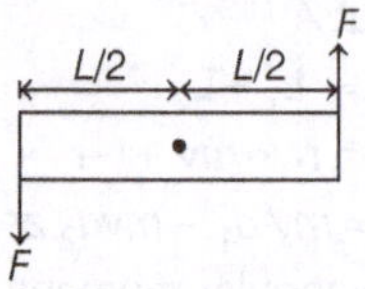

$$\tau = F \times \frac{L}{2} + F \times \frac{L}{2} = FL$$

In case II, net torque about its centre is

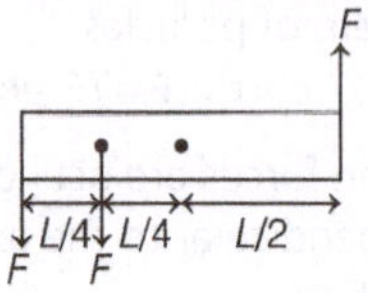

$$\tau = F \times \frac{L}{2} + F \times \frac{L}{4} + F \times \frac{L}{2}$$
$$= \frac{5}{4} FL$$

In case III, net torque about its centre is

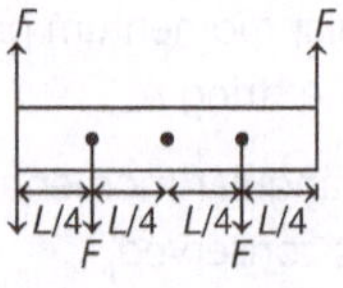

$$\tau = -F \times \frac{L}{2} + F \times \frac{L}{4} - F \times \frac{L}{4} + F \times \frac{L}{2}$$
$$= 0$$

41 (*c*) For rotational equilibrium,

$$M_1 g \times r_A = M_2 g \times x$$

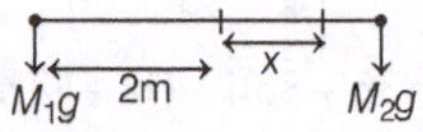

$$(40 \times 10) \times 2 = (60 \times 10)\, x$$
$$\Rightarrow \quad x = \frac{8}{6} = \frac{4}{3}\text{ m}$$

So, 60 kg boy has to be displaced

$$= 2 - \frac{4}{3} = \frac{2}{3}\text{ m}.$$

42 (*d*) As the weight w balances the normal reactions.

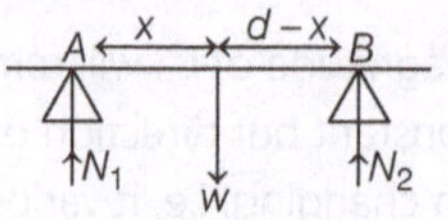

So, $\quad w = N_1 + N_2 \quad$ ...(i)

Now, balancing torque about the COM,

$$N_1 x = N_2 (d - x)$$

From Eq. (i), we get

$$N_1 x = (w - N_1)(d - x)$$
$$\Rightarrow \quad N_1 = \frac{w(d - x)}{d}$$

43 (*c*)

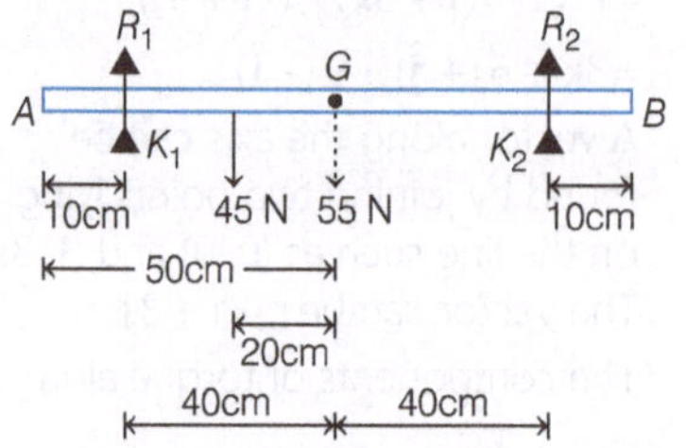

For the translational equilibrium of the rod,

$$R_1 + R_2 - 45\text{ N} - 55\text{ N} = 0$$
$$R_1 + R_2 = 45\text{ N} + 55\text{ N} = 100\text{ N} \quad \text{...(i)}$$

For the rotational equilibrium, taking moments about G, we get

$$-R_1(40) + 45(20) + R_2(40) = 0$$
$$R_1 - R_2 = \frac{900}{40} = 22.5\text{ N} \quad \text{...(ii)}$$

Solving (i) and (ii), we get

$$R_1 = 61.2\text{ N}$$
$$R_2 = 38.8\text{ N}$$

44 (*a*) Taking the moment of forces about centre of gravity G

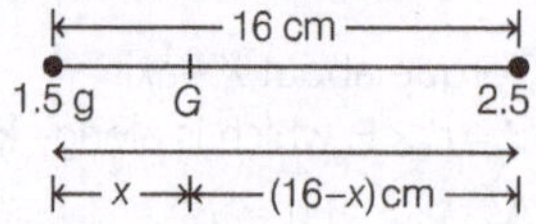

i.e. $\quad 1.5\,x = 2.5\,(16 - x)$

$$\Rightarrow \quad 8x = 80$$
$$\therefore \quad x = 10\text{ cm}$$

45 (*c*)

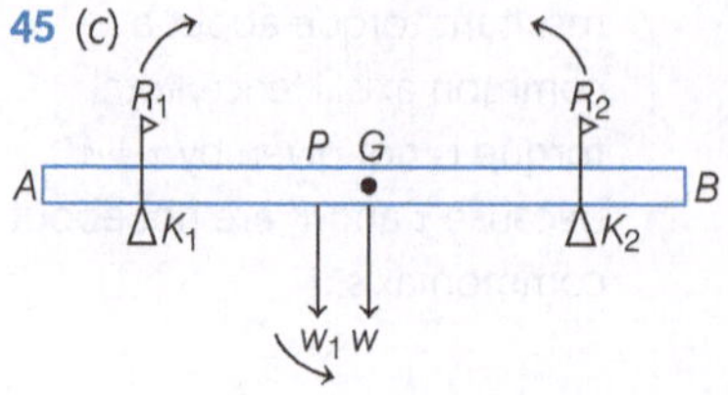

The rod is uniform in cross-section and homogeneous. Hence, G is at the centre of rod.

For translational equilibrium of the rod,

$$R_1 + R_2 - w_1 - w = 0$$

or $R_1 + R_2 - m_1 g - mg = 0 \quad$ ...(i)

For rotational equilibrium,

$$-R_1\,(K_1G) + w_1\,(PG) + R_2\,(K_2G) = 0 \quad \text{...(ii)}$$

we have, $w = 4.0\,g$ N and $w_1 = 6.0\,g$ N, where g = acceleration due to gravity.

Taking, $g = 9.8\text{ ms}^{-2}$.

With numerical values inserted in Eq. (i), we get

$$R_1 + R_2 - 4.0\,g - 6.0\,g = 0$$
$$\Rightarrow \quad R_1 + R_2 = 10.00\,g \quad \text{...(iii)}$$
$$= 98.00\text{ N}$$

From Eq. (ii), we get

$$-0.25\,R_1 + 0.05\,w_1 + 0.25\,R_2 = 0$$

or $\quad R_1 - R_2 = \dfrac{0.05 \times 6.0g}{0.25}$

$$= 1.2g\text{ N} = 11.76\text{ N} \quad \text{...(iv)}$$

From Eqs. (iii) and (iv),

$$R_1 = 54.88\text{ N} \simeq 55\text{ N}$$
$$\Rightarrow \quad R_2 = 43.12\text{ N}$$

47 (*a*) From Pythagoras theorem,

$$BC = \sqrt{AB^2 - AC^2}$$
$$= \sqrt{8} = 2\sqrt{2}\text{m}$$

For translational equilibrium,

$$N - w = 0 \quad \text{...(i)}$$

and $\quad F - F_1 = 0 \quad$ ...(ii)

For rotational equilibrium,

$$2\sqrt{2}\,F_1 - (1/2)\,w = 0 \quad \text{...(iii)}$$

Now,

$$w = 20 \times g = 20 \times 9.8\text{ N} = 196\text{ N}$$

From Eq. (i), $N = 196.0$ N

From Eq. (iii), reaction force of wall,

$$F_1 = w / 4\sqrt{2}$$
$$= 34.6\text{ N}$$

From Eq. (ii),

$$F = F_1 = 34.6\text{ N}$$

∴ Reaction force of floor,

$$F_2 = \sqrt{F^2 + N^2}$$
$$= \sqrt{(34.6)^2 + (196)^2}$$
$$= 199\text{ N}$$

48 (*b*) Total moment of inertia is

$$I = \frac{M}{2}\left(\frac{l}{2}\right)^2 + \frac{M}{2}\left(\frac{l}{2}\right)^2$$

$$= \frac{Ml^2}{8} + \frac{Ml^2}{8} = \frac{Ml^2}{4}$$

49 (*b*) Moment of inertia of the complete disc about O,

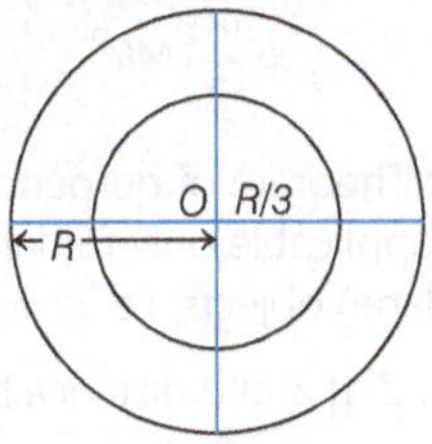

$$I_1 = \frac{1}{2}(9M)R^2 = \frac{9}{2}MR^2$$

Moment of inertia of removed portion,

$$I_2 = \frac{1}{2}M\left(\frac{R}{3}\right)^2 = \frac{L}{18}MR^2$$

∴Moment of inertia of the remaining portion of the disc about O,

$$I = I_1 - I_2$$

$$= \frac{40}{9}MR^2$$

50 (*d*) The angle between the rods will not make any difference.

∴ Net moment of inertia,

$$I = I_1 + I_2$$

$$= \frac{Ml^2}{12} + \frac{Ml^2}{12} = \frac{Ml^2}{6}$$

51 (*a*) For disc, moment of inertia about the diameter, $I_d = \frac{mr^2}{4}$ and moment of inertia about the tangential axis,

$$I_{disc} = \frac{mr^2}{4} + mr^2$$

$$I_{disc} = \frac{5mr^2}{4}$$

Let the radius of gyration of disc is k_{disc}.

$$\Rightarrow \quad I_{disc} = m\,k_{disc}^2$$

$$\Rightarrow \quad \frac{5mr^2}{4} = m\,k_{disc}^2$$

$$\Rightarrow \quad k_{disc} = \sqrt{\frac{5}{4}}r \quad \text{...(i)}$$

For ring, moment of inertia about the diameter,

$$I'_a = mr^2/2$$

and moment of inertia about the tangential axis,

$$I_{ring} = \frac{mr^2}{2} + mr^2$$

$$= \frac{3}{2}mr^2$$

Let the radius of gyration of ring, k_{ring}.

$$\Rightarrow \quad I_{ring} = m\,k^2_{ring}$$

$$\Rightarrow \quad \frac{3}{2}mr^2 = mk^2_{ring}$$

$$\Rightarrow \quad k_{ring} = \sqrt{\frac{3}{2}}r \quad \text{...(ii)}$$

From Eqs. (i) and (ii), we get

$$\therefore \quad \frac{k_{disc}}{k_{ring}} = \frac{\sqrt{\frac{5}{4}}r}{\sqrt{\frac{3}{2}}r} = \sqrt{\frac{5}{6}}$$

52 (*b*) As, moment of inertia of rod,

$$I_{rod} = \frac{ML^2}{12} \quad \text{...(i)}$$

Using radius of gyration,

$$I = Mk^2 \quad \text{...(ii)}$$

Comparing Eqs. (i) and (ii), we get

Radius of gyration,

$$k = L/\sqrt{12}$$

53 (*b*) I_{disc} about the axis along its diameter $= \frac{MR^2}{4}$ ...(i)

Using radius of gyration,

$$I = Mk^2 \quad \text{...(ii)}$$

Comparing Eqs. (i) and (ii), we get

$$k = \frac{R}{2}.$$

54 (*a*)

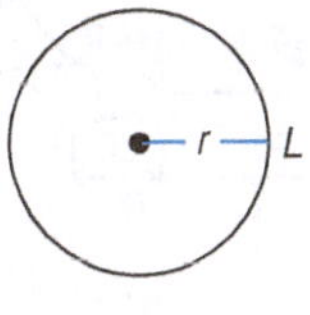

$$\Rightarrow \quad r = \frac{L}{2\pi} \quad \text{...(i)}$$

The moment of inertia of the ring about its axis,

$$I = Mr^2$$

$$\Rightarrow \quad I = M\left(\frac{L}{2\pi}\right)^2 \quad \left[\because r = \frac{L}{2\pi}\right]$$

$$\Rightarrow \quad I = \frac{ML^2}{4\pi^2}$$

55 (*b*) As two solid spheres are equal in masses, so

$$m_A = m_B$$

$$\Rightarrow \quad \frac{4}{3}\pi R_A^3 \rho_A = \frac{4}{3}\pi R_B^3 \rho_B$$

$$\Rightarrow \quad \frac{R_A}{R_B} = \left(\frac{\rho_B}{\rho_A}\right)^{1/3}$$

The moment of inertia of a solid sphere about diameter,

$$I = \frac{2}{5}mR^2$$

$$\Rightarrow \quad \frac{I_A}{I_B} = \left(\frac{R_A}{R_B}\right)^2 \quad (\text{as } m_A = m_B)$$

$$\therefore \quad \frac{I_A}{I_B} = \left(\frac{\rho_B}{\rho_A}\right)^{2/3}$$

$$\Rightarrow \quad \frac{I_B}{I_A} = \left(\frac{\rho_A}{\rho_B}\right)^{2/3}$$

56 (*a*) Moment of inertia of remaining solid

= Moment of inertia of complete solid

− Moment of inertia of removed portion

$$\therefore I = \frac{9MR^2}{2} - \left[\frac{M(R/3)^2}{2} + M\left(\frac{2R}{3}\right)^2\right]$$

$$= MR^2\left(\frac{9}{2} - \frac{1}{18} - \frac{4}{9}\right)$$

$$\Rightarrow I = 4MR^2$$

57 (*d*) Moment of inertia of a solid cylinder about its perpendicular bisector of length is

$$I = \frac{mR^2}{4} + \frac{ml^2}{12}$$

$$= \frac{m^2}{4\pi\rho l} + \frac{ml^2}{12} \quad [\because \rho\pi R^2 l = m]$$

For I to be maximum,

$$\frac{dI}{dl} = -\frac{m^2}{4\pi\rho}\left(\frac{1}{l^2}\right) + \frac{ml}{6} = 0$$

$$\Rightarrow \quad \frac{m^2}{4\pi\rho} = \frac{ml^3}{6}$$

Now, putting $m = \rho\pi R^2 l$

$$\therefore \quad l^3 = \frac{3}{2\pi\rho}\cdot\rho\pi R^2 l$$

$$\Rightarrow \quad \frac{l}{R} = \sqrt{\frac{3}{2}}$$

58 (a) Moment of inertia of hollow cylinder about its axis is

$$I_1 = \frac{M}{2}(R_1^2 + R_2^2)$$

where, R_1 = inner radius and

R_2 = outer radius.

Moment of inertia of thin hollow cylinder of radius R about its axis is

$$I_2 = MR^2$$

Given, $I_1 = I_2$ and both cylinders have same mass (M).

So, we have

$$\frac{M}{2}(R_1^2 + R_2^2) = MR^2$$

$$(10^2 + 20^2)/2 = R^2$$

$$R \approx 16 \text{ cm}$$

59 (a) Its moment of inertia of shell A about the XX'-axis is $I_A = \frac{2}{3} mr^2$

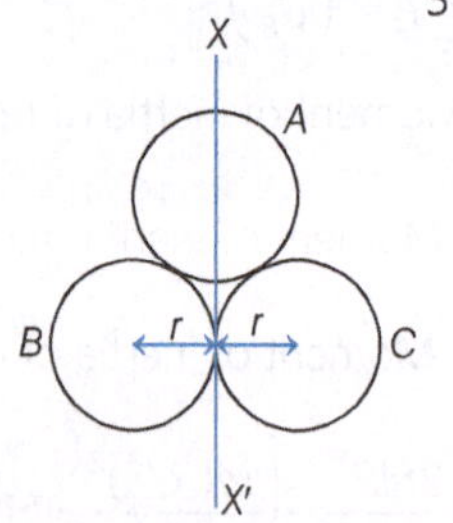

The moment of inertia of shell B about XX'-axis is

$$I_{B'} = I_B + mr^2$$

$$= \frac{2}{3} mr^2 + mr^2 = \frac{5}{3} mr^2$$

Similarly, the moment of inertia of the spherical shell C about the XX'-axis is

$$I_{C'} = \frac{5}{3} mr^2$$

Total moment of inertia is,

$$I = I_A + I_{B'} + I_{C'}$$

$$= 4\, mr^2$$

60 (a) The statement given in option (a) is incorrect and it can be corrected as,

Due to rotation, lower part has acceleration greater than g.

61 (b)

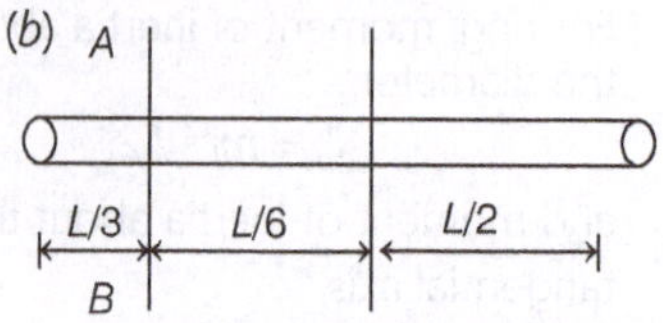

Applying parallel axes theorem, moment of inertia about an axis AB at a distance $\frac{L}{3}$ from one end is given as

$$I = I_{CM} + Mx^2$$

$$= \frac{ML^2}{12} + M\left(\frac{L}{6}\right)^2$$

$$\left(\because x = \frac{L}{2} - \frac{L}{3} = \frac{L}{6}\right)$$

$$\Rightarrow \quad I = \frac{ML^2}{9}$$

62 (d)

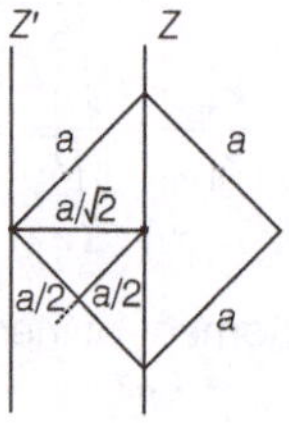

$$I_{Z'} = I_Z + m\left(\frac{a}{\sqrt{2}}\right)^2$$

$$= \frac{ma^2}{6} + \frac{ma^2}{2} = \frac{2}{3} ma^2$$

63 (d) Moment of inertia of an outer disc about the axis through centre is

$$= \frac{MR^2}{2} + M(2R)^2$$

$$= MR^2\left(4 + \frac{1}{2}\right)$$

$$= \frac{9}{2} MR^2$$

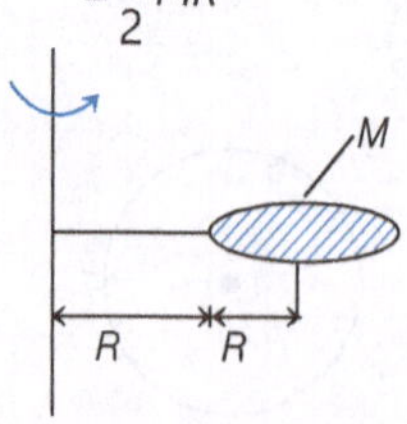

For 6 such discs,

Moment of inertia

$$= 6 \times \frac{9}{2} MR^2 = 27 MR^2$$

So, moment of inertia of system

$$I_0 = \frac{MR^2}{2} + 27MR^2$$

$$I_0 = \frac{55}{2} MR^2$$

Hence, $I_P = \frac{55}{2} MR^2 + (7M \times 9R^2)$

$$\Rightarrow \quad I_P = \frac{181}{2} MR^2$$

$$I_P = \frac{181}{2} MR^2$$

64 (b) Theorem of perpendicular axes is applicable only for lamina (plane) objects, i.e. $I_Z \neq I_X + I_Y$.

As, $Z' \,||\, Z$ and distance between

them $= a\frac{\sqrt{2}}{2} = \frac{a}{\sqrt{2}}$

Now, by theorem of parallel axes

$$I_{Z'} = I_Z + m\left(\frac{a}{\sqrt{2}}\right)^2 = I_Z + \frac{ma^2}{2}$$

Z'' is not parallel to Z, hence theorem of parallel axes cannot be applied, i.e. $I'_Z \neq I_Z + \frac{ma^2}{2}$

As, X and Y-axes are symmetrical.

Hence, $I_X = I_Y$

65 (d) Angular acceleration,

$$\alpha = \frac{\omega - \omega_0}{t} = \frac{2\pi(\nu - \nu_0)}{t}$$

Given, $\nu = 4500 \text{ rpm} = \frac{4500}{60} \text{ s}^{-1}$

$$\nu_0 = 1200 \text{ rpm} = \frac{1200}{60} \text{ s}^{-1}$$

$$t = 10 \text{ s}$$

Substituting the given values,we get

$$\alpha = \frac{\omega - \omega_0}{t}$$

$$= \frac{\frac{2\pi}{60}(4500 - 1200)}{10}$$

$$= 11\pi \text{ rads}^{-2} = \frac{11\pi \times 180}{\pi}$$

$$= 1980 \text{ degs}^{-2}$$

66 (d) Total angular displacement in 36 rotation,

$$\theta = 36 \times 2\pi$$

Using $\omega_2^2 - \omega_1^2 = 2\alpha\theta$, we get

$$(\omega/2)^2 - \omega^2 = 2\alpha(36\times 2\pi) \quad \text{...(i)}$$

Similarly,

$$0^2 - (\omega/2)^2 = 2\alpha\,(n\times 2\pi) \quad \text{...(ii)}$$

Dividing Eq. (i) by Eq. (ii), we get

$$\frac{-\frac{3}{4}\omega^2}{-\omega^2/4} = \frac{36}{n}$$

$$\Rightarrow \quad n = 12$$

67 (c) (i) $\omega_0 = \frac{2\pi\times 1200}{60}$ rads^{-1}

$$= 40\,\pi \text{ rads}^{-1}$$

Similarly, $\omega = \frac{2\pi\times 3120}{60}$

$$= 104\pi \text{ rads}^{-1}$$

∴ Angular acceleration,

$$\alpha = \frac{\omega-\omega_0}{t} = \frac{104\pi - 40\pi}{16} = 4\pi \text{ rads}^{-2}$$

(ii) As we know,

$$\theta = \omega_0 t + \frac{1}{2}\alpha t^2 = 40\,\pi\times 16 + \frac{1}{2}\times 4\pi\times 16^2 = 1152\,\pi \text{ rad}$$

Number of revolutions

$$= \frac{1152\pi}{2\pi} = 576$$

68 (d) As $\alpha = \frac{\omega-\omega_0}{t} = \frac{600\pi - 200\pi}{10} = 40\pi \text{ rad/s}^2$

Now, $\theta = \frac{\omega^2-\omega_0^2}{2\alpha} = \frac{(600\pi)^2-(200\pi)^2}{2\times 40\pi}$

$$\theta = 4000\,\pi$$

∴Number of revolution,

$$n = \frac{\theta}{2\pi} = \frac{4000\pi}{2\pi} = 2000$$

69 (a) Power of the engine,

$$P = \tau\omega = 100\times 100 = 10\times 10^3 \text{ W} = 10 \text{ kW}$$

70 (a) Torque, $\tau = FR = 25\times 0.20$

$$= 5.0 \text{ N-m}$$

$$I = \frac{MR^2}{2} = \frac{20\times(0.2)^2}{2}$$

$$= 0.4 \text{ kg-m}^2$$

∴Angular acceleration,

$$\alpha = \frac{\tau}{I} = 5.0/0.4 = 12.50 \text{ rad/s}^2$$

71 (c) $\mathbf{r}\times\mathbf{F} = I\alpha = I\frac{(\omega_2-\omega_1)}{t}$

[from $\tau = r\times F$ and $\tau = I\alpha$]

$$\Rightarrow \quad \omega_2 - \omega_1 = \frac{r\times F\times t}{I} = \frac{10\times 0.2\times 4}{0.4} = 20 \text{ rads}^{-1}$$

72 (a) For hollow cylinder,

$$\alpha_1 = \frac{\tau}{I_1} \text{ (as } \tau = I\alpha)$$

and for solid sphere

$$\alpha_2 = \frac{\tau}{I_2}$$

$$\therefore \quad \frac{\alpha_1}{\alpha_2} = \frac{I_2}{I_1} = \frac{\frac{2}{5}MR^2}{MR^2} = \frac{2}{5}$$

73 (d) $\tau = T\times r = T\times 0.5$

$$\tau = \frac{T}{2} \text{ N-m} \quad \text{...(i)}$$

As $\tau = I\alpha$ ...(ii)

From Eqs. (i) and (ii), we get

$$\frac{T}{2} = I\alpha = \left(\frac{mR^2}{2}\right)\times(2\times 2\pi)$$

$$\left(\because I_{\text{solid cylinder}} = \frac{mR^2}{2}\right)$$

$$\Rightarrow \quad T = 50\,\pi = 157 \text{ N}$$

74 (c) Moment of inertia of the insect-disc system,

$$\text{MI} = \frac{1}{2}MR^2 + mx^2$$

Clearly, as the insect moves along the diameter of the disc. Moment of inertia first decreases and then increases.

By conservation of angular momentum, angular speed first increases and then decreases.

75 (a) Work done

$$= \Delta\text{KE} = \frac{1}{2}I(\omega_1^2 - \omega_2^2)$$

In this case, $\omega_2 = 0$,

Work done $= \frac{1}{2}\times 10\times 50^2$

$$= 12500 \text{ J}$$

So, average power $= \frac{\text{Work done}}{\text{Time}}$

$$= \frac{12500}{10} = 1250 \text{ W}$$

76 (b) Final angular speed of system

$$\omega = \frac{I_1\omega_1 + I_2\omega_2}{I_1 + I_2}$$

Loss of energy

$$= \frac{1}{2}I\omega_1^2 + \frac{1}{2}I\omega_2^2 - \frac{1}{2}(2I)\omega^2 \quad (\because I_1 = I_2)$$

$$= \frac{1}{4}I(\omega_1-\omega_2)^2$$

77 (d) The point of contact P is momentarily at rest and the ring rotates about P.

$$\therefore \quad \alpha = \frac{\tau_P}{I_P} = \frac{F(2R)}{2MR^2} = \frac{F}{MR}$$

As $F + f = Ma = M(R\alpha) = F$

$$F + f = F \quad (\therefore f = 0)$$

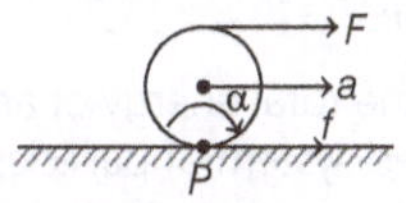

78 (c) Using $\omega = \omega_0 + \alpha t$

$$\Rightarrow \quad 0 = 2\pi - \alpha 60$$

$$\Rightarrow \quad \alpha = \frac{\pi}{30}$$

$$\therefore \quad \tau = I\alpha = 2\times\frac{\pi}{30} = \frac{\pi}{15} \text{ N-m}$$

79 (d) As, $I_2\omega_2 = I_1\omega_1$

$$\therefore \quad \omega_2 = \frac{I_1}{I_2}\times\omega_1 = \frac{I_1}{\frac{75I_1}{100}}\times 3\pi$$

$$= \frac{4}{3}\times 3\pi = 4\pi \text{ rad s}^{-1}$$

80 (c) As, $I_1\omega_1 + I_2\omega_2 = (I_1 + I_2)\,\omega$

or $2\times 8 + 4\times 4 = (2+4)\,\omega$

or $\omega = \frac{16+16}{6} = \frac{32}{6}$

$$= \frac{16}{3} \text{ rad/s}$$

82 (a) As the acrobat bends his body, then moment of inertia I will decrease and hence ω of acrobat will increase as no external torque is acting on the acrobat.

83 (*d*) $I_1\omega_1 = I_2\omega_2$

$$\omega_2 = \frac{I\omega \times 100}{60\,I} = \frac{5\omega}{3}$$

84 (*b*) According to law of conservation of angular momentum, $L = I\omega =$ constant, therefore when angular velocity increases, then moment of inertia of the system will decrease, so that L remains constant.

Assertion and Reason Questions

1 (*a*) If the external force acting on the system is zero, the centre of mass will remain at rest.

2 (*c*) It is not necessary that translational motion of body is always in straight line. A parabolic motion of an object without rotation is also translational motion.

3 (*a*) If the total energy of an isolated system of particles remains constant, then the centre of mass of the system will move along the same path as a single particle having same mass and same initial conditions.

7 (*a*) The total momentum of a system of particles is the vector sum of the momenta of all the particles in the system. If there is no external force acting on the system, the total momentum of the system will remain constant.

8 (*a*) The torque acting on a rigid body is given by $\tau = \frac{dL}{dt}$

Torque is a measurement of the rotational force acting on a rigid body.

9 (*d*) Due to melting of polar ice caps, more water is reacting near equator & so moment of inertia of earth is increasing. As, $L =$ constant,

$w \propto \frac{1}{T}$, so w is decreasing

$\therefore T$ is increasing.

Statement Based Questions

3 (*b*) Statement I is correct but Statement II is incorrect.

For a general translational motion, momentum $p = mv$, hence **p** and **v** are always parallel.

5 (*b*) Statement I is correct but Statement II is incorrect. Statement II can be corrected as, the shape of rigid body must not change on application of force.

6 (*b*) Statement I is correct but Statement II is incorrect. It can be corrected as, at equilibrium.

Load arm × Load

$$= \text{Effort} \times \text{Effort arm}$$

$$F_1 d_1 = F_2 d_2$$

$$\Rightarrow \quad \frac{F_1}{F_2} = \frac{d_2}{d_1}$$

The ratio of $\frac{F_1}{F_2}$ is called mechanical advantage (MA).

8 (*b*) Statement I is correct but Statement II is incorrect. It can be corrected as, moment of inertia of a body changes with changing the axis of rotation.

Numerical Type Questions

1. (8) The given situation is shown below

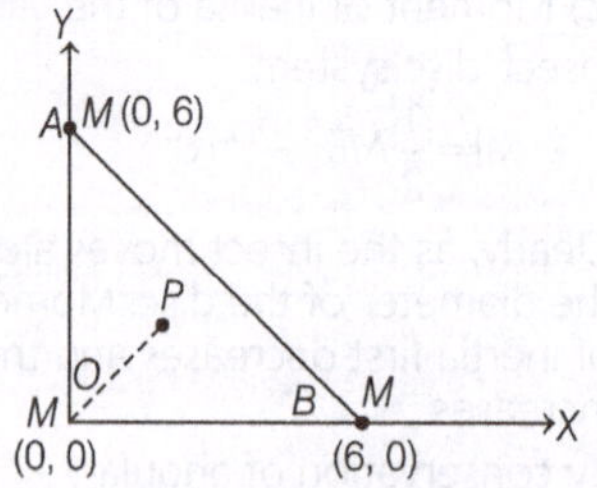

Now, $X_{COM} = \frac{x_1 m_1 + x_2 m_2 + x_3 m_3}{m_1 + m_2 + m_3}$

$$= \frac{0(M) + 6(M) + 0(M)}{M + M + M} = 2\hat{i}$$

and $Y_{COM} = \frac{y_1 m_1 + y_2 m_2 + y_3 m_3}{m_1 + m_2 + m_3}$

$$= \frac{0(M) + 0(M) + 6\hat{j}(M)}{M + M + M} = 2\,\hat{j}$$

$\therefore$ Position vector of COM,

$$\mathbf{OP} = 2\hat{i} + 2\hat{j}$$

$$|\mathbf{OP}| = \sqrt{2^2 + 2^2} = \sqrt{8} = \sqrt{x}$$

$\therefore \quad x = 8$

2. (200)

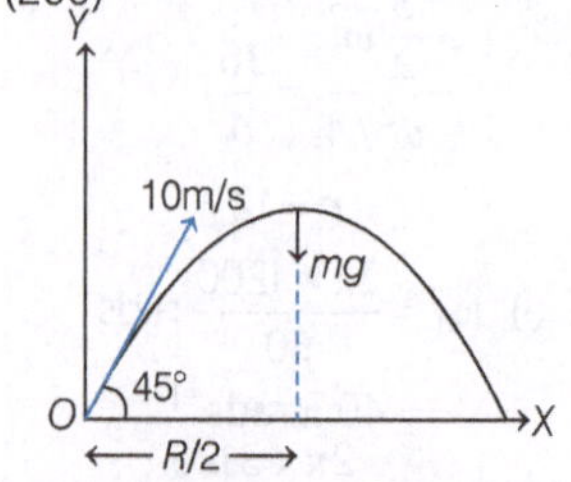

The range of particle is

$$R = \frac{u^2 \sin 2\theta}{g} = \frac{(10)^2 \sin 90^\circ}{10} = 10 \text{ m}$$

Now, torque of the weight of the particle about point of projection,

$$\tau = \mathbf{r} \times \mathbf{F}$$

Here, $\mathbf{r} = \frac{\mathbf{R}}{2}$, $\mathbf{F} = m\mathbf{g}$

$$\therefore \quad \tau = \frac{R}{2}\hat{i} \times (4 \times 10)(-\hat{j})$$

$$= \frac{10}{2} \times (40)(\hat{i} \times (-\hat{j}))$$

$$= -200\,\hat{\mathbf{k}} = -N\,\hat{\mathbf{k}}$$

$\therefore \quad N = 200$

3. (2) Mass of length $dx = \frac{m}{L} dx$

$\therefore$ Centripetal force $= \left(\frac{m}{L} dx\right) x\omega^2$

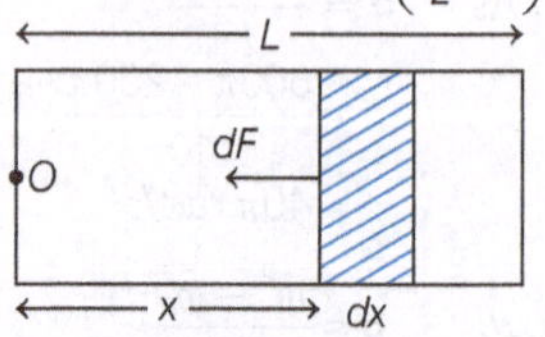

$$dF = \frac{m}{L}\omega^2 x\,dx$$

$$F = \int dF = \frac{m\omega^2}{L}\int_0^L x\,dx$$

$$= \frac{mL\omega^2}{2} = \frac{mL\omega^2}{n}$$

$\therefore \quad n = 2$

4. (5) Volume of sphere = Volume of disc

$$\frac{4}{3}\pi R_1^3 = \pi R^2 \times \frac{R}{6}$$

$$\Rightarrow \quad R_1 = \frac{R}{2}$$

Now, moment of inertia of sphere about its diameter,

$$I' = \frac{2}{5}MR_1^2$$

$$= \frac{2}{5}M\left(\frac{R}{2}\right)^2 = \frac{2}{5}\frac{MR^2}{4}$$

$$= \frac{1}{5}\left(\frac{MR^2}{2}\right)\left[\because I = \frac{MR^2}{2}\right]$$

$$= \frac{I}{5} = \frac{I}{n}$$

$\therefore \quad n = 5$

5. (4) As we know that,

Radius of gyration, $k \propto \sqrt{I}$

$$\therefore \quad \frac{k_1}{k_2} = \sqrt{\frac{I_1}{I_2}}$$

$$\Rightarrow \quad \frac{5}{x} = \sqrt{\frac{I_c + m(3)^2}{I_c}}$$

$$\Rightarrow \quad \frac{5}{x} = \sqrt{1 + \frac{9m}{mx^2}}$$

$$\Rightarrow \quad x = \sqrt{25 - 9}$$

$$\Rightarrow \quad x = \sqrt{16} = 4 \text{ cm}$$

6 (10) Here, time taken for the box to fall,

$$T = \sqrt{\frac{2h}{g}} = \sqrt{\frac{2 \times 20}{10}} = 2 \text{ s}$$

$\because$ The box is rotate about the corner,

Angular impulse = Change in angular momentum

$$\tau \times t = I\omega$$

$$\Rightarrow \quad mg \times \frac{l}{2} \times t = \frac{ml^2}{3}\omega$$

$$\Rightarrow \quad \omega = \frac{3gt}{2l}$$

$$= \frac{3 \times 10 \times 0.01}{2 \times 0.03} = 5 \text{ rad/s}$$

Now, angle of rotation, $= \omega \times T$

$$= 5 \times 2 = 10 \text{ rad}$$

7. (2) As bullet gets embedded at centre of door,

So, $r = \dfrac{1.2}{2} = 0.6$ m

Now, angular moment transferred by bullet to door

$$L = mv \times r$$

$$= 6 \times 10^{-3} \times 250 \times 0.6$$

$$= 0.98 \text{ J-s}$$

Moment of Inertia of door about the vertical axis at one end,

$$I = \frac{Ml^2}{3} = \frac{15 \times 1.2}{3} = 6 \text{ kg-m}^2$$

As we know,

$$L = I\omega$$

$$\omega = \frac{L}{I} = \frac{0.9}{6}$$

$$= 0.15 = 15 \times 10^{-2} \text{ rad/s}$$

$$= 15 \times 10^{-x} \text{ rad/s}$$

So, x is 2.

8. (33) According to law of conservation of angular momentum,

$$I_1\omega_1 = I_2\omega_2$$

$$\omega_2 = \frac{I_1}{I_2}\omega_1 = \frac{I}{(2/3)I} \times 22$$

$$= \frac{3}{2} \times 22 = 33 \text{ rad/s}$$

NCERT Exemplar Questions

3 (*b*) The initial velocity is $\mathbf{v}_i = v\hat{\mathbf{e}}_y$ and after reflection from the wall, the final velocity is $\mathbf{v}_f = -v\hat{\mathbf{e}}_y$. The trajectory is described as position vector $\mathbf{r} = y\hat{\mathbf{e}}_y + a\hat{\mathbf{e}}_z$.

Hence, the change in angular momentum is

$\mathbf{r} \times m(\mathbf{v}_f - \mathbf{v}_i) = 2mva\hat{\mathbf{e}}_x$.

4 (*d*) We know that, angular acceleration, $\alpha = \dfrac{d\omega}{dt}$

Given, ω = constant

$$\Rightarrow \quad \alpha = \frac{d\omega}{dt} = \frac{0}{dt} = 0$$

Hence, angular acceleration is zero.

6 (*a*) Coordinate of centre of mass of non-uniform body is given as,

$$R = \frac{\int x\,dm}{\int dm}$$

where, $dm = \rho(x)dx$

Here, $\rho(x) = a(1 + bx^2)$

$$\Rightarrow \quad R = \frac{\int_0^L xa(1 + bx^2) \cdot dx}{\int_0^L a(1 + bx^2) \cdot dx}$$

$$= \frac{\left[\dfrac{ax^2}{2} + \dfrac{abx^4}{4}\right]_0^L}{\left[ax + \dfrac{abx^3}{3}\right]_0^L}$$

$$= \frac{\dfrac{a}{2} + \dfrac{ab}{4}}{a + \dfrac{ab}{3}} \quad [\because \text{given, } L = 1 \text{ m}]$$

$$= \frac{3(2 + b)}{4(3 + b)}$$

7 (*a*) As no external torque acts on the system, angular momentum should be conserved.

Hence, $\quad I\omega$ = constant $\quad$ ...(i)

From Eq. (i), $I_1\omega_1 = I_2\omega_2$

where, ω_1 and ω_2 are angular velocities before and after jumping.

$$\omega_2 = \frac{I_1\omega_1}{I_2} = \frac{2MR^2\omega}{MR^2} = 2\omega$$

Past Exams Questions

1 (*a*) Given, moment of inertia $I = 2400$ g cm^2

mass of rod, $m = 400$ g

We know that, moment of inertia of a thin rod, $I = \dfrac{ml^2}{12}$

$$\Rightarrow \quad \frac{12 \times I}{m} = l^2$$

$$\Rightarrow \quad l^2 = \frac{12 \times 2400}{400}$$

$$\Rightarrow \quad l^2 = 12 \times 6$$

$$\Rightarrow \quad l = \sqrt{72}$$

$$= 8.48 \simeq 8.5 \text{ cm}$$

2 (*a*) The given situation is shown below.

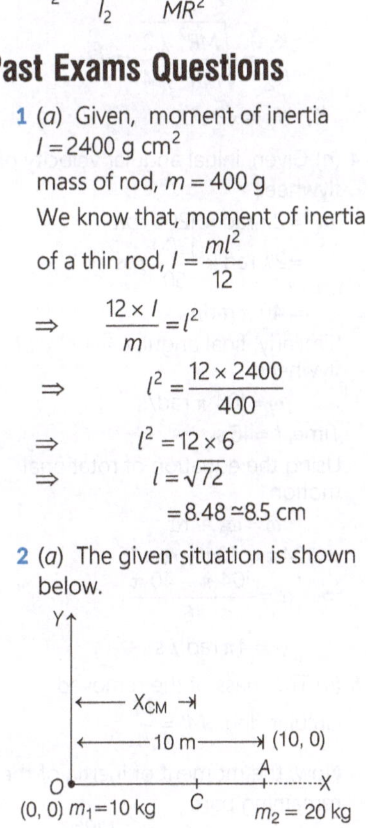

Let X_{CM} be the position of centre of mass from 10 kg mass.

$$\therefore \quad X_{CM} = \frac{m_1x_1 + m_2x_2}{m_1 + m_2}$$

$$= \frac{10 \times 0 + 20 \times 10}{10 + 20}$$

$$= \frac{200}{30} = \frac{20}{3} \text{ m}$$

3 (*a*) Radius of gyration of a body is given as $K = \sqrt{\frac{I}{m}}$

$$\therefore \quad \frac{K_1}{K_2} = \sqrt{\frac{I_1}{I_2}} \quad \text{...(i)}$$

I_1 = Moment of inertia of thin uniform disc about an axis passing through its centre and normal to plane.

$$I_1 = \frac{MR^2}{2}$$

I_2 = Moment of inertia of disc about its diameter.

$$I_2 = \frac{MR^2}{4}$$

$$\therefore \quad \frac{K_1}{K_2} = \sqrt{\frac{MR^2/2}{MR^2/4}} = \sqrt{2}$$

$$K_1 : K_2 = \sqrt{2} : 1$$

4 (*a*) Given, initial angular velocity of flywheel,

$$\omega_0 = 2\pi \text{ rad} \times 1200 \text{ rpm}$$

$$= 2\pi \text{ rad} \times \frac{1200}{60} \text{ rps}$$

$$= 40\,\pi \text{ rad/s}$$

Similarly, final angular velocity of flywheel,

$$\omega = 104\,\pi \text{ rad/s}$$

Time, $t = 16$ s

Using the equation of rotational motion,

$$\omega = \omega_0 + \alpha t$$

$$\Rightarrow 104\pi = 40\pi + \alpha \times 16$$

$$\Rightarrow \quad \alpha = \frac{104\,\pi - 40\,\pi}{16}$$

$$= 4\pi \text{ rad/s}$$

5 (*a*) The mass of the removed circular ring, $M' = \frac{M}{4}$

Now, the moment of inertia of the remaining part,

$$I'' = I - I' = MR^2 - \frac{MR^2}{4}$$

$$\Rightarrow \quad I'' = \frac{3MR^2}{4}$$

Comparing with $I'' = KMR^2$

The value of $K = 3/4$.

6 (*a*) Initial angular speed of wheel,

$$\omega_0 = 2\pi f_0 = 2\pi \times \frac{360}{60} \text{ rad/s}$$

$$= 12\pi \text{ rad/s}$$

Final angular speed of wheel,

$$\omega = 2\pi f$$

$$= 2\pi \times \frac{1200}{60} \text{ rad/s} = 40\pi \text{ rad/s}$$

and $\quad t = 14$ s

$$\omega = \omega_0 + \alpha t$$

$$\because \quad \alpha = \frac{\omega - \omega_0}{t}$$

$$= \frac{40\pi - 12\pi}{14} = \frac{28\pi}{14} = 2\pi \text{ rad/s}^2$$

7 (*c*) From third equation of motion for circular motion

$$\omega^2 - \omega_0^2 = 2\,\alpha\theta$$

$$\Rightarrow \left(\frac{v_0}{r}\right)^2 - 0 = 2\,\alpha(2\pi n)$$

$$\Rightarrow \quad \alpha = \frac{v_0^2}{4\pi n r^2} \text{ rad/s}^2$$

8 (*d*) Moment of force $= \mathbf{r} \times \mathbf{F}$

$$= (\mathbf{r}_1 - \mathbf{r}_2) \times \mathbf{F}$$

$$= [0\hat{\mathbf{i}} + 2\hat{\mathbf{j}} - 1\hat{\mathbf{k}}] \times [4\hat{\mathbf{i}} + 5\hat{\mathbf{j}} - 6\hat{\mathbf{k}}]$$

$$= \begin{vmatrix} \hat{\mathbf{i}} & \hat{\mathbf{j}} & \hat{\mathbf{k}} \\ 0 & 2 & -1 \\ 4 & 5 & -6 \end{vmatrix}$$

$$= \hat{\mathbf{i}}[(-6 \times 2) - (-1 \times 5)] - \hat{\mathbf{j}}[(-6 \times 0) - (-1 \times 4)] + \hat{\mathbf{k}}[(0 \times 5) - 2 \times 4]$$

$$= -7\hat{\mathbf{i}} - 4\hat{\mathbf{j}} - 8\hat{\mathbf{k}}$$

9 (*c*)

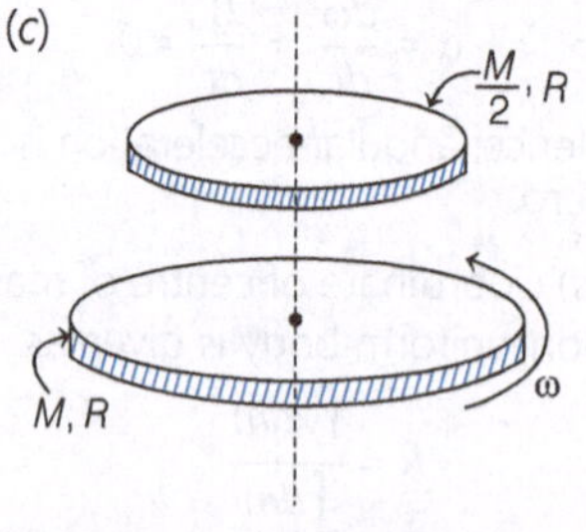

As there is no external torque, angular momentum of system is conserved.

$$\Rightarrow \quad I_1\omega_1 = I_2\omega_2 \quad \text{...(i)}$$

Here I_1 = moment of inertia of disc of mass M and radius $R = MR^2/2$

ω_1 = Angular speed of disc 1 = ω

I_2 = Moment of inertia of both discs combined.

$$= \frac{1}{2}\left(M + \frac{M}{2}\right) \times R^2 = \frac{3}{4}MR^2$$

So, from Eq. (i)

$$\frac{MR^2}{2} \times \omega = \frac{3}{4}MR^2 \times \omega_2$$

$$\text{or} \quad \omega_2 = \frac{2}{3}\omega$$

10 (*c*) For hollow sphere, moment of inertia,

$$I_1 = \frac{2}{3}mR^2 \text{ or } \left(\sqrt{\frac{2}{3}}R\right)^2 m$$

$$\therefore \quad K_1 = \sqrt{\frac{2}{3}}R \quad \text{...(i)}$$

[As $I = mK^2$]

For solid cylinder, moment of inertia,

$$I_2 = \frac{1}{4}mR^2 + \frac{m}{3}(4R)^2$$

$$= \left(\sqrt{\frac{67}{12}}R\right)^2 m$$

$$\therefore \quad K_2 = \sqrt{\frac{67}{12}}R \quad \text{...(ii)}$$

Taking the ratio of Eqs. (i) and (ii),

$$\frac{K_1}{K_2} = \sqrt{\frac{2}{3}}R \times \sqrt{\frac{12}{67}} \times \frac{1}{R} = \sqrt{\frac{8}{67}}$$

Matching with the given equation, the value of x is 67.

11 (*b*)

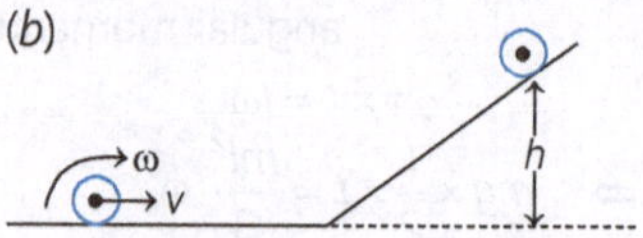

Energy conservation gives

$$\frac{1}{2}mv^2 + \frac{1}{2}I\omega^2 = mgh$$

For disc, $I = \frac{mr^2}{2}$ and $v = r\,\omega$, hence disc is not slipping.

So, we have

$$\frac{1}{2}mv^2 + \frac{1}{2}\frac{mr^2}{2} \times \frac{v^2}{r^2} = mgh$$

$$\Rightarrow \quad \left(\frac{1}{2} + \frac{1}{4}\right)mv^2 = mgh$$

$$\text{or} \quad h = \frac{3v^2}{4g}$$

12 (*b*) Given, $\mathbf{F} = 4\hat{\mathbf{i}} - 3\hat{\mathbf{j}}$

Resolving the components of position vector in horizontal and vertical direction

$\therefore$ Horizontal component,

$$r_x = r\cos\theta$$
$$= 10 \times \frac{1}{2} = 5 \text{ units}$$

Vertical component, $r_y = r\sin\theta$

$$= 10 \times \frac{\sqrt{3}}{2} = 5\sqrt{3} \text{ units}$$

$\therefore$ Position vector w.r.t. O,

$$\mathbf{r}_O = 5\hat{\mathbf{i}} + 5\sqrt{3}\,\hat{\mathbf{j}}$$

and position vector w.r.t. Q,

$$\mathbf{r}_Q = -5\hat{\mathbf{i}} + 5\sqrt{3}\,\hat{\mathbf{j}}$$

Torque at point P w.r.t. O,

$$\tau_O = \mathbf{r}_O \times \mathbf{F}$$
$$= (5\hat{\mathbf{i}} + 5\sqrt{3}\,\hat{\mathbf{j}}) \times (4\hat{\mathbf{i}} - 3\hat{\mathbf{j}})$$
$$= (15 + 20\sqrt{3})(-\hat{\mathbf{k}})$$
$$|\tau_O| = 15 + 20\sqrt{3}$$

Torque at point P w.r.t. Q,

$$\tau_Q = \mathbf{r}_Q \times \mathbf{F}$$
$$= (4\hat{\mathbf{i}} - 3\hat{\mathbf{j}}) \times (-5\hat{\mathbf{i}} + 5\sqrt{3}\hat{\mathbf{j}})$$
$$= (-15 + 20\sqrt{3})\hat{\mathbf{k}}$$
$$= (15 - 20\sqrt{3})(-\hat{\mathbf{k}})$$
$$|\tau_Q| = 15 - 20\sqrt{3}$$

13 (*d*) Let mass per unit area be σ.

$\therefore$ Mass of smaller disc, $M' = \pi r^2\sigma$

Mass of larger disc, $M = \pi R^2\sigma$

$\therefore$ Moment of inertia of smaller disc around one of its diameter lying on its plane,

$$I' = \frac{1}{4}M' r^2$$
$$\Rightarrow \quad I' = \frac{\pi\sigma r^4}{4}$$

and moment of inertia of bigger disc around axis AB (perpendicular to the plane) of disc and passing through its centre,

$$I = \frac{1}{2}MR^2 = \frac{\pi\sigma R^4}{2}$$
$$\therefore \quad \frac{I}{I'} = \frac{\frac{\pi\sigma R^4}{2}}{\frac{\pi\sigma r^4}{4}} = \frac{2R^4}{r^4}$$
$$\Rightarrow \quad \frac{I}{I'} = \frac{2R^4}{r^4}$$

14 (*d*)

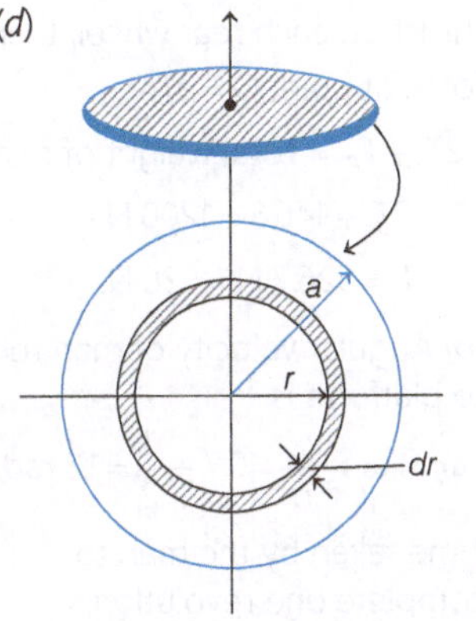

Given, mass per unit area,

$$\sigma(r) = A + Br$$

Mass of elemental ring,

$$dm = \sigma(r) \cdot dA = (A + Br)2\pi r\, dr$$

Moment of inertia of this elemental ring about axis,

$$dI = dm \cdot r^2$$
$$= 2\pi r^3\,(A + Br) \cdot dr$$

Moment of inertia of complete disc of radius a,

$$I = \int_0^a dI = \int_0^a 2\pi r^3 (A + Br)\, dr$$
$$= \left[2\pi A \frac{r^4}{4} + 2\pi B \frac{r^5}{5}\right]_0^a$$
$$= 2\pi a^4\left(\frac{A}{4} + \frac{aB}{5}\right)$$

15 (*b*)

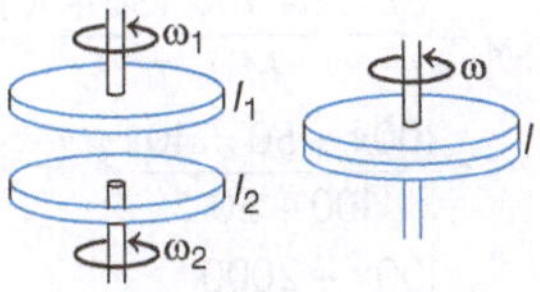

As there is no external torque, angular momentum of system is conserved

$$L_1 + L_2 = L_{\text{system}}$$
$$\Rightarrow I_1\omega_1 + I_2\omega_2 = (I_1 + I_2)\omega$$
$$\Rightarrow \quad \omega = \frac{I_1\omega_1 + I_2\omega_2}{I_1 + I_2}$$
$$\omega = \frac{0.1 \times 10 + 0.2 \times 5}{(0.1 + 0.2)}$$
$$\text{or} \quad \omega = \frac{20}{3} \text{ rad/s}$$

Kinetic energy of combined system is

$$K = \frac{1}{2} I_{\text{system}}\omega^2$$
$$= \frac{1}{2}(0.1 + 0.2) \times \left(\frac{20}{3}\right)^2 = \frac{20}{3}\text{ J}$$

16 (*a*) For a system of discrete masses, acceleration of centre of mass (CM) is given by

$$a_{\text{CM}} = \frac{m_A a_A + m_B a_B + m_C a_C + m_D a_D}{m_A + m_B + m_C + m_D}$$

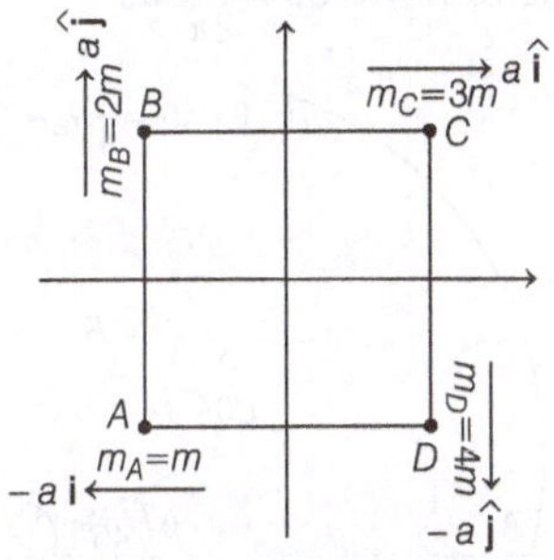

$$a_{\text{CM}} = \frac{-ma\hat{\mathbf{i}} + 2ma\hat{\mathbf{j}} + 3ma\hat{\mathbf{i}} - 4ma\hat{\mathbf{j}}}{m + 2m + 3m + 4m}$$
$$= \frac{2a\hat{\mathbf{i}} - 2a\hat{\mathbf{j}}}{10}$$
$$= \frac{a}{5} \cdot (\hat{\mathbf{i}} - \hat{\mathbf{j}}) \text{ ms}^{-2}$$

Skill Boosters

1 (*d*) As system is symmetrical about X-axis. Therefore CM of system will lie on along X-axis.

Mass of square plate,

$$m_1 = \sigma L^2$$
$$\text{and} \quad x_1 = -\frac{L}{2}$$

Mass of circular disc,

$$m_2 = \pi\left(\frac{L}{2}\right)^2 \sigma = \frac{\pi L^2\sigma}{4}$$
$$\text{and} \quad x_2 = +\frac{L}{2}$$

Now, centre of mass of the composite plate, relative to the point O,

$$x_{\text{cm}} = \frac{m_1x_1 + m_2x_2}{m_1 + m_2}.$$

$$= \frac{\sigma L^2\left(-\frac{L}{2}\right) + \frac{\pi L^2 \sigma}{4}\left(\frac{L}{2}\right)}{\sigma L^2 + \frac{\pi L^2 \sigma}{4}}$$

$$= \left(\frac{\pi - 4}{\pi + 4}\right)\frac{L}{2} \text{ along } X\text{-axis.}$$

2 (c) Let dm is the elementary mass of small arc length that makes an angle $d\theta$ at its centre of curvature, and λ is the mass per unit angle then $dm = \lambda \cdot d\theta = \frac{m}{2\pi} \cdot d\theta$

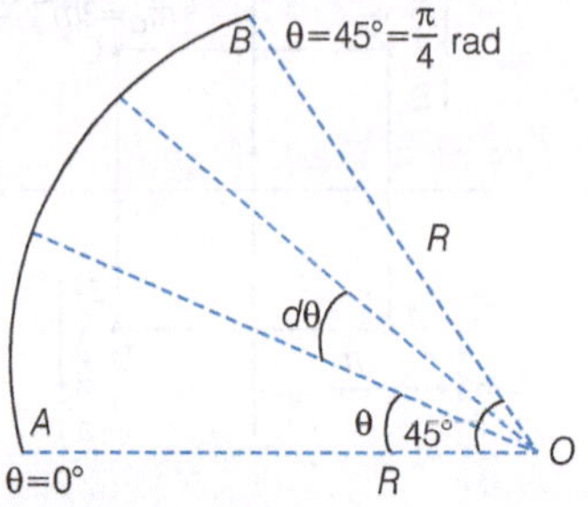

The moment of inertia of this elementary length about Z-axis is given by

$$dI = dmR^2 = \frac{m}{2\pi} R^2 d\theta$$

The moment of inertia of arc length AB about Z-axis is therefore.

$$I = \frac{m}{2\pi} R^2 \int_0^{\frac{\pi}{4}} d\theta$$

$$= \frac{m}{2\pi} \cdot R^2 \frac{\pi}{4} = \frac{1}{8} mR^2$$

3 (b) Force at $C_r = 70g = 700$ N

Force at $C_t = 50g = 500$ N

In the equilibrium position, the torque on the system about point O must be balanced.

So, Torque at P = Torque at C_r + Torque at C_t

$$F_P \times 1.5 = 700 \times 0.1 + 500 \times 0.3$$

$$F_P = \frac{70 + 150}{1.5} = 146.6 \text{ N}$$

Now, the force of rear wheel acts at the mid-point of AB. If T is the thrust on each rear wheel, then force at point $O = 2T$.

$\therefore 2T + F_P$ = Total weight of system

$$2T + 146.6 = 1200 \text{ N}$$

$$T = 526.7 \text{ N} \approx 526 \text{ N}.$$

4 (b) Angular velocity of man relative to platform is

$$\omega_r = \omega + \frac{v_0}{r} = 0.7 + \frac{1}{2} = 1.2 \text{ rad/s}.$$

Time taken by the man to complete one revolution,

$$T = \frac{2\pi}{\omega_r} = \frac{2\pi}{1.2} \text{ s}$$

Now, angular displacement of the man with respect to ground,

$$\theta = \omega_0 T = \frac{v_0 t}{r}$$

$$= \frac{1}{2}\left(\frac{2\pi}{1.2}\right) = \frac{5}{6}\pi \text{ rad}.$$

5 (c) Since no external force acts, the centre of mass of the system remains at rest even when the boy walks on the plank.

Let the seaboard be at the origin $O\,(x = 0)$. Initially x be the distance of the centre of mass of the plank from O. Then, the distance of the centre of mass of the system (plank + boy) from O will be

$$x_{CM} = \frac{M \times x + m \times (30 + 10)}{M + m}$$

$$= \frac{100x + 50 \times 40}{100 + 50}$$

$$= \frac{100x + 2000}{150}$$

Since the boy moves towards the seaboard and the centre of mass of the system has to remain at rest, the plank will move away from the seaboard. If x' is the distance moved by the plank, the distance of the centre of mass from the seaboard when the boy walks 6 m on the plank is given by

$$x'_{CM} = \frac{100\,(x + x') + 50\,(40 - 6 + x')}{100 + 50}$$

$$= \frac{100x + 150x' + 1700}{150}$$

Since $x_{CM} = x'_{CM}$

$$\frac{100x + 2000}{150} = \frac{100x + 150x' + 1700}{150}$$

$$\Rightarrow x' = \frac{300}{150} = 2 \text{ m}$$

$\therefore$ Distance of the boy from the seaboard $= 40 - 6 + 2 = 36$ m.

6 (b) Since the system (boy + plank) is initially at rest, its momentum is zero. Since no external force acts on the system, the momentum of the system will remain zero. Let us assume that the boy runs in the positive x-direction.

Velocity of boy relative to the plank is

$$\mathbf{v}_{bp} = v\hat{\mathbf{i}}$$

Now, $\mathbf{v}_{bp} = \mathbf{v}_b - \mathbf{v}_p$

where $\mathbf{v}_b$ = velocity of boy relative to ground

and $\mathbf{v}_p$ = velocity of plank relative to ground

Hence, $\mathbf{v}_b = \mathbf{v}_{bp} + \mathbf{v}_p$

$$= v\hat{\mathbf{i}} + v_p\hat{\mathbf{i}}$$

$$= (v + v_p)\hat{\mathbf{i}}$$

Total momentum of plank + boy $= 0$

$$\Rightarrow \quad M\mathbf{v}_p + m\mathbf{v}_b = 0$$

$$\Rightarrow \quad Mv_p\hat{\mathbf{i}} + mv_b\hat{\mathbf{i}} = 0$$

$$\Rightarrow \quad Mv_p\hat{\mathbf{i}} + m\,(v + v_p)\hat{\mathbf{i}} = 0$$

which gives $v_p = -\frac{mv}{M + m}$

$\therefore$ Velocity of boy is $\mathbf{v}_b$

$$= \left(v - \frac{mv}{M + m}\right)\hat{\mathbf{i}} = \frac{mv}{M + m}\hat{\mathbf{i}}$$

$$= \left(\frac{250 \times 6}{250 + 50}\right)\hat{\mathbf{i}}$$

$$\therefore |v_p| = 5 \text{ m/s}$$

7 (d) For uniform motion in a horizontal circle, the tension in the string is equal to the centripetal force.

$$T = \frac{mv^2}{r} = \frac{mv^2}{l} \qquad (\because r = l)$$

Angular momentum about the centre of the circle is

$L = mvr = mvl = \text{constant} = k$ (given)

$\therefore \quad v = \dfrac{k}{ml}$

$\therefore \quad T = \dfrac{m}{l}\left(\dfrac{k}{ml}\right)^2 = \dfrac{k^2}{ml^3}$

When $l' = \dfrac{l}{2}$,

$$T' = \dfrac{k^2}{m\left(\dfrac{l}{2}\right)^3} = \dfrac{8k^2}{ml^3} = 8T$$

8 (*d*)

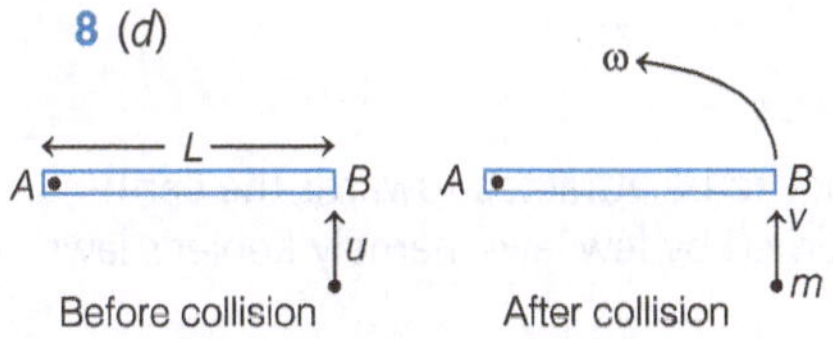

(a) Let v be the velocity of the ball just after collision. Since the collision is perfectly elastic, $e = 1$, i.e.

Velocity of approach = Velocity of separation

or $\quad u = \omega L - v$

$\Rightarrow \quad \omega = \dfrac{u + v}{L}$ ...(i)

$\because$ there is no external torque, the angular momentum about point A is conserved i.e.

$$muL = mvL + I\omega$$

$$\omega = \dfrac{3(u - v)m}{ML} \quad \text{... (ii)}$$

From Eqs. (i) and (ii)

$$v = \left(\dfrac{3m - M}{3m + M}\right)u \quad \text{... (iii)}$$

Now, from Eqs. (iii) and (i), we get

$$\omega = \dfrac{6mu}{(3m + M)L} = \dfrac{6 \times 0.2 \times 5}{(3 \times 0.2 + 0.4) \times 1}$$

$$= 6.0 \text{ rad/s}$$

9 (*b*) Let the mass of each dumb-bell be m then,

Total initial angular momentum

$$= mr_1^2\,\omega_1 + mr_1^2\omega_1 = 2mr_1^2\omega_1$$

When the body pulls the dumb bells towards his chest, then

Final angular momentum

$$= 2mr_2^2\omega_2$$

From the principle of conservation of angular momentum.

Initial angular momentum = Final angular momentum

$$2mr_1^2\omega_1 = 2mr_2^2\omega_2$$

$$\omega_2 = \dfrac{r_1^2}{r_2^2}\,\omega_1 = \dfrac{(0.8)^2}{(0.4)^2} \times 2 = \dfrac{0.64}{0.16} \times 2$$

$$= 4 \times 2 = 8 \text{ rad/s}$$

10 (*b*) Initially m_2 is at rest at a height h above the floor and m_1 and pulley are also at rest. Hence the total initial energy of the system is

$E_i = 0 + m_2gh = m_2gh$

When m_2 is released, it begins to fall and m_1 begins to rise. Let v be the speed of m_2 just before it hits the floor.

At this instant the speed of m_1 rising up is also v and height of m_1 at this instant is also h. Therefore, the final total energy of the system is

E_f = PE of m_1 at height h + KE of m_1 and m_2 + rotational KE of pulley

$$= m_1gh + \dfrac{1}{2}m_1v^2 + \dfrac{1}{2}m_2v^2 + \dfrac{1}{2}I\omega^2$$

$$= m_1gh + \dfrac{1}{2}v^2(m_1 + m_2) + \dfrac{1}{2} \times \left(\dfrac{1}{2}MR^2\right) \times \left(\dfrac{v}{R}\right)^2$$

$$= m_1gh + \dfrac{1}{2}v^2\left(m_1 + m_2 + \dfrac{M}{2}\right)$$

From conservation of energy,

$$E_f = E_i$$

$$\Rightarrow m_1gh + \dfrac{1}{2}v^2\left(m_1 + m_2 + \dfrac{M}{2}\right) = m_2gh$$

$$v = \left[\dfrac{2(m_2 - m_1)gh}{m_1 + m_2 + \dfrac{M}{2}}\right]^{\frac{1}{2}}$$

put, $m_1 = 2$ kg, $m_2 = 4$ kg,

$M = 8$ kg, $h = 1$ m

$g = 10 \text{ m/s}^2$, then

$$v = \sqrt{\dfrac{2 \times 2 \times 10 \times 1}{10}}$$

$$v = \sqrt{4} = 2 \text{ m/s}$$

07

Scan for **Physics Through Concept Master** Videos

Gravitation

Topicwise No. of Ques asked in 5 Years (NEET)

Topics	No. of Questions				
	2024	2023	2022	2021	2020
Kepler's Laws	–	–	–	–	–
Universal Law of Gravitation and The Gravitational Constant	–	–	–	–	–
Acceleration Due to Gravity and its Variation	1	–	1	–	2
Gravitational Potential Energy	1	1	–	–	–
Escape Velocity and Satellites	–	1	–	2	–

Special Type of Ques Asked In 5 Years (NEET)

Types	Years				
	2024	2023	2022	2021	2020
A-R	–	–	–	–	–
Statement Based	–	–	–	–	–
Matching	–	1	–	–	–

Last 5 Years Weigtage (NEET)

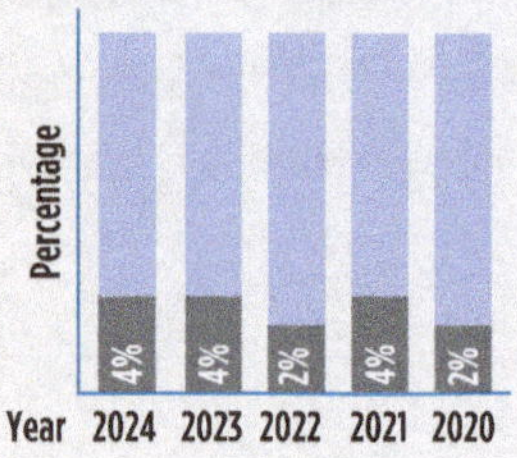

Each material object has a tendency to be attracted towards the earth. This tendency of an object is governed by few laws, namely Kepler's laws and gravitational law.

Kepler's Laws

These are three scientific laws describing the motion of planets around the sun as given below

1. **Law of Orbits** All planets move in elliptical orbit with sun situated at one of the foci of the ellipse as shown in figure below.

   The closest point P is called **perihelion** and the farthest point A is called **aphelion**.

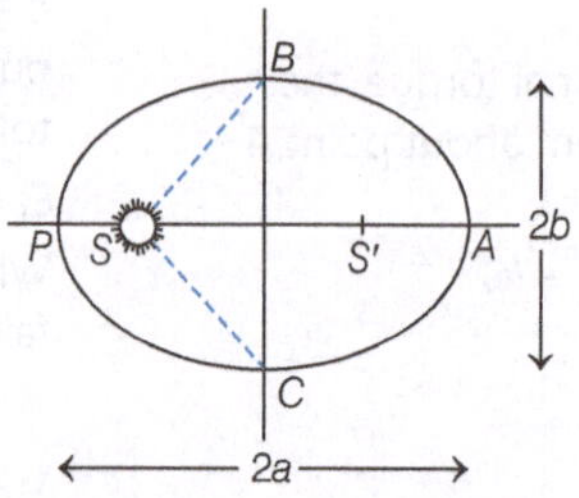

2. **Law of Areas** The line that joins any planet to the sun sweeps equal areas in equal intervals of time.

   The planet P as shown in figure below appears to move slower when it is farther from the sun than when it is nearer.

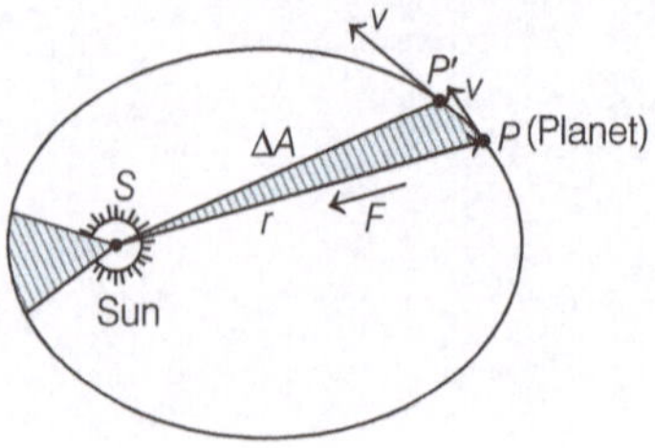

The area ΔA swept out by the planet of mass m in time interval Δt is given by $\Delta \mathbf{A} = \frac{1}{2}(\mathbf{r} \times \mathbf{v}\Delta t)$

Hence, $$\frac{\Delta \mathbf{A}}{\Delta t} = \frac{1}{2}\frac{\mathbf{r} \times \mathbf{p}}{m} = \frac{\mathbf{L}}{2m} \qquad \left(\because \mathbf{v} = \frac{\mathbf{p}}{m}\right)$$

where, **v** is the velocity and **L** is the angular momentum equal to $(\mathbf{r} \times \mathbf{p})$.

For a central force F, which is directed along **r**, **L** is a constant as the planet goes around the sun. Hence, $\Delta \mathbf{A}/\Delta t$ is a constant.

- The law of areas can be understood as a consequence of conservation of angular momentum, which is valid for any central force.
- A **central force** is such that the force on the planet is along the vector joining the sun and the planet.

3. **Law of Periods** The square of the time period of revolution of a planet is proportional to the cube of semi-major axis of the ellipse traced out by the planet,

i.e. $$T^2 \propto a^3$$

where, a = semi-major axis and T = time period. NEET 2019

Universal Law of Gravitation

- It states that every body in the universe attracts every other body with a force which is directly proportional to the product of their masses and inversely proportional to the square of the distance between them.
- The gravitational force F between two point masses m_1 and m_2 separated by r distance apart is given by

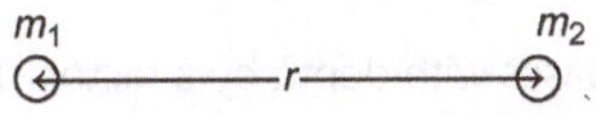

$$F \propto \frac{m_1 m_2}{r^2} \Rightarrow F = G\frac{m_1 m_2}{r^2}$$

where, G is a **universal gravitational constant** and assumed to have the same value everywhere for all matter.

- The force **F** on a point mass m_2 due to another point mass m_1 can be expressed in vector form as

$$\mathbf{F} = -G \cdot \frac{m_1 m_2}{r^2} \cdot \hat{\mathbf{r}} \text{ or } \mathbf{F} = -G\frac{m_1 m_2}{|\mathbf{r}|^3}\mathbf{r}$$

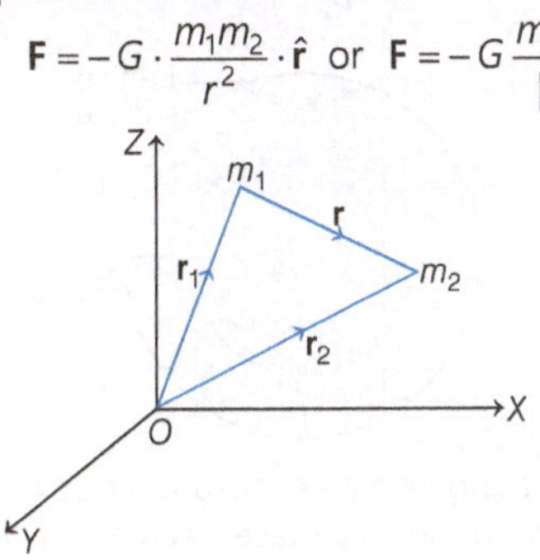

where, **r** is the unit vector from m_1 to m_2 and $\mathbf{r} = \mathbf{r}_2 - \mathbf{r}_1$.

- **Characteristics of the gravitational force**
  - The gravitational force is attractive in nature and directed along the line joining the point masses, i.e. the force **F** is along $-\mathbf{r}$.
  - The direction of gravitational force on m_1 due to m_2 is along **r**. So, by Newton's third law, this force is of course $-\mathbf{F}$.
  - If $\mathbf{F}_{12}$ is the gravitational force on body 1 due to body 2 and $\mathbf{F}_{21}$ is the gravitational force on body 2 due to body 1, then they are related as $\mathbf{F}_{12} = -\mathbf{F}_{21}$.
  - Gravitational force is a central as well as conservative force but the weakest force in nature.
  - It is independent of the nature of the medium in which point masses are present.
  - It holds good for long distances like interplanetary distance and also for short distances like interatomic distances.
  - It depends upon the initial and final positions of the particle. So, work done by gravity around a closed path is zero.
  - The universal law of gravitation refers to the **point masses**, whereas we deal with the extended objects which have finite size.
  - If we have collection of point masses, the force on any one of them is the vector sum of the gravitational forces exerted by the other point masses as shown below

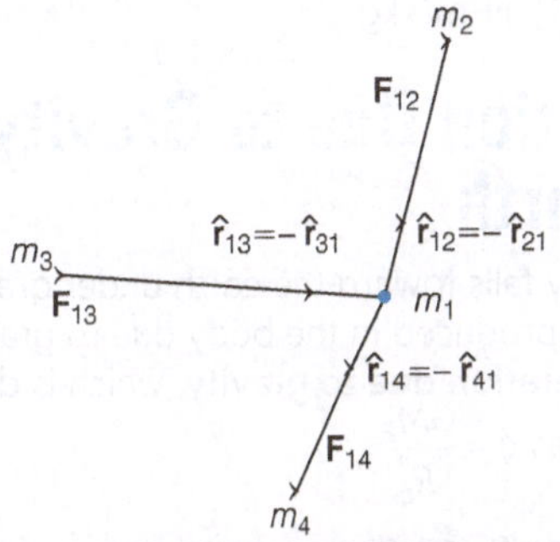

The total force on m_1 is

$$\mathbf{F}_1 = \frac{Gm_2 m_1}{r_{21}^2}\hat{\mathbf{r}}_{21} + \frac{Gm_3 m_1}{r_{31}^2}\hat{\mathbf{r}}_{31} + \frac{Gm_4 m_1}{r_{41}^2}\hat{\mathbf{r}}_{41}$$

- The force of attraction between a hollow spherical shell of uniform density and a point mass situated outside is just as if the entire mass of the shell is concentrated at the centre of the shell.
- The force of attraction due to a hollow spherical shell of uniform density, on a point mass situated inside it is zero.

The Gravitational Constant

- The value of the gravitational constant G was first calculated by English scientist **Henry Cavendish** in 1798.
- The apparatus used by him is schematically shown in figure below.

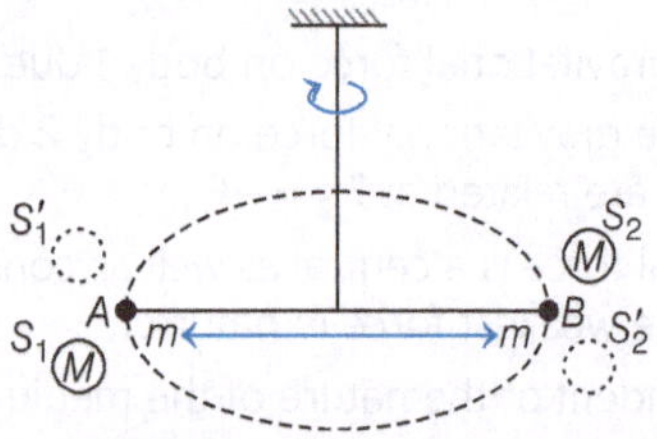

S_1 and S_2 are large spheres which are kept on either side of masses at A and B. When the big spheres S_1' and S_2' are taken to other side of the masses, then the bar AB rotates a little by an angle θ due to restoring torque per unit angle τ reverses its direction. This angle θ is measured experimentally.

- If M and m are the masses of big sphere and its neighbouring small ball with separation between them d, then the gravitational constant is determined by $G = \frac{\tau \theta d^2}{MmL}$, where L is the length of the bar AB.
- Observation of θ thus enables one to calculate G from the above equation and currently its accepted value is $G = 6.67 \times 10^{-11}$ N-m^2/kg^2.

Acceleration Due to Gravity of the Earth

- When a body falls toward the earth under gravity, then acceleration produced in the body due to gravity is called **acceleration due to gravity**, which is denoted by g and given as $g = \frac{GM_E}{R_E^2}$.

  where, M_E and R_E are the mass and radius of the earth, respectively.
- By putting the values of G, M_E and R_E, the acceleration due to gravity on the surface of the earth is calculated as

$$g = \frac{GM_E}{R_E^2} = \frac{6.67 \times 10^{-11} \times 6 \times 10^{24}}{(6400 \times 10^3)^2} = 9.8 \text{ m/s}^2$$

- The expression for g at the surface of the earth in **terms of density** ρ of the earth is given by

$$g = \frac{4}{3} \pi G \rho \cdot R_E$$

Acceleration Due to Gravity Below and Above the Surface of the Earth

- The value of g at point P at a certain height h from earth's surface as shown in figure below is given by

$$g(h) = \frac{GM_E}{(R_E + h)^2} = \frac{g}{\left(1 + \frac{h}{R_E}\right)^2}$$ NEET 2020

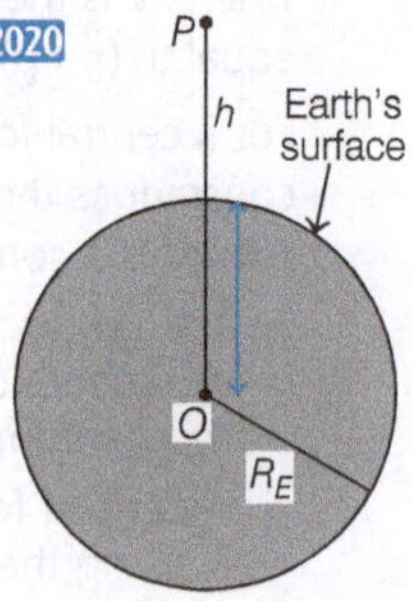

where, g = acceleration due to gravity on the surface of earth.

For $h << R_E$, $g(h) \approx g\left(1 - \frac{2h}{R_E}\right)$

Therefore, g decreases with height by a factor $(1 - 2h/R_E)$.

- The value of g at point P at a depth d from earth's surface as shown in figure below is given by

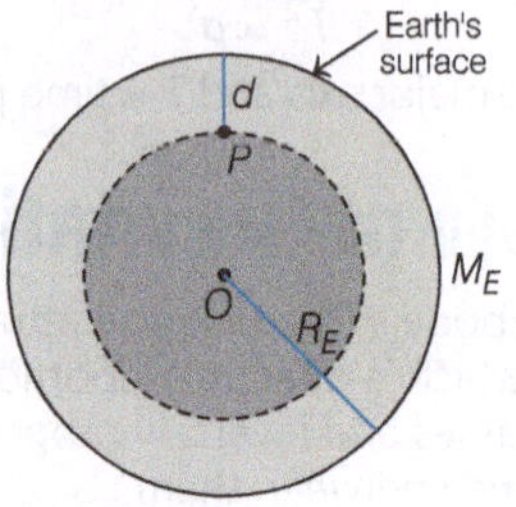

$$g(d) = g\left(1 - \frac{d}{R_E}\right)$$

Therefore, g decreases with depth by a factor $\left(1 - \frac{d}{R_e}\right)$ and becomes zero at earth's centre.

- The acceleration due to gravity inside the earth at point P at a distance r from the centre of the earth as shown in figure below is given by

$$g(r) = \left(\frac{GM_E}{R_E^3}\right) r$$

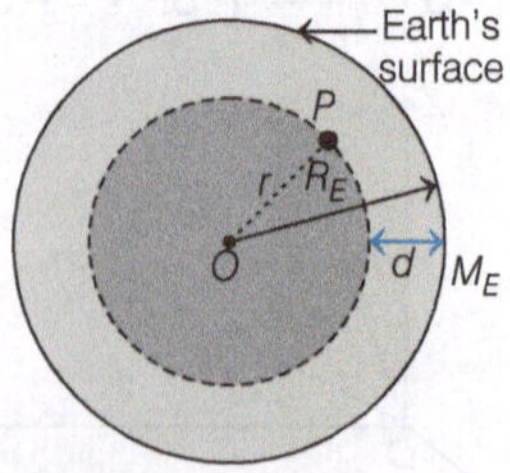

The remarkable thing about acceleration due to earth's gravity is that it is maximum on its surface decreasing whether you go up or down. NEET 2020

Gravitational Potential Energy

- **Gravitational potential energy** of a body at a point is the amount of work done in bringing a given body from infinity to a point against the gravitational force.
- If m_1 and m_2 are two masses separated by infinite distance, then gravitational potential energy of the system when they are brought to a separation of r is given by
$$U = -\frac{Gm_1m_2}{r}$$
where, the negative sign indicates that the two bodies are attracting each other.
- Gravitational potential energy is a scalar quantity. Its dimensional formula is $[ML^2T^{-2}]$ and SI unit is joule.
- **The change in gravitational potential energy of a body** of mass m when it is lifted along a vertical path by a distance r_1 to r_2 from the centre of the earth is given by
$$U_{12} = U(r_2) - U(r_1) = -GM_Em\left(\frac{1}{r_2} - \frac{1}{r_1}\right)$$
where, M_E = mass of the earth.
- The gravitational potential energy of a body of mass m at height h above the surface of the earth ($r_1 = 0$, $r_2 = R_E + h$) is given by
$$U_h = -\frac{GM_Em}{(R_E + h)}$$
where, R_E = radius of the earth.
- The gravitational potential energy of a body of mass m on the surface of the earth ($r_1 = 0$, $r_2 = R$) is given by
$$U_{\text{surface}} = -\frac{GM_Em}{R_E}$$
- The potential energy associated with a body of mass m when it is lifted through a height h above the earth surface is given by
$$U_h = \frac{mgh}{\left(1 + \frac{h}{R_E}\right)}$$
For $h << R_E$, $U_h = mgh$
- **The gravitational potential** due to the gravitational force of the earth is defined as the potential energy of a body of unit mass at that point.
- The gravitational potential at a point at a distance r from a body of mass m is given by
$$V = \frac{U}{m} = -\frac{Gm}{r} \quad \text{(if we choose } V = 0 \text{ as } r \to \infty)$$
NEET 2023

Marks Maximiser

- **Gravitational Potential of some Continuous Mass Distributions**
  - **Uniform ring of mass M and radius R** Gravitational potential on the axis, $V = -\frac{GM}{(R^2 + x^2)^{1/2}}$
  - **Uniform disc of mass M and radius R** Gravitational potential on the axis, $V = -\frac{2GM}{R^2}[x - \sqrt{R^2 + x^2}]$
  - **Thin spherical shell of mass M and radius R** Gravitational potential at a distance r from centre.
    (i) Inside the shell, $V(r < R) = -\frac{GM}{R}$
    (ii) On the surface of shell, $V(r = R) = -\frac{GM}{R}$
    (iii) Outside the shell, $V(r > R) = -\frac{GM}{r}$

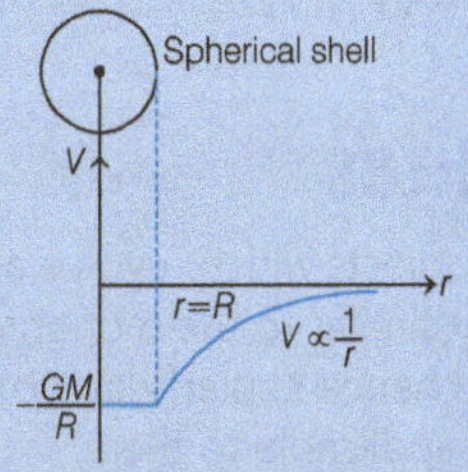

- **Gravitational Field**
  - The space around a material body in which its gravitational pull can be experienced is called its **gravitational field.**
  - **The intensity of gravitational field at** a point due to a body of mass M, at a distance r from the centre of the body,
  $$E = -\frac{GM}{r^2}$$
  where, negative sign shows that the gravitational intensity is of attractive nature.
  - Gravitational potential (V) is related with gravitational field intensity (E) by a relation
  $$E = -\frac{dV}{dr} \Rightarrow dV = -\mathbf{E} \cdot d\mathbf{r}$$

Escape Velocity

- The minimum speed required to project a body vertically upward from the earth surface, so that it reaches at infinity (i.e. escape from the earth) is called **escape velocity**.

It is given by
$$v_e = \sqrt{\frac{2GM_E}{R_E}} = \sqrt{2gR_E}$$
NEET 2021

- The escape speed on the surface of the earth in terms of density ρ of the earth is given by $v_e = \sqrt{\frac{8\pi\rho GR^2}{3}}$
- Escape velocity at the earth is 11.2 kms^{-1} and for the moon is 2.3 kms^{-1}, about five times smaller.
  This is the reason that **moon has no atmosphere**. Gas molecules if formed on the surface of the moon having velocities larger than this will escape from the gravitational pull of the moon.
- If a body is projected from a planet with a speed v which is smaller than the escape speed v_e $(v < v_e)$, then the body will reach a certain height may either move in an orbit around the planet or may fall back to the planet.
- If speed of projection (v) of the body from the surface of a planet is greater than the escape speed (v_e) of that planet, the body will escape out from the gravitational field of that planet and will move the interstellar space with speed v' and it is given by $v' = \sqrt{v^2 - v_e^2}$

Earth Satellites

- Earth satellites are objects which revolve around the earth. Their motion is very similar to the motion of planets around the sun and hence Kepler's laws of planetary motion are equally applicable to them.
- **Moon is the only natural satellite of the earth** moving in a nearly circular orbit with a time period of approximately 27.3 days which is also roughly equal to the rotational period of the moon about its own axis.
- **Orbital speed of a satellite** It is defined as the minimum speed required to put the satellite into a given orbit around the earth. Orbital speed of a satellite at a height h from surface of earth is given by $v_o = \sqrt{\frac{GM_E}{R_E + h}} = R_E\sqrt{\frac{g}{R_E + h}}$.

  When a satellite revolve near the earth's surface, i.e. $h << R_E$, then its orbital velocity, $v_o = \sqrt{gR_E} \approx 7.92$ km/h

  The orbital speed of a satellite is independent of the mass of the satellite.
- **Time period of a satellite** It is the time taken by satellite to complete one revolution around the earth and it is given by

$$T = \frac{2\pi(R_E + h)}{v_o} = \frac{2\pi(R_E + h)^{3/2}}{\sqrt{GM_E}}$$
$$= \frac{2\pi}{R_E}\sqrt{\frac{(R_E + h)^3}{g}}$$

When a satellite revolve near the earth's surface, i.e. $h << R_E$, then $T_o = 2\pi\sqrt{\frac{R_E}{g}} \approx 85$ min

For Concept Master Video

- **Height of satellite above the earth's surface**

  It can be given as $h = \left(\frac{T^2R_E^2g}{4\pi^2}\right)^{1/3} - R_E$ NEET 2021

Energy of an Orbiting Satellite

- **Kinetic energy of the satellite orbiting** in a circular orbit with speed v is $KE = \frac{1}{2}mv^2 = \frac{GmM_E}{2(R_E + h)}$
- **Potential energy** at distance $(R + h)$ from the centre of the earth is $PE = -\frac{GmM_E}{(R_E + h)}$

  Also, $KE = \frac{|PE|}{2}$
- **Total energy of a satellite**,

$$TE = KE + PE = \frac{GmM_E}{2(R_E + h)} - \frac{GmM_E}{(R_E + h)}$$
$$= -\frac{GmM_E}{2(R_E + h)} = \frac{PE}{2}$$

- For a satellite orbiting very close to the earth surface, i.e. $h << R_E$.

  Total energy, $TE = -\frac{GM_Em}{2R_E}$
- The total energy of a circularly orbiting satellite is thus negative, with the potential energy being negative but twice in magnitude of the positive kinetic energy.
- Kinetic energy of a satellite is equal to negative of total energy while potential energy is equal to twice the total energy. i.e.

  $KE = -(TE)$, $PE = 2(TE)$
- When the orbit of a satellite becomes elliptic, both the KE and PE vary from point-to-point, but TE remains constant and it is negative as in the circular orbit case.
- Satellites are always at finite distance from the earth and hence their TE cannot be positive or zero. If total energy is positive or zero, the satellites escape to infinity.
- The energy required to remove a satellite from its orbit to infinity is called **binding energy of the satellite**. It is negative of total energy of the satellite.

  Binding energy,

$$E_b = -(TE) = \frac{GM_Em}{2(R_E + h)}$$

Caution Points

- When an astronaut is inside a space satellite, they feel weightless, because both the astronaut and the satellite are free falling towards the earth.
- The gravitational potential energy of an object with respect to infinity (PE = 0) is negative. The total energy of a satellite is also negative, this implies a satellite is bonded to the earth.
- As the gravitational force between two bodies is central, the gravitational force might not necessarily line up with the line joining their centre of mass.
- The gravitational force experienced by a particle inside a spherical shell is zero. Unlike electrical shielding, the gravitational shielding is not possible, i.e. the spherical shell does not shield the effect of gravitational force due to the outside body on a body inside the shell.

PYQ Notes

1. The variation of acceleration due to gravity due to **rotation of the earth at latitude λ** is given by

$$g_\lambda = g - \omega^2 R \cos^2 \lambda$$

where, R = radius of the earth

and ω = angular speed of the rotation of the earth.

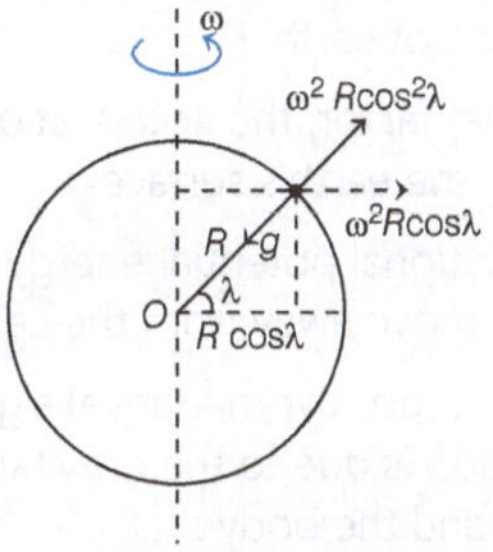

At pole, $\lambda = 90° \Rightarrow g_\lambda = g$

At equator, $\lambda = 0 \Rightarrow g_\lambda = (g - \omega^2 R)$

Hence, at pole, acceleration due to gravity is maximum and at equator, the acceleration due to gravity is minimum. **[JEE Main 2023, 21]**

2. The magnitude of gravitational field intensity at a point when a body of mass m experiences gravitational force F at that point is given by **[NEET 2022]**

$$I = \frac{F}{m} = -\frac{Gm}{r^2}$$

Negative sign shows that the gravitational field intensity is of attractive nature.

3. **The variation of acceleration due to gravity g with distance r inside and outside the earth from its centre** is given by

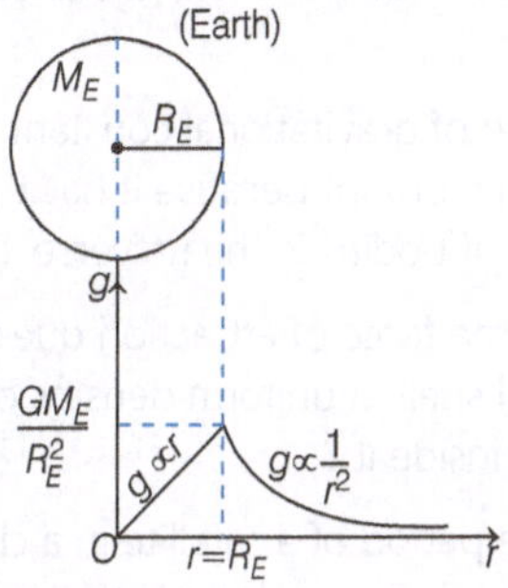

Inside the earth,

$$g = \left(\frac{GM_E}{R_E^3}\right) \cdot r, 0 < r < R_E$$

At the surface, $g = \dfrac{GM_E}{R_E^2}, r = R_E$

Outside the earth,

$$g = \frac{GM_E}{r^2}, r > R_E$$

[NEET 2016]

Step by Step

Mastering NCERT

- Concept Builders
- Topical Questions
- Assertion and Reason Questions
- Statement Based
- Matching Type
- Numerical Type
- NCERT Exemplar
- Past Exams MCQs
- Skill Boosters

Concept Builders

1 The ...... (square / cube) of the time period of revolution of a planet is proportional to the .... (square/ cube) of the semi-major axis of the ellipse traced out by the planet.

2 Which is fundamental quantity mass or weight ?

3 The force due to earth's gravity .... (increases / decreases) with increase in distance from earth's surface.

4 The value of gravitational constant G is called universal constant because it has the same value for any pair of bodies in the universe. [T/ F]

5 What is the force of attraction due to a hollow spherical shell of uniform density, on a point mass situated inside it ?

6 The time period of a satellite in a circular orbit of radius R is T. The period of another satellite in a circular orbit of radius 9 R is 27 T. [T/F]

7 What is the ratio of the force of attraction between two bodies kept in air and at the same distance apart in water ?

8 If the density of planet is doubled without changing its radius, then how does g change on the planet?

9 A planet revolving in elliptical orbit has to follow a trajectory such that the areal velocity is constant . [T/F]

10 The gravitational force acts .... (parallel/perpendicular) to the velocity of the moon.

11 The value of G depends on the nature and size of the masses. [T/F]

12 The value of acceleration due to gravity is ...... (maximum / zero) at the centre.

13 The value of acceleration due to gravity increases due to rotation of earth. [T/F]

14 By what factor, the acceleration due to gravity decreases below the earth's surface?

15 Gravitational potential energy .... (increases / decreases) as we move away from the centre of the solid sphere.

16 The ...... (positive/negative) sign in potential energy equation is due to the gravitational attraction between the earth and the body .

17 As the distance between two bodies increases, the gravitational potential energy decreases. [T/F]

18 The escape velocity depends on the mass and radius of the planet from the surface of which the body is projected, so value of escape velocity is different for different planets. [T/F]

19 The total energy of a circular orbiting satellite is ...... (positive / negative) in magnitude.

20 The kinetic energy of a satellite is twice the potential energy of satellite. [T/F]

Topical Questions

Kepler's Laws

1 A planet revolves in an elliptical orbit around the sun. If v_p and v_a are the velocities of the planet at the perigee and apogee respectively, then the eccentricity of the elliptical orbit is given by **NCERT Pg. 128**

(a) $\frac{v_p - v_a}{v_p + v_a}$ (b) $\frac{v_p + v_a}{v_p - v_a}$ (c) $\frac{v_p}{v_a}$ (d) $\frac{v_a - v_p}{v_a + v_p}$

2 The distance between the sun and the earth is R. The total duration of year, if the distance between the sun and earth becomes $3R$ will be **NCERT Pg. 128**

(a) 3 yr

(b) $\sqrt{3}$ yr

(c) $3\sqrt{3}$ yr

(d) 9 yr

3 A planet moves around the sun on an elliptical path as shown in the figure. If t_1 and t_2 are the time taken by the planet to cover equal area *SAB* and *SCD* respectively, then **NCERT Pg. 128**

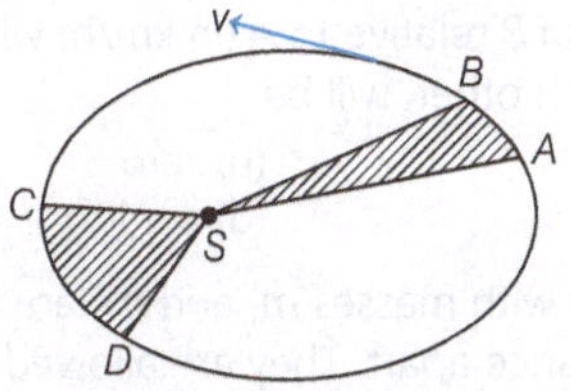

(a) $t_1 > t_2$ (b) $t_1 < t_2$ (c) $t_1 = t_2$ (d) $t_1 = \sqrt{t_2}$

4 Earth revolves round the sun in an elliptical path. The angular momentum of earth is L kg-m^2 s^{-1}, mass is M kg and period of revolution is T second. The area (in m^2) covered by radius vector in one revolution is **NCERT Pg. 128**

(a) $\frac{LT}{2M}$ (b) $\frac{LT}{3M}$ (c) $\frac{LT}{M}$ (d) $\frac{2LT}{M}$

5 A planet moving around sun sweeps area A_1 in 2 days, A_2 in 3 days and A_3 in 6 days, then $A_1 : A_2 : A_3$ is **NCERT Pg. 128**

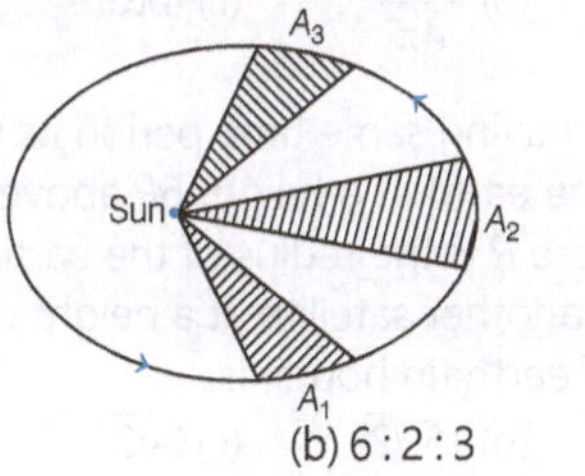

(a) 3 : 2 : 6 (b) 6 : 2 : 3
(c) 2 : 3 : 6 (d) 3 : 6 : 2

6 The law of areas can be interpreted as **NCERT Pg. 128**

(a) $\frac{\Delta A}{\Delta t} = \frac{L}{2m}$ (b) $\frac{\Delta A}{\Delta t} = \frac{L}{m}$

(c) $\frac{\Delta A}{\Delta t} = 2(r \times p)$ (d) $\frac{\Delta A}{\Delta t} = \frac{2L}{m}$

7 Let a planet is moving around the sun in an elliptical orbit as shown below. **NCERT Pg. 128**

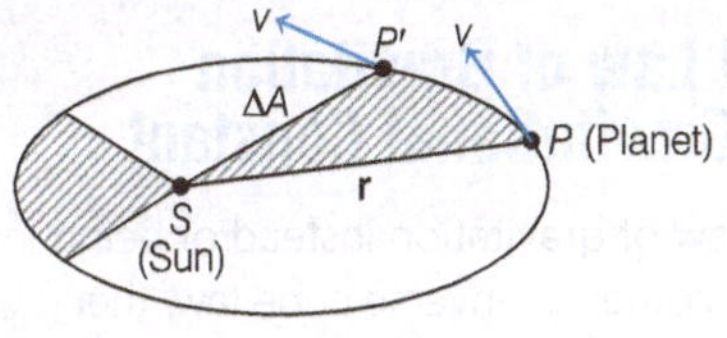

The area swept out by the planet of mass m in time interval Δt is given by

(a) $\Delta A = \frac{1}{2}|\mathbf{r} \times \mathbf{v}\, \Delta t|$ (b) $\Delta A = \frac{1}{2}|\mathbf{r} \times \mathbf{v}|$

(c) $\Delta A = \frac{1}{2}|\mathbf{r} \times \mathbf{p}|$ (d) $\Delta A = \frac{1}{3}|\mathbf{r} \times \mathbf{v}|$

8 In planetary motion, the areal velocity of position vector of a planet depends on angular velocity ω and the distance of the planet from sun r. So, the correct relation for areal velocity is **NCERT Pg. 128**

(a) $\frac{dA}{dt} \propto \omega r$ (b) $\frac{dA}{dt} \propto \omega^2 r$

(c) $\frac{dA}{dt} \propto \omega r^2$ (d) $\frac{dA}{dt} \propto \sqrt{\omega r}$

9 Let the speed of the planet at the perihelion P in figure be v_P and the sun-planet distance SP be r_P. The corresponding quantity at the aphelion A is (r_A, v_A). The mass of the planet is m_P. **NCERT Pg. 128**

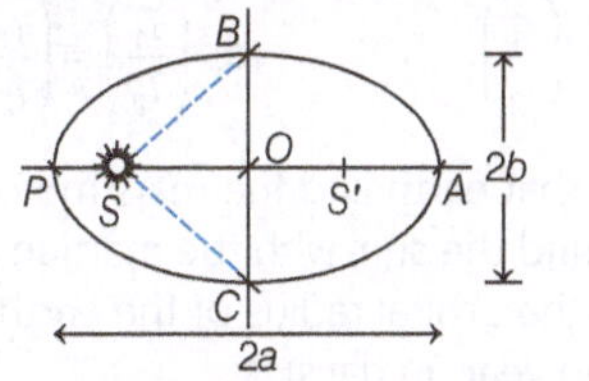

The magnitude of the angular momentum at P is

(a) $L_P = \frac{m_P r_P}{v_P}$ (b) $L_P = \frac{m_P v_P}{r_P}$

(c) $L_P = m_P r_P v_P$ (d) $L_P = m_P v_P$

10 A planet is moving around the sun in an elliptical path as shown in the figure. The linear speed of the planet is minimum at **NCERT Pg. 128**

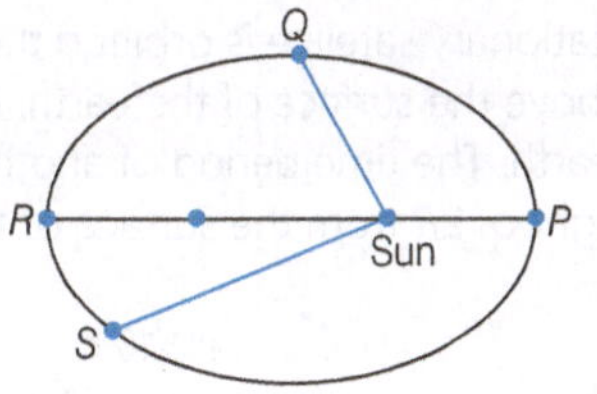

(a) P (b) S (c) Q (d) R

11 The maximum and minimum velocities of a planet are 3×10^4 m s^{-1} and 1×10^3 m s^{-1}, respectively. The minimum distance of the planet from the sun, if maximum distance is 4×10^4 km, is **NCERT Pg. 128**

(a) 4×10^3 km (b) 3×10^3 km
(c) $(4/3) \times 10^3$ km (d) 1×10^3 km

12 The kinetic energies of a planet in an elliptical orbit about the sun, at positions A, B and C are K_A, K_B and K_C, respectively. AC is the major axis and SB is perpendicular to AC at the position of the sun S as shown in the figure, then **NCERT Pg. 128**

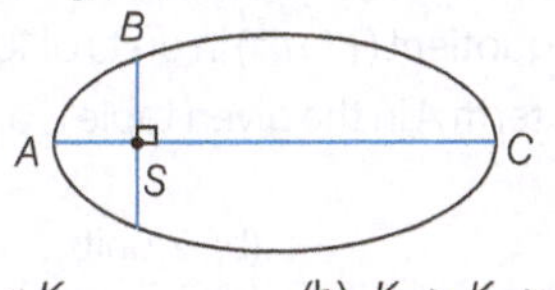

(a) $K_B < K_A < K_C$ (b) $K_A > K_B > K_C$
(c) $K_A < K_B < K_C$ (d) $K_B > K_A > K_C$

13 The time period of revolution T of planet in years (yr) is 84. The semi-major axis a in units of 10^{10} m is 287. The quotient (T^2/a^3) in units of 10^{-34} yr^{2}m^{-3} is approximately **NCERT Pg. 128**

(a) 3 units (b) 4 units
(c) 2 units (d) 1 unit

14 According to Kepler's law of planetary motion, if T represents time period and r is orbital radius, then for two planets, these are related as **NCERT Pg. 128**

(a) $\left(\frac{T_1}{T_2}\right)^3 = \left(\frac{r_1}{r_2}\right)^2$ (b) $\left(\frac{T_1}{T_2}\right)^{3/2} = \left(\frac{r_1}{r_2}\right)$

(c) $\left(\frac{T_1}{T_2}\right)^2 = \left(\frac{r_1}{r_2}\right)^3$ (d) $\left(\frac{T_1}{T_2}\right) = \left(\frac{r_1}{r_2}\right)^{2/3}$

15 Assuming that earth and the mars move in circular orbits around the sun, with the martian orbit being 1.52 times the orbital radius of the earth. The length of the martian year (in days) is **NCERT Pg. 128**

(a) $(1.52)^{2/3} \times 365$ (b) $(1.52)^{3/2} \times 365$
(c) $(1.52)^2 \times 365$ (d) $(1.52)^3 \times 365$

16 A planet of radius R has a time period of revolution T. Find the time period of a planet of radius $9R$. **NCERT Pg. 128**

(a) $3\sqrt{3}\,T$ (b) $9T$
(c) $27T$ (d) $9\sqrt{3}T$

17 A geostationary satellite is orbiting the earth at a height of $5R$ above the surface of the earth, R being the radius of the earth. The time period of another satellite in hour at a height of $2R$ from the surface of the earth is **NCERT Pg. 128**

(a) 5 h (b) 10 h
(c) $6\sqrt{2}$ h (d) $6/\sqrt{2}$ h

18 Following table shows the data from measurement of planetary motions to confirm Kepler's law of periods.

Planet	a	T	Q
Mercury	5.79	0.24	2.95
Venus	10.8	0.615	A
Earth	15.0	1.00	2.96
Mars	22.8	1.88	2.98

Here, a = semi-major axis in units of 10^{10} m for the elliptical orbits,

T = time period of revolution of the planet in years (yr) and Q = the quotient (T^2/a^3) in units of 10^{-34} y^{2}m^{-3})

The missing term A in the given table is approximately equal to **NCERT Pg. 128**

(a) 3 units (b) 2 units
(c) 2.5 units (d) 3.5 units

19 Two satellites A and B revolve around the same planet in coplanar circular orbits lying in the same plane. Their periods of revolutions are 1 h and 8 h, respectively and the radius of the orbit of A is 10^4 km.

The speed of B relative to A (in km/h) when they are close to each other, will be **NCERT Pg. 128**

(a) $3\pi \times 10^4$ (b) zero
(c) $2\pi \times 10^4$ (d) $\pi \times 10^4$

20 Two bodies with masses m_1 and m_2 are initially at rest at infinite distance apart. They are allowed to move towards each other under the mutual gravitational force, their relative velocity of approach at a separation r between them is **NCERT Pg. 128**

(a) $\sqrt{\frac{2G}{r}(m_1 m_2)}$ (b) $\sqrt{\frac{2G(m_1+m_2)}{r}}$

(c) $\sqrt{\frac{r}{2G(m_1 m_2)}}$ (d) $\sqrt{\frac{2G(m_1-m_2)}{r}}$

21 If a graph is plotted between T^2 and r^3 for a planet, then its slope will be (where M_S is the mass of the sun) **NCERT Pg. 128**

(a) $\frac{4\pi^2}{GM_S}$ (b) $\frac{GM_S}{4\pi}$ (c) $4\pi GM_S$ (d) GM_S

22 A satellite having same time period as that of earth is orbiting the earth at a height $6R$ above the surface of earth, where R is the radius of the earth. The time period of another satellite at a height of 2.5 R from the surface of earth (in hours) is **NCERT Pg. 128**

(a) $3\sqrt{2}$ (b) $1.5\sqrt{2}$ (c) $6\sqrt{2}$ (d) $12\sqrt{2}$

23. Average distance of the earth from the sun is L_1. If one year of the earth $=D$ days, one year of another planet whose average distance is L_2 from the sun , will be **NCERT Pg. 128**

(a) $D\left(\frac{L_2}{L_1}\right)^{1/2}$ days (b) $D\left(\frac{L_2}{L_1}\right)^{3/2}$ days

(c) $D\left(\frac{L_2}{L_1}\right)^{2/3}$ 0 days (d) $D\left(\frac{L_2}{L_1}\right)$ days

Universal Law of Gravitation and The Gravitational Constant

24 If the law of gravitation instead of being inverse square law, becomes an inverse cube law, then **NCERT Pg. 129**

(a) planets will have elliptical orbits.
(b) Kepler's law of areas does not hold good.
(c) projectile motion of a stone thrown by hand on the surface of the earth will be approximately parabolic.
(d) there will be no gravitational force inside a spherical shell of uniform density.

25 Kepler's third law states that square of period of revolution T of a planet around the sun, is proportional to third power of average distance r between sun and planet i.e. $T^2 = kr^3$, where k is constant. If the masses of sun and planet are M and m respectively, then as per Newton's law of gravitation force of attraction between them is $F = \frac{GMm}{r^2}$, where G is gravitational constant. The relation between G and k is described as **NCERT Pg. 129**

(a) $k = 1/G$ (b) $Gk = 4\pi^2$
(c) $GMk = 4\pi^2$ (d) $k = G$

26 Two point masses m_1 and m_2 having masses in the ratio of 4 : 3 are separated by a distance of 1 m. If another point mass M is placed in between m_1 and m_2, the force between m_1 and m_3 is $\left(\frac{1}{3}\right)$rd of the force between m_2 and m_3. Then, the distance between m_1 and m_3 is **NCERT Pg. 129**

(a) $\frac{2}{7}$ m (b) $\frac{1}{4}$ m
(c) $\frac{2}{3}$ m (d) $\frac{1}{3}$ m

27 Two identical spheres of radii R are kept touching each other. How gravitational force of attraction between them depends on R? **NCERT Pg. 129**

(a) $R^{\frac{1}{2}}$ (b) $\frac{1}{R^2}$ (c) R^3 (d) R^4

28 Newton arrived at an universal law based on his observation of an apple falling from a tree. Newton's reasoning was that the moon revolving in an orbit of radius R_m was subjected to a centripetal acceleration due to earth's gravity whose magnitude is given by **NCERT Pg. 129**

(a) $a_m = \frac{v^3}{R_m}$ (b) $a_m = \frac{4\pi^2 R_m}{T^2}$
(c) $a_m = \frac{mv^2}{R_m}$ (d) $a_m = \frac{\pi^2 R_m}{T^2}$

29 A planet is revolving around the sun in a circular orbit with a radius r and the time period is T. If the force between the planet and star is proportional to $r^{-3/2}$, then the square of time period is proportional to **NCERT Pg. 129**

(a) $r^{3/2}$ (b) r^2 (c) r (d) $r^{5/2}$

30 Four particles of masses m, $2m$, $3m$ and $4m$ are kept in sequence at the corners of a square of side a. The magnitude of gravitational force acting on a particle of mass m placed at the centre of the square will be **NCERT Pg. 129**

(a) zero (b) $\frac{4\sqrt{2}\, Gm^2}{a^2}$
(c) $\frac{6Gm^2}{a^2}$ (d) $\frac{24Gm^2}{a^2}$

31 The height at which the weight of a body becomes (1/16)th of its weight on the surface of the earth (radius R), is **NCERT Pg. 129**

(a) $5R$ (b) $15\,R$ (c) $3\,R$ (d) $4\,R$

32 If mass of a planet is 2% of mass of earth. The ratio of gravitational pull of earth on the planet and that of planet on the earth will be **NCERT Pg. 129**

(a) 1 : 20 (b) 2 : 5 (c) 1 : 1 (d) 1 : 50

33 Two equal point masses are separated by a distance d_1. The force of gravitation acting between them is F_1. If the separation is decreased to d_2, then the new force of gravitation F_2 is given by **NCERT Pg. 129**

(a) $F_2 = F_1$ (b) $F_2 = F_1\left(\frac{d_1}{d_2}\right)^2$
(c) $F_2 = F_1\left(\frac{d_2}{d_1}\right)^2$ (d) $F_2 = F_1\left(\frac{d_1}{d_2}\right)$

34 Two sphere of masses m and M are situated in air and the gravitational force between them is F. The space around the masses is now filled with a liquid of specific gravity 3. The gravitational force will now be **NCERT Pg. 129**

(a) F (b) $\frac{F}{3}$ (c) $\frac{F}{9}$ (d) $3\,F$

35 Three equal masses of m kg each are fixed at the vertices of an equilateral triangle ABC and a mass $2m$ is placed at centroid G of the triangle as shown below. **NCERT Pg. 129**

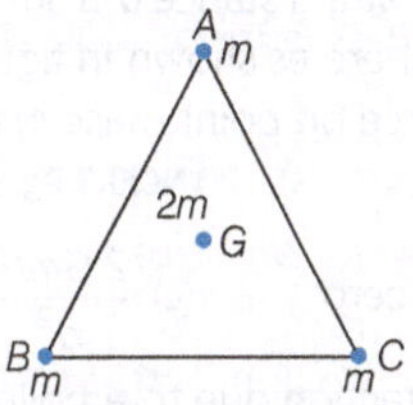

($AG = BG = CG =$ 1m)

The force acting on a mass $2m$ placed at the centroid G of the triangle is

(a) $\frac{2\,Gm^2}{\sqrt{2}}$ (b) $2Gm^2$ (c) $6Gm^2$ (d) zero

36 Three uniform spheres of mass M and radius R each are kept in such a way that each touches the other two. The magnitude of the gravitational force on any of the spheres due to the other two is **NCERT Pg. 129**

(a) $\frac{\sqrt{3}}{4}\frac{GM^2}{R^2}$ (b) $\frac{3}{2}\frac{GM^2}{R^2}$ (c) $\frac{\sqrt{3}\,GM^2}{R^2}$ (d) $\frac{\sqrt{3}}{2}\frac{GM^2}{R^2}$

37 A point mass m is placed at the centre of the square $ABCD$ of side a units as shown below.
NCERT Pg. 129

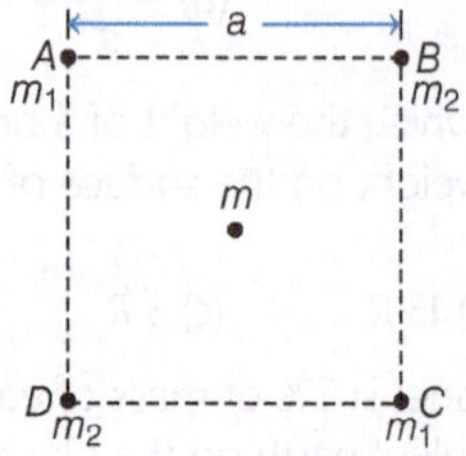

The resultant gravitational force on mass m due to masses m_1 and m_2 placed on the vertices of square is

(a) $\dfrac{Gm_1m_2}{(a\sqrt{2})^2}$ (b) $\dfrac{2Gm(m_1+m_2)}{a^2}$

(c) zero (d) $\dfrac{Gm(m_1+m_2)}{(a\sqrt{2})^2}$

38 A mass M is split into two parts, m and $(M-m)$, which are then separated by a certain distance. What ratio of m/M maximizes the gravitational force between the two parts? **NCERT Pg. 129**

(a) 1/3 (b) 1/2 (c) 1/4 (d) 1/5

39 Two spherical bodies of masses m and $5\,m$ and radii R and $2R$ are released in free space with initial separation between their centres equal to $12R$. If they attract each other due to gravitational force only, then the distance covered by the smaller body before collision is
NCERT Pg. 129

(a) $2.5\,R$ (b) $4.5\,R$ (c) $7.5\,R$ (d) $1.5\,R$

40 A point mass m is placed outside a hollow spherical shell of mass M and uniform density at a distance d from centre of the sphere as shown in figure. Gravitational force on point mass m at P is **NCERT Pg. 129**

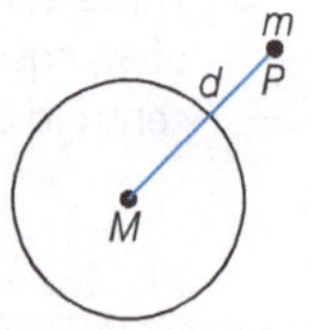

(a) $\dfrac{GmM}{d^2}$ (b) zero (c) $\dfrac{2\,GmM}{d^2}$ (d) $\dfrac{GmM}{2d^2}$

41 The force of attraction due to a hollow spherical shell of mass M, radius R and uniform density, on a point mass m situated inside it is **NCERT Pg. 129**

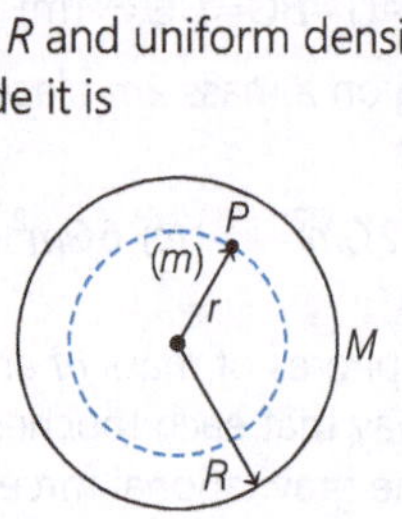

(a) $\dfrac{GmM}{r^2}$ (b) $\dfrac{Gm\,M}{R^2}$ (c) zero (d) $\dfrac{GmM}{2r^2}$

42 The figure shown is the schematic representation of Cavendish's experiment to determine the value of the gravitational constant. The bar AB has two small lead spheres attached at its ends. The bar is suspended from a rigid support by a fine wire. Two large lead spheres are brought close to the small ones but on opposite sides as shown.

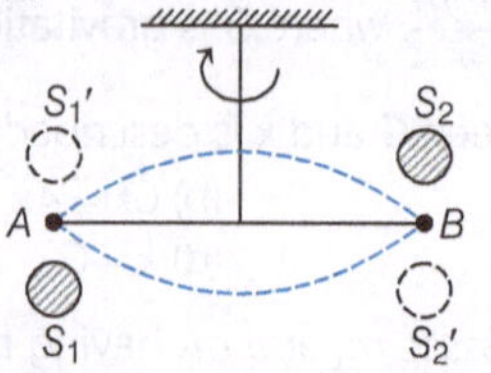

The big spheres attract the near by small ones by a force which is **NCERT Pg. 131**

(a) equal and opposite
(b) equal but in same direction
(c) unequal and opposite
(d) zero

Acceleration Due to Gravity and its Variation

43 If M_E is the mass of the earth and R_E its radius, the ratio of the acceleration due to gravity and the gravitational constant is **NCERT Pg. 132**

(a) $\dfrac{R_E^2}{M_E}$ (b) $\dfrac{M_E}{R_E^2}$ (c) $M_ER^2{}_E$ (d) $\dfrac{M_E}{R_E}$

44 The acceleration due to gravity g and density of the earth ρ are related by which of the following relations? where, G is the gravitational constant and R_E is the radius of the earth. **NCERT Pg. 132**

(a) $\rho = \dfrac{4\pi GR_E}{3g}$ (b) $\rho = \dfrac{3g}{4\pi GR_E}$

(c) $\rho = \dfrac{3G}{4\pi gR_E}$ (d) $\rho = \dfrac{4\pi gR_E}{3G}$

45 The mass of the moon is (1/8) of the earth but the gravitational pull is (1/6) of the earth. It is due to the fact that **NCERT Pg. 132**

(a) moon is the satellite of the earth
(b) the radius of the earth is (8/6) of the moon
(c) the radius of the earth is $(\sqrt{8/6})$ of the moon
(d) the radius of the moon is (6/8) of the earth

46 If g is the acceleration due to gravity at the surface of the earth, then the force acting on the particle of mass m placed at the surface is **NCERT Pg. 132**

(a) mg (b) $\dfrac{GmM_E}{R_E^2}$

(c) $\dfrac{GmM_E}{(1-2R_E)^2}$ (d) Both (a) and (b)

47 What will be the mass of a planet that has satellite whose time period is T and orbital radius is r? NCERT Pg. 132

(a) $\dfrac{4\pi^2 r^3}{GT^2}$ (b) $\dfrac{2\pi r^3}{GT^2}$

(c) $\dfrac{4\pi^2 r^2}{GT^2}$ (d) $\dfrac{2\pi^3 r^3}{GT^2}$

48 According to Newton's law of gravitation, let $\mathbf{F}_1$ and $\mathbf{F}_2$ be the forces between two masses m_1 and m_2 at positions $\mathbf{r}_1$ and $\mathbf{r}_2$, where

$$\mathbf{F}_1 = -\mathbf{F}_2 = -\frac{\mathbf{r}_{12}}{r_{12}^3} GM_0^2 \left(\frac{m_1 m_2}{M_0^2}\right)^n$$

where, M_0 is a constant of dimension of mass, $\mathbf{r}_{12} = \mathbf{r}_1 - \mathbf{r}_2$ and n is a number. In such a case, NCERT Pg. 132

(a) the acceleration due to gravity on the earth will be different for different objects

(b) None of the three laws of Kepler will be valid

(c) only the third law will be valid

(d) only the second law and third law will be valid

49 If the mass of the earth is doubled and its radius halved, then new acceleration due to gravity g' is NCERT Pg. 132

(a) $g' = 4g$ (b) $g' = 8g$

(c) $g' = g$ (d) $g' = 16g$

50 A planet has twice the density of earth but the acceleration due to gravity on its surface is exactly the same as on the surface of earth. Its radius in terms of radius of earth R will be NCERT Pg. 132

(a) $R/4$ (b) $R/2$ (c) $R/3$ (d) $R/8$

51 Suppose, the acceleration due to gravity at the earth's surface is 10 ms^{-2} and at the surface of mars, it is 4.0 ms^{-2}. A 60 kg passenger goes from the earth to the mars in a spaceship moving with a constant velocity. Neglect all other objects in the sky.

Which curve best represents the weight (net gravitational force) of the passenger as a function of time? NCERT Pg. 132

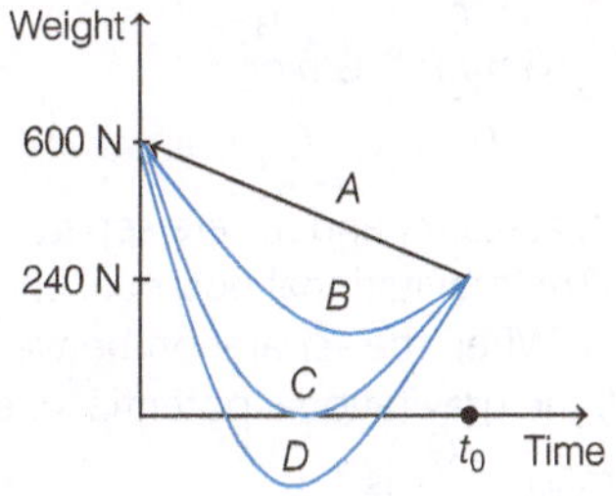

(a) A (b) B (c) C (d) D

52 If the mass of the sun becomes ten times smaller and gravitational constant G for the earth becomes ten times larger in magnitude. Then, for earth, NCERT Pg. 132

(a) walking on ground would become more easy.

(b) acceleration due to gravity on the earth will not change.

(c) raindrops will fall much slower.

(d) airplanes will have to travel much faster.

53 If one assumes that the gravitational force due to the earth decreases in proportion to the inverse square of the distance from the centre of the earth, then which of the following relation between a_m (centripetal acceleration of moon), R_m (distance of the moon from centre of the earth), g (acceleration due to gravity on the surface of the earth) and R_E (radius of earth) is correct? NCERT Pg. 132

(a) $\dfrac{g}{a_m} = \dfrac{R_m}{R_E}$ (b) $\dfrac{g}{a_m} = \left(\dfrac{R_m}{R_E}\right)^2$

(c) $\dfrac{g}{a_m} = \left(\dfrac{R_E}{R_m}\right)^2$ (d) $\dfrac{g}{a_m} = \dfrac{R_E}{R_m}$

54 The time period of the moon is $T = 27.3$ days and radius of orbit is $R_m = 3.84 \times 10^8$ m, the value of centripetal acceleration due to the earth's gravity is NCERT Pg. 132

(a) much smaller than the value of acceleration due to gravity g on the surface of the earth.

(b) is equal to the value of acceleration due to gravity g on the surface of the earth.

(c) much larger than the value of acceleration due to gravity g on the surface of the earth.

(d) is equal to the value of acceleration due to gravity g' on the surface of the moon.

55 Find the angular velocity of the earth, so that weight of a body becomes zero at the equator. NCERT Pg. 133

(a) 1.25 rad s^{-1} (b) 1.25×10^{-1} rad s^{-1}

(c) 1.25×10^{-2} rad s^{-1} (d) 1.25×10^{-3} rad s^{-1}

56 The value of acceleration due to gravity at earth's surface is 9.8 ms^{-2}. The altitude above its surface at which the acceleration due to gravity decreases to 4.9 ms^{-2}, is close to (Take, radius of earth $= 6.4 \times 10^6$ m) NCERT Pg. 133

(a) 9.0×10^6 m (b) 2.6×10^6 m

(c) 6.4×10^6 m (d) 1.6×10^6 m

57 A body weights w at the surface of the earth. Its weight at a height equals to half the radius of the earth will be NCERT Pg. 133

(a) $\dfrac{w}{2}$ (b) $\dfrac{2w}{3}$ (c) $\dfrac{4w}{9}$ (d) $\dfrac{8w}{27}$

58 At what height h above the surface of the earth, the value of g becomes $\left(\frac{g}{2}\right)$?
(Take, g = acceleration due to gravity at the surface of the earth and R = radius of the earth) NCERT Pg. 133

(a) $3R$ (b) $\sqrt{2}R$
(c) $(\sqrt{2}-1)R$ (d) $\frac{1}{\sqrt{2}}R$

59 The radius of earth is R. Height of a point vertically above the earth's surface at which acceleration due to gravity becomes 1% of its value at the surface is NCERT Pg. 133

(a) $8R$ (b) $9R$
(c) $10R$ (d) $20R$

60 The weight of a body on the surface of the earth is 45 N. What is the gravitational force on it due to the earth at a height equal to half the radius of the earth? NCERT Pg. 133

(a) 35 N (b) 20 N (c) 18 N (d) 40 N

61 The height at which the acceleration due to gravity decreases by 51% of its value at the surface of the earth is NCERT Pg. 133

(a) $\frac{2R}{5}$ (b) $\frac{3R}{7}$ (c) $\frac{4R}{9}$ (d) $\frac{3R}{11}$

62 The percentage decrease in weight of a body when it is taken 32 km below the earth surface is (Take, radius of the earth, R = 6400 km) NCERT Pg. 133

(a) 0.4% (b) 0.5%
(c) 0.6% (d) 0.7%

63 Find acceleration due to gravity at a distance of 2000 km from the centre of earth.
(Given, R_E = 6400 km, r = 2000 km and $M_E = 6 \times 10^{24}$ kg) NCERT Pg. 133

(a) 1.53 m/s^2 (b) 7.12 m/s^2
(c) 3.06 m/s^2 (d) 1.8 m/s^2

64 A body weighs 200 N on the surface of the earth. How much will it weigh half-way down to the centre of the earth? NCERT Pg. 133

(a) 200 N (b) 250 N
(c) 100 N (d) 150 N

65 A box weighs 196 N on a spring balance at the north pole. Its weight recorded on the same balance, if it is shifted to the equator is close to (Take, $g = 10\ ms^{-2}$ at the north pole and the radius of the earth = 6400 km) NCERT Pg. 133

(a) 195.66 N (b) 195.33 N
(c) 194.66 N (d) 194.33 N

66 The acceleration due to gravity at a height 1 km above the earth is the same as at a depth d below the surface of earth. Then, NCERT Pg. 133

(a) $d = \frac{1}{2}$ km (b) d = 1 km
(c) $d = \frac{3}{2}$ km (d) d = 2 km

67 Which of the following statements(s) is/are incorrect? NCERT Pg. 133

(a) Acceleration due to gravity decreases with altitude.
(b) Acceleration due to gravity increases with increasing depth (assume the earth to be a sphere of uniform density).
(c) Acceleration due to gravity increases with latitude.
(d) Acceleration due to gravity is independent of the mass of the object.

Gravitational Potential Energy

68 A body of mass m is released to a height nR above the surface of the earth. The change in the gravitational potential energy is NCERT Pg. 134

(a) $nMgR$ (b) $\left(\frac{n}{n+1}\right)mgR$
(c) $\frac{GMm}{R(n+1)}$ (d) $\left(\frac{n}{n-1}\right)mgR$

69 Gravitational potential energy of a system of particles as shown in the figure is NCERT Pg. 134

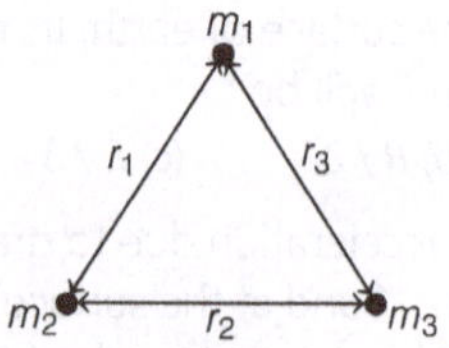

(a) $\frac{Gm_1m_2}{r_1} + \frac{Gm_2m_3}{r_3} + \frac{Gm_1m_3}{r_3}$
(b) $\left(\frac{-Gm_1m_2}{r_1}\right) + \left(\frac{-Gm_2m_3}{r_2}\right) + \left(\frac{-Gm_1m_3}{r_3}\right)$
(c) $\frac{-Gm_1m_2}{r_1} - \frac{Gm_2m_3}{r_2} + \frac{Gm_1m_3}{r_3}$
(d) $\frac{Gm_1m_2}{r_1} + \frac{Gm_2m_3}{r_2} - \frac{Gm_1m_3}{r_3}$

70 Two point masses m_1 and m_2 are separated by a distance r. The gravitational potential energy of the system is G_1. When the separation between the particles is doubled, the gravitational potential energy is G_2. Then, the ratio of $\frac{G_1}{G_2}$ is NCERT Pg. 134

(a) 1 (b) 2 (c) 3 (d) 4

71 The mass of the earth is 6×10^{24} kg and that of the moon is 7.4×10^{22} kg. The potential energy of the system is -7.79×10^{28} J. The mean distance between the earth and moon is $(G = 6.67 \times 10^{-11} N\text{-}m^2 kg^{-2})$ **NCERT Pg. 134**

(a) 3.8×10^8 m (b) 3.37×10^6 m
(c) 7.60×10^4 m (d) 1.9×10^2 m

72 The work done to raise a mass m from the surface of the earth to a height h, which is equal to the radius of the earth, is **NCERT Pg. 134**

(a) $2mgR$ (b) $\frac{1}{2} mgR$
(c) $\frac{3}{2} mgR$ (d) mgR

73 The gravitational potential at a distance r from the centre of the earth $(r > R)$ is given by (consider, mass of the earth $= M_E$ and radius of the earth $= R$) **NCERT Pg. 134**

(a) $\frac{-GM_E}{R}$ (b) $\frac{GM_E}{R}$
(c) $\frac{-GM_E}{r}$ (d) $\frac{+GM_E}{r}$

74 At what height from the surface of earth, the gravitational potential and the value of g are -5.4×10^7 J kg^{-2} and 6.0 ms^{-2}, respectively? (Take, radius of earth is 6400 km) **NCERT Pg. 134**

(a) 1600 km (b) 1400 km
(c) 2000 km (d) 2600 km

75 Three particles each of mass m are kept at vertices of an equilateral triangle of side L. The gravitational potential at the centre due to these particles is **NCERT Pg. 134**

(a) $-\frac{3Gm}{L}$ (b) $\frac{-8Gm}{\sqrt{3}L}$
(c) $-\frac{3\sqrt{3}Gm}{L}$ (d) $\frac{-4Gm}{\sqrt{3}L}$

76. If the gravitational force had varied as $r^{-\frac{5}{2}}$ instead of r^{-2}, the potential energy of a particle at a distance r from the centre of the earth would be proportional to **NCERT Pg. 134**

(a) r^{-1} (b) r^{-2}
(c) $r^{-\frac{3}{2}}$ (d) $r^{\frac{3}{2}}$

77. The minimum energy required to launch a satellite of mass m from the surface of a planet of mass M and radius R in a circular orbit at a altitude $2R$ is **NCERT Pg. 134**

(a) $\frac{GmM}{3R}$ (b) $\frac{2GMm}{R}$
(c) $\frac{3GMm}{2R}$ (d) $\frac{5GMm}{6R}$

Escape Velocity and Satellites

78. The escape velocity of a body from the earth depends on **NCERT Pg. 135**

(i) the mass of the body
(ii) the location from where it is projected
(iii) the direction of projection
(iv) the height of the location from where the body is launched

(a) (i) and (ii) (b) (ii) and (iv)
(c) (i) and (iii) (d) (iii) and (iv)

79 An object is thrown from the surface of the moon. The escape speed for the object is **NCERT Pg. 135**

(a) $\sqrt{2g' R_m}$, where g' = acceleration due to gravity on the moon and R_m = radius of the moon.
(b) $\sqrt{2g' R_E}$, where g' = acceleration due to gravity on the moon and R_E = radius of the earth.
(c) $\sqrt{2gR_m}$, where g = acceleration due to gravity on the earth and R_m = radius of the moon.
(d) $\sqrt{3gR_m}$, where g = acceleration due to gravity on the earth and R_m = radius of the moon.

80 The escape velocity of a body from the earth is v_e. If the radius of earth contracts to (1/4)th of its value, keeping the mass of the earth constant, escape velocity will be **NCERT Pg. 135**

(a) doubled (b) halved
(c) tripled (d) unaltered

81 A satellite is in a circular orbit of radius r close to surface of a plane. At some point, it is given an impulse along its direction of motion causing its velocity to increase n times. If now goes into an elliptical orbit with the planet at the centre of the ellipse. The maximum possible value of n could be **NCERT Pg. 135**

(a) $\sqrt{2}$ (b) 2 (c) $\sqrt{2}+1$ (d) $\frac{1}{\sqrt{2}-1}$

82 If escape velocity on earth's surface is 11.1 km/h, then find the escape velocity on moon's surface. Mass of the moon is $\left(\frac{1}{81}\right)$ times of the mass of earth and radius of the moon is $\left(\frac{1}{4}\right)$ times radius of the earth. **NCERT Pg. 135**

(a) 2.46 km/h (b) 3.46 km/h
(c) 4.4 km/h (d) None of these

83 The ratio of escape velocity at earth (v_e) to the escape velocity at a planet (v_p) whose radius and mean density are thrice as that of earth is **NCERT Pg. 135**

(a) $1:3\sqrt{3}$ (b) $1:4$ (c) $1:\sqrt{2}$ (d) $1:2$

84 If v_e is the escape velocity and v_o is orbital velocity of a satellite for orbit close to the earth's surface, then these are related by **NCERT Pg. 136**

(a) $v_o = \sqrt{2}\, v_e$

(b) $v_o = v_e$

(c) $v_e = \dfrac{v_o}{2}$

(d) $v_e = \sqrt{2}\, v_o$

85 A satellite is orbiting the earth in a circular orbit of radius r, its **NCERT Pg. 137**

(a) kinetic energy varies as r

(b) angular momentum varies as $\dfrac{1}{\sqrt{r}}$

(c) linear momentum varies as $\dfrac{1}{r}$

(d) frequency of revolution varies as $\dfrac{1}{r^{3/2}}$

86 Which one of the following statements is incorrect? **NCERT Pg. 137**

(a) The orbital velocity of a satellite increases with the radius of the orbit.

(b) The orbital velocity of a satellite is less than of its escape velocity.

(c) The escape velocity at the moon is less than that at the earth.

(d) If mass of the satellite increases, then its orbital velocity remains unchanged.

87 The orbital angular momentum of a satellite revolving at a distance r from the centre is L. If the distance is increased to $16r$, then the new angular momentum will be **NCERT Pg. 137**

(a) $16\,L$ (b) $64\,L$ (c) $\dfrac{L}{4}$ (d) $4\,L$

88 A satellite is revolving in a circular orbit at a height h from the earth surface such that $h << R$, where R is the radius of the earth. Assuming that the effect of earth's atmosphere can be neglected. The minimum increase in the speed required, so that the satellite could escape from the gravitational field of earth is **NCERT Pg. 137**

(a) $\sqrt{\dfrac{gR}{2}}$ (b) $\sqrt{gR}$

(c) $\sqrt{2\,gR}$ (d) $\sqrt{gR}\,(\sqrt{2}-1)$

89 The orbital velocity of a satellite close to the surface of the earth is v. If this satellite starts orbiting at an altitude of half the earth's radius, the orbital velocity will be **NCERT Pg. 137**

(a) $\sqrt{\dfrac{2}{3}}\,v$ (b) $\sqrt{\dfrac{2}{5}}\,v$

(c) $\sqrt{\dfrac{2}{7}}\,v$ (d) $\sqrt{\dfrac{2}{9}}\,v$

90 A satellite of mass M is in a circular orbit of radius R about the centre of the earth. A meteorite of the same mass falling towards the earth collides with the satellite completely inelastically. The speeds of the satellite and the meteorite are the same just before the collision. The subsequent motion of the combined body will be

(a) in the same circular orbit of radius R **NCERT Pg. 137**

(b) in an elliptical orbit

(c) such that it escapes to infinity

(d) in a circular orbit of a different radius

Energy of an Orbiting Satellite

91. Figure shows the variations of energy E with the orbit radius r of a satellite in circular motion. Choose the correct statement. **NCERT Pg. 138**

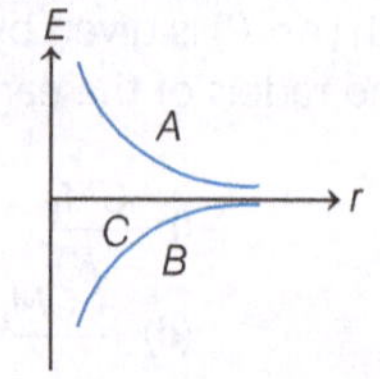

(a) A shows the kinetic energy, B shows the total energy and C the potential energy of the satellite.

(b) A and B are kinetic energy and potential energy respectively and C the total energy of the satellite.

(c) A and B are the potential energy and kinetic energy respectively and C the total energy of the satellite

(d) C and A are the kinetic and potential energies and B the total energy of the satellite.

92 Which one of the following statements is correct? **NCERT Pg. 138**

(a) The kinetic energy of an orbiting satellite is half of its total energy.

(b) The potential energy of an orbiting satellite increases with increases in radius of the orbit.

(c) Total energy of an orbiting satellite is positive.

(d) The potential energy of an orbiting satellite is half of its total energy.

93 An asteroid of mass m is approaching earth, initially at a distance $10\,R_E$ with speed v_i. It hits earth with a speed v_f (R_E and M_E are radius and mass of earth), then **NCERT Pg. 138**

(a) $v_f^2 = v_i^2 + \dfrac{2Gm}{R_E}\left(1+\dfrac{1}{10}\right)$

(b) $v_f^2 = v_i^2 + \dfrac{2GM_E}{R_E}\left(1+\dfrac{1}{10}\right)$

(c) $v_f^2 = v_i^2 + \dfrac{2GM_E}{R_E}\left(1-\dfrac{1}{10}\right)$

(d) $v_f^2 = v_i^2 + \dfrac{2Gm}{R_E}\left(1-\dfrac{1}{10}\right)$

94 The escape velocity of a body is v_e. A body is projected with velocity $2v_e$. With what constant velocity will it move in the inter planetary space? **NCERT Pg. 138**

(a) v_e (b) $\sqrt{5}\, v_e$
(c) $\sqrt{3}\, v_e$ (d) $\sqrt{2}\, v_e$

95 Two stars of masses 3×10^{31} kg each and at distance 2×10^{11} m rotate in a plane about their common centre of mass O. A meteorite passes through O moving perpendicular to the star's rotation plane. In order to escape from the gravitational field of this double star, the minimum speed that meteorite should have at O is (Take, gravitational constant, $G = 6.67 \times 10^{-11}$ N-m^{2}kg^{-2}) **NCERT Pg. 138**

(a) 2.8×10^5 m/s (b) 3.8×10^4 m/s
(c) 2.4×10^4 m/s (d) 1.4×10^5 m/s

96 Two satellites A and B have masses m and $2m$, respectively. A is in a circular orbit of radius R and B is in a circular orbit of radius $2R$ around the earth. The ratio of their kinetic energies, T_A / T_B is **NCERT Pg. 138**

(a) $\frac{1}{2}$ (b) 2 (c) $\sqrt{\frac{1}{2}}$ (d) 1

97 The kinetic energy of the satellite in a circular orbit with speed v is given as **NCERT Pg. 138**

(a) $KE = \frac{-GmM_E}{2(R_E + h)}$ (b) $KE = \frac{GmM_E}{(R_E + h)}$
(c) $KE = \frac{GmM_E}{2(R_E + h)}$ (d) $KE = -\frac{1}{2}mv^2$

98 The radius of the orbit of a satellite is r and its kinetic energy is K. If the radius of the orbit is doubled, then the new kinetic energy K' is **NCERT Pg. 138**

(a) $2K$ (b) $\frac{K}{2}$ (c) $4K$ (d) $\frac{K}{4}$

99 If the gravitational potential energy at infinity is assumed to be zero, the potential energy at distance $(R_E + h)$ from the centre of the earth is **NCERT Pg. 138**

(a) $PE = \frac{GmM_E}{(R_E + h)}$ (b) $PE = \frac{-GmM_E}{(R_E + h)}$
(c) $PE = mgh$ (d) $PE = \frac{-GmM_E}{2(R_E + h)}$

100 The potential energy of a satellite is given as

$$PE = \lambda\,(KE)$$

where, PE = potential energy of the satellite
and KE = kinetic energy of the satellite.
The value of the constant λ is **NCERT Pg. 138**

(a) -2 (b) 2
(c) $-1/2$ (d) $+1/2$

Assertion and Reason Questions

Direction (Q. Nos. 1-10) *In the following questions, a statement of Assertion is followed by a corresponding statement of Reason. Of the following statements, choose the correct one.*

(a) Both Assertion and Reason are correct and Reason is the correct explanation of Assertion.
(b) Both Assertion and Reason are correct but Reason is not the correct explanation of Assertion.
(c) Assertion is correct but Reason is incorrect.
(d) Assertion is incorrect but Reason is correct.

1 Assertion When a planet revolves in elliptical orbit around sun, its angular momentum about sun remains conserved.

Reason The total mechanical energy of a planet-sun system remains conserved. **NCERT Pg. 129**

2 Assertion Gravitational force between two masses in air is F. If they are immersed in water, the force will remain F.

Reason Gravitational force is independent of the medium in which masses are present. **NCERT Pg. 129**

3 Assertion The force of attraction due to a hollow spherical shell of uniform density, on a point mass situated inside it is zero.

Reason Various region of the spherical shell attract the point mass inside it in various directions. These forces cancel each other completely. **NCERT Pg. 129**

4 Assertion The acceleration due to gravity at the centre of the earth is zero.

Reason The mass of an object at the centre of the earth is zero. **NCERT Pg. 132**

5 Assertion As we go up the surface of the earth, we feel light weighed than on the surface of the earth.

Reason The acceleration due to gravity decreases on going up above the surface of the earth. **NCERT Pg. 133**

6 Assertion The escape speed for the moon is 2.3 kms^{-1} which is five times smaller than that for the earth.

Reason The escape speed depends on acceleration due to gravity on the moon and radius of the moon and both of them are smaller than that of earth. **NCERT Pg. 135**

7 **Assertion** The moon has no atmosphere. NCERT Pg. 135

Reason The escape speed for the moon is much smaller.

8 **Assertion** Escape velocity of a truck from the surface of the earth is equal the escape velocity of a bike.

Reason Escape velocity of a body depends on the mass of the body. NCERT Pg. 136

9 **Assertion** The velocity of the satellite decreases as its height above earth's surface increases and is maximum near the surface of the earth.

Reason The velocity of the satellite is inversely proportional to square root of its height above earth's surface. NCERT Pg. 137

10 **Assertion** The total energy of the satellite is always negative irrespective of the nature of its orbit, i.e. elliptical or circular and it cannot be positive or zero.

Reason If the total energy is positive or zero, the satellite would leave its orbit. NCERT Pg. 138

Statement Based Questions

Direction (Q. Nos. 1-10) *In the following questions, two statements (I & II) are given. In the light of the given statements, choose the correct option given below.*

(a) Both Statement I and Statement II are false.
(b) Statement I is true but Statement II is false.
(c) Statement I is false but Statement II is true.
(d) Both Statement I and Statement II are true.

1 **Statement I** The line that joins any planet to the sun sweeps equal areas in equal intervals of time.

Statement II The square of time period of revolution of a planet is proportional to the cube of major axis of the ellipse traced out by the planet. NCERT Pg. 128

2 **Statement I** For a planet orbiting around a sun, angular speed, angular momentum and kinetic energy changes with time.

Statement II No torque is acting on the rotating planet. NCERT Pg. 129

3 **Statement I** The plants move slower when they are farther from the sun than when they are nearer.

Statement II Angular velocity of a planet is constant quantity. NCERT Pg. 129

4 **Statement I** The acceleration due to gravity decreases with height from the surface of the earth.

Statement II The acceleration due to gravity at the earth surface is independent of the radius of the earth. NCERT Pg. 133

5 **Statement I** If the altitude of the satellite is increased by n times the radius of the earth, then the orbital velocity will become $\left(\frac{1}{\sqrt{1+n}}\right)$ times the orbital velocity near the surface of the earth.

Statement II If the radius of the orbit of a satellite is increased by n times the radius of the earth, then its orbital velocity will be $\left(\frac{1}{\sqrt{n}}\right)$ times the orbital velocity near the earth's surface. NCERT Pg. 133

6 **Statement I** The escape velocity of any object on the earth surface depends on the mass of object.

Statement II Escape velocity on the earth surface is five times smaller than that on the moon surface. NCERT Pg. 135

7 **Statement I** For a satellite orbiting in a circular orbit, the value of kinetic energy is less than potential energy.

Statement II If the total energy of a satellite becomes positive, the satellite will escape from the gravitational pull of the earth. NCERT Pg. 138

8 **Statement I** The magnitude of potential energy is half of the magnitude of total energy of orbiting satellite.

Statement II Total energy of orbiting satellite is negative which results the satellite bounded to the earth. NCERT Pg. 138

9 **Statement I** The geostationary satellites are launched, so as to revolve from west to east in an orbit concentric and coplanar with the equitorial plane and with a period of 24 h.

Statement II The time period of an earth satellite in a circular orbit is independent of the mass of the satellite. NCERT Pg. 137

10 **Statement I** A satellite S is moving in an elliptical orbit around the earth. The mass of the satellite is very small compared to the mass of the earth, then the acceleration of S is always directed towards the centre of the earth.

Statement II If the kinetic energy of the satellite orbiting around the earth is doubled, then it will rotate with a great speed. NCERT Pg. 138

Matching Type Questions

1 Two uniform solid spheres of equal radii R but mass M and $4M$ have a centre-to-centre separation $6R$ as shown in figure. The two spheres are held fixed. A projectile of mass m is projected from the surface of the sphere of mass M directly towards the centre of the second sphere. N is the point where net gravitational is zero. **NCERT Pg. 129**

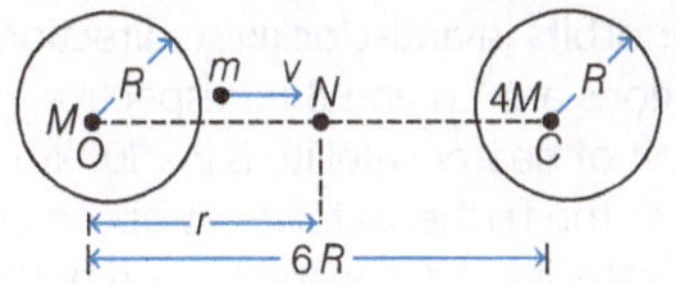

With reference to the above situation, match the Column I (quantities) with Column II (mathematical expressions) and select the correct answer from the codes given below.

Column I	Column II
A. Distance r of neutral point N	1. $\sqrt{\frac{3GM}{5R}}$
B. Minimum speed of the projectile v_{min}, so that it reaches the surface of the second sphere	2. $2R$
C. The speed with which the projectile hits the seconds sphere, if projected with v_{min}	3. $\sqrt{\frac{27GM}{5R}}$
D. Distance between points O and C	4. $6R$

Codes

	A	B	C	D
(a)	4	2	3	1
(b)	3	2	1	4
(c)	2	1	3	4
(d)	3	1	4	2

2 A satellite of mass m revolving with a velocity v around the earth. With reference to the above situation, match the Column I (types of energy) with Column II (expression) and select the correct answer from the codes given below. **NCERT Pg. 138**

Column I	Column II
A. Kinetic energy of the satellite	1. $-\frac{1}{2}mv^2$
B. Potential energy of the satellite	2. $\frac{1}{2}mv^2$
C. Total energy of the satellite	3. $-mv^2$
D. Binding energy of the satellite	4. mv^2

Codes

	A	B	C	D		A	B	C	D
(a)	4	2	3	1	(b)	2	3	1	4
(c)	3	4	1	2	(d)	3	4	2	1

3 Match the Column I (quantities) with Column II (relations) and select the correct answer from the codes given below. **NCERT Pg. 138**

Column I	Column II
A. Kinetic energy of orbiting satellite	1. $\sqrt{\frac{2GM}{R}}$
B. Orbital velocity of the orbiting satellite	2. $\frac{GM}{R^2}$
C. Acceleration due to gravity at the earth surface	3. $\sqrt{\frac{GM}{R}}$
D. Escape velocity at the earth surface	4. $\frac{GMm}{2R}$

Codes

	A	B	C	D		A	B	C	D
(a)	1	3	4	2	(b)	3	4	2	1
(c)	4	3	2	1	(d)	1	2	4	3

Numerical Type Questions

1 The planet jupiter is placed at a distance of 5.2 times of the radius of earth. The period of revolution of jupiter around the sun (in years) is .... **NCERT Pg. 128**

2 If the earth suddenly shrinks to $\frac{1}{27}$th times to its original volume, mass remaining unchanged, then the duration of the day (in h) will be .... **NCERT Pg. 128**

3 Estimate the mass of the sun in the unit of 10^{19} kg, assuming the orbit of the earth around the sun to be a circle. The distance between the sun and earth is 1.49×10^{11} m. ($G = 6.67 \times 10^{-11}$ N-m^2/kg^2) **NCERT Pg. 137**

4 If acceleration due to gravity on the planet x is 9 times on the planet y. A man jumps to height of 2m on the surface of planet x, then the maximum height, he can attain at planet y would be .... m. **NCERT Pg. 132**

5 If the earth were made of lead of relative density 11.3, then the value of acceleration due to gravity on the surface of earth is $\frac{x}{100}$ m/s^2. If radius of earth is 6.4×10^6 m and G is 6.67×10^{-11} N-m^2 kg^{-2}, then what is the value of x? **NCERT Pg. 137**

6 At what height (in km) above the surface of the earth, the value of acceleration due to gravity would be half of its value on the surface of earth? (R_e =6400 km) **NCERT Pg. 133**

7 If the radius of the earth is reduced by 4% keeping the mass same, the change in the escape velocity will be .... %. **NCERT Pg. 135**

8 If the planet A has a mass 9 times and radius 2 times of the planet B, then the minimum speed required by a rocket to pull out of the gravitational force of planet B is $\frac{x}{1000}$ km/s, the value of x is .... (Given, escape velocity of planet A is 11.2 km/s). **NCERT Pg. 135**

9 An spacecraft is launched with velocity 10 km/s from the earth's surface. The maximum height attained by the spacecraft will be xR, where R is the radius of the earth. Take, the value of x is .... **NCERT Pg. 138**

10 Two satellites revolve around a planet in coplanar circular orbits in anti-clockwise direction. Their period of revolutions are 1 h and 8 h, respectively. The radius of the orbit of nearer satellite is 2×10^3 km. The angular speed of the farther satellite as observed from the nearer satellite at the instant when both the satellites are closest is π/x rad h^{-1}, where x is .... **NCERT Pg. 138**

NCERT Exemplar Questions

1 The earth is an approximate sphere. If the interior contained matter which is not of the same density everywhere, then on the surface of the earth, the acceleration due to gravity

(a) will be directed towards the centre but not the same everywhere.

(b) will have the same value everywhere but not directed towards the centre.

(c) will be same everywhere in magnitude directed towards the centre.

(d) Cannot be zero at any point.

2 Different points in the earth are at slightly different distances from the sun and hence experience different forces due to gravitation. For a rigid body, we know that if various forces act at various points in it, the resultant motion is as if a net force acts on the CM (centre of mass) causing translation and a net torque at the CM causing rotation around an axis through the CM. For the earth-sun system (approximating the earth as a uniform density sphere),

(a) the torque is zero.

(b) the torque causes the earth to spin.

(c) the rigid body result is not applicable since the earth is not even approximately a rigid body.

(d) the torque causes the earth to move around the sun.

3 Satellites orbiting the earth have finite life and sometimes debris of satellites fall to the earth. This is because

(a) solar cells and batteries in satellites run out.

(b) laws of gravitation predict a trajectory spiralling inwards.

(c) of viscous forces causing the speed of satellite and hence height to gradually decrease.

(d) of collisions with other satellites.

4 Both the earth and the moon are subject to the gravitational force of the sun. As observed from the sun, the orbit of the moon

(a) will be elliptical.

(b) will not be strictly elliptical because the total gravitational force on it is not central.

(c) is not elliptical but will necessarily be a closed curve.

(d) deviates considerably from being elliptical due to influence of planets other than the earth.

5 In our solar system, the inter-planetary region has chunks of matter (much smaller in size compared to planets) called asteroids. They

(a) will not move around the sun, since they have very small masses compared to the sun.

(b) will move in an irregular way because of their small masses and will drift away into outer space.

(c) will move around the sun in closed orbits but not obey Kepler's laws.

(d) will move in orbits like planets and obey Kepler's laws.

6 Particles of masses $2M$, m and M are respectively at points A, B and C with $AB = 1/2(BC)$. m is much-much smaller than M and at time $t = 0$, they are all at rest as given in figure. At subsequent times before any collision takes place,

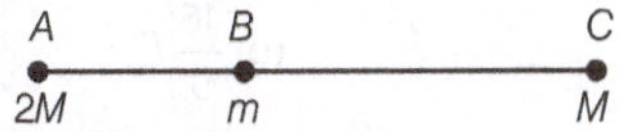

(a) m will remain at rest.
(b) m will move towards M.
(c) m will move towards $2M$.
(d) m will have oscillatory motion.

7 The centre of mass of an extended body on the surface of the earth and its centre of gravity
(a) are always at the same point for any size of the body.
(b) are always at the same point only for spherical bodies.
(c) can never be at the same point.
(d) is close to each other for objects, say of sizes less than 100 m.

Past Exams Questions

NEET

1. The mass of a planet is 1 / 10 th that of the earth and its diameter is half that of the earth. The acceleration due to gravity on that planet is **NCERT Pg. 132, NEET 2024**
(a) 19.6 ms^{-2} (b) 9.8 ms^{-2} (c) 4.9 ms^{-2} (d) 3.92 ms^{-2}

2. The minimum energy required to launch a satellite of mass m from the surface of earth of mass M and radius R in a circular orbit at an altitude of $2R$ from the surface of the earth is **NCERT Pg. 138, NEET 2024**
(a) $\frac{5GmM}{6R}$ (b) $\frac{2GmM}{3R}$ (c) $\frac{GmM}{2R}$ (d) $\frac{GmM}{3R}$

3. Two bodies of mass m and $9m$ are placed at a distance R. The gravitational potential on the line joining the bodies where the gravitational field equal zero, will be (G = gravitational constant) **NCERT Pg. 138, NEET 2023**
(a) $-\frac{12\,Gm}{R}$ (b) $-\frac{16\,Gm}{R}$
(c) $-\frac{20\,Gm}{R}$ (d) $-\frac{8\,Gm}{R}$

4. A body of mass 60 g experiences a gravitational force of 3.0 N when placed at a particular point. The magnitude of the gravitational field intensity at that point is **NCERT Pg. 129, NEET 2022**
(a) 50 N/ kg (b) 20 N / kg
(c) 180 N/kg (d) 0.05 N/kg

5 The escape velocity from the earth's surface is v. The escape velocity from the surface of another planet having a radius four times that of earth and same mass density is **NCERT Pg. 135, NEET 2021**
(a) v (b) $2v$ (c) $3v$ (d) $4v$

6 The ratio of escape velocity at earth (v_e) to the escape velocity at a planet (v_p) whose radius and mean density are twice as that of earth is **NCERT Pg. 135, NEET 2016**
(a) $1:2\sqrt{2}$ (b) 1: 4 (c) $1:\sqrt{2}$ (d) 1: 2

7 A satellite of mass m is orbiting the earth (of radius R) at a height h from its surface. The total energy of the satellite in terms of g_0, the value of acceleration due to gravity at the earth's surface is **NCERT Pg. 138, NEET 2016**
(a) $\frac{mg_0R^2}{2(R+h)}$ (b) $-\frac{mg_0R^2}{2(R+h)}$
(c) $\frac{2mg_0R^2}{R+h}$ (d) $-\frac{2mg_0R^2}{R+h}$

8 A remote sensing satellite of earth revolves in a circular orbit at a height of 0.25×10^6 m above the surface of earth. If earth's radius is 6.38×10^6 m and $g = 9.8$ ms^{-2}, then the orbital speed of the satellite is **NCERT Pg. 137, AIPMT 2015**
(a) 7.76 kms^{-1} (b) 8.56 kms^{-1}
(c) 9.13 kms^{-1} (d) 6.67 kms^{-1}

9 A satellite S is moving in an elliptical orbit around the earth. The mass of the satellite is very small as compared to the mass of the earth, then **NCERT Pg. 137, AIPMT 2015**
(a) the angular momentum of S about the centre of the earth changes in direction, but its magnitude remains constant.
(b) the total mechanical energy of S varies periodically with time.
(c) the linear momentum of S remains constant in magnitude.
(d) the acceleration of S is always directed towards the centre of the earth.

10 A black hole is an object whose gravitational field is so strong that even light cannot escape from it. To what approximate radius would earth (mass = 5.98×10^{24} kg) have to be compressed to be a black hole? **NCERT Pg. 135, AIPMT 2014**
(a) 10^{-9} m (b) 10^{-6} m
(c) 10^{-2} m (d) 10^{-7} m

JEE Main

11 Four identical particles of mass m are kept at the four corners of a square. If the gravitational force exerted on one of the masses by the other masses is $\left(\frac{2\sqrt{2}+1}{32}\right)\frac{Gm^2}{L^2}$, the length of the sides of the square is **NCERT Pg. 135, JEE Main 2024**

(a) $3L$ (b) $2L$
(c) $4L$ (d) $\frac{L}{2}$

12 The mass of the moon is $\frac{1}{144}$ times the mass of a planet and its diameter is 1/16 times the diameter of a planet. If the escape velocity on the planet is v, then the escape velocity on the moon will be **NCERT Pg. 135, JEE Main 2024**

(a) $\frac{v}{4}$ (b) $\frac{v}{3}$ (c) $\frac{v}{6}$ (d) $\frac{v}{12}$

13 The escape velocities of two planets A and B are in the ratio 1 : 2. If the ratio of their radii respectively is 1 : 3, then the ratio of acceleration due to gravity of planet A to the acceleration of gravity of planet B will be **NCERT Pg. 135, JEE Main 2023**

(a) 4/3 (b) 3/4 (c) 3/2 (d) 2/3

14 Two objects of equal masses placed at certain distance from each other attracts each other with a force of F. If one-third mass of one object is transferred to the other object, then the new force will be **NCERT Pg. 129, JEE Main 2022**

(a) $\frac{2}{9}F$ (b) $\frac{16}{9}F$
(c) $\frac{8}{9}F$ (d) F

15 A solid sphere of radius R gravitationally attracts a particle placed at $3R$ from its centre with a force F_1. Now, a spherical cavity of radius $(R/2)$ is made in the sphere (as shown in figure) and the force becomes F_2. The value of $F_1 : F_2$ is **NCERT Pg. 129, JEE Main 2021**

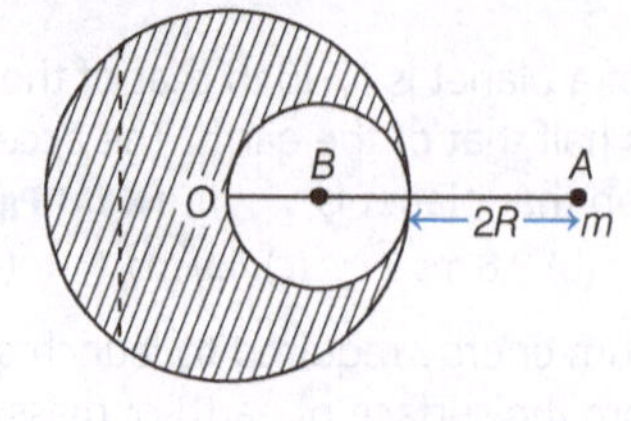

(a) 25 : 36 (b) 36 : 25
(c) 50 : 41 (d) 41 : 50

Skill Boosters

1 Mass density of gaseous planet varies according to distance r from the centre as $\rho(r)=\rho_0\left(1-\frac{r^2}{R^2}\right)$

A scientist want to land a spacecraft on the planet in study its properties. At which point, the spacecraft will experience the maximum attractive force?

(a) $x=\sqrt{\frac{1}{3}}R$ (b) $x=R$
(c) $x=\sqrt{\frac{3}{4}}R$ (d) $\sqrt{\frac{5}{9}}R$

2 A tunnel is dug along a chord of the earth at a perpendicular distance $\frac{R}{3}$ from the earth's centre. Assume wall of the tunnel is frictionless. Find the force exerted by the wall on mass m at distance x from the centre of the tunnel.

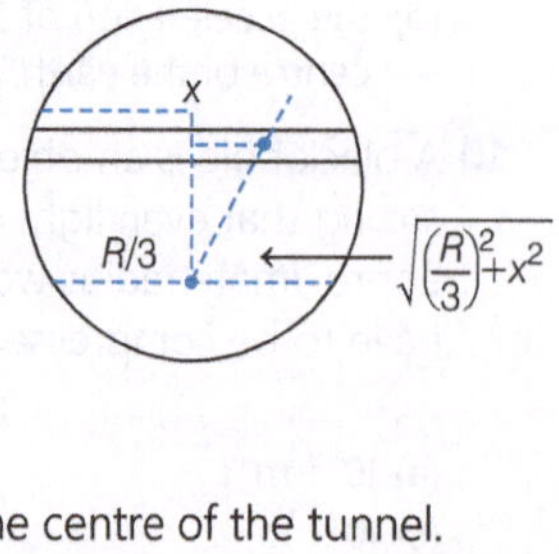

(a) $\frac{mg\sqrt{\frac{R^2}{9}+x^2}}{R}$ (b) $\frac{mgx}{\sqrt{\frac{R^2}{(a+x^2)}}}$ (c) $\frac{mg}{3}$ (d) $\frac{mgx}{R}$

3 A, B, C and D are four masses, each of mass m lying on the vertices of a square of side a. They always move along a common circle with velocity v. Find v so that they always remain on the vertices of the square.

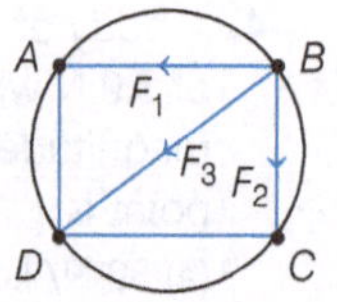

(a) $\sqrt{\frac{Gm\,(2\sqrt{2}+1)}{2\sqrt{2}\,a}}$

(b) $\sqrt{\frac{Gm\,(\sqrt{2}+1)}{2\,a}}$

(c) $\sqrt{\frac{Gm\,\sqrt{2}\,(2+1)}{a}}$

(d) $\sqrt{\frac{Gm\,(\sqrt{2}+5)}{2\,a}}$

4 An artificial satellite of a planet revolves in a circular orbit whose radius exceeds the radius of the planet 7 times. In the process of motion, the satellite experiences slight resistance due to cosmic dust. Assuming the resistive force depends on the speed of the satellite as $F = kv^2$ (where k is a constant), find how long the satellite will stay in orbit until it falls on to the planet's surface.

(Given, m = mass of the satellite, g = acceleration due to gravity at the surface of planet and R = radius of the planet)

(a) $\frac{m}{k\sqrt{2gR}}(\sqrt{7}-1)$

(b) $\frac{m}{k\sqrt{gR}}(\sqrt{7}-1)$

(c) $\frac{2m}{k\sqrt{2gR}}(\sqrt{7}-1)$

(d) $\frac{m}{2k\sqrt{gR}}(\sqrt{7}-1)$

5 Velocity of a point on the equator of a rotating spherical planet is v. The angular velocity of the planet is such that, the value of g at the equator is half of g at the pole. Determine the escape velocity for a polar particle on the planet as a function of v.

(a) $6v$ (b) $2v$ (c) $4v$ (d) $3v$

6 A double star is a system of two stars moving around the centre of mass of the system due to gravitation. The distance between the components of the double star is (Given, the total mass is M and time period is T)

(a) $\left(\frac{GMT^2}{\pi^2}\right)^{1/3}$ (b) $\left(\frac{GMT^2}{4\pi^2}\right)^{1/3}$

(c) $\left(\frac{GMT^2}{2\pi^2}\right)^{1/3}$ (d) $\left(\frac{GMT}{3\pi^2}\right)^{1/3}$

7 Let ω be the angular velocity of the earth's rotation about its axis. The acceleration due to gravity at the surface of earth near the poles is g. An object weighed at the equator gives the same reading as a reading taken at a depth d below earth's surface at a pole ($d << R$). The value of d is

(a) $\frac{\omega^2R^2}{g}$ (b) $\frac{\omega^2R^2}{2g}$

(c) $\frac{2\omega^2R^2}{g}$ (d) $\frac{\omega^2R^2}{\sqrt{2}g}$

8 Find the gravitational potential energy of a point mass m_0 and a thin uniform rod of mass m_0 and length l, if they are located along a straight line at a distance d measured from the centre of the rod.

(a) $-\frac{Gm_0^2}{l}\log_e\left(\frac{d+r}{d-r}\right)$

(b) $-\frac{Gm_0^2}{l}\log_e\left(\frac{d+2l}{d-2l}\right)$

(c) $-\frac{Gm_0^2}{l}\log_e\left(\frac{2d+l}{2d-l}\right)$

(d) $-\frac{Gm_0^2}{2l}\log_e\left(\frac{d+l}{d-l}\right)$

9 A ring of radius R, mass m and a solid sphere of same mass m and same radius R are placed with their centres on positive X-axis. The observer is moving from some finite distance on negative X-axis towards positive X-axis. The plane of the ring is perpendicular to X-axis. If the observer moves only up to the surface of the solid sphere, then the net gravitational field varies with the distance moved along X-axis as

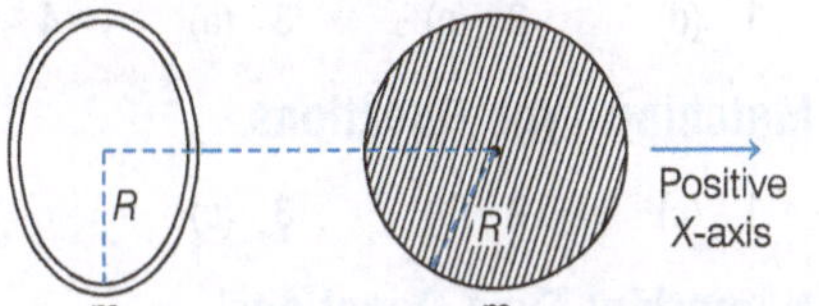

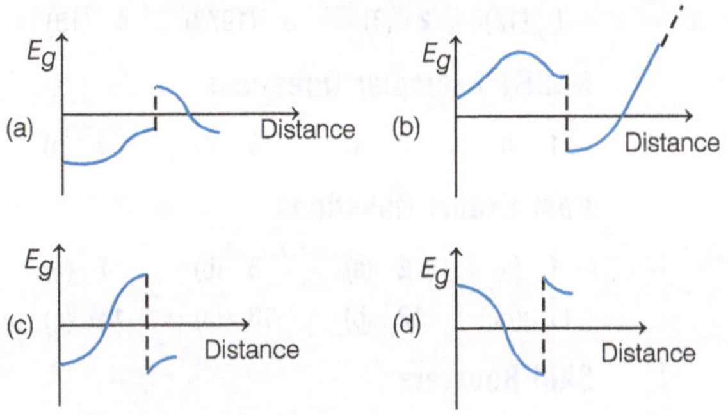

10 At some place gravitational field is

$$\mathbf{E}_g = 4\hat{\mathbf{i}} + \hat{\mathbf{j}}\left(\frac{\text{N}}{\text{Kg}}\right)$$

Work done by this field is zero when a particle is moved along path

(a) $x + y = 6$ (b) $x + 4y = 6$

(c) $4x + y = 6$ (d) $x - 4y = 6$

Correct Codes

Topical Questions

1 (a)	2 (c)	3 (c)	4 (a)	5 (c)	6 (a)	7 (a)	8 (c)	9 (c)	10 (d)
11 (c)	12 (b)	13 (a)	14 (c)	15 (b)	16 (c)	17 (c)	18 (a)	19 (d)	20 (b)
21 (a)	22 (c)	23 (b)	24 (c)	25 (c)	26 (c)	27 (d)	28 (b)	29 (d)	30 (b)
31 (c)	32 (c)	33 (b)	34 (a)	35 (d)	36 (a)	37 (c)	38 (b)	39 (c)	40 (a)
41 (c)	42 (a)	43 (b)	44 (b)	45 (c)	46 (d)	47 (a)	48 (a)	49 (b)	50 (b)
51 (c)	52 (d)	53 (b)	54 (a)	55 (d)	56 (b)	57 (c)	58 (c)	59 (b)	60 (b)
61 (b)	62 (b)	63 (c)	64 (c)	65 (b)	66 (d)	67 (b)	68 (b)	69 (b)	70 (b)
71 (a)	72 (b)	73 (c)	74 (d)	75 (c)	76 (c)	77 (d)	78 (b)	79 (a)	80 (a)
81 (a)	82 (a)	83 (a)	84 (d)	85 (d)	86 (a)	87 (d)	88 (d)	89 (a)	90 (d)
91 (b)	92 (b)	93 (c)	94 (c)	95 (a)	96 (d)	97 (c)	98 (b)	99 (b)	100. (a)

Assertion and Reason Questions

1 (b)	2 (a)	3 (a)	4 (c)	5 (a)	6 (a)	7 (a)	8 (c)	9 (a)	10 (a)

Statement Based Questions

1 (d)	2 (c)	3 (b)	4 (b)	5 (d)	6 (a)	7 (d)	8 (c)	9 (d)	10 (b)

Matching Type Questions

1 (c)	2 (b)	3 (c)

Numerical Type Questions

1 (12)	2 (3)	3 (1972)	4 (18)	5 (2221)	6 (2650)	7 (2)	8 (5279)	9 (4)	10 (3)

NCERT Exemplar Questions

1 (d)	2 (a)	3 (c)	4 (b)	5 (d)	6 (c)	7 (d)

Past Exams Questions

1 (d)	2 (a)	3 (b)	4 (a)	5 (d)	6 (a)	7 (b)	8 (a)	9 (d)	10 (c)
11 (c)	12 (b)	13 (b)	14 (c)	15 (c)					

Skill Boosters

1 (d)	2 (c)	3 (a)	4 (b)	5 (b)	6 (b)	7 (a)	8 (c)	9 (b)	10 (c)

Step by Step

Decoding the Questions

Concept Builders

1 square, cube
2 mass
3 decreases
4 True (T)
5 Zero
6 True (T)
7 1 : 1
8 It gets doubled
9 True (T)
10 Perpendicular
11 False
12 zero
13 False (F)
14 $1-\frac{d}{R_E}$
15 decreases
16 negative
17 False (F)
18 True (T)
19 negative
20 False (F)

Topical Questions

1 (*a*) As, $\frac{v_p}{v_a}=\frac{a(1+e)}{a(1-e)}$

$$e=\frac{v_p-v_a}{v_a+v_p}$$

2 (*c*) From Kepler's law,

$$\left(\frac{T_2}{T_1}\right)^2=\left(\frac{r_2}{r_1}\right)^3$$

$$T_2=3\sqrt{3}T_1=3\sqrt{3}\text{ yr}$$

4 (*a*) Here, $\frac{dA}{dt}=\frac{L}{2M}$

$$\Rightarrow \quad dA=\frac{L}{2M}\times dt$$

$$\Rightarrow \quad A=\frac{L}{2M}\times T$$

5 (*c*) By Kepler's law of planetary motion, $\frac{dA}{dt}=\text{constant}$

$$\therefore \quad \frac{A_1}{t_1}=\frac{A_2}{t_2}=\frac{A_3}{t_3}$$

$$\Rightarrow \quad \frac{A_1}{2}=\frac{A_2}{3}=\frac{A_3}{6}$$

$$\therefore A_1:A_2:A_3=2:3:6$$

6 (*a*) Area, $\Delta A=\frac{1}{2}r\,(v\Delta t)$

Then, areal velocity,

$$\frac{\Delta A}{\Delta t}=\frac{1}{2}\cdot\frac{rv\Delta t}{\Delta t}=\frac{1}{2}rv$$

$$=\frac{mvr}{2m}=\frac{L}{2m}=\text{constant}$$

7 (*a*) The area swept out by the given planet in time interval Δt is

$$\Delta A=\frac{1}{2}|\mathbf{r}\times\mathbf{PP'}|$$

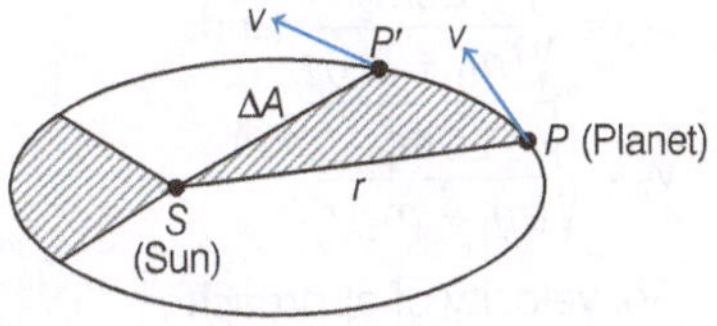

$$\Rightarrow \quad \Delta A=\frac{1}{2}|\mathbf{r}\times\mathbf{v}\Delta t|$$

8 (*c*) From Kepler's second law, the areal velocity can be given as

$$\frac{dA}{dt}=\frac{L}{2m}=\frac{I\omega}{2m}=\frac{mr^2\omega}{2m}$$

$$\Rightarrow \quad \frac{dA}{dt}\propto\omega r^2$$

9 (*c*) For a particle, angular momentum is $\mathbf{L}=\mathbf{r}\times\mathbf{p}$.

So, magnitude of angular momentum, $|\mathbf{L}|=|\mathbf{r}||\mathbf{p}|\sin\theta$

or $\quad L=mv\,r\sin\theta$

When $\theta=90°$, then

$$L_P=m_P r_P v_P$$

10 (*d*) $\quad m_1v_1r_1=m_2v_2r_2$

But $\quad m_1=m_2$

$$\Rightarrow \quad \frac{v_1}{v_2}=\frac{r_2}{r_1}$$

For points R and P, $\frac{v_R}{v_P}=\frac{r_P}{r_R}$

Since, $\quad r_R>r_P$

$\therefore \quad v_R<v_P$

11 (*c*) From conservation of angular momentum,

$$L=mvr=\text{constant}$$

$$m\,v_{max}\,r_{min}=m\,v_{min}\,r_{max}$$

$$\Rightarrow \quad v_{max}\cdot r_{min}=v_{min}\cdot r_{max}$$

or $\quad r_{min}=\frac{v_{min}\cdot r_{max}}{v_{max}}$

$$=\frac{1\times10^3\times4\times10^4}{3\times10^4}$$

$$=\frac{4}{3}\times10^3\text{ km}$$

12 (*b*) According to the question,

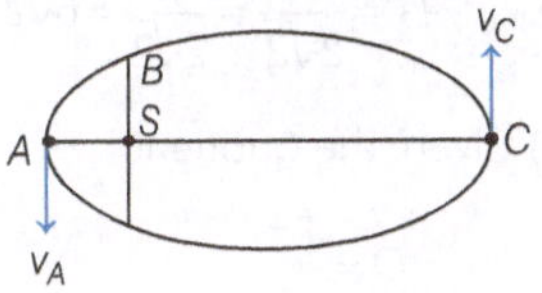

$$v_A=v_{max},\ v_C=v_{min}$$

Therefore, we can write

$$v_A>v_B>v_C \quad \text{...(i)}$$

Kinetic energy (K) of the planet at any point is given as

$$K=\frac{1}{2}mv^2$$

From Eq. (i), we can write

$$K_A>K_B>K_C$$

13 (*a*) $\frac{T^2}{a^3}=\frac{(84)^2}{(287\times10^{10})^3}$

$$=2.98\times10^{-34}\text{ yr}^2\text{m}^{-3}$$

$$\approx 3.00\times10^{-34}\text{ yr}^2\text{m}^{-3}$$

14 (*c*) From Kepler's third law of planetary motion,

$$\frac{T_1^2}{r_1^3}=\frac{T_2^2}{r_2^3}=\text{constant}$$

or $\quad \left(\frac{T_1}{T_2}\right)^2=\left(\frac{r_1}{r_2}\right)^3$

15 (*b*) If time period for the mars and the earth are T_m and T_e, respectively. Then, according to Kepler's third law, $\frac{T_m^2}{T_e^2}=\frac{R_{ms}^3}{R_{es}^3}$

$$\therefore \quad T_m=\left(\frac{R_{ms}}{R_{es}}\right)^{3/2}\cdot T_e$$

$$\therefore \quad T_m=(1.52)^{3/2}\times 365\text{ days}$$

16 (c) By Kepler's third law of planetary motion,

$$\frac{T_1}{T_2}=\left(\frac{a_1}{a_2}\right)^{3/2}$$

$$\therefore \quad \frac{T}{T_2}=\left(\frac{R}{9R}\right)^{3/2}$$

$$\Rightarrow \quad T_2=27T$$

17 (c) From Kepler's third law, $T^2 \propto r^3$

$$\text{So,} \quad \frac{T_2^2}{T_1^2}=\frac{r_2^3}{r_1^3}=\frac{(3R)^3}{(6R)^3}$$

$$\Rightarrow \quad T_2=\frac{T_1}{2\sqrt{2}}=\frac{24}{2\sqrt{2}}=6\sqrt{2}\text{ h}$$

18 (a) Given, the quotient,

$$Q=\frac{T^2}{a^3}$$

For venus,

$$a=10.8\text{ units}=10.8\times 10^{10}\text{ m},$$

$$T=0.615\text{ yr}$$

$$\Rightarrow \quad Q=\frac{T^2}{a^3}=\frac{(0.615)^2}{(10.8)^3\times 10^{30}}\frac{\text{y}^2}{\text{m}^3}$$

$$\Rightarrow \quad A=3.00\times 10^{-34}\text{ y}^2\text{m}^{-3}$$

$$=3\text{ units}$$

19 (d) Kepler's law,

$$\frac{T_A^2}{T_B^2}=\frac{r_A^3}{r_B^3}$$

$$\Rightarrow \quad \frac{1^2}{8^2}=\frac{(10^4)^3}{r_B^3}$$

$$\therefore \quad r_B=4\times 10^4\text{ km}$$

Speed of satellite A,

$$v_A=\frac{2\pi r_A}{T_A}=\frac{2\pi\times 10^4}{1}$$

$$=2\pi\times 10^4\text{ km/h}$$

Speed of satellite B,

$$v_B=\frac{2\pi r_B}{T_B}=\frac{2\pi\times 4\times 10^4}{8}$$

$$=\pi\times 10^4\text{ km/h}$$

The speed of B relative to A when they are close to each other is

$$v_{BA}=v_A-v_B$$

$$=2\pi\times 10^4-\pi\times 10^4$$

$$=\pi\times 10^4\text{ km/h}$$

20 (b) By conservation of momentum

$$m_1v_1=m_2v_2 \quad \text{(i)}$$

Change in PE of the system

= Total change in KE of the system

$$\Rightarrow U_f-U_i=K_f-K_i$$

$$0-\left(-\frac{Gm_1m_2}{r}\right)=\left(\frac{1}{2}m_1v_1^2+\frac{1}{2}m_2v_2^2\right)-0$$

$$\Rightarrow \frac{2Gm_1m_2}{r}=m_1v_1^2+m_2v_2^2 \quad \text{... (ii)}$$

From Eqs. (i) & (ii), we get

$$v_1=\sqrt{\frac{2Gm_2^2}{(m_1+m_2)r}} \text{ and}$$

$$v_2=\sqrt{\frac{2Gm_1^2}{(m_1+m_2)r}}$$

So, velocity of approach

$$=|v_{\text{relative}}|=|v_1|+|v_2|$$

$$=\sqrt{\frac{2G}{(m_1+m_2)r}}(m_1+m_2)$$

$$=\sqrt{\frac{2G(m_1+m_2)}{r}}$$

21 (a) By Kepler's law of period

$$T^2\propto r^3$$

$$\Rightarrow T^2=\left(\frac{4\pi^2}{GM_S}\right)r^3$$

$\therefore$ Slope of T^2 *versus* r^3 graph is $\frac{4\pi^2}{GM_S}$.

22 (c) $r_1=6R+R=7R$,

$r_2=2.5R+R=3.5R$

$T_1=24\text{h}$

By Kepler's law of period,

$$T_2=\left(\frac{r_2}{r_1}\right)^{3/2}\times T_1=\left(\frac{3.5R}{7R}\right)^{3/2}\times 24$$

$$=6\sqrt{2}\text{ h}$$

24 (c) $F=\frac{GMm}{a^3}=\frac{mv^2}{a}$

Orbital speed, $v=\frac{\sqrt{GM}}{a}$

Time period of revolution of a planet,

$$T=\frac{2\pi r}{v}$$

$$T=\frac{2\pi a}{\frac{\sqrt{GM}}{a}}=\frac{2\pi a^2}{\sqrt{GM}}$$

$$\Rightarrow \quad T\propto a^2$$

Hence, the orbit of the planet around the sun will not be elliptical because for elliptical orbit $T^2\propto a^3$.

As force $F=\left(\frac{GM}{a^3}\right)m=g'm$.

Since, g' = acceleration due to gravity is constant, hence path followed by a projectile will be approximately parabolic (as $T\propto a^2$).

25 (c) As we know that, period of revolution,

$$T=\frac{2\pi r}{v}=2\pi\frac{r}{\sqrt{GM/r}}=2\pi\frac{r^{3/2}}{\sqrt{GM}}$$

$$\Rightarrow T^2=\frac{4\pi^2}{GM}r^3=kr^3$$

$$\therefore \quad k=\frac{4\pi^2}{GM}$$

$$\Rightarrow \quad GMk=4\pi^2$$

26 (c) Let the point mass M is placed at a distance of x m from m_1.

Also, $\frac{m_1}{m_2}=\frac{4}{3}$

As given $F_{13}=\frac{1}{3}F_{23}$

$$\frac{Gm_1M}{x^2}=\frac{1}{3}\frac{Gm_2M}{(1-x)^2}$$

$$\Rightarrow \quad \frac{m_1}{m_2}=\frac{x^2}{3(1-x)^2}$$

$$\frac{4}{3}=\frac{x^2}{3(1-x)^2}$$

$$\therefore \quad x=\frac{2}{3}\text{ m}$$

27 (d) $M=\rho\times\frac{4}{3}\pi R^3$

$$\text{So, } F=\frac{GM^2}{4R^2}$$

$$=\frac{G\left(\rho\times\frac{4}{3}\pi R^3\right)^2}{4R^2}=\frac{4G\rho^2\pi^2R^4}{9}$$

$$\therefore F\propto R^4$$

28 (*b*) In a circular motion, the centripetal acceleration,

$$a = \frac{v^2}{R_m}$$

$$a = \left(\frac{2\pi R_m}{T}\right)^2 \times \frac{1}{R_m} = \frac{4\pi^2 R_m}{T^2}$$

29 (*d*) According to the question,

$$\text{force} = \frac{GMm}{r^{3/2}} = m\omega^2 r$$

$$\Rightarrow \quad \frac{GMm}{r^{3/2}} = \frac{4\pi^2 mr}{T^2}$$

$$\Rightarrow \quad T^2 = \left(\frac{4\pi^2}{GM}\right) \cdot r^{5/2}$$

$$\Rightarrow \quad T^2 \propto r^{5/2}$$

30 (*b*)

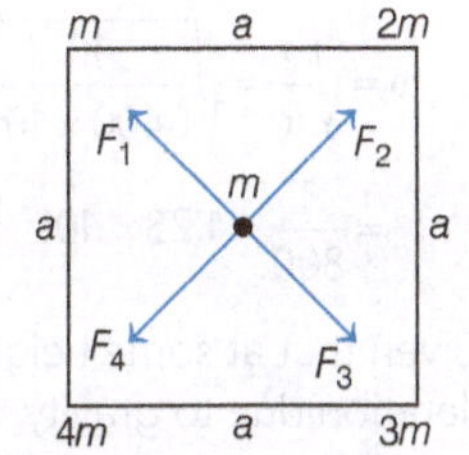

So, resultant force will be

$$F_{24} = F_4 - F_2$$

$$F_{24} = \frac{Gm\,4m}{\left(\frac{a}{\sqrt{2}}\right)^2} - \frac{Gm(2m)}{\left(\frac{a}{\sqrt{2}}\right)^2}$$

$$= \frac{4Gm^2}{a^2}$$

Similarly,

$$F_{13} = \frac{Gm(3m)}{\left(\frac{a}{\sqrt{2}}\right)^2} - \frac{Gm(m)}{\left(\frac{a}{\sqrt{2}}\right)^2}$$

$$= \frac{4Gm^2}{a^2}$$

Now, the angle between the forces is 90°. So, the resultant force will be $F = 4\sqrt{2}\,\frac{Gm^2}{a^2}$

31 (*c*) $\quad F = \frac{GMm}{(R+h)^2}$

Then, according to the question,

$$\frac{GMm}{(R+h)^2} = \frac{1}{16}\frac{GMm}{R^2}$$

$$h = 3R$$

33 (*b*)

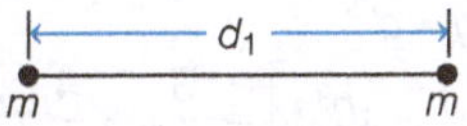

Gravitational force,

$$F_1 = \frac{Gm \cdot m}{d_1^2} = \frac{Gm^2}{d_1^2}$$

Similarly,

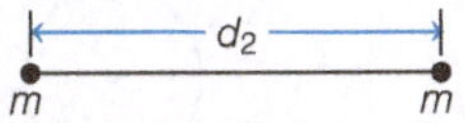

Gravitational force,

$$F_2 = \frac{Gm^2}{d_2^2}$$

$$\because \quad \frac{F_1}{F_2} = \left(\frac{d_2}{d_1}\right)^2$$

$$\therefore \quad F_2 = F_1\left(\frac{d_1}{d_2}\right)^2$$

35 (*d*)

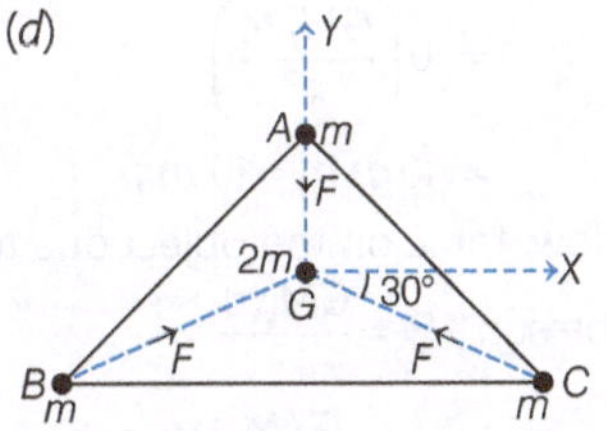

$$\Rightarrow |\mathbf{F}_{x\,(\text{net})}|$$

$$= |F\cos 30°\,\hat{\mathbf{i}} - F\cos 30°\,\hat{\mathbf{i}}| = 0$$

Similarly, along *Y*-axis,

$$|\mathbf{F}_{y(\text{net})}| = |-F\,\hat{\mathbf{j}} + (F\sin 30° + F\sin 30°)\,\hat{\mathbf{j}}|$$

$$= \left|-F\,\hat{\mathbf{j}} + \left(\frac{F}{2} + \frac{F}{2}\right)\hat{\mathbf{j}}\right|$$

$$= |F\hat{\mathbf{j}} - F\hat{\mathbf{j}}| = 0$$

F_{net} = Resultant force on mass at *G* due to masses at *A*, *B* and *C* $= \sqrt{F^2_{x\,(\text{net})} + F^2_{y\,(\text{net})}} = 0$

36 (*a*)

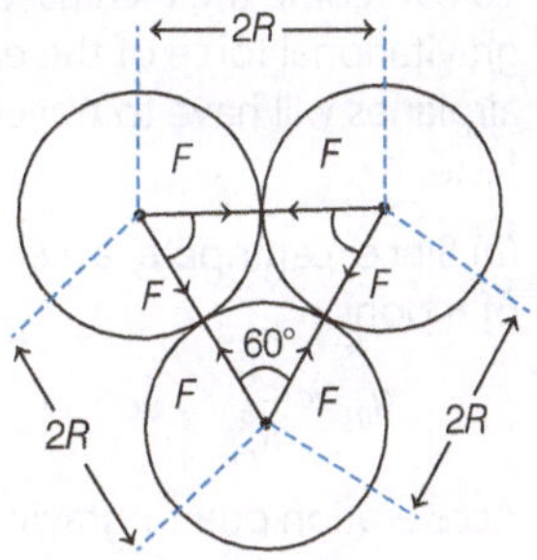

$$F = G \cdot \frac{M \cdot M}{(2R)^2} = \frac{GM^2}{4R^2}$$

$$F_{\text{net}} = \sqrt{F^2 + F^2 + 2F^2\cos 60°}$$

$$= \sqrt{3}\,F$$

$$\therefore F_{\text{net}} = \frac{\sqrt{3}}{4}\frac{GM^2}{R^2}$$

37 (*c*) $|\mathbf{F}_1| = \left[\frac{Gmm_1}{(a/\sqrt{2})^2}\right]$

$$|\mathbf{F}_2| = \left[\frac{Gmm_2}{(a/\sqrt{2})^2}\right]$$

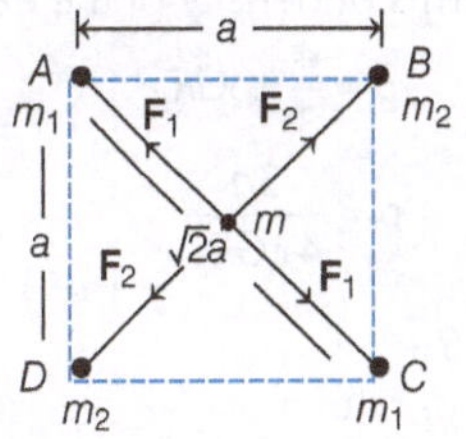

$$\mathbf{F}_{\text{net}\,(BD)} = \mathbf{F}_2 - \mathbf{F}_2 = 0$$

$$\mathbf{F}_{\text{net}\,(AC)} = \mathbf{F}_1 - \mathbf{F}_1 = 0$$

$\therefore$ Net force on *m* is $|\mathbf{F}_{\text{net}}|$ = zero

38 (*b*) $F = \frac{Gm(M-m)}{r^2}$

For maximum force, $\frac{dF}{dm} = 0$

$$\Rightarrow M - 2m = 0 \Rightarrow \frac{m}{M} = \frac{1}{2}$$

39 (*c*)

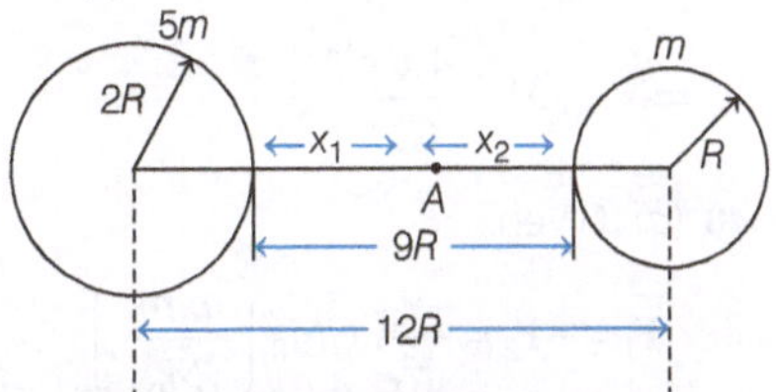

$$\therefore x_1 + x_2 = [12R - (R + 2R)] = 9R$$

$$F = G \cdot \frac{5m \cdot m}{(12R)^2}$$

$$a_1 = \frac{F}{5m} = \frac{Gm}{(12R)^2}$$

$$x_1 = \frac{1}{2}a_1 t^2 = \frac{1}{2} \cdot \frac{Gm}{(12R)^2} \cdot t^2$$

$$a_2 = \frac{F}{m} = \frac{5Gm}{(12R)^2}$$

$$x_2 = \frac{1}{2}a_2 t^2 = \frac{1}{2} \cdot \frac{5Gm}{(12R)^2} \cdot t^2$$

$$\frac{1}{2} \cdot \frac{Gm}{(12R)^2} \cdot t^2 + \frac{1}{2} \cdot \frac{5Gm}{(12R)^2} \cdot t^2 = 9R$$

$$\Rightarrow \quad t^2 = \frac{3R(12R)^2}{Gm}$$

$$\therefore \quad x_2 = \frac{1}{2} \cdot \frac{5Gm}{(12R)^2} \times \frac{3R(12R)^2}{Gm}$$
$$= 7.5R$$

43 (b) The acceleration due to gravity at the surface of the earth,

$$g = \frac{GM_E}{R_E^2} \Rightarrow \frac{g}{G} = \frac{M_E}{R_E^2}$$

44 (b) The acceleration due to gravity in terms of density of the earth is

$$g = \frac{4}{3}\pi\rho G R_E$$
$$\therefore \quad \rho = \frac{3g}{4\pi G R_E}$$

45 (c) $\frac{g_m}{g_E} = \frac{1}{6}$

$$g = \frac{GM}{R^2} \Rightarrow g \propto \frac{M}{R^2}$$
$$\therefore \quad \frac{g_m}{g_E} = \left(\frac{M_m}{M_E}\right)\left(\frac{R_E}{R_m}\right)^2 = \frac{R_E^2}{8R_m^2} = \frac{1}{6}$$
$$\therefore \quad R_E = \sqrt{\frac{8}{6}} R_m$$

47 (a) $F = G\frac{Mm}{r^2}$

Thus, $M\omega^2 r = \frac{4\pi M^2}{T^2} = \frac{GmM}{r^2}$

$$\Rightarrow \quad M = \frac{4\pi^2 r^3}{GT^2}$$

48 (a) Given,

$$\mathbf{F}_1 = -\mathbf{F}_2 = \frac{-\mathbf{r}_{12}}{r_{12}^3} GM_0^2 \left(\frac{m_1 m_2}{M_0^2}\right)^n$$
$$g = \frac{|\mathbf{F}_1|}{\text{mass}}$$
$$= \frac{GM_0^2 (m_1 m_2)^n}{r_{12}^2 (M_0)^{2n}} \times \frac{1}{(\text{mass})}$$

Since, g depends upon mass of the object. Hence, g is different for different objects.

49 (b) Acceleration due to gravity,

$$g' = \frac{GM'}{R'^2}$$
$$= \frac{G(2M)}{(R/2)^2} = \frac{8GM}{R^2}$$
$$\therefore \quad g' = 8g$$

50 (b) $g = g'$

$$\therefore \frac{G}{R^2}\left[\frac{4}{3}\pi R^3 \rho\right] = \frac{G}{R'^2} \times \frac{4}{3}\pi R'^3 (2\rho)$$
$$\Rightarrow \quad R' = \frac{R}{2}$$

52 (d) Consider the given diagram,

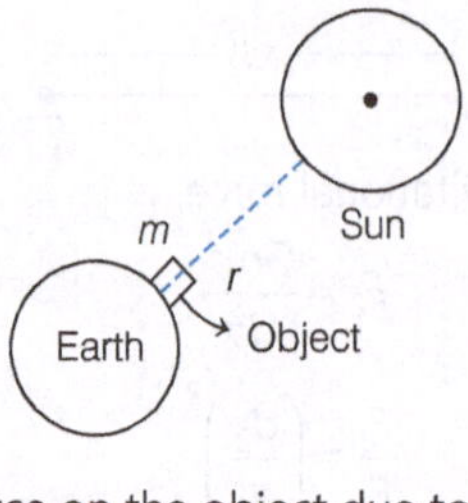

Force on the object due to the earth,

$$F = \frac{G' M_E m}{R^2} = \frac{10 GM_E m}{R^2}$$
$$= 10\left(\frac{GM_E m}{R^2}\right)$$
$$= (10g)\, m = 10\, mg \quad \text{...(i)}$$

Now, force on the object due to the sun, $F' = \frac{GM_s' m}{r^2}$

$$= \frac{G(M_s) m}{10 r^2}$$

As $r >> R$ (radius of the earth)

$\Rightarrow$ F' will be very small, so the effect of the sun will be neglected.

Now, as $g' = 10g$

$= mg' = 10\, mg$ [from Eq. (i)]

i.e. $v_e \propto g$

As, $g' > g$

$\Rightarrow$ $v_e' > v_e$

Hence, rain drops will fall much faster.

To overcome the increased gravitational force of the earth, the airplanes will have to travel much faster.

53 (b) Since, centripetal acceleration of moon,

$$a_m \propto \frac{1}{R_m^2} \quad \text{...(i)}$$

Acceleration due to gravity,

$$g \propto \frac{1}{R_E^2} \quad \text{...(ii)}$$

On dividing Eq. (ii) by Eq. (i), we get

$$\frac{g}{a_m} = \frac{R_m^2}{R_E^2} = \left(\frac{R_m}{R_E}\right)^2$$

54 (a) Centripetal acceleration is given as

$$a = \frac{4\pi^2 R_m}{T^2}$$
$$= \frac{4 \times \left(\frac{22}{7}\right)^2 \times (3.84 \times 10^8)}{(27.3 \times 24 \times 60 \times 60)^2}$$
$$\approx 0.0027 \text{ ms}^{-2}$$

55 (d) Here,

$$g' = g\left(1 - \frac{R\omega^2}{g}\right) = 0$$

or, $\omega = \sqrt{\frac{g}{R}} = \sqrt{\frac{10}{6400 \times 10^3}}$

$$= \frac{1}{800} = 1.25 \times 10^{-3} \text{ rad s}^{-1}$$

56 (b) Given that at some height h, acceleration due to gravity,

$$g_h = 4.9 \text{ m/s}^2 \approx \frac{g}{2} \quad \text{... (i)}$$

$\therefore$ The ratio of acceleration due to gravity at earth's surface and at some altitude h is

$$\left(1 + \frac{h}{R_e}\right) = \sqrt{\frac{g}{g_h}} = \sqrt{2} \text{ [from Eq. (i)]}$$
$$\therefore \quad \frac{h}{R_e} = \sqrt{2} - 1$$

or $h = 0.414 \times R_e$

$$h = 0.414 \times 6400 \text{ km}$$
$$= 2.6 \times 10^6 \text{ m}$$

57 (c) $w' = mg' \quad \text{...(i)}$

$$g' = g\left(\frac{R_E}{R_E + h}\right)^2$$

According to the question,

$$h = \left(\frac{R_E}{2}\right)$$
$$\therefore \quad g' = g\left[\frac{R_E}{\frac{3R_E}{2}}\right]^2 = \frac{4}{9} g \quad \text{...(ii)}$$

On substituting Eq. (ii) in Eq. (i), we get

$$w' = \frac{4\,mg}{9} = \frac{4}{9}w$$

58 (c) $g' = g\left(\frac{R}{R+h}\right)^2$

$\Rightarrow \quad \frac{g}{2} = g\left(\frac{R}{R+h}\right)^2$

$\Rightarrow \quad h = (\sqrt{2} - 1)\,R$

59 (b) $\frac{g'}{g} = \left(\frac{R}{R+h}\right)^2$

$\Rightarrow \quad \left(\frac{1}{100}\right) = \left(\frac{R}{R+h}\right)^2$

$\therefore \quad h = 10\,R - R = 9\,R$

60 (b) $g' = \frac{g}{\left(1 + \frac{h}{R_E}\right)^2} = \frac{g}{\left(1 + \frac{R_E/2}{R_E}\right)^2}$

$$= \frac{4g}{9} \quad \text{...(i)}$$

Weight of the body at the earth's surface,

$$w = mg = 45\text{ N} \quad \text{...(ii)}$$

Then, weight of the body at altitude h is

$$w' = mg' = \frac{4}{9}mg \quad \text{...(iii)}$$

From Eqs. (ii) and (iii), we get

$$w' = \frac{4}{9} \times 45 = 20\text{ N}$$

61 (b) $g_h = g\left(\frac{R}{R+h}\right)^2$

Given, $g_h = g - 0.51\,g = 0.49\,g$

$\therefore \quad \frac{49}{100}g = g\left(\frac{R}{R+h}\right)^2$

$\therefore \quad h = \frac{3R}{7}$

62 (b) $g_d = g\left(1 - \frac{d}{R}\right) = g\left(1 - \frac{32}{6400}\right)$

$$= \frac{199}{200}g$$

$\therefore$% decrease in weight

$$= \left(\frac{mg - mg_d}{mg} \times 100\right)\%$$

$$= \left(\frac{g - \frac{199}{200}g}{g} \times 100\right)\% = 0.5\%$$

63 (c) $d = R_E - r = 6400 - 2000$

$$= 4400\text{ km} = 4.4 \times 10^6\text{ m}$$

$$g' = g\left(1 - \frac{d}{R_E}\right)$$

$$= 9.8\left(1 - \frac{4.4 \times 10^6}{6.4 \times 10^6}\right)$$

$$= 3.06\text{ m/s}^2$$

64 (c) $mg' = mg\left(1 - \frac{d}{R}\right)$

Thus, the weight of the body at half way down $\left(\text{i.e. } d = \frac{R}{2}\right)$ to the centre of the earth is

$$mg' = 200 \times \left(1 - \frac{R/2}{R}\right)$$

$$= 200\left(1 - \frac{1}{2}\right) = 200 \times \frac{1}{2}$$

$$= 100\text{ N}$$

65 (b) Mass of box at pole,

$$m = \frac{w_p}{g_p} = \frac{196}{10} = 19.6\text{ kg}$$

Now, due to rotation of earth, acceleration due to gravity at equator,

$$g_e = g_p - R\omega^2 \quad \text{...(i)}$$

Here,

$$g_p = 10\text{ ms}^{-2},\ R = 6400 \times 10^3\text{ m},$$

$$\omega = \frac{2\pi}{T} \text{ and } T = 24 \times 3600\text{ s}$$

Now, substituting the given values in Eq. (i), we get

$$g_e = g_p - 0.034$$

$$= 10 - 0.034$$

$$= 9.966\text{ ms}^{-2}$$

So, weight of box at equator,

$$w_e = g_e \times m = 9.966 \times 19.6$$

$$= 195.33\text{ N}$$

66 (d) If $h << R$

$$gh = g\left(1 - \frac{2h}{R}\right)$$

and $g_d = g\left(1 - \frac{d}{R}\right)$

Given, when $h = 1$ km, so $g_d = g_h$

or $g\left(1 - \frac{d}{R}\right) = g\left(1 - \frac{2h}{R}\right)$

$\Rightarrow d = 2h$ or $d = 2$ km

68 (b) $\Delta U = U_H - U_E$

$$= -\frac{GMm}{R + nR} + \frac{GMm}{R}$$

$$= \left[\frac{n}{n+1}\right]mgR$$

69 (b) Total gravitational potential energy

$$= \frac{-Gm_1m_2}{r_1} - \frac{Gm_2m_3}{r_2} - \frac{Gm_1m_3}{r_3}$$

$$= \left(\frac{-Gm_1m_2}{r_1}\right) + \left(\frac{-Gm_2m_3}{r_2}\right) + \left(\frac{-Gm_1m_3}{r_3}\right)$$

70 (b)

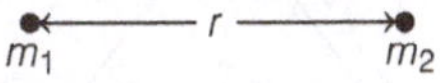

As we know,

$$G_1 = \frac{-Gm_1m_2}{r} \quad \text{...(i)}$$

When separation between the particle is doubled, i.e. $2r$, then

$$G_2 = -\frac{Gm_1m_2}{2r} \quad \text{...(ii)}$$

On dividing Eq. (i) by Eq. (ii), we get

$$\frac{G_1}{G_2} = 2$$

71 (a) The potential energy of the earth-moon system is

$$U = -\frac{GM_E \cdot M_m}{r}$$

$$\therefore \quad r = -\frac{GM_E\,M_m}{U}$$

$$= -\frac{6.67 \times 10^{-11} \times 6 \times 10^{24} \times 7.4 \times 10^{22}}{-7.79 \times 10^{28}}$$

$$= 3.8 \times 10^8\text{ m}$$

72 (b) As we know, the potential energy of body of mass m on the surface of earth is

$$U_1 = -\frac{GMm}{R}$$

$$U_2 = -\frac{GMm}{(R+h)}$$

Here, $h = R$ (given)

$$\Rightarrow \quad U_2 = -\frac{GMm}{2R}$$

Thus, the change in potential energy, $\Delta U = U_2 - U_1$

$$\Delta U = -\frac{GMm}{2R} + \frac{GMm}{R} = \frac{mgR}{2}$$

74 (*d*) $V_g = -\frac{GM}{R+h}$

$$g' = \frac{GM}{(R+h)^2}$$

$$\Rightarrow \frac{|V_g|}{g'} = R + h$$

$$\frac{5.4 \times 10^7}{6.0} = R + h$$

$$\Rightarrow h = 2600 \text{ km}$$

75 (*c*)

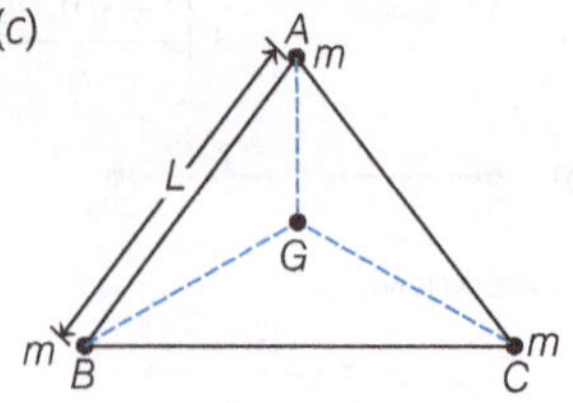

$$V_T = V_A + V_B + V_C$$

$$\Rightarrow V_T = -\frac{Gm}{AG} - \frac{Gm}{BG} - \frac{Gm}{CG}$$

Also, $AG = BG = CG = \frac{2}{3} \times \left(\frac{\sqrt{3}\,L}{2}\right)$

$$= \frac{\sqrt{3}\,L}{3}$$

$$\Rightarrow V_T = -Gm\left(\frac{1}{AG} + \frac{1}{BG} + \frac{1}{CG}\right)$$

$$= -Gm\left(\frac{3 \times 3}{\sqrt{3}\,L}\right) = \frac{-3\sqrt{3}\,Gm}{L}$$

76 (*c*) For $F \propto \frac{1}{r^{\frac{5}{2}}}$

$$U = -\int F \cdot dr$$

$$= \int \left(\frac{1}{r^{\frac{5}{2}}}\right) \cdot dr = -\frac{2}{3} r^{-3/2}$$

$$\therefore U \propto r^{-\frac{3}{2}}$$

77 (*d*) Gravitational potential energy is given by

$$U = -\frac{GMm}{r}$$

Orbital velocity, $v_o = \sqrt{\frac{GM}{R+h}}$

Total energy,

$$E_f = \frac{1}{2} m v_o^2 - \frac{GMm}{R+h}$$

$$= \frac{1}{2} m \frac{GM}{3R} - \frac{GMm}{3R} = -\frac{GMm}{6R}$$

Now, $E_i = -\frac{GMm}{R} + \text{KE}$

But $E_i = E_f$

$$-\frac{GMm}{6R} = -\frac{GMm}{R} + \text{KE}$$

$$\Rightarrow \text{KE} = \frac{5GMm}{6R}$$

80 (*a*) Given, escape velocity on the surface of earth,

$$v_e = \sqrt{\frac{2GM_E}{R_E}}$$

$$\Rightarrow v'_e = \sqrt{\frac{2GM_E}{R'}} = \sqrt{\left(\frac{2\,GM_E}{R_E/4}\right)}$$

$$= 2\sqrt{\frac{2\,GM_E}{R_E}}$$

or $v'_e = 2\,v_e$

81 (*a*) For satellite to revolve around the planet, $v_0 \le v_e$

and $v_e = \sqrt{2} v_0$

$$\therefore n \le \sqrt{2}$$

82 (*a*) $v_e = 11.1$ km/h

Also, $v_e = \sqrt{2gR_E}$

or $v_e = \sqrt{\frac{2\,GM_E}{R_E}}$

$\therefore$ Escape velocity on the surface of moon,

$$v_m = \sqrt{\frac{2G\,M_m}{R_m}} = \sqrt{\frac{2G\,\frac{M_E}{81}}{\frac{R_E}{4}}}$$

$$= \frac{2}{9} v_e = \frac{2}{9} \times 11.1 = 2.46 \text{ km/h}$$

83 (*a*) $v_e = \sqrt{2gR}$

$$g = \frac{4}{3} G\pi\rho R$$

$$\Rightarrow v_e = R\sqrt{\frac{8}{3}\pi G\rho} \quad \text{...(i)}$$

$$v_p = 3R\sqrt{\frac{8}{3}\pi G 3\rho} \quad \text{...(ii)}$$

Dividing Eq. (i) by Eq. (ii), we get

$$\frac{v_e}{v_p} = \frac{R\sqrt{\frac{8}{3}\pi G\rho}}{3R\sqrt{\frac{8}{3}\pi G 3\rho}}$$

$$\Rightarrow \frac{v_e}{v_p} = \frac{1}{3\sqrt{3}} = 1 : 3\sqrt{3}$$

84 (*d*) Escape velocity, $v_e = \sqrt{\frac{2GM_E}{R}}$

Orbital velocity, $v_o = \sqrt{\frac{GM_E}{R}} = \frac{v_e}{\sqrt{2}}$

$$\therefore v_e = \sqrt{2}\, v_o$$

87 (*d*) Angular momentum,

$$L = mvr = m\sqrt{\frac{GM}{r}}\, r = m\sqrt{GMr}$$

$$\therefore L \propto \sqrt{r}$$

If r is increased to $16r$, then new angular momentum,

$$L' \propto \sqrt{16r} \Rightarrow L' = 4L$$

88 (*d*) $v_o = \sqrt{\frac{GM}{R+h}}$

Since, $R >> h$

$$\therefore v_o = \sqrt{\frac{GM}{R}} = \sqrt{gR}$$

Escape velocity of the satellite,

$$v_e = \sqrt{\frac{2\,GM}{R+h}} = \sqrt{\frac{2\,GM}{R}} = \sqrt{2gR}$$

$\therefore$ Change in velocity,

$$\Delta v = v_e - v_o = \sqrt{gR}\,(\sqrt{2} - 1)$$

89 (*a*) Velocity of satellite at a distance R from the centre of the earth,

$$v = \sqrt{\frac{GM}{R}}$$

Now, velocity at an altitude $\frac{R}{2}$ will be

$$v' = \sqrt{\frac{GM}{R + \frac{R}{2}}} = \sqrt{\frac{2}{3}\frac{GM}{R}} = \sqrt{\frac{2}{3}}\, v$$

90 (*d*) Let initial momentum of the satellite and the meteorite are p_1 and p_2, respectively.

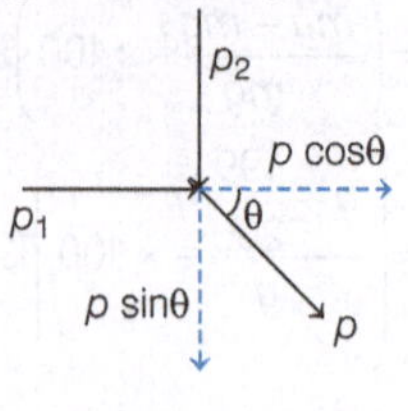

Now, magnitude of p,

$$p = \sqrt{p_1^2 + p_2^2}$$

$$p = \sqrt{2}\, mv \quad [\because p_1 = p_2 = mv]$$

$$2mv' = \sqrt{2}\, mv$$

$$v' = \frac{v}{\sqrt{2}}$$

Hence, the velocity can only decrease, if the height from the surface of the earth increases. Therefore, option (d) is correct.

93 (c) Initial energy of the asteroid is

$$E_i = K_i + U_i = \frac{1}{2} mv_i^2 - \frac{GM_E m}{10R_E}$$

Final energy of the asteroid is

$$E_f = \frac{1}{2} mv_f^2 - \frac{GM_E m}{R_E}$$

According to law of conservation of energy, $E_i = E_f$

$$\frac{1}{2} mv_i^2 - \frac{GM_E m}{10R_E} = \frac{1}{2} mv_f^2 - \frac{GM_E m}{R_E}$$

$$\Rightarrow \quad v_f^2 = v_i^2 + \frac{2GM_E}{R_E}\left(1 - \frac{1}{10}\right)$$

94 (c) Applying law of conservation of energy,

$$U_i + K_i = U_f + K_f$$

$$-\frac{GMm}{R} + \frac{1}{2} m(2v_e)^2 = 0 + \frac{1}{2} mv^2$$

$$v = \sqrt{3}\, v_e$$

95 (a)

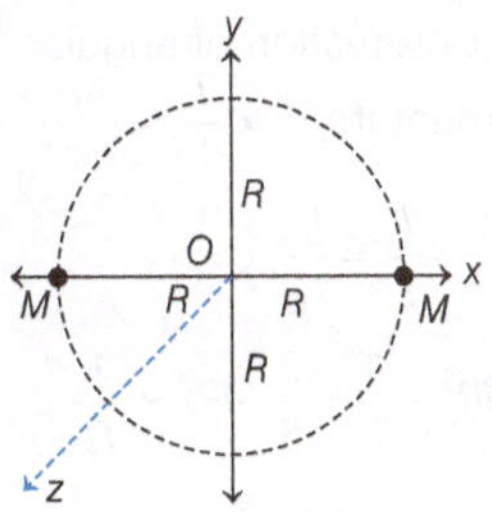

Diameter of circle,

$$2R = 2 \times 10^{11} \text{m}$$

$$\Rightarrow \quad R = 10^{11} \text{ m}$$

Potential energy of meteorite at O, origin $\hat{\mathbf{j}}$,

$$U_{\text{total}} = -\frac{2\,GMm}{R}$$

Kinetic energy K of the meteorite is

$$K = \frac{1}{2} mv^2$$

By conservation of energy, we have

$$\Rightarrow \frac{1}{2} mv^2 - \frac{2\,GMm}{R} = 0$$

$$\Rightarrow v^2 = \frac{4\,GM}{R}$$

$$= \frac{4 \times 6.67 \times 10^{-11} \times 3 \times 10^{31}}{10^{11}}$$

$$\Rightarrow \quad v = 2.83 \times 10^5 \text{ m/s}$$

96 (d) Orbital speed of a satellite in a circular orbit is

$$v_o = \sqrt{\left(\frac{GM}{r_o}\right)}$$

So, kinetic energies of satellites A and B are

$$T_A = \frac{1}{2} m_A v_{oA}^2 = \frac{GMm}{2R}$$

$$T_B = \frac{1}{2} m_B v_{oB}^2$$

$$= \frac{GM(2m)}{2(2R)} = \frac{GMm}{2R}$$

So, ratio of their kinetic energies is

$$\frac{T_A}{T_B} = 1$$

97 (c) KE of satellite, $K = \frac{1}{2} mv_o^2$

$$= \frac{1}{2} m \left(\sqrt{\frac{GM_E}{(R_E + h)}}\right)^2$$

$$= \frac{1}{2} \frac{GmM_E}{(R_E + h)}$$

98 (b) KE of a satellite, $K = \dfrac{GmM_E}{2\,(R_E + h)}$.

$$\Rightarrow \quad K = \frac{GmM_E}{2r}$$

Since, $K \propto \frac{1}{r} \Rightarrow \frac{K_1}{K_2} = \frac{r_2}{r_1}$

$$\Rightarrow \quad \frac{K}{K_2} = \left(\frac{2r}{r}\right)$$

$$\therefore \quad K_2 = \frac{K}{2}$$

Assertion and Reason Questions

1 (b) According to Kepler's second law, the angular momentum of planet is constant.

3 (a) A point P (mass m) is situated inside the hollow spherical shell is shown in the figure.

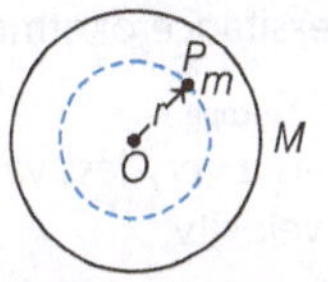

For point P inside the hollow spherical shell,

$$F_P = \text{zero}$$

The force of gravitation due to various region of the spherical shell be attractive and hence from symmetry, it can be seen that these forces cancel each other completely.

Therefore, Assertion and Reason are correct and Reason is the correct explanation of Assertion.

4 (c) The acceleration due to gravity at depth d below the earth surface,

$$g' = g\left(1 - \frac{d}{R}\right)$$

At the centre, $d = R \Rightarrow g' = 0$

The mass of an object remains constant any location, so it is not zero at the centre of the earth.

6 (a) Escape speed for moon $= \sqrt{2g'R_m}$, where g' and R_m both are much smaller than corresponding values on the earth, hence on substituting the values.

Escape speed on the moon comes out to be 2.3 kms^{-1} as calculated below

$$\because \quad g' = g/6$$

and $\quad R_m = 1760$ km

$\Rightarrow$ Escape speed

$$= \sqrt{2 \times \frac{9.8}{6} \times 1760 \times 10^3} \text{ ms}^{-1}$$

$$= 2.3 \text{ kms}^{-1}$$

$\because \quad (v_i)_{\min}$ (earth) = 11.2 kms^{-1}

and $\quad (v_i)_{\min}$ (moon) = 2.3 kms^{-1}

Thus, escape speed for the moon is five times smaller than that of earth.

Therefore, Assertion and Reason are correct and Reason is the correct explanation of Assertion.

7 (*a*) For exsitance of atmosphere

$$v_{\text{rms}} < v_{\text{escape}}$$

Moon has a very less value of escape velocity.

8 (*c*) Reason is not correct but it can be corrected as,

The escape velocity of a body is independent of the mass of the body is,

$$v_{\text{escape}} = \sqrt{2gR}$$

Statement Based Questions

2 (*c*) For a planet orbiting the sun, the angular momentum remains constant. The torque of the body is given by $\tau = \frac{d\mathbf{L}}{dt}$

$$\Rightarrow \frac{d\mathbf{L}}{dt} = 0 \quad (\because \mathbf{L} \text{ is constant})$$

3 (*b*) The areal velocity of the planet is constant, this is because the linear speed keeps changing. The linear speed is more when the planet is close to the sun and less when it is away from the sun.

7 (*d*) If the potential energy becomes equal to the kinetic energy, the satellite will escape away from the gravitational pull of the earth.

Matching Type Questions

1 (*c*)

A.

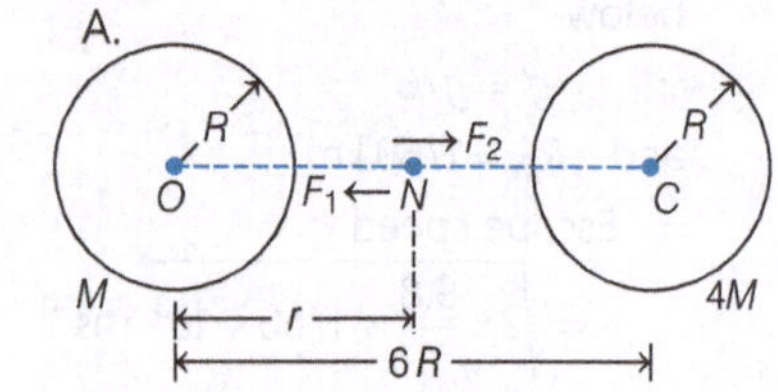

At N, $\quad F_1 = F_2$

$$\Rightarrow \frac{GmM}{r^2} = \frac{Gm(4M)}{(6R - r)^2}$$

$$\Rightarrow r = 2R$$

Thus, $ON = r = 2R$.

B. To project the projectile with minimum speed from M. It is sufficient to project the particle with a speed which would enable it to reach N. After N, projectile will be attracted by $4M$.

At the neutral point, speed approaches zero,

i.e. $\quad v_N = 0$

Total energy of the particle at $N = E_N$

$\Rightarrow \quad E_N =$ GPE due to M + GPE due to $4M$

$$E_N = \frac{-GmM}{2R} - \frac{4GMm}{4R} \quad \text{...(i)}$$

From the principle of conservation of mechanical energy,

$$\frac{1}{2}mv^2 - \frac{GmM}{R} - \frac{4GMm}{5R} = -\frac{GMm}{2R} - \frac{4GMm}{4R}$$

$$\Rightarrow v_{\min} = \sqrt{\frac{3GM}{5R}}$$

C. Applying principle of conservation of energy, we get

$$v_f = \sqrt{\frac{27GM}{5R}}$$

Hence, A → 2, B → 1, C → 3, D → 4.

2 (*b*)

A. If the velocity of satellite is v and mass m, then

$$\text{KE} = \frac{1}{2}mv^2 \quad \text{...(i)}$$

B. Since, potential energy of the satellite

$= -2 \times$ kinetic energy of satellite

$$\Rightarrow \quad \text{PE} = -mv^2 \quad \text{...(ii)}$$

C. Also, total energy

$$= \text{KE} + \text{PE}$$

$$= \frac{1}{2}mv^2 - mv^2$$

$$= -\frac{1}{2}mv^2$$

D. Binding energy = − (Total energy)

$$= mv^2$$

Hence, A → 2, B → 3, C → 1, D → 4.

3 (*c*) The orbital velocity of the orbiting satellite is $v_o = \sqrt{\frac{GM}{R}}$

∴ Kinetic energy,

$$K = \frac{1}{2}mv_o^2 = \frac{GMm}{2R}$$

Acceleration due to gravity at the earth surface, $g = \frac{GM}{R^2}$

The escape velocity at the earth surface,

$$v_e = \sqrt{\frac{2GM}{R}}$$

Numerical Type Questions

1 (12) From the Kepler's law,

$$T_2^2 = \left(\frac{R_2}{R_1}\right)^3 T_1^2$$

$$\Rightarrow T_2^2 = \left(\frac{5.2R}{R}\right)^3 \times 1$$

$$\Rightarrow T_2 = 11.86 \approx 12 \text{ yr}$$

2 (3) As given, $V_f = \frac{1}{27}V_i$

$$\frac{4}{3}\pi R_f^3 = \frac{1}{27} \times \frac{4}{3}\pi R_i^3$$

$$\Rightarrow R_f = \frac{R_i}{3}$$

By conservation of angular momentum, $L \propto \frac{I}{T}$

$$\therefore \frac{I_i}{T_i} = \frac{I_f}{T_f}$$

$$\frac{2}{5}MR_i^2 \times \frac{1}{T_i} = \frac{2}{5}MR_f^2 \times \frac{1}{T_f}$$

$$\therefore \quad T_f = \left(\frac{R_f}{R_i}\right)^2 \times T_i = \left(\frac{1}{3}\right)^2 \times 24$$

$$T_f = \frac{24}{9}$$

So, $\quad T_f = 2.66 \text{ h} \approx 3 \text{ h}$

3 (1972) The orbital speed of earth can be given as

$$v = \sqrt{\frac{GM}{r}}$$

Thus, $T = \frac{2\pi r}{v}$

$$T = 2\pi r\sqrt{\frac{r}{GM}}$$

$$\Rightarrow M = \frac{4\pi^2 r^3}{GT^2}$$

$$= \frac{4 \times (3.14)^2 \times (1.49 \times 10^{11})^3}{(6.67 \times 10^{-11})(365 \times 24 \times 3600)^2}$$

$$M = 1.972 \times 10^{22} \text{kg}$$
$$= 1972 \times 10^{19} \text{kg}$$
$$= 1972 \text{ unit}$$

4 (18) As given

$$g_x = 9g_y$$

We know that,

$$v^2 = 2gh \Rightarrow h = \frac{v^2}{2g}$$

$\therefore$ At planet x, $h_x = \frac{v^2}{2g_x}$

At planet y, $h_y = \frac{v^2}{2g_y}$

Now, $\frac{h_x}{h_y} = \frac{g_y}{g_x} = \frac{1}{9}$

$$\Rightarrow \quad h_y = 9h_x$$
$$\therefore \quad h_y = 9 \times 2$$
$$h_y = 18 \text{ m}$$

5 (2221) Given, density of earth,

$$\rho = 11.3 \times 10^3 \text{ kg m}^{-3}$$

Acceleration due to gravity on the surface of earth,

$$g = \frac{GM}{R^2} = \frac{G}{R^2} \cdot \frac{4}{3}\pi R^3 \cdot \rho$$
$$= \frac{4}{3} \times \frac{22}{7} \times 6.67 \times 10^{-11} \times 6.4 \times 10^6 \times 11.3 \times 10^3$$
$$= 22.21 \text{ m/s}^2$$
$$\therefore \frac{x}{100} = 22.21$$
$$\Rightarrow \quad x = 2221$$

6 (2650) Let g' is the acceleration due to gravity at height h.

So, $g' = \frac{g}{2}$

$$\therefore \quad g' = g\left(\frac{R}{R+h}\right)^2$$

$$\therefore \quad \frac{g}{2} = g\left(\frac{R}{R+h}\right)^2$$

$$h = 2649.6 \text{ km}$$
$$\simeq 2650 \text{ km}$$

7 (2) The escape velocity is given by

$$v_e = \sqrt{\frac{2GM}{R}}$$

Now, the radius is reduced by 4%, then $R_1 = (R - 0.04R)$

$$= 0.96R$$

$$\therefore \quad v_e' = \sqrt{\frac{2GM}{0.96R}}$$

$$\Rightarrow \quad \frac{v_e}{v_e'} = \sqrt{0.96}$$

$$\Rightarrow \quad v_e' = 1.02v_e$$

$\therefore$% change in escape velocity

$$= \frac{v_e' - v_e}{v_e} \times 100\% = 2\%$$

8 (5279) Escape velocity on the surface of planet A is

$$v_A = \sqrt{\frac{2GM}{R}} = 11.2 \text{ km/s}$$

$\therefore$ The escape velocity on the surface of planet B,

$$v_B = \sqrt{\frac{2G\left(\frac{M}{9}\right)}{\frac{R}{2}}}$$

$$= \sqrt{\frac{4}{9}\frac{GM}{R}} = \frac{\sqrt{2}}{3} \times v_A$$

$$\Rightarrow \quad v_B = \frac{1.414}{3} \times 11.2$$

$$\Rightarrow \quad v_B = 5.279 \text{ km/s}$$

$$\therefore \quad \frac{x}{1000} = 5.279 \Rightarrow x = 5279$$

9 (4) Initial energy of the spacecraft

$$= \frac{1}{2}mv_0^2 - \frac{GMm}{R}$$

$$\therefore \text{Final energy} = -\frac{GMm}{R+h}$$

By law of conservation of energy,

$$\frac{1}{2}mv_0^2 - \frac{GMm}{R} = -\frac{GMm}{R+h}$$

$$\Rightarrow \quad \frac{h}{R+h} = \frac{v_0^2}{2gR}$$

$$\Rightarrow \frac{h}{R+h} = \frac{(10 \times 10^3)^2}{2 \times 9.8 \times 6400 \times 10^3} = 0.8$$

$$\Rightarrow \quad h = 4R$$

10 (3) Applying the Kepler's third law,

$$\left(\frac{T_1}{T_2}\right)^2 = \left(\frac{R_1}{R_2}\right)^3$$

$$\Rightarrow \quad \frac{2000}{R_2} = \left(\frac{1}{8}\right)^{2/3}$$

$$\Rightarrow \quad R_2 = 8000 \text{ km}$$

$$\omega_1 = \frac{2\pi}{1} \text{ rad/h}$$

$$\omega_2 = \frac{2\pi}{8} = \frac{\pi}{4} \text{ rad/h}$$

The speed of the nearer satellite to orbit,

$$v_1 = \omega_1 R_1$$
$$= (2\pi) \times 2 \times 10^3 \text{ km/h}$$

The speed of the farther satellite to the orbit, $v_2 = \omega_2 R_2$

$$= \left(\frac{\pi}{4}\right) \times 8000$$
$$= \pi \times 2 \times 10^3 \text{ km/h}$$

Thus, the relative angular speed of the nearer satellite to the farther satellite, $\omega = \frac{v_1 - v_2}{R_2 - R_1}$

$$= \frac{2\pi \times 2 \times 10^3 - \pi \times 2 \times 10^3}{8000 - 2000}$$

$$= \frac{2\pi \times 10^3}{6000} = \frac{\pi}{3} \text{ rad/h}$$

Comparing with, $\omega = \frac{\pi}{x}$

$$\therefore \quad x = 3$$

NCERT Exemplar Questions

2 (*a*) The earth is revolving around the sun in a circular motion due to gravitational attraction. The force of attraction will be of radial nature, i.e. angle between position vector **r** and force **F** is zero. So, torque, $|\tau| = |\mathbf{r} \times \mathbf{F}| = rF\sin 0° = 0$

3 (*c*) As the total energy of the earth satellite bounded system is negative $\left(\text{i.e.} \frac{-GMm}{2a}\right)$. So, due to the viscous force acting on satellite, energy decreases continuously and radius of the orbit or height gradually decreases.

Therefore, debris of satellites fall to the earth.

6 (*c*) Particles of masses $2M, m$ and M are respectively at points A, B and C as shown below.

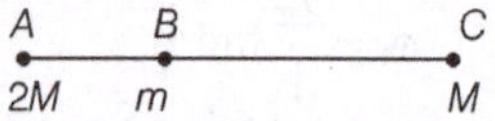

Force on B due to A,

$$F_{BA} = \frac{G(2Mm)}{(AB)^2} \text{ towards } BA$$

Force on B due to C,

$$F_{BC} = \frac{GMm}{(BC)^2} \text{ towards } BC$$

As, $BC = 2AB$

$$\Rightarrow \quad F_{BC} = \frac{GMm}{4(AB)^2} < F_{BA}$$

Hence, m will move towards A, i.e. $2M$.

Past Exams Questions

1 (*d*) We know that,

$$g = \frac{GM}{R^2}$$

According to question,

$$g = \frac{G\left(\frac{M}{10}\right)}{\left(\frac{R}{2}\right)^2} = \frac{GM \times 4}{R^2 \times 10} = \frac{GM}{R^2} \times \frac{2}{5}$$

Hence, $\dfrac{g'}{g} = \dfrac{\frac{GM}{R^2} \times \frac{2}{5}}{\frac{GM}{R^2}}$

$$\Rightarrow \quad g' = \frac{2}{5} \times g = \frac{2}{5} \times 9.8$$

$$= 3.92 \text{ ms}^{-2}$$

2 (*a*) Given altitude, $h = 2R$

From surface, $r_1 = R$

and $\quad r_2 = 2R + R = 3R$

Then, energy required to launch a satellite from orbit r_1 to r_2 is sum of difference in energies in the orbit (ΔE) and energy on the surface of the earth.

$$\Delta E = GMm\left(\frac{1}{r_1} - \frac{1}{r_2}\right)$$

$$= GMm\left(\frac{1}{R} - \frac{1}{3R}\right)$$

$$= \frac{2}{3}\left(\frac{GMm}{R}\right)$$

Energy on surface $= \frac{1}{2}mv^2$

$$v^2 = \frac{GM}{r_{\text{orbit}}} = \frac{GM}{3R}$$

$\therefore$ Minimum energy

$$= \Delta E + \frac{GMm}{6R}$$

$$= \frac{2}{3}\left(\frac{GMm}{R}\right) + \left(\frac{GMm}{6R}\right)$$

$$= \frac{5}{6}\frac{GMm}{R}$$

3 (*b*) The given situation is shown below.

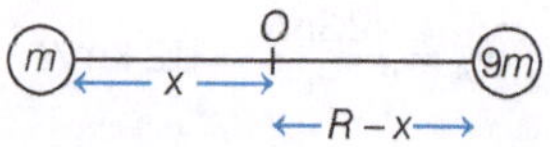

Since, gravitational field at point O is zero, hence $\dfrac{Gm}{x^2} = \dfrac{G(9m)}{(R-x)^2}$

$$\Rightarrow \left(\frac{1}{x}\right)^2 = \left(\frac{3}{R-x}\right)^2 \Rightarrow \frac{1}{x} = \frac{3}{R-x}$$

$$\Rightarrow \quad 3x = R - x \Rightarrow x = \frac{R}{4}$$

$\therefore$ Gravitational potential at point O,

$$V = \frac{-Gm}{x} + \left[\frac{-G(9m)}{R-x}\right]$$

$$= \frac{-Gm}{\frac{R}{4}} - \frac{9Gm}{R - \frac{R}{4}}$$

$$= -\frac{4Gm}{R} - \frac{12Gm}{R} = -\frac{16Gm}{R}$$

4 (*a*) Given , mass of body, $m = 60$g

$$= 6 \times 10^{-2} \text{ kg}$$

Gravitational force, $F = 3.0$ N

Magnitude of gravitational field intensity,

$$I = \frac{F}{m} = \frac{3}{6 \times 10^{-2}} = 50 \text{ N/kg}$$

5 (*d*) The escape speed is given by

$$v_e = R\sqrt{\frac{8}{3}\pi\rho G} = v$$

As, ρ = constant $\Rightarrow v_e \propto R$

$$\therefore \quad v_e' = \left(\frac{R'}{R}\right)v_e = \left(\frac{4R}{R}\right)v = 4v$$

6 (*a*) Since, the escape velocity of earth can be given as

$$v_e = \sqrt{2gR} = R\sqrt{\frac{8}{3}\pi G\rho}$$

$$\Rightarrow \quad v_e = R\sqrt{\frac{8}{3}\pi G\rho} \quad \text{...(i)}$$

$$v_p = 2R\sqrt{\frac{8}{3}\pi G 2\rho} \quad \text{...(ii)}$$

Dividing Eq. (i) Eq. (ii), we get

$$\frac{v_e}{v_p} = \frac{R\sqrt{\frac{8}{3}\pi G\rho}}{2R\sqrt{\frac{8}{3}\pi G 2\rho}}$$

$$\Rightarrow \quad \frac{v_e}{v_p} = \frac{1}{2\sqrt{2}}$$

7 (*b*) Total energy of a satellite at height h is

$$= \text{KE} + \text{PE} = \frac{GMm}{2(R+h)} - \frac{GMm}{(R+h)}$$

$$= \frac{-GMm}{2(R+h)} = \frac{-GMmR^2}{2R^2(R+h)} = \frac{-mg_0R^2}{2(R+h)}$$

8 (*a*) Orbital velocity of the satellite

$$v_o = \sqrt{\frac{GM_e}{R_e\left[1 + \frac{h}{R_e}\right]}}$$

$$\Rightarrow \quad v_o = \sqrt{\frac{gR_e}{1 + \frac{h}{R_e}}}$$

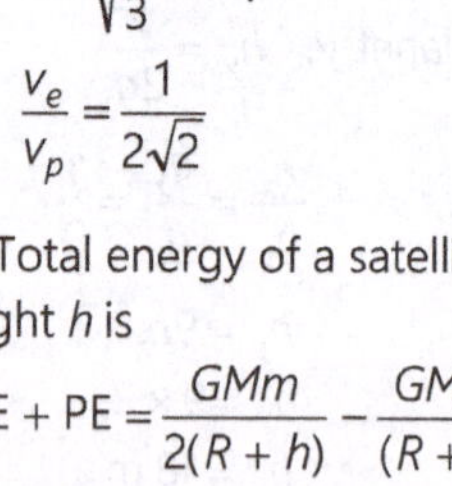

Substitutes the values of g, R_e and h, we get

$$v_o = \sqrt{60 \times 10^6} \text{ m/s}$$
$$= 7.76 \text{ km/s}$$

10 (*c*) $v_e = \sqrt{\dfrac{2GM}{R'}}$

$$c = \sqrt{\frac{2GM}{R'}}$$
$$R' = \frac{2GM}{c^2}$$
$$= \frac{2 \times 6.67 \times 10^{-11} \times 6 \times 10^{24}}{9 \times 10^{16}}$$
$$= 0.889 \times 10^{-2} \simeq 10^{-2} \text{ m}$$

11 (*c*) Let side of square be x.

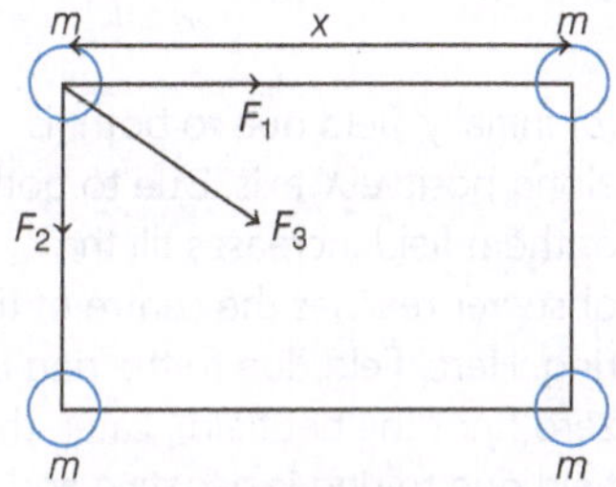

Gravitational force on any of mass due to other three masses is

$$F = \mathbf{F}_1 + \mathbf{F}_2 + \mathbf{F}_3$$
$$= \frac{\sqrt{2} \cdot Gm^2}{x^2} + \frac{Gm^2}{(\sqrt{2}x)^2}$$
$$= \frac{Gm^2}{x^2}\left(\sqrt{2} + \frac{1}{2}\right)$$
$$= \frac{Gm^2}{x^2}\left(\frac{2\sqrt{2}+1}{2}\right)$$

This force is given

$$F = \left(\frac{2\sqrt{2}+1}{32}\right)\frac{Gm^2}{L^2}$$

So, $\dfrac{1}{x^2}\left(\dfrac{2\sqrt{2}+1}{2}\right) = \dfrac{2\sqrt{2}+1}{(32)\,L^2}$

$$\Rightarrow \quad x = 4L$$

12 (*b*) Escape velocity on the surface of planet is, $v = \sqrt{\dfrac{2GM}{R}}$

Escape velocity on the surface of moon is,

$$v' = \sqrt{\frac{2GM'}{R'}}$$
$$= \sqrt{\left[\frac{2G\left(\frac{M}{144}\right)}{\left(\frac{R}{16}\right)}\right]} = \frac{1}{3}\sqrt{\frac{2GM}{R}} = \frac{v}{3}$$

13 (*b*) Escape velocity of any planet from surface is given as

$$v_e = \sqrt{2gR}$$

For two planets A and B,

$$\frac{(v_e)_A}{(v_e)_B} = \sqrt{\frac{g_A}{g_B}}\sqrt{\frac{R_A}{R_B}} \quad \text{...(i)}$$

From Eq. (i), $\dfrac{1}{2} = \sqrt{\dfrac{g_A}{g_B}}\sqrt{\dfrac{1}{3}}$.

or $\sqrt{\dfrac{g_A}{g_B}} = \dfrac{\sqrt{3}}{2}$ or $\dfrac{g_A}{g_B} = \dfrac{3}{4}$

14 (*c*) Initially, force between two masses

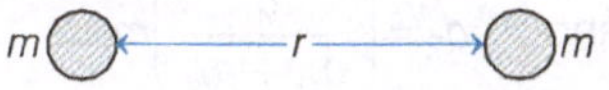

$$F = \frac{Gm \times m}{r^2} = \frac{Gm^2}{r^2}$$

When $\dfrac{1}{3}$rd of first mass is transferred to other, masses will be $\dfrac{4}{3}m$ and $\dfrac{2}{3}m$.

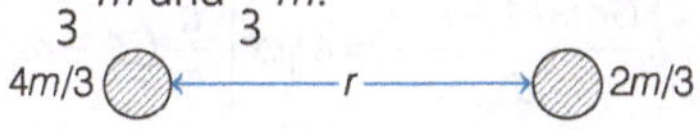

Now, force of attraction will be

$$F' = \frac{G\dfrac{4m}{3} \times \dfrac{2m}{3}}{r^2}$$
$$\Rightarrow \quad F' = \frac{8}{9}\frac{Gm^2}{r^2} \Rightarrow F' = \frac{8}{9}F$$

15 (*c*) $M' = \rho \cdot \dfrac{4}{3}\pi\left(\dfrac{R}{2}\right)^3 = \dfrac{M}{8}$

By using concept of gravitational force,

$$F_1 = \frac{GMm}{(3R)^2} = \frac{GMm}{9R^2} \quad \text{...(i)}$$

and $F_{\text{cavity}} = \dfrac{GM'm}{(AB)^2}$

$$= \frac{G(M/8)m}{(2R + R/2)^2}$$
$$= \frac{4GMm}{25 \times 8\, R^2} \quad \text{...(ii)}$$

$$\therefore \quad F_2 = F_1 - F_{\text{cavity}}$$
$$= \frac{GMm}{9R^2} - \frac{4}{25 \times 8}\frac{GMm}{R^2}$$
$$= \frac{41}{50 \times 9}\frac{GMm}{R^2}$$
$$\because \quad \frac{F_1}{F_2} = \frac{50}{41}$$

Skill Boosters

1 (*d*)

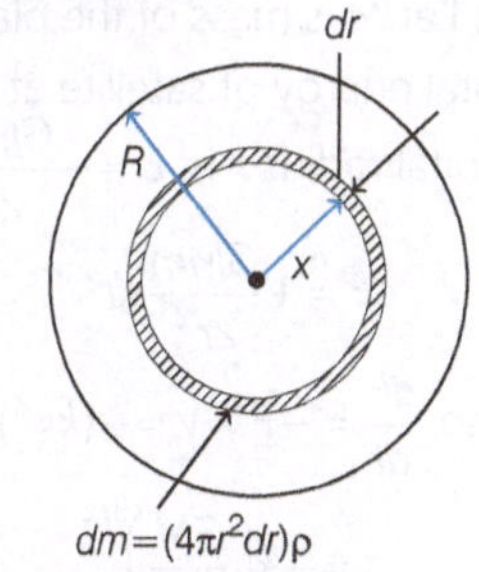

Gravitational field,

$$E = \frac{G}{x^2}\int_0^x (4\pi r^2 dr)(\rho(r))$$
$$= \frac{G}{x^2}\int_0^x (4\pi r^2)\,\rho_0\left(1 - \frac{r^2}{R^2}\right)dr$$
$$= \frac{4\pi G\rho_0}{x^2}\left[\frac{r^3}{3} - \frac{r^5}{5R^2}\right]_0^x$$
$$= 4\pi G\rho_0\left(\frac{x}{3} - \frac{x^3}{5R^2}\right)$$

For gravitational field to be maximum ,

$$\frac{d}{dx}\left[4\pi G\rho_0\left(\frac{x}{3} - \frac{x^3}{5R^2}\right)\right] = 0$$
$$\Rightarrow \quad 4\pi G\rho_0\left(\frac{1}{3} - \frac{3x^2}{5R^2}\right) = 0$$
$$\Rightarrow \quad x = \sqrt{\frac{5}{9}}R$$

2 (*c*) Here,

$$F = mg' = mg\left[1 - \frac{\sqrt{\dfrac{R^3}{9} + x^2}}{9}\right]$$

$$\frac{mg\sqrt{\dfrac{R^2}{9} + x^2}}{R} \times \frac{\dfrac{R}{3}}{\sqrt{\dfrac{R^2}{9} + x^2}} = \frac{mg}{3}$$

3 (*a*) Here, $F_{net} = \sqrt{2}\, F_1 + F_3 = \frac{mv^2}{R}$

$$\sqrt{2}\, a = 2R \text{ or } R = \frac{a}{\sqrt{2}}$$

Thus, $\sqrt{2}\frac{Gm^2}{a^2} + \frac{Gm^2}{2a^2} = \frac{mv^2}{a}\sqrt{2}$

or $\quad v = \sqrt{\frac{Gm(2\sqrt{2}+1)}{2\sqrt{2}\, a}}$

4 (*b*) Let M is mass of the planet. Total energy of satellite at an orbital radius r is $E = -\frac{GMm}{2r}$

$$\Rightarrow \quad dE = +\frac{GMm}{2r^2} dr \qquad \text{...(i)}$$

Also, $\frac{dE}{dt} = -F \times v = -(kv^2)v = -kv^3$

$$= -k\left(\frac{GM}{r}\right)^{3/2}$$

or $\quad dE = -k\left(\frac{GM}{r}\right)^{3/2} dt \qquad \text{...(ii)}$

From Eqs. (i) and (ii), we get

$$\frac{GMm}{2r^2} dr = -k\left(\frac{GM}{r}\right)^{3/2} dt$$

$$dt = -\frac{GMm}{2r^2} \cdot \left(\frac{r}{GM}\right)^{3/2} \cdot \frac{1}{k} dr$$

$$= -\frac{m}{2\sqrt{GM}} \cdot \frac{1}{k} \cdot \frac{1}{\sqrt{r}} dr$$

$$\int_0^t dt = -\frac{m}{2k\sqrt{GM}} \int_{7R}^{R} \frac{1}{\sqrt{r}} dr$$

$$t = -\frac{m}{k\sqrt{GM}} [\sqrt{r}]_{7R}^{R}$$

$$t = -\frac{mR}{k\sqrt{GM}}(\sqrt{7} - 1)$$

$$t = \frac{m}{k\sqrt{gR}}(\sqrt{7} - 1)$$

$$\left(\because g = \frac{GM}{R^2}\right)$$

5 (*b*) $mg_{pole} = \frac{GMm}{R^2} \Rightarrow GM = gR^2$

$$(\because g_{pole} = g)$$

At the equator,

$$\frac{GMm}{R^2} - mg' = \frac{mv^2}{R}$$

$$\Rightarrow mg - \frac{mg}{2} = \frac{mv^2}{R} \text{ or } g = \frac{2v^2}{R}$$

Now, at the pole, total energy of a particle is $E_T = U + K$

or $E_T = -\frac{GMm}{R} + 0$

$\therefore$ Binding energy

$$= |E_T| = \frac{GMm}{R} = mgR$$

$$\therefore \quad \frac{1}{2} mv_e^2 = mgR = m\frac{2v^2}{R} R$$

$$\Rightarrow \quad v_e = 2v$$

6 (*b*) Let d = distance between stars and d_1 and d_2 be the distances of stars form centre of mass of system.

$$\therefore \quad d_1 = \left(\frac{d}{m_1 + m_2}\right) m_2$$

and $\quad d_2 = \left(\frac{d}{m_1 + m_2}\right) m_1$

$$m_1 + m_2 = M \qquad \text{(given)}$$

$$\therefore \quad d_1 = \frac{d}{M} m_2 \text{ and } d_2 = \frac{d}{M} m_1$$

Also, $\frac{Gm_1 m_2}{d^2} = m_1\omega^2 d_1 = m_2\omega^2 d_2$

$$\therefore \frac{Gm_1(M - m_1)}{d^2} = m_1\omega^2\left[\frac{d}{M}(M - m_1)\right]$$

So, $GM = \omega^2 d^3 \Rightarrow GM = \left(\frac{2\pi}{T}\right)^2 d^3$

$$\therefore \quad d = \left[\frac{GMT^2}{4\pi^2}\right]^{1/3}$$

7 (*a*) $\left(1 - \frac{d}{R}\right) = g - \omega^2 R$

$$\Rightarrow \omega^2 R = \frac{gd}{R} \Rightarrow d = \frac{\omega^2 R^2}{g}$$

8 (*c*) Consider an element as shown in the figure.

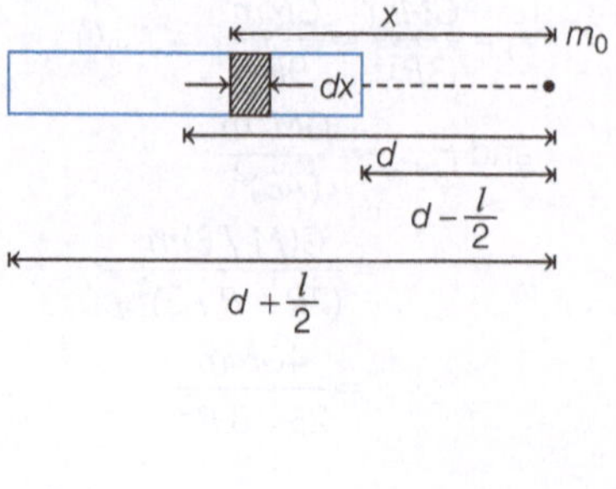

$$dm = \frac{m_0}{l} dx$$

Gravitational potential energy between dm and point mass is

$$dU = -\frac{Gm_0 dm}{x}$$

$$= -\frac{Gm_0^2}{l} \cdot \frac{1}{x} dx$$

Now, $U = \frac{Gm_0^2}{l} \int_{d-\frac{1}{2}}^{d+\frac{1}{2}} \frac{1}{x} dx$

$$= -\frac{Gm_0^2}{l} \ln\left(\frac{d + \frac{1}{2}}{d - \frac{1}{2}}\right)$$

or $\quad U = -\frac{Gm_0^2}{l} \ln\left(\frac{2d + l}{2d - l}\right)$

9 (*b*) Initially, field due to both is along positve X-axis. Due to both of them field increases till the observer reaches the centre of the ring. Here, field due to the ring is zero (not the net field). Later, the field due to ring is negative and due to sphere is positive. Somewhere, in the middle field becomes zero and later the influence of sphere will be greater than that of ring, field is positive and increases till the observer reaches the surface of sphere.

10 (*c*) Work done will be zero when particle is taken along a path perpendicular to field.

Now angle made by $\mathbf{E}_g$ with X-axis is given by

$$\tan\theta = \frac{E_y}{E_x} = \frac{1}{4}$$

A line perpendicular to field vector has a slope

$$m = -4 \; \{\therefore m_1 \times m_2 = -1 \text{ for perpendicular lines}\}$$

So, path of particle is along

$$y = -4x + c$$

or $\quad y + 4x = c$

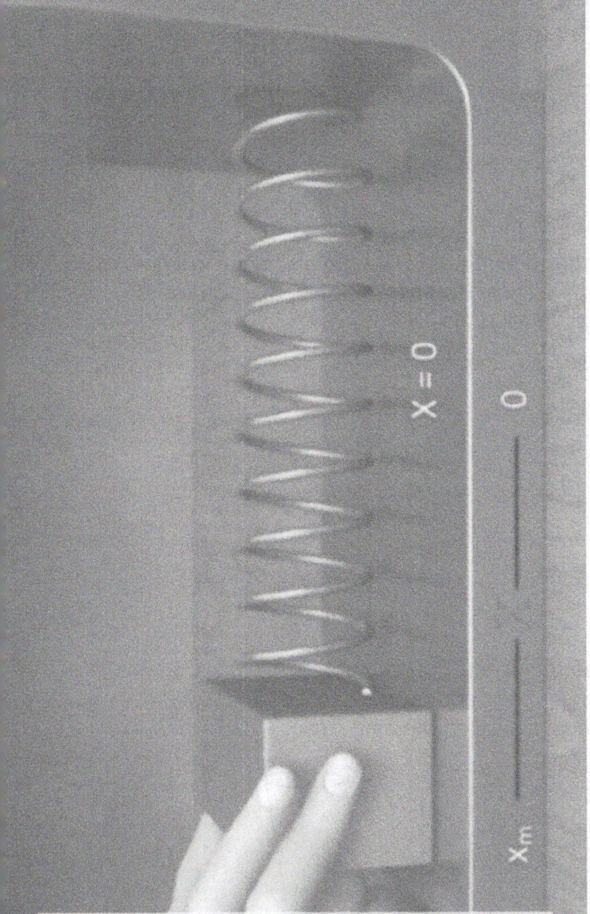

08

Mechanical Properties of Solids

Topicwise No. of Ques asked in 5 Years (NEET)

Topics	No. of Questions				
	2024	2023	2022	2021	2020
Elastic Behaviour of Solids	–	–	–	–	–
Stress and Strain	–	1	–	–	–
Stress-Strain Curve	–	–	–	–	–
Elastic Moduli	1	–	–	–	1
Applications of Elastic Behaviour of Materials	–	–	–	–	–

Special Type of Ques Asked In 5 Years (NEET)

Types	Years				
	2024	2023	2022	2021	2020
A-R	–	–	1	–	–
Statement Based	–	–	–	–	–
Matching	–	–	–	–	–

Last 5 Years Weigtage (NEET)

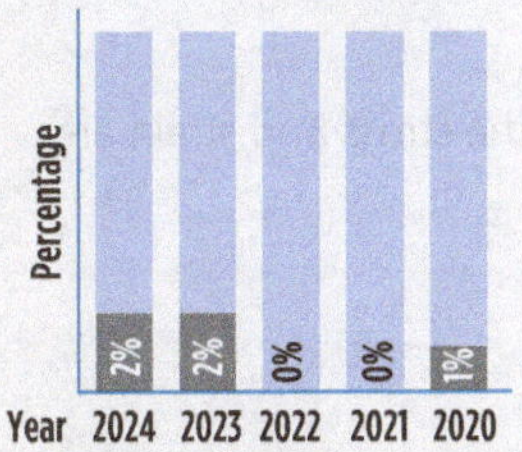

- A solid has definite shape and size. An external force is required to change the shape and size of solid body.
- A force acting on a body to produce a change in the shape of the body, is called **deforming force**.
- The property of a body by virtue of which it tends to regain its original size and shape when the applied force is removed is known as **elasticity**.
- The substances which regain their original shape and size after removal of deforming force are called **elastic substances**.
- The inability of a body to regain its original configuration is called **plasticity**. The substances possessing this feature are called **plastic substances**. e.g. Putty, mud, bakelite etc.

*Elastic Behaviour of Solids

- In solid, each atom or molecule is surrounded by neighbouring atoms or molecules. These are bonded together by interatomic or intermolecular forces and stay in a stable equilibrium position.
- When a solid is deformed, the atoms or molecules are displaced from their equilibrium positions causing a change in interatomic or intermolecular distances.
- When the deforming force is removed, the interatomic force tend to drive them back to their original position. **Thus, the body regains its original shape and size.**

**This topic is not included in rationalised NCERT. But it is given in latest NEET syllabus.*

- The restoring mechanism can be visualised by taking a model of **spring-ball system** as shown in figure. Here the balls represent atoms and springs represent interatomic forces.

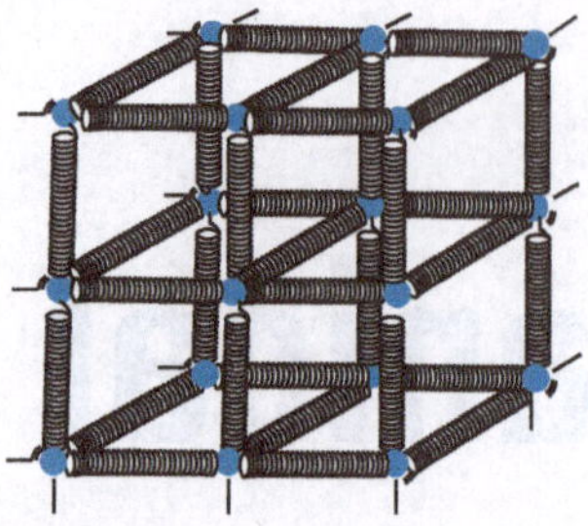

Stress and Strain

- When a body is subjected to a deforming force, a restoring force is developed in the body. The restoring force per unit cross-sectional area set-up within the body is called **stress**.

$$\text{Stress}(\sigma) = \frac{\text{Restoring force }(F)}{\text{Area of cross - section}(A)}$$

Its **SI unit** is Nm^{-2} or pascal (Pa) and **dimensional formula** of stress is $[ML^{-1}T^{-2}]$.

- Stresses are of three types as given below
  (i) **Longitudinal Stress** The restoring force acting per unit area along the length of the body is known as **longitudinal stress**. It is of two types NEET 2023
    (a) **Tensile Stress** When an object is stretched by two equal forces applied normal to its cross-sectional area, then restoring force per unit area is called tensile stress.
    (b) **Compressive Stress** If an object is compressed under the action of applied forces, the restoring force per unit area is known as **compressive stress.**
  (ii) **Tangential or Shearing Stress** The restoring force per unit area developed due to the applied tangential force is known as tangential or shearing stress.
  (iii) **Hydraulic or Volumetric Stress** If the equal normal forces are applied on an object all over its surfaces, then its volume changes. The internal restoring force per unit area in this case is known as hydraulic or volumetric stress and in magnitude is equal to the hydraulic pressure (applied force per unit area).
- The relative change in configuration of a body on applying deforming force is called **strain** of the body.

$$\text{i.e. Strain} = \frac{\text{Change in configuration }(\Delta x)}{\text{Original configuration}(x)}$$

It is a dimensionless quantity.

- Strains are of three types as given below
  (i) **Longitudinal Strain** The ratio of change in length (ΔL) to the original length (L) of the body is known as longitudinal strain.

$$\text{i.e. Longitudinal strain} = \frac{\Delta L}{L}$$

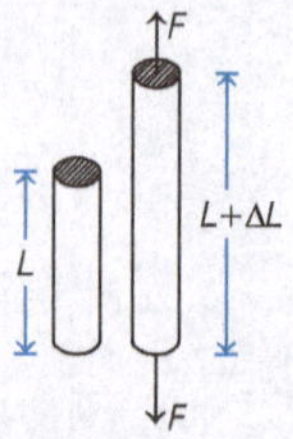

  (ii) **Shearing Strain** The ratio of relative displacement between the opposite faces to the length of the cylinder L is called shearing strain.

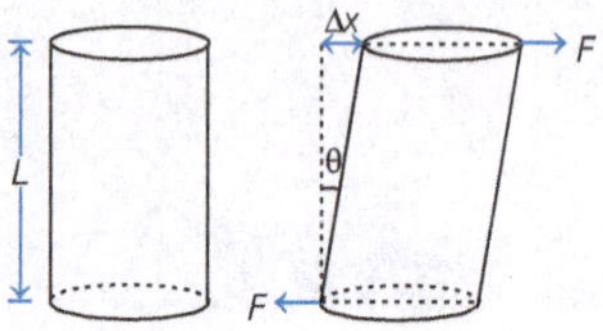

$$\text{i.e. Shearing strain} = \frac{\Delta x}{L} = \tan\theta$$

where, θ is the angular displacement of the cylinder from vertical. Usually θ is very small, i.e. $\tan\theta \simeq \theta$.

  (iii) **Volume Strain** The strain produced by a hydraulic pressure is called volume strain and is defined as the ratio of change in volume ΔV to the original volume V.

$$\text{i.e. Volume strain} = \frac{\Delta V}{V}$$

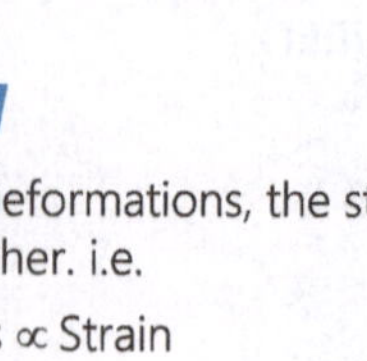

Note *The strain perpendicular to the applied force is known as* ***lateral strain.***

Hooke's Law

It states that for small deformations, the stress and strain are proportional to each other. i.e.

$$\text{Stress} \propto \text{Strain}$$

$\Rightarrow$ Stress $= k \times$ Strain

where, k is the proportionality constant and is known as **modulus of elasticity**.

SI unit of k is Nm^{-2} and dimension is $[ML^{-1}T^{-2}]$.

Stress-Strain Curve

The given graph between stress and strain tells us about simple case of metallic wire which is subjected to increasing tension.

- **From O to *A***, it is the initial part of the curve which is a straight line, indicating that stress is directly proportional to strain Hooke's law is obeyed.
- **From *A* to *B***, the stress is not proportional to strain. However, the body regains its original dimension after removing the load.
- **Point *B*** is known as yield point (or elastic limit) and the corresponding stress is known as yield strength (σ_y) of the material.

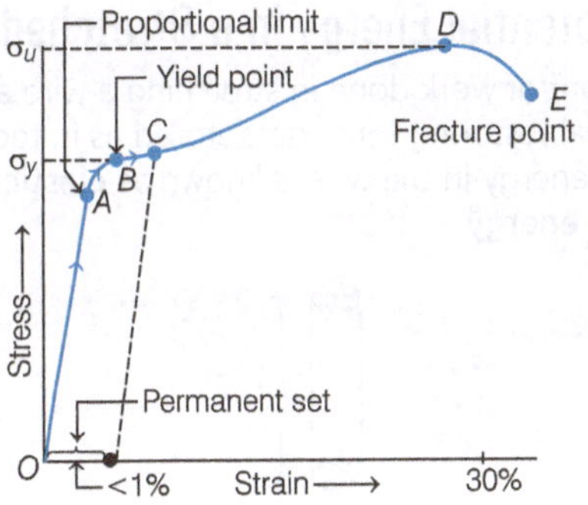

NEET 2019

- **Beyond *B*,** the strain increases more rapidly than stress.
- **From *B* to *C*** When the load is removed at some point *C* between *B* and *D*, the body does not regain its original dimension. In this case even when the stress is zero, the strain is not zero. The material is said to have permanent deformation.
- **Point *D***, this point on the graph is called the ultimate tensile strength (σ_u) of the material.
- **Point *E***, it is the fracture point, where the body breaks on applying further stress. It is also called breaking stress.
- Larger the separation between *C* and *E*, substance will be more **ductile**.
- Lesser the separation between *C* and *E*, substance will be more **brittle**.
- **Elastomer** Substances which can be stretched to cause large strains are called elastomers.
- Figure shows stress-strain curve for the elastic tissue of Aorta present in heart.

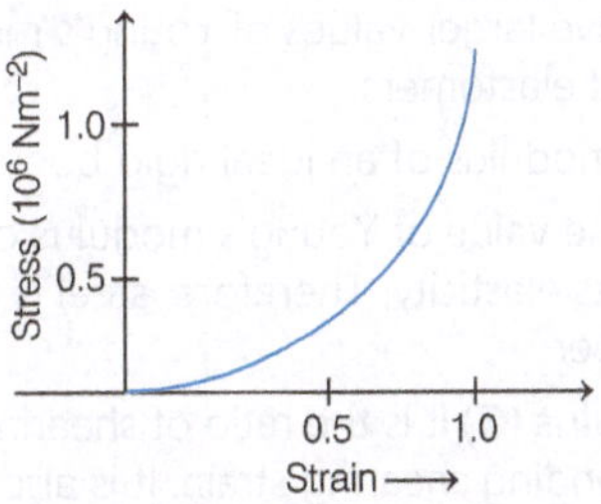

- The stress-strain behaviour varies from material to material, e.g. rubber can be pulled to several times its original length and still returns to its original shape.

Marks Maximiser

Variation in Elasticity

- **Effect of Temperature** Elasticity decreases as the temperature increases. On annealing, i.e. on alternate heating and cooling, elasticity decreases.
- **Effect of Impurities** If impurity is more elastic, the elasticity of the material increases. But if impurity is more plastic, the elasticity of the material decreases.
- **Elastic Relaxation Time** The time delay in restoring the original form after removal of deforming force is called elastic relaxation time. For quartz, it is minimum and for glass, it is high.

Elastic Moduli

The ratio of stress and strain is called **modulus of elasticity** or **elastic moduli.**

It is found to be a characteristic of the material. It has same units and dimensions as that of stress, i.e. $\mathbf{Nm^{-2}}$ or **Pa.**

- Depending on the types of stresses and strains, there are three types of modulus of elasticity as given below
  (i) **Young's Modulus (*Y*)** It is the ratio of tensile (or compressive) stress (σ) to the longitudinal strain (ε).

So, $$Y = \frac{\sigma}{\varepsilon} = \frac{FL}{A\,\Delta L} = \frac{MgL}{\pi r^2 \Delta L}$$ NEET 2020

where, M = mass of the body, A = area of the body,
ΔL = change in the length due to the strain,
g = acceleration due to gravity
and L = length of the body.

- Its unit is N/m^2 or pascal and its dimensional formula is $[ML^{-1}T^{-2}]$.
- Metals have larger values of Young's modulus than alloys and elastomers.
- Young's modulus of an ideal rigid body is infinity.
- Greater the value of Young's modulus of a material, larger is its elasticity. Therefore, steel is more elastic than rubber.

(ii) **Shear Modulus** (G) It is the ratio of shearing stress (σ_S) to the corresponding shearing strain. It is also called modulus of rigidity. NEET 2022

$$\therefore \quad \eta \text{ or } G = \frac{\text{Shearing stress}}{\text{Shearing strain}} = \frac{FL}{A\Delta x} = \frac{F}{A\tan\theta}$$

$$G = \frac{F}{A\theta} \quad [\because \tan\theta \simeq \theta \text{ for small radius of } \theta]$$

or $$\sigma_S = G \times \theta \quad \left[\because \sigma_s = \frac{F}{A}\right]$$

where, θ = shearing angle.

- SI unit of shear modulus is Nm^{-2}, its dimensional formula is $[ML^{-1}T^{-2}]$.
- For most materials, $Y > G$ and mostly $G \approx Y/3$.
- The Young's modulus and shear modulus are relevant only for solids, since only solids have lengths and shape.

(iii) **Bulk modulus (B)** It is the ratio of hydraulic stress to the corresponding hydraulic strain, $B = \dfrac{-p}{\left(\dfrac{\Delta V}{V}\right)}$

- The negative sign indicates the fact that with increase in pressure, a decrease in volume occurs.
- SI unit of bulk modulus is the same as pressure, i.e. Nm^{-2} or Pa, its dimensional formula is $[ML^{-1}T^{-2}]$.
- For a system in equilibrium, if p is positive, ΔV is negative, then bulk modulus B is always positive.
- The reciprocal of the bulk modulus is called **compressibility.** It is defined as the fractional change in volume per unit increase in pressure.

  Compressibility, $K = \dfrac{1}{B} = \dfrac{-\Delta V}{Vp}$
- Bulk modulus is relevant for solids, liquids and gases.
- Bulk moduli for solids are much larger than for liquids, i.e. $B_{solid} > B_{liquid} > B_{gas}$

Poisson's Ratio

- The strain perpendicular to the applied force is called **lateral strain.**
- Within the elastic limit, the ratio of the lateral strain to the longitudinal strain in a stretched wire is called **Poisson's ratio.**

$$\text{Poisson's ratio, } \sigma = \frac{\text{Lateral strain}}{\text{Longitudinal strain}} = -\frac{\Delta d/d}{\Delta L/L}$$

where, Δd = change in diameter, d = original diameter, ΔL = change in length and L = original length.

Here, negative sign shows that if the length increases, then radius of wire decreases.

- It is a pure number and has no dimensions or units. Its value depends only on the nature of material.

  For steels, its value is between 0.28 and 0.30 and for **aluminium alloys**, it is about 0.33.

Elastic Potential Energy in a Stretched Wire

- The amount of work done in stretching a wire against the internal restoring force gets stored as in the form of potential energy in the wire is known as **elastic potential energy**.

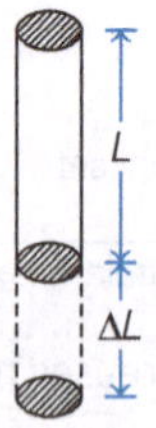

Work done, W = Average force × Increase length

$$W = \frac{F}{2} \times \Delta L = \frac{1}{2} \cdot \frac{F}{A} \frac{\Delta L}{L} \times AL$$ NEET 2019

where, L is the length of rod, ΔL is increase in length and F is deforming force.

Elastic potential energy in a stretched wire,

$$U = \frac{1}{2} \times \text{Stress} \times \text{Strain} \times \text{Volume of the wire}$$

- **Elastic potential energy per unit volume,**

$$u = \frac{U}{V} = \frac{1}{2} \times \text{Stress } (\sigma) \times \text{Strain } (\varepsilon) = \frac{1}{2}\sigma\varepsilon$$

Applications of Elastic Behaviour of Materials

- In figure, a beam is fixed at its ends and loaded with weight at its middle (as shown below), then depression at the centre, $\delta = \frac{w l^3}{4bd^3 Y}$

  where, Y = Young's modulus, w = weight of beam, l = length of beam, b = breadth of beam and d = thickness of beam.

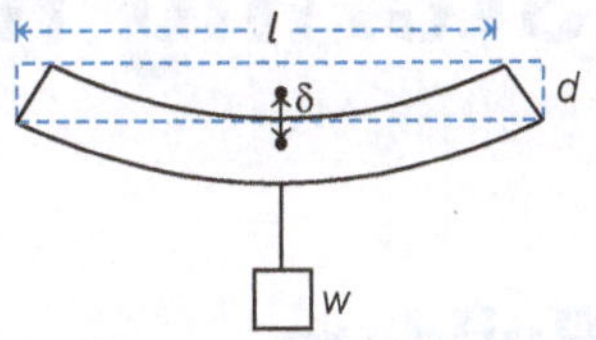

- To reduce the bending for a given load, one should use a material with a large Young's modulus Y.

Caution Points

- A deforming force applied in one direction can produce strain in other direction. In such situation, the proportionality between stress and strain cannot be described by just one elastic constant.
- Since stress is not a vector quantity like force, so stress can't be applied in a specific direction.

PYQ Notes

1. Elongation of a wire under its own weight $e = \frac{l^2 dg}{2Y}$ (where l is length of the wire, d is density and Y is the young's modulus of the wire). **[NEET 2022]**
2. If two wires of Young's moduli Y_1 and Y_2 with same length and radius are joined end-to-end and loaded with some force, then the combination behaves as a single wire and its Young's modulus is given by $Y = \frac{2Y_1Y_2}{Y_1 + Y_2}$ **[JEE Main 2021]**
3. If l_1, l_2 are the lengths of a wire under tensions T_1 & T_2, then the length of the unstretched wire, $l = \frac{l_1 T_2 - l_2 T_1}{T_2 - T_1}$ **[NEET 2021]**
4. The elongation produced in a wire when a body of mass M hung at the free end of the wire is immersed in a liquid $= \frac{(Mg - V\rho g) L}{AY}$ (where, L is length of the wire, V is volume of the body immersed in the liquid, A is area of cross-section of the wire and ρ = density of the liquid) **[JEE Main 2019]**

Step by Step

Mastering NCERT

- Concept Builders
- Topical Questions
- Assertion and Reason Questions
- Statement Based
- Matching Type
- Numerical Type
- NCERT Exemplar
- Past Exams MCQs
- Skill Boosters

Concept Builders

1 The forces working between two molecules in solid is called ....

2 The property of a body by virtue of which it tends to regain its original shape and size when applied forces are removed is called plasticity. [T/F]

3 If the applied stress is equal to the Young's modulus, then length of the wire becomes .... [double/triple].

4 The restoring force acting per unit area along the length of the body is called .... stress. (longitudinal/tangential)

5 The interatomic forces in solids are only attractive in nature. [T/F]

6 Tensile and compressive stress can also be termed as .... (tangential stress/longitudinal stress).

7 What does the slope of stress *versus* strain graph under elastic limit give?

8 What does the proportionality constant k in Hooke's law?

9 If a wire is stretched to double of its original length, then what will be the value of strain?

10 Which type of modulus of elasticity is present in solids?

11 What is the formula for the Young's modulus?

12 Young's modulus of the material of a wire .... (increases/decreases) with the increase in percentage of elastic impurity.

13 Young's modulus and shear modulus are relevant only for solids since solids have a definite shape. [T/F]

14 The bulk moduli of solids are much .... (larger/smaller) than for liquids.

15 The ratio of .... (lateral/longitudinal) strain to the .... (lateral/longitudinal) strain is called Poisson's ratio.

16 A piece of rubber under an ordinary stress can display 1000 % strain, yet when unloaded returns to its original length. This shows that the elastic restoring forces in a rubber piece are strictly conservative. [T/F]

17 The volume of the wire will not change on loading, if its Poisson's ratio is 0.5. [T/F]

18 When a wire is put under a tensile stress, work is done against the interatomic forces. This work is stored in the wire in the form of elastic potential energy. [T/F]

19 Due to deforming force, the separation between molecules either increases or decreases. This cause an .... (increase/decrease) in potential energy.

20 If a beam of metal having young modulus Y supported at the two edges is loaded at the centre, the depression at the centre is proportional to .... [$1/Y$/$1/Y^2$]

Topical Questions

Introduction

1 Those substances which do not have a tendency to regain its shape after removal of deforming force are known as **NCERT Pg. 167**

(a) plastic
(b) elastic
(c) non-plastic but elastic
(d) elastic Poisson's ratio

2 Two identical solid balls, one of ivory and the other of wet clay are dropped from the same height on the floor. After striking the floor, **NCERT Pg. 167**

(a) ivory ball will rise to a greater height than wet clay ball
(b) ivory ball will rise to a lesser height than wet clay ball
(c) Both balls will rise to the same height
(d) direction of ball will be random

Elastic Behaviour of Solids

3 When the distance between two atoms is less than the normal equilibrium distance r_0, repulsive forces between atoms exist which is zero at **Old NCERT Pg. 236**

(a) $r = r_0$
(b) $r < r_0$
(c) $r > r_0$
(d) $r = 0$

4 When a solid is deformed, the atoms or molecules are displaced from their equilibrium position causing **Old NCERT Pg. 236**
(a) change in the temperature
(b) change in the volume
(c) change in the kinetic energy
(d) change in the interatomic distances

5 In a solid, each atom is surrounded by neighbouring atoms, these are bounded together by **Old NCERT Pg. 236**
(a) covalent bond (b) interatomic forces
(c) nuclear forces (d) gravitational forces

Stress and Strain

6 A uniform bar of square cross-section is lying along a frictionless horizontal surface. A horizontal force is applied to pull it from one of its ends, then **NCERT Pg. 168**
(a) the bar is under same stress throughout its length
(b) the bar is not under any stress because force has been applied only at one end
(c) the bar simply moves without any stress in it
(d) the stress developed gradually reduces to zero at the end of the bar where no force is applied

7 *A* and *B* are two wires and the radius of *A* is twice that of *B*. They are stretched by the same load, then the stress on *B* is **NCERT Pg. 168**
(a) equal to that on *A* (b) four times that on *A*
(c) two times that on *A* (d) half that on *A*

8 A steel wire having a radius of 2.0 mm, carrying a load of 4 kg, is hanging from a ceiling. Given that $g = 3.1\pi\,ms^{-2}$, what will be the tensile stress that would be developed in the wire? **NCERT Pg. 168**
(a) $6.2 \times 10^6 Nm^{-2}$ (b) $5.2 \times 10^6 Nm^{-2}$
(c) $3.1 \times 10^6 Nm^{-2}$ (d) $4.8 \times 10^6 Nm^{-2}$

9 On suspending a mass *Mg* the length *l* of elastic wire having area of cross-section *A*, becomes double the initial length. The instantaneous stress action on the wire is **NCERT Pg. 168**
(a) Mg/A (b) $Mg/2A$ (c) $2Mg/A$ (d) $4Mg/A$

10 The breaking stress of a wire depends upon **NCERT Pg. 168**
(a) length of the wire
(b) radius of the wire
(c) material of the wire
(d) shape of the cross-sectional of wire

11 A cube of aluminium of side 0.1 m is subjected to a shearing force of 100 N. The top face of the cube is displaced through 0.02 cm with respect to the bottom face. The shearing strain would be **NCERT Pg. 168**
(a) 0.02 (b) 0.1 (c) 0.005 (d) 0.002

12 A uniform cube is subjected to volume compression. If each side is decreased by 1%, then bulk strain is **NCERT Pg. 168**
(a) 0.01 (b) 0.06
(c) 0.02 (d) 0.03

13 Two blocks of masses *m* and *M* are connected by means of a metal wire of cross-sectional area *A* passing over a frictionless fixed pulley as shown in the figure. The system is then released. If $M = 4\,m$, then the stress produced in the wire is **NCERT Pg. 168**

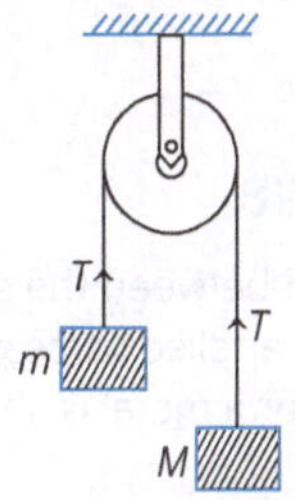

(a) $\frac{2mg}{3A}$ (b) $\frac{4mg}{3A}$ (c) $\frac{8mg}{5A}$ (d) $\frac{3mg}{4A}$

14 Wires *A* and *B* are connected with mass *m* as shown in figure. Wires are of same material and have radii r_A and r_B. End of *B* is pulled with a force of $mg/3$. With reference to the above situation, which of the following statement is correct? **NCERT Pg. 168**

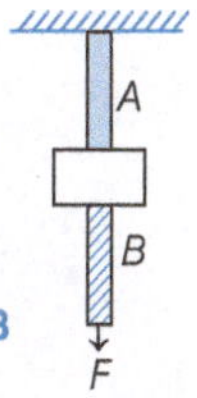

(a) *A* breaks before *B* when $r_A = r_B$
(b) *A* breaks after *B* when $r_A < 2r_B$
(c) Neither *A* nor *B* will break if $r_A = 2r_B$
(d) *A* break when 2 kg force applied

15 Two blocks are tied with a wire and are hanged over a pulley as shown. Masses of blocks are 1 kg and 4 kg and pulley is frictionless. With reference to the above situation, which of the following is an incorrect statement? **NCERT Pg. 168**

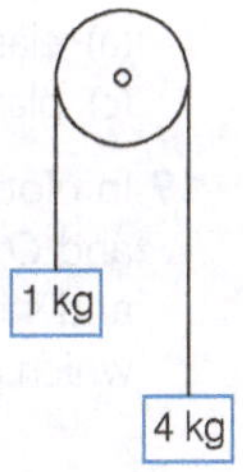

(a) Tension in wire is 10 N.
(b) Tension in wire is 16 N.
(c) If breaking stress is 3.18×10^9 Nm^{-2}, then wire must be of 4×10^{-5} m radius so that wire does not break.
(d) Breaking stress of wire depends on its material

Hooke's Law

16 If stress on a body is increased, then as per Hooke's law of elasticity, the ratio of stress to strain is **NCERT Pg. 169**
(a) increases (b) decreases
(c) becomes zero (d) remains constant

17 Within the limit of elasticity, which of the following graph obey Hooke's law? **NCERT Pg. 169**

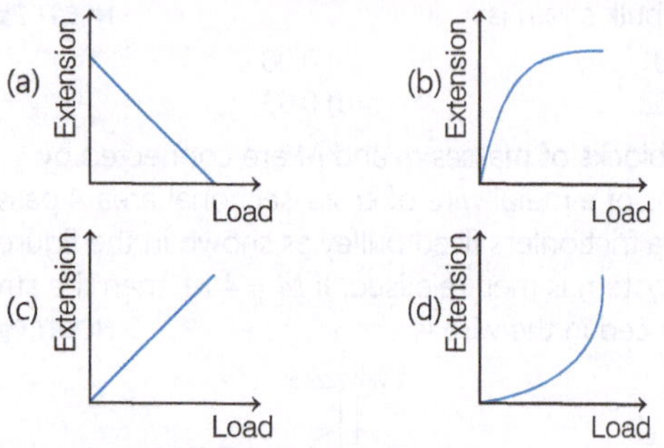

Stress-Strain Curve

18 A graph is plotted between the stress (which is equal in magnitude to the applied force per unit area) and the strain produced for a metal is shown in figure. **NCERT Pg. 169**

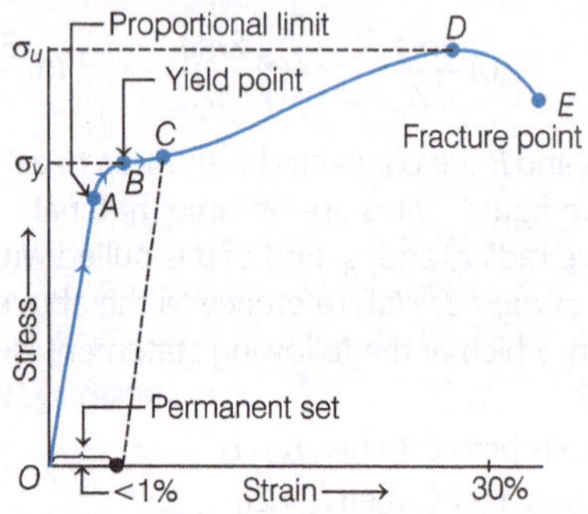

From the graph, we can see in the region from O to A, the curve is linear. In this region, Hooke's law is obeyed. Thus, from O to A, the solid body behaves as a/an

(a) elastic body (b) partially elastic body
(c) plastic body (d) inelastic body

19 In plotting stress *versus* strain curves for two materials P and Q, a student by mistake puts strain on the Y-axis and stress on the X-axis as shown in the figure. Then, which of the following statement is correct? **NCERT Pg. 169**

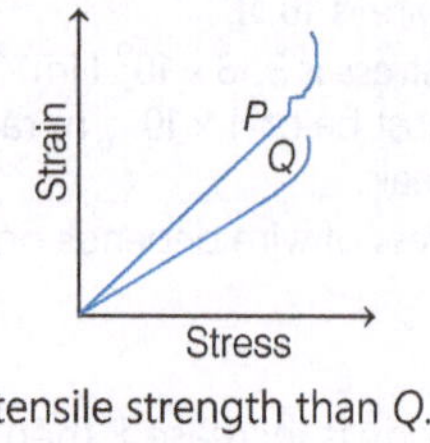

(a) P has more tensile strength than Q.
(b) P is more ductile than Q.
(c) P is more brittle than Q.
(d) The Young's modulus of P is more than that of Q.

20 Two stress-strain graphs A and B are drawn by a student (as shown below) but he forgets to specify what are the conditions for A and B. Which of the following statement shows the incorrect conditions for A and B? **NCERT Pg. 169**

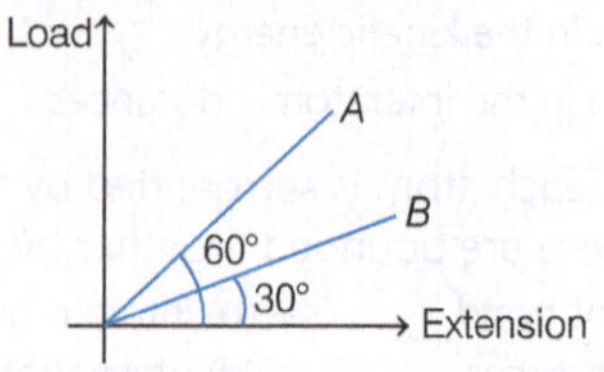

(a) If A and B are made for two different wires of identical dimensions, then $Y_A : Y_B = \sqrt{3} : 1$.
(b) If A and B are made for two different wires of equal length and of same material, then wire A is more thicker than B.
(c) Extension of A is less than that of B.
(d) None of the above

21 A copper and a steel wire of the same diameter are connected end-to-end. A deforming force F is applied to this composite wire which causes a total elongation of 1 cm. The two wires will have **NCERT Pg. 170**

(a) the same stress and strain
(b) the same stress but different strain
(c) the same strain but different stress
(d) different strains and stress

22 The elastic limit of brass is 379 MPa. What should be the minimum diameter of a brass rod, if it is to support a 400 N load without exceeding its elastic limit? **NCERT Pg. 169**

(a) 0.90 mm
(b) 1.00 mm
(c) 1.16 mm
(d) 1.36 mm

Elastic Moduli

23 A wire elongates by l mm when a load w is hanged from it. If the wire goes over a pulley and two weights $2w$ each are hung at the two ends, the elongation of the wire will be (in mm) **NCERT Pg. 170**

(a) l (b) $2l$
(c) zero (d) $\frac{l}{2}$

24 Young's moduli of two wires A and B are in the ratio 7:4. Wire A is 2 m long and has radius R. Wire B is 1.5 m long and has a radius of 2 mm. If the two wires stretch by the same length for a given load, then the value of R is close to **NCERT Pg. 170**

(a) 1.3 mm (b) 1.7 mm
(c) 1.5 mm (d) 1.9 mm

25 On applying a stress of 20×10^8 Nm^{-2}, the length of a perfectly elastic wire is doubled. Its Young's modulus will be **NCERT Pg. 170**

(a) 40×10^8 Nm^{-2} (b) 20×10^8 Nm^{-2}
(c) 10×10^8 Nm^{-2} (d) 5×10^8 Nm^{-2}

26 A wire of length 2 m is made from 10 cm^3 of copper. A force F is applied so that its length increases by 2 mm. Another wire of length 8 m is made from the same volume of copper. If the same force F is applied to it, its length will increase by **NCERT Pg. 170**

(a) 0.8 cm (b) 1.6 cm (c) 2.4 cm (d) 3.2 cm

27 The diameter of a brass rod is 4 mm and Young's modulus of brass is 9×10^{10} Nm^{-2}. The force required to stretch it by 0.1% of its length, is **NCERT Pg. 170**

(a) 360πN (b) 36 N
(c) $144\pi \times 10^3$ N (d) $36\pi \times 10^5$ N

28 The following four wires of length L and radius r are made of the same material. When they are under same tension, the largest extension is produced in **NCERT Pg. 170**

(a) $L = 200$ cm, $r = 0.5$ mm (b) $L = 150$ cm, $r = 0.3$ mm
(c) $L = 250$ cm, $r = 0.1$ mm (d) $L = 400$ cm, $r = 0.2$ mm

29 A wire of length L and area of cross-section A is stretched by a load. The elongation produced in the wire is l. If Y be the Young's modulus of the material of the wire, then force constant of the wire is **NCERT Pg. 170**

(a) $\frac{YL}{A}$ (b) $\frac{YA}{L}$ (c) $\frac{YA}{l}$ (d) $\frac{Yl}{A}$

30 Two wires of same material having radius in ratio 2 : 1 and lengths in ratio 1 : 2. If same force is applied on them, then ratio of their change in length will be **NCERT Pg. 170**

(a) 1 : 1 (b) 1 : 2
(c) 1 : 4 (d) 1 : 8

31 Two wires are made of the same material and have the same volume. The first wire has cross-sectional area A and the second wire has cross-sectional area $3A$. If the length of the first wire is increased by Δl on applying a force F, how much force is needed to stretch the second wire by the same amount? **NCERT Pg. 170**

(a) $4F$ (b) $6F$
(c) $9F$ (d) F

32 A 15 kg mass fastened to the end of a steel wire of unstretched length 2 m is whirled in a vertical circle with an angular velocity of 2 rev s^{-1} at the bottom of the circle. The cross-section of the wire is 0.02 cm^2. The elongation of the wire when the mass is at the lowest point of its path is **NCERT Pg. 170**

(Take, $g = 10$ ms^{-2}, $Y_s = 2 \times 10^{11}$ Nm^{-2})

(a) 2.4 cm (b) 1.52 mm
(c) 2.52 mm (d) 3.52 mm

33 The length of a rubber cord is l_1 m when the tension is 2 N and l_2 m when the tension is 8 N. The length when the tension is 14 N, is **NCERT Pg. 170**

(a) $(2.5l_2 - 1.5l_1)$ m (b) $(6l_2 - 1.5l_1)$ m
(c) $(2l_1 - l_2)$ m (d) $(2l_2 - l_1)$ m

34 Two wires are made of same material and have the same volume. However, wire 1 has cross-sectional area A and wire 2 has cross-sectional area $4A$. If the length of wire 1 increase by Δx on applying force F, how much force is needed to stretch wire 2 by the same amount? **NCERT Pg. 170**

(a) $4F_1$ (b) $8F_1$ (c) $12F_1$ (d) $16F_1$

35 A copper wire of length 3.2 m and a steel wire of length 1.6 m, both of diameter 4 mm, are connected end-to-end. When stretched by a load, the net elongation is found to be 1.3 mm. The load applied is **NCERT Pg. 170**

($Y_{copper} = 1.2 \times 10^{11}$ Nm^{-2}, $Y_{steel} = 2 \times 10^{11}$ Nm^{-2})

(a) 1.6×10^2 N (b) 1.8×10^2 N
(c) 3.2×10^2 N (d) 4.7×10^2 N

36 A copper wire and steel wire of the same diameter and of lengths 50 cm and 200 cm respectively are connected end-to-end and a force is applied, which stretches their combined length by 2 cm. The elongation in each wire, if Young's modulus for copper and steel are 12×10^{11} dyne cm^{-2} and 20×10^{11} dyne cm^{-2}, respectively **NCERT Pg. 170**

(a) 0.46 cm, 1.54 cm (b) 1.59 cm, 0.41 cm
(c) 1.32 cm, 0.68 cm (d) 0.58 cm, 1.42 cm

37 Two springs of equal lengths and equal cross-sectional area are made of material whose Young's moduli are in the ratio of 3 : 2. They are suspended and loaded with the same mass. The ratio of force constant of there spring is **NCERT Pg. 170**

(a) $\sqrt{3} : \sqrt{2}$ (b) 3 : 2 (c) $3\sqrt{3} : 2\sqrt{2}$ (d) 9 : 4

38 Two wires are made of copper and other of steel are joined end-to-end as shown in figure. The area of cross-section of copper wire is twice that of steel wire. They are placed under compressive force of magnitude F. The ratio of their lengths such that change in length of both wires are same is **NCERT Pg. 170**

($Y_C = 1.1 \times 10^{11}$ N/m^2, $Y_S = 2 \times 10^{11}$ N/m^2)

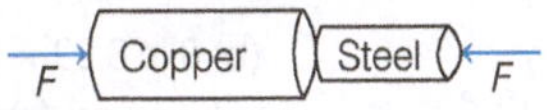

(a) 2.3 (b) 1.1 (c) 3 (d) 1.65

39 Two separate wires A and B are stretched by 2 mm and 3 mm respectively, when they are subjected to a force of 2 N. Assume that both the wires are made up of same material and the radius of wire B is 3 times that of the radius of wire A. The lengths of the wires A and B are in the ratio of $a : b$ is **NCERT Pg. 170**

(a) 2 : 25 (b) 2 : 27 (c) 27 : 2 (d) 25 : 2

40 A metal wire of length 6 m and area of cross-section A is attached to a rigid support. Another metal wire of length 10 m and of the same cross-sectional area is attached to the free end of the first wire. A body of mass 10 kg is then suspended from the free end of the second wire. If Y_1 and Y_2 are the Young's moduli of the wires are 1.2×10^{11} N/m^2 and 2×10^{11} N/m^2 respectively, the effective force constant of the system of two wires is **NCERT Pg. 170**

(a) $10^{12} A$ (b) $2 \times 10^{11} A$ (c) $2 \times 10^{12} A$ (d) $10^{10} A$

41 A steel bar $ABCD$ is 40 cm long is made up of three parts AB, BC and CD as shown in figure. The rod is subjected to a pull of 40 kN. Diameter of parts AB and CD is 60 mm while diameter of part BC is 25 mm. The total extension (in mm) of the rod is (Young's modulus for steel = 2×10^{11} Nm^{-2}) **NCERT Pg. 170**

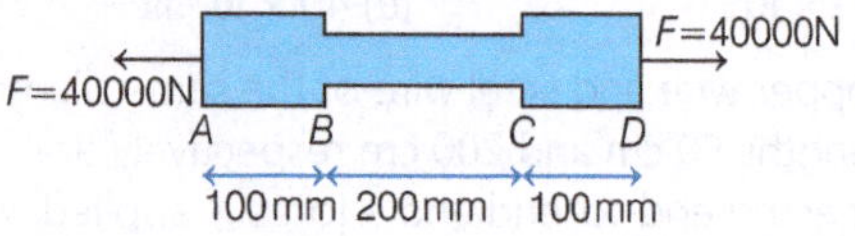

(a) 0.0637 (b) 0.084 (c) 0.0657 (d) 0.096

42 Two parallel steel wires A and B are fixed to rigid support at the upper ends and subjected to the same load at the lower ends. The lengths of the wires are in the ratio 4 : 7 and their radii are in the ratio 5 : 2. The increase in the length of the wire A is 1 mm. Calculate the increase in the length of the wire B. **NCERT Pg. 170**

(a) 10.94 mm (b) 3.42 mm
(c) 2.89 mm (d) 3.32 mm

43 Three equal masses of 5 kg are connected by massless string of cross-sectional area 0.002 cm^2 and Young's modulus 2×10^{11} N/m^2. In the absence of friction, the longitudinal strain in the wires is **NCERT Pg. 170**

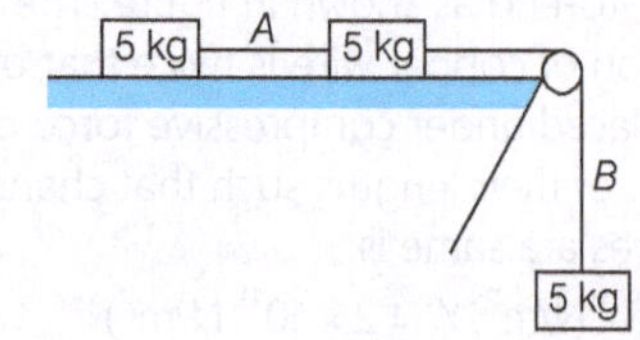

(a) A is 10^{-4} (b) B is 8.33×10^{-4}
(c) A is 4.16×10^{-4} (d) (b) and (c) both

44 If the ratio of diameters, lengths and Young's moduli of steel and brass wires as shown in the figure are p, q and r, respectively. Then, the corresponding ratio of increase in their lengths would be **NCERT Pg. 170**

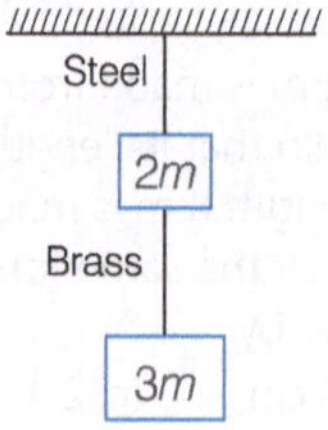

(a) $\frac{3q}{5p^2r}$ (b) $\frac{5q}{3p^2r}$
(c) $\frac{3q}{5pr}$ (d) $\frac{5q}{3pr}$

45 The Young's modulus of steel is twice that of brass. Two wires of same length and of same area of cross-section, one of steel and another of brass are suspended from the same roof. If we want the lower ends of the wires to be at the same level, then the weight added to the steel and brass wires must be in the ratio of **NCERT Pg. 170**

(a) 1 : 2 (b) 2 : 1
(c) 4 : 1 (d) 1 : 1

46 A stone of mass m is tied to one end of a wire of length L. The diameter of the wire is D and it is suspended vertically. The stone is now rotated in a horizontal plane and makes an angle θ with the vertical. If Young's modulus of the wire is Y, then the increase in the length of the wire is **NCERT Pg. 170**

(a) $\frac{4mgL}{\pi D^2 Y}$ (b) $\frac{4mgL}{\pi D^2 Y \sin\theta}$
(c) $\frac{4mgL}{\pi D^2 Y \cos\theta}$ (d) $\frac{4mgL}{\pi D^2 Y \tan\theta}$

47 One end of a horizontal thick copper wire of length $2L$ and radius $2R$ is welded to an end of another horizontal thin copper wire of length L and radius R. When the arrangement is stretched by applying forces at two ends, the ratio of the elongation in the thin wire to that in the thick wire is **NCERT Pg. 170**

(a) 0.25 (b) 0.50
(c) 2 (d) 4

48 For a perfectly rigid body, **NCERT Pg. 170**

(a) Young's modulus is infinite and bulk modulus is zero
(b) Young's modulus is zero and bulk modulus is infinite
(c) Young's modulus is infinite and bulk modulus is also infinite
(d) Young's modulus is zero and bulk modulus is also zero

49 A hollow cylindrical column of steel support a load of 12000 kg. The inner and outer radii of the column are 20 cm and 30 cm, respectively. Assuming the load distribution to be uniform. The compressional strain of the column will be ($Y_S = 2\times 10^{11}$ Pa) **NCERT Pg. 170**

(a) 3.75×10^{-6} (b) 375×10^{6}
(c) 3.75×10^{-4} (d) 3.75×10^{-3}

50 An iron bar of length l m and cross-section A m^2 is pulled by a force of F newton from both ends, so as to produce and elongation in metres. Which of the following statement is correct? **NCERT Pg. 170**

(a) Elongation is directly proportional to cross-section A
(b) Elongation is directly proportional to Young's modulus
(c) Elongation is inversely proportional to length l
(d) Elongation is inversely proportional to A

51 The upper end of a wire of radius 4 mm and length 100 cm is clamped and its other end is twisted through an angle of 30°. Then, angle of shear is **NCERT Pg. 172**

(a) 12° (b) 0.12°
(c) 1.2° (d) 0.012°

52 A square lead slab of side 30 cm and thickness 4 cm is subjected to a shearing force (on its narrow face) of magnitude 8×10^4 N. The lower edge is riveted to the floor. How much is the upper edge displaced, if the shear modulus of lead is 5.6×10^9 Pa? **NCERT Pg. 172**

(a) 3.6×10^{-5} m (b) 3.6×10^{-3} m
(c) 3.6×10^{-4} m (d) 3.6×10^{4} m

53 A cube of aluminium of each side 5 cm is subjected to a tangential force. The top face of the cube is sheared through 0.025 cm with respect to the bottom. The tangential force (in dyne) is
(Take, $G = 2.08\times10^{11}$ dyne cm^{-2}) **NCERT Pg. 172**

(a) 18×10^{8} (b) 25×10^{8}
(c) 26×10^{9} (d) 18×10^{9}

54 A square lead slab of side 40 cm and thickness 20 cm is subjected to a shearing force (on its upper face) of 12×10^4 N. The lower edge is riveted to the floor. How much will the upper edge be displaced?
(Shear modulus of lead = 5.6×10^9 N m^{-2}) **NCERT Pg. 172**

(a) 0.16 mm (b) 0.11 mm
(c) 0.11 cm (d) 1.6 cm

55 When a pressure of 100 atmosphere is applied on a spherical ball of rubber, then its volume reduces to 0.01%. The bulk modulus of the material of the rubber (in dyne cm^{-2}) is **NCERT Pg. 173**

(a) 10×10^{12} (b) 100×10^{12}
(c) 1×10^{12} (d) 20×10^{12}

56 A solid sphere of radius R made of a material of bulk modulus B is surrounded by a liquid in a cylindrical container. A massless piston of area A floats on the surface of the liquid. When a mass M is placed on the piston to compress the liquid, the fractional change in the radius of the sphere $\frac{\delta R}{R}$ is **NCERT Pg. 173**

(a) $\frac{Mg}{BA}$ (b) $\frac{Mg}{2BA}$ (c) $\frac{Mg}{3BA}$ (d) $\frac{Mg}{4BA}$

57 If compressibility of a material is 4×10^{-5} per atm, pressure is 100 atm and volume is 100 cm^3, then find ΔV. **NCERT Pg. 173**

(a) 0.4 cm^3 (b) 0.8 cm^3 (c) 0.6 cm^3 (d) 0.2 cm^3

58 The approximate depth of an ocean is 2700 m. The compressibility of water is 45.4×10^{-11} Pa^{-1} and density of water is 10^3 kg/m^3. What fractional compression of water will be obtained at the bottom of the ocean? **NCERT Pg. 173**

(a) 0.8×10^{-2} (b) 1.0×10^{-2}
(c) 1.2×10^{-2} (d) 1.4×10^{-2}

59 A uniform wire (Young's modulus, $Y = 2\times10^{11}$ N/m^2) is subjected to longitudinal stress of 4×10^6 N/m^2. If the overall volume change in wire is 0.01%, the fractional decrease in the radius of the wire is **NCERT Pg. 173**

(a) 0.4×10^{-4} (b) 0.6×10^{-4}
(c) 1.2×10^{-4} (d) 2.2×10^{-4}

60 A cube is subjected to pressure of 4×10^4 N/m^2. Each side of the cube is shortened by 2%. The bulk modulus of elasticity of cube is **NCERT Pg. 173**

(a) 5.2×10^4 N/m^2 (b) 7.4×10^4 N/m^2
(c) 2.6×10^4 N/m^2 (d) 6.67×10^5 N/m^2

61 Which of the following statement is incorrect? **NCERT Pg. 173**

(a) The bulk modulus for solid is much larger than for liquids.
(b) Gases are least compressible.
(c) For a system in equilibrium, the value of bulk modulus is always positive.
(d) The SI unit of bulk modulus is same as that of pressure.

62 Which of the following statement is incorrect? **NCERT Pg. 173**

(a) Young's modulus and shear modulus are relevant only for solids.
(b) Bulk modulus is relevant for liquids and gases.
(c) Metals have larger values of Young's modulus than elastomers.
(d) Alloys have larger values of Young's modulus than metals.

63 The Poisson's ratio of a material is 0.8. If a force is applied to a wire of this material, there is a decrease in cross-sectional area by 3%. The percentage increase in its length is **NCERT Pg. 174**

(a) 2.2% (b) 1.2% (c) 1.86% (d) 1.75%

64 A metal cylinder of length 10 m is subjected to a uniform compressive force F as shown in the figure. The change in length and volume of cylinder is 3% and 9%, respectively. The Poisson's ratio is **NCERT Pg. 174**

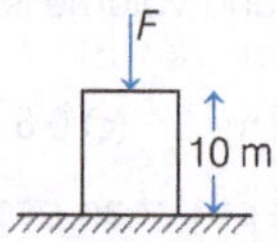

(a) 3% (b) 2% (c) 1% (d) 4%

65 If the volume of a wire remains constant when subjected to tensile stress, the value of Poisson's ratio of the material of the wire is **NCERT Pg. 174**

(a) 0.1 (b) 0.2 (c) 0.4 (d) 0.5

66 A material has Poisson's ratio 0.5. If a uniform rod suffers a longitudinal strain of 2×10^{-3}, then the percentage change in volume is **NCERT Pg. 174**

(a) 0.6 (b) 0.4 (d) 0.2 (d) zero

67 The Poisson's ratio of a material is 0.4. If a force is applied to a wire of this material, there is a decrease of cross-sectional area is 2%. The percentage increase in its length is **NCERT Pg. 174**

(a) 3% (b) 2.5% (c) 1% (d) 0.5%

68 Which of the following statement is correct regarding Poisson's ratio? **NCERT Pg. 174**

(a) It is the ratio of longitudinal strain to the lateral strain.
(b) Its value is independent of the nature of the material.
(c) It is a unitless and dimensionless quantity.
(d) The practical value of Poisson's ratio lies between 0 and 1.

69 Identical springs of steel and copper ($Y_{steel} > Y_{copper}$) are equally stretched. It implies, **NCERT Pg. 174**

(a) less work is done on copper spring
(b) less work is done on steel spring
(c) equal work is done on both the springs
(d) Data is incomplete

70 When the load on a wire is increased from 3 kg-wt to 5 kg-wt, the elongation increases from 0.61 mm to 1.02 mm. The required work done during the extension of the wire is **NCERT Pg. 174**

(a) 16×10^{-3} J (b) 8×10^{-2} J
(c) 20×10^{-2} J (d) 11×10^{-3} J

Applications of Elastic Behaviour of Materials

71 Overbridges are constructed with steel but not with aluminium because steel is **NCERT Pg. 174**

(a) more elastic than aluminium
(b) less elastic than aluminium
(c) more plastic than aluminium
(d) less plastic than aluminium

72 A wire of diameter 1 mm breaks under a tension of 1000 N. Another wire of same material as that of the first one, but of diameter 2 mm breaks under a tension of **NCERT Pg. 174**

(a) 500 N (b) 1000 N (c) 10000 N (d) 4000 N

73 In steel, the Young's modulus and the strain at the breaking point are 2×10^{11} Nm^{-2} and 0.15, respectively. The stress at the breaking point for steel is **NCERT Pg. 174**

(a) 1.33×10^{11} Nm^{-2} (b) 1.33×10^{12} Nm^{-2}
(c) 7.5×10^{-13} Nm^{-2} (d) 3×10^{10} Nm^{-2}

74 A uniform rod of length L and density ρ is being pulled along a smooth floor with a horizontal acceleration α. The magnitude of the stress at the transverse cross-section through the mid-point of the rod is **NCERT Pg. 174**

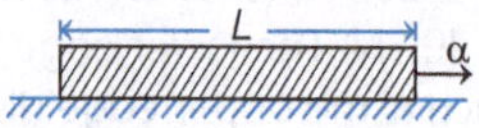

(a) $L\rho\alpha$ (b) $\frac{L\rho\alpha}{2}$
(c) $\frac{2}{3} L\rho\alpha$ (d) None of these

75 A metal bar is supported at two ends. If metal bar is loaded at centre with a heavy load, the depression in bar at the centre is proportional to [Y = Young's modulus of bar] **NCERT Pg. 174**

(a) $\frac{1}{Y^2}$ (b) $\frac{1}{Y}$ (c) Y (d) Y^2

76 If the load hanging from middle position of a metal beam is increased to double, then depression in the bar at the centre is **NCERT Pg. 174**

(a) increased to four times
(b) increased to three times
(c) increased to double
(d) increased to six times

77 The area of cross-section of the rope used to lift a load by a crane is 5×10^{-4} m^2. The maximum lifting capacity of the crane is 10 metric tonne. To increase the lifting capacity of the crane to 20 metric tonne, the required area of cross-section of the rops should be (Take, $g = 10$ ms^{-2}) **NCERT Pg. 174**

(a) 6.25×10^{-4} m^2 (b) 10×10^{-4} m^2
(c) 1×10^{-4} m^2 (d) 1.67×10^{-4} m^2

78 Assuming that shear stress at the base of a mountain is equal to the force per unit area due to its weight. Calculate the maximum possible height of a mountain on the earth, if breaking stress of a typical rock is 9×10^7 Nm^{-2} and its density is 1.5×10^3 kg m^{-3}. (Take, $g = 10$ ms^{-2}) NCERT Pg. 175

(a) 4 km (b) 8 km
(c) 10 km (d) 6 km

79 Two strips of metal are riveted together at their ends by four rivets, each of diameter 8 mm. Assume that each rivet is to carry one quarter of the load. If the shearing stress on the rivet is not to exceed 5.38×10^7 Pa, the maximum tension that can be exerted by the riveted strip is NCERT Pg. 175

(a) 101×10^2 N (b) 108×10^2 N
(c) 88×10^2 N (d) 120×10^2 N

80 A steel wire of 2 m in length is stretched through 4 mm. The cross-sectional area of wire is 2 mm^2. If Young's modulus of steel is 2×10^{11} N/m^2, then elastic potential energy stored in the wire will be NCERT Pg. 175

(a) 2 J (b) 4 J
(c) 0.5 J (d) 1.6 J

81 Two wires of the same material and length but diameter in the ratio 1 : 2 are stretched by the same load. The ratio of elastic potential energy per unit volume for the two wires is NCERT Pg. 175

(a) 1 : 1 (b) 2 : 1 (c) 4 : 1 (d) 16 : 1

82 When a block of mass M is suspended by a long wire of length L, the length of the wire becomes $(L + l)$. The elastic potential energy stored in the extended wire is NCERT Pg. 175

(a) MgL (b) $\frac{1}{2}Mgl$ (c) $\frac{1}{2}MgL$ (d) Mgl

83 A metal wire of length L is suspended vertically from a rigid support. When a body of mass M is attached to the lower end of wire, the elongation of the wire is l, then which of the following statement is incorrect? NCERT Pg. 175

(a) The loss of gravitational potential energy of mass m is mgl.
(b) The elastic potential energy stored in the wire is mgl.
(c) The elastic potential energy stored in the wire is $(1/2)\,mgl$.
(d) Heat produced is $\frac{1}{2}mgl$.

Assertion and Reason Questions

Direction (Q. Nos. 1-10) *In the following questions, a statement of Assertion is followed by a corresponding statement of Reason of the following statements, choose the correct one.*

(a) Both Assertion and Reason are correct and Reason is the correct explanation of Assertion.
(b) Both Assertion and Reason are correct but Reason is not the correct explanation of Assertion.
(c) Assertion is correct but Reason is incorrect.
(d) Assertion is incorrect but Reason is correct.

1 **Assertion** For rubber, strain is more as compared to steel.

Reason Rubber is less elastic than steel. NCERT Pg. 167

2 **Assertion** Spring balance shows incorrect readings after using it for a long time.

Reason Spring in the spring balance loses its elastic strength over the period of time. NCERT Pg. 168

3 **Assertion** Ropes are always made of a number of thin wires braided together.

Reason It helps to ease in manufacturing, flexibility and strength. NCERT Pg. 169

4 **Assertion** Elongation produced in a body is directly proportional to the applied force.

Reason Within the elastic limit, stress is inversely proportional to the strain. NCERT Pg. 170

5 **Assertion** Young's modulus for a perfectly plastic body is zero.

Reason For a perfectly plastic body, restoring force is zero. NCERT Pg. 170

6 **Assertion** When a spring is loaded, then shearing stress is produced in it.

Reason Shape of spring remains unchanged under the application of tangential stress. NCERT Pg. 172

7 **Assertion** The strain produced by a hydraulic pressure is volumetric in nature.

Reason It is a ratio of change in volume ΔV to the original volume V. NCERT Pg. 173

8 **Assertion** Gases have large compressibility.

Reason Compressibility is defined as the fractional change in volume per unit decrease in pressure. NCERT Pg. 173

9 **Assertion** Maximum height of a mountain on earth is ~ 10 km.
Reason A mountain base is not under uniform compression and provides some shearing stress to rock under which it can flow. **NCERT Pg. 173**

10 **Assertion** When a solid sphere is placed in the fluid under high pressure, then it is compressed uniformly on all sides.
Reason The force applied by fluids acts in perpendicular direction at each point of surface. **NCERT Pg. 174**

Statement Based Questions

Direction (Q. Nos. 1-8) *In the following questions, Statement I and Statement II are given. Read these statements and choose the most appropriate answer from the options given below.*

(a) Both Statement I and Statement II are incorrect.
(b) Statement I is correct but Statement II is incorrect.
(c) Statement I is incorrect but Statement II is correct.
(d) Both Statement I and Statement II are correct.

1. **Statement I** As a result of applied tangential force, there is a relative displacement between opposite face of the body.
Statement II The force applied by the fluid acts vertically at upper and lower points of the surface of a submerge body. **NCERT Pg. 169**

2. **Statement I** Hydraulic stress is equal and opposite to the applied force per unit area by the fluid.
Statement II Strain is a ratio of change in dimension to the original dimension of the body. **NCERT Pg. 169**

3. **Statement I** The ultimate strength and fracture points of a less ductile object are very far.
Statement II The stress-strain curves of different types of material are same. **NCERT Pg. 169**

4. **Statement I** Elastomers can be elastically stretched to a large value of strain.
Statement II Young's modulus of elastomers is very large. **NCERT Pg. 170**

5. **Statement I** Hollow shaft is much stronger than a solid rod of same length and same mass.
Statement II It is difficult to twist a long rod as compared to small rod. **NCERT Pg. 172**

6. **Statement I** Value of Poisson's ratio is independent of the nature of the material.
Statement II The practical value of Poisson's ratio lies between 0 and 1. **NCERT Pg. 174**

7. **Statement I** When a wire is put under a tensile stress, work is done against the interatomic forces.
Statement II A cube has side length L, elongation length ΔL and elastic potential energy W. If side length become double and elastic potential energy remain same, then changed elongation length is $\frac{1}{2}$ time of ΔL. **NCERT Pg. 174**

8. **Statement I** A pillar with rounded ends support less load than that with a distributed shape at ends.
Statement II A factor of safety of value 1 means that a structure or component can sustain a load beyond its designed load. **NCERT Pg. 174**

Matching Type Questions

1 Match the Column I (quantity) with Column II (units).

	Column I		Column II
A.	Stress × Strain	1.	J
B.	YA/l	2.	Nm^{-1}
C.	Yl^3	3.	Jm^{-3}
D.	Fl/AY	4.	m

Choose the correct answer from the options given below.
Codes **NCERT Pg. 170**

	A	B	C	D
(a)	3	2	1	4
(b)	2	1	3	4
(c)	3	4	1	2
(d)	1	2	4	3

2 A bar of cross-section A is subjected to equal and opposite tensile forces at its ends. Consider a plane section of the bar, whose normal makes an angle θ with the axis of the bar.

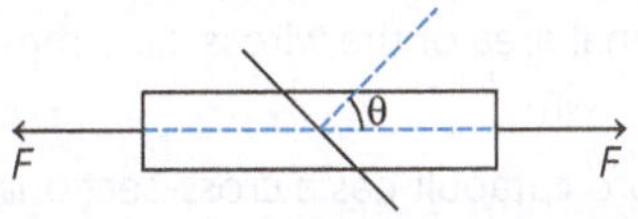

Match the Column I (stress) with Column II (value). **NCERT Pg. 172**

Column I		Column II	
A.	The tensile stress on this plane will be	1.	0°
B.	The shearing stress on this plane will be	2.	$(F/A)\cos^2\theta$
C.	The tensile strength will be maximum at θ =	3.	$\left(\frac{F}{2A}\right)\sin 2\theta$
D.	The shearing stress will be maximum at θ =	4.	45°

Choose the correct answer from the options given below.

Codes

	A	B	C	D
(a)	3	2	4	1
(b)	2	3	1	4
(c)	2	3	4	1
(d)	3	2	1	4

3 Match the Column I (stress) with Column II (characteristic). **NCERT Pg. 173**

Column I		Column II	
A.	Longitudinal stress	1.	Independent of area of cross-section of wire.
B.	Shear stress	2.	Change in pressure
C.	Breaking stress	3.	Length of wire increases or decreases
D.	Bulk stress	4.	Shape changes

Choose the correct answer from the options given below.

Codes

	A	B	C	D		A	B	C	D
(a)	3	4	2	1	(b)	4	3	1	2
(c)	3	4	1	2	(d)	1	2	3	4

4 Match the Column I (elastic moduli) with Column II (value). **NCERT Pg. 173**

Column I		Column II	
A.	Young's modulus for perfectly elastic body	1.	Maximum
B.	For most material, modulus of rigidity	2.	Minimum
C.	Bulk modulus for solid	3.	$Y/3$
D.	Bulk modulus for gas	4.	Infinite

Choose the correct answer from the options given below.

Codes

	A	B	C	D		A	B	C	D
(a)	4	1	2	3	(b)	4	3	1	2
(c)	1	2	4	3	(d)	3	4	1	2

Numerical Type Questions

1 The elastic behaviour of material for linear stress and linear strain, as shown in the figure. The energy density for a linear strain of 4×10^{-4} is .... kJ/m^3. Assume that material is elastic upto the linear strain of 4×10^{-4}.

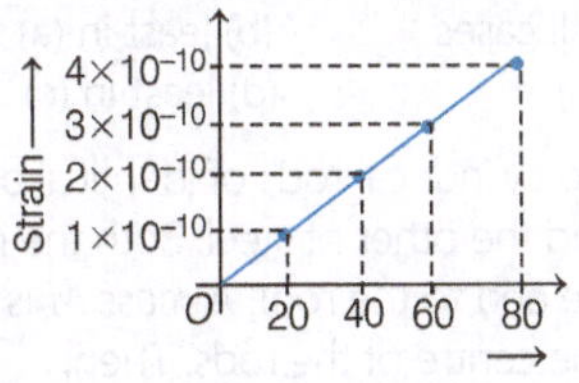

NCERT Pg. 169

2 A copper wire of length 2.2 m and a steel wire of length 1.6 m both of diameter 3.0 mm are connected end-to-end. When stretched by a load, the net elongation is found to be 0.70 mm and the load applied is .... (in N).
[Take, $Y_C = 1.1 \times 10^{11}$ N/m^2, $Y_S = 2 \times 10^{11}$ N/m^2] **NCERT Pg. 170**

3 The length of a wire becomes l_1 and l_2 when 60 N and 80 N tensions are applied, respectively. If $10 l_2 = 11 l_1$, the natural length of wire will be $7 l_1 / x$. Here the value of x is .... **NCERT Pg. 170**

4 A steel rod has a radius of 10 mm and a length of 5 m. A force of 6.28 kN stretches it along its length. Young's modulus of steel is 2.0×10^{11} N/m^2. The longitudinal strain produced in the wire is .... $\times 10^{-5}$. **NCERT Pg. 170**

5 Two wires made of same material are subjected to forces in the ratio of 1 : 3. Their lengths are in the ratio 3 : 1 and diameter are in the ratio 1 : 2. The ratio of their extensions is $\frac{x}{4}$. The value of x is .... **NCERT Pg. 170**

6 In an experiment to determine the Young's modulus of wire of a length exactly 2 m, the extension in the length of the wire is measured as 0.4 mm with an uncertainty of ± 0.02 mm when a load of 1 kg is applied. The diameter of the wire is measured as 0.4 mm with an uncertainty of $\pm$ 0.01 mm. The error in the measurement of Young's modulus (ΔY) is found be $x \times 10^{10}$ Nm^{-2}. The value of x is .... (Take, $g = 10$ ms^{-2}) **NCERT Pg. 170**

7 A metallic cube whose each side is 5 cm is subjected to a shearing force of 50 kgf. The top face is displaced through 0.2 cm with respect to the bottom. The shear modulus of elasticity is $x \times 10^5$ Nm^{-2}. The value of x is .... **NCERT Pg. 172**

8 A 10 kg of mass is attached to one end of a copper wire 4 m long and 2 mm in diameter. The Poisson ratio and Young's modulus of wire is 0.4 and 1.2×10^{11} Nm^{-2}, respectively. The lateral compression produce in wire is $x \times 10^{-8}$, then the value of x is .... **NCERT Pg. 174**

9 The elastic potential energy stored in a steel wire of length 10 m stretched through 2 cm is 80 J. The cross-sectional area of the wire is .... mm^2. (Take, $Y = 2.0 \times 10^{11}$ Nm^{-2}) **NCERT Pg. 174**

10 A rubber cord catapult has a cross-sectional area 2 mm^2 and total unstretched length 1 m. It is stretched to 1.1 m and the released to project a missile of mass 20 g. The Young's modulus of rubber is 4×10^8 Nm^{-2}. The velocity of projection of the projectile is .... ms^{-1}. **NCERT Pg. 174**

NCERT Exemplar Questions

1 Modulus of rigidity of ideal liquid is
(a) infinity
(b) zero
(c) unity
(d) some finite small non-zero constant value

2 The maximum load, a wire can withstand without breaking when its length is reduced to half of its original length, will
(a) be double
(b) be half
(c) be four times
(d) remain same

3 A spring is stretched by applying a load to its free end. The strain produced in the spring is
(a) volumetric
(b) shear
(c) longitudinal and shear
(d) longitudinal

4 A rigid bar of mass M is supported symmetrically by three wires each of length l. Those at each end are of copper and the middle one is of iron. The ratio of their diameters, if each is to have the same tension, is equal to

(a) $\frac{Y_{copper}}{Y_{iron}}$ (b) $\sqrt{\frac{Y_{iron}}{Y_{copper}}}$

(c) $\frac{Y^2_{iron}}{Y^2_{copper}}$ (d) $\frac{Y_{iron}}{Y_{copper}}$

5 A mild steel wire of length $2L$ and cross-sectional area A is stretched, well within elastic limit, horizontally between two pillars as shown in figure. A mass m is suspended from the mid-point of the wire, strain in the wire is

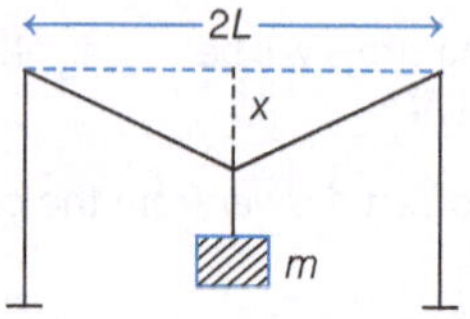

(a) $\frac{x^2}{2L^2}$ (b) $\frac{x}{L}$ (c) x^2 / L (d) $x^2 / 2L$

6 A rectangular frame is to be suspended symmetrically by two strings of equal length on two supports (figure). It can be done in one of the following three ways.

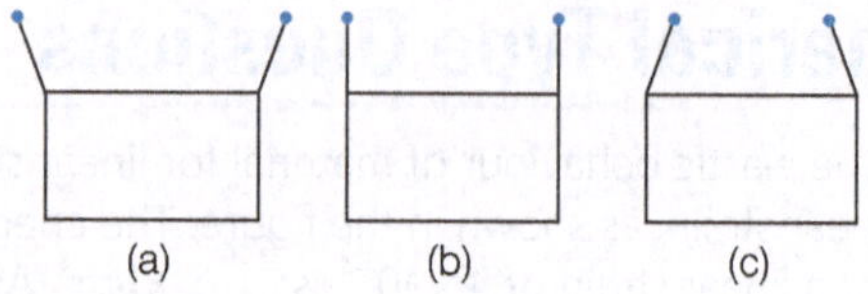

The tension in the strings will be
(a) same in all cases (b) least in (a)
(c) least in (b) (d) least in (c)

7 Consider two cylindrical rods of identical dimensions, one of rubber and the other of steel. Both the rods are fixed rigidly at one end to the roof. A mass M is attached to each of at the centre of the rods. Then,
(a) both the rods will elongate but there shall be no perceptible change in shape
(b) the steel rod will elongate and change shape but the rubber rod will only elongate
(c) only rubber rod will elongate

(d) the steel rod will elongate without any perceptible change in shape, but the rubber rod will elongate with the shape of the bottom edge tappered to a tip at the centre

8 The stress-strain graphs for two materials are shown in figure, then (assume same scale)

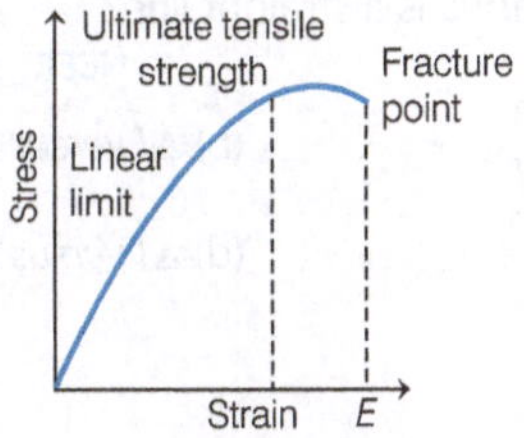

Material (i)

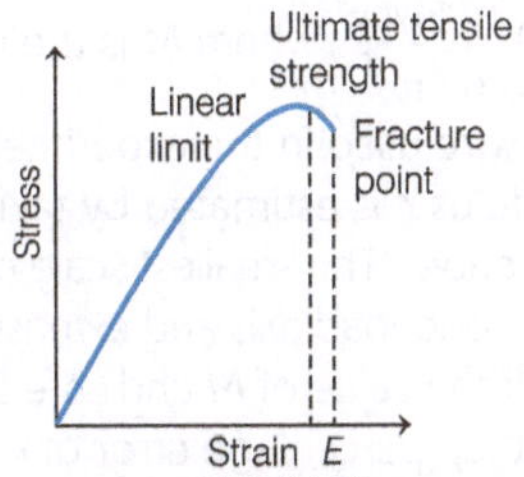

Material (ii)

(a) material (ii) is more elastic than material (i) and hence material (ii) is more ductile

(b) material (i) and (ii) have the same elasticity and the same brittleness

(c) material (ii) is elastic over a larger region of strain as compared to (i)

(d) material (ii) is less brittle than material (i)

9 A wire is suspended from the ceiling and stretched under the action of a weight F suspended from its other end. The force exerted by the ceiling on it is equal and opposite to the weight, then

(a) tensile stress at any cross-section A of the wire is $\dfrac{F}{2A}$

(b) tensile stress at any cross-section is zero

(c) tensile stress at any cross-section A of the wire is $2F/A$

(d) tension at any cross-section A of the wire is F

10 A rod of length l and negligible mass is suspended at its two ends by two wires of steel (wire A) and aluminium (wire B) of equal lengths (figure). The cross-sectional areas of wires A and B are 1.0 mm^2 and 2.0 mm^2, respectively.

Then, $(Y_{Al} = 70 \times 10^9 \text{Nm}^{-2}$ and $Y_{steel} = 200 \times 10^9 \text{Nm}^{-2})$

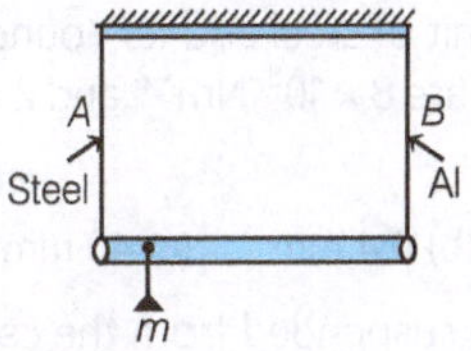

(a) Mass m should be suspended close to wire A to have equal stresses in both the wires

(b) Mass m should be suspended close to B to have equal stresses in both the wires

(c) Mass m should be suspended at the middle of the wires to have equal stresses in both the wires

(d) Mass m should be suspended close to wire B to have equal strain in both wires

11 A copper and a steel wire of the same diameter are connected end-to-end. A deforming force F is applied to this composite wire which causes a total elongation of 1 cm. The two wires will have

(a) the same stress

(b) the different stress

(c) the same strain

(d) None of the above

12 A wire of length L and radius r is rigidly fixed at one end. On stretching the other end of the wire with a force F, the increase in its length is l. If another wire of same material but of length $2L$ and radius $2r$ is stretched with a force of $2F$, the increase in its length will be

(a) l (b) $2l$

(c) $l/2$ (d) $l/4$

13 To what depth must a rubber ball be taken in deep sea, so that its volume is decreased by 0.1%?

(Take, density of sea water $= 10^3$ kgm^{-3}, bulk modulus of rubber $= 9 \times 10^8 \text{Nm}^{-2}$, $g = 10$ ms^{-2})

(a) 9 m (b) 18 m

(c) 90 m (d) 180 m

Past Exams Questions

NEET

1 The maximum elongation of a steel wire of 1 m length if the elastic limit of steel and its Young's modulus, respectively, are 8×10^8 Nm^{-2} and 2×10^{11} Nm^{-2}, is

NCERT Pg. 170, NEET 2024

(a) 4 mm (b) 0.4 mm (c) 40 mm (d) 8 mm

2 Let a wire be suspended from the ceiling (rigid support) and stretched by a weight w attached at its free end. The longitudinal stress at any point of cross-sectional area A of the wire is NCERT Pg. 168, NEET 2023

(a) $\frac{w}{A}$ (b) $\frac{w}{2A}$ (c) zero (d) $\frac{2w}{A}$

3 Given below are two statements: One is labelled as Assertion (A) and the other is labelled as Reason (R).

Assertion (A) The stretching of a spring is determined by the shear modulus of the material of the spring.

Reason (R) A coil spring of copper has more tensile strength than a steel spring of same dimensions.

In the light of the above statements, choose the most appropriate answer from the options given below

NCERT Pg. 172, NEET 2022

(a) Both A and R are true and R is not the correct explanation of A.

(b) A is true but R is false.

(c) A is false but R is true.

(d) Both A and R are true and R is the correct explanation of A.

4 A wire of length L, area of cross-section A is hanging from a fixed support. The length of the wire changes to L_1 when mass M is suspended from its free end. The expression for Young's modulus is

NCERT Pg. 170, NEET 2020

(a) $\frac{Mg(L_1 - L)}{AL}$ (b) $\frac{MgL}{AL_1}$

(c) $\frac{MgL}{A(L_1 - L)}$ (d) $\frac{MgL_1}{AL}$

5 The bulk modulus of a spherical object is B. If it is subjected to uniform pressure p, the fractional decrease in radius is NCERT Pg. 173, NEET 2017

(a) $\frac{p}{B}$ (b) $\frac{B}{3p}$

(c) $\frac{3p}{B}$ (d) $\frac{p}{3B}$

6 Copper of fixed volume V is drawn into wire of length l. When this wire is subjected to a constant force F, the extension produced in the wire is Δl. Which of the following graphs is a straight line?

NCERT Pg. 170, AIPMT 2014

(a) Δl versus $\frac{1}{l}$ (b) Δl versus l^2

(c) Δl versus $\frac{1}{l^2}$ (d) Δl versus l

JEE Main

7 Young's modulus is determined by the equation given by $Y = 49000 \frac{M}{l} \frac{\text{dyne}}{\text{m}^2}$, where M is the mass and l is the extension of wire used in the experiment. Now error in Young's modulus Y is estimated by taking data from M-l plot is graph paper. The smallest scale division are 5 g and 0.02 cm along load axis and extension axis respectively. If the value of M and l are 500 g and 2 cm respectively, then percentage error of Y is

NCERT Pg. 170, JEE Main 2024

(a) 0.5% (b) 0.2% (c) 2% (d) 0.02%

8 Under the same load, wire A having length 5.0 m and cross-section 2.5×10^{-5} m^2 stretches uniformly by the same amount as another wire B of length 6.0 m and a cross-section of 3.0×10^{-5} m^2 stretches. The ratio of the Young's modulus of wire A to that of wire B will be NCERT Pg. 170, JEE Main 2023

(a) 1: 2 (b) 1 : 4

(c) 1 : 1 (d) 1 : 10

9 Two wires of same length and same radius are joined end-to-end and loaded. The Young's moduli of the materials of the two wires are Y_1 and Y_2. The combination behaves as a single wire, then its Young's modulus is NCERT Pg. 170, JEE Main 2021

(a) $Y = \frac{2Y_1Y_2}{3(Y_1 + Y_2)}$ (b) $Y = \frac{2Y_1Y_2}{Y_1 + Y_2}$

(c) $Y = \frac{Y_1Y_2}{2(Y_1 + Y_2)}$ (d) $Y = \frac{Y_1Y_2}{Y_1 + Y_2}$

10 Two steel wires having same length are suspended from a ceiling under the same load. If the ratio of their energy stored per unit volume is 1 : 4, the ratio of their diameters is NCERT Pg. 174, JEE Main 2020

(a) $\sqrt{2} : 1$ (b) $1 : \sqrt{2}$

(c) 2 : 1 (d) 1 : 2

Skill Boosters

1 A reinforced concrete column consists of concrete filled with iron bars. If iron occupies one-sixth of the total cross-sectional area and Young's modulus of concrete is one-eighth of that of iron. The concrete column is under a compressive load *w*. The fraction of load on the concrete is

(a) 0.62 (b) 0.43 (c) 0.74 (d) 0.92

2 One end of a nylon rope of length 4.5 m and diameter 6 mm is fixed to a tree limb. A monkey weighing 100 N jumps to catch the tree end and stays there. Find the elongation of the rope (given, Young's modulus of nylon = 4.8×10^{11} Nm^{-2} and Poisson's ratio of nylon = 0.2).

(a) 0.332 μm (b) 0.521 μm (c) 0.285 μm (d) 0.712 μm

3 In an experiment, brass and steel wires of length 1 m each with areas of cross-section 1 mm^2 are used. The wires are connected in series and one end of the combined wire is connected to a rigid support and other end is subjected to elongation. The stress required to produce a net elongation of 0.2 mm is (Take, Young's moduli for steel and brass are respectively 120×10^9 N/m^2 and 60×10^9 N/m^2)

(a) 1.2×10^6 N/m^2 (b) 0.2×10^6 N/m^2
(c) 8×10^6 N/m^2 (d) 4.0×10^6 N/m^2

4 A stone of 0.5 kg mass is attached to one end of a 0.8 m long aluminium wire of 0.7 mm diameter and suspended vertically. The stone is now rotated in a horizontal plane at a rate such that the wire makes an angle of 85° with the vertical. The increase in the length of the wire is (Young's modulus of aluminium = 7×10^{10} Nm^{-2}, sin 85° = 0.9962, cos 85° = 0.0872)

(a) 1.60 mm (b) 0.16 mm (c) 1.67 mm (d) 0.61 mm

5 A bottle has an opening of radius *a* and length *b*. A cork of length *b* and radius $(a+\Delta a)$, where $(\Delta a << a)$ is compressed to fit into the opening completely (see figure). If the bulk modulus of cork is *B* and frictional coefficient between the bottle and cork is μ, then the force needed to push the cork into the bottle is

(a) $(\pi\mu Bb)a$ (b) $(2\pi\mu Bb)\,\Delta a$
(c) $(\pi\mu Bb)\,\Delta a$ (d) $(4\pi\mu Bb)\,\Delta a$

6 A light rod of length 2 m is suspended horizontally by means of two vertical wires of equal lengths tied to its ends. One of the wires is made of steel and is of cross-section A_1 = 0.1 cm^2 and the other is of brass and is of cross-section A_2 = 0.2 cm^2. Find out the position along the rod at which a weight must be suspended to produce equal stresses in both wires. For steel, $Y = 20\times 10^{10}$ Nm^{-2} and for brass, $Y = 10^{10}$ Nm^{-2}

(a) 1.33 m (b) 1 m (c) 2.33 m (d) 1.3 m

7 One end of a long metallic wire of length *L* is tied to the ceiling. The other end is tied to a massless spring of spring constant *k*. A mass *m* hangs freely from the free end of the spring. The area of cross-section and the Young's modulus of the wire are *A* and *Y*, respectively. If the mass is slightly pulled down and released, it will oscillate. Find the time period of oscillation.

(a) $2\pi\sqrt{\dfrac{m(YA+kL)}{YAk}}$ (b) $\dfrac{1}{2\pi}\sqrt{\dfrac{mYA+kL}{YAk}}$

(c) $2\pi\sqrt{\dfrac{YAk}{mYA+kL}}$ (d) $2\pi\sqrt{\dfrac{kL}{YAk+mYA}}$

8 A boy's catapult is made of rubber cord which is 42 cm long, with 6 mm diameter of cross-section and of negligible mass. The boy keeps a stone weighing 0.02 kg on it and stretches the cord by 20 cm by applying a constant force. When released the stone flies off with a velocity of 20 ms^{-1}. Neglect the change in the area of cross-section of the cord while stretched. The Young's modulus of rubber is closest to

(a) 10^6 Nm^{-2} (b) 10^4 Nm^{-2} (c) 10^8 Nm^{-2} (d) 10^3 Nm^{-2}

9 A pendulum made of uniform wire of cross-sectional area *A* has period *T*. When an additional mass *M* is added to its bob, the time period changes to T_M. If the Young's modulus of the material of the wire is *Y*, then $\dfrac{1}{Y}$ is equal to (g = gravitational acceleration)

(a) $\left[1-\left(\dfrac{T}{T_M}\right)^2\right]\dfrac{A}{Mg}$ (b) $\left[\left(\dfrac{T_M}{T}\right)^2-1\right]\dfrac{Mg}{A}$

(c) $\left[1-\left(\dfrac{T_M}{T}\right)^2\right]\dfrac{A}{Mg}$ (d) $\left[\left(\dfrac{T_M}{T}\right)^2-1\right]\dfrac{A}{Mg}$

10 A sphere of radius 10 cm and mass 25 kg is attached to the lower end of a steel wire of length 5m and diameter 4 mm which is suspended from the ceiling of a room. The point of support is 521 cm above the floor. When the sphere is set swinging as a simple pendulum, its lowest point just grazes the floor. Calculate the velocity of the ball as its lowest position.

Young's modulus of steel = 20×10^{10} Nm^{-2}
Unstretched length of wire = 500 cm
Radius of the steel wire = 0.05 cm

(a) 23. 31 m/s (b) 25.3 m/s
(c) 31.26 m/s (d) 24.1 m/s

Correct Codes

Topical Questions

1 (a)	2 (a)	3 (a)	4 (d)	5 (b)	6 (d)	7 (b)	8 (c)	9 (c)	10 (c)
11 (d)	12 (d)	13 (c)	14 (a)	15 (a)	16 (d)	17 (c)	18 (a)	19 (b)	20 (a)
21 (b)	22 (c)	23 (b)	24 (b)	25 (b)	26 (d)	27 (a)	28 (c)	29 (b)	30 (d)
31 (c)	32 (a)	33 (d)	34 (d)	35 (d)	36 (d)	37 (b)	38 (b)	39 (b)	40 (d)
41 (d)	42 (a)	43 (d)	44 (b)	45 (b)	46 (c)	47 (c)	48 (c)	49 (a)	50 (d)
51 (b)	52 (c)	53 (c)	54 (b)	55 (c)	56 (c)	57 (a)	58 (c)	59 (a)	60 (d)
61 (b)	62 (d)	63 (c)	64 (c)	65 (d)	66 (d)	67 (b)	68 (c)	69 (b)	70 (a)
71 (a)	72 (d)	73 (d)	74 (b)	75 (b)	76 (c)	77 (b)	78 (d)	79 (b)	80 (d)
81 (d)	82 (b)	83 (b)							

Assertion and Reason Questions

1 (a)	2 (a)	3 (a)	4 (c)	5 (a)	6 (c)	7 (a)	8 (a)	9 (a)	10 (a)

Statement Based Questions

1 (b)	2 (d)	3 (a)	4 (b)	5 (b)	6 (a)	7 (b)	8 (b)

Matching Type Questions

1 (a)	2 (b)	3 (c)	4 (b)

Numerical Type Questions

1 (16)	2 (176.78)	3 (10)	4 (100)	5 (1)	6 (4)	7 (49)	8 (20.81)	9 (20)	10 (40)

NCERT Exemplar Questions

1 (b)	2 (d)	3 (c)	4 (b)	5 (a)	6 (c)	7 (d)	8 (c)	9 (d)	10 (b)
11 (a)	12 (a)	13 (c)							

Past Exams Questions

1 (a)	2 (a)	3 (b)	4 (c)	5 (d)	6 (b)	7 (c)	8 (c)	9 (b)	10 (a)

Skill Boosters

1 (b)	2 (a)	3 (c)	4 (c)	5 (d)	6 (a)	7 (a)	8 (a)	9 (d)	10 (c)

Step by Step

Decoding the Questions

Concept Builders

1 intermolecular force

2 False (F)

3 double

4 longitudinal

5 False (F)

6 longitudinal stress

7 Modulus of elasticity

8 Modulus of elasticity

9 1

10 Young's modulus

11 $Y = \dfrac{F \times L}{A \times \Delta L}$

12 increases

13 True (T)

14 larger

15 lateral, longitudinal

16 False (F)

17 True (T)

18 True (T)

19 increase

20 $\dfrac{1}{Y}$

Topical Questions

3 (*a*) When distance of separation between the atoms decreases, the repulsive force increase, so repulsion exist at $r = r_0$.

6 (*d*) When a horizontal force is applied on uniform bar to pull it, then an acceleration is produced in the each cross-section of rod. Hence, each section of rod experiences a tension which is zero at other end. Therefore, stress in the rod developed gradually reduces to zero at the end of the bar where no force is applied.

7 (*b*) $\therefore \quad r_A = 2r_B$ (given)

Now, $\text{Stress} = \dfrac{\text{Force}}{\text{Area}} = \dfrac{F}{\pi r^2}$

$\therefore$ Stress $\propto \dfrac{1}{r^2}$

$$\frac{(\text{Stress})_B}{(\text{Stress})_A} = \left(\frac{r_A}{r_B}\right)^2 = (2)^2$$

$\Rightarrow (\text{Stress})_B = 4 \times (\text{Stress})_A$

8 (*c*) Given, radius of wire,

$r = 2\text{ mm} = 2 \times 10^{-3}\text{ m}$

Weight of load,

$m = 4\text{ kg}$ and $g = 3.1\,\pi\text{ms}^{-2}$

$$\therefore \quad \text{Tensile stress} = \frac{\text{Force }(F)}{\text{Area}(A)} = \frac{mg}{\pi r^2}$$

$$= \frac{4 \times 3.1 \times \pi}{\pi \times (2 \times 10^{-3})^2}$$

$$= 3.1 \times 10^6\text{ Nm}^{-2}$$

9 (*c*) When the length of wire becomes doubled, its area of cross-section will become half because volume of wire is constant ($V = AL$).

So, the instantaneous stress

$$= \frac{\text{force}}{\text{area}} = \frac{Mg}{A/2} = \frac{2Mg}{A}$$

11 (*d*) Given, length of cube, $L = 0.1$ m

Shearing force, $F = 100$ N

and displaced distance,

$x = 0.02\text{ cm} = 0.02 \times 10^{-2}\text{ m}$

Shearing strain,

$$\phi = \frac{x}{L} = \frac{0.02 \times 10^{-2}}{0.1} = 0.002$$

12 (*d*) % change in $V = 3 \times$ (% change in L)

$= 3(1\%) = 3\%$

$\therefore \quad \Delta V = 3\%$ of V

$\Rightarrow$ Volumetric strain

$$\frac{\Delta V}{V} = \frac{3}{100} = 0.03$$

13 (*c*) Tension in the wire,

$$T = \left(\frac{2mM}{m+M}\right)g$$

$$\text{Stress} = \frac{\text{Tension}}{\text{Area}}$$

$$= \frac{2mM}{A(m+M)}g$$

$$= \frac{2(m \times 4m)\,g}{A(m+4m)} = \frac{8mg}{5A}$$

14 (*a*) Given, radii of wires A and B are r_A and r_B, respectively.

Force, $F = \dfrac{mg}{3}$

$$\therefore \quad \text{Stress in } B = \frac{\text{Force}}{\text{Area}} = \frac{mg}{3\pi r_B^2}$$

[$\because$ Area of wire $B = \pi r_B^2$]

Similarly, stress in A

$$= \frac{F + mg}{\pi r_A^2} = \frac{\frac{mg}{3} + mg}{\pi r_A^2}$$

When $r_A = r_B$,

Stress in $B = \dfrac{mg}{3\pi r_B^2}$

and stress in

$A = \dfrac{4}{3}\dfrac{mg}{\pi r_A^2}$

$\therefore$ Stress in $A >$ Stress in B

So, wire A will break earlier.

If $r_A = 2r_B$, then stress in A = stress in B, it means either A or B may breaks.

If $r_A < 2r_B$, then stress in A is more than that of B.

$\therefore$ A may break earlier.

Thus, the statement given in option (a) is correct, rest are incorrect.

15 (*a*) Given, mass of blocks, $m_1 = 1$ kg and $m_2 = 4$ kg

$\because$ Tension, $T = \dfrac{2m_1m_2}{m_1 + m_2} \times g$

$= \dfrac{2 \times 1 \times 4}{1+4} \times 10 \, (\because \, g = 10 \text{ ms}^{-2})$

$= 16 \text{ N}$

If breaking stress is $3.18 \times 10^9 \text{ Nm}^{-2}$, then

Breaking force = Breaking stress × Area

$\Rightarrow \quad 16 = 3.18 \times 10^9 \times \pi r^2$

$\Rightarrow \quad r = \sqrt{\dfrac{16}{3.18 \times 10^9 \times 3.14}}$

$= 4 \times 10^{-5} \text{ m}$

Thus, the statement given in option (a) is incorrect, rest are correct.

17 (c) According to Hooke's law within the limit of elasticity,

Stress ∝ Strain

or $\dfrac{\text{Load}}{\text{Area}} \propto \dfrac{\text{Extension}}{\text{Original dimension}}$

or Load ∝ Extension

Hence, graph given in option (c) obeys Hooke's law.

19 (b) From given graph, P has more strain for same stress as on Q, so P is more ductile than Q.

Thus, the statement given in option (b) is correct, rest are incorrect.

20 (a) If A and B are prepared for identical wires of two different materials, then

Young's modulus, $Y = \dfrac{Fl}{A\Delta l}$

$\Rightarrow \quad F = \dfrac{YA}{l} \cdot \Delta l \Rightarrow \dfrac{F}{\Delta l} = \dfrac{YA}{l}$

So, slope of load-extension graph

$= \dfrac{F}{\Delta l} = \dfrac{YA}{l}$

As wires are identical,

$\dfrac{(\text{Slope})_A}{(\text{Slope})_B} = \dfrac{\tan \theta_A}{\tan \theta_B} = \dfrac{\tan 60°}{\tan 30°} = \dfrac{Y_A}{Y_B}$

$[\because \theta_A = 60° \text{ and } \theta_B = 30°]$

$\Rightarrow \quad Y_A : Y_B = 3 : 1$

As, extension, $\Delta l = \dfrac{Fl}{AY}$

$\Rightarrow \quad \Delta l \propto \dfrac{1}{Y}$

Then for wires A and B,

$\dfrac{\Delta l_B}{\Delta l_A} = \dfrac{Y_A}{Y_B} = \dfrac{3}{1}$

$\therefore \quad \Delta l_B > \Delta l_A$

As extension for wire A is less than that of B, so A is more thicker than B.

Thus, the statements given in option (a) is incorrect, rest are correct.

21 (b) Stress $= \dfrac{\text{Force}}{\text{Area}}$

Since each wire is of same diameter, hence the area of cross-section is same for both the wires. As both the wires have the same deforming force F and same area of cross-section A, therefore stress is same for both the wires.

But Young's modulus, $Y = \dfrac{\text{Stress}}{\text{Strain}}$

or Strain $= \dfrac{\text{Stress}}{Y}$

Since Y is different for both the wires, therefore strain is different for both the wires.

22 (c) Stress in brass rod is given by

$\sigma = \dfrac{F}{A} = \dfrac{4F}{\pi d_{\min}^2} \quad \left[\because A = \dfrac{\pi d^2}{4}\right]$

For stress not to exceed elastic limit, we have, $\sigma \le 379$ MPa

$\Rightarrow \quad \dfrac{4F}{\pi d_{\min}^2} \le 379 \times 10^6$

$\therefore \quad d_{\min}^2 = \dfrac{1600}{\pi \times 379 \times 10^6}$

$\Rightarrow d_{\min} = 1.16 \times 10^{-3} \text{ m} = 1.16 \text{ mm}$

23 (b)

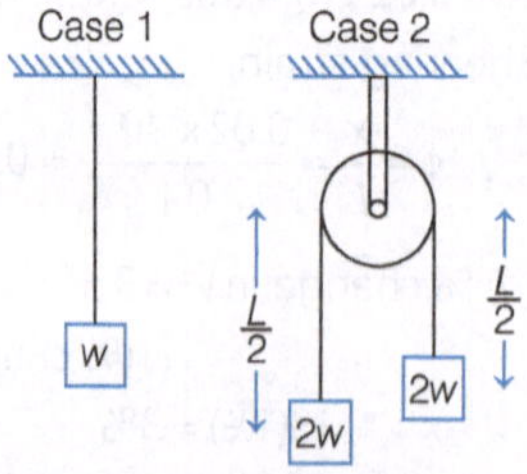

For 1st case, $Y = \dfrac{\left(\dfrac{W}{A}\right)}{\dfrac{l}{L}} = \dfrac{WL}{Al}$

For 2nd case, $Y = \dfrac{\dfrac{2w}{A}}{\dfrac{2l'}{L}} = \dfrac{WL}{Al'}$

$\Rightarrow l' = l$

So, total elongation of both sides

$\Rightarrow 2l' = 2l$

24 (b) Change in length of wire A

= Change in length of wire B

$\therefore \quad \Delta l_1 = \Delta l_2$

$\dfrac{Fl_1}{\pi r_1^2 Y_1} = \dfrac{Fl_2}{\pi r_2^2 Y_2}$

$\dfrac{2}{(R^2 \times 7)} = \dfrac{1.5}{(2^2 \times 4)}$

$\Rightarrow \quad R = 1.7 \text{ mm}$

25 (b) Given, stress, $F = 20 \times 10^8 \text{ Nm}^{-2}$

Young's modulus $= \dfrac{\text{Stress}}{\text{Strain}}$

$\because$ Strain $= \dfrac{\text{Change in length}}{\text{Original length}}$

$= \dfrac{2L - L}{L} = 1$

$\therefore \quad Y = \text{Stress} = 20 \times 10^8 \text{ Nm}^{-2}$

26 (d) Change in length, $l = \dfrac{FL}{AY} = \dfrac{FL^2}{VY}$

$\therefore \quad l \propto L^2$

$\dfrac{l_2}{l_1} = \left[\dfrac{L_2}{L_1}\right]^2 = \left(\dfrac{8}{2}\right)^2 = 16$

$\Rightarrow \quad l_2 = 16 l_1 = 16 \times 2 \text{ mm}$

$= 32 \text{ mm} = 3.2 \text{ cm}$

27 (a) Change in length, $l = 0.1\% \, L$

$= 0.001 \text{ L}$

$\Rightarrow \quad \dfrac{l}{L} = 0.001$

Young's modulus, $Y = \dfrac{F}{A} \cdot \dfrac{L}{l}$

$\therefore \quad F = YA \dfrac{l}{L}$

$= 9 \times 10^{10} \times \pi \times (2 \times 10^{-3})^2 \times 0.001$

$= 360 \pi \text{N}$

28 (c) Young's modulus,

$Y = \dfrac{FL}{A\Delta L} = \dfrac{TL}{\pi r^2 \Delta L}$

$\Rightarrow \quad \Delta L = \dfrac{TL}{\pi r^2 Y}$

As wires are of same material, so Y is same for all. Also T is same, so $\Delta L \propto \frac{L}{r^2}$.

Thus, $\frac{L}{r^2}$ is maximum for length, $L = 250$ cm and radius, $r = 0.1$ mm, i.e. 25×10^7 m, so its extension is largest.

29 (*b*) Young's modulus of a wire is

$$Y = \frac{F/A}{l/L} \Rightarrow F = \frac{YAl}{L}$$

Force constant, $k = \frac{F}{l} = \frac{YA}{L}$

30 (*d*) Given, ratio of radius of two wires, $r_1 : r_2 = 2 : 1$

$$\Rightarrow \quad \frac{r_1}{r_2} = \frac{2}{1}$$

and ratio of their lengths,

$$l_1 : l_2 = 1 : 2 \Rightarrow \frac{l_1}{l_2} = \frac{1}{2}$$

As, $Y = \frac{Fl}{A\Delta l} \Rightarrow \Delta l = \frac{Fl}{AY}$

$$\Delta l \propto \frac{l}{A}$$

$$\therefore \quad \frac{\Delta l_1}{\Delta l_2} = \frac{l_1 A_2}{l_2 A_1} \Rightarrow \frac{\Delta l_1}{\Delta l_2} = \frac{l_1}{l_2} \cdot \frac{r_2^2}{r_1^2}$$

$$= \frac{1}{2} \cdot \left(\frac{1}{2}\right)^2 = \frac{1}{8}$$

31 (*c*) For wire 1, $Y_1 = \frac{F_1 l_1}{A_1 \Delta l}$ ...(i)

For wire 2, $Y_2 = \frac{F_2 l_2}{A_2 \Delta l}$ ...(ii)

$\because$ Volume, $V = Al$ or $l = \frac{V}{A}$

Substituting the value of l in Eqs. (i) and (ii), we get

$$Y_1 = \frac{F_1 V}{A_1^2 \Delta l}$$

and $$Y_2 = \frac{F_2 V}{A_2^2 \Delta l}$$

As it is given that the wires are made up of same material, i.e.

$$Y_1 = Y_2$$

$$\Rightarrow \quad \frac{F_1 V}{A_1^2 \Delta l} = \frac{F_2 V}{A_2^2 \Delta l}$$

$$\Rightarrow \quad \frac{F_1}{F_2} = \frac{A_1^2}{A_2^2} = \frac{1}{9}$$

$(\because A_1 = A$ and $A_2 = 3A)$

or $F_2 = 9F_1 = 9F$ (given, $F_1 = F$)

32 (*a*) When the mass is at the lowest point of the vertical circle, the stretching force,

$$F = mg + mr\omega^2 = mg + mr(2\pi v)^2$$
$$= 15 \times 10 + 15 \times 2 \times (2\pi \times 2)^2$$
$$= 4887 \text{ N}$$

$\because \quad \Delta L = \frac{FL}{AY}$

$$\therefore \quad \Delta L = \frac{4887 \times 2}{0.02 \times 10^{-4} \times 2 \times 10^{11}}$$
$$= 2.4 \text{ cm}$$

33 (*d*) Let the original unstretched length be l.

$$\therefore \quad Y = \frac{T}{A} \frac{l}{\Delta l}$$

Now, $Y = \frac{2}{A} \frac{l}{(l_1 - l)} = \frac{8}{A} \frac{l}{(l_2 - l)}$

$$= \frac{14}{A} \frac{l}{(l_3 - l)}$$

$\therefore \quad 2(l_3 - l) = 14(l_1 - l)$

or $2l_3 + 12l = 14l_1$ ...(i)

Again, $8(l_3 - l) = 14(l_2 - l)$

$\Rightarrow \quad 8l_3 + 6l = 14l_2$ ... (ii)

To obtain l_3, solve Eqs. (i) and (ii), we get

$\therefore \quad l_3 = (2l_2 - l_1)$ m

34 (*d*) Here, volume is same for both wires.

$\therefore \quad A_1 l_1 = A_2 l_2$

$$\Rightarrow \quad l_2 = \frac{A_1 l_1}{A_2} = \frac{A l_1}{4A} = \frac{l_1}{4} \Rightarrow \frac{l_1}{l_2} = 4$$

Now, $\Delta x_1 = \frac{F_1 l_1}{AY}$ $(\because \Delta l = \Delta x)$

and $\Delta x_2 = \frac{F_2 l_2}{4AY}$

Given, $\Delta x_1 = \Delta x_2$

$$\Rightarrow \quad \frac{F_1 l_1}{AY} = \frac{F_2 l_2}{4AY}$$

$$\Rightarrow \quad F_2 = 4F_1 \times \frac{l_1}{l_2} = 4F_1 \times 4$$

$\therefore \quad F_2 = 16F_1$

35 (*d*) Both wires have the same tensile stress.

As, stress = Young's modulus × strain

$$\therefore \frac{w}{A} = Y_C \times \frac{\Delta L_C}{L_C} = Y_S \times \frac{\Delta L_S}{L_S} \quad \text{...(i)}$$

$$\therefore \quad \frac{\Delta L_C}{\Delta L_S} = \frac{L_C}{L_S} \times \frac{Y_S}{Y_C}$$

Here, for copper wire, $L_C = 3.2$ m,

$Y_C = 1.2 \times 10^{11}$ N m^{-2}

For steel wire, $L_S = 1.6$ m,

$Y_S = 2 \times 10^{11}$ Nm^{-2}

$$\therefore \frac{\Delta L_C}{\Delta L_S} = \left(\frac{3.2 \text{ m}}{1.6 \text{ m}}\right) \times \frac{(2 \times 10^{11} \text{ Nm}^{-2})}{(1.2 \times 10^{11} \text{ Nm}^{-2})}$$

$$= \frac{10}{3} \quad \text{...(ii)}$$

The total elongation is

$\Delta L_C + \Delta L_S = 1.3$ mm

$= 13 \times 10^{-4}$ m ...(iii)

Solving Eqs. (ii) and (iii), we get

$\Delta L_C = 10 \times 10^{-4}$ m

and $\Delta L_S = 3 \times 10^{-4}$ m

From Eq. (i),

$$w = A \times Y_C \times \frac{\Delta L_C}{L_C}$$

$$= \pi \times (2 \times 10^{-3})^2 \times 1.2 \times 10^{11} \times \frac{10 \times 10^{-4}}{3.2}$$

$$= 4.7 \times 10^2 \text{ N}$$

36 (*d*) Let L_1, L_2 be the lengths and Y_1, Y_2 be the values of Young's moduli of the copper and steel wires.

Then, $L_1 = 50$ cm; $L_2 = 200$ cm;

$Y_1 = 12 \times 10^{11}$ dyne cm^{-2},

$Y_2 = 20 \times 10^{11}$ dyne cm^{-2}

If l_1 and l_2 are respective increase in the lengths of the two wires, then $l_1 + l_2 = 2$ cm ...(i)

Let F be the force applied, then

$$l_1 = \frac{F \times L_1}{a \times Y_1} = \frac{F \times 50}{a \times 12 \times 10^{11}} \quad \text{...(ii)}$$

Also,

$$l_2 = \frac{F \times L_2}{a \times Y_2} = \frac{F \times 200}{a \times 20 \times 10^{11}} \quad \text{...(iii)}$$

Adding Eqs. (ii) and (iii), we have

$$l_1 + l_2 = \frac{F \times 50}{a \times 12 \times 10^{11}} + \frac{F \times 200}{a \times 20 \times 10^{11}}$$

or $l_1 + l_2 = \frac{F}{a} \times 14.16 \times 10^{-11}$ ...(iv)

From the Eqs. (i) and (iv), we have

$$\frac{F}{a} \times 14.16 \times 10^{-11} = 2$$

or $\frac{F}{a} = \frac{2}{14.16 \times 10^{-11}}$

In the Eq. (ii), substituting for $\frac{F}{a}$, we have

$$l_1 = 0.58 \text{ cm}$$

Also, $l_2 = 2 - l_1 = 2 - 0.58$
$= 1.42$ cm

37 (*b*) We know that, $Y = \frac{FL}{Al}$

Force constant, $k = \frac{F}{l} = Y\frac{A}{L}$

∴ $k \propto Y$

$$\frac{k_1}{k_2} = \frac{Y_1}{Y_2} = \frac{3}{2}$$

38 (*b*) Given, $A_C = 2A_S$, $l_C = l_S$

For steel, $Y_S = \frac{FL_S}{A_S l_S} \Rightarrow L_S = \frac{A_S l_S Y_S}{F}$

For copper, $Y_C = \frac{FL_C}{A_C l_C}$

$$\Rightarrow L_C = \frac{A_C l_C Y_C}{F}$$

$$\therefore \frac{L_C}{L_S} = \frac{A_C l_C Y_C}{A_S l_S Y_S}$$

$$\Rightarrow \frac{L_C}{L_S} = \frac{2A_S l_S (1.1 \times 10^{11})}{A_S l_S (2 \times 10^{11})}$$

($\because A_C = 2A_S, l_C = l_S$)

$$\Rightarrow \frac{L_C}{L_S} = \frac{2\,(1.1)}{2} = 1.1$$

39 (*b*) Given, $\Delta L_A = 2$ mm $= 0.002$ m

$\Delta L_B = 3$ mm $= 0.003$ m

Force, $F = 2$ N

$\because \frac{r_B}{r_A} = \frac{3}{1}$ ...(i)

Since, $Y_A = Y_B$

Using Hooke's law,

stress $= Y \times$ (strain)

$$\frac{F}{A} = Y\left(\frac{\Delta L}{L}\right)$$

$$\Rightarrow L = \frac{Y \Delta L A}{F}$$

$$\Rightarrow \frac{L_A}{L_B} = \frac{Y_A}{Y_B} \times \frac{\Delta L_A}{\Delta L_B} \times \frac{A_A}{A_B} \times \frac{F_B}{F_A}$$

$$\Rightarrow \frac{L_A}{L_B} = \frac{Y_A}{Y_A} \times \frac{0.002}{0.003} \times \frac{\pi r_A^2}{\pi r_B^2} \times \frac{2}{2}$$

$\Rightarrow \frac{L_A}{L_B} = \frac{0.002}{0.003} \times \frac{r_A^2}{9r_A^2}$ [using Eq.(i)]

$$\Rightarrow \frac{L_A}{L_B} = \frac{a}{b} = \frac{2}{27}$$

40 (*d*) Using the usual expression for the Young's modulus, the force constant for the wire can be written as $k = \frac{F}{\Delta L} = \frac{YA}{L}$

For series combination of wires,

$$k_{eq} = \frac{k_1 k_2}{k_1 + k_2}$$

Substituting the values, we get

$$k_{eq} = \frac{\left(\frac{Y_1 A}{L_1}\right)\left(\frac{Y_2 A}{L_2}\right)}{\frac{Y_1 A}{L_1} + \frac{Y_2 A}{L_2}} = \frac{(Y_1 Y_2) A}{Y_1 L_2 + Y_2 L_1}$$

$$\Rightarrow k_{eq} = \frac{(1.2 \times 10^{11} \times 2 \times 10^{11})\,A}{1.2 \times 10^{11} \times 10 + 2 \times 10^{11} \times 6}$$

$$= \frac{2.4 \times 10^{11}}{(24)} = 10^{10}$$

($\because L_1 = 6$ m and $L_2 = 10$ m)

$$\Rightarrow k_{eq} = 10^{10} A$$

41 (*d*) The axial force 40 kN is transmitted to each of the three parts of the bar.

Stress in part *AB*

$$= \frac{40000}{\frac{\pi}{4} \times (60)^2} = 14.15 \text{ N/mm}^2$$

Stress in part *BC*

$$= \frac{40000}{\frac{\pi}{4} \times (25)^2} = 81.48 \text{ N/mm}^2$$

Stress in part *CD* $= 14.15$ N/mm^2

Therefore, total extension of the rod = extension in parts *AB*, *BC* and *CA*

$$= \left(\frac{14.15}{2 \times 10^5} \times 100\right) 2 + \left(\frac{81.48}{2 \times 10^5} \times 200\right)$$

$= 0.096$ mm

42 (*a*) Let $L_A = 4L$ and $r_A = 5r$

Then, $L_B = 7L$ and $r_B = 2r$

Further, $l_A = 1$ mm

For steel wire *A*,

$$Y = \frac{F \times L_A}{\pi r_A^2 \times l_A} = \frac{F \times 4L}{\pi \times (5r)^2 \times 1}$$

or $Y = \frac{4FL}{25\pi r^2}$ ...(i)

For steel wire *B*,

$$Y = \frac{F \times L_B}{\pi r_B^2 \times l_B} = \frac{F \times 7L}{\pi \times (2r)^2 \times 1}$$

or $Y = \frac{7F \times L}{4\pi r^2 l_B}$ ...(ii)

From Eqs. (i) and (ii), we have

$$\frac{F \times 7L}{4\pi r^2 \times l_B} = \frac{4FL}{25\pi r^2}$$

or $l_B = \frac{7 \times 25}{4 \times 4} = 10.94$ mm

43 (*d*) The equations defining the motion are

$5g - T_B = 5a$, $T_A = 5a$

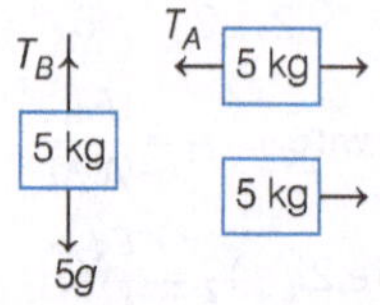

Solving, we get

$$a = \frac{5g}{15} = \frac{g}{3}, \; T_A = \frac{5}{3}g$$

and $T_B = \frac{10}{3}g$

So, strain in *A*

$$= \frac{T_A}{aY} = \frac{5}{3} \frac{g}{(0.002 \times 10^{-4})\,2 \times 10^{11}}$$

$= 4.16 \times 10^{-4}$

So, strain in *B*

$$= \frac{T_B}{aY} = \frac{10}{3} \frac{g}{(0.002 \times 10^{-4})\,2 \times 10^{11}}$$

$= 8.33 \times 10^{-4}$

44 (b)

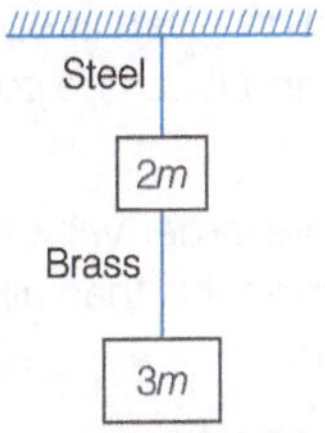

As, $Y = \frac{FL}{A\Delta L} = \frac{4FL}{\pi D^2 \Delta L}$ $\left(\because A = \frac{\pi D^2}{4}\right)$

$\therefore \quad \Delta L = \frac{4FL}{\pi D^2 Y}$

$\therefore \frac{\Delta L_s}{\Delta L_b} = \frac{F_s}{F_b} \frac{L_s}{L_b} \frac{D_b^2}{D_s^2} \frac{Y_b}{Y_s}$ ...(i)

Here, $F_s = (2m + 3m)\, g = 5mg$

$F_b = 3mg$

$\because \frac{D_s}{D_b} = p, \frac{L_s}{L_b} = q, \frac{Y_s}{Y_b} = r$ (given)

From Eq. (i), we get

$\therefore \frac{\Delta L_s}{\Delta L_b} = \left(\frac{5\, mg}{3\, mg}\right)(q)\left(\frac{1}{p}\right)^2\left(\frac{1}{r}\right)$

$= \frac{5q}{3p^2 r}$

45 (b) Given, $Y_s = 2Y_b,\ L_s = L_b,\ A_s = A_b$

As, $\Delta L = \frac{wL}{AY}$ [where, force $F = w$]

As $\Delta L_s = \Delta L_b \Rightarrow \frac{w_s L_s}{A_s Y_s} = \frac{w_b L_b}{A_b Y_b}$

$\Rightarrow \frac{w_s}{w_b} = \frac{Y_s}{Y_b} = \frac{2Y_b}{Y_b} = \frac{2}{1}$

46 (c) The situation is as shown in the figure

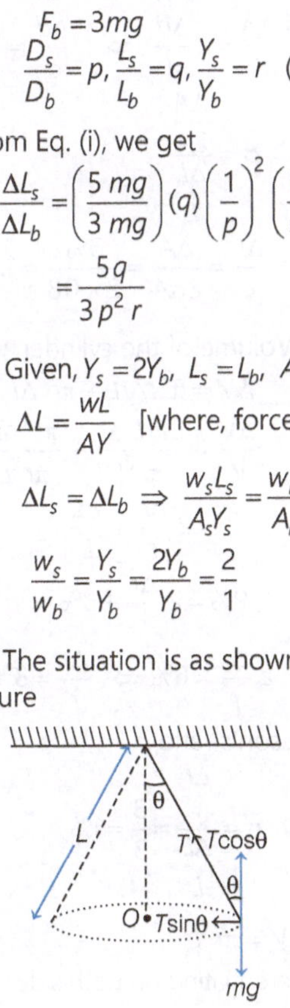

For vertical equilibrium of stone,

$T \cos\theta = mg$

or $T = \frac{mg}{\cos\theta}$ ...(i)

As, $Y = \frac{TL}{A\Delta L}$

$\Rightarrow \quad \Delta L = \frac{TL}{AY}$

$= \frac{mgL}{\cos\theta(\pi D^2/4)Y}$ [using Eq. (i)]

$= \frac{4mgL}{\pi D^2 Y \cos\theta}$

47 (c) Elongation in the wire,

$\Delta l = \frac{FL}{AY} = \frac{FL}{(\pi r^2)Y}$

$\therefore \quad \Delta l \propto \frac{L}{r^2}$

Ratio of elongation in the thin wire to that in the thick wire,

$\frac{\Delta l_1}{\Delta l_2} = \frac{L/R^2}{2L/(2R)^2} = 2$

48 (c) The perfectly rigid body won't yield any strain irrespective of the amount of stress.

$Y = \frac{\text{Stress}}{\text{Strain}} = \frac{\text{Stress}}{0} = \infty$

Bulk modulus for a rigid body is infinite because the rigid body is incompressible.

49 (a) Given, inner radius of column,

$r_1 = 20\text{ cm} = 0.2\text{ m}$

Outer radius of column,

$r_2 = 30\text{ cm} = 0.3\text{ m}$

$\therefore \quad A = \pi(r_2^2 - r_1^2) = 0.16\text{ m}^2$

Compressional force on column,

$F = Mg = 120000\text{ N}$

Now, $Y = \frac{FL}{Al}$

Strain $= \frac{l}{L} = \frac{F}{AY} = \frac{120000}{0.16 \times 2 \times 10^{11}}$

$= 3.75 \times 10^{-6}$

50 (d) As,

$\Delta l = \frac{Fl}{AY}$, thus elongation is inversely proportional to cross-section area.

51 (b) Given, radius of wire,

$r = 4\text{ mm} = 4 \times 10^{-3}\text{m}$,

twisted angle, $\theta = 30°$ and length of wire,

$L = 100\text{ cm} = 1\text{ m}$

$\therefore \ L\phi = r\theta$

$\Rightarrow \ \phi = \frac{r\theta}{L} = \frac{4 \times 10^{-3} \times 30°}{1} = 0.12°$

52 (c) Here, $\eta = 5.6 \times 10^9$ Pa,

$F = 8 \times 10^4$ N

Area of the narrow face is

$A = (30 \times 4)\text{ cm}^2$

$= 120 \times 10^{-4}\text{ m}^2$

Distance of the narrow face from the floor,

$L = 30\text{ cm} = 30 \times 10^{-2}\text{ m}$

If the upper edge of the slab gets displaced through a distance x, then

$x = \frac{FL}{A\eta} = \frac{8 \times 10^4 \times 30 \times 10^{-2}}{120 \times 10^{-4} \times 5.6 \times 10^9}$

$= 3.6 \times 10^{-4}$ m

53 (c) Given, $L = 5$ cm

Lateral displacement,

$x = 0.025$ cm

Shear modulus,

$G = 2.08 \times 10^{11}$ dyne cm^{-2}

Shearing strain,

$\theta = \frac{x}{L} = \frac{0.025}{5} = 0.005$

$\therefore \quad G = \frac{F}{A\theta}$

$\Rightarrow \quad F = GA\theta = 2.08 \times 10^{11} \times (5)^2 \times 0.005$

$= 26 \times 10^9$ dyne

54 (b) The lead slab is fixed and force is applied parallel to the narrow face as shown in the figure.

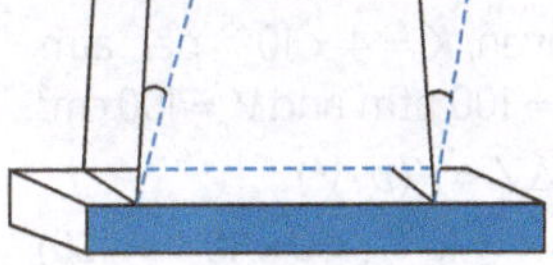

Area of the face parallel to which this force is applied,

$A = 40\text{ cm} \times 20\text{ cm}$

$= 0.08\text{ m}^2$

If ΔL is the displacement of the upper edge of the slab due to tangential force F, then $\Delta L = \frac{FL}{\eta A}$

$$\Rightarrow \Delta L = \frac{12 \times 10^4 \times 0.4}{5.6 \times 10^9 \times 0.08} = 0.11 \text{ mm}$$

55 (c) Here, $p = 100 \text{ atm} = 10^7 \text{ N/m}^2$ and $\Delta V = 0.01\% V$

$$\therefore \frac{\Delta V}{V} = 0.0001$$

$$|B| = \frac{p}{\Delta V / V} = \frac{10^7}{0.0001}$$

$$= 1 \times 10^{11} \text{ Nm}^{-2}$$

$$= 1 \times 10^{12} \text{ dyne cm}^{-2}$$

$[\because 1 \text{ N} = 10^5 \text{ dyne}]$

56 (c) We know that, $B = \frac{Mg / A}{\delta V / V}$

$$\Rightarrow \frac{\delta V}{V} = \frac{Mg}{BA} \quad \text{...(i)}$$

Now, $V = \frac{4}{3}\pi R^3$ ...(ii)

On differentiating,

$$\delta V = 4\pi R^2 \delta R \quad \text{...(iii)}$$

On dividing Eq. (iii) by Eq. (ii), we get

$$\frac{\delta V}{V} = \frac{3\delta R}{R}$$

$$\therefore \frac{\delta R}{R} = \frac{Mg}{3BA} \quad \text{[using Eq. (i)]}$$

57 (a) Compressibility,

$$|K| = \frac{1}{|\text{Bulk modulus of elasticity}|}$$

Bulk modulus, $|B| = \frac{pV}{\Delta V}$

$$\Rightarrow K = \frac{1}{\left(\frac{pV}{\Delta V}\right)} = \frac{\Delta V}{pV}$$

Given, $K = 4 \times 10^{-5}$ per atm, $p = 100$ atm and $V = 100 \text{ cm}^3$.

$$\therefore \Delta V = K(p \cdot V)$$

$$= 4 \times 10^{-5} (100 \times 10^{-6} \times 100)$$

$$= 0.4 \times 10^{-6} \text{m}^3 = 0.4 \text{ cm}^3$$

58 (c) Given, depth of ocean,

$$d = 2700 \text{ m}$$

Density of water, $\rho = 10^3 \text{ kg/m}^3$ and compressibility

$$= 45.4 \times 10^{-11} \text{ Pa}^{-1}$$

The pressure at the bottom of ocean is given by

$$p = \rho g d = 10^3 \times 10 \times 2700$$

$$= 27 \times 10^6 \text{ Pa}$$

So, fractional compression
$= \text{compressibility} \times \text{pressure}$
$= 45.4 \times 10^{-11} \times 27 \times 10^6 = 1.2 \times 10^{-2}$

59 (a) Given, $\frac{\Delta V}{V} = 0.01\% = 1 \times 10^{-4}$

$$\text{Strain} = \frac{\Delta l}{l} = \frac{\text{Stress}}{Y}$$

$$= \frac{4 \times 10^6}{2 \times 10^{11}} = 2 \times 10^{-5}$$

As we know that, $V = \pi r^2 l$

$$\Delta V = 2\pi r l \Delta r + \pi r^2 \Delta l$$

$$\Rightarrow \frac{\Delta V}{V} = \frac{2\pi r l \Delta r + \pi r^2 \Delta l}{\pi r^2 l}$$

$$= 2\frac{\Delta r}{r} + \frac{\Delta l}{l}$$

$$\Rightarrow 1 \times 10^{-4} = 2\frac{\Delta r}{r} + 0.2 \times 10^{-4}$$

$$\Rightarrow \frac{\Delta r}{r} = \frac{0.8 \times 10^{-4}}{2}$$

$$= 0.4 \times 10^{-4}$$

60 (d) Let initial length of each cube is l.

$$\text{Final length} = \left(1 - \frac{2}{100}\right)l = \frac{49}{50}l$$

Initial volume, $V_i = l^3$

Final volume, $V_f = \left(\frac{49}{50}l\right)^3$

$\therefore$ Change in volume, $\Delta V = V_f - V_i$

$$= \left(\frac{49}{50}l\right)^3 - l^3$$

$$\therefore \frac{\Delta V}{V} = \left(\frac{49}{50}\right)^3 - 1 = 0.058 \approx 0.06$$

$$\text{Bulk modulus, } B = \frac{-\Delta p}{\left(\frac{\Delta V}{V}\right)} = \frac{4 \times 10^4}{0.06}$$

$$= 6.67 \times 10^5 \text{ N/m}^2$$

61 (b) Statement given in option (b) is incorrect and it can be corrected as, Gases are about a million times compressible than solids. So, solids are least compressible.

62 (d) Statement given in option (d) is incorrect and it can be corrected as,

Metals have larger values of Young's modulus than alloy and elastomers.

63 (c) Poisson's ratio,

$$\sigma = \frac{\text{Lateral strain}}{\text{Longitudinal strain}} = \frac{\left(\frac{\Delta d}{d}\right)}{\left(\frac{\Delta l}{l}\right)}$$

$$A = \pi\left(\frac{d}{2}\right)^2$$

$$\Delta A = \frac{2\pi d \cdot \Delta d}{4}$$

$$\therefore \frac{\Delta A}{A} = 2\frac{\Delta d}{d} \Rightarrow \frac{\Delta d}{d} = \frac{\Delta A}{2A}$$

$$\text{So, } \sigma = \frac{\frac{\Delta A}{2A}}{\frac{\Delta L}{L}}$$

$$\therefore \frac{\Delta L}{L} = \frac{\Delta A}{2\sigma A} = \frac{3\%}{2 \times 0.8} = 1.86\%$$

64 (c) Volume of the cylinder, $V = \pi r^2 L$

$$\therefore \Delta V = \pi 2r\Delta r L + \pi r^2 \Delta L$$

$$\Rightarrow \frac{\Delta V}{V} = \frac{2\pi r L \,\Delta r}{\pi r^2 L} + \frac{\pi r^2 \Delta L}{\pi r^2 L}$$

$$= 2\frac{\Delta r}{r} + \frac{\Delta L}{L}$$

$$\Rightarrow 9\% = 2\frac{\Delta r}{r} + 3\%$$

$$\Rightarrow 2\frac{\Delta r}{r} = 6\% \Rightarrow \frac{\Delta r}{r} = 3\%$$

Poisson's ratio,

$$\sigma = \frac{\frac{\Delta r}{r}}{\frac{\Delta L}{L}} = \frac{3}{3} = 1\%$$

65 (d) $V = \pi r^2 L$

Differentiating on both sides, we get

$$\Delta V = \pi(2r\Delta r)L + \pi r^2 \Delta L$$

As, $\Delta V = 0$.

Hence, $0 = 2\pi r L \Delta r + \pi r^2 \Delta L$

$$\therefore \frac{\Delta r / r}{\Delta L / L} = -\frac{1}{2}$$

Poisson's ratio

$$= \frac{\text{Lateral strain}}{\text{Longitudinal strain}}$$

$$= \frac{\Delta r / r}{\Delta L / L} = \frac{1}{2} = 0.5$$

[neglecting negative sign]

67 (*b*) Poisson's ratio, $\sigma = 0.4$

Area, $A = \pi r^2 = \pi \left(\frac{d}{2}\right)^2 = \frac{\pi d^2}{4}$ ...(i)

or $d^2 = \frac{4A}{\pi}$

On differentiating both sides, we get

$$2d \cdot \Delta d = \frac{4}{\pi} \cdot \Delta A$$

So, $\Delta A = \frac{\pi d \cdot \Delta d}{2}$ ...(ii)

On dividing Eq. (ii) by Eq. (i), we get

$$\frac{\Delta A}{A} = \frac{\pi \cdot \frac{d}{2} \cdot \Delta d}{\pi \cdot d^2 / 4}$$

$= 2 \cdot \frac{\Delta d}{d}$ ...(iii)

Given, $\frac{\Delta A}{A} \times 100\% = 2\%$ ...(iv)

From Eqs. (iii) and (iv),

$$2\% = 2 \cdot \frac{\Delta d}{d} \text{ or } \frac{\Delta d}{d} = 1\%$$

Given, Poisson's ratio,

$$\sigma = \frac{\Delta d / d}{\Delta l / l} = 0.4$$

or $\frac{\Delta d}{d} = 0.4 \left(\frac{\Delta l}{l}\right)$

$\Rightarrow \frac{1}{0.4} \cdot \frac{\Delta d}{d} = \frac{\Delta l}{l}$

Percentage increase in its length,

i.e. $\left(\frac{\Delta l}{l}\right) \times 100\% = 2.5 \times 1\% = 2.5\%$

68 (*c*) Statement given in option (c) is correct, rest are incorrect and these can be corrected as

The ratio of the lateral strain to the longitudinal strain is called Poisson's ratio σ.

Its value depends only on the nature of the material.

It is the ratio of two similar quantities, so it is unitless and dimensionless quantity.

The practical value of Poisson's ratio lies between 0 and 0.5.

69 (*b*) Work done, $W = \frac{1}{2} \times F \times \Delta L$

For a given F, $W \propto \Delta L$ ...(i)

and $\Delta L = \frac{FL}{AY}$

$\Delta L \propto \frac{1}{Y}$ ...(ii)

From Eqs. (i) and (ii), we get

$$W \propto \frac{1}{Y}$$

$$\Rightarrow \frac{W_{steel}}{W_{copper}} = \frac{Y_{copper}}{Y_{steel}}$$

As, $Y_{copper} < Y_{steel}$

$\Rightarrow W_{steel} < W_{copper}$

So, less work is done on steel spring.

70 (*a*) Work done in stretching the wire through 0.61 mm under the load of 3 kg-wt,

$$W_1 = \frac{1}{2} \times \text{stretching force} \times \text{extension}$$

$$= \frac{1}{2} \times 3 \times 9.8 \times 0.61 \times 10^{-3}$$

$$= 8.967 \times 10^{-3} \text{ J}$$

Work done in stretching the wire through 1.02 mm under the load of 5 kg-wt.

$$W_2 = \frac{1}{2} \times 5 \times 9.8 \times 1.02 \times 10^{-3}$$

$$= 24.99 \times 10^{-3} \text{ J}$$

Hence, the work done in stretching the wire from 0.61 mm to 1.02 mm is

$$\Delta W = W_2 - W_1$$

$$= (24.99 - 8.967) \times 10^{-3}$$

$$\simeq 16 \times 10^{-3} \text{ J}$$

72 (*d*) Given, $d_1 = 1$ mm, $d_2 = 2$ mm, $F_1 = 1000$ N, $F_2 = ?$

Breaking force or tension $\propto$ area of cross-section

$$\therefore \frac{F_2}{F_1} = \left(\frac{d_2}{d_1}\right)^2$$

$$\Rightarrow \frac{F_2}{1000} = \left(\frac{2}{1}\right)^2$$

$$\Rightarrow F_2 = 1000 \times 4 = 4000 \text{ N}$$

73 (*d*) Given, Young's modulus $= 2 \times 10^{11}$ Nm^{-2}

Strain = 0.15

$$\therefore Y = \frac{\text{Stress}}{\text{Strain}}$$

$\Rightarrow$ Stress $= Y \times$ Strain

$$= 2 \times 10^{11} \times 0.15$$

$$= 3 \times 10^{10} \text{ Nm}^{-2}$$

74 (*b*) Force, $F = m\alpha = \rho V \alpha$

$\because m = \rho V$

$\therefore$ Volume

$(V) = \text{Area}(A) \times \text{Length}(L)$

$\therefore F = \rho A \frac{L}{2} \alpha$ $\left[\because \text{For mid-point of the rod, length} = \frac{L}{2}\right]$

$$\Rightarrow F = \frac{L}{2} A \rho \alpha$$

$$\therefore \text{Stress} = \frac{F}{A} = \frac{1}{2} L \rho \alpha$$

75 (*b*) A beam of length l, breadth b and depth d when loaded at the centre by a load w depresses by an amount given by

$$\delta = \frac{wl^3}{4bd^3Y}$$

i.e. $\delta \propto \frac{1}{Y}$

76 (*c*) Since, depression δ in the bar at centre is directly proportional to load.

i.e. $\delta \propto w$

$$\frac{\delta_2}{\delta_1} = \frac{w_2}{w_1} = \frac{2w_1}{w_1} = 2$$

$\therefore \delta_2 = 2\delta_1$

Hence, depression in the bar at the centre is increased to double.

77 (*b*) Given, $A_1 = 5 \times 10^{-4}$ m^2

Load, $F_1 = 10$ metric tonne $\times g$

$= 10^4 g$N

For second condition,

$F_2 = 20$ metric tonne $\times g$

$= 2 \times 10^4 g$N

For the condition of elastic limit,

$$\frac{F_1}{A_1} = \frac{F_2}{A_2} \Rightarrow A_2 = \frac{F_2}{F_1} A_1$$
$$= \frac{2 \times 10^4\, g}{10^4 g} \times 5 \times 10^{-4}$$
$$= 10 \times 10^{-4} \text{m}^2$$

78 (*d*) For a mountain of height h and base area A, weight, $w = Ah\rho g$

So, pressure at the base due to its own weight, $p = \frac{w}{A} = \frac{Ah\rho g}{A} = h\rho g$

The mountain will exist, if

$h\rho g \leq$ Breaking stress

$$\therefore \quad h \leq \frac{\text{Breaking stress}}{\rho g}$$
$$h \leq \frac{9 \times 10^7}{1.5 \times 10^3 \times 10} = 6 \text{ km}$$
$$\therefore h_{max} = 6 \text{ km}$$

79 (*b*) Radius of a rivet,

$$r = \frac{8}{2} \text{mm} = 4 \times 10^{-3} \text{ m}$$

Maximum stress $= 5.38 \times 10^7$ Pa

Maximum load on a rivet

= Maximum stress × Area of cross-section

$$= 5.38 \times 10^7 \times \pi \times (4 \times 10^{-3})^2$$
$$= 2700 \text{ N}$$

∴ Maximum tension that can be exerted by rivet strip

$$= 4 \times 2700 = 10800 \text{ N} = 108 \times 10^2 \text{ N}$$

80 (*d*) Given, $l = 2$ m

$$\Delta l = 4 \text{ mm} = 4 \times 10^{-3} \text{ m}$$
$$A = 2 \text{ mm}^2 = 2 \times 10^{-6} \text{ m}$$
$$Y = 2 \times 10^{11} \text{ N/m}^2$$

Elastic potential energy stored in wire,

$$u = \frac{1}{2} \times \text{Stress} \times \text{Strain} \times \text{Volume of the wire}$$
$$= \frac{1}{2} \times Y \times (\text{Strain})^2 \times \text{Volume of the wire}$$
$$= \frac{1}{2} \times 2 \times 10^{11} \times \left(\frac{4 \times 10^{-3}}{2}\right)^2 \times 2 \times 2 \times 10^{-6}$$
$$\therefore u = 1.6 \text{ J}$$

81 (*d*) Elastic potential energy per unit volume is

$$u = \frac{1}{2} \frac{(\text{stress})^2}{Y}$$
$$\Rightarrow u \propto (\text{stress})^2$$
$$\therefore \quad \frac{u_1}{u_2} = \frac{(\text{stress})_1^2}{(\text{stress})_2^2} = \frac{(F_1/A_1)^2}{(F_2/A_2)^2} \quad \left[\because \frac{F}{A} = \text{stress}\right]$$

As both the wires are stretched by the same load, therefore

$$F_1 = F_2$$
$$\therefore \quad \frac{u_1}{u_2} = \left(\frac{A_2}{A_1}\right)^2 = \left(\frac{D_2^2}{D_1^2}\right)^2 = \left(\frac{D_2}{D_1}\right)^4$$
$$= \left(\frac{2}{1}\right)^4 = \frac{16}{1}$$

82 (*b*) In stretching a wire, the work done against internal restoring force is stored as elastic potential energy in wire and given by

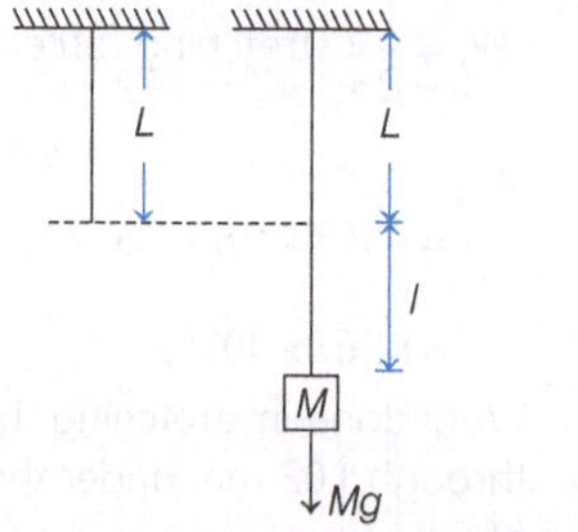

$$U = W = \frac{1}{2} \times \text{Force } (F) \times \text{Elongation } (l)$$
$$= \frac{1}{2} Fl = \frac{1}{2} \times Mg \times l = \frac{1}{2} Mgl$$

83 (*b*) Loss in gravitational potential energy of mass $m = mgl$

Elastic potential energy stored in wire = Work done

$$= \frac{1}{2} \times \text{Stretching force} \times \text{Extension}$$
$$= \frac{1}{2} mgl$$
$$\therefore \text{Heat produced} = \frac{1}{2} mgl$$

Thus, the statement given in option (b) is incorrect, rest are correct.

Assertion and Reason Questions

1 (*a*) The elasticity of a material is the ratio of stress and strain. In given case, the strain produced in the rubber is more than that in steel.

As rubber is less elastic than steel. Therefore, Assertion and Reason are correct and Reason is the correct explanation of Assertion.

2 (*a*) Spring balance shows incorrect reading after using it for a long time as with time the spring in it loses its elastic strength.

Therefore, Assertion and Reason are correct and Reason is the correct explanation of Assertion.

3 (*a*) A single wire of a radius would practically be a rigid rod. So, the ropes are always made of a number of thin wires braided together, like in pigtails, for ease in manufacturing, flexibility and strength.

Therefore, Assertion and Reason are correct and Reason is the correct explanation of Assertion.

4 (c) According to Hooke's law within the elastic limit, stress is directly proportional to the strain.

i.e. Stress ∝ Strain

$$\Rightarrow \frac{F}{A} \propto \frac{\Delta l}{l} \Rightarrow F \propto \Delta l$$

Hence, elongation produced in a body is directly proportional to the applied force.

Therefore, Assertion is correct but Reason is incorrect.

5 (*a*) Young's modulus of a material,

$$Y = \frac{\text{Stress}}{\text{Strain}}$$
$$\therefore \quad \text{Stress} = \frac{\text{Restoring force } (F)}{\text{Area } (A)}$$

As, restoring force is zero for a plastic body.

$$\therefore \quad Y = 0$$

Therefore, Assertion and Reason are correct and Reason is the correct explanation of Assertion.

6 (c) When a spring is loaded, then shearing stress is produced, which changes the shape of spring. Therefore, Assertion is correct but Reason is incorrect.

7 (a) The strain produced by a hydraulic pressure is called volumetric strain, as pressure creates a normal force on every point and is defined as the ratio of change in volume ΔV to the original volume V.

i.e. Volume strain $= \frac{\Delta V}{V}$

Therefore, Assertion and Reason are correct and Reason is the correct explanation of Assertion.

8 (a) Molecules in gases are very poorly coupled to their neighbours molecules.

Since, compressibility is defined as the fractional change in volume per unit increase or decrease in pressure.

$$K = 1/B = -(1/\Delta p) \times (\Delta V/V)$$

where, B is bulk modulus and Δp change in pressure.

So, in gases, fractional change in volume with per unit increase or decrease in pressure is not very prominent.

Thus, they have large compressibility.

Therefore, Assertion and Reason are correct and Reason is the correct explanation of Assertion.

9 (a) The maximum height of a mountain on the earth is ~10 km.

As a mountain base is not under uniform compression and this provides some shearing stress to the rocks under which they can flow.

Thus, mathematically, it has been calculated that under the elastic limit, maximum height of a mountain is ~10 km.

Therefore, Assertion and Reason are correct and Reason is the correct explanation of Assertion.

10 (a) If a solid sphere placed in the fluid under high pressure, then it is compressed uniformly on all sides. The force applied by the fluids acts in perpendicular direction at each point of the surface and the body is said to be under hydraulic compression.

This leads to decrease in its volume without any change of its geometrical shape.

Therefore, Assertion and Reason are correct and Reason is the correct explanation of Assertion.

Statement Based Questions

1 (b) Statement I is correct but Statement II is incorrect.

Relative displacement happens because tangential force applied only on the one face of the body. The force applied by the fluid acts in perpendicular direction at each point of the surface of a submerge body.

3 (a) Both Statement I and Statement II are incorrect.

If ultimate strength and fracture points of an object is very far apart, then object is ductile.

The stress-strain curve vary from material to material.

4 (b) Statement I is correct but Statement II is incorrect.

Elastomers are those materials which can be elastically stretched to a large value strain. Due to large strain for a given stress, Young's modulus of elastomers is very small.

5 (b) Statement I is correct but Statement II is incorrect.

It is difficult to twist a small rod as compared to long rod.

As we know,

For twisting angle of shear, $\phi \propto \frac{1}{L}$.

It means, L is always responsible for shear angle and if L is more than angle will be small.

6 (a) Both Statement I and Statement II are incorrect. Value of Poisson's ratio depends only on the nature of material.

The practical value of Poisson's ratio lies between 0 and 0.5.

7 (b) Statement I is correct but Statement II is incorrect.

Elastic potential energy of cube before increase in its side length,

$$W_1 = \frac{1}{2} \times Y \times \left(\frac{\Delta L}{L}\right)^2 \times L^3$$

Elastic potential energy of cube after increase in its side length,

$$W_2 = \frac{1}{2} \times Y \times \left(\frac{\Delta L_1}{2L}\right)^2 \times (2L)^3$$

$\because \; W_1 = W_2$

$$\Rightarrow \frac{1}{2} \times Y \times \left(\frac{\Delta L}{L}\right)^2 \times L^3 = \frac{1}{2} \times Y \times \left(\frac{\Delta L_1}{2L}\right)^2 \times (2L)^3$$

$$\Delta L_1 = \frac{1}{\sqrt{2}} \Delta L$$

8 (b) Statement I is correct but Statement II is incorrect.

A factor of safety of value 1 mean that a structure or component will fail exactly when it reaches the designed load and cannot support any additional load.

Matching Type Questions

1 (a) A. Stress × Strain $= Nm^{-2}$

$= (Nm)m^{-3} = Jm^{-3}$

B. $\frac{YA}{l} = \frac{Nm^{-2} \times m^2}{m} = Nm^{-1}$

C. $Yl^3 = Nm^{-2} \times m^3 = Nm = J$

D. $Fl/AY = \frac{N \times m}{m^2 \times Nm^{-2}} = m$

Hence, A → 3, B → 2, C → 1 and D → 4.

2 (*b*) The resolved part of F along the normal is the tensile stress on this plane and the resolved part parallel to the plane is the shearing stress on the plane as shown below.

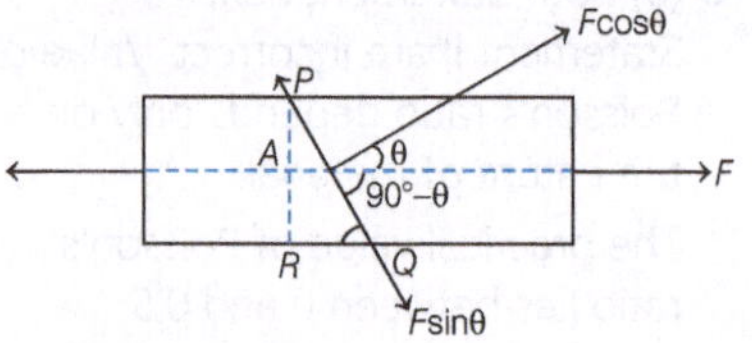

Given, cross-section area of bar = A

Let cross-section area of plane = A'

Then, from ΔPQR

$$\because \frac{A}{A'} = \sin(90° - \theta) = \cos\theta$$

$$\therefore \text{Area, } A' = \frac{A}{\cos\theta} = A\sec\theta$$

A. Tensile stress

$$= \frac{\text{Force}}{\text{Area}} = \frac{F\cos\theta}{A\sec\theta} = \frac{F}{A}\cos^2\theta$$

(area of plane section = $A\sec\theta$)

B. Shearing stress

$$= \frac{\text{Force}}{\text{Area}} = \frac{F\sin\theta}{A\sec\theta}$$

$$= \frac{F}{A}\sin\theta\cos\theta = \frac{F}{2A}\sin 2\theta$$

C. Tensile stress or strength will be maximum when $\cos^2\theta$ is maximum, i.e. $\cos\theta = 1$ or $\theta = 0°$.

D. Shearing stress will be maximum when $\sin 2\theta$ is maximum, i.e. or $2\theta = 90°$, i.e. $\theta = 45°$.

Hence, A → 2, B → 3, C → 1 and D → 4.

3 (*c*) A. Longitudinal stress can be a tensile or compressive. During tensile stress, length of wire increases and during compressive stress, length of wire decreases.

B. When deforming force is applied tangentially to a surface of the body, then tangential or shear stress is produced and shape of the body changes.

C. Breaking stress is independent of area of cross-section of wire.

D. Bulk stress is equal to change in pressure.

Hence, A → 3, B → 4, C → 1 and D → 2.

Numerical Type Questions

1 (*16*) From the graph, Young's modulus can be calculated as

$$Y = \frac{\text{Stress}}{\text{Strain}} = \frac{80 - 20}{4\times10^{-10} - 1\times10^{-10}}$$

$$= 20\times10^{10}\ \text{N/m}^2$$

Energy density,

$$E = \frac{1}{2}\times\text{Stress}\times\text{Strain}$$

$$= \frac{1}{2}\times Y\times(\text{Strain})^2$$

Given, strain = 4×10^{-4}

$$\therefore E = \frac{1}{2}\times20\times10^{10}\times(4\times10^{-4})^2$$

$$= 16\times10^3\ \text{J/m}^3$$

$$= 16\ \text{kJ/m}^3$$

2 (*176.78*) The copper and steel wires are under same tensile stress because they have same tension and same area of cross-section.

As, Stress = Strain × Young's modulus

$$\frac{W}{A} = \frac{\Delta L_C}{L_C}\times Y_C = \frac{\Delta L_S}{L_S}\times Y_S$$

where, C and S refer to copper and steel.

Now, $\dfrac{\Delta L_C}{\Delta L_S} = \dfrac{Y_S}{Y_C}\times\dfrac{L_C}{L_S}$

$$\Rightarrow \frac{\Delta L_C}{\Delta L_S} = \frac{2\times10^{11}}{1.1\times10^{11}}\times\frac{2.2}{1.6} = 2.5 \quad \text{...(i)}$$

and $\Delta L_C + \Delta L_S = 7\times10^{-4}$ m (given) ...(ii)

From Eqs. (i) and (ii), we get

$\Delta L_C = 5\times10^{-4}$ m, $\Delta L_S = 2\times10^{-4}$ m

$$Y = \frac{F\times L}{A\times\Delta L} \Rightarrow F = \frac{YA\Delta L}{L}$$

$$F = \frac{1.1\times10^{11}\times\pi\times(1.5)^2\times10^{-6}\times5\times10^{-4}}{2.2} = 176.78\ \text{N}$$

3 (*10*) We know that, $F = kx$

$$\therefore F = \frac{YA}{l_0}\cdot x$$

When $F = 60$ N,

$$60 = k(l_1 - l_0) \quad \text{...(i)}$$

When $F = 80$ N,

$$80 = k(l_2 - l_0) \quad \text{...(ii)}$$

So, $\dfrac{80}{60} = \dfrac{k(l_2 - l_0)}{k(l_1 - l_0)}$

Given, $10l_2 = 11l_1$, $l_2 = 1.1l_1$

$$\frac{80}{60} = \frac{(1.1l_1 - l_0)}{l_1 - l_0}$$

$$4l_1 - 4l_0 = 3.3l_1 - 3l_0 \Rightarrow 0.7l_1 = l_0$$

$$\Rightarrow l_0 = \frac{7}{10}l_1$$

So, $x = 10$

4 (*100*) We know that,

$$\text{Strain} = \frac{\text{Stress}}{Y} \qquad \left(\because \text{Stress} = \frac{F}{A}\right)$$

$$\text{Strain} = \frac{F}{A\cdot Y}$$

Longitudinal strain

$$= \frac{62.8\times1000}{\pi r^2\times2\times10^{11}}$$

$$= \frac{200}{2}\times10^{-5} = 100\times10^{-5}$$

So, $x = 100$

5 (*1*) Young modulus, $Y = \dfrac{F}{A}\times\dfrac{l}{\Delta l}$

$$\Rightarrow Y = \frac{F}{\pi r^2}\times\frac{l}{\Delta l}$$

$$\Rightarrow \Delta l = \frac{Fl}{\pi r^2 Y} \Rightarrow \Delta l \propto \frac{Fl}{r^2}$$

($\because$ Y is same for both wires)

$$\therefore \frac{\Delta l_1}{\Delta l_2} = \frac{F_1}{F_2}\times\frac{l_1}{l_2}\times\frac{r_2^2}{r_1^2}$$

$$= \frac{1}{3}\times\frac{3}{1}\times\frac{1}{4} = \frac{1}{4}$$

So, value of x is 1.

6 (*4*) Given, $L = 2$ m

$l = 0.4$ mm $= 0.4\times10^{-3}$ m

$d = 0.4$ mm $= 0.4\times10^{-3}$ m

Extension of the length,

$$\Delta l = \pm 0.02 \text{ mm}$$

Uncertainty in diameter of wire,

$$\Delta d = \pm 0.01 \text{ mm}$$

Young's modulus,

$$Y = \frac{mg \times L}{A \times l} = \frac{mgL}{\pi\left(\frac{d}{2}\right)^2 l} = \frac{4mgL}{\pi (d)^2 l} \quad \text{...(i)}$$

After putting the given values in Eq. (i), we get

$$Y = \frac{4 \times 1 \times 10 \times 2}{\pi \times (0.4 \times 10^{-3})^2 \times 0.4 \times 10^{-3}}$$

$$= 0.398 \times 10^{12} \text{ N/m}^2$$

$$\frac{\Delta Y}{Y} = \frac{\Delta l}{l} + 2\frac{\Delta d}{d}$$

$$= \frac{0.02}{0.4} + 2 \times \frac{0.01}{0.4} = 0.1$$

$$\Rightarrow \Delta Y = 0.1 \times Y = 0.1 \times 0.398 \times 10^{12}$$

$$\simeq 4 \times 10^{10} \text{ N/m}^2$$

So, value of x is 4.

7 (*49*) Given, $L = 5 \text{ cm} = 5 \times 10^{-2} \text{m}$,

$F = 50 \text{ kgf} = 490 \text{ N}$

$\Delta L = 0.2 \text{ cm} = 0.2 \times 10^{-2} \text{m}$

Shearing stress

$$= \frac{F}{A} = \frac{F}{L^2} = \frac{490}{(5 \times 10^{-2})^2}$$

$$= 19.6 \times 10^4 \text{ Nm}^{-2}$$

Shearing strain

$$= \frac{\Delta L}{L} = \frac{0.2 \times 10^{-2}}{5 \times 10^{-2}} = 0.04$$

Shear modulus of elasticity,

$$G = \frac{\text{Shearing stress}}{\text{Shearing strain}} = \frac{19.6 \times 10^4}{0.04}$$

$$= 49 \times 10^5 \text{ Nm}^{-2}$$

8 (*20.81*) Force, $F = mg = 98$ N

Diameter, $D = 2 \text{ mm} = 2 \times 10^{-3}$ m

Poisson ratio, $\sigma = 0.4$

Young's modulus,

$Y = 1.2 \times 10^{11} \text{ N/m}^2$, length of wire, $l = 4$ m

$$\text{As,} \quad Y = \frac{4F}{\pi D^2} \times \frac{l}{\Delta l} \Rightarrow \frac{\Delta l}{l} = \frac{4F}{\pi D^2 Y}$$

$$\text{Poisson's ratio, } \sigma = \frac{-\frac{\Delta D}{D}}{\frac{\Delta l}{l}}$$

$$\Rightarrow -\Delta D = \sigma \cdot \frac{\Delta l}{l} \cdot D$$

Lateral compression

$$= -\Delta D$$

$$= \sigma D \frac{\Delta l}{l} = \sigma D \times \frac{4F}{\pi D^2 Y} = \frac{4\sigma F}{\pi D Y}$$

$$= \frac{4 \times 0.4 \times 98}{3.14 \times 2 \times 10^{-3} \times 1.2 \times 10^{11}}$$

$$= 20.81 \times 10^{-8}$$

9 (*20*) Length of steel wire, $L = 10$ m

Change in length,

$\Delta L = 2 \text{ cm} = 2 \times 10^{-2}$ m

$Y = 2 \times 10^{11} \text{ Nm}^{-2}$

We know that, elastic potential energy,

$$U = \frac{1}{2} \times Y \times (\text{Strain})^2 \times (A \times L)$$

$$\Rightarrow A = \frac{2U}{Y \times (\text{Strain})^2 \times L}$$

$$= \frac{2U}{Y \times \left(\frac{\Delta L}{L}\right)^2 \times L} = \frac{2UL}{Y \times (\Delta L)^2}$$

$$= \frac{2 \times 80 \times 10}{2 \times 10^{11} \times (2 \times 10^{-2})^2}$$

$$= 2 \times 10^{-5} \text{ m}^2 = 20 \text{ mm}^2$$

10 (*40*) Given, $l = 1$ m,

$A = 2 \text{ mm}^2 = 2 \times 10^{-6} \text{ m}^2$,

$\Delta l = 1.1 - 1 = 0.1$ m,

$Y = 4 \times 10^8 \text{ Nm}^{-2}$

$$\text{Tension, } F = \frac{YA\Delta l}{l}$$

$$= \frac{4 \times 10^8 \times 2 \times 10^{-6} \times 0.1}{1} = 80 \text{ N}$$

Kinetic energy of the missile = Elastic potential energy

$$\frac{1}{2}mv^2 = \frac{1}{2} \times \text{tension} \times \text{extension}$$

$$v = \sqrt{\frac{F \times \Delta l}{m}} = \sqrt{\frac{80 \times 0.1}{0.02}}$$

$$(\because 20 \text{ g} = 0.02 \text{ kg})$$

$$\Rightarrow v = 40 \text{ m/s}$$

NCERT Exemplar Questions

2 (*d*) Breaking stress

$$= \frac{\text{Breaking force}}{\text{Area of cross - section}}$$

When length of the wire changes, area of cross-section remains same. Hence, breaking force will be same.

Thus, when the length of the wire is reduced to half of its original length, then the maximum load it can withstand without breaking remains same.

3 (*c*) Consider the diagram shown below, where a spring is stretched by applying a load to its free end. Clearly, the length and shape of the spring changes.

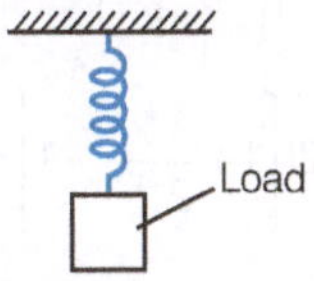

Thus, the change in length corresponds to longitudinal strain and change in shape corresponds to shearing strain.

4 (*b*) As, Young's modulus,

$$Y = \frac{\text{Stress}}{\text{Strain}} = \frac{FL}{A\Delta L}$$

$$= \frac{F}{\pi(D/2)^2} \times \frac{L}{\Delta L} = \frac{4FL}{\pi D^2 \Delta L}$$

where, D is the diameter of wire.

$$D^2 = \frac{4FL}{\pi \Delta L Y} \Rightarrow D = \sqrt{\frac{4FL}{\pi \Delta L Y}}$$

$$\text{Hence,} \quad D \propto \sqrt{\frac{1}{Y}}$$

(because F and $\frac{L}{\Delta L}$ are constants)

Then, ratio of diameters of copper and iron is $\frac{D_{copper}}{D_{iron}} = \sqrt{\frac{Y_{iron}}{Y_{copper}}}$

5 (*a*) Consider the diagram below

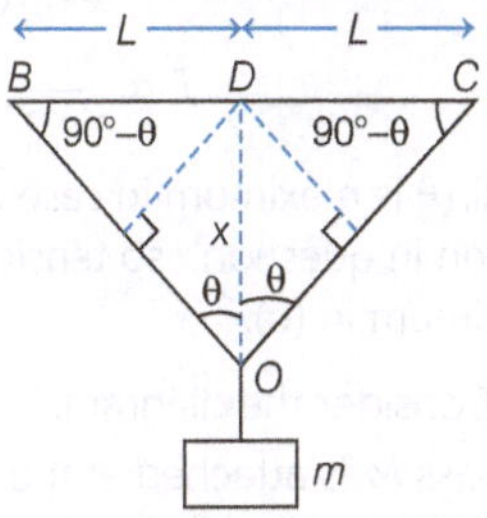

Given, length of wire $= 2L$

Cross-section area of wire $= A$

Length, $DO = x$

Hence, change in length,

$$\Delta L = BO + OC - (BD + DC)$$
$$= 2BO - 2BD \quad (\because BO = OC, BD = DC)$$
$$= 2\,(BO - BD)$$
$$= 2[(x^2 + L^2)^{1/2} - L]$$

$[\because$ In ΔBDO, $BO^2 = BD^2 + DO^2$ and $BD = L]$

$$= 2L\left[\left(1 + \frac{x^2}{L^2}\right)^{1/2} - 1\right]$$

$$= 2L\left[1 + \frac{1}{2}\frac{x^2}{L^2} - 1\right] = \frac{x^2}{L}$$

$(\because x << L)$

$$\therefore \quad \text{Strain} = \frac{\Delta L}{2L} = \frac{x^2/L}{2L} = \frac{x^2}{2L^2}$$

6 (c) Consider the FBD diagram of the rectangular frame.

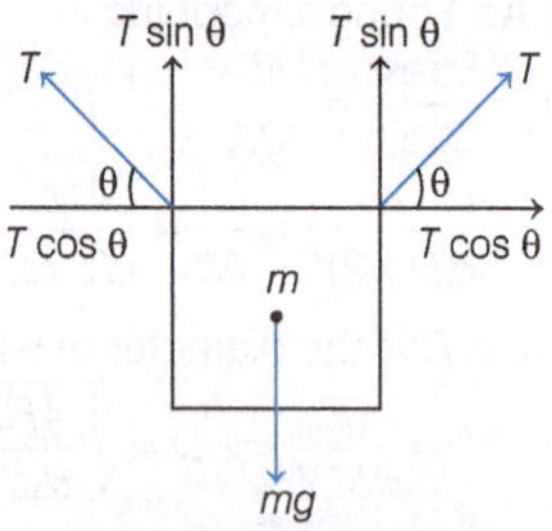

From above figure,

Balancing vertical forces

$$2T\sin\theta - mg = 0$$

(T is tension in the string)

$$\Rightarrow \quad 2T\sin\theta = mg \quad \text{...(i)}$$

Now, total horizontal force

$$T\cos\theta - T\cos\theta = 0$$

Now, from Eq. (i), $T = \dfrac{mg}{2\sin\theta}$

So, $$T \propto \frac{1}{\sin\theta}$$

As $\sin\theta$ is maximum in case (b) (given in question), so tension is minimum in (b).

7 (d) Consider the diagram.

A mass M is attached at the centre of the two cylindrical rods as shown below. As the mass is attached to both the rods, both rods will be elongated, but due to different elastic properties of material, there is no change in shape of steel rod, while for rubber rod, the shape of the bottom edge tappered to a tip at the centre.

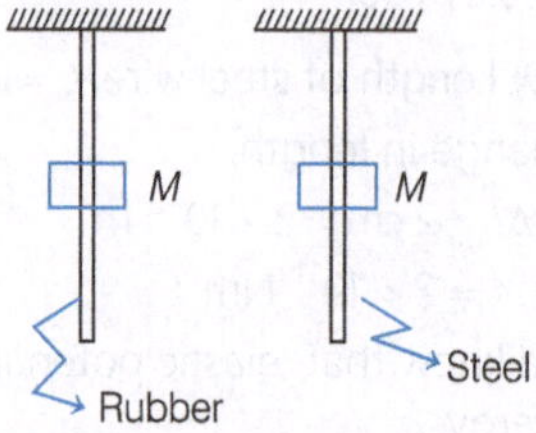

8 (c) It is clear from the two graphs, the ultimate tensile strength for material (ii) is greater, hence material (ii) is elastic over larger region as compared to material (i).

For material (ii), fracture point is nearer, so it is more brittle.

9 (d) A wire is suspended from the ceiling and stretched under the action of a weight F suspended from its other end as shown in the figure.

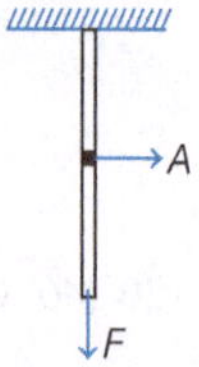

Clearly, force at cross-section is F.

$$\text{Stress} = \frac{\text{Tension}}{\text{Area}} = \frac{F}{A}$$

where, A is cross-section area of the wire

Tension at any cross-section A of the wire

= Applied force $= F$

10 (b) Let the mass m is placed at x from the end B.

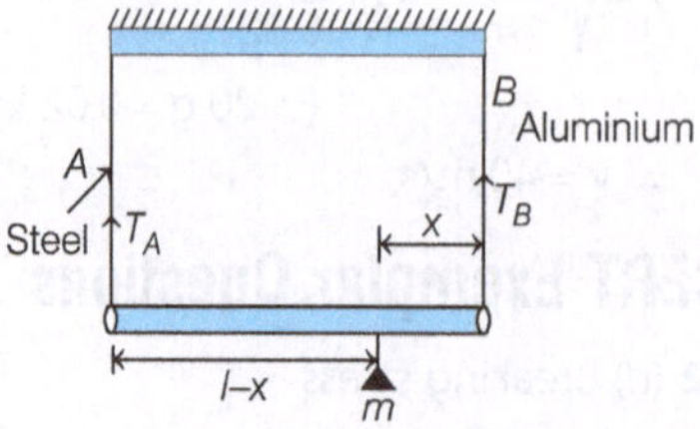

For the rotational equilibrium of the system,

$$\Sigma\tau = 0 \quad \text{(total torque = 0)}$$

$$\Rightarrow \quad T_B x - T_A(l - x) = 0$$

$$\Rightarrow \quad \frac{T_B}{T_A} = \frac{l - x}{x}$$

Stress in wire A, $S_A = \dfrac{T_A}{a_A}$

Stress in wire B, $S_B = \dfrac{T_B}{a_B}$

where, a_A and a_B are cross-sectional areas of wire A and B, respectively.

According to question, $a_B = 2a_A$

Now, for equal stress, $S_A = S_B$

$$\Rightarrow \quad \frac{T_A}{a_A} = \frac{T_B}{a_B} \Rightarrow \frac{T_B}{T_A} = \frac{a_B}{a_A} = 2$$

$$\Rightarrow \quad \frac{l - x}{x} = 2$$

$$\Rightarrow \quad \frac{l}{x} - 1 = 2 \quad \left[\because \frac{T_B}{T_A} = \frac{l - x}{x}\right]$$

$$\Rightarrow \quad x = \frac{l}{3}$$

$$\therefore \quad l - x = l - l/3 = \frac{2l}{3}$$

Hence, mass m should be placed closer to wire B.

For equal strain, $(\text{strain})_A = (\text{strain})_B$

$$\Rightarrow \quad \frac{S_A}{Y_A} = \frac{S_B}{Y_B}$$

(where, Y_A and Y_B are Young's moduli)

$$\Rightarrow \quad \frac{T_A/a_A}{Y_{\text{steel}}} = \frac{T_B/a_B}{Y_{\text{Al}}}$$

$$\Rightarrow \frac{Y_{\text{steel}}}{Y_{\text{Al}}} = \frac{T_A}{T_B} \times \frac{a_B}{a_A} = \left(\frac{x}{l - x}\right)\left(\frac{2a_A}{a_A}\right)$$

$$\Rightarrow \frac{200 \times 10^9}{70 \times 10^9} = \frac{2x}{l - x} \Rightarrow \frac{20}{7} = \frac{2x}{l - x}$$

$$\Rightarrow \quad \frac{10}{7} = \frac{x}{l - x}$$

$$\Rightarrow 10l - 10x = 7x$$

$$\Rightarrow \quad 17x = 10l$$

$$\Rightarrow \quad x = \frac{10l}{17}$$

$$\Rightarrow \quad l - x = l - \frac{10l}{17} = \frac{7l}{17}$$

Hence, mass m should be placed closer to wire A.

11 (*a*) Consider the diagram where a deforming force F is applied to the combination.

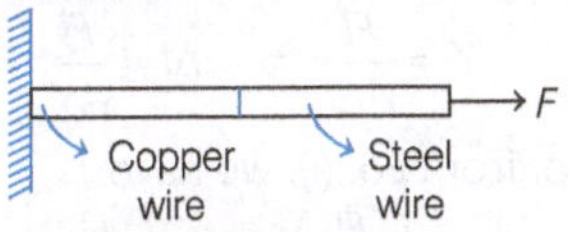

For steel wire,

$$Y_{steel}=\frac{\text{Stress}}{\text{Strain}}=\frac{F/A}{\text{Strain}}$$

As F and A are same for both the wires, hence stress will be same for both the wires.

$$(\text{Strain})_{steel}=\frac{\text{Stress}}{Y_{steel}},$$

$$(\text{Strain})_{copper}=\frac{\text{Stress}}{Y_{copper}}$$

As, $Y_{steel}\neq Y_{copper}$

Hence, the two wires will have different strains.

12 (*a*) Given, length of wires, $L_1=L$ and $L_2=2L$

Radius of wires, $r_1=r$ and $r_2=2r$

Force on the wires, $F_1=F$ and $F_2=2F$

Young's modulus, $Y=\frac{FL}{Al}$

[where, F = force, L = length, A = area and l = expansion in length]

$$l=\frac{FL}{\pi r^2 Y}$$

Ratio of expansion for both the wires

$$\frac{l_2}{l_1}=\frac{F_2}{F_1}\frac{L_2}{L_1}\left(\frac{r_1}{r_2}\right)^2=2\times 2\times\left(\frac{1}{2}\right)^2=1$$

$\therefore$ $l_2=l_1$, i.e. the increment in length will be same, i.e. l.

13 (*c*) Given, decrement in volume

$$\frac{\Delta V}{V}=0.1\,\%$$

Density of sea water $=10^3$ kg m^{-3}

Bulk modulus of rubber

$$=9\times 10^8\ \text{Nm}^{-2}$$

Gravitational acceleration,

$$g=10\ \text{ms}^{-2}$$

Let h be the depth at which the rubber ball be taken,

then $p=h\rho g$ ...(i)

By definition of bulk modulus,

$$B=-\frac{p}{\Delta V/V}$$

The negative sign shows that with increase in pressure, a decrease in volume occurs.

$$\therefore\quad p=|B|\frac{\Delta V}{V}$$

Using Eq. (i), we get

$$h\rho g=|B|\frac{\Delta V}{V}\ \text{or}\ h=\frac{|B|}{\rho g}\frac{\Delta V}{V}$$

Substituting the given values, we get

$$h=\frac{9\times 10^8}{10^3\times 10}\left(\frac{0.1}{100}\right)=90\ \text{m}$$

Past Exams Questions

1 (*a*) Length of wire $=1$ m

Elastic limit, $E=8\times 10^8$ Nm^{-2}

Young's modulus $Y=2\times 10^{11}$ Nm^{-2}

We know that, $Y=\frac{F}{A}\frac{l}{\Delta l}$

Here, $\frac{F}{A}$ = Elastic limit E

$$\Rightarrow\quad Y=E\frac{l}{\Delta l}$$

$$\Rightarrow\quad \Delta l=\frac{E}{Y}l$$

$$\Rightarrow\quad \Delta l=\frac{8\times 10^8}{2\times 10^{11}}\times 1$$

$$=4\times 10^{-3}\ \text{m}$$

$$=4\ \text{mm}$$

3 (*b*) When a coil spring is stretched, neither its length nor its volume changes, but there is only the change in its shape. Therefore, stretching of a coil spring is determined by shear modulus.

Young's modulus of steel spring is more than Young's modulus of copper spring, due to which tensile strength of steel spring is more than tensile strength of copper spring.

Hence, A is true but R is false.

4 (*c*) Here, change in length of wire,

$$\Delta L=(L_1-L)$$

Area of cross-section $=A$

Force, $F=Mg$

Young's modulus,

$$Y=\frac{(F/A)}{\left(\frac{\Delta L}{L}\right)}=\frac{\left(\frac{Mg}{A}\right)}{\left(\frac{L_1-L}{L}\right)}=\frac{MgL}{A(L_1-L)}$$

5 (*d*) Bulk modulus, $B=\frac{F/A}{\Delta V/V}$

$$\Rightarrow\quad \frac{\Delta V}{V}=\frac{p}{B}\Rightarrow\left|\frac{\Delta V}{V}\right|=\frac{p}{B}$$

Fractional decreases in volume,

$$\frac{\Delta V}{V}=3\frac{\Delta R}{R}\quad[\because V=\frac{4}{3}\pi R^3]$$

Volume of the sphere decreases due to the decrease in its radius.

Hence, $\frac{\Delta V}{V}=\frac{3\Delta R}{R}=\frac{p}{B}\Rightarrow\frac{\Delta R}{R}=\frac{p}{3B}$

6 (*b*) Youngs' modulus is given by

$$Y=\frac{F\times l}{A\times\Delta l}\quad\text{...(i)}$$

As, $V=A\times l=\text{constant}$ ...(ii)

From Eqs. (i) and (ii), we get

$$Y=\frac{F\times l^2}{V\times\Delta l}$$

$$\Rightarrow\quad \Delta l=\frac{F}{V\times Y}\times l^2\Rightarrow\Delta l\propto l^2$$

7 (*c*) Given,

$$Y=49000\times\frac{M}{l}\frac{\text{dyne}}{\text{m}^2}$$

$\therefore$ Percentage error in Y is,

$$\frac{\Delta Y}{Y}\times 100=\frac{\Delta M}{M}\times 100+\frac{\Delta l}{l}\times 100$$

$$=\frac{\Delta M}{M}\times 100+\frac{\Delta l}{l}\times 100$$

$$=\frac{5}{500}\times 100+\frac{0.02}{2}\times 100$$

$$=1+1=2\%$$

8 (*c*) Given, $L_A=5$ m,

$$A_A=2.5\times 10^{-5}\ \text{m}^2,$$

$$L_B=6\ \text{m},$$

$$A_B=3\times 10^{-5}\ \text{m}^2$$

As we know, from Hooke's law,

$$Y=\frac{FL}{A\Delta L}$$

If F and ΔL are same, then $Y\propto\frac{L}{A}$

For two wires A and B,

$$\frac{Y_A}{Y_B}=\frac{L_A}{L_B}\cdot\frac{A_B}{A_A}=\frac{5}{6}\cdot\frac{3\times 10^{-5}}{2.5\times 10^{-5}}$$

$$\Rightarrow \frac{Y_A}{Y_B}=\frac{1}{1}$$

9 (b) Given, length of two wires,

$$l_1=l_2=l$$

Radius of two wires, $r_1=r_2=r$

Since, Young's moduli are different.

$\therefore$ Change in length of wires 1 and 2 will be Δl_1 and Δl_2.

As we know that,

$$Y=\frac{Fl}{A\Delta l}\Rightarrow \Delta l=\frac{Fl}{YA}$$

As the wires are in series.

$\therefore$ Net change in length,

$$\Delta l=\Delta l_1+\Delta l_2$$

$$\frac{F(2l)}{Y\pi r^2}=\frac{Fl}{Y_1\pi r^2}+\frac{Fl}{Y_2\pi r^2}$$

$$\Rightarrow \frac{2}{Y}=\frac{1}{Y_1}+\frac{1}{Y_2}$$

$$\Rightarrow \frac{2}{Y}=\frac{Y_2+Y_1}{Y_1Y_2}\Rightarrow Y=\frac{2Y_1Y_2}{Y_1+Y_2}$$

This is the Young's modulus for the combination of wires.

10 (a) Elastic potential energy stored in a loaded wire,

$$U=\frac{1}{2}(\text{Stress}\times\text{Strain}\times\text{Volume})$$

$\therefore$ Energy stored per unit volume,

$$u=\frac{U}{\text{Volume}}=\frac{1}{2}\times\text{Stress}\times\text{Strain}$$

$$=\frac{1}{2}\left(\frac{F}{A}\right)^2\times\frac{1}{Y}$$

$$\therefore \frac{u_A}{u_B}=\frac{\frac{1}{2Y}\cdot\frac{F^2}{A_A^2}}{\frac{1}{2Y}\cdot\frac{F^2}{A_B^2}}=\frac{A_B^2}{A_A^2}$$

$$\Rightarrow \frac{u_A}{u_B}=\frac{d_B^4}{d_A^4}\quad\left(\because A=\pi\frac{d^2}{4}\right)$$

Here, $\dfrac{u_A}{u_B}=\dfrac{1}{4}$

So, $\dfrac{d_B^4}{d_A^4}=\dfrac{1}{4}$

or $\dfrac{d_B}{d_A}=\dfrac{1}{\sqrt{2}}$

$$\Rightarrow \frac{d_A}{d_B}=\sqrt{2}:1$$

Skill Boosters

1 (b) Since, strain $=\dfrac{\sigma_C}{Y_C}=\dfrac{\sigma_i}{Y_i}$

where, the subscript c and i refer to concrete and iron, respectively. Let x fraction of load w be shared be concrete, then

$$\frac{xw}{A_cY_c}=\frac{w-xw}{A_iY_i}$$

$$\Rightarrow x=\frac{A_cY_c}{A_iY_i+A_cY_c}$$

$$\Rightarrow x=\frac{A_cY_c}{\frac{1}{6}A_c\times 8Y_c+A_cY_c}$$

$$\left(\because A_i=\frac{1}{6}A_C, Y_i=8Y_C\right)$$

$$=\frac{3}{7}=0.43$$

2 (a) Given, $l=4.5$ m

$$r=\frac{6}{2}\text{ mm}=3\times 10^{-3}\text{ m}$$

According to the question,

$$F=w=100\text{ N}$$

and Young's modulus,

$$Y=4.8\times 10^{11}\text{ Nm}^{-2}$$

As, $Y=\dfrac{Fl}{A\Delta l}$

$$\Rightarrow \Delta l=\frac{Fl}{AY}=\frac{Fl}{\pi r^2 Y}$$

$$=\frac{100\times 4.5}{3.14\,(3\times 10^{-3})^2\times 4.8\times 10^{11}}$$

$$=3.32\times 10^{-5}\text{ m}=0.332\text{ μm}$$

3 (c) In given experiment, a composite wire is stretched by a force F.

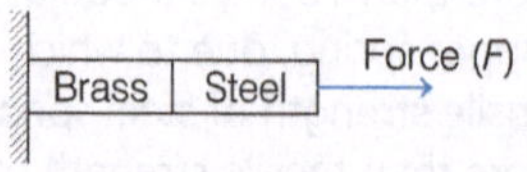

Net elongation in the wire = Elongation in brass wire + Elongation in steel wire ... (i)

Now, Young's modulus of a wire of cross-section (A) when some force (F) is applied,

$$Y=\frac{Fl}{A\Delta l}\Rightarrow \Delta l=\frac{Fl}{AY}$$

So, from Eq. (i), we have

$$\Delta l_{\text{net}}=\left(\frac{Fl}{AY}\right)_{\text{brass}}+\left(\frac{Fl}{AY}\right)_{\text{steel}}$$

As subjected to same force, so

$$\Delta l_{\text{net}}=\frac{F}{A}\left(\frac{l}{Y_{\text{brass}}}+\frac{1}{Y_{\text{steel}}}\right)$$

Here, $\Delta l_{\text{net}}=0.2$ mm
$=0.2\times 10^{-3}$ m

and $l=1$ m

$$Y_{\text{brass}}=60\times 10^9\text{ Nm}^{-2}$$

$$Y_{\text{steel}}=120\times 10^9\text{ Nm}^{-2}$$

On putting the values, we have

$$0.2\times 10^{-3}=\frac{F}{A}\left(\frac{1}{60\times 10^9}+\frac{1}{120\times 10^9}\right)$$

$$\Rightarrow \text{Stress}=\frac{F}{A}=8\times 10^6\text{ Nm}^{-2}$$

4 (c) On solving T in horizontal and vertical direction, we get

$$T\cos\theta=mg \quad \text{...(i)}$$

$$T\sin\theta=\frac{mv^2}{r} \quad \text{...(ii)}$$

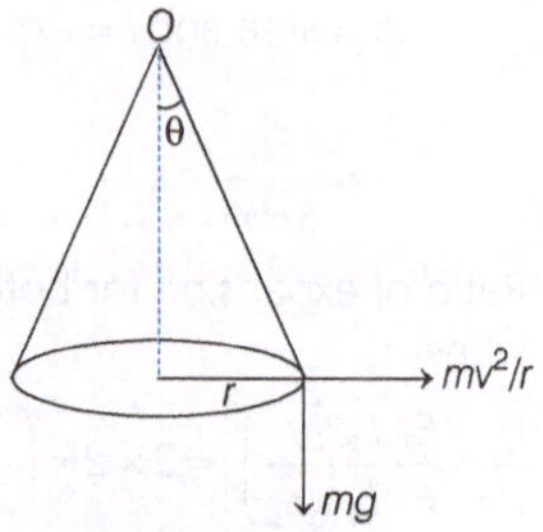

$$\therefore T=\frac{mg}{\cos\theta}=\frac{mg}{\cos 85°}$$

$$=\frac{0.5\times 9.8}{0.0872}=56.19\text{ N}$$

As, $Y=\dfrac{\frac{T}{A}}{\frac{\Delta l}{l}}\Rightarrow \Delta l=\dfrac{Tl}{YA}$

$$=\frac{56.19\times 0.8}{7\times 10^{10}\times\pi\times(0.35\times 10^{-3})^2}$$

$$=1.67\times 10^{-3}\text{ m}$$

$$=1.67\text{ mm}$$

5 (*d*) As, stress $= \dfrac{\text{normal force}}{\text{area}}$

$$= \frac{N}{A} = \frac{N}{(2\pi a)\, b},$$

$$V = \pi a^2 b$$

$$\Delta V = 2\pi ab\Delta a$$

$$\text{Stress} = B \times \text{Strain}$$

$$\frac{N}{(2\pi a)b} = B\frac{2\pi a\Delta a \times b}{\pi a^2 b} \quad \left[\because \text{Strain} = \frac{\Delta V}{V}\right]$$

$$\Rightarrow \quad N = B\frac{(2\pi a)^2 \Delta a b^2}{\pi a^2 b}$$

Force needed to push the cork,

$$F = \mu N = \frac{\mu \times B \times 4\pi^2 a^2 b^2 \Delta a}{\pi a^2 b}$$

$$= (4\pi\mu B b)\, \Delta a$$

6 (*a*) (i) Stress in steel wire $= \dfrac{T_1}{A_1}$

Stress in brass wire $= \dfrac{T_2}{A_2}$

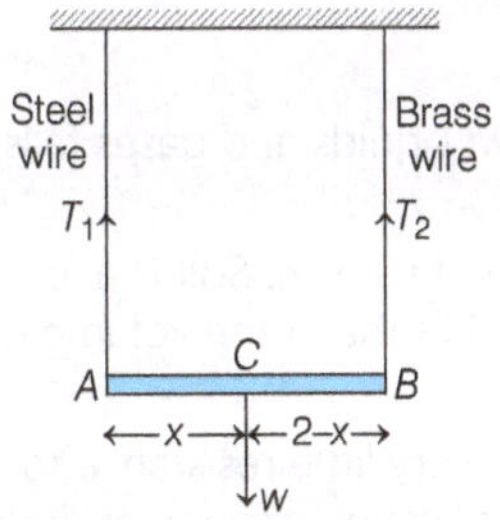

As both an equal.

$$\text{So,} \quad \frac{T_1}{A_1} = \frac{T_2}{A_2}$$

$$\Rightarrow \quad \frac{0.1}{0.2} = \frac{1}{2}$$

Let x be the distance from steel wire.

$$\therefore \quad T_1 x = T_2(2 - x)$$

$$\Rightarrow \quad \frac{T_1}{T_2} = \frac{2 - x}{x}$$

$$\Rightarrow \quad x = 4 - 2x \quad \left(\because \frac{T_1}{T_2} = \frac{1}{2}\right)$$

$$\therefore 3x = 4 \Rightarrow x = \frac{4}{3} = 1.33 \text{ m}$$

7 (*a*) Wire is equivalent to a spring of spring constant, $k' = \dfrac{AY}{L}$

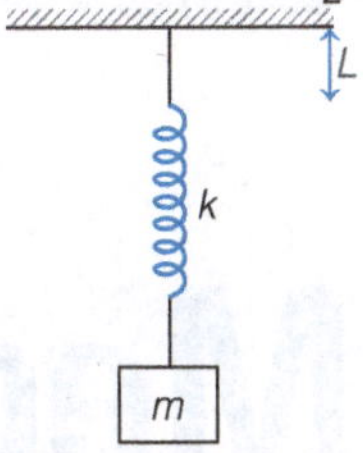

Here, k' and k are in series,

$$\text{So,} \quad k_{eq} = \frac{k'\, k}{k' + k}$$

$$= \frac{(AY / L)\, k}{\left(\frac{AY}{L}\right) + k}$$

$$= \frac{AYk}{AY + kL}$$

$$\therefore \quad T = 2\pi\sqrt{\frac{m}{k_{eq}}}$$

$$= 2\pi\sqrt{\frac{m\,(AY + kL)}{AYk}}$$

8 (*a*) When rubber cord is stretched, then it stores potential energy and when released, this potential energy is given to the stone as kinetic energy.

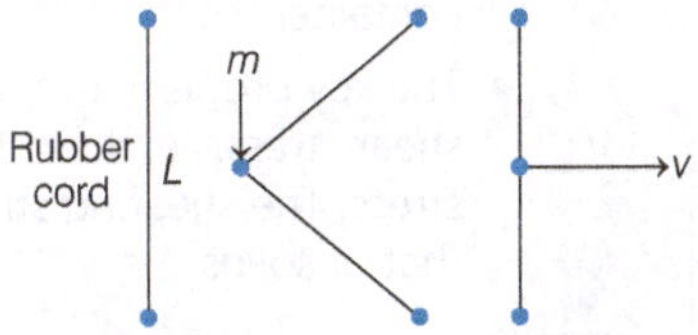

So, potential energy of stretched cord = kinetic energy of stone

$$\Rightarrow \frac{1}{2}Y\left(\frac{\Delta L}{L}\right)A \cdot L = \frac{1}{2}mv^2$$

Here, $\Delta l = 20$ cm $= 0.2$ m, $L = 42$ cm $= 0.42$ m

$$\therefore A = \pi r^2 = \pi\left(\frac{d}{2}\right)^2$$

$$= \pi\left(\frac{6 \times 10^{-3}}{2}\right)^2$$

$$= \pi(3 \times 10^{-3})^2 = 9\pi \times 10^{-6} \text{ m}^2$$

On substituting values, we get

$$Y = \frac{mv^2 L}{A(\Delta L)^2}$$

$$= \frac{0.02 \times (20)^2 \times 0.42}{9\pi \times 10^{-6} \times (0.2)^2}$$

$$\approx 3.0 \times 10^6 \text{ Nm}^{-2}$$

So, the closest value of Young's modulus is 10^6 Nm^{-2}.

9 (*d*) $T = 2\pi\sqrt{\dfrac{L}{g}}$ ...(i)

$$T_M = 2\pi\sqrt{\frac{L + \Delta L}{g}}$$

Here, $T_M = 2\pi\sqrt{\dfrac{L + \dfrac{MgL}{AY}}{g}}$ ...(ii)

Solving Eqs. (i) and (ii), we get

$$\frac{1}{Y} = \frac{A}{Mg}\left[\left(\frac{T_M}{T}\right)^2 - 1\right]$$

10 (*c*) $\because \Delta l = 521 - 500 - 20 = 1$ cm $= 0.01$ m

$$\because \quad T - mg = mv^2/R$$

$$\therefore \quad T = m\left(g + \frac{v^2}{R}\right)$$

$$= m$$

$$\left(g + \frac{v^2}{l}\right)\Delta l = \frac{Tl}{AY}$$

$$= \frac{m\left(g + \frac{v^2}{l}\right)l}{(\pi d^2 / 4)Y}$$

$$= \frac{mg\,l + mv^2}{(\pi d^2 / 4)Y}$$

$$\therefore \ v = \sqrt{\frac{\pi d^2\, \Delta l Y}{4m} - gl}$$

$$= \sqrt{\frac{(3.14)\,(4 \times 10^{-3})^2\,(0.01)\,(2 \times 10^{11})}{4 \times 25} - 9.8 \times 5}$$

$$= 31.26 \text{ m/s}$$

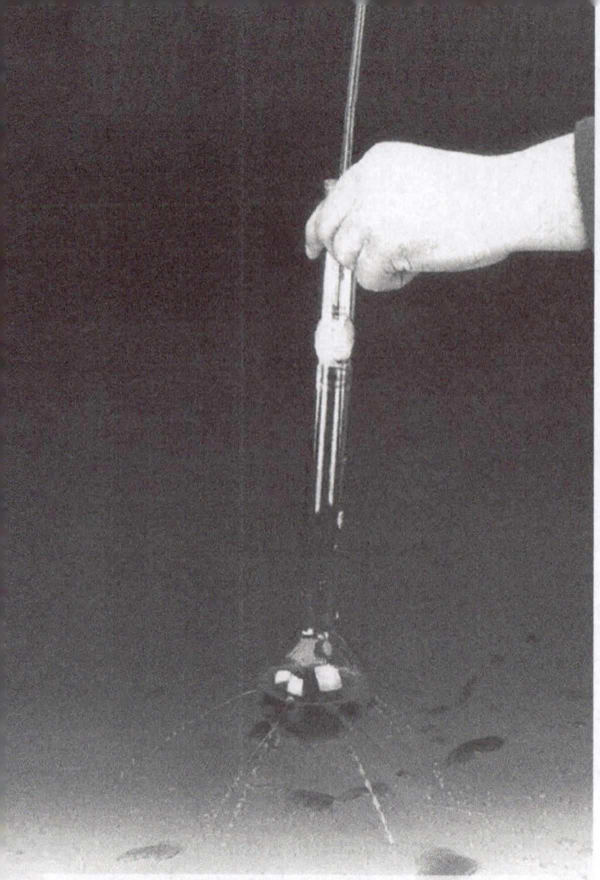

09

Scan for **Physics Through Concept Master** *Videos*

Mechanical Properties of Fluids

Topicwise No. of Ques asked in 5 Years (NEET)

Topics	No. of Questions				
	2024	2023	2022	2021	2020
Pressure	–	–	–	–	–
Flow of Liquids	–	–	–	–	–
Bernoulli's Principle	–	1	–	–	–
Viscosity	–	–	1	1	–
Surface Tension	1	1	1	–	1

Special Type of Ques Asked In 5 Years (NEET)

Types	Years				
	2024	2023	2022	2021	2020
A-R	–	–	–	–	–
Statement Based	–	–	–	–	–
Matching	–	–	–	–	–

Last 5 Years Weigtage (NEET)

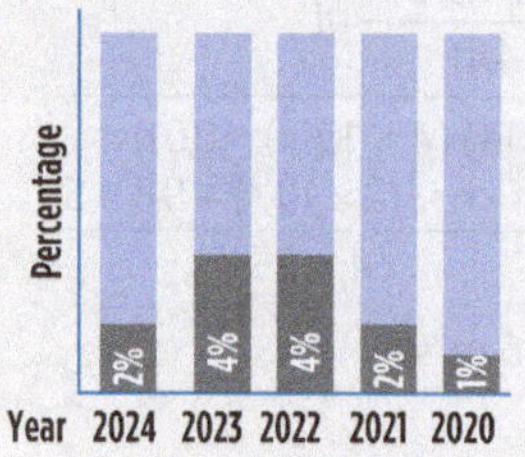

- **Fluids** are those substances which can flow. Liquids and gases falls in the category of fluids.
- Unlike a solid, a fluid has no definite shape of its own. Solids and liquids have a fixed volume, whereas a gas fills the entire volume of its container.
- The key property of fluids is that they offer very little resistance to shear stress. i.e. their shape changes by application of very small shear stress. The shearing stress of fluids is about million times smaller than that of solids.

Pressure and Pascal's Law

- The force exerted by a liquid at rest per unit area of the surface in contact with the liquid is called as **pressure**.
- When an object is submerged in a fluid at rest, the fluid exerts a force on its surface. This force is perpendicular to the surface in contact with it.
    - If F is the magnitude of normal force on area A, then we define

      $$\text{Pressure } (p_{av}) = \frac{\text{Force } (F)}{\text{Area } (A)}$$

    - If the area is very small, then we define **instantaneous pressure p**,

      $$p = \lim_{\Delta A \to 0} \frac{\Delta F}{\Delta A} = \frac{dF}{dA}$$

    - It is a **scalar quantity** and its **SI unit is Nm^{-2}**.

- **Density** is defined as the ratio of the mass of a body to its volume.

$$\rho = \frac{m}{V}$$

where, ρ = density, V = volume and m = mass.

  - It is a scalar quantity and its SI unit is kg m^{-3}.
- A liquid is largely incompressible and its density is therefore, nearly constant at all pressures. On the other hand, gases exhibit a large variation in densities with pressure.
- **Pascal's law** It states that, the change in pressure applied to an enclosed liquid at rest is transmitted equally to all other points of the liquid in all directions.
- **Pressure exerted by a liquid column,** $p = \rho g h$

where, h = height of liquid column,

g = acceleration due to gravity

and ρ = density of liquid.

- **Variation of pressure with depth** The pressure p at depth below the surface of a liquid open to the atmosphere is greater than atmospheric pressure p_a by an amount ρgh.

i.e. Pressure $p = p_a + \rho g h$

The effect of gravity illustrated through pressure on a vertical cylindrical column is shown below.

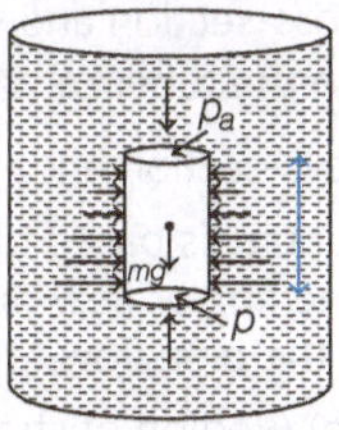

Variation of pressure

- The excess of pressure, $p - p_a$ at depth h is called a **gauge pressure**. i.e. $p - p_a = \rho g h$
- The pressure exerted by the atmosphere is called **atmospheric pressure.** Atmospheric pressure at any point is equal to the weight of a column of air of unit cross-sectional area extending from that point to the top of the atmosphere.
- The liquid pressure is same at all points x, y and z at the same horizontal level (same depth) shown in figure. The result is appreciated through the example of **hydrostatic paradox.**

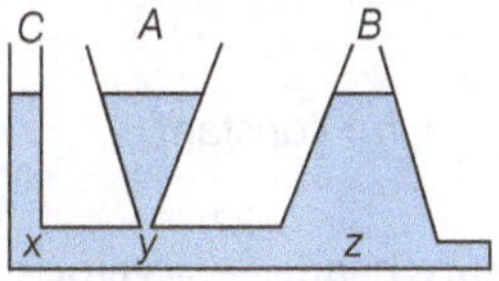

Hydrostatic paradox

- **Atmospheric pressure is measured with mercury barometer** accurately shown in the figure.

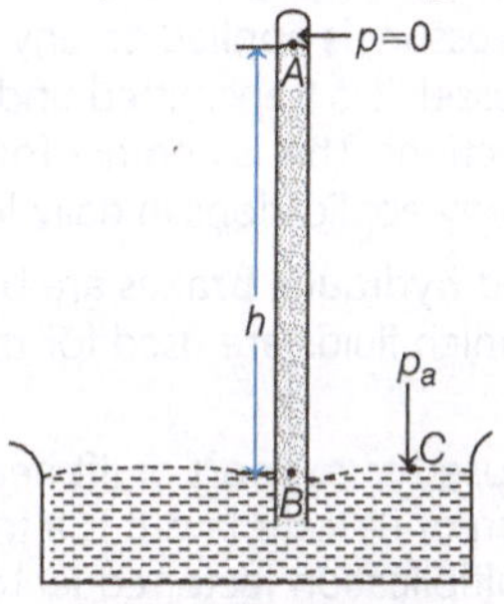

Mercury Barometer

At point A, there is only mercury vapour whose pressure is neglected *i.e.* $p_A = 0$

Pressure at point C which is atmospheric pressure p_a is equal to the pressure at point B. Pressure at B is equal to the pressure applied by the mercury present between point A and B. i.e. ρgh.

$$\therefore \quad p_B = p_C = p_a = \rho g h$$ **NEET 2020, 19**

where, p_a, ρ and h are atmospheric pressure, density of mercury and the height of mercury column in the tube, respectively.

- The mercury column in the barometer has a height of about 76 cm at sea level equivalent to one atmosphere (1 atm).
- $p_a = 1 \text{ atm} = 1.013 \times 10^5 \text{ Pa} = 76 \text{ cm of Hg}$

$1 \text{ torr} = 133 \text{ Pa} = 1 \text{ mm of Hg}$

$1 \text{ bar} = 10^5 \text{ Pa}$

- The unit mm of Hg and torr are used in medicine and physiology while bar is used in meteorology.
- An open tube manometer shown in figure below is a useful instrument for **measuring pressure differences.**

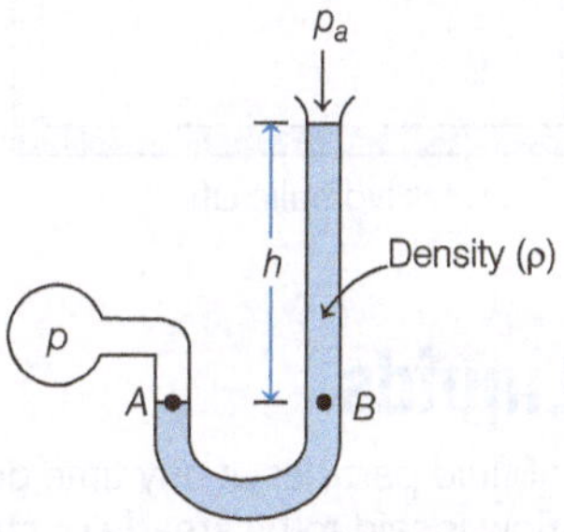

Open tube manometer

The pressure is same at the same levels A and B on both sides of U-tube containing a fluid

i.e., $p_A = p_B$

$\therefore \quad p = p_a + \rho g h$

$\therefore \quad p - p_a = \text{Gauge pressure} = \rho g h$

The open tube manometer measures gauge pressure $(p - p_a)$ i.e. ρgh.

Hydraulic Machines

- When external pressure is applied on any part of a fluid contained in a vessel, it is transmitted undiminished and equally in all directions. This is another form of the Pascal's law and it has many applications in daily life.
- **Hydraulic lift** and **hydraulic brakes** are based on the Pascal's law, in which fluids are used for transmitting pressure.
- **Hydraulic lift** is used to support or lift heavy objects based on the application of Pascal's law. It is a force multiplying device with a multiplication factor equal to the ratio of the areas of the two pistons.
- In hydraulic lift as shown in the figure below, two pistons are separated by the space filled with a liquid.

  Let the area of small piston $= A_1$

  The area of large piston $= A_2$

  Downward force applied on small piston $= F_1$

  Upward force exerted on large piston $= F_2$

  By Pascal's law, the external pressure p is equally transmitted throughout the liquid.

  $$\therefore \quad p = \frac{F_1}{A_1} = \frac{F_2}{A_2} \Rightarrow F_2 = \left(\frac{A_2}{A_1}\right) F_1$$

  As, $A_2 > A_1 \Rightarrow F_2 > F_1$

  Hence, the heavy loads like car, truck can be lifted by applying small force.

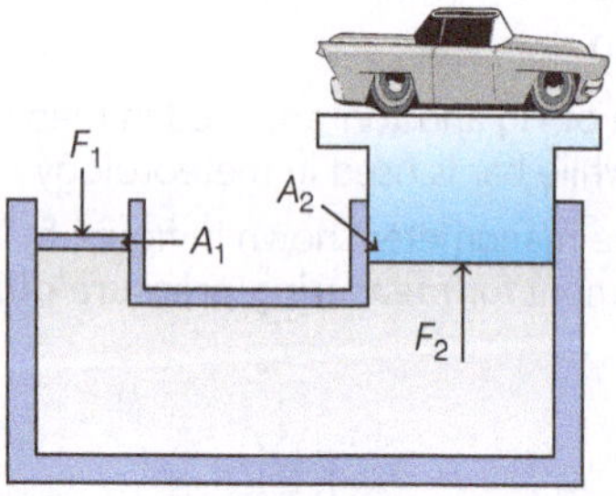

Hydraulic Lift

Flow of Liquids

- If the velocity of fluid particles at any time does not vary with time, the flow is said to be **steady** or **streamline flow**.
  - The path followed by a fluid particle in streamline flow is known as **streamlines**.
  - Velocity of particles in streamline is along the tangent to the curve at that point.
- If the liquid flows over a horizontal surface in the form of layers of different velocities, then the flow of liquid is called **laminar flow**.

(a) Trajectory of fluid particle in streamline flow

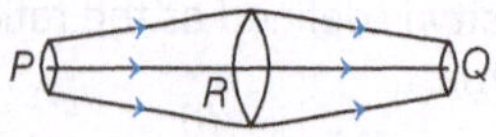

(b) Region of streamline flow

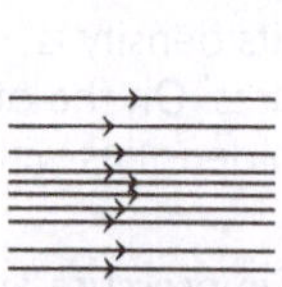

(c) Laminar flow

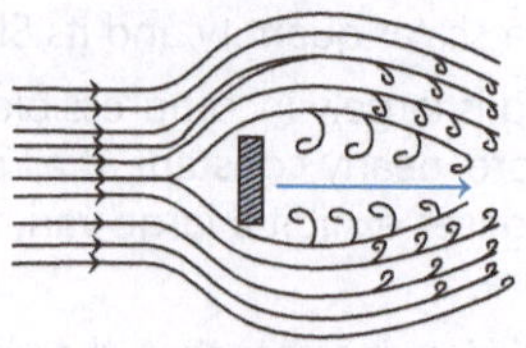

(d) Turbulent flow

- The flow in which velocity of fluid is greater than its critical velocity and the motion of particles becomes irregular is called **turbulent flow**. Figure (d) shows the example of turbulent flow for a jet of air striking a flat plate placed perpendicular to it.
- **Critical velocity** The velocity of fluid upto which the flow is streamlined and above which it becomes turbulent is called critical velocity.
- **Equation of continuity** It states that "when an incompressible and non-viscous fluid flows steadily through a tube of non-uniform cross-section, then the product of area of cross-section and velocity of flow is same at every point in the tube, i.e. $A_1 v_1 = A_2 v_2$

  where, $A =$ area of cross-section and $v =$ velocity of flow.
- The equation of continuity is based on law of conservation of mass i.e. the volume flux or flow rate Av remains constant throughout the pipe flow.
- In the above figure (b) (Region of streamline flow), as $A_R > A_Q$. So, $v_R < v_Q$ i.e. the fluid is accelerated while passing from R to Q.

Bernoulli's Principle

- According to this principle, "if an ideal fluid (incompressible and non-viscous fluid) is flowing in streamlined flow, then total energy, i.e. sum of pressure energy, kinetic energy and potential energy per unit volume of the liquid remains constant at every cross-section of the tube."

  $$p + \frac{1}{2}\rho v^2 + \rho g h = \text{constant}$$

  or $$\frac{p}{\rho g} + \frac{v^2}{2g} + h = \text{constant}$$

  where, $\frac{p}{\rho g} =$ **pressure head**, $\frac{v^2}{2g} =$ **velocity head** and h = **gravitational head.**

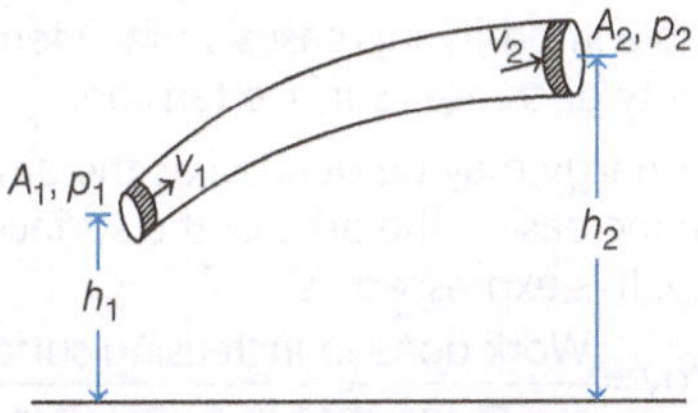

The flow of an ideal fluid in a pipe of varying cross section

For two different points in a ideal fluid flow, Bernoulli's equation can be written as

$$p_1 + \frac{1}{2}\rho v_1^2 + \rho g h_1 = p_2 + \frac{1}{2}\rho v_2^2 + \rho g h_2$$

For Concept Master Video

- Bernoulli's equation ideally applies to fluids with zero viscosity or non-viscous fluids.

Speed of Efflux : Torricelli's Law

- The outflow of a fluid is called **efflux** and the speed of the fluid coming out is called **speed of efflux.**
- When tank as shown below is closed, the speed of efflux is given by $v_1 = \sqrt{2gh + \frac{2(p - p_a)}{\rho}}$

  where, ρ = density of liquid.

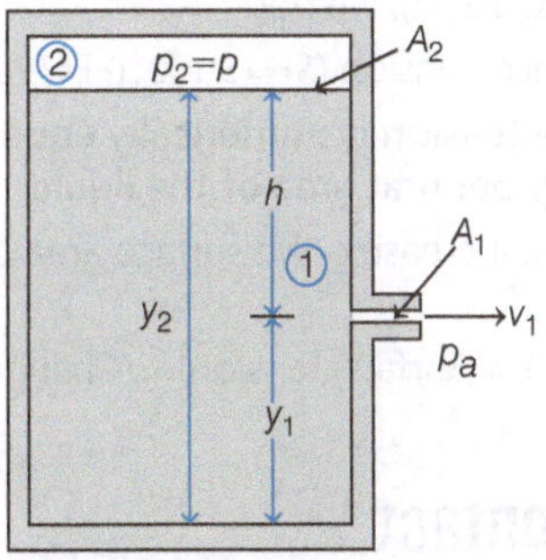

Torricelli's law applied on a container

- When the tank is open to the atmosphere, then

$$p = p_a \Rightarrow v_1 = \sqrt{2gh}$$

  This is also the speed of a freely falling body and this equation represents **Torricelli's law.**
- The horizontal distance covered by the liquid coming out of the hole is called **range** and is given by

$$R = 2\sqrt{hy_1}$$

  R will be maximum at $h = \frac{y_2}{2}$

$$\therefore \quad R_{max} = y_2$$

Marks Maximiser

Venturimeter It is a device which is used to measure the flow speed of incompressible fluid. According to given figure, speed of fluid at wide neck is given as

$$v_1 = \sqrt{\frac{2\rho_m g h}{\rho}} \cdot \left[\left(\frac{A}{a}\right)^2 - 1\right]^{-1/2}$$

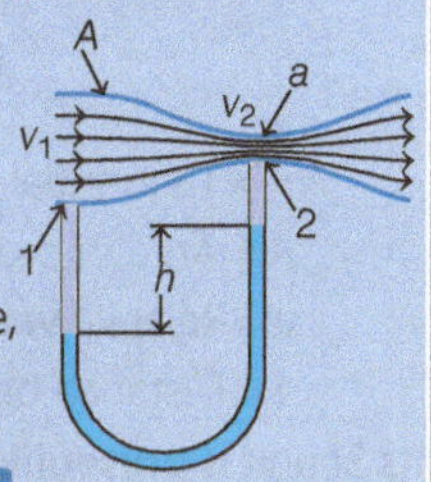

where, ρ_m = density of liquid contained in U-tube,

ρ = density of fluid

and h = difference in height in U-tube. NEET 2023

Dynamic Lift

- It is the force that acts on a body, by virtue of its motion through a fluid such as airplane wing, a hydrofoil or a spinning ball. The deviation of spinning ball from its parabolic trajectory can be explained on the basis of Bernoulli's principle.
  (i) **When ball is moving without spin in air,** then speed of air above and below the ball is same, hence pressure difference is zero. Therefore, air exerts no upward or downward force on the ball.
  (ii) **When ball is moving with spin in air,** then speed of air above and below to the ball is not same, hence, pressure difference is created due to which non-zero net force acts on the ball.
- **Magnus Effect** When a ball is moving in air with spin, then due to difference in the velocities of air results in the pressure difference between the lower and upper faces and there is net upward force on the ball.
  This dynamic lift due to spinning is called **Magnus effect.**
- **Aerofoil or Lift on Aircraft Wing** An aircraft wing is designed, so that air moves faster over the top of the wings that it does under the wings, thus making the air pressure less on top than underneath. This difference in pressure results in a net upward lifting force on the wings.

Viscosity

- The property of a fluid by virtue of which an internal frictional force acts between its different layers, which opposes their relative motion is called **viscosity.**

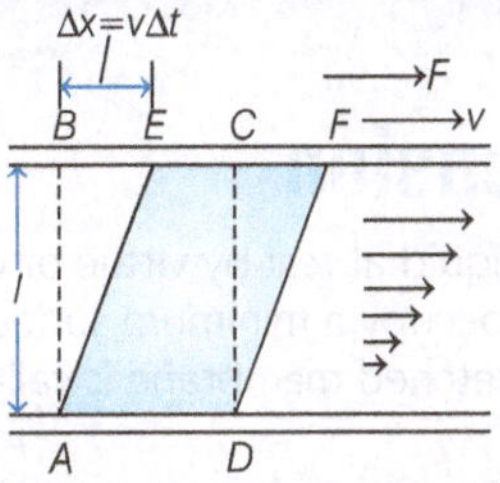

Velocity distribution of viscous flow between two parallel plates

- The velocities of layers increase uniformly from bottom (zero velocity) to the top layer (velocity v).
- The **coefficient of viscosity** for a fluid is defined as the ratio of shearing stress to the strain rate.

$$\eta = \frac{F/A}{v/l} = \frac{Fl}{vA}$$

F = Tangential force acting on the layers of liquid.
A = Area of cross-section
v = Relative velocity between two layers
l = Distance between two layers

Its SI unit is **poiseuille (Pl)**.

- The viscosity of liquids decreases with temperature, while it increases in the case of gases.
- **Stokes' Law** There is a viscous drag force F on a sphere of radius r moving with velocity v through a fluid of viscosity η. It can be expressed as $F = 6\pi\eta rv$
- **Terminal Velocity** The maximum constant velocity acquired by the body while falling through a viscous fluid is called terminal velocity.

$$v = \frac{2}{9} \times \frac{r^2(\rho - \sigma)g}{\eta}$$ NEET 2019

where, r = radius of the spherical body,
v = terminal velocity,
η = coefficient of viscosity of fluid,
ρ = density of the spherical body
and σ = density of fluid.

Marks Maximiser

- When a spherical ball is dropped in a viscous liquid, then the velocity of ball increases initially. After sometime, the ball acquires a constant velocity.
- The **velocity-time graph** of the body is given below.

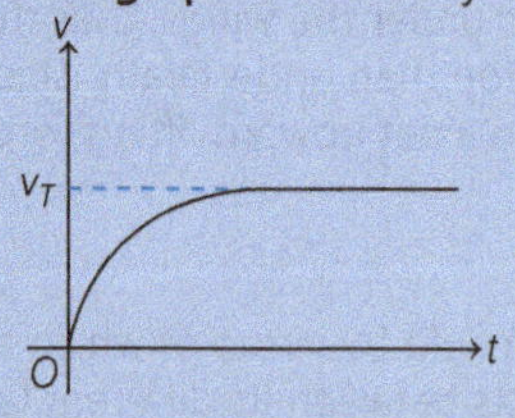

where, v_T = terminal velocity acquired by the ball.

Surface Tension

- The property of liquid at rest by virtue of which a liquid surface tends to occupy a minimum surface area and behaves like a stretched membrane is called **surface tension**.

It's SI unit is Nm^{-1} and dimensions is $[MT^{-2}]$

- Like viscosity, **the surface tension of a liquid usually falls with temperature.**
- A highly soluble impurity increases surface tension and in soluble impurity decreases surface tension.
- The **surface energy** may be defined as the amount of work done in increasing the area of the surface film through unity. It is expressed as

$$\text{Surface energy} = \frac{\text{Work done in increasing surface area}}{\text{Increase in surface area}}$$

It's SI unit is joule and dimension is $[ML^2T^{-2}]$

- **Relation between surface energy and surface tension**
Surface tension is force per unit length (or surface energy per unit area) acting in the plane of the interface between the plane of the liquid and any other substance.

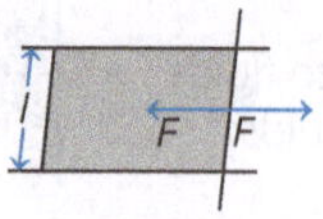

Surface film in equilibrium

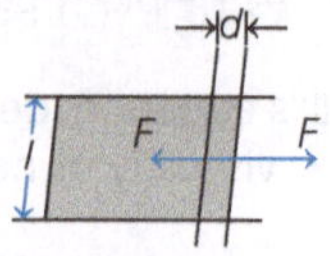

Surface film stretched extra displacement d

The surface tension of the liquid film shown in above figure is

$$S = \frac{F}{2l} \quad \text{...(i)}$$

The surface energy of the liquid film shown in above figure is

$$E = \frac{\text{Work}}{\text{Area}} = \frac{F \times d}{2 \times l \times d} = \frac{F}{2l} \quad \text{...(ii)}$$

From Eq. (i) and Eq. (ii), we get

Surface Tension (S) = Surface Energy (E)

Hence, **surface tension is numerically equal to the surface energy per unit area of the liquid.**

$\therefore$ Work done in increasing the surface area ΔA of a liquid of surface tension S is

Work done (W) = (Surface tension) × (Change in surface in area) = $S \cdot \Delta A$.

Angle of Contact

- When a liquid comes in contact with a solid surface, then its free surface becomes curved at the point of contact.
- The angle (θ) inside the liquid made by tangent of liquid surface and solid surface is known as angle of contact.
- Different shapes of water drops with interfacial tensions (i) on a lotus leaf (ii) on a clean plastic plate shown in figures. At the line of contact, the surface tensions between three media must be in equilibrium,

if $S_{la} \cos\theta + S_{sl} = S_{sa}$

where, S_{la} = surface tension of liquid-air interface,
S_{sl} = surface tension of solid-liquid interface
and S_{sa} = surface tension of solid-air interface.

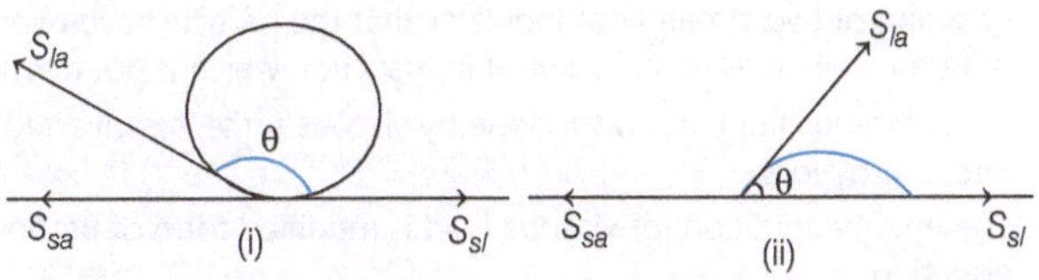

(i) If $S_{sl} > S_{la}$, i.e. $\theta > 90°$, then **liquid does not wet the solid.**

(ii) If $S_{sl} < S_{la}$, i.e. $\theta < 90°$, then **liquid wet the solid.**

(iii) If $S_{la} = S_{sa}$, i.e. $\theta = 90°$, then **liquid does not wet the solid.**

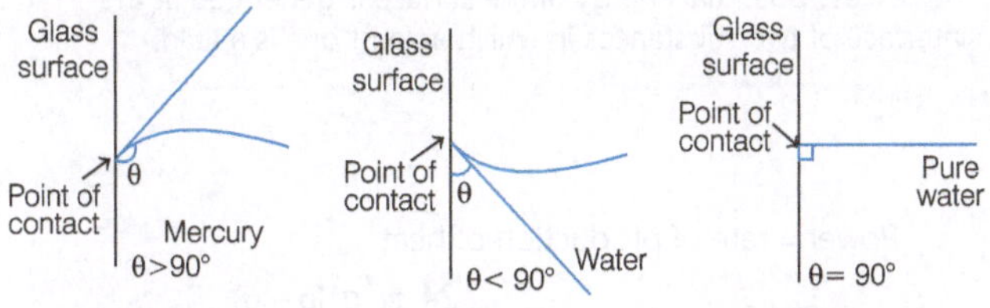

(i) Liquid does not wets the solid surface

(ii) Liquids wets the solid surface

(iii) Liquid does not wet the solid surface

Drops and Bubbles

One consequence of surface tension is that, the pressure p_i inside a spherical drop is more than the pressure p_o outside.

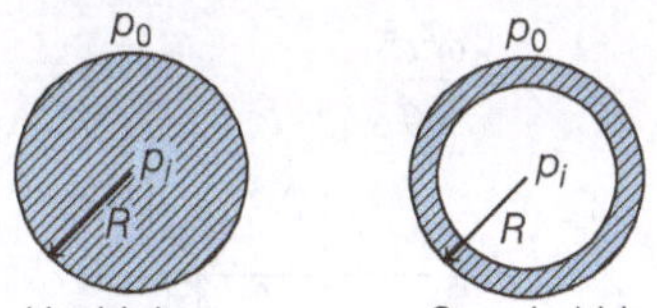

Liquid drop Soap bubble

Excess pressure inside a liquid drop, $(p_i - p_o) = \dfrac{2S}{R}$

Excess pressure inside a soap bubble, $(p_i - p_o) = \dfrac{4S}{R}$ NEET 2022, 19

A soap bubble has two surfaces which are in contact with air i.e. outer and inner layer of bubble. Hence, excess pressure of soap bubble is twice of the excess pressure of liquid drop.

Capillary Rise

The phenomenon of rising or falling of liquid in a capillary, when it is immersed in a liquid is called capillarity.

- When a capillary tube is inserted into water as shown in figure. The contact angle between water and glass is acute, thus the surface of water in the capillary is concave.
- The pressure difference between the two sides of top surface, $p_i - p_0 = \dfrac{2S}{r}\cos\theta$
- The height of liquid column in a capillary tube is given by $h = \dfrac{2S\cos\theta}{r\rho g}$ NEET 2020

  where, r is the radius of the capillary tube, θ is the angle of contact and ρ is density of liquid.

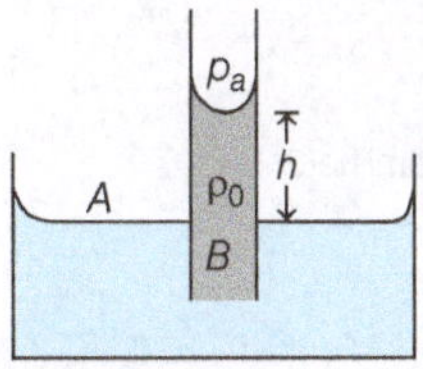

Capillary tube immerged in water

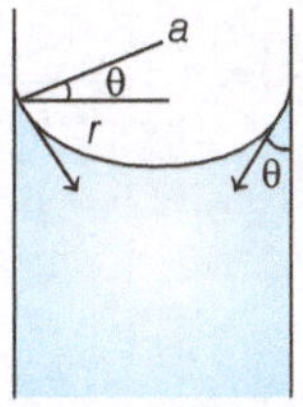

Enlarged picture of capillary tube

- The capillary rise h in terms of radius of the meniscus a.

$$h = \frac{2S\cos\theta}{r\rho g} \quad ...(i)$$

Also, $r = a\cos\theta$ ...(ii)

∴ From Eqs. (i) and (ii), we get

$$h = \frac{2S}{a\rho g}$$

- In capillary, there are following cases

  (i) **When the angle of contact between the liquid and glass is acute, then surface of liquid in the capillary is concave.**

  The pressure of the liquid inside the tube, just at the meniscus (air-liquid interface) is less than the atmospheric pressure.

  (ii) **When the angle of contact between the liquid and glass is obtuse, then surface of liquid in the capillary is convex.**

  The pressure of liquid inside the tube, just at the meniscus (air-liquid interface) is greater than the atmospheric pressure.

  (iii) **When the angle of contact between the liquid and glass is right angle, the surface of liquid in the capillary tube is plane.**

  The pressure of liquid inside the tube, just at the meniscus (air-liquid interface) is equal to the atmospheric pressure.

Caution Points

- Force is a vector quantity, but the ratio of force to area i.e. pressure is a scalar quantity.
The concept of fluid can be described by the fluid properties that varies from one point to another in the fluid.
- The pressure measuring instruments such as tyre pressure gauge and blood pressure gauge (sphygmomanometer) measures gauge pressure only.
- Two streamlines never intersect in a steady flow of the fluid.

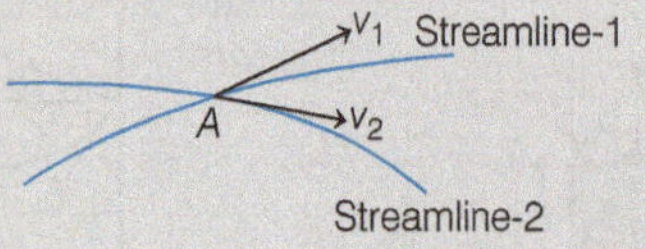

Crossing of two streamlines indicates that the particle have two different velocities at the point of intersection which is not possible.

- For viscous fluid, the work done by viscous force is converted into energy loss.
The energy equation for viscous fluid is modified form of Bernoulli's equation.

$$p_1 + \frac{1}{2}\rho v_1^2 + \rho g h_1 = p_2 + \frac{1}{2}\rho v_2^2 + \rho g h_2 + E_{\text{loss}}$$

- Surface tension is the surface energy present at the surface of fluid in the form of excess potential energy. It is not the potential energy of internal molecules of the fluid.
The excess potential energy of the surface is generated at the interface of two substances in which at least one is a fluid.

PYQ Notes

1. If a spherical body of mass m and density σ is dropped in a viscous liquid of density ρ. The body moves with constant velocity after sometime, then the viscous force on the body is given by

$$F_v = mg - \frac{\rho m}{\sigma} g = mg\left(1 - \frac{\rho}{\sigma}\right)$$

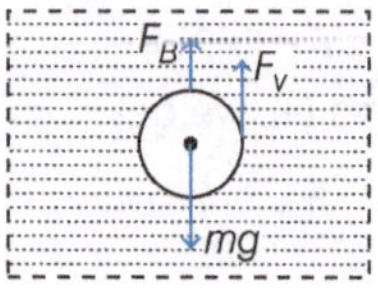

[NEET 2021]

2. When two soap bubbles of radii R_1 and R_2 are combined to form a common surface, the radius of curvature of common surface, $R = \frac{R_1 R_2}{R_2 - R_1}$. **[JEE Main 2021]**
3. If N small drops of liquids having each of radius r and terminal velocity v combined, then terminal velocity of new drop, $v' = vN^{\frac{2}{3}}$ **[NEET 2020]**
4. If a liquid of density ρ is coming out with velocity v from a pipe of cross-section area A and hits a plate, then the force exerted on the plate by the liquid is given by
$$F = v(\rho A v) = \rho A v^2$$ **[NEET 2019]**
5. When a spherical body of radius r falls in a viscous liquid, then

Power = rate of production of heat

$$P = F \cdot v_T = 6\pi\eta r v_T \cdot v_T = \frac{24}{81}\frac{\pi r^5 g^2(\rho - \sigma)}{\eta}$$ **[NEET 2017]**

6. If a long cylindrical vessel of radius r filled with a certain liquid. The vessel is rotated by angular velocity ω about its axis, then the height of liquid raise in the vessel is given by

$$p_0 + \frac{1}{2}\rho\omega^2 r^2 = p_0 + \rho g h$$

$$\therefore \quad h = \frac{\omega^2 r^2}{2g}$$ **[NEET 2016]**

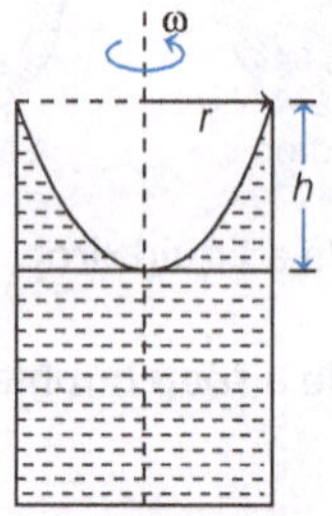

7. If length of capillary tube is less than or equal to height of liquid rises (h), then the liquid after reaching the upper end will increase the radius of its meniscus. **[NEET 2015]**

Step by Step

Mastering NCERT

- Concept Builders
- Topical Questions
- Assertion and Reason Questions
- Statement Based
- Matching Type
- Numerical Type
- NCERT Exemplar
- Past Exams MCQs
- Skill Boosters

Concept Builders

1 When an object is submerged in a fluid at rest, the fluid exerts a net force on its surface. This force is always normal to the object's surface. [T/F]

2 It is difficult for a man to walk on sand while a camel walks easily on sand. This is due to the fact that for small area, pressure is less. [T/F]

3 According to Pascal's law, the pressure in a fluid at rest is ...... (same / different) at all points at same height .

4 In a car brake system, piston connected with brake pedal is larger, whereas piston connected with brake shoe is of smaller area. [T/F]

5 The small force applied on the smaller piston will be appearing as a very large force on the larger piston. On which law this concept is based.

6 The pressure p at depth below the surface of a liquid open to the atmosphere is greater than atmospheric pressure. What does the excess pressure is called?

7 The liquid pressure .... (increases/decreases) with the decrease in depth.

8 The volume of liquid flowing per second out of an orifice at the bottom of a tank does not depend upon density of liquid. [T/F]

9 The pans of a physical balance are in equilibrium. The air is blown under the right side, then the right side pan will move .... (up/down)

10 In a steady flow two streamlines do not intersect as it means that the fluid particle will have two possible velocities at the point of intersection which is not possible. [T/F]

11 What forces makes mosquitoes float on the surface of water?

12 With rise in temperature, the viscosity for gases ...... (increases / decreases) and for liquid .... (increases/ decreases) .

13 The force required by a man to move his limbs immersed in water is smaller than the force for the same movement in air. This is due to the .... (pressure/ upthrust) by water.

14 A spaceship while entering the earth's atmosphere catch fire, this is due to .... (Surface tension/Viscosity) of air.

15 A closed compartment containing gas is moving with same acceleration in horizontal direction. Neglect the effect of gravity. What will be the pressure in the front compartment with respect to the rear compartment.

16 An iron needle slowly placed on the surface of water floats in it because of surface tension. [T/F]

17 The angle between tangent to the liquid surface at the point of contact and solid surface inside the liquid is termed as .... (angle of contact/angle of inclination).

18 When a glass capillary is dipped vertically in a mercury tank, the mercury level in capillary will ...... (remain same / fall)

19 What is the height to which a liquid rises or falls in a capillary is directly proportional to?

20 If two soap bubbles of different radii are connected by a tube, then the air flows from .... (bigger/smaller) bubble to .... (bigger/smaller) bubble.

Topical Questions

Pressure

1 The fluids offer very little resistance to **NCERT Pg. 180**

(a) pressure (b) normal stress
(c) shear stress (d) viscosity

2 Which of the following has the volume equal to the entire volume of its container? **NCERT Pg. 180**

(a) Nitrogen (b) Water
(c) Wood (d) Kerosene

3 The two thigh bones (femurs), each of cross-sectional area 10 cm^2 support the upper part of human body of mass 40 kg. Estimate the average pressure sustained by the femurs. **NCERT Pg. 181**

(a) 2×10^5 Nm^{-2} (b) 3×10^4 Nm^{-2}
(c) 2.5×10^3 Nm^{-2} (d) 6×10^4 Nm^{-2}

4 Pressure at half of the depth of lake is equal to 3/4 pressure at the bottom of the lake, then what is the depth of the lake? **NCERT Pg. 182**

$(p_{atm} = 10^5 N/m^2)$

(a) 20 m (b) 10 m
(c) 40 m (d) 5 m

5 Pressure at a point inside a liquid does not depend on **NCERT Pg. 182**

(a) the depth of the point below the surface of the liquid
(b) the nature of the liquid
(c) the acceleration due to gravity at that point
(d) total weight of fluid in the beaker

6 Figure given below shows an element in the interior of a fluid at rest. This elemental volume is in the shape of a right angled prism. Let the elemental volume is small enough that we can ignore the effect of gravity, but it is drawn in an enlarged scale for the sake of clarity. **NCERT Pg. 182**

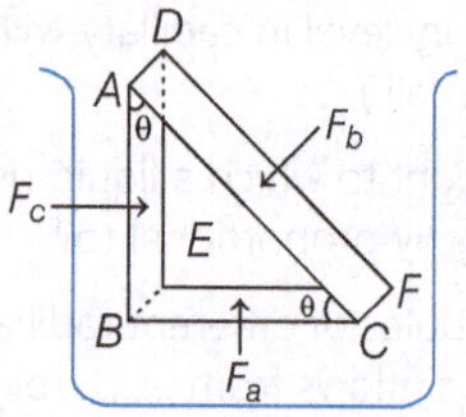

For equilibrium of elemental volume, which of these are correct?

(a) $F_b \sin\theta = F_c$ (b) $F_c \cos\theta = F_b$
(c) $F_b \cos\theta = F_c$ (d) $F_a \cos\theta = F_b$

7 An *L*-shaped tube containing liquid of density ρ is accelerated horizontally with acceleration as shown in the figure. The end of tube *B* is closed while end *A* is open. If the atmospheric pressure is p_0. Then, the pressure at *B* is **NCERT Pg. 183**

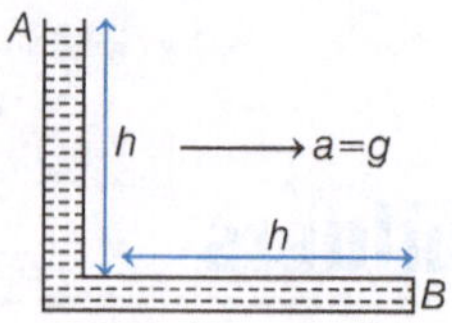

(a) $\frac{p_0}{2}$ (b) p_0 (c) $\frac{2}{3}p_0$ (d) $2p_0$

8 The liquids in U-tube of a uniform cross-section are water and mercury. If the difference of the height of the mercury columns is 2 cm, then the height *h* of the water column is **NCERT Pg. 184**

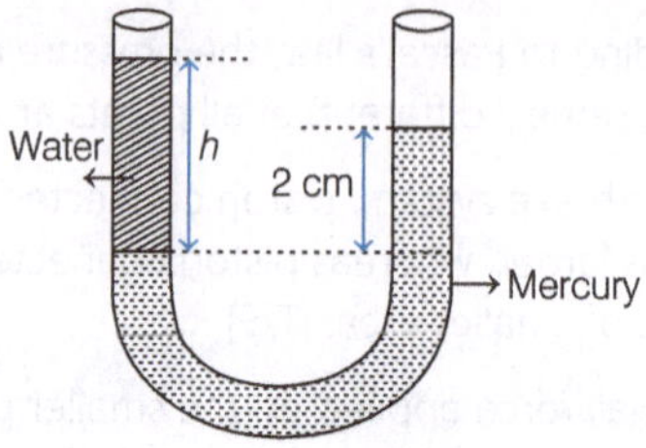

(a) 6.8 cm (b) 13.6 cm
(c) 27.2 cm (d) 54 cm

9 The pressure at a depth $\frac{1}{3}$ of the depth of the lake is equal to half of the pressure at the bottom of the lake. If the height of the water barometer is 10m, the depth of the lake is **NCERT Pg. 184**

(a) 60 m (b) 30 m
(c) 40 m (d) 20 m

10 The heart of a man pumps 5 L of blood through the arteries per minute at a pressure of 150 mm of mercury. If the density of mercury be 13.6×10^3 kg m^{-3} and $g = 10$ ms^{-2}, then the power of heart in watt is **NCERT Pg. 184**

(a) 1.70 (b) 2.35
(c) 3.0 (d) 1.50

11 A long cylindrical vessel is half-filled with a liquid. When the vessel is rotated about its own vertical axis, the liquid rises up near the wall. If the radius of vessel is 5 cm and its rotational speed is 2 rotations per second, then the difference in the heights between the centre and the sides (in cm) will be **NCERT Pg. 184**

(a) 0.1 (b) 1.2
(c) 0.4 (d) 2.0

12 Find density of ethyl alcohol. Using information given in the diagram below. **NCERT Pg. 184**

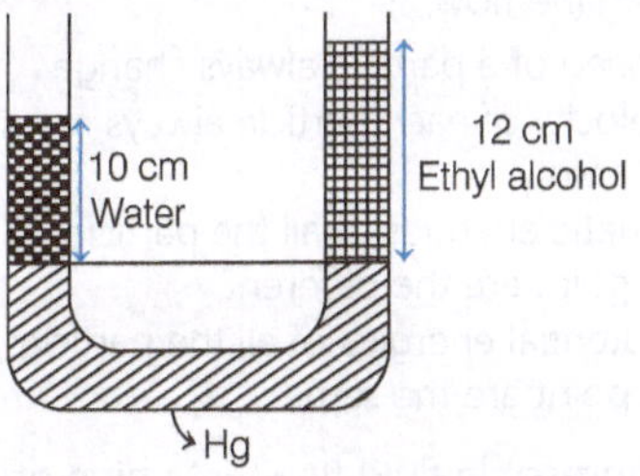

(a) 0.83 gcm^{-3} (b) 0.5 gcm^{-3}
(c) 1.83 gcm^{-3} (d) 0.12 gcm^{-3}

13 A liquid of density ρ is coming out of a hose pipe of radius a with horizontal speed v and hits a mesh. 50% of the liquid passes through the mesh unaffected 25% losses all of its momentum and, 25% comes back with the same speed. The resultant pressure on the mesh will be **NCERT Pg. 184**

(a) ρv^2 (b) $\frac{1}{2}\rho v^2$ (c) $\frac{1}{4}\rho v^2$ (d) $\frac{3}{4}\rho v^2$

14 A student measures pressure of a gas in a container using a mercury manometer and she also measures atmospheric pressure using a mercury barometer. She gave following representation **NCERT Pg. 184**

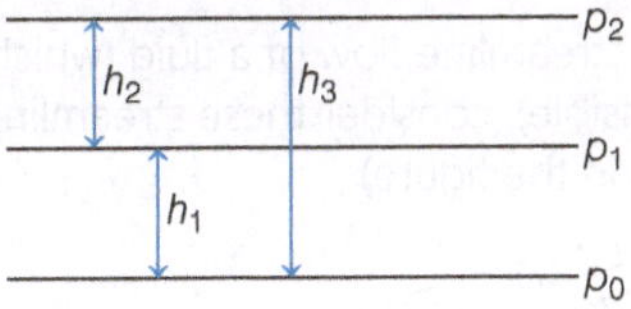

If p_1 = atmospheric pressure,
and p_2 = absolute pressure, then
(a) gauge pressure = $h_1 + h_2$
(b) gauge pressure = $h_3 - h_1$
(c) gauge pressure = h_3
(d) absolute pressure = h_1

15 A hydraulic lift is designed to lift a car with a maximum mass of 3000 kg. The area of cross-section of smaller piston carrying load is 425 cm^2. What maximum pressure would the smaller piston have to bear? **NCERT Pg. 185**

(a) $6.92 \times 10^5 Nm^{-2}$ (b) $3.68 \times 10^5 Nm^{-2}$
(c) $5.7 \times 10^5 Nm^{-2}$ (d) $2.1 \times 10^6 Nm^{-2}$

16 A hydraulic lift has limbs of areas A_1 and A_2 ($A_1 >> A_2$). A piston creates a force F_2 in small limb to balance a large force F_1. Which of the following statement is correct? **NCERT Pg. 185**

(a) $F_2 \propto \frac{A_1}{A_2}$.
(b) Work done by F_1 > Work done by F_2.
(c) Pressure in small area limb is more than pressure in large area limb.
(d) If piston of small area limb has velocity v_2 and piston of large area limb as velocity v_1, then $\frac{v_2}{v_1} = \frac{A_1}{A_2}$.

17 A hydraulic lift has 2 limbs of areas A and $2A$. Force F is applied over limb of area A to lift a heavy car. If distance moved by piston P_1 is x, then distance moved by piston P_2 is **NCERT Pg. 185**

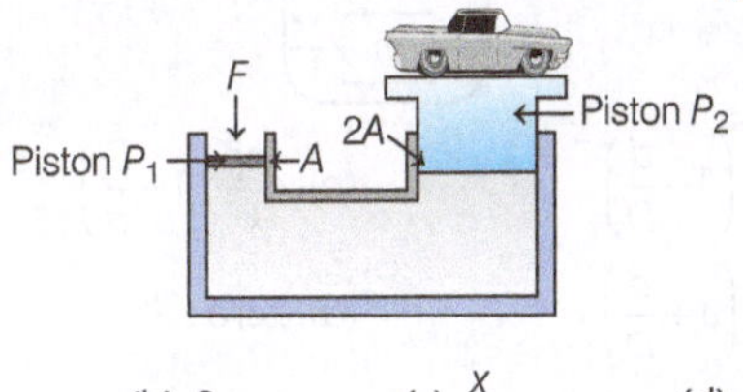

(a) x (b) $2x$ (c) $\frac{x}{2}$ (d) $4x$

18 Two syringes of different cross-sections (without needles) filled with water are connected with a tightly fitted rubber tube filled with water. Diameters of the smaller piston and larger piston are 1.0 cm and 3.0 cm, respectively. If the smaller piston is pushed in through 6.0 cm, how much does the larger piston move out? **NCERT Pg. 185**

(a) 0.67 cm (b) 0.5 cm
(c) 0.75 cm (d) 1.00 cm

19 A car of mass 500 kg is lifted by a hydraulic jack that consist of two pistons. If the diameter of large and small pistons are 2 m and 20 cm respectively, then force required to lift the car by smaller piston is (take, $g = 10\ m/s^2$) **NCERT Pg. 185**
(a) 5000 N (b) 25 N (c) 500 N (d) 50 N

20 A thin uniform cylindrical sheet, closed at both ends,is partially filled with water. It is floating vertically in water in half-submerged state. If ρ_c is the relative density of the material of the shell with respect to water, then the correct statement is that the shell is **NCERT Pg. 186**
(a) more than half filled, if ρ_c is less than 0.5.
(b) more than half filled, if ρ_c is more than 1.0.
(c) half filled, if ρ_c is more than 0.5.
(d) less than half filled, if ρ_c is less than 0.5.

21 A sphere of radius R has a concentric cavity of radius r. The relative density of the material of the sphere is σ. It just floats when placed in a tank full of water. The ratio $\frac{R}{r}$ is **NCERT Pg. 186**

(a) $\left(\frac{\sigma-1}{\sigma}\right)^{\frac{1}{3}}$ (b) $\left(\frac{\sigma}{\sigma-1}\right)^{\frac{1}{3}}$

(c) $\left(\frac{\sigma+1}{\sigma}\right)^{2}$ (d) $\left(\frac{\sigma}{\sigma+1}\right)^{3}$

22 A cube of mass m and density D is suspended from the point P, by a spring of stiffness k. The system is kept inside a beaker filled with a liquid of density d. The elongation in the spring (assuming $D > d$) is **NCERT Pg. 186**

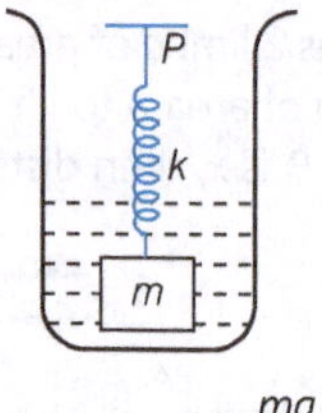

(a) $\frac{mg}{k}\left(1-\frac{d}{D}\right)$ (b) $\frac{mg}{k}\left(1-\frac{D}{d}\right)$

(c) $\frac{mg}{k}\left(1+\frac{d}{D}\right)$ (d) zero

23 A cubical block of wood 10 cm on a side floats at the interface between oil and water with its lower surface horizontal and 4 cm below the interface. The density of oil is $0.6 gcm^{-3}$. The mass of block is **NCERT Pg. 186**

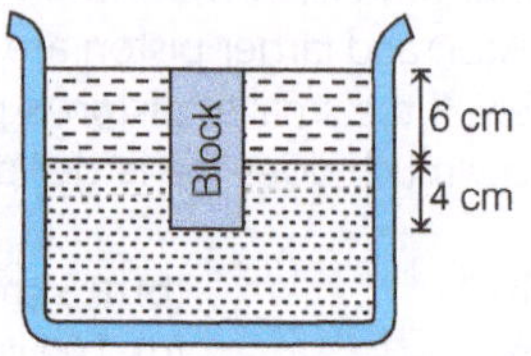

(a) 706 g (b) 607 g (c) 760 g (d) 670 g

24 A solid body floats in water has $\frac{1}{5}$ th of its volume immersed in it. What fraction of its volume will be immersed, if it floats in a liquid of specific gravity 1.4? **NCERT Pg. 186**

(a) $\frac{1}{6}$ (b) $\frac{1}{3}$ (c) $\frac{1}{5}$ (d) $\frac{1}{7}$

25 An ice cube floats on water in a beaker with (9/10)th of its volume submerged under water. What fraction of its volume will be submerged, if the beaker of water is taken to the moon where the gravity is (1/6)th that on the earth? **NCERT Pg. 186**

(a) $\frac{9}{10}$ (b) $\frac{27}{50}$ (c) $\frac{2}{3}$ (d) Zero

26 A cubical block of steel of each side equal to l is floating on mercury in a vessel. The densities of steel and mercury are ρ_s and ρ_m. The height of the block above the mercury level is given by **NCERT Pg. 186**

(a) $l\left(1+\frac{\rho_s}{\rho_m}\right)$ (b) $l\left(1-\frac{\rho_s}{\rho_m}\right)$

(c) $l\left(1+\frac{\rho_m}{\rho_s}\right)$ (d) $l\left(1-\frac{\rho_m}{\rho_s}\right)$

Flow of Liquids

27 In a streamline flow, **NCERT Pg. 186**

(a) the speed of a particle always change
(b) the velocity of each particle always remains same at a given point
(c) the kinetic energies of all the particles arriving at a given point are the different
(d) the potential energies of all the particles arriving at a given point are the same

28 An incompressible fluid flows in a pipe of uniform cross-section of area A which splits up into two outlets O_1 and O_2 of area of cross -section $\frac{A}{3}$ and $\frac{2A}{3}$ respectively as shown in the figure. The velocity of fluid flow at O_1 is 3 m/s and in the pipe is 6 m/s. The speed of fluid flow at O_2 is **NCERT Pg. 187**

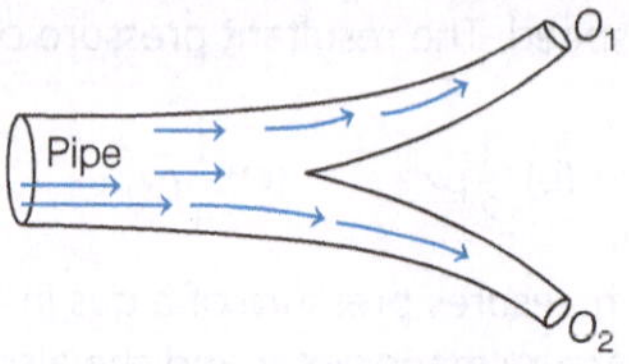

(a) 3 m/s (b) 7.5 m/s
(c) 4 m/s (d) 6 m/s

29 In case of streamline flow of a fluid (which is incompressible), consider these streamlines A, B and C (as shown in the figure) **NCERT Pg. 187**

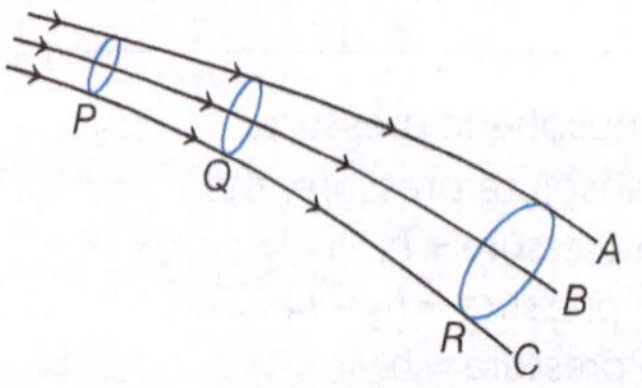

Let, P, Q and R are 3 planes perpendicular to the direction of flow of streamlines, then which of the following is correct?

(a) $m_P > m_Q > m_R$, where m = mass flow per second.
(b) $v_P > v_Q > v_R$
(c) $n_P > n_Q > n_R$, where n = number of fluid particles crossing area per unit time.
(d) $m_P < m_Q < m_R$

30 A liquid flows through a pipe of varying diameter. The velocity of the liquid is $2 ms^{-1}$ at a point, where the diameter is 6 cm. The velocity of the liquid at a point, where the diameter is 3 cm will be **NCERT Pg. 187**

(a) $1 ms^{-1}$ (b) $4 ms^{-1}$
(c) $8 ms^{-1}$ (d) $16 ms^{-1}$

31 An incompressible liquid flows through a horizontal tube as shown (areas of tubes is marked), then the velocity v of the fluid is **NCERT Pg. 187**

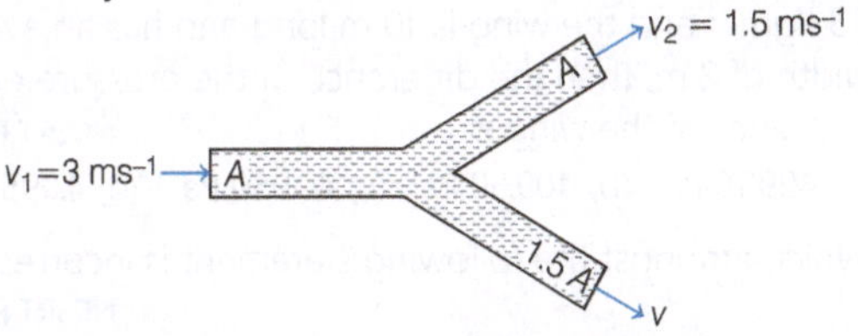

(a) $3.0\ ms^{-1}$ (b) $1.5\ ms^{-1}$
(c) $1.0\ ms^{-1}$ (d) $2.25\ ms^{-1}$

32 In a turbulent flow, the velocity of the liquid molecules in contact with the walls of the tube is **NCERT Pg. 187**
(a) zero (b) maximum
(c) equal to critical velocity (d) may have any value

33 In a laminar flow, the velocity of the liquid in contact with the walls of the tube is **NCERT Pg. 187**
(a) zero
(b) maximum
(c) in between zero and maximum
(d) equal to critical velocity

Bernoulli's Principle

34 According to Bernoulli's equation,

$$\frac{p}{\rho g} + h + \frac{1}{2}\frac{v^2}{g} = \text{constant}$$

The terms, $\frac{p}{\rho g}$, h and $\frac{1}{2}\frac{v^2}{g}$ are generally called respectively : **NCERT Pg. 188**
(a) Gravitational head, pressure head and velocity head
(b) Gravity, gravitational head and velocity head
(c) Pressure head, gravitational head and velocity head
(d) Gravity, pressure and velocity head

35 Determine the pressure difference in tube of non-uniform cross sectional area as shown in figure.
$\Delta p = ?, d_1 = 5$ cm, $v_1 = 4$ m/s, $d_2 = 2$ cm. **NCERT Pg. 188**

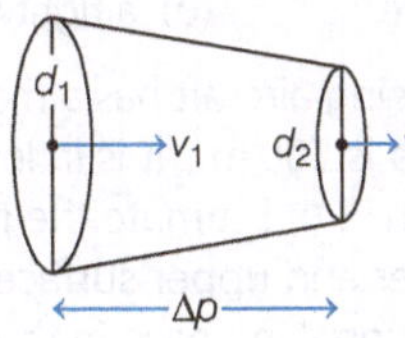

(a) 304200 Pa (b) 304500 Pa
(c) 302500 Pa (d) 303500 Pa

36 A sealed tank has 2-openings as shown below. One at near top and other at near bottom. Let height of water filled above the bottom opening is h and a compressor producing a pressure p is connected to top opening.

Velocity of water obtained from lower opening is (take, atmospheric pressure p_a such that $p - p_a = \rho g h$) **NCERT Pg. 188**

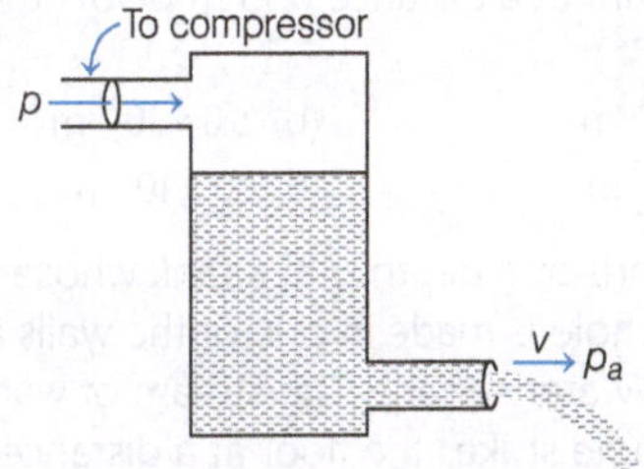

(a) $\sqrt{2gh}$ (b) $\sqrt{gh}$ (c) $2\sqrt{gh}$ (d) 0

37 A water tank standing on floor has two small holes punched in vertical wall one above the other. The holes are 2.4 cm and 7.6 cm above the floor. If the jet of water from holes hit the floor at the same point, then height of water in tank is **NCERT Pg. 189**

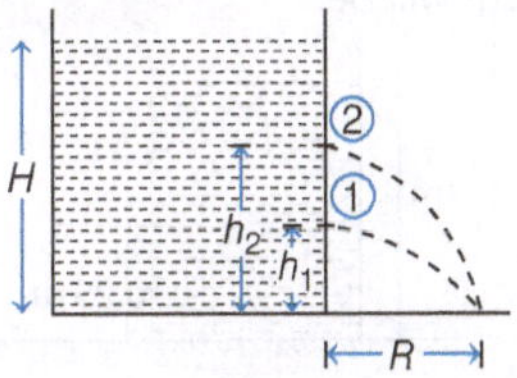

(a) 10 cm (b) 5 cm
(c) 2.5 cm (d) 6.8 cm

38 For the shown diagram, find range of liquid coming out from small hole ($g = 10 m/s^2$) **NCERT Pg. 189**

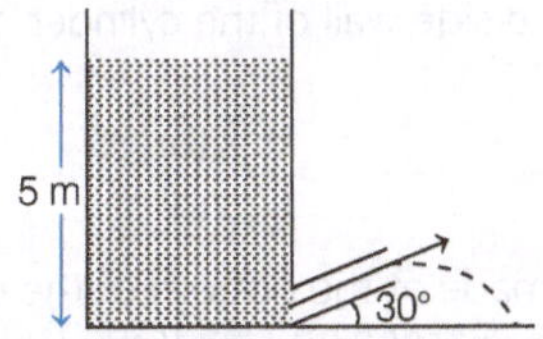

(a) 5m (b) 12.6 m
(c) 8.7m (d) 10m

39 As shown in the adjoining figure, water squirts horizontally out of two small holes in the side of the cylinder and the two streams strike the ground at the same point. If the hole Q is at a height h above the ground and the level of water stands at height H above the ground, then the height of P above ground level is **NCERT Pg. 189**

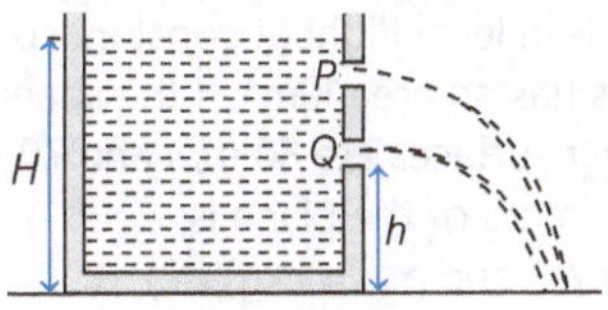

(a) $2h$ (b) H/h
(c) $H - h$ (d) $H/2$

40 Water is flowing continuously from a tap having cross-sectional area $10 \times 10^{-5}\,m^2$. The water velocity as it leaves the tap is $1\,ms^{-1}$. The cross-sectional area of the water stream at a distance 0.15 m below the tap is $(g = 10\,ms^{-2})$. **NCERT Pg. 189**

(a) $5.0 \times 10^{-4} m^2$ (b) $5.0 \times 10^{-5} m^2$
(c) $1.0 \times 10^{-5} m^2$ (d) $2.0 \times 10^{-5} m^2$

41 Water stands at a depth H in a tank whose side walls are vertical. A hole is made in one of the walls at a height h below the water surface. The stream of water emerging from the hole strikes the floor at a distance R from the tank, where R is given by **NCERT Pg. 189**

(a) $R = \sqrt{h(H-h)}$ (b) $R = \sqrt{h(H+h)}$
(c) $R = 2\sqrt{h(H-h)}$ (d) $R = 2\sqrt{h(H+h)}$

42 If a small orifice is made at a height of 0.25 m from the ground as shown in figure below, the horizontal range of water stream will be **NCERT Pg. 189**

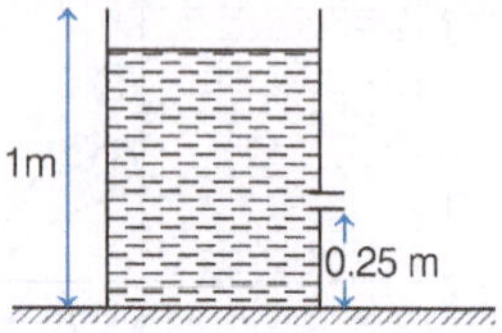

(a) 46.5 cm (b) 56.6 cm
(c) 76.6 cm (d) 86.6 cm

43 A cylinder of height 20 m is completely filled with water. The velocity of efflux of water (in ms^{-1}) through a small hole on the side wall of the cylinder near its bottom is **NCERT Pg. 189**

(a) 10 (b) 20
(c) 25.5 (d) 5

44 A hole is made at the bottom of the tank filled with water (density $1000\,kgm^{-3}$). If the total pressure at the bottom of the tank is 3 atm ($1\,atm = 10^5\,Nm^{-2}$), then the velocity of efflux is **NCERT Pg. 189**

(a) $\sqrt{200}\,ms^{-1}$ (b) $\sqrt{400}\,ms^{-1}$
(c) $\sqrt{500}\,ms^{-1}$ (d) $\sqrt{800}\,ms^{-1}$

45 Just before "Heart attack", velocity of blood flow through the affected "artery" **NCERT Pg. 189**

(a) increases (b) decreases
(c) remains same (d) stopped

46 A plane is in level flight at constant speed and each of its wings has an area $10 m^2$. If the speed of air on upper and lower surfaces are 80 m/s and 70 m/s, respectively, then the mass of the plane is $(g = 10\,m/s^2$ and $\rho_{air} = 1\,kg/m^3)$ **NCERT Pg. 190**

(a) 2500 kg (b) 1500 kg
(c) 3000 kg (d) 4000 kg

47 Air is streaming past a horizontal airplane's wing such that its speed is $120\,ms^{-1}$ over the upper surface and $90\,ms^{-1}$ at the lower surface. If the density of air is $1.3\,kgm^{-3}$ and the wing is 10 m long and has an average width of 2 m, then the difference of the pressure on the two sides of the wing is **NCERT Pg. 190**

(a) 4095.0 Pa (b) 409.50 Pa (c) 40.950 Pa (d) 4.0950 Pa

48 Which amongst the following statement is incorrect? **NCERT Pg. 190**

(a) A jet of air striking a plate placed perpendicular to it is an example of turbulent flow.
(b) The carburetor of automobile has a venturi channel (nozzle) through which air flows with a high speed.
(c) Ball moving without spinning inside a fluid experiences a net upward force.
(d) None of the above

49 A ball is moving without spinning in a straight line through a fluid (as shown)

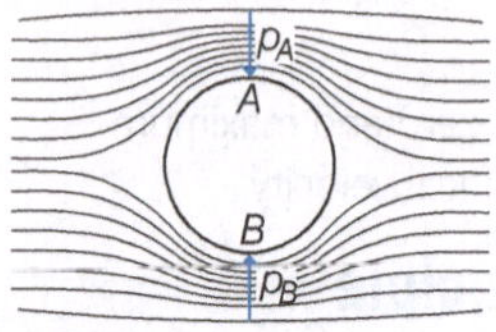

If p_A and p_B are pressure values at A and B, then **NCERT Pg. 190**

(a) $p_A < p_B$ (b) $p_B < p_A$ (c) $p_A \times p_B = 1$ (d) $p_A / p_B = 1$

50 A ball is moving in a straight line through a fluid which is spinning around its own centre of mass as shown.

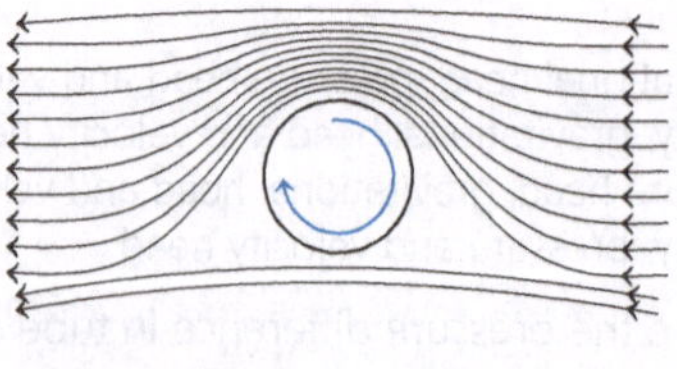

Then, the ball experiences **NCERT Pg. 190**

(a) an upward force (b) a downward force
(c) a leftward force (d) a rightward force

51 A fully loaded boeing aircraft has a mass of 3.3×10^5 kg. Its total wing area is $500\,m^2$. It is in level flight with a speed of $960\,kmh^{-1}$. (i) Estimate the pressure difference between the lower and upper surfaces of the wings (ii) Estimate the fractional increase in the speed of the air on the upper surface of the wing relative to the lower surface. The density of air is $\rho = 1.2\,kg\,m^{-3}$. **NCERT Pg. 190**

(a) $6.5 \times 10^{+3}\,Nm^{-2}$, 0.01
(b) $6.5 \times 10^3\,Nm^{-2}$, 0.09
(c) $6.5 \times 10^3\,Nm^{-2}$, 0.08
(d) $2.5 \times 10^3\,Nm^{-2}$, 0.02

52 The flow of blood in a large artery of an anesthetised dog is diverted through a venturimeter. The wider part of the meter has a cross-sectional area equal to that of the artery, $A = 8\ \text{mm}^2$.

The narrower part has an area, $a = 4\ \text{mm}^2$ and density of blood, $\rho = 1.06 \times 10^3\ \text{kg m}^{-3}$.

The pressure drop in the artery is 24 Pa, then what is the speed of the blood in the artery? **NCERT Pg. 191**

(a) $0.5\ \text{ms}^{-1}$

(b) $0.125\ \text{ms}^{-1}$

(c) $1.25\ \text{ms}^{-1}$

(d) $2.5\ \text{ms}^{-1}$

Viscosity

53 As the temperature of water increases, its viscosity **NCERT Pg. 191**

(a) remains unchanged

(b) decreases

(c) increases

(d) increases or decreases depending on the external pressure

54 The coefficient of viscosity for hot air is **NCERT Pg. 191**

(a) greater than the coefficient of viscosity for cold air

(b) smaller than the coefficient of viscosity for cold air

(c) same as the coefficient of viscosity for cold air

(d) increases or decreases depending on the external pressure

55 We have three beakers *A*, *B* and *C* containing three different liquids. They are stirred vigorously and placed on a table, then liquid which is **NCERT Pg. 191**

(a) most viscous comes to rest at the earliest

(b) most viscous comes to rest at the last

(c) most viscous slows down earliest but comes to rest at the last

(d) All of them come to rest at the same time

56 An object is moving through a viscous fluid. Which of the following statement is incorrect? **NCERT Pg. 194**

(a) Viscous force on object decreases with increase in temperature.

(b) Viscous force depends on velocity of object.

(c) Viscous force decreases if object is made pointed.

(d) Viscous force is directed anti-parallel to velocity of flow.

57 A metal block of area $0.10\ \text{m}^2$ is connected to a 0.010 kg mass *via* a string that passes over an ideal pulley (considered massless and frictionless), as in figure. A liquid with a film thickness of 0.30 mm is placed between the block and the table. When released the block moves to the right with a constant speed of $0.085\ \text{ms}^{-1}$, find the coefficient of viscosity of the liquid. **NCERT Pg. 191**

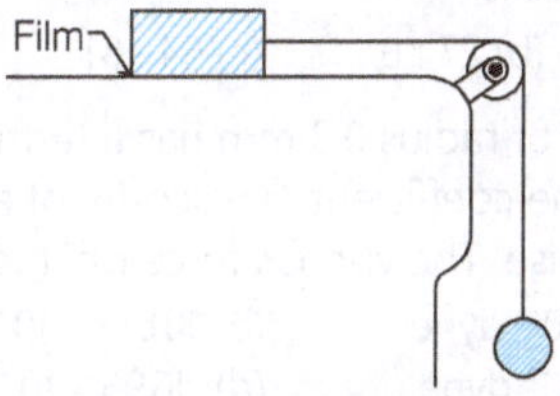

(a) 4×10^{-2} Pa-s

(b) 3.45×10^{-3} Pa-s

(c) 5×10^{-2} Pa-s

(d) 7×10^{-7} Pa-s

58 A body is moving in a viscous liquid with velocity more than terminal velocity, then find curve between acceleration *versus* velocity **NCERT Pg. 192**

(a) 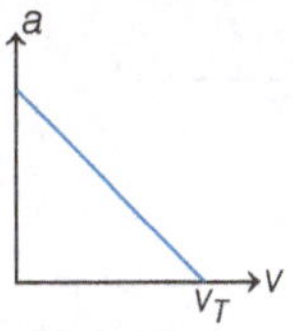

(b) 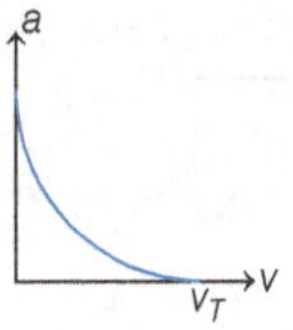

(c) 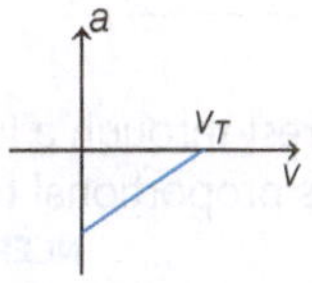

(d) 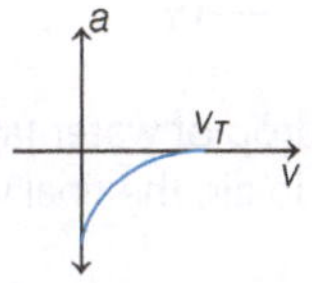

59 The velocity of a spherical ball of mass *m* and density ρ_1, when dropped in a container filled with glycerol becomes constant after some time. If the density of glycerol is ρ_2, then viscous force acting on the ball when it's velocity is constant will be **NCERT Pg. 192**

(a) $\dfrac{m\rho_1}{\rho_2} g$

(b) $\dfrac{m(\rho_1 + \rho_2)}{(\rho_1 - \rho_2)} g$

(c) $mg \dfrac{\rho_2}{\rho_1}$

(d) $mg\left[\dfrac{\rho_1 - \rho_2}{\rho_1}\right]$

60 A container filled with viscous liquid is moving vertically downwards with constant speed $3v_0$. At the instant shown, a sphere of radius *r* is moving vertically downwards (in liquid) has speed v_0. The coefficient of viscosity is η. There is no relative motion between the liquid and the container. Then at the shown instant, the magnitude of viscous force acting on sphere is **NCERT Pg. 192**

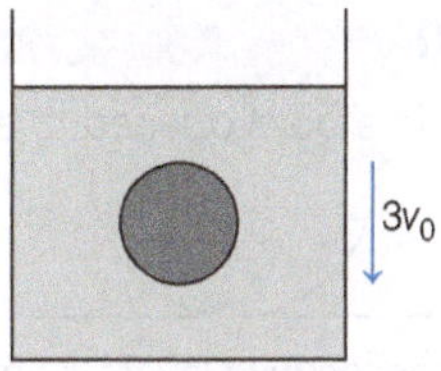

(a) $6\pi\eta r v_0$

(b) $12\pi\eta r v_0$

(c) $18\pi\eta r v_0$

(d) $24\pi\eta r v_0$

61 Two rain drops reach earth from clouds with different terminal velocities having ratio 9 : 4. Then, the ratio of their volumes is **NCERT Pg. 192**

(a) 3 : 2 (b) 27 : 8 (c) 64 : 81 (d) 8 : 27

62 A rain drop of radius 0.3 mm has a terminal velocity in air 1 m/s. The coefficient of viscosity of air is 18×10^{-5} poise. The viscous force on it is **NCERT Pg. 192**

(a) 101.73×10^{-4} dyne (b) 101.73×10^{-5} dyne
(c) 16.95×10^{-5} dyne (d) 16.95×10^{-4} dyne

63 Which one shows the variation of the velocity v with time t for a small sized spherical body falling in a column of a viscous liquid? **NCERT Pg. 192**

(a)
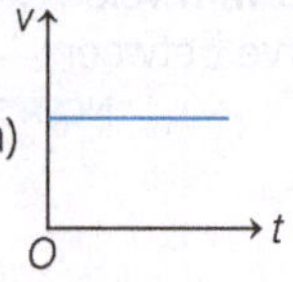

(b)
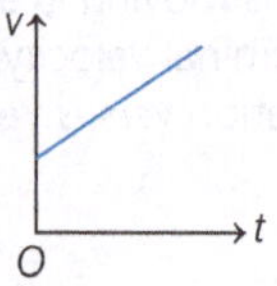

(c)
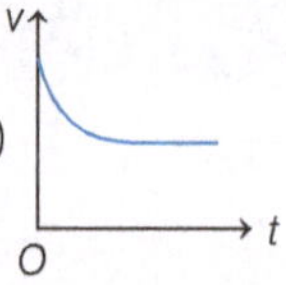

(d)
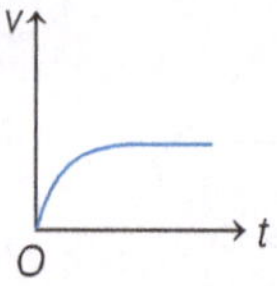

64 A small drop of water falls from rest through a large height h in air, the final velocity is proportional to **NCERT Pg. 192**

(a) $\sqrt{h}$ (b) h (c) $1/h$ (d) h^0

65 The terminal velocity of a copper ball of radius 2.0 mm falling through a tank of oil at 20°C is 6.5 cms^{-1}. Compute the viscosity of the oil at 20°C. Density of oil is $1.5 \times 10^3 \text{ kgm}^{-3}$, density of copper is $8.9 \times 10^3 \text{ kgm}^{-3}$ and $g = 9.8 \text{ m/s}^2$. **NCERT Pg. 192**

(a) 1×10^{-1} kg ms^{-1} (b) 9.9×10^{-1} kg ms^{-1}
(c) 24.3×10^{-2} kg ms^{-1} (d) 2×10^{-2} kg ms^{-1}

66 Consider two solid spheres P and Q each of density 8 gcm^{-3} and diameters 1 cm and 0.5 cm, respectively. Sphere P is dropped into a liquid of density 0.8 gcm^{-3} and viscosity $\eta = 3$ poiseuille. Sphere Q is dropped into a liquid of density 1.6 gcm^{-3} and viscosity $\eta = 2$ poiseuille. The ratio of the terminal velocities of P and Q is **NCERT Pg. 192**

(a) 3 : 1 (b) 9 : 1 (c) 2 : 4 (d) 4 : 2

Surface Tension

67 A liquid is kept in a bowl opened to atmosphere.

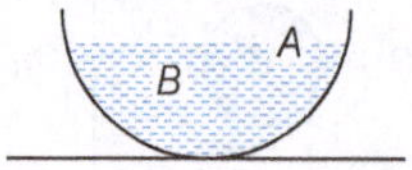

Consider two consecutive layers A and B as shown above, which of the following statement(s) is correct? **NCERT Pg. 193**

(a) Total energy of surface A = Total energy of surface B.
(b) Number of molecules in surface A > Number of molecules in surface B.
(c) Energy of a molecule of layer B is equal to energy of layer A.
(d) Net force on a molecule of surface B is zero.

68 The surface tension of a liquid at its boiling point **NCERT Pg. 191**

(a) becomes zero
(b) becomes infinity
(c) is equal to the value at room temperature
(d) is half to the value at room temperature

69 A liquid film is formed over a frame $ABCD$ as shown in figure. Wire CD can slide without friction. Maximum value of mass that can be hanged from CD without breaking the liquid film is **NCERT Pg. 194**

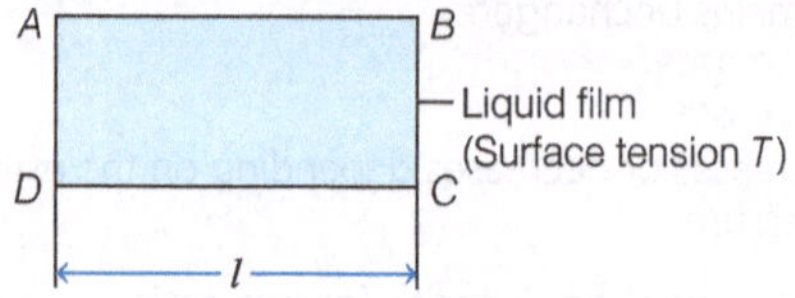

(a) $\frac{Tl}{g}$ (b) $\frac{2Tl}{g}$ (c) $\frac{g}{2Tl}$ (d) Tl

70 A small drop is formed using a dropper over a clean solid surface, then which of the following statement(s) is/are correct?

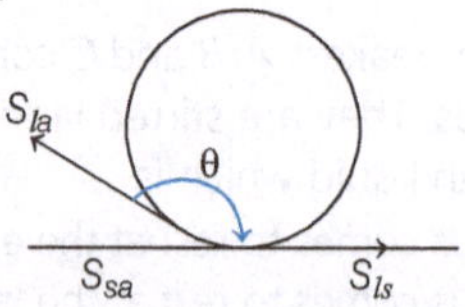

where, S_{la} = surface force of liquid and air,
S_{sa} = surface force of solid and air
and S_{ls} = surface force of liquid and solid. **NCERT Pg. 195**

(a) If $S_{ls} > S_{la}$, then angle of contact is less than 90°.
(b) If $S_{ls} > S_{la}$, then angle of contact is equal to 90°.
(c) If $S_{ls} > S_{la}$, then liquid spreads over solid surface.
(d) If $S_{ls} > S_{la}$, then liquid does not spread on solid surface

71 A 10 cm long wire is placed horizontally on the surface of water and is gently pulled up with a force of 2×10^{-2} N. To keep the wire in equilibrium, the surface tension in Nm^{-1} of water is **NCERT Pg. 195**

(a) 0.1 (b) 0.2
(c) 0.001 (d) 0.002

72 A wooden stick 2 m long is floating on the surface of water. The surface tension of water is 0.07 Nm^{-1}. By putting soap solution on one side of the stick, the surface tension is reduced to $0.06\ Nm^{-1}$. The net force on the stick will be **NCERT Pg. 195**

(a) 0.07 N (b) 0.06 N (c) 0.01 N (d) 0.02 N

73 The force required to separate two glass plates of $10^{-2}m^2$ with a film of water 0.05 mm thick between them, is (surface tension of water is $70 \times 10^{-3}\ Nm^{-1}$) **NCERT Pg. 195**

(a) 28 N (b) 14 N (c) 50 N (d) 38 N

74 A thin liquid film is formed between a U-shaped wire and a light slider, supporting a weight of 1.5×10^{-2} N as shown in the figure. The length of the slider is 30 cm and its weight is negligible. The surface tension of the liquid film is **NCERT Pg. 195**

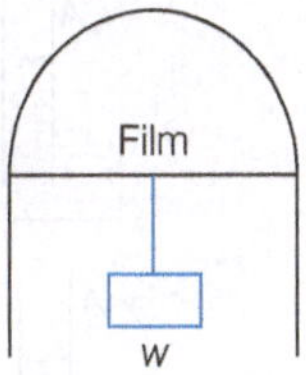

(a) $0.0125\ Nm^{-1}$ (b) $0.1\ Nm^{-1}$
(c) $0.05\ Nm^{-1}$ (d) $0.025\ Nm^{-1}$

75 If two soap bubbles of different radii are connected by a tube, **NCERT Pg. 196**

(a) Air flows from bigger bubble to the smaller bubble till the sizes become equal
(b) Air flows from bigger bubble to the smaller bubble till the sizes are interchanged
(c) Air flows from the smaller bubble to the bigger bubble
(d) There is no flow of air.

76 Pressure inside the two soap bubbles are 1.01 atm and 1.02 atm. The ratio of their free surface area is **NCERT Pg. 196**

(a) 2 : 1 (b) 1 : 8 (c) 101 : 102 (d) 4 : 1

77 If T be the surface tension, the amount of work done in blowing a soap bubble from a diameter d to diameter D is **NCERT Pg. 196**

(a) $\pi(D^2 - d^2)T$ (b) $2\pi(D^2 - d^2)T$
(c) $4\pi(D^2 - d^2)T$ (d) $8\pi(D^2 - d^2)T$

78 A soap bubble has radius R and thickness $d(<<R)$ as shown. It collapses into a spherical drop. The ratio of excess pressure in the drop to the excess pressure inside the bubble is **NCERT Pg. 196**

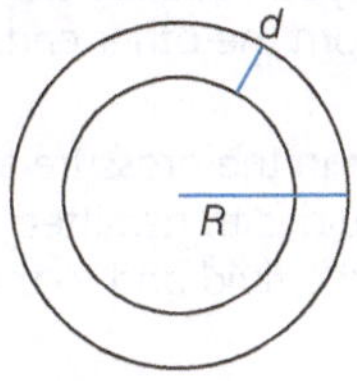

(a) $\left[\frac{R}{3d}\right]^{\frac{1}{3}}$ (b) $\left[\frac{R}{6d}\right]^{\frac{1}{3}}$ (c) $\left[\frac{R}{24d}\right]^{\frac{1}{3}}$ (d) $\left[\frac{R}{9d}\right]^{\frac{1}{3}}$

79 The shape of drops and bubbles are spherical due to its **NCERT Pg. 196**

(a) surface with minimum energy
(b) surface with maximum energy
(c) high pressure
(d) low pressure

80 A spherical drop of radius r is in equilibrium. The extra surface energy, if radius of bubble is increased by Δr, is (S = surface tension) **NCERT Pg. 196**

(a) $4\pi r\,\Delta r\,S$ (b) $8\pi r\,\Delta r\,S$
(c) $2\pi r\,\Delta r\,S$ (d) $10\pi r\,\Delta r\,S$

81 A small spherical droplet of density d is floating exactly half immersed in a liquid of density ρ and surface tension T. The radius of the droplet is (take note that, the surface tension applies an upward force on the droplet) **NCERT Pg. 196**

(a) $r = \sqrt{\frac{3T}{(2d - \rho)g}}$ (b) $r = \sqrt{\frac{T}{(d - \rho)g}}$

(c) $r = \sqrt{\frac{T}{(d + \rho)g}}$ (d) $r = \sqrt{\frac{2T}{3(d + \rho)g}}$

82 A soap bubble of radius r is blown up to form a bubble of radius $3r$ under isothermal conditions. If σ is the surface tension of soap solution, the energy spent in blowing is **NCERT Pg. 196**

(a) $3\pi\sigma r^2$ (b) $6\pi\sigma r^2$
(c) $12\pi\sigma r^2$ (d) $64\pi\sigma r^2$

83 Two small drops of mercury, each of radius r, coalesce to form a single large drop of radius R. The ratio of the total surface energies before and after the change is **NCERT Pg. 196**

(a) $1:2^{1/3}$ (b) $2^{1/3}:1$
(c) $2:1$ (d) $1:2$

84 The excess pressure inside an air bubble of radius r just below the surface of water is p_1. The excess pressure inside a drop of the same radius just outside the surface is p_2. If T is the surface tension, then **NCERT Pg. 196**

(a) $p_1 = 2p_2$ (b) $p_1 = p_2$
(c) $p_2 = 2p_1$ (d) $p_2 = 0, p_1 \neq 0$

85 The surface tension of water at temperature of the experiment is $7.30 \times 10^{-2}\ Nm^{-1}$. (1 atm pressure $= 1.01 \times 10^5$ Pa, density of water = 1000 kgm^{-3} and $g = 9.80\ ms^{-2}$). Calculate the pressure inside a bubble of radius 1mm. **NCERT Pg. 196**

(a) 3×10^2 Pa
(b) 8×10^4 Pa
(c) 1.01×10^5 Pa
(d) 7×10^3 Pa

86 A soap bubble, blown by a mechanical pump at the mouth of a tube, increases in volume, with time, at a constant rate. The graph that correctly depicts the time dependence of pressure inside the bubble is given by **NCERT Pg. 196**

(a) 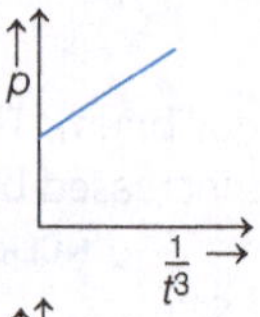

(b) 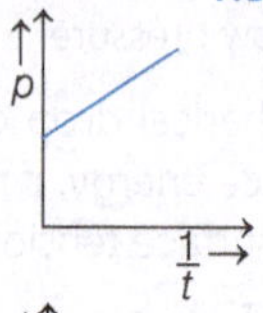

(c) 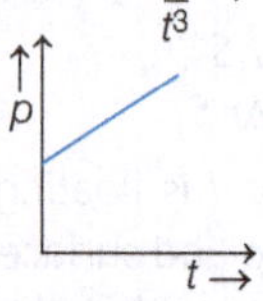

(d) 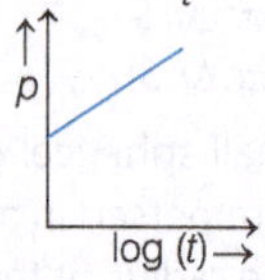

87 If the air bubble of radius r is formed at a depth h inside the container of soap solution of density ρ, the total pressure inside the bubble is (here, p_o denotes the atmospheric pressure and σ denotes surface tension) **NCERT Pg. 196**

(a) $\frac{2\sigma}{r} + h\rho g$ (b) $\frac{2\sigma}{r} - h\rho g$

(c) $\frac{2\sigma}{r} + p_o + h\rho g$ (d) $\frac{2\sigma}{r} + p_o - h\rho g$

88 Two capillary tube of radii 0.3 cm and 0.4 cm are dipped in the same liquid. The ratio of respective heights through which liquid will rise, is **NCERT Pg. 197**

(a) 3 : 4 (b) 4 : 3 (c) 1 : 1 (d) 1 : 2

89 A liquid rises to a height of 1.8 cm in a glass capillary *A*. Another glass capillary *B* having diameter 90% of capillary *A* is immersed in the same liquid. The rise of liquid in capillary *B* is **NCERT Pg. 197**

(a) 1.4 cm (b) 1.8 cm (c) 2.0 cm (d) 2.2 cm

90 The lower end of a capillary tube of diameter 2.00 mm is dipped 8.00 cm below the surface of water in a beaker. What is the pressure required in the tube in order to blow a hemispherical bubble at its end in water? **NCERT Pg. 197**

(a) 2×10^5 Pa (b) 1.01784×10^5 Pa

(c) 3×10^3 Pa (d) 2.438×10^5 Pa

91 A capillary tube *A* is dipped in water. Another identical tube *B* is dipped in soap-water solution. Which of the following shows the relative nature of the liquid columns in the two tubes? **NCERT Pg. 197**

(a) 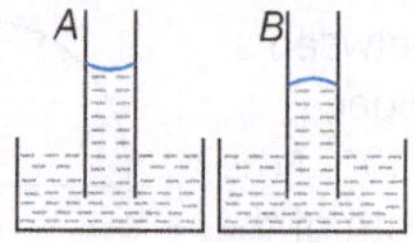

(b) 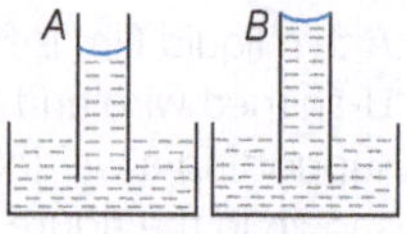

(c) 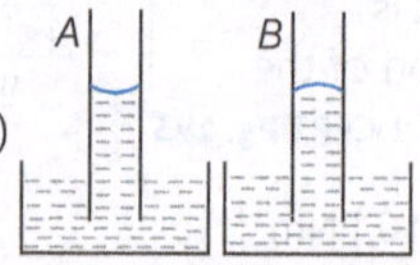

(d) 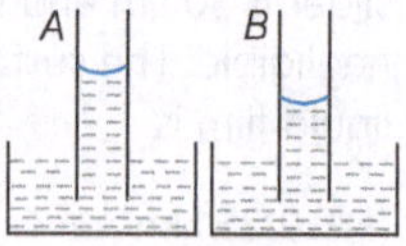

92 Two capillaries made of same material but of different radii are dipped in a liquid. The rise of liquid in one capillary is 2.2 cm and that in the other is 6.6 cm. The ratio of their radii is **NCERT Pg. 197**

(a) 9 : 1 (b) 1 : 9 (c) 3 : 1 (d) 1 : 3

93 If *M* is the mass of water that rises in a capillary tube of radius *r*, then mass of water which will rise in a capillary tube of radius 2*r* is **NCERT Pg. 197**

(a) 2*M* (b) 4*M* (c) $\frac{M}{2}$ (d) *M*

94 The lower end of a capillary tube of radius *r* is placed vertically in water. Then, with the rise of water in the capillary, heat evolved is **NCERT Pg. 197**

(a) $\frac{\pi^2 r^2 h^2}{2} dg$ (b) $\frac{\pi r^2 h^2 dg}{2}$

(c) $-\frac{\pi^2 h^2 dg}{2}$ (d) $-\frac{\pi r^2 h^2 dg}{2}$

Assertion and Reason Questions

Direction (Q. Nos. 1-10) *In the following questions, a statement of Assertion is followed by a corresponding statement of Reason. Of the following statements, choose the correct one.*

(a) Both Assertion and Reason are correct and Reason is the correct explanation of Assertion.

(b) Both Assertion and Reason are correct but Reason is not the correct explanation of Assertion.

(c) Assertion is correct but Reason is incorrect.

(d) Assertion is incorrect but Reason is correct.

1 Assertion When you squeeze one end of a tube to get toothpaste out from the other end, Pascal's principle is observed.

Reason A change in the pressure applied to enclosed incompressible fluid is transmitted undiminished to every portion of the fluid and to the walls of its container. **NCERT Pg. 182**

2 Assertion The stream of water flowing at high speed from a garden hose pipe tend to spread like a fountain when held vertically up, but tends to narrow down when held vertically down.

Reason Speed of upstream decreases as its area of cross-section increases and speed of downstream increases as its area of cross-section decreases. NCERT Pg. 187

3 **Assertion** The machine parts are jammed in winter.

Reason The viscosity of the lubricants used in the machine increases at low temperature. NCERT Pg. 190

4 **Assertion** The steady flow of a liquid over a horizontal surface in the form of layers of different velocity is called turbulent flow.

Reason When a fluid is flowing in a pipe, then velocity of the liquid layer along the axis of tube is maximum and decreases gradually as it move towards wall. NCERT Pg. 191

5 **Assertion** The shape of an automobile is so designed that its front resembles the streamline pattern of the fluid through which it moves.

Reason The resistance offered by the fluid is reduced. NCERT Pg. 191

6 **Assertion** No net force acts on a body falling in a liquid with a velocity equal to the terminal velocity.

Reason The weight of the body is balanced by the upward buoyant force. NCERT Pg. 192

7 **Assertion** A fluid will stick to a solid surface.

Reason Surface energy between fluid and solid is smaller than the sum of surface energies between solid-air and liquid-air interface. NCERT Pg. 193

8 **Assertion** Sometimes insects can walk on the surface of water.

Reason The gravitational force on insect is balanced by force due to surface tension. NCERT Pg. 195

9 **Assertion** A bubble differs from a drop as it has two interfaces.

Reason Excess pressure inside a drop is directly proportional to its surface area. NCERT Pg. 196

10 **Assertion** Due to surface tension, a liquid surface acts like a thin elastic film.

Reason Water rises in a narrow capillary tube due to its low surface tension. NCERT Pg. 196

Statement Based Questions

Direction (Q. Nos. 1-8) *In the following questions, two statements (I & II) are given. In the light of the given statements, choose the correct option given below.*

(a) Both Statement I and Statement II are false.
(b) Statement I is true but Statement II is false.
(c) Statement I is false but Statement II is true.
(d) Both Statement I and Statement II are true.

1 **Statement I** In streamline flow every fluid particle follows the path of its preceding particle with same velocity.

Statement II Speed of particle is less than the critical speed in streamline flow. NCERT Pg. 187

2 **Statement I** Turbulence like friction is sometimes desirable.

Statement II Turbulence promotes mixing and increases the rate of transfer of mass, momentum and energy. NCERT Pg. 187

3 **Statement I** Bernoulli's equation ideally applies to non-viscous fluids.

Statement II Fluid must be compressible in Bernoulli's theorem. NCERT Pg. 188

4 **Statement I** Viscous force is proportional to the velocity of the object.

Statement II Viscous is a dragging force which acts opposite to the direction of motion. NCERT Pg. 190

5 **Statement I** Atoms or molecules in a fluid are arranged in a random manner.

Statement II A fluid can withstand tangential or shearing stress for an indefinite period. NCERT Pg. 191

6 **Statement I** Stress depends on the rate of change of strain or strain rate.

Statement II The coefficient of viscosity for a fluid is defined as the ratio of shearing stress to the strain rate. NCERT Pg. 191

7 **Statement I** All the raindrops hit the surface of the earth with the same constant velocity.

Statement II An object falling through a viscous medium eventually attains a terminal velocity. NCERT Pg. 192

8 **Statement I** Soap bubbles are more stable than water because soap has lower surface tension.

Statement II Surface tension minimises the surface area of a liquid. NCERT Pg. 196

Matching Type Questions

1 Match the Column I (situation) with Column II (reason or principle). Choose the correct answer from the options given below.

	Column I		Column II
A.	Hydraulic lift	1.	Archimedes' principle
B.	A razor blade can be made to float on water surface in a tray.	2.	Pascal's law
C.	The dam of water reservoir is made thick at the bottom level.	3.	Surface tension
D.	Ship is floating on ocean water.	4.	Pressure

NCERT Pg. 192

Codes

	A	B	C	D		A	B	C	D
(a)	2	3	4	1	(b)	2	3	1	4
(c)	2	1	3	4	(d)	1	2	3	4

2 Match the Column I (situation) with Column II (value or changes). Choose the correct answer from the options given below.

	Column I		Column II
A.	When a single drop splits into *n*-identical drops, then	1.	Zero
B.	When a *n*-identical drops combine to form a single drop, then	2.	Temperature increase
C.	The surface tension of a liquid drop decreases, for	3.	Energy absorbed
D.	The surface tension of water at boiling temperature is	4.	Energy released

NCERT Pg. 192

Codes

	A	B	C	D		A	B	C	D
(a)	3	4	1	2	(b)	3	4	2	1
(c)	4	3	1	2	(d)	1	2	3	4

3 Match the Column I (terms or quantities) with Column II (dimensions). Choose the correct answer from the options given below.

	Column I		Column II
A.	Coefficient of viscosity	1.	$[ML^0T^{-2}]$
B.	Density	2.	$[M^0L^0T^0]$
C.	Surface tension	3.	$[ML^{-1}T^{-1}]$
D.	Specific gravity	4.	$[ML^{-3}T^0]$

NCERT Pg. 199

Codes

	A	B	C	D		A	B	C	D
(a)	2	3	4	1	(b)	1	4	3	2
(c)	3	4	1	2	(d)	1	2	3	4

Numerical Type Questions

1 A tube of length 50 cm is filled completely with an incompressible liquid of mass 200 g and closed at both ends. The tube is then rotated in horizontal plane about one of its ends with a uniform angular velocity $\sqrt{xF}$ rad s^{-1}, where F be the force exerted by the liquid at the other end, then the value of x will be .... **NCERT Pg. 183**

2 An ideal fluid of density 800 kg m^{-3} flows smoothly through a bent pipe (as shown in figure) that tapers in cross-sectional area from a to $\frac{a}{2}$. The pressure difference between the wide and narrow sections of pipe is 4800 Pa. At wider section, the velocity of fluid is $\sqrt{x}$ ms^{-1} for $x =$ ...... (Given, $g = 10\ m/s^2$) **NCERT Pg. 188**

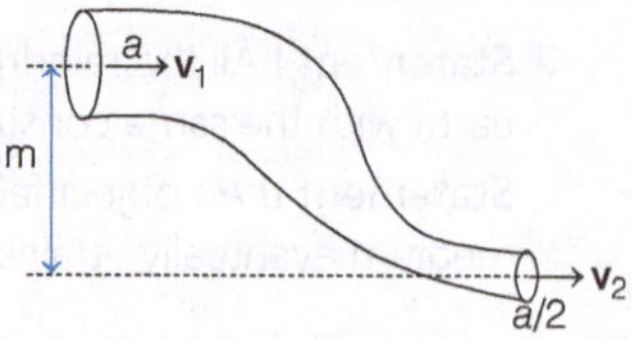

3 Consider a water tank as shown in the figure. It's cross-sectional area is 0.4 m^2. The tank has an opening B near the bottom whose cross-section area is 1 cm^2. A load of 28 kg is applied on the water at the top when the height of the water level is 73 cm above the bottom, the velocity of water coming out the opening B is v ms^{-1}. The value of v, to the nearest integer, is .... (Take, value of g to be 10 ms^{-2}) **NCERT Pg. 189**

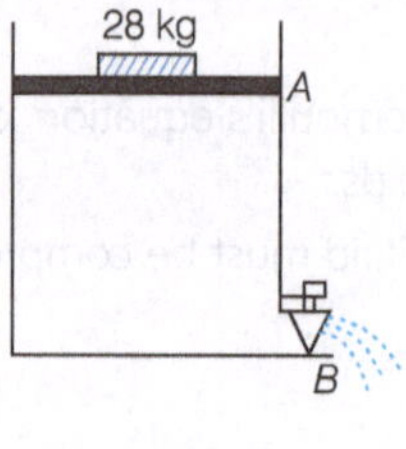

4 The velocity of a small ball of mass 80 g and density 8 g/cc when dropped in a container filled with glycerine becomes constant after some time. If the density of glycerine is 1.3 g/cc, then the value of viscous force acting on the ball will be $x \times 10^{-2}$N. The value of x is .... [use, $g = 10 \text{m/s}^2$] **NCERT Pg. 192**

5 Suppose you have taken a dilute solution of oleic acid in such a way that its concentration becomes 0.1 cm^3 of oleic acid per cm^3 of the solution. Then, you make a thin film of this solution (monomolecular thickness) of area 4 cm^2 by considering 10 spherical drops of radius $\left(\frac{3}{40\pi}\right)^{1/3} \times 10^{-3}$ cm. Then, the thickness of oleic acid layer will be $x \times 10^{-14}$ m, where x is .... **NCERT Pg. 194**

6 A soap bubble of radius 0.01m is formed inside the another soap bubble of radius 0.09 m. The radius of an equivalent soap bubble which has the same excess pressure as inside the smaller bubble with respect to the atmospheric pressure is $x \times 10^{-3}$m, then the value of x is...... . **NCERT Pg. 196**

7 When a long glass capillary tube of radius 0.01 cm is dipped in a liquid, the liquid rises to a height of 10 cm within it. If the contact angle between the liquid and glass is close to 0°, the surface tension of the liquid, (in millinewton m^{-1}) to the nearest integer is ....

(Take, $\rho_{(\text{liquid})} = 900 \text{ kgm}^{-3}$, $g = 10 \text{ ms}^{-2}$) **NCERT Pg. 197**

NCERT Exemplar Questions

1 A tall cylinder is filled with viscous oil. A round pebble is dropped from the top with zero initial velocity. From the plot shown in figure, indicate the one that represents the velocity v of the pebble as a function of time t.

(a) 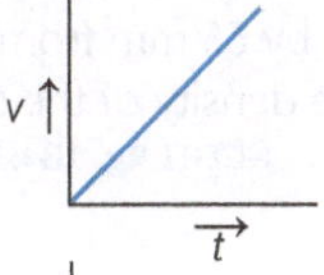

(b) 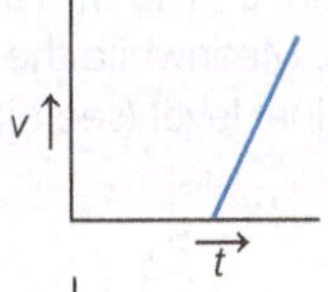

(c) 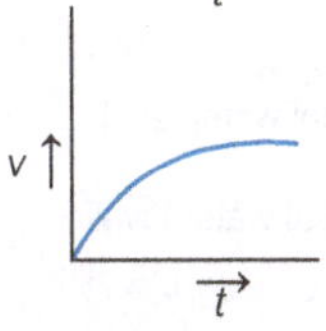

(d) 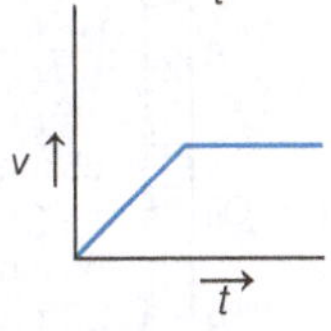

2 Which of the following diagram does not represent a streamline flow?

(a) 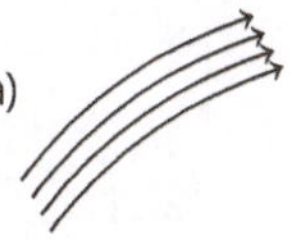

(b) 

(c) 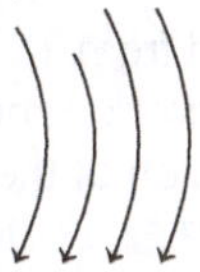

(d) 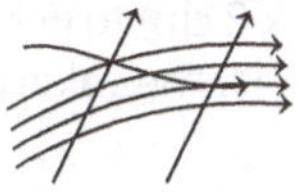

3 Along a streamline,
(a) the velocity of all fluid particles remains constant
(b) the velocity of all fluid particles crossing a given position is constant
(c) the velocity of all fluid particles at a given instant is constant
(d) the speed of all fluid particles remains constant

4 The angle of contact at the interface of water-glass is 0°, ethyl alcohol-glass is 0°, mercury-glass is 140° and methyliodide-glass is 30°. A glass capillary is put in a trough containing one of these four liquids.

It is observed that the meniscus is convex. The liquid in the trough is
(a) water
(b) ethylalcohol
(c) mercury
(d) methyliodide

5 For a surface molecule,
(a) the net force on it is zero
(b) there is a net downward force
(c) the potential energy is less than that of a molecule inside
(d) the potential energy is equal to that of a molecule inside

6 Pressure is a scalar quantity, because
(a) it is the ratio of force to area and both force and area are vectors
(b) it is the ratio of the magnitude of the force to area
(c) it is the ratio of the component of the force parallel to the area
(d) it does not depend on the size of the area chosen

7 If a drop of liquid breaks into smaller droplets, it results in lowering temperature of the droplets. Let a drop of radius R breaks into N small droplets each of radius r. Estimate the drop in temperature. (S = surface tension, s = specific heat)

(a) $\frac{3S}{\rho s}\left(\frac{1}{R^2}-\frac{1}{r^2}\right)$ (b) $\frac{3S}{\rho s}\left(\frac{1}{R}-\frac{1}{r}\right)$

(c) $\frac{2S}{\rho s}\left(\frac{1}{R}-\frac{1}{r}\right)^2$ (d) $\frac{4S}{\rho s}\left(\frac{1}{R^2}-\frac{1}{r^2}\right)$

8 The surface tension and vapour pressure of water at 20°C is 7.28×10^{-2} Nm^{-1} and 2.33×10^3 Pa, respectively. What is the radius of the smallest spherical water droplet which can be formed without evaporating at 20°C?

(a) 5×10^{-4} m
(b) 6.25×10^{-5}m
(c) 9×10^{-2} m
(d) 3×10^{-5} m

Past Exams Questions

NEET

1 A thin flat circular disc of radius 4.5 cm is placed gently over the surface of water. If surface tension of water is 0.07 Nm^{-1}, then the excess force required to take it away from the surface is **NCERT Pg. 194, NEET 2024**

(a) 19.8 mN (b) 198 N
(c) 1.98 mN (d) 99 N

2 The amount of energy required to form a soap bubble of radius 2 cm from a soap solution is nearly (surface tension of soap solution = 0.03 N m^{-1}) **NCERT Pg. 196, NEET 2023**

(a) 5.06×10^{-4} J
(b) 3.01×10^{-4} J
(c) 50.1×10^{-4} J
(d) 30.16×10^{-4} J

3 A barometer is constructed using a liquid (density = 760 kg/m^3). What would be the height of the liquid column, when a mercury barometer reads 76 cm? (Density of mercury = 13600 kg/m^3) **NCERT Pg. 184, NEET 2020**

(a) 1.36 m (b) 13.6 m
(c) 136 m (d) 0.76 m

4 A capillary tube of radius r is immersed in water and water rises in it to a height h. The mass of the water in the capillary tube is 5 g. Another capillary tube of radius $2r$ is immersed in water. The mass of water that will rise in this tube is **NCERT Pg. 197, NEET 2020**

(a) 5.0 g (b) 10.0 g
(c) 20.0 g (d) 2.5 g

5 A soap bubble, having radius of 1 mm, is blown from a detergent solution having a surface tension of 2.5×10^{-2} N/m. The pressure inside the bubble equals at a point Z_0 below the free surface of water in a container. Taking g = 10 m/s^2, density of water = 10^3kg/m^3, the value of Z_0 is **NCERT Pg. 196, NEET 2019**

(a) 10 cm (b) 1 cm
(c) 0.5 cm (d) 100 cm

6 A small sphere of radius r falls from rest in a viscous liquid. As a result, heat is produced due to viscous force. The rate of production of heat when the sphere attains its terminal velocity, is proportional to **NCERT Pg. 192, NEET 2018**

(a) r^5 (b) r^2
(c) r^3 (d) r^4

7 A U-tube with both ends open to the atmosphere, is partially filled with water. Oil, which is immiscible with water, is poured into one side until it stands at a distance of 10 mm above the water level on the other side. Meanwhile the water rises by 65 mm from its original level (see diagram). The density of the oil is **NCERT Pg. 184, NEET 2017**

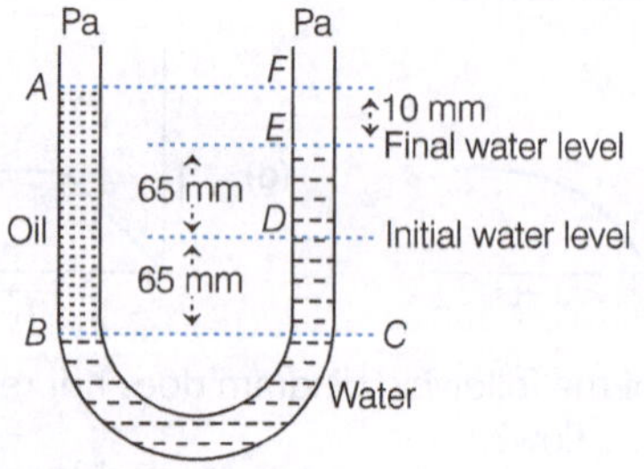

(a) 650 kg m^{-3}
(b) 425 kg m^{-3}
(c) 800 kg m^{-3}
(d) 928 kg m^{-3}

8 A rectangular film of liquid is extended from (4 cm × 2 cm) to (5 cm × 4 cm). If the work done is 3×10^{-4} J, the value of the surface tension of the liquid is **NCERT Pg. 194, NEET 2016**

(a) 0.250 Nm^{-1}
(b) 0.125 Nm^{-1}
(c) 0.2 Nm^{-1}
(d) 8.0 Nm^{-1}

9 Three liquids of densities ρ_1, ρ_2 and ρ_3 (with $\rho_1 > \rho_2 > \rho_3$), having the same value of surface tension T, rise to the same height in three identical capillaries. The angles of contact θ_1, θ_2 and θ_3 obey **NCERT Pg. 197, NEET 2016**

(a) $\frac{\pi}{2} > \theta_1 > \theta_2 > \theta_3 \geq 0$

(b) $0 \leq \theta_1 < \theta_2 < \theta_3 < \frac{\pi}{2}$

(c) $\frac{\pi}{2} < \theta_1 < \theta_2 < \theta_3 < \pi$

(d) $\pi > \theta_1 > \theta_2 > \theta_3 > \frac{\pi}{2}$

10 Water rises to height h in a capillary tube. If the length of capillary tube above the surface of water is made less than h, then **NCERT Pg. 197, AIPMT 2015**

(a) water rises upto the top of capillary tube and stays there without overflowing
(b) water rises upto a point a little below the top and stays there
(c) water does not rise at all.
(d) water rises upto the tip of capillary tube and then starts overflowing like fountain.

11 A certain number of spherical drops of a liquid of radius r coalesce to form a single drop of radius R and volume V. If T is the surface tension of the liquid, then **NCERT Pg. 196, AIPMT 2014**

(a) energy $= 4VT\left(\frac{1}{r} - \frac{1}{R}\right)$ is released

(b) energy $= 3VT\left(\frac{1}{r} + \frac{1}{R}\right)$ is absorbed

(c) energy $= 3VT\left(\frac{1}{r} - \frac{1}{R}\right)$ is released

(d) energy is neither released nor absorbed

JEE Main

12 The excess pressure inside a soap bubble is thrice the excess pressure inside a second soap bubble. The ratio between the volume of the first and the second bubble is **NCERT Pg. 196, JEE Main 2024**

(a) 1 : 9 (b) 1 : 81
(c) 1 : 3 (d) 1 : 27

13 A cube of ice floats partly in water and partly in kerosene oil. The ratio of volume of ice immersed in water to that in kerosene oil (specific gravity of kerosene oil = 0.8, specific gravity of ice = 0.9) **NCERT Pg. 188, JEE Main 2024**

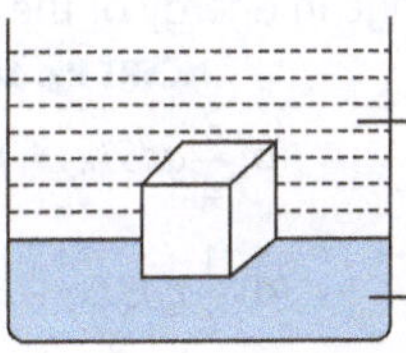

(a) 9 : 10 (b) 8 : 9
(c) 1 : 1 (d) 5 : 4

14 The figure shows a liquid of given density flowing steadily in horizontal tube of varying cross-section. Cross- sectional areas at A is 1.5 cm^2, and B is 25 mm^2, if speed of liquid at B is 60 cm/s then $(p_A - p_B)$ is

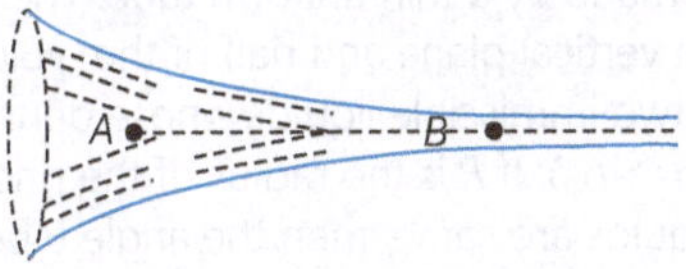

(Given, p_A and p_B are liquid pressure at A and B points. density, $\rho = 1000$ kg m^{-3} A and B are on the axis of tube) **NCERT Pg. 187, JEE Main 2023**

(a) 36 Pa (b) 135 Pa
(c) 175 Pa (d) 27 Pa

15 A drop of liquid of density ρ is floating half immersed in a liquid of density σ and surface tension 7.5×10^{-4} Ncm^{-1}. The radius of drop in cm will be (Take, $g = 10$ ms^{-2}) **NCERT Pg. 192, JEE Main 2022**

(a) $\frac{15}{\sqrt{(2\rho - \sigma)}}$ (b) $\frac{15}{\sqrt{(\rho - \sigma)}}$

(c) $\frac{3}{2\sqrt{(\rho - \sigma)}}$ (d) $\frac{3}{20\sqrt{(2\rho - \sigma)}}$

16 When two soap bubbles of radii a and $b (b > a)$ coalesce, the radius of curvature of common surface is **NCERT Pg. 196, JEE Main 2021**

(a) $\frac{ab}{b-a}$ (b) $\frac{a+b}{ab}$

(c) $\frac{b-a}{ab}$ (d) $\frac{ab}{a+b}$

17 Two identical cylindrical vessels are kept on the ground and each contains the same liquid of density d. The area of the base of both vessels is S but the height of liquid in one vessel is x_1 and in the other, x_2. When both cylinders are connected through a pipe of negligible volume very close to the bottom, the liquid flows from one vessel to the other until it comes to equilibrium at a new height. The change in energy of the system in the process is **NCERT Pg. 183, JEE Main 2020**

(a) $gdS(x_2^2 + x_1^2)$ (b) $\frac{3}{4}gdS(x_2 - x_1)^2$

(c) $gdS(x_2 + x_1)^2$ (d) $\frac{1}{4}gdS(x_2 - x_1)^2$

18 Water flows in a horizontal tube (see figure). The pressure of water changes by 700 Nm^{-2} between *A* and *B*, where the area of cross- section are 40 cm^2 and 20 cm^2, respectively. Find the rate of flow of water through the tube. (Take, density of water = 1000 kgm^{-3}) **NCERT Pg. 188, JEE Main 2020**

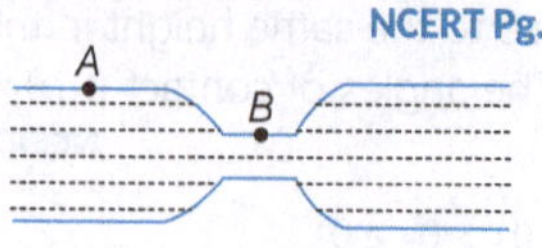

(a) 3020 cm^3/s
(b) 2420 cm^3/s (c) 2720 cm^3/s
(d) 1810 cm^3/s Skill Boosters

Skill Boosters

1 A ring is made by a thin uniform tube. The ring is placed in vertical plane and half of the volume of ring is filled by two immiscible liquids whose densities are ρ_1 and ρ_2 $(\rho_1 > \rho_2)$. If *R* is the radius of the ring and volume of two liquids are same, then the angle θ between the radius vector passing through the common interface and the vertical is

(a) $\theta = \tan^{-1}\frac{\pi}{2}\left(\frac{\rho_1}{\rho_2}\right)$ (b) $\theta = \tan^{-1}\frac{\pi}{2}\left(\frac{\rho_1 - \rho_2}{\rho_1 + \rho_2}\right)$

(c) $\theta = \tan^{-1}\left(\frac{\rho_1}{\rho_2}\right)$ (d) $\theta = \tan^{-1}\left(\frac{\rho_1 - \rho_2}{\rho_1 + \rho_2}\right)$

2

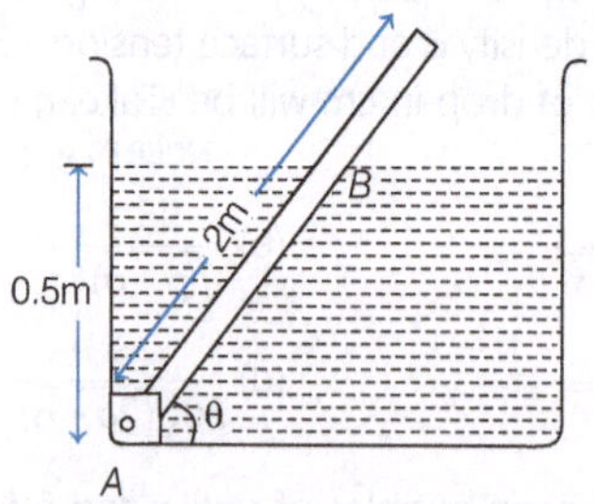

In the above diagram, a rod *AB* is mounted at point *A* and beaker is filled with water Assume that the cross - section is $10^{-2} m^2$ and buoyancy acts at the centre of the immersion part *AB* of the rod. The rod is allowed to drop from vertical position. The angle θ at which the rod will come to rest is (density of water $= 10^3$ kg/ m^3, weight of rod = 50 N, $g = 10 m/s^2$)

(a) 30° (b) 45°
(c) 60° (d) 37°

3 A vertical narrow glass tube of uniform cross - section, closed at one end has air filled in it upto 40 cm of height, with a column of mercury of height 10 cm above it. If the tube is gradually inclined in the vertical plane and brought to a position making an angle of 60° with the vertical, then new length of air column entrapped within the tube is (atmospheric pressure = 76 cm of Hg)

(a) 45.47 cm (b) 43.47 cm
(c) 42.47 cm (d) 44.47 cm

4 A drop of water of volume *V* is pressed between the two glasses placed, so as to spread to an area *A*. If *T* is the surface tension of water, the normal force required to separate the glass plates is

(a) $\frac{TA^2}{V}$ (b) $\frac{2TA^2}{V}$ (c) $\frac{4TA^2}{V}$ (d) $\frac{TA^2}{2V}$

5 There is a rectangular wire frame having a thin film of soap solution. A circular ring of massless thin wire of area of cross-section *A* is placed on the surface of the film. The radius of the ring is *R*. Now , inside portion of the ring is pricked. If the surface tension of soap solution is *T* and Young's modulus of wire is *Y*, then change in radius of the wire is

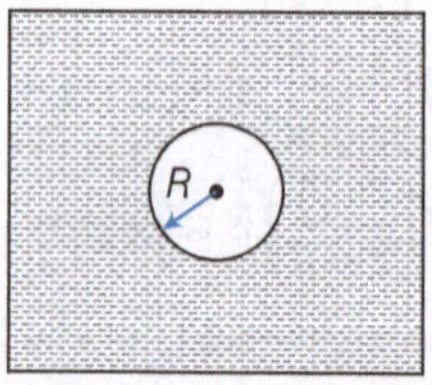

(a) $\frac{TR^2}{AY}$ (b) $\frac{2TR^2}{AY}$ (c) $\frac{TR^2}{3AY}$ (d) $\frac{TR^2}{2AY}$

6 A horizontal capillary tube with an internal radius *r* and a length of *l* is inserted into the side of a cylindrical vessel having a radius of *R*. The vessel is filled with castor oil whose viscosity is η . The level of the castor oil sinks in the cylindrical vessel with a velocity *v* and the height of this level from the capillary tube is *h*. Then, *v* is

(a) $\frac{r^4\rho gh}{R^2\eta l}$ (b) $\frac{r^4\rho gh}{4R^2\eta l}$ (c) $\frac{r^4\rho gh}{8R^2\eta l}$ (d) $\frac{r^4\rho gh}{16R^2\eta l}$

7 A water clock (clepsydra) used in ancient Greece is designed as a vessel with a small orifice *O* (see figure). The time is determined according to the level of water in the vessel. What should be the equation corresponding to the shape of the vessel for the time scale to be uniform ? (Vessel is symmetric about vertical axis and a = the area of orifice and v = speed with which water surface lower down)

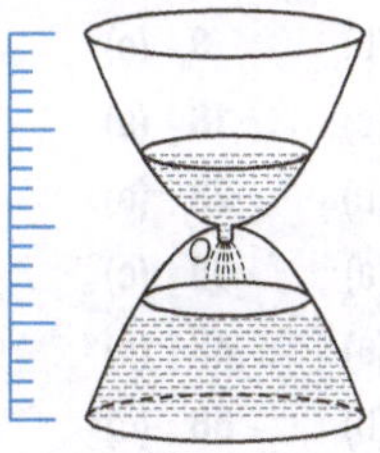

(a) $y = kx^4$, where $k = \dfrac{\pi^2 v^2}{ga^2}$

(b) $y = kx^4$, where $k = \dfrac{2\pi^2 v^2}{ga^2}$

(c) $y = kx^4$, where $k = \dfrac{\pi v^2}{ga^2}$

(d) $y = kx^4$, where $k = \dfrac{\pi^2 v^2}{2ga^2}$

8 Find the force acting on the blade of an undershot wheel (see figure), if the stream after impinging on the blade continues to move with the velocity of the blade. The height of the water head is h, the radius of the wheel is R and angular velocity of the wheel is ω and cross-sectional area of the stream is A.

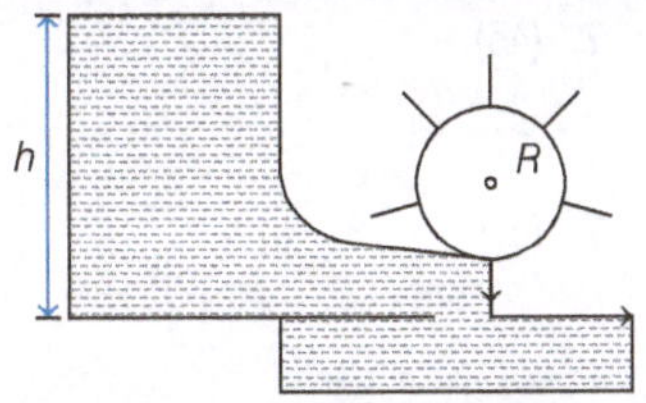

(a) $\rho A(\sqrt{2gh} - \omega R)^2$ (b) $\rho A(\sqrt{2gh} + \omega R)^2$

(c) $\dfrac{\rho A}{2}(\sqrt{2gh} - \omega R)^2$ (d) $\dfrac{\rho A}{2}(\sqrt{2gh} + \omega R)^2$

9 A cubical container with side 3 m has a small hole with a cap at point C as shown in the figure. The water level is upto D (BC = 0.5 cm and BD = 2 m).If container is given a constant acceleration a_0 = 9 ms^{-2} and the hole is simultaneously opened, then amount of water that will spill out is (Given, g = 10 ms^{-2})

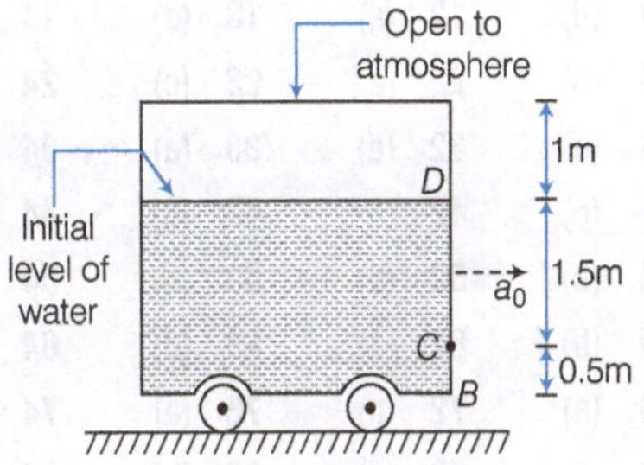

(a) 2150 L (b) 4150 L

(c) 3150 L (d) 2750 L

10 Water is contained in a rectangular tank, at rest, to a height H. Which of the following graphs best represents the variation of hydrostatic thrust F per unit width of the side of the vessel (width is measured perpendicular to paper) on the area measured from the top of a level, at a height y from the bottom level?

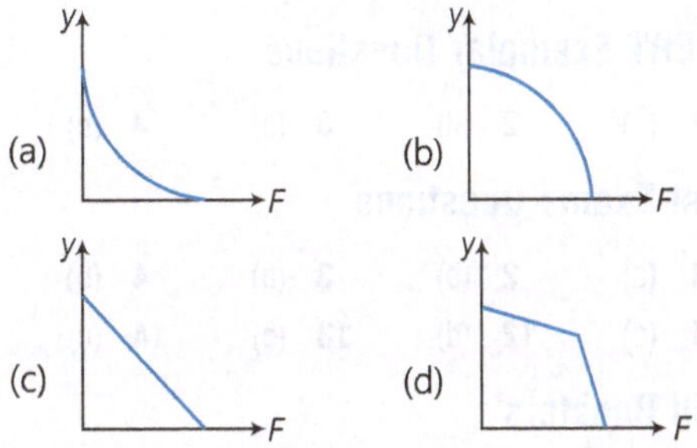

Correct Codes

Topical Questions

1 (c)	2 (a)	3 (a)	4 (b)	5 (d)	6 (a)	7 (b)	8 (c)	9 (b)	10 (a)
11 (d)	12 (a)	13 (d)	14 (b)	15 (a)	16 (d)	17 (c)	18 (a)	19 (d)	20 (a)
21 (b)	22 (a)	23 (c)	24 (d)	25 (a)	26 (b)	27 (b)	28 (b)	29 (b)	30 (c)
31 (c)	32 (d)	33 (a)	34 (c)	35 (b)	36 (c)	37 (a)	38 (c)	39 (c)	40 (b)
41 (c)	42 (d)	43 (b)	44 (b)	45 (a)	46 (b)	47 (a)	48 (c)	49 (d)	50 (a)
51 (c)	52 (b)	53 (b)	54 (a)	55 (a)	56 (a)	57 (b)	58 (c)	59 (d)	60 (b)
61 (b)	62 (a)	63 (d)	64 (d)	65 (b)	66 (a)	67 (d)	68 (a)	69 (b)	70 (d)
71 (a)	72 (d)	73 (a)	74 (d)	75 (c)	76 (d)	77 (b)	78 (c)	79 (a)	80 (b)
81 (a)	82 (d)	83 (b)	84 (b)	85 (c)	86 (b)	87 (c)	88 (b)	89 (c)	90 (b)
91 (d)	92 (c)	93 (a)	94 (b)						

Assertion and Reason Questions

1 (a)	2 (a)	3 (a)	4 (d)	5 (a)	6 (c)	7 (a)	8 (a)	9 (c)	10. (c)

Statement Based Questions

1 (d)	2 (d)	3 (b)	4 (d)	5 (b)	6 (d)	7. (c)	8. (d)

Matching Type Questions

1 (a)	2 (b)	3 (c)

Numerical Type Questions

1 (20)	2 (14)	3 (4)	4 (67)	5 (25)	6 (9)	7 (45)

NCERT Exemplar Questions

1 (c)	2 (d)	3 (b)	4 (c)	5 (b)	6 (b)	7 (b)	8 (b)

Past Exams Questions

1 (a)	2 (b)	3 (b)	4 (b)	5 (b)	6 (a)	7 (d)	8 (b)	9 (b)	10 (a)
11 (c)	12 (d)	13 (c)	14 (c)	15 (a)	16 (a)	17 (d)	18 (c)		

Skill Boosters

1 (d)	2 (a)	3 (c)	4 (b)	5 (b)	6 (c)	7 (d)	8 (a)	9 (c)	10 (b)

Step by Step

Decoding the Questions

Concept Builders

1. True (T)
2. False (F)
3. Same
4. False (F)
5. Pascal's law
6. Gauge pressure
7. decreases
8. True (T)
9. down
10. True (T)
11. Surface tension
12. Increases, decreases
13. Upthrust
14. Viscosity
15. lower than rear compartment.
16. True (T)
17. angle of contact
18. Fall
19. The surface tension of liquid
20. Smaller, bigger

Topical Questions

1 (c) The key property of fluids is that they offer very little resistance to shear stress i.e. their shapes changes by application of very small shear stress.

3 (a) The force acting on them is $F = 40$ kg wt $= 400$ N (take, $g = 10\ ms^{-2}$).

Thus, the average pressure is

$$p_{av} = \frac{F}{A} = \frac{400}{20 \times 10^{-4}} = 2 \times 10^5\ Nm^{-2}$$

4 (b) Given, $p_{h/2} = \frac{3}{4}(p_{bottom})$

$$\Rightarrow p_0 + \rho g \frac{h}{2} = \frac{3}{4}(p_0 + \rho g h)$$

$$\Rightarrow h = \frac{p_0}{\rho g} = \frac{10^5}{10^3 \times 10} = 10\ m$$

5 (d) Pressure at a point inside a liquid, $p = \frac{F}{A} = \rho g h$

It does not depend on the weight of fluid.

6 (a) In equilibrium,

$$\Sigma F_x = 0 \text{ and } \Sigma F_y = 0$$

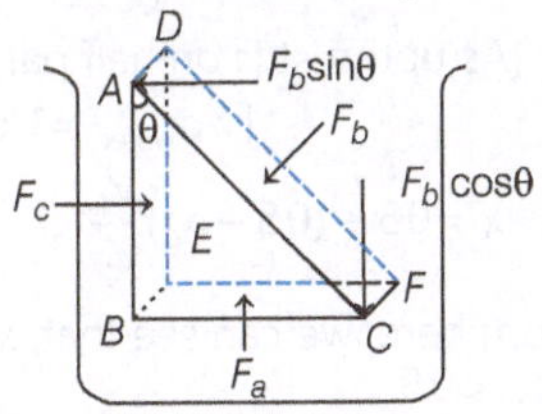

$$\Rightarrow F_b \sin\theta = F_c \text{ and } F_b \cos\theta = F_a$$

7 (b) The pressure exerted by liquid at end B is

$$p = p_0 + \rho g h - \rho g h = p_0$$

8 (c) $\rho_1 h_1 = \rho_2 h_2$, $13.6 \times 2 = 1 \times h$

$$h = 27.2\ cm$$

9 (b) $p_0 + \frac{h}{3} dg = \frac{1}{2}(hdg + p_0)$

$$p_0 + \frac{hdg}{3} = \frac{p_0}{2} + \frac{hdg}{2}$$

$$\frac{Hdg}{2} = hdg\left(\frac{1}{6}\right)$$

$$h = 3H = 30\ m$$

10 (a) Pumping rate of heart of a man

$$= \frac{dV}{dt} = \frac{5 \times 10^{-3}}{60}\ m^3\ s^{-1}$$

$$\text{Power of heart} = p \cdot \frac{dV}{dt} = \rho g h \cdot \frac{dV}{dt} \quad (\because p = \rho g h)$$

$$= \frac{(13.6 \times 10^3)(10) \times (0.15 \times 5 \times 10^{-3})}{60}$$

$$= 1.70\ W$$

11 (d)

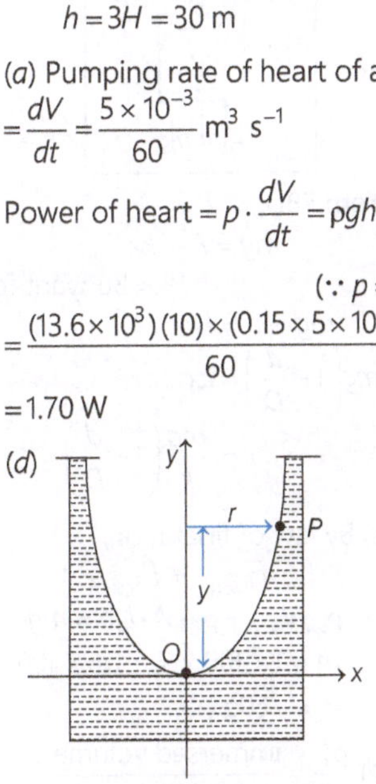

If p_0 is atmospheric pressure, then total pressure at point P is

$$p = p_0 + \frac{1}{2}\rho r^2\omega^2 - \rho g y$$

For any point on surface of rotating fluid,

$$p = p_0$$

Hence, for any surface point;

$$p_0 = p_0 + \frac{1}{2}\rho r^2\omega^2 - \rho g y$$

$$y = \frac{r^2\omega^2}{2g} = \frac{(4\pi)^2(0.05)^2}{2 \times 10}$$

$$= 0.02\ m = 2\ cm$$

12 (a) Pressure at left arm of U-tube,

$$p_1 = p_0 + \rho_1 g h_1$$

$$= p_0 + \rho_1 10(10 \times 10^{-2})$$

or $p_1 = p_0 + \rho_1$

Pressure at right arm of U-tube,

$$p_2 = p_0 + \rho_2 10(12 \times 10^{-2})$$

or $p_2 = p_0 + 1.2\ \rho_2$

$\therefore$ $p_1 = p_2$

$$\Rightarrow p_0 + \rho_1 = p_0 + 1.2\rho_2$$

$\therefore$ Density of ethyl alcohol,

$$\rho_2 = \frac{\rho_1}{1.2} = \frac{1000}{1.2} = 833.3\ kg/m^3$$

$$= 0.83\ gcm^{-3}$$

13 (d) Mass per unit time of a liquid flow is given by

$$\frac{dm}{dt} = \rho A v$$

$\therefore$ Rate of change in momentum of the 25% of liquid which loses all momentum is

$$\frac{dp_1}{dt} = \frac{1}{4}\left(\frac{dm}{dt}\right)v = \frac{1}{4}\rho A v^2 \quad \text{...(i)}$$

and the rate of change in momentum of the 25% of the liquid which comes back with same speed.

$$\frac{dp_2}{dt} = \frac{1}{4}\left(\frac{dm}{dt}\right) \times 2v = \frac{1}{2}\rho A v^2 \quad \text{...(ii)}$$

[$\because$ Net change in velocity is $= 2v$]

$\therefore$ Net pressure on the mesh is

$$p = \frac{F_{net}}{A}$$

From Eqs. (i) and (ii), we get

$$p = \frac{3}{4}\rho v^2 A / A = \frac{3}{4}\rho v^2$$

14 (b) From the given figure, we can write, $p_1 = \rho g h_1$

$\Rightarrow \quad p' = p_2$

$= \rho g(h_1 + h_2) = \rho g h_3$

Similarly, $p'' = p_2 - p_1$

$= \rho g(h_3 - h_1) = \rho g h_2$

$\therefore$ In terms of height, we can write,

Absolute pressure $= h_3 = h_1 + h_2$

Gauge pressure $= h_2 = h_3 - h_1$

15 (a) Pressure on smaller piston is given by

$$p = \frac{F}{A} = \frac{3000 \times 9.8}{425 \times 10^{-4}} = 6.92 \times 10^5 \text{ Nm}^{-2}$$

16 (d) By Pascal's law,

$$\Rightarrow \quad \frac{F_1}{A_1} = \frac{F_2}{A_2}$$

$$\Rightarrow \quad F_2 \propto A_2/A_1$$

Also, $\quad V_1 = V_2$

$$\Rightarrow \quad A_1 x_1 = A_2 x_2$$

$$\Rightarrow A_1 \cdot \frac{d}{dt} x_1 = A_2 \frac{d}{dt} x_2$$

$$\Rightarrow \quad A_1 v_1 = A_2 v_2$$

$$\Rightarrow \quad \frac{v_2}{v_1} = \frac{A_1}{A_2}$$

As pressure is same in both the limbs, so work done by force F_1 is equal to that of F_2.

Thus, the statement given in option (d) is correct, rest are incorrect.

17 (c) Since, the fluid in the lift is perfectly incompressible.

$$\therefore \quad V_1 = V_2 \Rightarrow A_1 x_1 = A_2 x_2$$

$$\Rightarrow x_2 = \frac{A_1}{A_2} x_1 = \frac{Ax}{2A} = \frac{x}{2}$$

18 (a) $V_1 = V_2$

$$L_1 A_1 = L_2 A_2$$

$$L_2 = \frac{A_1}{A_2} L_1$$

$$= \frac{\pi(1/2 \times 10^{-2})^2}{\pi(3/2 \times 10^{-2})^2} \times 6 \times 10^{-2}$$

$$= 0.67 \times 10^{-2} \text{m} = 0.67 \text{ cm}$$

19 (d) According to Pascal's law,

$$\frac{F_2}{\pi r_2^2} = \frac{w}{\pi r_1^2}$$

$$\Rightarrow \quad F_2 = w\left(\frac{r_2}{r_1}\right)^2 = 5 \times 10^3 \left(\frac{0.1}{1}\right)^2 = 50 \text{ N}$$

20 (a) In floating condition,

Total weight = Upthrust

$$\therefore V_1 \rho_c g + (x V_2)(1) g = \left(\frac{V_1 + V_2}{2}\right)(1) g$$

[As upthrust is on half part only]

[$\because \rho_{water} = 1 \text{ kgm}^{-3}$]

$$\Rightarrow \quad x = 0.5 + (0.5 - \rho_c)\frac{V_1}{V_2}$$

From here, we can see that, $x > 0.5$ if $\rho_c < 0.5$.

Thus, the statement given in option (a) is correct, rest are incorrect.

21 (b) $Mg = F_h$

$$\frac{4}{3}\pi(R^3 - r^3) d_s g = \frac{4}{3}\pi R^3 d_l g$$

(d_s = density of solids, d_l = density of liquid, $\frac{d_s}{d_l} = \sigma$)

$$\frac{R}{r} = \left(\frac{\sigma}{\sigma - 1}\right)^{\frac{1}{3}}$$

22 (a)

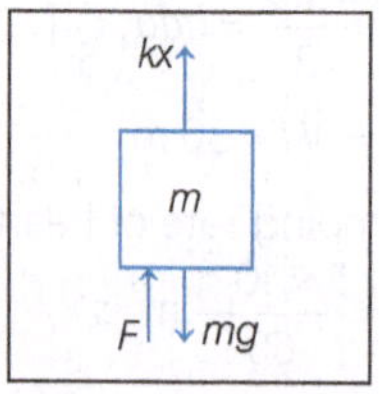

From FBD,

$$mg = F + kx$$

[F = Buoyant force]

$$mg - F = kx$$

$$mg\left(1 - \frac{d}{D}\right) = kx$$

$$x = \frac{mg}{k}\left(1 - \frac{d}{D}\right)$$

23 (c) By law of floatation,

$$F_{B_{water}} + F_{B_{Oil}} = w$$

$$\Rightarrow \rho_w A l_w g + \rho_0 \cdot A \cdot l_0 g = mg$$

$$\Rightarrow m = 1 \times 100 \times 4 + 0.6 \times 100 \times 6$$

$$= 760\text{g}$$

24 (d) $\frac{\rho_s}{\rho_w} = \frac{\text{immersed volume}}{\text{Total volume}}$ ... (i)

Here, ρ_s = density of solid, and ρ_w = density of water

$$\frac{\rho_s}{\rho_w} = \frac{1}{5}$$

In liquid of specific gravity 1.4,

$$\frac{\rho_s}{\rho_e} = \frac{V_s}{V}$$

ρ_l = density of liquid

$$\frac{\rho_s}{1.4\rho_w} = \frac{V_s}{V}$$

$$\therefore \quad \frac{V_s}{V} = \frac{1}{7}$$

25 (a) The fraction of the cube submerged under a liquid is independent of the value of g.

Therefore, the volume submerged will remain same.

26 (b)

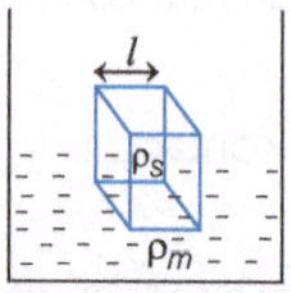

Let h be the height of the block above the surface of mercury and volume of mercury displaced $= (l - h) \cdot l^2$

$\therefore$ Weight of mercury displaced $= (l - h) \cdot l^2 \cdot \rho_m \cdot g$

This is equal to the weight of the block which is $\rho_s \cdot l^3 g$

Thus, according to Archimedes' principle,

$$(l - h)\, l^2 \cdot \rho_m \cdot g = \rho_s \cdot l^3 \cdot g$$

which gives, $h = l\left(1 - \frac{\rho_s}{\rho_m}\right)$

28 (b) By equation of continuity,

$$A_1 v_1 = A_2 v_2 + A_3 v_3$$

$$\Rightarrow A \times 6 = \frac{A}{3} \times 3 + \frac{2A}{3} \cdot v_3$$

$$\therefore \quad v_3 = 7.5 \text{ m/s}$$

29 (b) $\Delta m_P = \Delta m_Q = \Delta m_R$, we have

$$A_P v_P \rho_P \Delta t = A_Q v_Q \rho_Q \Delta t$$

$$= A_R v_R \rho_R \Delta t \quad \text{...(i)}$$

For flow of incompressible fluids, we have,

$$\rho_P = \rho_R = \rho_Q$$

Thus, Eq. (i) reduces to,

$$\Rightarrow \quad A_P v_P = A_R v_R = A_Q v_Q$$

Also, from the given figure we can also say that, $A_R > A_Q > A_P$

$$\therefore \quad v_P > v_Q > v_R$$

30 (*c*) According to equation of continuity of flow,

$$A_1v_1 = A_2v_2$$

$$(\because A_1 = \pi r_1^2 \text{ and } A_2 = \pi r_2^2)$$

$$\therefore \quad v_2 = v_1\left(\frac{r_1}{r_2}\right)^2$$

$$= 2\times\left(\frac{3}{3/2}\right)^2$$

$$= 2\times 2^2 = 8\ \text{ms}^{-1}$$

31 (*c*) $M = m_1 + m_2$

$$\Rightarrow \quad Av_1 = Av_2 + 1.5Av$$

$$\Rightarrow \quad A\times 3 = A\times 1.5 + 1.5Av$$

$$\Rightarrow \quad v = 1.0\ \text{ms}^{-1}$$

35 (*b*) By the principle of continuity,

$$A_1v_1 = A_2v_2$$

$$\pi r_1^2 v_1 = \pi r_2^2 v_2$$

$$(2.5\times 10^{-2})^2\times 4 = (10^{-2})^2\cdot v_2$$

$$\Rightarrow \quad v_2 = 25\ \text{m/s}$$

From Bernoulli's theorem,

$$p_1 + \frac{1}{2}\rho v_1^2 = p_2 + \frac{1}{2}\rho v_2^2$$

$$p_1 - p_2 = \frac{1}{2}\rho(v_2^2 - v_1^2)$$

$$[\because \text{density of water, } \rho = 10^3\ \text{kg/m}^3]$$

$$= \frac{1}{2}\times 10^3(25^2 - 4^2)$$

$$= 304500\ \text{Pa}$$

36 (*c*) Applying Bernoulli's theorem, at different parts of figure given below, $p_a + \frac{1}{2}\rho v^2 + \rho g y_1$

$$= p + \frac{1}{2}\rho v_2^2 + \rho g y_2$$

$$= p + \rho g y_2 \quad [\because v_2 = 0]$$

$$v^2 = \frac{2}{\rho}(p - p_a + \rho g(y_2 - y_1)) \quad \text{...(i)}$$

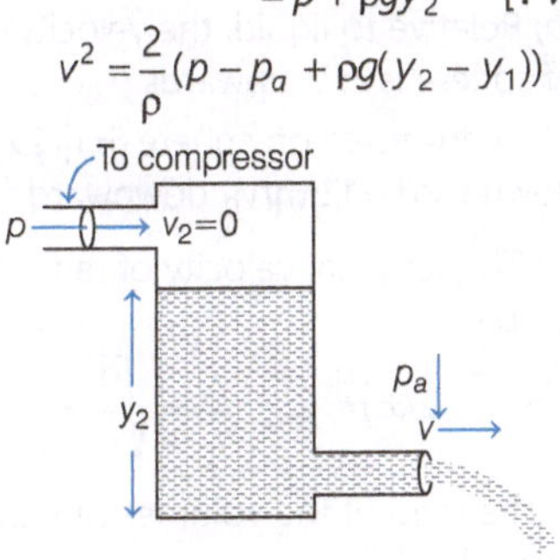

Given, $y_2 - y_1 = h$

hence, $v = 2\sqrt{gh}$

37 (*a*) For the water jet coming from orifice of container,

$$R = 2\sqrt{(H - h_1)\cdot h_1}$$

$$= 2\sqrt{(H - h_2)\cdot h_2}$$

$$\therefore (H - h_1)\cdot h_1 = (H - h_2)\cdot h_2$$

$$\Rightarrow (H - 2.4)\times 2.4 = (H - 7.6)\times 7.6$$

$$\therefore \quad H = 10\ \text{cm}$$

38 (*c*) Velocity of efflux,

$$v = \sqrt{2gh} = \sqrt{2\times 10\times 5} = 10\ \text{m/s}$$

Range, R

$$= \frac{u^2\sin 2\theta}{g} = \frac{(10)^2\sin 2\times 30^\circ}{10}$$

$$\approx 8.7\ \text{m}$$

39 (*c*) Range of water gets for point Q and P are as follows.

For point Q, $x = 2\sqrt{(H - h)h}$

For point P, $x = 2\sqrt{h'(H - h')}$

$$\therefore \quad 2\sqrt{h(H - h)} = 2\sqrt{h'(H - h')}$$

Solving it, we get $h' = (H - h)$

40 (*b*) Applying Bernoulli's principle at points 1 and 2.

$$p_0 + \rho gh + \frac{1}{2}\rho v_1^2 = p_0 + \frac{1}{2}\rho v_2^2$$

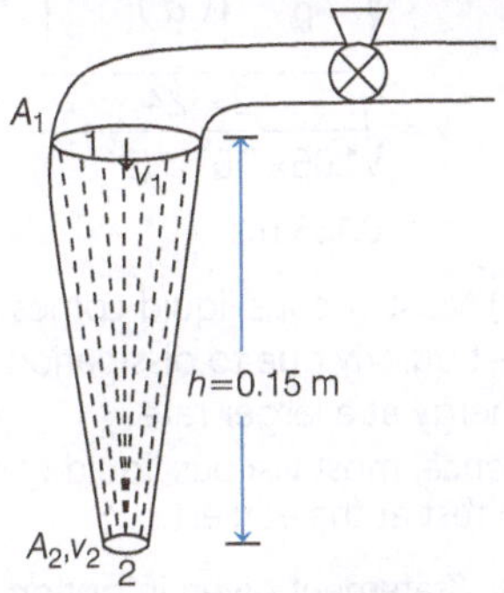

$$\Rightarrow \quad v_2^2 = v_1^2 + 2gh$$

$$\Rightarrow \quad v_2^2 = (1)^2 + 2\times 10\times 0.15 = 4$$

$$\therefore \quad v_2 = 2\ \text{m/s}$$

By equation of continuity,

$$A_1v_1 = A_2v_2$$

$$\Rightarrow \quad A_2 = \frac{A_1v_1}{v_2} = \frac{10\times 10^{-5}\times 1}{2}$$

$$= 5\times 10^{-5}\ \text{m}^2$$

41 (*c*) The velocity of efflux,

$$v = \sqrt{2gh} \quad \text{...(i)}$$

If t is the time taken by water to strike the floor, then

$$s = \frac{1}{2}gt^2$$

or $\quad (H - h) = \frac{1}{2}gt^2$

$$\Rightarrow \quad t = \sqrt{\frac{2(H - h)}{g}} \quad \text{...(ii)}$$

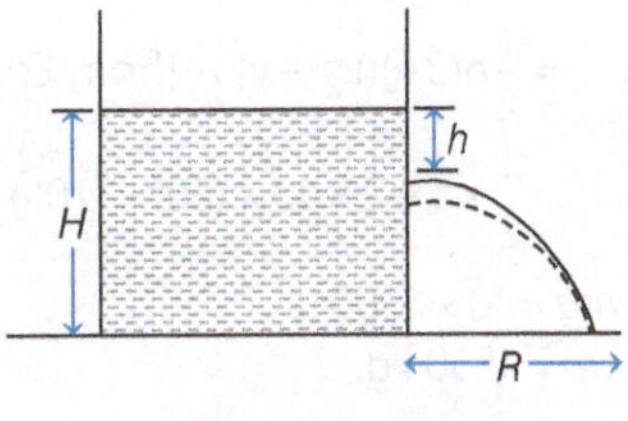

$$R = vt$$

From Eqs. (i) and (ii), we get

$$R = \sqrt{2g\cdot h}\times\sqrt{\frac{2(H - h)}{g}}$$

$$R = 2\sqrt{h(H - h)}$$

42 (*d*)

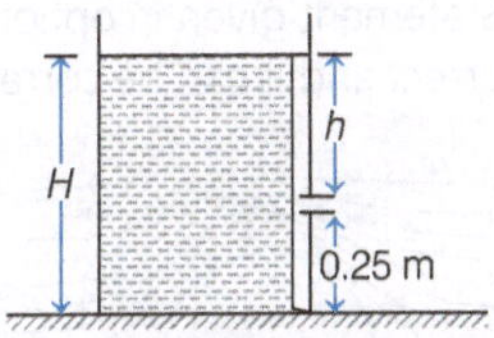

Range of water stream,

$$R = 2\sqrt{h(H - h)}$$

$$= 2\sqrt{(1 - 0.25)0.25}$$

$$= 86.6\ \text{cm}$$

43 (*b*) According to Torricelli's theorem, the velocity of efflux of water,

$$v = \sqrt{2gh} = \sqrt{2\times 10\times 20}$$

$$= 20\ \text{ms}^{-1}$$

44 (*b*) Using Torricelli's law,

Velocity, $v = \sqrt{2gh}$ ...(i)

and $p_2 - p_1 = \rho g(h_2 - h_1)$

Here, $h_2 = h$ and $h_1 = 0$ then

$$p_2 - p_1 = \rho gh$$

$$h = \frac{p_2 - p_1}{\rho g} \quad \text{...(ii)}$$

From Eq. (i) and Eq. (ii), we get

$$v = \sqrt{\frac{2g\times(p_2 - p_1)}{\rho g}}$$

$$= \sqrt{\frac{2\times(3\times 10^5 - 1\times 10^5)}{1000}}$$

$$= \sqrt{\frac{4\times 10^5}{1000}}$$

$$= \sqrt{400}\ \text{m/s}$$

46 (*b*) From Bernoulli's principle

$$p_1 + \frac{1}{2}\rho v_1^2 = p_2 + \frac{1}{2}\rho v_2^2$$

$$p_1 - p_2 = \frac{1}{2}\rho(v_2^2 - v_1^2) \quad \text{...(i)}$$

$$mg = (p_1 - p_2)2A$$

$$= \frac{1}{2}\rho(2A)(v_2^2 - v_1^2) \quad \text{[from Eq. (i)]}$$

$$= \frac{1}{2} \times 1 \times 2 \times 10 \times (80^2 - 70^2)$$

$$mg = 10 \times 1500$$

$$\therefore m = 1500 \text{ kg}$$

47 (*a*) From the Bernoulli's theorem,

$$p_1 - p_2 = \frac{1}{2}\rho(v_2^2 - v_1^2)$$

$$\Rightarrow p_1 - p_2 = \frac{1}{2} \times 1.3 \times [(120)^2 - (90^2)]$$

$$= 4095 \text{ Pa}$$

48 (*c*) Statement given in option (c) is incorrect and it can be corrected as,

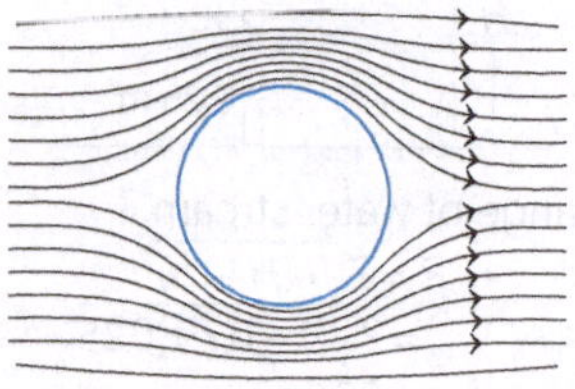

From the symmetry of streamlines, it is clear that the velocity of fluid above and below the ball at corresponding points is the same resulting in zero pressure difference. The fluid therefore, exerts no upward or downward force on the ball.

49 (*d*) As the ball is not spinning, then by Bernoulli's theorem, $p_A = p_B$.

$$\Rightarrow \quad (p_A / p_B) = 1$$

51 (*c*) The weight of the boeing aircraft is balanced by the upward force due to the pressure difference.

$$\Delta p \times A = mg$$

$$\Delta p = (3.3 \times 10^5 \times 9.8) / 500$$

$$= 6.5 \times 10^3 \text{ Nm}^{-2}$$

Bernoulli's equation,

i.e. $p_1 + \left(\frac{1}{2}\right)\rho v_1^2 + \rho g h_1$

$$= p_2 + \left(\frac{1}{2}\right)\rho v_2^2 + \rho g h_2$$

$$v_2 - v_1 = \frac{2\Delta p}{\rho(v_2 + v_1)}$$

$$(\Delta p = p_1 - p_2) \quad \text{...(i)}$$

Taking the average speed,

$$v_{av} = (v_2 + v_1)/2$$

$$= 960 \text{ kmh}^{-1}$$

$$= 267 \text{ ms}^{-1}$$

$$v_2 - v_1 / v_{av} = \frac{\Delta p}{\rho v_{av}^2}$$

$$\Rightarrow \quad \frac{v_2 - v_1}{v_{av}} = \frac{6.5 \times 10^3}{1.2 \times (267)^2} \approx 0.08$$

52 (*b*) $A = 8 \text{ mm}^2$, area of narrower part, $a = 4 \text{ mm}^2$ and density of blood, i.e. ρ is $1.06 \times 10^3 \text{ kgm}^{-3}$.

The ratio of the areas is $\frac{A}{a} = 2$.

The pressure drop in artery

$$= \rho_m g h = 24 \text{ Pa}$$

So, the speed of the blood in the artery,

$$v = \sqrt{\frac{2\rho_m gh}{\rho}}\left[\left(\frac{A}{a}\right)^2 - 1\right]^{-1/2}$$

$$\Rightarrow \quad v = \sqrt{\frac{2 \times 24}{1.06 \times 10^3 \times (2^2 - 1)}}$$

$$\simeq 0.125 \text{ ms}^{-1}$$

55 (*a*) Most viscous liquid comes to rest quickly due to dissipation of energy at a larger rate.
Hence, most viscous liquid comes to rest at the earliest.

56 (*a*) Statement given in option (a) is incorrect and it can be corrected as,
Viscous force decreases with decrease in viscosity. If fluid is a gas, its viscosity increases with increase in temperature.
Thus, viscous force on object decreases with decrease in temperature.

57 (*b*) The shear force,

$$F = \text{Tension}$$

$$= mg$$

$$= 9.8 \times 10^{-2} \text{ N}$$

Shear stress on the fluid

$$= F/A = \frac{9.8 \times 10^{-2}}{0.10}$$

$$\text{Velocity gradient} = \frac{v}{l} = \frac{0.085}{0.30 \times 10^{-3}}$$

$\Rightarrow$ Coefficient of viscosity,

$$\eta = \frac{\text{Stress}}{\text{Velocity gradient}}$$

$$= 3.45 \times 10^{-3} \text{ Pa-s}$$

58 (*c*) $F_{net} = F_v + F_u - w$

$$Ma = 6\pi r\eta v + \frac{4}{3}\pi r^3 \sigma g - \frac{4}{3}\pi r^3 \rho g$$

$$a = \left(\frac{6\pi r\eta}{M}\right)v - \frac{4}{3}\pi r^3 g(\rho - \sigma)$$

Comparing with $Y = mX + C$

$$m = \tan\theta = \frac{6\pi r\eta}{M} = +\text{ve}$$

and $C = -\frac{4}{3}\pi r^3 g(\rho - \sigma) = -\text{ve}$

59 (*d*)

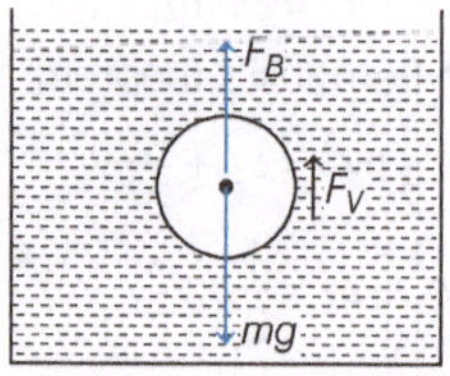

When the spherical ball moves with constant velocity, then

$$F_B + F_v = mg$$

$$\Rightarrow \quad \sigma_2 V_g + F_v = mg$$

$$\Rightarrow \rho_2 \cdot \frac{m}{\rho_1} g + F_v = mg$$

$\therefore$ Viscous force, F_v

$$= mg\left(\frac{\rho_1 - \rho_2}{\rho_1}\right)$$

60 (*b*) Relative to liquid, the velocity of sphere is $2v_0$ upwards.
$\therefore$ Viscous force on sphere $6\pi\eta r 2v_0$ downward $= 12\pi\eta r v_0$ downward

61 (*b*) The terminal velocity of rain drop is

$$v \propto r^2 \Rightarrow \quad \frac{r_1}{r_2} = \sqrt{\frac{9}{4}} = \frac{3}{2}$$

$\therefore$ The ratio of the volumes of rain drops is

$$\frac{V_1}{V_2} = \left(\frac{r_1}{r_2}\right)^3 = \left(\frac{3}{2}\right)^3 = \frac{27}{8}$$

62 (*a*) By Stokes' law, the viscous force on the rain drop is given by

$$F_v = 6\pi\eta r v_t$$
$$= 6 \times \pi \times 18 \times 10^{-5} \times 0.03 \times 100$$
$$= 101.73 \times 10^{-4} \text{ dyne.}$$

63 (*d*) According to Stokes' law, the retarding force is proportional to velocity. Initial velocity will increase. When viscous force plus buoyant force become equal to the force of gravity, the net force and hence acceleration become zero. The spherical body then moves with a constant velocity called terminal velocity.

65 (*b*) Terminal velocity,

$$v_T = \frac{2a^2(\rho - \sigma)g}{9\eta}$$

$$v_T = \frac{2 \times (2 \times 10^{-3})^2 \times (8.9 - 1.5) \times 10^3 \times 9.8}{9 \times 6.5 \times 10^{-2}}$$

$$= 9.9 \times 10^{-1} \text{ kg m s}^{-1}$$

66 (*a*) Terminal velocity is given by

$$v_T = \frac{2}{9}\frac{r^2}{\eta}(d - \rho)g$$

$$\frac{v_P}{v_Q} = \frac{r_P^2}{r_Q^2} \times \frac{\eta_Q}{\eta_P} \times \frac{(d - \rho_P)}{(d - \rho_Q)}$$

$$\Rightarrow \frac{v_P}{v_Q} = \left(\frac{1}{0.5}\right)^2 \times \left(\frac{2}{3}\right) \times \frac{(8 - 0.8)}{(8 - 1.6)}$$

$$\Rightarrow v_P : v_Q = 3 : 1$$

67 (*d*) As the liquid molecule inside the liquid is surrounded equally from all sides, so net force on a molecule of surface *B* will be zero.

Thus, the statement given in option (d) is correct, rest are incorrect..

69 (*b*) A liquid film has two surfaces, so upward force $= 2Tl$

According to question,

Weight of the body hanged from wire (mg)

= Upward force due to surface tension ($2Tl$)

$$\Rightarrow \quad m = \frac{2Tl}{g}$$

70 (*d*) According to question, the situation can be depicted as below,

From, this we have,

$$S_{la} \cos\theta + S_{ls} = S_{sa}$$

$\because \theta > 90°$ and $\cos\theta$ is negative.

This implies that $S_{ls} > S_{la}$. Hence, liquid does not spread on solid surface.

Thus, the statement given in option (d) is correct, rest are incorrect.

71 (*a*) Surface tension,

$$T = \frac{F}{2l} = \frac{2 \times 10^{-2}}{2 \times 10 \times 10^{-2}} = 0.1 \text{ Nm}^{-1}$$

72 (*d*) Force on one side of the stick

$$F_1 = T_1 \times L$$
$$= 0.07 \times 2 = 0.14 \text{ N}$$

and force on other side of the stick

$$F_2 = T_2 \times L = 0.06 \times 2 = 0.12 \text{ N}$$

So, net force on the stick

$$= F_1 - F_2 = 0.14 - 0.12$$
$$= 0.02 \text{ N}$$

73 (*a*) Force required to separate the two glass plates,

$$F = \frac{2TA}{t}$$

$$= \frac{2 \times 70 \times 10^{-3} \times 10^{-2}}{0.05 \times 10^{-3}} = 28 \text{ N}$$

74 (*d*) A liquid film has two free surfaces.

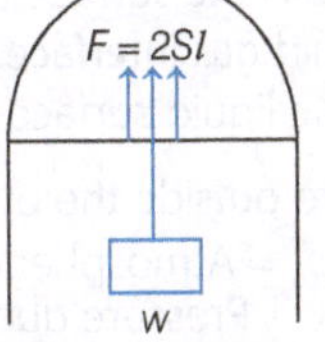

$$\therefore \quad 2Sl = w$$
$$\Rightarrow \quad S = w/2l$$
$$\Rightarrow \quad S = \frac{1.5 \times 10^{-2}}{2 \times 30 \times 10^{-2}}$$
$$\therefore \quad S = 0.025 \text{ Nm}^{-1}$$

75 (*c*) The excess pressure inside a soap bubble is

$$\Delta p = \frac{4S}{r}$$

$$\Rightarrow \quad \Delta p \propto \frac{1}{r}$$

As, fluid flow from high pressure to low pressure. So, air flow from smaller bubble to the bigger bubble.

76 (*d*) For soap bubble,

$$\Delta p = \frac{4T}{R}$$

$$\frac{\Delta p_1}{\Delta p_2} = \frac{R_2}{R_1}$$

$$\Rightarrow \quad \frac{R_2}{R_1} = \frac{0.01}{0.02}$$

$$\frac{S_1}{S_2} = \left(\frac{R_1}{R_2}\right)^2 = 4 : 1$$

77 (*b*) Work done

$$= 8\pi T[r_2^2 - r_1^2]$$
$$= 8\pi T\left[\frac{D^2}{4} - \frac{d^2}{4}\right]$$
$$= 2\pi[D^2 - d^2]\,T$$

78 (*c*) $p_1 = \frac{4T}{R}, p_2 = \frac{2T}{R'}$

But $4\pi R^2 d = \frac{4}{3}\pi R'^3$

$$R' = (3R^2 d)^{\frac{1}{3}}$$

$$\therefore \quad \frac{p_2}{p_1} = \frac{2T/R'}{4T/R} = \frac{R}{2R'}$$

$$\frac{p_2}{p_1} = \left(\frac{R}{24d}\right)^{1/3}$$

80 (*b*) If radius increases by Δr, then the extra surface energy is

$$= |4\pi(r + \Delta r)^2 - 4\pi r^2|\,S$$
$$= (4\pi r^2 + 4\pi\Delta r^2 + 8\pi r\Delta r - 4\pi r^2)\,S$$
$$= 8\pi r\,\Delta r\,S$$

(neglecting Δr^2 as it is very small)

81 (*a*) FBD of droplet

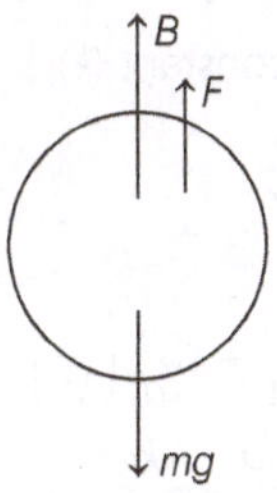

$$B + F = mg$$

[$B \to$ Buoyant force]

$$\left(\frac{2}{3}\pi r^3\right)\rho g + T(2\pi r) = d\left(\frac{4}{3}\pi r^3\right)g$$

$$T(2\pi r) = \left(\frac{2}{3}\pi r^3\right) g\,[2d - \rho]$$

$$r = \sqrt{\frac{3T}{(2d-\rho)g}}$$

82 (*d*) Increase in surface area

$= 36\pi r^2 - 4\pi r^2 = 32\pi r^2$

Since, a bubble has two surfaces, the total increase in surface area

$= 64\pi r^2$.

$\therefore$ Energy spent = Work done

= Surface tension × Area

$= 64\pi\sigma r^2$

83 (*b*) As, radius of bigger drop

$R = n^{1/3} r = 2^{1/3} r$

$$\Rightarrow \frac{r^2}{R^2} = 2^{-2/3}$$

$$\frac{\text{Initial surface energy}}{\text{Final surface energy}} = \frac{2(4\pi r^2 T)}{(4\pi R^2 T)} = 2\left(\frac{r^2}{R^2}\right)$$

$$= 2 \times 2^{-2/3} = 2^{1/3} = 2^{1/3} : 1$$

84 (*b*) Excess pressure inside an air bubble just below the surface of water, $p_1 = \frac{2T}{r}$, due to only one free surface

and excess pressure inside a drop,

$$p_2 = \frac{2T}{r}$$

$\therefore \quad p_1 = p_2$

85 (*c*) Pressure inside the bubble is

$p_i = p_o + 2S/r$

$= 1.01 \times 10^5 + (2 \times 7.30 \times 10^{-2}/10^{-3})$

$= 1.01146 \times 10^5$ Pa

86 (*b*) From Boyle's law

pV = constant (k)

$$\Rightarrow p = \frac{k}{V}$$

we get

$$\frac{dp}{dt} = k.\frac{d}{dt}\left(\frac{1}{V}\right)$$

So, $\frac{dp}{dt} = \frac{-kc}{V^2}$ ... (i)

Now, from $\frac{dV}{dt} = c$; we get

or $\int dV = \int c\,dt$ or $V = ct$ ... (ii)

From Eqs. (i) and (ii), we get

$$\frac{dp}{dt} = \frac{-kc}{c^2 t^2}$$

$$\Rightarrow dp = -\frac{k}{c}.t^{-2} dt$$

Integrating both sides, we get

$$\int dp = -\frac{k}{c}\int t^{-2} dt$$

$$\Rightarrow p \propto \frac{1}{t}$$

87 (*c*) The total pressure inside the air bubble is

$p_t = p + p_o + h\rho g$

$= \frac{2\sigma}{r} + p_o + h\rho g \quad \left(\because p = \frac{2\sigma}{r}\right)$

88 (*b*) The height of capillary rise is

$$h \propto \frac{1}{r}$$

$$\Rightarrow \frac{h_1}{h_2} = \left(\frac{r_2}{r_1}\right) = \frac{0.4}{0.3} = \frac{4}{3}$$

89 (*c*) For capillary tube,

$h_A = 1.8$ cm, $d_B = 0.9 d_A$

The height of capillary rise is given by

$$h = \frac{2S\cos\theta}{\rho r g} \Rightarrow h \propto \frac{1}{r} \propto \frac{1}{d}$$

$$\therefore \frac{h_B}{h_A} = \left(\frac{d_A}{d_B}\right) = \left(\frac{d_A}{0.9 d_A}\right) = \frac{10}{9}$$

$$\therefore h_B = \frac{10}{9} \times h_A = \frac{10 \times 1.8}{9} = 2 \text{ cm}$$

90 (*b*) The excess pressure in a bubble of gas in a liquid is given by $2S/r$, where S is the surface tension of the liquid gas interface. There is only one liquid surface in this case.

Pressure outside the bubble,

p_o = Atmospheric pressure + Pressure due to 8 cm of water column

$\therefore \quad p_o = (1.01 \times 10^5 + 0.08 \times 1000 \times 9.8)$

$= 1.01784 \times 10^5$ Pa

91 (*d*) Soap solution has lower surface tension, S as compared to pure water and capillary rise in tube,

$$h = \frac{2S\cos\theta}{\rho r g}$$

So, h is less for soap solution.

Also, angle of contact in both the cases will be acute.

92 (*c*) As, $h \propto \frac{1}{r}$

or $\frac{r_1}{r_2} = \frac{h_2}{h_1} = \frac{6.6}{2.2} = \frac{3}{1}$

93 (*a*) Height of liquid rise in capillary tube,

$$h = \frac{2S\cos\theta_c}{\rho r g}$$

$$\Rightarrow h \propto \frac{1}{r}$$

So, when radius is doubled, height becomes half.

$\therefore \quad h' = \frac{h}{2}$

$\Rightarrow \quad M = \rho \times \pi r^2 h$

$\therefore \quad M' = \rho \pi r'^2 h'$

$\therefore \quad \frac{M'}{M} = 2$

$\Rightarrow \quad M' = 2M$

94 (*b*) Height of water in capillary tube

$$h = \frac{2S\cos\theta}{rdg}$$

The increase in potential energy ΔE_P, of the raised water column

$= mg\frac{h}{2}$ ...(i)

and $m = \pi r^2 h d$

From Eq. (i), we get

$$\Delta E_p = (\pi r^2 hd)\left(\frac{hg}{2}\right) = \frac{\pi r^2 h^2 dg}{2}$$

Further, heat evolved = increase in potential energy

$$\Delta W = \Delta E_p = \frac{\pi r^2 h^2 dg}{2}$$

Assertion and Reason Questions

2 (*a*) As from equation of continuity, volume flow rate of fluid, i.e. $Q = Av$ = constant.

In this case,area of cross-section increases due to decrease in velocity of upstream while area of cross-section of downstream decreases due to increase in velocity of water.

3 (a) The machine parts are jammed in winter because the viscosity of the lubricants used in the machines increases at low temperature.

4 (d) Assertion is incorrect because this type of flow is known as laminar flow.
When a fluid is flowing in a pipe or a tube, then velocity of the liquid layer along the axis of the tube is maximum and decreases gradually as we move towards the walls.

5 (a) When a body moves through a fluid, its motion is opposed by the force of fluid friction called resistance of fluid. It acts normal to the surface and increases with increasing speed of body.
It is due to this reason, the shape of an automobile is, so designed that it resembles the streamline pattern of the fluid through which it moves, so that air friction is minimum.
Also, the resistance offered by the fluid is reduced.

6 (c) The weight of the body is balanced by two upward forces, namely the buoyant force and viscous force.
No net force acts on a body falling in a liquid with a velocity equal to the terminal velocity, because this force (viscous) is balanced by the weight of body.

7 (a) A fluid will stick to a solid surface, if the surface energy between fluid and the solid is smaller than the sum of surface energies between solid-air and liquid-air, interface.

9 (c) The excess pressure inside a liquid drop is given by $p = \frac{2\sigma}{R}$

i.e. $p \propto \frac{1}{R}$ or $p \propto \frac{1}{\text{surface area}}$

Statement Based Questions

2 (d) Turbulence is desired in heat exchangers for mixing fluids etc.

3 (b) A restriction on application of Bernoulli's theorem is that the fluids must be incompressible as the elastic energy of the fluid is also not taken into consideration.

5 (b) A fluid cannot withstand tangential or shearing stress for an indefinite period. It begins to flow when a shearing stress is applied.

Numerical Type Questions

1 (20) The given situation is shown below.

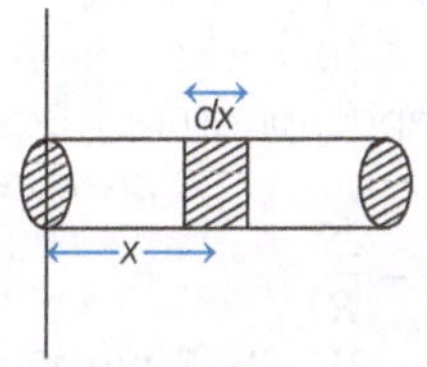

Force exerted by the liquid at the other end due to rotation,

$$F = \int (dm)\omega^2 x$$

where, $dm = \frac{m}{L} \cdot dx$

$$\therefore F = \int_0^L \frac{m}{L} dx \cdot \omega^2 x = \frac{m}{L} \cdot \omega^2 \left[\frac{x^2}{2}\right]_0^L$$

$$F = \frac{m\omega^2 L}{2}$$

$$\omega = \sqrt{20F} = \sqrt{xF} \quad \text{(given)}$$

$\therefore x = 20$

2 (14) From Bernoulli's theorem,

$$\frac{p_1}{\rho} + gh_1 + \frac{1}{2}v_1^2 = \frac{p_2}{\rho} + gh_2 + \frac{1}{2}v_2^2$$

$$\frac{p_1 - p_2}{\rho} = g(h_2 - h_1) + \frac{1}{2}(v_2^2 - v_1^2)$$

$$\frac{4800}{800} = 10 \times (0 - 1.5) + \frac{1}{2}(v_2^2 - v_1^2)$$

$$v_2^2 - v_1^2 = 42 \quad \text{...(i)}$$

From equation of continuity,

$$a_1 v_1 = a_2 v_2$$

$$a v_1 = \frac{a}{2} . v_2$$

$$\Rightarrow \quad v_2 = 2v_1$$

Substituting value in Eq. (i) and solving,we get

$$v_1 = \sqrt{14} = \sqrt{x} \quad \text{(given)}$$

$\therefore \quad x = 14$

3 (4)

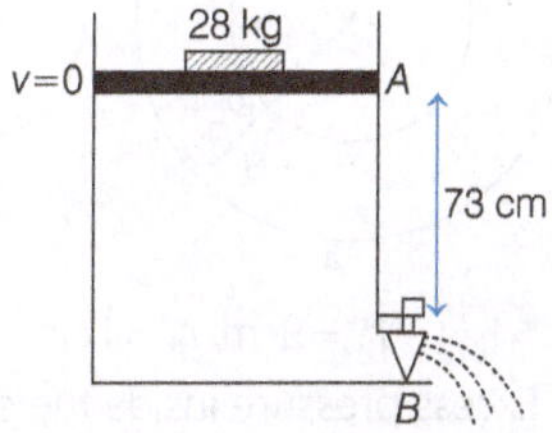

Using the Bernoulli's principle equation,

$$p_0 + \frac{mg}{A} + \rho g h + \frac{\rho v_A^2}{2} = p_0 + \frac{\rho v_B^2}{2}$$

$$\Rightarrow 0 + \frac{(28)10}{0.4} + 1000 \times 10 \times 0.73 + \frac{\rho(0)^2}{2}$$

$$= 0 + \frac{1000 \times v_B^2}{2}$$

$$v_B = 4 \text{ m/s}$$

4 (67) Viscous force,

$$F = mg - \text{Buoyant force,}$$

$$F = mg - V\sigma g$$

$$F = mg - \frac{m}{\rho}\sigma g,$$

$$F = 80 \times 10^{-3} \times 10\left[1 - \frac{1.3}{8}\right]$$

Thus, $F = 67 \times 10^{-2}$ N

$\because \quad F = x \times 10^{-2}$ N (given)

$\therefore \quad x = 67$

5 (25) Since we know,
Volume of film
= Area of film × Thickness
Also, we know, volume of film
= volume of 10 spherical drops

$$4t_T = 10 \times \frac{4}{3}\pi r^3 = 10^{-9} \text{ cm}^3$$

Hence, thickness of film,

$$t_T = \frac{10^{-9}}{4} \text{ cm}$$

Thickness of oleic acid layer

$= 0.1\, t_T$

$= 25 \times 10^{-14}$ m

On comparing with

$x \times 10^{-14}$ m, $x = 25$

6 (9) The given situation is shown below

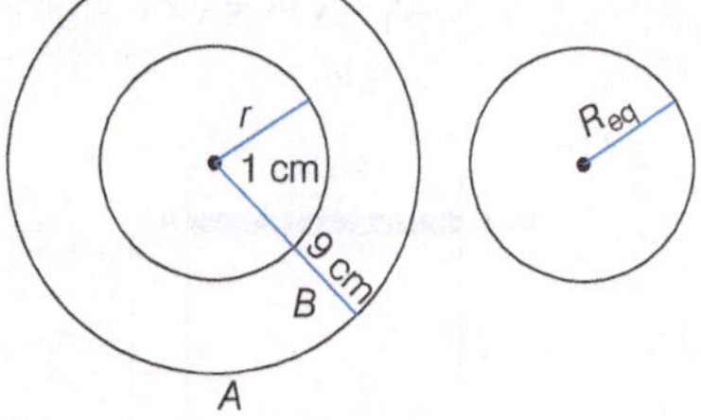

$r_A = 9\text{cm}, r_B = 1\text{ cm}$

Excess pressure inside the soap bubble is given by

$$(\Delta_p)_{\text{excess}} = \frac{4S}{r_A} + \frac{4S}{r_B}$$

According to the given question,

$$\frac{4S}{r_A} + \frac{4S}{r_B} = \frac{4S}{R_{\text{eq}}}$$

$$\Rightarrow \frac{1}{r_A} + \frac{1}{r_B} = \frac{1}{R_{\text{eq}}}$$

$$\Rightarrow R_{\text{eq}} = \frac{9}{10} = 0.9\text{ cm} = 9 \times 10^{-3}\text{m}$$

$$R_{\text{eq}} = x \times 10^{-3}\text{m} \quad \text{(given)}$$

$$\Rightarrow x = 9$$

7 (45) Height of liquid in capillary tube,

$$h = \frac{2S\cos\theta}{\rho g r}$$

$$\Rightarrow S = \frac{\rho g r h}{2\cos\theta}$$

$$S = \frac{900 \times 10 \times 10 \times 10^{-5} \times 10 \times 10^{-2}}{2 \times 1}$$

$$= 45 \times 10^{-3}\text{N/m}$$

$$= 45\text{ mN/m}$$

NCERT Exemplar Questions

1 (c) When the pebble is falling through the viscous oil, the viscous force is $F = 6\pi\eta r v$

First velocity increases due to gravity and then becomes constant known as terminal velocity.

3 (b) As we know for a streamline flow of a liquid, velocity of each particle at a particular position is constant, because Av = constant (law of continuity) between two cross-section of a tube of flow.

7 (b) $\frac{4}{3}\pi R^3 = N \times \frac{4}{3}\pi r^3$

$$\Rightarrow N = \frac{R^3}{r^3}$$

Now, change in surface area,

$$\Delta A = 4\pi(R^2 - Nr^2)$$

Energy released $= S \times \Delta A$

$$= S \times 4\pi(R^2 - Nr^2)$$

Energy released $= ms\Delta\theta$

$$S \times 4\pi(R^2 - Nr^2) = \left(\frac{4}{3}\pi R^3 \times \rho\right) s\Delta\theta$$

$$\Delta\theta = \frac{3S}{\rho s}\left(\frac{R^2}{R^3} - \frac{Nr^2}{R^3}\right)$$

$$= \frac{3S}{\rho s}\left(\frac{1}{R} - \frac{1}{r}\right)$$

8 (b) Vapour pressure = Excess pressure in drop

$$p = \frac{2S}{R}$$

$$\Rightarrow R = \frac{2S}{p} = \frac{2 \times 7.28 \times 10^{-2}}{2.33 \times 10^3}$$

$$= 6.25 \times 10^{-5}\text{m}$$

Past Exams Questions

1 (a) Radius of disc,

$$r = 4.5\text{ cm}$$

$$= 4.5 \times 10^{-2}\text{ m}$$

Surface tension, $S = 0.07\text{ Nm}^{-1}$

The force required to take away circular disc from the surface of water,

$$F = S \times 2\pi r$$

$$= 0.07 \times 2 \times 3.14 \times 4.5 \times 10^{-2}$$

$$= 1.9782 \times 10^{-2}\text{ N} = 19.8\text{ mN}$$

2 (b) Amount of energy required,

$$E = 2SA$$

$$= 2 \times 0.03 \times 4\pi(2 \times 10^{-2})^2$$

$$= 3.01 \times 10^{-4}\text{ J}$$

3 (b) $p_{\text{liquid}} = p_{\text{mercury}}$

$$\Rightarrow h_l\rho_l g = h_m\rho_m g$$

$$\Rightarrow h_l = \frac{h_m\rho_m}{\rho_l}$$

$$= \frac{0.76 \times 13600}{760}$$

$$= 13.6\text{ m}$$

4 (b) Relation for height of water in capillary tube is

$$h = \frac{2S\cos\theta}{\rho g r} \Rightarrow h \propto \frac{1}{r}$$

$$\Rightarrow \frac{h_1}{h_2} = \frac{r_2}{r_1} = \frac{2r}{r} = 2$$

As $\quad m = A \cdot h \cdot \rho$

$$\therefore \frac{m_2}{m_1} = \frac{A_2 h_2 \rho}{A_1 h_1 \rho}$$

$$= \frac{\pi(r_2)^2}{\pi(r_1)^2}\frac{h_2}{h_1}$$

$$= \frac{4}{2} = 2$$

$$\Rightarrow m_2 = 2 \times m_1 = 10\text{ g}$$

5 (b) Pressure inside the bubble

$$p_1 = p_0 + \frac{4S}{r} \quad \text{... (i)}$$

The pressure at the depth Z_0 below the water surface is

$$p_2 = p_0 + Z_0\rho g \quad \text{... (ii)}$$

From Eqs. (i) and (ii), we get

$$p_0 + \frac{4S}{r} = p_0 + Z_0\rho g$$

$$\Rightarrow Z_0 = \frac{4S}{r\rho g}$$

$$\Rightarrow Z_0 = \frac{4 \times 2.5 \times 10^{-2}}{1 \times 10^{-3} \times 10^3 \times 10}$$

$$= 1\text{ cm}$$

6 (a) Rate of heat produced,

$$\frac{dQ}{dt} = F \times v_T$$

where, F is the viscous force and v_T is the terminal velocity.

As, $\quad F = 6\pi\eta r v_T$

$$\Rightarrow \frac{dQ}{dt} = 6\pi\eta r v_T^2 \quad \text{...(i)}$$

From the relation for terminal velocity,

$$v_T \propto r^2 \quad \text{...(ii)}$$

From Eq. (ii), we can rewrite Eq. (i) as

$$\frac{dQ}{dt} \propto r \cdot (r^2)^2$$

or $\quad \frac{dQ}{dt} \propto r^5$

7 (d) $p_1 = p_2$

$$h_{\text{oil}} \cdot \rho_{\text{oil}}\, g = h_{\text{water}} \cdot \rho_{\text{water}} \cdot g$$

$$\rho_{\text{oil}} = \frac{h_{\text{water}} \cdot \rho_{\text{water}} \cdot g}{h_{\text{oil}} \cdot g}$$

From figure,

$$\rho_{oil} = \frac{(65+65)\times 1000}{(65+65+10)}$$
$$= 928 \text{ kgm}^{-3}$$

8 (*b*) Given, change in surface area,
$$\Delta A = (5\times 4 - 4\times 2)\times 2$$
($\because$ film has two surfaces)
$$= 24\times 10^{-4}\text{m}^2$$
So, work done,
$$W = S\cdot \Delta A$$
$$3\times 10^{-4} = S\times 24\times 10^{-4}$$
$$\therefore \quad S = \frac{1}{8} = 0.125 \text{ N/m}$$

9 (*b*) According to ascent formula for capillary tube, $h = \dfrac{2T\cos\theta}{\rho g r}$
$$\therefore \frac{\cos\theta_1}{\rho_1} = \frac{\cos\theta_2}{\rho_2} = \frac{\cos\theta_3}{\rho_3}$$
Thus, $\cos\theta \propto \rho$
$$\therefore \quad \rho_1 > \rho_2 > \rho_3$$
$$\therefore \cos\theta_1 > \cos\theta_2 > \cos\theta_3$$
$$0 \le \theta_1 < \theta_2 < \theta_3 < \frac{\pi}{2}$$

10 (*a*) $h = \dfrac{2\sigma}{\rho S R}$ or $R \propto \dfrac{1}{h}$

When height is reduced, then the radius of meniscus increases.

11 (*c*) As energy released
$$= (A_f - A_i)T$$
$$A_i = n\times 4\pi r^2$$
$$= \frac{R_3}{r^3}\times 4\pi r^2 = \frac{3V}{r}$$
$$A_f = 4\pi R^2 = \left(\frac{4}{3}\pi R^3\right)\frac{3}{R} = \frac{3V}{R}$$
Energy released
$$= T\times (A_i - A_f)$$
$$= 3VT\left(\frac{1}{r} - \frac{1}{R}\right)$$

12 (*d*) Given, $p_A = 3p_B$

We know that, excess pressure inside soap bubble, $\Delta p = \dfrac{4T}{r}$
$$\Rightarrow \quad \frac{p_A}{p_B} = \frac{r_B}{r_A} \Rightarrow \frac{3}{1} = \frac{r_B}{r_A}$$
$$\Rightarrow \quad \frac{r_A}{r_B} = \frac{1}{3}$$
Hence, $\dfrac{V_A}{V_B} = \dfrac{1}{27}$

13 (*c*)

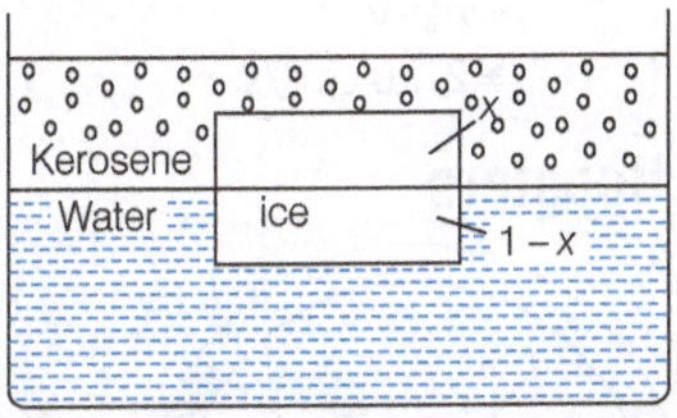

Let x part of ice is in kerosene and $1-x$ part is in water.
Then, weight of ice cube
= upthrust by kerosene
+ upthrust by water on ice
$$\Rightarrow V\cdot\rho_{ice}\cdot g = xV\cdot\rho_{kerosene}\cdot g + (1-x)V\cdot\rho_{water}\cdot g$$
$$\Rightarrow \quad \rho_{ice} = x\rho_{kerosene} + (1-x)\,\rho_{water}$$
$$\Rightarrow \quad \frac{\rho_{ice}}{\rho_{water}} = x\left(\frac{\rho_{kerosene}}{\rho_{water}}\right) + (1-x)$$
Substituting values,
$$0.9 = x0.8 + 1 - x$$
$$\Rightarrow \quad 0.2x = 0.1 \Rightarrow x = 1/2$$
So, remaining 1/2 is in water.
$\therefore$ Ratio of volume immersed
$$= \frac{1}{2} : \frac{1}{2} \text{ or } 1:1$$

14 (*c*) $A_1 v_1 = A_2 v_2$
$$\Rightarrow \quad v_1 = \frac{A_2 v_2}{A} = \frac{25\times 10^{-6}\times 0.6}{1.5\times 10^{-4}}$$
$$= 0.1 \text{ m/s}$$
According to Bernoulli's principle,
$$p_A - p_B = \frac{1}{2}\rho(v_2^2 - v_1^2)$$
$$= \frac{1}{2}\times 1000[(0.6)^2 - (0.1)^2]$$
$$= 500[0.35] = 175.00$$
$$= 175 \text{ Pa}$$

15 (*a*) Given, density of drop of liquid, $\rho_d = \rho$, density of liquid, $\rho_l = \sigma$ and surface tension of liquid,

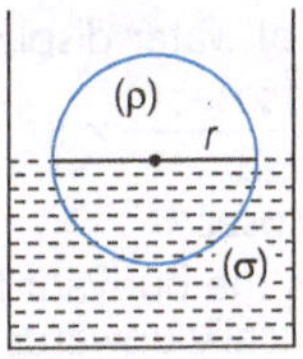

$$S = 7.5\times 10^{-4} \text{ N/cm}$$
$$= 7.5\times 10^{-2} \text{ N/m}$$

Buoyant force at surface tension = mg
$$\Rightarrow \quad \sigma\frac{V}{2}g + 2\pi RS = \rho vg$$
$$\Rightarrow \quad 2\times R = \frac{(2\rho-\sigma)}{2} - \frac{4}{3}\pi R^3 g$$
$$= \sqrt{\frac{3T}{g(2\rho-\sigma)}}$$
$$= \sqrt{\frac{3\times 7.5\times 10^{-2}}{10(2\rho-\sigma)}}$$
$$= \frac{15}{\sqrt{(2\rho-\sigma)}} \text{ cm}$$

16 (*a*)

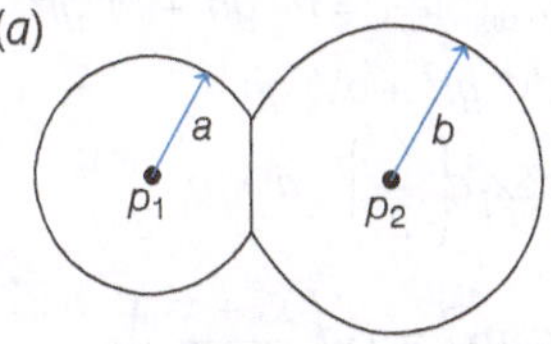

Pressure inside the bubble 1,
$$p_1 = p_0 + \frac{4S}{a}$$
where, p_0 is the initial pressure.
Pressure inside the bubble 2.
$$p_2 = p_0 + \frac{4S}{b}$$
Excess pressure at common surface is given by $p_{ex} = p_1 - p_2$
Let, r be the radius of common surface, then
$$\Rightarrow \quad \frac{4S}{r} = \left(p_0 + \frac{4S}{a}\right) - \left(p_0 + \frac{4S}{b}\right)$$
$$\Rightarrow \quad r = \frac{ab}{b-a}$$

17 (*d*)

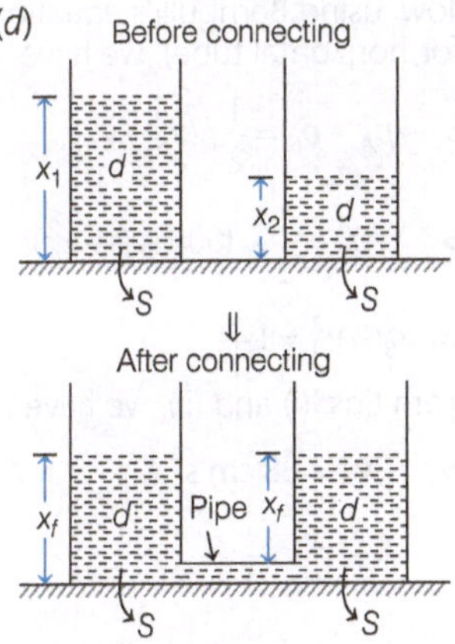

By conservation of volume,

$$(V_{\text{system}})_{\text{initial}} = (V_{\text{system}})_{\text{final}}$$

$$Sx_1 + Sx_2 = Sx_f + Sx_f$$

$$x_f = \frac{x_1 + x_2}{2} \quad \text{...(i)}$$

Now, initial energy of system,

$$(U_{\text{system}})_{\text{initial}} = M_1gh_1 + M_2gh_2$$

$$= dV_1gh_1 + dV_2gh_2$$

$$= dSx_1g\left(\frac{x_1}{2}\right) + dSx_2g\left(\frac{x_2}{2}\right)$$

$$= \frac{1}{2}dSg(x_1^2 + x_2^2) \quad \text{...(ii)}$$

and final energy of system,

$$(U_{\text{system}})_{\text{final}} = M'gh' + M'gh'$$

$$= dV'gh' + dV'gh'$$

$$= dSx_fg\left(\frac{x_f}{2}\right) + dSx_fg\left(\frac{x_f}{2}\right)$$

$$= dSgx_f^2 = dSg\left(\frac{x_1 + x_2}{2}\right)^2 \quad \text{...(iii)}$$

[Using Eq. (i)]

Therefore, the change in energy of system,

$$\Delta U_{\text{system}} = (U_{\text{system}})_{\text{final}} - (U_{\text{system}})_{\text{initial}}$$

$$= -\frac{1}{4}gdS(x_2 - x_1)^2$$

18 (c) By equation of continuity for sections A and B, we have

$$A_Av_A = A_Bv_B$$

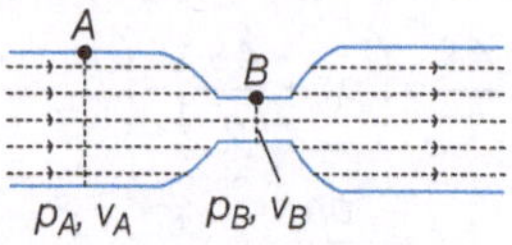

$$\Rightarrow \quad 2v_A = v_B \quad \text{...(i)}$$

Now, using Bernoulli's equation (for horizontal tube), we have

$$\Rightarrow \quad p_A - p_B = \frac{1}{2}\rho(v_B^2 - v_A^2)$$

$$\Rightarrow \quad 700 = \frac{1}{2} \times 1000\,(v_B^2 - v_A^2)$$

$$\Rightarrow v_B^2 - v_A^2 = 1.4 \quad \text{...(ii)}$$

From Eqs. (i) and (ii), we have

$$\Rightarrow \quad v_A = 68 \text{ cm s}^{-1}$$

So, volume flow rate of water

$$= A_A \cdot v_A$$

$$= 2720 \text{ cm}^3/\text{s}$$

Skill Boosters

1 (d)

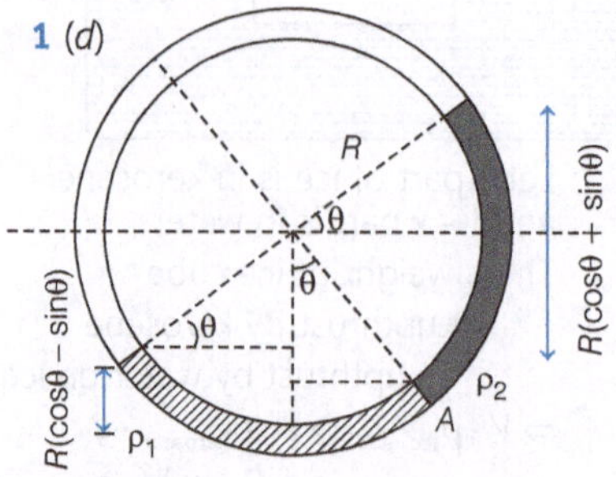

Balancing pressure at point A

$$\rho_1gR(\cos\theta - \sin\theta) = \rho_2gR(\sin\theta + \cos\theta)$$

$$\frac{\rho_1}{\rho_2} = \frac{\sin\theta + \cos\theta}{\cos\theta - \sin\theta} = \frac{\tan\theta + 1}{1 - \tan\theta}$$

$$\rho_1 - \rho_1\tan\theta = \rho_2 + \rho_2\tan\theta$$

$$(\rho_1 + \rho_2)\tan\theta = \rho_1 - \rho_2$$

$$\theta = \tan^{-1}\left(\frac{\rho_1 - \rho_2}{\rho_1 + \rho_2}\right)$$

2 (a) Let G is the mid-point of the rod and E is the mid point of AB

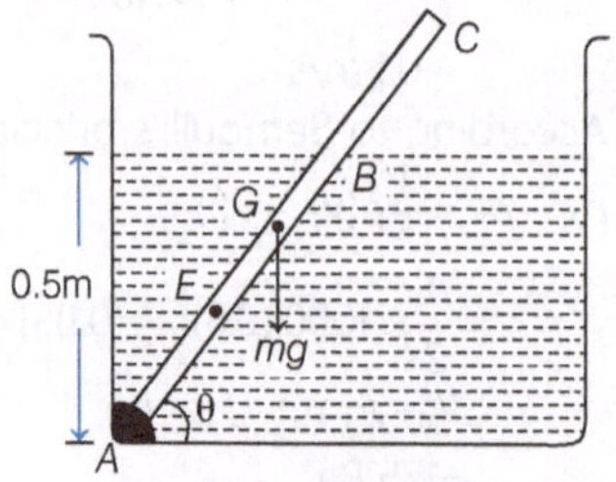

$$AB = \frac{0.5}{\sin\theta} = \frac{\operatorname{cosec}\theta}{2}$$

$$\text{Volume of } AB = \frac{10^{-2}}{2}\operatorname{cosec}\theta$$

Weight of water displaced by AB

$$w = \frac{(10^{-2}\operatorname{cosec}\theta)}{2} \times 10^3 \times 10$$

$$= 50 \operatorname{cosec}\theta$$

This w is the buoyant force acting at E vertically upwards. While weight of the rod mg acts at G vertically downwards. Now taking moments of both these forces about A.

$$(50\operatorname{cosec}\theta)(AE\cos\theta) = 50\,(AG\cos\theta)$$

$$\text{Here, } AE = \frac{1}{2}AB = \frac{1}{4}\operatorname{cosec}$$

$$\text{and } AG = 1$$

$$\therefore\ 50 \times \frac{1}{4}\operatorname{cosec}^2\theta\cos\theta = 50\cos\theta$$

$$\operatorname{cosec}^2\theta = 4$$

$$\operatorname{cosec}\theta = 2 \text{ or } \sin\theta = \frac{1}{2}$$

$$\text{or} \quad \theta = 30^\circ$$

3 (c) $p_1 = p_0 + 10$ (in cm of Hg)

and $p_2 = p_0 + 5$ (in cm of Hg)

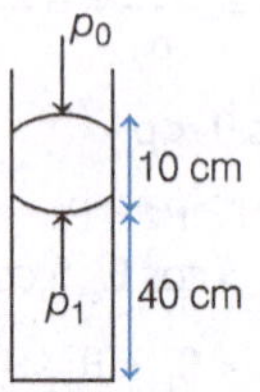

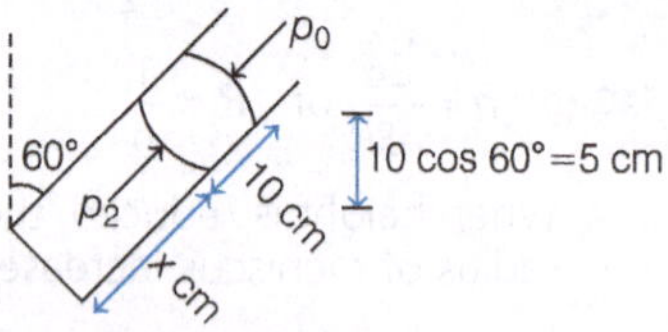

In this process, there is no temperature change. So,

$$p_1V_1 = p_2V_2$$

$$\therefore\ (p_0 + 10)\,40A = (p_0 + 5)xA$$

$$\Rightarrow\ (76 + 10)\,40 = (76 + 5)\,x$$

$$x = \frac{86}{81} \times 40 = 42.47 \text{ cm}$$

4 (b) $d = 2R\cos\theta$

For water- glass,

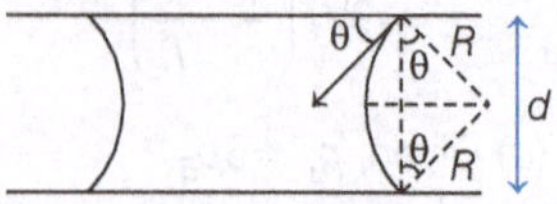

$$\therefore \quad d = 2R \ \Rightarrow\ R = \frac{d}{2}$$

Excess pressure is

$$\Delta p = T\left[\frac{1}{R_1} + \frac{1}{R_2}\right]$$

Here, for one surface,

$$R_1 = R$$

For other surface, $R_2 = \infty$

$$\therefore \quad \Delta p = \frac{T}{R} = \frac{2T}{d}$$

$$V = Ad$$

$$\Rightarrow \quad d = \frac{V}{A}$$

$$\therefore \quad \Delta p = \frac{2TA}{V}$$

$$\therefore \text{ Force, } F = A \cdot \Delta p = \frac{2TA^2}{V}$$

5 (*b*) F is the tension in the wire.

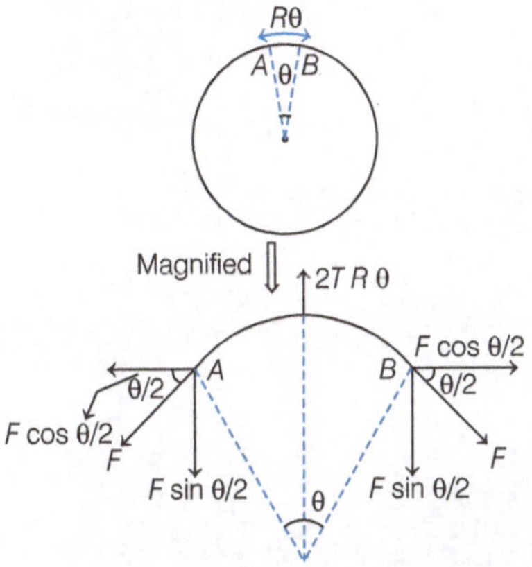

Force due to tension in the wire, on the element is $F_1 = 2F \sin\left(\frac{\theta}{2}\right)\downarrow$

Force on the element due to surface tension of soap film is

$F_2 = 2(T\,R\,\theta)\uparrow$

$\because$ The wire is in contact with the soap film along upper length $R\theta$ and along lower length $R\theta$ both of the element AB.

For equilibrium, $F_2 = F_1$

$$2(T\,R\,\theta) = 2F \sin\left(\frac{\theta}{2}\right)$$

$$2(T\,R\,\theta) = 2F\left(\frac{\theta}{2}\right)$$

$$\left(\because \theta \text{ is small}, \sin\frac{\theta}{2} = \frac{\theta}{2}\right)$$

$$F = 2TR$$

$$Y = \frac{FL}{A\Delta L} = \frac{FR}{A\Delta R}$$

$$\Delta R = \frac{FR}{AY} = (2TR)\frac{R}{AY}$$

$$\Delta R = \frac{2TR^2}{AY}$$

6 (*c*) Volume flow rate in capillary tube is $Q = \frac{V}{t} = \frac{\pi r^4}{8\eta i l}\Delta p$ ... (i)

$$\Delta p = \rho g h \quad \text{... (ii)}$$

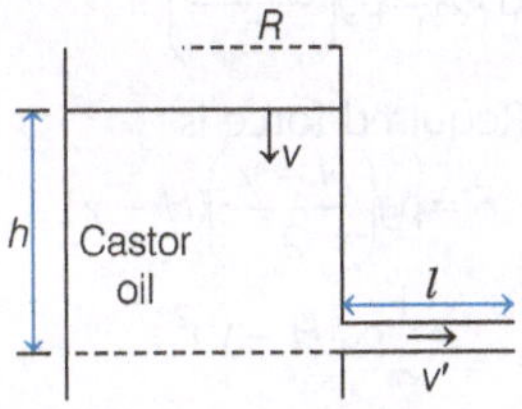

Also, volume flow rate in capillary tube

$$\frac{V}{t} = A' v' = \pi r^2 v' \quad \text{... (iii)}$$

Using, Eqs. (ii) and (iii) in Eq. (i) we get

$$\pi r^2 v' = \frac{\pi r^4}{8\eta l}.\rho g h \text{ or } v' = \frac{r^2 \rho g h}{8\eta l} \quad \text{...(iv)}$$

From equation of continuity

$$v' A' = vA$$

$$\pi r^2 v' = v.\pi R^2$$

$$\Rightarrow \quad v = \frac{r^2}{R^2}.v'$$

$$\text{or } v = \frac{r^2}{R^2}.\frac{r^2 \rho g h}{8\eta l} = \frac{r^4 \rho g h}{8R^2 \eta l}$$

7 (*d*) A snapshot of the system at an instant is shown in the figure

v = speed with which the water level lowers (this has to be constant)

$A = \pi x^2$ = area of surface of water

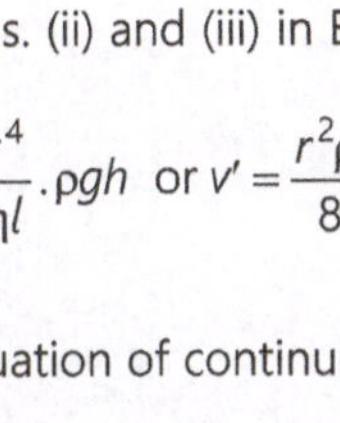

$v' = \sqrt{2gy}$ = Speed of water through orifice

a = area of orifice (given)

From equation of continuity, at this instant $Av = av'$

$$\pi x^2 v = a\sqrt{2gy}$$

$$2gy = \frac{\pi^2 x^4 v^2}{a^2}$$

$$\Rightarrow \quad y = \frac{\pi^2 v^2}{2ga^2}.x^4$$

If V has to be constant . $\frac{\pi^2 v^2}{2ga^2}$ = constant = k (say)

then equation required is $y = kx^4$

$$\text{where, } k = \frac{\pi^2 v^2}{2ga^2}$$

8 (*a*) Initial velocity of water blade is

$$v = \sqrt{2gh} - \omega R$$

So, the mass of water impinging on the blade in unit time is

$$m = \rho A v = \rho A(\sqrt{2gh} - \omega R)$$

After the impact. the velocity of water w.r.t. blade is zero (given)

$\therefore$ Change in momentum in unit time = mv

According to Newton's second law, the force required in unit time

$$= mv = \rho A(\sqrt{2gh} - \omega R)^2$$

9 (*c*) We know that

$$\tan\theta = \frac{a_0}{g} = \frac{9}{10}$$

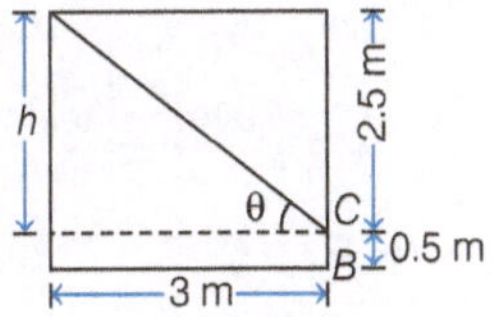

Also $\tan\theta = \frac{h}{3}$ (from figure)

$$\frac{h}{3} = \frac{9}{10}$$

$$\Rightarrow \quad h = 2.7 \text{ m}$$

So, when water level goes below C no water comes out through C. Initial volume of water is

$V_i = 3 \times 3 \times 2$

$= 18 \text{ m}^3$

Final Volume of water is

$V_f = \frac{1}{2} \times 3 \times 2.7 \times 3 + 3 \times 0.3 \times 3$

$= 14.85 \text{ m}^3$

$\therefore$ Volume of water spilled

$= V_i - V_f$

$= 18 - 14.85$

$= 3.15 \text{ m}^3$

$= 3150 \text{ L}$

10 (b) Pressure at Point $Q_2 = \rho g (H - y)$

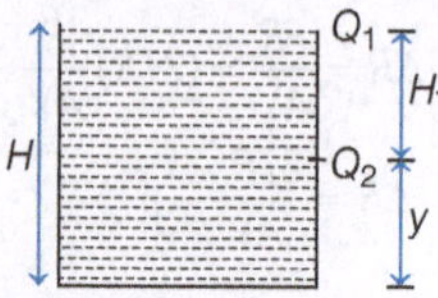

Area between Q_1 and $Q_2 = (H - y)(1) = H - y$

Average pressure between Q_1 and $Q_2 = \rho g \left(\frac{H - y}{2}\right)$

$\therefore$ Required force is

$F = \rho g \left(\frac{H - y}{2}\right)(H - y)$

$= \frac{1}{2} \rho g (H - y)^2$

So, $(H - y)^2 = \frac{2}{\rho g} F$

At $y = H$, $F = 0$ (here, depth $= 0$)

At $y = 0$, $F = \frac{\rho g H^2}{2}$ (Here, depth $= H$)

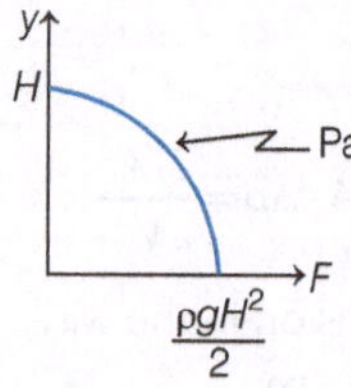

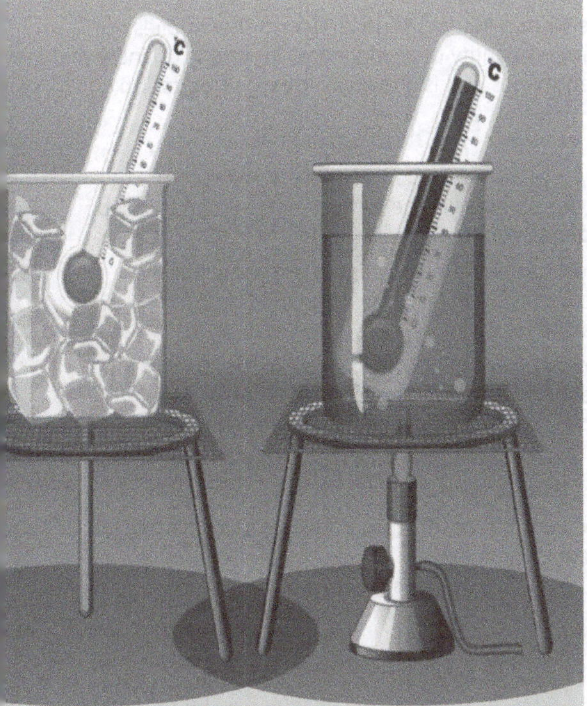

10

Scan for **Physics Through Concept Master** *Videos*

Thermal Properties of Matter

Topicwise No. of Ques asked in 5 Years (NEET)

Topics	No. of Questions				
	2024	2023	2022	2021	2020
Temperature and Heat	–	–	–	–	–
Measurement of Temperature	–	–	–	–	–
Ideal Gas Equation and Absolute Temperature	–	–	–	–	–
Thermal Expansion	1	–	–	–	–
Specific Heat Capacity	–	–	–	–	1
Calorimetry	–	–	–	–	–
Change of State	–	–	–	–	–
Heat Transfer	–	–	1	–	1
Newton's Law of Cooling	–	–	–	1	–

Special Type of Ques Asked In 5 Years (NEET)

Types	Years				
	2024	2023	2022	2021	2020
A-R	–	–	–	–	–
Statement Based	–	–	–	–	–
Matching	–	–	–	–	–

Last 5 Years Weigtage (NEET)

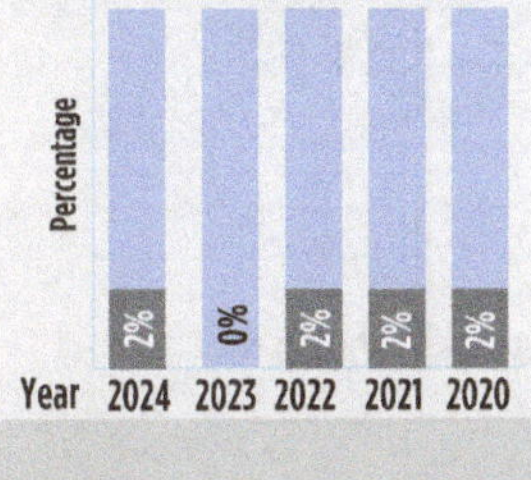

Temperature and Heat

- **Temperature** is the property by virtue of which we predict the hotness or coldness of a body relative to some other body.
- An object that has a higher temperature than another object is said to be **hotter**. A hot utensil is said to have a high temperature and ice cube to have a low temperature. **Hot and cold are relative terms**.
- Heat transfer takes place between the system and the surrounding medium, until the body and the surrounding medium are at the same temperature.
- Heat is the form of energy transferred between two (or more) systems or a system and its surroundings by virtue of temperature difference.
- **SI unit** of heat is **joule (J)**, while SI unit of **temperature is kelvin (K)** but **degree celsius (°C)** is commonly used unit.
- When an object is heated, many changes may take place. Its temperature may rise, it may expand or change state.

Measurement of Temperature

- The devices which are used to measure the temperature are termed as **thermometers**, while the science related to measurement of temperature is termed as **thermometry**.
- Many physical properties of materials change with temperature. Some of these properties are used as the basis for constructing thermometers. **The commonly used property is variation of the volume of a liquid with temperature**.

- **In glass thermometers,** liquid like mercury, alcohol etc. are used. Volume of such liquids varies linearly with temperature over a wide range.
- To define any standard scale, two fixed reference points are needed.
- The ice point and the steam point of water are two convenient fixed points and are known as the **freezing** and **boiling points**, respectively. These two points are the temperatures at which pure water freezes and boils under standard pressure.

Ice Point and Steam Point of Different Scales

Scale	Ice point/Lower reference point	Steam point/Upper reference point	Unit
Celsius	0	100	°C
Fahrenheit	32	212	°F
Kelvin	273.15	373.15	K

- A relationship for converting temperature on two scales, for Fahrenheit temperature t_F and Celsius temperature t_C is

$$\frac{t_F - 32}{180} = \frac{t_C}{100}$$

The variance of both two scales is shown below.

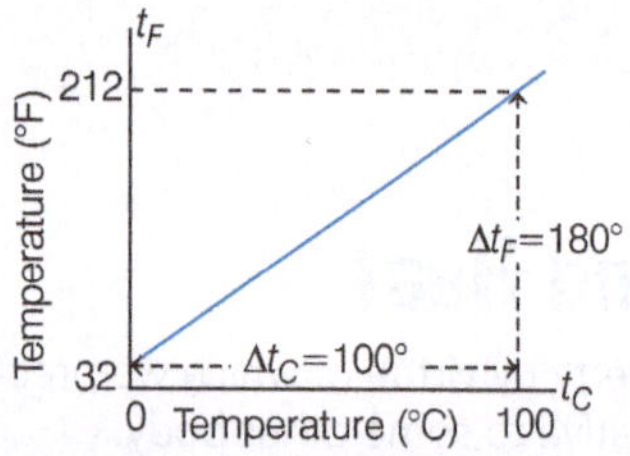

Marks Maximiser

Measuring the correct temperature from a faulty thermometer

$$\text{Temperature} = \frac{\text{Temperature reading on faulty scale} - \text{Lower fixed point}}{\text{Upper fixed point} - \text{Lower fixed point}}$$

Ideal Gas Equation and Absolute Temperature

- Experiments show that all the gases at low densities exhibit same expansion behaviour.
- The variables that describe the behaviour of a given quantity (mass) of gas are pressure, volume and temperature (p, V and T).
- As we know when temperature of the gas is held constant, then pV = constant **(Boyle's law)** and when pressure of the gas is constant, then $\frac{V}{T}$ = constant **(Charles' law)** for a given quantity of gas, then pV/T should also be constant. This relation is known as **ideal gas law.**
- It can be written in a more general form that applies not just to given quantity of a single gas but to any quantity of a low density gas and is known as **ideal gas equation.**

i.e. $$\frac{pV}{T} = \mu R \quad \text{or} \quad pV = \mu RT$$

where, p = pressure, T = temperature, V = volume, μ = number of moles in the sample of gas and R is called **universal gas constant**, i.e. $R = 8.31\ \text{J mol}^{-1}\ \text{K}^{-1}$.

- From ideal gas equation, we find that product of the pressure and volume are directly proportional to temperature, i.e. $pV \propto T$.
- The relation $pV \propto T$, allows a gas to be used to measure temperature in a constant volume gas thermometer. Holding the volume of gas constant, it gives $p \propto T$.

Thus, in a constant volume gas thermometer, temperature is read in terms of pressure.

- **Pressure *versus* temperature** graph by a low density gas kept at constant volume.

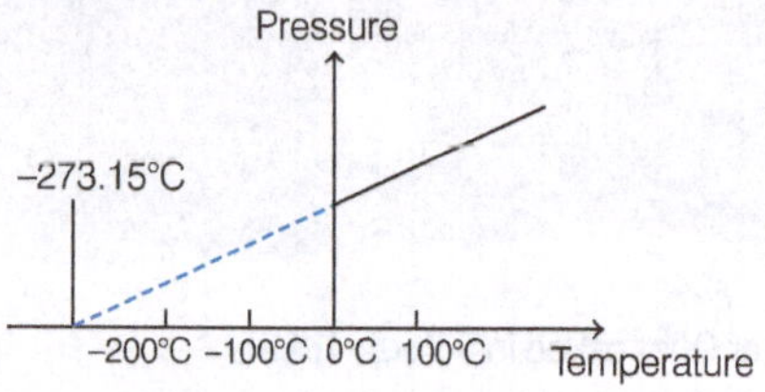

- At low temperature, measurements on real gases deviate from the values predicted by the ideal gas law.

But the relationship is linear over a large temperature range and it looks as though the pressure might reach zero with decreasing temperature, if the gas continued to be a gas.

- Extrapolation of lines for low density gases indicate the same temperature –273.15°C that is known as **absolute zero temperature.** Its value on Kelvin scale is 0K.

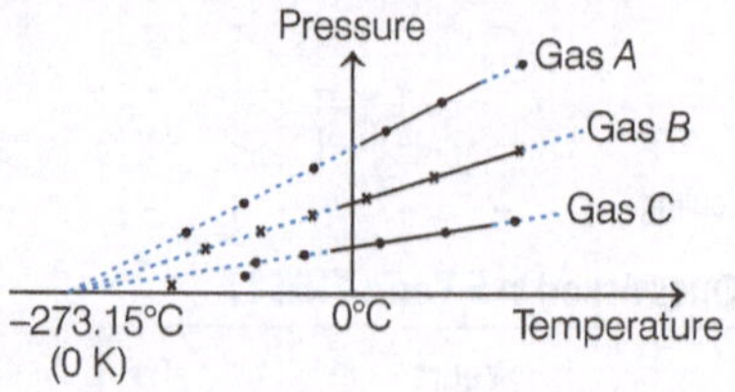

- Absolute zero temperature on Kelvin, Celsius and Fahrenheit temperature scale 0K, –273.15°C and –459.69°F, respectively.

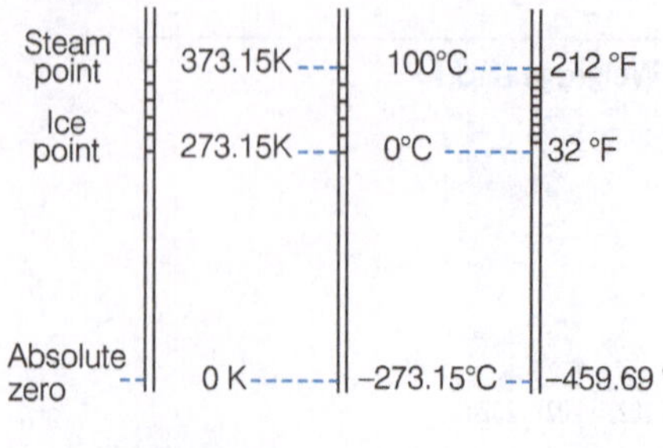

The figure shows comparison of Kelvin, Celsius and Fahrenheit temperature scales.

- The size of unit in Kelvin and Celsius temperature scales is same, so the temperature on these scales are related by $T = T_C + 273.15$

Thermal Expansion

- The increase in the dimensions of a body due to the increase in its temperature is called **thermal expansion.** It occurs in solids, liquids and gases.
- **In the case of solids**, thermal expansion occurs in length, area and volume.
- **In liquids and gases** only volume expansion occurs because they do not posses any fixed shape.
- **In the case of gases**, the state of a gas at any instant is dependent on its volume, temperature and pressure. Hence, a gas can be heated at constant volume or at constant pressure.

Types of Thermal Expansion in Solids

These are of three types as given below

(i) **Linear Expansion** The expansion in length due to increase of temperature of a body, is called linear expansion.

The expansion in length Δl of a body due to increase in temperature ΔT, is expressed as $\frac{\Delta l}{l} = \alpha \Delta T$

$$\Rightarrow \quad \alpha = \frac{\Delta l}{l \Delta T}$$

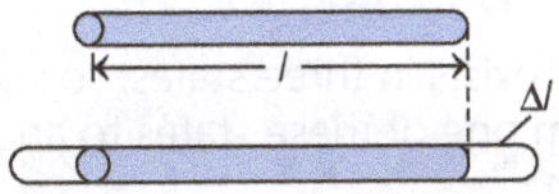

where, α is coefficient of linear expansion.

Normally, metals expands more and have relatively high values of α_l. NEET 2019

(ii) **Area Expansion** The expansion in area due to increase in temperature of a body is called area expansion.

The expansion in the area (ΔA) of a body due to increase in temperature (ΔT) is expressed as

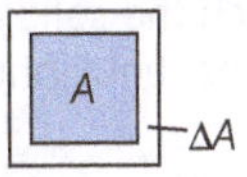

$$\frac{\Delta A}{A} = \beta \Delta T = 2\alpha \, \Delta T \qquad [\because \beta = 2\alpha]$$

$$\Rightarrow \quad \beta = \frac{\Delta A}{A \Delta T}$$

where, β is coefficient of area expansion.

(iii) **Volume Expansion** The expansion in volume due to increase of temperature of a body is called volume expansion.

The expansion in the volume (ΔV) of a body due to increase in temperature (ΔT) is expressed as,

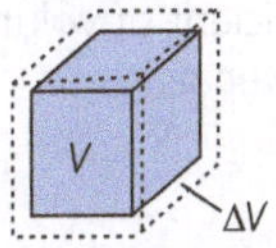

$$\frac{\Delta V}{V} = \gamma \Delta T = 3\alpha \, \Delta T \qquad [\because \gamma = 3\alpha]$$

$$\Rightarrow \quad \gamma = \frac{\Delta V}{V \Delta T}$$

where, γ is coefficient of volume expansion.

- The units of α, β and γ are same $°C^{-1}$ or K^{-1}.
- The value of α, β or γ depends on the nature of material.
- **The relation between** α, β **and** γ are given as, $\alpha : \beta : \gamma = 1 : 2 : 3$

Anomalous Expansion of Water

In normal situation, matter expands on heating and contracts on cooling. But in case of water, it contracts on heating between 0° C and 4° C (i.e. in this range, coefficient of volume expansion is negative), i.e. volume of a given amount of water decreases as it is cooled from room temperature as shown in Fig. (a).

Below 4°C, the volume increases and therefore density decreases as shown in Fig. (b).

Thus, it means that water exhibits an anomalous behaviour.

Density of water is maximum at 4°C.

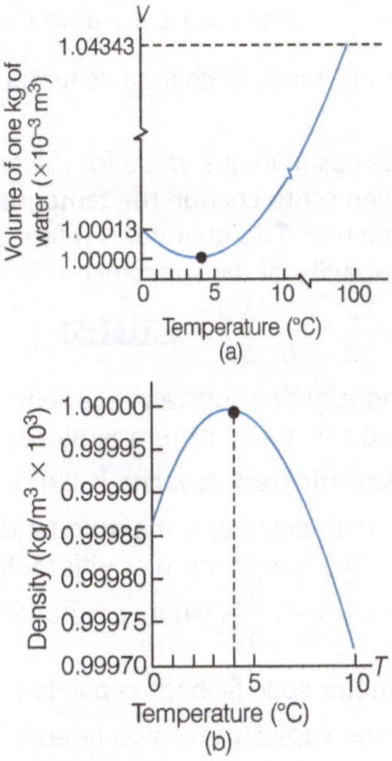

Thermal expansion of water

- At ordinary temperature, gases expand more than solids and liquids.
- For liquids, the coefficient of volume expansion is relatively independent of the temperature. However, for gases, it is dependent on temperature.
- For ideal gas, the coefficient of volume expansion at constant pressure is given as

$$\gamma = \frac{1}{T}$$

At 0°C, $\gamma = 3.7 \times 10^{-3}\ K^{-1}$, which is much larger than that for solids and liquids.

Thermal Stress

When a metal rod whose ends are fixed is heated, then compressive strain is produced in the rod. The stress set up in the rod due to increase of temperature is called **thermal stress**.

Thermal stress $= Y \dfrac{\Delta l}{l} = Y\alpha\,\Delta T$

where, Y = Young's modulus, ΔT = change in temperature, Δl = change in length and α = linear expansion coefficient of the material.

Specific Heat Capacity

- The change in temperature of a substance when given quantity of heat is absorbed or rejected by it, is characterised by a quantity called **heat capacity** of substance.

  It is given by $S = \dfrac{\Delta Q}{\Delta T}$, where ΔQ is the amount of heat supplied to the substance to change its temperature from T to $T + \Delta T$.
- Every substance has a unique value for the amount of heat absorbed or given off to change the temperature of unit mass of it by one unit. This quantity is referred to as the **specific heat capacity** of the substance.

  It is given by $s = \dfrac{S}{m} = \dfrac{1}{m}\cdot\dfrac{\Delta Q}{\Delta T}$ NEET 2020
- Specific heat capacity of a substance depends on the nature of the substance and its temperature.

  The **SI unit of specific heat capacity** is $Jkg^{-1}K^{-1}$.
- **Molar specific heat capacity** is the amount of heat required to raise the temperature of unit mole gas by 1°C and given by $c = \dfrac{S}{\mu} = \dfrac{1}{\mu}\cdot\dfrac{\Delta Q}{\Delta T}$, where μ = number of moles.

  The **SI unit of molar specific heat capacity** is $J\ mol^{-1}\ K^{-1}$.
- Molar specific heat capacity is of two types
  (i) **Molar specific heat at constant pressure** is the amount of heat required to raise the temperature of unit mole of gas by 1°C at constant pressure. It is denoted by C_p.
  (ii) **Molar specific heat at constant volume** is the amount of heat required to raise the temperature of unit mole of gas by 1°C at constant volume. It is denoted by C_V.
- Water has the highest specific heat capacity as compared to other substances. For this reason, water is also used as coolant in automobile radiators, as well as a heater in hot water bags.
- Due to high specific heat capacity, water warms up more slowly than land during summer and consequently wind from the sea has a cooling effect.

Calorimetry

- Calorimetry means measurement of heat, i.e. it is one of the method for the measurement of specific heat or latent heat of a substance. A device in which heat measurement can be done is called **calorimeter**.
- When a body at higher temperature is brought in contact with another body at lower temperature, the heat lost by the hot body is equal to the heat gained by the colder body provided no heat is allowed to escape to the surroundings.

  According to principle of calorimetry,

  Heat lost by hotter body = Heat gained by colder body

  $m_1 s_1 \Delta T_1 = m_2 s_2 \Delta T_2$

  where, m_1 = mass of hot body, m_2 = mass of cold body,
  s_1 = specific heat of hot body
  and s_2 = specific heat of cold body.

Change of State

- Matter normally exists in three states; solid, liquid and gas. A transition from one of these states to another is called a change of state.
- The change of state from solid to liquid without any rise in temperature is called **melting or fusion**.
- The change of state from liquid to solid without any change in temperature is called **freezing**.
- Both the solid and the liquid states of the substance co-exist in thermal equilibrium, during the change of states from solid to liquid.

  The temperature at which the solid and the liquid states of the substance is in thermal equilibrium with each other is called its **melting point**.
- The melting point of a substance at standard atmospheric pressure is called its **normal melting point**.
- The phenomenon in which ice melts when pressure is increased and freezes again when pressure is removed is called **regelation**.

- The change of state from liquid to vapour (or gas) without change in temperature is called **vaporisation**.
- During vaporisation, both the liquid and vapour states of the substance co-exist in the thermal equilibrium. The temperature at which the liquid and the vapour states of the substance co-exist is called its **boiling point**.
- The boiling point increases with increase in pressure and *vice-versa*.
- The boiling point of a substance at standard atmospheric pressure is called its **normal boiling point**.
- The change from solid state to vapour state without passing through the liquid state is called **sublimation** and the substance is said to sublime.
- During sublimation process both the solid and vapour states of a substance co-exist in thermal equilibrium.

  The temperature of a substance remains constant during its state change (phase change). The phase diagram of water is shown in the following figure

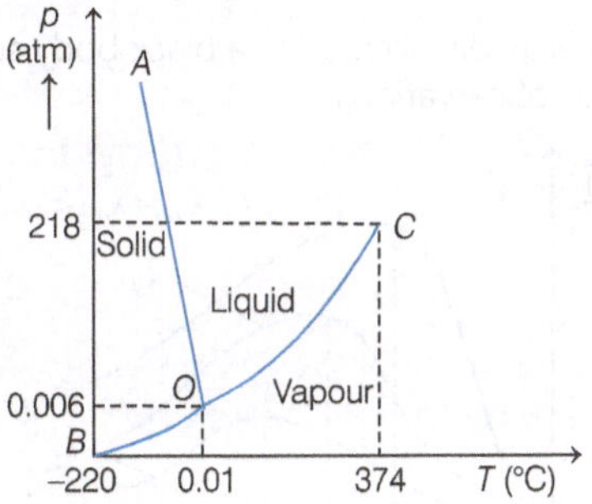

(i) The phase diagram divides the p-T plane into a **solid region**, the **vapour region** and the **liquid region**.

(ii) The regions are separated by the curve such as **sublimation curve** (BO), **fusion curve** (AO) and **vaporisation curve** (CO).

(iii) The points on sublimation curve BO represents states in which solid and vapour phases co-exist.

Points on the fusion curve AO represents states in which solid and liquid phases co-exist.

Points on vaporisation curve CO represents states in which the liquid and vapour phases co-exist.

(iv) The temperature and pressure at which the fusion curve, the vaporisation curve and the sublimation curve meet and all the three phases of a substance co-exist is called the **triple point of the substance**.

(v) The triple point of water is represented by the temperature 273.16K and pressure 6.11×10^{-3} Pa.

Latent Heat

- The amount of heat transferred per unit mass during the change of state of a substance without any change in its temperature is called **latent heat** of the substance.

$$Q \propto m \Rightarrow Q = mL$$

where, L = latent heat of the material.

- Its **SI unit is** J/kg and practical unit is cal/g.
- There are two types of latent heat of materials

  (i) The amount of heat required to change the state of unit mass of a substance from solid to liquid at its melting point is called the **latent heat of fusion** L_F. For water, its value is 3.33×10^5 J kg^{-1}.

  (ii) The amount of heat required to change the state of unit mass of a substance from liquid to vapour at its boiling point is called the **latent heat of vaporisation** L_V. For water, its value is 22.6×10^5 J kg^{-1}.

- The temperature *versus* heat for water at 1 atm pressure is shown below.

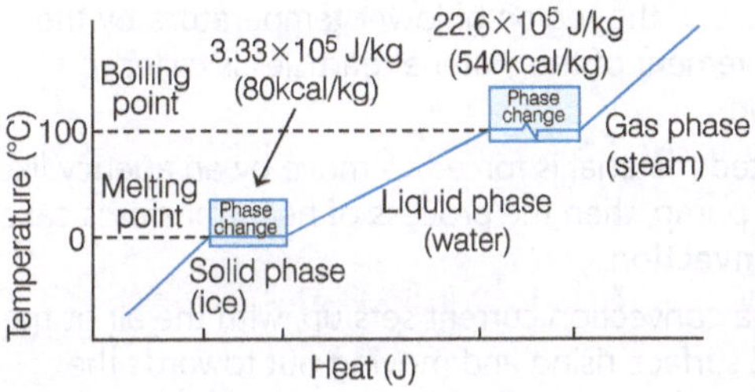

For **Concept Master** *Video*

- From the above figure, we see that the slopes of the phase lines are not all the same, which indicates that specific heats of various states are not equal.

Heat Transfer

- Heat is energy transfer from one system to another or from one part of a system to another part, arising due to temperature difference.
- Heat transfer takes place by three distinct modes, namely **conduction, convection** and **radiation**.

Conduction

- It is the mechanism of transfer of heat between two adjacent parts of a body because of their temperature difference.
- In this process, heat is transmitted from one part of the body to another at a lower temperature through molecular collision without any actual motion of particles of substance.
- Gases are poor thermal conductors while liquids have conductivities intermediate between solids and gases.
- The rate of flow of heat (or heat current) H is proportional to the temperature difference ΔT and the area of cross-section A and is inversely proportional to the length L,

i.e. $H = K \cdot A \dfrac{\Delta T}{L} = \dfrac{KA(T_1 - T_2)}{L}$

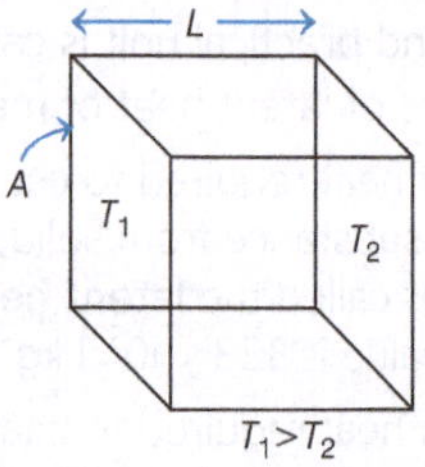

For Concept Master Video

where, K is called the **thermal conductivity** of the material. **The SI unit of K** is $Js^{-1}m^{-1}K^{-1}$ or $Wm^{-1}K^{-1}$. NEET 2019

Convection

- The process of heat transmission from the region of higher temperature to the region of lower temperature by the actual movement of the material particles is called **convection.**
- If the heated material is forced to move by an agency like blower or pump, then the process of heat transfer is called **forced convection.**
- On earth, a convection current sets up, with the air at the equatorial surface rising and moving out towards the poles, descending and streaming in towards the equator. This is called **trade wind.**
- Conduction and convection require some material as a transport medium.

Radiation NEET 2022

- The mechanism in which heat is transferred from one place to another without any medium is called **radiation.**
- The energy so transferred by electromagnetic waves is called **radiant energy.** It is the fastest mode of transfer of heat.
- The electromagnetic radiation emitted by a body by virtue of its temperature, like radiation by a red hot iron or light from a filament lamp is called **thermal radiation.**
- When thermal radiation falls on other bodies, it is partly reflected and partly absorbed. The amount of heat that a body can absorb by radiation depends on the colour of the body.

i.e. $Q = Q_a + Q_r + Q_t$

$\Rightarrow \dfrac{Q_a}{Q} + \dfrac{Q_r}{Q} + \dfrac{Q_t}{Q} = 1 \Rightarrow a + r + t = 1$

where, a, r and t are **coefficient of absorption, coefficient of reflection and coefficient of transmission, respectively.**

- A body will be
  - (i) **Perfect reflector**, if $a = t = 0$ and $r = 1$.
  - (ii) **Perfect absorber**, if $r = t = 0$ and $a = 1$.
  - (iii) **Perfect transmitter**, if $a = r = 0$ and $t = 1$.
- A good reflector is a bad absorber.
- We wear white or light coloured clothes in summer, so that they absorb the least heat from the sun. However, during winter, we use dark coloured clothes, which absorb heat from the sun and keep our body warm.
- The bottoms of utensils for cooking food are blackened, so that they absorb maximum heat from fire and transfer it to the food to be cooked.

Black Body Radiation

- A black body is an object which absorbs all the radiation falling on it.
- **Wien's displacement law** states that "as temperature of black body T increases, the wavelength λ_m corresponding to maximum emission decreases" such that

  $\lambda_m T = b$ (constant) NEET 2019

  where, b is known as **Wien's constant** and its value is 2.89×10^{-3} mK.
- From the energy distribution in a black body spectrum, we get following observations.

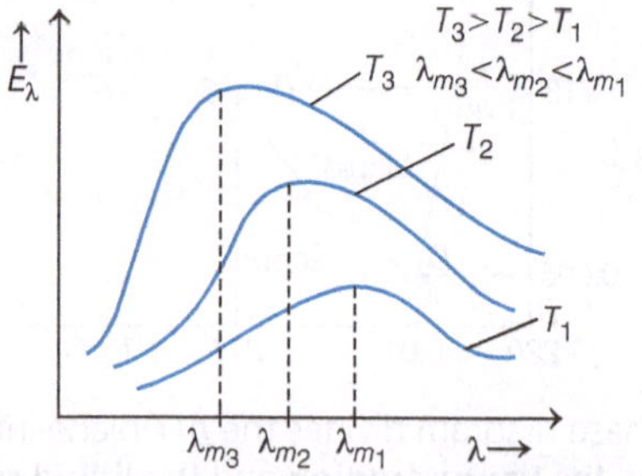

(i) As temperature of black body increases, the wavelength corresponding to maximum value of E_λ shifts towards left.

(ii) The energy associated with a radiation of particular wavelength increases with the increase in temperature.

(iii) The area under the curve is found to increase with fourth power of absolute temperature, i.e. $E \propto T^4$.

(iv) The most significant features of the black body radiation curve is that they are universal. They depend only on temperature and not on the size, shape or material of the black body.

Stefan-Boltzmann Law

- According to this law, the radiant energy emitted per unit area per second by a perfectly black body (i.e. emissive power of black body) is directly proportional to the fourth power of its absolute temperature, i.e. $H = A\sigma T^4$

  where, σ = **Stefan-Boltzmann constant** and its value in SI units is 5.67×10^{-8} $Wm^{-2} K^{-4}$, A is the surface area of body and T is the absolute temperature of the body.

- **For a body whose emissivity is e,** then energy emitted per unit time is given by $H = Ae\sigma T^4$.

  Here, $e = 1$ for perfect radiator.
- A body at temperature T, with surroundings at temperature T_s emits as well as receives energy.

  For a perfect radiator, the net rate of loss of radiant energy is

$$H = \sigma A(T^4 - T_s^4)$$

For a body with emissivity e, the relation modifies to

$$H = e\,\sigma A(T^4 - T_s^4)$$

Newton's Law of Cooling

- According to this law, "rate of cooling of a body is directly proportional to the temperature difference between the body and the surroundings, if the temperature difference is small."

  Mathematically, $-\dfrac{dQ}{dt} = k(T_2 - T_1)$ **NEET 2021, 19**

  where, k is a positive constant depending upon the area and nature of the surface of the body.
- According to Newton's law of cooling, when a body cools by radiation, then temperature of body decreases exponentially as shown in the graph.

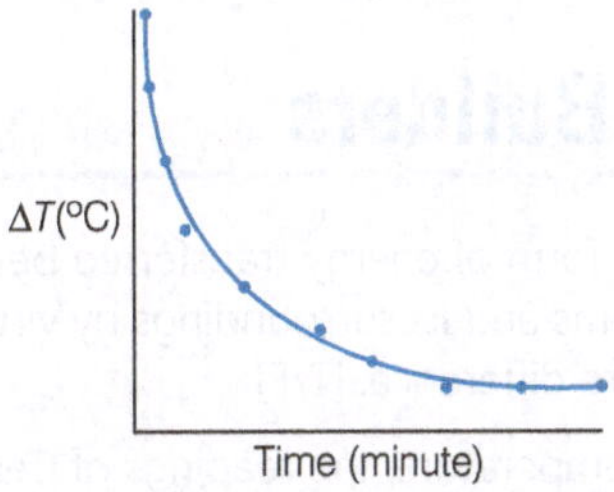

- If a body cools by radiation through a small temperature difference from T_1 to T_2 in a short time t when the surrounding temperature is T_0, then

$$\frac{dQ}{dt} = ms\frac{dT_2}{dt} = k\frac{T_1 - T_2}{t} = k\left[\frac{T_1 + T_2}{2} - T_0\right]$$

Caution Points

- When a liquid and its vapour are in equilibrium (like water and steam), they have same temperature and pressure throughout. The only thing which is different in two phases, is their molar volume (i.e. density) at equilibrium. This is true for a system with any number of phases in equilibrium.
- Convection takes place when the matter present in the fluid moves around because of temperature difference. For example, if we have a hot metal rod under a running water tap, it loses heat through direct contact with the water (conduction), not because the water starts swirling around (convection).

PYQ Notes

1. The following identity is used to convert temperature on any scale into the other scale.

$$\frac{\text{Reading on any scale } (T) - \text{lower fixed point (LFP)}}{\text{Upper fixed point} - \text{lower fixed point}} = \text{constant}$$

[JEE Main 2023]

2. When a bullet of mass m travelling with a speed of v m/s strikes with a fixed wooden target and n% of its total kinetic energy is converted into heat in the bullet while rest part is converted into heat in the wood, then rise in temperature (ΔT) of bullet is calculated by using following formula.

$$(ms\,\Delta T)_{\text{bullet}} = \frac{n}{100}\left(\frac{1}{2}mv^2\right)$$

where, s is the specific heat of the material of bullet.

[JEE Main 2022]

3. The ratio of heat required to raise the temperature of two metallic solid spheres of radii r_1 and r_2 through 1 K is given by

$$\frac{Q_1}{Q_2} = \left(\frac{r_1}{r_2}\right)^3$$

[NEET 2020]

4. **Combination of conducting slabs**

(i) **Series combination**

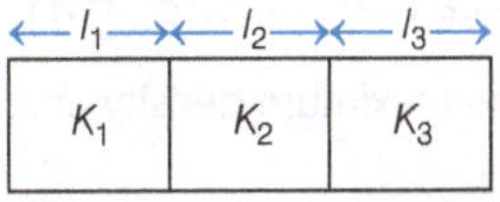

$T_1 > T_2$

$$H = \frac{Q}{t} = \frac{(T_1 - T_2)}{\dfrac{l_1}{K_1A} + \dfrac{l_2}{K_2A} + \dfrac{l_3}{K_3A}}$$

$\therefore$ Equivalent thermal conductivity, $K = \dfrac{l_1 + l_2 + l_3}{\dfrac{l_1}{K_1} + \dfrac{l_2}{K_2} + \dfrac{l_3}{K_3}}$

(ii) **Parallel combination**

$$H = \frac{Q}{t} = (K_1A_1 + K_2A_2 + K_3A_3)\frac{(T_1 - T_2)}{l}$$

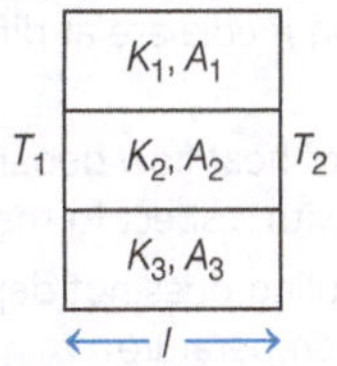

and equivalent thermal conductivity,

$$K = \frac{K_1A_1 + K_2A_2 + K_3A_3}{A_1 + A_2 + A_3}$$

[NEET 2016]

Step by Step

Mastering NCERT

- Concept Builders
- Topical Questions
- Assertion and Reason Questions
- Statement Based
- Matching Type
- Numerical Type
- NCERT Exemplar
- Past Exams MCQs
- Skill Boosters

Concept Builders

1 Heat is the form of energy transferred between two or more systems and its surroundings by virtue of temperature difference. [T/F]

2 At which temperature, the readings of Centigrade and Fahrenheit scales are the same?

3 The ice and steam point have values......... °F (38/32) and .... °F (212/100) respectively.

4 Fill in the blank space for given temperature in other units – 40°F=…°C=… K.

5 .... (Rubber/Wood) contracts on heating.

6 Test tubes and beakers are made up of pyrex glass or silica because they have very low value of coefficient of linear expansion. [T/F]

7 The size of hole in the metallic disc decreases on heating the metal disc. [T/F]

8 The materials having low specific heat cools .... (more/less) rapidly, then material having high specific heat.

9 Water exhibits on anomalous behaviour, it contracts on heating between 0°C and 4°C. [T/F]

10 Water has the maximum density at .... °C. [0/4]

11 Coefficient of volume expansion for a solid is a constant that does not change with temperature. [T/F]

12 Two bodies attains thermal equilibrium at temperature T, then $m_1 s_1 (T - T_1) = m_2 s_2 (T - T_2)$. [T/F]

13 Relegation occurs due to .... (lowering/elevation) of melting point of water.

14 Specific heat is .... (directly/inversely) proportional to the slope of temperature-time curve.

15 Name the process in which the solid state changes to vapour state without passing through the liquid state.

16 What is the value of triple point of water in kelvin?

17 Two identical metal wires of thermal conductivity K_1 and K_2 respectively are connected in series. The effective thermal conductivity of the combination is ....

18 Conduction and convection are the process, where heat is transferred by the collision of molecules. [T/F]

19 Ratio of emissivity and absorptivity of most of real bodies is .... (one / less than one)

20 Newton's law of cooling is valid for any temperature difference. [T/F]

Topical Questions

Temperature and Heat

1 A glass of ice-cold water left on a table on a hot summer day eventually warms up, whereas a cup of hot tea on the same table cools down because NCERT Pg. 202

(a) its surrounding media are at different temperature

(b) the direction of heat flow depends on the surrounding temperature with respect to the body

(c) heating or cooling does not depend on surrounding temperature

(d) Both (a) and (b)

2 Which of the following is essential in order to flow heat from one part of the solid to another? NCERT Pg. 202

(a) Uniform temperature (b) Density gradient

(c) Temperature gradient (d) Uniform density

Measurement of Temperature

3 In a thermometer with celcius scale, the level of mercury rises to $\left(\frac{3}{5}\right)$th of the total distance when thermometer taken from the melting ice to warm liquid. The temperature of liquid (in K) is

NCERT Pg. 203

(a) 313.15 (b) 330 (c) 333.15 (d) 217.15

4 A faulty thermometer has its fixed points at 5°C and 95°C. What is the correct temperature when the thermometer reads 64°C? **NCERT Pg. 203**

(a) 60°C (b) 75.5°C
(c) 60.5°C (d) 65.5°C

5 The graph of Fahrenheit temperature (F) *versus* Celsius temperature (C) is shown below. The correct relation between F and C which can be deduced from graph, is **NCERT Pg. 203**

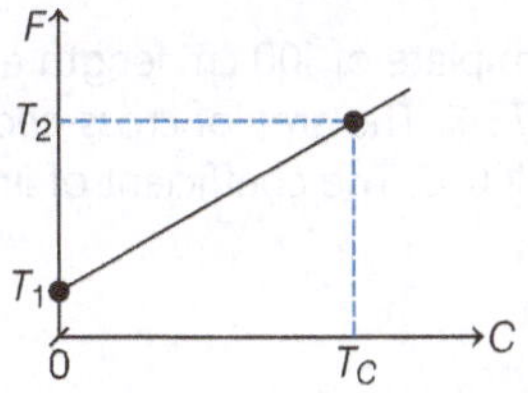

(a) $\frac{F-32}{T_2-T_1}=\frac{T_C}{C}$ (b) $\frac{F-T_1}{T_2-T_1}=\frac{C}{T_C}$

(c) $\frac{F-32}{T_2-T_1}=\frac{C}{T_C}$ (d) $\frac{C}{T_1-T_2}=\frac{F-32}{T_C}$

6 On Centigrade or Celsius scale (°C), the temperature of a body increases by 30° C. The increase in temperature on Fahrenheit scale (°F) is **NCERT Pg. 203**

(a) 50° (b) 40°
(c) 30° (d) 54°

7 A thermometer graduated according to a linear scale reads a value x_0 when in contact with boiling water and $x_0/3$ when in contact with ice. What is the temperature of an object in °C, if this thermometer in the contact with the object reads $x_0/2$? **NCERT Pg. 203**

(a) 35 (b) 60 (c) 40 (d) 25

8 Two absolute scales A and B have triple points of water defined to be 400 A and 300 B. The relation between T_A and T_B is (triple point of water is 273.16 K temperature and 6.11×10^{-3} atm pressure at which water co-exists in gas, liquid and solid states) **NCERT Pg. 203**

(a) $T_A=\frac{4}{3}T_B$ (b) $T_B=\frac{4}{7}T_A$ (c) $T_A=\frac{4}{7}T_B$ (d) $T_B=T_A$

Ideal Gas Equation and Absolute Temperature

9 A real gas obeys ideal gas equation more correctly when **NCERT Pg. 204**

(a) temperature is very low and pressure is very high
(b) temperature is very high and pressure is low
(c) temperature and pressure, both are very low
(d) temperature and pressure, both are very high

10 The equation of state for 5g of oxygen at pressure p, temperature T, when occupying a volume V, will be **NCERT Pg. 204**

(a) $pV=5RT$ (b) $pV=\frac{5}{2}RT$

(c) $pV=\frac{5}{16}RT$ (d) $pV=\frac{5}{32}RT$

11 If a gas at 27°C is allowed to expand three times of its original volume and pressure is halved. The new temperature of the gas is **NCERT Pg. 204**

(a) 390 K (b) 300 K (c) 250 K (d) 450 K

12 An ideal gas is contained in a cylinder at pressure p_1 and temperature T_1. The initial moles of the gas is n_1. The gas leaks from the cylinder and attains a final pressure p_2 and temperature T_2. The new moles of the gas present in the cylinder is **NCERT Pg. 204**

(a) $\frac{p_2T_1}{p_1n_1T_2}$ (b) $\frac{n_1T_2\,p_2}{T_1p_1}$

(c) $\frac{n_1T_1\,p_2}{T_2p_1}$ (d) Data insufficient

Thermal Expansion

13 A uniform metallic circular disc of mass M and radius R, mounted on frictionless bearings, is rotating (with angular frequency ω) about an axis passing through its centre and perpendicular to its plane. The temperature of the disc is then increased by Δt. If α is the coefficient of linear expansion of the metal, then which of the following statement is correct? **NCERT Pg. 205**

(a) The moment of inertia increases by $MR^2\alpha\Delta t$.
(b) The moment of inertia remains unchanged.
(c) The angular frequency increases by $2\,\alpha\,\omega\Delta t$.
(d) The angular frequency decreases by $\alpha\,\omega\Delta t$.

14 A bimetallic strip consists of metals X and Y. It is mounted rigidly at the base as shown in figure. The metal X has a higher coefficient of expansion compared to that of metal Y. When bimetallic strip is placed in a cold bath, then **NCERT Pg. 205**

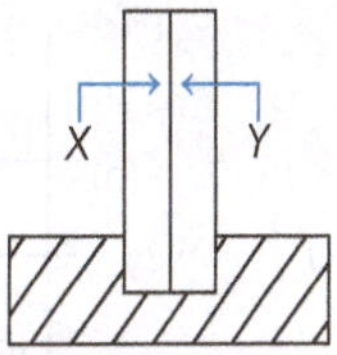

(a) it will bend towards the right
(b) it will bend towards the left
(c) it will not bend but shrink
(d) it will neither bend nor shrink

15 A bar of iron is 10 cm at 20°C. At 19°C, it will be (α of iron $= 11 \times 10^{-6} °C^{-1}$) **NCERT Pg. 205**
(a) 11×10^{-6} cm, longer
(b) 11×10^{-5} cm, shorter
(c) 11×10^{-6} cm, shorter
(d) 11×10^{-5} cm, longer

16 A surveyor's 30 m steel tape is correct at a temperature of 20°C. The distance between the two points, as measured by this tape on a day when the temperature is 35°C is 26 m . The true distance between the points is [α_l (steel) $= 1.2 \times 10^{-5}$ /°C] **NCERT Pg. 205**
(a) 25.9953 m (b) 26.0046 m
(c) 27.995 m (d) 24.0046 m

17 A copper rod of 88 cm and an aluminium rod of unknown length have same increase in length independent of increase in temperature. The length of aluminium rod is ($\alpha_{Cu} = 1.7 \times 10^{-5} K^{-1}$ and $\alpha_{Al} = 2.2 \times 10^{-5} K^{-1}$) **NCERT Pg. 205**
(a) 113.9 cm (b) 88 cm
(c) 68 cm (d) 6.8 cm

18 How much should the temperature of a brass rod be increased so as to increase its length by 1%? (Given, α for brass is $0.00002 °C^{-1}$) **NCERT Pg. 205**
(a) 300°C (b) 400°C (c) 500° C (d) 550° C

19 Two rods, one of aluminium and the other made of steel, having initial length l_1 and l_2 are connected together to form a single rod of length $l_1 + l_2$. The coefficients of linear expansion for aluminium and steel are α_a and α_s, respectively. If the length of each rod increases by the same amount when their temperatures are raised by t°C, then find the ratio of l_1 with $l_1 + l_2$. **NCERT Pg. 205**
(a) $\frac{\alpha_s}{\alpha_a}$ (b) $\frac{\alpha_a}{\alpha_s}$
(c) $\frac{\alpha_s}{\alpha_a + \alpha_s}$ (d) $\frac{\alpha_a}{\alpha_a + \alpha_s}$

20 Coefficient of volumetric expansion α_V is not a constant. It depends on temperature. Variation of α_V with temperature T for metals is **NCERT Pg. 205**

(a)
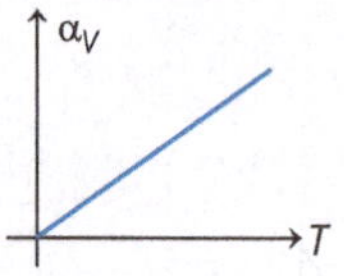

(b)
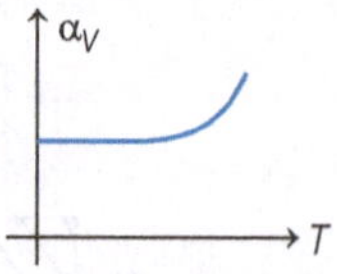

(c)
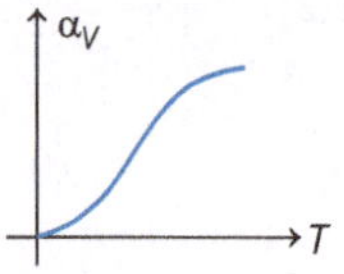

(d)
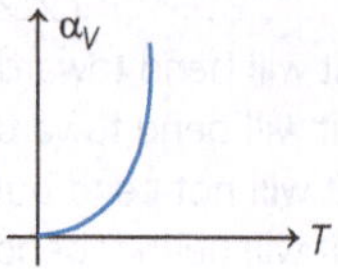

21 The coefficient of volume expansion of glycerine is $49 \times 10^{-5} °C^{-1}$. What is the fractional change in density for a 30°C rise in temperature? **NCERT Pg. 205**
(a) 0.0155 (b) 0.0143
(c) 0.0255 (d) 0.0355

22 For an ideal gas, coefficient of volume expansion is given by **NCERT Pg. 205**
(a) $\frac{nR\Delta T}{p}$ (b) $\frac{\Delta T}{T}$
(c) $\frac{R\Delta T}{T}$ (d) $\frac{1}{T}$

23 An aluminium plate of 100 cm length and 20 cm breadth at 273 K. The area of cross-section is increased by 2 cm^2 at 100°C. The coefficient of linear expansion of plate is **NCERT Pg. 205**
(a) 5×10^{-6}/°C
(b) 6.6×10^{-6}/°C
(c) 10^{-2}/°C
(d) 2×10^{-6}/°C

24 The coefficient of volume expansion of a liquid is $49 \times 10^{-5} K^{-1}$. When temperature is raised by 30°C, then which of the following statement is correct? **NCERT Pg. 206**
(a) Its density decreases.
(b) Its density increases.
(c) Its fractional decrease in density is 2.5×10^{-2}.
(d) Its fractional increase in density is 2.5×10^{-2}.

25 Which of the following graph shows the variation of volume of water with increase in temperature? **NCERT Pg. 206**

(a)
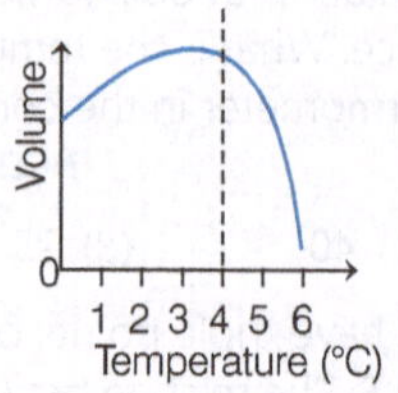

(b)
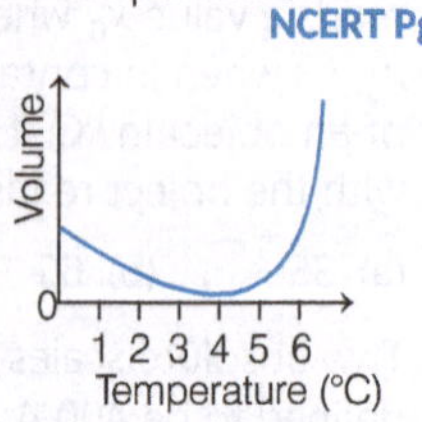

(c)
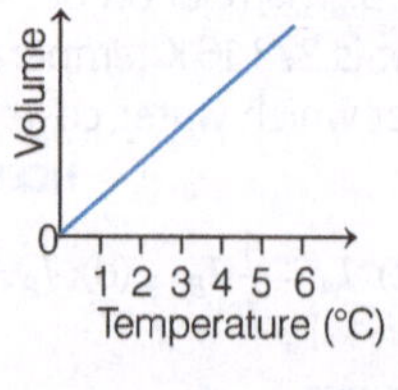

(d)
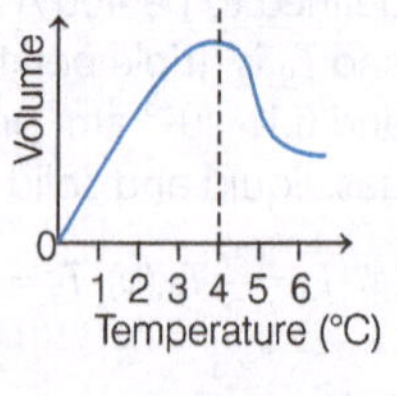

26 Temperature of atmosphere in Kashmir falls below – 10°C in winter. Due to this water, animal and plant life of Dal-lake **NCERT Pg. 206**
(a) is destroyed in winters
(b) frozen in winter and regenerated in summers
(c) survives as only top layer of lake is frozen
(d) None of the above

27 A brass wire 1.8 m long at 27°C is held taut with little tension between two rigid supports. If the wire is cooled to a temperature of – 39°C, what is the tension developed in the wire, if its diameter is 2.0 mm? Coefficient of linear expansion of brass = $2.0\times 10^{-5}\,°C^{-1}$ and Young's modulus of brass = $0.91\times 10^{11}\,Nm^{-2}$. **NCERT Pg. 207**

(a) 3.77×10^2 N (b) 5.3×10^2 N
(c) 2.5×10^2 N (d) 4.3×10^2 N

28 Two rods of different materials having coefficients of thermal expansion α_1 and α_2 and Young's modulii Y_1 and Y_2 respectively are fixed between two rigid walls. The rods are heated, such that they undergo the same increase in temperature. There is no bending of rods. If $\alpha_1/\alpha_2 = 2/3$ and stresses developed in the two rods are equal, then Y_1/Y_2 is **NCERT Pg. 207**

(a) 3/2 (b) 1 (c) 2/3 (d) 1/2

29 A wire 3 m in length and 1 mm in diameter at 30°C is kept in a low temperature – 170°C and is stretched by hanging a weight of 10 kg at one end, so the change in length of the wire is ($Y = 2\times 10^{11}\,Nm^{-2}$, $g = 10\,ms^{-2}$ and $\alpha = 1.2\times 10^{-5}\,°C^{-1}$) **NCERT Pg. 207**

(a) –5.3 mm (b) – 2.5 mm (c) – 52 mm (d) – 25 mm

30 A liquid is heated to the temperature of 353 K, due to heating the mass expelled is $\left(\frac{1}{50}\right)$th of mass still remaining, the coefficient of expansion of liquid is **NCERT Pg. 207**

(a) 1.6×10^{-5}/°C (b) 2.5×10^{-4}/°C
(c) 29×10^{-5}/°C (d) 3.2×10^{-4}/°C

Specific Heat Capacity

31 At normal temperature and pressure, which of the following has highest value of specific heat capacity? **NCERT Pg. 208**

(a) Water (b) Aluminium
(c) Ice (d) Mercury

32 If there is no change in temperature of substance irrespective of amount of heat given or released by the substance, then the value of specific heat capacity of substance is **NCERT Pg. 208**

(a) zero (b) negative
(c) 1 (d) infinite

33 A refrigerator converts 100 g of water at 20°C into ice at –10°C in one hour. What will be the quantity of heat removed per minute? (Specific heat of ice = 0.5 cal/g°C, latent heat of fusion = 80 cal/g) **NCERT Pg. 209**

(a) 150 cal/min (b) 145 cal/min
(c) 160.3 cal/min (d) 175 cal/min

34 Which of the substances *A*, *B* and *C* has the lowest heat capacity? If heat is supplied to all of them at equal rates, the temperature *versus* time graph is shown below. **NCERT Pg. 208**

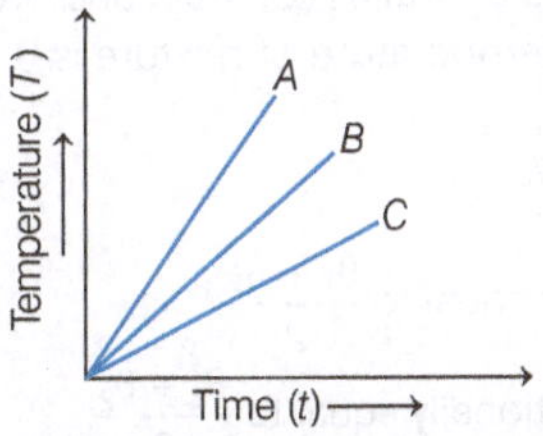

(a) *A* (b) *B*
(c) *C* (d) All have equal specific heat

35 A normal diet furnishes 200 kcal to a 60 kg person in a day. If this energy was used to heat the person with no losses to the surroundings, how much would the person's temperature increases? The specific heat of the human body is $0.83\,cal\,g^{-1}\,°C^{-1}$. **NCERT Pg. 208**

(a) 8.2°C (b) 4.01°C
(c) 6.0°C (d) 5.03°C

36 A certain substance has a mass of 50 g for 1 mole. When 300 J of heat is added to 25 g of sample of this material, its temperature rises from 25°C to 45°C. Calculate specific heat capacity and molar heat capacity of the sample. **NCERT Pg. 208**

(a) $600\,J\,kg^{-1}°C^{-1}$, $45\,J\,mol^{-1}\,°C^{-1}$
(b) $450\,J\,kg^{-1}°C^{-1}$, $30\,J\,mol^{-1}\,°C^{-1}$
(c) $600\,J\,kg^{-1}°C^{-1}$, $30\,J\,mol^{-1}\,°C^{-1}$
(d) $700\,J\,kg^{-1}°C^{-1}$, $80\,J\,mol^{-1}\,°C^{-1}$

37 A metal block is made from a mixture of 2.4 kg of aluminium, 1.6 kg of brass and 0.8 kg of copper. The amount of heat required to raise the temperature of this block from 20°C to 80°C is (specific heats of aluminium, brass and copper are 0.216, 0.0917 and $0.0931\,calkg^{-1}°C^{-1}$, respectively) **NCERT Pg. 208**

(a) 96.2 cal (b) 44.4 cal
(c) 86.2 cal (d) 62.8 cal

38 Two spheres made up of same material have diameter ratios 2 : 3. The ratio of their thermal capacities is **NCERT Pg. 208**

(a) 32 : 8 (b) 27 : 8
(c) 16 : 3 (d) 64 : 27

39 A helium bubble of 5 mol is submerged into water and the temperature of water is increased by 50°C. The amount of heat added to helium during expansion is ($R = 2\,cal/K\,mol^{-1}$) **NCERT Pg. 208**

(a) 1400 cal (b) 625 cal
(c) 1000 cal (d) 1250 cal

Calorimetry

40 Two similar bodies of equal masses are heated to temperatures θ_1 and θ_2 ($\theta_1 > \theta_2$) and are mixed together. If temperature of mixture is θ, then **NCERT Pg. 209**

(a) $\theta = \frac{\theta_1 + \theta_2}{2}$

(b) θ is never equal to $\frac{\theta_1 + \theta_2}{2}$

(c) θ is conditionally equal to $\frac{\theta_1 + \theta_2}{2}$

(d) $\theta > \frac{\theta_1 + \theta_2}{2}$

41 The temperature of equal masses of three different liquids *A*, *B* and *C* are 12°C, 19°C and 28°C, respectively. The temperature when *A* and *B* are mixed is 16°C and when *B* and *C* are mixed is 23°C. The temperature when *A* and *C* are mixed, is **NCERT Pg. 209**

(a) 18.2°C (b) 22°C
(c) 20.2°C (d) 25.2°C

Change of State

42 Refer to the plot of temperature *versus* time (figure) showing the changes in the state of ice on heating (not to scale). Which of the following statement is correct?

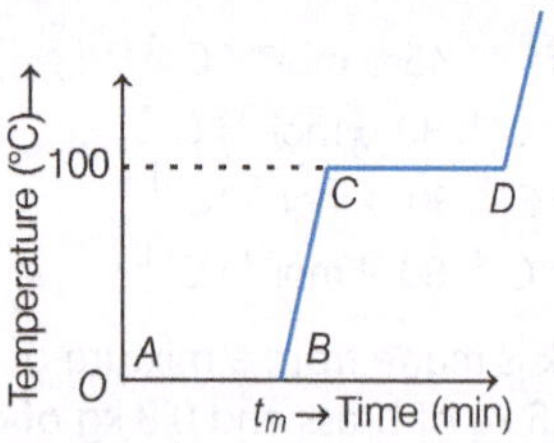

NCERT Pg. 210

(a) The region *AB* represents ice and water in thermal equilibrium.
(b) At *B* water starts boiling.
(c) At *C* all the water gets converted into steam.
(d) *C* to *D* represents water and steam in equilibrium below boiling point.

43 The graph shows the variation of temperature *T* of one kilogram of a material with the heat *H* supplied to it. At point *O*, the substance is in the solid state. From the graph, which of the following statement is correct? **NCERT Pg. 210**

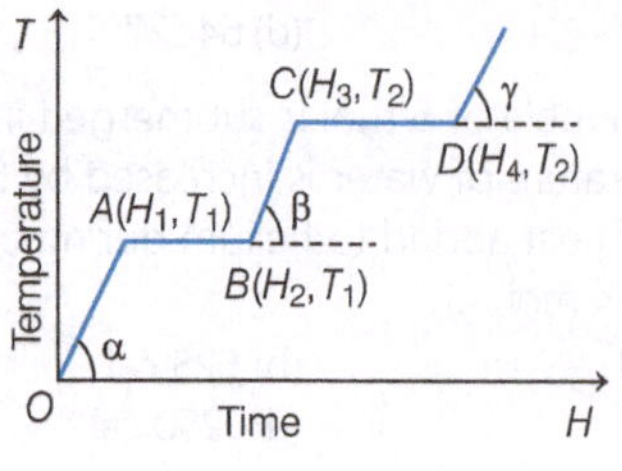

(a) T_2 is the melting point of the solid.
(b) *AB* represents the change of state from solid to liquid.
(c) $(H_2 + H_1)$ represents the latent heat of fusion of the substance.
(d) $(H_3 - H_1)$ represents the total latent heat of vaporisation of the liquid.

44 A block of ice at 0°C is slowly heated and converted into steam at 100°C. Which of these curves represent the phenomenon qualitatively? **NCERT Pg. 210**

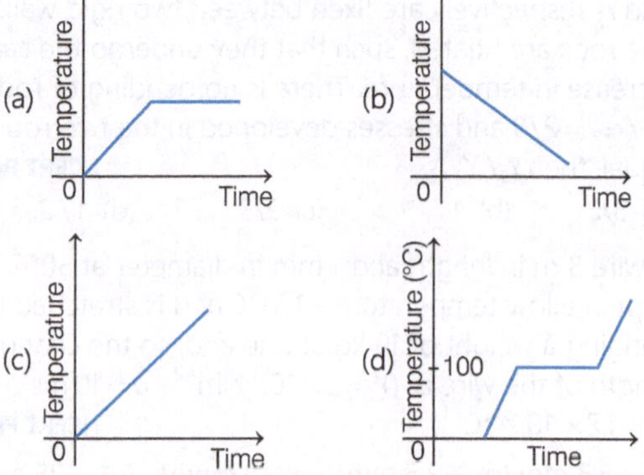

45 If a wire is pressed over a slab of ice as shown, then

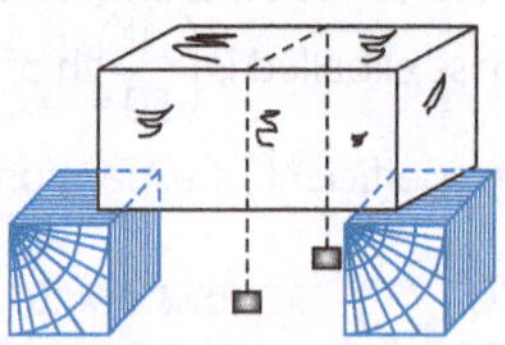

NCERT Pg. 210

(a) it cuts the slab into 2 parts and pass to other side after some time
(b) it passes through the ice slab and the slab does not split
(c) it remains over the slab (as initially placed)
(d) ice slab melts completely

46 For the phase diagram of water given in figure, curves *OA*, *AB* and *AC* are respectively **NCERT Pg. 210**

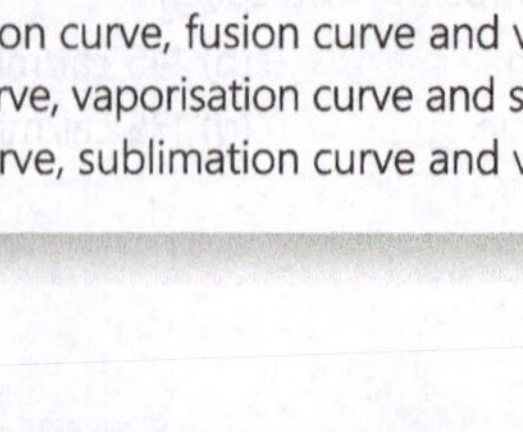

(a) sublimation curve, vaporisation curve and fusion curve
(b) sublimation curve, fusion curve and vaporisation curve
(c) fusion curve, vaporisation curve and sublimation curve
(d) fusion curve, sublimation curve and vaporisation curve

47 The latent heat of vaporisation of a substance is always NCERT Pg. 213
(a) greater than its latent heat of fusion
(b) greater than its latent heat of sublimation
(c) equals to its latent heat of sublimation
(d) less than its latent heat of fusion

48 Steam burns are more serious in comparison to those caused from boiling water because NCERT Pg. 213
(a) steam at 100°C carries same heat as that of water at 100°C
(b) steam is more reactive
(c) steam has less surface tension, so it burns surface more rapidly
(d) steam at 100°C carries more heat than water at 100°C

49 A piece of ice (heat capacity = 2100 J $kg^{-1}°C^{-1}$ and latent heat = 3.36×10^5 J kg^{-1}) of mass m grams is at – 5°C at atmospheric pressure.
It is given 420 J of heat, so that the ice starts melting. Finally, when the ice-water mixture is in equilibrium, it is found that 1 g of ice has melted. Assuming there is no other heat exchange in the process, then find the value of m. NCERT Pg. 213
(a) 8 g (b) 2 g (c) 4 g (d) 6 g

50 Calculate the heat required to convert 3 kg of ice at –12°C kept in a calorimeter to steam at 100°C at atmospheric pressure. Given specific heat capacity of ice is 2100 $Jkg^{-1}K^{-1}$, specific heat capacity of water is 4186 $Jkg^{-1}K^{-1}$, latent heat of fusion of ice is 3.35×10^5 Jkg^{-1} and latent heat of steam is 2.256×10^6 Jkg^{-1}. NCERT Pg. 213
(a) 8×10^4 J (b) 9.1×10^6 J
(c) 4×10^3 J (d) 7×10^6 J

Heat Transfer

51 A thermocol cubical icebox of side 20 cm has thickness of 5 cm. If 5 kg of ice is put in the box, the amount of ice remains in the box after 10 h is (The outside temperature is 50°C and the coefficient of thermal conductivity of thermocol is 0.01 $Js^{-1}m^{-1}°C^{-1}$ and the latent heat of fusion of ice is 335×10^3 J/kg) NCERT Pg. 215
(a) 2.42 kg (b) 3.7 kg
(c) 4.7 kg (d) 3.9 kg

52 The thermal conductivity of two rods of equal length and diameter is 3 and 7 units, respectively. If they are joined in series the thermal conductivity of the combination in the given units is NCERT Pg. 215
(a) 4.2 (b) 2.43
(c) 1.43 (d) 0.53

53 A composite slab made of two materials with different thermal conductivities of K and $2K$, and thickness t and $4t$, respectively. The outer surface of the slab have temperatures T_1 and T_2 ($T_2 > T_1$). The rate of heat flow through the slab in steady state is $\left(\frac{A(T_2 - T_1)K}{t}\right) f$. Find the value of f. NCERT Pg. 216

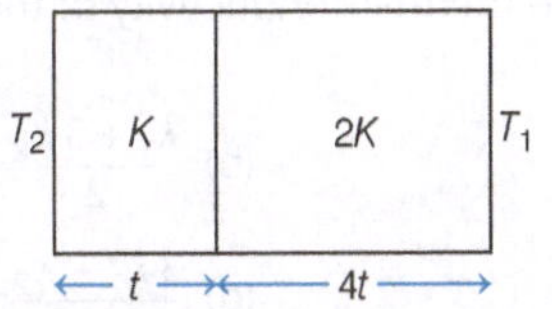

(a) 3 (b) $\frac{2}{3}$ (c) $\frac{1}{3}$ (d) 1

54 Calculate the rate of loss of heat through a glass window of area 1000 cm^2 and thickness 0.4 cm, when temperature inside is 37°C and outside is –5°C. Coefficient of thermal conductivity of glass is 2.2×10^{-3} cal $s^{-1}cm^{-1}K^{-1}$. NCERT Pg. 216
(a) 450 cal s^{-1} (b) 231 cal s^{-1}
(c) 439 cal s^{-1} (d) 650 cal s^{-1}

55 Heat is flowing steadily from A to B. Temperature T at P, at distance x from A is such that NCERT Pg. 216

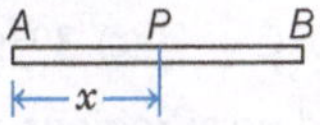

(a) T decreases linearly with x
(b) T increases linearly with x
(c) T decreases exponentially with x
(d) T increases with x as $T \propto x^2$

56 Water is boiled in a rectangular steel tank of thickness 2 cm by a constant temperature furnace. Due to vaporisation, water level falls at a steady rate of 1 cm in 9 min. Calculate the temperature of the furnace. Given, K for steel = 0.2 $cals^{-1}cm^{-1}°C^{-1}$. NCERT Pg. 216
(a) 150°C (b) 110°C (c) 130°C (d) 200°C

57 One rod of length 2m and thermal conductivity 50 units is attached to another rod of length 1 m and thermal conductivity 100 units. Temperature of free ends are 70°C and 50°C respectively, then temperature of junction point will be NCERT Pg. 216
(a) 60°C (b) 54°C (c) 64°C (d) 68°C

58 Two rods of same length and material transfer a given amount of heat in 12 s, when they are joined end-to-end (i.e. in series). But when they are joined in parallel, they will transfer same heat under same temperature difference across their ends in NCERT Pg. 216
(a) 24 s (b) 3 s (c) 38 s (d) 1.5 s

59 A solid cylinder of radius R, made of a material of thermal conductivity K_1 is surrounded by a hollow cylinder of inner radius R and outer radius $2R$ made of material of thermal conductivity K_2. The two ends of the combined system are maintained at two different temperatures. There is no loss of heat across the cylindrical surface and the system is in steady state.

The effective thermal conductivity of the system is **NCERT Pg. 216**

(a) $K_1 + K_2$ (b) $\frac{K_1 + 3K_2}{4}$

(c) $\frac{K_1 K_2}{K_1 + K_2}$ (d) $\frac{3K_1 + K_2}{4}$

60 Three rods made of the same material and having the same cross-section have been joined as shown in the figure. Each rod is of the same length. The left and right ends are kept at 0°C and 90°C, respectively. The temperature of the junction of the three rods will be **NCERT Pg. 216**

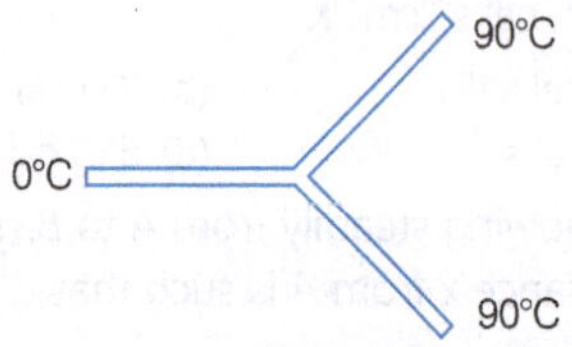

(a) 45°C (b) 90°C (c) 30°C (d) 60°C

61 The equatorial and polar regions of the earth receive unequal solar heat. The convection current arising is called **NCERT Pg. 217**

(a) land breeze (b) sea breeze
(c) trade wind (d) tornado

62 The amount of heat that a body can absorb by radiation **NCERT Pg. 217**

(a) depend on both colour and temperature of body
(b) depends on colour of body only
(c) depends on temperature of body only
(d) depends on density of body

63 Gulab jamuns (assumed to be spherical) are to be heated in an oven. They are available in two sizes, one twice bigger (in radius) than the other. Pizzas (assumed to be discs) are also to be heated in oven. They are also in two sizes, one twice bigger (in radius) than the other. All four are put together to be heated to oven temperature. Choose the correct statement from the following. **NCERT Pg. 218**

(a) Both size gulab jamuns will get heated in the same time.
(b) Smaller gulab jamuns are heated before bigger ones.
(c) Bigger pizzas are heated before smaller ones.
(d) Bigger pizzas are heated before smaller gulab jamuns .

64 The bottom of utensils for cooking food are blackened to **NCERT Pg. 218**

(a) absorb minimum heat from fire
(b) absorb maximum heat from fire
(c) emit radiations
(d) reflect heat to surroundings

65 The plots of intensity of radiation *versus* wavelength of three black bodies at temperature T_1, T_2 and T_3 are shown. Then, **NCERT Pg. 218**

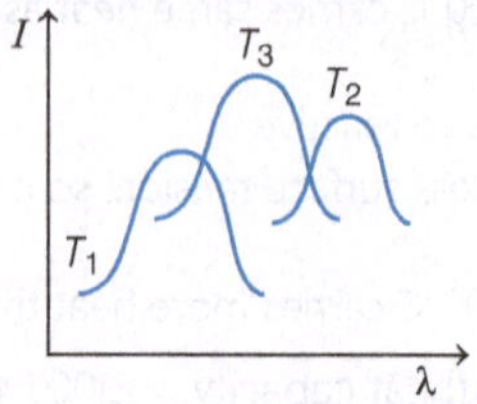

(a) $T_3 > T_2 > T_1$ (b) $T_1 > T_2 > T_3$
(c) $T_2 > T_3 > T_1$ (d) $T_1 > T_3 > T_2$

66 A black body is at a temperature of 5760 K. The energy of radiation emitted by the body at wavelength 250 nm is U_1, at wavelength 500 nm is U_2 and that at 1000 nm is U_3 and Wien's constant, $b = 2.88 \times 10^6$ nm-K. Which of the following is correct? **NCERT Pg. 218**

(a) $U_3 = 0$ (b) $U_1 > U_2$ (c) $U_2 > U_1$ (d) $U_1 = 0$

67 The wavelength $\lambda_m = 5.5 \times 10^{-7}$ m corresponds to a temperature of sun of 5500 K. If the furnace has wavelength λ_m equal to 11×10^{-7} m, then temperature of furnace is **NCERT Pg. 218**

(a) 5000 K (b) 1750 K (c) 3750 K (d) 2750 K

68 If the radius of a star is R and it acts as a black body, what would be the temperature of the star, in which rate of energy production is Q? (σ is Stefan's constant) **NCERT Pg. 219**

(a) $\frac{Q}{4\pi R^2 \sigma}$ (b) $\left[\frac{Q}{4\pi R^2 \sigma}\right]^{1/2}$

(c) $\left[\frac{Q}{4\pi R^2 \sigma}\right]^{1/4}$ (d) $\left[\frac{4\pi R^2 Q}{\sigma}\right]^{1/4}$

69 The temperature of two bodies A and B are 727°C and 327°C respectively, the ratio $H_A : H_B$ of the rates of heat radiated by them is **NCERT Pg. 219**

(a) 727 : 327 (b) 5 : 3 (c) 25 : 9 (d) 625 : 81

70 Calculate radiation power for sphere whose temperature is 227°C, radius is 2 m and emissivity is 0.8. **NCERT Pg. 219**

(a) 142.5 kW (b) 1500 W (c) 1255 W (d) 1575 W

71 At what temperature will the filament of 100 W lamp operate, if it is supposed to be perfectly black body of area 1. 0 cm^2? **NCERT Pg. 219**

(a) 3449 K (b) 2049 K (c) 3000 K (d) 3010 K

72 Due to the change in main voltage, the temperature of an electric bulb rises from 3000 K to 4000 K. What is the percentage rise in electric power consumed? **NCERT Pg. 219**
(a) 216 (b) 100 (c) 150 (d) 178

73 Three very large plates of same area are kept parallel and close to each other. They are considered as ideal black surfaces and have very high thermal conductivity. The first and third plate is maintained at temperature $2T$ and $3T$, respectively. The temperature of the middle (second) plate under steady state condition is **NCERT Pg. 219**
(a) $\left(\frac{65}{2}\right)^{1/4} T$ (b) $\left(\frac{97}{4}\right)^{1/4} T$
(c) $\left(\frac{97}{2}\right)^{1/4} T$ (d) $(97)^{1/4} T$

74 If temperature of sun $= 6000$ K, radius of sun $= 7.2 \times 10^5$ km, radius of earth $= 6000$ km and distance between earth and sun $= 15 \times 10^7$ km. Find intensity of radiation on earth in W/m^2. **NCERT Pg. 219**
(a) 1473 (b) 1540
(c) 1693 (d) 1841

Newton's Law of Cooling

75 A body cools in 7 min from 60°C to 40°C, then what will be its temperature after the next 7 min? The temperature of the surroundings is 10°C. **NCERT Pg. 220**
(a) 40°C (b) 30°C (c) 15°C (d) 28°C

76 A liquid in a beaker has temperature $\theta(t)$ at time t and θ_0 is temperature of surroundings, then according to Newton's law of cooling, the correct graph between $\log_e(\theta - \theta_0)$ and t is **NCERT Pg. 220**

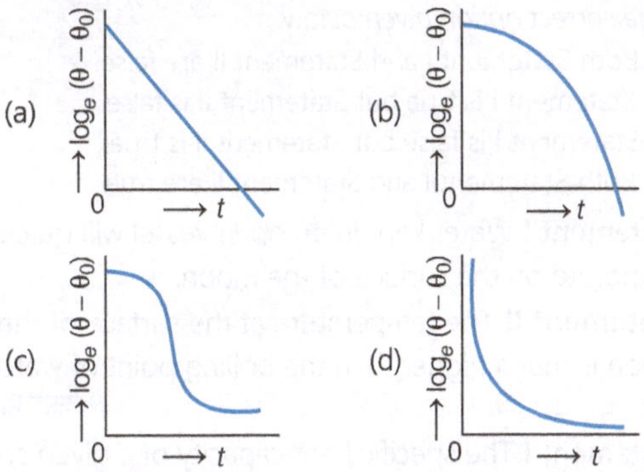

Assertion and Reason Questions

Direction (Q. Nos. 1-10) *In the following questions, a statement of Assertion is followed by a corresponding statement of Reason. Of the following statements, choose the correct one.*

(a) Both Assertion and Reason are correct and Reason is the correct explanation of Assertion.
(b) Both Assertion and Reason are correct but Reason is not the correct explanation of Assertion.
(c) Assertion is correct but Reason is incorrect.
(d) Assertion is incorrect but Reason is correct.

1 Assertion If equal amount of heat is added to equal masses of different substances, the resulting change in temperature is also equal.
Reason Every substance requires a unique value of heat to change its temperature per unit mass, per degree centigrade (or per kelvin). **NCERT Pg. 208**

2 Assertion The triple point of water is a standard fixed point in modern thermometry.
Reason Melting point of ice and the boiling point of water changes due to change in atmospheric pressure. **NCERT Pg. 211**

3 Assertion Houses made of concrete roofs get very hot during summer days.
Reason Thermal conductivity of concrete is much smaller than that of metal. **NCERT Pg. 214**

4 Assertion When temperature difference across the two sides of a wall is increased, its thermal conductivity increases.
Reason Thermal conductivity depends on the nature of material of the wall. **NCERT Pg. 214**

5 Assertion NH_3 is liquified more easily than CO_2.
Reason Critical temperature of NH_3 is more than CO_2. **NCERT Pg. 214**

6 Assertion A brass tumbler feels much colder than a wooden tray on a chilly day.
Reason The thermal conductivity of brass is less than that of wood. **NCERT Pg. 215**

7 Assertion The radiation from the sun's surface varies as the fourth power of its absolute temperature.
Reason Sun is not a black body. **NCERT Pg. 218**

8 Assertion For higher temperatures, the peak emission wavelength of a black body shifts to lower wavelengths.
Reason Peak emission wavelength of a black body is proportional to the four power of temperature. **NCERT Pg. 218**

9 **Assertion** The rate of loss of heat of a body at 300 K is *R*. At 900 K, the rate of loss becomes 81 *R*.
Reason This is as per Newton's law of cooling. NCERT Pg. 219

10 **Assertion** Bodies radiate heat at all temperatures.
Reason Rate of radiation of heat is proportional to the fourth power of absolute temperature. NCERT Pg. 219

Statement Based Questions

Direction (Q. Nos. 1-8) *In the following questions, two statements (I & II) are given. In the light of the given statements, choose the correct option given below.*
(a) Both Statement I and Statement II are false.
(b) Statement I is true but Statement II is false.
(c) Statement I is false but Statement II is true.
(d) Both Statement I and Statement II are true.

1 **Statement I** Water kept in an open vessel will quickly evaporate on the surface of the moon.
Statement II The temperature at the surface of the moon is much higher than the boiling point of water. NCERT Pg. 203

2 **Statement I** The specific heat capacity of a given solid can be determined by using the principle of calorimetry.
Statement II Heat gained is equal to the heat lost. NCERT Pg. 209

3 **Statement I** During vaporisation, the temperature remains constant.
Statement II During vaporisation, both liquid and vapour states co-exist in equilibrium. NCERT Pg. 211

4 **Statement I** Convection is a mode of heat transfer by actual motion of matter.
Statement II Convection is possible only in gases. NCERT Pg. 211

5 **Statement I** Conduction of heat takes places in solids and liquids like mercury and molten metals.
Statement II In radiation, energy directly flows from heat source to the given body at a speed of $3\times 10^{8}\ ms^{-1}$. NCERT Pg. 211

6 **Statement I** Thermos bottle consists of a double-walled glass vessel with inner and outer walls coated with silver.
Statement II In flask, space between the walls is evacuated to reduce conduction and convection losses. NCERT Pg. 217

7 **Statement I** While measuring the thermal conductivity of liquid experimentally, the upper layer is kept hot and the lower layer kept cold.
Statement II This avoids heating of liquid by convection. NCERT Pg. 217

8 **Statement I** According to Newton's law of cooling, the rate of loss of heat, $-\frac{dQ}{dt}$ of the body is directly proportional to the difference of temperature.
Statement II This law holds for all type of temperature differences. NCERT Pg. 220

Matching Type Questions

1 If 10g of oxygen are subjected to a pressure of 3 atm at a temperature of 10°C. Heating at a constant pressure, the gas is expanded to 10L. With reference to the given situation, match the Column I (physical quantity) with Column II (value). Choose the correct answer from the options given below.
($R = 0.0821$ atm-litre $K^{-1}\ mol^{-1}$) NCERT Pg. 206

Column I		Column II
A. The volume of the gas before expansion (in litres)	1.	4.13
B. The temperature of the gas after expansion (in kelvin)	2.	1.0
C. The density of the gas before expansion (in gL^{-1})	3.	2.42
D. The density of the gas after expansion (in gL^{-1})	4.	1169.4

	A	B	C	D
(a)	3	4	2	1
(b)	4	3	1	2
(c)	3	4	1	2
(d)	4	2	3	1

2 Match the Column I (mixture) with Column II (temperature). Choose the correct answer from the options given below. Three liquids *A*, *B* and *C* having same specific heat and masses *m*, 2*m* and 3*m* at temperatures 20°C, 40°C and 60°C, respectively. Temperature of the mixture when **NCERT Pg. 209**

Column I	Column II
A. *A* and *B* are mixed	1. 33.3°C
B. *A* and *C* are mixed	2. 52°C
C. *B* and *C* are mixed	3. 50°C
D. *A*, *B* and *C* all three are mixed	4. None of the above

	A	B	C	D
(a)	1	3	2	4
(b)	1	2	3	4
(c)	1	4	2	3
(d)	1	3	4	2

3 Match the Column I (quantity) with Column II (dimension). Choose the correct answer from the options given below. **NCERT Pg. 219**

Column I	Column II
A. Thermal resistance	1. $[MT^{-3} K^{-4}]$
B. Stefan's constant	2. $[M^{-1}L^{-2}T^{3} K]$
C. Wien's constant	3. $[ML^{2}T^{-3}]$
D. Heat current	4. [LK]

	A	B	C	D
(a)	1	2	3	4
(b)	1	4	3	2
(c)	2	1	4	3
(d)	2	1	3	4

Numerical Type Questions

1 A second pendulum clock has a steel wire. The clock is calibrated at 20°C. The time lost by the clock in one week is *x* s when the temperature rises to 30° C, the value of *x* is (nearest integer) (Take, $\alpha = 1.2 \times 10^{-5}\ °C^{-1}$) **NCERT Pg. 205**

2 50 g of water takes 2 min to cool down from 30° to 25°C in a closed vessel. If another liquid of mass 100 g takes same time to cool from 30°C to 25°C, then the specific heat of the liquid is $x \times 10^{-1}$ k cal/kg. The value of *x* is .... (the water equivalent of vessel is 30 g) **NCERT Pg. 208**

3 A bullet penetrates into a solid object and melts. If half of its kinetic energy was used to heat it, then the initial velocity of the bullet is *x* m/s. If the initial temperature of the bullet is 27°C and the melting point is 327°C, then the value of *x* is .... (Given, latent heat of fusion of lead $= 2.5 \times 10^{4}\ J\,kg^{-1}$ and specific heat capacity of lead $= 125\ J kg^{-1}K^{-1}$) **NCERT Pg. 209**

4 A water heater heats water flowing at a rate of 2 kg/min from 20°C to 60°C. If the heater operates on a burner, the rate of combustion of fuel will be *x* g/min, the value of *x* is .... (Heat of combustion $= 8 \times 10^{3}$ J/g and specific heat of water $= 4.2\ Jg^{-1}°C^{-1}$) **NCERT Pg. 208**

5 A beaker has volume capacity of 600 cc at 30°C, when it is partially filled with volume V_m at 30°C, it is found that unfilled volume of the beaker remains constant as the temperature is varied. If $\gamma_{beaker} = 6 \times 10^{-6}\ °C^{-1}$ and $\gamma_{mercury} = 1.5 \times 10^{-4}\ °C^{-1}$, where γ is coefficient of volume expansion, then V_m is ..... . **NCERT Pg. 207**

6 A double-pane window consists of two glass sheets each of area 1 m^2 and thickness 0.01 m separated by a 0.05 m thick stagnant air space. In the steady state, the room glass interface and the glass outdoor interface are at constant temperature of 27° C and 0° C, respectively. The rate of heat flow through the window pane is ....W (Given, $K_{glass} = 0.8\ W\ m^{-1}\ K^{-1}$, $K_{air} = 0.08\ W\ m^{-1}K^{-1}$) **NCERT Pg. 215**

7 The surface area of a metal ball is 200 cm^2 and temperature is 527°C. It is placed in a vessel at 27°C. If the emissivity of the metal is 0.4 and $\sigma = 5.67 \times 10^{-8}\ J\ m^{-2}\ s^{-2}\ K^{-1} m$, then the rate of loss of heat from the ball is approximately .... **NCERT Pg. 219**

NCERT Exemplar Questions

1 A uniform metallic rod rotates about its perpendicular bisector with constant angular speed. If it is heated uniformly to raise its temperature slightly, then
(a) its speed of rotation increases
(b) its speed of rotation decreases
(c) its speed of rotation remains same
(d) its speed increases because its moment of inertia increases

2 An aluminium sphere is dipped into water. Which of the following is true?
(a) Buoyancy will be less in water at 0°C than that in water at 4°C.
(b) Buoyancy will be more in water at 0°C than that in water at 4°C.
(c) Buoyancy in water at 0°C will be same as that in water at 4°C.
(d) Buoyancy may be more or less in water at 4°C depending on the radius of the sphere.

3 As the temperature is increased, the period of a pendulum
(a) increases as its effective length increases even though its centre of mass still remains at the centre of the bob
(b) decreases as its effective length increases even though its centre of mass still remains at the centre of the bob
(c) increases as its effective length increases due to shifting to centre of mass below the centre of the bob
(d) decreases as its effective length remains same but the centre of mass shifts above the centre of the bob

4 Heat is associated with
(a) kinetic energy of random motion of molecules
(b) kinetic energy of orderly motion of molecules
(c) total kinetic energy of random and orderly motion of molecules
(d) kinetic energy of random motion in some cases and kinetic energy of orderly motion in other

5 The radius of a metalic sphere at room temperature T is R and the coefficient of linear expansion of the metal is α. The sphere heated a little by a temperature ΔT, so that its new temperature is $T + \Delta T$. The increase in the volume of the sphere is approximately
(a) $2\pi R\alpha\,\Delta T$ (b) $\pi R^2\alpha\,\Delta T$
(c) $4\pi R^3\alpha\,\Delta T/3$ (d) $4\pi R^3\alpha\,\Delta T$

6 100 g of water is supercooled to –10°C. At this point, due to some disturbance mechanised or otherwise some of it suddenly freezes to ice. What will be the temperature of the resultant mixture and how much mass would freeze?
($s_W = 1$ cal/g°C and $L_{w(\text{Fusion})} = 80$ cal/g)
(a) 0°C, 12.5 g (b) 20°C, 50 g
(c) 30°C, 30 g (d) 50°C, 10 g

7 Find out the increase in moment of inertia I of a uniform rod (coefficient of linear expansion α) about its perpendicular bisector when its temperature is slightly increased by ΔT.
(a) $2I\alpha\Delta T$ (b) $4I\alpha\Delta T$ (c) $6I\alpha\Delta T$ (d) $3I\alpha T$

8 Calculate the stress developed inside a tooth cavity filled with copper when hot tea at temperature of 57°C is drunk. You can take body (tooth) temperature to be 37°C, $\alpha = 1.7 \times 10^{-5}$ /°C and bulk modulus for copper is 140×10^{9} Nm^{-2}.
(a) 5×10^{4} Nm^{-2}
(b) 3×10^{2} Nm^{-2}
(c) 1.428×10^{8} Nm^{-2}
(d) 3.46×10^{5} Nm^{-2}

Past Exams Questions

NEET

1 A metallic bar of Young's modulus, 0.5×10^{11} N m^{-2} and coefficient of linear thermal expansion 10^{-5} °C^{-1}, length 1 m and area of cross-section 10^{-3}m^2 is heated from 0°C to 100°C without expansion or bending. The compressive force developed in it is **NCERT Pg. 207, NEET 2024**
(a) 5×10^3 N (b) 50×10^3 N
(c) 100×10^3 N (d) 2×10^3 N

2 The energy that will be ideally radiated by a 100 kW transmitter in 1 hour is **NCERT Pg. 218, NEET 2022**
(a) 36×10^7 J (b) 36×10^4 J
(c) 36×10^5 J (d) 1×10^5 J

3 A cup of coffee cools from 90°C to 80°C in t minutes when the room temperature is 20°C. The time taken by a similar cup of coffee to cool from 80°C to 60°C at a room temperature same at 20°C, is **NCERT Pg. 220, NEET 2021**
(a) $\frac{13}{10}t$ (b) $\frac{13}{5}t$ (c) $\frac{10}{13}t$ (d) $\frac{5}{13}t$

4 The quantities of heat required to raise the temperature of two solid copper spheres of radii r_1 and r_2 ($r_1 = 1.5\, r_2$) through 1 K are in the ratio **NCERT Pg. 208, NEET 2020**

(a) $\frac{9}{4}$ (b) $\frac{3}{2}$
(c) $\frac{5}{3}$ (d) $\frac{27}{8}$

5 A deep rectangular pond of surface area A, containing water (density = ρ, specific heat capacity = s), is located in a region where the outside air temperature is a steady value at −26° C. The thickness of the frozen ice layer in this pond, at a certain instant is x.
Taking the thermal conductivity of ice as K, and its specific latent heat of fusion as L, the rate of increase of the thickness of ice layer, at this instant would be given by **NCERT Pg. 215, NEET 2019**
(a) $26\ K/\rho r\ (L-4s)$ (b) $26\ K/\ (\rho x^2 - L)$
(c) $26\ K/(\rho x L)$ (d) $26\ K/\rho r\ (L+4s)$

6 A metal rod at a temperature of 145°C radiates energy at a rate of 17W. If its temperature is increased to 273°C, then it will radiate at the rate of **NCERT Pg. 219, NEET 2017**
(a) 17.5 W (b) 50.3 W
(c) 49.6 W (d) 67.5 W

7 A body cools from a temperature $3T$ to $2T$ in 10 min. The room temperature is T. Assume that Newton's law of cooling is applicable. The temperature of the body at the end of next 10 min will be **NCERT Pg. 219, NEET 2016**
(a) $\frac{7}{4}T$ (b) $\frac{3}{2}T$
(c) $\frac{4}{3}T$ (d) T

8 A piece of ice falls from a height h, so that it melts completely. Only one-quarter of the heat produced is absorbed by the ice and all energy of ice gets converted into heat during its fall. The value of h is [Latent heat of ice is 3.4×10^5 J/kg and $g = 10$ N/kg] **NCERT Pg. 213, NEET 2016**
(a) 544 km (b) 136 km
(c) 68 km (d) 34 km

9 The two ends of a metal rod are maintained at temperatures 100°C and 110°C. The rate of heat flow in the rod is found to be 4.0 J/s. If the ends are maintained at temperatures 200°C and 210°C, the rate of heat flow will be **NCERT Pg. 215, AIPMT 2015**
(a) 44.0 J/s (b) 16.8J/s16.8
(c) 8.0 J/s (d) 4.0 J/s

10 Certain quantity of water cools from 70°C to 60°C in the first 5 min and to 54°C in the next 5 min. The temperature of the surroundings is **NCERT Pg. 220, AIPMT 2014**
(a) 45°C (b) 20°C
(c) 42°C (d) 10°C

JEE Main

11 On celcius scale, the temperature of body increases by 40°C. The increase in temperature on fahrenheit scale is **NCERT Pg. 203, JEE Main 2024**
(a) 72°F (b) 75°F
(c) 70°F (d) 68°F

12 A 100 g of iron nail is hit by a 1.5 kg hammer striking at a velocity of 60 ms^{-1}. What will be the rise in the temperature of the nail, if one-fourth of energy of the hammer goes into heating the nail?
[Specific heat capacity of iron = 0.42 $Jg^{-1}\ °C^{-1}$] **NCERT Pg. 213, JEE Main 2022**
(a) 675°C (b) 1600°C
(c) 16.07°C (d) 6.75°C

13 A copper block of mass 5.0 kg is heated to a temperature of 500°C and is placed on a large ice block. What is the maximum amount of ice that can melt? [Specific heat of copper = 0.39 $Jg^{-1}°C^{-1}$ and latent heat of fusion of water = 335 J g^{-1}] **NCERT Pg. 213, JEE Main 2022**
(a) 1.5 kg (b) 5.8 kg (c) 2.9 kg (d) 3.8 kg

14 At 40°C, a brass wire of 1 mm radius is hung from the ceiling. A small mass M is hung from the free end of the wire. When the wire is cooled down from 40°C to 20°C, it regains its original length of 0.2 m. The value of M is close to (coefficient of linear expansion and Young's modulus of brass are 10^{-5} °C and 10^{11} N / m^2 respectively, g = 10 m s^{-2}) **NCERT Pg. 207, JEE Main 2019**
(a) 1.5 kg (b) 9 kg
(c) 0.5 kg (d) 0.9 kg

15 Two rods A and B of identical dimensions are at temperature 30°C. If A is heated upto 180°C and B upto T°C, then new lengths are the same. If the ratio of the coefficients of linear expansion of A and B is 4 : 3, then the value of T is **NCERT Pg. 205, JEE Main 2019**
(a) 230°C (b) 270°C
(c) 200°C (d) 250°C

Skill Boosters

1. A body P is connected to a large body Q through a conducting rod of length L, cross-sectional area A and thermal conductivity K. This assembly is placed in an atmosphere of temperature T_A and body Q is also maintained at temperature T_A. Let heat capacity of body P is C and it is initially at temperature T_1. If in time t second, temperature of body P falls to T_2. Then, choose the correct option.

(a) $\log\left(\frac{T_2 - T_A}{T_1 - T_A}\right) = -\left(K_1 + \frac{KA}{LC}\right)t$

(b) $\log\left(\frac{T_2 - T_A}{T_1 - T_A}\right) = -\left(K_1 + \frac{KA}{LC}\cdot t\right)$

(c) $\log\left(\frac{T_1 - T_A}{T_2 - T_A}\right) = -\left(K_1 + \frac{KA}{LC}\cdot t\right)$

(d) $\log\left(\frac{T_1 - T_A}{T_2 - T_A}\right) = -\left(K_1 + \frac{KA}{LC}\right)t$

2. An isosceles triangle is formed using a thin rod of length l_1 and coefficient of linear expansion α_1 as the base and two thin rods of length l_2 and coefficient of linear expansion α_2 as two sides. If the distance between the apex and the mid-point of the base remains unchanged as the temperature changes, then correct relation is

(a) $\frac{l_1}{l_2} = \sqrt{\frac{\alpha_2}{\alpha_1}}$ (b) $\frac{l_1}{l_2} = \sqrt{\frac{\alpha_1}{\alpha_2}}$

(c) $\frac{l_1}{l_2} = 2\sqrt{\frac{\alpha_2}{\alpha_1}}$ (d) $\frac{l_1}{l_2} = 2\sqrt{\frac{\alpha_1}{\alpha_2}}$

3. Specific heat of a substance varies with temperature as,
$C = 0.2 + 0.14t + 0.023t^2$ (cal g^{-1} °C^{-1})
The heat required to raise the temperature of 2 g of substance from 5°C to 15°C will be

(a) 24 cal (b) 56 cal (c) 82 cal (d) 100 cal

4. Six identical conducting rods are joined as shown in the figure.

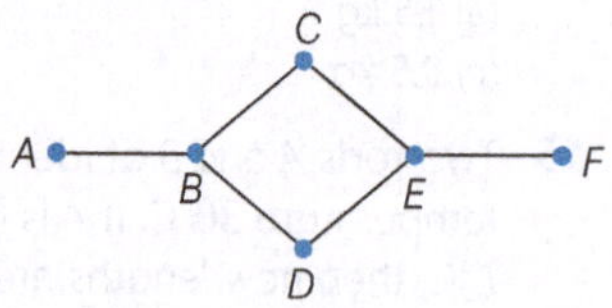

End A and F are maintained at 200°C and 0°C, respectively.
Temperature of point B in steady state will be

(a) 100°C (b) 55.56°C (c) 66.67°C (d) 80°C

5. Temperature of a heat source is 10^3 K. It is connected to a reservoir which is at temperature 10^2 K. The connecting slab is made up of copper of thickness 2 m. If conductivity of copper is 0.1 WK^{-1}m^{-1}, then energy flux through slab in the steady state is

(a) 90 Wm^{-2} (b) 65 Wm^{-2} (c) 45 Wm^{-2} (d) 180 Wm^{2}

6. The power radiated by a black body is P and it radiates maximum energy at wavelength λ_0. If the temperature of the black body is now changed, so that it radiates maximum energy at wavelength $\frac{3}{4}\lambda_0$, the power radiated by it becomes nP. The value of n is

(a) $\frac{256}{81}$ (b) $\frac{4}{3}$ (c) $\frac{3}{4}$ (d) $\frac{81}{256}$

7. Three bars of equal lengths and equal area of cross-sections are connected in series. Their thermal conductivities are in the ratio of 2 : 3 : 4. If the open ends of the first and the last bars are at temperature 200°C and 18° C respectively in the steady state, then calculate the temperatures of both the junctions.

(a) 116°C, 74°C (b) 120°C, 180°C
(c) 125°C, 50°C (d) 130°C, 40°C

8. Two blocks of metal with heat capacities C_1 and C_2 are interconnected by a rod of length l, cross-sectional area A and low heat conductivity K. Let the whole system is thermally isolated from the surrounding and the heat capacity of the rod is negligible. The difference in the temperature between the blocks as a function of time is $\left(\tau = \frac{KA(C_1 + C_2)}{C_1C_2}t\right)$

(a) $(T_0)\cdot e^{-\frac{t}{\tau}}$ (b) $(T_0)\, e^{\frac{t}{\tau}}$ (c) $(T_0)\cdot e^{\frac{t^2}{\tau^2}}$ (d) $(T_0)\cdot e^{-\frac{t^2}{\tau}}$

9. A large number of identical rods has length l cross-sectional area A and thermal conductivity K, are arranged as shown in the figure. Ends A and B are maintained at temperatures θ_1 and θ_2 ($< \theta_1$), respectively. If lateral surface of each rod is thermally insulated, the rate of heat transfer in the steady state will be

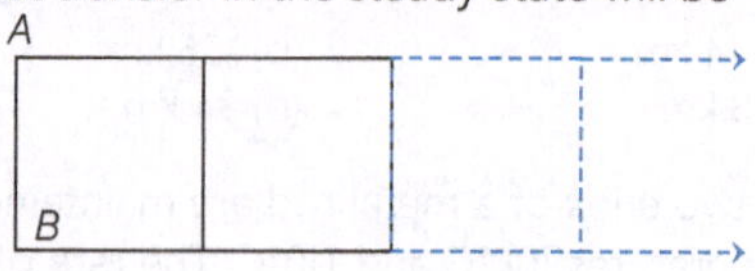

(a) $\frac{KA(\theta_1 - \theta_2)}{l}$ (b) $\frac{KA(\theta_1 - \theta_2)}{l(\sqrt{3} - 1)}$

(c) $\frac{KA(\theta_1 - \theta_2)}{2l}$ (d) $\frac{KA(\theta_1 - \theta_2)}{l(\sqrt{2} - 1)}$

10. Two spherical bodies of emissivity $e_1 = 0.8$ and $e_2 = 0.4$ are placed inside a perfectly black body which is maintained at temperature T. The energy radiated per second by this system is

(a) $E = 0.4\,\sigma AT^4$ (b) $E = 0.8\,\sigma AT^4$
(c) $E = 0.6\,\sigma AT^4$ (d) $E = \sigma AT^4$

Correct Codes

Topical Questions

1 (d)	2 (c)	3 (c)	4 (d)	5 (b)	6 (d)	7 (d)	8 (a)	9 (b)	10 (d)
11 (d)	12 (c)	13 (a)	14 (b)	15 (b)	16 (a)	17 (c)	18 (c)	19 (c)	20 (c)
21 (b)	22 (d)	23 (a)	24 (a)	25 (b)	26 (c)	27 (a)	28 (a)	29 (a)	30 (b)
31 (a)	32 (d)	33 (d)	34 (a)	35 (b)	36 (c)	37 (b)	38 (b)	39 (d)	40 (c)
41 (c)	42 (a)	43 (b)	44 (d)	45 (b)	46 (b)	47 (a)	48 (d)	49 (a)	50 (b)
51 (c)	52 (a)	53 (c)	54 (b)	55 (a)	56 (b)	57 (b)	58 (b)	59 (b)	60 (d)
61 (c)	62 (a)	63 (b)	64 (b)	65 (d)	66 (c)	67 (d)	68 (c)	69 (d)	70 (a)
71 (b)	72 (a)	73 (c)	74 (c)	75 (d)	76 (a)				

Assertion and Reason Questions

1 (d)	2 (a)	3 (b)	4 (d)	5 (a)	6 (c)	7 (c)	8 (c)	9 (c)	10 (d)

Statement Based Questions

1 (b)	2 (d)	3 (d)	4 (b)	5 (d)	6 (d)	7 (d)	8 (b)

Matching Type Questions

1 (c)	2 (a)	3 (c)

Numerical Type Questions

1 (36)	2 (5)	3 (500)	4 (42)	5 (24)	6 (41.5)	7 (182)

NCERT Exemplar Questions

1 (b)	2 (a)	3 (a)	4 (a)	5 (d)	6 (a)	7 (a)	8 (c)

Past Exams Questions

1 (b)	2 (a)	3 (b)	4 (d)	5 (c)	6 (c)	7 (b)	8 (b)	9 (d)	10 (a)
11 (a)	12 (c)	13 (c)	14 (b)	15 (a)					

Skill Boosters

1 (a)	2 (c)	3 (c)	4 (c)	5 (c)	6 (a)	7 (a)	8 (a)	9 (b)	10 (d)

Step by Step

Decoding the Questions

Concept Builders

1 True (T) **2** $-40°C$ **3** 32, 212 **4** -40, 233.15 **5** Rubber **6** True (T) **7** False (F) **8** more **9** True (T) **10** 4 **11** False (F) **12** True (T) **13** lowering **14** inversely **15** Sublimation **16** 273.16 **17** $\dfrac{2K_1K_2}{K_1+K_2}$ **18** True (T) **19** 1 **20** False (F)

Topical Questions

1 (*d*) When the temperature of a body and its surrounding medium are different, then heat transfer takes place between them.

3 (*c*) Given, $\Delta T = T_b - T_f = 100$

Temperature of liquid,

$T = \left(\frac{3}{5}\right)$th of distance between lower and upper fixed point

$\Rightarrow T = \frac{3}{5} \times 100 = 60°C$

On Kelvin scale,

$T_K = 273.15 + 60 = 333.15$ K

4 (*d*) For a thermometer

$$\frac{\text{Reading on any scale} - \text{Lower fixed point}}{\text{Upper fixed point} - \text{Lower fixed point}} = \text{constant}$$

i.e. $\dfrac{X - \text{LFP}}{\text{UFP} - \text{LFP}} = \dfrac{C-0}{100-0}$

$$\frac{C-0}{100-0} = \frac{64-5}{95-5} = \frac{59}{90} = 0.655$$

$\Rightarrow \quad C = 65.5\ °C$

5 (*b*)

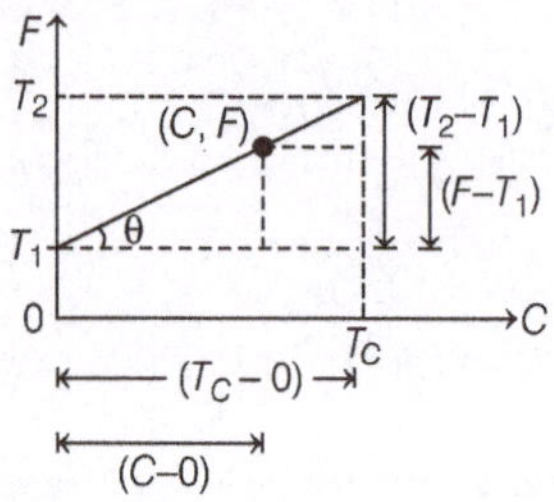

The slope of graph is given by

$$\tan\theta = \frac{T_2 - T_1}{T_C - 0} = \frac{T_2 - T_1}{T_C} \quad ...(i)$$

Similarly, for any arbitrary point (*C*, *F*), it is given by

$$\tan\theta = \frac{F - T_1}{C - 0} = \frac{F - T_1}{C} \quad ...(ii)$$

From Eqs. (i) and (ii), we get

$$\frac{T_2 - T_1}{T_C} = \frac{F - T_1}{C} \Rightarrow \frac{F - T_1}{T_2 - T_1} = \frac{C}{T_C}$$

6 (*d*) $$\frac{F_1 - 32}{180} = \frac{C_1}{100} \quad ...(i)$$

or $$\frac{F_2 - 32}{180} = \frac{C_2}{100} \quad ...(ii)$$

Subtracting Eq. (i) from Eq. (ii), we get

$$\frac{F_2 - F_1}{180} = \frac{C_2 - C_1}{100}$$

Given, $\quad C_2 - C_1 = 30°C$

$\Rightarrow \quad F_2 - F_1 = \frac{180}{100} \times 30°C$

$= 54°F$

7 (*d*) By principle of thermometry,

$$\frac{T-0}{100-0} = \frac{\frac{X_0}{2} - \frac{X_0}{3}}{X_0 - \frac{X_0}{3}}$$

or $\quad T = 25°C$

8 (*a*) As per the question, the triple point of water is 273.16 K on Kelvin scale, 400 *A* on scale *A* and 300 *B* on scale *B*, so

$273.16\text{ K} = 400\,A = 300\,B$

$\Rightarrow \quad A = \frac{273.16}{400}$ K

and $\quad B = \frac{273.16}{300}$ K

If T_A and T_B be the triple points of water, then

$$\frac{273.16}{400} T_A = \frac{273.16}{300} T_B$$

$\Rightarrow \quad T_A = \frac{4}{3} T_B$

10 (*d*) Number of moles in 5g of oxygen, $n = \frac{5}{32}$

Ideal gas equation is given by

$pV = nRT$

$\therefore \quad pV = \frac{5}{32} RT$

11 (*d*) Since, change in number of moles is zero.

$\therefore \quad n_i = n_f$

So, $\dfrac{p_i V_i}{RT_i} = \dfrac{p_f V_f}{RT_f}$

$$\Rightarrow \frac{p_i V_i}{300R} = \frac{\frac{p_i}{2} 3V_i}{RT_f} \Rightarrow T_f = 450\text{ K}$$

12 (*c*) Since, number of moles are changing but volume is constant, hence

$$\frac{p}{nT} = \frac{R}{V} = \text{constant}$$

$$\Rightarrow \frac{p_1}{n_1 T_1} = \frac{p_2}{n_2 T_2} \Rightarrow n_2 = \frac{n_1 T_1 p_2}{T_2 p_1}$$

13 (*a*) Moment of inertia of circular disc, $I = \frac{1}{2} MR^2$

$\therefore \quad \dfrac{\Delta I}{I} = \dfrac{2\Delta R}{R} = 2 \times \alpha\,\Delta t$

$\therefore \Delta I = (2\,\alpha\,\Delta t)\frac{1}{2} MR^2 = MR^2 \alpha\,\Delta t$

As angular momentum remains constant.

$\therefore \quad I\omega = \text{constant}$

$\therefore \quad I\Delta\omega + \omega\Delta I = 0$

$\Rightarrow \quad \Delta\omega = -\omega \times \dfrac{\Delta I}{I} = -\omega(2\,\alpha\,\Delta t)$

Thus, the statement given in option (a) is correct, rest are incorrect.

14 (*b*) The metal *X* has a higher coefficient of expansion compared to that of metal *Y*, so on placing bimetallic strip in a cold bath, *X* will shrink more than *Y*. Hence, the strip will bend towards the left.

15 (*b*) According to linear expansion,

we get $\frac{L_1}{L_2} = \frac{1+\alpha(\Delta\theta_1)}{1+\alpha(\Delta\theta_2)}$

$$\frac{10}{L_2} = \frac{1+11\times10^{-6}\times20}{1+11\times10^{-6}\times19}$$

$\Rightarrow \quad L_2 = 9.99989$ cm

Shortness in length

$= 10 - 9.99989 = 0.00011$

$= 11\times10^{-5}$ cm

16 (*a*) Let T be the rise in temperature from correct value, then

$T = 35°C - 20°C = 15°C$

Using the relation,

Measured length = Correct length $\times(1+\alpha_l T)$

$\Rightarrow 26 = l(1+1.2\times10^{-5}\times15)$

$\Rightarrow \quad l = \frac{26}{1.00018} = 25.9953$ m

17 (c) Since, the elongation is same for both the rods,

$(\Delta l)_{Cu} = (\Delta l)_{Al}$

$\Rightarrow L_{Cu}\alpha_{Cu}\Delta T = L_{Al}\alpha_{Al}\Delta T$ ... (i)

Substituting the given values,

$$L_{Al} = \frac{88\times1.7\times10^{-5}}{2.2\times10^{-5}} = 68 \text{ cm}$$

18 (c) $\Delta T = \frac{\Delta L}{L\alpha} = \frac{1}{100\times0.00002}$

$= 500°C$

19 (c) $\quad \Delta l_1 = \Delta l_2$

or $\quad l_1\alpha_a t = l_2\alpha_s t$

$\therefore \quad \frac{l_1}{l_2} = \frac{\alpha_s}{\alpha_a}$

or $\quad \frac{l_1}{l_1+l_2} = \frac{\alpha_s}{\alpha_a+\alpha_s}$

21 (*b*) Given, $\alpha_V = 49\times10^{-5}\ °C^{-1}$,

$\Delta T = 30°C$

$V' = V + \Delta V = V(1+\alpha_V\Delta T)$

$\therefore \quad V' = 1.0147V$

$$\rho' = \frac{m}{V'} = \frac{m}{1.0147V} = 0.9855\rho$$

Hence, fractional change in density

$$= \frac{\rho-\rho'}{\rho} = 0.0143$$

22 (*d*) $pV = \mu RT$ ...(i)

At constant pressure,

$p\Delta V = \mu R\Delta T$ ...(ii)

Divide Eq. (ii) by Eq. (i), we get

$$\frac{\Delta V}{V} = \frac{\Delta T}{T}$$

Also, $\frac{\Delta V}{V} = \alpha_V\Delta T$

i.e. $\quad \alpha_V = \frac{1}{T}$ for ideal gas

23 (*a*) Original area of the plate,

$A = (100\times20)\text{ cm}^2 = 2000\text{ cm}^2$

Now, coefficient of area expansion is given by

$$\beta = \frac{\Delta A}{A\Delta T} = \frac{2}{2000\times10^2}$$

$\beta = 1\times10^{-5}/°C$

But $\beta = 2\alpha$

$\Rightarrow \quad \alpha = 5\times10^{-6}/°C$

24 (*a*) Variation of density with temperature is given by

$$\rho' = \frac{\rho}{1+\alpha_V\Delta\theta}$$

So, its density decreases with temperature.

Fractional decrease is

$$\frac{\rho'-\rho}{\rho} = \left(\frac{1}{1+49\times10^{-5}\times30} - 1\right)$$

$= -1.5\times10^{-2}$

25 (*b*) Water contracts when it is heated from 0°C to 4°C. Thus, its density increases and volume decreases. Hence, correct graph is shown in option (c).

27 (*a*) Thermal strain in the wire,

$$\frac{\Delta l}{l} = \alpha\Delta T$$

The corresponding stress is,

$Y\times\text{strain} = Y\alpha\Delta T$

The tension F developed in the wire is

F = Stress × Cross-sectional area

$= Y\alpha\Delta T\times A = YA\alpha\Delta T$

Here, $A = \pi r^2 = 3.14\,(1.0\times10^{-3}\text{ m})^2$

$= 3.14\times10^{-6}\text{ m}^2$

and $\Delta T = 27° - (-39°) = 66°C$

$\therefore \quad F = 3.77\times10^2$ N

28 (*a*) Thermal stress $= Y\alpha\Delta T$

Both the rods are heated for equal stresses.

$\therefore\ Y_1\alpha_1\Delta T_1 = Y_2\alpha_2\Delta T_2$

Since, $\Delta T_1 = \Delta T_2$

$\Rightarrow \quad \frac{Y_1}{Y_2} = \frac{\alpha_2}{\alpha_1} = \frac{3}{2}$

29 (*a*) The contraction in the length of the wire due to change in temperature is given as

$\Delta L_1 = \alpha L\Delta T = 1.2\times10^{-5}\times3\times(-170-30)$

$= -7.2\times10^{-3}$ m

$$A = 3.14\times\left(\frac{1}{2}\times10^{-3}\right)^2$$

$= 0.785\times10^{-6}\text{ m}^2$

The expansion in the length,

$$\Delta L_2 = \frac{FL}{AY} = \frac{mgL}{AY}$$

$$= \frac{(10\times10)\times3}{(0.785\times10^{-6})(2\times10^{11})}$$

$= 1.91\times10^{-3}$ m

Resultant change in length

$= \Delta L_1 + \Delta L_2 \approx -5.3\times10^{-3}$

$= -5.3$ mm

30 (*b*) $\quad \Delta m = \rho\Delta V$

Volume expansion coefficient is given by

$$\gamma = \frac{\Delta V}{V\Delta T} = \frac{\Delta m}{m\Delta T} = \frac{\frac{x}{50}}{x(353-273)}$$

$\Rightarrow \gamma = 2.5\times10^{-4}/°C$

31 (*a*) Specific heat capacities are given as

Water $= 4.18\times10^3\text{ Jkg}^{-1}\text{ K}^{-1}$

Aluminium $= 9.01\times10^2\text{ Jkg}^{-1}\text{ K}^{-1}$

Ice $= 2.06\times10^3\text{ Jkg}^{-1}\text{ K}^{-1}$

Mercury $= 1.4\times10^2\text{ Jkg}^{-1}\text{ K}^{-1}$

Hence, water has highest value of specific heat capacity.

32 (*d*) Infinite thermal capacity implies that there would be practically no change in temperature whether heat is given or released by the substance.

33 (*d*) Heat removed in cooling water

$\Delta Q_1 = ms\Delta T = 100 \times 1 \times 20$
$= 2000$ cal

Heat of phase change,

$\Delta Q_2 = mL = 100 \times 80 = 8000$ cal

Now, heat removed in cooling ice from 0°C to −10°C.

$\Delta Q_3 = 100 \times 0.5 \times 10 = 500$ cal

Total heat removed in one hour,

$\Delta Q = 2000 + 8000 + 500$
$= 10500$ cal

∴Heat removed per minute

$= \dfrac{10500}{60} = 175$ cal/min

34 (*a*) Heat capacity $S = \dfrac{\Delta Q}{\Delta T}$

$\Rightarrow \quad \Delta T = \dfrac{\Delta Q}{S} = \dfrac{k\Delta t}{S}$

(k = rate of heat supply)

$\Rightarrow \quad \Delta T = \dfrac{k}{S} \cdot \Delta t$

Comparing with $y = mx$, slope of graph, $m = \dfrac{k}{S}$ or slope $(m) \propto \dfrac{1}{S}$

$S \propto \dfrac{1}{m}$

∴Line with largest slope has smallest heat capacity.

35 (*b*) $Q = ms\Delta T$

$\Rightarrow \quad \Delta T = \dfrac{Q}{ms} = \dfrac{2 \times 10^5}{60 \times 10^3 \times 0.83}$
$= 4.01$°C

36 (*c*) $\Delta T = 45°C - 25°C = 20°C$

Heat capacity of substance

$= \dfrac{\Delta Q}{\Delta T} = \dfrac{300}{20} = 15$ J° C^{-1}

Specific heat capacity,

$s = \dfrac{1}{m} \cdot \dfrac{\Delta Q}{\Delta T} = \dfrac{1}{0.025} \times 15$
$= 600$ Jkg^{-1} °C^{-1}

Number of moles in 25 g sample,

i.e. $\mu = \dfrac{25}{50} = 0.5$ mol

Molar heat capacity,

$C = \dfrac{1}{\mu} \cdot \dfrac{\Delta Q}{\Delta T} = \dfrac{1}{0.5} \times 15$

$= 30$ Jmol^{-1} °C^{-1}

37 (*b*) $\Delta T = T_2 - T_1$
$= (80 - 20)°C = 60°C$

$Q = m_1 s_1 \Delta T + m_2 s_2 \Delta T + m_3 s_3 \Delta T$
$= (2.4 \times 0.216 + 1.6 \times 0.0917 + 0.8 \times 0.0931)(60)$
$= 44.376$ cal ≈ 44.4 cal

38 (*b*) Specific capacity of a substance is given by

$s = \dfrac{\Delta Q}{m\Delta T}$

$\therefore \quad \dfrac{s_1}{s_2} = \dfrac{m_2}{m_1}$

As $m = \rho V$

$\therefore \quad \dfrac{m_1}{m_2} = \dfrac{V_1}{V_2} = \dfrac{\frac{4}{3} \cdot \pi (r_1)^3}{\frac{4}{3} \cdot \pi (r_2)^3} = \dfrac{(r_1)^3}{(r_2)^3}$

$\Rightarrow \quad \dfrac{m_1}{m_2} = \left(\dfrac{2}{3}\right)^3 = \dfrac{8}{27}$

$\therefore \quad \dfrac{s_1}{s_2} = \dfrac{m_2}{m_1} = \dfrac{27}{8}$

$\Rightarrow s_1 : s_2 = 27 : 8$

39 (*d*) As we know, $Q = nC_p\Delta T$

where, n = number of moles.

$\therefore \quad Q = 5 \times \dfrac{5R}{2} \times 50$

$= 25 \times \dfrac{2}{2} \times 50$

$\Rightarrow \quad Q = 1250$ cal

40 (*c*) By principle of calorimetry,

$m_1 s_1 (\theta_1 - \theta) = m_2 s_2 (\theta - \theta_2)$

$\Rightarrow \theta = \dfrac{m_1 s_1 \theta_1 + m_2 s_2 \theta_2}{m_1 s_1 + m_2 s_2}$

When $m_1 = m_2$ and $s_1 = s_2$, then

$\theta = \dfrac{\theta_1 + \theta_2}{2}$

41 (*c*) When liquids A and B are mixed, then

$s_A (16 - 12) = s_B (19 - 16)$

$\Rightarrow \quad \dfrac{s_A}{s_B} = \dfrac{3}{4}$

and when liquids B and C are mixed, then

$\dfrac{s_B}{s_C} = \dfrac{5}{4}$

$\Rightarrow \quad \dfrac{s_A}{s_C} = \dfrac{s_A}{s_B} \times \dfrac{s_B}{s_C}$

$= \dfrac{3}{4} \times \dfrac{5}{4} = \dfrac{15}{16}$ ...(i)

If θ is the temperature when A and C are mixed, then

$s_A (\theta - 12) = s_C (28 - \theta)$

$\Rightarrow \quad \dfrac{s_A}{s_C} = \dfrac{28 - \theta}{\theta - 12}$ ...(ii)

On solving Eqs. (i) and (ii), we have

$\theta = 20.2$°C

42 (*a*) During the process AB, temperature of the system is 0°C. Hence, it represents phase change that is transformation of ice into water while temperature remains 0°C.

BC represents rise in temperature of water from 0°C to 100°C, i.e. water starts boiling at C.

Now, water starts converting into steam which is represented by CD. Hence, C to D represents water and steam in thermal equilibrium at boiling point.

Thus, the statement given in option (a) is correct, rest are incorrect.

43 (*b*) Since in the region AB, temperature is constant, therefore at this temperature, phase of the material changes from solid to liquid and $(H_2 - H_1)$ heat will be absorbed by the material. This heat is known as the heat of melting of the solid.

Similarly, in the region CD, temperature is constant, therefore at this temperature, phase of the material changes from liquid to gas and $(H_4 - H_3)$ heat will be absorbed by the material. This heat is known as the heat of vaporisation of the liquid.

Thus, the statement given in option (b) is correct, rest are incorrect.

47 (*a*) As more energy is required for enormous expansion, so latent heat of vaporisation of a substance is always greater than latent heat of fusion.

49 (*a*) Heat required for melting of 1g of ice, $Q = mL = \frac{1}{1000} \times 3.36 \times 10^5$

$= 336$ J

Heat used for raising temperature of m gram ice from $-5°C$ to $0°C$,

$\Delta Q = 420 - 336 = 84$ J

But $\Delta Q = ms\Delta T$

$\Rightarrow 84 = m \times 2100 \times 5$

$\Rightarrow m = 0.008 \text{ kg} = 8 \text{ g}$

50 (*b*) Q_1 = Heat required to convert ice from $-12°C$ to ice at $0°C$

$= ms_i \Delta T_1$

$\Delta Q_1 = 3 \times 2100 \times [0 - (-12)]$

$= 75600$ J

Q_2 = Heat required to melt ice at $0°C$ to water at $0°C$.

$= mL_i = 3 \times (3.35 \times 10^5)$

$= 1005000$ J

Q_3 = Heat required to convert water at $0°C$ to water at $100°C$.

$= ms_w \Delta T_2 = (3)(4186) \times (100)$

$Q_3 = 1255800$ J

Q_4 = Heat required to convert water at $100°C$ to steam at $100°C$

$= mL_s$

$= 3 \times (2.256 \times 10^6)$

$= 6768000$ J

So, $Q = Q_1 + Q_2 + Q_3 + Q_4$

$= 9.1 \times 10^6$ J

51 (*c*) $A = 6l^2 = 6 \times (20 \times 10^{-2})^2$

$A = 24 \times 10^{-2} \text{ m}^2$

$\Delta T = 50 - 0 = 50°C$

Now, total heat entering the box through all faces is

$$Q = \frac{KA\Delta T}{x} \times t$$

(x = thickness of box)

$$Q = (0.01) \times \frac{(24 \times 10^{-2})(50) \times (36 \times 10^3)}{5 \times 10^{-2}}$$

$\Rightarrow Q = 86400$ J

Let amount of melt in the tin is m kg.

$\therefore Q = mL_f$

$$\Rightarrow m = \frac{86400}{335 \times 10^3} = 0.258 \text{ kg}$$

So, the amount of ice left

$= 5 - 0.258 = 4.7$ kg

52 (*a*) $R_{eq} = R_1 + R_2$

$$\therefore \frac{2L}{K_{eq}A} = \frac{L}{3 \times A} + \frac{L}{7 \times A}$$

$\Rightarrow K_{eq} = 4.2$

53 (*c*) The rate of heat flow through the composite slab in steady state is

$$\frac{Q}{T} = \frac{T_2 - T_1}{\frac{l_1}{K_1 A} + \frac{l_2}{K_2 A}}$$

$$\Rightarrow \frac{Q}{T} = \frac{A(T_2 - T_1)}{\frac{t}{K} + \frac{4t}{2K}} = \frac{A(T_2 - T_1)K}{3t}$$

On comparing with the given rate of heat flow equation,

$$f = \frac{1}{3}$$

54 (*b*) Rate of loss of heat,

$$H = \frac{Q}{t} = \frac{KA(T_1 - T_2)}{x}$$

$$= \frac{2.2 \times 10^{-3} \times 1000 \times 42}{0.4}$$

$= 231 \text{ cal s}^{-1}$

55 (*a*) As, heat is flowing from A to B, so

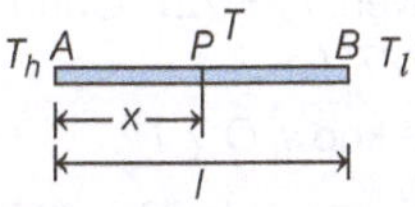

where, T_h = higher temperature

and T_l = lower temperature.

Heat current,

$$H = \frac{\Delta Q}{\Delta t} = \frac{KA(T_h - T_l)}{l} = \frac{KA(T_h - T)}{x}$$

$$\Rightarrow \frac{x}{l}(T_h - T_l) = T_h - T$$

$$\Rightarrow T = T_h - \left(\frac{T_h - T_l}{l}\right)x$$

Hence, T decreases linearly with x from T_h to T_l.

56 (*b*) Suppose area of the bottom of the tank $= A \text{ cm}^2$

Volume of water that vaporises in 9 min (or 540 s) $= (A \times 1) \text{ cm}^3$

Mass of water that vaporises in 540 s $= A \text{ cm}^3 \times 1\text{g cm}^{-3} = A\text{g}$

$\therefore Q = mL = A \times 540$ cal

But $Q = \frac{KA(T_1 - T_2)}{x} \times t$

or $T_1 - T_2 = \frac{Qx}{KAt}$

$$= \frac{A \times 540 \times 2}{0.2 \times A \times 540} = 10$$

Total temperature of the furnace, i.e.

$T_1 = T_2 + 10 = 100 + 10 = 110°C$

57 (*b*) Let θ be the junction temperature,

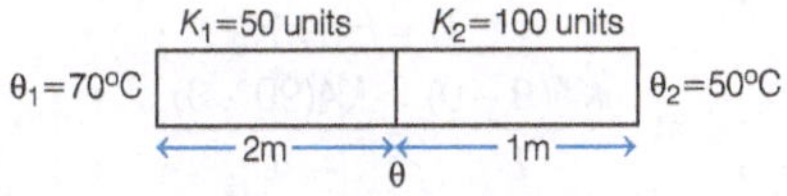

$H_1 = H_2$

$$\Rightarrow K_1 \frac{A\Delta\theta_1}{l_1} = K_2 \frac{A\Delta\theta_2}{l_2}$$

$$\Rightarrow K_1 \frac{\Delta\theta_1}{l_1} = K_2 \frac{\Delta\theta_2}{l_2}$$

$$50 \frac{(70 - \theta)}{2} = 100 \frac{(\theta - 50)}{1}$$

$\Rightarrow \theta = 54°C$

58 (*b*) Time required for heat transfer,

$$\Delta t = \frac{\Delta Q(\Delta x)}{KA(\Delta T)}$$

In parallel combination, $A \to 2$ times and length becomes half, i.e. $\Delta x \to 1/2$ times as shown in figure.

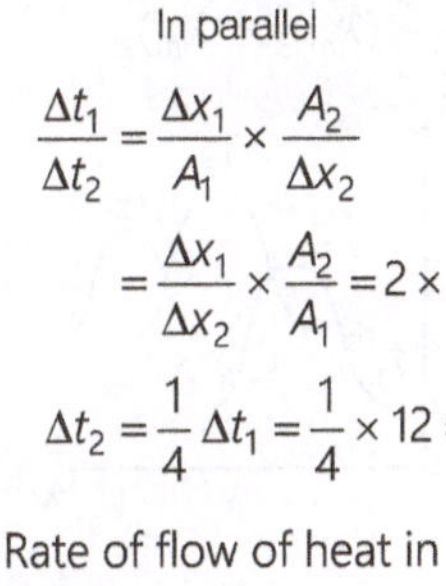

$$\therefore \frac{\Delta t_1}{\Delta t_2} = \frac{\Delta x_1}{A_1} \times \frac{A_2}{\Delta x_2}$$

$$= \frac{\Delta x_1}{\Delta x_2} \times \frac{A_2}{A_1} = 2 \times 2 = 4$$

$$\Rightarrow \Delta t_2 = \frac{1}{4}\Delta t_1 = \frac{1}{4} \times 12 = 3 \text{ s}$$

59 (*b*) Rate of flow of heat in the combined system

$$\Rightarrow \frac{KA(\theta_1-\theta_2)}{l} = \frac{K_1A_1(\theta_1-\theta_2)}{l} + \frac{K_2A_2(\theta_1-\theta_2)}{l}$$

$$\Rightarrow KA = K_1A_1 + K_2A_2$$

$$\Rightarrow K\pi(2R)^2 = K_1(\pi R^2) + K_2\pi[(2R)^2 - R^2]$$

$$\Rightarrow \pi R^2(K\times 4) = \pi R^2(K_1 + 3K_2)$$

$$\therefore \quad K = \frac{K_1 + 3K_2}{4}$$

60 (*d*) Let the temperature of junction be θ, then

$$H = H_1 + H_2$$

$$\Rightarrow \frac{KA(\theta - 0)}{L} = \frac{KA(90°-\theta)}{L} + \frac{KA(90°-\theta)}{L}$$

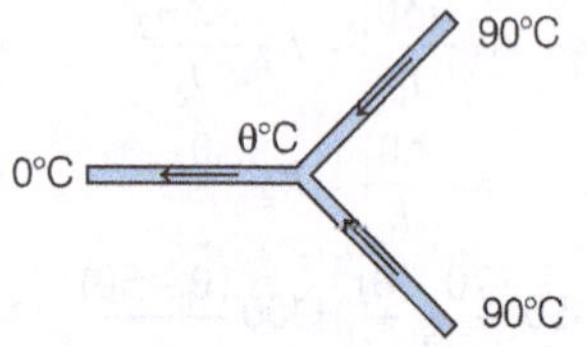

or $\theta = 90° - \theta + 90° - \theta$

or $\theta = 180° - 2\theta$

or $3\theta = 180°$ or $\theta = 60°C$

63 (*b*) For spheres, surface to volume ratio is more for small sphere than large sphere.
So, a small gulabjamun absorbs more heat (per unit volume) than large ones and becomes more hot.
For discus there is not much difference for small and large ones.

65 (*d*) According to Wien's law,

$$\lambda_m \propto \frac{1}{T}$$

and from the graph,
$(\lambda_m)_1 < (\lambda_m)_3 < (\lambda_m)_2$

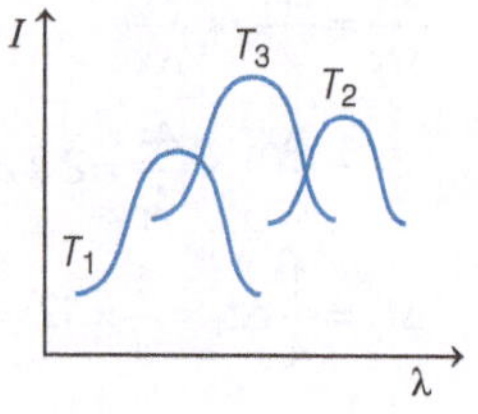

Therefore, $T_1 > T_3 > T_2$

66 (*c*) According to Wien's law, we get

$$\lambda_m = \frac{b}{T}$$

or $\lambda_m = \frac{2.88\times10^6 \text{ nm-K}}{5760 \text{ K}}$

$\Rightarrow \lambda_m = 500$ nm

$\because \lambda_m$ = wavelength corresponding to maximum energy,
so $U_2 > U_1$.

67 (*d*) According to Wien's displacement law,

$$\lambda_m T = b$$

or $\lambda_m \propto \frac{1}{T}$

$$\frac{(\lambda_m)_s}{(\lambda_m)_f} = \frac{T_f}{T_s}$$

or $T_f = T_s \times \frac{(\lambda_m)_s}{(\lambda_m)_f}$

$$= 5500 \text{ K} \times \frac{(5.5\times10^{-7}\text{ m})}{(11\times10^{-7}\text{ m})}$$

$$= 2750 \text{ K}$$

68 (*c*) According to Stefan's law,

$$Q = \sigma e A T^4$$

For black body, $e = 1$

$$\Rightarrow \quad T = \left[\frac{Q}{\sigma(4\pi R^2)}\right]^{1/4}$$

69 (*d*) Given, $T_A = 727°C$ and $T_B = 327°C$

As we know, $Q \propto T^4$

$$\Rightarrow \frac{Q_A}{Q_B} = \frac{H_A}{H_B} = \left(\frac{273+727}{273+327}\right)^4 = \frac{625}{81}$$

70 (*a*) Given, temperature of sphere,
$T = 227°$ C
$= 273 + 227 = 500$ K
Radius, $r = 2$ m
Emissivity, $e = 0.8$

$\therefore$ Radiation power of sphere = Radiated energy per second

$$= \sigma A e T^4$$

$$= 5.67\times10^{-8}\times4\pi\times2^2\times0.8\times(500)^4$$

$$= 142430.4 \text{ W}$$

$$= 142.4 \text{ kW} \approx 142.5 \text{ kW}$$

71 (*b*) $\sigma = 5.67\times10^{-5}$ erg cm^{-2} s^{-1} K^{-4}
Power of lamp = 100 W = 100 Js^{-1}
$\therefore$ Rate of emission of energy,

$$E = 100\times10^7 \text{ erg s}^{-1}$$

$(\because 1\text{J} = 10^7 \text{erg})$

Area, $A = 1$ cm^2, temperature, $T = ?$
According to Stefan-Boltzmann law, we get

$$E = \sigma T^4 \times A$$

$$\therefore T = \left(\frac{E}{\sigma A}\right)^{1/4}$$

$$= \left(\frac{100\times10^7}{5.67\times10^{-5}\times1}\right)^{1/4} = 2049 \text{ K}$$

72 (*a*) $P_1 = \sigma T_1^4 = \sigma(3000)^4$ ...(i)

$P_2 = \sigma T_2^4 = \sigma(4000)^4$ ...(ii)

$$\because \frac{P_2}{P_1} = \frac{(4000)^4}{(3000)^4} = \frac{256}{81}$$

As we know, percentage rise in power

$$= \frac{P_2 - P_1}{P_1}\times100 = 216\%$$

73 (*c*) Rate of energy received = Rate of energy emitted

$$\sigma A(3T)^4 - \sigma A(T')^4 = \sigma A(T')^4 - \sigma A(2T)^4$$

$$\Rightarrow (3T)^4 - (T')^4 = (T')^4 - (2T)^4$$

$$\Rightarrow \quad T' = \left(\frac{97}{2}\right)^{1/4} T$$

74 (*c*)

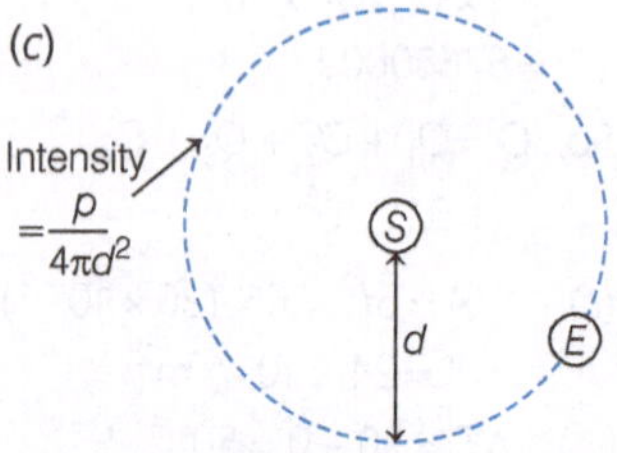

Intensity of radiation

$$= \frac{\text{Energy}}{\text{Area} \times \text{Time}}$$

Now, energy radiated by sun per unit time

$$= \sigma T^4 \times 4\pi R_s^2$$

This energy spreads over a sphere of $4\pi d^2$. So, intensity at earth

$$= \frac{\sigma T^4\times4\pi R_s^2}{4\pi d^2} = \frac{\sigma T^4 R_s^2}{d^2}$$

$$= \frac{5.67\times10^{-8}\times(6\times10^3)^4 \times(7.2\times10^8)^2}{(1.5\times10^{11})^2}$$

$$= \frac{5.67 \times 1296 \times 51.84}{2.25} \times 10^{-2}$$

$$= 1693 \frac{W}{m^2}$$

75 (*d*) **In first case**

$T_1 = 60°C, T_2 = 40°C$

$T_0 = 10°C, t = 7 \text{ min} = 420 \text{ s}$

According to Newton's law of cooling, we get

$$ms \frac{T_1 - T_2}{t} = k\left(\frac{T_1 + T_2}{2} - T_0\right)$$

$$ms \times \frac{20}{420} = k \times 40 \quad ...(i)$$

In second case

$$ms \times \frac{40 - T_2}{420} = k\left(\frac{40 + T_2}{2} - T_0\right) \quad ...(ii)$$

On dividing Eq. (ii) by Eq. (i), we get

$$20 + \frac{T_2}{2} - 10 = 80 - 2T_2$$

$$\Rightarrow T_2 = 28°C$$

76 (*a*) $$-\frac{d\theta}{dt} = k(\theta - \theta_0)$$

$$\Rightarrow \int \frac{d\theta}{\theta - \theta_0} = \int -k\, dt$$

$$\Rightarrow \ln(\theta - \theta_0) = -kt + C$$

which is a straight line with negative slope.

Thus, the graph given in option (a) is correct.

Assertion and Reason Questions

1 (*d*) If equal amount of heat is added to equal masses of different substances, then the resulting temperature changes will not be the same.

It implies that every substance has a unique value for the amount of heat absorbed or rejected to change the temperature of unit mass of it by one unit.

Therefore, Assertion is incorrect but Reason is correct.

3 (*b*) Houses made of concrete roofs get very hot during summer days, because thermal conductivity of concrete (though much smaller than that of a metal) is still not small enough.

Therefore, Assertion and Reason are correct but Reason is not the correct explanation of Assertion.

4 (*d*) Thermal conductivity of the wall depends only on nature of material of the wall and not on temperature difference across its two sides.

Therefore, Assertion is incorrect but Reason is correct.

5 (*a*) A gas can be liquified by applying pressure only when it is cooled below the critical temperature.

Critical temperature of NH_3 is more than CO_2, i.e.

$T_{NH_3} = 405$ K and $T_{CO_2} = 304.1$ K.

Hence, NH_3 is liquified more easily than CO_2.

Therefore, Both Assertion and Reason are correct and Reason is the correct explanation of Assertion.

6 (*c*) The thermal conductivity of brass is high, i.e. brass is a good conductor of heat. So, when a brass tumbler is touched, heat quickly flows from human body to tumbler. Consequently, the tumbler appears colder. On the other hand, wood is a bad conductor. So, heat does not flow from the human body to the wooden tray in this case. Thus, it appears comparatively hotter.

Therefore, Assertion is correct but Reason is incorrect.

7 (*c*) At a high temperature of 6000 K, the sun acts like a black body emitting complete radiation.

It follows from Stefan's law that $E \propto T^4$, i.e. the radiation from the sun's surface varies as the fourth power of its absolute temperature.

Therefore, Assertion is correct but Reason is incorrect.

8 (*c*) According to Wien's law, the peak emission wavelength of a body is inversely proportional to its absolute temperature.

$$\lambda_m = \frac{\text{constant}}{T}$$

Therefore, Assertion is correct but Reason is incorrect.

9 (*c*) Stefan's law is applied here not the Newton's law of cooling.

According to Stefan's law,

$$\frac{E_2}{E_1} = \left(\frac{T_2}{T_1}\right)^4 = \left(\frac{900}{300}\right)^4 = 81$$

$$\Rightarrow \frac{E_2}{R} = 81$$

Therefore, $E_2 = 81\, R$

Therefore, Assertion is correct but Reason is incorrect.

10 (*d*) Assertion is incorrect because at absolute zero (0 K), heat is neither radiates nor absorbed. Reason is the statement of Stefan's law, as $E \propto T^4$.

Therefore, Assertion is incorrect but Reason is correct.

Statement Based Questions

1 (*b*) On the surface of moon, the atmospheric pressure is low. This leads to a lower boiling point. Thus, water evaporates easily on moon compared to earth.

Therefore, Statement I is true but Statement II is false.

2 (*d*) Calorimetry means measurement of heat, the heat lost by the body is equal to the gained by the cold body provided no heat is allowed to escape to the surrounding.

Therefore, both Statement I and Statement II are true.

3 (*d*) Both the liquid and vapour states of the substance co-exist in thermal equilibrium, during the change of state from liquid to vapour.

Therefore, Both Statement I and Statement II are true.

4 (*b*) Statements II is incorrect and it can be corrected as,
Convection is possible only in fluids.

7 (*d*) We know that to measure thermal conductivity of liquids experimentally they must be heated from the top, i.e. upper layer is kept hot cold, so as to prevent convection in liquids. Therefore, both Statement I and Statement II are true.

8 (*b*) Statement II is incorrect and it can be corrected as, the Newton's law of cooling, holds good only for small difference of temperature.

Matching Type Questions

1 (*c*) Initial condition,
Given, $m = 10$ g
$\Rightarrow$ Number of moles, $n = \frac{M}{M_0} = \frac{10}{32}$

$\Rightarrow p_1 = 3$ atm
$T_1 = 10°C = 10 + 273 = 283$ K

A. Let volume of the gas before expansion $= V_1$
From ideal gas equation,
$$p_1V_1 = nRT_1$$
$$\Rightarrow V_1 = \frac{nRT_1}{p_1} = \frac{10 \times 0.0821 \times 283}{32 \times 3} = 2.42 \text{ L}$$

B. At constant pressure, applying Charles' law,
$$\frac{V_1}{T_1} = \frac{V_2}{T_2} \quad \text{...(i)}$$
Given, $V_2 = 10$ L, $T_2 = ?$
Using Eq. (i), we get
$$T_2 = \left(\frac{V_2}{V_1}\right) \times T_1 = \left(\frac{10}{2.42}\right) \times 283 = 1169.4 \text{ K}$$

C. Density before expansion,
$$d_1 = \frac{\text{Mass}}{V_1} = \frac{10}{2.42} = 4.13 \text{ gL}^{-1}$$

D. Density after expansion,
$$d_2 = \frac{\text{Mass}}{V_2} = \frac{10}{10} = 1 \text{ g L}^{-1}$$
Hence, A $\rightarrow$ 3, B $\rightarrow$ 4, C $\rightarrow$ 1 and D $\rightarrow$ 2.

2 (*a*)
A. When *A* and *B* having same specific heat and masses *m* and 2*m* are mixed together, we get
$$(m)(s)(\theta - 20°) = (2m)(s)(40° - \theta)$$
$$\Rightarrow \theta - 20° = 80° - 2\theta$$
$$\Rightarrow \theta = \frac{100°}{3} = 33.3°C$$

B. When liquids *A* and *C* are mixed together, we get
$$(m)(s)(\theta - 20°) = (3m)(s)(60° - \theta)$$
$$\Rightarrow \theta - 20° = 180° - 3\theta$$
$$\Rightarrow \theta = 50°C$$

C. When liquids *B* and *C* are mixed together, we get
$$(2m)(s)(\theta - 40°) = (3m)(s)(60° - \theta)$$
$$\Rightarrow 2\theta - 80 = 180 - 3\theta$$
$$\Rightarrow \theta = 52°C$$

D. When *A*, *B* and *C* are mixed, we get
$$(m)(s)(\theta - 20°) + (2m)(s)(\theta - 40°) = (3m)(s)(60° - \theta)$$
or $\theta = 46.67°C$
Hence, A $\rightarrow$ 1, B $\rightarrow$ 3, C $\rightarrow$ 2 and D $\rightarrow$ 4.

3 (*c*) A. Thermal resistance $= \frac{L}{KA}$
$$\text{Dimensions} = \frac{[\text{L}]}{\left[\frac{\text{ML}^2\text{T}^{-2}}{\text{T}} \times \frac{\text{L}}{\text{L}^2\text{K}}\right]\text{L}^2} = [\text{M}^{-1}\text{L}^{-2}\text{T}^3\text{K}]$$

B. Stefan-Boltzmann law,
Heat radiated per unit time by body
$$= \frac{\Delta Q}{\Delta t} = e\sigma AT^4$$
$$\Rightarrow \sigma = \frac{\Delta Q/\Delta t}{eAT^4}$$
e = emissivity (dimensionless constant)
Dimensions of σ (Stefan-Boltzmann constant)
$$= \frac{[\text{ML}^2\text{T}^{-2}]}{[\text{TL}^2\text{K}^4]} = [\text{MT}^{-3}\text{K}^{-4}]$$

C. From Wien's displacement law,
$\lambda_m T$ = constant
Here, 'constant' is called Wien's constant, its value is 2.9×10^{-3} m-K and dimensions [LK].

D. Heat current,
$$H = \frac{\Delta Q}{\Delta t} = \frac{KA(T_h - T_l)}{L}$$
Dimensions of H is $[\text{ML}^2\text{T}^{-3}]$.
Hence, A $\rightarrow$ 2, B $\rightarrow$ 1, C $\rightarrow$ 4 and D $\rightarrow$ 3.

Numerical Type Questions

1 (36) The time period of second's pendulum is $T = 2$s.
The change in time period due to increase in length of wire is
$$\Delta T = \frac{1}{2} T\alpha\Delta\theta$$
$$= \frac{1}{2} \times 2 \times 1.2 \times 10^{-5} \times 10$$
$$= 1.2 \times 10^{-4} \text{s}$$
The new time period,
$$T' = T + \Delta T = 2 + (1.2 \times 10^{-4})$$
$$\Rightarrow T' = 2.00012 \text{ s}$$
$\therefore$ Time lost in a week is
$$\Delta t = \left(\frac{\Delta T}{T'}\right)t$$
$$= \frac{1.2 \times 10^{-4}}{2.00012} \times (7 \times 24 \times 3600)$$
$$\Rightarrow \Delta t = 36.28 \text{ s} \approx 36 \text{ s}$$
So, the value of x is 36.

2 (5) As the surrounding is same for both liquids and both takes same time to cool, therefore
$$\left(\frac{dQ}{dt}\right)_w = \left(\frac{dQ}{dt}\right)_l$$
$$\Rightarrow \frac{(m_w C_w + w)\Delta T}{t} = \frac{(m_l C_l + w)\Delta T}{t}$$
where, w = water equivalent of the vessel
$$\Rightarrow m_w C_w = m_l C_l$$

$\Rightarrow \quad C_l = \dfrac{m_w C_w}{m_l} = \dfrac{50 \times 1}{100}$

$\Rightarrow \quad C_l = 0.5 \text{ kcal/kg}$

$= 5 \times 10^{-1} \text{kcal/kg}$

So, the value of x is 5.

3 (*500*) From calorimetry, heat required, $\Delta Q = ms\Delta\theta$

Let mass of bullet is m.

$\Delta\theta = 327° - 27° = 300°C$

$\Rightarrow \quad \Delta Q_1 = m \times 125 \times 300$

$\Rightarrow \quad \Delta Q_1 = m \times 3.75 \times 10^4$

Heat required to melt the bullet,

$\Delta Q_2 = mL_1$

$= m \times 2.5 \times 10^4$

Now, kinetic energy of the bullet,

$KE = \dfrac{1}{2} mv^2$

Half of kinetic energy $= \dfrac{1}{4} mv^2$

From principle of calorimetry,

Lost in KE $= \Delta Q_1 + \Delta Q_2$

$\dfrac{1}{4} mv^2 = m(3.75 + 2.5) \times 10^4$

$\Rightarrow \quad v = 500 \text{ m/s}$

So, the value of x is 500.

4 (*42*) According to question,

$\dfrac{\Delta Q}{\Delta t} = \dfrac{m}{\Delta t} \cdot s\Delta T$

Also, $\dfrac{\Delta Q}{\Delta t} = m' \times$ heat of combustion

$\Rightarrow \dfrac{2}{60} \times 4.2 \times 10^3 \times (60 - 20)$

$= m' \times 8 \times 10^3 \times 10^3$

$\Rightarrow m' = \dfrac{2 \times 4.2 \times 10^3 \times 40}{60 \times 8 \times 10^3 \times 10^3} \text{ kg/s}$

$= \dfrac{2 \times 4.2 \times 10^3 \times 40 \times 10^3 \times 60}{60 \times 8 \times 10^3 \times 10^3}$ g/min

$\Rightarrow m' = 42$ g/min

So, the value of x is 42.

5 (*24*) Change in volume of beaker = Change in volume of mercury

$\Rightarrow V_b \gamma_b \Delta T = V_m \gamma_m \Delta T$

$\Rightarrow \quad V_m = \dfrac{V_b \gamma_b}{\gamma_m} = \dfrac{600 \times 6 \times 10^{-6}}{1.5 \times 10^{-4}}$

$= 24 \text{ cm}^3$

$\Rightarrow \quad V_m = 24 \text{ cc}$

6 (*41.5*) The given situation is shown below.

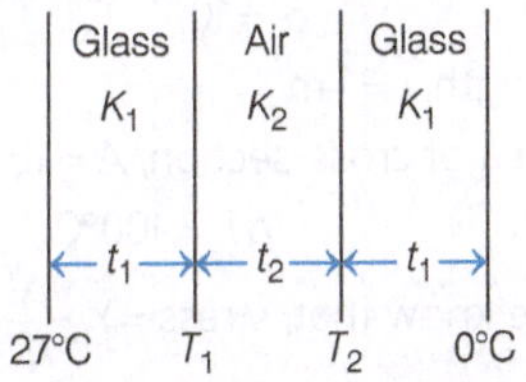

The rate of heat flow through the window pane is $H = \dfrac{\Delta T}{R}$

where, R is total thermal resistance

$\therefore \quad R = \dfrac{t_1}{K_1 A_1} + \dfrac{t_2}{K_2 A_2} + \dfrac{t_1}{K_1 A_1}$

$= \dfrac{2t_1}{K_1 A_1} + \dfrac{t_2}{K_2 A_2}$

$= \dfrac{2 \times 0.01}{0.8 \times 1} + \dfrac{0.05}{0.08 \times 1}$

$= 0.65 \text{ W}^{-1} \text{ K}$

$\therefore \quad H = \dfrac{27 - 0}{0.65} = 41.5 \text{ W}$

7 (*182*) From Stefan's law, the rate of loss of heat is given as

$\dfrac{Q}{t} = \sigma Ae(T_1^4 - T_2^4)$

As, $\quad T_1 = 273 + 527 = 800 \text{ K}$

$T_2 = 273 + 27 = 300 \text{ K}$

$\therefore \quad \dfrac{Q}{T} = 5.67 \times 10^{-8} \times 2 \times 10^{-2}$

$\times 0.4 \times ([(800)^4 - (300)^4]$

$= 182.12$

$\Rightarrow \quad \dfrac{Q}{T} \simeq 182 \text{ J/s}$

NCERT Exemplar Questions

1 (*b*) As the rod is heated, it expands. As no external torque is acting on the system, so angular momentum should be conserved.

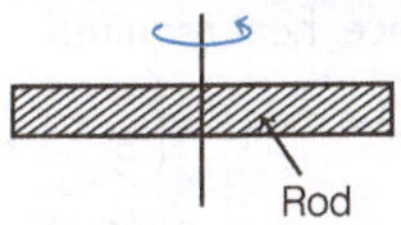

$L = I\omega = \text{constant} \Rightarrow I_1 \omega_1 = I_2 \omega_2$

Due to expansion of the rod,

$I_2 > I_1$

$\Rightarrow \quad \dfrac{\omega_2}{\omega_1} = \dfrac{I_1}{I_2} < 1$

$\Rightarrow \quad \omega_2 < \omega_1$

So, angular velocity (speed of rotation) decreases.

2 (*a*) Let volume of the sphere be V and ρ be its density, then we can write buoyant force, $F = V\rho g$

$F \propto \rho$

Hence, buoyancy will be less in water at 0°C than that in water at 4°C.

3 (*a*) A pendulum of length L is shown as

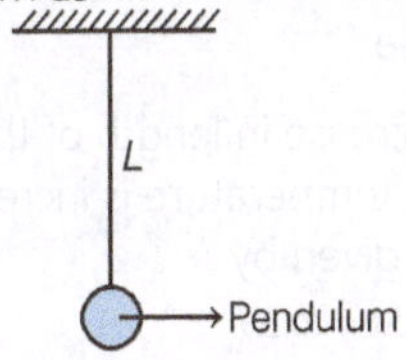

We know that, time period of pendulum,

$T = 2\pi \sqrt{\dfrac{L}{g}} \Rightarrow T \propto \sqrt{L}$

As the temperature is increased, the length of the pendulum increases.

The centre of mass of the system still remains at the centre of the bob.

5 (*d*) Let the radius of the sphere is R. As the temperature increases, radius of the sphere increases as shown in figure.

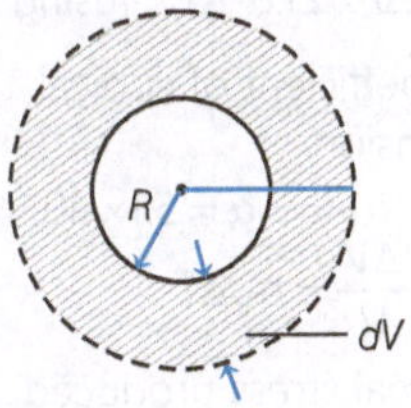

Original volume, $V = \dfrac{4}{3}\pi R^3$

Coefficient of linear expansion = α

$\therefore$ Coefficient of volume expansion $= 3\alpha$

$\therefore \quad \dfrac{1}{V}\dfrac{dV}{dT} = 3\alpha$

$\Rightarrow \quad dV = 3V\alpha dt$

$\simeq 4\pi R^3 \alpha \Delta T$

= Increase in the volume

6 (a) Heat required to bring water from −10°C to 0°C,

$$Q = ms_w \Delta T$$
$$= 100 \times 1 \times 10 = 1000 \text{ cal}$$

As it is water to ice conversion, heat will be released.

$$\therefore \quad Q = ml$$

or $$m = \frac{Q}{l} = \frac{1000}{80} = 12.5 \text{ g}$$

As small mass of ice is formed, therefore the temperature of the mixture will remain 0°C because water cannot remain at −10°C with 0°C ice.

7 (a) Increase in length of the rod when temperature is increased by ΔT is given by

$$\Delta l = l\alpha\Delta T \quad \text{...(i)}$$

∴ New moment of inertia of the rod,

$$I' = \frac{M}{12}(l + \Delta l)^2$$
$$I' = \frac{M}{12}(l^2 + 2l\Delta l) \quad (\because \Delta l^2 \approx 0)$$
$$I' = \frac{Ml^2}{12} + \frac{Ml\Delta l}{6} = I + \frac{Ml\Delta l}{6}$$

∴ Increase in moment of inertia,

$$\Delta I = I' - I = \frac{Ml \cdot \Delta l}{6}$$
$$= 2 \times \left(\frac{Ml^2}{12}\right)\frac{\Delta l}{l}$$
$$\Delta I = 2I\,\alpha\,\Delta T \quad \text{[using Eq. (i)]}$$

8 (c) Coefficient of cubical expansion,

$$\alpha_V = 3\alpha = 5.1 \times 10^{-5} /°\text{C}$$
$$\frac{\Delta V}{V} = \alpha_V \Delta T \quad \text{...(i)}$$

Thermal stress produced

$$= B \times \text{volumetric strain}$$
$$= B \times \frac{\Delta V}{V} = B \times \alpha_V \Delta T$$
$$= 140 \times 10^9 \times (5.1 \times 10^{-5} \times 20)$$
$$= 1.428 \times 10^8 \text{ N m}^{-2}$$

Past Exams Questions

1 (b) Given,

Young's modulus,

$$Y = 0.5 \times 10^{11} \text{Nm}^{-2}$$

Coefficient of linear thermal expansion,

$$\alpha = 10^{-5}\ °\text{C}^{-1}$$

Length, $l = 1$ m

Area of cross-section, $A = 10^{-3}$ m^2

$$\Delta T = 100°\text{C}$$

We know that, stress $= Y \cdot \frac{\Delta l}{l}$

Here, $$\Delta l = l\alpha\Delta T$$
$$= 1 \times 10^{-5} \times 100 = 10^{-3}$$
$$\Rightarrow \quad \frac{F}{A} = Y \cdot \frac{10^{-3}}{1}$$

Compressive force,

$$F = 0.5 \times 10^{11} \times 10^{-3} \times 10^{-3}$$
$$= 0.5 \times 10^5 = 50 \times 10^3 \text{ N}$$

2 (a) Given,

Power, $P = 100 \text{ kW} = 100 \times 10^3$ W

Time, $t = 1 \text{ h} = 3600$ s

Energy, E = Power × Time

$$= 100 \times 10^3 \times 3600$$
$$= 36 \times 10^7 \text{ J}$$

3 (b) In first conditions;

Using the Newton's law of cooling, rate of cooling

$$= \frac{dT}{dt} = K\left[\frac{T_i + T_f}{2} - T_0\right]$$
$$\Rightarrow \quad \frac{90 - 80}{t} = K\left[\frac{90 + 80}{2} - 20\right]$$
$$\Rightarrow \quad K = \frac{2}{13t}$$

In second condition;

$$\frac{80 - 60}{t_1} = \frac{2}{13t}\left[\frac{60 + 80}{2} - 20\right]$$
$$\frac{20}{t_1} = \frac{2}{13t}[50] \quad \Rightarrow t_1 = \frac{13}{5}t$$

4 (d) Since, heat required,

$$Q = mc\Delta T = \left(\frac{4}{3}\pi r^3 \cdot \rho\right)c\Delta T$$
$$[\because m = V_{\text{sphere}}\,\rho]$$

Since, π, ρ, c and T are constants.

$$\Rightarrow \quad Q \propto r^3$$

or $$\frac{Q_1}{Q_2} = \frac{r_1^3}{r_2^3}$$
$$= \left(\frac{r_1}{r_2}\right)^3 = \left(\frac{1.5\,r_2}{r_2}\right)^3 = \frac{27}{8}$$

5 (c) Given, $\theta_0 = 0°$ C, $\theta_1 = -26°$ C

$$\frac{dQ}{dt} = \frac{KA(\theta_0 - \theta_1)}{x}$$
$$\Rightarrow \frac{\rho A dx L}{dt} = \frac{KA(\theta_0 - \theta_1)}{x}$$
$$\Rightarrow \quad \frac{dx}{dt} = \frac{KA(\theta_0 \ \theta_1)}{\rho A x L}$$
$$= \frac{K[0 - (-26)]}{\rho x L} = \frac{26K}{\rho x L}$$

6 (c) From Stefan's law, $E \propto T^4$

$$\frac{E_1}{E_2} = \frac{P_1}{P_2} = \left(\frac{T_1}{T_2}\right)^4$$
$$\Rightarrow \frac{P_1}{P_2} = \left(\frac{418}{546}\right)^4 \Rightarrow P_2 = \frac{1}{0.343} \times 17$$
$$\Rightarrow P_2 = 49.6 \text{ W}$$

7 (b) According to Newton's law of cooling,

$$\Delta T = \Delta T_0\, e^{-\lambda t}$$
$$\Rightarrow \ 3T - 2T = (3T - T)e^{-\lambda \times 10} \quad \text{...(i)}$$

Again for next 10 min,

$$T' - T = (2T) \times e^{-\lambda(20)} \quad \text{...(ii)}$$

From Eqs. (i) and (ii), we get

$$T' - T = (2T)\,(e^{-\lambda \times 10})^2$$
$$= (2T)\left(\frac{1}{2}\right)^2 = \frac{T}{2}$$
$$\therefore \quad T' = T + \frac{T}{2} = \frac{3T}{2}$$

8 (b) As given, only one quarter of its energy is absorbed by the ice.

So, $$\frac{mgh}{4} = mL_f \Rightarrow h = \frac{mL_f \times 4}{mg}$$
$$= \frac{L_f \times 4}{g} = \frac{3.4 \times 10^5 \times 4}{10 \times 1000} \text{ km}$$
$$= 136 \text{ km}$$

9 (d) As, $$\frac{dQ}{dt} \propto \Delta T$$

Also, $$\Delta T_1 = \Delta T_2$$

Hence, $$\frac{dQ_2}{dt} = 4 \text{ J/s}$$

10 (a) Let the temperature of the surrounding be t°C.

For first case,

$$\frac{(70 - 60)}{5 \text{ min}} = K\,(65°\text{C} - t°\text{C})$$

(65° is average of 70°C and 60°C)

$$\frac{10}{5\,\text{min}} = K(65°\text{C} - t°\text{C}) \quad \text{...(i)}$$

For second case,

$$\frac{(60-54)}{5\,\text{min}} = K(57-t) \quad \text{...(ii)}$$

From Eqs. (i) and (ii), we get

$$t = 45°\,\text{C}$$

11 (*a*) The relation between fahrenheit and celsius scale is

$$\frac{F-32}{9} = \frac{C}{5}$$

Change in celsius and fahrenheit is related as,

$$\Delta C = \frac{5}{9}\Delta F$$

Now, $\Delta C = 40°\text{C}$ (given)

$$40 = \frac{5}{9}\Delta F$$

$$\Delta F = 72°\text{F}$$

Hence, option (a) is correct.

12 (*c*) Heat energy gain by nail

$$\frac{1}{4}\left[\frac{1}{2}m_2v^2\right] = m_1 s\Delta T$$

$$\Rightarrow \frac{1}{4}\left[\frac{1}{2}\times 1.5\times 60^2\right] = 0.1\times 420 \times \Delta T$$

$$\Rightarrow \quad \Delta T = \frac{675}{42} = 16.07\,°\text{C}$$

13 (*c*) Heat given by the block,

$$\Delta Q = ms\Delta T$$

$$= 5\times 0.39\times 10^3\times(500-0)$$

$$= 9.75\times 10^5\ \text{J}$$

Heat taken by ice to melt m kg of ice,

$$Q_2 = mL_f$$

$$Q_2 = m\times 335\times 10^3$$

Hence, according to principle of calorimetry,

$$m\times 335\times 10^3 = 9.75\times 10^5$$

$$\Rightarrow \quad m \simeq 2.9\ \text{kg}$$

14 (*b*) Extension due to the weight will be equal to contraction by cooling.

$$\Rightarrow \quad \frac{Mgl}{AY} = l\,\alpha\Delta T$$

$$\Rightarrow M = \frac{\alpha\Delta TAY}{g}$$

$$= \frac{10^{-5}\times 10^{11}\times 20\times \pi\times(10^{-3})^2}{10}$$

$M = 2\pi$ kg $= 6.28$ kg

Value of M will be close to 9 kg per options.

15 (*a*) New lengths are same,

i.e. $\Delta l_1 = \Delta l_2$

$$\Rightarrow l_0\,\alpha_1(180-30) = l_0\,\alpha_2(T-30)$$

or $$\frac{\alpha_1}{\alpha_2} = \frac{(T-30)}{150}$$

Given, $\alpha_1 : \alpha_2 = 4:3$

$$\therefore \quad \frac{T-30}{150} = \frac{4}{3}$$

or $T = 200 + 30 = 230°\text{C}$

Skill Boosters

1 (*a*) Rate of cooling = Cooling by radiation per second + Cooling by conduction per second.

$$\therefore \quad -\frac{dT}{dt} = K_1(T-T_A) + \frac{KA}{LC}(T-T_A)$$

$$\Rightarrow \int_{T_1}^{T_2}\frac{dT}{T-T_A} = -\left(K_1 + \frac{KA}{LC}\right)\int_0^t dt$$

$$\Rightarrow \log\left(\frac{T_2-T_A}{T_1-T_A}\right) = -\left(K_1+\frac{KA}{LC}\right)\cdot t$$

Note In conduction,

$$\frac{dQ}{dt} = \frac{KA(T-T_A)}{L} = C\left(-\frac{dT}{dt}\right)$$

$$\therefore \quad -\frac{dT}{dt} = \frac{KA}{LC}(T-T_A)$$

2 (*c*) Given condition is

Initially, $L = \sqrt{l_2^2 - \left(\frac{l_1}{2}\right)^2}$

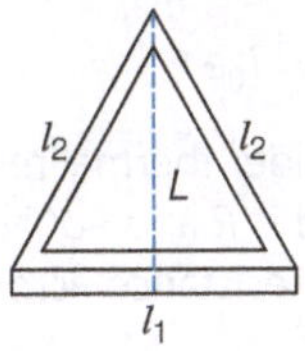

After temperature change,

$$L = \sqrt{l_2' - \left(\frac{l_1'}{2}\right)^2}$$

Equating $l_2^2 - \frac{l_1^2}{4} = l_2'^2 - \frac{l_1'^2}{4}$

$$\Rightarrow l_2^2 - \frac{l_1^2}{4} = l_2^2(1+\alpha_2\Delta T)^2 - \frac{l_1^2}{4}(1+\alpha_1\Delta T)^2$$

$$\Rightarrow \frac{l_1^2}{4}[(1+\alpha_1\Delta T)^2 - 1] = l_2^2[(1+\alpha_2\Delta T)^2-1]$$

$$\Rightarrow \frac{l_1^2}{4}(\alpha_1^2\Delta T^2 + 2\Delta T\cdot\alpha_1) = l_2^2(\alpha_2^2\Delta T^2 + 2\alpha_2\Delta T)$$

Neglecting $\alpha_1^2\Delta T^2$, $\alpha_2^2\Delta T^2$ as it is very small.

$$\Rightarrow \frac{l_1^2}{4}\cdot 2\Delta T\cdot\alpha_1 = l_2^2\cdot 2\alpha_2\Delta T$$

$$\Rightarrow \frac{l_1^2}{l_2^2} = 4\frac{\alpha_2}{\alpha_1} \quad \Rightarrow \quad \frac{l_1}{l_2} = 2\sqrt{\frac{\alpha_2}{\alpha_1}}$$

3 (*c*) $\frac{dQ}{dt} = mC$

$$\Rightarrow \quad dQ = mCdt$$

$$\Rightarrow \quad Q = \int mCdt = m\int Cdt$$

$$= m\int_5^{15}(0.2 + 0.14t + 0.023t^2)\,dt$$

$$= 2\left(0.2t + \frac{0.14t^2}{2} + \frac{0.023t^3}{3}\right)_5^{15}$$

$$= 82\ \text{cal}$$

4 (*c*) Let thermal resistance of each rod is R.

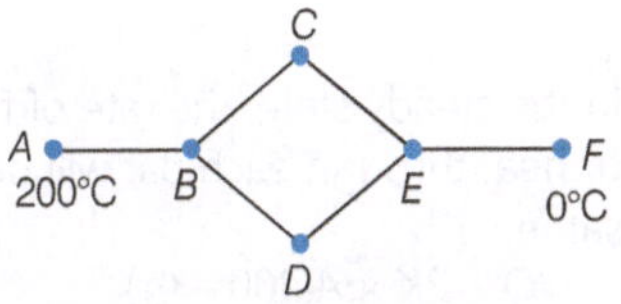

Equivalent combination is

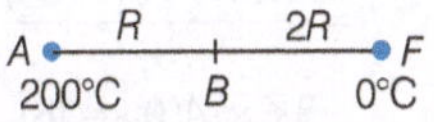

Effective resistance between B and F is $2R$.

If T is temperature of B, then

$$RT_2 + 2RT_1 = (R+2R)T$$

$$\Rightarrow \quad \frac{T_1+T_2}{3} = T$$

$$\Rightarrow \quad \frac{200+0}{3} = T$$

$$\Rightarrow \quad T = 66.67°\text{C}$$

5 (c) $\frac{\Delta Q}{\Delta t} = \frac{KA(T_1 - T_2)}{l}$

Energy flux, $\frac{\Delta Q}{A\Delta t} = \frac{K(T_1 - T_2)}{l}$

$= \frac{(0.1)(1000 - 100)}{2}$ $(\because l = 2\,\text{m})$

$= 45\ \text{Wm}^{-2}$

6 (a) $\lambda_{(\max_1)} T_1 = \lambda_{(\max_2)} T_2$

or $\frac{T_1}{T_2} = \frac{\lambda_{(\max_2)}}{\lambda_{(\max_1)}}$ ...(i)

$\frac{T_1}{T_2} = \frac{\frac{3}{4}\lambda_0}{\lambda_0} = \frac{3}{4}$ ...(ii)

$P \propto T^4$

$\Rightarrow \frac{P_1}{P_2} = \left(\frac{T_1}{T_2}\right)^4 = \left(\frac{3}{4}\right)^4 = \frac{81}{256}$

Given, $P_1 = P$ and $P_2 = nP$

$\Rightarrow \frac{P_1}{P_2} = \frac{P}{nP} = \frac{81}{256}$

$\Rightarrow n = \frac{256}{81}$

7 (a) Suppose θ_1 and θ_2 be the temperatures of junctions B and C, respectively.

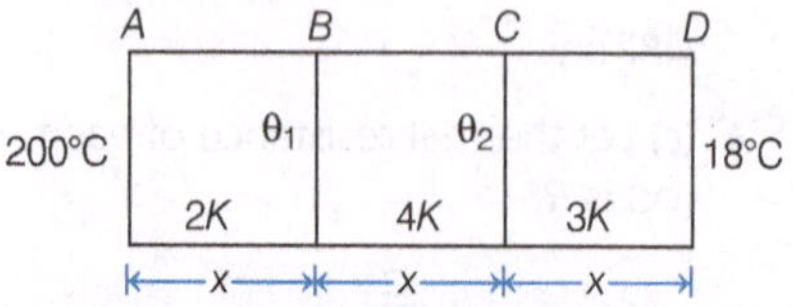

In the steady state, the rate of flow of heat through each bar will be same.

$\frac{Q}{t} = \frac{2K \times A(200 - \theta_1)}{x}$

$= \frac{4K \times A(\theta_1 - \theta_2)}{x}$

$= \frac{3K \times A(\theta_2 - 18)}{x}$

$2(200 - \theta_1) = 4(\theta_1 - \theta_2)$

$= 3(\theta_2 - 18)$

$200 - \theta_1 = 2\theta_1 - 2\theta_2$

and $4\theta_1 - 4\theta_2 = 3\theta_2 - 54$

$\Rightarrow 3\theta_1 - 2\theta_2 = 200$

and $4\theta_1 - 7\theta_2 = -54$

Solving the given expressions for θ_1 and θ_2, we get

$\theta_2 = 74°\,\text{C}$ and $\theta_1 = 116°\,\text{C}$.

8 (a) Temperatures T_1 and T_2 at time t and $T_1 + dT_1, T_2 + dT_2$ be the temperatures at time $dt + t$.

Now, heat transferred per second,

$\frac{dQ}{dt} = \frac{KAT}{l}$ ...(i)

Also, $dT = dT_1 + dT_2$ ...(ii)

As we know,

Heat lost = Heat gained

$\therefore C_1 dT_1 = C_2 dT_2$ ...(iii)

From Eqs. (ii) and (iii), we get

$dT = \left(\frac{C_1 + C_2}{C_2}\right) dT_1$ ...(iv)

As heat lost is given by

$dQ = -C_1 dT_1$

$\therefore \frac{dQ}{dt} = -C_1 \frac{dT_1}{dt} = \frac{KAT}{l}$

So, $\frac{-C_1C_2}{C_1 + C_2}\frac{dT}{dt} = \frac{KA}{l}T$

$\Rightarrow \frac{dT}{T} = \frac{-KA(C_1 + C_2)}{C_1C_2} dt$

Integrating on both sides,

$\int_{T_0}^{T} \frac{dT}{T} = \int_0^t \frac{-KA(C_1 + C_2)}{C_1C_2} dt$

$\ln \frac{T}{T_0} = \frac{-KA(C_1 + C_2)}{C_1C_2} \times t$

$\Rightarrow T = T_0 \exp\left[\frac{-KA(C_1 + C_2)}{C_1C_2} t\right]$

$\Rightarrow T = T_0 e^{\frac{-t}{\tau}}$

9 (b) Consider thermal resistance of each rod is R and equivalent thermal resistance across A and B as R'. The heat circuit will show the equivalent thermal resistance R' across C and D also.

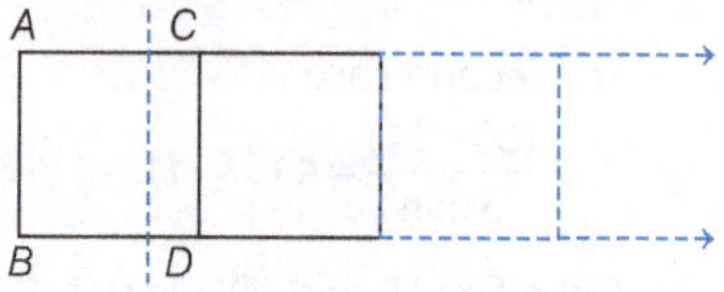

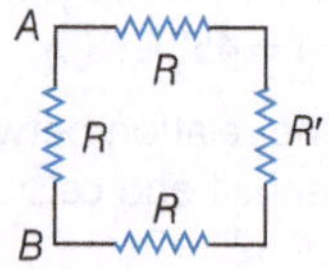

The equivalent resistance across AB is therefore,

$R' = \frac{R(R + R' + R)}{R + (R + R' + R)}$

$\left(\because R = \frac{R_1R_2}{R_1 + R_2}\right)$

$R'^2 + 2RR' - 2R^2 = 0 = (\sqrt{3} - 1)R$

The value of $(-\sqrt{3} - 1)R$ is not possible, because negative thermal resistance has no meaning here.

Now, since,

$R = \frac{l}{KA}$

$\therefore R' = \frac{(\sqrt{3} - 1)l}{KA}$

Temperature difference between A and $B = \theta_1 - \theta_2$.

Therefore, the rate of heat flow

$= \frac{\theta_1 - \theta_2}{R}$

$= \frac{KA(\theta_1 - \theta_2)}{(\sqrt{3} - 1)l}$

10 (d) Since, the two bodies are placed inside a perfectly black body of $e = 1$, hence the radiation of the system will be same as the radiation of the perfectly black body $E = \sigma AT^4$.

11

Scan for **Physics Through Concept Master** *Videos*

Thermodynamics

Topicwise No. of Ques asked in 5 Years (NEET)

Topics	No. of Questions				
	2024	2023	2022	2021	2020
Zeroth Law and First Law of Thermodynamics	–	–	–	–	–
Thermodynamic State Variables and Thermodynamic Processes	1	–	1	–	1
Second Law of Thermodynamics and Carnot Engine	–	1	–	–	–

Special Type of Ques Asked In 5 Years (NEET)

Types	Years				
	2024	2023	2022	2021	2020
A-R	–	–	–	–	–
Statement Based	–	–	–	–	–
Matching	–	–	–	–	–

Last 5 Years Weigtage (NEET)

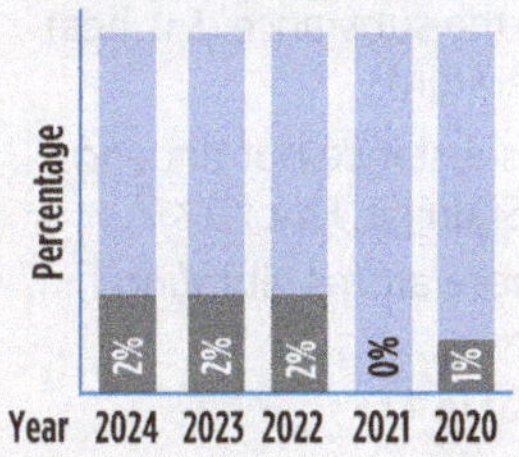

- Thermodynamics is the branch of Physics that deals with the concept of heat and temperature and the inter-conversion of heat and other forms of energy.
- Thermodynamics is a macroscopic science, it deals with bulk system and does not go into the molecular constitution of matter.
- The state of gas in thermodynamics is specified by macroscopic variables such as pressure, volume, temperature, internal energy and entropy.
- Unlike mechanics, thermodynamics is not concerned with the motion of the system as a whole.

Thermal Equilibrium

- A thermodynamic system is said to be in thermal equilibrium when macroscopic variables (like pressure, volume, temperature, mass, composition, etc.) that characterise the system do not change with time.
- Two systems are said to be in thermal equilibrium, if there is no net flow of heat between them when they are brought into thermal contact.
- There are types of boundries that separates thermodynamics system with its surroundings.
  - **Adiabatic wall** is an insulating wall (can be movable) separating the two systems that does not allow flow of energy (heat) from one system to another.
  - **Diathermic wall** is a conducting wall separating two systems, that allows energy flow (heat) from one system to another.

Zeroth Law of Thermodynamics

- Zeroth law of thermodynamics states that, if two systems *A* and *B* are in thermal equilibrium with a third system *C* separately, then *A* and *B* will be in thermal equilibrium with each other.

- If the two systems *A* and *B* are in contact with a third system *C* through diathermic wall, then the macroscopic variables of *A* and *B* will vary until both *A* and *B* come in thermal equilibrium with the third system *C*.

  This shows that two systems *A* and *B* are separately in thermal equilibrium with a third system *C*. This condition is shown in Fig. (a)

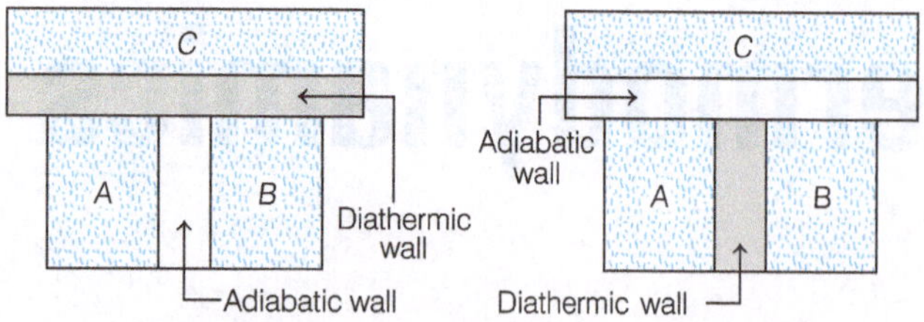

(a) (b)

- Now, the adiabatic wall between *A* and *B* is replaced by a diathermic wall and an adiabatic wall insulates *C* from *A* and *B*. *A* and *B* are found in thermal equilibrium with each other. This condition is shown in Fig. (b). **Both the above experiments prove the zeroth law of thermodynamics.**

Heat, Internal Energy and Work

- **Temperature** is the measurement of the hotness of a body. It determines the direction of flow of heat when two bodies are placed in thermal contact.
- **Heat** is the energy transfer due to temperature difference between the system and the surroundings.
- **Internal energy** (U) of a system is the sum of the kinetic energy due to the motion of molecules and the potential energy associated with the vibrational motion of molecules. Its value depends only on the given state of the system, not on the path taken to arrive at that state. Thus, the internal energy of a given mass of gas depends on its state described by specific values of pressure, volume and temperature.
- In case of ideal gas, internal energy depends only on temperature and in case of a real gas, internal energy depends on both temperature and volume.
- Heat and work in thermodynamics are not state variable. They are modes of energy transfer to a system resulting in change in its internal energy.
- Work is energy transfer brought about by means (e.g. moving the piston by raising or lowering some weight connected to it) that do not involve such a temperature difference.
- The state of a thermodynamic system is characterised by its internal energy, not heat. So, a certain amount of heat is supplied to the system or a certain amount of work is done by the system or on the system.

First law of Thermodynamics

- The first law of thermodynamics states that, the net heat energy supplied to a system is equal to sum of change in internal energy of the system and work done by the system. This means that heat energy cannot be created or destroyed but it can be converted. It is also known as the law of conservation of energy.

  i.e. Heat supplied, $\Delta Q = \Delta U + \Delta W$

  where, ΔQ = heat supplied to the system,

  ΔW = work done by the system

  and ΔU = change in internal energy. **NEET 2019**
- When internal energy $\Delta U = \Delta Q - \Delta W$, in general, ΔQ and ΔW depend on the path taken to go from initial to final states. But $\Delta Q - \Delta W$ is path independent.

Marks Maximiser

Sign conventions

$+Q$ if heat is transferred to the system

$-Q$ if heat is transferred from the system

$+W$ if work is done by the system

$-W$ if work is done on the system

Specific Heat Capacity

- The amount of heat required to raise the temperature of unit mass of substance through one degree is called the **specific heat capacity of the substance.** It may be expressed as $Q = ms\,\Delta T$

  Thus, $$s = \frac{Q}{m\Delta T} = \frac{Q}{m(T_2 - T_1)}$$

  Here, $ms = S$ = Heat capacity

  It depends on the nature of the substance and its temperature. Its SI unit is J kg^{-1} K^{-1}.
- **Molar specific heat capacity** The amount of heat required to raise the temperature of one mole of a substance through a unit degree is called the molar specific heat of the substance.

  $$C = \frac{S}{\mu} = \frac{1}{\mu}\frac{\Delta Q}{\Delta T}$$

  where, μ is the number of moles of the substance, S is heat capacity and ΔT is change in temperature.

  It is independent of the amount of substance but depends on the nature of the substance. Its SI unit is J mol^{-1} K^{-1}.
- Consider a solid of N atoms and these atoms vibrating about its mean position.

  Here, average energy of an oscillator in 1 D

  $$= \left(\frac{1}{2}k_B T\right)$$

  But in three dimension, average energy $= 3k_B T$

Thus, **total energy** is $U = 3k_BT \times N_A = 3RT$

For a solid, at a constant pressure,

$$\Delta Q = \Delta U + p\Delta V$$
$$C = \frac{\Delta Q}{\Delta T} = \frac{\Delta U}{\Delta T} = 3R$$

Note This is valid at room temperature and carbon is an exception to this.

- **Specific heat capacity at constant volume and specific heat capacity at constant pressure are related as**

$$C_p - C_V = R \quad \text{...(i)}$$

where, R is gas constant.

Eq. (i) is also known as **Mayer's relation**.

Specific Heat Capacity of Water

- The specific heat of water slightly varies with temperature.

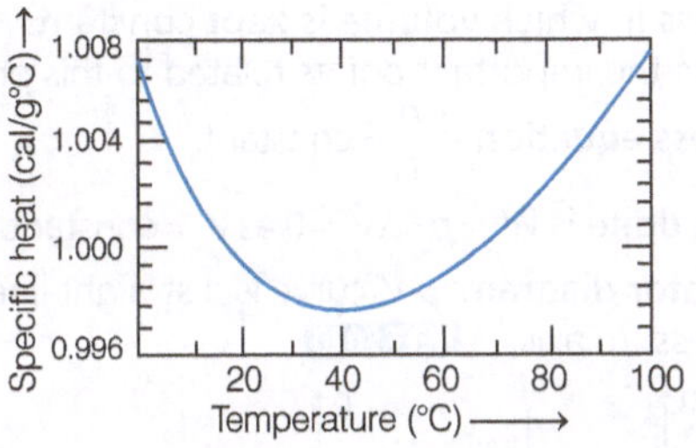

- In old time, **calorie** is used as a unit of heat. Earlier it was defined as the amount of heat required to raise the temperature of 1 g of water by 1°C.
- One calorie is defined as the amount of heat required to raise the temperature of 1g of water from 14.5°C to 15.5°C.
- In SI units, specific heat capacity of water is 4186 $\text{Jkg}^{-1}\ \text{K}^{-1}$, i.e. 4.186 $\text{Jg}^{-1}\text{K}^{-1}$.

Thermodynamic State Variables and Equation of State

- Every equilibrium state of a thermodynamic system is completely described by specific values of some macroscopic variables and these are called **state variables**.
- The thermodynamic state variables are of two kinds,
  (i) **Extensive variables** indicate the size of the system. e.g. Internal energy U, volume V, total mass M, heat energy ΔQ, etc.
  (ii) **Intensive variables** do not indicate the size of the system. e.g. Pressure p, temperature T and density ρ.
- The product of an intensive variable and an extensive variable is extensive.
- The connection between the state variables is called the **equation of state.** e.g. For an ideal gas, the equation of state is **ideal gas relation**, i.e. $pV = \mu RT$.

Thermodynamic Processes NEET 2022

Quasi-static Process

- **It is an idealised process in which at every stage, the system is in equilibrium state.** During this process, the system changes its variables (p, T, V), so slowly that it remains in (thermal and mechanical) equilibrium with its surroundings throughout.

Isothermal process

- **It is a process in which temperature of the system is kept constant during the change in state.**

Following are the important points related to this process :

(i) **Equation of state** In this process, p and V changes but T remains constant, i.e. change in temperature $\Delta T = 0$.

Thus, $p_1V_1 = p_2V_2$

(ii) **Work done** is $W = \mu RT \ln\left(\frac{V_2}{V_1}\right) = \mu RT \ln\left(\frac{p_1}{p_2}\right)$

There arises two cases for finding the nature of the work done.

Case I If $V_f > V_i$, then $W > 0$

Thus, it is an **isothermal expansion** which means the gas absorbs heat.

Case II If $V_f < V_i$, then $W < 0$

Thus, it is an **isothermal compression**, work is done on the gas by the environment and heat is released.

(iii) Since, for an ideal gas, U depends only on T.
Thus, there is no change in the internal energy $(\Delta U = 0)$ of an ideal gas in an isothermal process.

So, **first law of thermodynamics**, then implies $\Delta Q = \Delta W$, i.e. heat supplied in an isothermal change is used to do work against external surroundings.

(iv) ***p-V* curve or indicator diagram** The pressure-volume curve for a fixed temperature is called an **isotherm.** Two isotherms never intersect. p-V curve is a rectangular hyperbola.

Slope of isotherm curve $\tan\theta = \frac{dp}{dV} = \frac{-p}{V}$

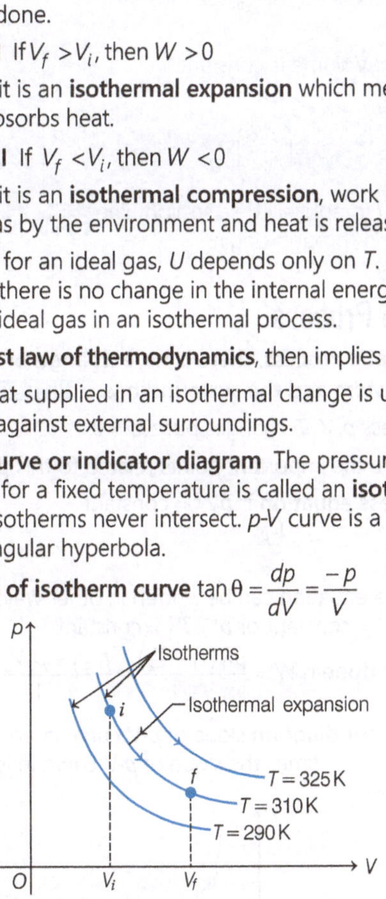

(v) The area between the isotherm and volume axis represents the work done in isothermal process.

(vi) **Specific heat** Specific heat of gas during isothermal change is infinite.

As, $\Delta T = 0 \quad \therefore \; C = \dfrac{Q}{m\Delta T} = \dfrac{Q}{m \times 0} = \infty$

Marks Maximiser

- **Conversion of *p-V* graph into *V-T* and *p-T* graph**

(i) Conversion of *p-V* graph into *V-T* graph, in *p-V* graph

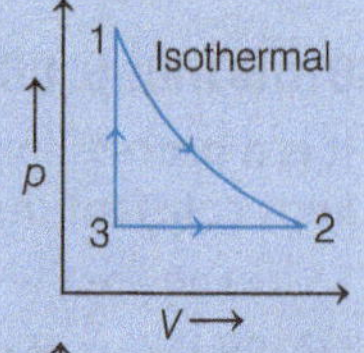

$1 \to 2$: Temperature is constant

$2 \to 3$: Pressure is constant

$\therefore$ Using ideal gas equation, we get

$$V = \left(\frac{nR}{p}\right)T$$

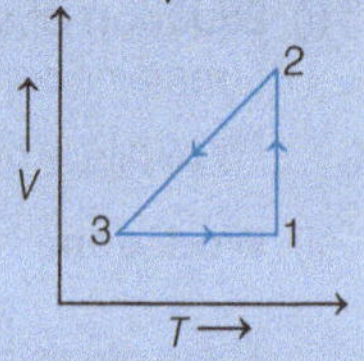

i.e. *V-T* graph is a straight line passing through origin.

$3 \to 1$: Volume is constant.

(ii) Conversion of *p-V* graph into *p-T* graph.

$3 \to 1$: Volume is constant.

$\therefore \qquad pV = nRT$

$\Rightarrow \qquad p = \left(\dfrac{nR}{V}\right)T$

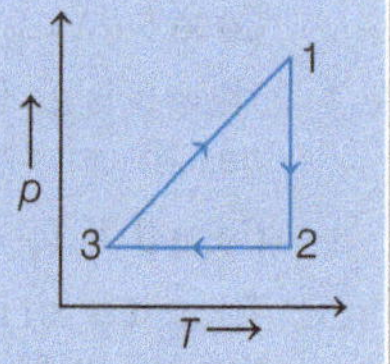

i.e. *p-T* graph will be a straight line passing through origin.

Adiabatic Process

In an adiabatic process, there is no exchange of heat between system and the surroundings. NEET 2019

In this process p, V, T changes but $\Delta Q = 0$.

Following are the important points related to this process

(i) **Process equation** is $pV^{\gamma} =$ constant.

where, $\gamma = \dfrac{C_p}{C_V}$

Above equation can be written in other ways as $TV^{\gamma-1} =$ constant or $p^{1-\gamma}T^{\gamma} =$ constant.

(ii) **Work done** is $W = \dfrac{\mu R(T_1 - T_2)}{\gamma - 1} = \dfrac{p_1V_1 - p_2V_2}{\gamma - 1}$

(iii) **Indicator diagram** slope of *p-V* curve in an adiabatic process is γ times the slope of *p-V* curve in isothermal process.

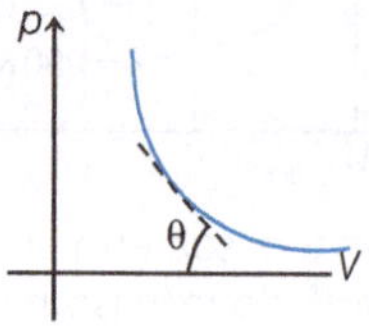

i.e. $\tan\theta = -\gamma\left(\dfrac{p}{V}\right)$

As $\gamma > 1$, therefore the curve in *p-V* diagram is steeper in an adiabatic process than in an isothermal process.

(iv) **First law in adiabatic process** In this process, $\Delta Q = 0$

$\therefore \qquad \Delta U = -\Delta W$

If $\Delta W =$ positive, then $\Delta U =$ negative, so temperature decreases, i.e. adiabatic expansion produces cooling.

If $\Delta W =$ negative, then $\Delta U =$ positive, so temperature increases, i.e. adiabatic compression produces heating.

(v) **Specific heat** As, $\Delta Q = 0$

$\therefore$ Specific heat of a gas during adiabatic change is zero.

Isochoric Process

It is a process in which volume is kept constant.

Following are the important points related to this process

(i) **Process equation** is $\dfrac{p}{T} =$ constant.

(ii) **Work done** is $W = p \cdot \Delta V = 0$ as $V =$ constant.

(iii) **Indicator diagram** *p-V* curve is a straight line parallel to pressure axis. NEET 2020

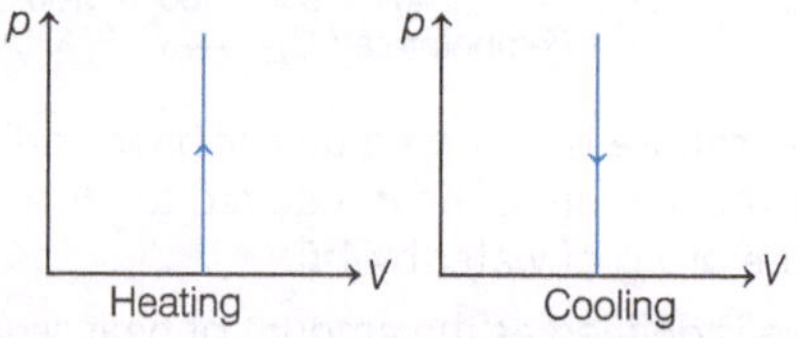

(iv) In isochoric cooling, pressure and temperature both decrease. Hence, ΔQ and ΔU both are negative.

(v) In isochoric expansion, pressure and temperature both increase. Hence, ΔQ and ΔU both are positive.

Isobaric Process

It is a process in which pressure is kept constant.

Following are the important points related to this process

(i) **Process equation** is $\dfrac{V}{T} =$ constant.

(ii) **Work done** is $W = p(V_2 - V_1) = \mu R(T_2 - T_1)$.

(iii) ***p-V* curve** is a straight line parallel to volume axis.

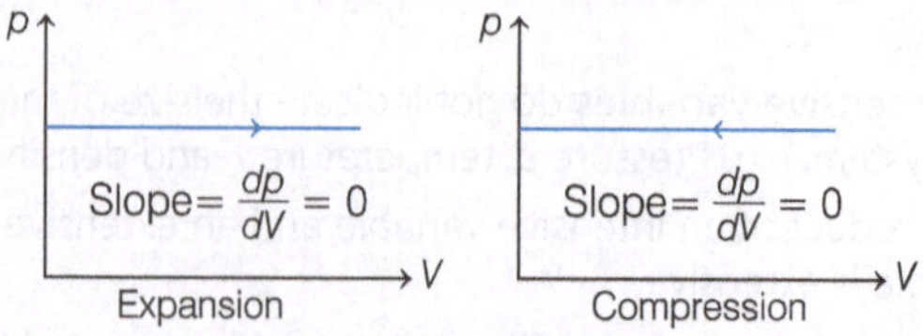

(iv) In isobaric process, due to change in temperature, internal energy changes. Thus, heat absorbed goes partly to increase internal energy and partly to do work.

(v) In isobaric expansion, temperature increases. So, change in internal energy is positive. Since, volume increases, hence work done and heat flow in the system is positive.

(vi) In isobaric compression due to decrease in temperature change in internal energy is negative. Also, due to decrease in volume, ΔW and ΔQ both are negative.

Cyclic Process

Is a process in which the system returns to its initial state.

Following are the important points related to this process

(i) As initial and final states are the same, so $\Delta U = 0$ for a cyclic process.

(ii) Total heat absorbed equals the work done by the system.

(iii) Work done during the cyclic process can be computed from area enclosed by the cycle on *p*-*V* curve.

For Concept Master Video

Note If the cycle is clockwise, work done by the system is positive and if the cycle is anti-clockwise, work done by the system is negative.

Marks Maximiser

Comparison between Isothermal and Adiabatic Curves

(i) When compressed to the same volume from the same initial state.

Final pressure : $p_a < p_b$

Final temperature : $T_a < T_b$

Work done : $W_a < W_b$

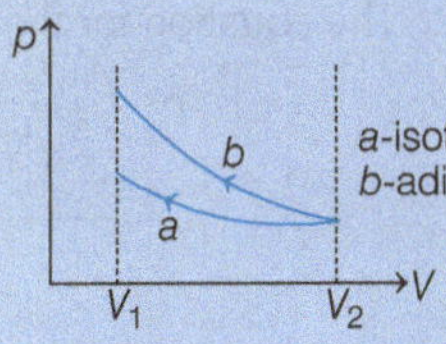

For Concept Master Video

(ii) When expanded to the same volume from the same initial state.

Final pressure : $p_a > p_b$

Final temperature : $T_a > T_b$

Work done : $W_a > W_b$

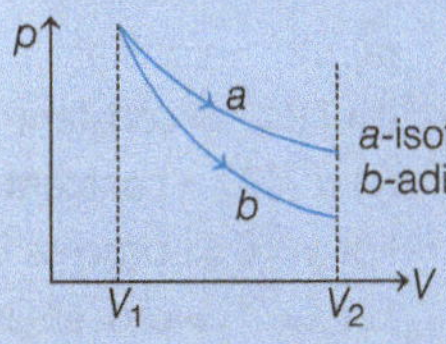

Second Law of Thermodynamics

It put a restriction on the first law of thermodynamics.

The second law implies that no heat engine can have efficiency η equal to 1 or no refrigerator can have coefficient of performance equal to infinity.

Two statements of Kelvin-Planck and Clausius put restrictions on the possibility of perfect heat engine and perfect refrigerator, respectively.

Kelvin-Planck statement No process is possible whose sole result is the absorption of heat from a reservoir and the complete conversion of the heat into work.

Clausius statement No process is possible whose sole result is the transfer of heat from a colder body to hotter body.

Reversible and Irreversible Processes

- **Reversible process** A reversible process is one which can be retraced in opposite direction by changing the external condition infinitesimally.
- **The conditions for reversible process are**
  (i) The pressure and temperature must not differ from those of the surrounding at any stage of the cycle of operation.
  (ii) All the processes taking place in the cycle must be infinitely slow.
  (iii) The dissipative forces such as friction, viscosity, inelasticity, etc., should be absent.
  (iv) There should not be any loss of energy due to conduction, convection or radiation during the cycle of operation.
- **Irreversible process** Any process which cannot be retraced in the reverse direction exactly is known as irreversible process.
- Most of the processes occurring in the nature are irreversible.
- **The conditions of irreversible process are**
  (i) The conditions for thermodynamics equilibrium, i.e. mechanical, thermal or chemical equilibrium are not satisfied because a natural process does not take place quasi-statically.
  (ii) Dissipative effects, such as inelasticity, viscosity, friction, eddy-formation, etc., are always present.

Carnot Engine

- Carnot engine is a theoretical engine which is free from all practical imperfections and it has maximum efficiency and it is an ideal heat engine.

  It is a reversible heat engine operating between two temperatures.
- As the engine works, the working substance of the engine undergoes a cycle known as **Carnot cycle**. A Carnot cycle is as shown in the figure below.

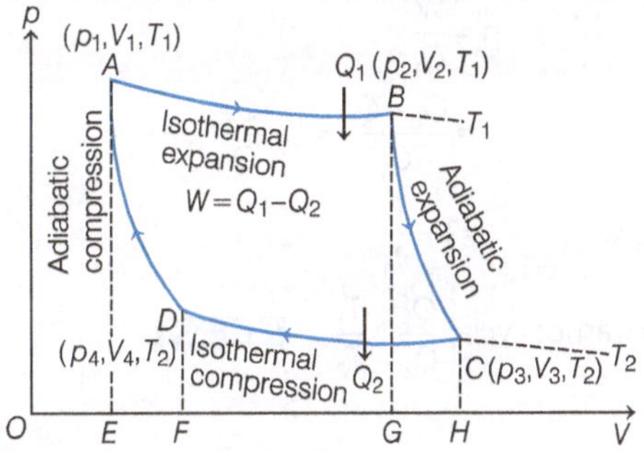

- A Carnot's cycle contains the following four processes
  (i) **Isothermal expansion (*AB*)** In process *AB*, the substance absorbs heat Q_1 from the source at T_1 and does work W_1 given by
  Isothermal expansion
  $$W_{A\to B} = W_1 = Q_1 = \mu RT_1 \ln\left(\frac{V_2}{V_1}\right)$$
  (ii) **Adiabatic expansion (*BC*)** This operation is represented by the adiabatic curve *BC*. In this process, there is no transfer of heat, the temperature of the substance falls to T_2 and it does some external work W_2 given by
  Adiabatic expansion, $W_{B\to C} = W_2 = \dfrac{\mu R(T_1 - T_2)}{\gamma - 1}$
  (iii) **Isothermal compression (*CD*)** This operation is represented by the isotherm *CD*. In this process, the substance rejects heat Q_2 to the sink at T_2 and work W_3, is done on the substance given by
  Isothermal compression, $W_{C\to D} = W_3$
  $$= Q_2 = \mu RT_2 \ln\left(\frac{V_3}{V_4}\right)$$
  (iv) **Adiabatic compression (*DA*)** This operation is represented by adiabatic curve *DA*. In this process, work W_4 is done on the substance and is given by
  Adiabatic compression,
  $$W_{D\to A} = W_4 = \mu R\left(\frac{T_1 - T_2}{\gamma - 1}\right)$$
- **Net work done during the complete cycle**,
  $$W = W_1 + W_2 + (-W_3) + (-W_4)$$
  $$= W_1 - W_3 = \text{Area } ABCD \text{ (As, } W_2 = W_4)$$
  $$= \mu RT_1 \ln\left(\frac{V_2}{V_1}\right) - \mu RT_2 \ln\left(\frac{V_3}{V_4}\right)$$
- The net work done per cycle by the engine is numerically equal to the area of the loop representing the Carnot's cycle.
- **Efficiency of Carnot cycle** The efficiency of engine is defined as the ratio of work done to the heat supplied, i.e.
  $$\eta = \frac{W}{Q_1}$$
  $$= \frac{Q_1 - Q_2}{Q_1} = 1 - \frac{Q_2}{Q_1}$$
  $$= 1 - \frac{T_2}{T_1}$$
  ∵ For a Carnot cycle, $\dfrac{Q_1}{Q_2} = \dfrac{T_1}{T_2}$ NEET 2023

- **Carnot's theorem** states that
  (i) A heat engine working between the two given temperatures T_1 of hot reservoir, i.e. source and T_2 of cold reservoir, i.e. sink cannot have efficiency more than that of the Carnot engine.
  (ii) The efficiency of the Carnot engine is independent of the nature of the working substance.
- All reversible heat engine working between same temperature are equally efficient and no heat engine can be more efficient than Carnot engine (as it is ideal).

Caution Points

- Temperature of a body depends on its average internal energy and not on its kinetic energy.
- Heat capacity depends on the process when heat is supplied to the system.

PYQ Notes

1. Work done is polytropic process, $W = \dfrac{-nRdT}{x-1}$, $x \neq 1$
   (Analogous to the work done in adiabatic process
   $W = \dfrac{nR(T_1 - T_2)}{x-1} = \dfrac{p_1V_1 - p_2V_2}{x-1}$ $(x \neq 1)$
   [NEET 2021]
2. The equation for the polytropic process are

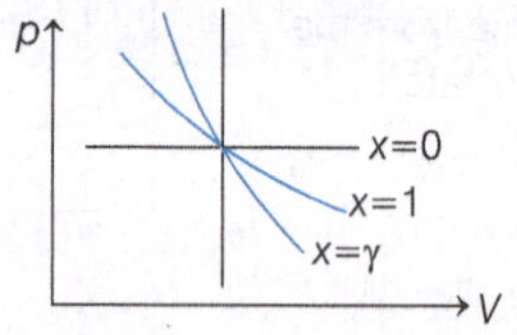

   (a) pV^x = constant
   (b) TV^{x-1} = constant
   (c) $p^{1-x}T^x$ = constant
   For $x = 0 \Rightarrow$ process is isobaric (p = constant)
   For $x = 1 \Rightarrow$ process is isothermal (pV = constant)
   For $x = \gamma \Rightarrow$ process is adiabatic (pV^γ = constant)
   [JEE Main 2019]
3. **Polytropic Process** The process that follows the given equation are called polytropic processes.
   i.e. pV^x = constant
   where, x is called the **polytropic index of compression or expansion** whose value lies between $-\infty$ to $+\infty$. **[NEET 2016]**
4. In isothermal quasi-static processes, heat is absorbed or given out by the system even though at every stage the gas has the same temperature as that of the surrounding reservoir. This is possible because of the infinitesimal difference in temperature between the system and the reservoir.
   [JEE Main 2016]

Step by Step

Mastering NCERT

- Concept Builders
- Topical Questions
- Assertion and Reason Questions
- Statement Based
- Matching Type
- Numerical Type
- NCERT Exemplar
- Past Exams MCQs
- Skill Boosters

Concept Builders

1 Which law suggest that when two systems A and B are in thermal equilibrium with a third system separately and both are in thermal equilibrium with each other too?

2 Which thermodynamic variable is defined by zeroth law?

3 Which type of molecular motion is responsible for internal energy of a monoatomic gas ?

4 In case of an ideal gas, internal energy depends only on the .... (pressure/temperature) but in case of a real gas, it depends on .... (pressure/volume) and temperature.

5 In a cyclic process, the total heat absorbed by a system is equal to the work done by the system because internal energy is a state function. [T/F]

6 Which law of thermodynamics tells about the conversion of mechanical energy into heat energy?

7 ΔQ and ΔW in general are path ...... (dependent / independent).

8 Molar specific heat capacity of a solid at constant pressure is $3R$. [T/F]

9 In an isothermal process, heat transferred from the reservoir to system does effect the temperature of the reservoir. [T/F]

10 A quasi-static isothermal expansion of an ideal gas in a cylinder fitted with a frictionless movable piston is a reversible process . [T/F]

11 In an isothermal quasi-static process, the gas has the same temperature throughout the change of volume. [T/F]

12 If an ideal gas is compressed isothermally, then the heat is .... (released / absorbed) by the system.

13 In an isothermal process, if the volume of an ideal gas is halved , then work done by the gas is .... (positive / negative)

14 What is the value of specific heat of a gas in a adiabatic process?

15 In an adiabatic process, the state of gas is changed from (p_1, V_1, T_1) to (p_2, V_2, T_2), so $T_1V_1^{\gamma-1} = T_2V_2^{\gamma-1}$. [T/F]

16 When a cyclic process is represented clockwise, work done in the process is .... (positive/negative).

17 In an adiabatic process, $W > 0$ and $T_2 < T_1$. [T/F]

18 A process is ...... (reversible / irreversible) only, if a system is in equilibrium with the surrounding at every stage.

19 The stirring of a liquid in thermal contact with a reservoir will increase the internal energy of reservoir. It is a reversible process. [T/F]

20 Which cycle is used as a standard of performance of all heat engines operating between a high and a low temperature.

Topical Questions

Thermal Equilibrium and Zeroth Law of Thermodynamics

1 In the figure below, two systems A and B are separated by an insulating fixed wall (adiabatic wall) and also insulated from surroundings by insulated wall.

NCERT Pg. 227

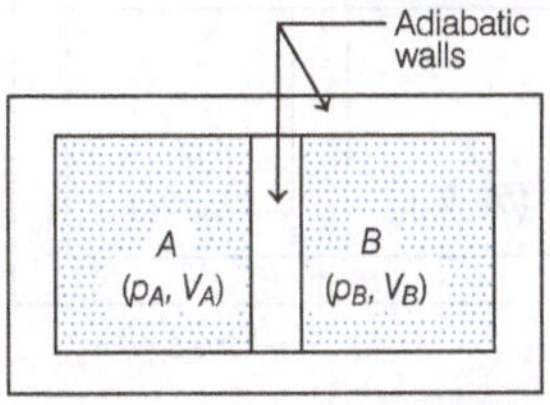

Choose the correct option regarding above information.
(a) The pressures of A and B will change with time.
(b) The temperatures of A and B will change with time.
(c) The thermodynamic states of A and B will not change with time.
(d) The temperatures of A change but not B.

2 If two systems are in thermal equilibrium with each other, it means their **NCERT Pg. 227**
(a) masses are equal, temperatures may be unequal
(b) temperatures are equal
(c) masses and temperatures both are equal
(d) masses are unequal but temperature is equal

3 If a system is in thermodynamic equilibrium with its surroundings, it means **NCERT Pg. 227**
(a) temperature of system and surroundings must be same
(b) pressure and volume of system and surroundings must be same
(c) pressure, volume and temperature of system and surroundings may be different
(d) there is no chemical change in system

4 Choose the correct option from the following. **NCERT Pg. 228**
(a) Zeroth law gives the concept of temperature.
(b) Temperature measures the 'hotness' of the body.
(c) Heat flows from the body at higher temperature to the one at a lower temperature, until thermal equilibrium is attained.
(d) All of the above

5 According to zeroth law, which physical quantity must have same value for the two systems to be in thermal equilibrium? **NCERT Pg. 228**
(a) Pressure (b) Temperature
(c) Volume (d) Composition

6 According to zeroth law of thermodynamics, if two systems A and B are separately in equilibrium with C, then **NCERT Pg. 228**
(a) $T_A = T_B$ (b) $T_A > T_C$, $T_B > T_C$ and $T_A = T_B$
(c) $T_A = T_C$ and $T_A \neq T_B$ (d) $T_A < T_C$, $T_B < T_C$ and $T_A = T_B$

7 The two gases are separated by a fixed diathermic wall with initial states as (p_A, V_A) and (p_B, V_B). **NCERT Pg. 228**

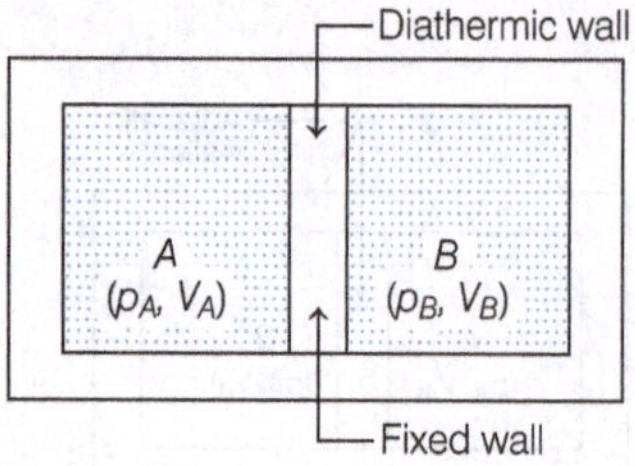

Choose the correct statement.
(a) The thermodynamic states of A and B will not change with time.
(b) There will be a flow of energy between the two systems until the equilibrium is attained.
(c) The states of the two systems will change until the equilibrium is attained.
(d) Both (b) and (c)

Heat, Internal Energy and Work : First Law of Thermodynamics

8 The internal energy of a gas contained in a movable box moving with a constant speed v **NCERT Pg. 229**

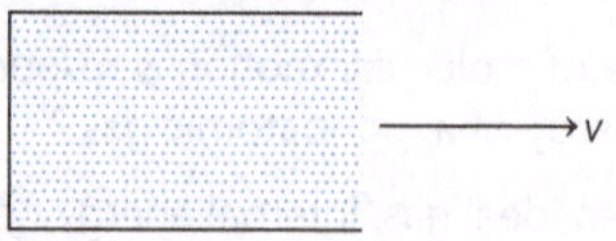

(a) depends on v
(b) does not depend on v
(c) depends only on molecular energies
(d) Both (b) and (c)

9 Consider a system to be a certain mass of gas contained in a cylinder with movable piston as shown in the figure.

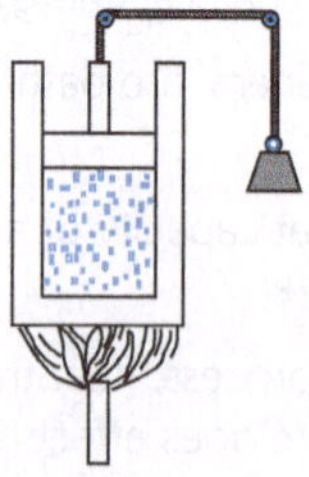

The state of the gas and hence its internal energy can be changed by **NCERT Pg. 229**
(a) putting the cylinder in contact with the body at a higher temperature than gas
(b) pushing the piston down
(c) Either (a) or (b)
(d) Neither (a) nor (b)

10 The internal energy of a system could be changed **NCERT Pg. 230**
(a) by extracting heat from the system
(b) by doing work on the system
(c) if the system does some work on the surroundings
(d) All of the above

11 A system is provided with 200 cal of heat and the work done by the system on the surroundings is 40 J. Then, its internal energy **NCERT Pg. 230**

(a) increases by 600 J (b) decreases by 800 J
(c) increases by 800 J (d) decreases by 50 J

12 A perfect gas goes from state 1 to state 2 by absorbing heat of 7×10^5 J and doing external work of 5.5×10^5 J. It is now transferred between the same two states in another process in which it absorbs 10^5 J of heat. In the second process, **NCERT Pg. 230**

(a) work done on the gas is 10^5 J
(b) work done on the gas is 0.5×10^5 J
(c) work done by the gas is 10^5 J
(d) work done by the gas is 0.5×10^5 J

13 An electric appliance supplies 6000 J/min heat to the system. If the system delivers a power of 90 W. How long it would take to increase the internal energy by 2.5×10^3 J? **NCERT Pg. 230**

(a) 2.5×10^2 s (b) 4.1×10^1 s
(c) 2.4×10^3 s (d) 2.5×10^1 s

14 A gas can be taken from A to B *via* two different processes ACB and ADB.

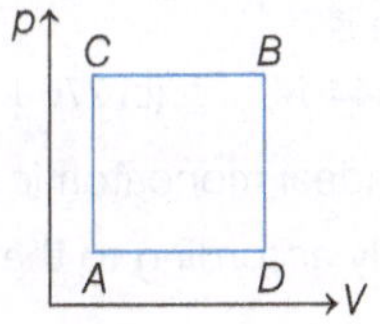

When path ACB is used 60 J of heat flows into the system and 30 J of work is done by the system. If path ADB is used work done by the system is 10 J, the heat flow into the system in path ADB is **NCERT Pg. 230**

(a) 80 J (b) 40 J (c) 100 J (d) 20 J

15 A gas is compressed at a constant pressure of 45 N/m^2 from a volume of 15 m^3 to 10 m^3. Also, 100 J of energy is added to the gas through heating. The internal energy of the gas is **NCERT Pg. 231**

(a) 325 J (b) 425 J
(c) 350 J (d) 450 J

16 1 cm^3 of water at its boiling point absorbs 550 cal of heat to become steam of volume 1700 cm^3 the atmospheric pressure is 1.013×10^5 Nm^{-2} and the mechanical equivalent of heat is 4.19 cal, the energy spent in this process in overcoming intermolecular forces is **NCERT Pg. 231**

(a) 499 cal (b) 508.9 cal
(c) 509.8 cal (d) 500 cal

17 If the system is a gas in a cylinder with a movable piston as shown in the figure, then **NCERT Pg. 231**

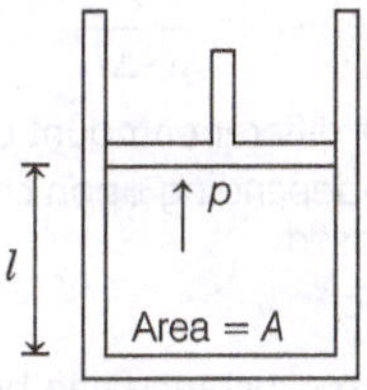

(a) $\Delta W = pV$
(b) $\Delta W = \Delta pV$
(c) $\Delta W = p\Delta V$
(d) $\Delta W = p\Delta V + V\Delta p$

18 An ideal monoatomic gas is taken from A to B by the following three ways p, q, r as shown in the given p-V curve. **NCERT Pg. 231**

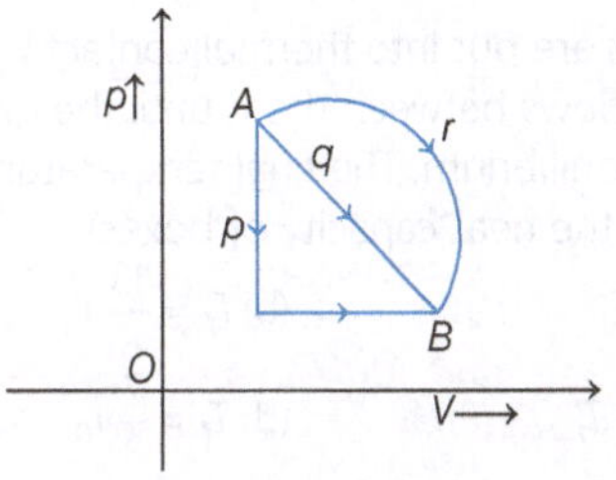

Then, amongst which of these ways, the internal energy change would be same?

(a) p and r (b) q and r
(c) p and q
(d) For all the ways internal energy change is same

Specific Heat Capacity

19 The specific heat of a gas at constant pressure is $C_p = 4.3 \times 10^3$ cal/kg°C and at constant volume is $C_V = 3.3 \times 10^3$ cal/kg°C. If 1 kg of the gas is heated from 10°C to 20°C at constant pressure, then the external work done on the gas to maintain it at constant pressure is **NCERT Pg. 231**

(a) 10^5 cal (b) 10^4 cal
(c) 5×10^3 cal (d) 10^{17} cal

20 A monoatomic gas is supplied the heat Q very slowly keeping the pressure constant. The work done by the gas will be **NCERT Pg. 231**

(a) $\frac{2}{3}Q$ (b) $\frac{3}{5}Q$
(c) $\frac{2}{5}Q$ (d) $\frac{1}{5}Q$

21 Molar specific heat capacity C of a substance having μ moles **NCERT Pg. 231**

(a) can be represented by $\frac{1}{\mu}\frac{\Delta Q}{\Delta T}$

(b) is different for different amount of substance

(c) can be varied depending upon change in the temperature rised

(d) Both (a) and (c)

22 Heat capacity of a substance can be increased

(a) by decreasing the mass of the substance **NCERT Pg. 231**

(b) by increasing the temperature

(c) by increasing the mass of the substance

(d) Both (b) and (c)

23 A rigid insulated box A containing one mole of nitrogen at temperature T_0 and another rigid insulated box B containing one mole of helium at temperature $\frac{8}{3}T_0$. The two boxes are put into thermal contact with each other and heat flows between them until the gases attain thermal equilibrium. The final temperature of the gases is (ignore the heat capacity of boxes) **NCERT Pg. 231**

(a) $T_f = \frac{3}{7}T_0$ (b) $T_f = \frac{13}{8}T_0$

(c) $T_f = \frac{8}{13}T_f$ (d) $T_f = \frac{7}{3}T_0$

24 The amount of heat required to raise the temperature of 40 g of oxygen at room temperature by 60°C at constant volume is ($R = 8.3$ J mol^{-1}K^{-1}) **NCERT Pg. 231**

(a) 1.52 kJ (b) 1.56 kJ (c) 1.62 kJ (d) 1.63 kJ

25 Mechanical equivalent of heat is equal to the amount of

(a) work done to produce 1 cal heat **NCERT Pg. 232**

(b) a conversion factor between calorie and joule

(c) Both (a) and (b)

(d) Neither (a) nor (b)

26 From the following graphs given in the options, variation of specific heat capacity of water with temperature is correctly respresented in **NCERT Pg. 232**

(a)

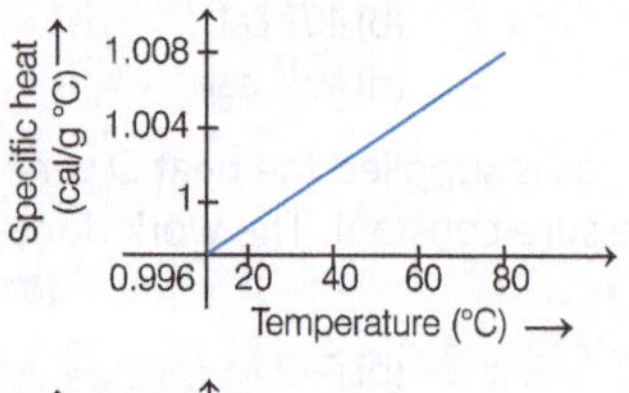

(b)

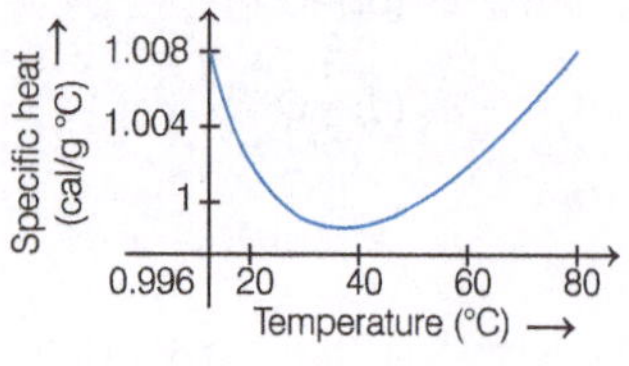

(c)

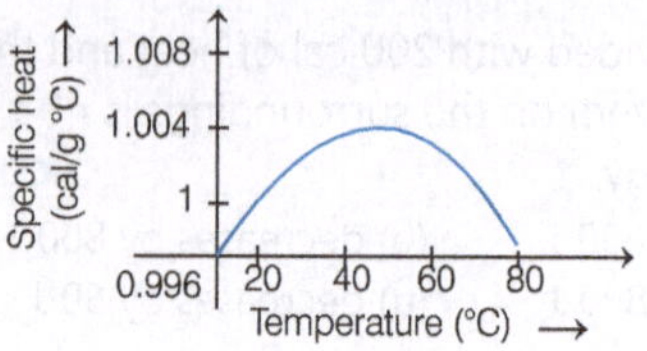

(d)

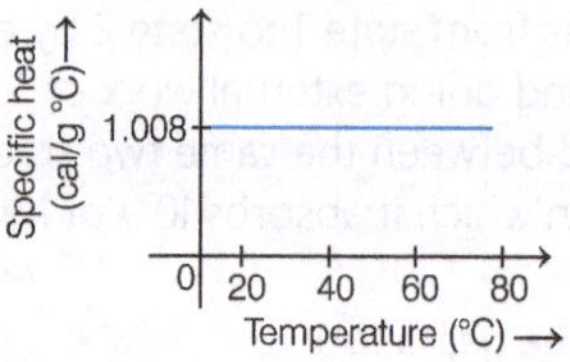

27 For an ideal gas, the molar specific heat capacity at constant pressure and volume are C_p and C_V, respectively. Choose the correct option. **NCERT Pg. 232**

(a) $C_V = \left(\frac{\Delta U}{\Delta T}\right)_V$ (b) $C_p = \left(\frac{\Delta U}{\Delta T}\right)_p + \left(\frac{p\Delta V}{\Delta T}\right)_p$

(c) $p\left(\frac{\Delta V}{\Delta T}\right)_p = R$ (d) All of these

28 310 J of heat is required to raise the temperature of 2 mol of an ideal gas at constant pressure from 25°C to 35°C. The amount of heat required to raise the temperature of the gas through the same range at constant volume is **NCERT Pg. 232**

(a) 384 J (b) 144 J (c) 276 J (d) 452 J

29 One mole of an ideal monoatomic gas at temperature T_0 expands slowly according to the law $\frac{p}{V}$ = constant. If the final temperature is $3T_0$, then amount of heat supplied is **NCERT Pg. 232**

(a) $2RT_0$ (b) $\frac{3}{2}RT_0$ (c) $\frac{1}{2}RT_0$ (d) $4RT_0$

30 An ideal gas having molar specific heat capacity at constant volume is $\frac{3}{2}R$, the molar specific heat capacity at constant pressure is **NCERT Pg. 232**

(a) $\frac{1}{2}R$ (b) $\frac{5}{2}R$ (c) $\frac{7}{2}R$ (d) $\frac{9}{2}R$

31 The pressure in a monoatomic gas increases from p_0 to $3p_0$ when its volume increases from V_0 to $2V_0$. **NCERT Pg. 232**

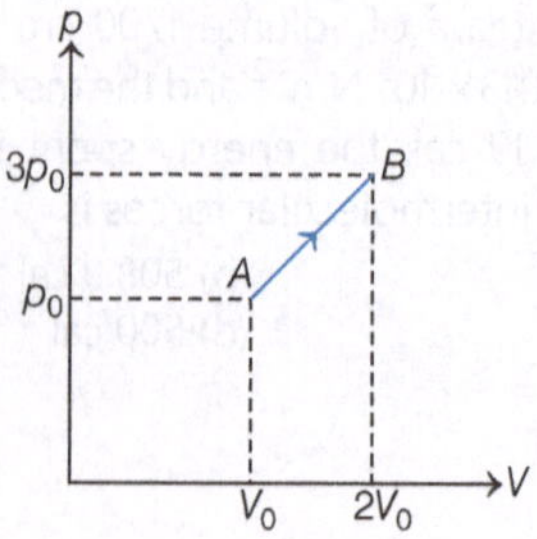

The increase in internal energy is

(a) $15p_0V_0$ (b) $7.5p_0V_0$
(c) $12.5p_0V_0$ (d) $5p_0V_0$

Thermodynamic State Variables and Equation of State

32 Amongst the following variables, state variable is (are) **NCERT Pg. 232**

(a) heat (b) work
(c) internal energy (d) All of these

33 Consider a situation in which a mixture of petrol vapour and air ignited by a spark. Then, the gases undergo explosion **NCERT Pg. 233**

(a) initially have non-uniform temperature and pressure
(b) cannot be described by state variables initially
(c) may eventually attains an equilibrium state with its surroundings after a certain time
(d) All of the above

34 A system in equilibrium is divided into two equal parts. The system before and after the division, with respective state variables are as shown below. **NCERT Pg. 233**

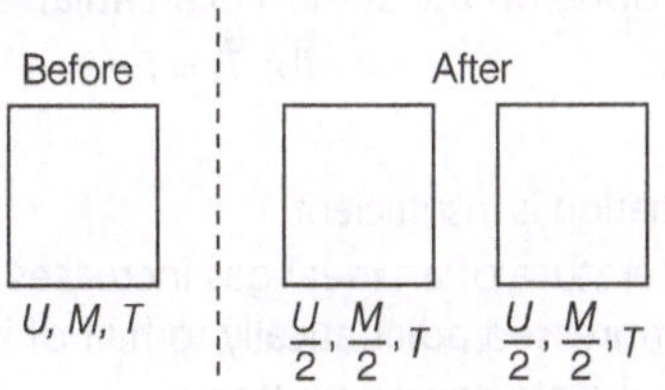

Then, from the above, we can say that

(a) U is an extensive state variable, whereas M and T are intensive state variables
(b) T is an extensive state variable, whereas U and M are intensive state variables
(c) U and M are extensive state variables, whereas T is intensive state variable
(d) U, M and T all are extensive state variables

35 The value of $\frac{pV}{T}$ for 2 moles of an ideal gas is nearly equal to **NCERT Pg. 233**

(a) R (b) $2R$ (c) $\frac{R}{2}$ (d) $3R$

36 Which is an intensive property? **NCERT Pg. 233**

(a) Volume (b) Mass
(c) Refractive index (d) Weight

37 Choose the correct statement from the following. **NCERT Pg. 233**

(a) Neglecting the small intermolecular forces in gas, its internal energy is just the sum of kinetic energies associated with various random motion of its molecules.
(b) A gas in a given state has a certain amount of heat.
(c) A gas in a given state has a certain amount of work.
(d) Both (b) and (c)

38 A system as shown in figure below, initially at state (p, T) is taken to state at (p', T') *via* a quasi-static process. Then, choose the correct statement. **NCERT Pg. 233**

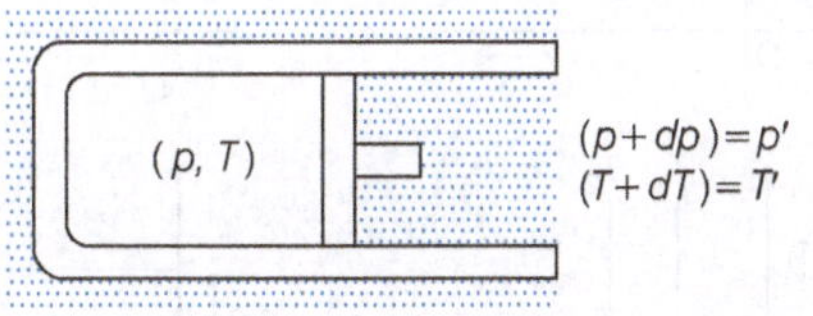

(a) External pressure of the system should be changed abruptly.
(b) Quasi-static process is not a hypothetical concept and can never be achieved by any way.
(c) Temperature can be changed by introducing an infinitesimal temperature difference between the system and surrounding reservoir.
(d) Various stages of the process will be in non-equilibrium state.

Thermodynamic Processes

39 A quasi-static process means **NCERT Pg. 233**

(a) a nearly static process
(b) that the change in p, V and T of the system occur in such a way that it remains in equilibrium at every instant with its surroundings
(c) Both (a) and (b)
(d) Neither (a) nor (b)

40 When heat is given to a gas in an isothermal change, the result will be **NCERT Pg. 234**

(a) increase in internal energy
(b) rise in temperature
(c) external work done by the gas
(d) external work done as well as increase in internal energy

41 For the given isothermal process $A \to B$ of an ideal gas, area under the graph is 20 J, then **NCERT Pg. 234**

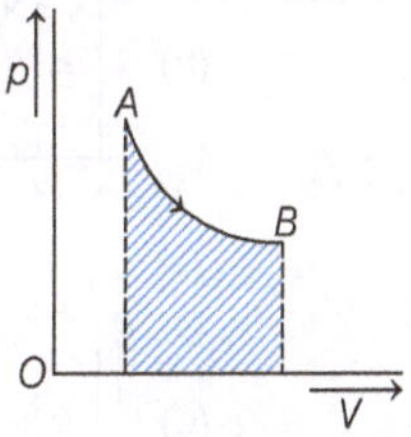

(a) $\Delta Q = 0$ (b) $\Delta Q = +20$ J
(c) $\Delta U = -20$ J (d) $\Delta U = 20$ J

42 Identity the graph which correctly represents an isotherm at temperatures T_1 and $T_2 (T_2 > T_1)$. **NCERT Pg. 234**

(a)
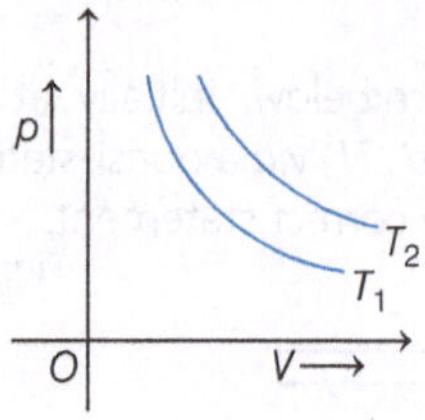

(b)
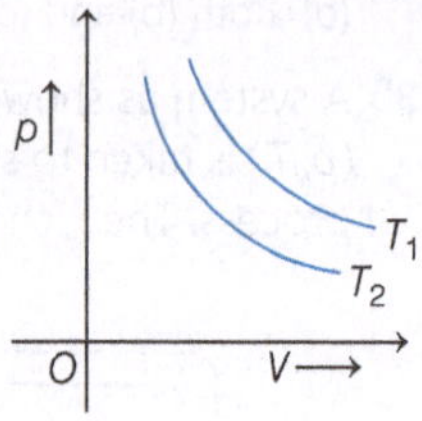

(c)
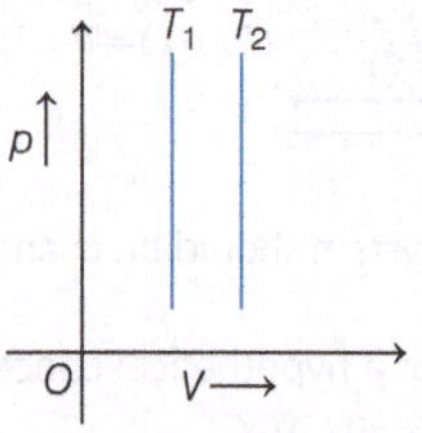

(d)
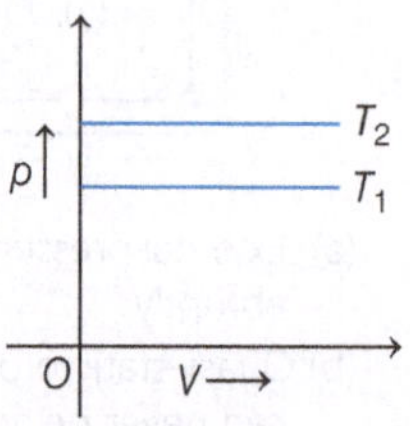

43 Among given curves, which one could represent isothermal process? **NCERT Pg. 234**

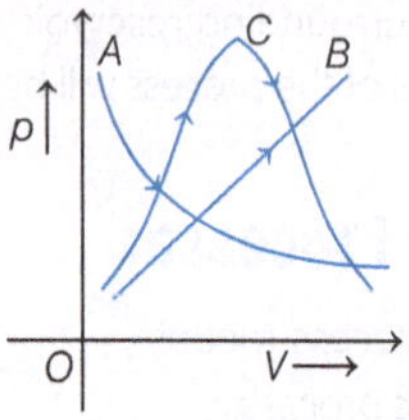

(a) Curve A (b) Curve B
(c) Curve C
(d) None of the curves could represent isothermal process

44 10 mol of an ideal gas at constant temperature 500 K is compressed from 50 L to 5 L. Work done in the process is (given, $R = 8.31 \text{ J mol}^{-1} \text{ K}^{-1}$) **NCERT Pg. 234**

(a) -1.2×10^4 J (b) -2.4×10^4 J
(c) -4.8×10^4 J (d) -9.6×10^4 J

45 1 mol of an ideal gas goes from an initial state A to final state B *via* two processes. It first undergoes isothermal expansion from volume V to $3V$ and then its volume is reduced from $3V$ to V at constant pressure. The correct p-V diagram representing the two processes is **NCERT Pg. 234**

(a)
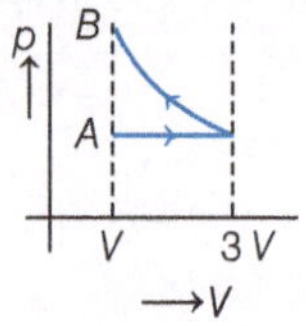

(b)
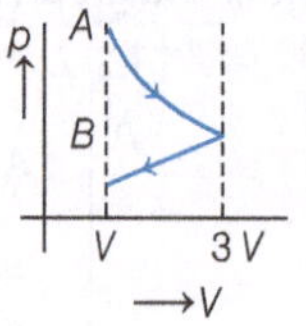

(c)
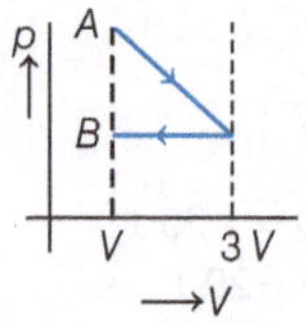

(d)
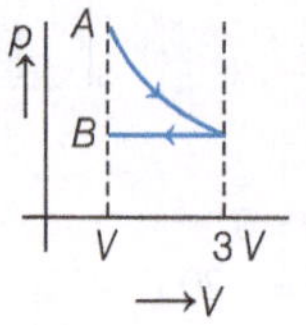

46 The slopes of isothermal and adiabatic curves are related as **NCERT Pg. 234**

(a) $\left(\frac{dp}{dV}\right)_{\text{iso}} = \left(\frac{dp}{dV}\right)_{\text{ad}}$ (b) $\left(\frac{dp}{dV}\right)_{\text{iso}} = \gamma \left(\frac{dp}{dV}\right)$

(c) $\left(\frac{dp}{dV}\right)_{\text{ad}} = \frac{3}{2}\left(\frac{dp}{dV}\right)_{\text{iso}}$ (d) $\left(\frac{dp}{dV}\right)_{\text{ad}} = \gamma \left(\frac{dp}{dV}\right)_{\text{iso}}$

47 Two identical cylinders A and B contains same ideal gas at same temperature T and volume V. The mass of gas A is m_A and that of B is m_B. The gas in each cylinder is now allowed to expand isothermally to the same final volume $3V$. The change in the pressure in A and B are Δp and $2\Delta p$ respectively, then **NCERT Pg. 234**

(a) $3m_A = 2m_B$ (b) $2m_A = m_B$
(c) $5m_A = m_B$ (d) $4m_A = 3m_B$

48 For an isothermal expansion or compression, (where ΔW_1 and ΔW_2 are the net work for expansion and compression, respectively) **NCERT Pg. 235**

(a) $\Delta W_1 = -\text{ve}\,;\, \Delta W_2 = +\text{ve}$
(b) $\Delta W_1 = \Delta W_2 ;\, \Delta W_2 = -\text{ve}$
(c) $\Delta W_1 = +\text{ve}\,;\, \Delta W_2 = -\text{ve}$
(d) $\Delta W_1 = \Delta W_2$, at every stage

49 If work is done on the system in an adiabatic process, **NCERT Pg. 235**

(a) $T_f < T_i$ (b) $T_f = T_i$
(c) $T_f > T_i$
(d) information is insufficient

50 The temperature of an ideal gas increases to 2 times when compressed adiabatically to half of its volume. Its equation of state can be written as **NCERT Pg. 235**

(a) $pV^{3/2} = \text{constant}$ (b) $pV^{4/3} = \text{constant}$
(c) $pV^{1/2} = \text{constant}$ (d) $pV^2 = \text{constant}$

51 Amongst the following relations which is true in the case of an adiabatic process, where $\gamma = C_p/C_V$. **NCERT Pg. 235**

(a) $p^{1-\gamma}T^{\gamma} = \text{constant}$ (b) $p^{\gamma}T^{1-\gamma} = \text{constant}$
(c) $pT^{\gamma} = \text{constant}$ (d) $p^{\gamma}T = \text{constant}$

52 In an adiabatic process, when pressure is increased by $\frac{2}{3}$%. If $\frac{C_p}{C_V} = \frac{3}{2}$, then the volume decreases by about **NCERT Pg. 235**

(a) $\frac{4}{9}$% (b) $\frac{2}{3}$% (c) 4% (d) $\frac{9}{4}$%

53 A gas is taken from V_i to V_f by two processes, one is isothermal and other is adiabatic.

Choose the correct option regarding the p-V diagram for two processes. **NCERT Pg. 235**

(a) $(\text{Slope})_{\text{isothermal}} = (\text{Slope})_{\text{adiabatic}}$
(b) $(\text{Slope})_{\text{isothermal}} > (\text{Slope})_{\text{adiabatic}}$
(c) $(\text{Slope})_{\text{isothermal}} < (\text{Slope})_{\text{adiabatic}}$
(d) Information is insufficient

54 In an isothermal reversible expansion, the volume of 128 g of oxygen at 25°C is increased from 75 L to 150 L. The amount of work done by the gas is **NCERT Pg. 235**

(a) $2.3 \times 900\, R \log_{10} 2$ (b) $R \log_{10} 2$
(c) $2.3 \times 1192\, R \log_{10} 2$ (d) $900\, R \log_{10} 2$

55 One mole of an ideal gas at temperature T_0 expands according to the law $\frac{p}{V^2}$ = constant. The work done by the gas till the temperature of gas becomes $2T_0$ is **NCERT Pg. 235**

(a) $\frac{1}{2}RT_0$ (b) $\frac{1}{3}RT_0$
(c) $\frac{2}{3}RT_0$ (d) $\frac{1}{3}R(5T_0)$

56 In an isobaric process, the work done by a diatomic gas is 10 J, the heat given to the gas will be [C_p for diatomic gas $= \frac{7}{2}R$] **NCERT Pg. 235**

(a) 35 J (b) 30 J
(c) 45 J (d) 60 J

57 An ideal gas at a pressure of 1 atm and temperature of 27°C is compressed adiabatically until its pressure becomes 8 times the initial pressure, then the final temperature is $\left(\gamma = \frac{3}{2}\right)$ **NCERT Pg. 235**

(a) 627°C (b) 527°C
(c) 427°C (d) 327°C

58 An ideal gas undergoes a process in which pressure and density varies as shown in the graph. **NCERT Pg. 235**

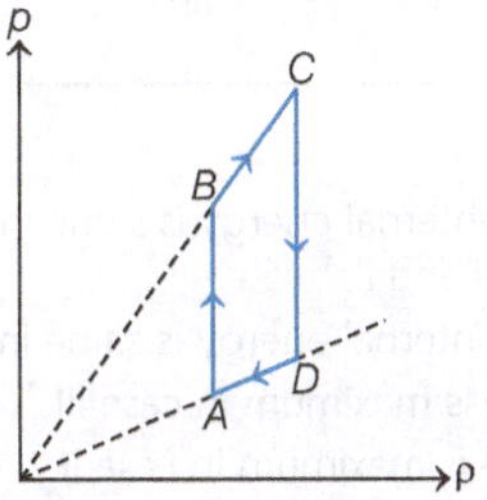

(a) In the process *BC*, internal energy of the gas remains constant
(b) In the process *AB*, work done by the gas is negative
(c) In the process *AB*, work done by the gas is positive
(d) None of the above

59 If a gas is heated at constant pressure, then the fraction of heat supplied used for external work is given by **NCERT Pg. 235**

(a) $\left(\frac{1}{\gamma^2} - 1\right)$ (b) $\left(1 - \frac{1}{\gamma}\right)$ (c) $\left(\frac{1}{\gamma} - 1\right)$ (d) $\frac{1}{\gamma}$

60 Diatomic gas at pressure 2 atm is compressed adiabatically, so that its temperature rises from 25°C to 919°C. The pressure of the gas in its final state is ($\gamma = 1.4$) **NCERT Pg. 235**

(a) 68.7 atm (b) 256 atm
(c) 8 atm (d) 225 atm

61 One mole of a gas expands with temperature according to relation $V = AT^{3/2}$. Work done when the temperature changes by 80 K is **NCERT Pg. 235**

(a) 100 R (b) 80 R (c) 120 R (d) 70 R

62 For a gas, $p = \frac{AT^2 - 2BT}{V}$, where p is the pressure, V is volume and A, B are constants. The work done by the gas as its temperature changes from T_1 to T_2, while pressure remaining constant is **NCERT Pg. 235**

(a) $A - \frac{B}{2}(T_2 - T_1)$
(b) $A(T_2^2 - T_1^2) - 2B(T_2 - T_1)$
(c) $A(T_1^2 - T_2^2) - 2B(T_1 - T_2)$
(d) $A(T_1 - T_2)^2 - B(T_1 - T_2)$

63 One mole of perfect gas is contained in a cylindrical container. The *p-V* diagram for the path followed by the gas from state *A* to state *B* is shown below. The work done when the gas taken from state *A* to state *B* is **NCERT Pg. 235**

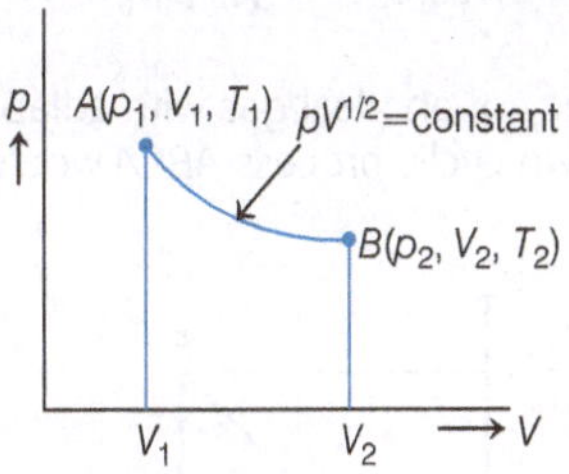

(a) $2p_1V_1^{1/2}[\sqrt{V_2} - \sqrt{V_1}]$
(b) $2p_1V_1^{3/2}[\sqrt{V_2} - \sqrt{V_1}]$
(c) $2p_1V_1^{-1/2}[\sqrt{V_2} - \sqrt{V_1}]$
(d) $2p_1V_1^{-3/2}[\sqrt{V_2} - \sqrt{V_1}]$

64 A certain quantity of O_2 $\left(\gamma = \frac{7}{5}\right)$ is compressed isothermally until its pressure is doubled (p_2) the gas is then allowed to expand adiabatically until its original volume is restored, then the final pressure (p_3) in terms of initial pressure (p_1) is **NCERT Pg. 235**

(a) $p_3 = \frac{p_1}{(2)^{3/5}}$ (b) $p_3 = \frac{p_1}{(2)^{2/5}}$
(c) $p_3 = \frac{p_1}{(2)^{1/5}}$ (c) $p_3 = \frac{p_1}{(2)^{4/5}}$

65 Following figure shows two processes A and B for a gas. If ΔQ_A and ΔQ_B are the amount of heat absorbed by the system in two cases, and ΔU_A and ΔU_B are changes in internal energies respectively, then **NCERT Pg. 235**

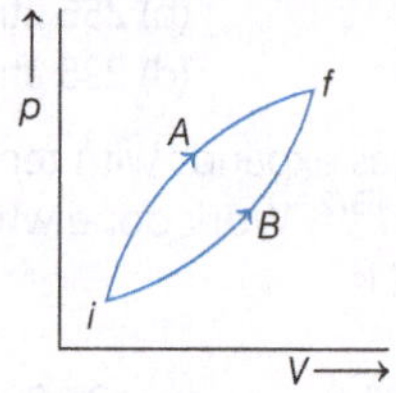

(a) $\Delta Q_A > \Delta Q_B,\ \Delta U_A > \Delta U_B$
(b) $\Delta Q_A < \Delta Q_B,\ \Delta U_A < \Delta U_B$
(c) $\Delta Q_A > \Delta Q_B,\ \Delta U_A = \Delta U_B$
(d) $\Delta Q_A = \Delta Q_B,\ \Delta U_A = \Delta U_B$

66 A thermodynamic system undergoes cyclic process $ABCDA$ as shown in figure. The work done by the system in the cycle is **NCERT Pg. 235**

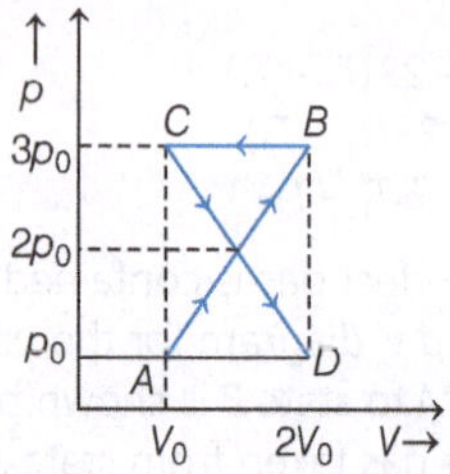

(a) $\frac{p_0V_0}{2}$ (b) zero (c) p_0V_0 (d) $2p_0V_0$

67 The efficiency of an ideal gas with adiabatic exponent γ for the shown cyclic process $ABCA$ would be **NCERT Pg. 235**

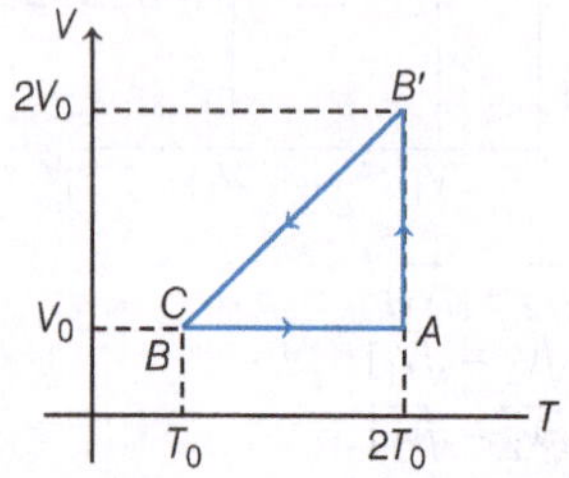

(a) $\frac{(2\ln 2 - 1)}{\gamma/(\gamma - 1)}$ (b) $\frac{(1 - 1\ln 2)}{\gamma/(\gamma - 1)}$
(c) $\frac{(2\ln 2 + 1)}{\gamma/(\gamma - 1)}$ (d) $\frac{(2\ln 2 - 1)}{\gamma/(\gamma + 1)}$

68 Choose the correct statement regarding isobaric process. **NCERT Pg. 235**
(a) $pV =$ constant.
(b) Heat absorbed by the gas goes partly to increase internal energy and partly to do work.
(c) The system returns to its initial state.
(d) Both (a) and (b)

69 The p-V graph shown below, shows the cycle followed by an engine. In this, the curve 1 to 2 is isothermal, 2 to 3 is adiabatic and 3 to 1 is also adiabatic. **NCERT Pg. 235**

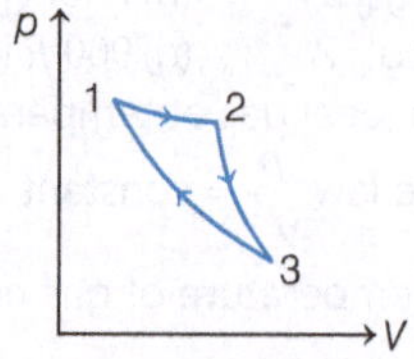

There is/are some condition(s) under which, this process does not exist. Choose the correct statement.
(a) Heat is completely converted to mechanical energy in such a process, which is not possible.
(b) Curves representing two adiabatic processes do not intersect.
(c) Curves representing an adiabatic process and an isothermal process do not intersect.
(d) Both (a) and (b)

70 Figure shows the p-V diagram of an ideal gas undergoing a change of state from A to B. Four different parts I, II, III and IV as shown in the figure may lead to the same change of state. Then, which of the following statement is correct? **NCERT Pg. 235**

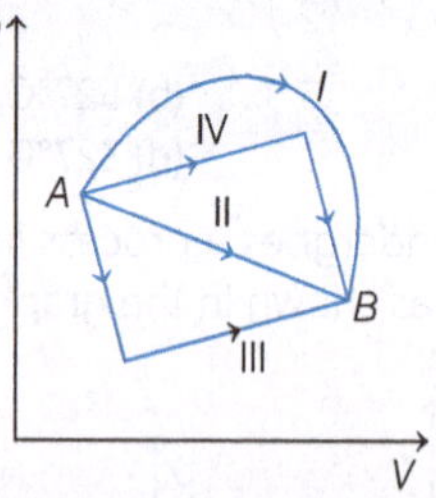

(a) Change in internal energy is same in IV and III cases, but not in I and II.
(b) Change in internal energy is same in all the four cases.
(c) Work done is maximum in case III.
(d) Work done is maximum in case II.

71 Figure below shows two paths that may be taken by a gas to go from a state A to a state C.

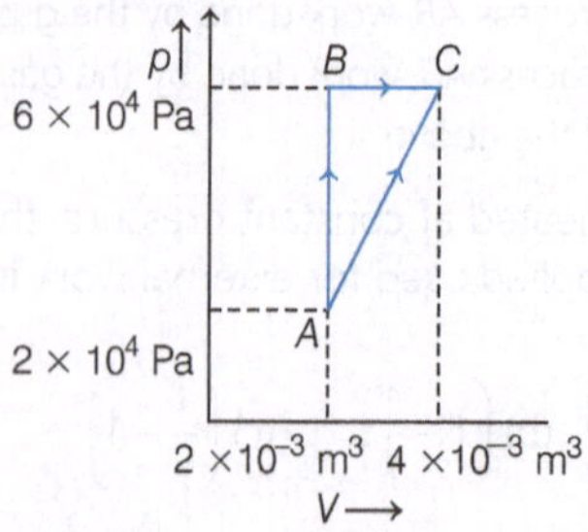

In process AB, 400 J of heat is added to the system and in process BC, 100 J of heat is added to the system. The heat absorbed by the system in the process AC will be **NCERT Pg. 235**

(a) 300 J (b) 380 J
(c) 500 J (d) 460 J

72 A sample of an ideal gas is taken through the cyclic process $abca$ as shown in the figure. The change in the internal energy of the gas along the path ca is –180 J. The gas absorbs 250 J of heat along the path ab and 60 J along the path bc. The work done by the gas along the path abc is **NCERT Pg. 235**

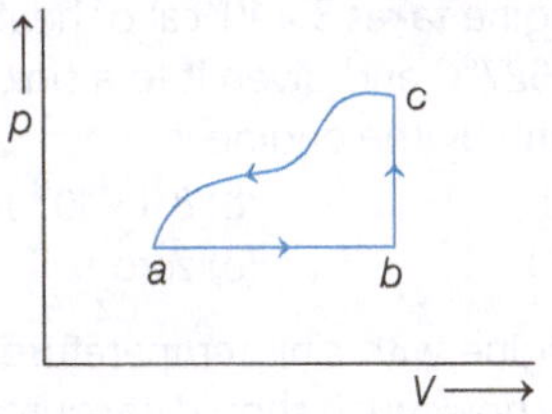

(a) 120 J (b) 130 J
(c) 100 J (d) 140 J

73 A container having 1 mole of a gas at a temperature 27°C has a movable piston which maintains at constant pressure of 1 atm in container. The gas is compressed until temperature becomes 127°C. The work done is (C_p for gas is 7.03 cal/mol-K) **NCERT Pg. 235**

(a) 703 J (b) 831 J
(c) 121 J (d) 2035 J

74 In a particular experiment an ideal gas undergoes adiabatic expansion satisfying the equation VT^3 = constant. The ratio of specific heats γ is **NCERT Pg. 235**

(a) 1.5 (b) 3
(c) $\frac{5}{3}$ (d) $\frac{4}{3}$

75 One mole of an ideal gas having initial volume V_1 pressure $2p$ and temperature T undergoes a cyclic process $ABCDA$ as shown below. The net work done in the complete cycle is **NCERT Pg. 235**

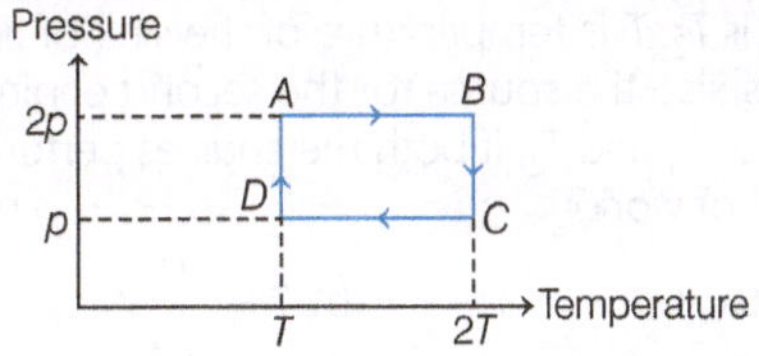

(a) Zero (b) $\frac{1}{2}RT\ln 2$
(c) $RT\ln 2$ (d) $\frac{3}{2}RT\ln 2$

76 One mole of an ideal diatomic gas undergoes a transition from A to B along a path AB as shown in the figure. **NCERT Pg. 235**

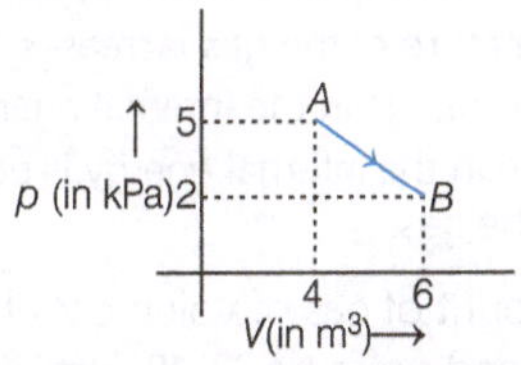

The change in internal energy of the gas during the transition is

(a) 20 kJ (b) – 20 kJ (c) 20 J (d) – 12 kJ

77 An ideal gas is compressed to half its initial volume by means of several process. Which of the process results in the maximum work done on the gas? **NCERT Pg. 235**

(a) Adiabatic (b) Isobaric
(c) Isochoric (d) Isothermal

78 A monoatomic gas at a pressure p, having a volume V expands isothermally to a volume $2V$ and then adiabatically to a volume $16V$. The final pressure of the gas is $\left(\text{take } \gamma = \frac{5}{3}\right)$ **NCERT Pg. 235**

(a) $64p$ (b) $32p$ (c) $\frac{p}{64}$ (d) $16p$

79 An ideal gas is taken through the cycle $A \rightarrow B \rightarrow C \rightarrow A$, as shown in figure. If the net heat supplied to the gas in the cycle is 5J, the work done by the gas in the process $C \rightarrow A$ is **NCERT Pg. 235**

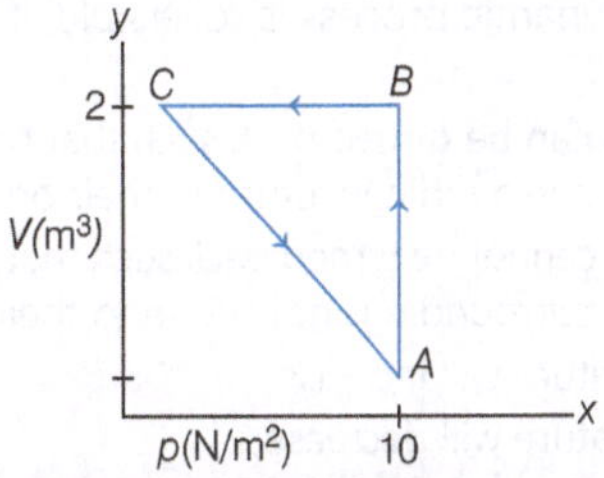

(a) –5 J (b) –10 J (c) –15 J (d) –20 J

80 An ideal gas is taken along the path AB as shown in the figure. The work done by the gas is **NCERT Pg. 235**

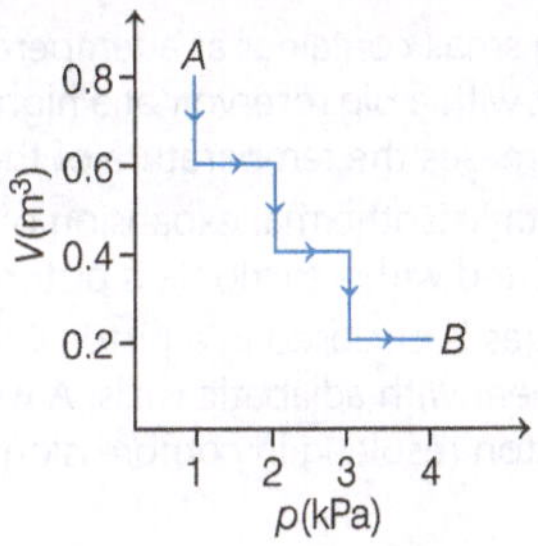

(a) 600 J (b) 1200 J (c) –600 J (d) –1200 J

81 A gas is compressed adiabatically, which one of the following statement is not true? **NCERT Pg. 235**

(a) There is no heat supplied to the system
(b) The temperature of the gas increases.
(c) There is no change in the internal energy
(d) The change in the internal energy is equal to the work done on the gas.

82 A certain amount of gas of volume V at 27°C temperature and pressure $2 \times 10^7 \text{ Nm}^{-2}$ expands isothermally until its volume gets doubled. Later it expands adiabatically until its volume gets redoubled. The final pressure of the gas will be (Use, $\gamma = 1.5$) **NCERT Pg. 235**

(a) 3.536×10^5 Pa
(b) 3.536×10^6 Pa
(c) 1.25×10^6 Pa
(d) 1.25×10^5 Pa

83 A litre of dry air at STP expands adiabatically to a volume of 3 L.
If $\gamma = 1.40$, the work done by air is ($3^{1.4} = 4.6555$) [Take, air to be an ideal gas] **NCERT Pg. 235**

(a) 100.8 J
(b) 86.0 J
(c) 48 J
(d) 60.7 J

Second Law of Thermodynamics and Carnot Engine

84 A thermodynamic process is reversible, if the **NCERT Pg. 236**

(a) process can be turned back such that both the system and the surroundings return to their original state
(b) process cannot be turned back such that both the system and the surroundings not return to their original state
(c) temperature will increase
(d) temperature will decrease

85 Which of the processes described below is/are reversible? **NCERT Pg. 236**

(a) The increase in temperature of an iron rod by hammering it.
(b) A gas in a small container at a temperature T_1 is brought in contact with a big reservoir at a higher temperature T_2 which increases the temperature of the gas.
(c) A quasi-static isothermal expansion of an ideal gas in cylinder fitted with a frictionless piston.
(d) An ideal gas is enclosed in a piston cylinder arrangement with adiabatic walls. A weight w is added to the piston resulting in compression of gas.

86 According to second law of thermodynamics, **NCERT Pg. 236**

(a) a heat engine cannot have efficiency equal to 1
(b) a refrigerator (or heat pump) could have infinite value of coefficient of performance
(c) a heat engine can fully convert heat into work
(d) None of the above

87 For Carnot engine, which process should be chosen to take the working substance from T_1 to T_2 or *vice-versa*? **NCERT Pg. 237**

(a) Isochoric (b) Isothermal
(c) Adiabatic (d) Isobaric

88 A Carnot engine takes 3×10^6 cal of heat from hot reservoir at 627°C and given it to a sink at 27°C. Then, the work done by the engine is **NCERT Pg. 238**

(a) 4.2×10^6 J (b) 8.4×10^6 J
(c) 16.8×10^6 J (d) zero

89 A Carnot engine with sink temperature at 17°C has 50% efficiency. By how much should its source temperature be changed to increase its efficiency to 60%? **NCERT Pg. 238**

(a) 225 K (b) 145 K
(c) 75 K (d) 250 K

90 A Carnot engine absorbs 6×10^5 cal at 227°C. The work done per cycle by the engine, if its sink is maintained at 127°C is **NCERT Pg. 238**

(a) 15×10^8 J (b) 15×10^4 J
(c) 5×10^5 J (d) 2×10^4 J

91 A Carnot engine has an efficiency of 1/6. When the temperature of the sink is reduced by 62°C, its efficiency is doubled. The temperatures of the source and the sink are respectively **NCERT Pg. 238**

(a) 62°C, 124°C (b) 99°C, 37°C
(c) 124°C, 62°C (d) 37°C, 99°C

92 Two ideal Carnot engines operate in cascade (all heat given up by one engine is used by the other engine to produce work) between temperatures T_1 and T_2. The temperature of the hot reservoir of the first engine is T_1 and the temperature of the cold reservoir of the second engine is T_2. T is temperature of the sink of first engine which is also the source for the second engine. How is T related to T_1 and T_2, if both the engines perform equal amount of work? **NCERT Pg. 238**

(a) $T = 0$ (b) $T = \dfrac{2T_1T_2}{T_1 + T_2}$

(c) $T = \sqrt{T_1 T_2}$ (d) $T = \dfrac{T_1 + T_2}{2}$

93 Given below figure shows a Carnot cycle, where a Carnot engine is operating between two temperatures T_1 and T_2. Here, working substance is an ideal gas. **NCERT Pg. 238**

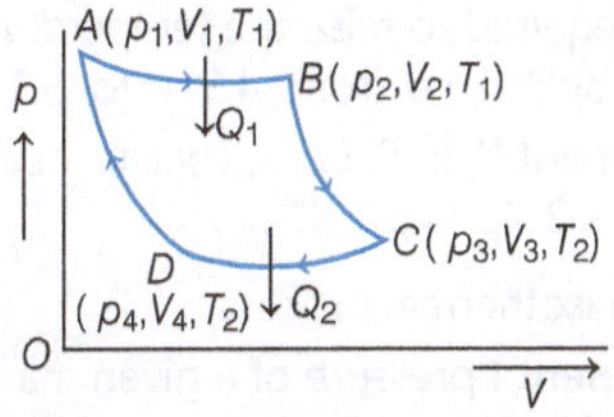

Total work done by the gas in one complete cycle,

(a) $\mu RT_2 \log \frac{V_2}{V_1} - \mu RT_1 \log \frac{V_3}{V_4}$

(b) $\mu RT_1 \log \frac{V_2}{V_1} - \mu RT_2 \log \frac{V_3}{V_4}$

(c) $\mu RT_1 \log \frac{V_2}{V_1} + \mu RT_2 \log \frac{V_3}{V_4}$

(d) zero

94 A Carnot engine has efficiency of $\frac{1}{4}$. Efficiency becomes $\frac{1}{3}$ when temperature of sink is decreased by 50 K (keeping source fixed). What is the original temperature of the sink? **NCERT Pg. 238**

(a) 350 K (b) 400 K
(c) 425 K (d) 450 K

Assertion and Reason Questions

Direction (Q. Nos. 1-10) *In the following questions, a statement of Assertion is followed by a corresponding statement of Reason. Of the following statements, choose the correct one.*

(a) Both Assertion and Reason are correct and Reason is the correct explanation of Assertion.
(b) Both Assertion and Reason are correct but Reason is not the correct explanation of Assertion.
(c) Assertion is correct but Reason is incorrect.
(d) Assertion is incorrect but Reason is correct.

1 Assertion In equation $\Delta Q = \Delta U + p\Delta V$, quantities on the both sides are intensive.

Reason The product of an intensive variable like p and an extensive quantity ΔV is extensive. **NCERT Pg. 233**

2 Assertion In isothermal process, whole of the heat energy supplied to the body is converted into internal energy.

Reason According to the first law of thermodynamics, $\Delta Q = \Delta U + \Delta W$. **NCERT Pg. 234**

3 Assertion In adiabatic process, work is independent of the path.

Reason In adiabatic process, work done is equal to negative of change in internal energy. **NCERT Pg. 235**

4 Assertion Heat absorbed by the gas during an isochoric process goes entirely to change its internal energy and its temperature.

Reason In an isochoric process, volume is constant. **NCERT Pg. 235**

5 Assertion In cyclic process, $\Delta U = 0$.

Reason Cyclic process means a reversible process. **NCERT Pg. 236**

6 Assertion First law of thermodynamics is based on energy conservation.

Reason Second law of thermodynamics put limitations on first law. **NCERT Pg. 236**

7 Assertion Rotating blade in a liquid stops after a certain time is an irreversible process.

Reason Irreversibility arises as the system attains a non-equilibrium state. **NCERT Pg. 236**

8 Assertion Reversible Carnot engine with one particular substance cannot be more efficient than the one using another substance.

Reason Efficiency of Carnot engine $= T_2/T_1$. **NCERT Pg. 238**

9 Assertion The efficiency of Carnot engine can be 100%.

Reason Carnot engine is reversible engine. **NCERT Pg. 238**

10 Assertion Consider I as an irreversible heat engine and R as a reversible heat engine working between the same source and sink at temperatures T_1 and T_2, respectively. If they are coupled such that I acts as a heat engine and R as a refrigerator $(T_1 > T_2)$, then $\eta_R < \eta_I$.

Reason According to second law of thermodynamics, efficiency of reversible Carnot engine is maximum. **NCERT Pg. 239**

Statement Based Questions

Direction (Q. Nos. 1-8) *In the following questions, two statements (I & II) are given choose the correct option given below.*

(a) Both Statement I and Statement II are false.
(b) Statement I is true but Statement II is false.
(c) Statement I is false but Statement II is true.
(d) Both Statement I and Statement II are true.

1 Statement I Temperature is related to the motion of particles as a whole, not to energy of the internal (disordered) motion of particles.

Statement II Whether or not a system is in a state of equilibrium, it is independent of the surroundings and nature of the wall that separates the system from the surroundings. **NCERT Pg. 227**

2 A gas is enclosed in a box with a partition as shown in the Fig. (a).

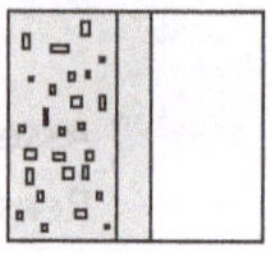
(a)

If this partition in the box is suddenly removed [as shown in Fig. (b)] leading to free expansion of the gas, then

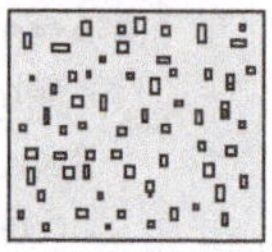
(b)

Statement I it is not an equilibrium state.

Statement II state variables can be used to describe the situation. **NCERT Pg. 228**

3 Statement I ΔQ and ΔW are path independent.

Statement II $\Delta Q - \Delta W$ is path dependent. **NCERT Pg. 230**

4 Statement I One calorie is equal to the amount of heat required to raise the temperature of 1 g of water by 1° C, i.e. from 14.5° C to 15.5° C.

Statement II In SI units, specific heat capacity of water is 2148 J kg^{-1} K^{-1}. **NCERT Pg. 232**

5 For an isothermal process,

Statement I pressure of a given mass of a gas varies inversely as its volume.

Statement II during expansion of gas, work is done by the gas on environment. **NCERT Pg. 234**

6 Statement I Kelvin and Planck's statements deny the possibility of a perfect refrigerator or heat pump.

Statement II Clausius statement denys the possibility of a perfect heat engine. **NCERT Pg. 236**

7 Statement I A process is reversible, if it is quasi-static.

Statement II A process is reversible, if there are no dissipative effects. **NCERT Pg 236**

8 Statement I The combustion reaction of a mixture of petrol and air ignited by a spark is an irreversible process.

Statement II The transfer of heat from one heated part of a liquid to the other colder part is an irreversible process. **NCERT Pg. 236**

Matching Type Questions

1 Match the Column I (quantity) with Column II (value) and select the correct answer from the options given below. **NCERT Pg. 234**

	Column I		Column II
A.	1 cal =	1.	4.186 J/gK
B.	$p\left(\frac{\Delta V}{\Delta T}\right)_p =$	2.	R
C.	Specific heat capacity of solids	3.	ΔQ
D.	For isothermal process, ΔW	4.	$3R$

Codes

	A	B	C	D
(a)	4	1	2	3
(b)	1	2	4	3
(c)	1	4	2	4
(d)	2	1	2	3

2 Match the Column I (thermodynamic process) with Column II (characteristic) and choose the correct answer from the option given below. **NCERT Pg. 235**

	Column I		Column II
A.	Isothermal	1.	Volume constant
B.	Isobaric	2.	Temperature constant
C.	Isochoric	3.	No heat flow between the system and surrounding
D.	Adiabatic	4.	Pressure constant

Codes

	A	B	C	D
(a)	1	2	3	4
(b)	4	2	3	1
(c)	2	4	1	3
(d)	3	1	2	4

3 Match the process in Column I with the predictions of first law given in Column II.

Column I		Column II	
A.	Isothermal	1.	$Q = W = \Delta E_{int} = 0$
B.	Adiabatic	2.	$\Delta E_{int} = -W$
C.	Isobaric	3.	$\Delta E_{int} = 0, Q = W$
D.	Free expansion	4.	$\Delta E_{int} + W = \Delta E_{int} + p\Delta V$

Choose the correct option. **NCERT Pg. 235**

Codes

	A	B	C	D
(a)	3	2	4	1
(b)	2	3	1	4
(c)	4	3	2	1
(d)	4	2	3	1

4 With respect to figure below match the Column I with Column II.

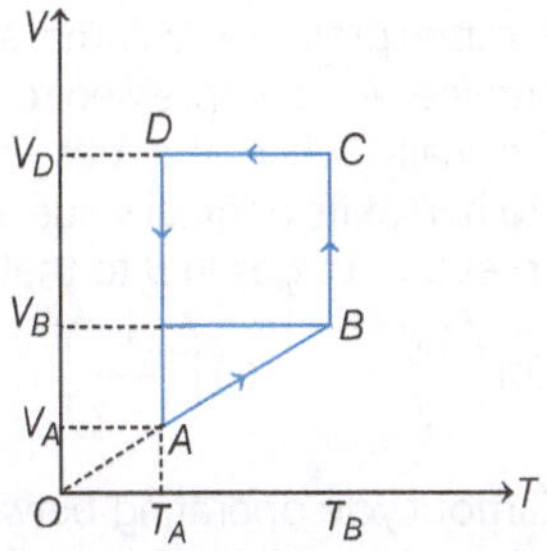

The volume ratios are $\frac{V_B}{V_A} = 2$ and $\frac{V_D}{V_A} = 4$

Temperature at point A,

$$T_A = 27°C \text{ and } R = 8.314.$$

Column I		Column II
A.	Temperature of gas at point B (in K)	1. 12471
B.	Heat absorbed in the process $A \to B$ (in J)	2. −7483
C.	Heat released in the process $C \to D$ (in J)	3. 6914
D.	Heat absorbed in the process $B \to C$ (in J)	4. 600

Choose the correct answer from the options given below. **NCERT Pg. 238**

Codes

	A	B	C	D
(a)	1	4	3	2
(b)	4	1	3	2
(c)	4	1	2	3
(d)	3	2	1	4

Numerical Type Questions

1 The amount of work done (nearest integer) to raise the temperature of one mole of an ideal gas by 35°C, if it is expanding under the condition $V = aT^{1/3}$ is ... J **NCERT Pg. 232**

2 In a thermodynamical process, the pressure depends on its volume as AV^3. The work done when the temperature changes from 100°C to 300°C will be ... μR, where μ denotes number of moles of gas. **NCERT Pg. 231**

3 The molar specific heat for the process $p = \frac{a}{T}$ for monoatomic gas is $\frac{x}{2}R$. If a is a constant, then the value of x is ... **NCERT Pg. 232**

4 One mole of an ideal gas requires 207 J heat to raise the temperature by 10K, when heated at constant pressure. If the same gas is heated at constant volume to raise the temperature by the same 10 K, then the heat required is ...... J. (Take, $R = 8.3$ J mol K) **NCERT Pg. 232**

5 A gas is compressed at a constant pressure of 35 N/m^2 from a volume of 20 m^3 to 15 m^3. Energy of 100 J is thus added to gas by heating. The internal energy is .... J. **NCERT Pg. 233**

6 A gas is taken through adiabatic process with $\gamma = 1.5$, in which the volume is compressed from 1600 cm^3 to 400 cm^3. If the initial pressure is 200 kPa. The absolute value of the work done by the gas in the process is ... J. **NCERT Pg. 235**

7 A Carnot engine operates between two reservoirs of temperatures 1200 K and 400 K. The engine performs 1200 J of work per cycle. The heat (in J) delivered by the engine to the low temperature reservoir in a cycle is ...... J. **NCERT Pg. 232**

8 An ideal Carnot engine, whose efficiency is 40% receives heat at 500 K. If its efficiency is 50%, then the intake temperature for the same exhaust temperature is ...... K. **NCERT Pg. 238**

NCERT Exemplar Questions

1 Consider p-V diagram for an ideal gas shown in figure.

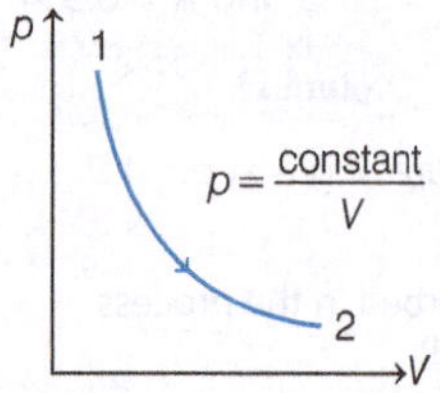

Out of the following diagrams, which figure represents the T-p diagram?

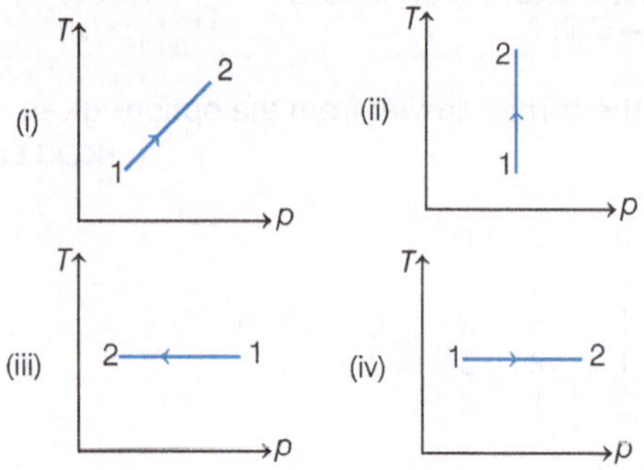

(a) (iv)
(b) (ii)
(c) (iii)
(d) (i)

2 An ideal gas undergoes cyclic process $ABCDA$ as shown in given p-V diagram. The amount of work done by the gas is

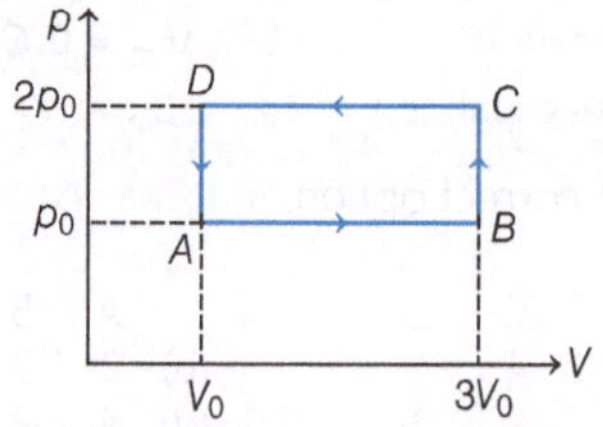

(a) $6p_0V_0$ (b) $-2p_0V_0$ (c) $+2p_0V_0$ (d) $+4p_0V_0$

3 Consider two containers A and B containing identical gases at the same pressure, volume and temperature. The gas in container A is compressed to half of its original volume isothermally while the gas in container B is compressed to half of its original value adiabatically. The ratio of final pressure of gas in B to that of gas in A is

(a) $2^{\gamma-1}$ (b) $\left(\frac{1}{2}\right)^{\gamma-1}$ (c) $\left(\frac{1}{1-\gamma}\right)^2$ (d) $\left(\frac{1}{\gamma-1}\right)^2$

4 Consider a Carnot cycle operating between $T_1 = 500$ K and $T_2 = 300$ K producing 1 kJ of mechanical work per cycle. Find the heat transferred to the engine by the reservoirs.

(a) 1000 J (b) 2000 J (c) 1500 J (d) 2500 J

Past Exams Questions

NEET

1 A thermodynamic system is taken through the cycle $abcda$. The work done by the gas along the path bc is **NCERT Pg. 238, NEET 2024**

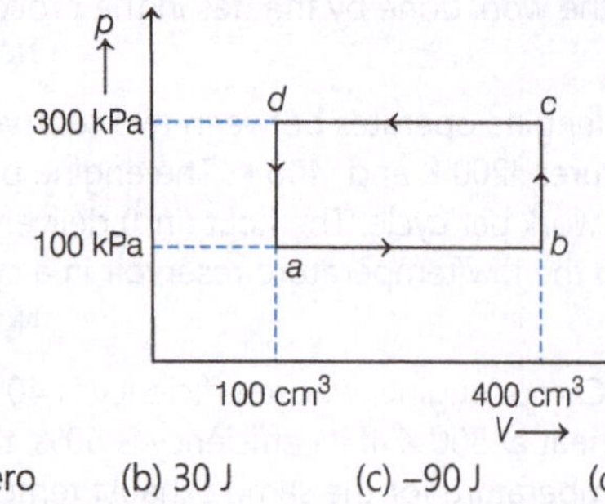

(a) zero (b) 30 J (c) −90 J (d) −60 J

2 A Carnot engine has an efficiency of 50% when its source is at a temperature of 327°C. The temperature of the sink is **NCERT Pg. 238, NEET 2023**

(a) 15°C (b) 100°C (c) 200°C (d) 27°C

3 An ideal gas undergoes four different processes from the same initial state as shown in the figure below. Those processes are adiabatic, isothermal, isobaric and isochoric. The curve which represents the adiabatic process among 1, 2, 3 and 4 is

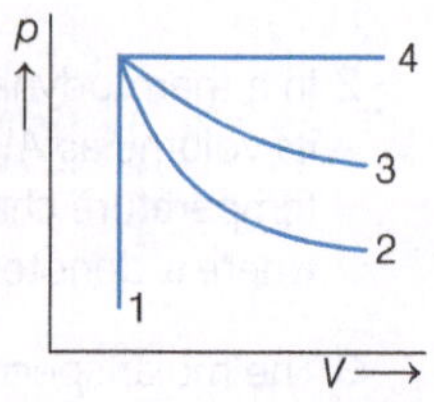

NCERT Pg. 235, NEET 2022

(a) 2 (b) 3 (c) 4 (d) 1

4 The p-V diagram for an ideal gas in a piston cylinder assembly undergoing a thermodynamic process is shown in the figure. The process is **NCERT Pg. 235, NEET 2020**

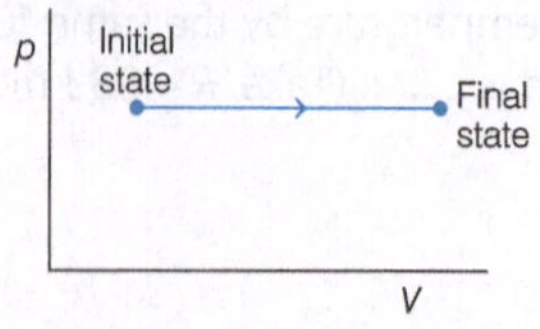

(a) adiabatic (b) isochoric
(c) isobaric (d) isothermal

5 1g of water of volume 1 cm^3 at 100°C is converted into steam at same temperature under normal atmospheric pressure ($\simeq 1 \times 10^5$ Pa). The volume of steam formed equals 1671 cm^3. If the specific latent heat of vaporisation of water is 2256 J/g, the change in internal energy is **NCERT Pg 231, NEET 2019**

(a) 2423 J (b) 2089 J
(c) 167 J (d) 2256 J

6 In which of the following processes, heat is neither absorbed nor released by a system? **NCERT Pg. 235, NEET 2019**

(a) Adiabatic
(b) Isobaric
(c) Isochoric
(d) Isothermal

7 A sample of 0.1 g of water at 100°C and normal pressure ($1.013 \times 10^5 Nm^{-2}$) requires 54 cal of heat energy to convert to steam at 100°C. If the volume of the steam produced is 167.1 cc, the change in internal energy of the sample is **NCERT Pg. 230, NEET 2018**

(a) 42.2 J (b) 208.8 J
(c) 104.3 J (d) 84.5 J

8 A gas is compressed isothermally to half of its initial volume. The same gas is compressed separately through an adiabatic process until its volume is again reduced to half. Then, **NCERT Pg. 235, NEET 2016**

(a) compressing the gas through adiabatic process will require more work to be done.
(b) compressing the gas isothermally or adiabatically will require the same amount of work.
(c) which of the case (whether compression through isothermal or through adiabatic process) requires more work will depend upon the atomicity of the gas.
(d) compressing the gas isothermally will require more work to be done.

9 One mole of an ideal monoatomic gas undergoes a process described by the equation $pV^3 =$ constant. The heat capacity of the gas during this process is **NCERT Pg. 235, NEET 2016**

(a) $\frac{3}{2}R$ (b) $\frac{5}{2}R$
(c) $2R$ (d) R

JEE Main

10 A real gas within a closed chamber at 27°C undergoes the cyclic process as shown in figure. The gas obeys $pV^3 = RT$ equation for the path A to B. The net work done in the complete cycle is (assuming $R = 8$ J/mol K) **NCERT Pg. 235, JEE Main 2024**

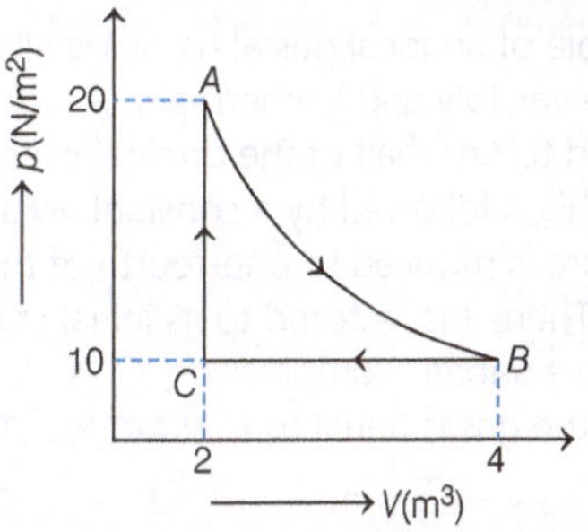

(a) – 20 J (b) 20 J (c) 205 J (d) 225 J

11 The heat absorbed by a system in going through the given cyclic process is **NCERT Pg 235, JEE Main 2024**

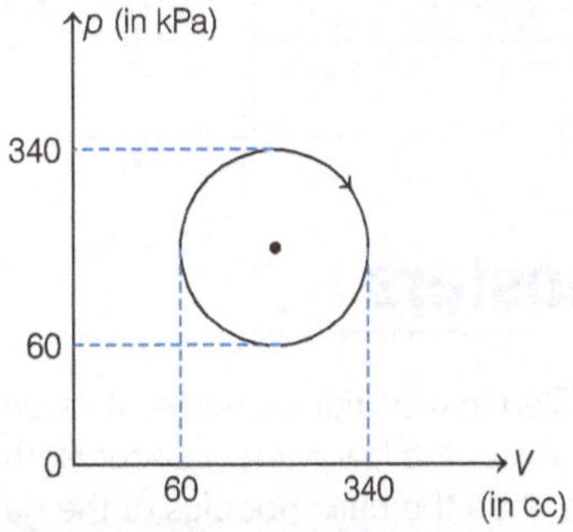

(a) 616 J (b) 431.2 J (c) 19.6 J (d) 61.6 J

12 Consider two containers A and B containing monoatomic gases at the same pressure (p), volume (V) and temperature (T). The gas in A is compressed isothermally to $\frac{1}{8}$ of its original volume, while the gas in B is compressed adiabatically to 1/8 of its original volume. The ratio of final pressure of gas in B to that of gas in A is **NCERT Pg 235, JEE Main 2023**

(a) $\frac{1}{8}$ (b) 4 (c) $8^{\frac{3}{2}}$ (d) 8

13 A sample of an ideal gas is taken through the cyclic process $ABCA$ as shown in figure. It absorbs 40 J of heat during the part AB, no heat during BC and rejects 60 J of heat during CA. A work 50 J is done on the gas during the part BC. The internal energy of the gas at A is 1560 J. The work done by the gas during the part CA is **NCERT Pg. 235, JEE Main 2022**

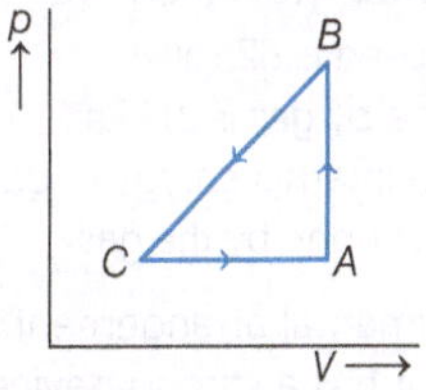

(a) 20 J (b) 30 J (c) – 30 J (d) – 60 J

14 If one mole of an ideal gas at (p_1, V_1) is allowed to expand reversibly and isothermally (A to B), its pressure is reduced to one-half of the original pressure (see figure). This is followed by a constant volume cooling till its pressure is reduced to one-fourth of the initial value ($B \to C$). Then, it is restored to its initial state by a reversible adiabatic compression ($C \to A$). The net work done by the gas is equal to **NCERT Pg. 234, JEE Main 2021**

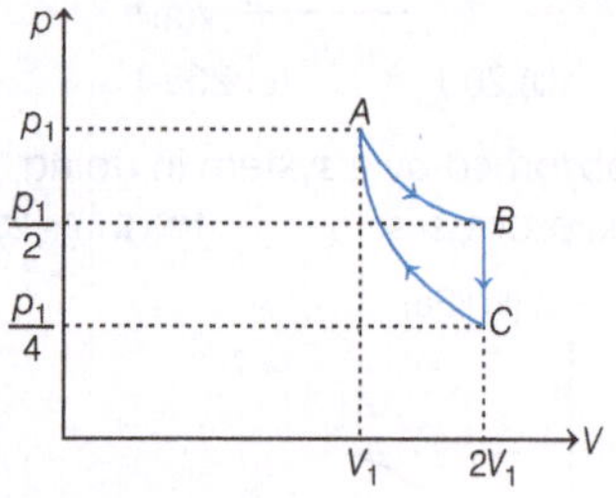

(a) $RT\left(\ln 2 - \frac{1}{2(\gamma - 1)}\right)$

(b) $-\frac{RT}{2(\gamma - 1)}$

(c) 0

(d) $RT \ln 2$

15 Two Carnot engines A and B are operated in series. The first one, A receives heat at $T_1 (= 600 \text{ K})$ and rejects to a reservoir at temperature T_2. The second engine B receives heat rejected by the first engine and in turn rejects to a heat reservoir at T_3 (= 400 K). Calculate the temperature T_2. If the work outputs of the two engines are equal. **NCERT Pg 237, JEE Main 2019**

(a) 600 K (b) 500 K

(c) 400 K (d) 300 K

Skill Boosters

1 A gas is filled in a cylindrical vessel. If its pressure and volume follows the law $p \propto V^{-3}$ under isothermal condition, then the bulk modulus of the gas at constant temperature is

(a) $2p$ (b) $\frac{p}{3}$

(c) $3p$ (d) $\frac{p}{2}$

2 A sample of monoatomic gas is inside a cubical box such that gas fills half of the box. Now, the gas is expended to fill the complete box such that its temperature remains constant throughout the process. The work done by the gas in the process is

(a) $RT(2 - \sqrt{2})$ (b) $\frac{2}{3}RT\left(2^{\frac{2}{3}} - 1\right)$

(c) $\frac{3}{2}RT\left(1 - \frac{1}{2^{\frac{2}{3}}}\right)$ (d) $\frac{R}{T}(2 - \sqrt{2})$

3 A sample of 10 g of oxygen is heated through 100°C at a constant pressure. If $C_V = 0.03$ cal mol^{-1}-K^{-1} and $R = 1.98$ cal mol^{-1}-K^{-1}, then

(a) heat supplied is 62 cal

(b) work done by gas is 219 cal

(c) change in internal energy of gas is 157 cal

(d) no work is done by the gas

4 In an experimental arrangement, a piston and cylinder arrangement has a stirring device. Piston is frictionless and is held down by the atmospheric pressure (101.3 kPa). Stirring device makes 9500 revolutions with an average torque of $\frac{1}{2\pi}$ N-m churning the fluid. The piston of diameter $\frac{1}{\sqrt{\pi}}$ m^2 moves out by 10 cm due to churning of fluid. Net work transfer for the system is

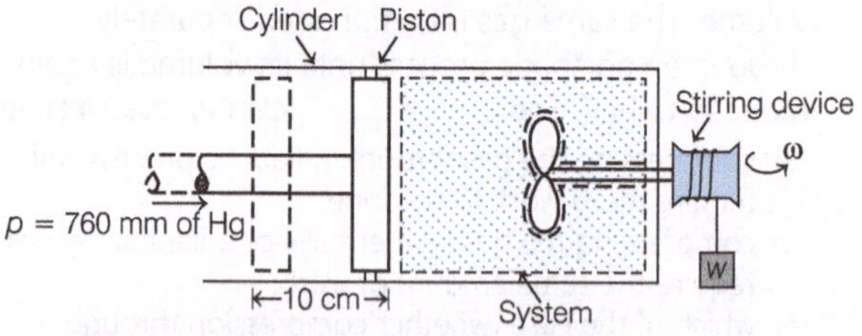

(a) 2.53 kJ (b) – 2.53 kJ

(c) 9497.47 kJ (d) – 9497.47 kJ

5 A cylinder contains compressed helium, is used to inflate in an elastic flexible balloon originally folded completely flat, to a volume of 0.6 m^3. If barometer reads 760 mm of Hg, then the work done by the atmosphere on the balloon is

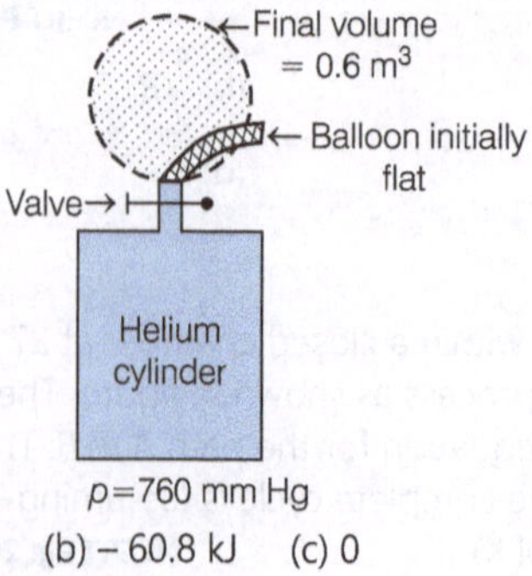

(a) 60.8 kJ (b) – 60.8 kJ (c) 0 (d) 60.8 J

6 A non-conducting piston of mass m and area of cross-section A is placed on a non-conducting cylinder.

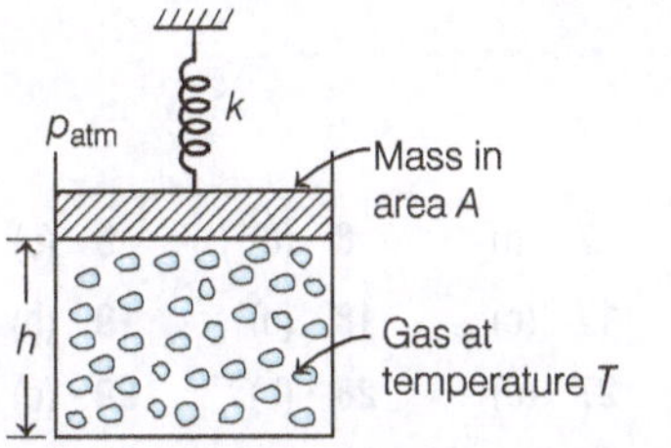

Initial height of piston is h and spring is relaxed with a spring constant k. Then,

(a) number of moles present, $n = \dfrac{\left(p_{atm} - \dfrac{mg}{A}\right)Ah}{RT}$

(b) number of moles present, $n = \dfrac{\left(p_{atm} + \dfrac{mg}{A}\right)Ah}{RT}$

(c) work done in displacing piston by heating gas $= mgx + p_{atm}Ax + kx^2$ (x = displacement of piston)

(d) Work done in displacing piston by heating gas $= mgx + p_{atm}Ax - kx^2$

7 A large object at 273 K and another large object at 373 K. For a small amount of energy of about 8 J be spontaneously transferred from cold object to hot object. Then,

(a) $\Delta S_{hot\ object} = 0.0256\ J\ K^{-1}$ (b) $\Delta S_{cold\ object} = -0.0263\ JK^{-1}$
(c) $\Delta S_{hot} + \Delta S_{cold} < 0$ (d) $\Delta S_{hot} + \Delta S_{cold} > 0$

8 At atmospheric pressure, 1 g of water becomes 1671 cm^3 of steam, when boiled. Latent heat of vaporisation of water is 539 cal g^{-1}. (1 cal = 4.18 J and 1 atm = 1.013×10^5 Nm^{-2})

If the sum of all form of energy of 1 g of water is E, then what is the sum of all form of energy of 1 g of steam?

(a) $E + 170$ J (b) $E + 2235$ J
(c) $E + 2083$ J (d) $E + 539$ J

9 A stone of mass 20 kg is dropped in a tank containing 200 kg water from a height of 15 m. Initially, stone and water are at same temperature.

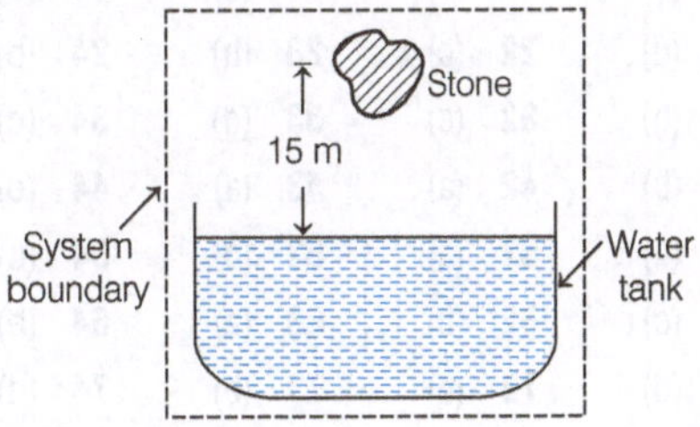

ΔQ, ΔW and ΔU when the stone is about to enter the water are respectively

(a) 2943 J, – 2943 J, 0
(b) – 2943 J, 2943 J, 0
(c) 0, 2943 J, 0
(d) 0, 0, 0

10 Two cylinders A and B are fitted with pistons contains equal amounts of an ideal diatomic gas at 300 K. The piston A is free to move while that of B is held fixed. The same amount of heat is given to gas in each cylinder. If rise of temperature of the gas in A is 30 K, then the rise of temperature of gas in B is

(a) 30 K
(b) 18 K
(c) 50 K
(d) 42 K

Correct Codes

Topical Questions

1 (c)	2. (b)	3 (a)	4 (d)	5 (b)	6 (a)	7 (d)	8 (d)	9 (c)	10 (d)
11 (c)	12 (b)	13 (a)	14 (b)	15 (a)	16 (b)	17 (c)	18 (d)	19 (b)	20 (c)
21 (d)	22 (c)	23 (b)	24 (b)	25 (b)	26 (b)	27 (d)	28 (b)	29 (d)	30 (b)
31 (b)	32 (c)	33 (d)	34 (c)	35 (b)	36 (c)	37 (a)	38 (c)	39 (c)	40 (c)
41 (b)	42 (a)	43 (a)	44 (d)	45 (d)	46 (d)	47 (b)	48 (c)	49 (c)	50 (d)
51 (a)	52 (a)	53 (c)	54 (c)	55 (b)	56 (a)	57 (d)	58 (a)	59 (b)	60 (b)
61 (c)	62 (b)	63 (a)	64 (b)	65 (c)	66 (b)	67 (a)	68 (b)	69 (d)	70 (b)
71 (d)	72 (b)	73 (b)	74 (d)	75 (c)	76 (b)	77 (a)	78 (c)	79 (a)	80 (d)
81 (c)	82 (b)	83 (b)	84 (a)	85 (c)	86 (a)	87 (c)	88 (b)	89 (b)	90 (c)
91 (b)	92 (d)	93 (b)	94 (d)						

Assertion and Reason Questions

1 (d)	2 (d)	3 (a)	4 (a)	5 (c)	6 (b)	7 (b)	8 (c)	9 (d)	10 (d)

Statement Based Questions

1 (a)	2 (b)	3 (a)	4 (b)	5 (d)	6 (a)	7 (d)	8 (d)

Matching Type Questions

1 (b)	2 (c)	3 (a)	4 (c)

Numerical Type Questions

1 (291)	2 (50)	3 (7)	4 (124)	5 (275)	6 (320)	7 (600)	8 (600)

NCERT Exemplar Questions

1 (c)	2 (b)	3 (a)	4 (d)

Past Exams Questions

1 (a)	2 (d)	3 (a)	4 (c)	5 (b)	6 (a)	7 (b)	8 (a)	9 (d)	10 (c)
11 (d)	12 (b)	13 (b)	14 (a)	15 (b)					

Skill Boosters

1 (c)	2 (c)	3 (c)	4 (d)	5 (b)	6 (b)	7 (c)	8 (c)	9 (d)	10 (d)

Step by Step

Decoding the Questions

Concept Builders

1 Zeroth law of thermodynamics

2 Temperature

3 Random translational motion

4 temperature, volume

5 True (T)   6 First law

7 dependent   8 True (T)

9 False (F)   10 True (T)

11 True (T)   12 released

13 negative   14 Zero

15 True (T)   16 positive

17 True (T)   18 reversible

19 False (F)   20 Carnot cycle

Topical Questions

8 (*d*) The internal energy of a gas contained in a movable box, depends only on the molecular energies, i.e. it is the sum of the kinetic energies and potential energies of the molecules of gas.

The kinetic energy of the moving box is not included in the internal energy.

Thus, internal energy does not depend on the speed *v* of the box.

9 (*c*) When the cylinder is put in contact with a body at a higher temperature than that of gas, then the temperature difference will cause a flow of energy (heat) from hotter body to gas. This increases the internal energy of the gas.

Similarly, if we push the piston down, i.e. do some work on the system, it also results in increasing the internal energy of the gas.

Thus, internal energy or state of the gas can be changed by either of the ways mentioned in options (a) and (b).

11 (*c*) Given, $dQ = +200$ cal

$$= 200 \times 4.2 = 840 \text{ J}$$

and $dW = +40$ J

From first law of thermodynamics,

$$dQ = dU + dW$$

$$\Rightarrow \quad dU = dQ - dW$$

$$\therefore \quad = 840 - 40 = 800 \text{ J}$$

So, the internal energy of the system increases by 800 J.

12 (*b*) From the first law of thermodynamics,

$$\therefore \; dU = dQ - dW$$

In the first process,

$$dU = 7 \times 10^5 - 5.5 \times 10^5$$

$$= 1.5 \times 10^5 \text{ J}$$

Now, *dU* being a state function, remains the same in the second process,

$$\therefore dW = dQ - dU = 1 \times 10^5 - 1.5 \times 10^5$$

$$\Rightarrow dW = -0.5 \times 10^5 \text{ J}$$

$\therefore$ The negative sign shows that work is done on the gas.

13 (*a*) Given, heat supplied to the system,

$$\frac{\Delta Q}{\Delta t} = 6000 \text{ J/min}$$

$$= \frac{6000}{60} = 100 \text{ J/s}$$

Power delivered,

$$P = \frac{\Delta W}{\Delta t} = 90 \text{ W}$$

Increase in internal energy,

$\Delta U = 2.5 \times 10^3$ J

From first law of thermodynamics, we have

$$\Delta Q = \Delta U + \Delta W$$

$$\text{or} \quad \frac{\Delta Q}{\Delta t} = \frac{\Delta U}{\Delta t} + \frac{\Delta W}{\Delta t} \quad \text{...(i)}$$

Putting values in Eq. (i),

$$100 = \frac{2.5 \times 10^3}{\Delta t} + 90$$

$$\Rightarrow \quad \Delta t = 2.5 \times 10^2 \text{ s}$$

14 (*b*) For the path *ACB* as shown in the figure below,

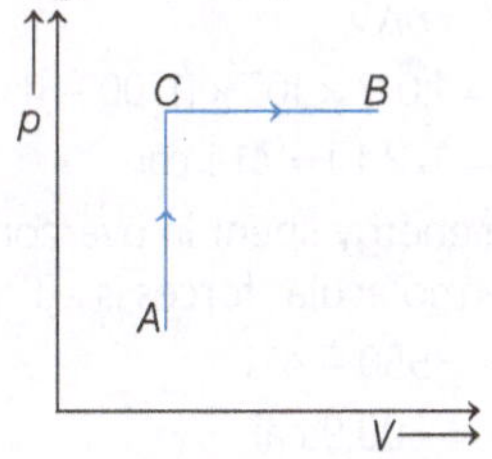

According to the first law of thermodynamics, heat supplied,

$$\Delta Q = (\Delta W) + (\Delta U)$$

$$\Rightarrow \quad \Delta Q_{ACB} = \Delta W_{ACB} + (U_B - U_A)$$

Substituting the given values,

$$U_B - U_A = 60 - 30 = 30 \text{ J} \quad \text{...(i)}$$

Similarly for the path *ADB* as shown in the figure below,

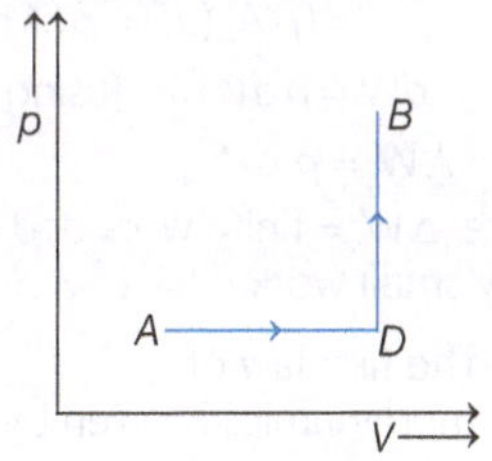

$$\Delta Q_{ADB} = \Delta W_{ADB} + (U_B - U_A)$$

$$\Rightarrow \quad \Delta Q_{ADB} = 10 + 30 \quad \text{[using Eq. (i)]}$$

$$= 40 \text{ J}$$

15 (*a*) Given, $p = 45$ N/m^2

$$V_1 = 15 \text{ m}^3$$

$$V_2 = 10 \text{ m}^3$$

$$Q = 100 \text{ J}$$

From the first law of thermodynamics,

$$W = p\Delta V = 45\,(15 - 10)$$

$$= 45 \times 5 = 225 \text{ J}$$

As the volume is decreased, the work done on the gas will be negative.

$$\therefore \quad W = -225 \text{ J}$$

Now, energy added,

$$Q = 100 \text{ J}$$

$$\therefore \quad Q = \Delta U + W$$

$\Rightarrow \quad \Delta U = Q - W$

$= 100 - (-225) = 325$ J

16 (b) Given, $p = 1.013 \times 10^5$ Nm^{-2}

$V_1 = 1$ cm^3 and $V_2 = 1700$ cm^3

Now, the work done by the steam is given by

$\Delta W = p\Delta V$

$= 1.013 \times 10^5 \times [1700 - 1] \times 10^{-6}$

$= 172.1$ J $= 41.1$ cal

The energy spent in overcoming intermolecular forces is

$= 550 - 41.1$

$= 508.9$ cal

17 (c) For the given system,

Volume $(V) = (l)(A)$

Let piston moves a distance dl.

$\Rightarrow \quad dV = A\, dl$, for constant A ...(i)

Force on piston = (pressure) (area) = pA

So, work = force × distance

$= (pA)(dl) = p(A\, dl)$

$\Rightarrow \quad dW = p\, dV$ [using Eq. (i)]

$\Rightarrow \quad \Delta W = p\,\Delta V$

Here, ΔW = finite work and dW = very small work.

19 (b) The first law of thermodynamics is given by

$\Delta Q = \Delta U + \Delta W$

Now, work done at constant pressure,

$(\Delta W)_p = (\Delta Q)_p - \Delta U$

$= (\Delta Q)_p - (\Delta Q)_V$

$[\because (\Delta Q)_V = \Delta U]$

Also, $(\Delta Q)_p = mC_p\Delta T$

$(\Delta Q)_V = mC_V\Delta T$

$\Rightarrow \quad (\Delta W)_p = m(C_p - C_V)\Delta T$

$= 1 \times (4.3 \times 10^3 - 3.3 \times 10^3) \times (20 - 10)$

$= 1 \times 1 \times 10^3 \times 10$

$(\Delta W)_p = 10^4$ cal

20 (c) $W = p\Delta V = \mu R\Delta T$

$Q = \mu C_p T$

$= \mu \times \frac{5}{2} R\Delta T = \frac{5}{2} W$

$\Rightarrow W = \frac{2}{5} Q$

22 (c) As, heat capacity of a substance given as

$$S = \frac{\text{Heat consumed by given mass}}{\text{Temperature raised}}$$

So, if given mass is increased or its temperature is decreased, then its heat capacity increases.

23 (b) Change in internal energy of a system is given by

$\Delta U = nC_V\Delta T = nC_V(T_f - T_i)$

For nitrogen gas,

$C_V = \frac{5}{2} R$

$\therefore \quad \Delta U = 1 \times \frac{5}{2} R(T_f - T_0)$

For helium gas, $C_V = \frac{3}{2} R$

$\therefore \Delta U = 1 \times \frac{3}{2} R\left(T_f - \frac{8}{3} T_0\right)$

Since, $\Delta U_{\text{system}} = 0$

$\therefore \Delta U_N + \Delta U_{He} = 0$

$\Rightarrow \frac{5}{2} R(T_f - T_0) + \frac{3}{2} R\left(T_f - \frac{8}{3} T_0\right) = 0$

$\Rightarrow \frac{5}{2} RT_f - \frac{5}{2} RT_0 + \frac{3}{2} RT_f - 4RT_0 = 0$

$\Rightarrow \quad T_f = \frac{13}{8} T_0$

24 (b) Given, mass of oxygen,

$m = 40$ g

$\Delta T = 60°$C

Now, molar mass of oxygen molecule,

$M = 32$ g/mol

$\therefore$ Number of moles,

$n = \frac{m}{M} = \frac{40}{32} = 1.25$ mol

The molar specific heat of O_2,

$C_V = \frac{5}{2} R$

Now, the amount of heat required,

$\Delta Q = nC_V\Delta T$

$= 1.25 \times \frac{5}{2} R \times 60$

$= 1558.125$ J

$= 155.8$ kJ

$= 156$ kJ

25 (b) The mechanical equivalent of heat is a constant that relates mechanical work to heat energy. Specifically, it quantifies how much work is equivalent to the calorie of heat energy. This constant allows us to convert between calories and joules (SI unit of energy) in thermodynamics calculations.

28 (b) At constant pressure,

Heat required, $\Delta Q = nC_p\Delta T$

$\Rightarrow 310 = 2 \times C_p \times (35 - 25)$

$\Rightarrow \quad C_p = \frac{310}{20} = 15.5$ J/mol-K

Similarly, at constant volume,

Heat required, $\Delta Q = nC_V\Delta T$

$= 2(C_p - R) \times (35 - 25)$

$(\because C_p - C_V = R)$

$= 2 \times (15.5 - 8.3) \times 10$

$= 2 \times 7.2 \times 10 = 144$ J

29 (d) Given, pV^{-1} = constant

We know that, pV^x = constant

$\Rightarrow \quad x = -1$

The molar heat capacity is given by

$C = C_V + \frac{R}{1 - x}$

$= \frac{R}{\gamma - 1} + \frac{R}{1 - x}$

For an ideal monoatomic gas,

$\gamma = \frac{5}{3}$

$\therefore \quad C = \frac{R}{\frac{5}{3} - 1} + \frac{R}{1 - (-1)}$

$\Rightarrow \quad C = 2R$

$\Delta Q = \mu C\Delta T$

$= 1(2R)(3T_0 - T_0)$

$\Rightarrow \quad \Delta Q = 4RT_0$

So, the heat supplied is $4RT_0$.

30 (b) Here, $C_V = \frac{3}{2} R$

Since, $C_p - C_V = R$

$\Rightarrow \quad C_p = C_V + R$

$= \frac{3}{2} R + R = \frac{5}{2} R$

31 (b) $\because \quad \Delta U = nC_V\Delta T$

$= \frac{3}{2}(nR\Delta T)$

$= \frac{3}{2}(p_2V_2 - p_1V_1)$

$= \frac{3}{2}(6p_0V_0 - p_0V_0)$

$= 7.5p_0V_0$

33 (*d*) When a mixture of petrol vapour and air is ignited by a spark, then an explosive chemical reaction takes place. During the initial stage of this reaction, the temperature and the pressure will not be uniform.

Thus, it represents a non-equilibrium state. Therefore, its initial state cannot be described by state variables.

However, with time the gas may attain a uniform temperature and pressure. Thus, it comes to thermal and mechanical equilibrium with time.

34 (*c*) Extensive state variables indicate the size of the system, whereas intensive do not.

So, if the system in equilibrium, it is divided into two equal parts, the variables that remain unchanged for each part are intensive.

On contrary, the variables whose values get halved in each part are extensive.

So, from the given values, we can say that U (internal energy) and M (mass) are extensive state variables and T (temperature) is an intensive state variable.

35 (*b*) We know that,

$$pV = nRT$$

$$\Rightarrow \frac{pV}{T} = nR = 2R \qquad [\because n = 2]$$

37 (*a*) As heat and work in thermodynamics are not state variables. They are modes of energy transfer to a system resulting in change in its internal energy. Thus, statement, like a gas in a given state has a certain amount of heat or a gas in a given state has a certain amount of work are meaningless.

In contrast, a gas in a given state has a certain amount of internal energy and a certain amount of heat is supplied to the system or a certain amount of work was done by the system are perfectly meaningful.

38 (*c*) In order to take the gas from the state (p, T) to (p', T') *via* a quasi-static process, the external pressure should be changed by a very small amount, that allow this system to equalise its pressure with surroundings.

This process is continued infinitely slowly until the system achieves the pressure p'. Similarly, temperature can be changed by introducing an infinitesimal temperature difference between the system and surrounding reservoir. Also, by choosing reservoirs of progressively different temperatures T to T', the system achieves the temperature T'.

40 (*c*) When heat is given to a gas in an isothermal change, the result will be external work done by the gas, because when there is an isothermal change, the temperature remains the same.

Hence, $\Delta U = 0$

41 (*b*) In isothermal process of an ideal gas, $\Delta U = 0$

So, $\Delta Q = \Delta W$ (from first law of thermodynamics)

As the area under the curve represents the amount of the work done, i.e.

$$\Delta W = +20 \text{ J}$$

$$\Rightarrow \quad \Delta Q = +20 \text{ J}$$

42 (*a*) For isothermal process, $pV =$ constant.

Therefore, p-V graph is a rectangular hyperbola.

Since, $\quad T_2 > T_1$

$$\Rightarrow \quad (pV)_{\text{at } T_2} > (pV)_{\text{at } T_1}$$

Thus, the graph given in option (a) correctly represents the given situation.

43 (*a*) In isothermal process, temperature is constant.

From ideal gas equation,

$pV = \mu RT$

At constant temperature,

$pV =$ constant

So, with decreasing pressure p, V must increase to keep product pV constant. This inverse relation between p and V is depicted correctly by curve A, where p decreases with increasing V.

44 (*d*) Given, $\mu = 10$ mol, $T = 500$ K,

$$V_1 = 50 \text{ L and } V_2 = 5 \text{ L}$$

Work done at constant temperature (i.e. isothermal process),

$$W = 2.3\mu RT \log_{10}\left(\frac{V_2}{V_1}\right)$$

$$= 2.3 \times 10 \times 8.31 \times 500 \times \log_{10}\left(\frac{5}{50}\right)$$

$$= -9.5565 \times 10^4 \text{ J}$$

$$\approx -9.6 \times 10^4 \text{ J}$$

45 (*d*) At first, the gas undergoes isothermal expansion from V to $3V$. For such a process, the equation of gas will be

$$pV = \text{constant.}$$

This means pressure is inversely proportional to volume. Thus, p-V curve for such a process will be as shown.

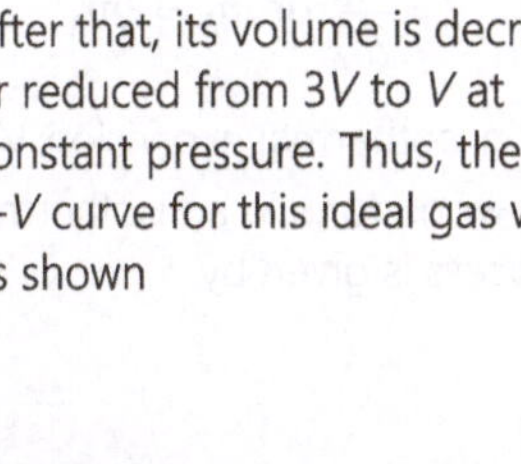

After that, its volume is decreased or reduced from $3V$ to V at constant pressure. Thus, the final p-V curve for this ideal gas will be as shown

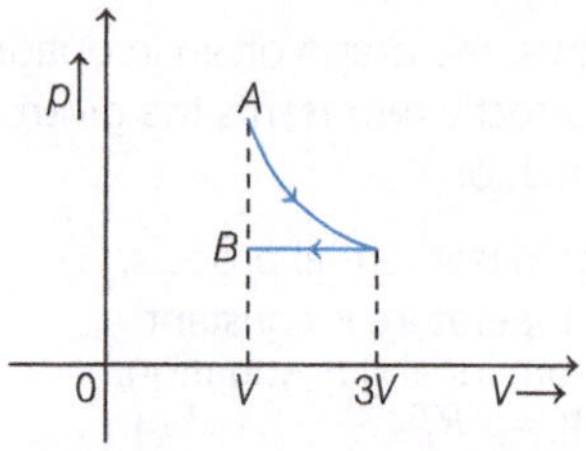

46 (d) For an isothermal process,

$$pV = \text{constant}$$

Slope is given by

$$\left(\frac{dp}{dV}\right)_{iso} = -\frac{p}{V} \quad \text{...(i)}$$

For an adiabatic process,

$$pV^\gamma = \text{constant}$$

∴ Slope is given by

$$\left(\frac{dp}{dV}\right)_{ad} = \frac{-\gamma p}{V} \quad \text{...(ii)}$$

From Eqs. (i) and (ii),

$$\left(\frac{dp}{dV}\right)_{ad} = \gamma\left(\frac{dp}{dV}\right)_{iso}$$

47 (b) From ideal gas equation,

$$pV = \mu RT$$

For gas A,

$$p_1V_1 = \frac{m}{M}RT$$

$$p_1 = \left(\frac{RT}{M}\right)\frac{m_A}{V_1}$$

and $p_2 = \left(\frac{RT}{M}\right)\frac{m_A}{V_2}$

$$\therefore \Delta p = p_1 - p_2$$

$$= \frac{RT}{M}m_A\left[\frac{1}{V_1} - \frac{1}{V_2}\right]$$

$$= \frac{RT}{M}m_A\left[\frac{1}{V} - \frac{1}{3V}\right]$$

$(\because V_1 = V, V_2 = 3V)$

$$\Rightarrow \Delta p = \left(\frac{RT}{M}\right)\frac{2m_A}{3V} \quad \text{...(i)}$$

Similarly, for gas B,

$$2\Delta p = \left(\frac{RT}{M}\right)\frac{2m_B}{3V} \quad \text{...(ii)}$$

Dividing Eq. (ii) by Eq. (i), we have

$$2 = \frac{m_B}{m_A} \text{ or } m_B = 2m_A$$

48 (c) In isothermal expansion, $V_2 > V_1$

As, work done in an isothermal process is given by

$$\Delta W = \mu RT \ln\frac{V_2}{V_1}$$

In this case, $\Delta W_1 > 0$

$\Rightarrow \Delta W_1 = +\text{ve}$

Similarly, in isothermal compression, $V_1 > V_2$

$\Rightarrow \Delta W_2 < 0$

$\Rightarrow \Delta W_2 = -\text{ve}$

49 (c) In adiabatic process, heat remains constant. So, from first law of thermodynamics,

$$\Delta Q = \Delta U + \Delta W$$

$$\Rightarrow \Delta U + \Delta W = 0$$

When work is done on system,

$$\Delta W = -\text{ve}$$

$$\Rightarrow \Delta U = -\Delta W = +\text{ve}$$

As, $\Delta U = \mu C_V \Delta T = +\text{ ve}$

$\Rightarrow \Delta T = +\text{ ve}$

$\Rightarrow T$ increases or $T_f > T_i$.

50 (d) For adiabatic process,

$$pV^\gamma = TV^{\gamma-1} = \text{constant}$$

$$\Rightarrow \frac{T_1}{T_2} = \left(\frac{V_2}{V_1}\right)^{\gamma-1}$$

Here, $T_2 = 2T_1$

and $V_2 = \frac{V_1}{2}$

$$\left(\frac{1}{2}\right)^{\gamma-1} = \left(\frac{1}{2}\right)$$

$$\Rightarrow \gamma - 1 = 1 \text{ or } \gamma = 2$$

$$\Rightarrow pV^\gamma = pV^2 = \text{constant}$$

51 (a) For adiabatic change, the equation of state is

$$pV^\gamma = \text{constant}$$

Also, for ideal gas,

$$pV = \mu RT$$

$$\Rightarrow V = \frac{\mu RT}{p}$$

So, $p\left(\frac{\mu RT}{p}\right)^\gamma = \text{constant}$

$$\Rightarrow \frac{p}{p^\gamma}T^\gamma = \frac{\text{constant}}{(\mu R)^\gamma} = \text{constant}$$

$$\Rightarrow p^{1-\gamma}T^\gamma = \text{constant}$$

52 (a) In an adiabatic process,

$$pV^\gamma = \text{constant} = k \text{ (say)}$$

Given, $\frac{C_p}{C_V} = \gamma = \frac{3}{2}$

$$\therefore pV^{3/2} = k$$

Taking logarithm on both sides, we get

$$\log p + \frac{3}{2}\log V = \log k$$

$$\therefore \frac{\Delta p}{p} + \frac{3}{2}\frac{\Delta V}{V} = 0$$

$$\Rightarrow \frac{\Delta V}{V} = -\frac{2}{3}\frac{\Delta p}{p}$$

$$\Rightarrow \frac{\Delta V}{V} \times 100 = -\frac{2}{3}\left(\frac{\Delta p}{p} \times 100\right)$$

$$= -\frac{2}{3} \times \frac{2}{3} = -\frac{4}{9}\%$$

Negative sign implies that volume decreases by 4/9%.

53 (c) Slope of isothermal curve

$$\tan\phi = \frac{dp}{dV} = -\frac{p}{V}$$

$\left[\because \text{for isothermal process, } pV = \text{constant} \Rightarrow pdV + Vdp = 0 \text{ or } \frac{dp}{dV} = -\frac{p}{V}\right]$

Similarly, slope of adiabatic curve,

$$\tan\phi = \frac{d}{dV}\left(\frac{\text{constant}}{V^\gamma}\right) = -\gamma\left(\frac{p}{V}\right)$$

$[\because \text{for adiabatic process, } pV^\gamma = \text{constant}]$

As we know, $\gamma > 1$

Thus, $(\text{Slope})_{\text{adiabatic}} > (\text{Slope})_{\text{isothermal}}$

54 (c) ∴ No. of moles of oxygen,

$$\mu = \frac{128}{32} = 4 \text{ mol}$$

For an isothermal process,

$$W = \mu RT \log_e\frac{V_2}{V_1}$$

$$= 2.3\,\mu RT \log_{10}\left(\frac{V_2}{V_1}\right)$$

$$= 2.3 \times 4 \times RT \times \log_{10}\frac{150}{75}$$

$$= 2.3 \times 1192\, R \log_{10} 2$$

55 (b) As $\frac{p}{V^2} = \text{constant} = k$

$$\Rightarrow p = kV^2$$

Work done is given by

$$W = \int_{V_1}^{V_2} p\,dV = \int_{V_1}^{V_2} kV^2 dV$$

$$W = k\left[\frac{V^3}{3}\right]_{V_1}^{V_2} = \frac{k}{3}[V_2^3 - V_1^3]$$

As $p = kV^2$

$$W = \frac{1}{3}[p_2V_2 - p_1V_1]$$

$$= \frac{1}{3}[\mu R\Delta T]$$

$$= \frac{1}{3}[\mu R(T_2 - T_1)]$$

$$= \frac{1}{3}R(2T_0 - T_0)$$

$$= \frac{1}{3}RT_0$$

56 (*a*) Ideal gas equation at constant pressure is given by

$$p\,\Delta V = nR\Delta T \quad \text{...(i)}$$

$\therefore$ Work done, $W = p\,\Delta V$

$$W = nR\,\Delta T \quad \text{...(ii)}$$

At constant pressure, heat given to gas is given by

$$Q = nC_p\Delta T \quad \text{...(iii)}$$

From Eqs. (ii) and (iii), we get

$$\frac{W}{Q} = \frac{nR\,\Delta T}{nC_p\,\Delta T}$$

$$= \frac{R}{C_p} = \frac{R}{(7/2)R} = \frac{2}{7}$$

Given, $W = 10$ J

$$\Rightarrow \frac{10}{Q} = \frac{2}{7} \Rightarrow Q = 35 \text{ J}$$

57 (*d*) Using relation,

$$\frac{T_2}{T_1} = \left(\frac{p_2}{p_1}\right)^{\frac{\gamma-1}{\gamma}}$$

$$\Rightarrow \frac{T_2}{T_1} = \left(\frac{8}{1}\right)^{\frac{1.5-1}{1.5}} = \left(\frac{8}{1}\right)^{\frac{1}{3}} = 2$$

$$\Rightarrow T_2 = 2T_1$$

$$\Rightarrow T_2 = 2(273 + 27)$$

$$= 600 \text{ K} = 327^\circ\text{C}$$

58 (*a*) $\rho = \dfrac{pM}{RT}$ and $\rho \propto \dfrac{1}{V}$

During AB, ρ is constant and hence volume is constant. So, work done is zero.

During BC, $p \propto \rho$

i.e. T = constant and hence U is constant.

59 (*b*) $dQ = nC_p dt \quad \text{...(i)}$

$$dW = dQ - dU$$

From Eq. (i),

$$dW = nC_p dt - nC_V dt$$

$$dW = ndt\,(C_p - C_V)$$

Dividing by dQ on both sides, we get

$$\frac{dW}{dQ} = \frac{ndt\,(C_p - C_V)}{dQ}$$

$$\Rightarrow \frac{dW}{dQ} = \frac{ndt\,(C_p - C_V)}{nC_p\,dt} \quad \text{[from Eq. (i)]}$$

$$= 1 - \frac{C_V}{C_p}$$

$$\Rightarrow \frac{dW}{dQ} = 1 - \frac{1}{\gamma} \quad \left(\because \frac{C_p}{C_V} = \gamma\right)$$

60 (*b*) Given, $T_i = 25^\circ\text{C} = 298$ K

$$T_f = 919^\circ\text{C} = 1192 \text{ K}$$

$$p_i = 2 \text{ atm}, \gamma = 1.4$$

$$pV^\gamma = \text{constant}$$

$$\Rightarrow \frac{T^\gamma}{p^{\gamma-1}} = \text{constant} \quad (\because pV = nRT)$$

$$\therefore \left(\frac{T_i}{T_f}\right)^\gamma = \left(\frac{p_i}{p_f}\right)^{\gamma-1}$$

$$\Rightarrow p_f = p_i\left(\frac{T_f}{T_i}\right)^{\frac{\gamma}{\gamma-1}}$$

$$\Rightarrow p_f = 2\left(\frac{1192}{298}\right)^{\left(\frac{1.4}{1.4-1}\right)} = 256 \text{ atm}$$

61 (*c*) Given, $V = AT^{3/2}$

$$\therefore \frac{dV}{V} = \frac{\frac{3}{2}AT^{1/2}dT}{AT^{3/2}}$$

$$= \frac{3}{2}\frac{dT}{T} \quad \text{... (i)}$$

Now, $dW = p\,dV = \dfrac{RT}{V}dV$

From Eq. (i),

$$dW = RT\,\frac{3}{2}\frac{dT}{T}$$

$$W = \int_{T_1}^{T_2} R\frac{3}{2}dT$$

$$W = \frac{3}{2}R(T_2 - T_1)$$

$$= \frac{3}{2}R \times 80$$

$$W = 120R$$

62 (*b*) Given, $p = \dfrac{AT^2 - 2BT}{V}$

$$\Rightarrow pV = AT^2 - 2BT$$

Since, pressure is constant.

$$\therefore p\,dV = (2AT - 2B)\,dT \quad \text{...(i)}$$

$$W = \int_{V_1}^{V_2}(2AT - 2B)\,dT$$

$$[\because W = \int p\,dV]$$

$$= [AT^2 - 2BT]_{T_1}^{T_2}$$

$$W = A(T_2^2 - T_1^2) - 2B(T_2 - T_1)$$

63 (*a*) For path A to B,

$$pV^{1/2} = \text{constant} = k$$

$$\Rightarrow p = kV^{-1/2}$$

$$W = \int_{V_1}^{V_2} p\,dV = \int_{V_1}^{V_2} kV^{-1/2}dV$$

$$= k\left[\frac{V^{1/2}}{1/2}\right]_{V_1}^{V_2}$$

$$= 2k\,[\sqrt{V_2} - \sqrt{V_1}]$$

$$W = 2p_1V_1^{1/2}[\sqrt{V_2} - \sqrt{V_1}]$$

64 (*b*)

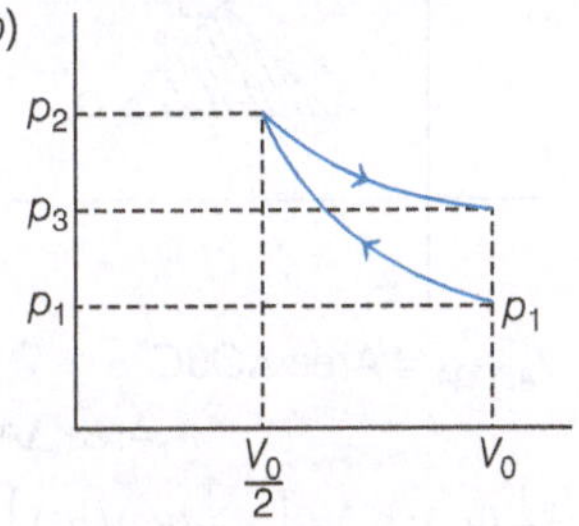

$$p_1V_0 = 2p_1V'$$

$$\Rightarrow V' = \frac{V_0}{2} \text{ (isothermal)}$$

Adiabatic expansion,

$$2p_1\left(\frac{V_0}{2}\right)^{7/5} = p_3V_0^{7/5}$$

$$\Rightarrow p_3 = \frac{p_1}{2^{2/5}}$$

65 (*c*) For process A,

$$\Delta Q_A = \Delta U_A + W_A$$

Similarly, for process B,

$$\Delta Q_B = \Delta U_B + W_B$$

Now, we know that,

Work done for a process = Area under it's p-V curve

Here,

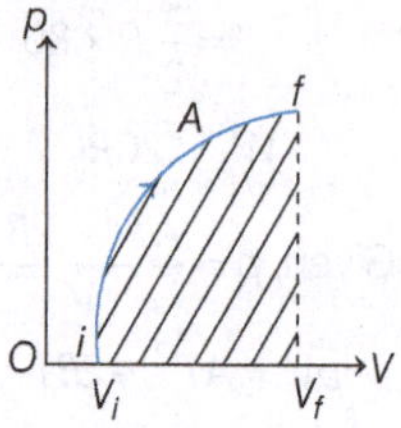

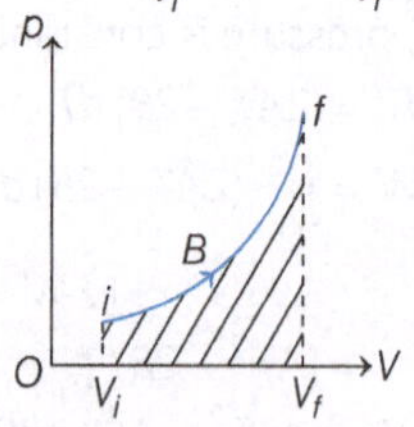

From the above graphs,

$$W_A > W_B \quad \text{...(i)}$$

Also, since the initial and final state are same in both process, so

$$\Delta U_A = \Delta U_B \quad \text{...(ii)}$$

So, from Eqs. (i) and (ii), we can conclude that

$$\Delta Q_A > \Delta Q_B$$

66 (*b*)

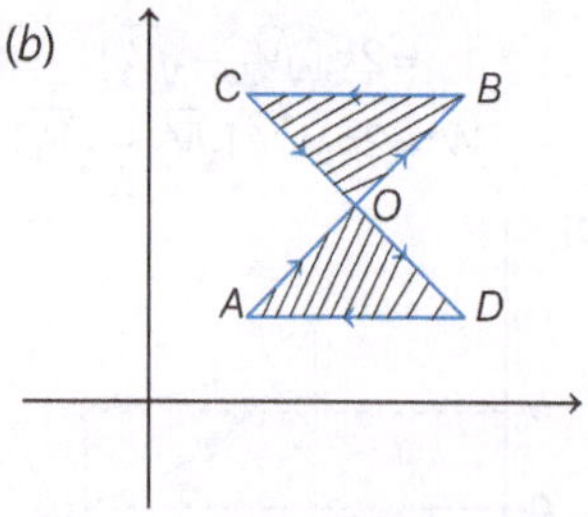

W_{ABCDA} = Area ΔOBC + Area ΔAOD

$$= \frac{1}{2}(V_0)(p_0) + \left(-\frac{1}{2}(V_0)(p_0)\right) = 0$$

67 (*a*) As, $W_{BC} = p\Delta V = nR\Delta T$

$$= -nR(2T_0 - T_0) = -nRT_0$$

$$W_{AB} = p\Delta V = 0 \quad (\because \Delta V = 0)$$

and $\quad W_{CA} = nRT \ln\left(\frac{V_2}{V_1}\right)$

$$= 2nRT_0 \ln\left(\frac{2V_0}{V_0}\right)$$

$$= +2nRT_0 \ln 2$$

Work done $= W_{CA} + W_{BC} + W_{AB}$

$$= 2nRT_0 \ln 2 - nRT_0 + 0$$

$$= nRT_0(2\ln 2 - 1)$$

Also, input heat,

$$\Delta Q_{BC} = nC_p\Delta T = \frac{nR\gamma T_0}{\gamma - 1}$$

$\therefore$ Efficiency

$$= \frac{\text{Work done}}{\text{Input heat}}$$

$$= \frac{(2\ln 2 - 1)}{\gamma/(\gamma - 1)}$$

68 (*b*) In an isobaric process,

$$\frac{V}{T} = \text{constant}$$

Work done by gas,

$$W = p(V_2 - V_1)$$

$$= nR(T_2 - T_1).$$

Since, temperature changes, so does internal energy. Thus, from the first law of thermodynamics, we can say that, heat absorbed goes partly to increase internal energy and partly to do work.

69 (*d*) The given process is a cyclic process, i.e. it returns to the original state 1.

Hence, $\quad dU = 0$

From first law of thermodynamics,

$$dQ = dU + dW$$

$$= 0 + dW = dW$$

Hence, total heat supplied is converted to work done by the gas (mechanical energy) which is not possible by second law of thermodynamics.

When the gas expands adiabatically from 2 to 3.In this case, it is not possible to return to the same state without heat being supplied to the gas, hence the process 3 to 1 cannot be adiabatic.

This implies that curves representing two adiabatic processes do not intersect.

70 (*b*) $dU_{A\to B} = \mu C_V\, dT$

$$= \mu C_V(T_B - T_A)$$

which depends only on temperatures at A and B that are fixed.

It means, internal energy is same for all the cases.

$dW_{A\to B}$ = Area under the p-V curve, which is maximum for the path I.

71 (*d*)

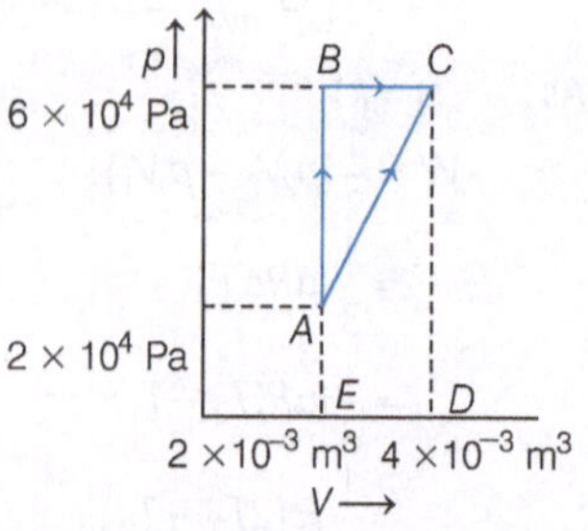

Process AB is isochoric, i.e. $\Delta V = 0$, so no work is done.

Heat added to the system in the process AB is

$$\Delta Q = 400\text{ J}$$

Now, $\quad \Delta Q = \Delta U + \Delta W$

Since, $\quad \Delta W = 0$

$\Rightarrow \quad \Delta U = \Delta Q = 400$ J

Work done in BC,

$$\Delta W = p(V_2 - V_1)$$

$$= 6 \times 10^4 (4 \times 10^{-3} - 2 \times 10^{-3})$$

$$= 6 \times 10^4 \times 2 \times 10^{-3} = 120\text{ J}$$

ΔU for process BC,

$$\Delta U = \Delta Q - \Delta W$$

$$= (100 - 120)\text{ J} = -20\text{ J}$$

Total increase in internal energy is going from state A to state C is $400 - 20 = 380$ J.

Work done in process AC,

Area of the trapezium $ACDEA$

$$= \frac{1}{2}(p_2 + p_1) \times (V_2 - V_1)$$

$$= \frac{1}{2}(6 \times 10^4 + 2 \times 10^4) \times (4 \times 10^{-3} - 2 \times 10^{-3})$$

$$= 80\text{ J}$$

Again, by using $\Delta Q = \Delta U + \Delta W$, where $\Delta U = 380$ J and $\Delta W = 80$ J

$$= 380 + 80 = 460\text{ J}$$

Thus, the heat absorbed by the system in the process AC will be 460 J.

72 (*b*) **In process** $a \to b$

Given, $\Delta Q_{ab} = 250\ \text{J}$ ...(i)

$\therefore \quad 250\ \text{J} = \Delta U_{ab} + \Delta W_{ab}$ ...(ii)

In process $b \to c$

Given, $\Delta Q_{bc} = 60\ \text{J}$

Also, V is constant, so $\Delta V = 0$

$\Rightarrow \quad \Delta W_{bc} = p(\Delta V)_{bc} = 0$

$\therefore \quad 60\ \text{J} = \Delta U_{bc} + 0$

$\Rightarrow \quad \Delta U_{bc} = 60\ \text{J}$ ...(iii)

In process $c \to a$

Given, $\Delta U_{ca} = -180\ \text{J}$ ...(iv)

Now, for complete cycle,

$\Delta U_{abca} = \Delta U_{ab} + \Delta U_{bc} + \Delta U_{ca} = 0$ ...(v)

From Eqs. (iii), (iv) and (v), we get

$\Delta U_{ab} = -60 + 180 = 120\ \text{J}$ ...(vi)

From Eqs. (ii) and (vi), we get

$\Delta dW_{ab} = 130\ \text{J}$ ...(vii)

From Eqs. (i) and (vii), we get

Work done by the gas along the path *abc*,

$\Delta W_{abc} = \Delta W_{ab} + \Delta W_{bc} = 130\ \text{J} + 0 = 130\ \text{J}$

73 (*b*) $W = p\Delta V = \mu R\,\Delta T$

$R = 8.31$ J/mol-K

$\therefore \quad W = 1 \times 8.31 \times (400 - 300)$

$\Rightarrow \quad W = 831\ \text{J}$

74 (*d*) $VT^3 = \text{constant}$

$\Rightarrow \quad T(V)^{\frac{1}{3}} = \text{constant}$ ...(i)

For adiabatic process,

$TV^{\gamma-1} = \text{constant}$ ...(ii)

Comparing Eqs. (i) and (ii),

$\gamma - 1 = \frac{1}{3} \Rightarrow \gamma = \frac{4}{3}$

75 (*c*) $\Delta W_{AB} = 1 \times R(2T - T) = RT$

$\Delta W_{BC} = 1 \times R2T \ln \frac{2p}{p} = 2RT \ln 2$

$\Delta W_{CD} = 1 \times R(T - 2T) = -RT$

$\Delta W_{DA} = -RT \ln 2$

$\therefore \quad \Delta W = \Delta W_{AB} + \Delta W_{BC} + \Delta W_{CD} + \Delta W_{DA} = RT \ln 2$

76 (*b*) The change in internal energy of gas in the transition from A to B is

$$\Delta U = nC_V dT = n\left(\frac{5R}{2}\right)(T_B - T_A)$$

$$= nR\frac{5}{2}\left(\frac{p_B V_B}{nR} - \frac{p_A V_A}{nR}\right)$$

$$= -\frac{4 \times 10^4}{2} = -20\ \text{kJ}$$

77 (*a*) Given, ideal gas is compressed to half its initial volume, i.e.

$$V_0 = \frac{V}{2}$$

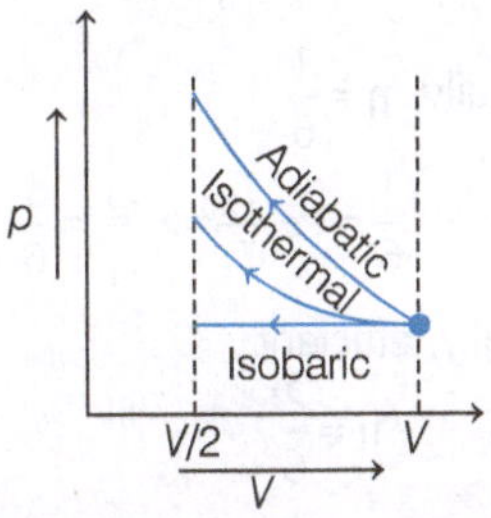

The isochoric process is one in which volume is kept constant, meaning that work done by the system will be zero, i.e. $W_{\text{isochoric}} = 0$

As we know, work done on the gas = Area under curve, i.e.

$$W_{\text{adiabatic}} > W_{\text{isothermal}} > W_{\text{isobaric}}$$

78 (*c*) For isothermal expansion process,

$pV = p' \times 2V \qquad [\because V' = 2V]$

$\Rightarrow \quad p' = \frac{p}{2}$

For adiabatic expansion

$pV^\gamma = \text{constant}$

$\Rightarrow \quad p'V^\gamma = p''V''^\gamma$

$\Rightarrow \quad \frac{p}{2}(2V)^{5/3} = p''(16V)^{5/3}$

$\Rightarrow \quad p'' = \frac{p}{2}\left[\frac{2V}{16V}\right]^{5/3} = p/64$

79 (*a*) $dQ = 5\ \text{J}$

$dU = 0$ (cyclic process)

$\Rightarrow \quad dQ = dW_{AB} + dW_{BC} + dW_{CA}$

$\Rightarrow \quad 5 = 10 + 0 + dW_{CA}$

$\Rightarrow \quad dW_{CA} = -5\ \text{J}$

80 (*d*) Note the volume has been plotted along Y-axis.

$W = \int p\,dV = \text{Area}$

$= (0.6 - 0.8) \times 10^3 + (0.4 - 0.6) \times 2 \times 10^3 + (0.2 - 0.4) \times 3 \times 10^{-3}$

$= -1200\ \text{J}$

81 (*c*) Since, the given process is adiabatic, hence $\Delta Q = 0$.

From first law of thermodynamics, we get

$$\Delta Q = \Delta U + \Delta W$$

$\Rightarrow \quad \Delta U = -\Delta W$

The process is adiabatic compression, therefore volume decreases. Hence,

$\Delta W = -\text{ve}$

$\Rightarrow \quad \Delta U = +\text{ve}$

Thus, internal energy of the system increases positively with change in temperature as gas is compressed adiabatically.

82 (*b*)

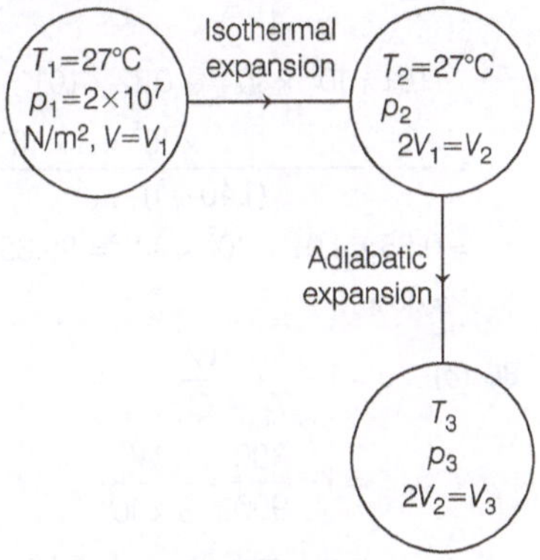

When gas is expanded isothermally,

$$p_1V_1 = p_2V_2$$

Given, $\quad V_2 = 2V_1$

$\Rightarrow \quad p_2 = p_1 \times \frac{V_1}{V_2}$

or $\quad p_2 = p_1 \times \frac{V_1}{2V_1} = \frac{p_1}{2}$

or $\quad p_2 = \frac{2 \times 10^7}{2} = 1 \times 10^7\ \text{Nm}^{-2}$

Now, gas is expanded adiabatically,

$\Rightarrow \quad p_2V_2^\gamma = p_3V_3^\gamma$

Given $\quad V_3 = 2V_2$

So, $\quad p_2 \cdot V_2^\gamma = p_3(2V_2)^\gamma$

$\Rightarrow \quad p_3 = \frac{p_2}{2^\gamma} = \frac{1\times 10^7}{2^{1.5}}$

$\Rightarrow \quad p_3 = \frac{1\times 10^7}{(2^{3/2})}$

$= 3.536\times 10^6$ Pa

83 (*b*) The given expansion process is adiabatic in nature and we have

$V_1 = 1\text{ L} = 10^{-3}\text{ m}^3$

$V_2 = 3\text{ L} = 3\times 10^{-3}\text{m}^3$

$p_1 = 1\text{ atm} = 1.01\times 10^5\text{ Pa}$

Using, $p_1V_1^\gamma = p_2V_2^\gamma$, we have

$p_1 \times 1^\gamma = p_2 \times (3)^\gamma$

Here, $\gamma = 1.40$ and $(3)^{1.4} = 4.6555$

So, $p_2 = \frac{p_1}{4.6555} \approx 0.22$ atm

$= 0.22\times 1.01\times 10^5$ Pa

Work done in an adiabatic expansion is given by

$W = \frac{(p_1V_1 - p_2V_2)}{\gamma - 1}$

$= \frac{(1.01\times 10^5 \times 10^{-3} - 0.22\times 1.01 \times 10^5 \times 3\times 10^{-3})}{(1.40-1)}$

$= 0.85\times 1.01\times 10^5\times 10^{-3} = 85.85$ J

≈ 86 J

88 (*b*) $\eta = 1 - \frac{T_2}{T_1} = \frac{W}{Q}$

$= 1 - \frac{300}{900} = \frac{W}{3\times 10^6}$

$\Rightarrow W = 2\times 10^6$ cal

$= 2\times 4.2\times 10^6$ J

$= 8.4\times 10^6$ J

89 (*b*) $\frac{50}{100} = 1 - \frac{290}{T_1} \quad \left(\because \eta = 1 - \frac{T_2}{T_1}\right)$

$\Rightarrow \quad T_1 = 580$ K

$\frac{60}{100} = 1 - \frac{290}{T_1'}$

$\Rightarrow \quad T_1' = 725$ K

$\therefore \quad \Delta T = T_1' - T_1$

$= 725 - 580$

$= 145$ K

90 (*c*) Given, $Q_1 = 6\times 10^5$ cal

$T_1 = 227°\text{C} = 227 + 273 = 500$ K

$T_2 = 127°\text{C} = 127 + 273 = 400$ K

As, $\quad \frac{Q_2}{Q_1} = \frac{T_2}{T_1}$

$\Rightarrow \quad Q_2 = \frac{T_2}{T_1}\times Q_1 = \frac{400}{500}\times 6\times 10^5$

$= 4.8\times 10^5$ cal

As, $W = Q_1 - Q_2$

$= (6\times 10^5 - 4.8\times 10^5)\times 4.2$ J

$= 5.04\times 10^5 \text{ J} \simeq 5\times 10^5$ J

91 (*b*) $\quad \eta = 1 - \frac{T_2}{T_1}$

Initially, $\eta = \frac{1}{6}$

$\therefore \quad \frac{1}{6} = 1 - \frac{T_2}{T_1} \Rightarrow \frac{T_2}{T_1} = \frac{5}{6}$

Finally, efficiency

$\eta = \frac{2}{6}$,

$T_{\text{sink}} = T_2' = T_2 - 62$

So, $\quad \eta = 1 - \frac{T'_2}{T'_1}$

$\Rightarrow \quad \frac{2}{6} = 1 - \frac{T_2 - 62}{T_1} \quad [\because T_1' = T_1]$

$\Rightarrow \frac{T_2}{T_1} - \frac{62}{T_1} = \frac{4}{6}$

$\Rightarrow \frac{5}{6} - \frac{62}{T_1} = \frac{4}{6} \quad \left[\because \frac{T_2}{T_1} = \frac{5}{6}\right]$

$= 99°$ C

$\Rightarrow \quad T_2 = \frac{5}{6}\times T_1 = 310$ K

$= 37°$ C

92 (*d*) Carnot engines given are operating in cascade configuration as shown in the figure.

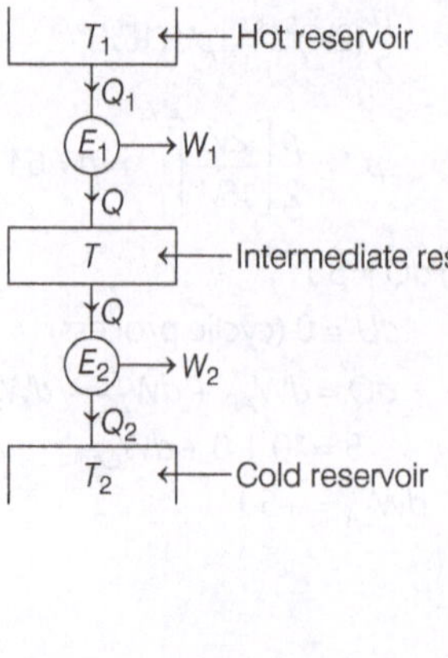

Work done by engine 1,

$W_1 = Q_1 - Q = k(T_1 - T)$

Work done by engine 2,

$W_2 = Q - Q_2 = k(T - T_2)$

So, $\quad \frac{W_1}{W_2} = \frac{T_1 - T}{T - T_2}$

As, $\frac{W_1}{W_2} = 1 \quad$ (given)

$\Rightarrow T - T_2 = T_1 - T$

$\Rightarrow \quad T = \frac{T_1 + T_2}{2}$

93 (*b*) $W_{\text{total}} = W_{A\to B} + W_{B\to C} + W_{C\to D} + W_{D\to A}$

By observing the isothermal process $A \to B$,

W_{iso} by gas $= \mu RT \log \frac{V_f}{V_i}$

$\Rightarrow W = \mu RT_1 \log\left(\frac{V_2}{V_1}\right) \quad$ ...(i)

Here, W is positive as $V_2 > V_1$.

By observing the adiabatic process $B \to C$,

W_{adia} by gas $= \frac{\mu R(T_i - T_f)}{\gamma - 1}$

$\Rightarrow W = \frac{\mu R(T_1 - T_2)}{(\gamma - 1)} \quad$ ...(ii)

Here, W is positive as T_2 is less than T_1.

By observing the isothermal process $C \to D$,

W_{iso} on gas $= \mu RT_2 \log\left(\frac{V_4}{V_3}\right)$

$\Rightarrow W = -\mu RT_2 \log\left(\frac{V_3}{V_4}\right) \quad$ ...(iii)

By observing the adiabatic process $D \to A$,

W_{adia} on gas $= \frac{\mu R(T_2 - T_1)}{\gamma - 1}$

$W = -\mu R\frac{(T_1 - T_2)}{\gamma - 1} \quad$ ...(iv)

Adding Eqs. (i), (ii), (iii) and (iv), we get

$\Rightarrow \quad W_{\text{total}} = \mu RT_1 \log\frac{V_2}{V_1} - \mu RT_2 \log\frac{V_3}{V_4}$

94 (*d*) $\eta = \frac{T_1 - T_2}{T_1}$

$$\frac{1}{4} = \frac{T_1 - T_2}{T_1} \quad \text{...(i)}$$

As the sink temperature is reduced by 50 K and then efficiency becomes $\frac{1}{3}$.

$$\therefore \frac{1}{3} = \frac{T_1 - (T_2 - 50)}{T_1}$$

$$\Rightarrow \frac{1}{3} = \left(\frac{T_1 - T_2}{T_1}\right) + \frac{50}{T_1}$$

From Eq. (i),

$$\frac{1}{3} = \frac{1}{4} + \frac{50}{T_1}$$

$$\Rightarrow \frac{50}{T_2} = \frac{1}{12}$$

$$\Rightarrow T_1 = 600 \text{ K}$$

Substituting the value of T_1 in Eq. (i), we get

$$T_2 = 450 \text{ K}$$

So, the original temperature is 450 K.

Assertion and Reason Questions

1 (*d*) In equation $\Delta Q = \Delta U + p\Delta V$, ΔQ is proportional to the total mass of the system and hence it is extensive. On the right hand side, ΔU is an extensive variable. Also, the product of an intensive variable like p and an extensive quantity ΔV is extensive.

4 (*a*) In an isochoric process, volume is constant. So, work done, $\Delta W = p\Delta V = 0$

Thus, according to first law of thermodynamics,

$$\Delta Q = \Delta U + \Delta W \Rightarrow \Delta Q = \Delta U$$

Therefore, heat absorbed by the gas goes entirely to change its internal energy and its temperature.

5 (*c*) In cyclic process, the system returns to its initial state as shown below, so $\Delta U = 0$.

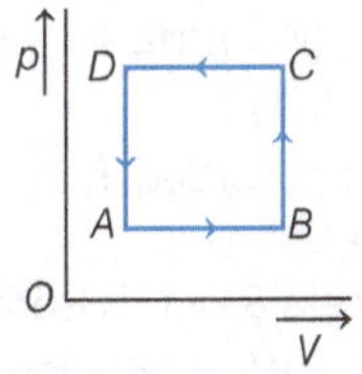

In cyclic process $A \rightarrow B \rightarrow C \rightarrow D \rightarrow A$, the system returns back its initial state but some work is done on system and system releases heat. Work done on the system is not reversed back. Thus, reversibility has nothing to do with cyclic process.

7 (*b*) Irreversibility mainly arises due to

(i) dissipative factor like friction, viscosity, etc.

(ii) and as many processes takes the system to non-equilibrium state.

So, when the blade is rotated in a liquid, then due to the viscosity, the system becomes irreversible as it stops after a certain time.

Thus, it is an irreversible process.

8 (*c*) Efficiency of Carnot engine,

$$\eta = 1 - \frac{T_2}{T_1}$$

where, T_2 = sink temperature

and T_1 = source temperature.

This expression of η does not include working substance information.

So, η is independent of working substance.

$\therefore$ Reversible Carnot engine with one particular substance cannot be more efficient than the one using another substance because it does not matter what substance is being used.

9 (*d*) A reversible heat engine operating between two temperature is called a Carnot engine. The efficiency of this engine is maximum but not 100%.

Efficiency of Carnot engine,

$\eta = 1 - \frac{T_2}{T_1}$, here T_1 and T_2 are in kelvin.

or $\quad \eta = 1 - \frac{Q_2}{Q_1}$

As all heat supplied cannot be fully converted to work (by second law of thermodynamics).

So, $Q_2 \neq 0$

$\Rightarrow \eta \neq 1$, i.e. $\eta \neq 100\%$.

10 (*d*) Efficiency of reversible process is always greater than an irreversible process. Hence, Assertion is incorrect but Reason is correct.

Statement Based Questions

3 (*a*) Since U is a state variable, ΔU depends only on the initial and final states and not on the path taken by the gas to go from one state to other.

However, ΔQ and ΔW, in general depend on the path taken to go from the initial to final states.

$$\Delta Q - \Delta W = \Delta U$$

It is clear that the combination $\Delta Q - \Delta W$ is however path independent.

4 (*b*) The Statement I is correct but Statement II is incorrect and it can be corrected as,

In SI units, specific heat capacity of water is 4186 J $kg^{-1}K^{-1}$, i.e. 4.186 J $g^{-1}K^{-1}$.

5 (*d*) For an isothermal process, temperature is fixed, so the ideal gas equation is given by pV = constant.

i.e. pressure of a given mass of gas varies inversely as its volume.

In an isothermal expansion, gas absorbs heat and does work on the environment.

6 (*a*) Kelvin and Planck's statements deny the possibility of perfect heat engine and Clausius statement denys the possibility of a perfect refrigerator.

Matching Type Questions

1 (b)

A. 1 cal = 4.186 J/gK = heat required to raise temperature of 1 g water from 14.5°C to 15.5° C.

B. $p\left(\frac{\Delta V}{\Delta T}\right)_p = R$

C. Specific heat capacity of solids = 3 R. (assuming three dimensional oscillator atoms)

D. For isothermal process, $\Delta T = 0$

$\Rightarrow \Delta U = 0$

From first law of thermodynamics,

$$\Delta W + \Delta U = \Delta Q$$

$$\Rightarrow \quad \Delta W = \Delta Q$$

Hence, A → 1, B → 2, C → 4 and D → 3.

3 (a) For isothermal process,

T = constant, $\Delta E_{int} = 0$

$\Rightarrow \Delta Q = \Delta W$

For adiabatic process,

$$\Delta Q = 0$$

$$\Rightarrow \quad \Delta E_{int} = -\Delta W$$

For free expansion,

$$\Delta Q = \Delta W = \Delta E_{int} = 0$$

Hence,

A → 3, B → 2, C → 4 and D → 1.

4 (c)

A. Process $A \to B$ is isobaric

V/T = constant

Hence, $\frac{V_A}{T_A} = \frac{V_B}{T_B}$

$\Rightarrow T_B = \frac{V_B}{V_A} \cdot T_A = 2 \times 300 = 600$ K

B. Heat absorbed in the process, $A \to B$

$$Q_1 = nC_p dT$$

$$= 2\left(\frac{5R}{2}\right)(600 - 300) = 1500\,R$$

$$= 1500 \times 8.314 = 12471 \text{ J}$$

C. Heat released in the process $C \to D$

The process $C \to D$ is isochoric.

$$Q_2 = nC_V dT$$

$$= 2 \times \frac{3}{2} R \times (300 - 600) = -900R$$

$$= -900 \times 8.314 = -7482.6 \text{ J}$$

$$\approx -7483 \text{ J}$$

D. Heat absorbed in the process $B \to C$

Process $B \to C$ is isothermal.

$$Q_3 = W_2 = nRT_B \log (V_D / V_B)$$

$$= 2 \times R \times 600 \log_e 2$$

$$= 1200\,R \times 0.693$$

$$= 831.6\,R$$

$$= 831.6 \times 8.314$$

$$= 6913.9 \text{ J} = 6914 \text{ J}$$

Hence, A → 4, B → 1, C → 2 and D → 3.

Numerical Type Questions

1 (291) Given, $V = aT^{1/3}$

$\Rightarrow \quad dV = \frac{1}{3} aT^{-2/3} dT$

Work done is given by

$$dW = pdV$$

But $pV = nRT$

$\Rightarrow \quad p = \frac{nRT}{V}$

$\therefore \quad dW = \frac{nRT}{aT^{1/3}} \times \frac{1}{3} aT^{-2/3} dT$

$$W = R\int_{T_1}^{T_2} dT$$

$$= R(T_2 - T_1)$$

$$= 8.31 \times 35 = 290.85 \text{ J}$$

$$W \approx 291 \text{ J}$$

2 (50) Given, $p = AV^3$

$T_1 = 100°C, T_2 = 300°C,$

$\Delta T = 200°C$

By using ideal gas equation,

$$pV = \mu RT$$

$$AV^3 \cdot V = \mu RT$$

Differentiating both sides,

$$4AV^3 dV = \mu R dT$$

$$4pdV = \mu R dT$$

$$pdV = \frac{\mu R dT}{4}$$

As, work done is given by

$$W = pdV$$

$$= \frac{\mu R dT}{4} = \frac{\mu R}{4} \Delta T$$

$$= \frac{\mu R}{4} \times 200$$

$$W = 50\,\mu R$$

3 (7) $\Delta Q = \Delta W + \Delta U$

$\Rightarrow C = \frac{\Delta Q}{\Delta T} = \frac{\Delta W}{\Delta T} + \frac{\Delta U}{\Delta T}$

or $C = \frac{\Delta W}{\Delta T} + C_V \; (\because \Delta U = C_V \Delta T)$

$C = \frac{p\Delta V}{\Delta T} + C_V \quad (\because \Delta W = p\Delta V)$ ...(i)

For the process $pV = RT$,

($\because \mu = 1$ for monoatomic gas)

$$V = \frac{RT}{p} = \frac{RT^2}{a}$$

$\Rightarrow \quad \frac{dV}{dT} = \frac{2RT}{a}$ ...(ii)

Substituting the values of Eq. (ii) in Eq. (i), we get

$$p\left(\frac{2RT}{a}\right) + C_V = \frac{a}{T}\left(\frac{2RT}{a}\right) + C_V$$

$$\left(\because p = \frac{a}{T}\right)$$

$\Rightarrow \quad C = 2R + C_V$

$$= 2R + \frac{3}{2}R$$

($\because C_V = \frac{3}{2}R$ for monoatomic gas)

$$C = \frac{7}{2}R$$

So, the value of x is 7.

4 (124) As we know that,

$C_p - C_V = R$

C_p is heat required to raise by 10K.

$\therefore \quad C_p = 20.7$ J/mol K

$C_V = 20.7 - 8.3 = 12.4$ J/mol K

So, for raising the temperature by 10 K, heat required will be

$$Q = 12.4 \times 10 = 124 \text{ J}$$

5 (275) From the first law of thermodynamics,

$$W = p\Delta V$$

$$= 35 \times (20 - 15)$$

$$= 175 \text{ J}$$

The work done on the gas will be negative as the volume is decreasing.

$\therefore \quad W = -175$ J

Energy added to the system is 100 J.

So, $\quad Q = \Delta U + W$

$\Rightarrow \Delta U = Q - W$

$= 100 - (-175) = 275$ J

6 (*320*) Given, sample of an ideal gas with ($\gamma = 1.5$) is taken from adiabatic process, when

$V_1 = 1600 \text{ cm}^3 = 16 \times 10^{-2} \text{ cm}^3$

$V_2 = 400 \text{ cm}^3 = 4 \times 10^{-2} \text{ cm}^3$

$p_1 = 200 \text{ kPa} = 2 \times 10^5$ Pa

Using the equation of adiabatic process,

$p_1 V_1^\gamma = p_2 V_2^\gamma$

$\therefore \quad p_2 = 16 \times 10^5$

Work done in adiabatic process,

$W = \dfrac{p_1 V_1 - p_2 V_2}{\gamma - 1}$

$= \dfrac{320 - 480}{0.5}$

$W = -320$ J

Hence, the work done in the adiabatic compression is 320 J.

7 (*600*) For the given Carnot engine, we have work output,

$W = Q_1 - Q_2$ ...(i)

and heat rejected,

$\Rightarrow \dfrac{Q_1}{Q_2} = \dfrac{T_1}{T_2}$

$\Rightarrow \dfrac{Q_1}{Q_2} = \dfrac{1200}{400}$

$\therefore \quad Q_1 = 3Q_2$ ...(ii)

From Eqs. (i) and (ii),

$W = 3Q_2 - Q_2$

$\Rightarrow 1200 = 2Q_2$

$\Rightarrow \quad Q_2 = 600$ J

8 (*600*) Given, efficiency of Carnot engine,

$\eta_1 = 40\% = 0.4$

Now, efficiency,

$\eta_2 = 50\% = 0.5$

$\eta = 1 - \dfrac{T_2}{T_1}$

For case I

$0.4 = 1 - \dfrac{T_2}{500}$

$\Rightarrow \dfrac{T_2}{500} = 0.6$

$\Rightarrow \quad T_2 = 300$ K

For case II

$\dfrac{300}{T_1} = 1 - 0.5$

$\Rightarrow \quad T_1 = 600$ K

NCERT Exemplar Questions

1 (*c*) According to the question, the equation of the gas is pV = constant.

Hence, we can say that the gas is going through an isothermal process.

From given graph p-V, it is also seen that the gas is expanding as with increasing volume, the pressure of gas decreasing, i.e. $p_2 < p_1$ at constant temperature.

This situation is correctly shown in T-p diagram of option (iii).

2 (*b*) Consider the p-V diagram given in the question.

Work done in the process $ABCDA$

= Area under the curve $ABCDA$

$W_{total} = W_{AB} + W_{BC} + W_{CD} + W_{DA}$ ...(i)

Here, $W_{BC} = W_{DA} = 0 \quad (\because \Delta V = 0)$

$W_{AB} = p_0(3V_0 - V_0) = 2p_0V_0$

$W_{CD} = 2p_0(V_0 - 3V_0) = -4p_0V_0$

Putting the values in Eq. (i), we get

$W_{total} = 2p_0V_0 + 0 - 4p_0V_0 + 0 = -2p_0V_0$

So, work done by the gas is $-2\,p_0V_0$.

3 (*a*) According to the given question, both the processes involves compression of the gas.

For isothermal process (gas A),

$p_1V_1 = p_2V_2$

$\Rightarrow p_0\,(2V_0) = p_2\,(V_0) \Rightarrow p_2 = 2p_0$

For adiabatic process (gas B),

$p_1V_1^\gamma = p_2V_2^\gamma$

$\Rightarrow \quad p_0\,(2V_0)^\gamma = p_2\,(V_0)^\gamma$

$\Rightarrow \quad p_2 = \left(\dfrac{2V_0}{V_0}\right)^\gamma p_0$ or $p_2 = (2)^\gamma p_0$

Hence, $\dfrac{(p_2)_B}{(p_2)_A}$ = Ratio of final pressures

$= \dfrac{(2)^\gamma p_0}{2p_0} = 2^{\gamma - 1}$

where, γ is ratio of specific heat capacities for the gas.

4 (*d*) Given, temperature of the source, $T_1 = 500$ K

Temperature of the sink, $T_2 = 300$ K

Work done per cycle,

$W = 1$ kJ $= 1000$ J

Heat transferred to the engine per cycle, $Q_1 = ?$

Efficiency of a Carnot engine,

$\eta = 1 - \dfrac{T_2}{T_1} = 1 - \dfrac{300}{500} = \dfrac{2}{5}$

Also, $\eta = \dfrac{W}{Q_1}$

or $\quad Q_1 = \dfrac{W}{\eta} = \dfrac{1000}{(2/5)} = 2500$ J

Past Exams Questions

1 (*a*) Work done in an isochoric process is always zero.

2 (*d*) Efficiency of Carnot engine,

$\eta = 50\% = 0.5$

Temperature of source,

$T_1 = 327°\text{C}$

$= (327 + 273)\text{ K} = 600$ K

If T_2 be the temperature of sink, then

$\eta = 1 - \dfrac{T_2}{T_1} \Rightarrow 0.5 = 1 - \dfrac{T_2}{600}$

$\Rightarrow \dfrac{T_2}{600} = 0.5$

$\Rightarrow \quad T_2 = 300\text{ K} = 27°\text{C}$

3 (*a*) Curve 1 is isochoric process because volume is constant. Whereas, in curves 2 and 3, curve 3 has smaller slope than curve 2. Hence, curve 3 represents isothermal process and curve 2 represents adiabatic process.

5 (*b*) Given, mass of water,

$m = 1$ g

Volume of 1 g of water

$= 1 \text{ cm}^3 = 10^{-6} \text{ m}^3$

Volume of 1 g of steam

$= 1671\ cm^3$

$= 1671 \times 10^{-6} m^3$

Pressure, $p = 1 \times 10^5$ Pa

Latent heat of vaporisation of water,

$L = 2256$ J/g

Change in volume,

$\Delta V = (1671 - 1) \times 10^{-6}\ m^3$

$= 1670 \times 10^{-6}\ m^3$ ...(i)

Heat supplied,

$\Delta Q = mL = 1 \times 2256$

$= 2256$ J ...(ii)

As the steam expands, the work done in expansion is

$\Delta W = p\Delta V$

$= 1 \times 10^5 \times 1670 \times 10^{-6}$

$= 167$ J ...(iii)

According to first law of thermodynamics,

$\Delta Q = \Delta U + \Delta W$

$\Rightarrow \Delta U = \Delta Q - \Delta W$

$= 2256 - 167$

$= 2089$ J

7 (*b*) Heat spent during the conversion of sample of water at 100°C to steam is,

$\Delta Q = 54$ cal

$= 54 \times 4.18$ J

$= 225.72$ J

Normal pressure,

$p = 1.013 \times 10^5\ Nm^{-2}$

Net work done during the conversion would be given as

$\Delta W = p\Delta V$

$= p[V_{steam} - V_{water}]$

Here, $V_{steam} = 167.1$ cc

$= 167.1 \times 10^{-6} m^3$

$V_{steam} = 0.1$ g

$= 0.1$ cc $= 0.1 \times 10^{-6}\ m^3$

$\therefore\ \Delta W = 1.013 \times 10^5$ $[(167.1 - 0.1) \times 10^{-6}]$

$= 16.917$ J

Now, by the first law of thermodynamics,

$\Delta Q = \Delta U + \Delta W$

$\Rightarrow \Delta U = \Delta Q - \Delta W$

$\Rightarrow \Delta U = 225.72 - 16.917$

$= 208.8$ J

8 (*a*)

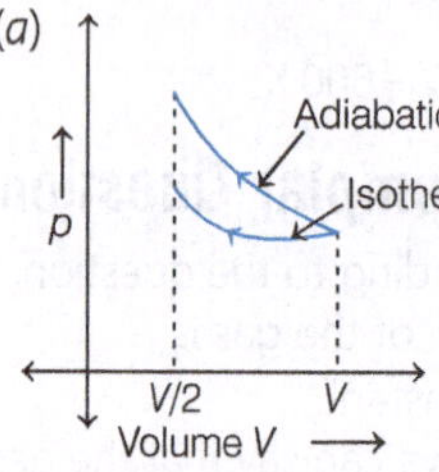

Since, the isothermal curve is less steeper than the adiabatic curve. So, area under the p-V curve for adiabatic process has more magnitude than isothermal curve.

Hence, work done in adiabatic process will be more than in isothermal process.

9 (*d*) Given, $pV^3 =$ constant

For a polytropic process,

$pV^{\alpha} =$ constant

$$\Rightarrow C = C_V + \frac{R}{1-\alpha} = \frac{3}{2}R + \frac{R}{1-3} = R$$

10 (*c*) $W_{AB} = \int p dV$

(Assuming T to be constant)

$$= \int \frac{RT}{V^3} dV$$

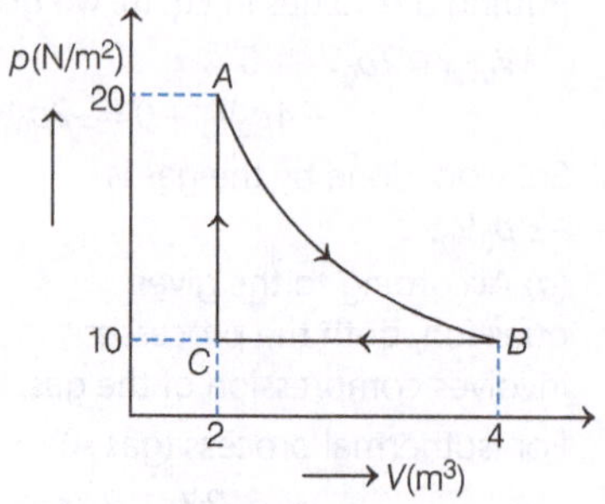

$$= RT \int_2^4 V^{-3} dV$$

$$= 8 \times 300 \times \left[-\frac{1}{2}\left(\frac{1}{4^2} - \frac{1}{2^2}\right)\right]$$

$= 225$ J

$$W_{BC} = p\int_4^2 dV = 10(2-4) = -20 \text{ J}$$

$W_{CA} = 0$

$\therefore W_{cycle} = 205$ J

11 (*d*)

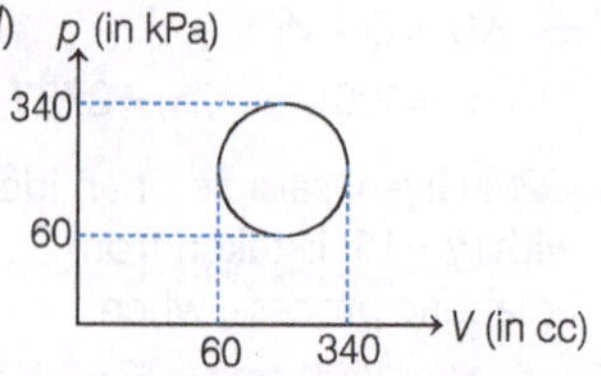

From thermodynamic equation,

$W = \Delta U + \Delta Q$

$\Delta U = 0$ for cyclic process

$\therefore \Delta Q = W =$ Area of p-V curve

$= \pi \times (140 \times 10^3$ Pa$)$ $\times (140 \times 10^{-6}\ m^3)$

$\Delta Q = 61.6$ J

The heat absorbed is 61.6 J.

12 (*b*) For container *A*, change is isothermal.

$$p, V, T \text{ to } p', \frac{V}{8}, T$$

Using Boyle's law,

$$p'\frac{V}{8} = pV$$

or $p' = 8p$ ...(i)

For container *B*, change is adiabatic $\left(\gamma = \frac{5}{3}\right)$.

$$p, V, T \text{ to } p'', \frac{V}{8}, T'$$

Using $p \cdot V^{\gamma} = p''\left(\frac{V}{8}\right)^{\gamma}$

We have,

So, $p'' = p \cdot (8)^{\gamma}$

$= p(8)^{\frac{5}{3}}$ ...(ii)

Ratio of final pressures of *B* and *A* samples is;

$$\frac{p''}{p'} = \frac{p \cdot 8^{\frac{5}{3}}}{p \cdot 8} = 8^{\frac{5}{3}-1}$$

$$= 8^{\frac{2}{3}} = 2^2 = 4$$

13 (*b*) For the given cyclic process :

AB is isochoric process, hence work done is zero.

$\Rightarrow \Delta Q_{AB} = \Delta U_{AB}$

$\Rightarrow \Delta U_{AB} = \Delta Q_{AB} = 40$ J (given)

BC is adiabatic process and

$\Delta Q_{BC} = 0$ (given)

$\Rightarrow \Delta U_{BC} + \Delta W_{BC} = 0$

$\Rightarrow \quad \Delta U_{BC} = -\Delta W_{BC} = -(-50)$

(given, $\Delta W_{BC} = -50$ J)

$\Rightarrow \quad \Delta U_{BC} = 50$ J

Now, as process is cyclic,

$\Delta U_{ABCA} = 0$

$\Rightarrow \Delta U_{AB} + \Delta U_{BC} + \Delta U_{CA} = 0$

$\Rightarrow \quad \Delta U_{CA} = -(\Delta U_{AB} + \Delta U_{BC})$

$= -(40 + 50) = -90$ J

Now, for process CA,

$\Delta U_{CA} + \Delta W_{CA} = \Delta Q_{CA}$

$\Rightarrow -90 + \Delta W_{CA} = -60$

Given, $\quad \Delta Q_{CA} = -60$

So, $\quad \Delta W_{CA} = 90 - 60 = 30$ J

14 (*a*) Let p_i, p_f, V_i and V_f be the initial and final pressure and volume.

Given, AB is isothermal ($\Delta T = 0$), BC is isochoric ($\Delta V = 0$) and CA is adiabatic ($\Delta Q = 0$).

Since, isothermal work

$(W_{AB}) = p_i V_i \ln \frac{V_f}{V_i}$

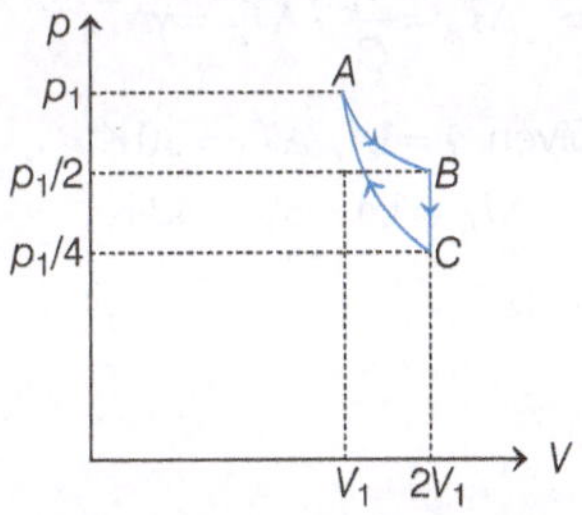

where, V_i and V_f are volume at A and B, respectively.

$\therefore \quad W_{AB} = p_1 V_1 \ln \frac{2V_1}{V_1} = p_1 V_1 \ln 2$

$\therefore \quad \Delta V = 0$

$\therefore \quad W_{BC} = 0$

Since, W_{CA} is an adiabatic work done, i.e.

$$W_{CA} = \frac{1}{1-\gamma}(p_f V_f - p_i V_i)$$

$$\Rightarrow \quad W_{CA} = \frac{1}{1-\gamma}\left(p_1 V_1 - \frac{p_1}{4} \times 2V_1\right)$$

$$= \frac{1}{1-\gamma}\frac{p_1 V_1}{2}$$

$\therefore$ Net work done,

$$W_{\text{net}} = W_{AB} + W_{BC} + W_{CA}$$

$$= p_1 V_1 \ln 2 + 0 + \frac{1}{1-\gamma}\frac{p_1 V_1}{2}$$

$$= p_1 V_1 [\ln 2 + 1/2(1-\gamma)]$$

From ideal gas law, $pV = nRT$

$$\therefore \quad W_{\text{net}} = RT\left[\ln 2 - \frac{1}{2(\gamma - 1)}\right]$$

$(\because n = 1)$

15 (*b*)

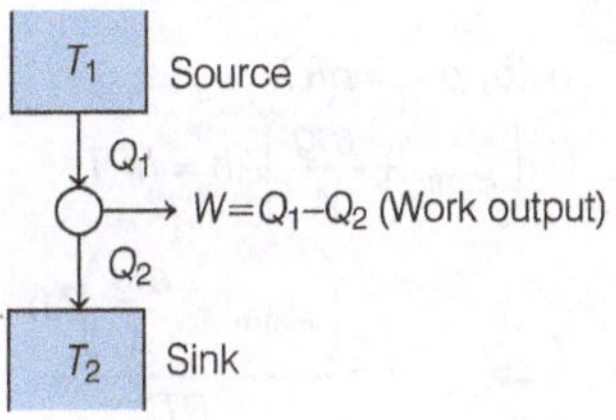

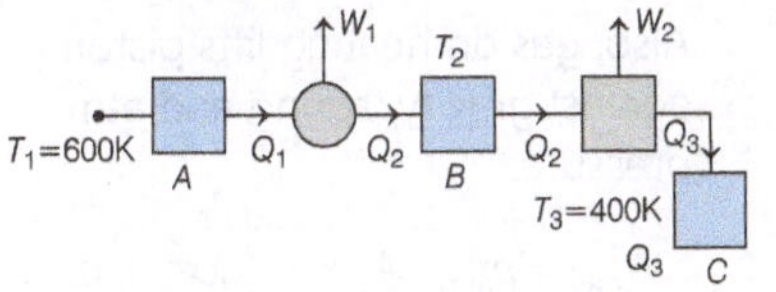

According to Carnot engine principle, $W_1 = Q_1 - Q_2$

(work output from sources A and B)

$W_2 = Q_2 - Q_3$

(work output from sources B and C)

As per the given condition, if the work outputs of the two engines are equal, then

$$Q_1 - Q_2 = Q_2 - Q_3$$

$$\Rightarrow \quad \frac{Q_1}{Q_2} + \frac{Q_3}{Q_2} = 2 \qquad \text{...(i)}$$

Therefore, $\frac{T_1}{T_2} + \frac{T_3}{T_2} = 2$

$$\Rightarrow \quad T_2 = \frac{T_1 + T_3}{2}$$

$$= \frac{600 + 400}{2}$$

$$T_2 = 500 \text{ K}$$

Skill Boosters

1 (*c*) Given pressure under isothermal condition,

$pV^3 =$ constant.

Differentiating w.r.t. pressure,

$$V^3 + p3V^2\frac{dV}{dp} = 0$$

$$\Rightarrow \quad V = -3\frac{pdV}{dp} = 0$$

$$\Rightarrow \quad V = -3\frac{pdV}{dp}$$

$$\frac{dp \cdot V}{dV} = -3p$$

$$\left[\because \text{Bulk modulus, } B = -\frac{dp}{\frac{dV}{V}}\right]$$

$$\therefore \quad B = -\left(\frac{dpV}{dV}\right) = -(-3p) = 3p$$

2 (c) Consider initial volume of gas $V_1 = V$ and final volume $V_2 = 2V$

Let initial temperature $T_1 = T$

$$T_1 V_1^{\gamma - 1} = T_2 V_2^{\gamma - 1}$$

$$TV^{\frac{2}{3}} = T_2 (2V)^{\frac{2}{3}}$$

$$T_2 = \frac{T}{2^{\frac{2}{3}}}$$

The work done by the gas in a process is

$$W = \frac{R(T_1 - T_2)}{\gamma - 1}$$

$$= \frac{R\left(T - \frac{T}{2^{\frac{2}{3}}}\right)}{\left(\frac{5}{3} - 1\right)} = \frac{3}{2}RT\left(1 - \frac{1}{2^{\frac{2}{3}}}\right)$$

3 (c) $pV = nRT \Rightarrow pdV = nRdT$

$\Rightarrow \quad W = nRdT$

$$= \frac{10}{32} \times 1.98\left(\frac{\text{cal}}{\text{mol - K}}\right) \times 100\,(\text{K})$$

Note that, $\Delta T = 100°\text{C} = 100\text{K}$

$\therefore \quad W = 62$ cal

As, $C_V = 5.03 \frac{\text{cal}}{\text{mol - K}}$ and

$$R = 1.98 \frac{\text{cal}}{\text{mol-K}}$$

$$C_p = C_V + R = 5.03 + 1.98$$

$$= 7.01 \frac{\text{cal}}{\text{mol-K}}$$

So, heat supplied is

$$Q = nC_p \Delta T = \frac{10}{32} \times 7.01 \times 100$$

$$= 219 \text{ cal}$$

So, $\Delta U = \Delta Q - \Delta W$

$$= 219 - 62$$

$$= 157 \text{ cal}$$

157 cal is used to increase the temperature of the gas.

4 (*d*) Work done by stirring device upon the system (negative work for system)

$= W_1 = -2\pi NT$

$= -2\pi \times 9500 \times \frac{1}{2\pi}$ (N-m)

$= -9500$ N-m

Work done by the system on surroundings

= Piston work (positive work for system)

$= (p \cdot A) \times l = p \times \frac{\pi d^2}{4} \times l$

$= 101.3 \times \frac{\pi}{4} \times \frac{1}{\pi} \times 10 \times 10^{-2}$

$= \frac{1013 \times 10^{-2}}{4} = 2.53$ kJ

Hence, net work transfer for the system,

$W_{net} = -9500 + 2.53$

$= -9497.47$ kJ

5 (*b*) Displacement work

$= \underset{\text{cylinder}}{\int pdV} + \underset{\text{balloon}}{\int pdV} = 0 + \underset{\text{balloon}}{\int pdV}$

$= 101.3 \text{ kPa} \times 0.6 \text{ m}^3$

$= 60.795 \text{ kJ} = 60.8$ kJ

As, balloon pushes the atmosphere.

$\therefore$ Work done by the atmosphere

$= -60.8$ kJ

6 (*b*) $pV = nRT$

$\left(p_{atm} + \frac{mg}{A}\right)Ah = nRT$

$\Rightarrow \quad n = \frac{\left(p_{atm} + \frac{mg}{A}\right)Ah}{RT}$

Also, gas on heating lifts piston against gravity, spring and atm pressure.

$\therefore W_{gas} = p_{atm} \cdot A \cdot x + \frac{1}{2}kx^2 + mgx$

7 (*c*) $\Delta S_{hot} = \frac{Q}{T_h} = \frac{R}{373} = -0.0214 \text{JK}^{-1}$

$\Delta S_{cold} = \frac{Q}{T_c} = \frac{-8}{273} = -0.0293 \text{ JK}^{-1}$

$\therefore \Delta S_{hot} + \Delta S_{cold} = -0.0507 \text{ JK}^{-1}$.

8 (*c*) $\Delta W = p\Delta V$

$= 1.013 \times 10^5 (1671 \times 10^{-6} - 1 \times 10^{-6})$

$= 169.2 \text{J} \approx 170 \text{J}$

$\Delta Q = 539 \times 4.18 = 2253$ J

$\Delta U = \Delta Q - \Delta W$

$= 2253 - 170$

$= 2083$ J

Hence, sum of all form of energy of 1 g steam is $E + 2083$ J.

9 (*d*) When the stone is about to enter the water,

$\Delta \text{KE} = mgh = 2943$ J

$\Delta \text{PE} = -2943$ J

$\Delta U = 0$

Also, $\Delta Q = \Delta W = 0$

10 (*d*) Piston of *A* is free to move.

$\therefore$ Heat is supplied at constant pressure,

$\Delta Q_A = nC_p(\Delta T)_A$

When piston of *B* is fixed, heat is supplied at constant volume,

$\Delta Q_B = nC_V(\Delta T)_B$

$\Delta Q_A = \Delta Q_B$

$\Rightarrow \quad nC_p\Delta T_A = nC_V\Delta T_B$

$\Rightarrow \quad \Delta T_B = \frac{C_p}{C_V} \cdot \Delta T_A = \gamma \Delta T_A$

Given, $\gamma = 1.4$, $\Delta T_A = 30$ K

$\therefore \quad \Delta T_B = 1.4 \times 30 = 42$ K

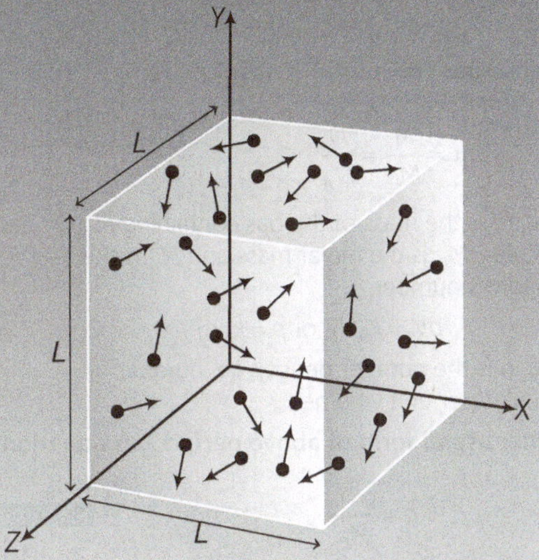

Topicwise No. of Ques asked in 5 Years (NEET)

Topics	No. of Questions				
	2024	2023	2022	2021	2020
Molecular Nature of Matter	–	–	–	–	–
Behaviour of Gases	1	–	1	–	2
Kinetic Theory of an Ideal Gas	–	–	1	–	–
Law of Equipartition of Energy	–	–	–	–	1
Specific Heat Capacity	–	–	–	–	–
Mean Free Path	–	–	–	–	2

Special Type of Ques Asked In 5 Years (NEET)

Types	Years				
	2024	2023	2022	2021	2020
A-R	–	–	–	–	–
Statement Based	–	–	–	–	–
Matching	–	–	1	–	–

Last 5 Years Weigtage (NEET)

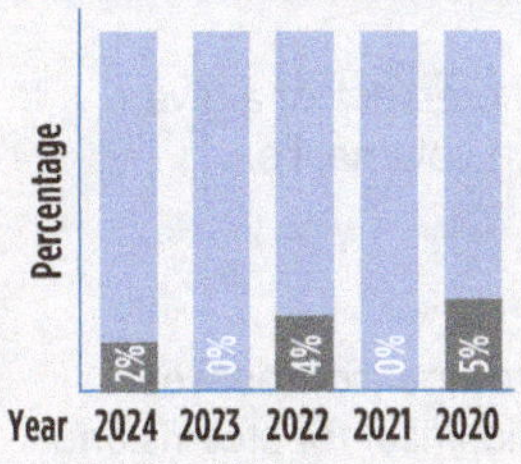

12

Scan for **Physics Through Concept Master** Videos

Kinetic Theory

- Kinetic theory explains the behaviour of gases based on the idea that the gas consists of rapidly moving atoms or molecules. This is possible as the interatomic forces between two gas molecules can be neglected.
- It was developed by Maxwell, Boltzmann and others, and gives a molecular interpretation of pressure and temperature of a gas and is consistent with gas laws and Avogadro's hypothesis.

  It correctly explains specific heat capacities of many gases. It also relates measurable properties of gas such as viscosity, conduction and diffusion with molecular parameters like molecular sizes and molecular masses.

Molecular Nature of Matter

- The molecular nature of matter can be explained by atomic hypothesis given by some scientists such as Feynman, Dalton, Gay-Lussac etc. in 19th century.
- **Feynman's atomic hypothesis :** All things are made of atoms which are little particles that move around in perpetual motion, attracting each other when they are a little distance apart, but repelling upon being squeezed into one another.
- **John Dalton atomic hypothesis :** The scientific atomic theory is usually credited to John Dalton. It is also referred as **molecular theory of matter**. He proposed two laws based on laws of definite and multiple proportions obeyed by elements when they combine into compounds.
  - (i) **First Law** The first law says that any given compound has a fixed proportion by mass of its constituents.
  - (ii) **Second Law** The second law says that when two elements form more than one compound, for a fixed mass of one element, the masses of the other elements are in ratio of small integers.
- **Gay-Lussac's Law** When gases combine chemically to yield another gas, their volumes are in the ratios of small integers.

- **According to the molecular theory of matter**
  (i) The atoms are much free in gases and can travel long distances without colliding. If they are not enclosed, gases disperse away. The average distance, a molecule can travel without colliding is called the **mean free path**. In gases, the mean free path is of the order of thousands of angstroms.
  (ii) In solids and liquids, the closeness makes the interatomic force important. The force has a long range attraction and a short range repulsion. **The atoms attract when they are at a few angstroms but repel when they come closer.**
  (iii) In dynamic equilibrium, molecules collide with each other and change their speeds during the collision. However, only the average properties remain constant.

Behaviour of Gases

- **Behaviour of gases can be stated as follows**
  (i) Gases at low pressure and much higher temperature above which they liquify (or solidify) satisfy a simple relation between their pressure, temperature and volume given by

$$pV = kT$$

where, T is the temperature in kelvin or absolute scale and k is constant for a given sample but varies with the volume of gas.

  (ii) With respect to atoms or molecules, k is proportional to the number of molecules (N) in a sample of gas.

i.e. $$k = Nk_B$$

It has been observed that, the value of k_B is same for all gases and it is called **Boltzmann constant.**

$$k_B = \frac{pV}{NT}$$

  (iii) According to **Avogadro's hypothesis**, the number of molecules per unit volume is the same for all gases at fixed temperature and pressure.

i.e. $$\frac{p_1V_1}{N_1T_1} = \frac{p_2V_2}{N_2T_2} = k_B$$

The number of molecules in 22.4 L of any gas is 6.02×10^{23}. This is known as **Avogadro number** and is **denoted by N_A**.

  (iv) The mass of 22.4 L of any gas is equal to its molecular weight in grams at STP (Standard Temperature 273 K and Pressure 1 atm). This amount of substance is called one **mole.**
  (v) The **perfect gas equation** can be written as

$$pV = \mu RT$$ NEET 2022

where, μ is the number of moles, $R = N_A k_B$ which is a **universal gas constant**, T is **absolute temperature** in kelvin and $R = 8.314 \text{J mol}^{-1}\text{K}^{-1}$.

Also, $$\mu = \frac{M}{M_0} = \frac{N}{N_A}$$

where, M is the mass of the gas containing N molecules, M_0 is the molar mass and N_A is the Avogadro's number.

$\therefore$ $$pV = k_B NT \text{ or } p = k_B nT$$

where, n is the number density, i.e. number of molecules per unit volume.

Another useful form of above perfect gas equation is

$$p = \frac{\rho RT}{M_0}$$ NEET 2020

where, ρ is the mass density of the gas.

  (vi) If a gas that satisfies the relation, $pV = \mu RT$ exactly at all pressures and temperatures, then it is defined to be an **ideal gas**.
  — **Real gases approach to ideal gas behaviour at low pressure and high temperature** It is shown in the following graph.

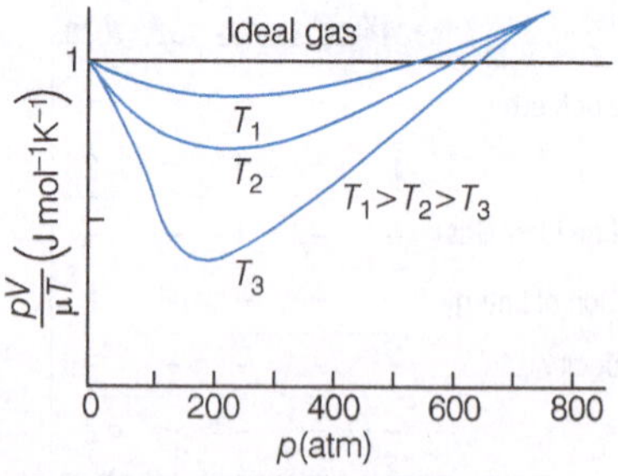

At three different temperatures T_1, T_2 and T_3, a real gas deviates from ideal gas behaviour shown in above figure.

  — An ideal gas is a simple theoretical model of gas. No real gas is truely ideal. At low pressure and high temperature, the molecules of a real gas are far apart and molecular interactions among them are negligible.
  — Without molecular interaction a real gas behaves like an ideal gas.

  (vii) Keeping temperature constant, pressure of a given mass of gas varies inversely with volume, i.e.

$pV = \text{constant}$ or $p \propto 1/V$.

This is called **Boyle's law**.

  — Following graph shows the comparison between experimental p-V curves (solid lines) for steams and the theoretical curves (dotted line) predicted by

Boyle's law at different temperatures. p is in unit of 22 atm and V in unit of 0.09 L.

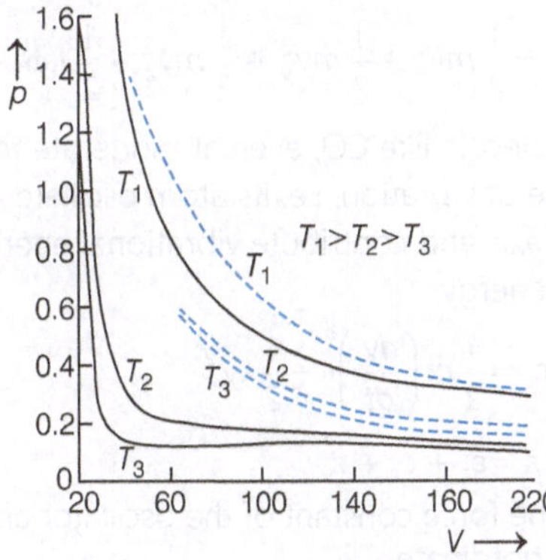

(viii) For a fixed pressure, the volume of a gas is proportional to its absolute temperature T.

i.e. $V \propto T$

This is called **Charles' law.**

— Following graph shows the experimental T-V curve (solid lines) for CO_2 at three pressures compared with Charles' law (dotted lines). T is in unit of 300 K and V in units of 0.13 L.

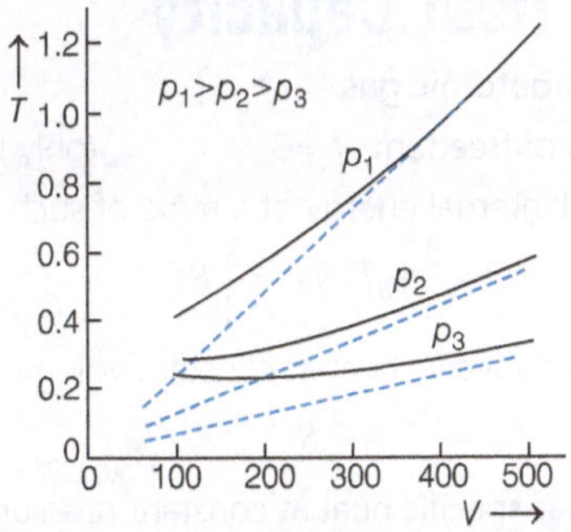

(ix) The total pressure of a mixture of ideal gases is equal to the sum of the partial pressures of the individual gases.

i.e. $$p = p_1 + p_2 + \dots = \frac{\mu_1 RT}{V} + \frac{\mu_2 RT}{V} + \dots$$

This is called **Dalton's law of partial pressure.**

Kinetic Theory of an Ideal Gas

It is based on the molecular picture of matter. **It correlates the macroscopic properties like pressure and temperature of gases to microscopic properties like speed and kinetic energy of gas molecules.**

- At ordinary pressure and temperature, the average distance between molecules is a factor of 10 or more than the typical size of a molecule (2Å). Thus, interaction between molecules is negligible.
- When the molecules come close to each other, they experience intermolecular forces and their velocities change. These interactions are called **collisions.**
- All collisions between molecules among themselves or between molecules and the walls of the container are **elastic, i.e. total kinetic energy and momentum remain conserved.**
- **Total pressure exerted by a gas** is

$$p = \frac{1}{3} nm\overline{v}^2 = \frac{1}{3}\rho\overline{v}^2$$ NEET 2021

where, $$\rho = nm = \frac{Nm}{V} = \text{density of gas}$$

Here, $\overline{v}^2$ denotes the **mean of the squared speed.**

- The **kinetic interpretation of temperature** of gas is given by the equation

$$pV = \frac{2}{3}E$$

- The **internal energy E of an ideal gas** which is purely kinetic energy can be given as

$$E = N \times \frac{1}{2} m\overline{v}^2$$

where, $N\,(= nV)$ is the number of molecules in the sample.

- The **average kinetic energy of one mole** of an ideal gas is

$$E = \frac{3}{2} k_B NT$$

or $$\frac{E}{N} = \frac{1}{2} m\overline{v}^2 = \frac{3}{2} k_B T$$

- Average kinetic energy of a gas molecule is proportional to the absolute temperature of the gas. It is independent of pressure, volume or the nature of an ideal gas.
- In equilibrium, the average kinetic energy of the molecules of different gases will be equal.

i.e. $$\frac{1}{2} m_1\overline{v}_1^2 = \frac{1}{2} m_2\overline{v}_2^2 = \frac{3}{2} k_B T$$

- For a mixture of non-reactive ideal gases, the total pressure gets contribution from each gas in mixture and given by

$$p = \frac{1}{3}\left[n_1 m_1 \overline{v}_1^2 + n_2 m_2 \overline{v}_2^2 + \dots\right]$$

$$\Rightarrow \quad p = (n_1 + n_2 + \dots) k_B T$$

(Dalton's law of partial pressure)

Marks Maximiser

- The mean square speed of a molecule is

$$\bar{v}^2 = \frac{3k_BT}{m} = \frac{3\,RT}{M_0}.$$

The square root of $\bar{v}^2$ is known as **root mean square (rms) speed** and is denoted by v_{rms}.

i.e. $$v_{rms} = \sqrt{\frac{3k_BT}{m}} = \sqrt{\frac{3RT}{M_0}}$$ NEET 2020, 2021

- The speed which is possessed by maximum number of molecules of the gas is called **most probable speed** of the gas molecules,

$$v_{mp} = \sqrt{\frac{2kT}{m}} = \sqrt{\frac{2RT}{M_0}}$$

- The arithmetic mean of the speeds of molecules of a gas at a given temperature is called **average speed** of the molecules.

$$v_{av} = \sqrt{\frac{8kT}{\pi m}} = \sqrt{\frac{8RT}{\pi M_0}}$$

- The relation among v_{rms}, v_{av} and v_{rmp} is

$$v_{rms} > v_{av} > v_{mp}$$

Law of Equipartition of Energy

- It states that for any system in thermal equilibrium, **the total energy is equally distributed in all possible energy modes, with each mode having an average energy equal to $\frac{1}{2}k_BT$.**
- The kinetic energy of a single molecule is

$$\varepsilon_t = \frac{1}{2}mv_x^2 + \frac{1}{2}mv_y^2 + \frac{1}{2}mv_z^2$$

- For a gas in thermal equilibrium at temperature T, the average value of energy denoted by $<\varepsilon_t>$ is $\frac{3}{2}k_BT$.

Since, there is no preferred direction, hence

$$<\frac{1}{2}mv_x^2> = <\frac{1}{2}mv_y^2> = <\frac{1}{2}mv_z^2> = \frac{1}{2}k_BT.$$

NEET 2020, 2021

- A molecule has one degree of freedom for motion in a line, two for motion in a plane and three for motion in space.
- Motion of a body as a whole from one point to another is called **translation.** Thus, a molecule free to move in space has **three translational degrees of freedom.**
- Molecules of a monoatomic gas have **only translational degrees of freedom.**
- Molecules of diatomic gas are made up of two atoms joined rigidly to one another through a bond. Thus, diatomic molecule has **5 degree of freedom**, i.e. 3 translational and 2 rotational. Hence, **total energy consists of translational energy ε_t and rotational energy ε_r.**

$$\text{i.e. } \varepsilon_t + \varepsilon_r = \frac{1}{2}mv_x^2 + \frac{1}{2}mv_y^2 + \frac{1}{2}mv_z^2 + \frac{1}{2}I_1\omega_1^2 + \frac{1}{2}I_2\omega_2^2$$

- Diatomic molecule like CO, even at moderate temperature have a mode of vibration, i.e. its atom oscillate along the interatomic axis and contribute vibrational energy terms ε_v to the total energy,

$$\varepsilon_v = \frac{1}{2}m\left(\frac{dy}{dt}\right)^2 + \frac{1}{2}ky^2$$

$$\Rightarrow \qquad \varepsilon = \varepsilon_t + \varepsilon_r + \varepsilon_v$$

where, k is the force constant of the oscillator and y is the vibrational coordinate.

- Each translational and rotational degrees of freedom of a molecule contributes $\frac{1}{2}k_BT$ to the energy, while each vibrational frequency contributes $2 \times \frac{1}{2}k_BT = k_BT$, since a vibrational mode has both kinetic and potential energy modes.

For Concept Master Video

Specific Heat Capacity

(i) **For monoatomic gas**

Degree of freedom, $f = 3$ (only translational)

The total internal energy of a mole of such a gas is

$$U = \frac{3}{2}k_BT\,N_A = \frac{3}{2}RT$$

The molar specific heat at constant volume,

$$C_V = \frac{dU}{dT} = \frac{3}{2}R$$

The molar specific heat at constant pressure,

$$C_p = C_V + R = \frac{5}{2}R \qquad [\because C_p - C_V = R]$$

$\therefore$ Ratio of specific heats, $\gamma = \frac{C_p}{C_V} = \frac{5}{3}$

(ii) **For diatomic gas** (for rigid diatomic)

$f = 5$ (3 translational + 2 rotational)

Similarly, $$U = \frac{5}{2}k_B\,T \times N_A = \frac{5}{2}RT$$

The molar specific heats are

$$C_V = \frac{5}{2}R,\ C_p = \frac{7}{2}R \Rightarrow \gamma = \frac{C_p}{C_V} = \frac{7}{5}$$

If the diatomic molecule is not rigid but in addition has a vibrational mode, then

$$U = \left(\frac{5}{2}k_BT + k_BT\right)N_A = \frac{7}{2}RT$$

$$\Rightarrow \qquad C_V = \frac{7}{2}R,\ C_p = \frac{9}{2}R \text{ and } \gamma = \frac{9}{7}$$

(iii) **For polyatomic gas**

Generally, degree of freedom $= (6 + f)$
(3 translational + 3 rotational + f vibrational)

Total internal energy,

$$U = \left(\frac{3}{2}k_BT + \frac{3}{2}k_BT + f\,k_BT\right)N_A$$

$$\Rightarrow \quad C_V = (3 + f)\,R \text{ and } C_p = (4 + f)\,R$$

where, f = number of vibrational modes.

$$\gamma = \frac{(4 + f)}{(3 + f)}$$

- **Specific heat capacity of solid** is $C = \frac{\Delta Q}{\Delta T} = \frac{\Delta U}{\Delta T} = 3R$

Hence, total energy, $U = 3k_BTN_A = 3RT$

Marks Maximiser

For Concept Master Video

- If n_1 moles of one gas is mixed with n_2 molesof another gas and so on ...., then

$$C_{V_{\text{mix}}} = \frac{n_1 C_{V_1} + n_2 C_{V_2} + \ldots\ldots\ldots}{n_1 + n_2 + \ldots\ldots\ldots}$$

where, $C_{V\text{mix}} \to$ molar specific heat of mixture at constant volume

- C_{V_1} and $C_{V_2} \to$ molar specific heats at constant volume of first and second gas, respectively.

So, $C_{p_{\text{mix}}} = C_{V_{\text{mix}}} + R$

Mean Free Path

- The average distance travelled by a molecule between two successive collisions is known as the **mean free path (l) of the molecule.**

The volume swept by a molecule in time Δt in which any molecule will collide with it, is shown below.

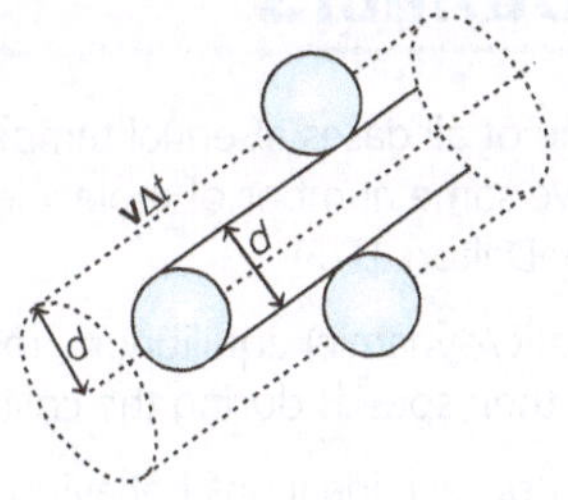

Mean free path, $l = \frac{1}{\sqrt{2}\, n\pi d^2}$

where, d = diameter of each molecule

and n = number of molecules per unit volume.

- The **rate of collision** of gas molecule is $n\pi d^2 < v >$ or the time between two successive collisions is on the average,

$$\tau = \frac{1}{n\pi < v > d^2}$$

- The mean free path in gases is of the order of thousands of angstroms.

Caution Points

- Pressure exists throughout a fluid, not only on the walls of container. A layer of gas inside a container is in equilibrium due to same amount of pressure exerted on both sides of the layer.
- The mean free path in a gas is 100 times the interatomic distance and 1000 times the size of the molecule. Generally, at ordinary pressures and temperatures, the intermolecular distances in solids and liquids is only 10 times of their interatomic distances.
- Molecules of air in a room do not fall and settle on the ground due to gravity because of their high speed and collisions.

  In equilibrium, there is a very slight increase in density at lower heights. This effect is small, since the potential energy for ordinary heights is much less than the average kinetic energy.
- The average of certain square quantity is not always equal to the square of average quantity. i.e. $< v^2 > \neq (< v >)^2$

PYQ Notes

1. When two ideal polyatomic gases at temperatures T_1 and T_2 are mixed, so that there is no loss of energy. If f_1 and f_2, m_1 and m_2, n_1 and n_2 are the degree of freedom, masses, number of moles of first and second gas respectively, then the temperature of mixture of these two gases is given by

$$T_{\text{mix}} = \frac{n_1 f_1 T_1 + n_2 f_2 T_2}{n_1 f_1 + n_2 f_2}$$

[JEE Main 2021]

2. For a gas of n moles having number of degree of freedom f at temperature T,

- The total internal energy of the gas is given by

$$U = nC_VT = \frac{nfRT}{2}$$

[NEET 2021]

- The change in internal energy of the gas is given by

$$\Delta U = \frac{nfR\Delta T}{2} = \frac{f}{2}(nR\Delta T) = \frac{f}{2}(W_{p\,=\,\text{constant}})$$

where, $W_{p=\text{constant}} = nR\Delta T$ = work done by the gas at constant pressure.

[NEET 2019]

Step by Step

Mastering NCERT

- Concept Builders
- Topical Questions
- Assertion and Reason Questions
- Statement Based
- Matching Type
- Numerical Type
- NCERT Exemplar
- Past Exams MCQs
- Skill Boosters

Concept Builders

1 Equal volume of all gases at equal temperature and pressure have same number of molecules. This law was proposed by Dalton. [T/F]

2 In .... (static/dynamic) equilibrium, molecules collide and change their speeds during the collision.

3 Real gases approach ideal gas behaviour at .... (low/high) pressure and .... (low/high) temperature.

4 When temperature of a given mass of a gas is kept constant, its pressure varies .... (directly/inversely) as the volume of the gas.

5 An ideal gas is heated at constant volume until its pressure doubles, then the mean square speed of the molecules become .... (half/double).

6 If the volume of a gas is doubled at constant pressure , then average translational kinetic energy of its molecule will also get doubled. [T/F]

7 The rms velocity of a gas is doubled when temperature of gas becomes .... (half/four) times.

8 The mean free path of a gas varies directly as density and pressure of the gas. [T/F]

9 What is the simplest evidence in nature that you can think of to suggest that atoms are not point masses.

10 The air pressure in a car tyre .... (increases/decreases) during driving.

11 As the bubble comes from the bottom of a lake to the top, its radius increases. [T/F]

12 What is the degree of freedom of a diatomic molecule?

13 In equilibrium, the total energy is equally distributed in all possible energy modes, with each mode having an average energy equal to .... $k_B T$. This is know as law of equipartition of energy.

14 How is the average kinetic energy of a gas molecule is related to the temperature of the gas?

15 Helium gas is filled in a closed vessel whose coefficient of thermal expansion is negligible. When it is heated from 300 K to 600 K, then the average kinetic energy of helium atom becomes ...... (half/double)

16 What is the relation between degree of freedom (n) and γ of a gas?

17 The ratio of kinetic energy of oxygen molecule and hydrogen molecule at temperature 27°C is ....

18 If μ_1 mole of a non-reactive gas in thermodynamical state (p_1, V_1, T_1) are mixed with μ_2 moles of another non-reactive gas at (p_2, V_2, T_2) and resultant mixture is at (p, V, T), then $\frac{\mu_1 p_1 V_1}{T_1} + \frac{\mu_2 p_2 V_2}{T_2} = \frac{pV}{T} \mu$. [T/F]

19 The average energy of a molecule or atom of a solid in three dimension is $3k_B T$. [T/F]

20 The mean free path of a gas molecule is defined as the average distance travelled by the molecules between two successive collisions. [T/F]

Topical Questions

Molecular Nature of Matter

1 Kinetic theory of gases relates viscosity of gases with **NCERT Pg. 244**

(a) temperature (b) velocity
(c) molecular size (d) pressure

2 The laws of definite and multiple proportions obeyed by elements when they combine to form a compound is proposed by **NCERT Pg. 244**

(a) Maxwell (b) John Dalton
(c) Avogadro (d) Newton

Behaviour of Gases

3 From the given V-T figure, find the relation between p_1 and p_2. **NCERT Pg. 246**

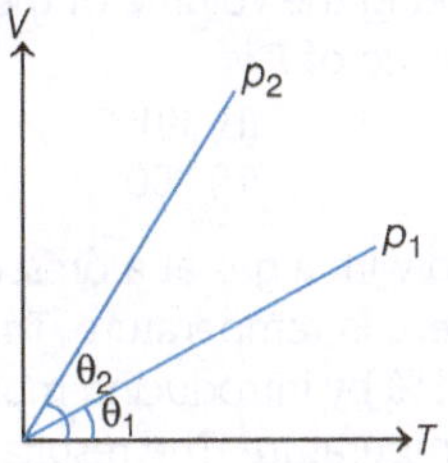

(a) $p_1 = p_2$ (b) $p_2 > p_1$
(c) $p_1 > p_2$ (d) $p_1 \geq p_2$

4 A 4.0 L sample at 27°C and 1.2 atm of pressure contains 0.75 mol of a gas. If an additional 0.25 mol of gas at the same temperature and pressure are added, then total volume of the gas is **NCERT Pg. 246**

(a) 1.5 L (b) 5.33 L
(c) 3 L (d) 4.5 L

5 The ratio of the molecular masses of two gases is 7/8. What is the ratio of the number of moles of two gases, if they are in two different containers and have same mass for each gas? **NCERT Pg. 246**
(a) 8/7 (b) 7/8
(c) 7/5 (d) 5/7

6 The equation of state for 5g of oxygen at a pressure p and temperature T when it occupies a volume V will be **NCERT Pg. 246**

(a) $pV = (5/32)RT$ (b) $pV = 5RT$
(c) $pV = (5/2)RT$ (d) $pV = (5/16)RT$

7 A vessel contains 32 g of O_2 at a temperature T. The pressure of the gas is p. An identical vessel containing 4g of H_2 at a temperature $2T$ has a pressure of **NCERT Pg. 246**

(a) $8p$ (b) $4p$
(c) p (d) $\frac{p}{8}$

8 Two identical vessels A and B with frictionless pistons contain the same ideal gas at the same temperature T and same volume V. The masses of gas in A and B are m_A and m_B, respectively. The gases are allowed to expand isothermally to same final volume $2V$. The change in pressures of the gas in A and B are found to be Δp and $1.5\,\Delta p$, respectively. Then, **NCERT Pg. 246**
(a) $9m_A = 4m_B$ (b) $3m_A = 2m_B$
(c) $2m_A = 3m_B$ (d) $4m_A = 9m_B$

9 $pV = \mu RT$ can be rewritten as **NCERT Pg. 246**
(a) $pV = k_B NT$ (N = total number of molecules in the perfect gas)
(b) $p = k_B nT$ (n = number density)
(c) $p = \rho RT/M_0$ (ρ = mass density and M_0 = molar mass)
(d) All of the above

10 Two vessels separately contains two ideal gases A and B at the same temperature, the pressure of A being twice that of B. Under such conditions, the density of A is found to be 1.5 times the density of B. The ratio of molecular weight of A and B is **NCERT Pg. 246**
(a) $\frac{2}{3}$ (b) $\frac{3}{4}$ (c) 2 (d) $\frac{1}{2}$

11 A gas is filled in a vessel. Its temperature is increased by 25% on Kelvin scale and volume is decreased by 10%. How much percentage of the gas has to leak for pressure to remain constant? **NCERT Pg. 246**
(a) 25% (b) 20% (c) 28% (d) 30%

12 Which one of the following graphs represents the behaviour of an ideal gas? **NCERT Pg. 246**

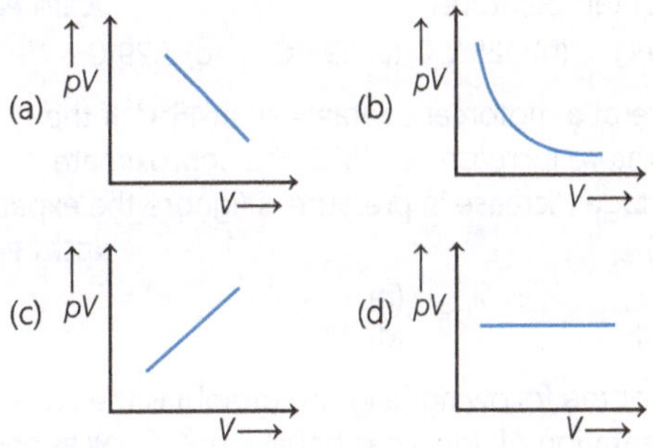

13 Saturated vapour is compressed to half of its volume without any change in temperature, then the pressure will be **NCERT Pg. 246**
(a) doubled (b) halved
(c) same (d) zero

14 1 mole of gas occupies a volume of 200 mL at 100 mm pressure. What is the volume occupied by two moles of gas at 400 mm pressure and at same temperature? **NCERT Pg. 246**

(a) 50 mL (b) 100 mL (c) 200 mL (d) 400 mL

15 For an ideal gas, keeping the temperature constant, the pressure of gas is decreased by 20%. The percentage change in volume is **NCERT Pg. 246**
(a) increases by 20%
(b) decreases by 20%
(c) increases by 25%
(d) decreases by 25%

16 Volume-temperature graph at atmospheric pressure for a monoatomic gas (V in m^3, T in °C) is **NCERT Pg. 246**

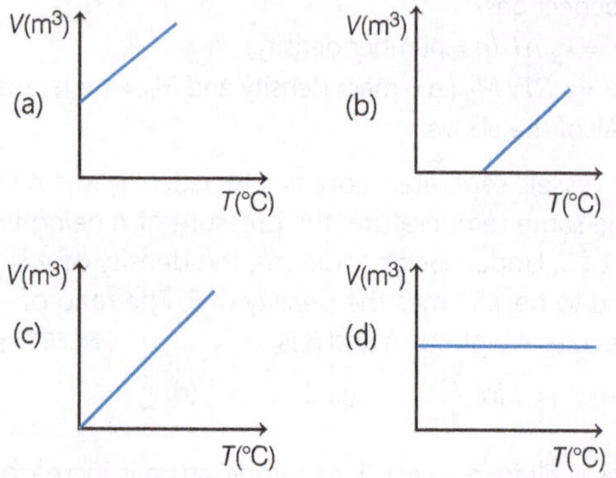

17 A perfect gas at 27°C is heated at constant pressure, so as to double its volume. The increase in temperature of the gas will be **NCERT Pg. 246**

(a) 300°C (b) 54°C (c) 327°C (d) 600°C

18 When the temperature of a gas increases by 1°C at constant volume, its pressure increases by 0.4%. What is its initial temperature? **NCERT Pg. 246**

(a) 250°C (b) 125°C (c) 195°C (d) 329°C

19 The tyre of a motorcar contains air at 15°C. If the temperature increases to 35°C, the approximate percentage increase in pressure is (ignore the expansion of tyre) **NCERT Pg. 246**

(a) 7 (b) 9
(c) 11 (d) 13

20 Which of the following diagram (graph) is the correct representation of ideal gas behaviour? **NCERT Pg. 246**

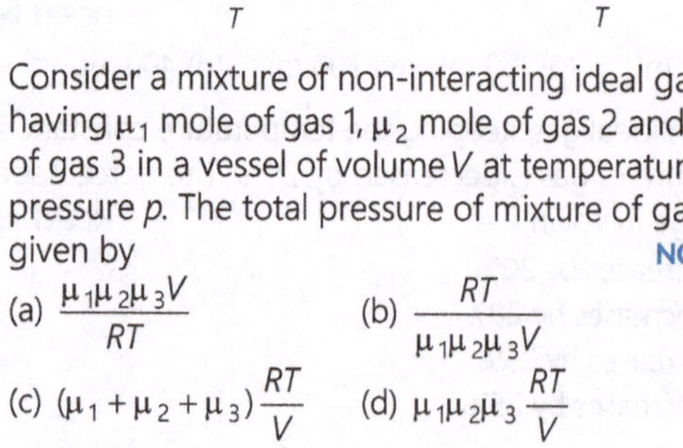

21 Consider a mixture of non-interacting ideal gases having μ_1 mole of gas 1, μ_2 mole of gas 2 and μ_3 mole of gas 3 in a vessel of volume V at temperature T and pressure p. The total pressure of mixture of gases is given by **NCERT Pg. 246**

(a) $\frac{\mu_1\mu_2\mu_3 V}{RT}$ (b) $\frac{RT}{\mu_1\mu_2\mu_3 V}$

(c) $(\mu_1+\mu_2+\mu_3)\frac{RT}{V}$ (d) $\mu_1\mu_2\mu_3\frac{RT}{V}$

Kinetic Theory of an Ideal Gas

22 Air is filled at 75°C in a vessel of open mouth. The vessel is heated to a temperature T, so that 25% of the air escapes. Assuming the volume of the vessel remaining constant, the value of T is **NCERT Pg. 248**

(a) 444°C (b) 191°C
(c) 171°C (d) 200°C

23 A vessel is filled with a gas at a pressure 76 cm of mercury at a certain temperature. The mass of the gas is increased by 75% by introducing more gas in the vessel at the same temperature. The resultant pressure of the gas is **NCERT Pg. 248**

(a) 114 cm of mercury (b) 112 cm of mercury
(c) 133 cm of mercury (d) 122 cm of mercury

24 Total rotational kinetic energy of two moles of rigid diatomic gas is **NCERT Pg. 248**

(a) RT (b) $\frac{RT}{2}$ (c) $\frac{5RT}{2}$ (d) $2RT$

25 In collision of a molecule of an ideal gas with the wall of container, **NCERT Pg. 248**

(a) only total kinetic energy remains conserved.
(b) only total momentum remains conserved.
(c) total kinetic energy and total momentum remains conserved.
(d) Neither total kinetic energy nor total momentum is conserved.

26 A gas at 300K is enclosed in a container. Now, the container is placed on a fast moving train. While the train is in motion, the temperature of the gas **NCERT Pg. 248**

(a) rises above 300 K (b) falls below 300K
(c) remains unchanged (d) becomes unsteady

27 When molecules of an isotropic gas travelling in cubical box along + x-direction collides with the wall of box elastically, the pressure exerted on the walls due to gas is (where, n = number of molecules per unit volume, m = mass and $\bar{v}^2$ = mean of squared speed) **NCERT Pg. 248**

(a) $3nm\bar{v}^2$ (b) $\frac{1}{3}nm\bar{v}^2$
(c) $nm\bar{v}^2$ (d) None of these

28 The internal energy of an ideal gas is in the form of **NCERT Pg. 248**

(a) kinetic energy of molecules
(b) potential energy of molecules
(c) Both kinetic and potential energy of molecules
(d) gravitational potential energy of molecules

29 The average translational kinetic energy of the molecule of a gas is **NCERT Pg. 248**

(a) $\frac{3}{2}k_BT$ (b) k_BT (c) $\frac{1}{2}k_BT$ (d) $\frac{2}{3}k_BT$

30 Oxygen and hydrogen are at the same temperature T. The ratio of the mean kinetic energy of oxygen molecules to that of the hydrogen molecules will be **NCERT Pg. 248**

(a) 16 : 1 (b) 1 : 1 (c) 4 : 1 (d) 1 : 4

31 At what temperature, the kinetic energy of gas molecule is half of the value at 27°C? **NCERT Pg. 248**

(a) 13.5°C (b) 150°C
(c) 75 K (d) – 123°C

32 The ratio of molecular masses of two gases in a container at a temperature T is 3 : 2. The ratio of the kinetic energies of the molecule of two gases is **NCERT Pg. 248**

(a) 3 : 2 (b) 9 : 4 (c) 1 : 1 (d) 4 : 9

33 At constant pressure, which of the following is true for an ideal gas? (where, ρ = density of the gas and $\bar{v}$ = rms speed of the gas) **NCERT Pg. 248**

(a) $\bar{v} \propto \sqrt{\rho}$ (b) $\bar{v} \propto \frac{1}{\rho}$
(c) $\bar{v} \propto \rho$ (d) $\bar{v} \propto \frac{1}{\sqrt{\rho}}$

34 The root mean square speed of a nitrogen molecule at 300K is (take, $k_B = 1.38 \times 10^{-23}$ JK^{-1} and $N_A = 6.02 \times 10^{23}$) **NCERT Pg. 248**

(a) $\sqrt{534}$ ms^{-1} (b) 534 ms^{-1}
(c) 16.34 ms^{-1} (d) $\sqrt{216}$ ms^{-1}

35 The rms velocity of a gas molecule is 300 ms^{-1}. The rms velocity of the molecules of gas with twice the molecular weight and half the absolute temperature, is **NCERT Pg. 248**

(a) 300 ms^{-1} (b) 600 ms^{-1}
(c) 75 ms^{-1} (d) 150 ms^{-1}

36 For a given gas at 1 atm pressure, rms speed of the molecules is 200 m/s at 127°C. At 2 atm pressure and at 227°C, the rms speed of the molecules will be **NCERT Pg. 248**

(a) $100\sqrt{5}$ m/s (b) 80 m/s
(c) 100 m/s (d) $80\sqrt{5}$ m/s

37 If the mass of He is 4 times that of hydrogen, then mean velocity of He at the same temperature is **NCERT Pg. 248**

(a) 2 times of H-mean value.
(b) (1 / 2) times of H-mean value.
(c) 2 times of H-mean value.
(d) same as H-mean value.

38 The molecules of a given mass of a gas have rms velocity of 200 ms^{-1} at 27°C and 1.0×10^5 Nm^{-2} pressure. When the temperature and pressure of the gas are respectively, 127°C and 0.05×10^5 Nm^{-2}, the rms velocity of its molecules (in ms^{-1}) is **NCERT Pg. 248**

(a) $\frac{400}{\sqrt{3}}$ (b) $\frac{100\sqrt{2}}{3}$
(c) $\frac{100}{3}$ (d) $100\sqrt{2}$

39 An ideal gas ($\gamma = 1.5$) is expanded adiabatically. How many times the gas has to be expanded to reduce the root mean square velocity of the molecules 2.0 times? **NCERT Pg. 248**

(a) 4 times (b) 16 times (c) 8 times (d) 2 times

40 At 0°C temperature, root mean square speed of which of the following gas will be maximum? **NCERT Pg. 248**

(a) H_2 (b) N_2
(c) O_2 (d) Same for all gases

41 Given below are plots of Maxwell's distribution of velocity of gas at different temperatures. Identify the true relation. **NCERT Pg. 248**

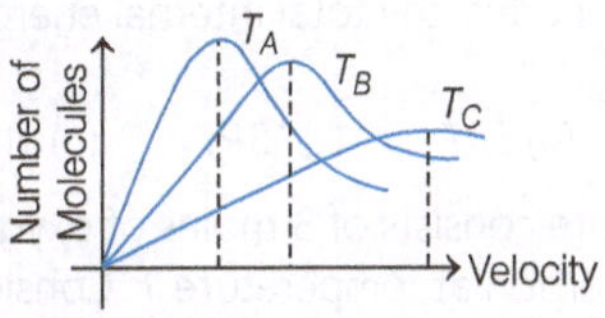

(a) $T_A > T_B > T_C$ (b) $T_A < T_B < T_C$
(c) $T_A = T_B = T_C$ (d) $T_A < T_B > T_C$

42 RMS speed of oxygen gas molecules at 27°C is v. Its value at 327°C will be **NCERT Pg. 248**

(a) v (b) $\sqrt{2}\,v$
(c) $\frac{3v}{\sqrt{2}}$ (d) $\frac{v}{\sqrt{2}}$

43 The root mean square speed of molecules of a gas is 1260 m/s. The average speed of the gas molecules is **NCERT Pg. 248**

(a) 1161 m/s (b) 1671 m/s
(c) 912 m/s (d) 1040 m/s

Law of Equipartition of Energy

44 The amount of heat energy required to raise the temperature of 1 g of helium at NTP, from T_1 kelvin to T_2 kelvin is **NCERT Pg. 252**

(a) $\frac{3}{8}N_Ak_B(T_2 - T_1)$ (b) $\frac{3}{2}N_Ak_B(T_2 - T_1)$
(c) $\frac{3}{4}N_Ak_B(T_2 - T_1)$ (d) $\frac{3}{4}N_Ak_B\left(\frac{T_2}{T_1}\right)$

45 A balloon has 5.0 g mol of helium at 7°C. Calculate the total internal energy of the system. NCERT Pg. 252

(a) 5×10^4 J (b) 2.9×10^4 J
(c) 1.74×10^4 J (d) 8×10^4 J

46 1 kg of a diatomic gas is at a pressure of 8×10^4 Nm^{-2} and the density of the gas is 4 kgm^{-3}. What is the energy of the gas due to its thermal motion? NCERT Pg. 252

(a) 3×10^4 J (b) 5×10^4 J
(c) 6×10^4 J (d) 7×10^4 J

47 Molecule of CO at moderate temperature have energy NCERT Pg. 252

(a) $\frac{7}{2} k_BT$ (b) $\frac{5}{2} k_BT$ (c) $\frac{3}{2} k_BT$ (d) $\frac{1}{2} k_BT$

48 The value of total energy two moles of polyatomic molecules is NCERT Pg. 252

(a) $\left(\frac{3}{2} k_BT + \frac{f}{2} k_BT\right) N_A$ (b) $\left(3 k_BT + \frac{f}{2} k_BT\right) N_A$

(c) $(3 k_BT + fk_BT) N_A$ (d) $\left(\frac{3}{2} k_BT + fk_BT\right) N_A$

49 A gas mixture consists of 2 moles of nitrogen and 4 moles of xenon at temperature T. Neglecting all vibrational modes, the total internal energy of the system is NCERT Pg. 252

(a) $4RT$ (b) $5RT$ (c) $15RT$ (d) $11RT$

50 A gas mixture consists of 3 moles of oxygen and 5 moles of argon at temperature T. Considering only translational and rotational modes, the total internal energy of the system is NCERT Pg. 252

(a) 12 RT (b) 15 RT (c) 20 RT (d) 4 RT

Specific Heat Capacity

51 If γ is the ratio of specific heats and R is the universal gas constant, then the molar specific heat at constant volume C_V is given by NCERT Pg. 253

(a) γR (b) $\frac{(\gamma - 1) R}{\gamma}$ (c) $\frac{R}{\gamma - 1}$ (d) $\frac{\gamma R}{\gamma - 1}$

52 A gas consisting of rigid diatomic molecules was initially under standard condition, then gas was compressed adiabatically to one-fifth of its initial volume. What will be the mean kinetic energy of a rotating molecule in the final state? NCERT Pg. 253

(a) 1.44 J (b) 4.55 J
(c) 787.98×10^{-23} J (d) 757.3×10^{-23} J

53 The specific heats C_p and C_V of a gas of diatomic molecules, A are given (in units of $J\,mol^{-1}\,K^{-1}$) by 29 and 22, respectively. Another gas of diatomic molecules B, has the corresponding values 30 and 21. If they are treated as ideal gases, then NCERT Pg. 253

(a) A has a vibrational mode but B has none.
(b) Both A and B have a vibrational mode each.
(c) A has one vibrational mode and B has two.
(d) A is rigid but B has a vibrational mode.

54 The ratio of molar specific heats $\frac{C_p}{C_V} = \gamma$ can be expressed in terms of degree of freedom (f) as NCERT Pg. 253

(a) $\left(1+\frac{f}{3}\right)$ (b) $\left(1+\frac{2}{f}\right)$ (c) $\left(1+\frac{f}{2}\right)$ (d) $\left(1+\frac{1}{f}\right)$

55 As temperature tends to zero, i.e. $T \to 0K$ NCERT Pg. 253

(a) specific heat of all substances approaches zero.
(b) specific heat of all substances approaches infinity.
(c) specific heat of all substances may be zero or infinity.
(d) specific heat of some substances approaches to zero.

56 The degree of freedom of an ideal gas molecule is 5. The gas perform 50 J work in expansion at constant pressure. The heat absorbed by the gas during this expansion is NCERT Pg. 253

(a) 100 J (b) 125 J (c) 150 J (d) 175 J

Mean Free Path

57 We took two separate gases with the same number densities for both. If the ratio of the diameters of their molecules is 4 : 1, then ratio of their mean free paths is NCERT Pg. 254

(a) 1 : 4 (b) 4 : 1
(c) 2 : 1 (d) 1 : 16

58 The mean free path for air molecule at STP is ($d = 2 \times 10^{-10}$ m and $n = 2.7 \times 10^{25} m^{-3}$) NCERT Pg. 254

(a) 3.5×10^{-7} m (b) 4×10^{-7} m
(c) 2.05×10^{-7} m (d) 5×10^{-7} m

59 Consider an ideal gas confined in an isolated closed chamber. As the gas undergoes an adiabatic expansion, the average time of collision between molecules increases as V^q, where V is the volume of the gas. The value of q is $\left(\gamma = \frac{C_p}{C_V}\right)$ NCERT Pg. 254

(a) $\frac{3\gamma + 5}{6}$ (b) $\frac{3\gamma - 5}{6}$ (c) $\frac{\gamma + 1}{2}$ (d) $\frac{\gamma - 1}{2}$

60 In an isobaric process, the absolute temperature is doubled. The mean free path (λ) and the relaxation time (τ) will become respectively NCERT Pg. 254

(a) $\frac{1}{2}$ times and 2 times (b) 2 times and $\sqrt{2}$ times

(c) $\sqrt{2}$ times and $\frac{1}{\sqrt{2}}$ times (d) 2 times and $\frac{1}{2}$ times

Assertion and Reason Questions

Direction (Q. Nos. 1-10) *In the following questions, a statement of Assertion is followed by a corresponding statement of Reason. Of the following statements, choose the correct one.*

(a) Both Assertion and Reason are correct and Reason is the correct explanation of Assertion.
(b) Both Assertion and Reason are correct but Reason is not the correct explanation of Assertion.
(c) Assertion is correct but Reason is incorrect.
(d) Assertion is incorrect but Reason is correct.

1 Assertion In gases, the molecules move faster and long distances without colliding.

Reason In gases, the interatomic forces are negligible. **NCERT Pg. 246**

2 Assertion A gas that satisfy $pV = \mu RT$ at all pressures and temperatures is known as ideal gas.

Reason A real gas at low pressure and high temperature behaves like ideal gas. **NCERT Pg. 246**

3 Assertion Gases do not settle to the bottom of a container.

Reason Gases have high kinetic energy **NCERT Pg. 246**

4 Assertion The total translational kinetic energy of all the molecules of a given mass of an ideal gas is 1.5 times the product of its pressure and volume.

Reason The molecules of a gas collide with each other and the velocities of the molecules change due to the collision. **NCERT Pg. 248**

5 Assertion If a gas chamber containing a gas is moved translationally, then temperature of gas will increase.

Reason Total kinetic energy of the chamber will increase by the translational motion. **NCERT Pg. 248**

6 Assertion Pressure of an ideal gas is equal to $(1/3)\, nm\bar{v}^2$.

Reason Pressure of an ideal gas increases with increase of volume. **NCERT Pg. 248**

7 Assertion The root mean square velocity of molecules of a gas having Maxwellian distribution of velocities is higher than their most probable velocity, at any temperature.

Reason A very small number of molecules of a gas possesses very large velocities. **NCERT Pg. 249**

8 Assertion Degree of freedom of a monoatomic gas is always three, whether we consider vibrational effect or not.

Reason At all temperatures (low or high), vibrational kinetic energy of an ideal gas is zero. **NCERT Pg. 252**

9 Assertion The number of degrees of freedom of a linear triatomic molecules is 7.

Reason The number of degree of freedom depends on number of particle in the system. **NCERT Pg. 252**

10 Assertion Mean free path of gas molecules does not depend on the density of the gas.

Reason Mean free path of gas molecules is defined as the average distance travelled by a molecule between two successive collisions. **NCERT Pg. 254**

Statement Based Questions

Direction (Q. Nos. 1-8) *In the following questions, two statement (I & II) are given. In the light of the given statements, choose the correct option given below.*

(a) Both Statement I and Statement II are incorrect.
(b) Statement I is correct but Statement II is incorrect.
(c) Statement I is incorrect but Statement II is correct.
(d) Both Statement I and Statement II are correct.

1 Statement I Atomic theory relates molecular properties with bulk properties of a gas.

Statement II According to kinetic theory, the interatomic forces are negligible in gases. **NCERT Pg. 244**

2 Statement I At low pressure and high temperature,a real gas behaves as an ideal gas.

Statement II According to Boyle's law, the graph of pressure *versus* volume is straight line. **NCERT Pg. 246**

3 Statement I The average kinetic energy of a molecule of the gas is independent of absolute temperature of the gas.

Statement II The collision between molecules of the gas and the wall of the container is elastic. **NCERT Pg. 248**

4 Statement I In the kinetic theory of gases, collisions between gas particles and the walls of the container are considered elastic.

Statement II Gas molecules are considered point like, volumeless particles with no intermolecular forces and in constant random motion. **NCERT Pg. 248**

5 Statement I If a gas sample is left for a long time, it will eventually reach a steady state.

Statement II The density and distribution of molecules do not depend on distance, position and time. **NCERT Pg. 248**

6 Statement I The product of pressure and volume of an ideal gas will be equal to translational kinetic energy of its molecules.

Statement II Molecules of diatomic gas have only translational degree of freedom. **NCERT Pg. 252**

7 Statement I According to the law of equipartition of energy, the energy for each degree of freedom in thermal equilibrium is $\frac{1}{2}k_bT$.

Statement II Each vibrational mode gives only 1 degree of freedom. **NCERT Pg. 252**

8 Statement I The average distance between two successive collisions of the gas molecules is inversely proportional to its number density.

Statement II The time between two successive collisions of the gas molecules is independent of the diameter of the molecules of gas. **NCERT Pg. 254**

Matching Type Questions

1 Match the Column I (relation of p, V and T) with Column II (related laws). **NCERT Pg. 246**

Column I	Column II
A. $pV = k_BNT$	1. Dalton's law
B. $p \propto 1/V, T =$ constant	2. Boyle's law
C. $V \propto T, p =$ constant	3. Ideal gas equation
D. $p = p_1 + p_2 + ...$	4. Charles' law

Choose the correct answer from the options given below.

Codes

	A	B	C	D
(a)	3	2	1	4
(b)	2	3	1	4
(c)	3	2	4	1
(d)	3	4	1	2

2 A molecule of gas collide with the wall of a container elastically as shown in figure below

Match the Column I (physical quantity) with Column II (formula). **NCERT Pg. 248**

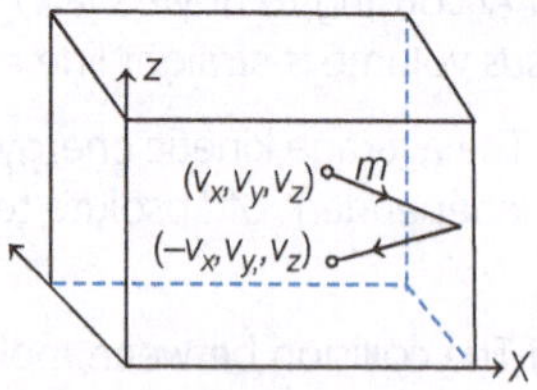

Column I	Column II
A. Change in momentum on the wall	1. $nm\bar{v}_x^2$
B. Total momentum due to v_x	2. $2mv_x$
C. Pressure due to collision along X-axis	3. $(nmv_x^2)A\Delta t$
D. Total pressure along X-axis	4. nmv_x^2

Choose the correct answer from the options given below.

Codes

	A	B	C	D
(a)	2	3	1	4
(b)	2	3	4	1
(c)	1	4	2	3
(d)	1	2	4	3

3 In Column I gases of different nature are given, then match Column I with the respective adiabatic constant (γ) in Column II. **NCERT Pg. 253**

Column I	Column II
A. Non-rigid diatomic gas	1. 1.67
B. Non-linear triatomic gas	2. 1.4
C. Rigid diatomic gas	3. 1.33
D. Monoatomic gas	4. 1.28

Choose the correct answer from the options given below.

Codes

	A	B	C	D
(a)	4	3	2	1
(b)	4	1	3	2
(c)	1	4	2	3
(d)	4	2	1	3

Numerical Type Questions

1 The average degree of freedom per molecule for a gas is 6. The gas performs 30J of work when it expands at constant pressure. The heat absorbed by the gas is ...... J. NCERT Pg. 253

2 The molar heat capacity of a gas is 37.35 J $mol^{-1}K^{-1}$ in the process $pT = A$, where A is a constant. The number of degree of freedom of the molecule of gas is .... NCERT Pg. 253

3 A monoatomic gas performs a work $\frac{2Q}{3}$, where Q is the heat supplied to it. The molar heat capacity of the gas will be ...... $\frac{R}{2}$, during this transformation (where, R is the gas constant). NCERT Pg. 253

4 The change in the magnitude of the volume of an ideal gas when a small additional pressure Δp is applied at a constant temperature, is the same as the change when the temperature is reduced by a small quantity ΔT at constant pressure. The initial temperature and pressure of the gas are 340 K and 2 atm, respectively. If $|\Delta T| = C|\Delta p|$, then value of C (in K/atm) is .... NCERT Pg. 246

5 An engine takes in 5 mol of air at 20°C and 1 atm and compresses it, adiabatically to (1/10)th of the original volume. Assuming air to be a diatomic ideal gas made up of rigid molecules, the change in its internal energy during this process comes out to be X kJ. The value of X to the nearest integer is .... NCERT Pg. 253

6 The temperature, at which the root mean square velocity of hydrogen molecules equals their escape velocity from the earth, is closest to ...... $\times 10^4$ K. Boltzmann constant $k_B = 1.38 \times 10^{-23}$ J/K, Avogadro number $N_A = 6.02 \times 10^{26}$/kg, radius of earth $= 6.4 \times 10^6$ m, gravitational acceleration on earth $= 10\ ms^{-2}$. NCERT Pg. 248

7 The mean free path of a gas molecule at STP is 2×10^{-7} m. The diameter of the molecule is ...... Å (nearest integer). (Given, Boltzmann constant is 1.4×10^{-23} J/K) NCERT Pg. 254

8 2 kg of a diatomic gas is at pressure of $12 \times 10^4\ N/m^2$. It has a density of 8 kg m^{-3}. The energy of the gas due to thermal motion is $x \times 10^3$ J, the value of x is ... . NCERT Pg. 252

9 The velocity of sound in air at a certain temperature is 350 m/s. The velocity of sound in helium at the same temperature is .... m/s.
(Take $\gamma_{air} = \frac{7}{5}$, molecular mass of air = 29u) NCERT Pg. 253

10 14 g nitrogen is filled in a vessel at 300 K temperature. The amount of heat to be transferred to the gas to double the rms speed of its molecule is .... J.
(Take, $R = 8.32$ J $mol^{-1}K^{-1}$) NCERT Pg. 253

NCERT Exemplar Questions

1 A cubic vessel (with face horizontal and vertical) contains an ideal gas at NTP. The vessel is being carried by a rocket which is moving at a speed of 500 ms^{-1} in vertical direction. The pressure of the gas inside the vessel as observed by us on the ground
(a) remains the same because 500 ms^{-1} is very much smaller than v_{rms} of the gas
(b) remains the same because motion of the vessel as a whole does not affect the relative motion of the gas molecules w.r.t. the walls
(c) will increase by a factor equal to $(v_{rms}^2 + (500)^2) / v_{rms}^2$, where v_{rms} was the original mean square velocity of the gas
(d) will be different on the top wall and bottom wall of the vessel

2 1 mol of an ideal gas is contained in a cubical volume V, $ABCDEFGH$ at 300K (see figure). One face of the cube $EFGH$ is made up of a material which totally absorbs any gas molecule incident on it. At any given time,

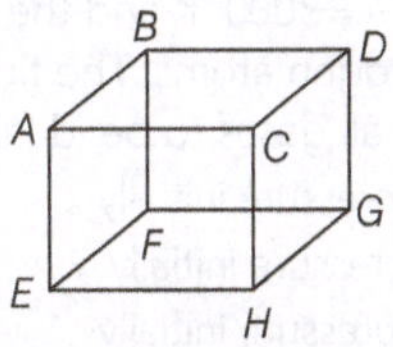

(a) the pressure on $EFGH$ would be zero
(b) the pressure on all the faces will the equal
(c) the pressure of $EFGH$ would be double of the pressure on $ABCD$
(d) the pressure on $EFGH$ would be half of that on $ABCD$

3 Boyle's law is applicable for an
(a) adiabatic process (b) isothermal process
(c) isobaric process (d) isochoric process

4 A cylinder containing an ideal gas is in vertical position and has a piston of mass M that is able to move up or down without friction (see figure). If the temperature is increased, then

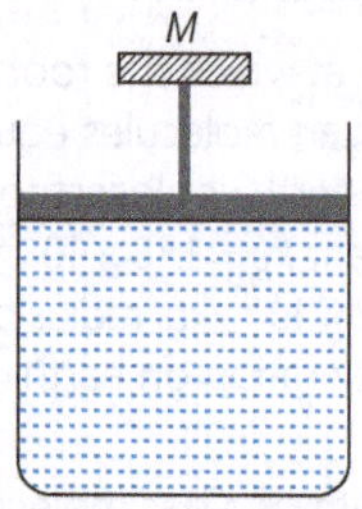

(a) both p and V of the gas will change
(b) only p will increase according to Charles' law
(c) V will change but not p
(d) p will change but not V

5 Volume *versus* temperature graphs for a given mass of an ideal gas are shown in figure, at two different values of constant pressure. What can be inferred about relation between p_1 and p_2?

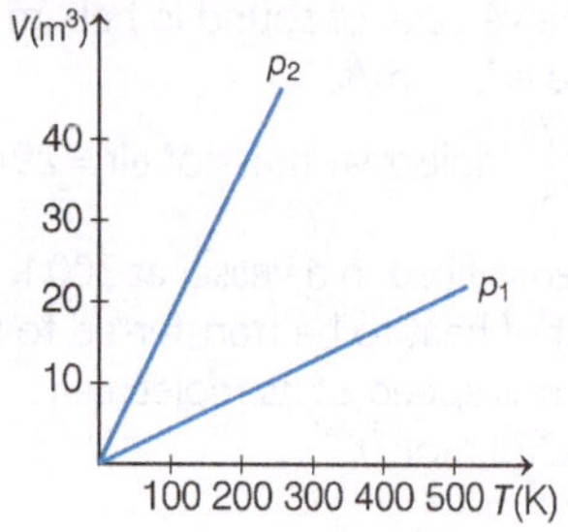

(a) $p_1 > p_2$ (b) $p_1 = p_2$
(c) $p_1 < p_2$ (d) Data is insufficient

6 1 mol of H_2 gas is contained in a box of volume $V = 1.00\ m^3$ at $T = 300$ K. The gas is heated to a temperature of $T = 3000$ K and the gas gets converted to a gas of hydrogen atoms. The final pressure would be (considering all gases to be ideal)
(a) same as the pressure initially
(b) 2 times the pressure initially
(c) 10 times the pressure initially
(d) 20 times the pressure initially

7 A vessel of volume V contains a mixture of 1 mol of hydrogen and 1 mol oxygen (both considered as ideal). Let $f_1(v)dv$ denote the fraction of molecules with speed between v and $(v + dv)$ with $f_2(v)dv$, similarly for oxygen. Then,
(a) $f_1(v) + f_2(v) = f(v)$ obeys the Maxwell's distribution law
(b) $f_1(v)$ and $f_2(v)$ will obey the Maxwell's distribution law separately
(c) Neither $f_1(v)$ nor $f_2(v)$ will obey the Maxwell's distribution law
(d) $f_2(v)$ and $f_1(v)$ will be the same

8 An inflated rubber balloon contains one mole of an ideal gas, has a pressure p, volume V and temperature T. If the temperature rises to 1.1 T and the volume is increased to 1.05 V, the final pressure will be
(a) 1.1 p (b) p
(c) less than p (d) between p and 1.1p

9 Diatomic molecules like hydrogen have energies due to both translational as well as rotational motion. From the equation in kinetic theory $pV = \frac{2}{3}E$, E is
(a) the total energy per unit volume
(b) only the translational part of energy because rotational energy is very small compared to the translational energy
(c) only the translational part of the energy because during collisions with the wall pressure relates to change in linear momentum
(d) the translational part of the energy because rotational energies of molecules can be of either sign and its average over all the molecules is zero

10 When an ideal gas is compressed adiabatically, its temperature rises and the molecules on the average have more kinetic energy than before. The kinetic energy increases,
(a) because of collisions with moving parts of the wall only
(b) because of collisions with the entire wall
(c) because the molecules gets accelerated in their motion inside the volume
(d) because of redistribution of energy amongst the molecules

Past Exams Questions

NEET

1 The following graph represents the T-V curves of an ideal gas (where T is the temperature and V the volume) at three pressures p_1, p_2 and p_3 compared with those of Charles's law represented as dotted lines.

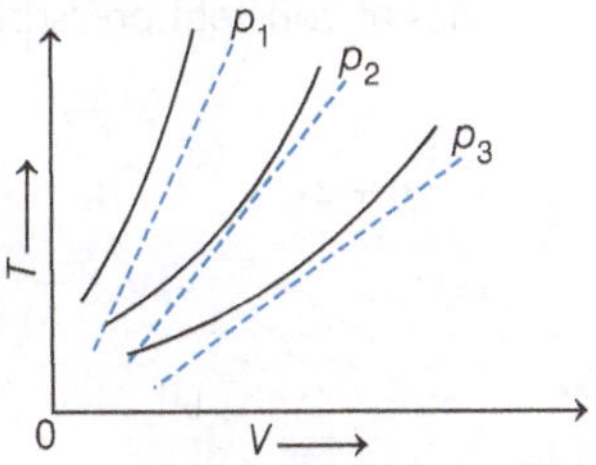

NCERT Pg. 246, NEET 2024

Then, the correct relation is

(a) $p_3 > p_2 > p_1$ (b) $p_1 > p_3 > p_2$
(c) $p_2 > p_1 > p_3$ (d) $p_1 > p_2 > p_3$

2 The volume occupied by the molecules contained in 4.5 kg water at STP, if the intermolecular forces vanish away is NCERT Pg. 246, NEET 2022

(a) 5.6×10^3 m^3 (b) 5.6×10^{-3} m^3
(c) 5.6 m^3 (d) 5.6×10^6 m^3

3 Match the Column I with Column II and choose the correct answer from the codes given below. NCERT Pg. 248, NEET 2021

Column I		Column II	
A.	Root mean square of gas molecules	1.	$\frac{1}{3}nm\bar{v}^2$
B.	Pressure exerted by ideal gas	2.	$\sqrt{\frac{3RT}{M}}$
C.	Average kinetic energy of a molecule	3.	$\frac{5}{2}RT$
D.	Total internal energy of 1 mole of a diatomic gas	4.	$\frac{3}{2}k_BT$

Codes

	A	B	C	D		A	B	C	D
(a)	3	1	4	2	(b)	2	3	4	1
(c)	2	1	4	3	(d)	3	2	1	4

4 A cylinder contains hydrogen gas at pressure of 249 kPa and temperature 27°C, its density is ($R = 8.3$ J mol^{-1} K^{-1}) NCERT Pg. 246, NEET 2020

(a) 0.2 kg/m^3 (b) 0.1 kg/m^3
(c) 0.02 kg/m^3 (d) 0.5 kg/m^3

5 An ideal gas equation can be written as $p = \frac{\rho RT}{M_0}$, where ρ and M_0 are respectively NCERT Pg. 246, NEET 2020

(a) mass density, mass of the gas
(b) number density, molar mass
(c) mass density, molar mass
(d) number density, mass of the gas

6 The mean free path l for a gas molecule depends upon diameter d of the molecule as NCERT Pg. 254, NEET 2020

(a) $l \propto \frac{1}{d^2}$ (b) $l \propto d$ (c) $l \propto d^2$ (d) $l \propto \frac{1}{d}$

7 Increase in temperature of a gas filled in a container would lead to NCERT Pg. 252, NEET 2019

(a) increase in its kinetic energy
(b) decrease in its pressure
(c) decrease in intermolecular distance
(d) increase in its mass

8 At what temperature will the rms speed of oxygen molecules become just sufficient for escaping from the earth's atmosphere?
(Given, mass of oxygen molecule $m = 2.76 \times 10^{-26}$ kg, Boltzmann's constant $k_B = 1.38 \times 10^{-23}$ J K^{-1}) NCERT Pg. 248, NEET 2018

(a) 5.016×10^4 K (b) 8.326×10^4 K
(c) 2.508×10^4 K (d) 1.254×10^4 K

9 A gas mixture consists of 2 moles of O_2 and 4 moles of Ar at temperature T. Neglecting all vibrational modes, the total internal energy of the system is NCERT Pg. 252, NEET 2017

(a) $4RT$ (b) $15RT$ (c) $9RT$ (d) $11RT$

10 A given sample of an ideal gas occupies a volume V at a pressure p and absolute temperature T. The mass of each molecule of the gas is m. Which of the following gives the density of the gas? NCERT Pg. 248, NEET 2016

(a) p/kT (b) pm/kT
(c) p/kTV (d) mkT

11 One mole of an ideal monoatomic gas undergoes a process described by the equation pV^3 = constant. The heat capacity of the gas during this process is NCERT Pg. 253, NEET 2016

(a) $\frac{3}{2}R$ (b) $\frac{5}{2}R$ (c) $2R$ (d) R

JEE Main

12 The parameter that remains the same for molecules of all gases at a given temperature is NCERT Pg. 252, NEET 2024

(a) speed (b) mass
(c) momentum (d) kinetic energy

13 A gas mixture consists of 8 moles of argon and 6 moles of oxygen at temperature T. Neglecting all vibrational modes, the total internal energy of the system is NCERT Pg. 250, NEET 2024

(a) $21RT$ (b) $29RT$ (c) $27RT$ (d) $20RT$

14 The pressure p and temperature T relationship of an ideal gas obeys the equation $pT^2 =$ constant. The volume expansion coefficient of the gas will be **NCERT Pg. 246, JEE Main 2023**

(a) $3T^2$ (b) $3/T$ (c) $3/T^3$ (d) $3/T^2$

15 Sound travels in a mixture of two moles of helium and n moles of hydrogen. If rms speed of gas molecules in the mixture is $\sqrt{2}$ times the speed of sound, then the value of n will be **NCERT Pg. 253, JEE Main 2022**

(a) 1 (b) 2
(c) 3 (d) 4

16 A gas has n degrees of freedom. The ratio of specific heat of gas at constant volume to the specific heat of gas at constant pressure will be **NCERT Pg. 253, JEE Main 2022**

(a) $\frac{n}{n+2}$ (b) $\frac{n+2}{n}$ (c) $\frac{n}{2n+2}$ (d) $\frac{n}{n-2}$

Skill Boosters

1 If we assume that, ideal gases behaves as follows.

I. At constant temperature, pressure is inversely proportional to the square of volume.

II. At constant pressure, the volume varies directly with the $\frac{2}{3}$ power of the temperature.

III. At 273 K and 1 atm pressure, 1 mole of ideal gas occupies 22.4 L volume.

Then, the ideal gas equation is

(a) $pV = nRT$ (b) $pV^2 = n^2RT$
(c) $pV^2 = n^2RT^2$ (d) $pV^2 = n^2RT^{\frac{4}{3}}$

2 Two identical vessels A and B with frictionless pistons contain the same ideal gas at the same temperature T and same volume V. The masses of gas nA and B are m_A and m_B, respectively. The gases are allowed to expand isothermally to same final volume $2V$. The change in pressures of the gas in A and B are found to be Δp and $15\Delta p$, respectively. Then,

(a) $9m_A = 4m_B$ (b) $3m_A = 2m_B$
(c) $2m_A = 3m_B$ (d) $4m_A = 9m_B$

3 A thin tube of uniform cross-section area A contain air at pressure p. The middle part of $2\sqrt{3}$ cm length contains mercury and both sides of air have same pressure at horizontal position. When the tube is held at angle of 30° with the vertical, then the length of air columns above and below the mercury column are 44 cm and 40 cm, respectively. If the system is kept at 30°C, then pressure p (in cm) of mercury is

(a) 45.8 (b) 31.4
(c) 58.6 (d) 52.8

4 A rectangular block of wood moving with velocity 2 m/s. In a gas at temperature T and mass density ρ. Assume that the velocity is along X-axis and the area of cross-section of the block perpendicular to direction of velocity is 50 cm. If mass of the gas molecule is m, then drag force on the block is

(a) $2\rho\sqrt{\frac{kT}{m}}$ (b) $4\rho\sqrt{\frac{kT}{m}}$
(c) $8\rho\sqrt{\frac{kT}{m}}$ (d) $6\rho\sqrt{\frac{kT}{m}}$

5 If 15 g mass of nitrogen gas is enclosed in a vessel at temperature 300 K, so that it does not loose any energy to external system. The amount of heat required to double the root mean square speed of Nitrogen molecules is

(a) 10 kJ (b) 20 kJ
(c) 30 kJ (d) 25 kJ

6 When 0.44 kg of air at 180°C expands adiabatically to three times its original volume and during the process, there is a fall in temperature to 15°C. Work done during the process is 52.5 kJ.
Then, the values of C_V and C_p are

(a) 1.01 kJ/kg-K and 0.72 kJ/kg-K, respectively.
(b) 0.72 kJ/kg-K and 1.01 kJ/kg-K, respectively.
(c) 0.52 kJ/kg-K and 1.01 kJ/kg-K, respectively.
(d) 0.72 kJ/kg-K and 0.52 kJ/kg-K, respectively.

7 Consider an ideal gas confined in an isolated closed chamber. As the gas undergoes an adiabatic expansion, the average time of collision between molecules increases as V^q, where V is the volume of the gas. The value of q is $\left(\gamma = \frac{C_p}{C_V}\right)$

(a) $\frac{3\gamma+5}{6}$ (b) $\frac{3\gamma-5}{6}$
(c) $\frac{\gamma+1}{2}$ (d) $\frac{\gamma-1}{2}$

8 A hollow 40 cm long cylinder of negligible mass rests over a frictionless horizontal surface. The cylinder contains nitrogen in one section and oxygen in other section. The nitrogen and oxygen volumes are

separated by a vertical non-porous membrane. Pressure of the nitrogen is twice that of oxygen.
If the membrane breaks, the cylinder moves

(a) 17.2 cm (b) 7.2 cm (c) 2.7 cm (d) 4.2 cm

9 An ideal monoatomic gas is heated from temperature T_1 to T_2 at constant volume. The gas is expanded back to its initial temperature as per the law pV^n = constant. It is found that entropy change in both process are equal. Then, specific heat of expansion of

(a) $\frac{3}{2}R$ (b) $\frac{5}{2}R$ (c) $\frac{7}{2}R$ (d) $\frac{1}{3}R$

10 A cubical box of 10.35 m side length having a pressure about $\sqrt{2} \times 10^{-3}$ Pa at 27°C. The box contains an ideal gas with molecular radius $\frac{1}{\sqrt{\pi}}$ (Å).
If atom/molecule of gas makes n intermolecular collisions, then the wall collisions of atom/molecule of gas is

(a) $3n$ (b) $5n$

(c) $2n$ (d) $\frac{1}{2}n$

Correct Codes

Topical Questions

1 (c)	2 (b)	3 (c)	4 (b)	5 (a)	6 (a)	7 (b)	8 (b)	9 (d)	10 (b)
11 (c)	12 (d)	13 (c)	14 (b)	15 (c)	16 (a)	17 (a)	18 (a)	19 (a)	20 (a)
21 (c)	22 (b)	23 (c)	24 (c)	25 (c)	26 (c)	27 (b)	28 (a)	29 (a)	30 (b)
31 (d)	32 (c)	33 (d)	34 (c)	35 (d)	36 (a)	37 (b)	38 (a)	39 (b)	40 (a)
41 (b)	42 (b)	43 (a)	44 (a)	45 (c)	46 (b)	47 (a)	48 (c)	49 (d)	50 (b)
51 (c)	52 (c)	53 (a)	54 (b)	55 (a)	56 (d)	57 (d)	58 (c)	59 (c)	60 (b)

Assertion and Reason Questions

1 (a)	2 (b)	3 (a)	4 (b)	5 (d)	6 (c)	7 (b)	8 (c)	9 (b)	10 (d)

Statement Based Questions

1 (c)	2 (b)	3 (c)	4 (d)	5 (d)	6 (a)	7 (b)	8 (b)

Matching Type Questions

1 (c)	2 (b)	3 (a)

Numerical Type Questions

1 (120)	2 (5)	3 (9)	4 (170)	5 (46)	6 (1)	7 (2)	8 (75)	9 (1029)	10 (9360)

NCERT Exemplar Questions

1 (b)	2 (d)	3 (b)	4 (c)	5 (a)	6 (d)	7 (b)	8 (d)	9 (c)	10 (a)

Past Exams Questions

1 (d)	2 (c)	3 (c)	4 (a)	5 (a)	6 (a)	7 (a)	8 (b)	9 (d)	10 (b)
11 (d)	12 (d)	13 (c)	14 (b)	15 (b)	16 (a)				

Skill Boosters

1 (d)	2 (b)	3 (b)	4 (b)	5 (a)	6 (b)	7 (c)	8 (c)	9 (a)	10 (b)

Step by Step

Decoding the Questions

Concept Builders

1 False (F)
2 dynamic
3 low, high
4 inversely
5 double
6 True (T)
7 four
8 False (F)
9 Brownian motion
10 increases
11 True (T)
12 5
13 $\frac{1}{2}k_BT$
14 $\frac{1}{2}mv^2 = \frac{3}{2}kT$
15 double
16 $\gamma = \left(1+\frac{2}{n}\right)$
17 1 : 1
18 True (T)
19 True (T)
20 True (T)

Topical Questions

3 (c) Slope $= \frac{V}{T}$

But $pV = nRT$

$\Rightarrow \quad \frac{V}{T} \propto \frac{1}{p}$

$\therefore$ Slope $\propto \frac{1}{p}$

From the figure,

$\tan\theta_2 > \tan\theta_1$

i.e. $\frac{1}{p_2} > \frac{1}{p_1}$

$\Rightarrow \quad p_1 > p_2$

4 (b) Given, $V_1 = 4.0\,\text{L}, \mu_1 = 0.75$ mol

When 0.25 mol of gas is added,

then $\quad \mu_2 = \mu_1 + 0.25$

$= 0.75 + 0.25 = 1$ mol

At constant p and T,

$$\frac{V_1}{\mu_1} = \frac{V_2}{\mu_2}$$

$$\Rightarrow \frac{4}{0.75} = \frac{V_2}{1}$$

$$\Rightarrow V_2 = \frac{4}{0.75} = 5.33\,\text{L}$$

5 (a) The number of moles of a gas,

$$\mu = \frac{M}{M_0} = \frac{\text{Total mass}}{\text{Molecular mass}}$$

Given, for two gases $\frac{(M_0)_1}{(M_0)_2} = \frac{7}{8}$

and M is same, so ratio of number of moles of two gases

$$\frac{\mu_1}{\mu_2} = \frac{M/(M_0)_1}{M/(M_0)_2} = \frac{(M_0)_2}{(M_0)_1} = \frac{8}{7}$$

6 (a) Number of moles,

$$\mu = \frac{M}{M_0} = \frac{5}{32}$$

So, from ideal gas equation,

$$pV = \mu RT = \frac{5}{32}RT$$

7 (b) For first vessel having O_2, number of moles,

$$\mu_1 = \frac{m_1}{M_1} = \frac{32}{32} = 1$$

When volume $= V$ and temperature $= T$, then

$$p_1V = RT \quad \text{...(i)}$$

For second vessel having H_2, number of moles,

$$\mu_2 = \frac{m_2}{M_2} = \frac{4}{2} = 2$$

When volume $= V$ and temperature $= 2T$, then

$$p_2V = 2R(2T) = 4RT \quad \text{...(ii)}$$

From Eqs. (i) and (ii), we get

$$p_2 = 4p_1 = 4p$$

$[\because p_1 = p \text{ (given)}]$

8 (b) Let p_1 and p_2 are the initial and final pressures of the gas filled in vessel A, then

$$p_1 = \frac{\mu_A RT}{V}$$

and $\quad p_2 = \frac{\mu_A RT}{2V}$

$$\therefore \quad \Delta p = p_2 - p_1 = -\frac{\mu_A RT}{2V}$$

$$\Rightarrow \quad \Delta p = -\left(\frac{m_A}{M}\right)\frac{RT}{2V} \quad \text{...(i)}$$

Similarly, for gas in vessel B,

$$1.5\,\Delta p = -\left(\frac{m_B}{M}\right)\frac{RT}{2V} \quad \text{...(ii)}$$

On dividing Eq. (ii) by Eq. (i), we get

$$1.5 = \frac{m_B}{m_A} \text{ or } \frac{3}{2} = \frac{m_B}{m_A}$$

$$\Rightarrow 3\,m_A = 2\,m_B$$

9 (d) The perfect gas equation can be written as

$$pV = \mu RT \quad \text{...(i)}$$

and $\quad R = N_A k_B =$ universal gas constant ... (ii)

Here, $\quad \mu = \frac{m}{M_0} = \frac{N}{N_A}$ ... (iii)

Using Eqs. (i), (ii) and (iii), we get

$$pV = k_B NT \quad \text{... (iv)}$$

or $\quad p = k_B nT$

where, $n =$ number density $= \frac{N}{V}$

From Eq. (iv), we get

Also, $\quad p = \frac{\rho RT}{M_0} \quad \left[\because V = \frac{M_0}{\rho}\right]$

Hence, all given options are correct.

10 (b) According to given situation,

$$\rho_A = 1.5\,\rho_B$$

$$p_A = 2\,p_B$$

According to ideal gas equation, we have

Pressure, $p = \frac{\rho RT}{M} \Rightarrow M = \frac{\rho RT}{p}$

where, R and T are constants.

So, $M \propto \frac{\rho}{p} \Rightarrow \frac{M_A}{M_B} = \frac{\rho_A}{\rho_B} \times \frac{p_B}{p_A}$

$$= 1.5 \times \frac{1}{2} = 0.75 = \frac{3}{4}$$

11 (c) From ideal gas equation,

Initially, $pV = \mu RT$ ... (i)

Finally, $p\Delta V = \mu_1 R \Delta T$

Given, $\Delta V = \left(1 - \frac{10}{100}\right)V = \frac{9}{10}V$

and $\Delta T = \left(1 + \frac{25}{100}\right)T = \frac{5}{4}T$

$\therefore \quad p \times \frac{9}{10}V = \mu_1 R \times \frac{5}{4}T$ ... (ii)

On dividing Eq. (ii) by Eq. (i), we get

$$\frac{9}{10} = \frac{\mu_1}{\mu} \times \frac{5}{4} \Rightarrow \frac{\mu_1}{\mu} = \frac{18}{25}$$

$\therefore$ Percentage of gas leaked

$$= \frac{\mu - \mu_1}{\mu} \times 100$$

$$= \left(1 - \frac{18}{25}\right) \times 100 = 28\%$$

13 (c) Pressure will be same on compressing because some of the vapour will change into liquid due to increased pressure.

14 (b) Using gas equation,

$$\frac{p_1V_1}{n_1} = \frac{p_2V_2}{n_2}$$

$\Rightarrow \frac{100 \times 200}{1} = \frac{400 \times V_2}{2}$

$\Rightarrow V_2 = 100$ mL

15 (c) According to Boyle's law,

$$p_1V_1 = p_2V_2$$

As the pressure is decreased by 20%, so $p_2 = \frac{80}{100}p_1$

$$p_1V_1 = \frac{80}{100}p_1V_2$$

$\Rightarrow V_2 = \frac{100}{80}V_1$

$\therefore$ Percentage increase in volume

$$= \frac{V_2 - V_1}{V_1} \times 100$$

$$= \frac{100 - 80}{80} \times 100 = 25\%$$

17 (a) According to Charles' law,

$$\frac{V_1}{V_2} = \frac{T_1}{T_2}$$

Given, $T_1 = 27°C + 273 = 300$ K,

$V_1 = V, V_2 = 2V$

$\therefore \quad \frac{1}{2} = \frac{300}{T_2}$

$\Rightarrow \quad T_2 = 600 \text{ K} = 600 - 273$

$= 327°C$

Increase in temperature,

$$\Delta T = 327 - 27 = 300°C$$

18 (a) At constant volume, $\frac{p_1}{p_2} = \frac{T_1}{T_2}$

$\Rightarrow \quad \frac{p}{p + \frac{0.4}{100}p} = \frac{T}{T+1}$

$\therefore \quad T = 250°C$

19 (a) As, volume remains constant.

$\therefore \quad \frac{p_1}{T_1} = \frac{p_2}{T_2} \Rightarrow \frac{p_1}{p_2} = \frac{T_1}{T_2}$

$\Rightarrow \quad \frac{p_2}{p_1} = \frac{308}{288}$

$\therefore$ Percentage increase in pressure

$$= \frac{p_2 - p_1}{p_1} \times 100$$

$$= \frac{308 - 288}{288} \times 100$$

$$= 6.94\% \simeq 7\%$$

20 (a) We know that, ideal gas equation is $pV = nRT$

At constant pressure, $V \propto T$

So, the graph is a straight line passing from origin.

21 (c) The total pressure of mixture of gases,

$p = p_1 + p_2 + p_3$ ...(i)

From Eq. (i),

$$p = \mu_1 \frac{RT}{V} + \mu_2 \frac{RT}{V} + \mu_3 \frac{RT}{V}$$

$$= (\mu_1 + \mu_2 + \mu_3)\frac{RT}{V}$$

22 (b) Given, $T_1 = 75°C = 348$ K

From the ideal gas equation,

$$pV = nRT = pV = \frac{m}{M}RT$$

$\Rightarrow \quad T \propto \frac{1}{m} \Rightarrow \frac{T_1}{T_2} = \frac{m_2}{m_1}$

As 25% gas escapes, $m_2 = 75\%$

$m_1 = \frac{3}{4}m_1$

$\Rightarrow \quad \frac{T_1}{T_2} = \frac{\frac{3}{4}m_1}{m_1}$

$$T_2 = \frac{4}{3} \times 348 = 464 \text{ K}$$

$\Rightarrow \quad T_2 = 191°C$

23 (c) Given, $p_1 = 76$ cm of Hg

Pressure exerted by M mass of a gas is given by

$$p = \frac{1}{2}\frac{M}{V}\bar{v}^2$$

At constant temperature, $\bar{v}^2$ and V are also constants.

$\therefore \quad p \propto M \Rightarrow \frac{p_2}{p_1} = \frac{M_2}{M_1}$

$\Rightarrow \frac{p_2}{76} = \frac{M_1 + \frac{3}{4}M_1}{M_1} \Rightarrow p_2 = \frac{7}{4} \times 76$

$\Rightarrow \quad p_2 = 133$ cm of Hg

29 (a) We know that,

or $\quad pV = \frac{2}{3}E$ ...(i)

We know that, ideal gas equation,

$pV = k_BNT$ ...(ii)

From Eqs. (i) and (ii), we get

$$\frac{2}{3}E = k_BNT \Rightarrow \frac{E}{N} = \frac{3}{2}k_BT$$

$\therefore$ Average translational kinetic energy of the molecule of gas

$$= \frac{3}{2}k_BT$$

30 (b) The mean kinetic energy for gas molecules,

$$E = \frac{3}{2}k_BT \Rightarrow E \propto T$$

$\therefore \quad \frac{E_O}{E_H} = \frac{T_1}{T_2}$ ...(i)

According to the question, both gases are at the same temperature T.

So, $\frac{E_O}{E_H} = \frac{T}{T} = \frac{1}{1} \Rightarrow E_O : E_H = 1:1$

31 (*d*) Kinetic energy of a gas molecule, $E = (3/2)\, k_B T$

$\therefore \quad E \propto T$ or $\dfrac{E_1}{E_2} = \dfrac{T_1}{T_2}$

$\Rightarrow \quad \dfrac{E}{E/2} = \dfrac{300}{T_2}$

$\therefore \quad T_2 = 150\text{ K}$

$= -123°\text{C}$

32 (*c*) Average kinetic energy of a molecule is

$$\text{KE} = \frac{3}{2} k_B T$$

As temperature T is same for two gases, so ratio of KE is

$$\frac{(\text{KE})_1}{(\text{KE})_2} = \frac{1}{1}$$

33 (*d*) Pressure due to an ideal gas is given by

$$p = \frac{1}{3} \rho \bar{v}^2 N \Rightarrow \bar{v} = \sqrt{\left(\frac{3p}{\rho N}\right)}$$

As N and p are constants, so

$$\bar{v} \propto \frac{1}{\sqrt{\rho}}$$

34 (*c*) For one molecule, $v_{rms} = \sqrt{\dfrac{3k_B T}{m}}$

and $\quad m = \dfrac{M_{N_2}}{N_A} = \dfrac{28}{6.02 \times 10^{23}}$

$= 4.65 \times 10^{-23}$ kg

$\therefore \quad v_{rms} = \sqrt{\dfrac{3 \times 1.38 \times 10^{-23} \times 300}{4.65 \times 10^{-23}}}$

$\simeq 16.34\text{ ms}^{-1}$

35 (*d*) Given, $v_{rms} = 300\text{ ms}^{-1}$

Root mean square velocity,

$$v_{rms} = \sqrt{\frac{3k_B T}{m}} \quad \text{...(i)}$$

$$v'_{rms} = \sqrt{\frac{3k_B (T/2)}{2m}} = \frac{1}{2}\sqrt{\frac{3k_B T}{m}}$$

$= \dfrac{v_{rms}}{2} \quad$ [from Eq. (i)]

$= \dfrac{300}{2} = 150\text{ ms}^{-1}$

36 (*a*) Since, $v_{rms} \propto \sqrt{T}$

$\therefore \quad \dfrac{v_{rms,2}}{v_{rms,1}} = \sqrt{\dfrac{T_2}{T_1}} \quad$ ...(i)

$\therefore \quad v_{rms,\,2} = \sqrt{\dfrac{500}{400}} \times 200$ m/s

$= 100\sqrt{5}$ m/s

37 (*b*) At same temperature, the average speed is given by

$$\bar{v} \propto \frac{1}{\sqrt{M}}$$

$\Rightarrow \quad \dfrac{\bar{v}_H}{\bar{v}_{He}} = \sqrt{\dfrac{M_{He}}{M_H}}$

Given, $M_{He} = 4\, M_H$

$\therefore \quad \dfrac{\bar{v}_H}{\bar{v}_{He}} = \sqrt{\dfrac{4}{1}} = 2$

$\Rightarrow \quad \bar{v}_{He} = \dfrac{1}{2}\bar{v}_H$

39 (*b*) As, $v_{rms} \propto \sqrt{T}$

$$\frac{T'}{T} = \left(\frac{v'_{rms}}{v_{rms}}\right)^2 = \left(\frac{v_{rms}/2}{v_{rms}}\right)^2 = \frac{1}{4}$$

During adiabatic process,

$$TV^{\gamma - 1} = T'V'^{\gamma - 1}$$

$\Rightarrow \quad \dfrac{V'}{V} = (4)^{\frac{1}{1.5-1}} = 4^2 = 16$

$\therefore \quad V' = 16V$

41 (*b*) Maxwell's law of distribution,

$$v \propto \sqrt{T}$$

As, temperature is increased the value of most probable speed increases but fraction of particles possessing most probable speed decreases.

42 (*b*) We know that,

$$v_{rms} = \sqrt{\frac{3RT}{M}}$$

Hence, $v_{rms} \propto \sqrt{T}$

$\Rightarrow \quad \dfrac{(v_{rms})_1}{(v_{rms})_2} = \sqrt{\dfrac{T_1}{T_2}}$

$\Rightarrow \quad \dfrac{v}{(v_{rms})_2} = \sqrt{\dfrac{300}{600}} = \dfrac{1}{\sqrt{2}}$

$\Rightarrow \quad (v_{rms})_2 = v\sqrt{2}$

43 (*a*) Root mean square speed of a gas molecule is given by

$$v_{rms} = \sqrt{\frac{3RT}{M}}$$

and $\quad v_{av} = \sqrt{\dfrac{8RT}{\pi M}}$

We have, $v_{rms} = 1260$ m/s

So, $\dfrac{v_{av}}{v_{rms}} = \dfrac{\sqrt{\dfrac{8RT}{\pi M}}}{\sqrt{\dfrac{3RT}{M}}} \Rightarrow \dfrac{v_{av}}{1260} = \sqrt{\dfrac{8}{3\pi}}$

$\Rightarrow v_{av} = 1260 \times \sqrt{\dfrac{8}{3\pi}}$

$\Rightarrow v_{av} = 1161$ m/s

44 (*a*) Energy of a gas, $E = \dfrac{3}{2} N k_B T$

$\because \quad N = \mu N_A$

$\therefore \quad E = \dfrac{3}{2} \cdot \mu \cdot N_A \cdot k_B T$

For helium molecule, $\mu = \dfrac{m}{M} = \dfrac{1}{4}$

$\therefore$ Heat energy required to raise temperature from T_1 to T_2 is

$$\Delta E = \frac{3}{8} N_A\, k_B\, \Delta T$$

$$= \frac{3}{8} N_A\, k_B (T_2 - T_1)$$

45 (*c*) Given, number of moles of helium = 5

Number of atoms (He is monoatomic)

$= 5 \times 6.023 \times 10^{23}$

$= 30.015 \times 10^{23}$

$= 3.0 \times 10^{24}$ atoms

Now, average kinetic energy per molecule $= \dfrac{3}{2} k_B T$

Temperature, $T = 273 + 7 = 280$ K

$\therefore$ Total energy of all the atoms

= Total internal energy

$= \dfrac{3}{2} k_B T \times$ Number of atoms

$= \dfrac{3}{2} \times 1.38 \times 10^{-23} \times 280 \times 3.0 \times 10^{24}$

$= 1.74 \times 10^4$ J

46 (*b*) Given, mass = 1 kg, density = 4 kgm^{-3}

$\therefore$ Volume $= \dfrac{\text{Mass}}{\text{Density}} = \dfrac{1}{4}\text{ m}^3$

Pressure $= 8 \times 10^4\text{ Nm}^{-2}$

Internal energy of diatomic gas,

$$E = \frac{5}{2} k_B N T = \frac{5}{2} p \times V$$

$$= \frac{5}{2} \times 8 \times 10^4 \times \frac{1}{4} = 5 \times 10^4\text{ J}$$

47 (*a*) Vibrational energy

$$=\frac{1}{2}m\left(\frac{dy}{dt}\right)^2+\frac{1}{2}ky^2$$

∴Total energy,

$$E=\underbrace{3\left(\frac{1}{2}k_BT\right)}_{\text{Translational mode}}+\underbrace{2\left(\frac{1}{2}k_BT\right)}_{\text{Rotational mode}}+\underbrace{2\left(\frac{1}{2}k_BT\right)}_{\text{Vibrational mode}}$$

$$=\frac{7}{2}k_BT$$

48 (*c*) $U=\left(\frac{3}{2}k_BT+\frac{f}{2}k_BT\right)N_A\times 2$

$$=(3k_BT+f\,k_BT)N_A$$

49 (*d*) The internal energy of n moles of a gas is given by

$$U=\frac{1}{2}nfRT$$

Degree of freedom of nitrogen is 5.

$$U_N=\frac{1}{2}\times 2\times 5RT=5RT$$

Degree of freedom of xenon is 3.

$$U_{X_e}=\frac{1}{2}\times 4\times 3RT=6RT$$

So, the total internal energy,

$$U=U_N+U_{X_e}$$
$$=5RT+6RT=11RT$$

50 (*b*) Internal energy of a gas with f degree of freedom is

$$U=\frac{nfRT}{2}$$

Internal energy due to O_2 gas which is a diatomic gas is

$$U_1=\frac{n_1f_1RT}{2}=3\times\frac{5}{2}RT$$

Internal energy due to Ar gas which is a monoatomic gas is

$$U_2=\frac{n_2f_2RT}{2}=5\times\frac{3}{2}RT$$

∴Total internal energy $=U_1+U_2$

$$\Rightarrow \quad U=15\,RT$$

51 (*c*) From Mayer's formula,

$$C_p-C_V=R \quad \text{...(i)}$$

and $\gamma=\frac{C_p}{C_V} \Rightarrow \gamma C_V=C_p$ ...(ii)

On substituting Eq. (ii) in Eq. (i), we get

$$\gamma C_V-C_V=R$$
$$\Rightarrow \quad C_V(\gamma-1)=R$$
$$\therefore \quad C_V=\frac{R}{\gamma-1}$$

52 (*c*) For diatomic gas, $\gamma=\frac{7}{5}$

For adiabatic process,

$$T_1V_1^{\gamma-1}=T_2V_2^{\gamma-1}$$

$$(300)V_1^{\frac{7}{5}-1}=T_2\left(\frac{V_1}{5}\right)^{\frac{7}{5}-1}$$

$\Rightarrow T_2=570.9\simeq 571$ K

Mean kinetic energy of a rotating molecules

$$=k_BT=1.38\times10^{-23}\times 571$$
$$=787.98\times10^{-23}\text{ J}$$

53 (*a*) Now, in given case,

For gas *A*, $C_p=29$, $C_V=22$

For gas *B*, $C_p=30$, $C_V=21$

By using $\gamma=\frac{C_p}{C_V}=1+\frac{2}{f}$,

we have

For gas *A*,

$$1+\frac{2}{f}=\frac{29}{22}\approx 1.3$$

$\Rightarrow f=6.67\approx 7$

So, gas *A* has vibrational mode of degree of freedom.

For gas *B*,

$$1+\frac{2}{f}=\frac{30}{21}\approx 1.4$$

$$\Rightarrow \quad f=5$$

54 (*b*) For one mole of a gas, the internal energy is given as

$$U=\frac{f}{2}RT$$

where, f = degree of freedom.

$$\because \quad C_V=\frac{dU}{dT}=\frac{f}{2}R$$

$$C_p=R+C_V$$

$$\Rightarrow \quad C_p=\left(1+\frac{f}{2}\right)R$$

$$v=\frac{C_p}{C_V}=1+\frac{2}{f}$$

56 (*d*) At constant pressure,

Work done is given by

$$W=nR\Delta T$$
$$\therefore \quad 50=nR\Delta T$$
$$\Rightarrow \quad \Delta T=\frac{50}{nR}$$

For $f=5$,

$$C_p=\left(1+\frac{f}{2}\right)R$$
$$=\left(1+\frac{5}{2}\right)R$$
$$C_p=\frac{7}{2}R$$

Heat absorbed $=nC_p\Delta T$

$$=n\times\frac{7}{2}R\times\frac{50}{nR}$$
$$=175\text{ J}$$

57 (*d*) As, mean free path,

$$l=\frac{1}{\sqrt{2}\,n\pi d^2}$$

$$\Rightarrow \quad l\propto\frac{1}{d^2} \qquad (\because n_1=n_2)$$

$$\Rightarrow \quad \frac{l_1}{l_2}=\frac{d_2^2}{d_1^2}=\left(\frac{1}{4}\right)^2=\frac{1}{16}$$

58 (*c*) Mean free path, $l=\frac{1}{\sqrt{2}\,n\pi d^2}$

On putting values, we get

$$l=\frac{1}{\sqrt{2}\times2.7\times10^{25}\times3.14\times(2\times10^{-10})^2}$$
$$=2.05\times10^{-7}\text{ m}$$

Assertion and Reason Questions

1 (*a*) The interatomic forces are negligible in gases. Therefore, in gases, the molecules are free and move long distances without colliding, with faster speed. Therefore, Assertion and Reason are correct and Reason is the correct explanation of Assertion.

2 (*b*) A real gas at low pressure and high temperature behaves like ideal gas and satisfies $pV=\mu RT$. Therefore, Assertion and Reason are correct but Reason is not the correct explanation of Assertion.

3 (*a*) Both the Assertion and Reason are correct and Reason is the correct explanation of the Assertion. As gases have kinetic energy, they don't settle at the bottom because of their small mass, the effect of gravity is negligible on them.

4 (*b*) Total translational kinetic energy of all molecules (*n* moles) of a given mass of an ideal gas

$$=\frac{3}{2}\mu RT=\frac{3}{2}pV \quad [\because pV=\mu RT]$$

$$=1.5\,pV$$

Due to collision of molecules of gas with each other, their velocities continuously change.

Therefore, Assertion and Reason are correct but Reason is not the correct explanation of Assertion.

5 (*d*) The translational motion of the gas chamber increases the total kinetic energy of the chamber but it does not contribute to the internal energy of the system. So, the temperature of gas in the chamber remains same.

Therefore, Assertion is incorrect but Reason is correct.

6 (*c*) Pressure of an ideal gas

$$=\frac{1}{3}nm\bar{v}^2$$

Also, pressure of an ideal gas,

$$p=\frac{\mu RT}{V}$$

If μ and T are constants, then

$$p\propto\frac{1}{V}$$

So, pressure of an ideal gas increases with the decrease of volume.

Therefore, Assertion is correct but Reason is incorrect.

8 (*c*) If the gas is monoatomic, no vibrational energy is there, so the degree of freedom is always three. Therefore, Assertion is correct but Reason is incorrect.

9 (*b*) Number of degrees of freedom of a linear triatomic molecule is 7. So, Assertion is correct.

10 (*d*) Mean free path of gas molecules varies inversely as density of the gas.

Statement Based Questions

1 (*c*) Statement II is correct but Statement I is incorrect and it can be corrected as,

The kinetic theory relates the molecular properties like viscosity, conduction and diffusion with bulk properties of a gas.

2 (*b*) Statement I is correct and Statement II is incorrect and it can be corrected as

By Boyle's law,

$$p\propto\frac{1}{V}$$

$\Rightarrow\quad pV=\text{constant}$

$\therefore$ The graph of *p*-*V* diagram is rectangular hyperbola.

3 (*c*) The average kinetic energy of the gas molecules is

$$\text{KE}=\frac{3}{2}k_BT\Rightarrow\text{KE}\propto T$$

The collision between gas molecules and wall of the container is elastic.

4 (*d*) Both the Statements are correct as gas particles are constantly colliding with each other and walls of their container and the total volume occupied by gas molecules is negligible relative to the total volume of their container. Also, gas molecules are considered as incompressible, hence collision is elastic.

6 (*a*) Translational kinetic energy of the molecules of gas is $k=\frac{3}{2}pv$

For diatomic gas, degree of freedom is association with 3 translational and 2 rotational motion.

7 (*b*) Statement I is correct but Statement II is incorrect as each vibrational mode gives 2 degrees of freedom i.e., kinetic and potential energies modes.

8 (*b*) Statement I is correct but Statement II is incorrect and it can be correct as,

The time between two successive collisions of the gas molecules is inversely proportional to square of the diameter of the gas molecule.

Matching Type Questions

2 (*b*)

A. As only *x*-component of velocity changes, so change in momentum of molecule

$$=-mv_x-(mv_x)$$

As collision is elastic, the total momentum of molecule and wall is conserved. So, change in momentum of wall (momentum imparted to wall) $=2mv_x$.

B. In time Δt, the number of molecules with velocity v_x that could reach the wall is $nAv_x\Delta t$ within volume of cylinder of length $v_x\Delta t$ as shown below, where *n* is number density.

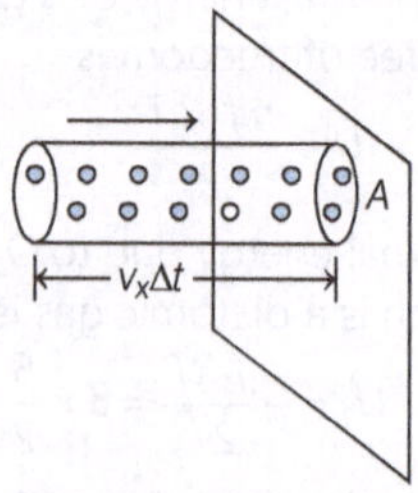

But on an average half of these molecules will hit the wall in time,

$$\Delta t=\frac{1}{2}n\,Av_x\Delta t$$

The total momentum transferred to the wall in time Δt

$$=(2mv_x)\left(\frac{1}{2}n\,Av_x\Delta t\right)$$

$$=(nmv_x^2)A\,\Delta t$$

C. Pressure $= \frac{F}{A} = \frac{\text{Momentum}}{\text{Area} \times \text{Time}}$

$$= \frac{(nmv_x^2)A\,\Delta t}{A\,\Delta t} = nmv_x^2$$

D. As the x-component of velocities of all the molecules are not same. So, we take average of $\overline{v}_x^2$.

$\therefore$ Total pressure, $p = nm\overline{v}_x^2$

Hence, A $\rightarrow$ 2, B $\rightarrow$ 3, C $\rightarrow$ 4 and D $\rightarrow$ 1.

3 (a) A-(4), B-(3), C-(2), D-(1)

As we know that, adiabatic constant (γ) is given as,

$\gamma = 1 + (2/f)$

f = Number of degrees of freedom.

For monoatomic gas, $f = 3$

$$\gamma = 1 + (2/3) = 1.67$$

For rigid diatomic gas, $f = 5$

$$\gamma = 1 + (2/5) = 1.4$$

For non-rigid diatomic gas, $f = 7$

$$\gamma = 1 + (2/7) = 1.28$$

For non-linear triatomic gas, $f = 6$

$$\gamma = 1 + (2/6) = 1.33$$

Numerical Type Questions

1 (120) Given, $f = 6$

As we know that,

$$\gamma = 1 + \frac{2}{f} = 1 + \frac{2}{6} = \frac{4}{3}$$

The amount of energy given for external work,

$$\frac{\Delta W}{\Delta Q} = \left(1 - \frac{1}{\gamma}\right)$$

$$\Rightarrow \quad \frac{30}{\Delta Q} = \left(1 - \frac{1}{4/3}\right)$$

$$= 1 - \frac{3}{4} = \frac{1}{4}$$

$$\Rightarrow \quad \Delta Q = 30 \times 4 = 120 \text{ J}$$

2 (5) Given, $C = 37.35$ J mol^{-1}K^{-1}

$$pT = A$$

As we know that,

$$pV = RT$$

$$\Rightarrow \quad p = \frac{RT}{V}$$

$$\Rightarrow \quad \frac{A}{T} = \frac{RT}{V} \qquad (\because pT = A)$$

$$\Rightarrow \quad V = \frac{RT^2}{A}$$

So, $\frac{dV}{dT} = \frac{2RT}{A}$ or $dV = \frac{2RT}{A} \cdot dT$

Work done when temperature changes by dT is

$$dW = pdV$$

$$= \frac{A}{T} \cdot \frac{2RT}{A} \cdot dT = 2RdT$$

Now, by first law of thermodynamics, $dQ = dU + dW$

$$\Rightarrow \quad CdT = C_V \cdot dT + 2RdT$$

$$\Rightarrow \quad C = C_V + 2R$$

$$\text{or} \quad C_V = C - 2R$$

As, $C_V = \frac{f}{2}R$; f = degrees of freedom,

$$\frac{f}{2}R = C - 2R$$

$$\text{or} \quad f = (C - 2R)\frac{2}{R}$$

$$= \left(\frac{37.35 - 2 \times 8.3}{8.3}\right) \times 2 = 5$$

3 (9) Work done, $W = \frac{2Q}{3}$

According to first law of thermodynamics,

$$Q = \Delta U + W \Rightarrow Q = \Delta U + \frac{2Q}{3}$$

$$\Rightarrow \Delta U = \frac{Q}{3} \qquad \text{...(i)}$$

But $\Delta U = nC_V \Delta T$

$$\Rightarrow \quad \Delta U = n\left(\frac{3R}{2}\right)\Delta T \qquad \text{...(ii)}$$

[for monoatomic gas, $C_V = \frac{3R}{2}$]

From Eqs. (i) and (ii), we get

$$n\left(\frac{3R}{2}\right)\Delta T = \frac{Q}{3}$$

$$n\left(\frac{9R}{2}\right)\Delta T = Q$$

$$n\left(\frac{9R}{2}\right)\Delta T = nC\Delta T$$

$$\Rightarrow \quad C = \frac{9R}{2}$$

4 (170) From ideal gas equation,

$$pV = nRT$$

At constant temperature, for small changes in p and V,

$$\Delta(pV) = \Delta(nRT)$$

$$\Rightarrow \quad p\Delta V + V\Delta p = 0$$

$$\Rightarrow \quad |\Delta p| = \frac{p\Delta V}{V} \qquad \text{...(i)}$$

Again, from ideal gas equation,

$$pV = nRT$$

At constant pressure, for small changes in V and T,

$$\Delta(pV) = \Delta(nRT)$$

$$\Rightarrow \quad |\Delta T| = \frac{p\Delta V}{nR} \qquad \text{...(ii)}$$

$$\therefore \quad \frac{|\Delta T|}{|\Delta p|} = \frac{\left(\frac{p\Delta V}{nR}\right)}{\left(\frac{p\Delta V}{V}\right)} = \frac{V}{nR}$$

$$\Rightarrow \quad |\Delta T| = \frac{V}{nR}|\Delta p| = \frac{T}{p}|\Delta p|$$

$$\Rightarrow \quad |\Delta T| = \frac{340}{2}|\Delta p|$$

$$\Rightarrow \quad |\Delta T| = 170\,|\Delta p|$$

Given that, $|\Delta T| = C\,|\Delta p|$

$$\therefore \quad C = 170 \text{ K/atm}$$

5 (46) Given, air is diatomic gas.

$$\gamma = 1 + \frac{2}{f} = \frac{7}{5}$$

As for adiabatic change,

$$T_i V_i^{\gamma-1} = T_f V_f^{\gamma-1}$$

$$\Rightarrow \quad 293 \cdot V^{\frac{7}{5}-1} = T_f \cdot \left(\frac{V}{10}\right)^{\frac{7}{5}-1}$$

$$\Rightarrow \quad T_f = 293 \times 10^{2/5} \text{ K}$$

Change in internal energy,

$$\Delta U = \frac{n \cdot f \cdot R(T_f - T_i)}{2}$$

$$= \frac{5 \times 5 \times \frac{25}{3} \times (293 \times 10^{2/5} - 293)}{2}$$

$$= 46144 \text{ J} \approx 46 \text{ kJ}$$

So, value of X is 46.

6 (1) We know that, rms velocity,

$$v_{\text{rms}} = \sqrt{\frac{3k_BT}{m}}$$

Escape velocity, $v_e = \sqrt{2gR_e}$

Given, $v_{\text{rms}} = v_e$

or $\sqrt{\frac{3k_BT}{m}} = \sqrt{2gR_e} \Rightarrow T = \frac{2gR_em}{3 \times k_B}$

Substituting the given values, we get

$$T = \frac{2 \times 10 \times 6.4 \times 10^6 \times 2}{3 \times 1.38 \times 10^{-23} \times 6.02 \times 10^{26}}$$
$$\approx 10^4 \text{ K}$$

7 (2) Mean free path is given by

$$\lambda = \frac{1}{\sqrt{2}\pi n d^2}$$

Thus, $\lambda = \dfrac{1}{\sqrt{2}\pi d^2\left(\dfrac{p}{k_BT}\right)}$

$$\Rightarrow \quad d^2 = \frac{k_BT}{\sqrt{2}\,\pi p \lambda}$$
$$= \frac{1.4 \times 10^{-23} \times 273}{\sqrt{2} \times 3.14 \times 1.01 \times 10^5 \times 2 \times 10^{-7}}$$
$$\Rightarrow d \approx 2 \times 10^{-10} = 2 \text{ Å}$$

8 (75) Volume, $V = \frac{m}{\rho} = \frac{2}{8} = \frac{1}{4} \text{ m}^3$

For diatomic gas, energy due to thermal motion is given by

$$\text{KE} = \frac{5}{2}nRT = \frac{5}{2}pV$$
$$= \frac{5}{2} \times 12 \times 10^4 \times \frac{1}{4}$$
$$= 7.5 \times 10^4 \text{ J}$$
$$\text{KE} = 75 \times 10^3 \text{ J}$$

So, the value of x is 75.

9 (1029) As we know that,

$$v = \sqrt{\frac{\gamma RT}{M}}$$

For air, $v_a = \sqrt{\dfrac{\gamma_a RT}{M_a}}$

For helium,

$$v_{He} = \sqrt{\frac{\gamma_{He} RT}{M_{He}}}$$

Now, $\dfrac{v_a}{v_{He}} = \sqrt{\dfrac{\gamma_a M_{He}}{\gamma_{He} M_a}}$

$$\frac{350}{v_{He}} = \sqrt{\frac{\frac{7}{5} \times 4}{\frac{5}{3} \times 29}}$$

$\therefore \quad v_{He} \approx 1029 \text{ m/s}$

10 (9360) As $v_{rms} \propto \sqrt{T}$

$$\frac{(v_{rms})_2}{(v_{rms})_1} = \sqrt{\frac{T_2}{T_1}}$$
$$\frac{2v_{rms}}{v_{rms}} = \sqrt{\frac{T_2}{300}} = 1200 \text{ K}$$

Now, the amount of heat required is given by

$$Q = \frac{f}{2}nR(T_2 - T_1)$$

For diatomic gas, $f = 5$

$$Q = \frac{5}{2} \times \frac{14}{28} \times 8.32 \times (1200 - 300)$$
$$\Rightarrow \quad Q = 9360 \text{ J}$$

NCERT Exemplar Questions

3 (b) Boyle's law is applicable when temperature is constant,

i.e. $\quad pV = \mu RT = \text{constant}$

$\Rightarrow \quad pV = \text{constant}$ (at constant temperature)

$\Rightarrow \quad p \propto \frac{1}{V}$ (where,

$p =$ pressure and $V =$ volume)

As, this process is called as isothermal process, so Boyle's law is applicable for isothermal process.

4 (c)

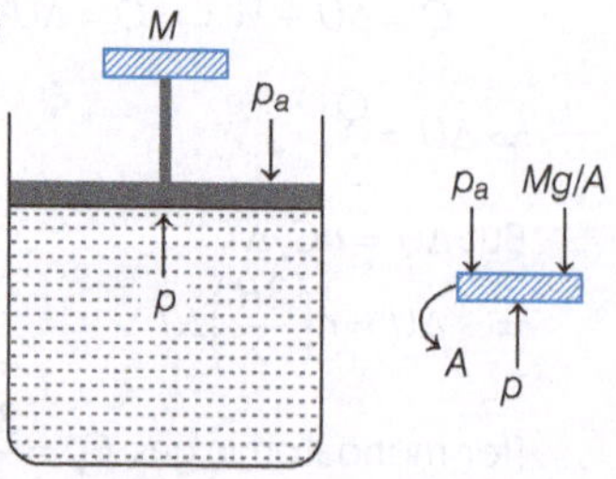

As $\quad pV = \mu RT$

$\Rightarrow \quad V \propto T$

So, when temperature T increases, volume V increases at constant pressure.

Hence, V will change but not p.

5 (a) We know for an ideal gas,

$$pV = \mu RT$$
$$\Rightarrow \quad V = \left(\frac{\mu R}{p}\right)T$$

Slope of the V-T graph,

$$m = \frac{dV}{dT} = \frac{\mu R}{p}$$

or $\quad p \propto \frac{1}{m}$

Hence, $\quad \frac{p_1}{p_2} = \frac{m_2}{m_1} > 1$ or $\quad p_1 > p_2$

6 (d) $\quad \mu_2 = 2\mu_1$

Now, by ideal gas equation,

$$pV = \mu RT$$

As volume V of the container is constant.

So, $\quad p \propto \mu\, T$

$$\Rightarrow \quad \frac{p_2}{p_1} = \frac{\mu_2\, T_2}{\mu_1\, T_1}$$
$$= \frac{(2\mu_1)(3000)}{\mu_1(300)} = 20$$
$$\Rightarrow \quad p_2 = 20p_1$$

8 (d) We know for an ideal gas,

$$\frac{p_1V_1}{T_1} = \frac{p_2V_2}{T_2}$$
$$\Rightarrow \quad p_2 = p_1V_1\left(\frac{T_2}{V_2T_1}\right)$$
$$\Rightarrow \quad p_2 = \frac{(p)(V)(1.1\,T)}{(1.05)\,V(T)} \approx 1.05\,p$$

Past Exams Questions

1 (d) Charles's law states that volume of a gas is proportional to its temperature on Kelvin scale at constant pressure.

It is clear for p_1, T is higher.

Thus, $p_1 > p_2 > p_3$.

Alternate Solution

We know that $pV = nRT$

$$\frac{T}{V} = \frac{p}{nR}$$
$$\text{Slope} = \frac{p}{nR}$$

i.e., slope $\propto p$

Hence, $p_1 > p_2 > p_3$

2 (c) $\quad n = \dfrac{4.5}{1.8 \times 10^{-2}} = 250$

$$\therefore \quad V = \frac{nRT}{p} = \frac{250 \times 8.3 \times 273}{10^5}$$
$$= 5.6 \text{ m}^3$$

3 (*c*) The average kinetic energy of a molecule,

$$KE_{av} = \frac{3}{2} k_B T$$

As, total internal energy of 1 mole of diatomic gas,

$$\Delta U = \frac{nfRT}{2}$$

$$\Rightarrow \quad \Delta U = \frac{5RT}{2}$$

The correct match is A $\rightarrow$ 2, B $\rightarrow$ 1, C $\rightarrow$ 4 and D $\rightarrow$ 3.

4 (*a*) As, from ideal gas,

$$\rho = \frac{pM}{RT} = \frac{249 \times 10^3 \times 2 \times 10^{-3}}{8.3 \times 300}$$

$$\Rightarrow \quad \rho = 0.2 \text{ kg/m}^3$$

5 (*a*) Ideal gas equation is given as

$$p = \frac{\rho RT}{M_0} \Rightarrow p \cdot \frac{M_0}{\rho} = RT$$

$$\Rightarrow \quad pV = RT$$

$$\text{where, } \quad V = \frac{M_0}{\rho}$$

Hence, ρ and M_0 are mass density and mass of gas, respectively.

6 (*a*) The mean free path l for a gas molecule is given as

$$l = \frac{1}{\sqrt{2}\pi n d^2} \Rightarrow l \propto \frac{1}{d^2}$$

where, d = diameter of molecule of gas.

7 (*a*) As the temperature of gas in the container is increased, the kinetic energy also increases. This is because the average kinetic energy of a gas is given by

$$KE = \frac{f}{2} nRT \qquad \text{... (i)}$$

From Eq. (i), KE $\propto T$

8 (*b*) Escape velocity on surface of earth is given by

$$v_e = \sqrt{2gR}$$

$$\Rightarrow \quad v_e = \sqrt{2 \times 9.8 \times 6.4 \times 10^6}$$

$$= 11200 \text{ ms}^{-1}$$

According to the question,

$$v_{rms} = v_e \Rightarrow \sqrt{\frac{3k_B T}{m_{O_2}}} = 112 \times 10^3$$

$$\text{or } T = \frac{(11.2 \times 10^3)^2 (m_{O_2})}{(3k_B)}$$

$$T = \frac{(11.2 \times 10^3)^2 (2.76 \times 10^{-26})}{(3 \times 1.38 \times 10^{-23})}$$

$$= 8.326 \times 10^4 \text{ K}$$

9 (*d*) Total internal energy of system
= Internal energy of oxygen molecules + Internal energy of argon molecules

$$= \frac{f_1}{2} n_1 RT + \frac{f_2}{2} n_2 RT$$

$$= \frac{5}{2} \times 2RT + \frac{3}{2} \times 4RT$$

$$= 11RT$$

10 (*b*) As we know that,

$$p = \frac{1}{3} \rho v_{rms}^2 = \frac{1}{3} \rho \frac{3RT}{M_0} = \frac{\rho RT}{M_0}$$

$$\Rightarrow \rho = \frac{pM_0}{RT} = \frac{pmN_A}{k N_A T}$$

$$\Rightarrow \rho = \frac{pm}{kT}$$

11 (*d*) As we know that, for polytropic process of index α, specific heat capacity $= C_V + \dfrac{R}{1-\alpha}$

$\because$ Process, pV^3 = constant

$$\Rightarrow \quad \alpha = 3$$

$$\therefore \quad C = C_V + \frac{R}{1-\alpha} = \frac{fR}{2} + \frac{R}{1-3}$$

$$\text{where, } C_V = \frac{fR}{2} = \frac{3R}{2}$$

For monoatomic gas, $f = 3$

$$\Rightarrow \quad C = \frac{3R}{2} - \frac{R}{2} = R$$

12 (*d*) At a given temperature, kinetic energy remains the same for the molecules of all gases.

13 (*c*) Argon is monoatomic, its degree of freedom is 3.

Oxygen is diatomic with 5 degrees of freedom.

Total internal energy of mixture
= Internal energy of Ar + Internal energy of O_2

$$= 8 \times \frac{3}{2} RT + 6 \times \frac{5}{2} RT$$

$$= (12 + 15) RT = 27RT$$

14 (*b*) Given for a process,

$$pT^2 = \text{constant}$$

$$\frac{nRT}{V} \cdot T^2 = \text{constant } (k)$$

$$\text{or} \quad T^3 = \frac{k}{nR} \cdot V$$

$$\text{or} \quad 3T^2 = \frac{k}{nR} \cdot \left(\frac{dV}{dT}\right)$$

$$\Rightarrow \quad \frac{1}{V} \cdot \left(\frac{dV}{dT}\right) = \frac{3}{T}$$

15 (*b*) For diatomic gas of H_2,

$$C_{p_2} = \frac{7}{2} R, C_{V_2} = \frac{5}{2} R$$

For monoatomic gas of He,

$$C_{p_1} = \frac{5}{2} R, C_{V_1} = \frac{3}{2} R$$

Specific heat ratio,

$$\gamma = \frac{n_1 C_{p_1} + n_2 C_{p_2}}{n_1 C_{V_1} + n_2 C_{V_2}}$$

$$= \frac{2 \times \frac{5}{2} R + n \times \frac{7}{2} R}{2 \times \frac{3}{2} R + n \times \frac{5}{2} R}$$

$$\gamma = \frac{10 + 7n}{6 + 5n} \qquad \text{... (i)}$$

It is given that,

$$v_{rms} = \sqrt{2} \times v_{sound}$$

$$\Rightarrow \quad \sqrt{\frac{3RT}{M}} = \sqrt{2} \times \sqrt{\frac{\gamma RT}{M}}$$

$$\Rightarrow \quad \gamma = \frac{3}{2}$$

$$\text{From Eq. (i), } \frac{3}{2} = \frac{10 + 7n}{6 + 5n}$$

$$\Rightarrow \quad n = 2$$

16 (*a*) $\therefore$ Internal energy of one mole of the gas,

$$U = \frac{n}{2} k_B T \times N_A = \frac{n}{2} RT$$

$$\therefore \quad C_V = \frac{dU}{dT} = \frac{d}{dt} \frac{n}{2} RT = \frac{nR}{2}$$

and $C_p = C_V + R$

$$= \frac{nR}{2} + R = R\left(\frac{n}{2} + 1\right)$$

$$\therefore \quad \frac{C_V}{C_p} = \frac{\frac{nR}{2}}{R\left(\frac{n}{2} + 1\right)} = \frac{n}{n+2}$$

Skill Boosters

1 (*d*) At constant temperature,

$$p \propto \frac{1}{V^2} \quad ...(i)$$

At constant pressure,

$$V \propto T^{\frac{2}{3}} \quad ...(ii)$$

Also, for constant pressure and temperature,

$$V \propto n \quad ...(iii)$$

Now, combining the Eqs. (i), (ii) and (ii), we get

$$pV^2 \propto n^2 T^{\frac{4}{3}}$$

$$pV^2 = n^2 R T^{\frac{4}{3}}$$

2 (*b*) Let p_1 and p_2 are the initial and final pressures of the gas filled in vessel *A*, then

$$p_1 = \frac{\mu_A RT}{V}$$

and $$p_2 = \frac{\mu_A RT}{2V}$$

$\therefore$ $$\Delta p = p_2 - p_1 = -\frac{\mu_A RT}{2V}$$

$\Rightarrow$ $$\Delta p = -\left(\frac{m_A}{M}\right)\frac{RT}{2V} \quad ...(i)$$

Similarly, for gas in vessel *B*,

$$1.5\Delta p = -\left(\frac{m_B}{M}\right)\frac{RT}{2V} \quad ...(ii)$$

On dividing Eq. (i). by Eq. (ii), we get

$$1.5 = \frac{m_B}{m_A} \text{ or } \frac{3}{2} = \frac{m_B}{m_A} \Rightarrow 3m_A = 2m_B$$

3 (*b*) When mercury is in middle, the length of air column on either side

$$= \frac{44 + 40}{2} = 42 \text{ cm}$$

When tube is held at 30° with vertical. If p_1 and p_2 are pressure at bottom and top of tube, then

$$p_1 - p_2 = 2\sqrt{3}\cos 30°$$

$$= 2\sqrt{3} \times \frac{\sqrt{3}}{2} = 3 \text{ cm of Hg} \quad ...(i)$$

Now, using Boyle's law,

$$p_1V_1 = p_2V_2 = pV$$

$$p_1 \times A \times 40 = p_2 \times A \times 44 = p \times A \times 42$$

$$p_1 \times 40 = p_2 \times 44 = p \times 42 \quad ...(ii)$$

From Eqs. (i) and (ii), we get

$$\frac{p \times 42}{40} - \frac{p \times 42}{44} = 3$$

$$p\left[\frac{42}{40} - \frac{42}{44}\right] = 3$$

$$p\left[\frac{21}{20} - \frac{21}{22}\right] = 3$$

$$p\left[\frac{21}{220}\right] = 3$$

$$p = 31.4 \text{ cm of Hg}$$

4 (*b*) Let *n* be the number of molecular per unit volume and rms speed of gas is *v*.

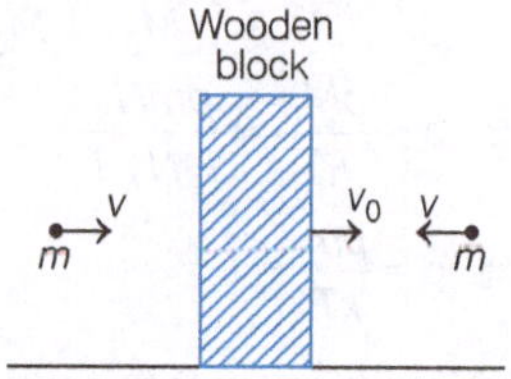

The relative speed of the molecular with respect to first face of block

$$= v + v_0$$

Momentum transferred to block per collision

$$= 2m(v + v_0)$$

Number of collision in time *t*

$$= \frac{1}{2}(v + v_0)nAT$$

Now, total momentum in time *t*

$$= m(v + v_0)^2 nAt$$

Similarly for second face, total momentum in time,

$$t = m(v - v_0)^2 nAt$$

So, net force $= \frac{dP}{dt} = (4mnAv)v_0$

$$= (4\rho Av)v_0 \quad [\because mn = \rho]$$

$$= 4\rho\sqrt{\frac{kT}{m}} \quad \left[\because v = \sqrt{\frac{kT}{m}}\right]$$

5 (*a*) As we know that,

$$v_{\text{rms}} = \sqrt{\frac{3RT}{m}}$$

or $$v_{\text{rms}} \propto \sqrt{T}$$

So, to double the rms speed, temperature must be raised four times.

$\therefore$ $$T_f = 1200 \text{ K}$$

The initial internal energy for diatomic gas, $U_i = \frac{5}{2}nRT$

$$= \frac{5}{2} \times \frac{15}{28} \times 8.314 \times 300 \quad \left[\because n = \frac{m}{M}\right]$$

$$= 3340.45 \text{ J}$$

Now, when gas temperature raised to 1200 K, its internal energy,

$$U_f = \frac{5}{2} \times \frac{15}{28} \times 8.314 \times 1200$$

$$= 13361.6 \text{ J}$$

Amount of heat supplied,

$$\Delta Q = U_f - U_i$$

$$= 13361.6 - 3340.45$$

$$= 10021.35 \text{ J}$$

$$\simeq 10 \times 10^3 \text{ J} = 10 \text{ kJ}$$

6 (*b*) $m = 0.44$ kg,

$$T_1 = 180 + 273 = 453 \text{ K}$$

$$\frac{V_2}{V_1} = 3, T_2 = 15 + 273 = 288 \text{ K}$$

$$W_{12} = 52.5 \text{ kJ}, \frac{C_P}{C_V} = 1.41$$

Now, adiabatic process

$$W_{12} = \frac{mR(T_1 - T_2)}{\gamma - 1}$$

$$52.5 = \frac{0.44 \times R(453 - 288)}{1.41 - 1}$$

$\Rightarrow$ $$R = 0.296 \text{ units}$$

$$\therefore C_p - C_V = 0.296 \text{ units}$$

$$\frac{C_P}{C_V} = 1.41$$

$\Rightarrow$ $$(1.41 - 1)C_V = 0.296$$

$\Rightarrow$ $$C_V = 0.722 \text{ kJ kg}^{-1}\text{K}^{-1}$$

$$C_p = 1.018 \text{ kJ kg}^{-1}\text{K}^{-1}$$

7 (*c*) We know that, average time of collision between molecules,

$$\tau = \frac{1}{n\pi\sqrt{2}\, v_{\text{rms}} d^2}$$

$\Rightarrow$ $$\tau \propto \frac{1}{n v_{\text{rms}}}$$

As, $$n \propto \frac{1}{V}$$

and $v_{rms} \propto \sqrt{T}$

Thus, we can write

$$n = kV^{-1} \text{ and } v_{rms} = k_2 T^{\frac{1}{2}}$$

where, k_1 and k_2 are constants.

$$\Rightarrow \qquad \tau \propto \frac{V}{\sqrt{T}}$$

For adiabatic process,

$V^{\gamma - 1}$ = constant or $T \propto V^{1-\gamma}$

Thus, we can write

$$\tau \propto VT^{-\frac{1}{2}} \propto V(V^{1-\gamma})^{-\frac{1}{2}}$$

$$\Rightarrow \qquad \tau \propto V^{\frac{\gamma+1}{2}}$$

As, given that average time of collision between molecules increases as V^q, on comparing, we get

$$q = \frac{\gamma + 1}{2}$$

8 (c) Cylinder before removal of membrane

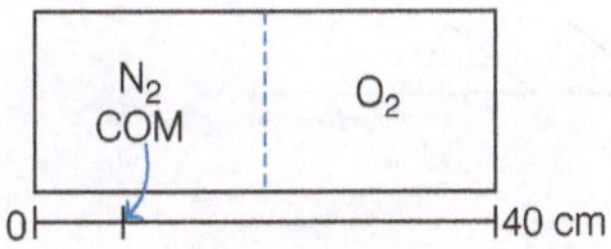

We assume temperature is same. COM of system must be on N_2 side (or $p_{N_2} > p_{O_2}$)

As, there is no external force is involved.

$$\Delta X = X_{\substack{\text{COM}\\\text{(final}}} - X_{\substack{\text{COM}\\\text{(initial)}}}$$

Now, $p_{N_2} V_{N_2} = n_{N_2} kT$

and $p_{O_2} V_{O_2} = n_{O_2} kT$

$$\Rightarrow \quad \frac{p_{N_2}}{p_{O_2}} = \frac{n_{N_2}}{n_{O_2}}$$

$$\Rightarrow \quad \frac{n_{N_2}}{n_{O_2}} = \frac{2}{1}$$

As, $\quad p_{N_2} = 2p$

and mass of given volumes of gases is

$$m_{N_2} = n_{N_2} M_{N_2}$$

$$\Rightarrow \quad m_{O_2} = n_{O_2} M_{O_2}$$

$$\text{Now, } X_{\substack{\text{COM}\\\text{(initial)}}} = \frac{\Sigma Xm}{\Sigma m}$$

$$= \frac{n_{N_2} M_{N_2} X_{N_2} + n_{O_2} M_{O_2} X_{O_2}}{(n_{N_2} M_{N_2} + n_{O_2} M_{O_2})}$$

$$= \frac{(1 \times 28.01 \times 10 + 1 \times 32 \times 30)}{2 \times 28.01 + 1 \times 32}$$

$$= 17.27 \text{ cm}$$

and

$$X_{\substack{\text{COM}\\\text{(final}}} = \frac{2 \times 28.01 \times 20 + 1 \times 32 \times 20}{2 \times 28.01 + 32}$$

$$= 20 \text{ cm}$$

$\therefore \Delta x$ = distance moved by cylinder

$$= X_{\text{final}} - X_{\text{initial}} = 20 - 17.27$$

$$= 2.7 \text{cm}$$

As, COM moves to right, the cylinder moves to the left.

9 (a) ΔS_1 (constant volume process)

$$= mC_V \ln\left(\frac{T_2}{T_1}\right)$$

ΔS_2 (polytropic process, pV^n = constant) $= mC_v \times \left(\frac{\gamma - n}{n - 1}\right) \ln\left(\frac{T_2}{T_1}\right)$

As change in entropy is same for both process,

$$\frac{\Delta S_2}{\Delta S_1} = 1 \Rightarrow \frac{\gamma + n}{n + 1} = 1$$

For monoatomic gas, $\gamma = \frac{5}{3}$

$$\frac{\frac{5}{3} - n}{n - 1} = 1 \Rightarrow \frac{5}{3} - n = n - 1$$

$$\Rightarrow \quad 2n = \frac{5}{3} + 1 = \frac{8}{3} \Rightarrow n = \frac{4}{3}$$

For monoatomic ideal gas,

C_V = molar specific heat at constant volume $= \frac{3}{2}R$

$\therefore$ Molar specific heat for polytropic process is

$$C_n = C_V \left|\left(\frac{\gamma - n}{1 - n}\right)\right|$$

$$= C_V \left|\left(\frac{\frac{5}{3} - \frac{4}{3}}{1 - \frac{4}{3}}\right)\right| = C_V \left|\left(\frac{\frac{1}{3}}{\frac{-1}{3}}\right)\right|$$

$$= C_V = \frac{3}{2}R$$

10 (b) $\therefore \lambda$ = mean free path

$$= \frac{kT}{4\pi\sqrt{2} \cdot r^2 \cdot p}$$

$$= \frac{1.38 \times 10^{-23} \times 300}{4\pi\sqrt{2}\left(\frac{1}{\sqrt{\pi}} \times 10^{-10}\right)^2 \times (\sqrt{2} \times 10^{-3})}$$

$$= \frac{1.38 \times 300 \times 10^{-23}}{8 \times 10^{-23}} = 51.75 \text{ m}$$

Also, side length of box = 10.35 m

$\therefore$ Collision frequency is given by

$$\bar{v} = \frac{\lambda}{t_{\text{molecular collisions}}}$$

$$= \frac{l_{\text{box}}}{t_{\text{wall collision}}}$$

$$\therefore \quad \frac{t_{\text{wall collision}}}{t_{\text{molecular collision}}} = \frac{\lambda}{l_{\text{box}}}$$

$$= \frac{51.75}{10.35} = 5$$

So, wall collisions are nearly 5 times more frequent than the intermolecular collisions.

Hence, wall collisions = 5 × intermolecular collisions = $5n$

13

Scan for **Physics Through Concept Master** *Videos*

Oscillations

Topicwise No. of Ques asked in 5 Years (NEET)

Topics	No. of Questions				
	2024	2023	2022	2021	2020
Periodic and Oscillatory Motions	–	–	–	–	1
Simple Harmonic Motion	1	1	–	–	1
Simple Harmonic Motion and Uniform Circular Motion	–	–	–	–	–
Velocity and Acceleration in SHM	–	–	–	–	–
Force Law for SHM	–	–	–	1	–
Energy in Simple Harmonic Motion	–	–	–	1	–
Simple Pendulum	1	–	1	–	–

Special Type of Ques Asked In 5 Years (NEET)

Types	Years				
	2024	2023	2022	2021	2020
A-R	1	–	–	–	–
Statement Based	1	–	–	–	–
Matching	1	–	–	–	–

Last 5 Years Weigtage (NEET)

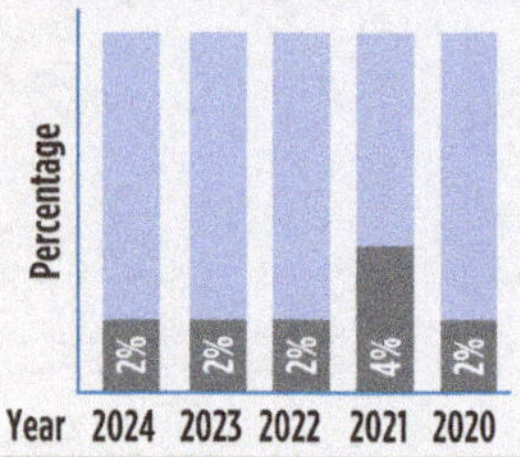

Periodic and Oscillatory Motion

- A motion that repeats itself at regular intervals of time is called **periodic motion**, e.g. revolution of earth around sun. NEET 2020
- Given graph shows the periodic motion for the time period T.

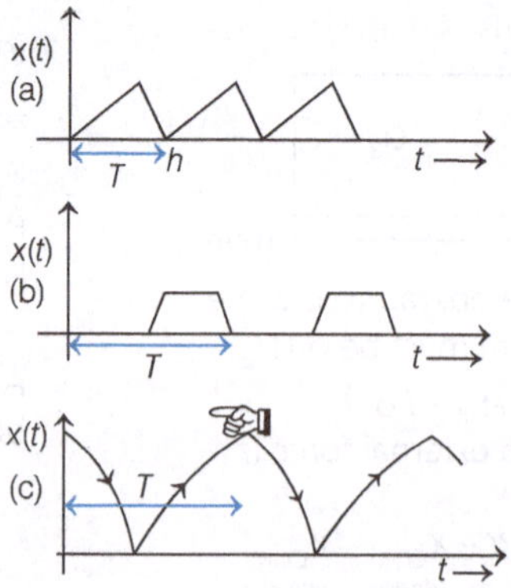

- A motion in which a body moves to and fro about a mean position or back and forth about a mean position, termed as **oscillatory motion**.
- If a body is given a small displacement from the equilibrium position, a force comes into play which tries to bring the body back to the equilibrium position, giving rise to **oscillations** or **vibrations**.
- Oscillatory or vibratory motion of a body is periodic and bounded about a fixed point.
- Every oscillatory motion is periodic but every periodic motion need not to be oscillatory. e.g. Circular motion is a periodic motion, but it is not oscillatory.

Time Period and Frequency

- The smallest interval of time after which the motion is repeated is called its **time period**. It is denoted by T and its SI unit is second.
- The reciprocal of time period T gives the number of repetitions that occur per unit time. This quantity is called the **frequency** of the periodic motion. It is denoted by symbol ν.

- The **relation between frequency ν and time period T** is given as

$$\nu = 1/T$$

- The SI unit of frequency is **hertz**.

1 hertz = 1 Hz = 1 oscillation per second = $1 s^{-1}$

- **Angular frequency**, $\omega = 2\pi\nu = \frac{2\pi}{T}$

Its SI unit is rad s^{-1}.

Displacement

- Displacement represents the change in position [see Fig. (a)] or angle [see Fig. (b)] with respect to mean position (or equilibrium position) of oscillation.

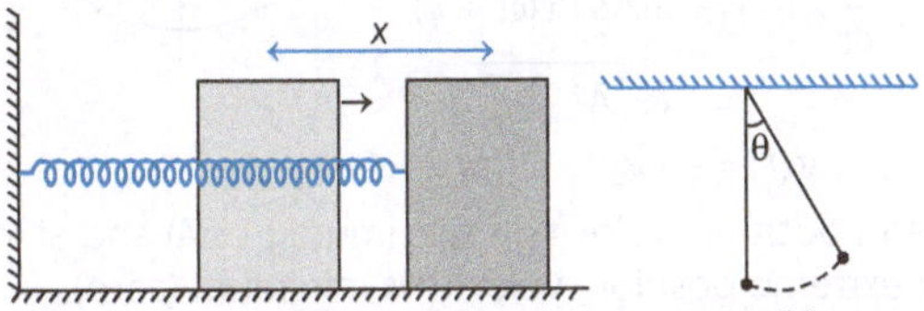

(a) (b)

- For a simple pendulum, the angle θ measured from the vertical as a function of time is a displacement variable.
- Displacement can have positive as well as negative values depending on its direction.
- The displacement can be represented by a mathematical function of time.
- In case of periodic motion, this function is periodic in time. One of the simplest periodic function is given by

$$x = f(t) = A\cos \omega t$$

If the argument of this function ωt is increased by an integral multiple of 2π radians, the value of function remains the same.

Periodic function

- A mathematical function which represents a periodic motion is called a periodic function.

A function $f(t)$ is said to be periodic, if $f(t) = f(t+T)$

where, T is the time period of the periodic function. T is given by

$$T = \frac{2\pi}{\omega}$$

- Any periodic function can be expressed as a superposition of sine and cosine functions of different time periods with suitable coefficients.
- A linear combination of sine and cosine functions like

$$f(t) = A\sin \omega t + B\cos \omega t \quad \text{...(I)}$$

is also a periodic function with same period T.

It can be written as

$$f(t) = D\sin(\omega t + \phi)$$

where, $D = \sqrt{A^2 + B^2}$ and $\phi = \tan^{-1}\left(\frac{B}{A}\right)$. **NEET 2019**

Simple Harmonic Motion

- It is the simplest form of oscillatory motion. It is a particular type of periodic motion in which a particle moves to and fro under the influence of a restoring force about a mean position.
- This motion arises when the acceleration of the oscillating body is directly proportional to its displacement from the mean position and its direction is always towards the mean position.

Acceleration, $a \propto -x \Rightarrow a = -kx$

or $\frac{d^2x}{dt^2} = -kx$

where, x = displacement at instant of time t.

- A particle oscillating back and forth about the origin of X-axis between the limits $+A$ and $-A$ is as shown in figure.

This oscillatory motion is said to be **simple harmonic**, if the displacement x of the particle from the origin varies with time as

$$x(t) = A\cos(\omega t + \phi)$$

where, $x(t)$ = displacement x as a function of time t,

A = amplitude,

ω = angular frequency $\left(\frac{2\pi}{T}\right)$,

$(\omega t + \phi)$ = phase (time-dependent)

and ϕ = initial phase constant.

- **Displacement as a continuous function of time** for simple harmonic motion is shown below.

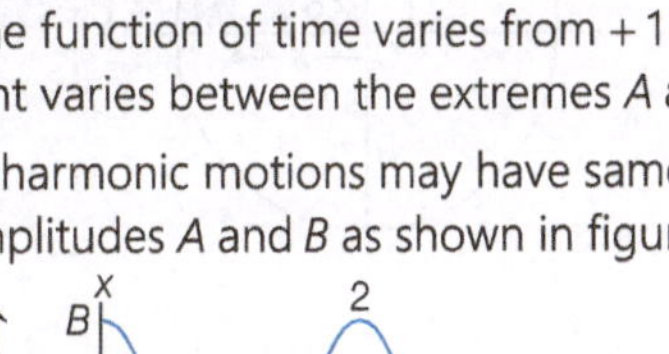

- The **amplitude** of SHM is the magnitude of maximum displacement of the particle.
- As the cosine function of time varies from +1 to −1, the displacement varies between the extremes A and $-A$.
- Two simple harmonic motions may have same ω and ϕ but different amplitudes A and B as shown in figure.

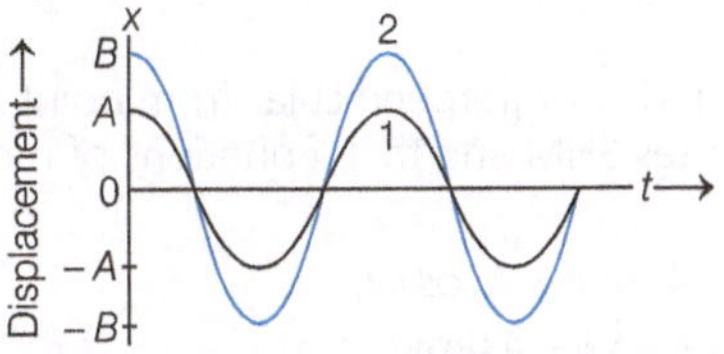

- When the amplitude A is fixed for a given SHM, the state of motion (position and velocity) of the particle at any time t is determined by the argument $(\omega t + \phi)$ in the cosine function. This time-dependent quantity, $(\omega t + \phi)$ is called the **phase of the motion**.

- The value of phase at $t = 0$ is ϕ and is called the **phase constant** (or phase angle). If the amplitude is known, ϕ can be determined from the displacement at $t = 0$.
- Two simple harmonic motions may have the same A and ω but different phase angle ϕ as shown in figure below

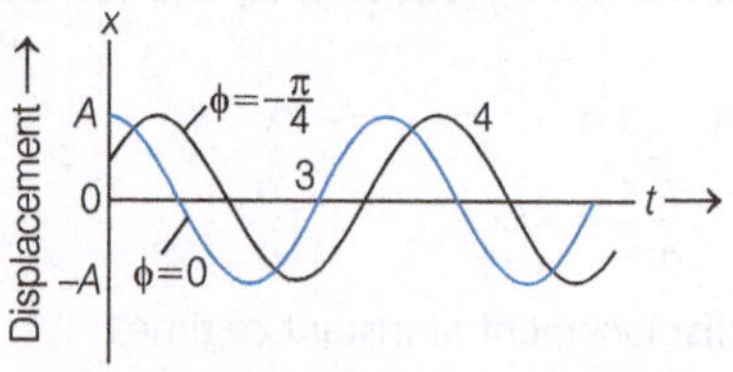

- Two simple harmonic motions may have the same A and ϕ but different ω, as seen in figure. In this plot, the curve b has half the period and twice the frequency of the curve a.

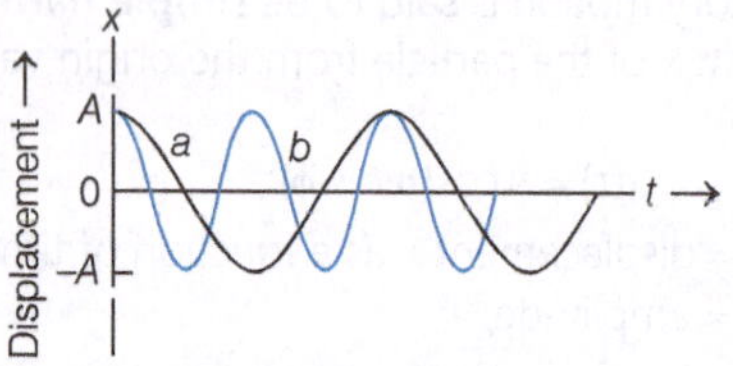

Simple Harmonic Motion and Uniform Circular Motion

- The projection of uniform circular motion on any diameter of a circle follows simple harmonic motion.
- The given figure describes the same situation graphically for a particle P moving uniformly on a circular path of radius A with angular speed ω in anti-clockwise direction.

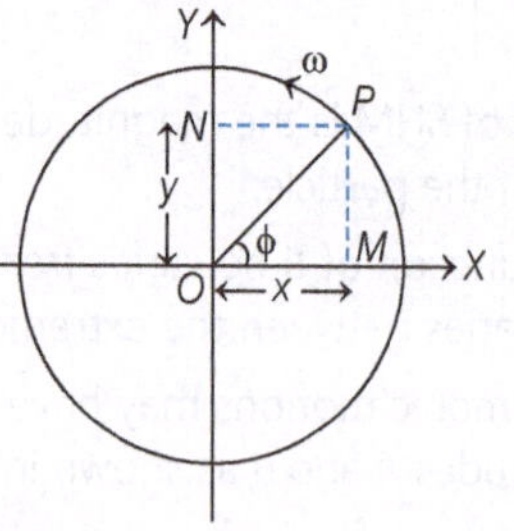

- The foot M and N of perpendicular from point P on X and Y-axes executes SHM and their equations of motion are given as

$$x = A\cos\phi = A\cos\omega t$$
$$y = A\sin\phi = A\sin\omega t$$

NEET 2019

- The phase difference between two SHM of M and N is $\frac{\pi}{2}$.

Velocity and Acceleration in Simple Harmonic Motion

- **Velocity** The rate of change of displacement with respect to time at any instant by a particle executing SHM is known as its velocity.
- The velocity $v(t)$ of the particle P' is the projection of the velocity **v** of the reference particle P is shown in the figure.

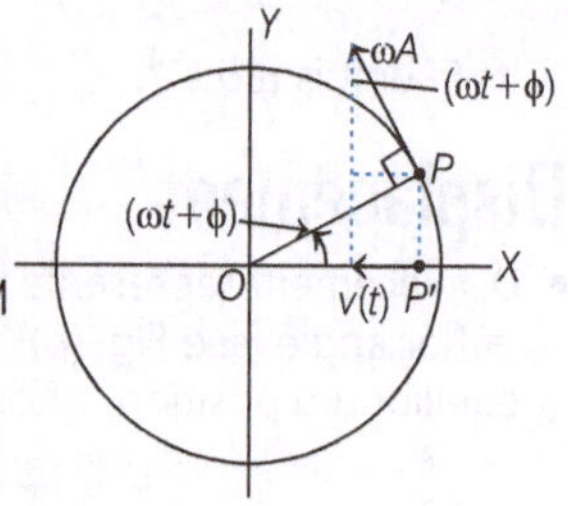

- The particle velocity during SHM as function of time is given by

$$v(t) = \frac{d}{dt}x(t) = -\omega A\sin(\omega t + \phi)$$
$$= -\omega\sqrt{A^2 - x^2}$$
$$v(t) = -\omega A \qquad (\text{for } x = 0)$$

- At mean position, velocity is maximum $(-\omega A)$ and at $x = A$, i.e. at extreme position, velocity is minimum (zero).
- **Acceleration** The rate of change of velocity with respect to time at any instant of a particle executing simple harmonic motion is known as acceleration.
- The acceleration $a(t)$ of the particle P' is the projection of the acceleration **a** of the reference particle P.

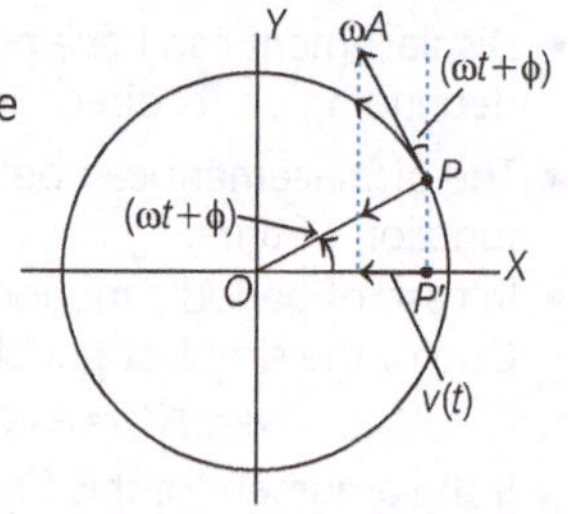

- The particle acceleration during SHM as function of time is given by

$$a(t) = \frac{d}{dt}v(t)$$
$$= -\omega^2 A\cos(\omega t + \phi) = -\omega^2 x(t)$$

NEET 2023

- At $x = 0$, i.e. at mean position acceleration is zero $[(a(t) = 0)]$.
- At $x = A$, i.e. at extreme position $a(t) = -\omega^2 A$.
- The displacement, velocity and acceleration of a particle in SHM are shown in figure below. They have same time period, but they are differ in phase. **NEET 2020**

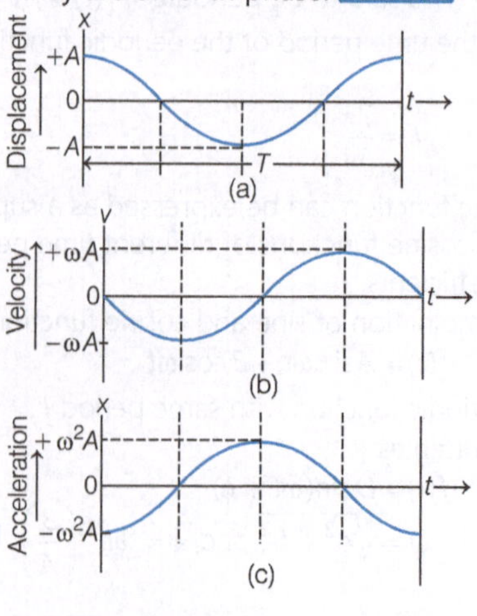

Force Law For Simple Harmonic Motion

- The force acting on a particle of mass m in SHM is given as

$$F(t) = ma = -m\omega^2 x(t)$$

i.e. $$F(t) = -kx(t)$$

where, $$k = m\omega^2$$

$$\Rightarrow \quad \omega = \sqrt{\frac{k}{m}}$$

- Like acceleration, force is always directed towards the mean position, hence it is sometimes called the **restoring force in SHM**.
- When a particle oscillating under such a force which is linearly proportional to displacement $x(t)$, then it is called **linear harmonic oscillator**.
- In the real world, the force may contain small additional terms proportional to x^2, x^3, etc. these are called **non-linear oscillators**.

Oscillations Due to a Spring*

- When a linear simple harmonic oscillator consisting of a block of mass m attached to a spring is pulled or pushed and released as shown in figure below, it starts oscillating back and forth about its equilibrium position under the action of a restoring force

$$F = -kx, \text{ where } k = \text{spring constant}$$

The above equation is same as the force law of SHM and therefore the system executes simple harmonic motion of angular frequency,

$$\omega = \sqrt{\frac{k}{m}} \text{ and time period, } T = 2\pi\sqrt{\frac{m}{k}}$$ NEET 2021

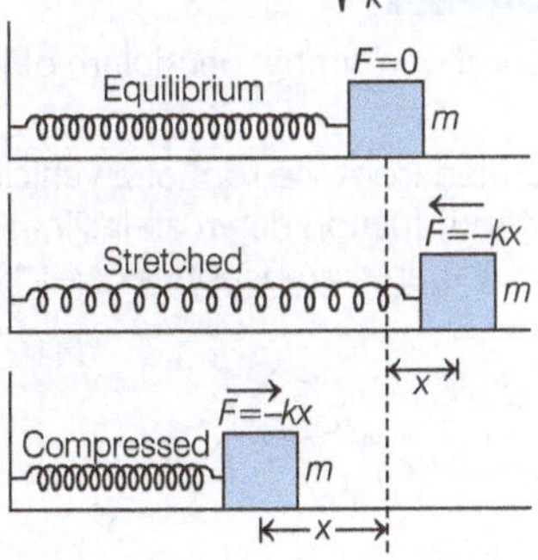

- Stiff springs have high value of k, while soft springs have low value of k.

Combination of Springs

(i) **Springs Connected in Parallel** For parallel combination of springs, the spring constant is given by

$$k_P = k_1 + k_2$$

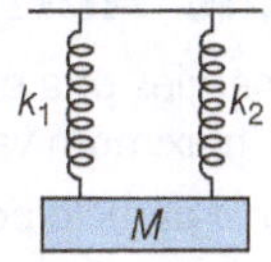

The frequency of vibration of parallel combination is given by

$$\nu_P = \frac{1}{2\pi}\sqrt{\frac{k_P}{m}} = \frac{1}{2\pi}\sqrt{\frac{k_1 + k_2}{m}}$$

(ii) **Springs Connected in Series** For series combination of springs, the spring constant is given by

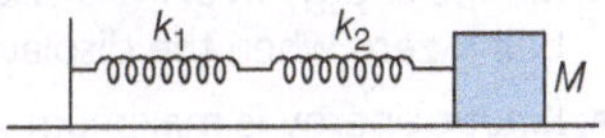

$$k_s = \frac{k_1 k_2}{k_1 + k_2}$$

Frequency of oscillation of the series combination is given by

$$\nu_s = \frac{1}{2\pi}\sqrt{\frac{k_s}{m}} = \frac{1}{2\pi}\sqrt{\frac{k_1 k_2}{m(k_1 + k_2)}}$$

- The spring-mass system as shown in figure below, when it is released with some extension, then time period is given by

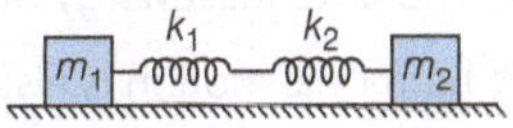

$$T = 2\pi\sqrt{\frac{m_{eq}}{k_{eq}}}$$

where, m_{eq} = reduced mass of the system $= \dfrac{m_1 m_2}{m_1 + m_2}$

$$k_{eq} = \frac{k_1 k_2}{k_1 + k_2}$$

- The time period of oscillation of the spring-mass system shown in figure below, when it is released with some distance from equilibrium position.

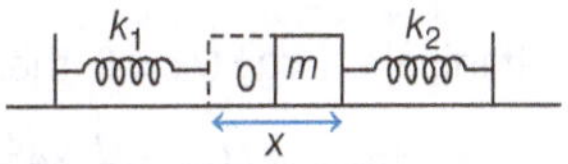

$$T = 2\pi\sqrt{\frac{m}{k}}$$

Marks Maximiser

Cases of Equivalent Spring

- If the length of spring of spring constant k is made n times, then its effective spring constant $k' = \dfrac{k}{n}$

  and time period becomes, $T' = \sqrt{n}T$
- If the spring of spring constant k is cut into n equal parts, the spring constant of each part,

  $$k' = nk$$

  Time period of each spring, $T' = \dfrac{T}{\sqrt{n}}$

* *This topic is not included in latest rationalised NCERT. But it is given in latest NEET syllabus.*

Energy in Simple Harmonic Motion

- Kinetic and potential energies of a particle in SHM vary between zero and their maximum values.
- The **kinetic energy** K of a particle performing SHM is given by

$$K = \frac{1}{2}mv^2 = \frac{1}{2}m\omega^2 A^2 \sin^2(\omega t + \phi)$$
$$= \frac{1}{2}kA^2 \sin^2(\omega t + \phi) = \frac{1}{2}k(A^2 - x^2)$$

- Kinetic energy in SHM is also a periodic function of time, being zero when the displacement is maximum.
- Kinetic energy is maximum when the particle is at the mean position.
- Period of kinetic energy is $T/2$.
- The **potential energy** of a particle executing simple harmonic motion is given by

$$U = \frac{1}{2}kx^2 = \frac{1}{2}kA^2 \cos^2(\omega t + \phi)$$

- The potential energy of a particle executing simple harmonic motion is also periodic, with period $\frac{T}{2}$. **NEET 2021**
- **Total energy of a particle** in SHM is given as

$$E = U + K = \frac{1}{2}kA^2 = \frac{1}{2}m\omega^2 A^2$$

- If initial energy $U_0 = 0$, then

$$E_{max} = U_{max} = K_{max} = \frac{1}{2}kA^2$$

If initial energy $U_0 \neq 0$, then

$$E_{max} = U_{max} = \frac{1}{2}kA^2 + U_0 \quad \text{but} \quad K_{max} = \frac{1}{2}kA^2$$

- The total mechanical energy of a harmonic oscillation is independent of time as expected for motion under any conservative force.
- The time and displacement dependence of the potential and kinetic energies of a linear simple harmonic oscillator are shown in figure.

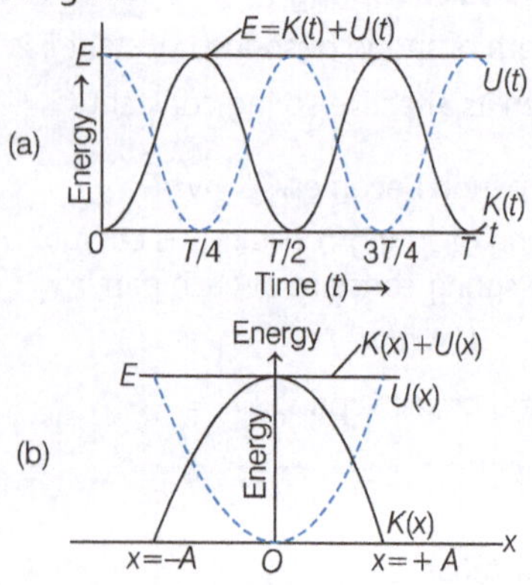

- Both kinetic and potential energies peak twice during each period of SHM.
- For $x = 0$ (mean position), the energy is kinetic and at the extremes $x = \pm A$, it is all potential energy. This means, in the course of motion between these limits, kinetic energy increases at the expense of potential energy or *vice-versa*.

Simple Pendulum

- A simple pendulum in practice, consists of a heavy but small sized metallic bob suspended by a light, inextensible and flexible string.

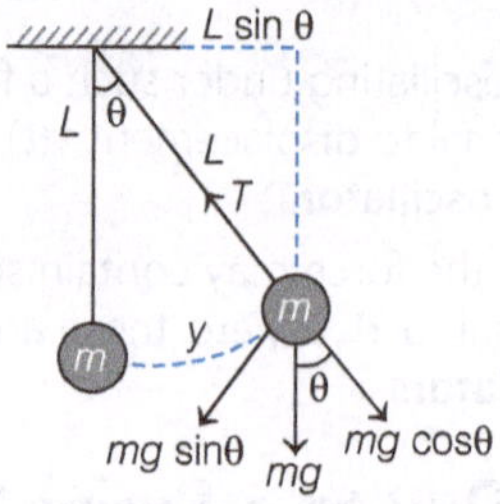

- For small angular displacement θ, restoring torque,

$$\tau = -mg(L\sin\theta) = I\alpha$$

Restoring acceleration, $\alpha = \frac{-mgL}{I}\sin\theta$

Angular frequency, $\omega = \sqrt{\frac{g}{L}} = \sqrt{\frac{mgL}{I}}$

and time period, $T = 2\pi\sqrt{\frac{I}{mgL}} = 2\pi\sqrt{\frac{L}{g}}$ **NEET 2022**

Marks Maximiser

- The time period of a simple pendulum of length l, when
  (i) it is suspended from the roof of a vehicle, which moves without friction down an inclined plane of inclination θ, then time period is given by

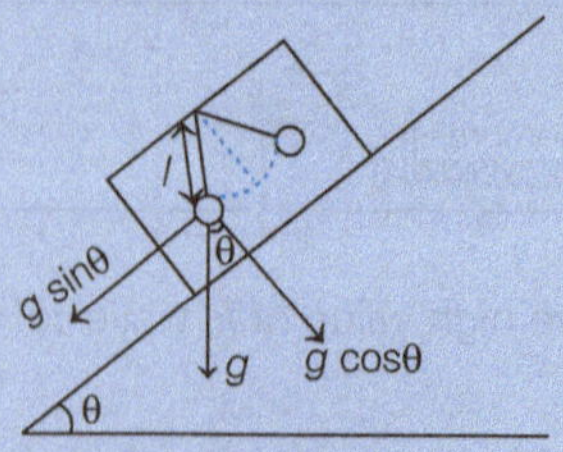

$$T = 2\pi\sqrt{\frac{l}{g_{eff}}},$$

where, $g_{eff} = g\cos\theta$

(ii) Its bob of density ρ is immersed in a liquid of density σ, then time period is given by

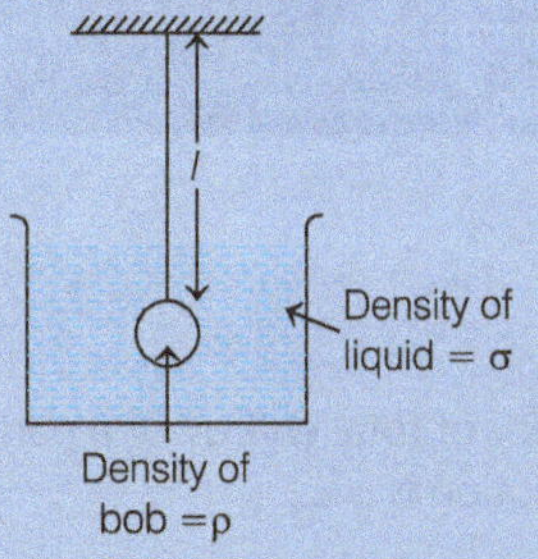

$$T = 2\pi\sqrt{\frac{l}{g_{\text{eff}}}}, \text{ where } g_{\text{eff}} = g\left(1 - \frac{\sigma}{\rho}\right)$$

(iii) It is suspended from the roof of a lift, which moves vertically upward or downward with acceleration '*a*', then time period is given by

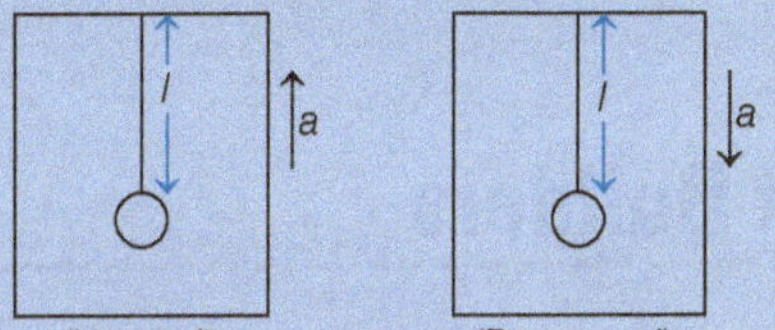

(Upward) (Downward)

For Concept Master Video

$$T = 2\pi\sqrt{\frac{l}{g_{\text{eff}}}}, \text{ where } g_{\text{eff}} = (g + a)$$

$$T = 2\pi\sqrt{\frac{l}{g_{\text{eff}}}}, \text{ where } g_{\text{eff}} = (g - a)$$

Caution Points

- Circular motion can arise due to an inverse-square law force (like planetary motion) as well as due to simple harmonic force in two dimensions equal to $-m\omega^2 r$.
- A particle subject to a simple harmonic force with initial velocity ωA will move uniformly in a circle of radius A.
- To fully describe linear simple harmonic motion with a given speed ω, two initial conditions needed, which could be either (i) initial position and initial velocity or (ii) amplitude and phase or (iii) energy and phase.
- The combination of two simple harmonic motions with arbitrary amplitude and phases is not necessarily periodic.
- A periodic motion can always be expressed as sum of infinite number of harmonic motions with appropriate amplitudes.
- The period of SHM is independent of its amplitude, energy and phase while the period of planetary orbits depends on their distance from central body.
- For small angular displacement, simple pendulum motion is simple harmonic motion.

PYQ Notes

1. When a particle executes SHM with amplitude A, then the distance from the mean position at which its kinetic energy becomes equal to its potential energy is given by **[JEE Main 2023]**

$$x = \pm\frac{A}{\sqrt{2}}$$

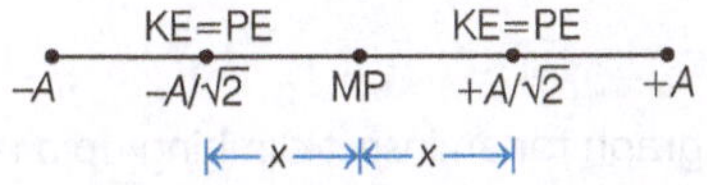

2. The average kinetic energy in one time period is equal to average potential energy in one time period for a body executing SHM and is given by

$$< KE > = < PE > = \frac{1}{4}m\omega^2 A^2$$

where m, ω and A are mass of the body, angular frequency and amplitude of SHM, respectively. **[JEE Main 2021]**

3. The sum of two periodic function is also a periodic function.
sin ω*t* + cos ω*t* is a periodic function. **[NEET 2020]**

4. Time of fall of an object from height h is given by
$$t = \sqrt{\frac{2h}{g}}$$
[NEET 2019]

5. The average velocity in complete cycle is zero in SHM. **[NEET 2019]**

Step by Step

Mastering NCERT

- Concept Builders
- Topical Questions
- Assertion and Reason Questions
- Statement Based
- Matching Type
- Numerical Type
- NCERT Exemplar
- Past Exams MCQs
- Skill Boosters

Concept Builders

1 Oscillatory motion is that motion, which is repeated after a fixed interval of time but not to and fro. [T/F]

2 What is the relation between frequency and time period of the periodic motion of the object ?

3 A mathematical function $f(t)$ is called periodic function if $f(t)=f(t+T)$. (T/F)

4 The function $e^{-\omega t}$ is a periodic but log (ωt) is not a periodic function. (T/F)

5 If a function is represented by a single sine or cosine function, then what will be the function called?

6 What is the mathematical expression of the force law for simple harmonic motion?

7 The projection of a uniform circular motion on any diameter of a circle is called .... motion.

8 In simple harmonic motion, a particle moves ...... (faster/slower) near the mean position and .... (faster/slower) near the extreme position.

9 The acceleration in SHM is always in same phase to that of displacement. [T/F]

10 What is the total distance travelled by a body exerting SHM in a time equal to its time period, if its amplitude is A?

11 What provides the restoring force for simple harmonic motion in a spring?

12 The frequency of total energy of a particle in simple harmonic motion is ....

13 Potential energy of a particle in SHM repeat after a period $\frac{T}{2}$ but kinetic energy repeat after a period $\frac{T}{4}$. [T/F]

14 What is the formula for the kinetic energy of a particle at an instant in SHM?

15 The displacement, velocity and acceleration have the same time period but they differ in phase. [T/F]

16 In one complete oscillation, an average value of kinetic energy of a particle of mass m, having angular frequency ω while moving with amplitude of oscillation A is ....

17 The pendulum clock runs faster due to ...... (increase/decrease) in its time period.

18 Clock based on spring pendulum give same time everywhere on a hill or moon or in satellite. [T/F]

19 When a pendulum taken to the top of a mountain, then will time period of the pendulum decrease ?

20 Tension in the string of pendulum at mean position is $\left(mg+\frac{mv^2}{l}\right)$. [T/F]

Topical Questions

Periodic and Oscillatory Motions

1 Which one of the following is both periodic and oscillatory ? NCERT Pg. 260

(a) A freely suspended bar magnet displaced from its N-S direction and released

(b) The piston in steam engine moves back and forth inside a cylinder

(c) Rotation of the earth about its axis

(d) An arrow released from a bow

2 Choose x-t graph for an insect climbing up a ramp uniformly and sliding down then comes back to initial point and repeats the process identically. NCERT Pg. 260

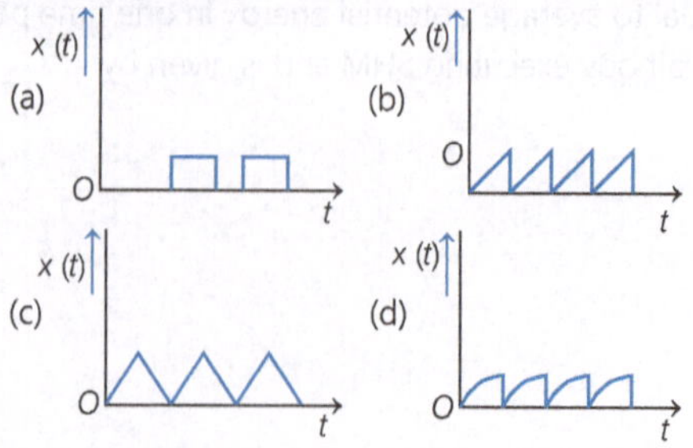

3 On an average, a human heart is found to beat 75 times in a minute. The beat frequency and period of human heart are respectively **NCERT Pg. 260**

(a) 1 Hz, 0.8 s (b) 1 Hz, 1 s
(c) 1.25 Hz, 0.8 s (d) 2 Hz, 0.5 s

4 The periodic function $f(t) = A\sin\omega t$ repeats itself after **NCERT Pg. 261**

(a) 2π (b) 3π (c) π (d) $\pi/2$

5 A particle perform oscillatory motion with amplitude 4 cm. If the time period of particle is 1 s, then time taken by the particle to reach 2 cm from the mean position is given by **NCERT Pg. 261**

(a) $(1/2)$ s (b) $(1/4)$ s
(c) $(1/12)$ s (d) $(1/6)$ s

6 Displacement of a particle in periodic motion is expressed as $x(t) = 20\cos\omega t$. If the time period of particle is 4s, then displacement of the particle in 1 s will be **NCERT Pg. 261**

(a) 10 m (b) 15 m (c) 0 (d) 20 m

7 The function $\log \omega t$ **NCERT Pg. 261**

(a) is a periodic function
(b) is a non-periodic function
(c) could represents oscillatory motion
(d) can represents circular motion

8 Choose the periodic function from the following. **NCERT Pg. 261**

(a) $A\sin^3(\omega t)^2$ (b) $\sin\omega t + \cos\omega t$
(c) $\tan(\omega t)^3$ (d) $e^{\omega t}$

Simple Harmonic Motion

9 Motion of a ball bearing inside a smooth curved bowl when released from a point slightly above the lower point, is **NCERT Pg. 262**

(a) simple harmonic motion (SHM)
(b) non-periodic motion
(c) parabolic
(d) periodic but not SHM

10 The relation between the time period of two simple harmonic motions represented by two curves is **NCERT Pg. 262**

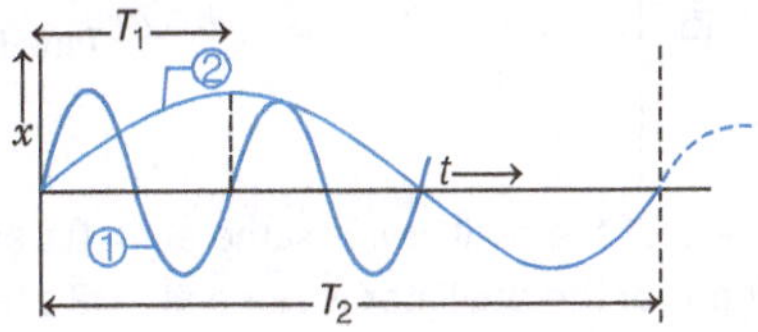

(a) $T_1 = 4T_2$ (b) $T_2 = 4T_1$
(c) $T_2 = 2T_1$ (d) $T_1 = 2T_2$

11 The displacement of a particle is given by $x = k\sin^2\omega t$. The motion of the particle corresponds to **NCERT Pg. 262**

(a) SHM of frequency $\frac{\omega}{\pi}$

(b) SHM of frequency $\frac{3\omega}{2\pi}$

(c) non-simple harmonic motion

(d) SHM of frequency $\frac{\omega}{2\pi}$

12 Figure shows snapshots of a particle moving between $+A$ and $-A$ about origin (at $x = 0$) at different instants. The particle moves in a way that velocity is maximum at $x = 0$ and minimum at $x = \pm A$. **NCERT Pg. 262**

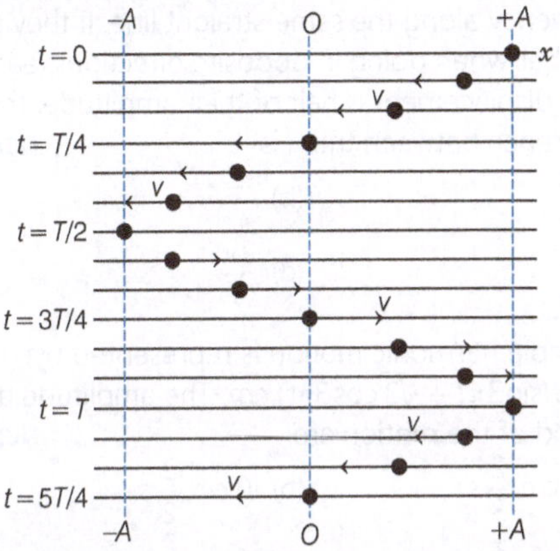

The correct displacement equation for the motion of the particle is

(a) $A\sin\omega t$
(b) $A\cos\omega t$
(c) $A\tan\omega t$
(d) $A\cot\omega t$

13 When two displacements represented by $y_1 = a\sin\omega t$ and $y_2 = b\cos\omega t$ are superimposed, the motion is **NCERT Pg. 262**

(a) not a simple harmonic
(b) simple harmonic with amplitude $\frac{a}{b}$
(c) simple harmonic with amplitude $\sqrt{a^2 + b^2}$
(d) simple harmonic with amplitude $\frac{(a+b)}{2}$

14 Two simple harmonic motions are represented by

$$y_1 = 5(\sin 2\pi t + \sqrt{3}\cos 2\pi t)$$

and $$y_2 = 5\sin\left(2\pi t + \frac{\pi}{4}\right).$$

The ratio of their amplitudes is **NCERT Pg. 262**

(a) 1 : 1 (b) 2 : 1
(c) 1 : 3 (d) $\sqrt{3}$: 1

15 Which of the following is incorrect when function $x = A\sin^2 \omega t + B\cos^2 \omega t + C\sin \omega t \cos \omega t$ represents SHM? **NCERT Pg. 262**

(a) If $A = 0, B = 0$, it will be in SHM

(b) If $A = -B, C = 2B$, amplitude $= |B\sqrt{2}|$

(c) If $A = B, C = 0$, amplitude $= |B|$

(d) If $A = B, C = 2B$, it will be in SHM

16 A body executing simple harmonic motion has a periodic time of 3 s. After how much time from $t = 0$, its displacement will be half of its amplitude? **NCERT Pg. 262**

(a) (1/8) s (b) (1/6) s

(c) (1/4) s (d) (1/3) s

17 Two particles execute SHM of the same amplitude and frequency along the same straight line. If they pass one another when going in opposite directions, each time their displacement is half of their amplitude, the phase difference between them is **NCERT Pg. 262**

(a) $\frac{\pi}{3}$ (b) $\frac{\pi}{4}$

(c) $\frac{\pi}{6}$ (d) $\frac{2\pi}{3}$

18. A simple harmonic motion is represented by: $y = 5(\sin 3\pi t + \sqrt{3}\cos 3\pi t)$ cm. The amplitude and time period of the motion are **NCERT Pg. 262**

(a) 5 cm, $\frac{2}{3}$ s (b) 10 cm, $\frac{3}{2}$ s

(c) 5 cm, $\frac{3}{2}$ s (d) 10 cm, $\frac{2}{3}$ s

19. If x, v and a represent the displacement, the velocity and the acceleration of a particle executing simple harmonic motion of time period T, then which of the following does not change with time ? **NCERT Pg. 262**

(a) $\frac{aT}{v}$ (b) $aT + 2\pi v$

(c) $\frac{aT}{x}$ (d) $a^2T + 4\pi^2 v^2$

20. If a simple harmonic motion is represented by $\frac{d^2x}{dt^2} + \alpha x = 0$, its time period is **NCERT Pg. 262**

(a) $2\pi\sqrt{\alpha}$ (b) $2\pi\alpha$

(c) $\frac{2\pi}{\sqrt{\alpha}}$ (d) $\frac{2\pi}{\alpha}$

21. Which of the following expressions does not represent simple harmonic motion? **NCERT Pg. 262**

(a) $x = A\cos \omega t + B\sin \omega t$

(b) $x = A\cos(\omega t + \alpha)$

(c) $x = B\sin(\omega t + \beta)$

(d) $x = A\sin \omega t \cos^2 \omega t$

22. The equation of motion of a simple harmonic motion is **NCERT Pg. 262**

(a) $\frac{d^2x}{dt^2} = -\omega^2 x$

(b) $\frac{d^2x}{dt^2} = -\omega^2 t$

(c) $\frac{d^2x}{dt^2} = -\omega x^2$

(d) $\frac{d^2x}{dt^2} = -\omega t$

23 Two simple harmonic motions given by $x = a\sin(\omega t + \delta)$ and $y = a\sin\left(\omega t + \delta + \frac{\pi}{2}\right)$ act on a particle simultaneously, then the motion of particle will be **NCERT Pg. 262**

(a) circular, anti-clockwise

(b) circular clockwise

(c) elliptical anti-clockwise

(d) elliptical clockwise

24. Which of the following is not a characteristics of simple harmonic motion? **NCERT Pg. 262**

(a) The motion is periodic

(b) The motion is along a straight line about the mean position

(c) The oscillations are responsible for the energy conversion

(d) The acceleration of the particle is directed towards the extreme position

25 The displacement y of a particle is given by $y = 4\cos^2\left(\frac{t}{2}\right)\sin(1000t)$. This expression may be considered to be a result of the superposition of how many simple harmonic motions **NCERT Pg. 262**

(a) 2 (b) 3

(c) 1 (d) 4

26 Displacement *versus* time curve for a particle executing SHM is shown in figure. Choose the correct statements. **NCERT Pg. 263**

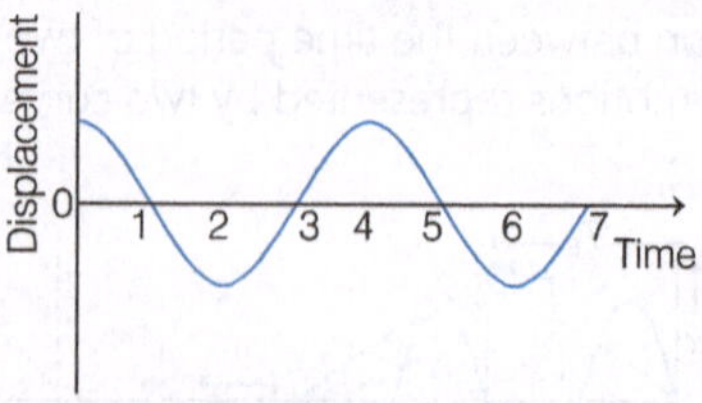

(a) Phase of the oscillator is same at $t = 0$ s and $t = 2$ s.

(b) Phase of the oscillator is same at $t = 2$ s and $t = 6$ s.

(c) Phase of the oscillator is same at $t = 1$ s and $t = 7$ s.

(d) Phase of the oscillator is same at $t = 3$ s and $t = 5$ s.

27 The displacement-time graph of a particle executing SHM is shown in figure. Which of the following statement is/are incorrect? **NCERT Pg. 263**

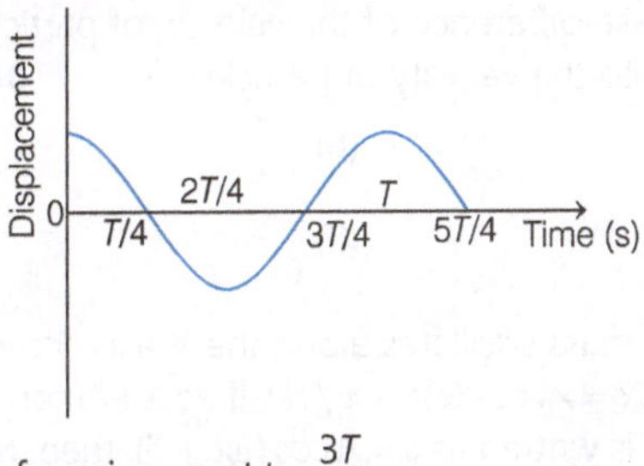

(a) The force is zero at $t = \frac{3T}{4}$.

(b) The acceleration is maximum at $t = \frac{4T}{4}$.

(c) The velocity is maximum at $t = \frac{T}{4}$.

(d) The PE is equal to KE of oscillation at $t = \frac{T}{2}$.

Simple Harmonic Motion and Uniform Circular Motion

28 A ball is moving in uniform circular motion in a horizontal plane, the shadow of ball on the wall will execute **NCERT Pg. 264**

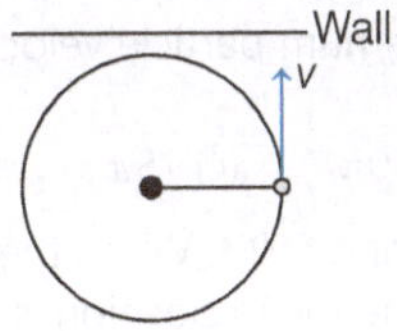

(a) projectile motion
(b) uniform circular motion
(c) simple harmonic motion
(d) non-uniform circular motion

29 Figure depicts a circular motion. The radius of the circle, period of revolution, initial position and the sense of revolution are indicated on the figure. **NCERT Pg. 264**

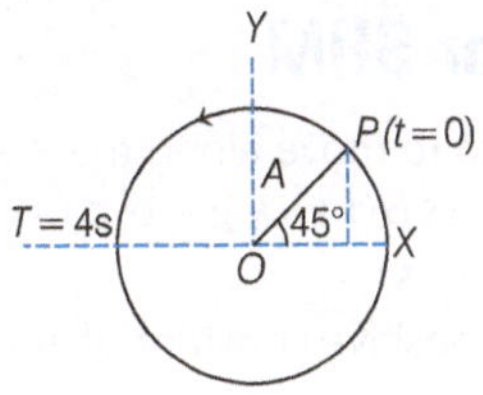

The simple harmonic motion of the X-projection of the radius vector of the rotating particle P is

(a) $A\cos\left(\frac{2\pi}{4}t + \frac{\pi}{4}\right)$ (b) $A\cos\left(\frac{\pi}{4}t + \frac{\pi}{4}\right)$
(c) $A\cos\left(\frac{\pi}{3}t + \frac{\pi}{2}\right)$ (d) $A\cos\left(\frac{2\pi}{3}t + \frac{\pi}{2}\right)$

30 In 1610, Galileo found four moons of planet jupiter. He observe the motion of one moon callisto from earth and his data in graph as shown below suggests that its motion is simple harmonic. **NCERT Pg. 264**

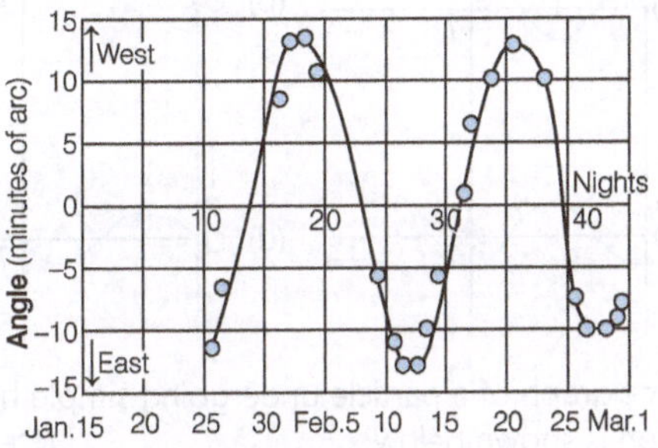

Now, choose the incorrect statement.

(a) The motion of moon callisto is not simple harmonic in real.

(b) The motion of moon callisto is actually uniform circular motion.

(c) Galileo observed projections of uniform circular motion in a line of plane of motion.

(d) The motion of moon callisto is SHM in real

Velocity and Acceleration in SHM

31 The equation of a simple harmonic motion is given by $y = 3\sin(50t - x)$, where x and y are in metres and t is in seconds, the maximum particle velocity (in ms^{-1}) is **NCERT Pg. 266**

(a) 3 (b) 50
(c) 150 (d) 25

32 The piston in the cylinder head of a locomotive has a stroke (twice the amplitude) of 2.0 m. If the piston moves with simple harmonic motion with an angular frequency of 100 rad min^{-1}, what is its maximum speed? **NCERT Pg. 266**

(a) 50 m min^{-1} (b) 100 m min^{-1}
(c) 200 m min^{-1} (d) 75 m min^{-1}

33 Two simple harmonic motions of angular frequency 100 $rads^{-1}$ and 1000 $rads^{-1}$ have the same displacement amplitude. The ratio of their maximum accelerations is **NCERT Pg. 266**

(a) $1:10$ (b) $1:10^2$
(c) $1:10^3$ (d) $1:10^4$

34 The oscillation of a body on a smooth horizontal surface is represented by the equation $x = A\cos\omega t$, **NCERT Pg. 266**

where x = displacement at time t and

ω = frequency of oscillation.

Which one of the following graphs shows correctly the variation of a with t?

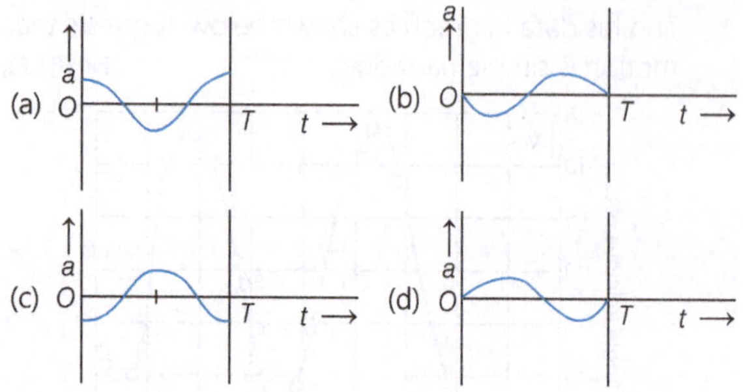

35 The x-t graph of a particle undergoing simple harmonic motion is shown below. **NCERT Pg. 266**

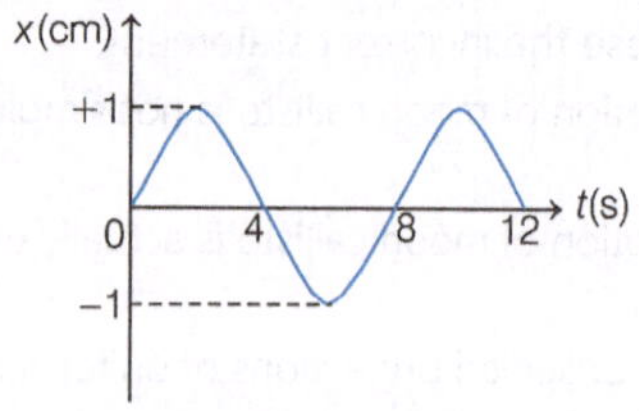

The acceleration of the particle at $t = \frac{4}{3}$ s is

(a) $\frac{\sqrt{3}}{32}\pi^2\ \text{cms}^{-2}$ (b) $-\frac{\pi^2}{32}\text{cms}^{-2}$

(c) $\frac{\pi^2}{32}\text{cms}^{-2}$ (d) $-\frac{\sqrt{3}}{32}\pi^2\text{cms}^{-2}$

36 A particle is executing a simple harmonic motion. Its maximum acceleration is α and maximum velocity is β, then its time period of vibration will be **NCERT Pg. 266**

(a) $\frac{\beta^2}{\alpha^2}$ (b) $\frac{\alpha}{\beta}$

(c) $\frac{\beta^2}{\alpha}$ (d) $\frac{2\pi\beta}{\alpha}$

37 A particle starts simple harmonic motion from the mean position. Its amplitude is a and time period is T. What is its displacement when its speed is half of its maximum speed? **NCERT Pg. 266**

(a) $\frac{\sqrt{2}}{3}a$ (b) $\frac{\sqrt{3}}{2}a$

(c) $\frac{2}{\sqrt{3}}a$ (d) $\frac{a}{\sqrt{2}}$

38 The displacement of an object attached to a spring and executing SHM is given by equation $x = 2\cos(2\pi t)$, where x is in cm and t in second. The time at which maximum speed first occurs is **NCERT Pg. 266**

(a) 0.2 s (b) 0.25 s

(c) 0.3 s (d) 0.4 s

39 Two simple harmonic motions are represented by the equations $y_1 = 0.1\sin\left(100\pi t + \frac{\pi}{3}\right)$ and $y_2 = 0.1\cos \pi t$.

The phase difference of the velocity of particle 1 with respect to the velocity of particle 2 is **NCERT Pg. 266**

(a) $-\frac{\pi}{6}$ (b) $-\frac{\pi}{3}$

(c) $\frac{\pi}{3}$ (d) $\frac{\pi}{6}$

40 A point mass oscillates along the X-axis according to the law $x = x_0\cos(\omega t - \pi/4)$. If acceleration of the particle is written as $a = A\cos(\omega t + \delta)$, then **NCERT Pg. 266**

(a) $A = x_0,\ \delta = -\frac{\pi}{4}$ (b) $A = x_0\omega^2,\ \delta = \frac{\pi}{4}$

(c) $A = x_0\omega^2,\ \delta = -\frac{\pi}{4}$ (d) $A = x_0\omega^2,\ \delta = \frac{3\pi}{4}$

41 The phase difference between the instantaneous velocity and acceleration of a particle executing simple harmonic motion is **NCERT Pg. 266**

(a) π (b) $0.707\ \pi$

(c) zero (d) $0.5\ \pi$

42 The equation of a simple harmonic motion is given by $y = 3\sin\left[\frac{\pi}{2}(50t - \phi)\right]$, where y is in metres and t is in second, the maximum particle velocity (in ms^{-1}) is **NCERT Pg. 266**

(a) 3π (b) 50π (c) 75π (d) 25π

43 A body is executing SHM. When the displacement of the body from the mean position is 4 cm and 5 cm, the values of the corresponding velocity of the body are 10 cm s^{-1} and 8 cm s^{-1}, respectively. The time period of the body is **NCERT Pg. 266**

(a) 2π s (b) $\frac{\pi}{2}$ s

(c) π s (d) $\frac{3\pi}{2}$ s

Force Law for SHM

44 A particle free to move along the X-axis has potential energy given as $U(x) = k[1 - \exp(-x^2)]$ (for $-\infty < x < +\infty$)

where, k is a positive constant of appropriate dimensions. Then, **NCERT Pg. 267**

(a) at points away from origin, the particle is in equilibrium

(b) for any finite non-zero value of x, there is a force directed away from the origin

(c) its total mechanical energy is $k/2$ and it is equal to its kinetic energy at origin

(d) the motion of the particle is simple harmonic

45 A particle of mass m oscillates with a potential energy $U = U_0 + \alpha x^2$, where U_0 and α are constants and x is the displacement of particle from equilibrium position. The time period of oscillation is **NCERT Pg. 267**

(a) $2\pi\sqrt{\frac{m}{\alpha}}$ (b) $\pi\sqrt{\frac{m}{2\alpha}}$ (c) $\pi\sqrt{\frac{2m}{\alpha}}$ (d) $2\pi\sqrt{\frac{m}{\alpha^2}}$

46 A body of mass m is placed in a potential field of $U(x) = U(1 - \cos ax)$, where U and a are constants. The time period of oscillation is **NCERT Pg. 267**

(a) $2\pi\sqrt{\frac{2m}{Ua^2}}$ (b) $2\pi\sqrt{\frac{m}{Ua^2}}$

(c) $2\pi\sqrt{m^2Ua}$ (d) $2\pi\sqrt{\frac{m}{Ua}}$

47 A particle is in linear simple harmonic motion between two points A and B, 10 cm apart (figure). Take the direction from A to B as the positive direction and choose the incorrect statements. **NCERT Pg. 267**

$AO = OB = 5$ cm,

$BC = 8$ cm

(a) The sign of velocity, acceleration and force on the particle when it is 3 cm away from A going towards B are positive.

(b) The sign of velocity of the particle at C going towards B is negative.

(c) The sign of velocity, acceleration and force on the particle when it is 4 cm away from B going towards A are negative.

(d) The sign of acceleration and force on the particle when it is at point B is negative.

48 A block is left in the equilibrium position as shown in the figure. If now it is stretched by $\frac{mg}{k}$, the net stretch of the spring is **Old NCERT Pg. 352**

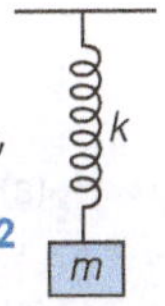

(a) $\frac{mg}{k}$ (b) $\frac{mg}{2k}$ (c) $\frac{2mg}{k}$ (d) $\frac{mg}{4k}$

49 A block is in SHM on a frictionless surface as shown in the figure. The position $x = 0$ show the unstretched position of the spring. If the spring is, then stretched and the block is released at $x = A$. Then, the speed of block at $x = 0$ is **Old NCERT Pg. 352**

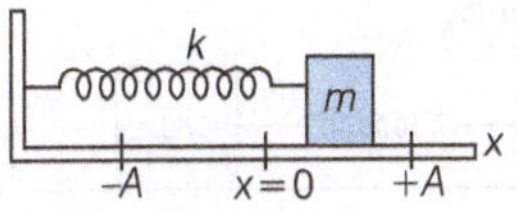

(a) 0 (b) $A^2\sqrt{\frac{k}{m}}$ (c) $A^2\sqrt{\frac{2k}{m}}$ (d) $A\sqrt{\frac{k}{m}}$

50 The mass m as shown in the figure oscillates in simple harmonic motion with amplitude A. The extension in the spring with spring constant k_1 is **Old NCERT Pg. 352**

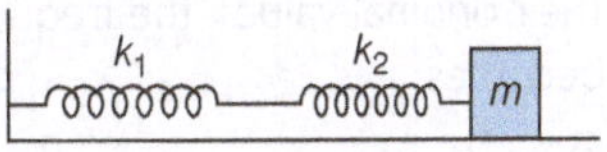

(a) $\frac{k_1A}{k_2}$ (b) $\frac{k_2A}{k_2}$ (c) $\frac{k_1A}{k_1 + k_2}$ (d) $\frac{k_2A}{k_1 + k_2}$

51 In the figure shown, the block is moved side ways by a distance A. The magnitude of net force on the block is **Old NCERT Pg. 352**

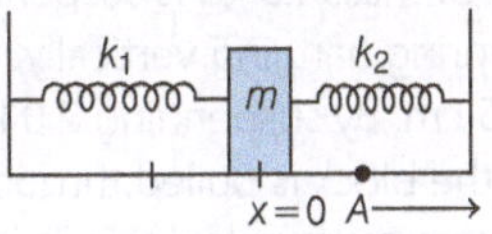

(a) $(k_1 - k_2)A$ (b) $(k_2 - k_1)A$

(c) $(k_1 + k_2)A$ (d) $\left(\frac{k_1 + k_2}{2}\right)A$

52 A spring mass system is hanging from a ceiling of an elevator in equilibrium as shown. The elevator suddenly starts accelerating with acceleration 9 ms^{-2}, then the frequency of oscillation is **Old NCERT Pg. 352**

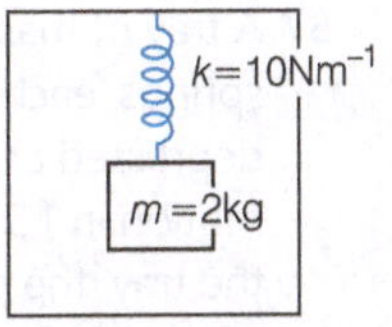

(a) 10 Hz (b) 4 Hz (c) 2.8 Hz (d) 0 Hz

53 The time period of system shown below is **Old NCERT Pg. 352**

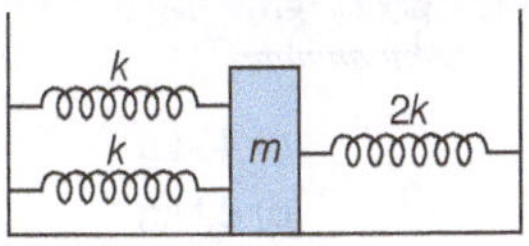

(a) $2\pi\sqrt{\frac{m}{3k}}$ (b) $2\pi\sqrt{\frac{2m}{k}}$ (c) $2\pi\sqrt{\frac{m}{4k}}$ (d) $2\pi\sqrt{\frac{m}{k}}$

54 The time period of the given spring mass system is equal to that of system **Old NCERT Pg. 352**

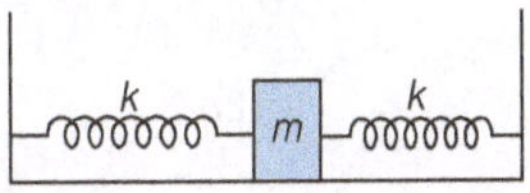

(a) 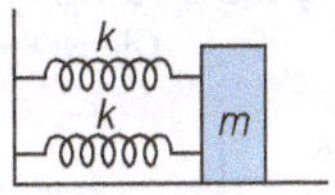

(b) 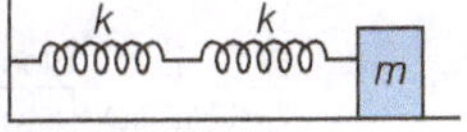

(c) 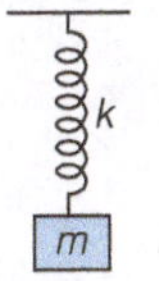

(d) 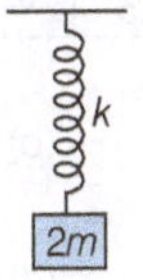

55 Two spring of force constants k_1 and k_2 are connected to a mass m as shown in figure. The frequency of oscillation of the mass is f. If both k_1 and k_2 are made four times their original values, the frequency of oscillation becomes **Old NCERT Pg. 352**

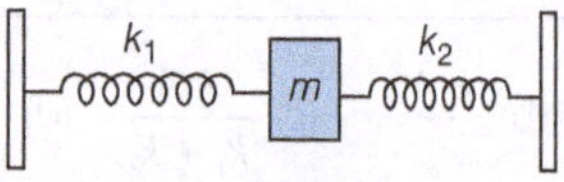

(a) $f/2$ (b) $f/4$
(c) $4f$ (d) $2f$

56 When a body of mass 1.0 kg is suspended from a certain light spring hanging vertically, its length increases by 5 cm. By suspending 2.0 kg block to the spring and if the block is pulled through 10 cm and released, the maximum velocity in it (in ms^{-1}) is (use, acceleration due to gravity = 10 ms^{-2}) **Old NCERT Pg. 352**

(a) 0.5 (b) 1
(c) 2 (d) 4

57 A tray of mass 20 kg is supported on two identical springs, each of spring constant k. When tray is depressed and released, it executes simple harmonic motion in 1.5 s. When a block of mass m is placed on the tray, the period of oscillation becomes 3s. The mass of the block is **Old NCERT Pg. 352**

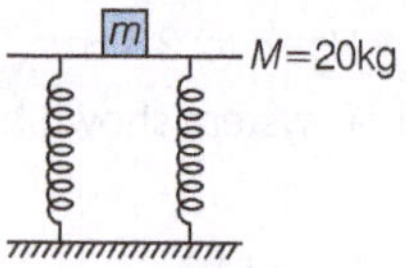

(a) 20 kg (b) 40 kg
(c) 60 kg (d) 80 kg

58 A mass m is vertically suspended from a spring of negligible mass, the system oscillates with a frequency of n, what will be the frequency of the system, if a mass $4m$ is suspended from the same spring? **Old NCERT Pg. 352**

(a) $\frac{n}{4}$ (b) $4n$
(c) $\frac{n}{2}$ (d) $2n$

59 The time period of a given spring-mass string system is **Old NCERT Pg. 352**

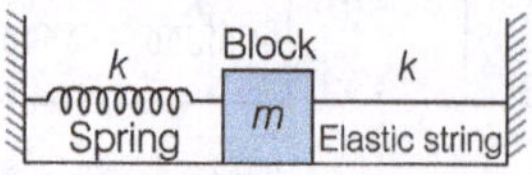

(a) $2\pi\sqrt{\frac{m}{2k}}$ (b) $2\pi\sqrt{\frac{m}{k}}$

(c) $(\sqrt{2}+1)\pi\sqrt{\frac{m}{2k}}$ (d) $(\sqrt{2}+1)\pi\sqrt{\frac{m}{k}}$

60 A clock P is based on oscillation of spring A and other clock Q is based on oscillation of spring B. Both clocks are taken to moon ($k_A = k_B$) **Old NCERT Pg. 352**

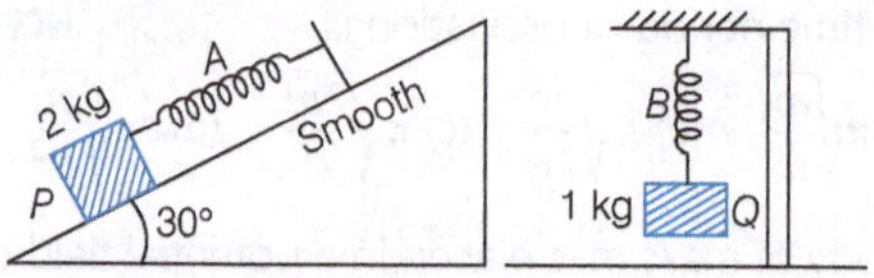

(a) P will run faster than Q
(b) P will run slower than Q
(c) Both will run at same rate on moon
(d) More information is required

61 As shown in figure, a simple harmonic oscillator having identical four springs has time period **Old NCERT Pg. 352**

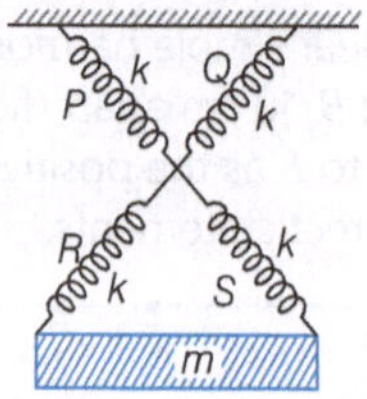

(a) $T = 2\pi\sqrt{\frac{m}{4k}}$ (b) $T = 2\pi\sqrt{\frac{m}{2k}}$

(c) $T = 2\pi\sqrt{\frac{m}{k}}$ (d) $T = 2\pi\sqrt{\frac{2m}{k}}$

62 Four massless springs whose force constants are $2k, 2k, k$ and $2k$ respectively, are attached to a mass M kept on a frictionless plane (as shown in figure). If the mass M is displaced in the horizontal direction, then the frequency of oscillation of the system is **Old NCERT Pg. 352**

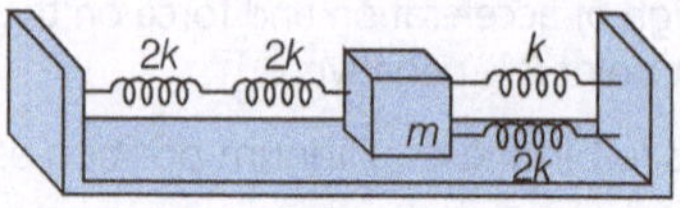

(a) $\frac{1}{2\pi}\sqrt{\frac{k}{4M}}$ (b) $\frac{1}{2\pi}\sqrt{\frac{4k}{M}}$

(c) $\frac{1}{2\pi}\sqrt{\frac{k}{7M}}$ (d) $\frac{1}{2\pi}\sqrt{\frac{7k}{M}}$

63 One end of a spring of force constant k is fixed to a vertical wall and the other to a block of mass m resting on a smooth horizontal surface. There is another wall at a distance x_0 from the block. The spring is then compressed by $2x_0$ and released. The time taken to strike the wall is **Old NCERT Pg. 352**

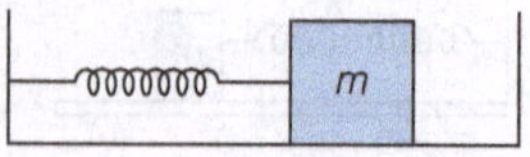

(a) $\frac{1}{6}\pi\sqrt{\frac{k}{m}}$ (b) $\sqrt{\frac{k}{m}}$ (c) $\frac{2\pi}{3}\sqrt{\frac{m}{k}}$ (d) $\frac{\pi}{4}\sqrt{\frac{k}{m}}$

64 Two identical particles each of mass m are interconnected by a light spring of stiffness k, the time period for small oscillation is equal to **Old NCERT Pg. 352**

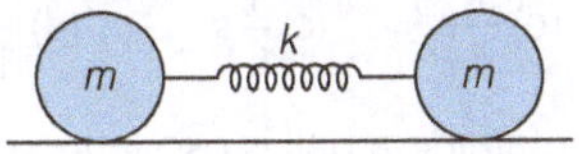

(a) $2\pi\sqrt{\frac{m}{k}}$ (b) $\frac{\pi}{2}\sqrt{\frac{m}{k}}$
(c) $\pi\sqrt{\frac{m}{2k}}$ (d) $\pi\sqrt{\frac{2m}{k}}$

65 A block of mass m is connected with two identical springs S_1 and S_2 as shown in the figure. The frequency of oscillation of the block is f. If spring S_2 is removed, then new frequency of oscillation of block will be **Old NCERT Pg. 352**

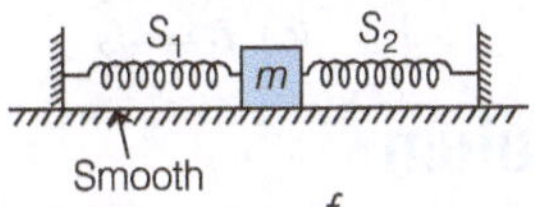

(a) f (b) $2f$ (c) $\frac{f}{\sqrt{2}}$ (d) $\sqrt{2}f$

66 A spring executes SHM with mass of 4 kg attached to it. The force constant of spring is 100 N/m. If at any instant, its velocity is 40 cm/s, the displacement from the mean position will be (Here, amplitude is 0.5 m) **Old NCERT Pg. 352**

(a) 0.06 m (b) 0.3 m (c) 0.49 m (d) 1.0 m

67 A vertical spring mass system is taken on moon. It starts oscillating on the moon. Choose the correct statements. **Old NCERT Pg. 352**

(a) The time period will become $\frac{T_{Earth}}{\sqrt{6}}$.
(b) The equilibrium position about which spring-mass system oscillates in vertical direction is $\frac{mg}{6k}$ from the unstretched position.
(c) k on moon decreases.
(d) k on moon increases.

Energy in Simple Harmonic Motion

68 A mass of 1 kg is executing SHM which is given by $x = 6.0\cos\left(100t + \frac{\pi}{4}\right)$ cm. What is the maximum kinetic energy? **NCERT Pg. 268**

(a) 3 J (b) 6 J (c) 9 J (d) 18 J

69 The expression for displacement of an object in SHM is $x = A\cos\omega t$. The potential energy at $t = T/4$ is **NCERT Pg. 268**

(a) $\frac{1}{2}kA^2$ (b) $\frac{1}{8}kA^2$ (c) $\frac{1}{4}kA^2$ (d) zero

70 In simple harmonic motion, let the time period of variation of potential energy is T_1 and time period of variation of position is T_2, then relation between T_1 and T_2 is **NCERT Pg. 268**

(a) $T_1 = T_2$ (b) $T_1 = 2T_2$ (c) $2T_1 = T_2$ (d) $T_1 = 3T_2$

71 For a particle executing SHM, a graph is plotted between its kinetic energy and potential energy against its displacement d. Which one of the following represents these correctly? (Graphs are schematic and not drawn to scale) **NCERT Pg. 268**

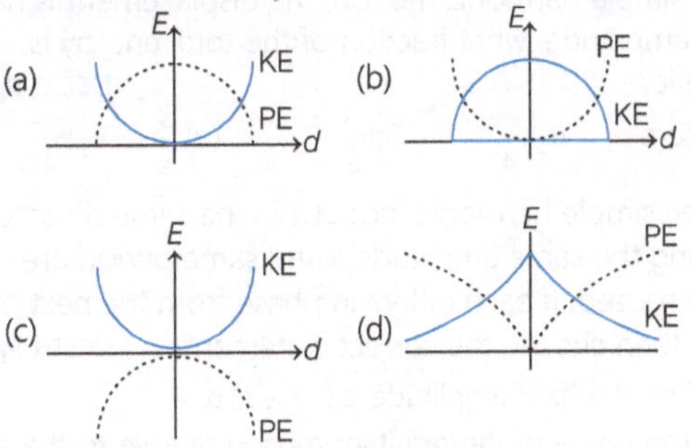

72 If the mass and diameter of a planet are twice that of earth, then the time period of oscillation of seconds pendulum on this plane will be **NCERT Pg. 268**

(a) $\frac{1}{\sqrt{2}}$ s (b) $2\sqrt{2}$ s (c) 1 s (d) 2 s

73 A is the amplitude of a particle executing SHM. If the potential energy of the particle is half of its total energy, then the displacement of the particle is **NCERT Pg. 268**

(a) $\frac{A}{4}$ (b) $\frac{A}{3}$ (c) $\frac{A}{2}$ (d) $\frac{A}{\sqrt{2}}$

74 When the displacement of a particle executing SHM is one-fourth of its amplitude, what fraction of the total energy is the kinetic energy? **NCERT Pg. 268**

(a) $\frac{16}{15}$ (b) $\frac{15}{16}$ (c) $\frac{5}{4}$ (d) $\frac{3}{4}$

75 A spring balance has a scale that reads 0 to 50 kg. The length of the scale is 20 cm. A block of mass m is suspended from this balance when it is displaced and released, it oscillates with a period of 0.5 s. The value of m is (Take, $g = 10\ ms^{-2}$) **NCERT Pg. 268**

(a) 16 kg (b) 24 kg
(c) 20 kg (d) 10 kg

76 A block of mass 1 kg is fastened to a spring with spring constant of 100 Nm^{-1}. The block is pulled to a distance of 10 cm from the equilibrium position. The kinetic energy of the block when it is 5 cm away from the equilibrium position, is **NCERT Pg. 268**

(a) 0.375 J (b) 0.0125 J
(c) 0.125 J (d) 0.0375 J

77 The angular velocity and the amplitude of a simple pendulum is ω and a, respectively. At a displacement x from the mean position, if its kinetic energy is K and potential energy is U, then the ratio K to U is **NCERT Pg. 268**

(a) $\left(\frac{a^2 - x^2\omega^2}{x^2\omega^2}\right)$ (b) $\frac{x^2\omega^2}{(a^2 - x^2\omega^2)}$

(c) $\left(\frac{a^2 - x^2}{x^2}\right)$ (d) $\frac{x^2}{a^2 - x^2}$

78 In a simple harmonic motion, the displacement is half of the amplitude, what fraction of the total energy is kinetic? **NCERT Pg. 268**

(a) Zero (b) $\frac{1}{4}$ (c) $\frac{1}{2}$ (d) $\frac{3}{4}$

79 Three simple harmonic motions in the same direction having the same amplitude a and same period are superposed. If each differs in phase from the next by 45°, then choose the correct statement. **NCERT Pg. 268**

(a) The resultant amplitude is $(1+\sqrt{2})\,a$.
(b) The phase of the resultant motion relative to the first is 90°.
(c) The energy associated with the resulting motion is $(3-2\sqrt{2})$ times the energy associated with any single motion.
(d) The resulting motion is not simple harmonic.

80 A body executes simple harmonic motion. Its Potential Energy (PE), the Kinetic Energy (KE) and Total Energy (TE) were measured as function of displacement x. Then, which of the following statement regarding the body is correct? **NCERT Pg. 268**

(a) KE is maximum, when $x=0$.
(b) TE is zero, when $x=0$.
(c) KE is maximum, when x is maximum.
(d) PE is maximum, when $x=0$.

81 The graph below shows the variation of potential energy $U(t)$, kinetic energy $K(t)$ with time t for a particle executing SHM. Choose the correct statement(s). **NCERT Pg. 268**

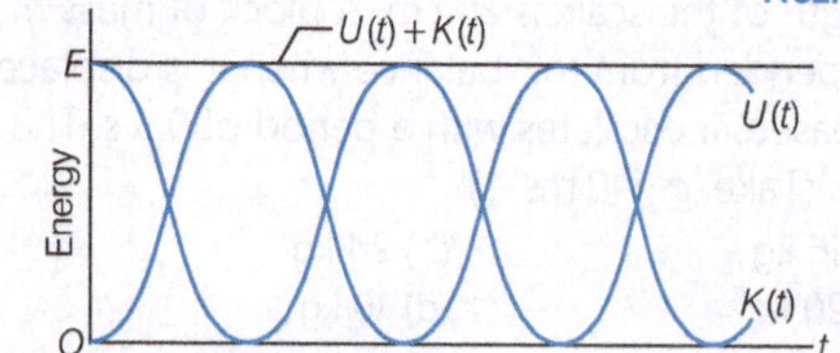

(a) The time periods of variation of potential and kinetic energies are same.
(b) The total mechanical energy is maximum at $t = T/2$.
(c) Kinetic energy is negative and potential energy is positive.
(d) Potential energy is negative and kinetic energy is positive.

82 Starting from the origin, a body oscillates simple harmonically with a period of 2 s. After what time will its kinetic energy be 75% of total energy? **NCERT Pg. 268**

(a) $\frac{1}{3}$ s (b) $\frac{1}{4}$ s (c) $\frac{1}{6}$ s (d) $\frac{1}{12}$ s

83 A system containing a ball is oscillating on a frictionless horizontal plane. The position of the mass when its potential energy and its kinetic energy both are equal, is (let A is the amplitude of oscillation) **NCERT Pg. 268**

(a) A (b) $A/\sqrt{2}$ (c) $A/2$ (d) $A/\sqrt{3}$

84 A block attached to a spring is executing SHM. Let the time period of variation of velocity is T_1 and time period of variation of kinetic energy is T_2. The relation between T_1 and T_2 is **NCERT Pg. 268**

(a) $T_1 = T_2$ (b) $T_1 = 2T_2$
(c) $T_1 = T_2/2$ (d) $T_1 = 4T_2$

Simple Pendulum

85 The ratio of frequencies of two pendulums are 2 : 3, then their lengths are in ratio **NCERT Pg. 270**

(a) $\sqrt{2/3}$ (b) $\sqrt{3/2}$ (c) 4/9 (d) 9/4

86 A simple pendulum is suspended from the ceiling of a lift. When the lift is at rest, its time period is T. With what acceleration should the lift be accelerated upwards in order to reduce its period to $T/2$? **NCERT Pg. 270**

(Take, g is acceleration due to gravity)

(a) $2g$ (b) $3g$ (c) $4g$ (d) g

87 A simple pendulum has a time period T_1 when it is on the earth's surface and T_2 when it is taken to a height $2R$ above the earth's surface, where R is the radius of the earth. The value of T_1/T_2 is **NCERT Pg. 270**

(a) 1/9 (b) 1/3 (c) $\sqrt{3}$ (d) 3

88 A uniform rod of mass m and length l_0 is pivoted at one end and is hanging in the vertical direction. The period of small angular oscillations of the rod is **NCERT Pg. 270**

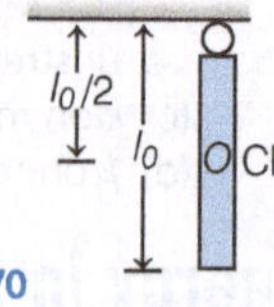

(a) $3\pi\sqrt{\frac{2l_0}{3g}}$ (b) $4\pi\sqrt{\frac{l_0}{3g}}$ (c) $4\pi\sqrt{\frac{2l_0}{3g}}$ (d) $2\pi\sqrt{\frac{2l_0}{3g}}$

89 A simple pendulum oscillating in air has period T. The bob of the pendulum is completely immersed in a non-viscous liquid. The density of the liquid is $\frac{1}{16}$th of the material of the bob. If the bob is inside liquid all the time, its period of oscillation in this liquid is **NCERT Pg. 270**

(a) $2T\sqrt{\frac{1}{10}}$ (b) $2T\sqrt{\frac{1}{14}}$ (c) $4T\sqrt{\frac{1}{14}}$ (d) $4T\sqrt{\frac{1}{15}}$

90 The length of a simple pendulum executing simple harmonic motion is increased by 21%. The percentage increase in the time period of the pendulum of increased length is **NCERT Pg. 270**

(a) 10%
(b) 11%
(c) 21%
(d) 42%

91 The bob of a simple pendulum executes simple harmonic motion in water with a period t, while the period of oscillation of the bob is to in air. Neglecting frictional force of water and given that the density of the bob is (4/3) × 1000 kg m^{-3}. What is the relation between t and t_0? **NCERT Pg. 270**

(a) $t = \frac{t_0}{2}$ (b) $t = t_0$ (c) $t = 2t_0$ (d) $t = 4t_0$

Assertion and Reason Questions

Direction (Q. Nos. 1-12) *In the following questions, a statement of Assertion is followed by a corresponding statement of Reason. Of the following statements, choose the correct one.*

(a) Both Assertion and Reason are correct and Reason is the correct explanation of Assertion.
(b) Both Assertion and Reason are correct but Reason is not the correct explanation of Assertion.
(c) Assertion is correct but Reason is incorrect.
(d) Assertion is incorrect but Reason is correct.

1 Assertion Vibrations and oscillations are two different types of motion.
Reason For vibration, frequency is more and for oscillation, the frequency is less. **NCERT Pg. 260**

2 Assertion $x(t) = A \sin \omega t$ is periodic in nature but cannot represent an oscillatory motion.
Reason $\sin \theta$ is a sinusoidal periodic function. **NCERT Pg. 260**

3 Assertion For an oscillatory motion, the equilibrium position can be represented by saying that it is a point for periodic motion, where net external force on the body is zero.
Reason For an oscillatory motion, if the body is displaced from the equilibrium position, a restoring force will arise that will try to bring back the body to equilibrium position. **NCERT Pg. 260**

4 Assertion $x = A \cos \omega t$ and $x = A \sin \omega t$ can represent same motion depending on initial position of particle.
Reason If the argument of $x = A \cos \omega t$, i.e. ωt is increased by 2π radian, the value of x remains same. **NCERT Pg. 261**

5 Assertion If the amplitude of SHM of a spring mass system is increased, then time period of SHM will remain constant.
Reason If amplitude is increased, body will have to travel more distance to complete one oscillation. **NCERT Pg. 263**

6 Assertion Simple harmonic motion is the projection of uniform circular motion on the diameter of the circle in which the latter motion occurs.
Reason Simple harmonic motion is a uniform motion. **NCERT Pg. 266**

7 Assertion The maximum velocity of a particle executing SHM, having amplitude 0.05 m and period of 2 s is 0.157 m/s.
Reason The velocity of a particle is minimum at the mean position. **NCERT Pg. 266**

8 Assertion A block of mass m attached to a stiff spring have large oscillation frequency.
Reason Stiff spring have high value of spring constant k. **Old NCERT Pg. 352**

9 Assertion The graph of total energy of a particle in SHM with respect to position is a straight line with zero slope.
Reason Total energy of particle in SHM remains constant throughout its motion. **NCERT Pg. 268**

10 Assertion If the amplitude of a simple harmonic oscillator is doubled, its total energy becomes double.
Reason The total energy is directly proportional to the square of the amplitude of vibration of the harmonic oscillator. **NCERT Pg. 268**

11 Assertion If a pendulum is falling freely, then its time period becomes zero.
Reason Freely falling body has the acceleration equal to g. **NCERT Pg. 270**

12 Assertion A pendulum clock is taken to a mountain top from normal plane, it becomes fast.
Reason The value of acceleration due to gravity is low at mountain top than at planes. **NCERT Pg. 270**

Statement Based Questions

Direction (Q Nos 1 - 6) *In the following questions Statement I and Statement II are given. Read these statements and choose the most appropriate answer from the options given below.*

(a) Both Statement I and Statement II and incorrect.
(b) Statement I is correct but Statement II is incorrect.
(c) Statement I is incorrect but Statement II is correct.
(d) Both Statement I and Statement II are correct.

1 Statement I The phase difference between displacement and acceleration of a particle in a simple harmonic motion is π rad.

Statement II In SHM, total mechanical energy is conserved. NCERT Pg. 266

2 Statement I If a hole were drilled through the centre of earth, i.e. along the diameter and a ball is dropped into the hole at one end, it will not get out of the other end of the hole.

Statement II It will execute SHM and will be seen at the other end after 43.2 min from the time it is dropped. NCERT Pg. 267

3 Statement I In SHM of a particle with angular frequency ω, kinetic energy and potential energy vary simple harmonically with angular frequency 2ω.

Statement II Kinetic energy and potential energy vary periodically but not simple harmonically with angular frequency 2ω. NCERT Pg. 268

4 Statement I In SHM, potential energy is always zero at mean position and maximum at extreme position.

Statement II In SHM, kinetic energy is maximum at mean position and zero at extreme position. NCERT Pg. 268

5 Statement I When a boy sitting on a swing stand up, the time period of swing will increase.

Statement II In standing position of the body, the effective length of the swing decreases. NCERT Pg. 270

6 Statement I If the length of a simple pendulum is increased by 4%, then the corresponding decrease in the period will be 2%.

Statement II Time period of simple pendulum is proportional to under root of length. NCERT Pg. 270

Matching Type Questions

1 A simple harmonic oscillator consists of a block attached to a string with $k = 200$ N/m.

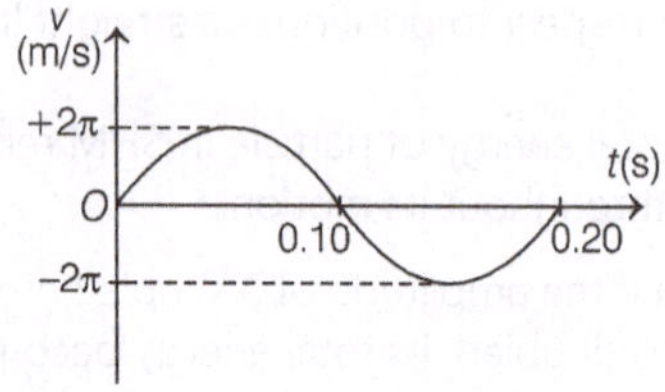

The block slides on a frictionless horizontal surface, with equilibrium $x = 0$. A graph of block's velocity (v) as function of time t is shown below. Then, match Column I with respective values in Column II. NCERT Pg. 262

	Column I		Column II
A.	Block's mass (kg)	1.	− 0.20
B.	Block's acceleration at $t = 0.105$ (m/s^2)	2.	0.20
C.	Block's maximum kinetic energy (J)	3.	− 200
D.	Block's displacement at $t = 0$ (m)	4.	4.0

Choose the correct answer from the options given below.

Codes

	A	B	C	D		A	B	C	D
(a)	2	3	1	4	(b)	1	2	4	3
(c)	2	3	4	1	(d)	3	2	4	1

2 Match the Column I (quantity) with Column II (value) for an object executing simple harmonic motion in a horizontal plane with displacement given as $x = A\cos\omega t$. NCERT Pg. 263

	Column I		Column II
A.	v_{max} / amplitude is equal to	1.	$T/8$
B.	a_{max} / amplitude is equal to	2.	$T/12$
C.	If object starts from $x = +A$, then time to reach at $+A/\sqrt{2}$	3.	ω
D.	If object starts from $x = 0$ and move towards right, then the time to reach at $+A/2$	4.	ω^2

Choose the correct answer from the options given below.

Codes

	A	B	C	D		A	B	C	D
(a)	3	1	4	2	(b)	3	4	1	2
(c)	4	3	2	1	(d)	3	4	2	1

3 A spring compressed by 30 cm develops a restoring force of 30 N. A body of 5 kg is placed over it. Match the different quantities given in column I with the respective value in column II.
[Take, $g = 10 \text{ m/s}^2$] **NCERT Pg. 267**

	Column I		Column II
A.	Force constant of spring (in N/m)	1.	50
B.	Displacement under the weight of body (in cm)	2.	100
C.	Angular frequency of oscillation when body is disturbed (in s^{-1})	3.	$2\sqrt{5}$
D.	Time period of oscillation when body is disturbed (in rad/s)	4.	$\frac{\pi}{\sqrt{5}}$

Choose the correct answer from the options given below.

Codes

	A	B	C	D		A	B	C	D
(a)	2	1	4	3	(b)	1	3	2	4
(c)	2	4	3	1	(d)	2	1	3	4

Numerical Type Questions

1 A particle executes simple harmonic motion with amplitude A and time period T. The displacement of the particle when its speed is half the maximum speed is $\sqrt{x}\, A/2$. The value of x is ...... **NCERT Pg. 266**

2 A point performs simple harmonic oscillation of time period T and the equation of motion is given by $x = a\sin\left(\omega t + \frac{\pi}{6}\right)$. After the elapse of $\frac{T}{x}$, the velocity of the point will be equal to half of its maximum velocity. The value of x is .... **NCERT Pg. 266**

3 A particle executes simple harmonic motion with an amplitude of 5 cm. When the particle is at 4 cm from the mean position, the magnitude of its velocity in SI units is equal to that of its acceleration. Then, its periodic time is $\frac{x}{3}\pi$ s. The value of x is .... **NCERT Pg. 266**

4 A man of mass 60 kg is standing on a platform executing SHM in vertical direction. The displacement from mean position of platform varies as $y = 0.5\sin(2\pi ft)$. The man will feel weightlessness at the highest point having frequency $\sqrt{\frac{g}{n\pi^2}}$. The value of n is .... **NCERT Pg. 263**

5 A rectangular block of mass 8 kg attached to a horizontal spiral spring executes simple harmonic motion of amplitude 2 m and time period 3.14 s. The maximum force exerted by spring on block is .... N. **Old NCERT Pg. 352**

6 A heavy brass sphere is hung from a weightless inelastic spring and as a simple pendulum its time period of oscillation is T. When the sphere is immersed in a non-viscous liquid of density 1/10 that of brass, it will act as a simple pendulum of period $\sqrt{\frac{x}{9}}T$. The value of x is ...... **Old NCERT Pg. 352**

7 A block of mass 1 kg is attached to a spring that vibrates with a frequency of 1 Hz on a frictionless horizontal table. Two springs identical to the original spring are attached in parallel to a block of mass 4 kg placed on the same table. So, the frequency of vibration of the 4 kg block is ...... Hz. **Old NCERT Pg. 352**

8 A particle of mass 0.2 kg executes SHM with frequency $\frac{25}{\pi}$ Hz. At position 4 cm, the particle has kinetic energy 0.5 J and potential energy of 0.4 J, then amplitude of oscillation is ...... cm. **NCERT Pg. 268**

9 The mass and diameter of a planet are twice those of earth. The period of oscillation of pendulum on this planet is $x\sqrt{2}$ s. The value of x is ....
[If it is a second pendulum on earth.] **NCERT Pg. 270**

NCERT Exemplar Questions

1 The displacement of a particle is represented by the equation $y = 3\cos\left(\frac{\pi}{4} - 2\omega t\right)$. The motion of the particle is

(a) simple harmonic with period $2\pi/\omega$
(b) simple harmonic with period π/ω
(c) periodic but not simple harmonic
(d) non- periodic

2 The displacement of a particle is represented by the equation $y = \sin^3 \omega t$. The motion is

(a) non-periodic
(b) periodic but not simple harmonic
(c) simple harmonic with period $2\pi/\omega$
(d) simple harmonic with period π/ω

3 The relation between acceleration and displacement of four particles are given below. Which of the particle is executing SHM?

(a) $a_x = +2x$ (b) $a_x = +2x^2$
(c) $a_x = -2x^2$ (d) $a_x = -2x$

4 The displacement of a particle varies with time according to the relation $y = a\sin\omega t + b\cos\omega t$.

(a) The motion is oscillatory but not SHM
(b) The motion is SHM with amplitude $a + b$
(c) The motion is SHM with amplitude $a^2 + b^2$
(d) The motion is SHM with amplitude $\sqrt{a^2 + b^2}$

5 Four pendulums *A*, *B*, *C* and *D* are suspended from the same elastic support as shown in figure. *A* and *C* are of the same length, while *B* is smaller than *A* and *D* is larger than *A*. If *A* is given a transverse displacement, then

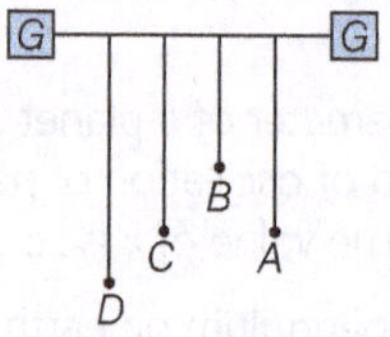

(a) *D* will vibrate with maximum amplitude
(b) *C* will vibrate with maximum amplitude
(c) *B* will vibrate with maximum amplitude
(d) All the four will oscillate with equal amplitude

6 Figure shows the circular motion of a particle. The radius of the circle, the period, sense of revolution and the initial position are indicated on the figure. The simple harmonic motion of the x-projection of the radius vector of the rotating particle *P* is

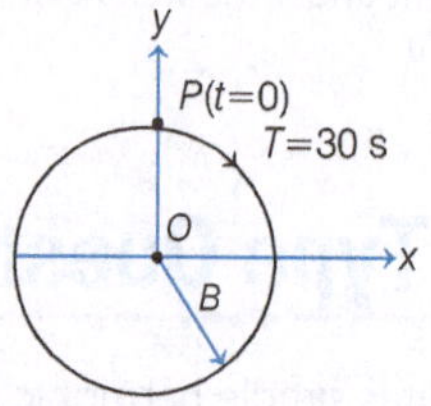

(a) $x(t) = B\sin\left(\frac{2\pi t}{30}\right)$ (b) $x(t) = B\cos\left(\frac{\pi t}{15}\right)$
(c) $x(t) = B\sin\left(\frac{\pi t}{15} + \frac{\pi}{2}\right)$ (d) $x(t) = B\cos\left(\frac{\pi t}{15} + \frac{\pi}{2}\right)$

7 The equation of motion of a particle is $x = a\cos(\alpha t)^2$. The motion is

(a) periodic but not oscillatory
(b) periodic and oscillatory
(c) oscillatory but not periodic
(d) Neither periodic nor oscillatory

8 A particle executing SHM has a maximum speed of 30 cms^{-1} and a maximum acceleration of 60 cms^{-2}. The period of oscillation is

(a) π s (b) $\frac{\pi}{2}$ s
(c) 2π s (d) $\frac{\pi}{t}$ s

9 When a mass *m* is connected individually to two springs having spring constants k_1 and k_2, the oscillation frequencies are ν_1 and ν_2. If the same mass is attached to the two springs as shown in figure, the oscillation frequency would be

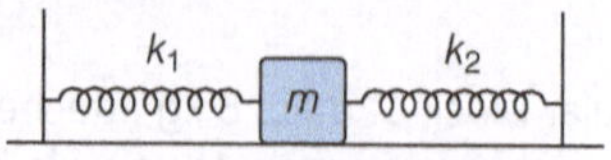

(a) $\nu_1 + \nu_2$ (b) $\sqrt{\nu_1^2 + \nu_2^2}$
(c) $\left(\frac{1}{\nu_1} + \frac{1}{\nu_2}\right)^{-1}$ (d) $\sqrt{\nu_1^2 - \nu_2^2}$

Past Exams Questions

NEET

1 If $x = 5\sin\left(\pi t + \frac{\pi}{3}\right)$ m represents the motion of a particle executing simple harmonic motion, the amplitude and time period of motion, respectively are **NCERT Pg. 262, NEET 2024**

(a) 5 cm, 2 s
(b) 5 m, 2 s
(c) 5 cm, 1 s
(d) 5 m, 1 s

2 If the mass of the bob in a simple pendulum is increased to thrice its original mass and its length is made half its original length, then the new time period of oscillation is $x/2$ times its original time period. Then, the value of x is **NCERT Pg. 270, NEET 2024**

(a) $\sqrt{3}$ (b) $\sqrt{2}$
(c) $2\sqrt{3}$ (d) 4

3 The x-t graph of a particle performing simple harmonic motion is shown in the figure. The acceleration of the particle at $t = 2$ s is **NCERT Pg. 262, NEET 2023**

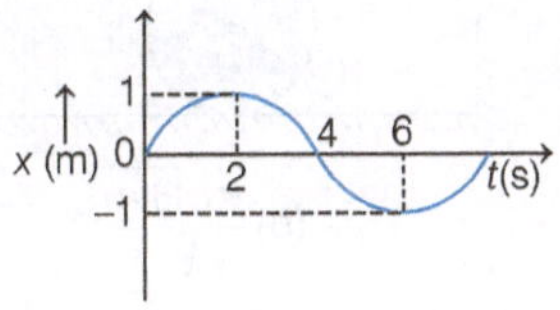

(a) $-\frac{\pi^2}{8}$ ms^{-2} (b) $\frac{\pi^2}{16}$ ms^{-2}
(c) $-\frac{\pi^2}{16}$ ms^{-2} (d) $\frac{\pi^2}{8}$ ms^{-2}

4 Two pendulums of length 121 cm and 100 cm start vibrating in phase. At some instant, the two are at their mean position in the same phase. The minimum number of vibrations of the shorter pendulum after which the two are again in phase at the mean position is **NCERT Pg. 270, NEET 2022**

(a) 9 (b) 10
(c) 8 (d) 11

5 A body is executing simple harmonic motion with frequency n, the frequency of its potential energy is **NCERT Pg. 261, NEET 2021**

(a) n (b) $2n$
(c) $3n$ (d) $4n$

6 The phase difference between displacement and acceleration of a particle in a simple harmonic motion is **NCERT Pg. 261, NEET 2020**

(a) $\frac{3\pi}{2}$ rad (b) $\frac{\pi}{2}$ rad
(c) zero (d) π rad

7 Average velocity of a particle executing SHM in one complete vibration is **NCERT Pg. 266, NEET 2019**

(a) $A\omega$ (b) $\frac{A\omega^2}{2}$
(c) zero (d) $\frac{A\omega}{2}$

8 A pendulum is hung from the roof of a sufficiently high building and is moving freely to and fro like a simple harmonic oscillator. The acceleration of the bob of the pendulum is 20 m/s^2 at a distance of 5 m from the mean position. The time period of oscillation is **NCERT Pg. 270, NEET 2018**

(a) 2 s (b) π s
(c) 2π s (d) 1 s

9 A particle executes linear simple harmonic motion with an amplitude of 3 cm. When the particle is at 2 cm from the mean position, the magnitude of its velocity is equal to that of its acceleration. Then, its time period (in seconds) is **NCERT Pg. 276, NEET 2017**

(a) $\frac{\sqrt{5}}{\pi}$ (b) $\frac{\sqrt{5}}{2\pi}$
(c) $\frac{4\pi}{\sqrt{5}}$ (d) $\frac{2\pi}{\sqrt{3}}$

10 A body of mass m is attached to the lower end of a spring whose upper end is fixed. The spring has negligible mass. When the mass m is slightly pulled down and released, it oscillates with a time period of 3 s. When the mass m is increased by 1 kg, the time period of oscillations becomes 5 s. The value of m (in kg) is **NCERT Pg. 270, NEET 2016**

(a) $\frac{3}{4}$ (b) $\frac{4}{3}$
(c) $\frac{16}{9}$ (d) $\frac{9}{16}$

JEE Main

11 A simple pendulum doing small oscillations at a place R height above earth surface has time period of $T_1 = 4$ s. T_2 would be it's time period if it is brought to a point which is at a height $2R$ from earth surface. Choose the correct relation [R = radius of earth]

NCERT Pg. 270, NEET 2024

(a) $2T_1 = T_2$ (b) $T_1 = T_2$
(c) $2T_1 = 3T_2$ (d) $3T_1 = 2T_2$

12 A particle executes simple harmonic motion between $x = -A$ and $x = +A$. If time taken by particle to go from $x = 0$ to $\frac{A}{2}$ is 2 s; then time taken by particle in going from $x = \frac{A}{2}$ to A is

NCERT Pg. 260, JEE Main 2023

(a) 3 s (b) 1.5 s
(c) 4 s (d) 2 s

13 The time period of oscillation of a simple pendulum of length L suspended from the roof of a vehicle, which moves without friction down an inclined plane of inclination α, is given by **NCERT Pg. 270, JEE Main 2022**

(a) $2\pi\sqrt{L/(g\cos\alpha)}$
(b) $2\pi\sqrt{L/(g\sin\alpha)}$
(c) $2\pi\sqrt{L/g}$
(d) $2\pi\sqrt{L/(g\tan\alpha)}$

Skill Boosters

1 The bob of a simple pendulum is a spherical hollow ball filled with water. A plugged hole near the bottom of the oscillating bob gets suddenly unplugged. During observation, till. Water is coming out, the time period of oscillation would

(a) first increase and then decrease to the original value
(b) first decrease and then increase to the original value
(c) remain unchanged
(d) increase towards a saturation value

2 Two identical blocks A and B, each of mass m resting on smooth floor, are connected by a light spring of natural length L and the spring constant k, with the spring at it natural length. A third identical block at C (mass m) moving with a speed v along the line joining A and B collides with A (Consider the collision to be elastic in nature). The maximum compression in the spring is equal to

(a) $v\sqrt{\frac{m}{2k}}$ (b) $m\sqrt{\frac{v}{2k}}$ (c) $\sqrt{\frac{mv}{k}}$ (d) $\frac{mv}{2k}$

3 A block of mass m is displaced from its equilibrium position and then released for the system as shown. The time period will be

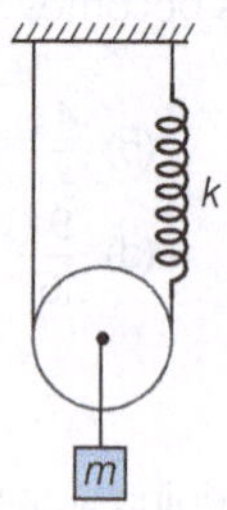

(a) $2\pi\sqrt{\frac{m}{2k}}$ (b) $2\pi\sqrt{\frac{m}{k}}$
(c) $2\pi\sqrt{\frac{m}{4k}}$ (d) $2\pi\sqrt{\frac{2m}{k}}$

4 A solid uniform cylinder of mass m performs small oscillations in horizontal plane, if slightly displaced from its mean position as shown in the figure. Initially springs are in natural lengths and cylinder does not slip on ground during oscillations due to friction between ground and cylinder. Force constant of each spring is k. The time period of oscillations is

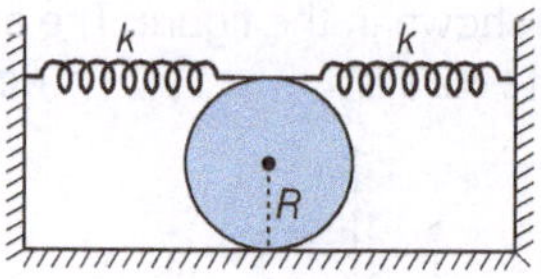

(a) $\pi\sqrt{\frac{3m}{k}}$ (b) $\frac{\pi}{4}\sqrt{\frac{3m}{k}}$
(c) $\frac{\pi}{2}\sqrt{\frac{3m}{k}}$ (d) $2\pi\sqrt{\frac{m}{2k}}$

5 The natural period of vibration of a 50 N disc (semicircular) is (The centre of mass of the semicircular disc lies at a distance of $\frac{4r}{3\pi}$ from the centre. Assume pure rolling.)

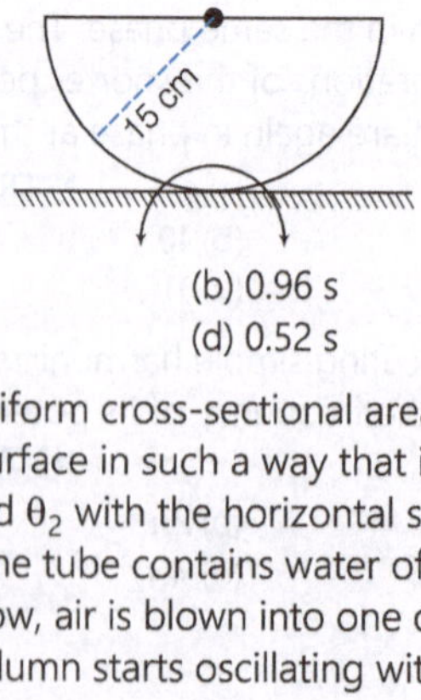

(a) 0.71 s (b) 0.96 s
(c) 0.85 s (d) 0.52 s

6 A tube of uniform cross-sectional area A is fixed to a horizontal surface in such a way that its two arms make angles θ_1 and θ_2 with the horizontal surface as shown in the figure. The tube contains water of mass m and density ρ. Now, air is blown into one of the arms and the water column starts oscillating with small amplitude.

The period of oscillation of water column is (consider water to be ideal

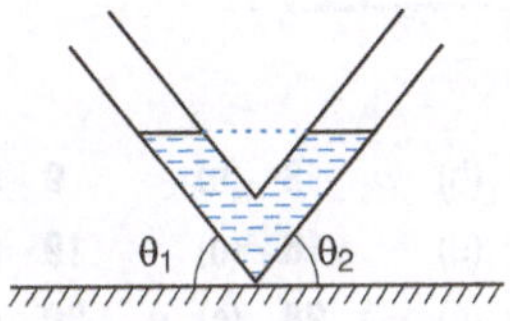

(a) $2\pi\sqrt{\dfrac{m}{2\rho g A(\sin\theta_1+\sin\theta_2)}}$

(b) $2\pi\sqrt{\dfrac{m}{\rho g A(\sin\theta_1+\sin\theta_2)}}$

(c) $\pi\sqrt{\dfrac{2m}{\rho g A(\sin\theta_1+\sin\theta_2)}}$

(d) None of the above

7 A smooth piston of mass m, area of cross-section A is in equilibrium in a gas jar when the pressure of the gas is p_0.
When the piston is disturbed slightly, the angular frequency of oscillation of the piston is
(Assume adiabatic change of state of the gas and γ is ratio of specific heats of the gas)

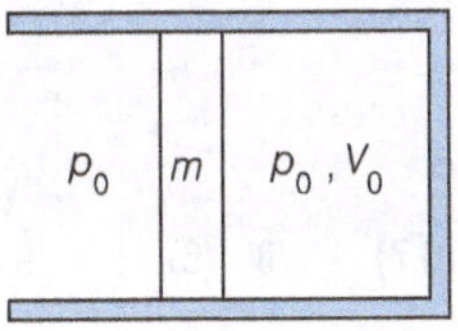

(a) $\sqrt{\dfrac{\gamma p_0 A^2}{3mV_0}}$ (b) $\sqrt{\dfrac{\gamma p_0 A^2}{\sqrt{2}\,mV_0}}$

(c) $\sqrt{\dfrac{\gamma p_0 A^2}{mV_0}}$ (d) $\sqrt{\dfrac{2\gamma p_0 A^2}{mV_0}}$

8 In the figure is shown a vessel filled with a liquid whose density varies with height h from the bottom as $\rho=\rho_0\left(4-\dfrac{3h}{h_0}\right)$ where ρ_0 is a constant and h_0 is the height of the liquid in the container. A solid block of small dimensions of density $\dfrac{5}{2}\rho_0$ and mass m is released from the bottom of the tank. The block performs SHM having the frequency of oscillation

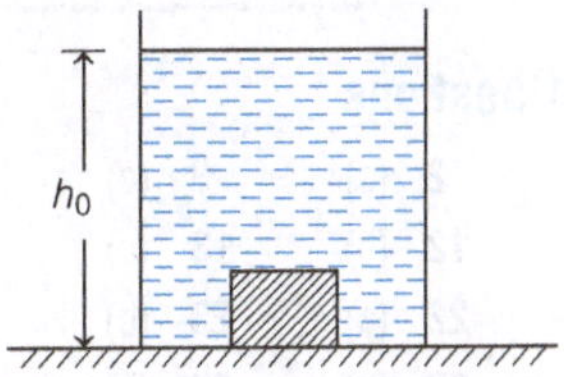

(a) $\dfrac{1}{2\pi}\sqrt{\dfrac{3g}{4h_0}}$ (b) $\dfrac{1}{2\pi}\sqrt{\dfrac{6g}{5h_0}}$

(c) $\dfrac{1}{2\pi}\sqrt{\dfrac{2g}{3h_0}}$ (d) $\dfrac{1}{2\pi}\sqrt{\dfrac{3g}{5h_0}}$

9 A uniform plank of mass m free to move in the horizontal direction only, is placed at the top of a solid cylinder of mass $2m$ and radius R. The plank is attached to a fixed wall by means of a light spring of spring constant k. There is no slipping between the cylinder and the plank as well as between the cylinder and ground. The time period of oscillations of the system is

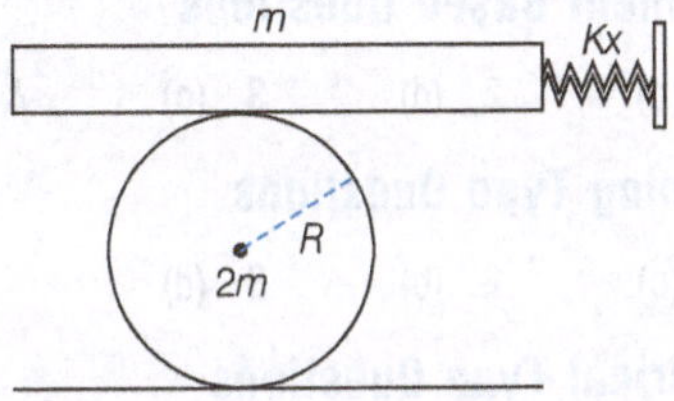

(a) $2\pi\sqrt{\dfrac{m}{k}}$ (b) $\pi\sqrt{\dfrac{7m}{k}}$

(c) $2\pi\sqrt{\dfrac{5m}{k}}$ (d) $\pi\sqrt{\dfrac{m}{k}}$

10 A uniform horizontal plank is resting on two cylindrical drums, which are spinning in opposite direction about their horizontal axes with equal angular velocity. The distance between the axes is $2L$ and the coefficient of friction between the plank and drums is μ.
If the plank is displaced slightly from the equilibrium position along its length and released, it performs SHM having the time period

(a) $4\pi\sqrt{\dfrac{L}{\mu}}$ (b) $4\pi\sqrt{\dfrac{L}{\mu g}}$ (c) $2\pi\sqrt{\dfrac{L}{\mu}}$ (d) $2\pi\sqrt{\dfrac{L}{\mu g}}$

Correct Codes

Topical Questions

1 (b)	2 (c)	3 (c)	4 (a)	5 (c)	6 (c)	7 (b)	8 (b)	9 (a)	10 (b)
11 (c)	12 (b)	13 (c)	14 (b)	15 (c)	16 (c)	17 (d)	18 (d)	19 (c)	20 (c)
21 (d)	22 (a)	23 (b)	24 (d)	25 (b)	26 (b)	27 (d)	28 (c)	29 (a)	30 (d)
31 (c)	32 (b)	33 (b)	34 (c)	35 (d)	36 (d)	37 (b)	38 (b)	39 (a)	40 (d)
41 (d)	42 (c)	43 (c)	44 (d)	45 (c)	46 (b)	47 (b)	48 (c)	49 (d)	50 (d)
51 (c)	52 (c)	53 (c)	54 (a)	55 (d)	56 (b)	57 (c)	58 (c)	59 (c)	60 (b)
61 (c)	62 (b)	63 (c)	64 (d)	65 (c)	66 (c)	67 (b)	68 (d)	69 (d)	70 (c)
71 (b)	72 (b)	73 (d)	74 (b)	75 (a)	76 (a)	77 (c)	78 (d)	79 (a)	80 (a)
81 (a)	82 (c)	83 (b)	84 (b)	85 (d)	86 (b)	87 (b)	88 (d)	89 (d)	90 (a)
91 (c)									

Assertion and Reason Questions

1 (d)	2 (d)	3 (b)	4 (b)	5 (c)	6 (c)	7 (c)	8 (a)	9 (a)	10 (d)
11 (d)	12 (d)								

Statement Based Questions

1 (d)	2 (d)	3 (c)	4 (c)	5 (c)	6 (c)

Matching Type Questions

1 (c)	2 (b)	3 (d)

Numerical Type Questions

1 (3)	2 (12)	3 (8)	4 (2)	5 (64)	6 (10)	7 (0.7)	8 (6)	9 (2)

NCERT Exemplar Questions

1 (b)	2 (b)	3 (d)	4 (d)	5 (b)	6 (a)	7 (c)	8 (a)	9. (b)

Past Exams Questions

1 (b)	2 (b)	3 (c)	4 (d)	5 (b)	6 (d)	7 (c)	8 (b)	9 (c)	10 (d)
11 (d)	12 (c)	13 (a)							

Skill Boosters

1 (a)	2 (a)	3 (c)	4 (c)	5 (b)	6 (b)	7 (c)	8 (b)	9 (b)	10 (d)

Step by Step

Decoding the Questions

Concept Buliders

1 False (F)

2 Frequency $= \dfrac{1}{\text{Time period}}$

3 True (T)

4 False (F)

5 Harmonic function

6 $F = -kx$

7 periodic

8 faster, slower

9 False (F)

10 4 A

11 Elasticity

12 zero

13 False (F)

14 $E_k = \dfrac{kA^2}{2}\cos^2 \omega t$

15 True (T)

16 $\dfrac{1}{4} m\omega^2 A^2$

17 decrease

18 True (T)

19 No

20 True (T)

Topical Questions

3 (c) The beat frequency of heart

$$= \frac{75}{1 \text{ min}} = \frac{75}{60} \text{s}^{-1}$$

$$= 1.25 \text{ Hz}$$

Time period, $T = \dfrac{1}{\text{Frequency}}$

$$= \frac{1}{1.25} = 0.8 \text{ s}$$

5 (c) Since, particle perform oscillatory motion, and its displacement equation is

$$y = a \sin \omega t$$

$$2 = 4 \sin \omega t$$

$$\frac{1}{2} = \sin \omega t$$

$$\sin \frac{\pi}{6} = \sin \omega t$$

$$\Rightarrow \quad \omega t = \frac{\pi}{6}$$

$$\Rightarrow \quad \frac{2\pi}{T} \cdot t = \frac{\pi}{6} \qquad \left(\because \omega = \frac{2\pi}{T}\right)$$

$$\Rightarrow \quad t = \frac{T}{12} = \frac{1}{12} \text{s}$$

6 (c) Given, $x(t) = 20 \cos \omega t$

$$x(t) = 20 \cos \frac{2\pi}{T} \cdot t \quad \text{... (i)}$$

$$\left(\because \omega = \frac{2\pi}{T}\right)$$

Given, $T = 4$s and $t = 1$ s

Substituting the given values in Eq. (i), we get

$$\therefore \quad x(t) = 20 \cos \frac{2\pi}{4} \cdot 1 = 0$$

7 (b) It may be noted that as $t \to \infty$, log ωt diverges to ∞. Therefore, it cannot represents any kind of repeated motion.

8 (b) Function ($\sin \omega t + \cos \omega t$)

represents a periodic function with period $2\pi / \omega$

In option (a), $A \sin^3 (\omega t)^2$ is not periodic function due to cube of sine value and square of t value.

In option (c), $\tan(\omega t)^3$ is not periodic function due to cube of t value.

In option (d), the function $e^{\omega t}$ is not periodic, as it increases with decreasing time.

10 (b) From graph, it is clear that time taken to complete one oscillation by curve 1 is equal to time taken to complete one-fourth oscillation by curve 2.

i.e. $\quad T_1 = \dfrac{T_2}{4} \Rightarrow T_2 = 4T_1$

11 (c) For a particle executing SHM,

$$x = k \sin^2 \omega t$$

$$\Rightarrow \quad \frac{dx}{dt} = 2k\omega (\sin \omega t)(\cos \omega t)$$

$$\Rightarrow \quad \frac{d^2x}{dt^2} = 2k\omega^2 \cos 2\,\omega t$$

but $\dfrac{d^2x}{dt^2} = a$

$$\therefore \quad a = 2k\omega^2 \cos 2\omega t$$

The given equation does not satisfy the SHM condition.

12 (b) By observing snapshots we can draw position-time graph for the given motion.

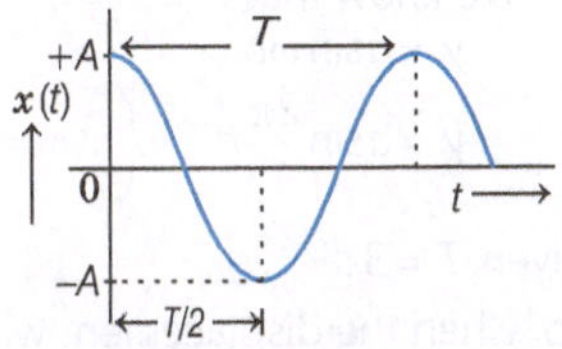

From figure, at $t = 0$ particle is at $x = +A$ and crosses mean position at $t = T/4$ and reaches other end in negative direction ($-A$) at $t = T/2$.

So, $\quad x(t) = A \cos \omega t$

13 (c) The resultant displacement is given by

$$y = y_1 + y_2 = \sqrt{a^2 + b^2} \sin(\omega t + \phi)$$

Here, amplitude $= \sqrt{a^2 + b^2}$

14 (b) Given equation,

$$y_1 = 5 (\sin 2\pi t + \sqrt{3} \cos 2\pi t)$$

$$= 10 \left(\frac{1}{2} \sin 2\pi t + \frac{\sqrt{3}}{2} \cos 2\pi t \right)$$

$$= 10 \left(\cos \frac{\pi}{3} \sin 2\pi t + \sin \frac{\pi}{3} \cos 2\pi t \right)$$

$$= 10 \left[\sin \left(2\pi t + \frac{\pi}{3} \right) \right]$$

$$\Rightarrow \quad A_1 = 10$$

Similarly, $y_2 = 5 \sin \left(2\pi t + \dfrac{\pi}{4} \right)$

$$\Rightarrow \quad A_2 = 5$$

Hence, $\frac{A_1}{A_2} = \frac{10}{5} = \frac{2}{1} = 2:1$

15 (c) Given function

$$x = A\sin^2 \omega t + B\cos^2 \omega t + C\sin \omega t \cos \omega t$$

$$x = \frac{A}{2}(1-\cos 2\omega t) + \frac{B}{2}(1+\cos 2\omega t) + \frac{C}{2}\sin 2\omega t$$

For $A = B; C = 0;$

$$x = \frac{B}{2}(1-\cos 2\omega t) + \frac{B}{2}(1+\cos 2\omega t) = B$$

In this case, the particle is at rest at $x = B$. B is not the amplitude.

16 (c) We know that,

$$y = a\sin \omega t$$

$$y = a\sin \frac{2\pi}{T}t \qquad \left(\because \omega = \frac{2\pi}{T}\right)$$

Given, $T = 3$ s

So, when the displacement will be half of its amplitude, i.e.

$$\frac{a}{2} = a\sin \frac{2\pi t}{3}$$

$$\frac{1}{2} = \sin \frac{2\pi t}{3}$$

$$\sin \frac{\pi}{6} = \sin \frac{2\pi t}{3}$$

$$\Rightarrow \quad t = \frac{1}{4}\text{ s}$$

17 (d) Equation for a particle executing simple harmonic motion is $x = A\sin(\omega t + \phi)$

$$A\sin(\omega t + \phi) = \frac{A}{2} \qquad \left[\because \text{Given, } x = \frac{A}{2}\right]$$

$$\sin(\omega t + \phi) = \frac{1}{2}$$

$$\sin(\omega t + \phi) = \sin \frac{\pi}{6}$$

Since, $\omega t + \phi = \frac{\pi}{6}$ or $\frac{5\pi}{6}$

So, the phase difference of the two particles when they are crossing each other at $x = \frac{A}{2}$ in opposite directions is,

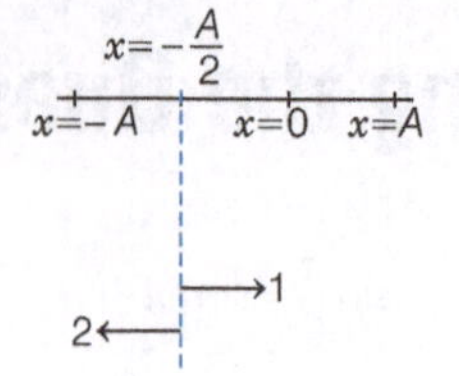

$$\Delta\phi = \frac{5\pi}{6} - \frac{\pi}{6} = \frac{2\pi}{3}$$

18 (d) Given equation,

$$y = 5(\sin 3\pi t + \sqrt{3}\cos 3\pi t)$$

$$= 10\left(\frac{1}{2}\sin 3\pi t + \frac{\sqrt{3}}{2}\cos 3\pi t\right)$$

$$= 10\left(\cos \frac{\pi}{3}\sin 3\pi t + \sin \frac{\pi}{3}\cos 3\pi t\right)$$

$$= 10\left[\sin\left(3\pi t + \frac{\pi}{3}\right)\right]$$

Compare the above equation with

$$y = A\sin(\omega t + \phi)$$

$\Rightarrow$ Amplitude $= 10$ cm,

$$\omega = 3\pi$$

Now, time period,

$$T = \frac{2\pi}{\omega} = \frac{2\pi}{3\pi} = \frac{2}{3}\text{ s}$$

19 (c) $\frac{aT}{x} = \frac{\omega^2 xT}{x} = \omega^2 T$

$$= \frac{4\pi^2}{T^2}T \qquad \left(\because \omega = \frac{2\pi}{T}\right)$$

$$= \frac{4\pi^2}{T} = \text{constant}$$

20 (c) The equation of SHM,

$$\frac{d^2x}{dt^2} + \alpha x = 0 \text{ or } \frac{d^2x}{dt^2} = -\alpha x$$

Comparing it with the equation of SHM

$$\frac{d^2x}{dt^2} = -\omega^2 x;$$

$$\omega^2 = \alpha \text{ or } \omega = \sqrt{\alpha}$$

$$\therefore T = \frac{2\pi}{\omega} = \frac{2\pi}{\sqrt{\alpha}}$$

21 (d) Simple harmonic motion is represented by a sine function or a cosine function or a linear combination of both.

Hence, options (a), (b) and (c) represent simple harmonic motion while option (d) is a product of the two functions (sine and cosine) and does not represent a simple harmonic motion.

23 (b) Given, $x = a\sin(\omega t + \delta)$ ... (i)

$$y = a\sin\left(\omega t + \delta + \frac{\pi}{2}\right)$$

$$\Rightarrow \quad y = a\cos(\omega t + \delta) \quad \text{...(ii)}$$

Squaring and adding Eqs. (i) and (ii), we get

$$x^2 + y^2 = a^2$$

This is the equation of a circle

At $(\omega t + \delta) = 0$; $x = 0$, $y = a$

At $(\omega t + \delta) = \frac{\pi}{2}$, $x = a$, $y = 0$

At $(\omega t + \delta) = \pi$, $x = 0$, $y = -a$

At $(\omega t + \delta) = \frac{3\pi}{2}$, $x = -a$, $y = a$

Thus, it is obvious that motion of particle is transversed in clockwise direction.

25 (b) $y = 4\cos^2\left(\frac{t}{2}\right)\sin(1000t)$

$$y = 2[1 + \cos t]\sin 1000t$$

$$y = 2\sin 1000t + 2\cos t \sin 1000t$$

$$= 2\sin 1000t + \sin(1001)t + \sin(999)t$$

Therefore, it carries 3 SHM's.

26 (b) It is clear from the curve that points corresponding to $t = 2$ s and $t = 6$ s are separated by a distance λ belongs to one time period. Hence, these points must be in same phase.

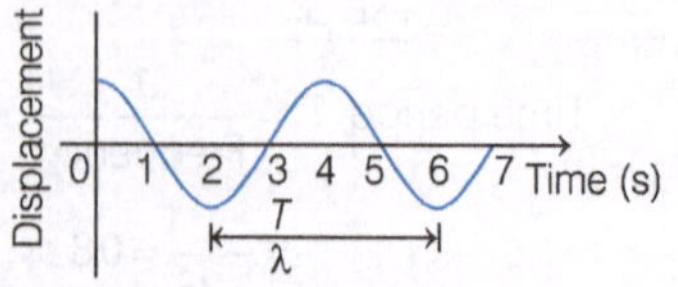

27 (d) Consider the figure given below

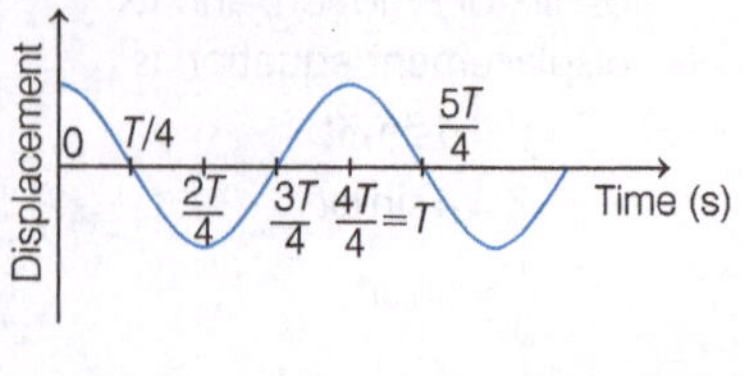

From this figure, it is clear that at, $t = \frac{2T}{4} = \frac{T}{2}$, the particle will be at extreme position, so KE = 0 and PE = maximum.

28 (c) The shadow will execute SHM on the wall as shown below

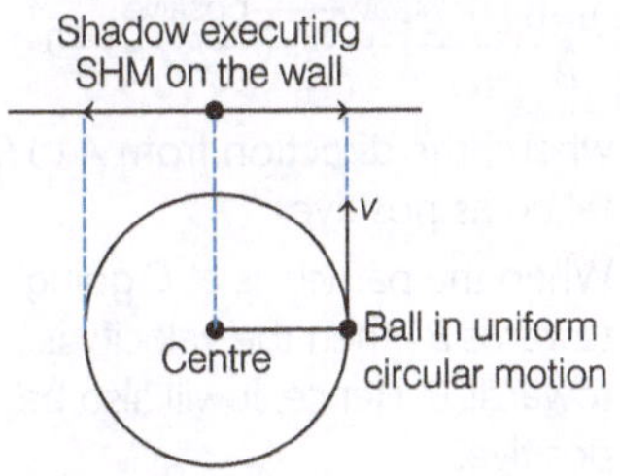

29 (a) At $t = 0$, OP makes an angle of $45° = (\pi/4)$ rad with the (positive direction of) X-axis. After time t, it covers an angle $\frac{2\pi}{T}t$ in the anti-clockwise sense and makes an angle of $\frac{2\pi}{T}t + \frac{\pi}{4}$ with the X-axis.

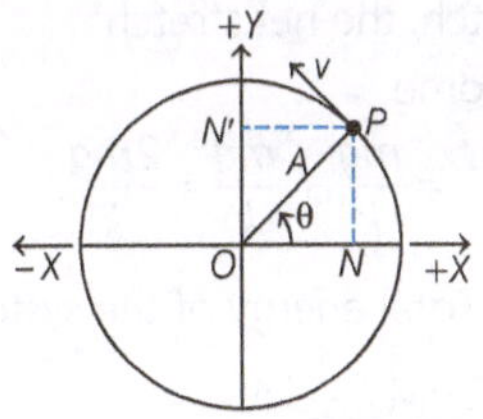

∴ The projection of OP on the X-axis at time t is given by

$$x(t) = A\cos\left(\frac{2\pi}{T}t + \frac{\pi}{4}\right)$$

For $T = 4$ s,

$$x(t) = A\cos\left(\frac{2\pi}{4}t + \frac{\pi}{4}\right)$$

30 (d) Actually, the motion of moon callisto is uniform circular motion. However, what Galileo observed the projection of that uniform circular motion in a line of plane of motion.

Hence, when it was viewed from the earth, it looked like to and fro motion, i.e. a simple harmonic motion.

Thus, the statements given in options (a), (b) and (c) are all correct.

31 (c) Maximum particle velocity,

$$v_{max} = A\omega = 3 \times 50 = 150 \text{ ms}^{-1}$$

32 (b) Given, angular frequency of the piston,

$$\omega = 100 \text{ rad min}^{-1}$$

and stroke length = 2 m

∴ Amplitude of SHM,

$$A = \frac{\text{Stroke length}}{2} = \frac{1}{2} = 1 \text{ m}$$

Now, $v_{max} = \omega A = 100 \times 1 = 100 \text{ m min}^{-1}$

33 (b) $\frac{(a_{max})_1}{(a_{max})_2} = \frac{\omega_1^2}{\omega_2^2} = \frac{(100)^2}{(1000)^2} = 1 : 10^2$

34 (c) As $x(t) = A\cos\omega t$

$$\Rightarrow v(t) = \frac{d}{dt}\{x(t)\} = -\omega A\sin\omega t$$

and $a(t) = \frac{d}{dt}\{v(t)\} = -\omega^2 A\cos\omega t$

If $t = 0$, then $a = -\omega^2 A$

If $t = \frac{T}{4}$, then $a = 0$

If $t = \frac{T}{2}$, then $a = +\omega^2 A$

We can see that only graph (c) will satisfy the above results.

35 (d) From the given graph, we have

Given, $T = 8$s

Angular frequency,

$$\omega = \frac{2\pi}{T} = \frac{2\pi}{8} = \left(\frac{\pi}{4}\right) \text{rads}^{-1}$$

As $x = A\sin\omega t$

∴ Acceleration, $a = \frac{d^2x}{dt^2} = -\omega^2 x$

$$= -\left(\frac{\pi^2}{16}\right)\sin\left(\frac{\pi}{4}t\right) \quad (\because A = 1)$$

On substituting $t = \frac{4}{3}$ s, we get

$$a = -\frac{\sqrt{3}}{32}\pi^2 \text{ cms}^{-2}$$

36 (d) $\frac{\alpha}{\beta} = \frac{A\omega^2}{A\omega}$

$$\Rightarrow \omega = \frac{\alpha}{\beta}$$

But $\omega = \frac{2\pi}{T}$

$$\therefore \frac{2\pi}{T} = \frac{\alpha}{\beta}$$

$$\Rightarrow T = \frac{2\pi\beta}{\alpha}$$

Thus, its time period of vibration,

$$T = \frac{2\pi\beta}{\alpha}$$

37 (b) Let displacement of the particle at any instant t is given by

$$x = a\sin\omega t$$
$$v = \omega\sqrt{a^2 - x^2}$$

At mean position, $x = 0$

$$\therefore v_{max} = \omega a$$

According to the question,

$$v = \frac{v_{max}}{2} = \frac{a\omega}{2}$$

But $v = \omega\sqrt{a^2 - x^2}$

$$\therefore \frac{a\omega}{2} = \omega\sqrt{a^2 - x^2}$$

$$\Rightarrow x = \frac{\sqrt{3}}{2}a$$

38 (b) $v = \frac{dx}{dt} = -4\pi \times \sin(2\pi t)$

$$v = v_{max} \rightarrow \sin(2\pi t) = \sin 90°$$

$$\therefore 2\pi t = \frac{\pi}{2}$$

$$\Rightarrow t = \frac{1}{4} = 0.25 \text{ s}$$

39 (a) Given, $y_1 = 0.1\sin\left(100\pi t + \frac{\pi}{3}\right)$

$$v_1 = \frac{dy_1}{dt} = 0.1 \times 100\pi\cos\left(100\pi t + \frac{\pi}{3}\right)$$

$$v_1 = 10\pi\sin\left(100\pi t + \frac{5\pi}{6}\right)$$

and $y_2 = 0.1\cos\pi t$

$$v_2 = \frac{dy_2}{dt} = -0.1\sin\pi t$$

$$\Rightarrow v_2 = 0.1\sin(\pi t + \pi)$$

Hence, phase difference

$$\Delta\phi = \phi_1 - \phi_2$$

$$= \left(100\pi t + \frac{5\pi}{6}\right) - (\pi t + \pi)$$

$$= \frac{5\pi}{6} - \pi \quad (\text{at } t = 0)$$

$$\Delta\phi = -\frac{\pi}{6}$$

40 (d) Given, $x = x_0 \cos\left(\omega t - \frac{\pi}{4}\right)$

Acceleration, $a = \frac{d^2x}{dt^2}$

$$= -\omega^2 x_0 \cos\left(\omega t - \frac{\pi}{4}\right)$$

$$= \omega^2 x_0 \cos\left(\omega t + \frac{3\pi}{4}\right)$$

So, $A = \omega^2 x_0$ and $\delta = \frac{3\pi}{4}$

41 (d) For particle executing SHM,

$$x = A \sin \omega t$$

$$\therefore \quad v = \frac{dx}{dt} = A\omega \cos \omega t$$

$$= A\omega \sin\left(\omega t + \frac{\pi}{2}\right)$$

Acceleration is given by

$$a = \frac{dv}{dt} = -A\omega^2 \sin \omega t$$

$$= A\omega^2 \sin(\omega t + \pi)$$

Phase difference between acceleration and velocity is

$$\left(\pi - \frac{\pi}{2}\right) = \frac{\pi}{2} = 0.5\,\pi$$

42 (c) $y = 3 \sin\left[\frac{\pi}{2}(50t - \phi)\right]$

Velocity, $v = \frac{dy}{dt}$

$$v = 3(25\pi) \cos\left[\frac{\pi}{2}(50t - \phi)\right]$$

So, $v_{max} = 75\pi$

43 (c) As force is always in the direction of acceleration

$$10 = \omega\sqrt{a^2 - 16} \quad \text{...(i)}$$

$$8 = \omega\sqrt{a^2 - 25} \quad \text{...(ii)}$$

$$\left(\frac{5}{4}\right)^2 = \frac{a^2 - 16}{a^2 - 25}$$

$$\Rightarrow \quad a^2 = \frac{369}{9} = 41$$

From Eq. (i),

$$10 = \omega\sqrt{41 - 16} = \omega \times 5$$

or $\omega = 2$

$$\frac{2\pi}{T} = 2$$

or $T = \pi$ s

44 (d) $F(x) = -\frac{dU}{dx}$

Given, $U(x) = k\,[1 - \exp(-x^2)]$

$$\therefore \quad F = -\frac{dU}{dx} = -2kx \exp(-x^2)$$

Here, negative sign implies that for any finite non-zero value of x, the force is directed towards the origin. This means there is a restoring force acting on the particle.

Hence, the motion of the particle is simple harmonic.

At $x = 0, F = 0$.

Hence, at equilibrium position force exerted on particle is zero.

Also, potential energy of the particle is minimum at $x = 0$ and at $x = \pm\infty$, the potential energy is maximum.

45 (c) $U = U_0 + \alpha x^2$

$$F = -\frac{dU}{dx} = -2\alpha x$$

$$\Rightarrow m\omega^2 x = -2\alpha x \Rightarrow \omega = \sqrt{\frac{2\alpha}{m}}$$

Time period, $T = \frac{2\pi}{\omega} = 2\pi\sqrt{\frac{m}{2\alpha}}$

$$\Rightarrow \quad T = \pi\sqrt{\frac{2m}{\alpha}}$$

46 (b) Given, $U(x) = U(1 - \cos ax)$

As we know that,

$$F = -\frac{dU}{dx} = -Ua \sin ax$$

ax is very small, so $\sin ax \sim ax$

$$\therefore \quad F = -Ua^2 x \quad \text{...(i)}$$

Thus, the body executes SHM.

So, for SHM,

$$F = -kx \quad \text{...(ii)}$$

From Eqs. (i) and (ii), we get

$$k = Ua^2$$

So, the time period oscillation,

$$T = 2\pi\sqrt{\frac{m}{k}}$$

$$= 2\pi\sqrt{\frac{m}{Ua^2}}$$

47 (b) Consider the diagram,

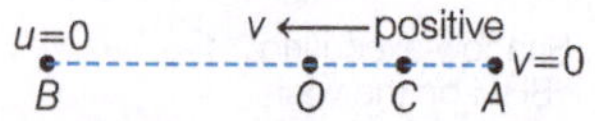

where, the direction from A to B is taken as positive.

When the particle is at C going towards B, then the velocity is towards B. Hence, it will also be positive.

48 (c) At equilibrium, the FBD of the block can be shown as alongside.

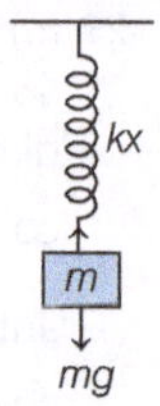

$$\therefore \quad mg = kx$$

$\Rightarrow$ Stretch, $x = mg/k$

Now, with the extra $\frac{mg}{k}$ stretch, the net stretch become

$$= \frac{mg}{k} + \frac{mg}{k} = \frac{2mg}{k}.$$

49 (d) Total energy of the system in

$$\text{SHM} = \frac{1}{2}kA^2 \quad \text{...(i)}$$

Kinetic energy of the system in

$$\text{SHM} = \frac{1}{2}mv^2 \quad \text{...(ii)}$$

Since, at equilibrium position, i.e. at $x = 0$, the energy of the system would be kinetic only.

$\therefore$ From Eqs. (i) and (ii), we get

$$\frac{1}{2}kA^2 = \frac{1}{2}mv^2$$

$$\Rightarrow \quad v = \sqrt{\left(\frac{k}{m}\right)A^2}$$

$$= A\sqrt{\frac{k}{m}}$$

50 (d) Let x_1 and x_2 be the extensions in the spring with spring constants k_1 and k_2, respectively.

Then, $x_1 + x_2 = A$ ...(i)

and $k_1x_1 = k_2x_2$ or $\frac{x_1}{x_2} = \frac{k_2}{k_1}$ ...(ii)

From Eq. (ii) substitute the value of x_2 in Eq. (i), we get

$$x_1 + \frac{k_1}{k_2}x_1 = A \quad \text{...(iii)}$$

$$k_2x_1 + k_1x_1 = Ak_2$$

On solving these equations, we get

$$x_1 = \left(\frac{k_2}{k_1 + k_2}\right)A$$

51 (c) The situation can be depicted as

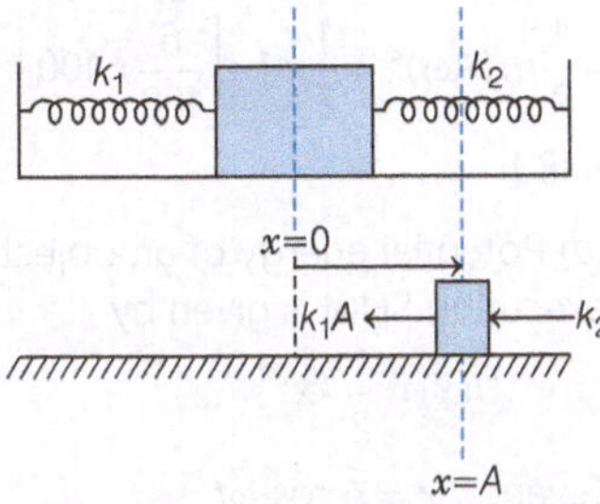

As, restoring force of a spring, $F = -kx$

From FBD, $\mathbf{F}_{net} = -(k_1 + k_2)A$

The magnitude of net force,

$|\mathbf{F}_{net}| = (k_1 + k_2)A$

52 (c) Frequency of oscillation of a spring mass system is given

as $\quad \nu = 2\pi\sqrt{\frac{m}{k}}$

This means, it is independent of acceleration due to gravity.

Given, $m = 2$kg, $k = 10$ Nm^{-1}

$$\Rightarrow \quad \nu = 2\pi\sqrt{\frac{2}{10}}$$

$$= 2.8 \text{ Hz}$$

53 (c) Since, the three springs are in parallel. So, net spring constant

$$= k + k + 2k = 4k$$

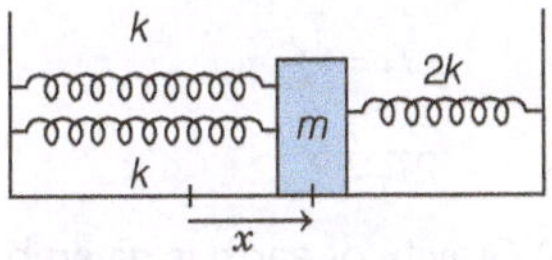

∴The net restoring force on mass m,

$$|\mathbf{F}_{net}| = -4kx \quad \text{...(i)}$$

As, force in SHM,

$$|\mathbf{F}_{SHM}| = -m\omega^2 x \quad \text{...(ii)}$$

On comparing Eqs. (i) and (ii), we get

$$m\omega^2 = 4k$$

$$\Rightarrow \quad \omega = \sqrt{\frac{4k}{m}}$$

$$\therefore \quad T = \frac{2\pi}{\omega} = 2\pi\sqrt{\frac{m}{4k}}$$

54 (a) For systems,

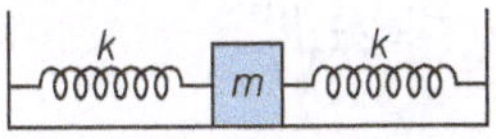

and

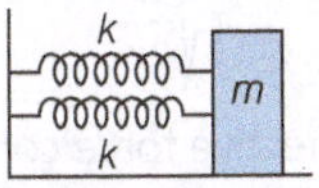

there are two springs of same spring constants k, attached to mass m in parallel. So, both systems have same time periods.

55 (d) Initially frequency of oscillation,

$$= \frac{1}{2\pi}\sqrt{\frac{k_1 + k_2}{m}} \quad \text{...(i)}$$

Now, when k_1 and k_2 are made four times their original value, then

$$= \frac{1}{2\pi}\sqrt{\frac{4k_1 + 4k_2}{m}} = 2f$$

[∵ using Eq. (i)]

56 (b) Given, $m_1 = 1$ kg

Extension in length,

$l_1 = 5$ cm $= 5 \times 10^{-2}$ m

$\therefore \quad m_1g = kl_1$

$$\Rightarrow k = \frac{m_1g}{l_1} = \frac{1 \times 10}{5 \times 10^{-2}} = 200 \text{ Nm}^{-1}$$

Now, if 2 kg block is suspended to this spring and pulled, then

Time period of the block,

$$T = 2\pi\sqrt{\frac{m}{k}} = 2\pi\sqrt{\frac{2}{200}}$$

$$= \frac{\pi}{5} \text{ s}$$

As, maximum velocity, $v_{max} = A\omega$

where, $A =$ amplitude

$= 10$ cm $= 10 \times 10^{-2}$ m(given)

$$\Rightarrow \quad v_{max} = A \times \frac{2\pi}{T}$$

$$= 10 \times 10^{-2} \times \frac{2\pi}{\pi/5}$$

$$= 1 \text{ ms}^{-1}$$

57 (c) The effective spring constant of the parallel spring combination is given by

$$k_{eff} = k + k = 2k$$

The time period is given by

$$T = 2\pi\sqrt{\frac{M}{k_{eff}}}$$

$$= 2\pi\sqrt{\frac{M}{2k}} \quad \text{...(i)}$$

When a block of mass m is placed on the tray, then

$$T' = 2\pi\sqrt{\frac{M + m}{2k}} \quad \text{...(ii)}$$

From Eqs. (i) and (ii),

$$\frac{T'}{T} = \sqrt{\frac{M + m}{M}}$$

$$\frac{3}{1.5} = \sqrt{\frac{20 + m}{20}}$$

$$\Rightarrow \quad m = 60 \text{ kg}$$

58 (c) Frequency of spring mass system is

$$n = \frac{1}{2\pi}\sqrt{\frac{k}{m}}$$

or $\quad n \propto \frac{1}{\sqrt{m}}$

or $\quad \frac{n_1}{n_2} = \sqrt{\frac{m_2}{m_1}}$

But $m_1 = m$, $m_2 = 4m$, $n_1 = n$

$$\therefore \quad \frac{n}{n_2} = \sqrt{\frac{4m}{m}} = 2$$

or $\quad n_2 = \frac{n}{2}$

59 (c) When a string is compressed, then it does not provide any restoring force.

Hence, $T = \frac{T_1}{2} + \frac{T_2}{2}$

$$T = \frac{2\pi}{2}\sqrt{\frac{m}{2k}} + \frac{2\pi}{2}\sqrt{\frac{m}{k}}$$

$$= (\sqrt{2} + 1)\pi\sqrt{\frac{m}{2k}}$$

60 (*b*) Time period of spring pendulum is independent of gravity and inclination of plane, but dependent on M and k,

$$T = 2\pi\sqrt{\frac{M}{k}}$$

$$T_A > T_B$$

As $M_A = 2\text{ kg}, M_B = 1\text{ kg}$

$$k_A = k_B$$

So, P will be slow.

61 (*c*) $x = k + k = 2k$ [for P, Q]

and $y = k + k = 2k$ [for R, S]

x and y both are in series.

$$\therefore \frac{1}{k'} = \frac{1}{x} + \frac{1}{y} = \frac{1}{k}$$

TIme period, $T = 2\pi\sqrt{\frac{m}{k'}} = 2\pi\sqrt{\frac{m}{k}}$

62 (*b*) The two springs on left side are in series, equivalent constant is

$$\frac{1}{\left(\frac{1}{2k} + \frac{1}{2k}\right)} = k.$$

The two springs on right hand side of mass M are in parallel. Their effective spring constant is $(k + 2k) = 3k$.

Equivalent spring constants of value k and $3k$ are in parallel is $k + 3k = 4k$

$\therefore$Frequency of mass is

$$n = \frac{1}{2\pi}\sqrt{\frac{4k}{M}}.$$

63 (*c*) We know that, the time needed to cover from compressed position to mean position $= T/4$

As $Y = A\sin\omega t$

$\therefore$ $x_0 = 2x_0 \sin\omega t$

But $\omega = \frac{2\pi}{T}$ or $x_0 = 2x_0 \sin\frac{2\pi}{T}t$

or $\frac{1}{2} = \sin\frac{2\pi}{T}t$

or $\frac{2\pi}{T}t = \frac{\pi}{6}$; $t = \frac{T}{12}$

Time taken to hit the wall,

$$\frac{T}{4} + \frac{T}{12} = \frac{T}{3}$$

If mass m is attached to the spring of force constant k,

$$T = 2\pi\sqrt{\frac{m}{k}}$$

$\therefore$Time taken to hit the wall

$$= \frac{T}{3} = \frac{2\pi}{3}\sqrt{\frac{m}{k}}$$

64 (*d*) The reduced mass,

$$\mu = \frac{(m)(m)}{m + m} = \frac{m}{2}$$

The required period of oscillation,

$$T = 2\pi\sqrt{\frac{\mu}{k}}$$

$$= \pi\sqrt{\frac{2m}{k}}$$

65 (*c*) Effective force constant is given by

$$k_{\text{eff}} = 2k$$

$$f = \frac{1}{2\pi}\sqrt{\frac{2k}{m}}$$

When one spring is removed, k_{eff} will become k and new frequency will be

$$f' = \frac{1}{2\pi}\sqrt{\frac{k}{m}} \Rightarrow f' = \frac{f}{\sqrt{2}}$$

66 (*c*) $v = \omega\sqrt{A^2 - x^2}$

$$v = \sqrt{\frac{k}{m}}\sqrt{A^2 - x^2}$$

$$v = 5\sqrt{A^2 - x^2} = 40 \times 10^{-2}$$

$$\frac{40^2}{5^2} \times 10^{-4} = (0.50)^2 - x^2$$

$$\Rightarrow \quad x = 0.49\text{ m}$$

67 (*b*) If g is the acceleration due to gravity on earth, then acceleration due to gravity on moon is $\frac{g}{6}$.

So, when the spring-mass system is taken to the moon, then the FBD is as shown below.

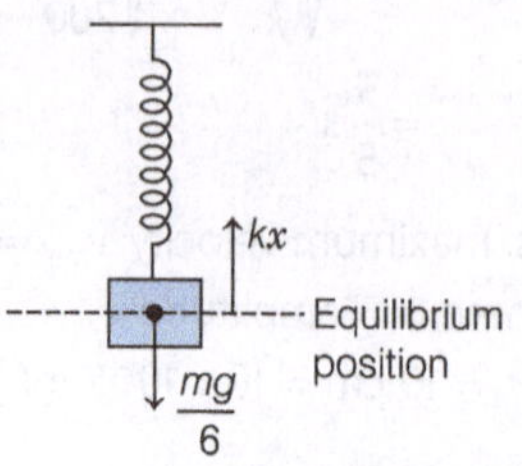

In equilibrium, $kx = \frac{mg}{6}$

where, k is spring constant and x is the extension in the spring.

$$\Rightarrow \quad x = \frac{mg}{6k}$$

68 (*d*) Given, $m = 1\text{ kg}$

The given equation of SHM is

$$x = 6.0\cos\left(100t + \frac{\pi}{4}\right)$$

We have, $A = 6.0\text{ cm} = \frac{6}{100}\text{ m}$

and $\omega = 100\text{ rad/s}$

Maximum kinetic energy

$$= \frac{1}{2}m(A\omega)^2 = \frac{1}{2} \times 1 \times \left[\frac{6}{100} \times 100\right]^2$$

$$= 18\text{ J}$$

69 (*d*) Potential energy of an object executing SHM is given by

$$U(x) = \frac{1}{2}kx^2$$

Given, $x = A\cos\omega t$

$$\Rightarrow \quad U(x) = \frac{1}{2}kA^2\cos^2\omega t$$

At $t = \left(\frac{T}{4}\right)$,

$$U(x) = \frac{1}{2}kA^2\cos^2\left(\frac{2\pi}{T} \times \frac{T}{4}\right)$$

$$= 0 \qquad \left(\because \omega = \frac{2\pi}{T}\right)$$

70 (*c*) For SHM,

Displacement,

$$x(t) = A\cos(\omega t + \phi) \qquad \text{...(i)}$$

$$\Rightarrow \quad T_2 = 2\pi/\omega$$

Potential energy,

$$\text{PE} = \frac{1}{2}kx^2 = \frac{1}{2}kA^2\cos^2(\omega t + \phi) \text{...(ii)}$$

$$= \frac{1}{2}kA^2\frac{[1 + \cos 2(\omega t + \phi)]}{2}$$

$$\therefore \quad T_1 = \frac{2\pi}{2\omega} = \frac{\pi}{\omega}$$

$$\Rightarrow \quad T_1 = \frac{T_2}{2}$$

$$\Rightarrow \quad 2T_1 = T_2$$

72 (*b*) Gravity of earth is given by

$$g_e = \frac{GM_e}{R^2}$$

Gravity of the planet.

$$g_P = \frac{G\cdot(2M_e)}{(2R_e)^2} = \frac{GM}{2R^2} = \frac{g_e}{2}$$

$$(\because M_P = 2M_e,\ R_P = 2R_e)$$

So, the time period is given by

$$T_P = 2\pi\sqrt{\frac{l}{g_P}} = 2\pi\sqrt{\frac{l}{g_e/2}}$$

$$= 2\pi\sqrt{\frac{l}{g_e}\times 2} = \sqrt{2}\times T_e$$

$$\Rightarrow \quad T_P = \sqrt{2}\times 2$$

$$\Rightarrow \quad T_P = 2\sqrt{2}\ \text{s}$$

73 (*d*) As given,

$$U = \frac{1}{2}E$$

$$\therefore \frac{1}{2}m\omega^2x^2 = \frac{1}{2}\left(\frac{1}{2}m\omega^2A^2\right)$$

$$\Rightarrow \quad x^2 = \frac{A^2}{2}$$

$$\Rightarrow \quad x = \frac{A}{\sqrt{2}}$$

74 (*b*) For SHM, the kinetic energy is given by

$$K = \frac{1}{2}m\omega^2(A^2 - x^2)$$

At $x = \frac{A}{4}$,

$$K = \frac{1}{2}m\omega^2\left[A^2 - \left(\frac{A}{4}\right)^2\right]$$

$$= \frac{1}{2}\left(\frac{15}{16}m\omega^2A^2\right)$$

Total energy of the particle,

$$E = \frac{1}{2}m\omega^2A^2$$

$$\therefore \quad \frac{K}{E} = \frac{\frac{1}{2}\left(\frac{15}{16}m\omega^2A^2\right)}{\frac{1}{2}m\omega^2A^2}$$

$$\Rightarrow \quad \frac{K}{E} = \frac{15}{16}$$

75 (*a*) The length of scale is 20 cm and scale reads upto 50 kg.

$$\therefore \quad F = mg = 50\times 10$$

$$= 500\ \text{N}$$

Spring constant is given by

$$k = \frac{F}{x} = \frac{500}{0.2} = 2500\ \text{Nm}^{-1}$$

or $\quad T = 2\pi\sqrt{\frac{m}{k}}$

$$\Rightarrow \quad m = \frac{T^2k}{4\pi^2}$$

$$= \frac{(0.5)^2\times(2500)}{4\times(3.14)^2} = 16\ \text{kg}$$

76 (*a*) For SHM, the angular frequency,

$$\omega = \sqrt{\frac{k}{m}} = \sqrt{\frac{100}{1}} = 10\ \text{rad s}^{-1}$$

Now, velocity of the block at $x = 0.05$ m is

$$v = \omega\sqrt{A^2 - x^2}$$

$$= 10\sqrt{(0.1)^2 - (0.05)^2}$$

$$= 10\sqrt{7.5\times 10^{-3}}\ \text{ms}^{-1}$$

So, the kinetic energy is given by

$$K = \frac{1}{2}mv^2$$

$$= \frac{1}{2}\times 1\times 0.75$$

$$\Rightarrow \quad K = 0.375\ \text{J}$$

77 (*c*) Kinetic energy of a particle in SHM is given by

$$K = \frac{1}{2}m\omega^2(a^2 - x^2) \quad \text{...(i)}$$

Potential energy is given by

$$U = \frac{1}{2}m\omega^2x^2 \quad \text{...(ii)}$$

From Eqs. (i) and (ii), we get

$$\frac{K}{U} = \frac{\frac{1}{2}m\omega^2(a^2 - x^2)}{\frac{1}{2}m\omega^2(x^2)}$$

$$\frac{K}{U} = \frac{a^2 - x^2}{x^2}$$

78 (*d*) The total energy of the particle executing SHM at instant *t* is given by

$$E = \frac{1}{2}m\omega^2a^2 \quad \text{... (i)}$$

and kinetic energy of the particle at instant *t* is given by

$$K = \frac{1}{2}m\omega^2(a^2 - x^2) \quad \text{... (ii)}$$

When $x = \frac{a}{2}$,

$$K = \frac{1}{2}m\omega^2\left(a^2 - \frac{a^2}{4}\right)$$

$$= \frac{1}{2}m\omega^2\times\frac{3}{4}a^2 \quad \text{... (iii)}$$

From Eqs. (i) and (iii), we get

$$\frac{K}{E} = \frac{3}{4}$$

$$\Rightarrow \quad K = \frac{3}{4}E$$

79 (*a*) Let simple harmonic motions be represented by

$$y_1 = a\sin\left(\omega t - \frac{\pi}{4}\right);\ y_2 = a\sin\omega t$$

and $y_3 = a\sin\left(\omega t + \frac{\pi}{4}\right)$

On superimposing, resultant SHM will be

$$y = a\left[\sin\left(\omega t - \frac{\pi}{4}\right) + \sin\omega t + \sin\left(\omega t + \frac{\pi}{4}\right)\right]$$

$$= a\left[2\sin\omega t\cos\frac{\pi}{4} + \sin\omega t\right]$$

$$= [a(1+\sqrt{2})\sin\omega t]$$

Thus, resultant amplitude,

$A = (1+\sqrt{2})a.$

80 (*a*) For a body executing SHM, its kinetic energy,

$$\text{KE}(x) = \frac{1}{2}m\omega^2(A^2 - x^2)$$

where, *A* is the amplitude.

So, KE at $x = 0$,

$$\text{KE}(0) = \frac{1}{2}m\omega^2A^2 = (\text{KE})_{\text{max}}$$

81 (*a*) Kinetic energy and potential energy of a particle executing SHM are periodic with period $\frac{T}{2}$.

Time periods of variation of potential and kinetic energies are same.

82 (*c*) From given information

$$\text{KE} = (\text{TE})\times\frac{75}{100}$$

$$\Rightarrow \frac{m\omega^2A^2}{2}\cos^2\omega t = \frac{m\omega^2A^2}{2}\times\frac{3}{4}$$

$\Rightarrow \cos \omega t = \frac{\sqrt{3}}{2}$

$\Rightarrow \omega t = \frac{\pi}{6}$

or $\frac{2\pi}{T} \times t = \frac{\pi}{6}$

$\Rightarrow t = \frac{T}{12}$

$\Rightarrow t = \frac{1}{6}$ s

83 (b) Total kinetic energy of the system

$$= \text{KE} + \text{PE} = \frac{1}{2}kA^2 \quad ...(i)$$

If KE = PE, then Eq. (i) can be written as,

$$\frac{1}{2}kA^2 = 2 \times \text{PE}$$

$$= 2\left(\frac{1}{2}kx^2\right)$$

or $\frac{1}{2}kx^2 = \frac{1}{2}\left[\frac{1}{2}kA^2\right]$

$\Rightarrow x = A/\sqrt{2}$

84 (b) For a block executing SHM, its velocity, $v = -A\omega \sin(\omega t + \phi)$ ...(i)

$\Rightarrow T_1 = \frac{2\pi}{\omega}$

$$\text{KE} = \frac{1}{2}mv^2$$

$$= \frac{1}{2}mA^2\omega^2 \sin^2(\omega t + \phi)$$

$$= mA^2\omega^2[1 - \cos(2\omega + 2\phi)]$$

$\Rightarrow T_2 = \frac{2\pi}{2\omega}$ ...(ii)

$\therefore T_2 = \frac{T_1}{2}$

So, $T_1 = 2T_2$

85 (d) The time period T of a simple pendulum of length l is given by

$$T = 2\pi\sqrt{\frac{l}{g}} = \frac{1}{\text{frequency}(n)}$$

$\therefore \frac{n_1}{n_2} = \sqrt{\frac{l_2}{l_1}}$

$\Rightarrow \frac{l_1}{l_2} = \left(\frac{n_2}{n_1}\right)^2$

$\Rightarrow \frac{l_1}{l_2} = \left(\frac{3}{2}\right)^2 = \frac{9}{4}$

86 (b) Time period of a simple pendulum which is initially at rest is given by

$$T = 2\pi\sqrt{\frac{l}{g}} \quad ...(i)$$

When the lift is moving up with an acceleration a, then time period becomes

$$T' = 2\pi\sqrt{\frac{l}{g+a}}$$

Given, $T' = \frac{T}{2}$

$\Rightarrow T' = \frac{T}{2} = 2\pi\sqrt{\frac{l}{g+a}}$ ...(ii)

On dividing Eq. (ii) by Eq. (i), we get

$$\frac{1}{2} = \sqrt{\frac{g}{g+a}}$$

$\Rightarrow a = 3g$

87 (b) Acceleration due to gravity at a height h is

$$g' = g\left(1 + \frac{h}{R}\right)^{-2}$$

$$= g\left(1 + \frac{2R}{R}\right)^{-2}$$

(given, $h = 2R$)

$$= g(3)^{-2}$$

$\because \frac{T_1}{T_2} = \sqrt{\frac{g'}{g}}$

$\therefore \frac{T_1}{T_2} = \sqrt{\frac{g(3)^{-2}}{g}} = \sqrt{\frac{1}{3^2}}$

$\Rightarrow T_2 = 3T_1 \Rightarrow \frac{T_1}{T_2} = \frac{1}{3}$

88 (d) The moment of inertia of rod about the point of oscillation is

$$I = \frac{1}{3}ml_0^2$$

Moreover, length l of the pendulum = distance from the oscillation axis to centre of mass of rod $= l_0/2$

$\therefore$ Time period of oscillation,

$$T = 2\pi\sqrt{\frac{I}{mgl}} = 2\pi\sqrt{\frac{\frac{1}{3}ml_0^2}{mg\left(\frac{l_0}{2}\right)}}$$

$\Rightarrow T = 2\pi\sqrt{\frac{2l_0}{3g}}$

89 (d) Initial time period,

$$T = 2\pi\sqrt{\frac{L}{g}} \quad ...(i)$$

Here,

$$\rho_{\text{liquid}} = \frac{\rho_{\text{bob}}}{16} = \frac{\rho}{16} \quad \text{(given)}$$

$\therefore$ Net force on the bob is

$$F_{\text{net}} = V\rho g - V \cdot \frac{\rho}{16} \cdot g \quad ...(ii)$$

Net force on the bob can also be written as

$$F_{\text{net}} = V\rho g_{\text{eff}} \quad ...(iii)$$

Equating Eqs. (ii) and (iii), we have

$$V\rho g_{\text{eff}} = V\rho g - V\rho g/16$$

$\Rightarrow g_{\text{eff}} = \frac{15}{16}g$ ...(iv)

The new time period of the bob will be

$$T' = 2\pi\sqrt{\frac{16\,L}{15\,g}}$$

$\Rightarrow T' = \frac{4}{\sqrt{15}} \times T$ [using Eq. (i)]

90 (a) $T = 2\pi\sqrt{\frac{l}{g}}$

$$l = \left(\frac{g}{4\pi^2}\right)T^2$$

$\therefore$ % change $= x + y + \frac{xy}{100}$

(valid only for two variables in terms of percentage)

$x \rightarrow$ % change in both variables

$\therefore$ % increase in length

$$= x + x + \frac{x^2}{100}$$

$$21 = 2x + \frac{x^2}{100}$$

$\Rightarrow x = 10\%$

91 (c) The time period of simple pendulum in air,

$$T = t_0 = 2\pi\sqrt{\frac{l}{g}} \quad ...(i)$$

In water, effective weight of bob is,

$w' =$ weight of bob in air − upthrust

$\Rightarrow \rho V g_{eff} = (\rho - \rho')Vg$

where, $\rho' =$ density of water

$\rho =$ density of bob

$$\therefore \quad g_{eff} = \left(1 - \frac{\rho'}{\rho}\right)g$$

$$\therefore \quad t = 2\pi\sqrt{\frac{l}{\left(1 - \frac{\rho'}{\rho}\right)g}} \quad \text{...(ii)}$$

From Eqs. (i) and (ii),

$$\frac{t}{t_0} = \sqrt{\left(\frac{1}{1 - \frac{\rho'}{\rho}}\right)}$$

$$= \sqrt{\frac{1}{1 - \frac{1000}{(4/3) \times 1000}}}$$

$$\Rightarrow \quad t = 2t_0$$

Assertion and Reason Questions

1 (*d*) There is no significant difference between oscillations and vibrations. It seems that, when frequency is small, then it is called oscillations (like, the oscillation of branch of a tree), while when frequency is high, then it is called vibration (like, the vibration of a string of musical instrument).

2 (*d*) $x(t) = A\sin\omega t$ is a sinusoidal periodic function that can represent an oscillatory motion.

3 (*b*) In oscillatory or vibratory motion, an object moves about an equilibrium position due to a restoring force.

When the body is at equilibrium position, no net external force acts on it, i.e. $F_{net} = 0$. Therefore, if it is left there at rest, it remains there forever.

If the body is then given then a small displacement from that position, a force comes into play, i.e. restoring force which tries to bring the body back to the equilibrium point giving rise to oscillation or vibrations.

4 (*b*) $x = A\cos\omega t$ and $x = A\sin\omega t$ both represent the displacement of particle undergoing periodic motion.

At $t = 0$,

If $x = A$, we can represents its displacement by

$$x = A\cos\omega t$$

and if $x = 0$, we can represent its displacement by

$$x = A\sin\omega t$$

This implies, both $x = A\cos\omega t$ and $x = A\sin\omega t$, represents the same motion depending on initial position of particle.

Since, $x = A\cos\omega t$ represents a periodic function with time period of 2π rad. So, if the argument of this function ωt is increased by an integral multiple of 2π rad, the value of the function remains the same.

5 (*c*) Time period of oscillation of spring mass system is

$$T = 2\pi\sqrt{\frac{m}{k}}$$

which is independent of the amplitude.

Thus, if the amplitude of the system is increased, then T will remain same.

6 (*c*) Simple harmonic motion is expressed by $v = \omega\sqrt{a^2 - y^2}$. With change in displacement y, velocity v changes. Thus, simple harmonic motion is not a uniform motion.

7 (*c*) The maximum velocity of a particle,

$$v_{max} = \omega A$$

$$= \frac{2\pi}{T} \times A$$

$$v_{max} = \frac{2\pi}{2} \times 0.05$$

$$v_{max} = 0.157 \text{ m/s}$$

The velocity of particle is minimum at extreme position.

8 (*a*) As, frequency of oscillation, for a spring mass system,

$$f = \frac{1}{2\pi}\cdot\sqrt{\frac{k}{m}} \quad \text{... (i)}$$

This means, a block of mass m attached to stiff spring have large frequency of oscillation according to Eq. (i).

10 (*d*) The total mechanical energy of a simple harmonic oscillator oscillating with amplitude a is

$E = \frac{1}{2}m\omega^2a^2$, i.e. $E \propto a^2$

Therefore, energy is directly proportional to the square of amplitude of vibration of harmonic oscillator.

11 (*d*) Time period of simple pendulum when it is falling under acceleration of a is

$$T = 2\pi\sqrt{\frac{l}{g - a}} \quad \text{...(i)}$$

In the case of freely falling,

$$a = g$$

$\therefore$ From Eq. (i),

$$T = 2\pi\sqrt{\frac{l}{g - g}}$$

$$\Rightarrow \quad T = \infty$$

12 (*d*) At mountain top, the value of acceleration due to gravity (g) is less than the planes.

Since, $T \propto \frac{1}{\sqrt{g}}$, so the time period of vibration of pendulum clock increase and due to this, it start taking more time to complete each vibration. Therefore, the pendulum clock becomes slow.

Matching Type Questions

1 (*c*) Period of oscillation, $T = 0.20$ s (given from the graph)

By definition, $\omega = \sqrt{\frac{k}{m}} = \frac{2\pi}{T}$

$$\therefore \quad m = \frac{kT^2}{4\pi^2}$$

$$= \frac{200 \times (0.20)^2}{4 \times 10} = 0.20 \text{ kg}$$

Also, $v_{max} = \omega a = 2\pi$ (given from the graph)

$$a = \frac{2\pi}{\omega} = \frac{2\pi}{\left(\frac{2\pi}{T}\right)}$$

$$= T = 0.20 \text{ m}$$

At $t = 0$, velocity is zero. Hence, the block is at its extreme left position, i.e. $x = -0.20$ m.

Block acceleration $= -\omega^2 a$

$$= -\frac{4\pi^2}{T^2} a$$

$$= -\frac{4 \times 10 \times 0.20}{(0.20)^2} = -200 \text{ m/s}^2$$

Maximum kinetic energy of the block,

$$K_{max} = \frac{1}{2} m v_{max}^2 = \frac{1}{2} m\omega^2 a^2$$

$$= \frac{1}{2} m \left(\frac{4\pi^2}{T^2}\right) a^2$$

$$= \frac{1}{2} \times 0.20 \times \frac{4 \times 10}{(0.20)^2} \times (0.20)^2$$

$$= 4 \text{ J}$$

2 (*b*) For an object executing SHM,

A. $v_{max} = A\omega$

$$\Rightarrow \quad \frac{v_{max}}{\text{Amplitude}} = \frac{A\omega}{A} = \omega$$

B. $a_{max} = A\omega^2$

$$\text{So,} \quad \frac{a_{max}}{\text{Amplitude}} = \frac{A\omega^2}{A} = \omega^2$$

C. If object starts from $x = +A$, its equation is

$$x = A\cos \omega t$$

For $x = +A/\sqrt{2}$

$$\frac{A}{\sqrt{2}} = A\cos \omega t$$

$$\cos \omega t = \frac{1}{\sqrt{2}} = \cos\left(\frac{\pi}{4}\right)$$

$$\Rightarrow \frac{2\pi}{T} \times t = \frac{\pi}{4} \Rightarrow t = T/8$$

D. If object starts from $x = 0$, its equation is

$$x = A\sin \omega t$$

For $x = +A/2 \Rightarrow \frac{A}{2} = A\sin \omega t$

$$\therefore \quad \frac{1}{2} = \sin \omega t$$

$$\Rightarrow \quad \sin\frac{\pi}{6} = \sin \omega t$$

$$\Rightarrow \quad \omega t = \frac{\pi}{6}$$

$$\frac{2\pi}{T} \cdot t = \frac{\pi}{6}$$

$$\Rightarrow \quad t = \frac{T}{12}$$

3 (*d*) Force constant,

$$k = \frac{F}{y} = \frac{30}{0.3} = 100 \text{ N/m}$$

When 5 kg weight is placed, force, $F' = mg = 5 \times 10 = 50$N

$$\therefore \text{Displacement} = \frac{F'}{k} = \frac{50}{100} = 0.5 \text{ m}$$

$$= 50 \text{ cm}$$

$$\text{Time period, } T = 2\pi\sqrt{\frac{m}{k}} = 2\pi\sqrt{\frac{5}{100}}$$

$$= \frac{\pi}{\sqrt{5}} \text{ s.}$$

Angular frequency,

$$\omega = \frac{2\pi}{T} = \frac{2\pi}{\frac{\pi}{\sqrt{5}}} = 2\sqrt{5} \text{rad / s}$$

Numerical Type Questions

1 (*3*) Given, amplitude of particle in SHM $= A$

Maximum velocity, $v = A\omega$

Let displacement be y when speed, $v_2 = \frac{v}{2}$

$$\Rightarrow \quad v_2 = \frac{A\omega}{2}$$

By equation of wave velocity,

$$v_2^2 = \omega^2(A^2 - y^2)$$

$$\because \quad \left(\frac{\omega A}{2}\right)^2 = \omega^2(A^2 - y^2)$$

$$\Rightarrow \quad \frac{\omega^2 A^2}{4} = \omega^2(A^2 - y^2)$$

$$\Rightarrow \quad \frac{A^2}{4} = A^2 - y^2$$

$$\Rightarrow \quad y = \frac{\sqrt{3}}{2} A$$

$$= \frac{A\sqrt{x}}{2}$$

Hence, $x = 3$

2 (*12*) Given, equation of motion of SHM,

$$x = a\sin\left(\omega t + \frac{\pi}{6}\right)$$

Velocity is given by,

$$v = \frac{dx}{dt}$$

$$\frac{a\omega}{2} = a\omega\cos\left(\omega t + \frac{\pi}{6}\right)$$

$$\frac{1}{2} = \cos\left(\omega t + \frac{\pi}{6}\right)$$

$$\omega t + \frac{\pi}{6} = \frac{\pi}{3} \qquad \left[\because \cos\frac{\pi}{3} = \frac{1}{2}\right]$$

$$\Rightarrow \quad \omega t = \frac{\pi}{6}$$

$$\frac{2\pi}{T} t = \frac{\pi}{6} \qquad \left[\because \omega = \frac{2\pi}{T}\right]$$

$$t = \frac{T}{12}$$

$\therefore$ The value of x is 12.

3 (*8*) For SHM,

$$v = \omega\sqrt{A^2 - x^2}$$

$$a = -\omega^2 x$$

Given, amplitude, $A = 5$ cm and displacement, $x = 4$ cm

At this time (when $x = 4$ cm),

$$|v_{x=4}| = |a_{x=4}|$$

$$\text{or } |\omega\sqrt{5^2 - 4^2}| = |-4\omega^2|$$

$$\Rightarrow \quad 3\omega = +4\omega^2$$

$$\Rightarrow \quad \omega = \frac{3}{4} \text{ rad s}^{-1}$$

So, time period,

$$T = \frac{2\pi}{\omega}$$

$$= 2\pi \times \frac{4}{3}$$

$$= \frac{8\pi}{3} \text{ s}$$

$\therefore$ The value of x is 8.

4 (2) As, $y = 0.5\sin(2\pi ft)$

For weightlessness, $a = g$

$$\therefore \quad g = |-\omega^2 A|$$

$$\omega^2 = \frac{g}{A}$$

$$4\pi^2 f^2 = \frac{g}{A}$$

$$\Rightarrow \quad f^2 = \frac{g}{A \times 4\pi^2}$$

$$\Rightarrow \quad f = \sqrt{\frac{g}{A \times 4\pi^2}}$$

$$= \sqrt{\frac{g}{0.5 \times 4 \times \pi^2}}$$

$$= \sqrt{\frac{g}{2\pi^2}} = \sqrt{\frac{g}{n\pi^2}} \quad \text{(given)}$$

$$\therefore \quad n = 2$$

5 (*64*) Given, $A = 2$ m, $T = 3.14$ s and $M = 8$ kg

$$T = 3.14 \text{ s} = \pi \text{s}$$

$$\Rightarrow \quad T = \frac{2\pi}{\omega}$$

$$\Rightarrow \quad \omega = 2$$

Maximum force exerted by spring is given by

$$F_{max} = Ma_{max} = M \times (A\omega^2)$$

$$= 8 \times 2 \times 2^2$$

$$F_{max} = 64 \text{ N}$$

6 (*10*) The time period of a pendulum in air is given by

$$T = 2\pi\sqrt{\frac{l}{g}} \quad \text{...(i)}$$

In liquid, effective weight of sphere,

w' = weight of bob in air – upthrust

$$\rho V g_{eff} = mg - m' g$$

$$= (\rho - \rho')Vg$$

where, ρ' = density of liquid,

ρ = density of sphere.

$$\rho' = \frac{\rho}{10}$$

$$\therefore \quad g_{eff} = \left(\frac{\rho - \rho/10}{\rho}\right) g = \frac{9}{10} g$$

Thus, $T' = 2\pi\sqrt{\frac{l}{g_{eff}}} = 2\pi\sqrt{\frac{l}{\frac{9}{10}g}}$

$$\frac{T'}{T} = \sqrt{\frac{10}{9}}$$

$$T' = \sqrt{\frac{10}{9}}\, T$$

So, the value of x is 10.

7 (0.7) As we know, the frequency of a spring is given by

$$\nu = \frac{1}{2\pi}\sqrt{\frac{k}{m}}$$

$$\Rightarrow \quad 1 = \frac{1}{2\pi}\sqrt{\frac{k}{1}} \qquad (\because \nu = 1, m = 1)$$

$$\Rightarrow \quad k = 4\pi^2 \text{ Nm}^{-1}$$

Now, when the 4 kg block is attached to 2 parallel springs, then

$$k_{eq} = k + k = 2k$$

$$\text{Frequency, } \nu' = \frac{1}{2\pi}\sqrt{\frac{k_{eq}}{m'}}$$

$$= \frac{1}{2\pi}\sqrt{\frac{2k}{4}}$$

$$= \frac{1}{2\pi}\sqrt{\frac{2 \times 4\pi^2}{4}} \qquad (\because k = 4\pi^2)$$

$$\nu' = 0.7 \text{ Hz}$$

8 (6) $\therefore$ Frequency is given by

$$f = \frac{1}{2\pi}\sqrt{\frac{k}{m}}$$

$$\frac{25}{\pi} = \frac{1}{2\pi}\sqrt{\frac{k}{0.2}}$$

$$\Rightarrow \quad k = 500 \text{ Nm}^{-1}$$

Total energy of the system is given by

$$T = \frac{1}{2}kA^2$$

$$\text{KE} + \text{PE} = \frac{1}{2}kA^2$$

$$0.5 + 0.4 = \frac{1}{2} \times 500 \times A^2$$

$$\Rightarrow \quad A^2 = \frac{2 \times 0.9}{500}$$

$$\Rightarrow \quad A = 0.06 \text{ m}$$

$$\Rightarrow \quad A = 6 \text{ cm}$$

9 (2) Given, $m_p = 2M_e$,

$$R_p = 2R_e$$

$$\text{Hence, } g_p = \frac{GM_p}{(R_p)^2} = \frac{2GM_e}{4R_e^2} = \frac{g_e}{2}$$

Time period of pendulum on this planet,

$$T_p = 2\pi\sqrt{\frac{l}{g_p}} = 2\pi\sqrt{\frac{2l}{g_e}} = \sqrt{2} \times T_e$$

$$= \sqrt{2} \times 2 = 2\sqrt{2} \text{ s} = x\sqrt{2} \quad \text{(given)}$$

$$\therefore x = 2$$

NCERT Exemplar Questions

1 (*b*) Given, $y = 3\cos\left(\frac{\pi}{4} - 2\omega t\right)$

Velocity of the particle,

$$v = \frac{dy}{dt}$$

$$= 6\,\omega \sin\left(\frac{\pi}{4} - 2\omega t\right)$$

Acceleration,

$$a = \frac{dv}{dt} = 12\omega^2 \cos\left(\frac{\pi}{4} - 2\omega t\right)$$

$$\Rightarrow \quad a = -4\,\omega^2 y$$

$\Rightarrow$ As acceleration, $a \propto -y$

Hence, motion is SHM.

Clearly, from the equation,

$$\omega' = 2\omega$$

$$\Rightarrow \quad \frac{2\pi}{T'} = 2\omega$$

$$\Rightarrow \quad T' = \frac{2\pi}{2\omega} = \frac{\pi}{\omega}$$

So, motion is SHM with period $\frac{\pi}{\omega}$.

2 (*b*) Given equation of motion is

$$y = \sin^3 \omega t$$

$$= (3\sin \omega t - \sin 3\omega t)/4$$

$$(\because \sin 3\theta = 3\sin\theta - 4\sin^3\theta)$$

$$\Rightarrow \quad \frac{dy}{dt} = \left[\frac{d}{dt}(3\sin \omega t) - \frac{d}{dt}(\sin 3\,\omega t)\right] / 4$$

$$\Rightarrow \quad 4\frac{dy}{dt}$$

$$= 3\,\omega\cos \omega t - [3\,\omega\cos 3\,\omega t]$$

$$\Rightarrow \quad 4 \times \frac{d^2y}{dt^2} = -3\,\omega^2 \sin \omega t + 9\,\omega^2 \sin 3\,\omega t$$

$$\Rightarrow \quad \frac{d^2y}{dt^2} = \frac{9\omega^2 \sin 3\omega t - 3\omega^2 \sin \omega t}{4}$$

$\Rightarrow \dfrac{d^2y}{dt^2}$ is not proportional to y.

Hence, motion is not SHM.

As the expression is involving sine function, hence it will be periodic.

3 (d) For a particle executing SHM,

acceleration $a \propto -$ displacement x

which is correctly given in option (d) only.

4 (d) According to the question,

$$y = a \sin \omega t + b \cos \omega t \quad \text{...(i)}$$

Let $a = A \sin \phi$ and $b = A \cos \phi$

Now, $a^2 + b^2 = A^2 \sin^2 \phi + A^2 \cos^2 \phi = A^2$

$$\Rightarrow \quad A = \sqrt{a^2 + b^2}$$

Now, substituting the values of a, b and A in Eq. (i), we get

$$\Rightarrow \quad y = A \sin \phi \cdot \sin \omega t + A \cos \phi \cdot \cos \omega t$$

$$= A \sin (\omega t + \phi)$$

$$\Rightarrow \frac{dy}{dt} = A\omega \cos (\omega t + \phi)$$

$$\Rightarrow \frac{d^2y}{dt^2} = -A\omega^2 \sin (\omega t + \phi)$$

$$= -Ay\omega^2 = (-A\omega^2)y$$

$$\Rightarrow \frac{d^2y}{dt^2} \propto -y$$

Hence, it is an equation of SHM with amplitude, $A = \sqrt{a^2 + b^2}$.

5 (b)

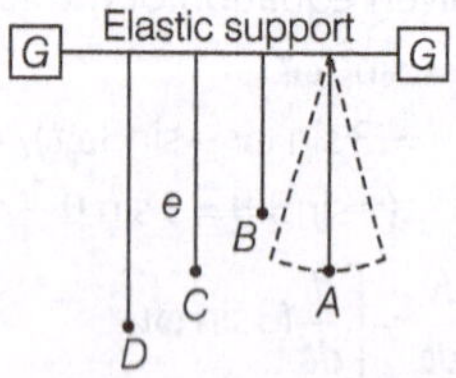

A and C are having same length, hence they will be in resonance, it is because their time period of oscillation,

$T = 2\pi \sqrt{\dfrac{l}{g}}$ will be same and hence frequency will be same.

So, C will vibrate with maximum amplitude.

6 (a) Let angular velocity of the particle executing circular motion is ω and when it is at Q, it makes an angle θ as shown in the diagram.

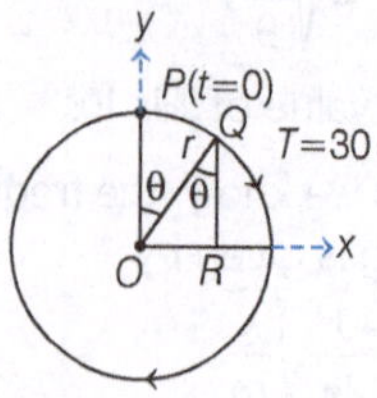

Clearly, $\theta = \omega t$

Now, we can write

$$OR = OQ \cos (90° - \theta)$$

$$= OQ \sin \theta = OQ \sin \omega t$$

$$= r \sin \omega t \quad (\because OQ = r)$$

$$\Rightarrow \quad x = r \sin \omega t = B \sin \omega t \quad (\because r = B)$$

$$= B \sin \frac{2\pi}{T} t = B \sin \left(\frac{2\pi}{30} t \right)$$

Clearly, this equation represents SHM.

7 (c) As $x = a \cos (\alpha t)^2$

is a cosine function, hence it is an oscillatory motion.

Now, putting $t + T$ in place of t,

$$x(t + T) = a \cos [\alpha (t + T)]^2$$

$$= a \cos (\alpha t^2 + \alpha T^2 + 2\alpha t T)$$

$$\neq x(t)$$

where, T is supposed to be the period of the given function.

Hence, it is not periodic.

8 (a) Let equation of the particle executing SHM is represented by

$$y = A \sin \omega t$$

Particle's speed,

$$v = \frac{dy}{dt} = A \omega \cos \omega t$$

$\Rightarrow$ Maximum speed,

$$(v)_{max} = A\omega = 30 \text{ cms}^{-1} \quad \text{(given) ...(i)}$$

Particle's acceleration,

$$a = \frac{dx^2}{dt^2} = -A\omega^2 \sin \omega t$$

Maximum acceleration,

$$|a_{max}| = \omega^2 A$$

$$= 60 \text{ cms}^{-2} \quad \text{(given) ...(ii)}$$

From Eqs. (i) and (ii), we get

$$\omega(\omega A) = 60$$

$$\Rightarrow \quad \omega(30) = 60$$

$$\Rightarrow \quad \omega = 2 \text{ rads}^{-1}$$

$$\Rightarrow \quad \frac{2\pi}{T} = 2 \text{ rads}^{-1}$$

$$\Rightarrow \quad T = \pi \text{ s}$$

9 (b)

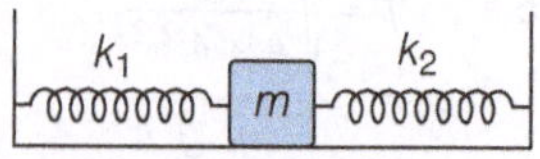

Equivalent spring constant $= k_{eq} = k_1 + k_2$.

Time period of oscillation of the spring-block system,

$$T = 2\pi \sqrt{\frac{m}{k_{eq}}}$$

$$= 2\pi \sqrt{\frac{m}{k_1 + k_2}}$$

$$\Rightarrow \quad \nu = \frac{1}{T} = \frac{1}{2\pi} \times \sqrt{\frac{k_1 + k_2}{m}} \quad \text{...(i)}$$

= equivalent oscillation frequency.

Initially when the mass is connected to the two springs individually as shown below, then

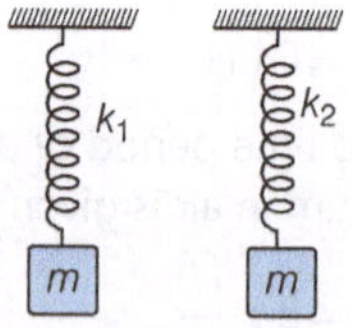

$$\nu_1 = \frac{1}{2\pi} \sqrt{\frac{k_1}{m}} \quad \text{...(ii)}$$

and $$\nu_2 = \frac{1}{2\pi} \sqrt{\frac{k_2}{m}} \quad \text{...(iii)}$$

From Eq. (i), we get

$$\nu = \frac{1}{2\pi} \left[\frac{k_1}{m} + \frac{k_2}{m} \right]^{1/2}$$

$$= \frac{1}{2\pi} \left[\frac{4\pi^2 \nu_1^2}{1} + \frac{4\pi^2 \nu_2^2}{1} \right]^{1/2}$$

$$\left[\begin{array}{l} \because \text{from Eq. (ii)}, \dfrac{k_1}{m} = 4\pi^2 \nu_1^2 \\ \text{and from Eq. (iii)}, \dfrac{k_2}{m} = 4\pi^2 \nu_2^2 \end{array} \right]$$

$$= \frac{2\pi}{2\pi} [\nu_1^2 + \nu_2^2]^{1/2}$$

$$\Rightarrow \quad \nu = \sqrt{\nu_1^2 + \nu_2^2}$$

Past Exams Questions

1 (*b*) Given, $x = 5\sin\left(\pi t + \frac{\pi}{3}\right)$ m ...(i)

The standard equation for SHM is

$x = A\sin(\omega t + \phi)$ ...(ii)

Thus, comparing Eqs. (i) and (ii), we get

$A = 5$ m and $\omega = \pi$

$\Rightarrow \frac{2\pi}{T} = \pi \Rightarrow T = 2$ s

Hence, option (b) is correct.

2 (*b*) Time period of a bob is given by,

$$T = 2\pi\sqrt{\frac{l}{g}}$$

According to question, $T' = 2\pi\sqrt{\frac{l}{2g}}$

$$= \frac{2\pi\sqrt{l}}{\sqrt{2g}}$$

Thus, $\frac{T'}{T} = \frac{T}{\sqrt{2}} = \frac{x}{2}T$

Hence, $x = \sqrt{2}$

4 (*d*) Let T_1 and T_2 be the time periods of longer and shorter pendulum, respectively.

Since, $T = 2\pi\sqrt{l/g}$

$$\Rightarrow \frac{T_1}{T_2} = \sqrt{\frac{l_1}{l_2}} = \sqrt{\frac{1.21}{1}}$$

$$= 1.1 = \frac{11}{10}$$

$\Rightarrow 10\,T_1 = 11\,T_2$

$\therefore$ 10 vibrations of longer pendulum = 11 vibrations of shorter pendulum

$\therefore$ Minimum number of vibrations of shorter pendulum = 11

5 (*b*) Frequency of kinetic energy and potential energy is 2 for one complete oscillation.

So, the frequency of the potential energy of a body executing SHM with frequency n is $2n$.

6 (*d*) In SHM, equation of displacement of a particle is

$y = a\sin\omega t$ and equation of acceleration of a particle is

$$A = a\omega^2\sin\omega t = a\omega^2\sin(\omega t + \pi)$$

$\therefore$ Phase difference between displacement and acceleration of a particle is

$= (\omega t + \pi) - \omega t = \pi$ rad

7 (*c*) The average velocity of a particle executing simple harmonic motion (SHM) is

$$v_{av} = \frac{\text{Total displacement}}{\text{Time interval}}$$

$$= \frac{x_f - x_i}{T}$$

$\because$ Displacement,

$x_f - x_i = 0$

$\therefore \quad v_{av} = \frac{0}{T} = 0$

8 (*b*) The acceleration of particle executing SHM at any instant (at position x) is given as

$a = -\omega^2 x$

$\Rightarrow |a| = \omega^2 x$ ...(i)

Here, $x = 5$ m, $|a| = 20$ ms^{-2}

On substituting the given values in Eq. (i), we get

$20 = \omega^2 \times 5$

$\Rightarrow \omega^2 = \frac{20}{5} = 4$

or $\omega = 2$ rad s^{-1}

As, we know that

Time period, $T = \frac{2\pi}{\omega}$ ...(ii)

On substituting the value of ω in Eq. (ii), we get

$$T = \frac{2\pi}{2} = \pi \text{ s}$$

9 (*c*) Given, when $x = 2$ cm

$|\mathbf{v}| = |\mathbf{a}|$

$\Rightarrow \omega\sqrt{A^2 - x^2} = \omega^2 x$

$$\Rightarrow \omega = \frac{\sqrt{A^2 - x^2}}{x} = \frac{\sqrt{9-4}}{2}$$

$\Rightarrow$ Angular velocity,

$$\omega = \frac{\sqrt{5}}{2}$$

$\therefore$ Time period of motion,

$$T = \frac{2\pi}{\omega} = \frac{4\pi}{\sqrt{5}} \text{ s}$$

10 (*d*) As we know that

Time period, $T = 2\pi\sqrt{\frac{m}{k}}$

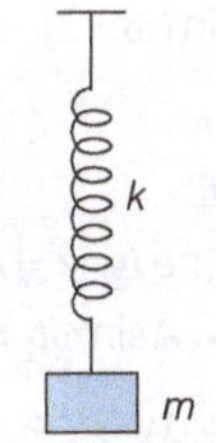

Case I $T_1 = 2\pi\sqrt{\frac{m}{k}}$ ...(i)

Case II When the mass m is increased by 1 kg, then

$T_2 = 2\pi\sqrt{\frac{m+1}{k}}$ ...(ii)

From Eqs. (i) and (ii), we get

$$\frac{T_2}{T_1} = \sqrt{\frac{m+1}{m}}$$

$\therefore \quad m = \frac{9}{16}$ kg

11 (*d*) The time period of simple pendulum is given by

$$T = 2\pi\sqrt{\frac{l}{g}}$$

and acceleration due to gravity is given by

$$g = \frac{GM}{r^2}$$

$T = 2\pi\sqrt{\frac{lr^2}{GM}}$ or $T \propto r$ ...(i)

Now, for height R above,

$T_1 \propto (R + R)$ ...(ii)

For height $2R$ above

$T_2 \propto (R + 2R)$ ...(iii)

From Eqs. (ii) and (iii),

$$\frac{T_1}{T_2} = \frac{R+R}{R+2R} = \frac{2}{3}$$

$\Rightarrow 3T_1 = 2T_2$

12 (*c*) Let equation of particle executing simple harmonic motion be

$$y = A \sin \omega t$$

At time t_1, $y = A/2$

$$\therefore \quad \frac{A}{2} = A \sin \omega t_1$$

$$\Rightarrow \quad \frac{1}{2} = \sin \omega t_1$$

$$\Rightarrow \quad \frac{1}{2} = \sin(\omega \times 2) \quad (\because t_1 = 2\text{ s})$$

$$\Rightarrow \quad \omega = \frac{\pi}{12} \quad \text{...(i)}$$

Again, at time t_2, $y = A$

$$\therefore \quad A = A \sin \omega t_2 \Rightarrow 1 = \sin \omega t_2$$

$$\sin \frac{\pi}{2} = \sin \omega t_2 \Rightarrow t_2 = \frac{\pi}{2\omega}$$

$\therefore$ Time taken by particle in going from $\frac{A}{2}$ to A

$$t = t_2 - t_1 = \frac{\pi}{2\omega} - 2$$

$$= \frac{\pi}{2(\pi/12)} - 2 \quad \text{[From Eq. (i)]}$$

$$= 4\text{ s}$$

13 (*a*) The situation given in the question can be depicted as shown below

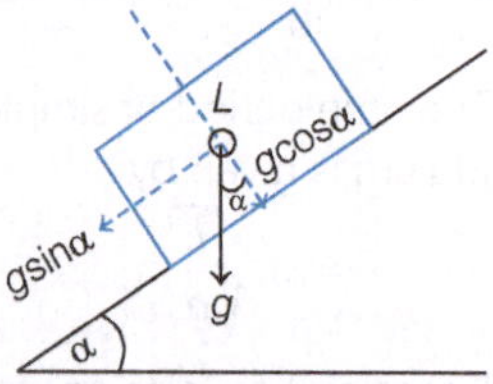

$$\therefore g_{\text{effective}} = g \cos \alpha$$

$$\therefore \quad T = 2\pi \sqrt{\frac{L}{g_{\text{effective}}}}$$

$$= 2\pi \sqrt{\frac{L}{g \cos \alpha}}$$

Skill Boosters

1 (*a*)

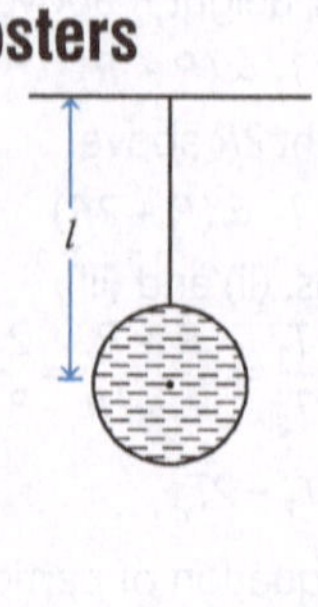

Spherical hollow ball filled with water,

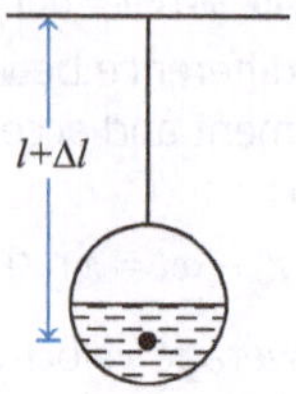

Spherical hollow ball half filled with water,

$$T_1 = 2\pi \sqrt{\frac{l + \Delta l}{g}}$$

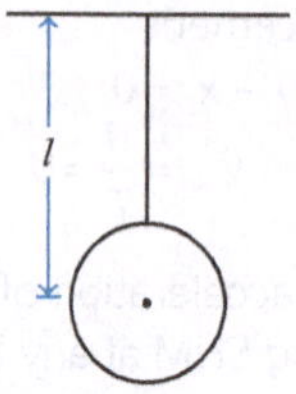

Spherical hollow ball,

$$T_2 = 2\pi \sqrt{\frac{l}{g}}$$

and $T_1 > T_2$

Hence, time period first increases and then decreases to the original value.

2 (*a*) Given condition can be seen in the figure given below

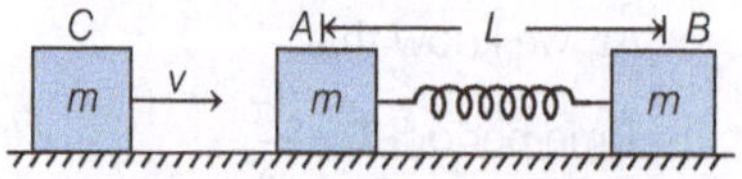

If collisions is elastic, C will stop and A will start moving with speed v towards B.

At maximum compression (say x), both A and B will move with same speed $v/2$.

$\therefore$ At maximum compression, applying the conservation of energy, we get

$$\frac{1}{2}mv^2 = \frac{1}{2}(2m)\left(\frac{v}{2}\right)^2 + \frac{1}{2}kx^2$$

$$\Rightarrow \quad x = v\sqrt{\frac{m}{2k}}$$

3 (*c*) Let l be the length through which mass m moves down before it comes to rest. In this case, the spring and string both will be stretched by length. Since, string is inextensible. So, spring is stretched by length $2l$.

The tension along the string and spring is same. In equilibrium,

$$mg = 2(k \times 2l)$$

It the block is pulled down through small distance x, then

$$F = mg - 2k(2l + 2x) = -4kx$$

As, $F \propto x$ and negative sign shows that is directed towards mean position. Hence, it executes SHM.

For SHM,

$$F = -k_{\text{eq}} x \quad \text{...(ii)}$$

From Eqs. (i) and (ii), we get

$$k_{\text{eq}} = 4k$$

$\therefore$ Time period,

$$T = 2\pi \sqrt{\frac{m}{4k}}$$

4 (*c*) A snapshot during oscillations of the cylinder is shown in the figure. Its displacement is x and velocity v. Its angular velocity is $\omega = \frac{v}{R}$ (due to pure rolling).

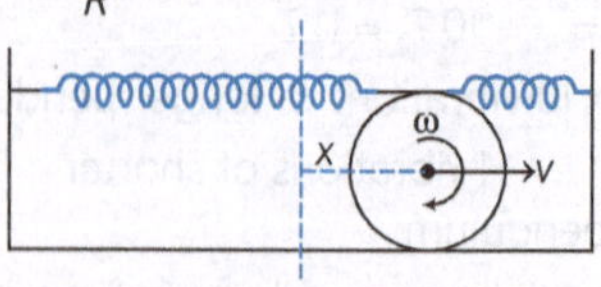

As the centre of the cylinder is at a distance x from the initial position, the springs which are connected at a point on its rim must be compressed and stretched by a distance $2x$. Thus, at this intermediate position, total energy of the oscillating system can be given as

$$E_T = \frac{1}{2}mv^2 + \frac{1}{2}\left(\frac{mR^2}{2}\right)\omega^2 + \left[\frac{1}{2}k(2x)^2\right]2$$

$$= \frac{1}{2}mv^2 + \frac{1}{4}mv^2 + 4kx^2$$

$$= \frac{3}{4}mv^2 + 4kx^2$$

$$\frac{dE_T}{dt} = \frac{3}{4}m \cdot 2v \cdot a + 4k \cdot 2x \cdot v = 0$$

[$\because E_T$ is constant]

$$\Rightarrow \frac{3}{2}ma = -8kx$$

$$\Rightarrow \quad a = -\left(\frac{16k}{3m}\right)x$$

$$\therefore \quad \omega = \sqrt{\frac{16k}{3m}}$$

$$\Rightarrow T = \frac{2\pi}{\omega} = 2\pi\sqrt{\frac{3m}{16k}} = \frac{\pi}{2}\sqrt{\frac{3m}{k}}$$

5 (*b*) Restoring torque is

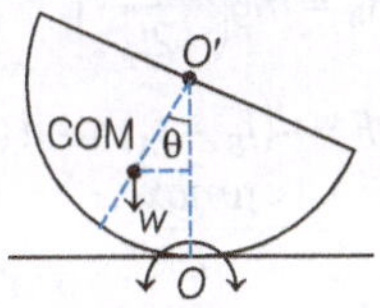

$$\tau = -w\left(\frac{4r}{3\pi}\sin\theta\right)$$

or $\tau = -\left(w\frac{4r}{3\pi}\right)\theta \quad (\because \theta \text{ is small})$

$$I\alpha = -w\frac{4r}{3\pi}\theta \qquad (\text{here, } I = I_0)$$

$$I'_0 = \frac{1}{2}mr^2, \; I'_0 = I_{COM} + m\left(\frac{4r}{3\pi}\right)^2$$

$$\because I_{COM} = \frac{1}{2}mr^2 - m\left(\frac{4r}{3\pi}\right)^2$$

$$\therefore \quad I_0 = \frac{1}{2}mr^2 - m\left(\frac{4r}{3\pi}\right)^2 + m\left(r - \frac{4r}{3\pi}\right)^2$$

$$= \frac{1}{2}mr^2 - m\left(\frac{4r}{3\pi}\right)^2 + mr^2 + m\left(\frac{4r}{3\pi}\right)^2 - 2mr \cdot \frac{4r}{3\pi}$$

$$= \frac{3}{2}mr^2 - \frac{8}{3\pi}mr^2$$

$$= \frac{9\pi - 16}{6\pi}mr^2$$

$$= 0.651\,mr^2$$

$$\therefore \alpha = -w\frac{4r}{3\pi} \cdot \frac{1}{0.65\,mr^2} \cdot \theta$$

$$= -50 \times \frac{4 \times 0.15}{3 \times 3.14} \times \frac{1}{0.65 \times 5 \times (0.15)^2}\theta$$

$$= -(43.55)\,\theta$$

$$\therefore \omega = \sqrt{43.55} = 6.6\ \text{s}^{-1}$$

$$\Rightarrow T = \frac{2 \times 3.14}{6.6} \simeq 0.96\ \text{s}$$

6. (*b*) An intermittent snap-shot of oscillating water column is shown below.

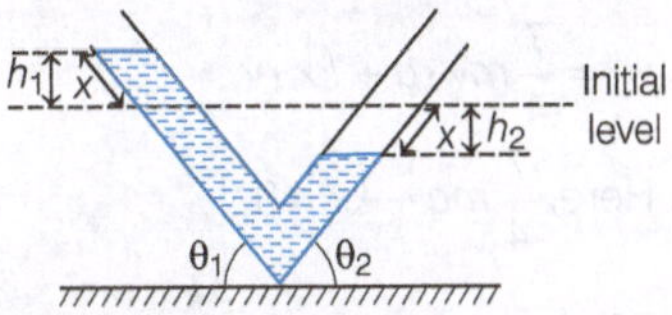

Pressure acting is

$$dp = \rho g(h_1 + h_2)$$

$$= \rho g(\sin\theta_1 + \sin\theta_2)x$$

Restoring force is

$$F = -\rho g(\sin\theta_1 + \sin\theta_2)Ax$$

Acceleration is

$$a = -\frac{\rho g(\sin\theta_1 + \sin\theta_2)}{m}Ax$$

Comparing this with $a = -\omega^2 x$, we have

$$\omega = \sqrt{\frac{\rho g(\sin\theta_1 + \sin\theta_2)A}{m}}$$

$\therefore$ Time period of oscillation of water column is

$$T = 2\pi\sqrt{\frac{m}{\rho gA(\sin\theta_1 + \sin\theta_2)}}$$

7 (*c*) In adiabatic process,

$$pV^\gamma = C$$

$$\ln p + \gamma \ln V = \ln C$$

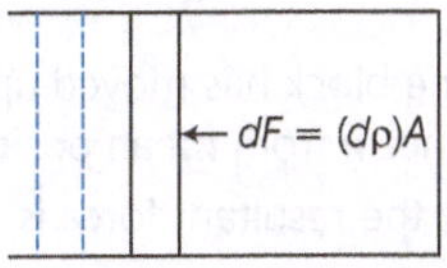

Taking differentials on both sides,

$$\frac{dp}{p} + \frac{\gamma dV}{V} = 0$$

or $$dp = \frac{-\gamma p}{V}dV$$

where, dV = change in volume of the gas = Adx.

Substituting $dp = \frac{dF}{A}$, $p = p_0$, $V = V_0$ and $dV = Adx$ in the above equation, we have

$$\left|\frac{dF}{A}\right| = \frac{\gamma p_0}{V_0}Adx$$

$$\Rightarrow \left|\frac{dF}{dx}\right| = \frac{\gamma p_0 A^2}{V_0}$$

$$\therefore \; k_{eff} = \frac{\gamma p_0 A^2}{V_0}$$

$$\therefore \quad \omega = \sqrt{\frac{k_{eff}}{m}} = \sqrt{\frac{\gamma p_0 A^2}{mV_0}}$$

8 (*b*) Density of block is $\rho_{block} = \frac{5}{2}\rho_0$.

Resultant force acting on the block at the height h from bottom is

$$F = \left[\frac{m}{\frac{5}{2}\rho_0}\right]\rho_0\left[4 - \frac{3h}{h_0}\right]g - mg$$

When the block is in equilibrium position, $F = 0$

$$\therefore \; \frac{2}{5}\left(4 - \frac{3h}{h_0}\right) = 1$$

$$\Rightarrow \quad 4 - \frac{3h}{h_0} = \frac{5}{2}$$

$$\frac{3h}{h_0} = 4 - \frac{5}{2} = \frac{3}{2}$$

$$\Rightarrow \qquad h = \frac{h_0}{2}$$

Let the block has moved up by a distance x from mean position.

Now, the resultant force is

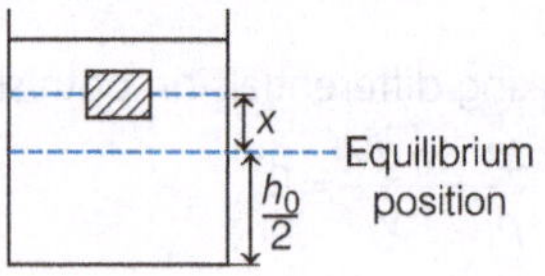

$$F_R = \left[\frac{m}{\frac{5}{2}\rho_0}\right]\rho_0\left\{4 - \frac{3\left(\frac{h_0}{2} + x\right)}{h_0}\right\}g - mg$$

$$= -\left[\frac{6\,mg}{5\,h_0}\right]x$$

Acceleration of the block is

$a = \frac{F_R}{m} = -\left(\frac{6g}{5h_0}\right)x$. So, the block performs SHM and $\omega = \sqrt{\frac{6g}{5h_0}}$

$$f = \frac{1}{2\pi}\sqrt{\frac{6g}{5h_0}}$$

9 (*b*) Let the plank is displaced by x distance, the centre of the cylinder is displaced by $\frac{x}{2}$.

Now, mechanical energy of the system is, E = KE (Plank) + PE (Spring) + KE (Cylinder)

$$= \frac{1}{2}mv^2 + \frac{1}{2}kx^2 + \frac{1}{2}I_P\omega^2 \quad \text{...(i)}$$

As $I_P = 3mR^2$, the velocity of centre of cylinder will be half of the velocity of the plank, i.e.

$$V_{\text{Cylinder}} = \frac{v}{2}$$

$$\omega R = \frac{v}{2}$$

$$\Rightarrow \quad \omega = \frac{v}{2R}$$

Substituting the value of ω in Eq. (i), we get

$$E = \frac{1}{2}mv^2 + \frac{1}{2}kx^2 + \frac{1}{2}(3mR^2)\left(\frac{v}{2R}\right)^2$$

$$= \frac{1}{2}mv^2 + \frac{1}{2}kx^2 + \frac{3}{8}mv^2$$

$$= \frac{7}{8}mv^2 + \frac{1}{2}kx^2 \quad \text{... (ii)}$$

Differentiating Eq.(ii) w.r.t. time,

$$\frac{dE}{dt} = \frac{7}{8}m\cdot 2v\left(\frac{dv}{dt}\right) + \frac{1}{2}k\cdot 2x\cdot\frac{dx}{dt}$$

$$= \frac{7}{4}mv\cdot a + kx\cdot v$$

Here, $\frac{7}{4}ma + kx = 0$

or $\qquad a = -\frac{4k}{7m}x$

Comparing with $a = -\omega^2 r$

$$\Rightarrow \quad T = 2\pi\sqrt{\frac{7m}{4k}} = \pi\sqrt{\frac{7m}{k}}$$

10 (*d*) As plank be in equilibrum along vertical as well as horizontal direction .

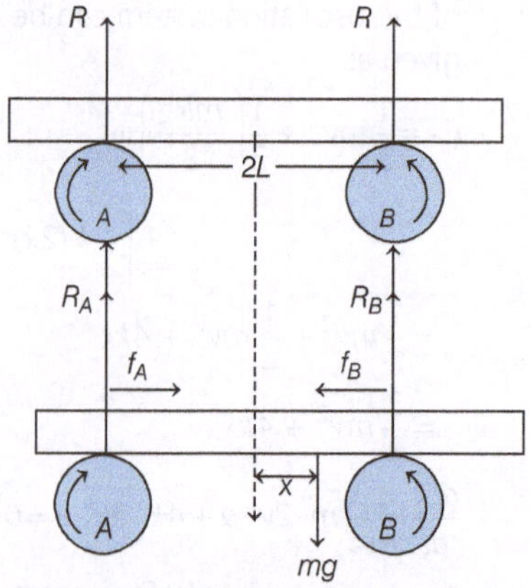

When plank is displaced by x to the right, the vertical equilibrium of the plank,

$$R_A + R_B = mg \quad \text{... (i)}$$

For rotational equilibrium ,

$$R_A(L + x) = R_B(L - x) \quad \text{... (ii)}$$

Solving Eqs. (i) and (ii), we get

$$R_A = mg\left(\frac{L - x}{2L}\right)$$

and $\quad R_B = mg\left(\frac{L + x}{2L}\right)$

Now, $F = -(f_B - f_A) = -\mu(R_B - R_A)$

$$= -\frac{\mu mgx}{L}$$

$$\therefore \quad k = \frac{\mu\, mg}{L}$$

So, $\quad T = 2\pi\sqrt{\frac{m}{k}} = 2\pi\sqrt{\frac{L}{\mu g}}$

14

Scan for **Physics Through Concept Master** Videos

Waves

Topicwise No. of Ques asked in 5 Years (NEET)

Topics	No. of Questions				
	2024	2023	2022	2021	2020
Transverse and Longitudinal Waves	–	–	–	–	–
Displacement Relation in a Progressive Wave	–	–	–	–	–
The Speed of a Travelling Wave	–	–	1	–	–
Principle of Superposition of Waves	–	–	–	–	–
Reflection of Waves	–	1	–	–	1
Beats	–	–	–	–	1

Special Type of Ques Asked In 5 Years (NEET)

Types	Years				
	2024	2023	2022	2021	2020
A-R	–	–	–	–	–
Statement Based	–	–	–	–	–
Matching	–	–	–	–	–

Last 5 Years Weigtage (NEET)

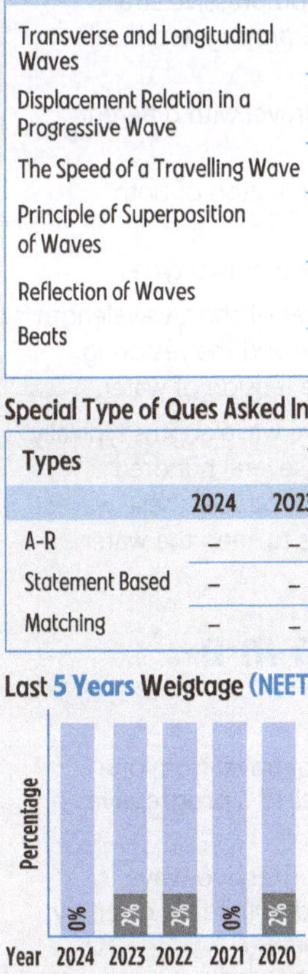

Introduction

- **Wave** is a pattern which moves through material medium by repeated vibration of the particles of the medium about their mean positions and without the actual physical transfer or flow of matter as a whole.
- Waves transport energy and the pattern of disturbance propagates from one point to another.
- When a pebble is thrown in a pond of still water, circular ripples called **waves** or **pulses** move outward on the surface of water without the movement of particles of the medium (water) from one point to another point as shown in figures (a) and (b).

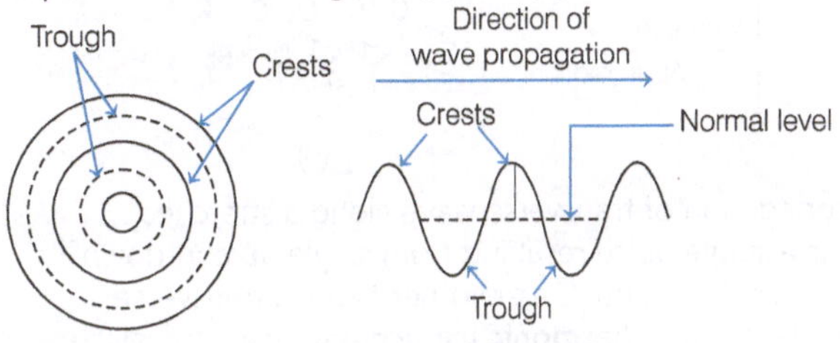

(a) Top view (b) Vertical section

- **There are mainly three types of waves**, which are as follows
  - (i) **Mechanical Waves** These waves require a medium for their propagation, i.e. they cannot propagate through vacuum, e.g. waves on string, water wave, sound wave, seismic wave, etc. These waves are governed by Newton's laws and can exist in material mediums, such as water, air, rock, etc.

    They involve oscillations of constituent particles and depend on the elastic properties of the medium.

    These waves are either of transverse or longitudinal nature.
  - (ii) **Electromagnetic Waves** These waves do not necessarily require a medium for their propagation and thus they can travel through vacuum, e.g. light, radio waves, X-rays, etc.

These waves travel in the form of oscillating electric and magnetic fields perpendicular to each other and are also called **non-mechanical waves**.

Light from the sun and distant stars reaches us through inter-stellar space, which is almost vacuum.

In vacuum, all electromagnetic waves have the same speed c, where $c = 299{,}792{,}458 \text{ ms}^{-1}$.

(iii) **Matter Waves** These waves are associated with constituents of matter namely, electrons, protons, neutrons, atoms and molecules, etc. When they are in motion, are called matter waves or **de-Broglie waves**. These waves become important in quantum mechanical description of matter.

Example Electron microscopes make use of the matter waves associated with fast moving electrons. An electron revolving around nucleus has a matter wave associated with it, as shown in figure below.

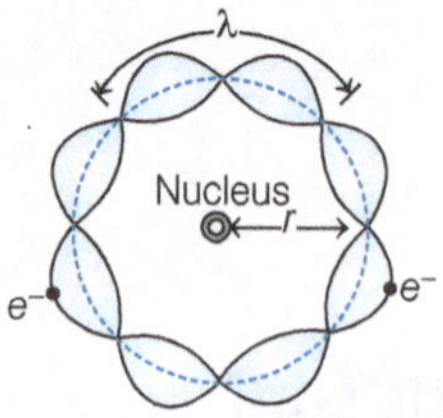

Transverse and Longitudinal Waves

- **Transverse waves** If the constituent particles of the medium oscillate perpendicular to the direction of wave propagation, then the wave is called transverse wave. These waves are propagated through a medium in the form of crests(C) and troughs(T) as shown in figure below.

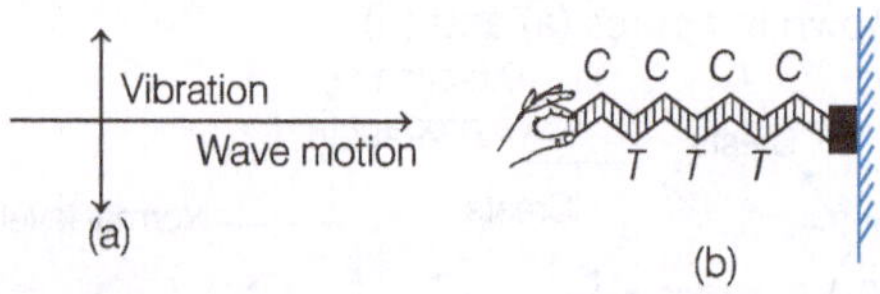

- The propagation of transverse wave along a stretched string as a single pulse resulting from single up and down jerk is shown in Fig. (a). On the other hand, a transverse wave in the form of **harmonic (sinusoidal) wave** travels along the stretched string as shown in Fig. (b), when we give a continuous periodic sinusoidal up and down jerk to one end of the string.

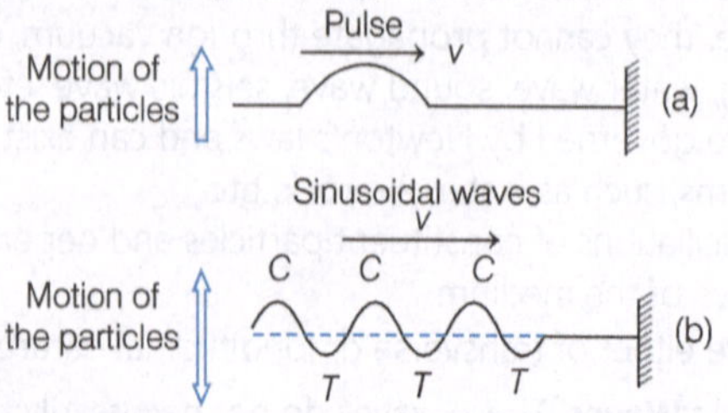

- Transverse waves can propagate only in those media, which can sustain shearing stress, such as solids not in fluids.

- **Longitudinal waves** If the constituent particles of the medium oscillate along the direction of wave propagation, the wave is called longitudinal wave. These waves are propagated in the form of **compressions (*C*)** and **rarefactions (*R*)** and the waves are also known as **pressure** or **compressional waves**.
- Pressure is force per unit area, so there is a restoring force proportional to the disturbance produced by sound waves.
- The compression or rarefaction moves from one region to another, making the propagation of a disturbance (sound waves) possible in air.

  The propagation of sound waves in air as shown in Fig. (a) and the waves on springs as shown in Fig. (b) are examples of longitudinal waves.

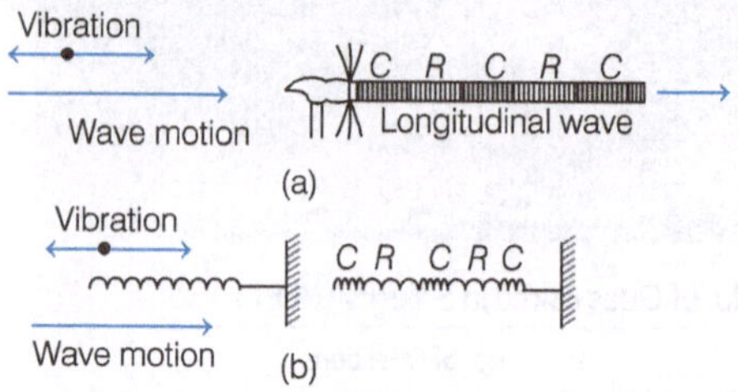

- Fluids as well as solids can sustain compressive strain, therefore longitudinal waves can be propagated in all elastic media.
- Transverse and longitudinal waves travel with different speed in the same medium.
- The waves in an ocean are the combination of both longitudinal and transverse waves.
- The waves on the surface of water are of two types
  (i) **Capillary Waves** These are ripples of short wavelength (not more than a few centimetre) and the restoring force is produced due to surface tension of water.
  (ii) **Gravity Waves** These waves have wavelengths typically ranging from few millimetres to several hundred metres. The restoring force that produces these waves is the pull of gravity, which tends to keep the water surface at its lowest level.

Displacement Relation in a Progressive Wave

- A transverse or longitudinal wave that travel from one point of the medium to another is called a **progressive wave**.
- The **displacement relation of a progressive wave** in positive x-direction at position x and at time t is given by

$$y(x,t) = a\sin(kx - \omega t + \phi_0)$$

$y(x,t)$ → Displacement; a → Amplitude; k → Angular wave number; ω → Angular frequency; ϕ_0 → Initial phase

- If **displacement equation can be considered to be a linear combination of sine and cosine function,**

$$y(x, t) = A\sin(kx - \omega t) + B\cos(kx - \omega t)$$

Then amplitude, $a = \sqrt{A^2 + B^2}$ and phase, $\phi = \tan^{-1}\left(\frac{B}{A}\right)$

- In a transverse progressive wave, the **crest** is the point of maximum positive displacement and the **trough** is the point of maximum negative displacement.

Some important definitions related to displacement of progressive wave motion are given below

- **Amplitude** The magnitude of maximum displacement of the constituent particle of the medium from their equilibrium position is called amplitude. It is denoted by a.
- **Phase** Argument of sine or cosine in equation for displacement is called phase. It is denoted by ϕ.
- **Wavelength** Minimum distance between two points having same phase or it is the distance between two consecutive crests or troughs in a wave. It is denoted by λ.
- **Angular Wave Number** Rate of change of phase per unit distance along the direction of propagation is known as angular wave number.

Angular wave number, $k = \frac{2\pi}{\lambda}$ (in rad m^{-1})

- **Period of Oscillation** The time takes for a particle to complete one full oscillation. It is given by $T = \frac{2\pi}{\omega}$
- **Frequency** Number of oscillations per second and given by $\nu = \frac{1}{T} = \frac{\omega}{2\pi}$ (in Hz)
- **Angular Frequency** The rate of change of phase with time is called angular frequency of the wave.

It is clearly equal to $\frac{2\pi}{T}$ because the phase change in T is 2π.

Its SI unit is rads^{-1}.

$$\omega = \frac{2\pi}{T} = 2\pi f$$

- A harmonic wave progressing along the positive direction of X-axis at different times is shown in figure below.

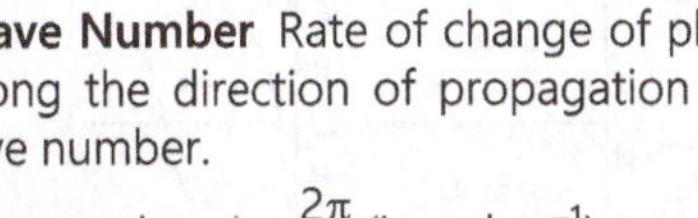

(a)

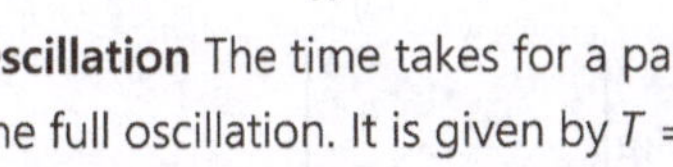

(b)

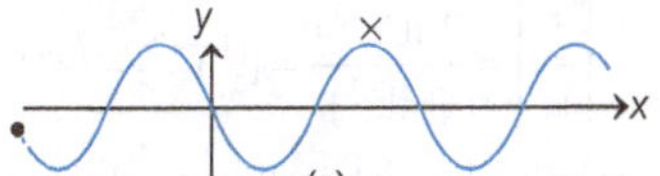

(c)

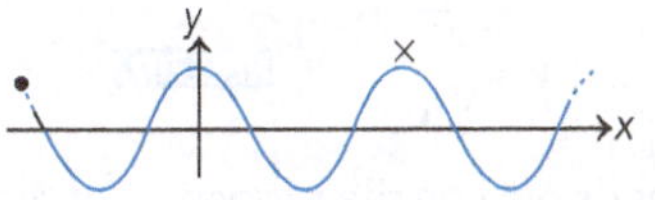

(d)

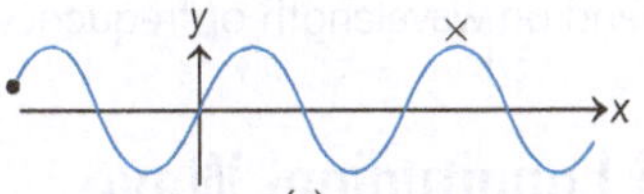

(e)

The solid dot (•) represents particle of the medium and it oscillates about its mean position as wave progresses. It can be observed that with time, the crest (×) progresses along the positive x-direction. Thus, the wave travels along the positive x-direction.

The Speed of a Travelling Wave

- A travelling or progressive wave pattern remains fixed, if all the points on the wave pattern moves with same speed, i.e. the phases of any point on it remains constant.
- Let a progression of a harmonic wave from time t to $t + \Delta t$, where Δt is a small interval. The wave pattern as a whole shifts to the right. The crest of the wave (or a point with any fixed phase) moves right by the distance Δx in time Δt.

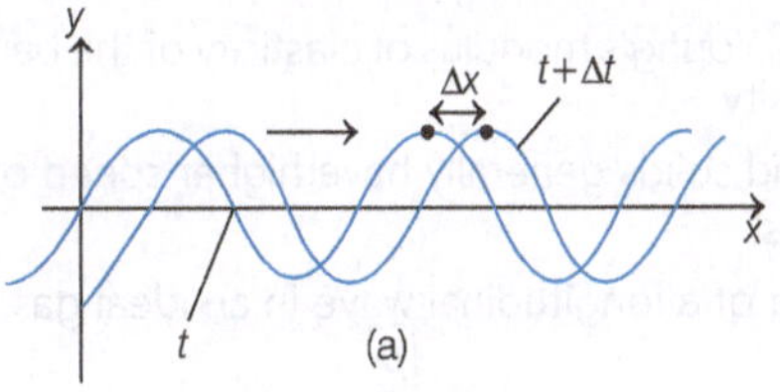

(a)

So, the speed of the wave is $\frac{\Delta x}{\Delta t}$.

- The motion of a fixed phase point on the wave is given by

$$kx - \omega t = \text{constant}$$

$$kx - \omega t = k(x + \Delta x) - \omega(t + \Delta t)$$

or $\quad k\Delta x - \omega\Delta t = 0$

Taking Δx, Δt vanishingly small, $\frac{dx}{dt} = \frac{\omega}{k} = v$

$$\Rightarrow \quad v = \frac{2\pi/T}{2\pi/\lambda} = \frac{\lambda}{T}$$

This is general relation for all progressive waves.

Speed of a Transverse Wave on Stretched String

- Velocity of wave through a medium (string) depends on its inertia (linear mass density μ, which is mass m of string divided by its length L) and elastic (restoring force) properties.

Here, the dimension of μ is $[ML^{-1}]$ and that of tension (T) is like force $[MLT^{-2}]$. We need to combine these dimensions to get speed v $[LT^{-1}]$

$$\left[\frac{T}{\mu}\right] = \frac{[MLT^{-2}]}{[ML^{-1}]} = [L^2T^{-2}] = [v^2]$$

If T and μ assumed to be only relevant physical quantities, then

$$v = \sqrt{\frac{T}{\mu}}$$ NEET 2022

Speed v depends only on the properties of the medium T (due to restoring force) and μ (due to inertial property). It does not depend on wavelength or frequency of the wave itself.

Speed of a Longitudinal Wave (Speed of Sound)

- The general formula for speed of longitudinal waves (sound) in a medium is $v = \sqrt{\frac{B}{\rho}}$
  where, B is the bulk modulus of liquid and ρ is its mass density.
- The speed of longitudinal waves (sound) in a solid bar is
  $$v = \sqrt{\frac{Y}{\rho}}$$
  where, Y is Young's modulus of elasticity of the bar and ρ is its mass density.
- Liquids and solids generally have higher speed of sound than gases.
- The speed of a longitudinal wave in an ideal gas is given by $$v = \sqrt{\frac{p}{\rho}}$$
  where, p is the pressure of the gas and ρ is its density.
  This relation is known as **Newton's formula.**
- Modified Newton's formula for speed of sound in an ideal gas for adiabatic change is $v = \sqrt{\frac{\gamma p}{\rho}}$
  where, γ is the ratio of specific heat of the gas at constant pressure to that at constant volume, i.e. $\gamma = C_p / C_V$.
  This modification of Newton's formula is known as the **Laplace correction.**
  For air, $\gamma = \frac{7}{5}$ $\therefore$ v (at STP) $= 331.3$ m/s
  which agrees with the actual speed of sound in air.

Principle of Superposition of Waves

- When two or more than two waves travel in same medium, then the resultant displacement is the algebraic sum of the displacements due to each wave. This is known as the **principle of superposition of waves.**
- If $y_1(x - vt)$, $y_2(x - vt)$, $y_3(x - vt)$, ..., $y_n(x - vt)$ the displacements due to n waves disturbances in the medium, then the resultant displacement $y(x, t)$ is given by
  $$y(x,t) = \sum_{i=1}^{n} y_i(x - vt)$$
- It is basic to the phenomenon of interference.
- For two waves differing only in their phases, the resultant displacement is given by
  $$y\,(x,t) = a\sin(kx - \omega t) + a\sin(kx - \omega t + \phi)$$
  $$= 2a\cos\frac{\phi}{2}\sin\left(kx - \omega t + \frac{\phi}{2}\right)$$
  Here, amplitude, $A(\phi) = 2\,a\cos\frac{\phi}{2}$
- According to principle of superposition, the resultant of two harmonic wave of equal amplitude and wavelength are shown in figures(a) and (b).

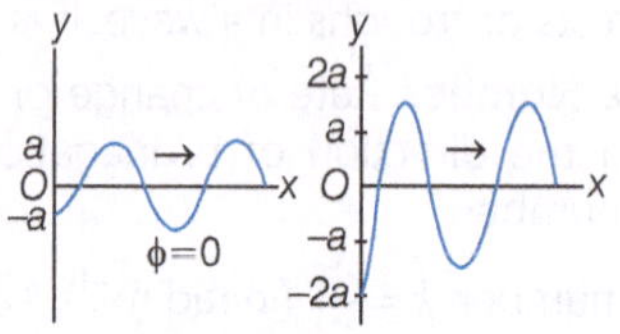

(a)

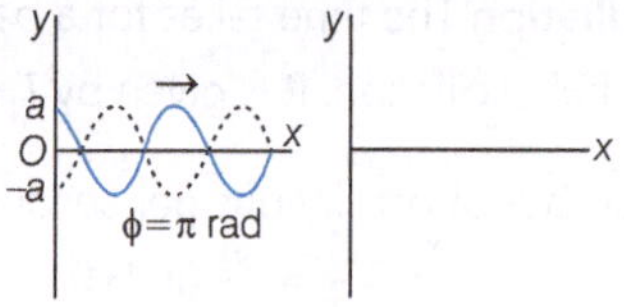

(b)

- The resultant wave has amplitude $2a$ for the phase difference, $\phi = 0$ i.e. the waves are in same phase as shown in Fig (a).
- On the other hand, the resultant wave has zero displacement everywhere at all times for the phase difference, $\phi = \pi$ i.e, the waves are completely out of phase as shown in Fig. (b).

Reflection of Waves

- When a progressive wave travelling through a medium reaches a rigid boundary, it gets reflected and the phenomena is called reflection of waves.

Reflection from a Fixed End

- If the reflecting end is a fixed or rigid boundary, then the reflected wave has the same shape as the incident pulse, but it suffers a phase change of π or 180° on reflection.
- If equation of incident travelling wave is
  $$y_i(x,t) = a\sin(kx - \omega t)$$

At a rigid boundary, the reflected wave is given by

$$y_r(x, t) = a\sin(kx - \omega t + \pi) = -a\sin(kx - \omega t)$$

- By principle of superposition, if the incident and reflected waves differ by phase of π superpose, then the resultant displacement is zero.
- The reflection of a pulse at a rigid boundary is shown in figure below.

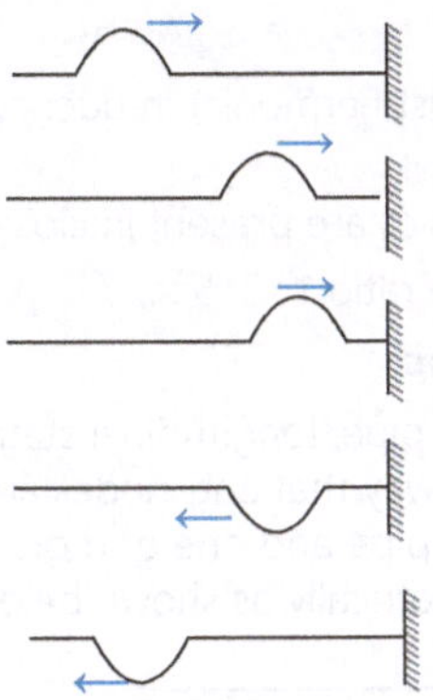

Reflection from a Free End

- If the reflecting end is not rigid but completely free to move (such as in case of string tied to a freely moving ring on a rod), then the reflected pulse has same phase and amplitude as that of incident pulse.
- In this case, the equations of incident wave y_i and reflected wave y_r are given by

$$y_i = A\sin(\omega t - kx), \quad y_r = A\sin(\omega t - kx + \pi)$$

The net maximum resultant displacement at the boundary is the twice of the amplitude of each pulse.

The reflection of a pulse at a free end is shown in figure below

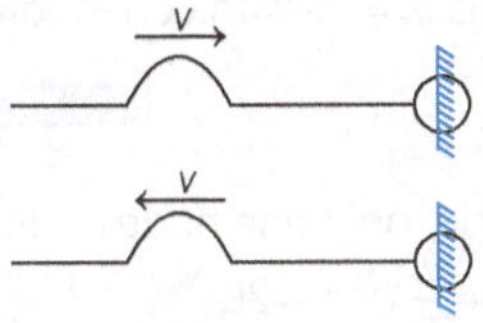

- If the boundary is not completely rigid or is an interface between two different elastic media, then a part of the incident wave is reflected and a part is transmitted into second media as shown in figure.

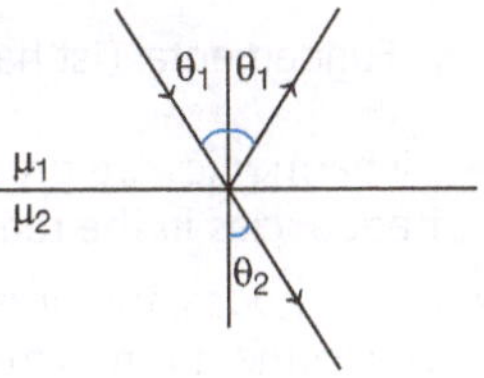

Stationary Waves and Normal Modes

- A **stationary wave** can be formed by the superposition of two travelling waves moving in opposite directions having same amplitude, frequency, wavelength and speed.
- Consider two waves moving are in opposite directions having same amplitude, frequency, wavelength and speed.

$$y_1(x,t) = a\sin(\omega t - kx)$$
$$y_2(x,t) = a\sin(\omega t + kx)$$

Principle of superposition gives the resultant displacement

$$y(x,t) = y_1(x,t) + y_2(x,t)$$
$$= a\sin(kx - \omega t) + a\sin(kx + \omega t)$$
$$y(x, t) = 2a\sin kx\cos\omega t$$

where, amplitude $= 2a\sin kx$.

These waves have following characteristics

(i) The amplitude varies from point to point, but each element of the string oscillates with the same angular frequency ω or time period.

(ii) There is no phase difference between oscillations of different elements of the wave.

(iii) The wave pattern is neither moving to the right nor to the left. Hence, they are called standing or stationary waves.

- In stationary waves, the system cannot oscillate with any arbitrary frequency, but is characterised by a set of natural frequencies or **normal modes** of oscillation.
- The points at which the amplitude is zero (i.e. where there is no motion at all) are **nodes** and the points at which the amplitude is largest are called **anti-nodes**.
- **Position of nodes** is given by

$$x = \frac{n\lambda}{2}; \qquad \text{where } n = 0, 1, 2, 3, \ldots$$

- **Position of anti-nodes** is given by

$$x = \left(n + \frac{1}{2}\right)\frac{\lambda}{2}; \qquad \text{where } n = 0, 1, 2, \ldots.$$

- The distance between any two successive nodes and two successive anti-nodes is $\lambda / 2$.

Stationary Waves in a String Fixed at both Ends

- In a stretched string of length L fixed at both ends, stationary waves are formed such a way that node is formed at rigid end and anti-node is formed in between them.
- Length L of string is related to λ as

$$L = \frac{n\lambda}{2}; \qquad \text{where } n = 1, 2, 3, \ldots .$$

Possible wavelengths, $\lambda = \frac{2L}{n}$ with corresponding

frequencies, $\nu = \frac{nv}{2L}$; where $n = 1, 2, 3, \ldots\ldots .$

- The lowest possible natural frequency of a system is called its **fundamental mode** or the **first harmonic**.

∴ For a stretched string fixed at either end, frequency is given by

$$\nu = \frac{v}{2L} \qquad \text{(for } n = 1\text{)}$$

- The first six harmonics of a stretched string fixed at both ends are shown in figure below.

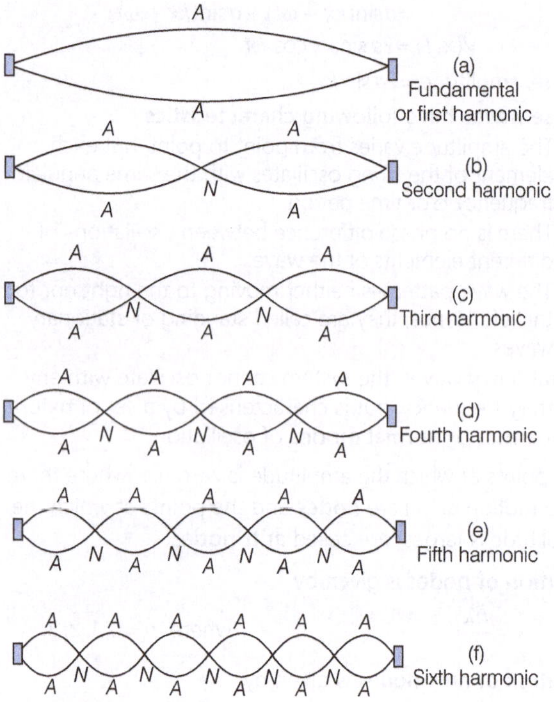

Closed Organ Pipe

- In a closed organ pipe, longitudinal stationary waves are formed in such a way that open end of pipe behaves as an anti-node and a node is formed at the closed end of pipe as shown below.

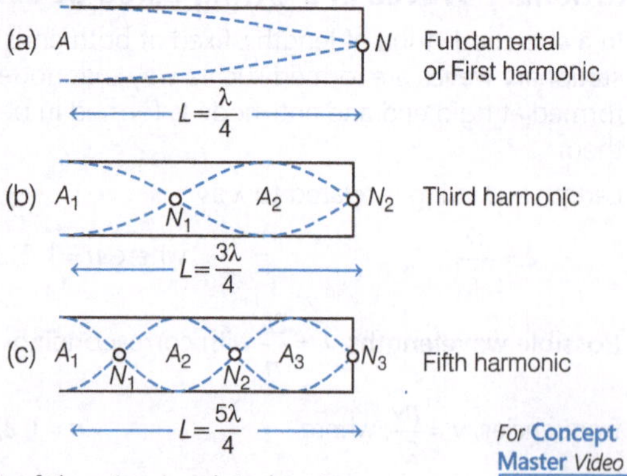

For Concept Master Video

- Length L of the pipe is related to λ as

$$L = \left(n + \frac{1}{2}\right)\frac{\lambda}{2}; \quad \text{for } n = 0, 1, 2, 3, \ldots\ldots$$

The possible wavelengths are then restricted by the relation

$$\lambda = \frac{2L}{(n + 1/2)},$$

$$\nu = \left(n + \frac{1}{2}\right)\frac{v}{2L}$$ NEET 2023

- For fundamental mode ($n = 0$), $L = \frac{\lambda}{4}$

or $$\lambda = 4L$$

∴ Fundamental (1st harmonic) frequency, $\nu = \frac{v}{\lambda} = \frac{v}{4L}$

- Only odd harmonics are present in closed pipe with their frequencies in the ratio 1 : 3: 5 : ... .

Open Organ Pipe

- In an open organ pipe, longitudinal stationary waves are formed in such a way that anti-nodes are formed at both the open ends of pipe and one or more nodes are formed in between symmetrically as shown below.

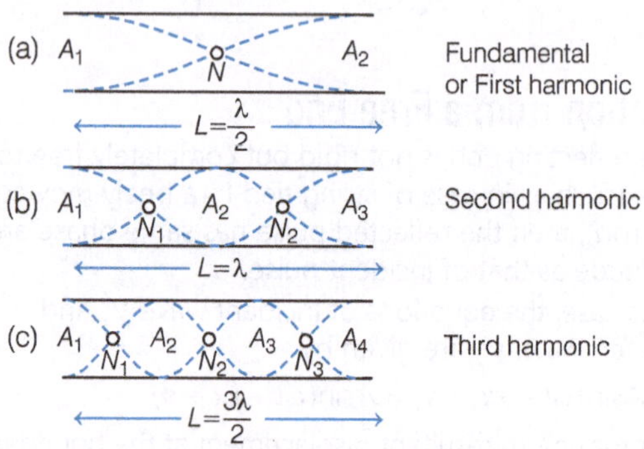

Length of the pipe is $L = \frac{n\lambda}{2}$, where $n = 1, 2, 3, \ldots$.

Possible wavelengths, $\lambda = \frac{2L}{n}$ with corresponding

frequencies, $\nu = \frac{nv}{2L}$. NEET 2023

- In fundamental mode, only one nodes is formed at the centre of pipe, so $L = \frac{\lambda}{2}$ or $\lambda = 2L$.

∴ Fundamental (1st harmonic) frequency, $\nu = \frac{v}{\lambda} = \frac{v}{2L}$.

- All harmonics are present in open pipe with their frequencies in the ratio 1 : 2 : 3 : 4 ... .
- At the nodes, the pressure changes are largest, while the diplacement is minimum (zero).
- At the anti-nodes (open end), pressure change is least and the displacement is maximum.
- If the external frequency is close to one of the natural frequencies, the system shows **resonance**.

Marks Maximiser

- In organ pipe, the anti-node is not formed exactly at the open end. The reflection takes place little above the open end. If length of organ pipe is L and end-correction is e, then length of air column in open pipe will be $(L + 2e)$ and in closed pipe, $(L + e)$.

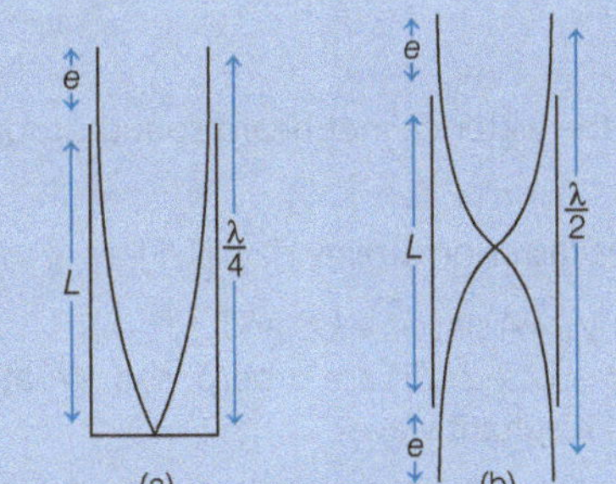

(a) For closed organ pipe (b) For open organ pipe

For Concept Master Video

- For open organ pipe, $f = \dfrac{nv}{2(L + 2e)}$, where $n = 1, 2, 3 \ldots\ldots$
- For closed organ pipe,

$$f = (2n + 1)\frac{v}{4(L + e)}, \text{ where } n = 0, 1, 2, 3 \ldots.$$

Beats

- The variation in intensity of sound with time at a particular position due to principle of superposition of two sound waves of slightly different frequencies is called **beats**.
- Let consider two harmonic waves of nearly equal frequency

$$y_1 = a \sin \omega_1 t = a \sin 2\pi\nu_1 t$$

and $$y_2 = a \sin \omega_2 t = a \sin 2\pi\nu_2 t$$

$\therefore$ $$y = 2a \cos \pi(\nu_1 - \nu_2)t \cdot \sin \pi(\nu_1 + \nu_2)t$$

- **Beat Frequency** Number of beats formed per second are expressed as $|\nu_1 - \nu_2|$, i.e. either $(\nu_1 - \nu_2)$ or $(\nu_2 - \nu_1)$, where ν_1 and ν_2 are frequencies of two sound waves.
- **Beat Period** It is the reciprocal of beat frequency expressed as

$$T = \frac{1}{|\nu_1 - \nu_2|}$$

- Essential condition for hearing beats is that $|\nu_1 - \nu_2|$ should not exceed 10 Hz.
- Superposition of two harmonic waves, one of frequency 11Hz in Fig. (a) and other of 9 Hz in Fig. (b), giving rise to beats of frequency 2Hz, as shown in Fig. (c)

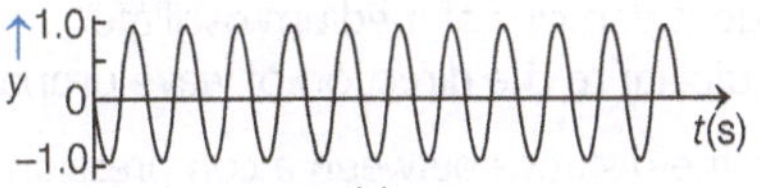

(a)

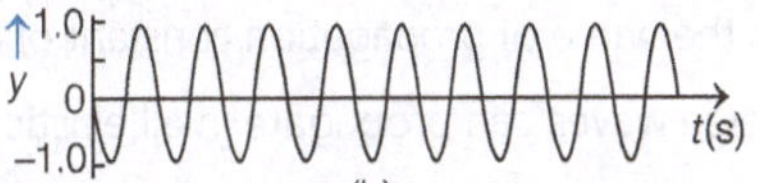

(b)

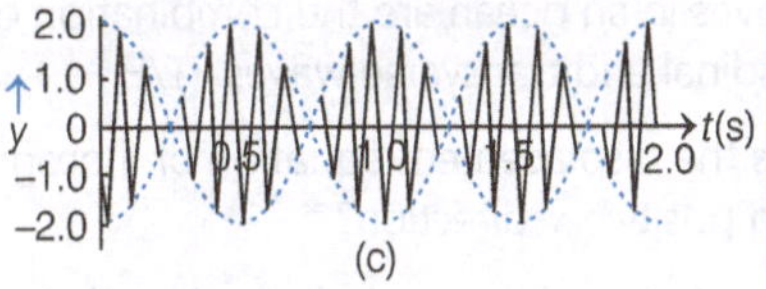

(c)

For Concept Master Video

Caution Points

- A sound wave is a series of compressions and rarefactions of air molecules. On the other hand, a wind is the bulk movement of air molecules.
- A harmonic progressive wave is a wave in which the particles of the medium oscillate with the same frequency but with different phases at an instant of time.
- In a stationary wave, all of the particles between two nodes have the same phase at a given time. However, the particles do not have the same amplitude.

PYQ Notes

1. A heavy ball of mass M is suspended from the ceiling of a car by a light string of mass $m (m <<< M)$. When car is at rest, the speed of transverse waves in the string is v. The speed of car increases to v' when the car has acceleration a, then

$$\frac{v}{v'} = \sqrt{\frac{g}{(g^2 + a^2)^{1/2}}}$$

[NEET 2019]

2. Difference between successive frequency in closed organ pipe $= \dfrac{2v}{4l}$ **[NEET 2017]**
3. A uniform string of length l is suspended from a rigid support. A short wave pulse is introduced at its lower end and t is the time taken to reach the support end, then

$$\int_0^l \frac{dx}{\sqrt{x}} = \int_0^t \sqrt{g}\, dt$$

[JEE Main 2016]

Step by Step

Mastering NCERT

- Concept Builders
- Topical Questions
- Assertion and Reason Questions
- Statement Based
- Matching Type
- Numerical Type
- NCERT Exemplar
- Past Exams MCQs
- Skill Boosters

Concept Builders

1 A wave .... (can/ can not) transfer angular momentum.

2 Name two important properties of a material medium responsible for the propagation of waves through it.

3 .... [Mechanical/Non-mechanical] waves do not necessarily require a medium for their propagation.

4 In a .... (transverse/longitudinal) wave, the constituent particles of medium oscillate perpendicular to the direction of wave propagation.

5 What is the distance between a compression and adjoining rarefaction in a longitudinal wave?

6 What is the name of propagation constant of a wave?

7 Transverse waves can propagate in all elastic media. [T/F]

8 The waves in an ocean are the combination of both longitudinal and transverse waves. [T/F]

9 What is the displacement equation of a progressive wave in positive x-direction?

10 The speed of sound wave in a medium depends on frequency of that wave. [T/F]

11 Diver inside the water cannot heard sound produced in air. [T/F]

12 Sound travels faster on a rainy day. [T/F]

13 If two waves $y_1 = A\sin(\omega t - kx)$ and $y_2 = A\sin(\omega t - kx + 2\pi/3)$ are superposed. What is the amplitude of resultant wave?

14 The modified Newton's formula for speed of sound in an ideal gas for adiabatic condition is known as ....

15 A string is vibrating in n loops. What is the number of nodes in that string?

16 What does a combination of tones of different frequencies is called ....

17 What is the relation between length of closed organ pipe and wavelength?

18 For open end organ pipe, at the anti-nodes position, pressure change is least and the displacement is maximum. [T/F]

19 The essential condition for hearing beats is that frequency beat should more than 10 Hz. [T/F]

20 Beats ...... (can/cannot) be observed by two light sources.

Topical Questions

Introduction

1 The correct possible order of interconversion of waves when our sound is transferred to the receiver *via* a mobile phone is **NCERT Pg. 279**
(a) sound waves $\rightarrow$ electric current signal $\rightarrow$ electromagnetic waves (radio waves)
(b) sound waves $\rightarrow$ electromagnetic waves $\rightarrow$ electric current signal
(c) sound waves $\rightarrow$ electric current signal $\rightarrow$ sound wave
(d) electromagnetic waves $\rightarrow$ sound waves $\rightarrow$ electric current signal

2 Which of the following waves require a medium for their propagation? **NCERT Pg. 279**
(a) Light waves (b) Radiowaves
(c) X-rays (d) Seismic waves

3 Which of the following statement is incorrect for mechanical waves? **NCERT Pg. 279**
(a) These waves require a medium for propagation, they cannot propagate through vacuum.
(b) They involve oscillations of constituent particles.
(c) They depend on the elastic properties of the medium.
(d) They have the same speed in all the media.

4 A collection of springs connected to one another is fixed at one end is as shown in figure below. If the other end *A* is pulled suddenly and released, then which of the following statement is correct? **NCERT Pg 279**

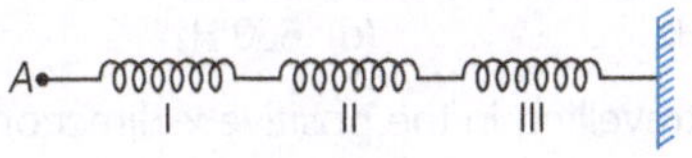

(a) The disturbance generating at end *A* will propagate to the other end but each spring will only executes small oscillations about its equilibrium position.
(b) Since, the spring II is connected to the I, it will also be stretched or compressed and so on.
(c) Springs I and III will displace from its equilibrium position while spring II will execute small oscillations about its equilibrium position.
(d) Both (a) and (b).

Transverse and Longitudinal Waves

5 The particles of the medium in a transverse wave vibrate **NCERT Pg. 280**

(a) in circular path
(b) in elliptical path
(c) in perpendicular to the direction of the propagation.
(d) in parallel to the direction of the propagation.

6. Ultrasonic waves produced by a vibrating quartz crystal are **NCERT Pg. 280**

(a) only longitudinal
(b) only transverse
(c) both longitudinal and transverse
(d) neither longitudinal nor transverse

7 The wave produced on the surface of water are of two types; capillary waves and gravity waves. Which of the following statement is incorrect about them? **NCERT Pg. 281**

(a) Capillary waves are ripples of fairly short wavelength (few centimetre).
(b) Gravity waves have wavelength typically ranging from several metre to several hundered metres.
(c) The restoring force in gravity waves is surface tension while in capillary waves is the pull of gravity.
(d) The particle motion in water waves involves both motion up & down and back & forth.

Displacement Relation in a Progressive Wave

8 The displacement of an elastic wave is given by the function $y = 3 \sin \omega t + 4 \cos \omega t$, where y is in cm and t is in second. The resultant amplitude will be **NCERT Pg. 281**

(a) 15 cm (b) 4 cm
(c) 5 cm (d) 3 cm

9 A simple wave motion is represented by $y = 5\,(\sin 4\pi t + \sqrt{3} \cos 4\pi t)$. Its amplitude is **NCERT Pg. 281**

(a) 5 (b) $5\sqrt{3}$
(c) $10\sqrt{3}$ (d) 10

10 The propagation of a harmonic wave is shown in figure below along positive *X*-axis at different times. **NCERT Pg. 282**

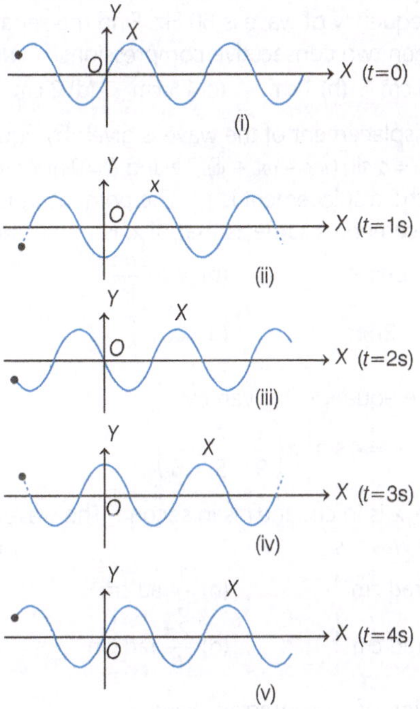

Then, the number of waves or oscillations crossed origin *O* in 4 s are

(a) 1 (b) 2
(c) 3 (d) 4

11 The displacement as a function of position x and time t is given by $y\,(x, t) = a \sin(kx - \omega t + \phi)$.
The range of possible value of $y(x, t)$, if a is a positive constant, is **NCERT Pg. 282**

(a) $-a \le y\,(x, t) \le a$
(b) $-\frac{a}{2} \le y\,(x, t) \le \frac{a}{2}$
(c) $-1 \le y\,(x, t) \le +1$
(d) $0 \le y\,(x, t) \le a$

12 The equation of a wave is given by $y = 10 \sin\left(\frac{2\pi}{45} t + \alpha\right)$.

If the displacement is 5 cm at $t = 0$, then the total phase at $t = 7.5$ s is **NCERT Pg. 282**

(a) π (b) $\pi/6$
(c) $\pi/2$ (d) $\pi/3$

13 The phase difference between the two given waves is

$$y_1 = a_1 \sin\left(\omega t - \frac{2\pi}{\lambda}x\right)$$

$$y_2 = a_2 \cos\left(\omega t - \frac{2\pi}{\lambda}x + \phi\right)$$ NCERT Pg. 282

(a) $\frac{2\pi}{\lambda}(\phi)$ (b) ϕ (c) $\frac{\pi}{2} + \phi$ (d) $\phi - \frac{\pi}{2}$

14 A longitudinal wave travels at a speed of 0.6 ms^{-1} and the frequency of wave is 60 Hz. Find the separation between two consecutive compressions. NCERT Pg. 283

(a) 0.5 cm (b) 1 cm (c) 1.5 cm (d) 2 cm

15 The displacement of the wave is given by equation $y(x,t) = a\sin(kx - \omega t + \phi)$. Taking $\phi = 0$ at point x and $t = 0$, the displacement is y'. The point at which the displacement is same as that of x, is NCERT Pg. 283

(a) $x + 2n\pi$ (b) $x + \frac{2n\pi}{k}$

(c) $kx + 2n\pi$ (d) $kx + \frac{\pi}{2}$

16 A wave equation is given by

$$y = 4\sin\left[\pi\left(\frac{x}{9} - \frac{t}{5} + \frac{1}{6}\right)\right]$$

where, x is in cm and t is in second. The wave number of the wave is NCERT Pg. 283

(a) $\frac{\pi}{9}$ rad cm^{-1} (b) $\frac{1}{6}$ rad cm^{-1}

(c) $\frac{\pi}{5}$ rad cm^{-1} (d) $\frac{2\pi}{9}$ rad cm^{-1}

17 Equation of a progressive wave is

$$y = a\sin\left(10\pi x + 11\pi t + \frac{\pi}{3}\right)$$

The wavelength of the wave is NCERT Pg. 283

(a) 0.2 unit (b) 0.1 unit

(c) 0.5 unit (d) 1 unit

18 A plane progressive wave equation is given by

$$y = 2\cos 2\pi(330t - x)$$

What is the period of the wave? NCERT Pg. 283

(a) $\frac{1}{330}$ s (b) $2\pi \times 330$ s

(c) $(2\pi \times 330)^{-2}$ s (d) $\frac{6.284}{330}$ s

19 In a sinusoidal wave, the time required for a particular point to move from maximum displacement to zero displacement is 0.14 s. The frequency of the wave is NCERT Pg. 283

(a) 0.42 Hz (b) 2.75 Hz

(c) 1.79 Hz (d) 0.56 Hz

20 The equation of a progressive wave can be given by $y = 15\cos(660\pi t - 0.02\pi x)$ cm. The frequency of the wave is NCERT Pg. 283

(a) 330 Hz (b) 342 Hz

(c) 365 Hz (d) 660 Hz

21 A wave travelling in the positive x-direction having displacement along y-direction 1 m, wavelength (2π) m and frequency of $(1/\pi)$ Hz is represented by NCERT Pg. 283

(a) $y = \sin(x - 2t)$ (b) $y = \sin(2\pi x - 2\pi t)$

(c) $y = \sin(10\pi x - 20\pi t)$ (d) $y = \sin(2\pi x + 2\pi t)$

22 Calculate the wave number of the wave. NCERT Pg. 283

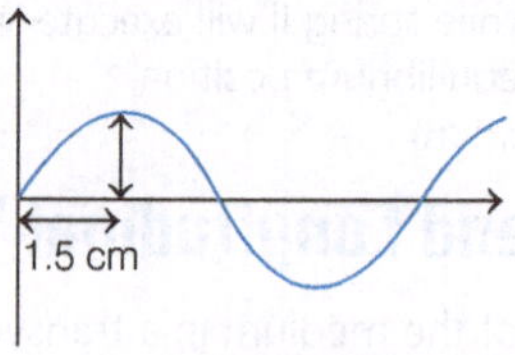

(a) 1.5 cm^{-1} (b) 0.16 cm^{-1}

(c) 3 cm^{-1} (d) 2 cm^{-1}

The Speed of a Travelling Wave

23 The displacement y of a particle in a medium can be expressed as $y = 10^{-6}\sin\left(100t + 20x + \frac{\pi}{4}\right)$ m, where t is in second and x is in metre. The speed of the wave is NCERT Pg. 284

(a) 2000 ms^{-1} (b) 5 ms^{-1}

(c) 20 ms^{-1} (d) 5π ms^{-1}

24 The equation of progressive wave is $y = 0.2\sin 2\pi\left(\frac{t}{0.01} - \frac{x}{0.3}\right)$, where x and y are in metres and t is in second. The velocity of propagation of the wave is NCERT Pg. 284

(a) 30 ms^{-1} (b) 40 ms^{-1}

(c) 300 ms^{-1} (d) 400 ms^{-1}

25 The displacement y of a wave travelling in the x-direction is given by $y = 10^{-4}\sin\left(600t - 2x + \frac{\pi}{3}\right)$ m, where x is expressed in metres and t in seconds. The speed of the wave motion (in ms^{-1}) is NCERT Pg. 284

(a) 300 (b) 600

(c) 1200 (d) 200

26 A transverse wave described by $y = 0.02\sin(x + 30t)$ propagates on a stretched string of linear density 12 gm^{-1}. The tension in the string is NCERT Pg. 285

(a) 2.16 N (b) 1.08 N

(c) 10.8 N (d) 0.0108 N

27 A 20 m long steel wire has mass 10 g. If the wire is under a tension of 125 N, the speed of transverse waves on the wire is **NCERT Pg. 285**

(a) 100 ms^{-1} (b) 200 ms^{-1}
(c) 400 ms^{-1} (d) 500 ms^{-1}

28 Figure shows a sinusoidal wave on a string. If the frequency of the wave is 100 Hz, the velocity and wavelength of the given wave is **NCERT Pg. 285**

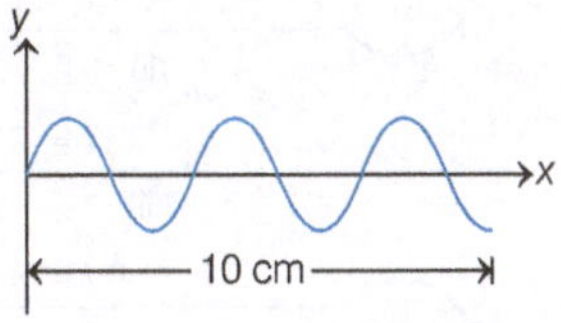

(a) 0.04 m, 4 ms^{-1} (b) 0.06 m, 6 ms^{-1}
(c) 0.08 m, 12 ms^{-1} (d) 0.06 m, 10 ms^{-1}

29 The operating frequency of an ultrasonic scanner is 3.2 MHz. If the speed of sound in a tissue is 1.6 km s^{-1}. The wavelength of sound (in mm) in the tissue is **NCERT Pg. 285**

(a) 0.25 (b) 0.5 (c) 0.75 (d) 1

30 A body sends waves 100 mm long through medium *A* and 0.25 m long in medium *B*. If the velocity of waves in medium *A* is 80 cm^{-1}, the velocity of waves (in m/s) in medium *B* is **NCERT Pg. 285**

(a) 1 (b) 2 (c) 3 (d) 4

31 Sound waves travel at 350 ms^{-1} through a warm air and at 3500 ms^{-1} through brass. The wavelength of a 700 Hz acoustic wave as it enters brass from warm air **NCERT Pg. 285**

(a) decrease by a factor 10
(b) increase by a factor 20
(c) increase by a factor 10
(d) decrease by a factor 20

32 An earthquake generates both transverse (*S*) and longitudinal (*P*) sound waves in the earth. The speed of *S* wave is about 4 kms^{-1} and that of *P* wave is about 8 kms^{-1}. A seismograph records *P* and *S* waves from an earthquake. The first *P* wave arrives 4 min before the first *S* wave. The epicentre of the earthquake is located at a distance (in km) of about **NCERT Pg. 285**

(a) 192 (b) 384
(c) 1920 (d) 3840

33 A string wave equation is given by $y = 0.002\cos(300t - 15x)$ and mass density is $\mu = 0.1$ kg/m. Then find the tension force in the string. **NCERT Pg. 285**

(a) 30 N (b) 20 N
(c) 40 N (d) 45 N

34 Two strings *A* and *B*, made of same materials are stretched by same tension. The radius of string *A* is double the radius of *B*. A transverse wave travels on *A* with speed v_A and on *B* with speed v_B. The ratio of v_A/v_B is **NCERT Pg. 285**

(a) 1/2 (b) 2
(c) 1/4 (d) 4

35 If the mass of 1 mol of air is 29.0×10^{-3} kg, then the speed of sound in air at standard temperature and pressure (using Newton's formula) is **NCERT Pg. 285**

(a) 250 ms^{-1} (b) 280 ms^{-1}
(c) 300 ms^{-1} (d) 380 ms^{-1}

36 The correct order of speed of sound in different media is (consider the speed at constant temperature) **NCERT Pg. 285**

(a) $v_{air} > v_{\substack{solid \\ (aluminium)}} > v_{\substack{liquid \\ (water)}}$

(b) $v_{\substack{solid \\ (aluminium)}} > v_{air} > v_{\substack{liquid \\ (water)}}$

(c) $v_{\substack{solid \\ (aluminium)}} > v_{\substack{liquid \\ (water)}} > v_{air}$

(d) $v_{\substack{liquid \\ (water)}} > v_{\substack{solid \\ (aluminium)}} > v_{air}$

37 A transverse wave travels on a taut steel wire with a velocity of *v* when tension in it is 2.06×10^4 N. When the tension is changed to *T*, the velocity changed to $v/2$. The value of *T* is close to **NCERT Pg. 285**

(a) 10.2×10^2 N (b) 5.15×10^3 N
(c) 2.50×10^4 N (d) 30.5×10^4 N

38 A string of length *L* is clamped between two points and speed of transverse wave in it is 500 m/s. Now the tension is increased to four times just by making the string more tight. Neglect variation in length while increasing the tension. The new speed of transverse wave is **NCERT Pg. 285**

(a) 125 m/s (b) 250 m/s
(c) 500 m/s (d) 1000 m/s

39 A string is under tension so that its length is increased by $\frac{1}{n}$ times its original length. The ratio of fundamental frequency of longitudinal vibrations and transverse vibrations will be **NCERT Pg. 286**

(a) $1:n$ (b) $n^2:1$
(c) $\sqrt{n}:1$ (d) $n:1$

40 The temperature at which the speed of sound in air be double of its value at 0°C is **NCERT Pg. 286**

(a) 800°C (b) 819°C
(c) 846°C (d) 750°C

41 If the initial velocity of sound in a gas is 340 m/s and the gas experiences a temperature increase of 20°C, then calculate the new velocity of sound in the gas (Assume STP conditions for initial state) **NCERT Pg. 286**

(a) 352 m/s
(b) 390 m/s
(c) 380 m/s
(d) 360 m/s

42 The bulk modulus of a liquid of density 6000 kg m^{-3} is 1.5×10^9 Nm^{-2}. The speed of sound in that liquid is **NCERT Pg. 286**

(a) 400 ms^{-1}
(b) 600 ms^{-1}
(c) 500 ms^{-1}
(d) 450 ms^{-1}

43 Speed of sound wave in a fluid depends **NCERT Pg. 286**

(a) directly on density of the medium
(b) directly on square of bulk modulus of the medium
(c) inversely on the square root of density
(d) inversely on the square root of bulk modulus of the medium

44 Two solid bars having Young's modulus Y_1 and Y_2 is in the ratio of $Y_1/Y_2 = 4$. If the bars are made up of materials with same density, then the ratio of the speeds of longitudinal waves in the solid bars i.e. v_1/v_2 is **NCERT Pg. 286**

(a) 2 (b) 1
(c) 3 (d) 4

45 A student plotted the following four graphs representing the variation of velocity of sound in a gas with the pressure p at constant temperature. Which one is correct? **NCERT Pg. 286**

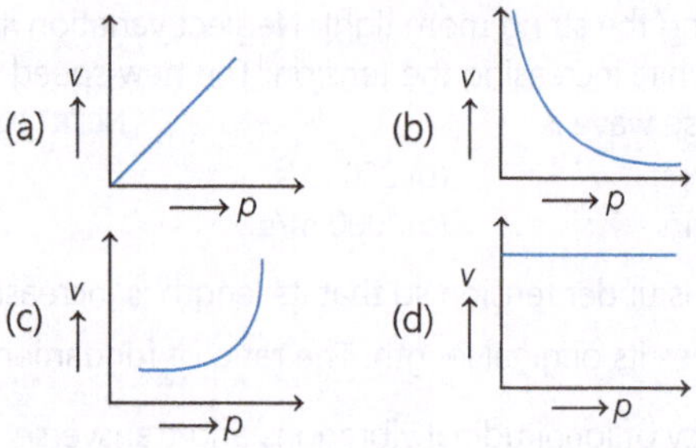

46 According to Laplace correction, the pressure variations in the medium during propagation of sound waves are **NCERT Pg. 287**

(a) adiabatic
(b) isothermal
(c) isobaric
(d) isochoric

Principle of Superposition of Waves

47 Two pulses having equal and opposite displacements moving in opposite directions overlap at $t = t_1$ as shown in figure. The resultant displacement of the wave at $t = t_1$ is **NCERT Pg. 287**

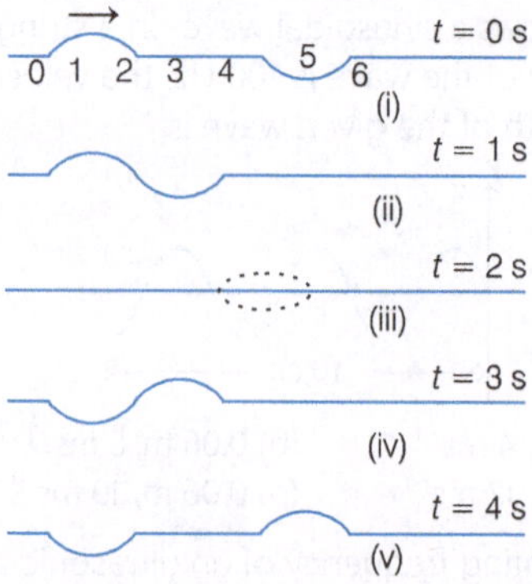

(a) twice the displacement of each pulse
(b) half the displacement of each pulse
(c) zero
(d) $\frac{4}{3}$th displacement of the wave

48 Let a wave $y(x,t) = a\sin(kx - \omega t)$ is reflected from an open boundary and then the incident and reflected waves overlap. Then the amplitude of resultant wave is **NCERT Pg. 287**

(a) $2a\cos kx$ (b) $2a\sin kx$
(c) $2a\sin\left(\frac{kx}{2}\right)$ (d) $a\sin kx$

49 Two waves of equal amplitude A and equal frequency travel in the same direction in a medium having phase difference of ϕ. The amplitude of the resultant wave is **NCERT Pg. 288**

(a) 0 (b) A
(c) $2A$ (d) between 0 to $2A$

50 Two sine waves having equal frequency travel in the same direction in a medium. The amplitude of each wave is A and the phase difference between the two waves is 120°. The resultant amplitude will be **NCERT Pg. 288**

(a) A (b) $2A$ (c) $4A$ (d) $\sqrt{2}A$

51 Two waves are passing through a region in the same direction at the same time. If the equations of these waves are $y_1 = a\sin\frac{2\pi}{\lambda}(vt - x)$ and $y_2 = b\sin\frac{2\pi}{\lambda}[(vt - x) + x_0]$, then the amplitude of the resulting wave for $x_0 = \frac{\lambda}{2}$ is **NCERT Pg. 288**

(a) $|a-b|$ (b) $|a+b|$
(c) $\sqrt{a^2+b^2}$ (d) $\sqrt{a^2+b^2+2ab\cos x}$

Reflection of Waves

52 When a wave is reflected normally from a rigid boundary, the reflected wave suffers a phase change of (assuming no absorption) NCERT Pg. 289
(a) $\pi/2$ (b) $\pi/4$
(c) π (d) 2π

53 To decrease the fundamental frequency of a stretched string fixed at both ends. Which of the following option is correct? NCERT Pg. 289
(a) Increase its tension
(b) Increase the wave velocity in it
(c) Increase its length
(d) Decrease its linear mass density

54 Two strings AB and BC having mass densities μ_1 and μ_2 are tied at B and are stretched between A and C. A wave pulse is generated at end A and progresses towards junction B. It is given that $(\mu_2 > \mu_1)$.

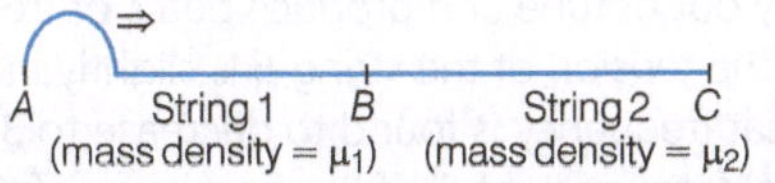

If the magnitude of velocity of the reflected wave and transmitted wave are v_r and v_t respectively, then the correct relation is NCERT Pg. 289
(a) $v_r > v_t$ (b) $v_r < v_t$
(c) $v_r > v_t$ and $v_t = 0$ (d) $v_r \le v_t$

55 If a propagating wave meets a boundary which is not completely rigid or is an interface between two different elastic media, then which of the statement is correct? NCERT Pg. 289
(a) A part of the incident wave is reflected and a part is transmitted into the second medium.
(b) The incident wave is completely reflected from the boundary.
(c) Only a part of the wave is reflected and the remaining part disappears.
(d) None of the above

56 At nodes in stationary waves, change in NCERT Pg. 290
(a) pressure is maximum
(b) pressure is minimum
(c) displacement is maximum
(d) density is minimum

57 A standing wave is generated on a string. Which of the following statement is correct for the stationary waves? NCERT Pg. 290
(a) The amplitude of stationary wave varies from point-to-point but each element of the string oscillates with the same angular frequency ω or time period.
(b) The string as a whole vibrates in phase with differing amplitudes at different points.
(c) The wave pattern in neither moving to the right nor to the left.
(d) All of the above

58 The fundamental frequency of a string stretched with a weight of 4 kg is 256 Hz. The weight required to produce its octave is (Neglect change in linear mass density) NCERT Pg. 291
(a) 4 kg-wt (b) 12 kg-wt
(c) 16 kg-wt (d) 24 kg-wt

59 A wire under tension vibrates with a fundamental frequency of 600 Hz. If the length of the wire is doubled, the radius is halved and the wire is made to vibrate under one-ninth of the tension, then the fundamental frequency will become NCERT Pg. 291
(a) 400 Hz (b) 600 Hz
(c) 300 Hz (d) 200 Hz

60 A string 2.0 m long and fixed at its ends is driven by a 240 Hz vibrator. The string vibrates in its third harmonic mode. The speed of the wave and its fundamental frequency is NCERT Pg. 291
(a) 180 m/s, 80 Hz (b) 320 m/s, 80 Hz
(c) 320 m/s, 120 Hz (d) 180 m/s, 120 Hz

61 An open tube is in resonance with string. If tube is dipped in water, so that 75% of length of tube is inside water, then the ratio of the frequency v_0 of tube to string is NCERT Pg. 292
(a) 1 (b) 2
(c) 2/3 (d) 3/2

62 An open pipe of sufficient length is dipping in water with a speed v vertically. If at any instant l is length of tube above water, then the rate at which fundamental frequency of pipe changes, is (speed of sound $= c$) NCERT Pg. 292

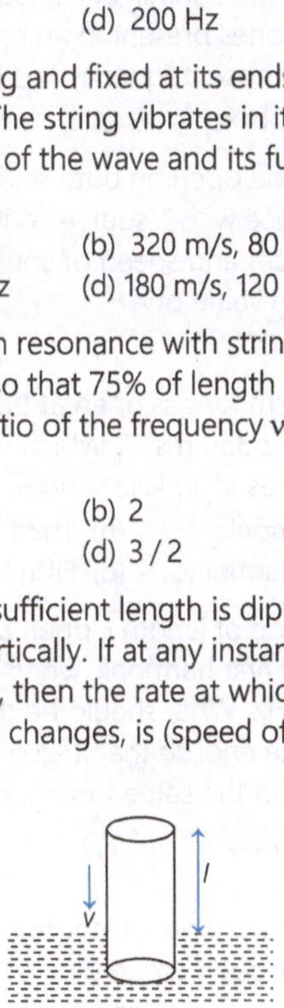

(a) $\frac{cv}{2l^2}$ (b) $\frac{cv}{4l^2}$
(c) $\frac{c}{2(vl^2)}$ (d) $\frac{c}{4(vl^2)}$

63 The fundamental frequency of a closed organ pipe is same as the first overtone frequency of the open pipe. The length of open pipe is 50 cm. The length of closed pipe is NCERT Pg. 292

(a) 25 cm (b) 100 cm
(c) 200 cm (d) 12.5 cm

64 A pipe of length 85 cm is closed from one end. Find the number of possible natural oscillations of air column in the pipe whose frequencies lie below 1250 Hz. The velocity of sound in air is 340 ms^{-1}. NCERT Pg. 292

(a) 12 (b) 8 (c) 6 (d) 4

65 The air column in a pipe open at both ends is oscillating with certain frequency. Which of the given statement is correct for the open air column at both ends? NCERT Pg. 292

(a) Each end of the pipe acts as an anti-node.
(b) An air column open at both ends generates all harmonics.
(c) Each end of the pipe is a node.
(d) Both (a) and (b)

66 If the speed of sound in air is 330 m/s, then find the number of tones present in an open organ pipe of length 1 m whose frequency is $\leq$1000 Hz. NCERT Pg. 293

(a) 2 (b) 4 (c) 8 (d) 6

67 An organ pipe open on both ends in the nth harmonic is in resonance with a source of 1000 Hz. The length of pipe is 16.6 cm and speed of sound in air is 332 m/s, then find the value of n. NCERT Pg. 293

(a) 3 (b) 2 (c) 1 (d) 4

68 An pipe 30 cm long is open at both ends. The speed of sound in air is 330 ms^{-1}. Which harmonic mode of the pipe resonates at 1.1 kHz source? NCERT Pg. 293

(a) First harmonic (b) Third harmonic
(c) Second harmonic (d) Fifth harmonic

69 An organ pipe of length L open at both ends is found to vibrate in its first harmonic when sounded with a tuning fork of 480 Hz. What should be the length of a pipe closed at one end, so that it also vibrates in its first harmonic with the same tuning fork? NCERT Pg. 293

(a) $\frac{L}{4}$ (b) $\frac{L}{2}$ (c) L (d) $2L$

70 An open organ pipe of length l is sounded together with another open organ pipe of length $(l + x)$ in their fundamental tones. Speed of sound in air is v. If $x << l$, the beat frequency heard will be NCERT Pg. 293

(a) $\frac{vx}{2l^2}$ (b) $\frac{vx}{4l^2}$
(c) $\frac{vl^2}{2x}$ (d) $\frac{vx^2}{2l}$

71 A person blows into an open end of a long pipe. As a result, a high pressure pulse of air travels down the pipe. When this pulse reaches the other end of the pipe, NCERT Pg. 293

(a) a high pressure pulse starts travelling up the pipe, if the other end of the pipe is open
(b) a low pressure pulse starts travelling up the pipe, if the other end of the pipe is open
(c) a low pressure pulse starts travelling down the pipe, if the other end of the pipe is closed
(d) a high pressure pulse starts travelling up the pipe, if the other end is half closed.

72 Two open organ pipes give 4 beats/s when sounded together in their fundamental mode. If the length of the pipes are 100 cm and 102.5 cm respectively, then the velocity of sound is NCERT Pg. 293

(a) 496 m/s (b) 328 m/s
(c) 49600 m/s (d) 32800 m/s

Beats

73 Two sitar strings A and B playing the note 'Dha' are slightly out of tune and produce beats of frequency 5 Hz. The tension of the string B is slightly increased and the beat frequency is found to decrease to 3 Hz. The original frequency of B, if the frequency of A is 427 Hz, is NCERT Pg. 293

(a) 422 Hz (b) 420 Hz
(c) 424 Hz (d) 419 Hz

74 A source of unknown frequency gives 4 beats/s when sounded with a source of known frequency 250 Hz. The second harmonic of the source of unknown frequency gives 5 beats/s when sounded with a source of frequency 513 Hz. The unknown frequency is NCERT Pg. 293

(a) 254 Hz (b) 246 Hz (c) 240 Hz (d) 260 Hz

75 When two tuning forks (fork 1 and fork 2) are sounded simultaneously, 4 beats/s are heard. Now, some tape is attached on the prong of the fork 2. When the tuning forks are sounded again, 6 beats/s are heard. If frequency of fork 1 is 200 Hz, then what was the original frequency of fork 2? NCERT Pg. 293

(a) 200 Hz (b) 202 Hz
(c) 196 Hz (d) 204 Hz

76 A tuning fork P is sounded with another tuning fork Q of frequency 500 Hz and 4 beats is observed. Now P is slightly loaded and 100% increased beat frequency is observed. The original frequency of P is NCERT Pg. 293

(a) 504 Hz (b) 508 Hz
(c) 496 Hz (d) 492 Hz

77 Two waves of wavelengths 2 m and 2.02 m respectively, moving with the same velocity and superimpose to produce 2 beats per second. The velocity of the waves is **NCERT Pg. 293**

(a) 400 m/s (b) 402 m/s
(c) 404 m/s (d) 406 m/s

78 Wavelength of two notes in air are $\frac{80}{175}$ m and $\frac{80}{173}$ m. Each note produces 4 beats with a third note of a fixed frequency. The speed of sound in air is **NCERT Pg. 293**

(a) 400 m/s (b) 300 m/s
(c) 280 m/s (d) 320 m/s

79 Two sound sources with wavelength 5.0 m and 5.5 m respectively, each propagate in a gas with velocity 330 m/s. We expect the following number of beats per second **NCERT Pg. 293**

(a) 1 (b) 6 (c) 12 (d) 0

80 Two tuning forks of frequencies n_1 and n_2 produce n beats per second. If n_2 and n are known, n_1 may be given by **NCERT Pg. 293**

(a) $\frac{n_2}{n} + n_2$ (b) $n_2 n$
(c) $n_2 \pm n$ (d) $\frac{n_2}{n} - n_2$

81 Two vibrating tuning forks produce progressive waves given by $y_1 = 4\sin 500\pi t$ and $y_2 = 2\sin 506\pi t$. Number of beats produced per minute is **NCERT Pg. 293**

(a) 360 (b) 180 (c) 3 (d) 60

Assertion and Reason Questions

Direction (Q. Nos. 1-10) *In the following questions, a statement of Assertion is followed by a corresponding statement of Reason. Of the following statements, choose the correct one.*

(a) Both Assertion and Reason are correct and Reason is the correct explanation of Assertion.
(b) Both Assertion and Reason are correct but Reason is not the correct explanation of Assertion.
(c) Assertion is correct but Reason is incorrect.
(d) Assertion is incorrect but Reason is correct.

1 Assertion Transverse waves are possible in solids and strings (under tension) but not in fluids.
Reason Solids and strings have non-zero shear modulus, but fluids have approximately zero shear modulus. **NCERT Pg. 280**

2 Assertion Longitudinal waves can be propagated through solids and fluids both.
Reason Solids as well as fluids have non-zero bulk modulus, i.e. they can sustain compressive stress. **NCERT Pg. 280**

3 Assertion Speed of sound at the top of a mountain is greater than the speed of sound near the surface of Earth.
Reason Speed of sound is directly proportional to the square root of pressure. **NCERT Pg. 285**

4 Assertion Fundamental frequency of a narrow pipe is more than that of broad diameter pipe of same length.
Reason According to Laplace end correction, if radius of pipe is less, frequency should be more. **NCERT Pg. 287**

5 Assertion The amplitude $A(\phi)$ of the resultant of the two travelling light waves given by equations

$$y_1(x,t) = A\sin(kx - \omega t) \text{ and}$$
$$y_2(x,t) = A\sin(kx - \omega t + \phi)$$

decreases as ϕ increases from 0 to π.
Reason The amplitude of the resultant of the two above mentioned waves is given by $A(\phi) = 2A\cos(\phi/2)$. **NCERT Pg. 287**

6 Assertion Variation in air pressure do not affect the speed of sound when temperature remains constant.
Reason Speed of sound is directly proportional to square of pressure. **NCERT Pg. 285**

7 Assertion Interference between two incoherent waves is not possible.
Reason It's not necessary to have constant phase difference between two waves interference to occur. **NCERT Pg. 293**

8 Assertion Superposition of two harmonic waves, one of frequency 11 Hz and the other of frequency 9 Hz give rise to beats of frequency 2 Hz.
Reason Harmonic waves of nearly equal frequencies interfere to give rise to beat having beat frequency, $\nu_{beat} = |\nu_1 - \nu_2|$. **NCERT Pg. 293**

9 Assertion Transverse wave travel through air in an organ pipe.
Reason Air possesses only volume elasticity. **NCERT Pg. 292**

10 Assertion To hear different beats, difference of the frequencies of two sources should be less than 10.
Reason More the number of beats more is the confusion. **NCERT Pg. 293**

Statement Based Questions

Direction (Q. Nos. 1-8) *In the following questions, Statement I and Statement II are given. Read the statements and choose the most appropriate answer from the options given below.*

(a) Both Statement I and Statement II are incorrect.
(b) Statement I is correct but Statement II is incorrect.
(c) Statement I is incorrect but Statement II is correct.
(d) Both Statement I and Statement II are correct.

1 Statement I A steel bar can propagate both longitudinal as well as transverse waves having different speeds.
Statement II Air can propagate both longitudinal and transverse wave. NCERT Pg. 280

2 Statement I Transverse sound wave does not occur in gases.
Statement II Gases cannot sustain shearing strain. NCERT Pg. 280

3 Statement I Waves produced by a motor boat sailing in water are both longitudinal and transverse waves.
Statement II The longitudinal and transverse waves cannot be produced simultaneously. NCERT Pg. 280

4 Statement I The velocity of sound increases with increase in humidity.
Statement II Velocity of sound does not depends upon the medium. NCERT Pg. 284

5 Statement I On a rainy day sound travel slower than on a dry day.
Statement II When moisture is present in air the density of air increases. NCERT Pg. 284

6 Statement I The velocity of sound in hydrogen gas is less than the velocity of sound in oxygen gas.
Statement II The density of hydrogen is more than the density of oxygen. NCERT Pg. 286

7 Statement I Sound produced by an open organ pipe is richer than the sound produced by a closed organ pipe.
Statement II Outside air can enter the pipe from both ends, in case of open organ pipe. NCERT Pg. 292

8 Statement I To hear distinct beats, the difference in frequencies of the sounding bodies should be less than 10 Hz.

Statement II The persistence of hearing of sound is 0.1 s, so the ear cannot distinguish between sounds of frequency more than 10 Hz. NCERT Pg. 293

Matching Type Questions

1 A wave travelling along a string is described by

$$y(x,t) = 0.005 \sin(80x - 3t)$$

in which the numerical constants are in SI units. With reference to the above equation of wave motion, match the Column I (characteristics of wave) with Column II (respective value). NCERT Pg. 283

	Column I		Column II
A.	Wave number of the wave	1.	0.0785 SI units
B.	Wavelength of the wave	2.	0.48 SI units
C.	Frequency of the wave	3.	0.005 SI units
D.	Displacement y of the wave at a distance $x = 30$ cm and time $t = 20$s	4.	80 SI units

Choose the correct answer from the options given below.

Codes

	A	B	C	D		A	B	C	D
(a)	4	1	2	3	(b)	2	1	3	4
(c)	1	4	3	2	(d)	3	1	2	4

2 If the incident travelling wave is given by $y(x,t) = a\sin(kx - \omega t)$, then match the Column I (condition) with Column II (equation of displacement). NCERT Pg. 289

	Column I		Column II
A.	Reflected wave from rigid boundary	1.	$a\sin(kx - \omega t)$
B.	Reflected wave from open boundary	2.	$-a\sin(kx - \omega t)$
C.	The resultant displacement at the rigid boundary	3.	$2a\sin(kx - \omega t)$
D.	The resultant displacement at the open boundary	4.	0

Choose the correct answer from the options given below.

Codes

	A	B	C	D		A	B	C	D
(a)	2	1	4	3	(b)	1	2	3	4
(c)	2	1	3	4	(d)	1	2	4	3

3 Column I has figures showing different modes of oscillation of the system (a string tied at both the ends) and Column II has name of the corresponding modes. Match the Column I with Column II. **NCERT Pg. 291**

Column I		Column II
A.	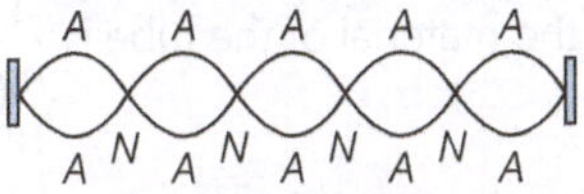	1. Fundamental mode
B.	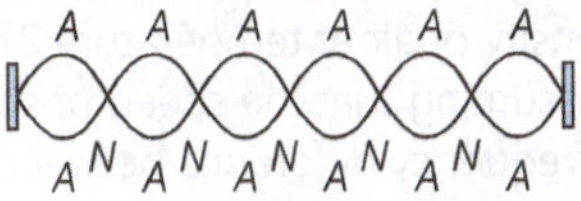	2. Second harmonic
C.	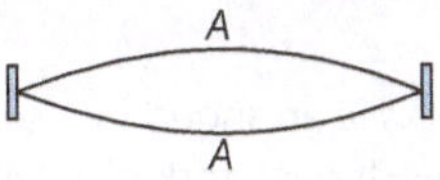	3. Sixth harmonic
D.	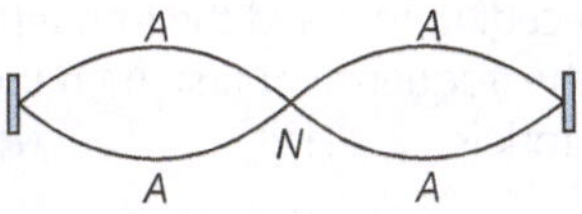	4. Fifth harmonic

Choose the correct answer from the options given below.

Codes

	A	B	C	D
(a)	4	2	3	1
(b)	4	3	1	2
(c)	3	2	1	4
(d)	2	3	1	4

4 Considering the length of the vibrating air column (which is closed at one end) as L, the possible wavelengths of the standing waves as λ, wave velocity as v and the normal nodes or the natural frequencies of the system as ν. Match the Column I (characteristics) with Column II (respective value). **NCERT Pg. 292**

Column I	Column II
A. ν	1. $\frac{2L}{(n+1/2)}$; $n = 0, 1, 2, 3, \cdots$
B. λ	2. $\left(n+\frac{1}{2}\right)\frac{v}{2L}$; $n = 0, 1, 2, 3, \cdots$
C. ν_0 (fundamental mode)	3. $v/4L$
D. Longest wavelength	4. $4L$

Choose the correct answer from the options given below.

Codes

	A	B	C	D		A	B	C	D
(a)	2	1	3	4	(b)	4	2	3	1
(c)	3	4	2	1	(d)	2	3	1	4

5 Column I lists the figure for odd harmonic of air column and Column II names the corresponding harmonics. Match the Column I with Column II. **NCERT Pg. 292**

Column I		Column II
A.		1. Third harmonic
B.		2. Fifth harmonic
C.	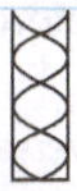	3. Ninth harmonic
D.		4. Seventh harmonic

Choose the correct answer from the options given below.

Codes

	A	B	C	D		A	B	C	D
(a)	1	2	3	4	(b)	4	3	2	1
(c)	2	3	4	1	(d)	3	2	1	4

Numerical Type Questions

1 A uniform rope of length 18 m and mass 8 kg hangs vertically from a rigid support. A block of mass 1 kg is attached at the lower end of it. A transverse wave of wavelength 3 cm is created at the lower end A of the rope. When wave reached at top, the wavelength is .... cm. **NCERT Pg. 285**

2 A wire of density 2×10^{-3} kg/cm^3 is stretched between two clamps 1 m apart. The resulting strain in the wire is 40.5×10^{-4}. The lowest frequency of the transverse vibrations in the wire is .... Hz. (Young's modulus of wire, $Y = 9 \times 10^{19}$ Nm^{-2}) **NCERT Pg. 286**

3 A guitar string of length 90 cm vibrates with a fundamental frequency of 120 Hz. The length of the string producing a fundamental frequency of 180 Hz will be .... cm. **NCERT Pg. 291**

4 A string fixed at both ends is vibrating in the lowest mode of vibration for which a point at 1/4 of its length from one end is a point of maximum displacement.

The frequency of vibration in this mode is 78 Hz. When it vibrates in the next higher mode such that this point is again a point of maximum displacement, then frequency at this point is .... Hz. **NCERT Pg. 291**

5 A string is clamped at both the ends and it is vibrating in its 4th harmonic. The equation of the stationary wave is $y = 0.3 \sin(0.157x) \cos(200\pi t)$. The length of the string is ...... m. (Rounding off to the nearest integer) **NCERT Pg. 291**

6 A vibrating tuning fork of frequency f is placed near the open end of a cylindrical tube. The other end of tube is fitted with a movable reflecting piston as shown in given figure. **NCERT Pg. 292**

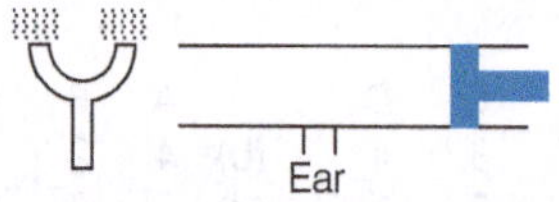

As the piston is moved through 6.25 cm, the intensity of sound changes from a maximum to minimum. If the speed of sound in air is 320 m/s, then the value of f is .... Hz.

7 An organ pipe is closed at one end has fundamental frequency of 1600 Hz. The maximum number of overtones generated by this pipe which a normal person can hear is .... **NCERT Pg. 292**

8 The temperature at which the fundamental frequency of an open organ pipe is independent of small variation in temperature in terms of the coefficient of linear expansion (α) of the material of the tube is $\frac{1}{n\alpha}$. The value of n is .... **NCERT Pg. 293**

9 A 1 m long open organ pipe is kept in a gas that has four times the density of air at temperature 27°C and pressure 1 atm. Assuming that the speed of sound in air is 320 m/s, then frequency difference between the fundamental and second harmonic of this pipe is .... Hz. **NCERT Pg. 293**

10 A set of 20 tuning forks is arranged in a series of increasing frequencies. If each fork gives 4 beats with respect to the preceding fork and the frequency of the last fork is twice the frequency of first, then the frequency of last fork is......... Hz. **NCERT Pg. 293**

NCERT Exemplar Questions

1 Water waves produced by a motorboat sailing in water are
(a) neither longitudinal nor transverse
(b) both longitudinal and transverse
(c) only longitudinal
(d) only transverse

2 Sound waves of wavelength λ travelling in a medium with a speed of v ms^{-1} enter into another medium where its speed in $2v$ ms^{-1}. Wavelength of sound waves in the second medium is
(a) λ (b) $\frac{\lambda}{2}$ (c) 2λ (d) 4λ

3 Speed of sound wave in air
(a) is independent of temperature
(b) increases with pressure
(c) increases with increase in humidity
(d) decreases with increase in humidity

4 Change in temperature of the medium changes
(a) frequency of sound waves
(b) amplitude of sound waves
(c) wavelength of sound waves
(d) loudness of sound waves

5 With propagation of longitudinal waves through a medium, the quantity transmitted is
(a) matter
(b) energy
(c) energy and matter
(d) energy, matter and momentum

6 A sound wave is passing through air column in the form of compression and rarefaction. In consecutive compressions and rarefaction,
(a) density remains constant
(b) Boyle's law is obeyed
(c) bulk modulus of air oscillates
(d) there is no transfer of heat

7 Equation of a plane progressive wave is given by $y_i = 0.6 \sin 2\pi\left(t - \frac{x}{2}\right)$. On reflection from a denser medium, its amplitude becomes (2/3) of the amplitude of the incident wave. The equation of the reflected wave is
(a) $y_r = 0.6 \sin 2\pi\left(t + \frac{x}{2}\right)$
(b) $y_r = -0.4 \sin 2\pi\left(t + \frac{x}{2}\right)$
(c) $y_r = 0.4 \sin 2\pi\left(t + \frac{x}{2}\right)$
(d) $y_r = -0.4 \sin 2\pi\left(t - \frac{x}{2}\right)$

Past Exams Questions

NEET

1 The ratio of frequencies of fundamental harmonic produced by an open pipe to that of closed pipe having the same length is NCERT Pg. 292, NEET 2023

(a) 2 : 1 (b) 1 : 3
(c) 3 : 1 (d) 1 : 2

2 If the initial tension on a stretched string is doubled, then the ratio of the initial and final speeds of a transverse wave along the string is NCERT Pg. 285, NEET 2022

(a) $\sqrt{2} : 1$ (b) $1 : \sqrt{2}$
(c) 1 : 2 (d) 1 : 1

3 The length of the string of a musical instrument is 90 cm and has a fundamental frequency of 120 Hz. Where should it be pressed to produced fundamental frequency of 180 Hz? NCERT Pg. 290, NEET 2020

(a) 75 cm (b) 60 cm
(c) 45 cm (d) 80 cm

4 In a guitar, two strings *A* and *B* made of same material are slightly out of tune and produce beats of frequency 6 Hz. When tension in *B* is slightly decreased, the beat frequency increases to 7 Hz. If the frequency of *A* is 530 Hz, the original frequency of *B* will be NCERT Pg. 293, NEET 2020

(a) 524 Hz (b) 530 Hz
(c) 537 Hz (d) 523 Hz

5 A tuning fork with frequency 800 Hz produces resonance in a resonance column tube with upper end open and lower end closed by water surface. Successive resonance are observed at length 9.75 cm, 31.25 cm and 52.75 cm. The speed of sound in air is NCERT Pg. 292, NEET 2019

(a) 500 m/s (b) 156 m/s
(c) 344 m/s (d) 172 m/s

6 The fundamental frequency in an open organ pipe is equal to the third harmonic of a closed organ pipe. If the length of the closed organ pipe is 20 cm, the length of the open organ pipe is NCERT Pg. 293, NEET 2018

(a) 12.5 cm (b) 8 cm
(c) 13.3 cm (d) 16 cm

7 A tuning fork is used to produce resonance in a glass tube. The length of the air column in this tube can be adjusted by a variable piston. At room temperature of 27°C, two successive resonances are produced at 20 cm and 73 cm of column length. If the frequency of the tuning fork is 320 Hz, the velocity of sound in air at 27°C is NCERT Pg. 292, NEET 2018

(a) 350 m/s (b) 339 m/s
(c) 330 m/s (d) 300 m/s

8 The two nearest harmonics of a tube closed at one end and open at other end are 220 Hz and 260 Hz. What is the fundamental frequency of the system? NCERT Pg. 292, NEET 2017

(a) 10 Hz (b) 20 Hz (c) 30 Hz (d) 40 Hz

9 The second overtone of an open organ pipe has the same frequency as the first overtone of a closed pipe *L* metre long. The length of the open pipe will be NCERT Pg. 293, NEET 2016

(a) L (b) $2L$ (c) $\frac{L}{2}$ (d) $4L$

10 Three sound waves of equal amplitudes have frequencies $(n-1)$, n, $(n+1)$. They superimpose to give beats. The number of beats produced per second will be NCERT Pg. 293, NEET 2016

(a) 1 (b) 4 (c) 3 (d) 2

11 A uniform rope of length L and mass m_1 hangs vertically from a rigid support. A block of mass m_2 is attached to the free end of the rope. A transverse pulse of wavelength λ_1 is produced at the lower end of the rope. The wavelength of the pulse when it reaches the top of the rope is λ_2. The ratio $\frac{\lambda_2}{\lambda_1}$ is NCERT Pg. 285, NEET 2016

(a) $\sqrt{\frac{m_1 + m_2}{m_2}}$ (b) $\sqrt{\frac{m_2}{m_1}}$
(c) $\sqrt{\frac{m_1 + m_2}{m_1}}$ (d) $\sqrt{\frac{m_1}{m_2}}$

12 A string is stretched between fixed points separated by 75.0 cm. It is observed to have resonant frequencies of 420 Hz and 315 Hz. There are no other resonant frequencies between these two. The lowest resonant frequency for this string is NCERT Pg. 291, AIPMT 2015

(a) 155 Hz (b) 205 Hz
(c) 10.5 Hz (d) 105 Hz

13 An air column, closed at one end and open at the other, resonates with a tunning fork when the smallest length of the column is 50 cm. The next larger length of the column resonating with the same tunning fork is NCERT Pg. 292, AIPMT 2015

(a) 100 cm (b) 150 cm
(c) 200 cm (d) 66.7 cm

14 The fundamental frequency of a closed organ pipe of length 20 cm is equal to the second overtone of an organ pipe open at both the ends. The length of organ pipe open at both the ends is **NCERT Pg. 292, AIPMT 2015**

(a) 80 cm (b) 100 cm
(c) 120 cm (d) 140 cm

15 If n_1, n_2 and n_3 are the fundamental frequencies of three segments into which a string is divided, then the original fundamental frequency n of the string is given by **NCERT Pg. 292, AIPMT 2014**

(a) $\frac{1}{n} = \frac{1}{n_1} + \frac{1}{n_2} + \frac{1}{n_3}$

(b) $\frac{1}{\sqrt{n}} = \frac{1}{\sqrt{n_1}} + \frac{1}{\sqrt{n_2}} + \frac{1}{\sqrt{n_3}}$

(c) $\sqrt{n} = \sqrt{n_1} + \sqrt{n_2} + \sqrt{n_3}$

(d) $n = n_1 + n_2 + n_3$

JEE Main

16 The fundamental frequency of a closed organ pipe is equal to the first overtone frequency of an open organ pipe. If length of the open organ pipe is 60 cm, then the length of the closed pipe will be **NCERT Pg. 292, JEE Main 2024**

(a) 60 cm (b) 30 cm (c) 45 cm (d) 15 cm

17 A plane progressive wave is given by $y = 2\cos 2\pi(330t - x)$ m. The frequency of the wave is **NCERT Pg. 281, JEE Main 2024**

(a) 330 Hz (b) 340 Hz (c) 165 Hz (d) 660 Hz

18 A steel wire with mass per unit length 7.0×10^{-3} kg m^{-1} is under tension of 70 N. The speed of transverse waves in the wire will be **NCERT Pg. 285, JEE Main 2023**

(a) 10 m/s
(b) 200π m/s
(c) 100 m/s
(d) 50 m/s

19 Which of the following equations correctly represents a travelling wave having wavelength $\lambda = 4.0$ cm, frequency $\nu = 100$ Hz and travelling in positive X-axis direction? **NCERT Pg. 283, JEE Main 2022**

(a) $y = A\sin[(0.50\pi\ \text{cm}^{-1})x - (100\pi\ \text{s}^{-1})t]$

(b) $y = A\sin 2\pi[(0.25\ \text{cm}^{-1})x - (50\ \text{s}^{-1})t]$

(c) $y = A\sin\left[\left(\frac{2\pi}{4}\ \text{cm}^{-1}\right)x - \left(\frac{2\pi}{100}\ \text{s}^{-1}\right)t\right]$

(d) $y = A\sin\pi[(0.5\ \text{cm}^{-1})x - (200\ \text{s}^{-1})t]$

20 A tuning fork A of unknown frequency produces 5 beats/s with a fork of known frequency 340 Hz. When fork A is filled, the beat frequency decreases to 2 beats/s. What is the frequency of fork A? **NCERT Pg. 291, JEE Main 2021**

(a) 342 Hz (b) 345 Hz (c) 335 Hz (d) 338 Hz

21 A progressive wave travelling along the positive x-direction is represented by $y(x,t) = A\sin(kx - \omega t + \phi)$. Its snapshot at $t = 0$ is given in the figure. **NCERT Pg. 285, JEE Main 2019**

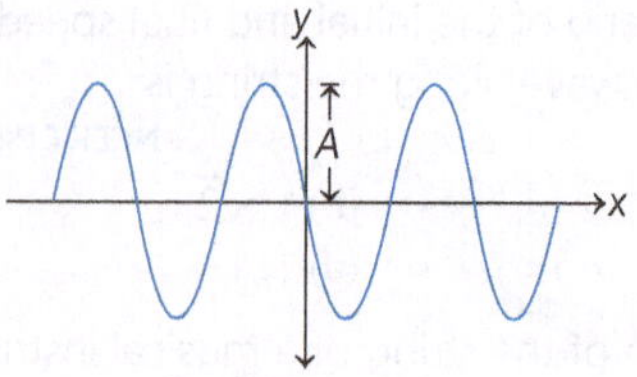

For this wave, the phase ϕ is

(a) $-\frac{\pi}{2}$ (b) π (c) 0 (d) $\frac{\pi}{2}$

22 A travelling harmonic wave is represented by the equation $y(x,t) = 10^{-3}\sin(50t + 2x)$, where x and y are in metre and t is in second. Which of the following is a correct statement about the wave? **NCERT Pg. 285, JEE Main 2019**

(a) The wave is propagating along the negative X-axis with speed 25 ms^{-1}.

(b) The wave is propagating along the positive X-axis with speed 25 ms^{-1}.

(c) The wave is propagating along the positive X-axis with speed 100 ms^{-1}.

(d) The wave is propagating along the negative X-axis with speed 100 ms^{-1}.

23 A wire of length $2L$, is made by joining two wires A and B of same length but different radii r and $2r$ are made of the same material. It is vibrating at a frequency such that the joint of the two wires forms a node. If the number of anti-nodes in wire A is p and that in B is q, then the ratio $p:q$ is **NCERT Pg. 285, JEE Main 2019**

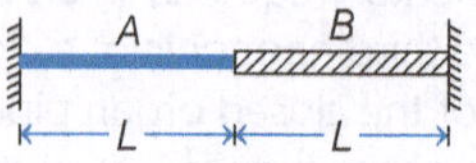

(a) 3 : 5 (b) 4 : 9
(c) 1 : 2 (d) 1 : 4

Skill Boosters

1 Ram was sitting in isolated room filled with two diatomic gases having masses m_2 and m_2. A pot was dropped in the corner of room. Calculate the speed through which sound will travel towards Ram if the separate speed of sound in two gases is v_1 and v_2, respectively.
[Take temperature as constant]

(a) $\sqrt{\dfrac{m_1v_1^2 + m_2v_2^2}{2(m_1 + m_2)}}$

(b) $\sqrt{\dfrac{2(m_1v_1^2 + m_2v_2^2)}{m_1 + m_2}}$

(c) $\sqrt{\dfrac{m_1v_1^2 + m_2v_2^2}{m_1 + m_2}}$

(d) $\sqrt{\dfrac{m_1v_1^2 + m_2v_2^2}{m_1 + m_2}}$

2 A progressive simple harmonic wave is moving in air along the X-axis. The part of this wave at a given point $x = x_0$ from the source and at a certain instant $t = t_0$ has the waveform shown below in the displacement-time (y-t) graph and velocity-time (v-t) graph, respectively. Velocity of the wave has value v_0 and its angular frequency is ω. Which of the following equations will correctly represent the complete wave at $x = x_0$, agreeing with above waveforms ?

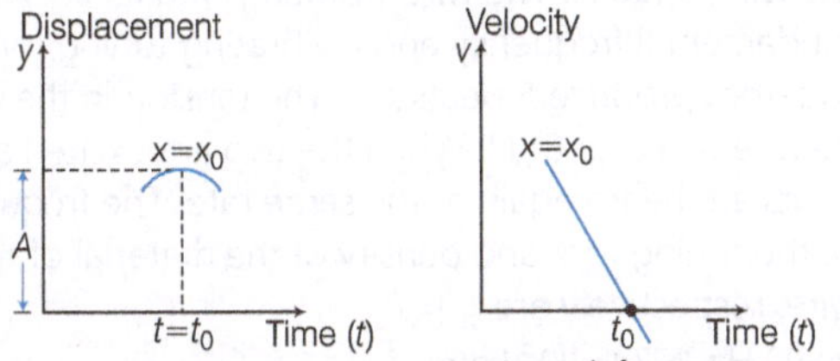

y-t graph v-t graph for $x = x_0$

(a) $y = -A\left[\cos\left\{\dfrac{2\pi}{T}(t - t_0) - \dfrac{\pi}{2}\right\}\right]$

(b) $y = -A\left[\sin\left\{\dfrac{2\pi}{T}(t - t_0) + \dfrac{\pi}{2}\right\}\right]$

(c) $y = A\left[\sin\left\{\dfrac{2\pi}{T}(t - t_0) + \dfrac{\pi}{2}\right\}\right]$

(d) $y = A\left[\cos\left\{\dfrac{2\pi}{T}(t - t_0) - \dfrac{\pi}{2}\right\}\right]$

3 A string has a mass 10 g and a length $L = 3$ m. Its two ends are tied to two walls a distance $d = 2$ m apart. Two blocks, each of mass $m = 2$ kg, are suspended from the string as shown in the figure. In what time will a wave pulse sent from a point P_1 reach point P_2?

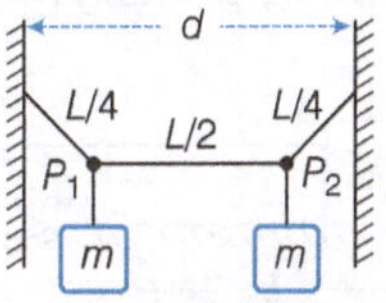

(a) 52.9 ms (b) 42.9 ms
(c) 32.9 ms (d) 22.9 ms

4 A block of mass m is attached to a vertical string of mass m_0 and length L_0 as shown in the figure. The whole system is placed on a planet whose mass is three times that of the earth and whose radius is 3 times that of the earth. Acceleration due to gravity on the earth is g. The time taken by a wave pulse to travel from one end A to other end B of the string is

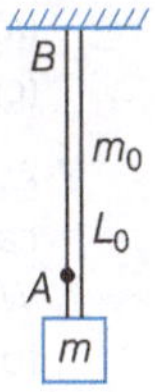

(a) $\left[\dfrac{\sqrt{m + m_0} - \sqrt{m}}{\sqrt{m_0}}\right]\sqrt{\dfrac{2L_0}{g}}$

(b) $\left[\dfrac{\sqrt{m + m_0} - \sqrt{m}}{\sqrt{m_0}}\right]\sqrt{\dfrac{3L_0}{g}}$

(c) $\left[\dfrac{\sqrt{m + m_0} - \sqrt{m}}{\sqrt{m_0}}\right]\sqrt{\dfrac{L_0}{2g}}$

(d) $2\left[\dfrac{\sqrt{m + m_0} - \sqrt{m}}{\sqrt{m_0}}\right]\sqrt{\dfrac{3L_0}{g}}$

5 In the figure is shown, a metal wire having a linear mass density 2.25×10^{-2} kg m^{-1}, with a block of mass 5 kg attached to the free end. Determine the speed of transverse wave in the string, if the block is immersed completely in a liquid, whose density bears a ratio of $\dfrac{17}{81}$ with that of the block.

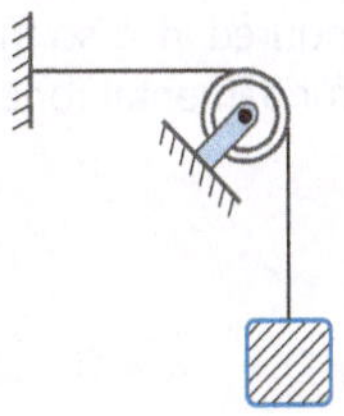

(a) 46.7 ms^{-1} (b) 41.5 ms^{-1}
(c) 37.2 ms^{-1} (d) 31.7 ms^{-1}

6 In the shown arrangement, the horizontal surface is smooth and pulley is ideal. Mass per unit length of the string is μ and its mass is much less than the masses of blocks. At $t = 0$, the system is released from rest (the initial distance between block m_2 and pulley is L_0) and a transverse pulse is produced at point A. The time required by the pulse to reach pulley is (Given, $m_1 = 10$ kg, $m_2 = 10$ kg, $\mu = 20$ gm^{-1}, $L_0 = 4$ m and $g = 10$ ms^{-2})

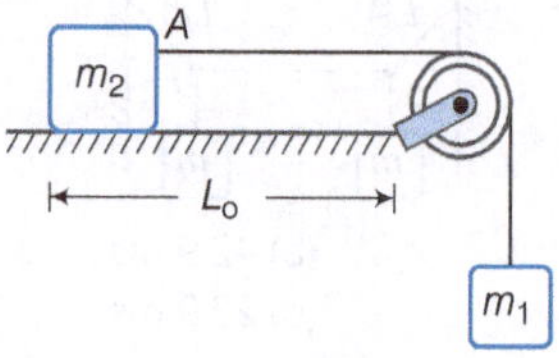

(a) 0.01 s (b) 0.06 s
(c) 0.08 s (d) 0.02 s

7 A certain string fixed to one end on a rigid support, carries a load at its other end passing through a pulley. When a length L of the wire is made to vibrate, it is found to resonate with a certain tuning fork. Upon immersing the load completely in water and kerosene separately, the corresponding lengths are found to be L_w and L_k. The specific gravity of the load (solid) is

(a) $\left[1 + \left(\frac{L_w}{L}\right)^2\right]^{-1}$

(b) $\frac{L_w}{L} + 1$

(c) $1 + \frac{L}{L_w}$

(d) $\left[1 - \left(\frac{L_w}{L}\right)^2\right]^{-1}$

8 A U-tube having uniform cross-section, but unequal arm lengths L_1 and $L_2 (< L_1)$ has a liquid of density ρ_1 filled in it upto a height h as shown in the figure. Another liquid of density $\rho_2 \left(= \frac{\rho_1}{2}\right)$ is poured in arm A. Both liquids are immiscible. What length of the second liquid should be poured in A, so that first overtone of A is in unison with fundamental tone of B?

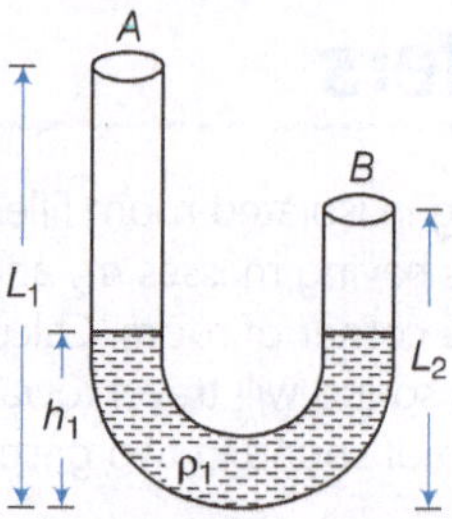

(a) $\frac{L_1 - 3L_2 + 2h}{3}$ (b) $\frac{2(L_1 - 3L_2 + 2h)}{3}$

(c) $\frac{L_1 - 3L_2 + 2h}{2}$ (d) $\frac{3(L_1 - 3L_2 + 2h)}{4}$

9 A metal rod of length 1m is clamped at two points as shown in the figure. Distance of the clamps from two ends are 5 cm and 15 cm, respectively. Find the minimum frequency of natural longitudinal oscillations of the rod. Given that, Young's modulus and density of the material of the rod are $Y = 1.6 \times 10^{11}$ Pa and $\rho = 2500$ kg m^{-3} respectively.

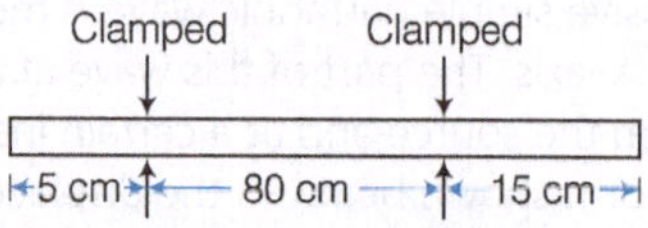

(a) 30 kHz (b) 40 kHz
(c) 50 kHz (d) 25 kHz

10 A metal wire of diameter 1 mm is held on two knife edges separated by a distance of 50 cm. The tension in the wire is 100 N. The wire vibrating with its fundamental frequency and a vibrating tuning fork together produce 5 beats s^{-1}. The tension in the wire is then reduced to 81 N. When the two are excited again, beats are heard again at the same rate. The frequency of the tuning fork and density of the material of the wire, respectively are

(a) 90 Hz, 1.274×10^4 kg m^{-3}
(b) 100 Hz, 1.724×10^4 kg m^{-3}
(c) 95 Hz, 1.724×10^4 kg m^{-3}
(d) 95 Hz, 1.274×10^4 kg m^{-3}

Correct Codes

Topical Questions

1 (a)	2 (d)	3 (d)	4 (d)	5 (c)	6 (a)	7 (c)	8 (c)	9 (d)	10 (a)
11 (a)	12 (c)	13 (c)	14 (b)	15 (b)	16 (a)	17 (a)	18 (a)	19 (c)	20 (a)
21 (a)	22 (b)	23 (b)	24 (a)	25 (a)	26 (c)	27 (d)	28 (a)	29 (b)	30 (b)
31 (c)	32 (c)	33 (c)	34 (a)	35 (b)	36 (c)	37 (b)	38 (d)	39 (c)	40 (b)
41 (a)	42 (b)	43 (c)	44 (a)	45 (d)	46 (a)	47 (c)	48 (b)	49 (d)	50 (a)
51 (a)	52 (c)	53 (c)	54 (a)	55 (a)	56 (a)	57 (a)	58 (c)	59 (d)	60 (b)
61 (b)	62 (b)	63 (d)	64 (c)	65 (d)	66 (d)	67 (c)	68 (c)	69 (b)	70 (a)
71 (b)	72 (d)	73 (a)	74 (a)	75 (c)	76 (c)	77 (c)	78 (d)	79 (b)	80 (c)
81 (b)									

Assertion and Reason Questions

1 (d)	2 (a)	3 (d)	4 (a)	5 (a)	6 (c)	7 (a)	8 (a)	9 (d)	10 (c)

Statement Based Questions

1 (b)	2 (d)	3 (b)	4 (b)	5 (a)	6 (a)	7 (d)	8 (d)

Matching Type Questions

1 (a)	2 (a)	3 (b)	4 (a)	5 (c)

Numerical Type Questions

1 (9)	2 (67.5)	3 (60)	4 (234)	5 (80)	6 (1280)	7 (6)	8 (2)	9 (80)	10 (152)

NCERT Exemplar Questions

1 (b)	2 (c)	3 (c)	4 (c)	5 (b)	6 (d)	7 (b)

Past Exams Questions

1 (a)	2 (b)	3 (b)	4 (a)	5 (c)	6 (c)	7 (b)	8 (b)	9 (b)	10 (a)
11 (a)	12 (d)	13 (b)	14 (c)	15 (a)	16 (d)	17 (a)	18 (c)	19 (d)	20 (c)
21 (b)	22 (a)	23 (c)							

Skill Boosters

1 (d)	2 (c)	3 (c)	4 (d)	5 (b)	6 (c)	7 (d)	8 (b)	9 (b)	10 (d)

Step by Step

Decoding the Questions

Concept Builders

1 Cannot

2 properties of elasticity and inertia

3 Non-mechanical

4 Transverse

5 $\frac{\lambda}{2}$

6 Angular wave number.

7 False (F) 8 True (T)

9 $y(x,t)=a\sin(kx-\omega t+\phi)$

10 False (F) 11 True (T)

12 True (T) 13 A

14 Laplace correction

15 $n+1$ 16 Note

17 $L\left(\frac{n+1}{2}\right)\frac{\lambda}{2}, n=0,1,2,3$

18 True (T)

19 False (F)

20 Cannot

Topical Questions

1 (*a*) In a mobile phone, initially sound waves are converted into an electric current signal which in turn generate electromagnetic waves (radio waves).

2 (*d*) Seismic waves are mechanical waves and hence require a material medium for their propagation.

3. (*d*) Statement given in option (d) is incorrect and it can be corrected as,

Mechanical waves have different speeds in different medium.

Rest statements are correct.

4 (*d*) When end A is pulled suddenly and released spring I gets disturbed from its equilibrium length.

Since, the spring II is connected to the spring I, it will also be stretched or compressed and so on.

The disturbance generated at end A will propagate to the other end but each spring will only execute small oscillations about its equilibrium position.

7 (*c*) Statement given in option (c) is incorrect and it can be corrected as,

The restoring force that produces gravity waves is the pull of gravity, which tends to keep the water surface at its lowest level. These waves extends to the very bottom with diminishing amplitude.

8 (*c*) Given, displacement of an elastic wave,

$$y=3\sin\omega t+4\cos\omega t$$

Assume, $3=a\cos\phi$ ...(i)

$4=a\sin\phi$ ...(ii)

Squaring and adding Eqs. (i) and (ii), we get

$$a^2\cos^2\phi+a^2\sin^2\phi=3^2+4^2$$

$$\Rightarrow a^2(\cos^2\phi+\sin^2\phi)=25$$

$$a^2\cdot 1=25$$

$$\Rightarrow a=5$$

Hence,

$$y=5\cos\phi\sin\omega t+5\sin\phi\cos\omega t$$

$$=5(\cos\phi\sin\omega t+\sin\phi\cos\omega t)$$

$$=5\sin(\omega t+\phi)$$

[using the trigonometric identity, $\sin(A+B)=\sin A\cos B+\cos A\sin B$]

Comparing the above equation with the general equation $y=A\sin(\omega t+\phi)$, we get resultant amplitude $=5$ cm

9 (*d*) $y=5(\sin 4\pi t+\sqrt{3}\cos 4\pi t)$

$=[5\sin 4\pi t+5\sqrt{3}\cos 4\pi t]$ ...(i)

For a left travelling wave, general equation for its motion is

$y=A\sin(kx+\omega t)+B\cos(kx+\omega t)$ ...(ii)

$=a\sin(kx+\omega t+\phi)$

where, $a=\sqrt{A^2+B^2}$ and $\phi=\tan^{-1}(B/A)$

On comparing both Eqs. (i) and (ii), we can say Eq. (i) represents Eq. (ii), where $x=0$

Also, we get $A=5$ and $B=5\sqrt{3}$

$\therefore$ Amplitude, $a=\sqrt{5^2+(5\sqrt{3})^2}$

$=\sqrt{25+75}=\sqrt{100}=10$

10 (*a*) In the given figure, notice the position of X w.r.t. time.

At $t=0$, the crest X is at a displacement of one quarter of wave from origin. With time it progresses along $+X$-axis and at $t=4$s, it is displaced by a full wave or oscillation, i.e. one crest and one trough. Thus, only one wave crosses the origin in 4s.

11 (*a*) The wave equation is $y(x,t)=a\sin(kx-\omega t+\phi)$ is a sine function. Since, the sine function varies between −1 and +1, so the displacement $y(x,t)$ varies between a and $-a$.

The range of possible values of $y(x,t)$ is

$$-a\le y(x,t)\le a$$

12 (*c*) Given, wave equation,

$$y=10\sin\left(\frac{2\pi}{45}t+\alpha\right)$$

the total phase of the $\left(\frac{2\pi}{45}t+\alpha\right)$

At $t=0$, $y=5$ cm, then from the above equation, we can write

$$5=10\sin\alpha$$

$$\sin\alpha=\frac{1}{2}\Rightarrow \alpha=\frac{\pi}{6}$$

If $t=7.5\text{ s}=(15/2)\text{ s}$, then

total phase $= \frac{2\pi}{45} \times \frac{15}{2} + \frac{\pi}{6}$

$= \frac{\pi}{3} + \frac{\pi}{6} = \frac{\pi}{2}$

13 (c) Given,

$$y_1 = a_1 \sin\left(\omega t - \frac{2\pi}{\lambda} x\right) \quad ...(i)$$

$$y_2 = a_2 \cos\left(\omega t - \frac{2\pi}{\lambda} x + \phi\right)$$

$$y_2 = a_2 \sin\left(\omega t - \frac{2\pi}{\lambda} x + \phi + \frac{\pi}{2}\right) \quad ...(ii)$$

The phase difference between the waves is given by

$$\Delta\phi = \left[\omega t - \frac{2\pi x}{\lambda} + \phi + \frac{\pi}{2}\right] - \left[\omega t - \frac{2\pi x}{\lambda}\right]$$

$$= \phi + \frac{\pi}{2} = \frac{\pi}{2} + \phi$$

14 (b) Given,

$v = 0.6\ \text{ms}^{-1}$

$f = 60$ Hz

As we know that,

$$\lambda = \frac{v}{f}$$

$$\Rightarrow \lambda = \frac{0.6}{60} \Rightarrow \lambda = 0.01\ \text{m}$$

i.e. $\lambda = 1$ cm

15 (b) Taking $\phi = 0$ in the given equation, the displacement at $t = 0$ becomes $y'(x, 0) = a \sin kx$

$= a \sin(kx + 2n\pi)$

($\because$ sine function repeats its value after every 2π change in angle)

$$= a \sin k\left(x + \frac{2n\pi}{k}\right)$$

$\Rightarrow$ The displacement at points x and $x + \frac{2n\pi}{k}$ are the same, where $n = 1, 2, 3, \ldots$.

16 (a) Given, wave equation

$$y(x,t) = 4 \sin\left[\pi\left(\frac{x}{9} - \frac{t}{5} + \frac{1}{6}\right)\right] \quad ...(i)$$

The general equation of a wave is

$y(x,t) = a \sin(kx - \omega t + \phi)$

Comparing Eq. (i) with general equation, we get

$$k = (\pi/9)\ \text{rad cm}^{-1}$$

Where k is the angular wave number.

17 (a) Given, wave equation

$$y(x,t) = a \sin(10\pi x + 11\pi t + \pi/3) \quad ...(i)$$

Comparing Eq. (i) with the general equation of wave

$$y = A \sin(kx + \omega t + \phi),$$

we get

$k = 10\pi$

As, $\lambda = \frac{2\pi}{k}$

$$\Rightarrow \lambda = \frac{2\pi}{10\pi} = 0.2 \text{ unit}$$

18 (a) Given, wave equation,

$$y = 2\cos 2\pi(330t - x)$$

It can be expressed as

$y = 2\cos(2\pi \times 330t - 2\pi x)$ ... (i)

On comparing Eq. (i) with $y = A\cos(\omega t - kx + \phi)$, we get

$\omega = 2\pi \times 330$

$\Rightarrow$ Period,

$$T = 2\pi/\omega = \frac{2\pi}{2\pi \times 330} = \left(\frac{1}{330}\right)\text{s}$$

19 (c) Let the time taken by a particle of the wave to complete one full oscillation is T.

$\Rightarrow T = 4 \times$ (time to travel from maximum displacement to zero by a particle)

$\Rightarrow T = 4 \times 0.14$ s $= 0.56$ s

$$\text{Frequency, } \nu = \frac{1}{T} = \frac{1}{0.56} = \frac{100}{56}$$

$= 1.79$ Hz

20 (a) Given, wave equation

$y = 15\cos(660\pi t - 0.02\pi x)$

On comparing with general equation of progressive wave,

$y(x,t) = a\cos(\omega t - kx)$

$$= a\cos\left(\frac{2\pi}{T}t - \frac{2\pi}{\lambda}x\right), \text{ we get}$$

$$\frac{2\pi}{T} = 660\pi \text{ or } \frac{1}{T} = 330$$

or $\nu = \frac{1}{T} = 330$ Hz

21 (a) Given, $a = 1$ m, $\lambda = 2\pi$ m and $\nu = \left(\frac{1}{\pi}\right)$ Hz

As, $y = a\sin(kx - \omega t)$

$$= \sin\left(\frac{2\pi}{2\pi} \times x - 2\pi \times \frac{1}{\pi} t\right)$$

$$\left(\because k = \frac{2\pi}{\lambda} \text{ and } \omega = 2\pi\nu\right)$$

$y = \sin(x - 2t)$

22 (b) As we know, wavelength λ can be defined as the distance between two successive crests or troughs of a wave.

So, here $\lambda = 1.5 \times 4 = 6$ cm

Hence, $\bar{v} = \frac{1}{\lambda}$

$\bar{v} = \frac{1}{6}$

$\bar{v} = 0.16\ \text{cm}^{-1}$

23 (b) The given wave equation,

$y = 10^{-6} \sin(100t + 20x + \pi/4)$ ...(i)

On comparing Eq. (i) with standard wave equation

$y = a\sin(\omega t + kx + \phi)$, we get

$\omega = 100\ \text{rad s}^{-1}$, $k = 20\ \text{rad m}^{-1}$, $\phi = \pi/4$

$\Rightarrow$ Wave velocity,

$$v = \frac{\omega}{k} = \frac{100}{20} = 5\ \text{ms}^{-1}$$

24 (a) The given wave equation is

$$y = 0.2 \sin 2\pi\left[\frac{t}{0.01} - \frac{x}{0.3}\right]$$

$$= 0.2 \sin\left[\frac{2\pi t}{0.01} - \frac{2\pi x}{0.3}\right]$$

$$= 0.2 \sin\left[\pi + \left(\frac{2\pi x}{0.3} - \frac{2\pi t}{0.01}\right)\right]$$

$$= 0.2 \sin\left(\frac{2\pi x}{0.3} - \frac{2\pi t}{0.01} + \pi\right) \quad ...(i)$$

Comparing Eq. (i) with standard wave equation

$y = a\sin(kx - \omega t + \phi)$, we get

$\omega = \frac{2\pi}{0.01}\ \text{rad s}^{-1}$,

$k = \frac{2\pi}{0.3}\ \text{rad m}^{-1}$ and $\phi = \pi$

$\Rightarrow$ Wave velocity,

$$v = \frac{\omega}{k} = \frac{2\pi/0.01}{2\pi/0.3}$$

$$= \frac{0.3}{0.01} = 30\ \text{ms}^{-1}$$

25 (a) Given, wave equation,

$$y = 10^{-4} \sin\left(600t - 2x + \frac{\pi}{3}\right)\text{m}$$

Standard wave equation,

$$y = a\sin(\omega t - kx + \phi)$$

Compare them,

Angular speed, $\omega = 600\ \text{s}^{-1}$

Propagation constant, $k = 2\ \text{m}^{-1}$

$\therefore$ Velocity $= \frac{\omega}{k} = \frac{600}{2} = 300$ m/s

26 (c) As we know,

$$v = \frac{\omega}{k} = \frac{30}{1} = 30\ \text{m/s}$$

and $T = v^2\mu = (30)^2 \times 12 \times 10^{-3}$

$= 10.8$ N

27 (d) Given, length $(L) = 20$ m

Mass $(M) = 10\text{g} = 10^{-2}$ kg

Tension $(T) = 125$ N

Mass per unit length of the wire,

$$\mu = \frac{M}{L} = \frac{10^{-2}}{20} = 5 \times 10^{-4}\ \text{kg/m}$$

Speed of the transverse wave on the wire,

$$v = \sqrt{\frac{T}{\mu}}$$

$$= \sqrt{\frac{125}{5 \times 10^{-4}}} = 5 \times 10^2\ \text{m/s}$$

$\Rightarrow v = 500$ m/s

28 (a) Given, frequency of the wave

$\nu = 100$ Hz

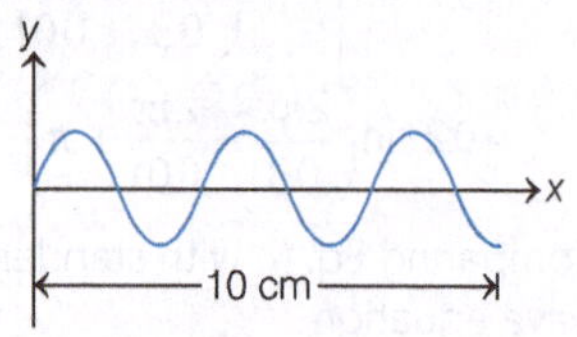

From the above figure, $\frac{5}{2}\lambda = 10$ cm

$\Rightarrow \lambda = 4$ cm

So, wavelength of the wave,

$\lambda = 4$ cm $= 0.04$ m

Now, velocity of the wave, $v = \nu\lambda$

$v = 100 \times 0.04$

$= 4\ \text{ms}^{-1}$

29 (b) Here, $\nu = 3.2\ \text{MHz} = 3.2 \times 10^6$ Hz $= 3.2 \times 10^6\ \text{s}^{-1}$, $v = 1.6\ \text{km s}^{-1}$ $= 1.6 \times 10^3\ \text{ms}^{-1}$ Wavelength,

$$\lambda = \frac{v}{\nu} = \frac{1.6 \times 10^3 \text{ms}^{-1}}{3.2 \times 10^6 \text{s}^{-1}}$$

$= 0.5 \times 10^{-3}$ m

$= 0.5$ mm

30 (b) Here, $\lambda_A = 100\ \text{mm} = 0.10$ m

$\lambda_B = 0.25$ m, $v_A = 80\ \text{cms}^{-1}$

$= 0.80\ \text{ms}^{-1}$

As the frequency of the wave remains same in the two media

$$\therefore \quad \nu = \frac{v_A}{\lambda_A} = \frac{v_B}{\lambda_B}$$

$$\therefore \quad v_B = \frac{\lambda_B}{\lambda_A} \times v_A = \frac{0.25}{0.10} \times 0.80$$

$\Rightarrow \quad v_B = 2\ \text{ms}^{-1}$

31 (c) Here, $v_{air} = 350\ \text{ms}^{-1}$,

$v_{brass} = 3500\ \text{ms}^{-1}$

When a sound wave goes from one medium to another medium, its frequency (ν) remains the same.

Frequency, $\nu = \frac{\text{Velocity}}{\text{Wavelength}} = \frac{v}{\lambda}$

Since, ν remains the same in both the media, so $\frac{v_{air}}{\lambda_{air}} = \frac{v_{brass}}{\lambda_{brass}}$

or $\lambda_{brass} = \lambda_{air} \times \frac{v_{brass}}{v_{air}}$

$$= \lambda_{air} \times \frac{3500}{350} = 10\lambda_{air}$$

32 (c) Let v_1, v_2 be speeds of S and P waves and t_1, t_2 be the time taken by these waves to travel to reach the seismograph. Let the epicentre of the earthquake is located at a distance d from the seismograph, then

$$d = v_1t_1 = v_2t_2 \quad \text{...(i)}$$

Here, $v_1 = 4\ \text{km s}^{-1}$

and $v_2 = 8\ \text{km s}^{-1}$

$\therefore \quad 4t_1 = 8t_2 \Rightarrow t_1 = 2t_2$ ...(ii)

and $t_1 - t_2 = 4\ \text{min} = 240$ s

$\therefore\ 2t_2 - t_2 = 240$ [using Eq. (ii)]

or $\quad t_2 = 240$ s

Put in Eq. (ii), we get

$t_1 = 2 \times 240\text{s} = 480$ s

$d = 4 \times 480 = 1920$ km

33 (c) Given, wave equation,

$y = 0.002\cos(300t - 15x)$

Mass density, $\mu = 0.1$ kg/m

Comparing the given wave equation with

$y = a\cos(\omega t - kx)$, we have

$\omega = 300\ \text{rad s}^{-1}$, $k = 15\ \text{rad m}^{-1}$

$\therefore$ Velocity of wave,

$$v = \frac{\omega}{k} = \frac{300}{15} = 20\ \text{m/s}$$

Wave speed in string is also given by

$$v = \sqrt{\frac{T}{\mu}} \quad \text{...(i)}$$

Substituting the values in Eq. (i), we get

$$20 = \sqrt{\frac{T}{0.1}}$$

$\Rightarrow \quad T = 40$ N

34 (a) Given, radius of wire $A = 2$ (radius of wire B)

i.e. $\quad r_A = 2r_B$

Also, tension $T_B = T_A$

Mass of string A, m_A = volume × density

$= (\pi r_A^2) \times l_A \times \rho_A$ ...(i)

and $\quad m_B = (\pi r_B^2) \times l_B \times \rho_B$ ...(ii)

Dividing Eq. (i) by Eq. (ii), we get

$$\therefore \quad \frac{m_A}{m_B} = \frac{r_A^2\, l_A}{r_B^2\, l_B} \quad (\because \rho_A = \rho_B)$$

$$\Rightarrow \quad \frac{m_A / l_A}{m_B / l_B} = \frac{r_A^2}{r_B^2} \quad \text{...(iii)}$$

Since, linear mass density,

$$\mu = \frac{m}{l}$$

$$\Rightarrow \quad \frac{\mu_A}{\mu_B} = \frac{m_A / l_A}{m_B / l_B} = \left(\frac{r_A}{r_B}\right)^2$$

[using Eq. (iii)]

We know, speed of transverse wave, $v = \sqrt{\frac{T}{\mu}}$

$$\Rightarrow \frac{v_A}{v_B} = \sqrt{\frac{\mu_B}{\mu_A}} = \frac{r_B}{r_A} = \frac{1}{2} \quad (\because r_A = 2r_B)$$

35 (b) We know that, 1 mol of any gas occupies 22.4 L at standard temperature and pressure (STP), therefore density of air at STP is

$$\rho_0 = \frac{\text{Mass of one mole of air}}{\text{Volume of one mole of air at STP}}$$

$$= \frac{29.0 \times 10^{-3}}{22.4 \times 10^{-3}} = 1.29 \text{ kg m}^{-3}$$

Also, at STP, pressure of air is $1.01 \times 10^5 \text{ Nm}^{-2}$.

So, according to Newton's formula for the speed of sound in medium, we get speed of sound in air at STP as

$$v = \sqrt{\frac{p}{\rho_0}} = \left[\frac{1.01 \times 10^5}{1.29}\right]^{1/2}$$

$$= 279.81 \text{ ms}^{-1} \cong 280 \text{ ms}^{-1}$$

36 (c) $v_{\substack{\text{solid} \\ \text{(aluminium)}}} = 6420 \text{ms}^{-1}$

$v_{\substack{\text{liquid} \\ \text{(water)}}} = 1482 \text{ ms}^{-1}$,

$v_{\text{air}} = 343 \text{ ms}^{-1}$

$\therefore$ Correct order is

$$v_{\substack{\text{solid} \\ \text{(aluminium)}}} > v_{\substack{\text{liquid} \\ \text{(water)}}} > v_{\text{air}}$$

37 (b) Transverse wave speed over a string is given by

$$v = \sqrt{T/\mu} \quad \text{... (i)}$$

Here, when velocity is v, then tension, $T_1 = 2.06 \times 10^4$ N

Let when velocity is $\frac{v}{2}$, then tension is T, hence from Eq. (i), we get

$$\frac{v}{\frac{v}{2}} = \sqrt{\frac{T_1}{T}}$$

$$\Rightarrow \quad T = \frac{T_1}{4} = \frac{2.06 \times 10^4}{4}$$

or $\quad T = 5.15 \times 10^3$ N

38 (d) $v = \sqrt{\frac{T}{\mu}}$; μ = mass per unit length of string.

$$v \propto \sqrt{T}$$

$$\frac{v_2}{v_1} = \sqrt{\frac{T_2}{T_1}}$$

$$v_2 = v_1\sqrt{\frac{T_2}{T_1}}$$

$$= 500\sqrt{\frac{4T}{T}}$$

$$= 1000 \text{ m/s}$$

39 (c) As we know,

Velocity of longitudinal wave,

$$v_1 = \sqrt{\frac{Y}{\rho}}$$

and velocity of transverse wave,

$$v_2 = \sqrt{\frac{T}{m}} = \sqrt{\frac{T}{\rho s}}$$

$$\therefore \quad \frac{v_1}{v_2} = \sqrt{\frac{Ys}{T}} = \sqrt{\frac{Y}{T/s}}$$

$$= \sqrt{\frac{Y}{Y\left(\frac{\Delta l}{l}\right)}} = \sqrt{n}$$

40 (b) The speed of sound in air is given as

$$v = \sqrt{\frac{\gamma RT}{M}}$$

where, T = absolute temperature,

γ = adiabatic constant,

R = gas constant

and M = molecular mass of air.

Since, γ and M are constants.

$$\therefore \quad v \propto \sqrt{T} \Rightarrow \frac{v_t}{v_0} = \sqrt{\frac{273 + t}{273}}$$

$$v_t = 2v_0 \text{ (Given)}$$

$$\frac{2v_0}{v_0} = \sqrt{\frac{273 + t}{273}}$$

$$2 = \sqrt{\frac{273 + t}{273}}$$

Squaring both sides, we get

$$4 = \frac{273 + t}{273}$$

$$1092 = 273 + t$$

$$819°\text{C} = t$$

41 (a) The velocity of sound (v) in a gas due to a temperature change is given by

$$\frac{v'}{v} = \sqrt{\frac{T'}{T}}$$

$$\frac{v'}{v} = \sqrt{\frac{20 + 273}{273}}$$

$$\frac{v'}{340} = \sqrt{\frac{293}{273}}$$

$$v' = 340 \times \sqrt{1.073}$$

$$= 340 \times 1.036$$

$$v' = 352.24 \text{ m/s}$$

$$v' \approx 352 \text{ m/s}$$

42 (b) Given, bulk modulus of liquid (B)

$$= 1.5 \times 10^9 \text{ Nm}^{-2}$$

Density (ρ) $= 6000 \text{ kgm}^{-3}$

So, the speed of sound in liquid is given by

$$v = \sqrt{\frac{B}{\rho}}$$

$$\therefore \quad v = \sqrt{\frac{1.5 \times 10^9}{6000}} = 600 \text{ ms}^{-1}$$

43 (c) Speed of sound waves in a fluid is given by

$v = \sqrt{\frac{B}{\rho}}$, where B is bulk modulus and ρ is density of the medium.

Clearly, $\quad v \propto \frac{1}{\sqrt{\rho}}$

($\because$ for any fluid, B = constant)

and $\quad v \propto \sqrt{B}$

($\because$ for medium, ρ = constant)

Hence, speed of sound wave depends on inversely square root of density and directly on square root of bulk modulus of the medium.

44 (a) The speed of wave in a bar,

$$v = \sqrt{\frac{Y}{\rho}}$$

So, the ratio of the speed of longitudinal waves in the solid bars is

$$\frac{v_1}{v_2} = \sqrt{\frac{Y_1\rho_2}{Y_2\rho_1}}$$

Since, solid bars are made up of the materials with same density, i.e. $\quad \rho_1 = \rho_2$

$$\Rightarrow \quad \frac{v_1}{v_2} = \sqrt{\frac{Y_1}{Y_2}} = \sqrt{4} = 2$$

$$\left[\text{given}, \frac{Y_1}{Y_2} = 4\right]$$

45 (*d*) The speed of sound in a gas does not depend upon pressure of the gas, till temperature remains constant, i.e. speed remains the same whatever be the pressure.

46 (*a*) The Laplace correction shows that the pressure variations in the propagation of sound waves are so fast that there is a short time for the heat flow to maintain constant temperature.

So, these variations are adiabatic in nature.

47 (*c*) Due to the principle of superposition, the displacement due to two pulses will exactly cancel out each other, i.e. at $t = t_1$ second, resultant displacement is zero.

48 (*b*) We have, incident wave,

$y_1 = a \sin(kx - \omega t)$

So the reflected wave,

$y_2 = a \sin(kx + \omega t)$

From principle of superposition,

The standing wave equation is obtained as

$$y(x,t) = y_1 + y_2$$
$$= a[\sin(kx - \omega t) + \sin(kx + \omega t)]$$
$$= 2a \sin kx \cos \omega t \quad \text{...(i)}$$

On comparing Eq. (i) with $y(x,t) = A(x) \cos \omega t$, we get

Amplitude, $A(x) = 2a \sin kx$

49 (*d*) Consider the two waves of equal amplitude A and equal frequency travelling in the same direction as follows

$$y_1(x,t) = A \sin(kx - \omega t)$$
$$y_2(x,t) = A \sin(kx - \omega t + \phi)$$
$$y(x,t) = A \sin(kx - \omega t) + A \sin(kx - \omega t + \phi)$$
$$= A\left[2 \sin\left[\frac{(kx - \omega t) + (kx - \omega t + \phi)}{2}\right] \cos \frac{\phi}{2}\right]$$
$$= 2A \cos \frac{\phi}{2} \sin\left(kx - \omega t + \frac{\phi}{2}\right)$$

∴ The resultant amplitude

$$= 2A \cos \frac{\phi}{2}$$

Since, the given cosine function will vary from 0 to π and hence, magnitude of wave varies between 0 to $2A$.

50 (*a*) Amplitude of the resultant of the two waves of same amplitude and equal frequency when they travel in the same direction in a medium having phase difference of ϕ is given as

$$A(\phi) = 2A \cos\left(\frac{\phi}{2}\right)$$

Given, $\phi = 120°$

$$\Rightarrow \quad A(\phi) = 2A \cos\left(\frac{120°}{2}\right)$$

or $\quad A(\phi) = 2A \times \frac{1}{2} = A$

51 (*a*) Let ϕ_1 and ϕ_2 represent angle of the first and second waves, then

$$\phi_2 = \frac{2\pi}{\lambda}[(vt - x) + x_0]$$

and $\quad \phi_1 = \frac{2\pi}{\lambda}(vt - x)$

But $x_0 = \frac{\lambda}{2} \Rightarrow \phi_2 - \phi_1 = \pi$

$$\left(\because \Delta\phi = \frac{2\pi}{\lambda}\Delta x\right)$$

Hence, phase difference $\phi = \pi$, so amplitude of the resultant wave is

$$R = \sqrt{a^2 + b^2 + 2ab \cos \phi}$$
$$= \sqrt{a^2 + b^2 + 2ab \cos \pi}$$
$$= \sqrt{(a - b)^2} = a - b$$

$\therefore R = |a - b|$

52 (*c*) The reflected wave has the same shape as the incident wave but it suffers a phase change of π or 180° on reflection.

This is because the boundary is rigid and the disturbance must have zero displacement at all times at the boundary.

53 (*c*) The string is undergoing standing waves.

Here, $\quad v = \sqrt{\frac{T}{\mu}} \quad$ ...(i)

and $\quad \lambda = kL \quad$ ...(ii)

where, k is a constant

Now, $\quad f = \frac{v}{\lambda}$

Using Eqs. (i) and (ii), we get

$$f = \frac{\sqrt{\frac{T}{\mu}}}{kL}$$

Here, T, μ and k are constants.

$$\therefore \quad f \propto \frac{1}{L}$$

Hence, to decrease the frequency, length can be increased.

55 (*a*) If a boundary is an interface between two different elastic media which means that the boundary is not completely rigid, then a part of the incident wave is reflected and a part is transmitted into the second medium.

Thus, the statement given in option (a) is correct but rest are incorrect.

56 (*a*) In stationary waves, change in pressure and density are maximum at nodes while displacement is minimum (zero).

58 (*c*) Octave means, the frequency is in the ratio of 2 : 1.

i.e., $\quad \frac{f'}{f} = \frac{2}{1}$

We know that, $f \propto \sqrt{T}$

$$\therefore \quad \frac{f'}{f} = \sqrt{\frac{T'}{T}} = \frac{2}{1} \Rightarrow T' = 4T$$

So, final weight,

$$T' = 4 \times 4 = 16 \text{ kg-wt}$$

59 (*d*) Possible frequencies of waves in a wire is given as

$$\nu_n = \frac{nv}{2l}$$

Fundamental frequency,

$$\nu_0 = \frac{v}{2L} \quad ...(i)$$
$$(\because n = 1)$$

Wave velocity,

$$v = \sqrt{\frac{T}{\mu}} = \sqrt{\frac{T}{(m/L)}} \quad ...(ii)$$
$$\left(\because \mu = \frac{m}{L}\right)$$

$\because$ Mass of the string,

$$m = \text{Volume} \times \text{Density}$$
$$= (\pi r^2 \times L) \times \rho$$
$$\Rightarrow \quad \mu = \frac{m}{L} = \pi r^2 \rho$$

On substituting the value of μ in Eq. (ii), we get

$$\Rightarrow \quad v = \sqrt{\frac{T}{\pi r^2 \rho}} = \frac{1}{r}\sqrt{\frac{T}{\pi\rho}}$$

Substituting the value of v in Eq. (i), we get

$$\nu_0 = \frac{1}{2rL}\sqrt{\frac{T}{\pi\rho}}$$
$$\therefore \quad \frac{\nu_{01}}{\nu_{02}} = \frac{L_2}{L_1} \times \frac{r_2}{r_1}\sqrt{\frac{T_1}{T_2}}$$
$$\Rightarrow \quad \frac{600}{\nu_{02}} = \frac{2}{1} \times \frac{1}{2} \times \sqrt{\frac{T}{T/9}} = 3$$
$$\therefore \quad \nu_{02} = \frac{600}{3} = 200 \text{ Hz}$$

60 (*b*) Frequency of vibration of a string in nth harmonic is given by

$$f_n = n \cdot \frac{v}{2l} \quad ... (i)$$

Here, $f_3 = 240$ Hz, $l = 2$ m and $n = 3$

Substituting these values in Eq. (i), we get

$$\therefore \quad 240 = 3 \times \frac{v}{2 \times 2}$$
$$\Rightarrow \quad v = \frac{4 \times 240}{3} = 320 \text{ ms}^{-1}$$

Also, fundamental frequency,

$$f = \frac{f_n}{n} = \frac{f_3}{3} = \frac{240}{3} = 80 \text{ Hz}$$

61 (*b*) When open tube is dipped in water, it becomes a tube closed at one end as shown below,

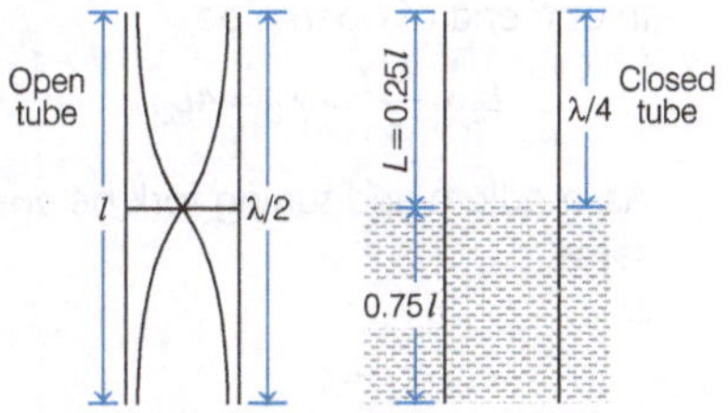

Fundamental frequency for open tube is $v/2l$.

Fundamental frequency of string

$$(\nu_0) = \frac{v}{2l}$$

Fundamental frequency for closed tube,

$$\nu_{0(\text{closed tube})} = \frac{v}{4L}$$

Length available for resonance for closed tube is 0.25 l.

$$\Rightarrow \quad L = 0.25\, l$$
$$\therefore \nu_{0\,(\text{closed tube})} = \frac{v}{4\,(0.25l)} = \frac{v}{2l} \times 2$$
$$= 2 \times \text{frequency of string}$$
$$\Rightarrow \quad \frac{\nu_{0(\text{closed tube})}}{\nu_{0(\text{string})}} = 2$$

62 (*b*) At time t, length of tube above water, $l = (l_1 - vt) = \frac{\lambda}{4}$

Fundamental frequency, $f_0 = \frac{c}{4l}$

$$f_0 = \frac{c}{4(l_1 - vt)}$$
$$\frac{df_0}{dt} = \frac{-c(-v)}{4(l_1 - vt)^2} = \frac{+cv}{4l^2}$$
$$\left|\frac{df_0}{dt}\right| = \frac{cv}{4l^2}$$

63 (*d*) Given, length of open organ pipe, $l = 50$ cm

For first overtone, $n = 2$

$$f_o = \frac{nv}{2l} = \frac{2v}{2 \times 50} = \frac{v}{50}$$

Length of closed organ pipe, $l_2 = l$

Fundamental frequency,

$$f_c = \frac{v}{4l}$$

As given, $f_o = f_c$

$$\therefore \quad \frac{v}{50} = \frac{v}{4l}$$
$$l = \frac{50}{4}$$
$$l = 12.5 \text{ cm}$$

64 (*c*) For an organ pipe, closed from one end frequency of nth harmonic oscillation is given as

$$\nu = \frac{(2n+1)\,v}{4L}$$

Given, $v = 340$ ms^{-1},

$L = 85$ cm $= 0.85$ m

and $\nu = 1250$ Hz

According to question,

$$\frac{(2n+1)v}{4L} < 1250$$

Substituting the given values in the above relation, we get

$$\Rightarrow \quad (2n+1) < 1250 \times \frac{4 \times 0.85}{340}$$
$$(2n+1) < 12.5$$
$$\Rightarrow \quad 2n < 11.50$$
$$n < 5.75$$

So, n can be 0, 1, 2, 3, 4, 5.

Therefore, we have 6 possible number of natural oscillations whose frequencies lie below 1250 Hz.

65 (*d*) In case of air column in a pipe open at both ends, each end acts an as anti-node.

The frequency of the possible nth harmonics in this pipe is given as $\nu_n = \frac{nv}{2L}$, where $n = 0, 1, 2, \ldots$.

Thus, an air column open at both ends generates all harmonics.

Thus, statements given in options (a) and (b) are correct but option (c) is incorrect.

66 (*d*) Given, speed of sound in air, $v = 330$ m/s

Length of organ pipe, $L = 1$ m and frequency, $\nu = 1000$ Hz

For an open organ pipe,

Fundamental frequency, $\nu_1 = \frac{v}{2L}$

$$= \frac{330}{2 \times 1} = 165 \text{ Hz}$$

$\therefore$ Number of tones present in the open organ pipe

$$= \frac{\nu}{\nu_1} = \frac{1000}{165} = 6.06 \simeq 6$$

67 (c) Given, $\nu = 1000$ Hz, $v = 332$ m/s and $L = 16.6$ cm$= 16.6 \times 10^{-2}$ m

Frequency of nth harmonic in an organ pipe open on both ends,

$$\nu = \frac{nv}{2L} \quad \text{or} \quad n = \frac{2\nu L}{v}$$

Substituting the given values in the above relation, we get

$$n = \frac{2 \times 1000 \times 16.6 \times 10^{-2}}{332} = 1$$

68 (c) In an open organ pipe, the frequency of its nth harmonic,

$$\nu_n = \frac{nv}{2L}, \text{ where } n = 1, 2, 3, \cdots \quad \text{...(i)}$$

Given, $L = 30$ cm $= 0.3$ m

and $v = 330$ ms^{-1}

Substituting the given values in Eq. (i), we get

$$\nu_n = \frac{n \times 330}{2 \times 0.3} = \left(\frac{n \times 330}{0.6}\right) = n550 \text{ s}^{-1}$$

Thus, few modes of an open pipe are

I. For $n = 1$, fundamental mode

$$\nu_1 = 550 \times 1 = 550 \text{ s}^{-1}$$
$$\Rightarrow \nu_1 = 550 \text{ Hz}$$

II. For $n = 2$, second harmonic

$$\nu_2 = 2\nu_0 = 2 \times 550 = 1100 \text{ Hz} = 1.1 \text{ kHz}$$

Thus, a source of frequency 1.1 kHz will resonate at second harmonic.

69 (b) As the medium, frequency and number of harmonics in open and closed pipes are same. So, number of nodes and waves in both cases will be same

In both ends of open pipe,

$$L_1 = \frac{2 \times \lambda_1}{4} \Rightarrow \lambda_1 = 2L_1$$

and $\quad V_1 = \frac{c}{\lambda_1} = \frac{c}{2L_1}$

In one end of open pipe,

$$L_2 = \frac{\lambda_2}{4} \Rightarrow \lambda_2 = 4L_2$$

As, medium and tuning fork be are same.

$\therefore \quad V_1 = V_2$

$$c_1 = c_2 = c$$
$$V_1 = \frac{c}{4L_1}$$

or $\quad \frac{c}{2L_1} = \frac{c}{4L_2}$

$\Rightarrow \quad L_2 = \frac{L_1}{2}$

So, length of one end closed pipe will be half of both end open pipe for first resonant harmonic.

70 (a) Number of beats/s $= n_1 - n_2$

$$= \frac{v}{2l} - \frac{v}{2(l+x)} = \frac{v(l+x-l)}{2l(l+x)}$$
$$= \frac{vx}{2l(l+x)} = \frac{vx}{2l^2} \quad (\because x << l)$$

71 (b) At open end, phase of pressure wave changes by 180°, so compression returns as rarefaction. At closed end, there is no phase change. So, compression returns as compression and rarefaction as rarefaction.

Hence, for an open pipe blown with high pressure pulse, low pressure pulse starts travelling up. Similarly, for closed pipe, high pressure pulse starts travelling up and down the pipe.

72 (d) $\Delta n = n_1 - n_2 = \frac{v}{2}\left(\frac{1}{l_1} - \frac{1}{l_2}\right)$

$$4 = \frac{v}{2}\left(\frac{1}{100} - \frac{1}{102.5}\right)$$
$$4 = \frac{v}{2}\left(\frac{2.5}{100 \times 102.5}\right)$$
$$v = \frac{4 \times 2 \times 100 \times 102.5}{2.5}$$
$$= 32800 \text{ ms}^{-1}$$

73 (a) Increase in the tension of a string increases its frequency. If the original frequency of $B\,(\nu_B)$ were greater than that of $A\,(\nu_A)$, further increase in ν_B should have resulted in an increase in the beat frequency. But the beat frequency is found to decrease. This shows that $\nu_B < \nu_A$.

Since, $\nu_A - \nu_B = 5$ Hz

and $\quad \nu_A = 427$ Hz,

we get $\quad \nu_B = 422$ Hz.

74 (a) Given, known frequency is 250 Hz and unknown frequency gives 4 beats/s, so there are two possible cases as shown

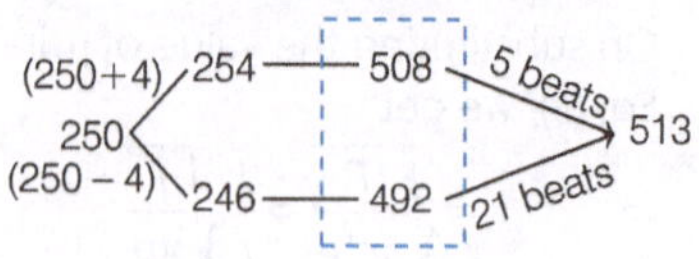

Hence, unknown frequency is 254 Hz.

75 (c) The frequency of fork 2 = frequency of fork 1 ± beat frequency

$$= 200 \pm 4 = 196 \text{ or } 204 \text{ Hz}$$

Since, on attaching the tape on the prong of fork 2, its frequency decreases, but now the number of beats per second is 6, i.e. the frequency difference now increases. It is possible only when before attaching the tape, the frequency of fork 2 is less than the frequency of tuning fork 1. Hence, the original frequency of fork 2 was 196 Hz.

76 (c) $n_Q = 500$ Hz

$$n_P = 496 \text{ Hz or } 504 \text{ Hz}$$

When loaded its frequency will decrease when $n_P = 496$, the difference with n_B will increase. This will give 8 beats when its frequency will decrease to 492 Hz. Therefore, 496 Hz is original frequency of P.

77 (c) $b = n_2 - n_1$

$$2 = \frac{v}{\lambda_2} - \frac{v}{\lambda_1}$$

$$2 = v\left(\frac{1}{2.02} - \frac{1}{2}\right)$$
$$2 = v\left(\frac{100}{202} - \frac{1}{2}\right)$$
$$2 = v\left(\frac{200 - 202}{404}\right)$$
$$2 = v \times \frac{2}{404}$$
$$v = 404 \text{ m/s}$$

78 (*d*) Let speed of sound in air be v and frequency of third note is f.

Given, $f_1 = \dfrac{v}{\frac{80}{175}} = \dfrac{175v}{80}$

$$f_2 = \frac{v}{\frac{80}{173}} = \frac{173v}{80}$$

According to condition,

$$\frac{175v}{80} - f = 4 \quad \text{...(i)}$$
$$f - \frac{173v}{80} = 4 \quad \text{...(ii)}$$

Adding Eqs. (i) and (ii), we get

$$\frac{175v}{80} - \frac{173v}{80} = 8$$
$$\Rightarrow \quad \frac{175v - 173v}{80} = 8$$
$$\Rightarrow \quad 2v = 8 \times 80$$
$$\Rightarrow \quad v = 320 \text{ m/s}$$

79 (*b*) Frequency $= \dfrac{\text{Velocity}}{\text{Wavelength}}$

$$\therefore \quad f_1 = \frac{v}{\lambda_1} = \frac{330}{5} = 66 \text{ Hz}$$
and $f_2 = \dfrac{v}{\lambda_2} = \dfrac{330}{5.5} = 60$ Hz

Number of beats per second
$$= f_1 - f_2$$
$$= 66 - 60 = 6$$

80 (*c*) Beat frequency = Number of beats/ second

$$n = n_2 \sim n_1$$
$$\therefore \quad n_1 = n_2 \pm n$$

81 (*b*) From the given equations of progressive wave, $\omega_1 = 500\pi$ and $\omega_2 = 506\pi$

$$\therefore \quad n_1 = 250, n_2 = 253$$

So, beat frequency

$$= n_2 - n_1 = 253 - 250 = 3$$
beats per second

$\therefore$ Number of beats per min $= 180$

Assertion and Reason Questions

1 (*d*) Ripples seen on water surface are transverse waves.
Transverse waves are possible on open fluid surface.

2 (*a*) Longitudinal waves involves compressions and they can propagate through both solids and fluids.
Since, solids and fluids both have bulk modulus, i.e. they can sustain compressive stress.

Therefore, both Assertion and Reason are correct and Reason is the correct explanation of Assertion.

3 (*d*) Speed of sound is given by
$$v = \sqrt{\frac{\gamma p}{\rho}}$$
i.e. $\quad v \propto \sqrt{p}$

So, the speed of sound is directly proportional to the square root of pressure.
Therefore, Assertion is incorrect but Reason is correct.

4 (*a*) Let speed of sound be v.
Length and radius of pipe are L and r, respectively.
Fundamental frequency of a pipe
$$\nu = \frac{v}{4(L+e)}, \text{ for closed organ pipe}$$
Here, $e = 0.6r$
$$\nu = \frac{v}{2(L+e)}, \text{ for open organ pipe}$$
Here, $e = 1.2r$
Thus, Reason is the correct explanation of Assertion.

5 (*a*) From the principle of superposition of waves,
the net displacement of two travelling light waves
$$y_1(x,t) = A\sin(kx - \omega t)$$
and $y_2(x,t) = A\sin(kx - \omega t + \phi)$ is
$$y(x,t) = 2A\cos\frac{\phi}{2}\sin\left(kx - \omega t + \frac{\phi}{2}\right)$$
The initial phase angle $= \dfrac{\phi}{2}$

The resultant amplitude of the given wave is $A(\phi) = 2A\cos\dfrac{\phi}{2}$

As, from $0 \le \phi \le \pi$, cosine function decreases.
Thus, resultant amplitude also decreases for $0 \le \phi \le \pi$.
Therefore, both Assertion and Reason are correct and Reason is the correct explanation of Assertion.

7 (*a*) Two waves interfere only when the phase difference between them remains constant throughout.

Therefore, both Assertion is correct but Reason is incorrect.

8 (*a*) $\nu_{beat} = |\nu_1 - \nu_2|$
Given, $\nu_1 = 11$ Hz
and $\quad \nu_2 = 9$ Hz
$\Rightarrow \quad \nu_{beat} = |11 - 9| = 2$ Hz
Therefore, both Assertion and Reason are correct and Reason is the correct explanation of Assertion.

9 (*d*) Since transverse wave can propagate through a medium which posses elasticity of shape. Air posses only volume elasticity therefore transverse wave cannot propagate through air. So, Assertion is incorrect but Reason is correct.

10 (*c*) According to the property of persistence of hearing, the impression of a sound heard persists on our mind for $\left(\dfrac{1}{10}\right)$ s. So, in order to hear distinct beats the time interval between the two successive beats should be greater than $\left(\dfrac{1}{10}\right)$ s. Thus, the difference between two frequencies must be less than 10. Also, the number of beats per second gives the difference of frequencies. So, more the number of beats, lesser would be the confusion.

Therefore, Assertion is correct but Reason is incorrect.

Statement Based Questions

1 (*b*) Statement I is correct but Statement II is incorrect. Statement II can be corrected as

Air can propagates only longitudinal waves, e.g. sound waves.

2 (*d*) Both Statement I and Statement II are correct.

In gases, sound waves are always longitudinal because gases cannot sustain shearing strain.

3 (*b*) Statement I is correct but Statement II is incorrect.

The propeller of a motor boat cuts the water surface laterally and also pushes it in backward direction. Hence, it will result in both longitudinal and transverse waves.

4 (*b*) Statement I is correct but Statement II is incorrect.

An expression for the speed of sound in any medium (derived by Newton) is given as

speed

$$= \sqrt{\frac{\text{elastic modulus of medium}}{\text{density of medium}}}$$

Velocity of sound in gas medium is

$$v = \sqrt{\frac{K}{\rho}}$$

where, K is bulk modulus of gas. $K = \gamma p$, where p is pressure of gas and γ is ratio of its principal heat capacities $\left(\frac{C_p}{C_V}\right)$. For moist air ρ is less than that for dry air and γ is slightly greater.

$\therefore$ Velocity of sound increases with increase in humidity.

5 (*a*) Both Statement I and Statement II are incorrect.

When moisture is present in the air, the density of water vapours is less than that of dry air. The velocity of sound is inversely proportional to the square root of density, hence sound travel faster in moist air than in the dry air. Therefore, on a rainy day sound travels faster than on a dry day.

6 (*a*) Both Statement I and Statement II are incorrect.

The velocity of sound in gaseous medium is given by

$$v = \sqrt{\frac{\gamma p}{\rho}}$$

Clearly, the velocity of sound in a gas is inversely proportional to the square root of density of the gas. The density of oxygen is 16 times the density of hydrogen, therefore, the velocity of sound in hydrogen is four times the velocity of sound in oxygen.

7 (*d*) Both Statement I and Statement II are correct.

Sound produced by an open organ pipe is richer because (i) It contains all harmonics. No harmonic is missing. (ii) Frequency of fundamental note in an open organ pipe is twice the fundamental frequency in a closed organ pipe of same length. [fundamental frequency of open pipe, $f_0 = \frac{v}{2L}$, fundamental frequency in closed pipe,

$$f_c = \frac{v}{4L}$$

$$\therefore \quad f_0 = 2f_c$$

8 (*d*) According to the property of persistence of hearing the impression of a sound heard persists on our mind for $\frac{1}{10}$ s.

Therefore, the number of beats per second should be less than 10.

Hence the difference in frequency of the two sources must be less than 10.

Therefore, Both Statement I and Statement II are correct.

Matching Type Questions

1 (*a*) Given,wave equation is

$$y(x,t) = 0.005 \sin(80x - 3t) \quad \text{...(i)}$$

A. The standard wave equation for a right travelling wave is given by

$$y(x,t) = a \sin(kx - \omega t) \quad \text{...(ii)}$$

On comparing Eq. (ii) with Eq. (i), we get

Amplitude, $a = 0.005$ SI units

Wave number, $k = 80$ SI units,

Angular frequency, $\omega = 3$ SI units

B. Wavelength, $\lambda = \frac{2\pi}{k} = \frac{2\pi}{80}$

$= 0.0785$ SI units

C. Frequency, $\nu = \frac{1}{T}$

As, $T = \frac{2\pi}{\omega} = \frac{2\pi}{3} = 2.09$ s

$\Rightarrow \nu = \frac{1}{2.09 \text{ s}} = 0.48$ SI units

D. The displacement y at $x = 30$ cm and time $t = 20$ s is given by

$$y = (0.005)\sin(80.0 \times 0.3 - 3 \times 20)$$

$$= 0.005 \sin(-36)$$

$$\approx 0.005 \text{ SI unit}$$

Hence, A $\rightarrow$ 4, B $\rightarrow$ 1, C $\rightarrow$ 2 and D $\rightarrow$ 3.

2 (*a*) Given, incident wave equation,

$$y(x,t) = a \sin(kx - \omega t)$$

A. Reflected wave from a rigid boundary suffers a phase change of π radians.

$$\Rightarrow y_{r_1}(x,t) = a \sin(kx - \omega t + \pi)$$

$$= -a \sin(kx - \omega t)$$

B. Reflected wave from an open boundary (non-rigid) will be in same phase with the incident wave.

$$y_{r_2}(x,t) = a \sin(kx - \omega t)$$

C. At the rigid boundary, the resultant displacement

$$= y(x,t) + y_{r_1}(x,t)$$

$= [a \sin(kx - \omega t)] + [-a \sin(kx - \omega t)]$

$= 0$

D. At the open boundary, the resultant displacement $= y\ (x, t) + y_{r_2}\ (x, t)$

$= a \sin(kx - \omega t) + a \sin(kx - \omega t)$

$= 2a \sin(kx - \omega t)$

Hence, $A \to 2$, $B \to 1$, $C \to 4$ and $D \to 3$.

3 (*b*) For a string tied at both the ends, the fixed end points behave as nodes.

A. From figure, number of nodes $= 6$

Distance between consecutive nodes $= \dfrac{\lambda}{2}$

Length of the string,

$$L = 5\left(\frac{\lambda}{2}\right) = \frac{5\lambda}{2} \quad \text{...(i)}$$

Also, we know, $L = \dfrac{n\lambda}{2}$;

$$n = 1, 2, 3, \cdots \quad \text{...(ii)}$$

On comparing Eqs. (i) and (ii), we get

$n = 5$

Thus, the figure represents fifth harmonic.

B. Number of nodes $= 7$

$$\Rightarrow \quad L = 6\left(\frac{\lambda}{2}\right) \quad \text{...(i)}$$

Again, comparing with $L = n\lambda / 2$, we get $n = 6$

Thus, the figure represents sixth harmonic.

C. Number of nodes $= 2$,

$\Rightarrow \quad L = \dfrac{\lambda}{2}$

$\Rightarrow \quad n = 1$

Thus, the figure represents first harmonic or fundamental mode.

D. Number of nodes $= 3$

or $\quad L = 2\left(\dfrac{\lambda}{2}\right) = \lambda$

So, $\quad n = 2$

Thus, the figure represents second harmonic.

Hence, $A \to 4$, $B \to 3$, $C \to 1$ and $D \to 2$.

4 (*a*) For closed organ pipe (one end closed)

B. Taking the end of the pipe to be at $x = 0$, which is the node condition. Then, the other end $x = L$ is an anti-node.

where, $L = \left(n + \dfrac{1}{2}\right)\dfrac{\lambda}{2}$; where, $n = 0, 1, 2, \cdots$.

So, the possible wavelengths of the waves in this pipe is given as

$$\lambda = \frac{2L}{\left(n + \frac{1}{2}\right)};$$

where $n = 0, 1, 2, 3, \cdots$ ...(i)

A. The normal modes or natural frequencies of the system are

$$\nu = \frac{v}{\lambda} = \left(n + \frac{1}{2}\right)\frac{v}{2L};$$

where $n = 0, 1, 2, 3, \cdots$ ...(ii)

C. For fundamental mode, put $n = 0$ in Eq. (ii), we get

$$\nu_0 = \frac{v}{4L}$$

D. For longest wavelength, $(n = 0)$,

$$\lambda = \frac{2L}{0 + \frac{1}{2}} = 4L$$

Hence, $A \to 2$, $B \to 1$, $C \to 3$ and $D \to 4$.

5 (*c*) Distance between consecutive anti-nodes $= \dfrac{\lambda}{2}$

Distance between node and anti-node $= \dfrac{\lambda}{4}$

A. From figure,

$\Rightarrow \quad L = \lambda + \dfrac{\lambda}{4}$

$= \dfrac{5\lambda}{4}$ ...(i)

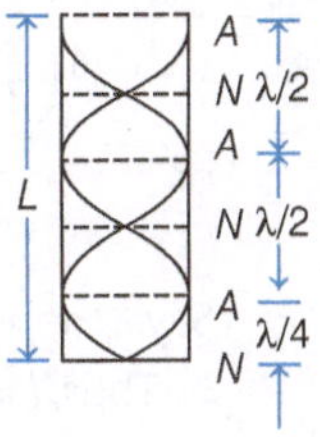

Since, for an air column closed at one end,

$$L = \left(n + \frac{1}{2}\right)\frac{\lambda}{2} = (2n + 1)\frac{\lambda}{4} \quad \text{...(ii)}$$

On comparing Eqs. (i) and (ii), we get

$(2n + 1) = 5$

or $\quad n = 2$

So, 5th harmonic occurs.

B. Similarly, $\quad L = 2\lambda + \dfrac{\lambda}{4} = \dfrac{9\lambda}{4}$

$$\Rightarrow \quad \frac{(2n + 1)\lambda}{4} = \frac{9\lambda}{4} \Rightarrow n = 4$$

Hence, it represents 9 th harmonic.

C. $\quad L = \dfrac{3\lambda}{2} + \dfrac{\lambda}{4} = \dfrac{7\lambda}{4}$

$$\Rightarrow \quad \frac{(2n + 1)\lambda}{4} = \frac{7\lambda}{4} \Rightarrow n = 3$$

Hence, it represents 7th harmonic.

D. $L = \dfrac{\lambda}{2} + \dfrac{\lambda}{4} = \dfrac{3\lambda}{4}$

$$\Rightarrow \quad \frac{(2n + 1)\lambda}{4} = \frac{3\lambda}{4} \Rightarrow n = 2$$

Hence, it represents 3rd harmonic.

Hence, $A \to 2$, $B \to 3$, $C \to 4$ and $D \to 1$.

Numerical Type Questions

1 (9) Since, tension is variable. So, velocity of wave at ends A and B will be different.

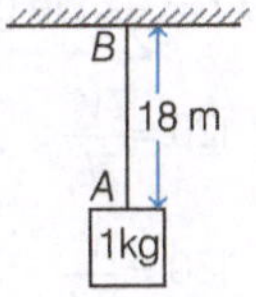

Given, $T_A = g$ and

$T_B = (8 + 1)\, g = 9\,g$

As we know, $v = \sqrt{\dfrac{T}{\mu}}$

$\therefore \quad v_A = \sqrt{\dfrac{T_A}{\mu}}$ and $v_B = \sqrt{\dfrac{T_B}{\mu}}$

Now, $\quad \dfrac{v_A}{v_B} = \sqrt{\dfrac{T_A}{\mu} \times \dfrac{\mu}{T_B}}$

$$= \sqrt{\frac{T_A}{T_B}} = \sqrt{\frac{g}{9g}} = \frac{1}{3}$$

$$\frac{v_A}{v_B} = \frac{1}{3}$$

$\Rightarrow \quad v_B = 3v_A$

Frequency of a wave depends only on source.

$\therefore$ Frequency of wave at A and B must be equal.

$$f_A = f_B$$

$$\Rightarrow \quad \frac{v_A}{\lambda_A} = \frac{v_B}{\lambda_B} \qquad [\because v = \lambda_f]$$

$$\Rightarrow \quad \lambda_B = \frac{v_B}{v_A} \times \lambda_A = 3 \times 3$$

$[\because \lambda_A = 3 \text{ cm (given)}]$

$= 9 \text{ cm}$

2 (67.5) Given, density of wire,

$$d = 2 \times 10^{-3} \text{ kg / cm}^3$$
$$= 2 \times 10^3 \text{ kg / m}^3$$

Strain in the wire,

$$\varepsilon = 40.5 \times 10^{-4}$$

and $Y = 9 \times 10^9 \text{ N / m}^2$

The lowest frequency of vibration in wire will be

$$f = \frac{1}{2L}\sqrt{\frac{Y \times \varepsilon}{d}}$$

$$= \frac{1}{2 \times 1}\sqrt{\frac{9 \times 10^9 \times 40.5 \times 10^{-4}}{2 \times 10^3}}$$

$$= \frac{135}{2} = 67.5 \text{ Hz}$$

3 (60) Using $f = \frac{v}{2L}$, we get

$$120 = \frac{v}{2L_1} \qquad \text{...(i)}$$

and $$180 = \frac{v}{2L'} \qquad \text{...(ii)}$$

Dividing Eq. (ii) by Eq. (i),

we get $\frac{L'}{L} = \frac{120}{180} = \frac{2}{3}$

$$L' = 90 \times \frac{2}{3} = 60 \text{ cm}$$

4 (234) In a string fixed at both ends, the point of maximum displacement is at $\frac{1}{4}$ of its length, when $n = 2, 6, \ldots$

For $n = 2$,

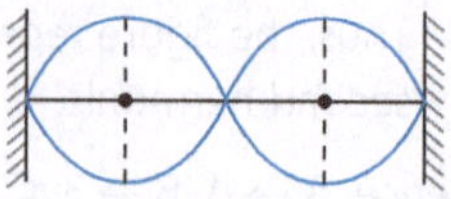

$$f_1 = \frac{2v}{2L} \qquad \text{...(i)}$$

and for $n = 6$

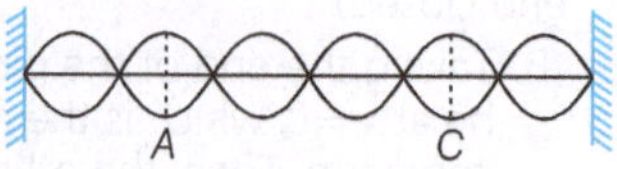

$$f_2 = \frac{6v}{2L} \qquad \text{...(ii)}$$

Dividing Eq. (ii), by Eq. (i), we get

$$\frac{f_2}{f_1} = \frac{\frac{6v}{2L}}{\frac{2v}{2L}} = 3$$

$$f_2 = 3f_1 = 3 \times 78 = 234 \text{ Hz}$$

5 (80) Given equation of stationary wave,

$y = 0.3 \sin (0.157\, x) \cos (200\pi t)$

Comparing it with general equation of stationary wave, i.e.

$y = a \sin kx \cos \omega t$, we get

$$k = (2\pi / \lambda) = 0.157$$

$$\Rightarrow \quad \lambda = \frac{2\pi}{0.157} = 4\pi^2$$

$$\left(\because \frac{1}{2\pi} \approx 0.157\right) \text{...(i)}$$

and $\omega = 200\,\pi = \frac{2\pi}{T}$

$\Rightarrow \quad T = \frac{1}{20} \text{ s}$

As the possible wavelength associated with nth harmonic of a vibrating string, i.e. fixed at both ends is given as

$$\lambda = \frac{2l}{n} \text{ or } l = n\left(\frac{\lambda}{2}\right)$$

Now, according to question, string is fixed from both ends and oscillates in 4th harmonic, so

$$4\left(\frac{\lambda}{2}\right) = l \Rightarrow 2\lambda = l$$

or $$l = 2 \times 4\pi^2 = 8\pi^2$$

[using Eq. (i)]

Say, $\pi^2 \approx 10$

$\Rightarrow$ Thus, $l \approx 80$ m

6 (1280) Here, when the piston is moved through 6.25 cm, then the path difference change $= 2 \times 6.25$

$= 12.50$ cm

Since, the intensity of sound changes from maximum to minimum, the change in path difference is $\frac{\lambda}{2}$.

$$\therefore \quad \frac{\lambda}{2} = 12.50 \text{ cm}$$

$$\Rightarrow \quad \lambda = 12.50 \times 2$$
$$= 25 \text{ cm}$$

Given, velocity of sound in air,

$v = 320 \text{ m/s} = 32000 \text{ cm/s}$

Now, the frequency of vibrating tuning fork, $f = \frac{v}{\lambda}$

$$= \frac{32000}{25} = 1280 \text{ Hz}$$

7 (6) Here, critical hearing frequency of a person = 20000 Hz.

If a closed pipe vibrates in Nth mode, then frequency of vibration,

$$n = \frac{(2N-1)v}{4l} = (2N-1)n_1$$

where, n_1 is fundamental frequency of vibration of closed pipe.

$\therefore 20000 = (2N-1) \times 1600$

$$\frac{200}{16} = 2N - 1$$

$\Rightarrow \quad N = 6.75$

$N \approx 7$

Also, in a closed organ pipe,

Number of overtone = (Number of mode of vibration) -1

$= 7 - 1 = 6$

8 (2) The fundamental frequency of an open organ pipe,

$$f = \frac{v}{2L}$$

where, L is the length of open organ pipe.

As we know that,

$$L = L_0\,[1 + \alpha(T - T_0)]$$

and velocity of sound, $v = \sqrt{\frac{\gamma RT}{M}}$

Now, for small $(T - T_0)$,

$$f(T) = f(T_0)$$

$$\frac{v}{2L} = \frac{v_0}{2L_0}$$

$$\Rightarrow \frac{\sqrt{\frac{\gamma RT}{M}}}{2L_0[1+\alpha(T-T_0)]} = \frac{\sqrt{\frac{\gamma RT_0}{M}}}{2L_0}$$

$$\Rightarrow \frac{\sqrt{T}}{1+\alpha(T-T_0)} = \sqrt{T_0}$$

$$\Rightarrow \sqrt{\frac{T}{T_0}} = 1 + \alpha(T - T_0)$$

$$\Rightarrow \left[1 + \left(\frac{T - T_0}{T_0}\right)\right]^{1/2} = 1 + \alpha(T - T_0)$$

Using binomial approximation,

$$\Rightarrow 1 + \frac{1}{2}\left(\frac{T - T_0}{T_0}\right) = 1 + \alpha(T - T_0)$$

$$\Rightarrow \quad \alpha = \frac{1}{2T_0}$$

or $\quad T_0 = \frac{1}{2\alpha} = \frac{1}{n\alpha}$

$\therefore \quad n = 2$

9 (80) Given, speed of sound in air,

$$v_{air} = 320 \text{ m/s}$$

and $\frac{\rho_{air}}{\rho_{gas}} = \frac{1}{4}$

Now, using Laplace formula, the speed of sound in medium is,

$$v = \sqrt{\frac{\gamma p}{\rho}}$$

$$\Rightarrow \frac{v_{gas}}{v_{air}} = \sqrt{\frac{\rho_{air}}{\rho_{gas}}} = \sqrt{\frac{1}{4}} = \frac{1}{2}$$

$$\Rightarrow \quad v_{gas} = \frac{v_{air}}{2} = \frac{320}{2} = 160 \text{ m/s}$$

Now, for open organ pipe,

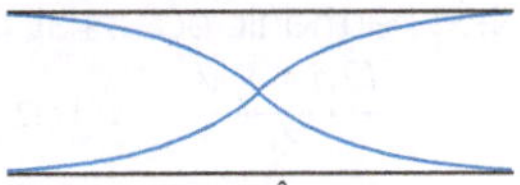

$L = \frac{\lambda}{2}$

$\therefore$ Fundamental frequency,

$$f_1 = \frac{v}{\lambda} = \frac{v}{2L} \quad \text{...(i)}$$

Second harmonic frequency,

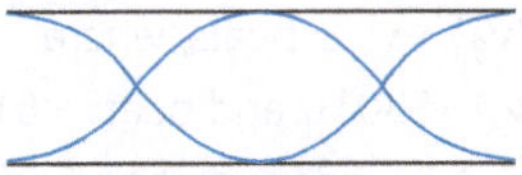

$L = \lambda$

$$f_2 = \frac{v}{\lambda} = \frac{v}{L} \quad \text{...(ii)}$$

$$\therefore \quad \Delta f = f_2 - f_1 = \frac{v}{L} - \frac{v}{2L}$$

$$= \frac{v}{2L} = \frac{160}{2 \times 1}$$

$$= 80 \text{ Hz}$$

10 (152) Let $f_1 = f_0$, then

$$f_2 = f_0 + 4$$

$$f_3 = f_0 + 2 \times 4$$

$$f_4 = f_0 + 3 \times 4$$

$$\vdots \quad \vdots \quad \vdots$$

$$f_{20} = f_0 + 19 \times 4$$

Now, $f_{20} = 2f_1$

$\Rightarrow \quad f_0 + 19 \times 4 = 2f_0$

$\Rightarrow \quad f_0 = 76 \text{ Hz}$

So, $f_{20} = 76 + 19 \times 4 = 152$ Hz

NCERT Exemplar Questions

1 (*b*) Water waves produced by a motor boat sailing in water are both longitudinal and transverse. The waves produced on the surface of water are transverse waves. Inside the water, longitudinal waves are produced due to vibrations of the rudder of the boat.

2 (*c*) Given, $v' = 2v$

Let the frequency of the sound waves in the first medium is ν and in the second medium is ν'.

Since, frequency remains same in both the medium,

so $\quad \nu = \nu'$

$$\Rightarrow \quad \frac{v}{\lambda} = \frac{v'}{\lambda'} \quad (\because v = \nu\lambda)$$

$$\Rightarrow \quad \lambda' = \left(\frac{v'}{v}\right)\lambda$$

where, λ & λ' are wavelengths and v & v' are the speeds of sound waves in first & second medium, respectively.

So, $\quad \lambda' = \left(\frac{2v}{v}\right)\lambda = 2\lambda$

3 (*c*) Speed of sound in air is given by $\quad v = \sqrt{\frac{\gamma p}{\rho}}$

For air, γ and p are constants.

$\therefore \quad v \propto \frac{1}{\sqrt{\rho}}$, where ρ is density of air.

$$\Rightarrow \quad \frac{v_2}{v_1} = \sqrt{\frac{\rho_2}{\rho_1}}$$

where, ρ_1 is density of dry air and ρ_2 is density of moist air.

As, $\rho_2 < \rho_1 = \frac{v_2}{v_1} > 1 \Rightarrow v_2 > v_1$

Hence, speed of sound wave in air increases with increase in humidity.

4 (*c*) Speed of sound wave in a medium, $\quad v \propto \sqrt{T} \quad$ ...(i)

where, T is temperature of the medium.

As, $\quad v = \nu\lambda$

If frequency ν remains fixed, so

$$v \propto \lambda \text{ or } \lambda \propto v$$

$$\Rightarrow \quad \lambda \propto \sqrt{T} \quad \text{[from Eq. (i)]}$$

5 (*b*) There is no physical movement of any part of the medium during the transmission of longitudinal waves, therefore only energy is transmitted to the mediums particles.

6 (*d*) Due to compression and rarefaction, density of the medium (air) changes. At compressed regions, density is maximum and at rarefactions, density is minimum.

As density is changing, so Boyle's law is not obeyed.

Bulk modulus remains same.

The time of compression and rarefaction is too small, i.e., we can assume adiabatic process and hence, no transfer of heat.

7 (*b*) Given, equation of incident wave,

$$y_i = 0.6 \sin 2\pi\left(t - \frac{x}{2}\right)$$

Equation of reflected wave,

$$y_r = A_r \sin 2\pi\left(t + \frac{x}{2} + \pi\right)$$

[$\because$ at denser medium, phase changes by π]

The positive sign is due to reversal of direction of propagation,

Amplitude of reflected wave,

$$A_r = \frac{2}{3} \times A_i$$

$$= \frac{2}{3} \times 0.6 = 0.4 \text{ units}$$

$$\therefore \quad y_r = -0.4 \sin 2\pi\left(t + \frac{x}{2}\right)$$

[$\because \sin(\pi + \theta) = -\sin\theta$]

Past Exams Questions

1 (a) Fundamental frequency of an open pipe, $f_o = \frac{v}{2l}$

and fundamental frequency of an closed pipe,

$$f_c = \frac{v}{4l}$$

$$\frac{f_o}{f_c} = \frac{v/2l}{v/4l} = \frac{2}{1}$$

$\therefore f_o : f_c = 2:1$

2 (b) Velocity of transverse wave in the string, $v \propto \sqrt{T}$

$$\therefore \quad \frac{v_1}{v_2} = \sqrt{\frac{T_1}{T_2}} = \sqrt{\frac{T_1}{2T_1}}$$

[$\because T_2 = 2T_1$]

$$= \frac{1}{\sqrt{2}}$$

$v_1 : v_2 = 1 : \sqrt{2}$

3 (b) We know that, $f \propto \frac{1}{l}$

$$\Rightarrow \quad \frac{f_1}{f_2} = \frac{l_2}{l_1}$$

$$\Rightarrow \quad l_2 = \frac{f_1 l_1}{f_2} = \frac{120 \times 0.9}{180}$$

$$= \frac{2}{3} \times 0.9 = 0.6 \text{ m}$$

$$= 60 \text{ cm}$$

4 (a) In case of beats formation unknown frequency

$(\nu_B) = \nu_A \pm$ beats, where

$\nu_A = 530$ Hz and beats $= 6$ Hz

$\Rightarrow \nu_A = 530 \pm 6 = 536$ or 524 Hz

When tension in B is slightly decreased, then beats frequency increases to 7 Hz.

This is possible, if we take original frequency of B as 524 Hz.

5 (c) For vibrating tuning fork over a resonance tube, the first resonance is obtained at the length.

$$l_1 = \frac{\lambda}{4}$$

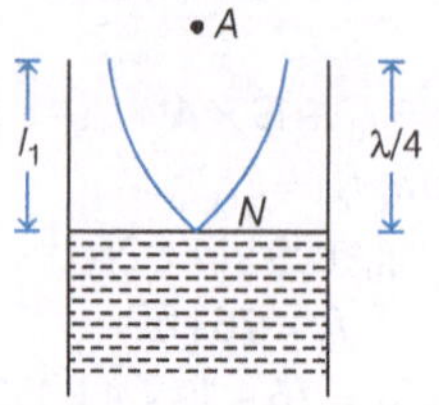

and for second resonance,

$$l_2 = \frac{\lambda}{4} + \frac{\lambda}{2} = \frac{3\lambda}{4} \quad \text{...(ii)}$$

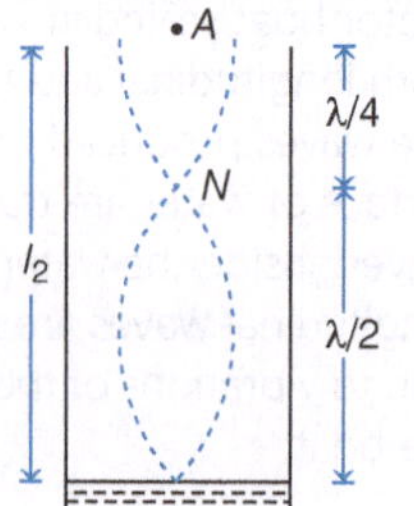

From Eqs. (i) and (ii), we get

$$l_2 - l_1 = \frac{3\lambda}{4} - \frac{\lambda}{4} = \frac{\lambda}{2}$$

$$\Rightarrow \quad \lambda = 2(l_2 - l_1)$$

$$\Rightarrow \quad v = 2f(l_2 - l_1) \quad \text{...(iii)}$$

$$\left(\because \lambda = \frac{v}{f}\right)$$

Here, $f = 800$ Hz, $l_1 = 9.75$ cm, $l_2 = 31.25$ cm.

$$\Rightarrow \quad v = 2 \times 800\,(31.25 - 9.75)$$

$$= 34400 \text{ cm/s}$$

$$= 344 \text{ m/s}$$

6 (c) Fundamental frequency for an open organ pipe is given as

$$f = \frac{v}{2L}$$

Third harmonic for a closed organ pipe is given as $f' = \frac{3v}{4L'}$

According to the question,

$$f = f'$$

$$\Rightarrow \quad \frac{v}{2L} = \frac{3v}{4L'}$$

$$L = \frac{2}{3}L'$$

Given, $L' = 20$ cm

$$\Rightarrow \quad L = \frac{2}{3} \times 20$$

$$= \frac{40}{3} \text{ cm} = 13.3 \text{ cm}$$

7 (b) For first resonance, $l_1 = \frac{\lambda}{4}$

For second resonance, $l_2 = \frac{3\lambda}{4}$

$$\therefore \quad (l_2 - l_1) = \frac{3\lambda}{4} - \frac{\lambda}{4}$$

or $\quad \lambda = 2(l_2 - l_1) \quad$ ...(i)

As, velocity of sound wave is given as,

$$v = \nu\lambda$$

where, ν is the frequency,

$$\Rightarrow \quad v = \nu\,[2(l_2 - l_1)]$$

[from Eq. (i)]

Here, $\nu = 320$ Hz,

$l_2 = 0.73$ m, $l_1 = 0.20$ m

$$\Rightarrow \quad v = 2\,[320\,(0.73 - 0.20)]$$

$$= 339.2 \text{ ms}^{-1}$$

$$\simeq 339 \text{ ms}^{-1}$$

8 (b) Now, given two nearest harmonics are of frequencies 220 Hz and 260 Hz.

$$\therefore \quad \frac{(2n-1)v}{4l} = 220 \text{ Hz} \quad \text{...(i)}$$

Next harmonic occurs at

$$\frac{(2n+1)v}{4l} = 260 \text{ Hz} \quad \text{...(ii)}$$

On subtracting Eq. (i) from Eq. (ii), we get

$$\frac{v[(2n+1)-(2n-1)]}{4l} = 260 - 220$$

$$2\left(\frac{v}{4l}\right) = 40 \Rightarrow \frac{v}{4l} = 20 \text{ Hz}$$

$\therefore$ Fundamental frequency of the system

$$= \frac{v}{4l} = 20\text{ Hz}$$

9 (*b*) For an open organ pipe,

$$v_n = \frac{n}{2L} v, \text{ where } n = 1, 2, 3, \ldots$$

For second overtone $n = 3$,

$$v_{2_o} = \frac{3v}{2L_1} \quad \ldots\text{(i)}$$

For closed organ pipe,

$$v_n = \left(\frac{2n+1}{4L}\right) v$$

where, $n = 0, 1, 2, 3, \ldots$

Ist overtone for closed organ pipe, $n = 1$

$$v_{1_c} = \frac{3v}{4L} \quad \ldots\text{(ii)}$$

$$\therefore \quad v_{2o} = v_{1c}$$

$$\Rightarrow \quad \frac{3v}{2L_1} = \frac{3v}{4L} \Rightarrow \quad L_1 = 2L$$

10 (*a*) Beat frequency $= f_1 - f_2$

$$= n - (n-1) = 1$$

and similarly for n and $n+1$,

Beat frequency $= n + 1 - n = 1$

11 (*a*) Wavelength of transverse pulse, $\lambda = \frac{v}{f}$ ...(i)

As we know, $v = \sqrt{\frac{T}{\mu}}$ ...(ii)

From Eqs. (i) and (ii), we get

$$\lambda = \frac{1}{f}\sqrt{\frac{T}{\mu}} \Rightarrow \lambda \propto \sqrt{T}$$

So, for two different cases, we get

$$\frac{\lambda_2}{\lambda_1} = \sqrt{\frac{T_2}{T_1}} = \sqrt{\frac{m_1 + m_2}{m_2}}$$

12 (*d*) Given, $l = 75$ cm,

$f_1 = 420$ Hz and $f_2 = 315$ Hz

As, two consecutive resonant frequencies for a string fixed at both ends will be $f_1 = \frac{nv}{2l}$

and $\quad f_2 = \frac{(n+1)v}{2l}$

$$\Rightarrow \quad f_2 - f_1 = 420 - 315$$

$$\Rightarrow \quad \frac{(n+1)v}{2l} - \frac{nv}{2l} = 105\text{ Hz}$$

$$\Rightarrow \quad \frac{v}{2l} = 105\text{ Hz}$$

13 (*b*) The smallest length of the air column is associated with fundamental mode of vibration of the air column as shown in the diagram.

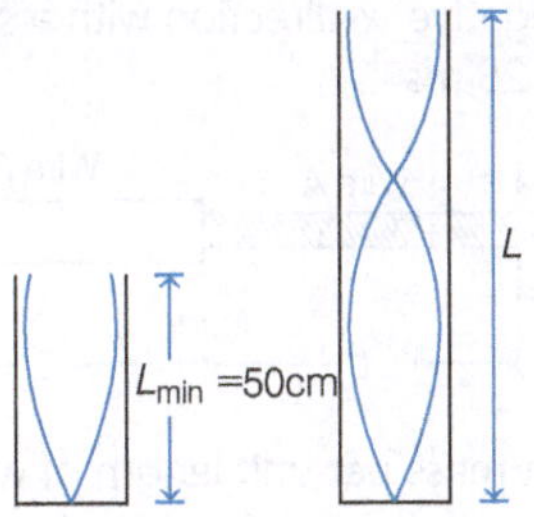

$$\because \quad L_{min} = \frac{\lambda}{4} \Rightarrow 50 = \frac{\lambda}{4}$$

$$\Rightarrow \quad \lambda = 200\text{ cm}$$

The next higher length of the air column,

$$L = \frac{\lambda}{4} + \frac{\lambda}{2} = \frac{\lambda + 2\lambda}{4} = \frac{3\lambda}{4}$$

$$= \frac{3}{4} \times 200 = 150\text{ cm}$$

14 (*c*) The fundamental frequencies of closed and open organ pipes are given as

$$v_c = \frac{v}{4l} \Rightarrow v_o = \frac{v}{2l'}$$

Given, the second overtone (one-third harmonic) of open pipe is equal to the fundamental frequency of closed pipe,

i.e. $\quad 3v_o = v_c$

$$\Rightarrow \quad 3\frac{v}{2l'} = \frac{v}{4l}$$

$$\Rightarrow \quad l' = 6l = 6 \times 20 = 120\text{ cm}$$

15 (*a*) Given,

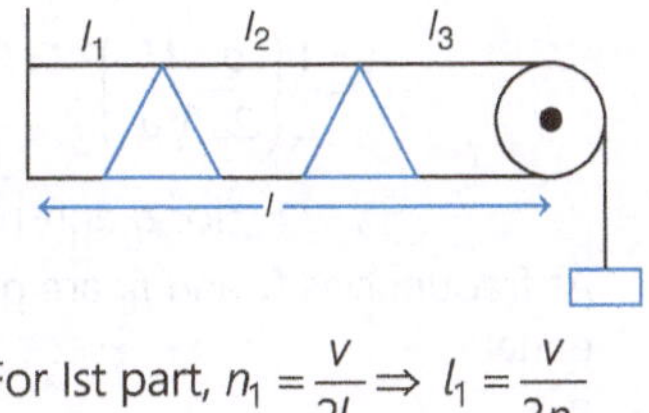

For Ist part, $n_1 = \frac{v}{2l_1} \Rightarrow l_1 = \frac{v}{2n_1}$

For IInd part, $n_2 = \frac{v}{2l_2} \Rightarrow l_2 = \frac{v}{2n_2}$

For IIIrd part, $n_3 = \frac{v}{2l_3} \Rightarrow l_3 = \frac{v}{2n_3}$

For the complete wire,

$$n = \frac{v}{2l} \Rightarrow l = \frac{v}{2n}$$

We have, $l = l_1 + l_2 + l_3$

$$\frac{v}{2n} = \frac{v}{2n_1} + \frac{v}{2n_2} + \frac{v}{2n_3}$$

$$\frac{1}{n} = \frac{1}{n_1} + \frac{1}{n_2} + \frac{1}{n_3}$$

16 (*d*) Fundamental frequency of closed organ pipe is,

$f_1 = \frac{v}{4L_1}$, v = Speed of sound and

L_1 = Length of closed organ pipe

First overtone of open organ pipe has frequency,

$$f_2 = 2 \cdot \frac{v}{2L_2},$$

L_2 = Length of open organ pipe

Given, $f_1 = f_2$ and $L_2 = 60$ cm

$$\therefore \quad \frac{v}{4L_1} = 2 \cdot \frac{v}{2L_2}$$

$$\Rightarrow \quad L_1 = \frac{L_2}{4} = \frac{60}{4} = 15\text{ cm}$$

17 (*a*) Wave equation is,

$$y = 2\cos 2\pi(330t - x)$$

$$y = 2\cos(2\pi \times 330t - 2\pi x)$$

Compare with standard wave equation,

$$y = A\cos(\omega t - kx)$$

So, angular frequency,

$$\omega = 2\pi \times 330 \frac{\text{rad}}{\text{s}}$$

$\therefore$ Linear frequency is,

$$f = \frac{\omega}{2\pi} = \frac{2\pi \times 330}{2\pi}$$

$$= 330\text{ Hz}$$

18 (*c*) Speed of transverse wave,

$$v = \sqrt{\frac{T}{\mu}} = \sqrt{\frac{70}{7.0 \times 10^{-3}}}$$

$$v = 100\text{ m/s}$$

19 (*d*) We know that,

$$k=\frac{2\pi}{\lambda}=\frac{2\pi}{4}=0.5\pi\,\text{cm}^{-1}$$

$$\omega=2\pi\nu=2\pi\times100=200\,\pi\text{s}^{-1}$$

and equation of wave,

$$y=A\sin(kx-\omega t)$$

putting the values of k and ω, then

$$y=A\sin\pi[(0.5)x-200t]$$

Hence, option (d) is correct answer.

20 (*c*) Given, $f=340$ Hz

Let beat frequency of tuning fork A be f_A and f_A' be the frequency of tuning fork A after filling.

In first case, beat frequency $=5$

$$\Rightarrow\quad f_A=340\pm5$$

$$\Rightarrow\quad f_A=345\text{ Hz or }335\text{ Hz}$$

After filling tuning fork A,

$$f_A'=340\pm2$$

$$\Rightarrow\quad f_A'=342\text{ ro }338\text{ Hz}$$

As on filling, frequency of A increases.

Hence, original frequency of tuning fork A is 335 Hz.

21 (*b*) From the given snapshot at $t=0$,

$$y=0\text{ at }x=0$$

and $y=-$ve when x increases from zero.

Standard expression of any progressive wave is given by

$$y=A\sin(kx-\omega t+\phi)$$

Here, ϕ is the phase difference, we need to get at $t=0$,

$$y=A\sin(kx+\phi)$$

Clearly $\phi=\pi$, so that

$$y=A\sin(kx+\pi)$$

$$y=-A\sin(kx)$$

$$\Rightarrow\quad y=0\text{ at }x=0$$

and $\quad y=-$ ve at $x>0$

Which satisfies the given snapshot.

22 (*a*) Wave equation is given by,

$$y=10^{-3}\sin(50t+2x)$$

Speed of wave is obtained by differentiating phase of wave.

Now, phase of wave from given equation is $\phi=50t+2x=$ constant.

Differentiating ϕ w.r.t. t, we get

$$\frac{d}{dx}(50t+2x)=\frac{d}{dt}(\text{constant})$$

$$\Rightarrow\ 50+2\left(\frac{dx}{dt}\right)=0$$

$$\Rightarrow\ \frac{dx}{dt}=\frac{-50}{2}$$

$$=-25\,\text{ms}^{-1}$$

So, wave is propagating in negative x-direction with a speed of 25 ms^{-1}.

23 (*c*)

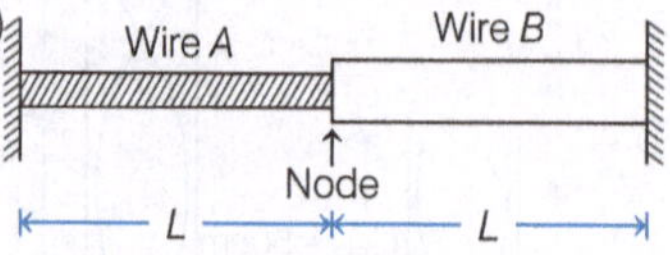

Let mass per unit length of wires are μ_A and μ_B, respectively.

∵ For same material, density is also same.

So, $\mu_A=\frac{\rho\pi r^2L}{L}=\mu$

and $\mu_B=\frac{\rho4\pi r^2L}{L}=4\mu$

Tension (T) in both connected wires are same.

So, speed of wave in wires are

$$v_A=\sqrt{\frac{T}{\mu_A}}=\sqrt{\frac{T}{\mu}}$$

and $\quad v_B=\sqrt{\frac{T}{\mu_B}}=\sqrt{\frac{T}{4\mu}}$

$$[\because\mu_A=\mu\text{ and }\mu_B=4\mu]$$

So, nth harmonic in such wires system is $f_{nth}=\frac{pv}{2L}$

$$\Rightarrow\quad f_A=\frac{pv_A}{2L}=\frac{p}{2L}\sqrt{\frac{T}{\mu}}$$

(for p anti-nodes)

Similarly, $f_B=\frac{qv_B}{2L}=\frac{q}{2L}\sqrt{\frac{T}{4\mu}}$

$$=\frac{1}{2}\left(\frac{q}{2L}\sqrt{\frac{T}{\mu}}\right)$$

(for q anti-nodes)

As frequencies f_A and f_B are given equal.

So, $\quad f_A=f_B$

$$\Rightarrow\ \frac{p}{2L}\sqrt{\frac{T}{\mu}}=\frac{q}{2}\left[\frac{1}{2L}\sqrt{\frac{T}{\mu}}\right]$$

$$\frac{p}{q}=\frac{1}{2}\ \Rightarrow\ p:q=1:2$$

Skill Boosters

1 (*d*) Number of moles of first gas is

$$n_1=\frac{m_1}{M_{01}}$$

Number of moles of second gas is

$$n_2=\frac{m_2}{M_{02}}$$

where, M_{01}, M_{02} are molecular masses of gases. Let $M_{0\text{ mix}}$ is the molecular mass of mixture.

Then,

$$m_1+m_2=\left(\frac{m_1}{M_{01}}+\frac{m_2}{M_{02}}\right)M_{0\text{ mix}}$$

$$\therefore\ M_{0\text{mix}}=\frac{m_1+m_2}{\frac{m_1}{M_{01}}+\frac{m_2}{M_{02}}}\quad\text{...(i)}$$

We know that,

$$v_1=\sqrt{\frac{\gamma RT}{M_{01}}},\ v_2=\sqrt{\frac{\gamma RT}{M_{02}}}$$

and $v_{\text{mix}}=\sqrt{\frac{\gamma RT}{M_{\text{0mix}}}}$

$$\therefore M_{01}=\frac{\gamma RT}{v_1^2},\ M_{02}=\frac{\gamma RT}{v_2^2}$$

and $M_{0\text{ mix}}=\frac{\gamma RT}{v_{\text{mix}}^2}$

Using these in Eq. (i), we get

$$\frac{\gamma RT}{v_{\text{room}}^2}=\frac{m_1+m_2}{\frac{m_1v_1^2}{\gamma RT}+\frac{m_2v_2^2}{\gamma RT}}$$

$$\Rightarrow v_{\text{room}}^2=\frac{m_1v_1^2+m_2v_2^2}{m_1+m_2}$$

∴ Speed of sound in room,

$$v_{\text{room}}=\sqrt{\frac{m_1v_1^2+m_2v_2^2}{m_1+m_2}}$$

2 (*c*) At $t=t_0$, $\frac{dy}{dt}=0$ and $y=A$

(from the first graph)

For $t>t_0$, v is negative and for $t<t_0$, v is positive (from the second graph).

We have to check these conditions in case of each option. Let us do it with the correct option (c).

$$\frac{dy}{dt} = A\frac{2\pi}{T}\cos\left[\frac{2\pi}{T}(t-t_0)+\frac{\pi}{2}\right]$$

$$= -\frac{2\pi}{T}A\sin\left\{\frac{2\pi}{T}(t-t_0)\right\}$$

$\therefore$ For $t < t_0$, $\frac{dy}{dt}$ is positive and for $t > t_0$, $\frac{dy}{dt}$ is negative.

3 (c) In the figure,

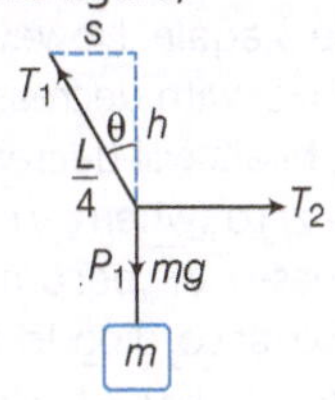

$$s = \frac{0.5}{2} = 0.25 \text{ m}$$

$$\frac{L}{4} = \frac{3}{4} = 0.75 \text{ m}$$

$$h = \sqrt{(0.75)^2 - (0.25)^2} = 0.707 \text{ m}$$

From Lami's theorem,

$$\frac{mg}{\sin(90° + \theta)} = \frac{T_2}{\sin(180° - \theta)}$$

$$T_2 = mg\tan\theta = (2)(9.8)\left(\frac{0.25}{0.707}\right)$$

$$= 6.93 \text{ N}$$

Mass per unit length of the string is

$$\mu = \frac{10\times10^{-3}}{3} = 3.33\times10^{-3}\text{ kg m}^{-1}$$

$\therefore$ Speed of pulse,

$$v = \sqrt{\frac{T_2}{\mu}} = \sqrt{\frac{6.93}{3.33\times10^{-3}}}$$

$$= 45.62 \text{ ms}^{-1}$$

$$\therefore \text{Time taken} = \frac{P_1P_2}{v} = \frac{L/2}{v}$$

$$= \frac{1.5}{45.62} = 0.0329 \text{ s}$$

$$= 32.9 \text{ ms}$$

4 (d) $g_p = \frac{G\cdot 3M}{(3R)^2} = \frac{g}{3}$

$\mu = \frac{m_0}{L_0}$. At the location of differential element tension is

$$F = \left[m + \frac{m_0}{L_0}y\right]g_p$$

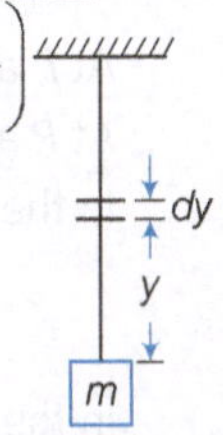

$$\text{and } v = \sqrt{\frac{F}{\mu}} = \sqrt{\frac{\left(m+\frac{m_0}{L_0}y\right)g}{3\left(\frac{m_0}{L_0}\right)}}$$

$$\therefore \frac{dy}{dt} = \sqrt{\frac{\left(m+\frac{m_0}{L_0}y\right)g}{3\left(\frac{m_0}{L_0}\right)}}$$

$$\Rightarrow \int_0^{L_0}\frac{dy}{\sqrt{mL_0 + m_0y}} = \sqrt{\frac{g}{3m_0}}\int_0^t dt$$

$$\therefore t = 2\left[\frac{\sqrt{m+m_0} - \sqrt{m}}{\sqrt{m_0}}\right]\sqrt{\frac{3L_0}{g}}$$

5 (b) $\rho_{\text{liquid}} = \frac{17}{81}\rho$, where $\rho = \rho$ (density of the block)

Volume of the block is

$$V = \frac{m}{\rho} = \frac{5}{\rho}$$

Buoyant force, B_F

$$= V\rho_L g = \frac{5}{\rho}\cdot\frac{17}{81}\rho\cdot g = \frac{85}{81}g$$

$\therefore$ Tension in the string is

$$T = \text{weight} - B_F = 5g - \frac{85}{81}g$$

$$= \frac{320\,g}{81}$$

$\therefore$ Speed of transverse wave in the string is $v = \sqrt{\frac{T}{\mu}}$

$$\text{or} \quad v = \sqrt{\frac{\frac{320\,g}{81}}{2.25\times10^{-2}}}$$

$$= \sqrt{1722} = 41.5 \text{ ms}^{-1}$$

6 (c) Let the acceleration of the system is a. Then,

$m_1g - T = m_1a$

$\Rightarrow 100 - T = 10\,a$ ...(i)

and $T = m_2a \Rightarrow T = 10a$ ...(ii)

From Eqs. (i) and (ii),

$$a = 5\text{ ms}^{-2}, T = 50\text{ N}$$

$$v = \sqrt{\frac{T}{\mu}} = \sqrt{\frac{50}{0.02}} = 50\text{ ms}^{-1}$$

In ground frame, speed of transverse pulse $= v + at$ (at time t)

$$\therefore \frac{dl}{dt} = v + at$$

$$\Rightarrow \int_0^t (v+at)\,dt = L_0$$

$$L_0 = vt + \frac{1}{2}at^2$$

$$\Rightarrow 4 = 50t + 2.5t^2$$

$$2.5t^2 + 50t - 4 = 0$$

$$\Rightarrow t = \frac{-50 \pm \sqrt{2500+40}}{5}$$

$$= 0.08 \text{ s}$$

7 (d) Initially $F_1 = V\rho_s g$

and $F_2 = V(\rho_s - \rho_w)g$,

$F_3 = V(\rho_s - \rho_k)g$

Now, $f \propto \frac{\sqrt{F}}{L}$ (other things remaining constant) $\left[\because f = \frac{n}{2L}\sqrt{\frac{F}{\mu}}\right]$

The wire resonates with the same tuning fork, so

$$\frac{\sqrt{F}}{L} = \text{constant or } \frac{F}{L^2} = \text{constant}$$

$$\therefore \frac{F_1}{L^2} = \frac{F_2}{L_w^2} = \frac{F_3}{L_k^2}$$

$$\therefore \frac{V\rho_s g}{L^2} = \frac{V(\rho_s - \rho_w)g}{L_w^2} \quad \text{...(i)}$$

$$\text{and } \frac{V\rho_s g}{L^2} = \frac{V(\rho_s - \rho_k)g}{L_k^2} \quad \text{...(ii)}$$

$$\text{From Eq. (i), } \frac{\rho_s}{L^2} = \frac{\rho_s - \rho_w}{L_w^2}$$

$$1 - \frac{\rho_w}{\rho_s} = \left(\frac{L_w}{L}\right)^2$$

$$\Rightarrow \frac{\rho_w}{\rho_s} = 1 - \left(\frac{L_w}{L}\right)^2$$

$$\frac{\rho_s}{\rho_w} = \left[1 - \left(\frac{L_w}{L}\right)^2\right]^{-1}$$

, which is specific gravity of solid.

8 (b) Let h' be the length of second liquid poured in A.

Now, let the first liquid comes down a level y in arm A and rises up the same level y in arm B.

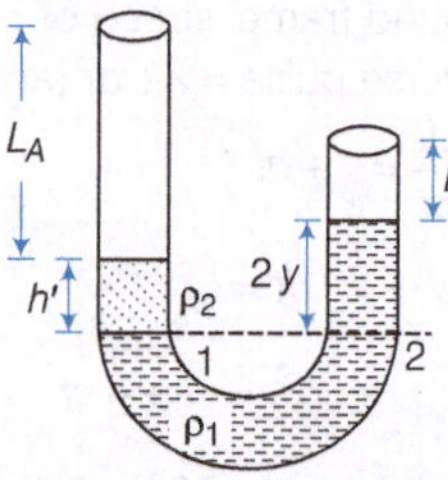

Pressure at 1 = Pressure at 2

$$\rho_2 gh' = \rho_1 g(2y)$$

$$y = \frac{\rho_2}{2\rho_1} h' = \frac{h'}{4} \qquad \left[\because \frac{\rho_2}{\rho_1} = \frac{1}{2}\right]$$

Length of air column in A is

$$L_A = (L_1 - h) - (h' - y)$$

or $\quad L_A = L_1 - h - \left(h' - \frac{h'}{4}\right)$

$$= L_1 - h - \frac{3h'}{4}$$

Length of air column B is

$$L_B = L_2 - h + y = L_2 - h + \frac{h'}{4}$$

It is given that first overtone of A is in unison with fundamental tone of B. Thus, $3\left[\frac{v}{4L_A}\right] = \frac{v}{4L_B}$

or $\quad L_A = 3L_B$

$$\therefore L_1 - h - \frac{3h'}{h} = 3\left[L_2 - h + \frac{h'}{4}\right]$$

$$\Rightarrow L_1 - h - \frac{3h'}{4} = 3L_2 - 3h + \frac{3h'}{4}$$

$$\frac{3h'}{2} = L_1 - 3L_2 + 2h$$

$$\Rightarrow h' = \frac{2(L_1 - 3L_2 + 2h)}{3}$$

9 (b) $v = \sqrt{\frac{Y}{\rho}} = \sqrt{\frac{1.6 \times 10^{11}}{2500}}$

$$= \frac{4}{5} \times 10^4 = 8000 \text{ ms}^{-1}$$

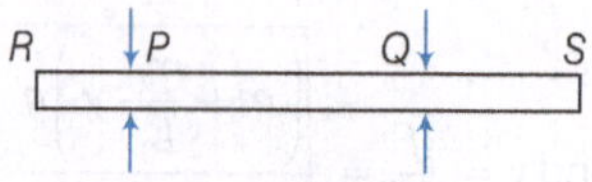

At P and Q, nodes are formed.

At R and S, anti-nodes are formed.

In the region PQ,

$$n_1\lambda = 80 \text{ cm} \qquad \text{...(i)}$$

$$(n_1 = 1, 2, 3, \cdots)$$

In the region RP,

$$(2n_2 - 1)\frac{\lambda}{4} = 5 \text{ cm}$$

$$\Rightarrow \quad (2n_2 - 1)\lambda = 20 \text{ cm} \qquad \text{...(ii)}$$

$$(n_2 = 1, 2, 3, \cdots)$$

In the region QS,

$$(2n_3 - 1)\frac{\lambda}{4} = 15 \text{ cm}$$

$$\Rightarrow \quad (2n_3 - 1)\lambda = 60 \text{ cm} \qquad \text{...(iii)}$$

$$(n_3 = 1, 2, 3, \cdots)$$

From Eqs. (i) and (ii), we get

$$\frac{n_1}{2n_2 - 1} = 8 \qquad \text{...(iv)}$$

From Eqs. (i) and (iii), we get

$$\frac{n_1}{2n_3 - 1} = \frac{8}{3} \qquad \text{...(v)}$$

For minimum frequency, n_1, n_2 and n_3 should be least.

So, $n_1 = 8$, $n_2 = 1$, $n_3 = 2$

From Eqs. (iv) and (v) for minimum frequency.

From Eq. (ii), $\lambda = \frac{20}{2(1) - 1} = 20 \text{ cm}$

or $\quad \lambda = 0.2 \text{ m}$

$$\therefore \quad f_{min} = \frac{v}{\lambda} = \frac{8000}{0.2} = 40 \text{ kHz}$$

10 (d) Here, only tension (F) in the vibrating string is changed. So, we write, $f_0 = \frac{1}{2L}\sqrt{\frac{F}{\mu}} = c\sqrt{F}$, where

constant, $c = \frac{1}{2L\sqrt{\mu}}$ and F is tension.

According to given problem, $f - c\sqrt{F} = 5$ or $c\sqrt{F} - f = 5$. If $f - c\sqrt{F} = 5$, on decreasing the tension, beats will increase and can never be 5 again. However, if $c\sqrt{F} - f = 5$, with decrease in tension, beats will decrease, become zero (when $c\sqrt{F} = f$) and will increase $c\sqrt{F}$ becomes smaller than f. So, according to the given problem, $\quad c\sqrt{100} - f = 5$

and $\qquad f - c\sqrt{81} = 5$

or $\quad f + 5 = 10c$

and $\quad f - 5 = 9c$

$$\therefore \quad \frac{f+5}{f-5} = \frac{10}{9}$$

$$\Rightarrow \quad f = 95 \text{ Hz}$$

Now, using $f + 5 = 10c$, we have

$$95 + 5 = 10c$$

or $\quad c = 10$

$$\Rightarrow \quad \frac{1}{2L\sqrt{\mu}} = 10$$

$$\mu = \frac{1}{4 \times 100 \times (0.5)^2} = 0.01$$

or $\rho \times$ cross-sectional area $= 0.01$

$$\rho = \frac{0.01}{\pi\left(\frac{10^{-3}}{2}\right)^2}$$

or $\quad \rho = 1.274 \times 10^4 \text{ kg m}^{-3}$

Chapter at a Glance

Completely Coloured Glorified Infographics to map all the Key points of the chapters for quick review.

Units and Measurement (Chapter at a Glance)

System of Units

A complete set of the fundamental units and derived units, is called as the system of units.

Three such systems of units are as follows:

- **CGS System** This system is also called Gaussian system. The base units for length, mass and time in this system are centimetre, gram and second, respectively.
- **FPS System** This system is a British system which uses foot, pound and second as base units of length, mass and time, respectively.
- **MKS System** This system is a French system which uses metre, kilogram and second as base units of length, mass and time, respectively.

SI Units

- The SI units is internationally accepted system of units.
- There are seven base units and two supplementary units in this system.

Derived Units

- The units of measurement of all other physical quantities which can be obtained from fundamental units are called derived units.

Fundamental Units

- Those physical quantities which are independent of other physical quantities and not defined in terms of other physical quantities are called fundamental or base quantities.

Units

- Reference standard used to measure a physical quantity is called unit.

Supplementary Units

- **Plane angle** It is the ratio of length of arc to the radius of circle. Its unit is radian with symbol rad.
  i.e, $d\theta = \frac{dS}{r}$

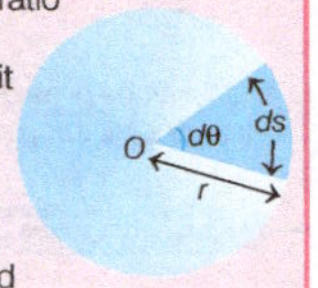

- **Solid angle** It is the ratio of the intercepted area dA of the spherical surface to the square of its radius. Its unit is steradian with symbol sr.
  $d\Omega = \frac{dA}{r^2}$

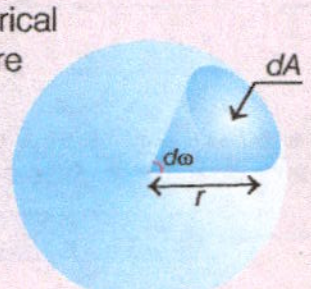

Significant Figures

- All the non-zero digits are significant.
- All the zeros in between two non-zero digit are significant no matter, where the decimal points is.
- If the number is less than 1, the zero on the right of decimal point and to the left of first non-zero digit are not significant.
- Zeroes after the last non-zero digit are significant, if number is less than 1.
- In a number without decimal point, say terminal zeroes - such as 1500 have two significant figure.

Accuracy and Precision

- The accuracy of a measurement is a measure of how close the measured value is to the true value of the quantity.
- Precision tells us to what resolution or limit the quantity is measured.

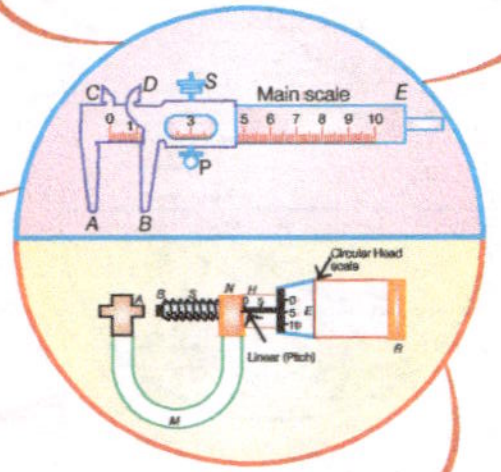

Limitations

- It cannot establish the formulae containing trigonometrical exponential and logarithmic terms.
- If a physical quantity depends on three physical quantities out of which two quantities have same dimension, we cannot establish relation among them.

Dimensional Formula

The expression which shows how and which of the fundamental quantities represent the dimension of physical quantity.

e.g. Acceleration = $[M^0L^1T^{-2}]$

Mass density = $[ML^{-3}T^0]$

Dimensions of a Physical Quantity

The dimensions of a physical quantity are the power to which the units of base quantities are raised to represent a derived unit of that quantity.

Uses of Dimensional Analysis

- **Conversion of units from one system to another**

  $$n_2 = n_1\left[\frac{M_1}{M_2}\right]^a\left[\frac{L_1}{L_2}\right]^b\left[\frac{T_1}{T_2}\right]^c$$

- **To check dimensional correctness of an equation.**

  A physical quantity equation will be dimensionally correct, if the dimensions of all terms occuring on the both sides of the equation are same.

- **Deducing relation among the physical quantities.**

  Say, $Q = f(x, y, z)$

  Let, $Q \propto X^a$, $Q \propto Y^b$, $Q \propto Z^c$

  Thus $Q \propto X^a Y^b Z^c$

Error of a Product

Assumed $Z = AB$, measured value of A and B are $A \pm \Delta A$ and $B \pm \Delta B$, then maximum relative error of product, $\left(\frac{\Delta Z}{Z}\right) = \pm\left[\frac{\Delta A}{A} + \frac{\Delta B}{B}\right]$

Percentage Error

When fractional error or relative error is expressed in percentage, then

Percentage error,

$$(\delta a) = \frac{\Delta a_{mean}}{a_m} \times 100\ \%$$

Error of a Quotient

Assumed $Z = A/B$, then measured value

$$Z \pm \Delta Z = \frac{A \pm \Delta A}{B \pm \Delta B} = Z\left(1 \pm \frac{\Delta A}{A}\right)\left(1 \pm \frac{\Delta B}{B}\right)^{-1}$$

∴ The maximum relative error of quotient $\frac{\Delta Z}{Z} = \pm\left(\frac{\Delta A}{A} + \frac{\Delta B}{B}\right)$

Error in Case of Measured Quantity Raised to a Power

Assumed the nth power of A and B,

then $Z = \frac{A^n}{B^n}$

$\pm\frac{\Delta Z}{Z} = \pm n\frac{\Delta A}{A} \pm n\frac{\Delta B}{B}$

∴ The maximum relative error

$$\frac{\Delta Z}{Z} = \pm\left(n\frac{\Delta A}{A} + \frac{n\Delta B}{B}\right)$$

Error of a Sum or Difference

- The limiting errors in two physical quantities A and B are $\pm \Delta A$ and $\pm \Delta B$ respectively, then
- **For sum** $Z = A + B$, the maximum possible error, $\Delta Z = \Delta A + \Delta B$
- **For difference** $Z = A - B$, maximum possible error, $\Delta Z = \Delta A + \Delta B$

Combination of Errors

While performing a mathematical operations such as addition, substraction, division, multiplication, etc, the error combination depends on the type of mathematical operation performed on physical quantities.

Relative Error/Fractional Error

- The ratio of mean absolute error to the mean value of the quantity measured.
- Relative error $(\delta a) = \frac{\text{Mean absolute error}}{\text{Mean value}}$

  $$\delta a = \frac{\Delta a_{mean}}{a_m}$$

Gross Error

- These errors can be arise due to extreme carelessness of the observer.
- Recording the observations with an instrument without adjusting it properly.
- Reading an observation wrongly.

Error in Measurement

- The difference between true and measured value of a quantity is called error of measurement.
  Error = True value – Measured value

Random Errors

- The random errors are those errors which occur irregularly in the measurement. Their sign and magnitude both are random.
- There is no exact cause of such errors. These errors arise due to random and unpredictable fluctuations in experimental condition.
  e.g. Fluction in voltage supply, mechanical vibration of experimental set ups.

Systematic Error

- **Instrumental error** They occur due to imperfect design or manufacture of calibration of the measuring instrument.
- **Imperfection in experimental technique** It occur due to the experimental arrangement limitation.
- **Personal error** These errors arise due to inexperience of the observer, such as lack of proper setting of apparatus and taking observations without proper precaution.
- **Error due to external causes**
  Various parameter such as change in temperature, pressure, volume, etc.

Mean Absolute Error

The arithmetic mean of the magnitudes of absolute error in all the measurements.

- $\Delta a_{mean} = \sum_{i=1}^{n} \frac{|\Delta a_i|}{n}$

Least Count Error

– This error is due to the limitation imposed by the least count of the measuring instrument.

– It is a uncertainty associated with the resolution of the measuring instrument.

Absolute Error

- The magnitude of the difference between the true value of a quantity and the individual measured value is called the absolute error.
- It is denoted by $|\Delta a|$.
- $|\Delta a|$ = Actual value – Measured value

Motion in a Straight Line (Chapter at a Glance)

Uniform and Non-Uniform Speed

- **Uniform Speed**
  The speed at which an object covers equal distance in equal time interval.
- **Non-Uniform Speed**
  The speed at which an object covers equal distance in unequal interval of time.

Instantaneous Speed

- The limit of the average speed as the time interval (Δt) becomes infinitesimally small or approaches to zero.
  Instantaneous speed, $s_i = \underset{\Delta t \to 0}{\text{Lim}} \dfrac{\Delta s}{\Delta t}$ or $s_i = \dfrac{ds}{dt}$

Instantaneous Velocity

- The limit of average velocity as the time interval becomes infinitesimally small or approaches to zero.
- $v_i = \lim\limits_{\Delta t \to 0} \dfrac{\Delta x}{\Delta t}$ or $v_i = \dfrac{dx}{dt}$

Uniform and Non-Uniform Velocity

- **Uniform Velocity**
  An object could have uniform velocity, if it covers equal displacement in equal interval of time.
- **Non-Uniform Velocity**
  If an object is moving with a non-uniform velocity, then it will have unequal displacement in equal time interval.

Frame of Reference

- The frame of reference is a coordinate system with a clock w.r.t which, an observer can describe the position, displacement, acceleration of an object.
- **Inertial Frame of Reference**
  It is that frame of reference which is either at rest or in the stare of uniform motion.
- **Non-Inertial Frame of Reference**
  It is that form of reference which performs accelerated motion with respect to an inertial frame of reference.

Displacement

- The change in position of an object in a particular direction.
- Displacement, $\Delta x = x_2 - x_1$
- **Case I** $x_2 > x_1$, Δx is positive
- **Case II** $x_1 > x_2$, Δx is negative
- **Case III** $x_1 = x_2$, Δx is zero

Speed

- The distance covered by an object divided by the time taken by it to cover that distance is called speed.
  $\text{Speed} = \dfrac{\text{Distance travelled}}{\text{Time taken}}$
- Speed is a scalar quantity.
- **Average Speed**
- The total distance travelled by the object divided by the total time taken.
  $\text{Average speed} = \dfrac{\text{Total distance travelled}}{\text{Total time taken}}$
  $V_{avg} = \dfrac{S_1 + S_2}{t_1 + t_2}$

Velocity

- The rate of change of position of an object with time is called the velocity of that object.
  $\text{Velocity} = \dfrac{\text{Displacement}}{\text{Time}}$
- It is a vector quantity.
- **Average Velocity**
- The change in position or displacement divided by the time interval in which that displacement occur.

Position

- The point where an object is situated, called position.
- Position determined by the coordinate axis that is, marked in units of length and that has positive and negative direction.

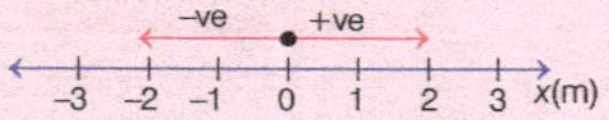

Position in + ve and – ve directions.

Distance

- Length of the path covered by an object in a given time-interval is known as its path length or distance travelled.
- Its SI unit is metre.
- **Example**

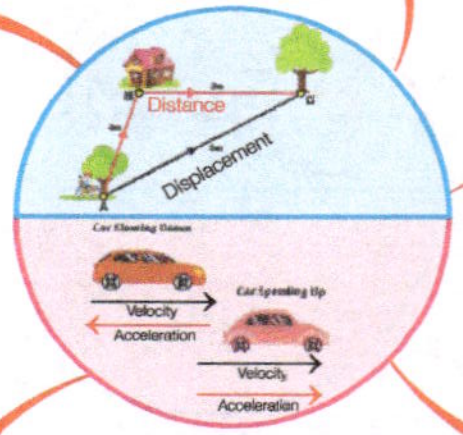

Kinematic Equations

- For uniformly accelerated motion, the displacement, time, initial velocity, final velocity and acceleration are related by three simple equations called kinematic equations of motion.
- **Velocity-Time Relation**
  $v = u + at$
- **Position-Time Relation**
  $x = ut + \dfrac{1}{2}at^2$
- **Position-Velocity Relation**
  $v^2 = u^2 + 2ax$

Uniform Motion

- An object travels equal distance in equal intervals along a straight line.

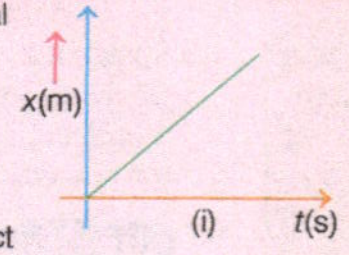

- **When object is stationary**
- Suppose that an object is at rest at a distance a from the origin.
- From the graph (ii); it is clear that, the position of the object remain same w.r.t. time.

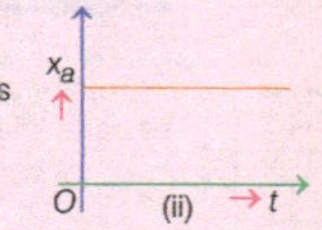

Non-Uniform Motion

- An object travel equal displacement in unequal interval of time.
- The speed of the body or its direction of motion or both change with time.
- **When Object is in Variable Motion**
- Object cover unequal distance in equal interval of time.
- The position-time graph of varying motion will not be a straight line.

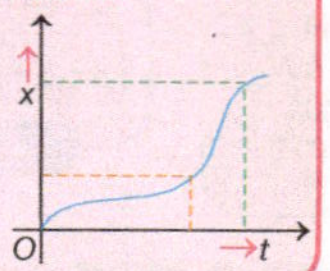

Relative Velocity

- The velocity of an object with respect to another object is called relative velocity.

Motion of an Object Under Gravity

- When an object is thrown vertically upwards or fall towards the earth, then its motion is called motion under gravity.
  $v = u + (\pm g)t$
  $h = ut + \dfrac{1}{2}(\pm g)t^2$
  $v^2 = u^2 + 2(\pm g)h$
- In case of upward motion, acceleration due to gravity (g) is taken as negative and for downward motion, g taken as positive.

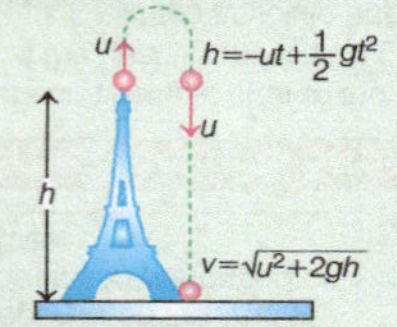

Free Fall

- Free fall is defined as situation in which an object moves only under the influence of gravity.
- Free fall is just a downward movement with no initial force or velocity.
- The free fall of any object is just a natural phenomenon on earth without support.

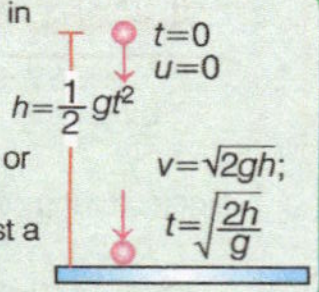

Acceleration

- The rate of change of velocity with time.
- It is a vector quantity.
- SI unit is metre per second square (m/s²).
- The dimensional formula is $[M^0L^1T^{-2}]$.
- **Average Acceleration**
- The change in velocity divided by time interval.
- Average acceleration $= \dfrac{\Delta v}{\Delta t} = \dfrac{\mathbf{v}_2 - \mathbf{v}_1}{t_2 - t_1}$

Uniform and Non-Uniform Acceleration

- **Uniform Acceleration** If an object is moving with uniform acceleration, it means that the object velocity is equal for equal interval of time.
- **Non-Uniform Acceleration** If an object has variable or non-uniform acceleration, it means that the change in velocity is unequal in equal interval of time.

Instantaneous Acceleration

- The acceleration of a body at a certain instant or the limiting value of average acceleration when time interval becomes very small or tends to zero.
- Instantaneous acceleration,
  $\mathbf{a}_{in} = \lim\limits_{\Delta t \to 0} \dfrac{\Delta \mathbf{v}}{\Delta t} = \dfrac{dv}{dt}$

Example of Relative Velocity

- If a bus A is moving with velocity vector $\mathbf{v}_A$ and another bus B with velocity vector $\mathbf{v}_B$, then velocity of object A relative to bus B is given as $\mathbf{v}_{AB} = \mathbf{v}_A - \mathbf{v}_B$
  The relative velocity of bus B, w.r.t, bus A,
  $\mathbf{v}_{BA} = \mathbf{v}_B - \mathbf{v}_A$
- **Case I** If $\mathbf{v}_B - \mathbf{v}_A = 0$, then the two objects A and B stay at a constant distance.

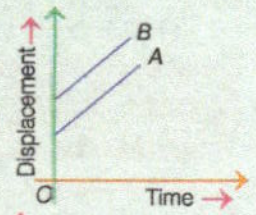

- **Case II** If $\mathbf{v}_A > \mathbf{v}_B$, Then one graph is steeper than other and they meet at common point.

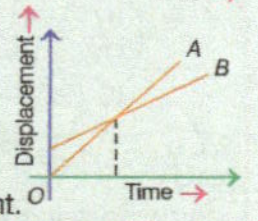

Position -Time Graphs

- **Positive Acceleration**
  When distance covered by moving object goes on increasing with time, then object said to have positive acceleration.

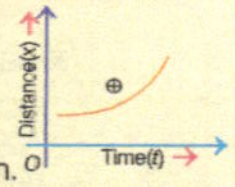

- **Negative Acceleration**
  When distance covered by moving object goes on decreasing with time. then object said to have negative acceleration.

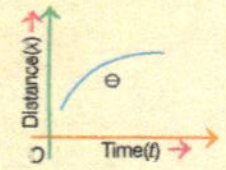

- **Zero Acceleration**
  When the moving object covers equal distance in equal time, the object is said to have zero acceleration.

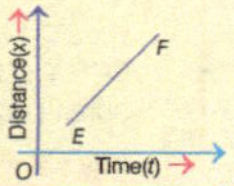

Velocity-Time Graphs

- **Positive Acceleration**
- If an object is moving with positive acceleration having zero initial velocity, then its volocity goes on increasing with time.

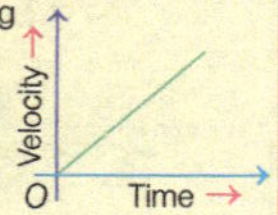

- **Negative Acceleration**
- If an object is moving with negative acceleration have some positive initial velocity, then its velocity goes an decreasing with time.
- The graph is a straight line having negative slope.

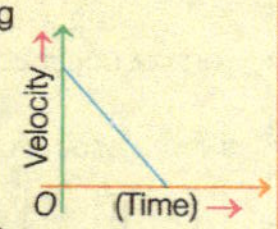

- **Zero Acceleration**
  The velocity of the object does not change with time.

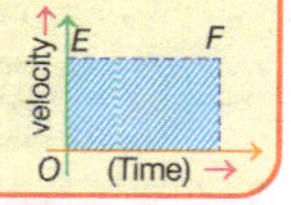

Motion in Plane (Chapter at a Glance)

Co-initial Vector
- The vector which has the same initial point are called co-initial vectors.

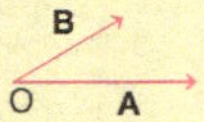

- Two vectors **A** and **B** have been drawn from the initial point *O*, therefore *A* and *B* are called co-initial vectors.

Equal Vectors
- Two vectors are said to be equal, if they have equal magnitude and same direction.

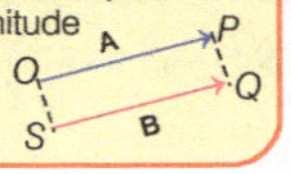

Unit Vector
- A vector having magnitude equal to unity but having a specific direction is called a unit vector.

$$\hat{\mathbf{A}} = \frac{\mathbf{A}}{|\mathbf{A}|} = \frac{\text{Vector}}{\text{Magnitude of the vector}}$$

Vector Multiplied by a Real Number
- If a vector multiplied by a real number, then the resultant vector is also a vector whose magnitude is changed but the direction remain same.

$$|\lambda \mathbf{A}| = \lambda\, |\mathbf{A}|, \text{ if } \lambda > 0$$

where, λ is a scalar number.

Resolution of Vectors
- Any vector can be resolved into components along two given vectors **a** and **b** lying in the same plane. $\mathbf{A} = \lambda_1 \mathbf{a} + \lambda_2 \mathbf{b}$ where, λ_1 and λ_2 real numbers.

Parallelogram Law
- If two vectors acting on a particle at the same time, are represented in magnitude and direction by the adjacent side of a parallelogram drawn from same point, then their resultant vector is along the diagonal of parallelogram.

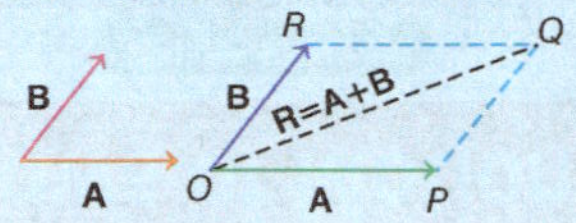

Collinear Vector
- The two or more vectors are said to be collinear, when they act along the same line or parallel lines.
- e.g. Tug of war

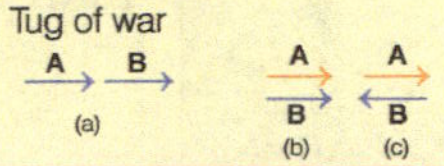

Vector Quantities
- Those physical quantities which have both magnitude and direction.
- These obey the triangular law or parallelogram law of addition and subtraction.
- e.g. Velocity, acceleration, momentum, etc.

Physical Quantities
- It is a physical property of a material or system that can be quantified by measurement.

Scalar Quantities
- Those physical quantities which have only magnitude but no direction.
- It is specified completely by a single number along with proper unit.
- e.g. Time, mass, length, etc.

Addition of Vectors
- Two vectors can be added, if both of them are of same nature.
- **Triangle law of vector addition**
  If two vectors can be represented both in magnitude and direction by the two sides of triangle taken in same order, then their resultant is represented by the third side of the triangle taken in the opposite order.

Resultant vector,
R = A + B

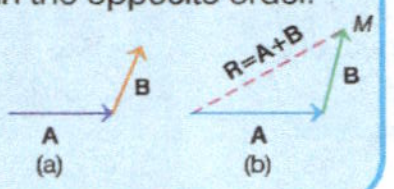

Properties of Addition of Vectors
(I) It follows commutative law, i.e.
A + B = B + A
(ii) It follows associative law, i.e.,
(A + B) + C = A + (B + C)
(iii) It obeys distributive law, i.e.
$\lambda\,(\mathbf{A} + \mathbf{B}) = \mathbf{A}\lambda + \lambda \mathbf{B}$
(iv) It follows identity law i.e., **A + 0 = A**

Uniform Circular Motion
When an object follows a circular path at a constant speed, the motion of the object is called uniform circular motion.
- **Angular Displacement**
  The angle traced out by the radius vector at the centre of the circular path in the given time. It is a vector quantity.
- **Angular Acceleration**
  The time rate of change of angular velocity of a particle.It is denoted by α.
  $$\alpha = \lim_{\Delta t \to 0} \frac{\Delta\omega}{\Delta t} = \frac{d\omega}{dt}$$
- **Centripetal Acceleration**
  The acceleration associated with uniform circular motion is called a centripetal acceleration.
  Centripetal acceleration $a = \dfrac{v^2}{r}$

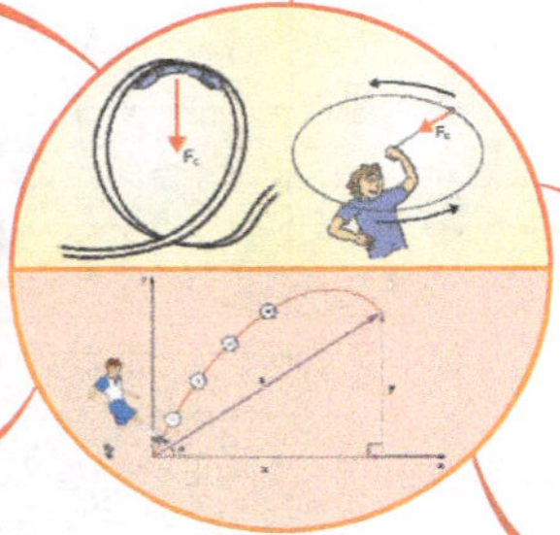

Subtraction of Vectors
It is expressed as
R = A + (– B)
R = A – B

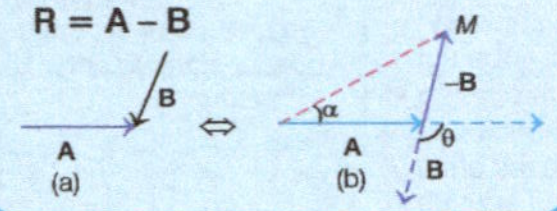

Properties of Subtraction of Vector
(I) It does not follow commutative properties, i.e., **A – B ≠ B – A**
(ii) It does not follow associative law, i.e., **A – (B – C) ≠ (A – B) – C**
(iii) It follows distributive law, i.e,
$\lambda\,(\mathbf{A} - \mathbf{B}) = \lambda \mathbf{A} - \lambda \mathbf{B}$
(iv) It follows identity law, i.e., **A – 0 = A**

Relative Velocity
The relative velocity of an object *A* w.r.t. object *B*,
$$\mathbf{v}_{AB} = \mathbf{v}_A - \mathbf{v}_B$$
Relative velocity of object *B* w.r.t. *A*,
$$\mathbf{v}_{BA} = \mathbf{v}_B - \mathbf{v}_A$$
Clearly, $\mathbf{v}_{AB} = -\,\mathbf{v}_{BA}$

Maximum Height
The maximum vertical height attained by an object above the point of projectile during its flight.
Maximum height, $H = \dfrac{u^2 \sin^2\theta}{2g}$

Horizontal Range
The horizontal range is distance covered by the projectile during its time of flight.
Horizontal range, $R = \dfrac{u^2 \sin 2\theta}{g}$
Here, maximum horizontal range,
$$R_{max} = \frac{u^2}{g} \quad [\because \theta = 45^\circ]$$

Time of Flight
Total time for which projectile is in flight, i.e. time during the motion of projectile.
Total time of flight, $T = \dfrac{2u \sin\theta}{g}$

Projectile Motion
Projectile motion is a form of motion in which an object is thrown with some initial velocity near the earth's surface and it moves along a curved path under the action of gravity alone.

Rain Problem
Relative velocity of rain,
$$v_{rm} = \sqrt{v_r^2 + v_m^2 + 2v_r v_m \cos 90^\circ}$$
$$= \sqrt{v_r^2 + v_m^2}$$
$$\tan\theta = \frac{BD}{OB} = \frac{v_m}{v_r}$$
$$\theta = \tan^{-1}\left(\frac{v_m}{v_r}\right)$$

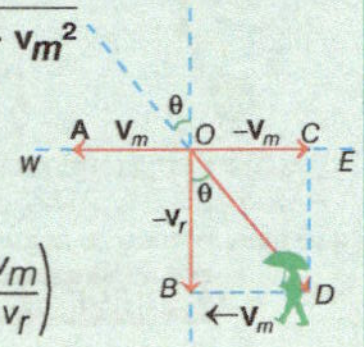

Equation of Projectile
- **Motion along horizontal direction (OX)**
  Time, $t = \dfrac{x}{u \cos\theta}$
- **Motion along vertical direction (OY)**
  Total vertical distance,
  $$y = x \tan\theta - \left(\frac{1}{2}\,\frac{g}{u^2 \cos^2\theta}\right) x^2$$

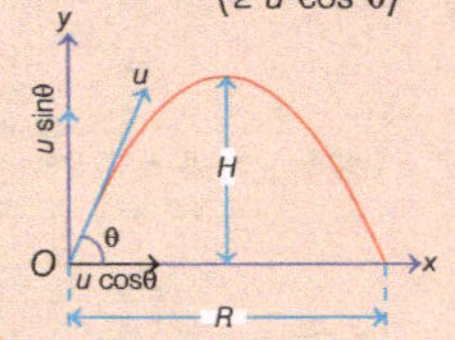

Position Vector
- It tells us about the minimum distance of an object from origin *O*.
- It also tells about the direction of the object with respect to origin *O*.

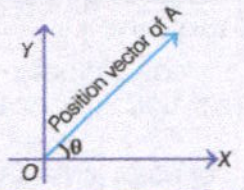

Displacement
The position vectors of an object in *XY*-plane are $\mathbf{r}_1 = x_1 \hat{\mathbf{i}} + y_1 \hat{\mathbf{j}}$ and $\mathbf{r}_2 = x_2 \hat{\mathbf{i}} + y_2 \hat{\mathbf{j}}$, then displacement is given by
$$\Delta \mathbf{r} = \mathbf{r}_2 - \mathbf{r}_1 = \Delta x \hat{\mathbf{i}} + \Delta y \hat{\mathbf{j}}$$

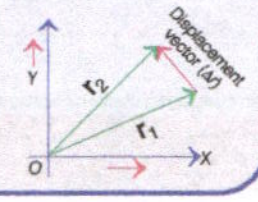

Instantaneous Acceleration
This instantaneous acceleration of an object is given by
$$\mathbf{a} = \lim_{\Delta t \to 0} \frac{\Delta \mathbf{v}}{\Delta t} = \frac{d\mathbf{v}}{dt}$$

Average Acceleration
The average acceleration of an object is the ratio of average velocity and time interval. i.e.
$$\mathbf{a} = \frac{\Delta \mathbf{v}}{\Delta t} = \bar{a}_x \hat{\mathbf{i}} + \bar{a}_y \hat{\mathbf{j}}$$

Instantaneous Velocity
The instantaneous velocity is given by
$$\mathbf{v} = \lim_{\Delta t \to 0} \frac{\Delta \mathbf{r}}{\Delta t} = \frac{d\mathbf{r}}{dt}$$

Average Velocity
The average velocity of an object is the ratio of the displacement and time interval.
i.e., $\mathbf{v} = \dfrac{\Delta \mathbf{r}}{\Delta t} = v_x \hat{\mathbf{i}} + v_y \hat{\mathbf{j}}$

Laws of Motion (Chapter at a Glance)

Rolling Friction

- When an object rolls on a surface without slipping, then the friction force between the surface, is called rolling friction.

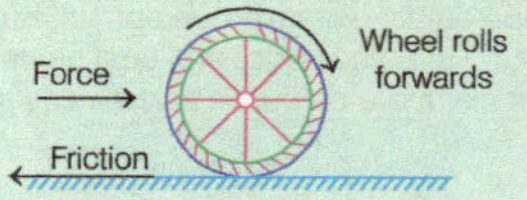

Example

- Ball bearings are used to reduce the friction between the rolling part.

Kinetic Friction

- If the object is sliding, then friction forces between their surfaces is called **kinetic friction** or **sliding friction**.
- If applied force exceeds the limiting value of friction force, i.e. $F > (f_s)_{max}$, then block starts slipping over the inclined plane. So, $f_K < f_L$ (slightly) $f_K < (f_s)_{max}$

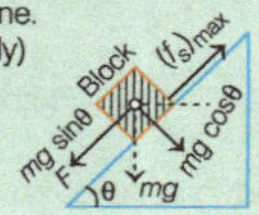

Static Friction

- If a body tends to slip over the surface of another body, then it is frictional force acting between their surfaces.
- When applied force is less than static friction, then block does not move.

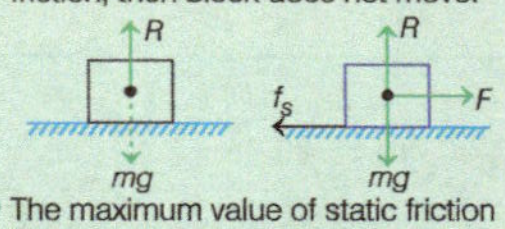

- The maximum value of static friction between two surfaces in contact is called **limiting friction**.

Friction

- When a body slips or tends to slip over the surface of another body, then a force develops parallel to surface in contact, in opposite direction. This is friction force.
- It is non-conservative force, i.e. work done by this forces depends on the path.

Angle of Repose

- Value of angle of inclination at which the force of static friction equal to limiting friction.
- If angle of friction be α(block tend to slip), then $\tan\alpha = \mu_s$
  Angle of repose = Angle of friction

Angle of Friction

- The angle made by the resultant of normal reaction and limiting friction with normal reaction is called angle of friction.
- Angle of friction, $\alpha = \tan^{-1} \mu_s$

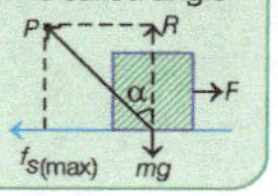

Circular Motion of Car on a Level Road

- When a vehicle goes round a curved road, it requires some centripetal force. While rounding the curve, the wheels of the vehicle have a tendency to leave the curved path and regain the straight line path.

- For the car to stay on the road, the maximum force of friction must be equal to or greater than the centripetal force.

$$\frac{mv^2}{r} \le \mu_s mg \Rightarrow v \le \sqrt{\mu_s r g}$$

Maximum velocity, $v_{max} = \sqrt{\mu_s r g}$

- Maximum velocity with which a vehicle can go round a level curve without skidding, $v = \sqrt{\mu_s r g}$

Dynamics of Circular Motion

- When an object moves on a circular path, a force acts on it, whose direction is towards the centre of the path, this force is called centripetal force.
- It is given as

$$F = \frac{mv^2}{r}$$

Example

- Condition for v_A to be minimum, for which the body just completes the circular path

$v_A = \sqrt{5gR}, T_A = 6mg$

$v_B = \sqrt{gR}, T_B = 0$

$v_C = \sqrt{3gR}, T_C = 3mg$

$v_P = \sqrt{gR(3+2\cos\theta)}$

$T_P = 3mg(1+\cos\theta)$

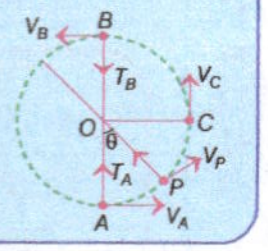

Motion of a Car on a Banked Road

- The large amount of friction between the tyres and the road produces considerable wear and tear of tyres. To avoid this, the curved road is given an inclined sloping upwards towards outer circumference.
- The system of raising outer edge of curved road above its inner edge called banking of the curved road. Maximum velocity of vehicle on banked road,

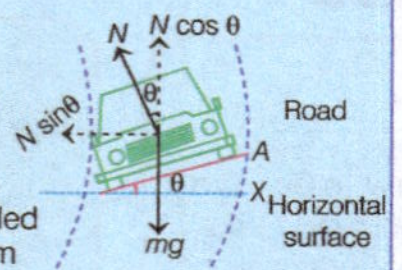

$$v_{max} = \sqrt{\frac{rg(\mu_s + \tan\theta)}{(1 - \mu_s \tan\theta)}}$$

- **Special case** When $\mu_s = 0$, then $v_{max} = \sqrt{rg \tan\theta}$

  i.e. Banking angle $\theta = \tan^{-1}\left(\frac{v^2}{rg}\right)$

Bending of a Cyclist

- When a cyclist takes turn along a circular path on a level road, he requires necessary centripetal force towards the centre of path.

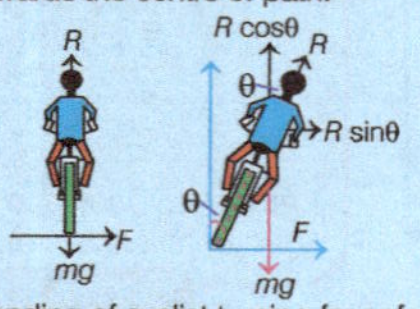

- Bending of cyclist turning for safe going, $R \sin\theta = mv^2/r$ and $R \cos\theta = mg$
  Maximum speed without slipping, $v = \sqrt{rg \tan\theta}$

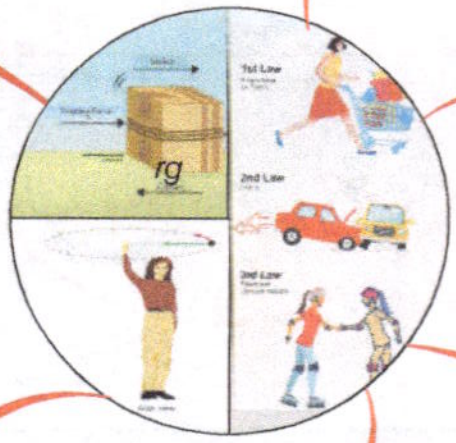

Aristotle's Fallacy

- Aristotle states that an external force is required to keep an object in motion.
- His statement is based on the fact that ever presenting resistive forces will always stop the motion.

Example

- Rolling ball that stops due to friction.
- The opposing force such as friction and viscous forces are always present in the nature.

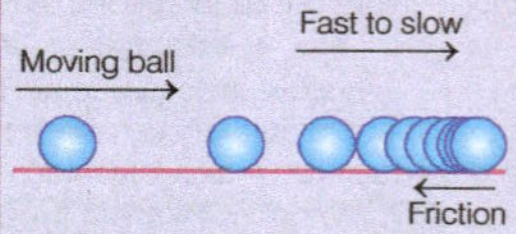

If there were no friction, no external force needed to maintain the state of uniform motion, then law of inertia proposed.

Law of Inertia

- A property of an object by virtue of which it cannot change its state of rest or motion or direction in the absence of external force.

First Law of Newton

- Every body continues in its state of rest or of uniform motion in a straight line unless it is compelled by some external force to change that state.
- If the net external force on a body is zero, its acceleration is zero. Acceleration can be non-zero, if there is net external force.
- **Example**
  If a body at rest, continues in its state of rest, a book on the table will continue to remain there unless we displace it.

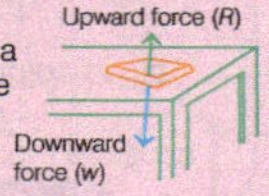

- A bullet fired on a window passes through it making a clean hole while a stone breaks the whole window.

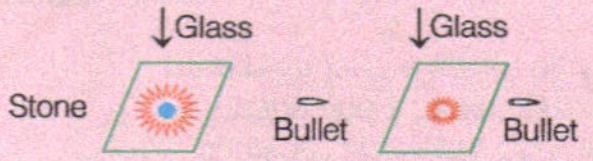

Second Law of Newton

- Rate of change in linear momentum of a body is directly proportional to applied force and takes place in the direction in which the force acts.
- $\mathbf{F} = \frac{\Delta \mathbf{p}}{\Delta t}$ (on the basis of experiment)
- For constant mass,
  $\mathbf{F} = m\mathbf{a}$

Third Law of Newton

- When a body exerts a force on second body, the second body also exert force on first body. The two forces are equal in magnitude and opposite in direction.

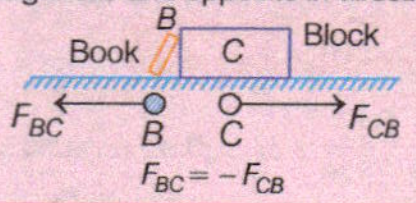

$F_{BC} = -F_{CB}$

Equilibrium of a Particle

- The body under the action of concurrent forces will be in equilibrium only when the vector sum of forces is zero.
- Mathematically, $\Sigma \mathbf{F}_{net} = 0$

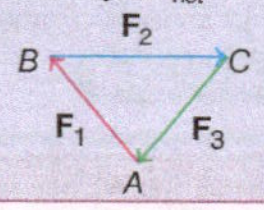

Impulse

- A large force acting for a short time to produce a finite change in momentum.

Impulse $= F \cdot \Delta t = \Delta p$

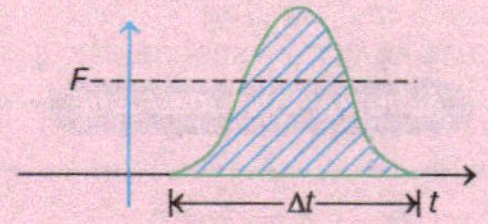

Linear Momentum

The linear momentum of a particle is defined as product of its mass and velocity.

$\mathbf{p} = m\mathbf{v}$

- Its SI unit is kilogram-metre/second.
- It is a vector quantity.
- Its dimensional formula is $[MLT^{-1}]$.
- If p=constant, then $v \propto \frac{1}{m}$.
- Heavier is the body, smaller will be its velocity.

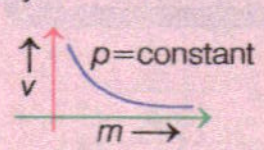

- If v=constant, then $p \propto m$.
  The heaviest body will have largest momentum.

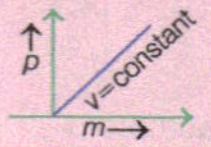

Law of Conservation of Linear Momentum

- Total momentum,

$$\mathbf{p} = \mathbf{p}_1 + \mathbf{p}_2 + \ldots + \mathbf{p}_n = \sum_{i=1}^{N} \mathbf{p}_i$$

- If resultant external force acting on a system is zero, then linear momentum of system remains conserved.
  i.e. $p_i = p_f$

Static Equilibrium

The physical state in which all components of a system are at rest and the net force and net torque are both zero throughout the system.

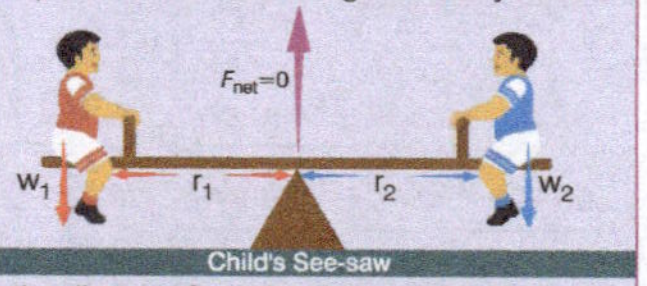

Child's See-saw

r is the distance from the pivot point to the point where the force is applied,
F is magnitude of the force and w is weight.

$w_1 r_1 = w_2 r_2$

Work, Energy and Power (Chapter at a Glance)

Nature of Positive Work Done
- When applied force and displacement has same direction, then the work is said to be positive work.
- When θ is acute, then cosθ is positive $0 \le \theta < 90°$.
- Work done $(W) = Fs \cos\theta$ = Positive

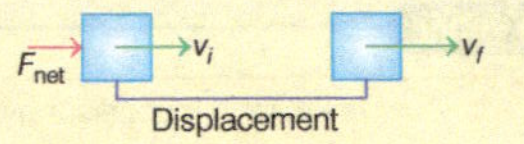

Nature of Negative Work Done
- When force applied and displacement has opposite direction, then it is said to be negative work.
- When θ is obtuse, then cos θ is negative $90° < \theta < 180$.

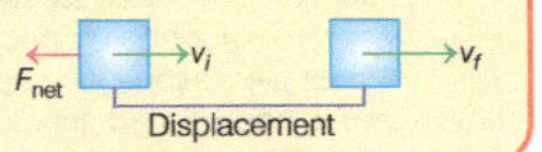

Zero Work
If a body gets displaced in the direction perpendicular to the direction of the applied force.
Work done $(W) = Fs \cos 90° = \text{Zero}$

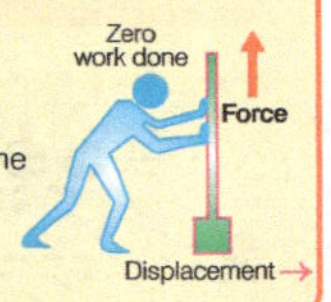

Conservative Force
Work done by the force in displacing an object depends only on the initial and final positions of an object.

Non-Conservative Force
If the work done by a force in displacing an object from one position to another, depends upon the path between the two positions.

Cases
(i) If p = constant, This is shown in $KE \propto \frac{1}{m}$

(ii) If KE = constant, $p^2 \propto m$ or $p \propto \sqrt{m}$

(iii) If mass = constant, $p^2 \propto KE$

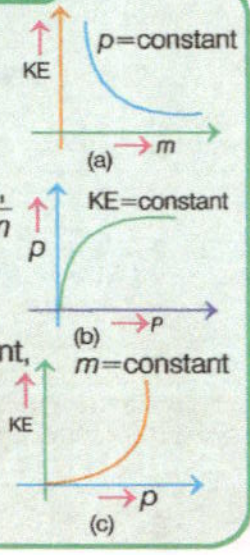

Work Done by Constant Force
- The product of component of force in the direction of the displacement and the magnitude of the displacement.
- The work done by a constant force is given by

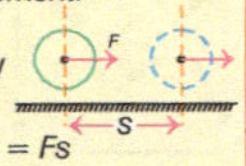

$W = \mathbf{F} \cdot \mathbf{s} \Rightarrow Fs \cos\theta$

(i) If $\theta = 0°$, $W = Fs \cos 0° = Fs$

(ii) If $\theta = 90°$; $W = Fs \cos 90° = 0$

(iii) If $\theta = 180°$; $W = Fs \cos 180 = -Fs$

Scalar Product
- The product of the magnitude of vectors **A** and **B** and the cosine of the angle θ between them. Then,

$\mathbf{A} \cdot \mathbf{B} = AB \cos\theta$

- It is a scalor quantity.
- It is also called dot product.

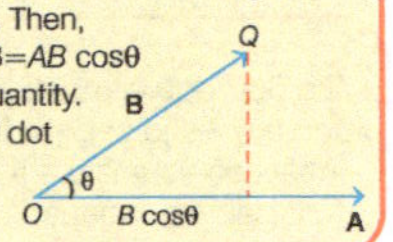

Work
If a force applied on a body displaces it, then the work is said to be done.

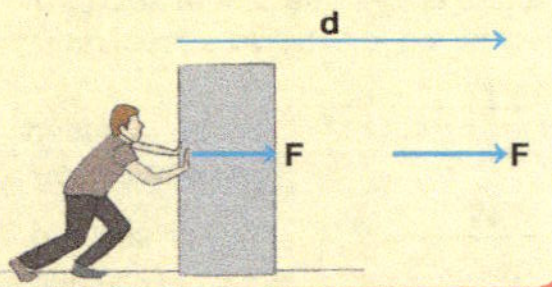

Work done by a Variable Force
Let a variable force F acts on a body along the fixed direction, say X– axis.
The magnitude of force F depends on x.
- The work done is

$\Delta W = F(x)\, \Delta x$ = Area of rectangle $abcd$

- $W_{x_i - x_f}$ = Area under the F-x curve

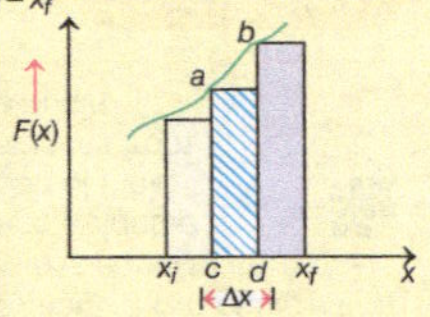

Kinetic Energy
- The energy possessed by a body by virtue of its motion is called kinetic energy.

i.e. $KE = \frac{1}{2} mv^2$

- **Relation between kinetic energy and linear momentum**
- Linear momentum, $p = \sqrt{2mKE}$

Conservation of Mechanical Energy
If only the conservative forces are doing work on a body, then its mechanical energy (KE + PE) remains constant.

Work-Energy Theorem
- **For constant force**

We use the equation of motion,
$v^2 - u^2 = 2as$

or $\frac{1}{2} mv^2 - \frac{1}{2} mu^2 = mas$

or $\frac{1}{2} mv^2 - \frac{1}{2} mu^2 = W$ or $K_f - K_i = W$

- **For variable force**

Variable force acts on a body of mass m and produce displacement in its own direction $(\theta = 0°)$, then small work done,
$dW = \mathbf{F} \cdot d\mathbf{s} = Fds \cos 0° = Fds$
Change in kinetic energy, $K_f - K_i = \int_{x_i}^{x_f} Fds$

Energy
- The energy of a body is defined as its capacity for doing work.
- It is a scalar quantity.
- Its dimensional formula is $[ML^2T^{-2}]$.
- It is measured in the same units as work. i.e., joule in SI and erg in CGS system.

Potential Energy
- The energy possessed by the body by virtue of its position or configuration in same field.
- Dimensional formula of potential energy is $[ML^2T^{-2}]$.
- The SI unit of potential energy is joule (J).

Gravitational Potential Energy
It is the energy possessed by the body due to its position above the earth's surface.
i.e. Gravitational potential energy, $U = mgh$

Conservation of Energy in an Elastic Spring
The kinetic energy is converted to potential energy and *vice-versa*. However, the total mechanical energy remains constant.

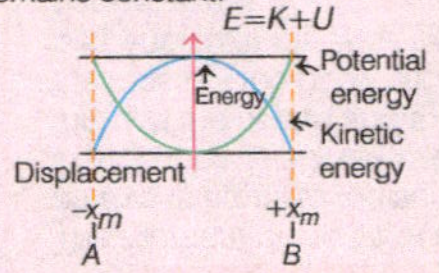

Mechanical Energy of a Stretched Spring
If the block of mass m is extended to position, x_m and released from rest, then total mechanical energy at any orbitary point x,
$\frac{1}{2} kx_m^2 = \frac{1}{2} kx^2 + \frac{1}{2} mv^2$

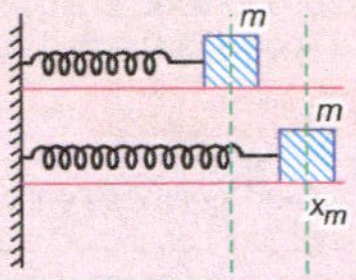

Collision
Collision between two bodies is defined as mutual interaction of the bodies for a short interval of time as a result of which the energy and momentum of the interacting bodies change.

Power
The rate of doing work is called the power.
Average power (P_{av}) = Rate of doing work.

$P_{av} = \frac{W}{t}$

- **Instantaneous power** $P_{av} = \frac{dW}{dt} = F \cdot \frac{ds}{dt} = \mathbf{F} \cdot \mathbf{v}$
- Power is a scalar quantity.
- The dimensional formula of power is $[ML^2T^{-3}]$.
- SI unit of power is watt (W)
- 1 horse power = 746 W

Perfectly Inelastic Collision in Two Dimensions
Consider two bodies A and B of masses M_1 and M_2 moving with velocities u_1 and u_2 along oblique direction.
After collision, two bodies stick together and move along a direction, so as to conserve momentum.
Conservation along X-axis,
$M_1 u_1 \cos\theta + M_2 u_2 = (M_1 + M_2)\, v \cos\phi$
Y-axis $M_1 u_1 \sin\theta = (M_1 + M_2)\, v \sin\phi$
- M_1 moving with velocity v_1 making angle θ with the horizontal.
- Both bodies making angle ϕ with the horizontal after collision.

Freely Falling Body
The mechanical energy of a freely falling body remains constant at all positions.
$E_A = E_B = E_C$ = Constant

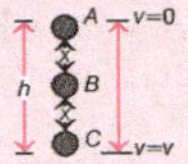

Elastic Collision in One Dimension
- Consider two perfectly elastic bodies A and B of masses M_1 and M_2 moving along the same straight line with velocities u_1 and u_2 respectively.
- If velocity of A is greater than B i.e., $u_1 > u_2$, then two bodies collides.

$\frac{1}{2} M_1 u_1^2 + \frac{1}{2} M_2 u_2^2 = \frac{1}{2} M_1 v_1^2 + \frac{1}{2} M_2 v_2^2$

Elastic Collision in One Dimension
In this type of collision, both momentum and kinetic energy are conserved and the colliding bodies continue to move along the same straight line after collision.

$$v_1 = \frac{(m_1 - m_2)\, u_1 + 2m_2 u_2}{m_1 + m_2}, \quad v_2 = \frac{(m_2 - m_1)\, u_2 + 2m_1 u_1}{m_1 + m_2}$$

Elastic Collision
Those collisions, in which both momentum and kinetic energy of the system are conserved, are called elastic collisions.

Inelastic Collision
Those collisions, in which the momentum of the system is conserved but the kinetic energy is not conserved are called inelastic collisions.

Perfectly Inelastic Collision
Those collisions, in which the colliding bodies stick together after the collision and then move with a common velocity, are called perfectly inelastic collision.

Inelastic Collision in One Dimension
- The collision, in which momentum is conserved with some loss of kinetic energy and the colliding bodies continue to move along the same straight line after collision.
- For a perfectly inelastic collision, $v_2 - v_1 = 0$ and therefore, $e = 0$.

Elastic Collision in Two Dimensions
Consider two bodies A and B of masses M_1 and M_2 moving along the same straight line with velocities u_1 and u_2, respectively. After the collision, two bodies move with velocities v_1 and v_2 along the direction of making angle θ and ϕ.
Here, $M_1 u_1 + M_2 u_2 = M_1 v_1 \cos\theta + M_2 v_2 \cos\phi$
$0 = M_1 v_1 \sin\theta + (-M_2 v_2 \sin\phi)$
$\Rightarrow M_1 v_1 \sin\theta - M_2 v_2 \sin\phi = 0$

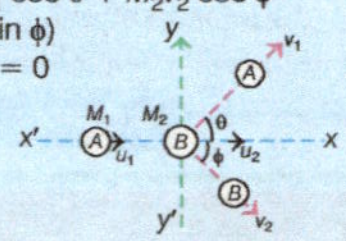

System of Particles and Rotational Motion (Chapter at a Glance)

Centre of Mass of a Uniform Thin Rod

- A uniform thin rod AB, mass M and length L.
- For X-axis: $X_{cm} = \frac{L}{2}$

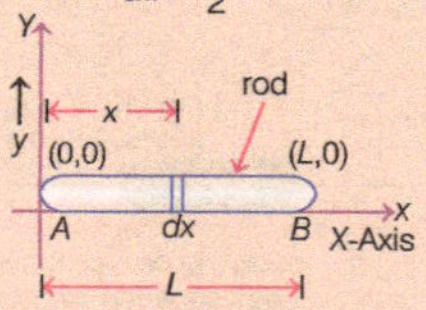

For Y-axis: $Y_{cm} = \frac{1}{M}\int y\, dm = 0$

$\therefore\ y = 0$, for thin rod

For a System of Two Particles

- For two particles,

$$X_{cm} = \frac{m_1x_1 + m_2x_2}{m_1 + m_2}$$

- The distance of the centre of mass of a system of two particle from the origin is equal to the mass weighted mean of their distances from the origin.

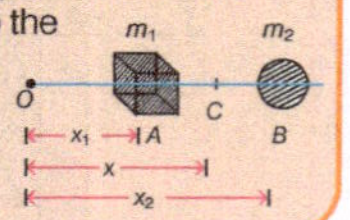

Centre of Mass

- The point in the system, where the whole mass of the system can be supposed to be concentrated.

For a System of n-Particles

- Suppose a system of n-particles having masses m_1, m_2, m_3 occupying. x-coordinate x_1, x_2, x_3, x_n
- Centre of mass, $x_{cm} = \frac{\sum_{i=1}^{n} m_i x_i}{\sum m_i}$

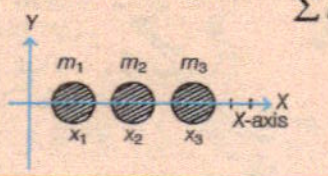

Motion of Centre of Mass

- Velocity of centre of mass, $v_{CM} = \frac{\sum_{i=1}^{n} m_i v_i}{M}$
- Acceleration of centre of mass $A_{CM} = \frac{\sum_{i=1}^{n} m_i a_i}{M}$
- Here, centre of mass of a system of particles moves as if whole mass of the system is concentrated at that point.

Angular Momentum

- It is defined as the moment of the linear momentum of the particle about fixed axis.
- Angular momentum, $\mathbf{L} = (\mathbf{r} \times \mathbf{v})m$
- SI unit of angular momentum is kg m^2s^{-1}
- It is a vector quantity.

Moment of Force (Torque)

- The turning effect of a force about the axis of rotation is called **moment of force** and measured as product of magnitude of force and the perpendicular distance of the line of force from the axis of rotation.

$$\tau = r \times F$$

- Torque or moment of force is a vector quantity.

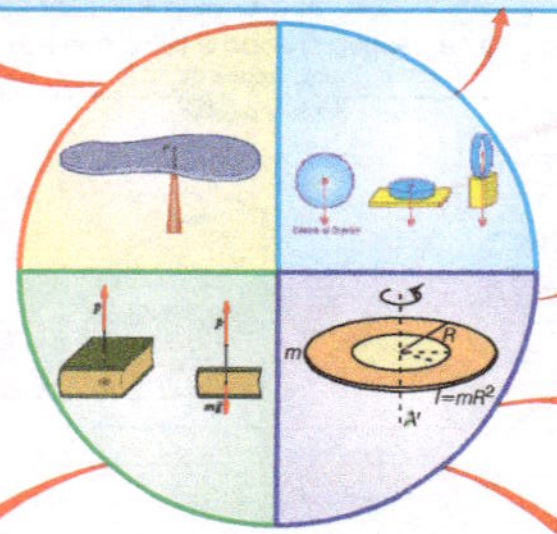

Principle of Conservation of Angular Momentum

- If the net external torque acting on a body is zero, then its angular momentum remains constant. $\frac{dL}{dt} = \tau_{ext}$

If $\tau_{ext} = 0$; $\frac{d\mathbf{L}}{dt} = 0$; $\mathbf{L}$ = constant.

Example

- When a diver jumps into water from a certain height, then he develops angular velocity and angular momentum about an axis passes through his centre of mass. He folds his body in air so that moment of inertia of body decreases. This result in increasing angular velocity. Thus, he tumbles in the air. On reaching near the water, he unfold his arm to decrease ω.

Properties of Couple

- The moment of couple is a vector quantity.
- A couple can only be balanced by an equal and opposite couple.
- A couple can be shifted as such without affecting its moment.
- The moment of couple about any point in its plane is always constant.

Principle of Moments

- If a body is in rotational equilibrium then algebraic sum of the moments of all these forces is zero.
- Mechanical advantage,

$$MA = \frac{F_1}{F_2} = \frac{d_2}{d_1}$$

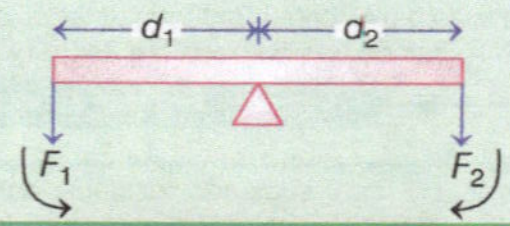

Couple/Torque

A pair of force of equal magnitude but acting in opposite direction with different lines of action. Let a couple force $-F$ and F acting at A and B, the moment of couple equal to torque.

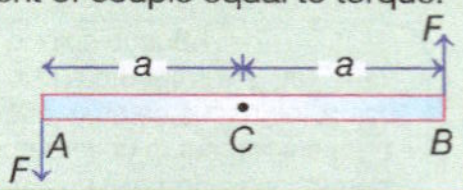

Centre of Gravity

- If the total weight of the body is supposed on a point such that total gravitational torque about this point is zero.

Theorem of Perpendicular Axis

- A planar body about an axis perpendicular to its plane is equal to the sum of moment of inertia about two perpendicular axis.
- $I_z = I_x + I_y$

Here, I_x, I_y, I_z are the moments of inertia of the plane body.

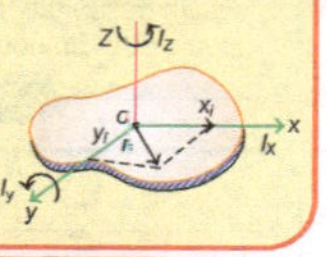

Moment of Inertia

- The property of a body by virtue of which it opposes the torque tending to change its state of rest or of uniform rotation about axis.
- The moment of inertia is given by $I = \sum_{i=1}^{n} m_i r_i^2$
- Radius of Gyration $K = \sqrt{\frac{I}{m}}$

Moment of Inertia of Regular Shaped

(i) Thin rod of length L,

$I = \frac{1}{12} ML^2$

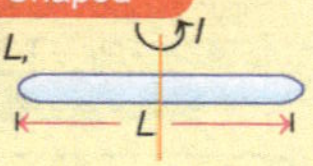

(ii) Circular ring of radius R,

$I = MR^2$

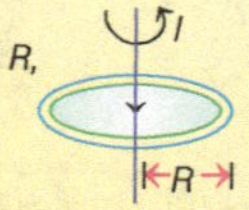

(iii) Solid sphere of radius R,

$I = \frac{2}{5} MR^2$

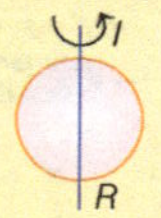

(iv) Circular disc of radius R,

$I = \frac{1}{4} MR^2$

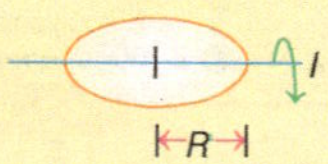

Theorem of Parallel Axis

- The moment of inertia of a body about an axis is equal to the sum of moment of inertia of body about the axis passing through the centre and the product of the mass of the body and square of perpendicular distance between the two parallel axes.
- $I = I_{cm} + mr^2$
- Here, I_{cm} is moment of inertia about centre of mass, m is mass of lamina, r is distance between two parallel axis.

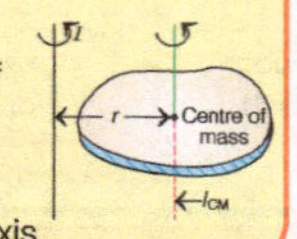

Equilibrium of Rigid Body

- A rigid body is said to be in equilibrium, if both of its linear momentum and angular momentum are not changing with time.
- A body in equilibrium does not possess linear acceleration or angular acceleration.

A Rigid Body

- A body with perfectly defined shape and the distance between all pairs of particles of such a body do not change while applying any force on it.

Translational Equilibrium

- If the net force acting on the rigid body is zero but net torque is non-zero, then rigid body is called in translational equilibrium.

Rotational Equilibrium Only

- If the net torque acting on the rigid body is zero but net force is non-zero, then rigid body is in rotational equilibrium only.

Vector Product of Two Vectors

- The vector product of two vectors is given by
  $\mathbf{R} = \mathbf{A} \times \mathbf{B}$
  $\mathbf{R} = AB \sin\theta$

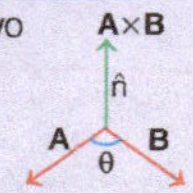

Properties of Vector Products

(i) $\mathbf{A} \times \mathbf{B} = -\mathbf{B} \times \mathbf{A}$

(ii) $\mathbf{A} \times (\mathbf{B} + \mathbf{C}) = (\mathbf{A} \times \mathbf{B}) + (\mathbf{A} \times \mathbf{C})$

(iii) $\mathbf{A} = a_x\hat{\mathbf{i}} + a_y\hat{\mathbf{j}} + a_z\hat{\mathbf{k}}$ and

$\mathbf{B} = b_x\hat{\mathbf{i}} + b_y\hat{\mathbf{j}} + b_z\hat{\mathbf{k}}$

Then,

$$\mathbf{A} \times \mathbf{B} = \begin{vmatrix} \mathbf{i} & \mathbf{j} & \mathbf{k} \\ a_x & a_y & a_z \\ b_x & b_y & b_z \end{vmatrix}$$

Relation between Angular and Linear Velocities

The linear velocity of a particle rotating about a fixed axis is given by,

$$v = \omega r$$

where, ω is angular velocity of particle.

Types of Motion

- **Pure Translational Motion** All the particles of the body have same velocity and move along parallel paths at any instant of time.
- **Pure Rotational Motion** Every particle of the body moves in a circle, which lies in a plane perpendicular to the axis of rotation and has its centre on the axis.
  The line or fixed axis about which the body is rotating is known as axis of rotation.
- **Rolling Motion.** The combination of pure translational motion and pure rotational motion is called rolling motion.

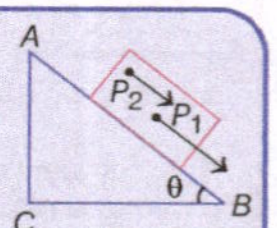

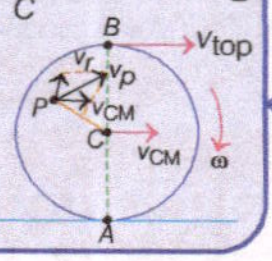

Gravitation (Chapter at a Glance)

Kepler's Third law : Law of Periods

- Square of time period of revolution T of a planet about the sun is directly proportional to cube of the semi-major axis a of their elliptical orbit.
  i.e. $T^2 \propto a^3$
- For circular orbit, $a = b = r$ (radius)
  $\therefore \quad T^2 \propto r^3$

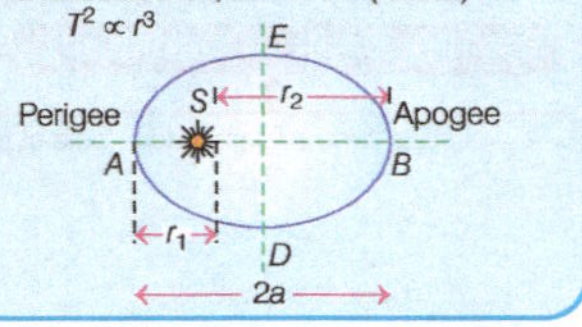

Kepler's Second Law: Law of Areas

- The line joining a planet to the sun sweeps equal area in equal time interval, i.e., areal speed of the planet remain constant in its orbit.
- When a planet is at the farthest position from the sun, its velocity is minimum and when it is nearest to the sun, its velocity is maximum.

Here, $\frac{dA}{dt} = \frac{L}{2m}$ = constant

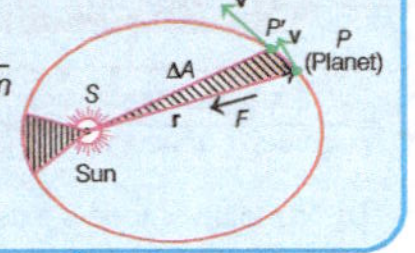

Newton's Universal Law

- Every material particle in the universe exerts an attractive force on another particle which is called gravitational force.
- The gravitational force acting between two particles is directly proportional to the product of their masses and inversely proportional to the square of the distance between the bodies.
- $F = \frac{-Gm_1m_2}{r^2}$
- Vector form,
  $\mathbf{F} = \frac{-G\,m_1m_2}{r^2}\,\hat{\mathbf{r}}$

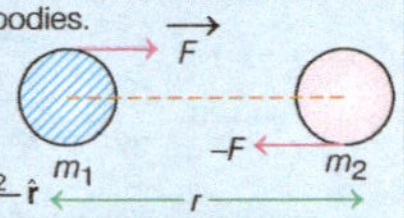

- Gravitational force acting between two particles does not depend on the nature of the particle and medium.
- This force is always attractive.
- This force is conservative in nature.
- Here, $F \propto \frac{1}{r^2}$,
  then graph between F and r will be hyperbola.

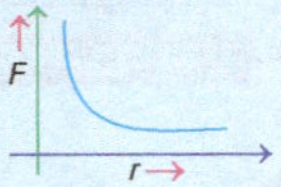

Gravitational Potential

- Gravitational potential at a point is the potential energy associated with a unit mass due to its position in the gravitational field of another body.
- At infinity, gravitational potential is zero as gravitational force is zero there.
- Here, $V = -\frac{W}{m}$

Gravitational Potential Energy

The energy of a system of two masses is equal to negative of work done by the gravitational field of one mass in bringing other mass from infinity to its present position.

A Body Placed in Earth's Gravitational Field

- Potential energy, $U = -\frac{GM_em}{r}$
- $W_{BA} = -GM_em\left[\frac{1}{r} - \frac{1}{r_1}\right]$

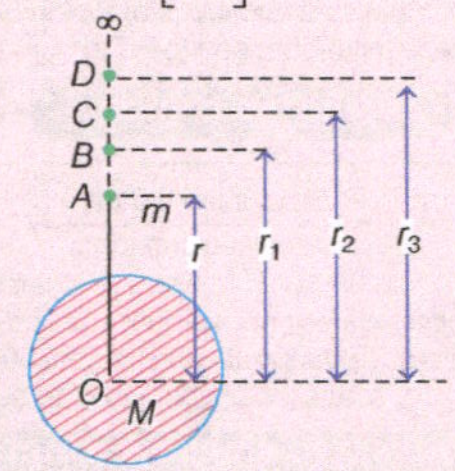

Graph of Energy

- Total energy of satellite,
  $E = -\frac{GM_em}{2r}$
- For a satellite revolving close to the earth's surface,
  $U = -\frac{GM_em}{R_e}$; $K = \frac{GM_em}{2R_e}$; $E = -\frac{GM_em}{2R_e}$

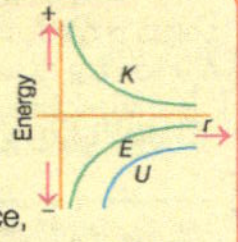

Variation in g due to Axial Rotation

If the observed value of g at the latitude λ is represented by g_λ, then

$g_\lambda = g_e - R_e\omega^2 \cos^2\lambda$

At equator, $\lambda = 0°$, $\cos\lambda = 1$

$\therefore g_\lambda = g_e - R_e\omega^2$

At poles, $\lambda = 90°$, $\cos\lambda = 0°$

$\therefore g_\lambda = g_e$ i.e, $g_p > g_e$

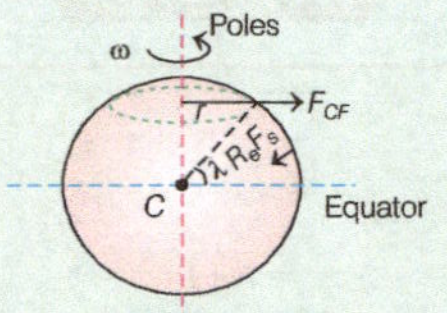

Kepler's First Law : Law of Orbits

- All planets revolve around the sun in elliptical orbits and the sun lies at one of the foci of ellipse.
- Eccentricity of ellipse, $e = \sqrt{1 - \frac{b^2}{a^2}}$

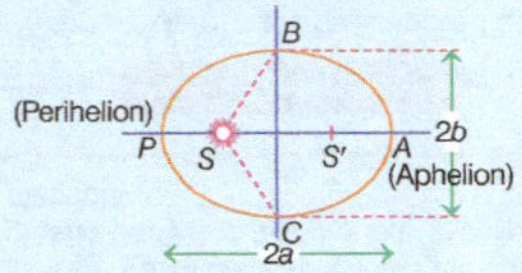

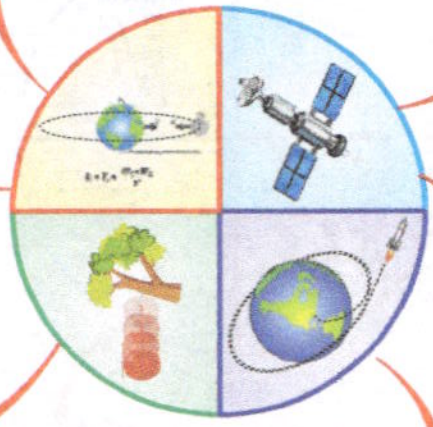

Energy

In a circular orbit of radius r around the earth (planet), gravitational potential energy of a satellite,

$$U = -\frac{GM_em}{r}$$

- Kinetic energy, $K = \frac{1}{2}mv_0^2 = \frac{1}{2}m\left(\sqrt{\frac{GM_e}{r}}\right)^2$
  $K = \frac{GM_em}{2r}$
- Total energy, $E = -\frac{GM_em}{2r}$

Orbital Speed

- Here, orbital speed

$v_o = \sqrt{\frac{Gm_e}{r}}$ (due to centripetal force)

$v_o = \sqrt{\frac{GM_e}{R_e + h}}$ ($\because r = R_e + h$)

Thus, $v_o = \sqrt{\frac{gR_e^2}{(R_e + h)}}$

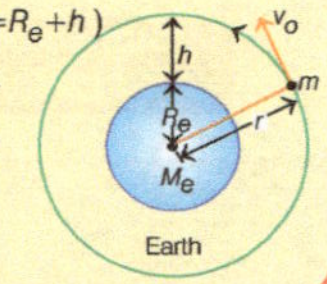

Satellites

- Those bodies which revolve around a planet are called satellites.

Acceleration due to Gravity of the Earth

- The force of gravity acting on a body having unit mass is known as acceleration due to gravity.
- According to Newton's second law, the acceleration due to gravity,
  $g = \frac{F}{m}$ or $\frac{GM}{R^2} = g$ or $g = \frac{4}{3}\pi G R\rho$
- **Gravitation**
  – The acceleration due to gravity is directed towards the centre of the earth.
  – It is a vector quantity.
  – Near the surface of the earth, the standard value for acceleration due to gravity is approximately 9.81 m/s^2.

Variation in g due to Shape of the Earth

- Earth is not in perfect shape. It is flat at the poles and bulged at the equator.
- Equatorial radius is about 21 km greater than the polar radius.
- On the earth's surface
  $g = \frac{GM_e}{R_e^2}$ or $g \propto \frac{1}{R_e^2}$

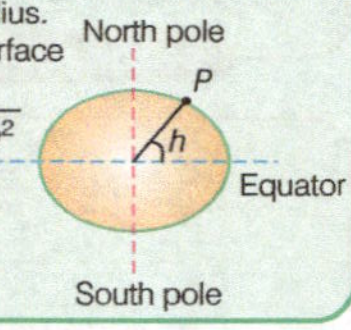

Escape Speed

- That minimum speed with which a body has to be projected vertically upward from the surface of the earth, so that it just crosses the gravitational field of the earth and never return back to earth.
- At infinity, $U_\infty = 0$ and $K_\infty = 0$

Then, $v_e = \sqrt{\frac{2GM_e}{R_e}}$

In terms of acceleration due to gravity, $v_e = \sqrt{2gR_e}$

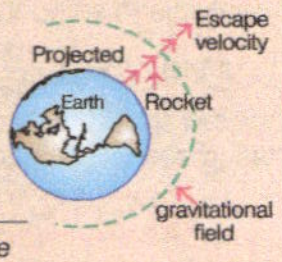

Thus, v_e = 11.2 × 10^3 m/s or 11.2 km / s

Time Period

- Time taken by a satellite to complete one cycle around the earth is called its time period or period of revolution (T).
  Here,
  $T = \frac{2\pi r^{3/2}}{\sqrt{GM_e}}$
  $T = 2\pi\sqrt{\frac{(R_e + h)^3}{gR_e^2}}$

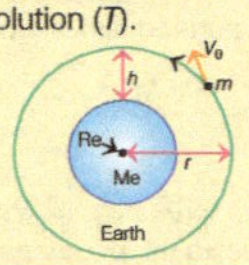

Graph of Orbital Speed

- The variation of orbital speed is given by
  $v_o = \sqrt{\frac{GM}{r}}$

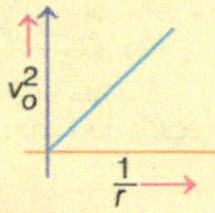

Variation in g due to Depth

- $g' = \frac{GM_e}{R_e^3}(R_e - d)$
- $g' = g\left(\frac{R_e - d}{R_e}\right)$
  or $g' = g\left(1 - \frac{d}{R_e}\right)$

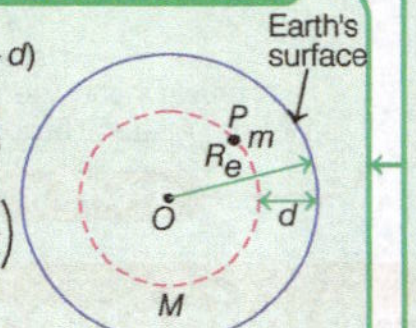

Variation in g due to Height

- Acceleration due to gravity at height h,
  $g' = \frac{GM_e}{(R_e + h)^2}$
  $\therefore \quad g' = g\left(1 - \frac{2h}{R_e}\right)$ (if $h << R_e$)
- The decrease in the value of g on going up at height h above the surface of earth by a factor. $\left(1 - \frac{2h}{R_e}\right)$.

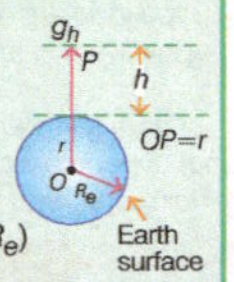

Escape Energy

- The minimum kinetic energy with which the body should be projected upward from earth surface, so that it may move to infinity, crossing gravitational field of earth.
- $U_e = \frac{1}{2}mv_e^2 = \frac{GM_em}{R_e} = mgR_e$

Facts

- There is no atmosphere at the moon :
  Escape speed on the moon surface:
  $v_e = \sqrt{2g_mR_m} = \sqrt{2 \times 1.63 \times 1.74 \times 10^6}$
  = 2.38 km/s
  which is less than the velocity of gas molecular on moon
- **Black hole** In black hole, escape velocity is greater than the speed of light.
  Then, $v_e = \sqrt{\frac{2GM}{R}} \geq c$
  Here, $c = 3 \times 10^8$ m/s

Graph of Time Period

- The variation of time period is $T^2 \propto r^3$
- Therefore, satellite obeys Kepler's third law of planetary motion.
- Greater is the distance of satellite from the earth's surface greater will be its time period of revolution.

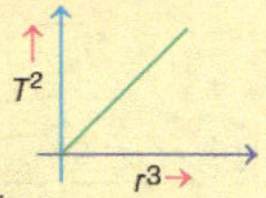

Mechanical Properties of Solids (Chapter at a Glance)

Normal Stress

- Restoring force acting normally on any surface inside a body per unit area is called normal stress.

Normal stress $= \frac{F_N}{A}$

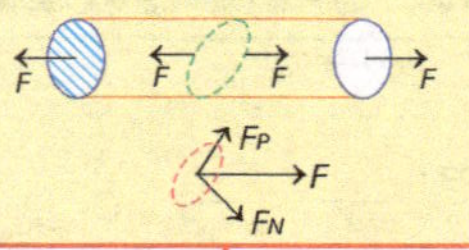

Longitudinal Stress

- When a deforming force is acting on the cross-sectional area along the length of a body, then it changes length of the body.
- Tensile stress $= \frac{F}{A}$

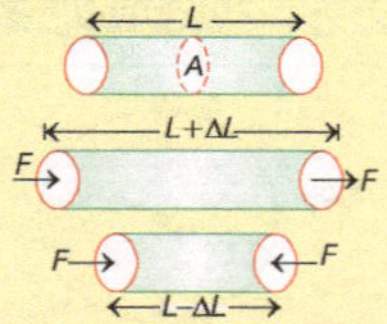

Volume Stress

- When a deforming force acting on a body is uniformly acting on each point of the body normal to the surface, then volume of this body is changed.
- Volume stress $= \frac{F}{ds}$

= Excess pressure on the body (Δp)

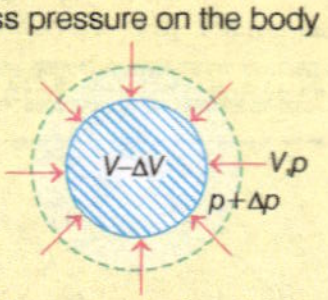

- It is also known as hydraulic stress.

Tangential or Shear Stress

- When a force acting tangentially on the surface of a body, then it changes shape of the body and the body is said to sheared.
- If the cross-sectional area of the cylinder is A and tangential force F, then Tangential stress $= \frac{F}{A}$

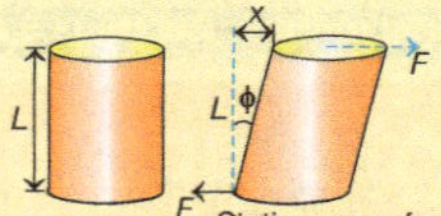

Stress

- When a body is subjected to a deforming force, a restoring force is developed in the body. This restoring force per unit area is known as stress.
- This restoring force is equal in magnitude but opposite in direction to the applied force.

Stress $= \frac{\text{Restoring force } (F)}{\text{Area of cross-section } (A)}$

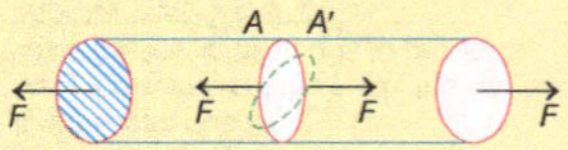

- SI unit is N/m^2 or pascal (Pa) and CGS system unit is dyne/cm^2.

Elastic and Plastic Behaviour of Solids

- A body that returns to its original shape and size on the removal of deforming force is called **elastic body** and this property is called **elasticity**.
- If a body does not show any tendency to regain its original shape and size even after the removal of deforming force are called **plastic body** and this property is called **plasticity**.

Strain

- When a deforming force is applied on a body, then shape and size of the body changes. The fractional change in the shape and size of the body is known as strain.

Longitudinal Strain

- The change in length per unit original length, when the body is deformed by external forces.

Longitudinal strain $= \frac{\text{Change in length}}{\text{Original length}} = \frac{\Delta L}{L}$

Volume Strain

- Fractional change in the volume of a body due to applied deforming force is called volume strain.

Volume strain $= \frac{\text{Change in volume}}{\text{Initial volume}} = \frac{\Delta V}{V}$

Shearing Strain

- If the deforming forces produce a change in the shape of the body, then the strain is called shear strain

Shearing strain $= \frac{\Delta x}{L} = \tan\theta$

Elastomers

- Materials which has very large elastic region but does not obey Hooke's law. There is no well defined plastic region.

Example : tissue of aorta, rubber, etc.

Hooke's Law

- According to this law, for small values of strain, the stress produced in a body is directly proportional to strain. $\frac{\text{Stress}}{\text{Strain}} = E = \text{constant}$
- Greater is the value of modulus of elasticity of the body, then it will be more elastic.
- Hooke's law is an empirical law and is found to be valid for most materials. However, there are some materials which do not exhibit this linear relationship.

Example Foams and gels, Biological tissues such as tendons, ligament and cartilage, etc.

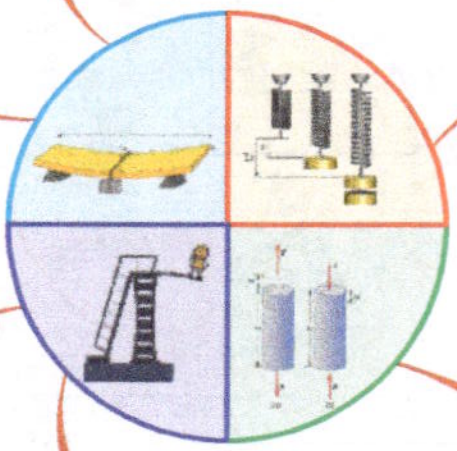

Stress-Strain Curve

- When a wire is stretched (breaking stress) by a load, it is seen that for small value of load, the extension produced in the wire is proportional to the load.
- If the weight is gradually increased, then length of the wire also increases gradually.

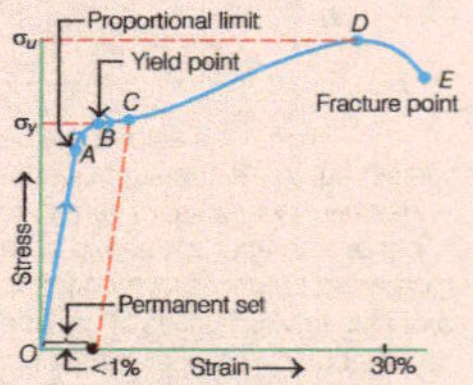

Here, S_u = ultimate tensile strength and S_y = yield strength

- If the ultimate strength and fracture points are closed, the material is said to be brittle.
- If they are far apart, the material is said to be ductile.

Applications of Elastic Behaviour of Materials

- A mild steel has a yield strength (σ_y) and has a lifting capacity M kg, then area of cross-section of the rope should at least be $A \geq \frac{Mg}{\sigma_y}$
- A bar of length l, breadth b, and depth d when loaded at the centre by a load w sags by $\delta = \frac{Wl^3}{4bd^3Y}$

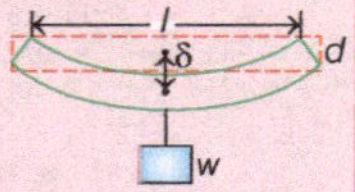

Energy Stored in a Deformed Body

- When a wire is stretched, an external work is done against internal restoring force produced in the wire. This work is stored in the form of elastic potential energy in the wire.
- Potential energy,

$$U = W = \frac{1}{2} \times \text{Weight} \times \text{Extension in length}$$

- Energy stored in the wire per unit volume Energy density is given by

$$U' = \frac{U}{V} = \frac{1}{2} \times \text{Stress} \times \text{Strain}$$

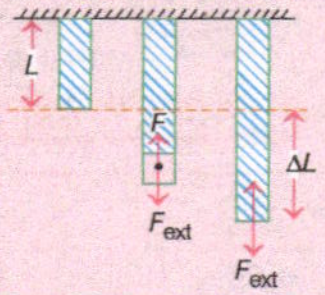

Poisson's Ratio

- Within the elastic limit, the ratio of lateral strain to the longitudinal strain is called poisson's ratio.

Poisson's ratio,

$$\sigma = \frac{\text{Lateral strain}}{\text{Longitudinal strain}} = \frac{-L}{D} \cdot \frac{\Delta D}{\Delta L}$$

- Poisson's ratio is a constant provided a material remains elastic, homogeneous and isotropic in nature.
- It's is a pure number and has no dimensions or units.
- It's value depends only on the nature of material.

Factors Affacting of Poisson's Ratio

- Hammering and rolling will increase elasticity of material.
- Annealing will decrease elasticity of material.
- **Temperature:** Elasticity of most of the materials decreases with increase in temperature.

Elastic Moduli

- The ratio of stress and strain is called modulus of elasticity.
- It has great importance for structural and manufacturing engineering designs.

Young's Modulus of Elasticity

- The ratio of longitudinal stress to longitudinal strain produced in the body is called Young's modulus of elasticity of material of body.

$$Y = \frac{\text{Longitudinal stress}}{\text{Longitudinal strain}} = \frac{FL}{A\Delta L}$$

Bulk Modulus of Elasticity

- The ratio of volume stress to the volume strain produced in a substance is called bulk modulus of elasticity of that substance.

$$B = \frac{\text{Volume or Normal stress}}{\text{Volume strain}}$$

$$B = \frac{-F/A}{\Delta V/V} = -\frac{pV}{\Delta V}$$

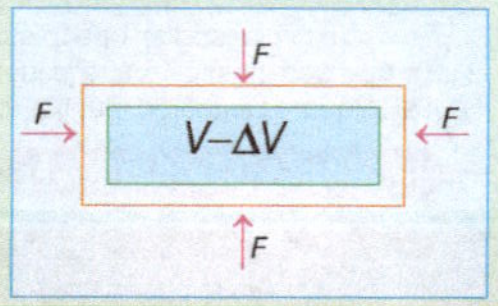

Modulus of Rigidity

- The ratio of produced tangential stress in an object to shear strain called modulus of rigidity. It is denoted by G or η.
- Tangential stress (Shear stress) $= \frac{F}{A}$
- Modulus of rigidity is given by

$$\eta \text{ or } G = \frac{\text{Tangential stress}}{\text{Shear strain}}$$

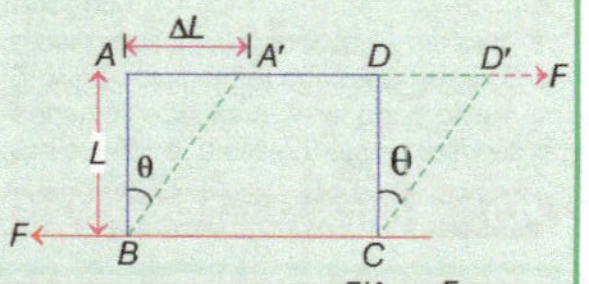

or shear modulus, $\eta = \frac{F/A}{\theta} = \frac{F}{A\theta}$

Mechanical Properties of Fluids (Chapter at a Glance)

Applications of Pascal's Law

- **Hydraulic Lift**
  It is used to lift the heavy loads. This is made by connecting two cylindrical vessels of different cross-sections. Each cylindrical vessel contains air tight frictionless pistons.
  An incompressible liquid is filled inside the vessel.
  $p = \frac{F_1}{A_1}; F_2 = pA_2 = \frac{F_1}{A_1}A_2$
  $A_2 >> A_1$, therefore $F_2 >>> F_1$

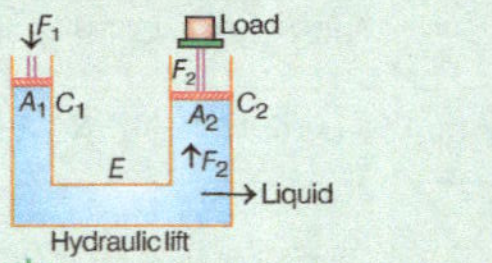

- **Hydraulic Brake**
  The working of the hydraulic brakes is also based on the Pascal's law.

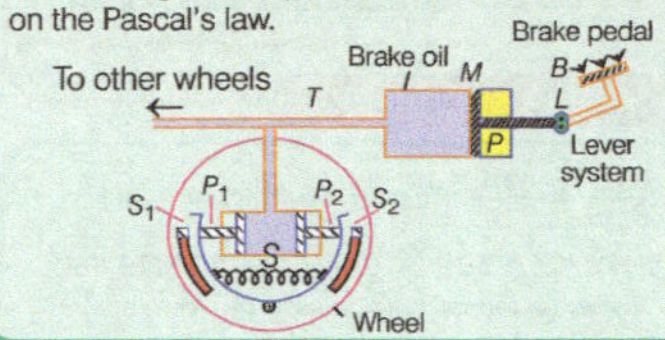

Hydrostatic Paradox

The pressure exerted by a liquid depends only on the height of fluid column and is independent of the shape of the containing vessel.

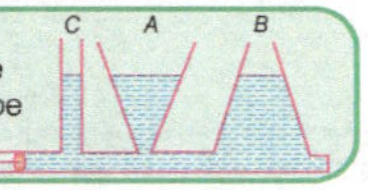

Variation of Pressure with Depth

- Consider a fluid at rest having density contained in a cylindrical vessel.
  So, pressure will distributed all side but depend on height of the vessel.
- Pressure difference, $p_2 - p_1 = h\rho g$
- Pressure, if we shift point A to the liquid surface.
  $p = p_a + h\rho g$
- Gauge pressure $= p - p_a = h\rho g$

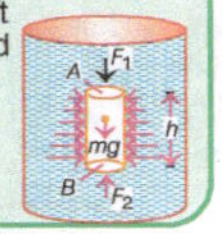

Bernoulli's Principle

- In streamlined flow of an incompressible and non-viscous fluid, the sum of pressure energy, kinetic energy and potential energy remain constant at each point of the flow,
  $p + \frac{1}{2}\rho v^2 + \rho g h = \text{Constant}$
- In terms of pressure head, velocity head and gravitational head,
  $\frac{p}{\rho g} + \frac{v^2}{2g} + h = \text{Constant}$

Pressure

- The pressure of liquid at a point is the thrust exerted by the liquid at rest per unit area. Pressure, $p = F/A$
- The SI unit of pressure is Nm^{-2}. It has been named as pascal (Pa)
- CGS unit of pressure is dyne/cm^2.

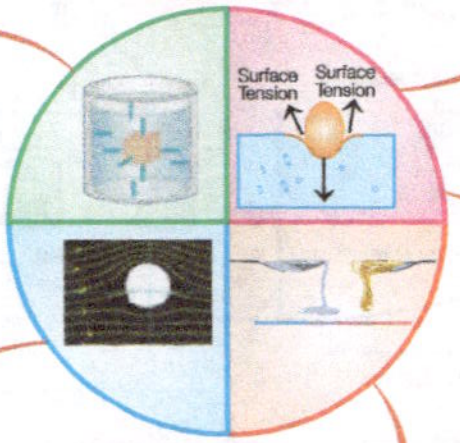

Pascal's Law

The pressure is applied on any part of the fluid placed in equilibrium inside a vessel, then this pressure is transmitted to each part of the fluid in all directions without decay in magnitude.

Atmospheric Pressure

The gaseous envelope surrounding the earth is called earth's atmosphere. The pressure exerted by the atmosphere is called atmospheric pressure.

Laminar Flow

If the liquid flows over a horizontal surface in the form of layers of different velocities, then the flow of liquid is called laminar flow.

Streamline Flow

Steady flow of a fluid is the flow in which every particle of the fluid follows exactly the same path as its preceding particle and same velocity at every point.

Turbulent Flow

When a liquid moves with a velocity greater than its critical velocity, the motion of the particles of fluid becomes disordered and irregular.

Equation of Continuity

During the steamline flow of the non-viscous and incompressible fluid through a pipe of varying cross-section, the product of area of cross-section and normal fluid velocity remains constant throughout the flow.

Critical Velocity

The maximum velocity of fluid upto which its flow remains streamlined and beyond which its flow becomes turbulent is called critical velocity.

Terminal velocity

The constant velocity attained by a freely falling body inside a viscous medium is called terminal velocity.

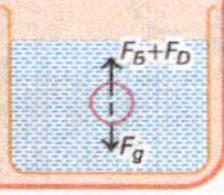

Viscosity

The property of fluid by virtue of which it opposes the relative motion between its different layers.

- The SI unit of viscosity is Nsm^{-2} and is called Poiseuille.

Coefficient of viscosity

Newton found that the viscous force acts between two layers of fluid is

(i) $F \propto A$

(ii) $F \propto \frac{dv}{dz}$

Hence, $F = -\eta A \frac{dv}{dz}$

$\eta = \frac{F/A}{dv/dz}$ or $\frac{F/A}{v/z}$

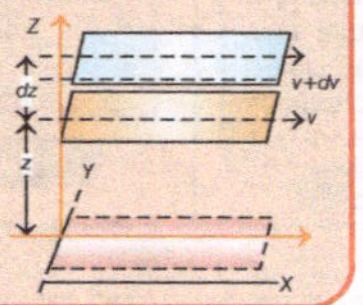

Stoke's Law

When a small sphere of radius r is moving with v velocity inside a homogeneous fluid, then retarding viscous force acting on the sphere, $F = 6\pi\eta rv$

Surface Energy

At a constant temperature, the amount of work done in expanding of the area of the free surface of liquid by unity against the cohesive force called surface energy.

$$\text{Surface energy} = \frac{\text{Work done in increasing the surface area}}{\text{Increase in surface area}}$$

Surface Energy Density

The surface tension of a liquid is numerically equal to the surface energy of unit surface area of a liquid.

$$T = \frac{E_S}{A} = \frac{\text{Surface energy}}{\text{Surface area}}$$

Surface Tension

It is the tendency of liquid surfaces at rest to shrink into the minimum surface area possible and behaves as a streched membrane. $S = \frac{F}{l}$

- **Measurement of Surface Tension**
  Let an imaginary line PQ is drawn tangentially anywhere on the liquid surface. This lines divides into two parts. One side of line exert force of attraction on the other part. This is perpendicular to the line and plane of surface of liquid.
  - SI unit of surface tension is N/m and dimensional formula is $[MT^{-2}]$.
  - This is a scalar quantity (magnitude is constant and direction is not defined)
  - CGS unit of surface tension is dyne/cm.

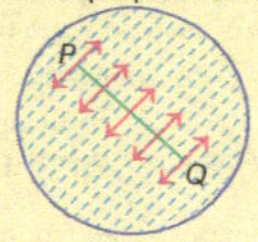

Factors Affecting of Surface Tension

- **Temperature**
  - Surface tension of liquids decrease with increase in temperature and attains zero value at particular temperature, called **critical temperature**
  - For small temperature differences, surface tension decreases almost linear by as $S_t = S_0(1 - \alpha t)$
- **Addition of impurities**
  Surface tension of liquid changes, with addition of impurities. Surface tension decreases in presence of contaminated substances such as dust particles on the surface of liquid.

Example of Surface Tension

Spraying of liquid results cooling, when a liquid is sprayed the large number of small drops are formed. As a result, surface area or surface energy increases. Thus, internal energy decreases, which depends on temperature.

Angle of Contact

The angle between tangent to liquid surface at the point of contact and the solid surface inside the liquid is called angle of contact (θ) of that liquid with that solid.

- **Value of angle of contact depend**
  - Nature of the solid and liquid in contact.
  - Cleanliness of the surface in contact.
  - Temperature of the liquid.
- Those liquids which wet the solid (water wets glass) have angle of contact θ < 90° (acute angle)
  - Ordinary water with glass, θ=8°
  - Pure water with glass, θ = 0°
- Those liquid which do not wet the solid (glass and mercury) have angle of contact θ > 90° (obtuse angle).
  - Mercury with glass, θ = 135°

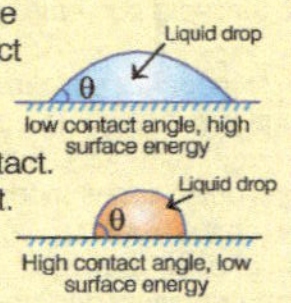

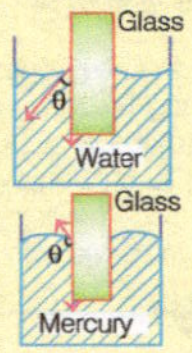

Capillarity

- The phenomena of fall or rise of liquid in a capillary narrow tube is known as capillarity.
  - When angle of contact of liquid with capillary tube is acute, then liquid rises in the capillary tube.
  - When angle of contact of liquid with capillary tube is obtuse (θ>90°), then liquid falls in capillary tube.
- Liquid in equilibrium, $h = \frac{2S\cos\theta}{r\rho g}$

Drops and Bubbles

- **Excess pressure**
  In equilibrium, the pressure inside a drop or bubble is more than pressure on its outer surface. Difference of these two pressures is called excess pressure.
- **Excess pressure inside a liquid drop**
  $\Delta p = \frac{2S}{R}$
  - In ordinary conditions,
    $p = p_0 =$ Atmospheric pressure
    $p_i = p + \frac{2S}{R} = p_0 + \frac{2S}{R}$
  - Pressure difference of the pressure on both side of a curved surface of liquid is called excess pressure.

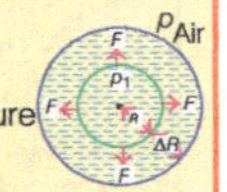

- **Excess pressure inside a soap bubble**
  $\Delta p = \frac{4S}{R}$
  - In ordinary conditions,
    $p = p_0 =$ Atmospheric pressure
    $p_i = p + \frac{4S}{R} = p_0 + \frac{4S}{R}$

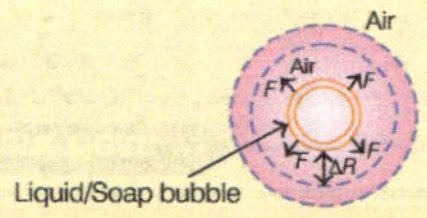

Thermal Properties of Matter (Chapter at a Glance)

Heat

Heat is the form of energy transferred between two (or more) systems or a system and its surrounding by virtue of temperature difference.

- **Transmission of Heat**
  When two bodies at different temperatures are brought in contact with each other, then heat flows from higher temperature to lower temperature. This flow of heat is called transmission of heat.
- **One Calorie**
  One calorie is equal to the amount of heat energy required to raise the temperature of one gram of water through 1°C (e.g. From 14.5°C to 15.5°C)

Temperature

Temperature is the measure of degree of hotness or coldness of a body and it is the condition of body which determines the direction of heat flow.

- **Measurement of Temperature**
  – A measure of temperature is obtained using a thermometer on some specified scales. These scales commonly called unit of temperature.
  – It measure the temperature of body in Kelvin (K), degree centigrade (°C) and degree Fahrenheit (°F).
- **Graph**
  The graph of Fahrenheit temperature (T_F) *versus* celsius or centigrade temperature (T_C)

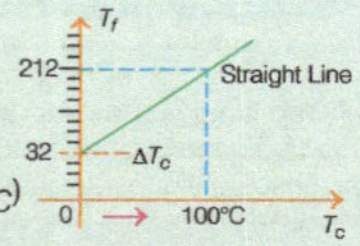

- **Conversion of Temperature**
  The ice and steam point of water are 32° F and 212° F, respectively on Fahrenheit scale and 0° and 100°C, respectively on Celsius scale. There are 100 equal interval between two reference points in celsius scale and 180 divisions in Fahrenheit scale.
  For Fahrenheit : $T_f = \frac{9}{5} T_c + 32$, **For Kelvin** : $T_k = T_c + 273.15$
- **Relation of Different Scales** $\frac{C}{100} = \frac{F-32}{180} = \frac{R}{80} = \frac{K-273.15}{100}$

Relation among Coefficients of Expansion

- The coefficient of expansion can be given as
  $\alpha_l = \frac{\Delta l}{l \Delta T}, \alpha_A = \frac{\Delta A}{A \Delta T}, \alpha_V = \frac{\Delta V}{V \Delta T}$
- The relation among coefficient of expansion is given by
  $\alpha_l : \alpha_A : \alpha_V = 1 : 2 : 3$

Area Expansion

- The expansion in the area of surface due to increase in its temperature is called area expansion.
- Expansion in area, $A = A_0(1 + \alpha_A \Delta T)$

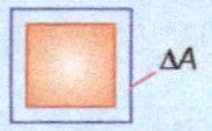

Volume Expansion

The expansion in the volume of an object due to increase in its temperature is known as volume expansion.
Expansion in volume, $V = V_0(1 + \alpha_V \Delta T)$

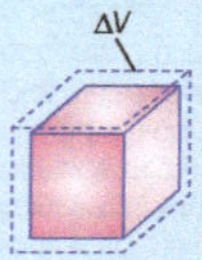

Thermal Expansion

The phenomenon of change in dimensions of an object due to heat supplied is known as thermal expansion.

Linear Expansion

- The expansion in length of a body due to increase in its temperature is called the linear expansion.
- Expansion in length, $L = L_0(1 + \alpha_l \Delta T)$

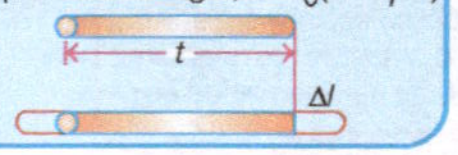

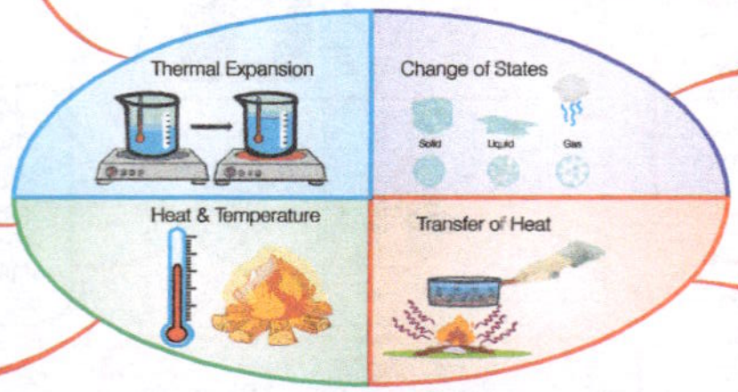

Latent Heat

The amount of heat transferred per unit mass during the change of phase of a substance without any change in its temperature.

- $Q = mL \Rightarrow L = \frac{Q}{m}$
- Latent heat of fusion, $L_f = \frac{Q}{m}$
- Latent heat of vaporisation, $L_v = \frac{Q}{m}$
- SI unit is Jkg^{-1}
- $L_{\text{fusion of ice}} = 80$ cal/g
- $L_{\text{vaporisation of water}} = 540$ cal/g

Change of State

The process of conversion of one state of a substance into another state is known as change of state.

- **Fusion and Melting Point** The process of change of state from solid to liquid is called **fusion**. The temperature at which solid states liquify is called melting point.
- **Freezing and Freezing Point** The process of change of state from liquid to solid is called **freezing**. The temperature at which liquid starts to freeze is known as the **freezing point**.
- **Vaporisation and Boiling Point** The process of change of state from liquid to vapour is called vaporisation. The temperature at which the liquid and the vapour states of the substance co-exist is called boiling point.
- **Sublimation** The process of change of state directly from solid to vapour is known as sublimation.
- The temperature and pressure at which all three phases of a substance co-exist simultaneously is known as the triple point.

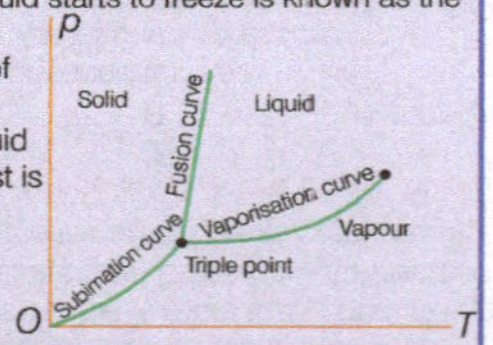

Calorimetry

Heat lost by hotter body = Heat gained by colder body.
$m_1 s_1 \Delta T = m_2 s_2 \Delta T$
Calorimeter is a device used for measuring the quantity of heat .

Ideal Gas Equation

- **Ideal Gas Equation**
  The ideal gas relationship as
  $pV = R \times (nT) \Rightarrow \frac{pV}{T} = nR$ (Constant)

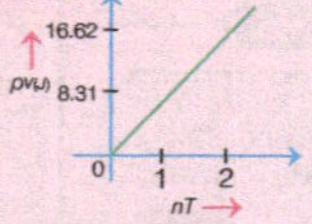

For two variables,
$\frac{p_f V_f}{T_f} = \frac{p_i V_i}{T_i}$ ∵ $R = 8.314$ J/mol K^{-1}

- **Boyle's Law**
  It is given by English Chemist Robert Boyle. Here, pressure is inversely proportional to the volume at constant temperature.
  i.e., $p \propto \frac{1}{V}$

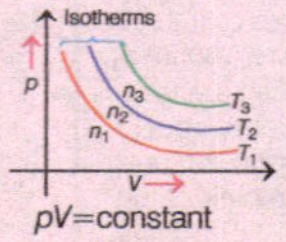

- **Charles' Law**
  It is given by French Scientist Jacques Charles. Here, volume of gas is directly proportional to the temperature at constant pressure.
  i.e., $V \propto T$

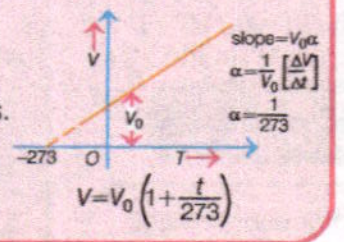

Absolute Temperature

- Theoretically, there is no limit for maximum temperature but there is a sharp point for minimum temperature called absolute temperature.
- The graph is extrapolated, – 273.15°C

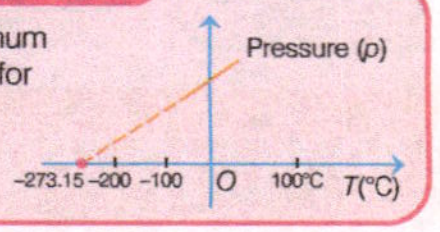

Anomalous Expansion of Water

- Water contracts on heating between the temperature 0°C to 4°C.
  When water cooled below the room temperature, the volume of given amount of water decreases until its temperature reaches to 4°C and below 4°C the volume again increases.
- If temperature of the top layer of water decreases below 4°C it becomes less dense and remains at the surface.

Heat Capacity

The amount of heat needed to change the temperature by unity i.e., 1°C, it is denoted by S and SI unit JK^{-1}

Heat capacity, $S = \frac{\Delta Q}{\Delta T}$

- **Specific Heat Capacity**
  The amount of heat needed to raise the temperature of unit mass of a substance by unity is known as the specific heat capacity or specific heat.
  SI unit of specific heat capacity $\text{Jkg}^{-1}\ \text{K}^{-1}$.
  Specific heat capacity, $s = \frac{1}{m}\frac{\Delta Q}{\Delta T}$
- **Relation between specific heat and molar specific heat capacity**
  Molar specific heat capacity, $C = \frac{\Delta Q}{n \Delta T}$
- $C = Ms$ (Here, M=Molecular mass of the substance)

Heat Transfer

- **Conduction** The transfer of heat taking place due to molecular vibration (i.e., molecular collisions).
- **Thermal conductivity** The ability of material to conduct the heat through it is known as thermal conductivity.
  Heat transfer, $Q = KA \frac{\Delta T}{L} t$
- **Convection** Convection is the process in which heat is transferred from one point to another by the actual motion of matter from a region of higher to lower temperature. e.g. Land breeze, sea breeze.
- **Radiation** A mode of transfer of heat from one place to another without heating the intervening medium. Heat transferred by thermal radiation.

Black Body Radiation

A body that absorbs all the radiation falling on it is known as **Black body**. It emits the electromagnetic wave at the fastest rate called black body radiation.

- **Stefan-Boltzmann's Law** Total energy emitted per second by a unit area of perfect black body is proportional to fourth power of its absolute temperature. i.e. $E = \sigma T^4$.
- **Wien's Displacement Law** The wavelength (λ_m) corresponding to which the energy emitted by a black body is maximum and inversely proportional to absolute temperature. $\lambda_m \propto 1/T$ or $\lambda_m T = b$.

Newton's Law of Cooling

The rate of cooling of a body is directly proportional to temperature difference between the body and its surroundings,

$-\frac{dQ}{dt} \propto (T - T_0)$ or Rate of loss of heat, $-\frac{dQ}{dt} = k(T - T_0)$

Thermodynamics (Chapter at a Glance)

Internal Energy of an Ideal Gas

- There are no molecular forces of attraction, so that the intermolecular forces are zero and gas does not posseses intermolecular potential energy.
  Thus, $U = U_K + U_P$; $U_P = 0$
  $U = U_K$

Internal Energy of Real Gases

- Intermolecular forces are not negligible.
- The molecules of real gas exert mutual force of attraction on one another, thus internal energy of real gas is less than the ideal gas under the same conditions.

Heat

- The energy that exchanged between a system and its surrounding because the temperature difference between them.
- SI unit of heat is joule.

Work

- By work, we mean work done by the system or on the system.
- Work done, $W = \int_{V_i}^{V_f} dW = \int_{V_i}^{V_f} p\,dV$
- If system expands, $V_f > V_i$ i.e., W = positive
- If system contracts, $V_f < V_i$ i.e., W = negative

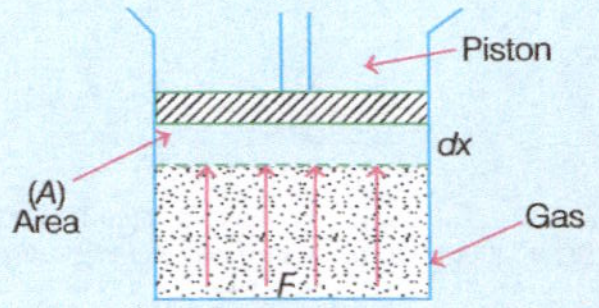

Internal Energy

- Energy due to the configuration and motion of the molecules of thermodynamical system is called internal energy.
- **Internal kinetic energy U_K** This is due to the motion of molecules.
- **Internal potential energy U_P** This is due to the configuration of molecules.
  Thus, total internal energy, $U = U_K + U_P$

Zeroth Law

- If two systems A and B are in thermodynamic equilibrium with a system C, they will also be in thermodynamic equilibrium mutually.

Thermodynamics Equilibrium

- When macroscopic variables (like pressure, volume, temperature, mass, composition, etc) that characterise the system do not change with time then system is said to be in equilibrium.

Thermodynamic System

- Thermodynamic system is an assembly of an extremely large number of particles, so that the assembly has a certain value of pressure, volume and temperature.
- There are three types of thermodynamic systems, which are open system, closed system and isolated system.

Thermodynamic State Variables

- It describes equilibrium states of systems by specific values of some macroscopic variables.
  - The connection between the state variable is called the equation of state.
  - For an ideal gas, the equation of state is the ideal gas relation,
    $pV = nRT$
  - The pressure - volume curve for fixed temperature is called an **isotherm**.

First Law of Thermodynamics

- Heat given to a system is equal to the sum of work done by the system and increase in the internal energy of the system.
  $Q = \Delta U + W$
- **Change in internal energy,**
  $dU = dQ - dW$
- **Limitation** This law does not explain the direction of flow of heat, whether it flows from hot rod to cold rod or *vice-versa*.
  - It is impossible to convert entire heat into work.

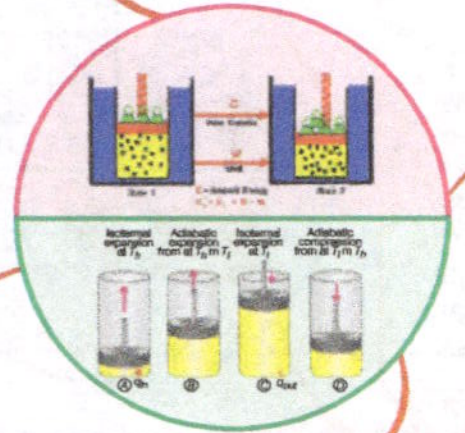

Specific Heat Capacity

- The amount of heat required to change the temperature of unit mass of a substance by unity. $s = \frac{1}{m}\left(\frac{\Delta Q}{\Delta T}\right)$

Molar Specific Heat Capacity

- Heat capacity per mole is known as molar specific heat capacity.
  $C = \frac{S}{n} = \frac{1}{n}\left(\frac{\Delta Q}{\Delta T}\right)$
- SI unit of molar specific heat capacity is J/mol-K

Relation Between C_p and C_V

- For an ideal gas, the relation between C_p and C_V is given as,
  $C_p - C_V = R$
  This is called **Mayer's formula**.
- The ratio of C_p and C_V is notified by γ.
  i.e., $\gamma = C_p/C_V$
  Here, $C_p = \left(\frac{\Delta Q}{\Delta T}\right)_p$ and $C_V = \left(\frac{\Delta Q}{\Delta T}\right)_V$

Specific Heat Capacity of Water

- The amount of heat required to raise the temperature of one gram of water by one degree centigrade.
- The specific heat of water varies slightly with temperature.

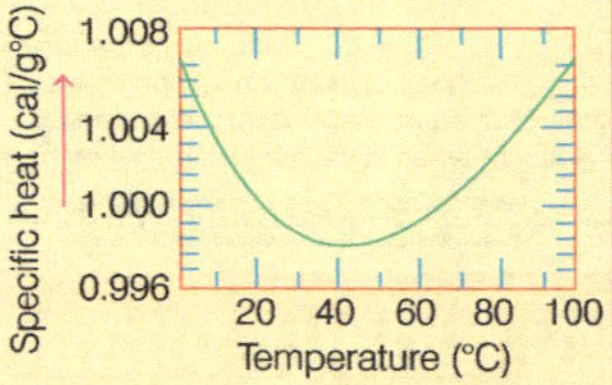

Quasi-Static Process

- A hypothetical process in which at every stage the system remains in equilibrium. Practically, a process that are sufficiently slow are consider as quasi-static process.

Isothermal Process

- That process in which temperature of a thermodynamical system remains constant.
  Example Melting of ice (or any solid) at melting point.
- **p-V Diagram**
  Follows Boyle's law,
  $p_iV_i = p_fV_f$
  Thus, pV = constant

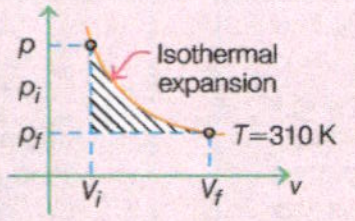

- **Work done**
  - Work done=Area under p-V graph
  $W_{iso} = 2.303\,nRT \log\left(\frac{V_f}{V_i}\right)$
  - If $V_f > V_i$, then $W > 0$ (Isothermal expansion)
  - If $V_f < V_i$, then $W < 0$ (Isothermal compression)

Carnot Engine

- Carnot engine is an ideal heat engine which is proposed by Sadi Carnot in 1824. The reversible engine which operates between two temperatures.

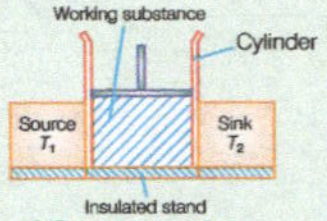

- **Efficiency of Carnot engine**
  - The ratio of work done to the heat supplied
  i.e., $\eta = \frac{\text{Work done}}{\text{Heat input}} = \frac{W_{net}}{Q_1}$
  - In cyclic process $\Delta U = 0$, therefore $\Delta W = \Delta Q$
  - Final efficiency of Carnot engine,
  $\eta = 1 - \frac{T_2}{T_1} = 1 - \frac{Q_2}{Q_1}$

Second Law of Thermodynamics

- The principle that put a restriction on the first law of thermodynamics is known as second law of thermodynamics.
  Mathematically, this law is represented as
  $\Delta S_{uni} > 0$
  where, ΔS_{uni} is the change in the entropy of the universe.
  Example The process of decaying organisms is showcase the tendency of nature towards increasing entropy.

Kelvin-Planck's Statement

- Total energy taken from an object cannot be converted into work (although total work can be converted into heat).

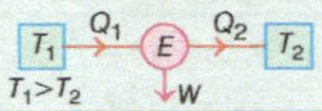

Adiabatic Process

- The process, in which there is no exchange of heat between system and surrounding take place.

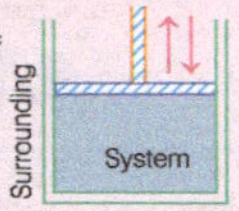

- **p-V Diagram**
  From first law of thermodyamics,
  $\Delta Q = \Delta U + \Delta W$
  - Adiabatic process,
  pV^γ = Constant
  Thus, $p_iV_i^\gamma = p_fV_f^\gamma$

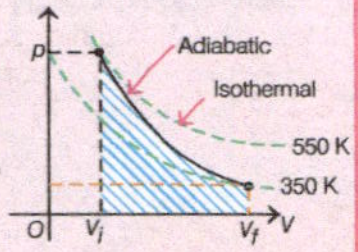

- **Work done**
  - Work done in an adiabatic process, $W = \int_{V_i}^{V_f} p\,dV = \int_{V_i}^{V_f} \frac{K}{V^\gamma}dV$
  - Work done, $W = \frac{nR\,(T_i - T_f)}{\gamma - 1}$

Carnot Cycle

- Working substance (ideal gas) in Carnot engine allow to undergo through a reversible cycle which is called Carnot cycle.

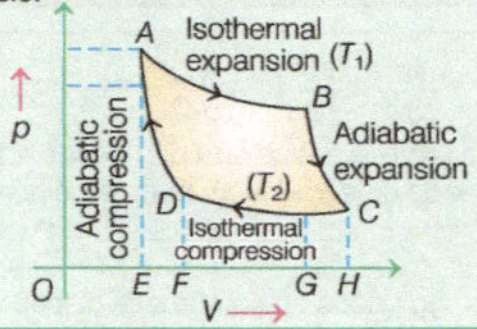

Carnot Theorem

- Efficiencies of all reversible engines working between the same temperatures are equal and their efficiencies cannot be greater than Carnot engine working between the same temperature.
  Carnot refrigerator, $\frac{Q_1}{Q_2} = \frac{T_1}{T_2}$
  Coefficient of performance, $K = \frac{Q_2}{Q_1 - Q_2} = \frac{T_2}{T_1 - T_2}$

Clausius's Statement

- Heat cannot flow from low temperature to high temperature automatically.
  $T_1 < T_2$

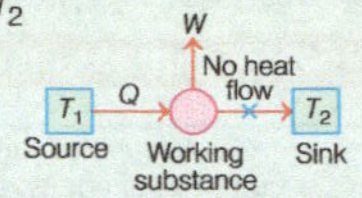

Isochoric Process

- Volume of the system remains constant. If heat added to system, its pressure increase and if heat extracted, pressure will be reduced.
- Work done, $\Delta W = 0$
- Change in internal energy, $\Delta U = nC_V\Delta T$

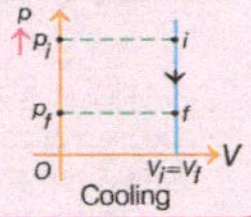

Isobaric Process

- Pressure of the system remains constant.
- Work done, $W = nR\,(T_f - T_i)$
- As temperature of gas changes, so its internal energy also changes.

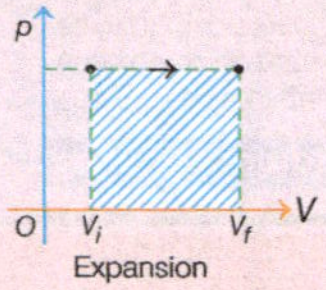

Kinetic Theory (Chapter at a Glance)

Avogadro's Hypothesis

- Equal volumes of all gases under identical conditions of pressure and temperature will contain equal number of molecules.
- Avogadro's number,
  $N_A = 6.023 \times 10^{23}$
- Density, $\rho = \frac{PM_0}{RT}$

Behaviour of Real Gas and Ideal Gas

- A real gas behaves as an ideal gas most closely at low pressure and high temperature.
  $pV = \mu RT \Rightarrow \frac{pV}{\mu T} = R$
- Behaviour of real gas approach ideal gas at low pressure $(T_1 > T_2 > T_3)$

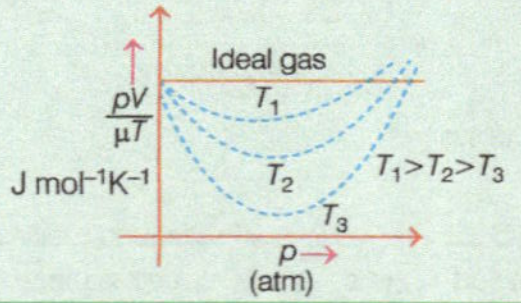

Boyle's Law

- According to this law, at constant temperature, volume of definite quantity of a gas is inversely proportional to its pressure (p).
  Therefore, $V \propto \frac{1}{p}$ (constant temperature)
- $p_1V_1 = p_2V_2 =$ Constant
- p-V curve for temperatures T_1 and T_2 is as shown.

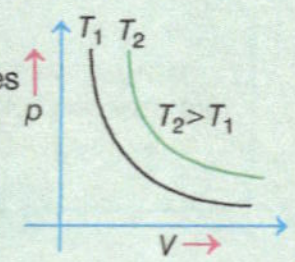

Charles' Law

- According to this law, at constant pressure, volume of definite quantity of a gas is directly proportional to absolute temperature (T) of the gases.
  Therefore,
  $V \propto T$ (constant pressure)
- $\frac{V_1}{T_1} = \frac{V_2}{T_2}$ and $V_t = V_0 \left(\frac{273 + t}{273}\right)$
  $p_2 > p_1$

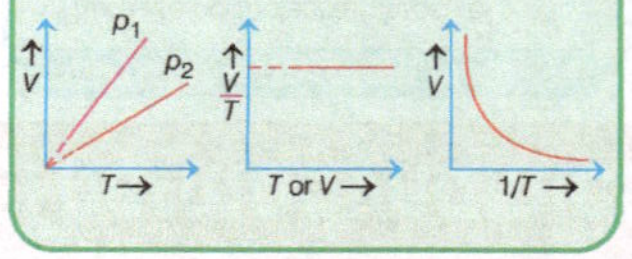

Atomic Hypothesis

- All things are made of atoms. The atoms are little particles that moves around in perpetual motion, attracting each other when they are a little distance apart, but repelling upon being squeezed into another.

Molecular Nature of Matter

- **Richard Feynman** In 20th century, Richard Feynman discovered that matter is made up of atoms.
- **John Dalton** He proposed the atomic theory to explain the laws of definite and multiple proportions.
- **Gay Lussac** When gases combine chemically to yield another gas, their volumes are in the ratio of small integers.
- The size of an atom is about an angstrom (10^{-10}m).
- In gases the interatomic distance are in tens of angstroms.
- In dynamic equilibrium, molecules collide and change their speed during collision. Only the average properties are constant.

Behaviour of Gases

- In a gas, molecules are far from each other and their mutual interactions are negligible except when two molecules collide.
- Gases at low pressures and high temperatures, much above the temperature that at which they liquify satisfy. $pV = Nk_BT$, observation tells that k_B is same for all gases.
- **For different gases**
  $\frac{p_1V_1}{N_1T_1} = \frac{p_2V_2}{N_2T_2} = \frac{p_3V_3}{N_3T_3} .....$
  $= k_B =$ constant.
  Boltzmann's constant,
  $k_B = 1.38 \times 10^{-23}$ J/K

Gay-Lussac's Law

- At constant volume, pressure of a definite quantity of gas is directly proportional to absolute temperature.
- Therefore, $p \propto T$
  $\frac{p_1}{T_1} = \frac{p_2}{T_2}$ and $p_t = p_0 + p_0 \times \frac{t}{273}$

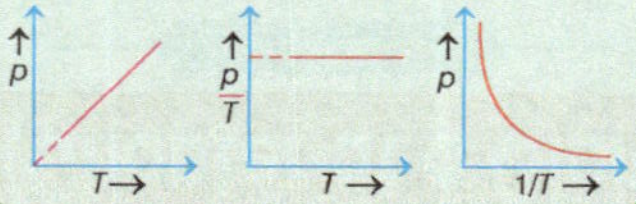

Internal Energy of Gases

- **Monoatomic Gases**
  Total internal energy of one mole of monoatomic gas,
  $U = \frac{3}{2}RT$
- **Diatomic Gases**
  Total internal energy of one mole of diatomic gas,
  $U = \frac{5}{2}RT$
- **Triatomic Gases**
  Total internal energy of one mole of triatomic gas,
  $U = \frac{7}{2}RT$
- **Solids**
  Total internal energy of one mole of solid,
  $U = 3RT$

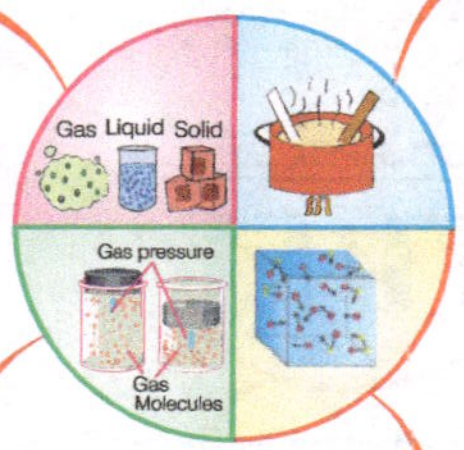

Kinetic Theory of an Ideal Gas

- It explains the behaviour of gases using this theory various properties of gas like pressure, temperature, energy etc,

Assumption of Kinetic Theory of Gases

- The density and the distribution of molecules is uniform throughout the gas.
- There is no intermolecular forces between molecules of gas except during collision.
- Specific heat capacities C_p and C_V of an ideal gas do not depend on the temperature.

Dalton's Law of Partial Pressure

- Total pressure of mixture of non-interacting ideal gas is equal to the sum of partial pressures exerted by individual gases in the mixture.
  $p = p_1 + p_2 + p_3 + ...$

Mean Free Path

- The average distance travelled by a molecule between two successive collisions is known as the mean free path of molecule.
- Mean free path, $\lambda = \frac{1}{\sqrt{2}n\pi d^2}$
  Here,
  d = Diameter of each molecule and
  n = Number of molecules per unit volume.
- The mean free path in gases is of the order of thousand of angstroms.

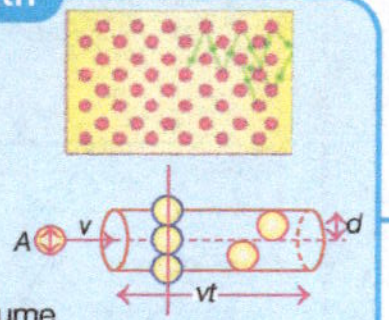

Law of Equipartition of Energy

- For a dynamic system in thermal equilibrium, the total energy is distributed equally amongst all the degree of freedom and the energy associated with each molecule per degree of freedom is (1/2) k_BT.
- Translational energy $< E_t > = (3/2)\, k_B T$.

Kinetic Interpretation of Temperature

- In kinetic theory, the kinetic interpretation of temperature states that the average kinetic energy of the gas molecules of an ideal gas is directly proportional to absolute temperature of the molecules.
- Molecular arrangements in solid, liquids and gases.

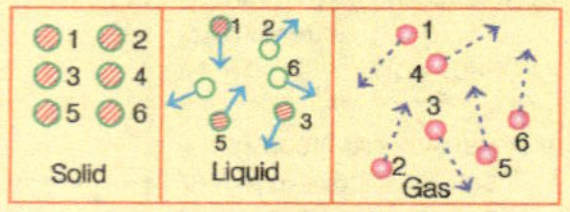

Pressure of an Ideal Gas

- The force exerted by the gas molecules on unit area of the walls of container is called pressure of gas.
- Impulse = Change in momentum
  $F\Delta t = \Delta p_x = -2mv_x$
- Average force exerted,
  $F = -\frac{2mv_x}{\Delta t} = \frac{(-2mv_x)}{\left(\frac{2l}{v_x}\right)}$
  $F = -\frac{mv_x^2}{l}$

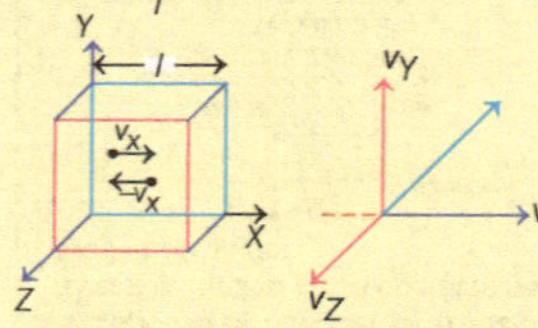

- Pressure of an ideal gas, $p = \frac{1}{3}\frac{mn}{V}v_{rms}^2$
  $n \rightarrow$ number of molecules

Basic Assumptions

- The molecule of gas are considered as hard spheres each of diameter d.
- All the molecules of gas except the molecule under consideration are at rest.

Degree of Freedom

Total number of condition or coordinates or independent quantities required to describe completely the position and configuration of a dynamical system.
Degree of freedom, $f = 3N$-k

- **For monoatomic gas**, such as helium, neon, argon, have translational degree of freedom.
  If $N = 1$ and $k = 0$, then $f = 3 \times 1 - 0 = 3$
- **For diatomic gas**, such as oxygen, hydrogen, nitrogen etc. $\therefore f = 5$
- **For triatomic gas**, such as H_2S, SO_2 have translational degree of freedom.
  $f = 7, f = 6$ (for non-linear)

Most Probable Speed

The speed with which most of the molecules move is called most probable speed.

$v_{mp} = \sqrt{\frac{2RT}{M}} = \left(\sqrt{\frac{2}{3}}\right) v_{rms} = 0.816 v_{rms}$

Concept of Temperature

- **Relation between temperature and rms speed** $\frac{1}{3}Mv_{rms}^2 = RT \Rightarrow v_{rms} = \sqrt{\frac{3RT}{M}}$
- **Relation between temperature and molecular kinetic energy** $E = \frac{3}{2}kT$
- Root mean square velocity of gas molecules is directly proportional to the square root of its absolute temperature.

Average Speed

This is equal to average of the speed of molecules
i.e., $v_{av} = \frac{v_1 + v_2 + ... + v_n}{n}$

- The relation among most probable speed, average speed and rms speed is given by
  $v_{mp} : v_{av} : v_{rms} = \sqrt{\frac{2RT}{M}} : \sqrt{\frac{8RT}{\pi M}} : \sqrt{\frac{3RT}{M}}$

Root Mean Square Speed

This speed is equal to the square root of the mean value of square of the velocities.

$v_{rms} = \sqrt{\left(\frac{v_1^2 + v_2^2 + v_3^2 + ... v_n^2}{n}\right)}$

Oscillations (Chapter at a Glance)

Period and Frequency

- The smallest interval of time after which a periodic motion is repeated is called its period.

Examples

- Period of revolution of the planet mercury is 88 earth days.
- Period of vibration of a quartz crystal is expressed in units of microsecond (10^{-6}), i.e. μs.
- The number of oscillations per unit time is called frequency. The relation between frequency and period is given by $\text{frequency} = \frac{1}{\text{Period}}$
- The SI unit of frequency is hertz (Hz). 1Hz = 1 Oscillation per second

Displacement

- Change in position of a particle with respect to origin but in oscillation, we use term displacement as the change in position with respect to mean position or reference point.

Examples

- Consider a block is attached to a spring at one of its end, the other end of which is fixed to rigid wall. Genenally, it is convenient to measure the displacement variable as the block from mean position of the oscillation with time.

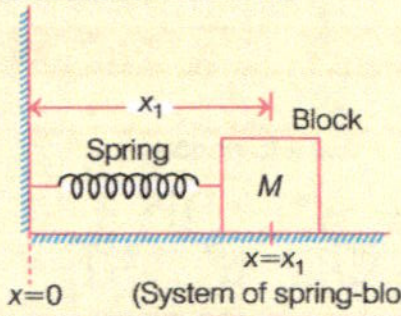

(System of spring-block)

Periodic Function

- The function which repeats its value in regular interval of time or period is called periodic function
  $f(t) = A\cos\omega t$ (cosine function)
  $f(t) = A\sin\omega t$ (sine function)
  Also $f(t) = A\sin\omega t + B\cos\omega t$
- Any periodic function can be expressed as a superposition of sine and cosine function of different time period with suitable coefficient.

Restoring Force

- The force which tend to bring the particle to its equilibrium position when particle is displaced from its equilibrium position is called restoring force.
- In equilibrium position, value of restoring force is zero.

Oscillatory Motion

- In periodic motion in which a particle (or object) undergoes back and forth or to and fro motion about a definite point along the same path is called oscillatory or vibratory motion.

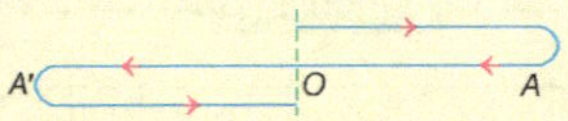

- Each oscillatory motion is essentially a periodic motion but each periodic motion is not essentially oscillatory.

Examples

- Motion of piston of an engine.
- Motion of molecules in solids.

Periodic Motion

- When a particle (or a body) moves, along a definite path such that it repeats its motion after a definite time interval, motion is called periodic motion.
- If $y(t)$ is the displacement of particle, then $y(t) = y(t+T) = y(t+2T) = ...$

Examples

- Rotational motion of the earth about its own axis.
- Motion of the earth about the sun in an elliptical orbit.

Simple Harmonic motion

- If a particle undergoes a motion to and fro about a fixed point (equilibrium position) such that
  - Motion remains along a straight line.
  - Force or acceleration acting on the particle must always be directed towards equilibrium position.
  - In SHM, if force acting on the particle is F and its displacement is y, then $F \propto -y$ or $F = -ky$

Equations of SHM

The motion of a particle executing SHM can be expressed by the following equations

$x(t) = A\cos(\omega t + \phi)$
$y(t) = A\sin(\omega t + \phi)$

SHM and Uniform Circular Motion

When a particle is moving with uniform speed on the circumference of circle, then the motion of the foot of perpendicular dropped from the position of particle on any diameter along the diameter is simple hamonic motion.

Oscillation of a Liquid in a U-tube

- Force, $F = -mg = -(A \cdot 2y \cdot \sigma)g$
- Mass of entire liquid, $M = A.2h.\sigma$
- Acceleration, $a = -\omega^2 y$
- Time period, $T = 2\pi\sqrt{\frac{h}{g}}$

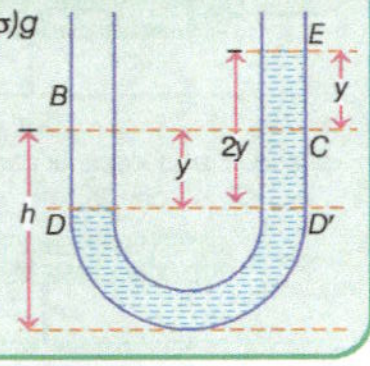

Damped Oscillation

- Oscillation of a body whose amplitude goes on decreasing with time.
  - Damped force $F_d = -br$, $r = dx/dt$
  - Displacement of damped oscillator. $x = x_m e^{-bt/2m}\cos(\omega t + \phi)$

  Amplitude decrease with time as $x = x_m e^{-(bt/2m)}$

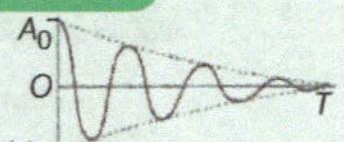

Characteristics of SHM

- **Amplitude** The maximum displacement of particle executing SHM.

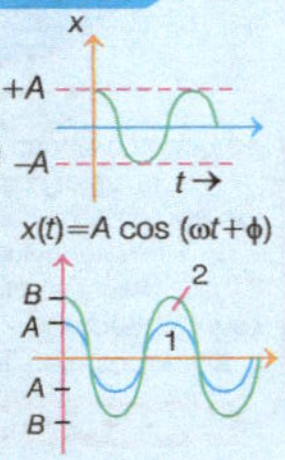

- **Phase**- Phase of a oscillating particle is that quantity which refers to the position and direction of motion of the particle at that instant.
  $x = A\cos(\omega t + \phi)$
  where, ϕ is phase difference.
- **Velocity** At any instant, the rate of change of displacement with respect to time of particle executing SHM is known as its velocity.
  $v = \omega\sqrt{A^2 - x^2}$
  - At mean position, $x = 0$, $v = \omega A$
  - At extreme position, $x = A$, $v = 0$ (Minimum velocity)
  $v(t) = -\omega A\sin(\omega t + \phi)$
- **Acceleration** At any instant, the rate of change of velocity with respect to time of particle executing SHM is known as acceleration.
  $a = \omega^2 A$
  - At mean position, $x = 0$, $a = 0$
  - At extreme position, $x = A$, $a = -\omega^2 A$
  $a(t) = -\omega^2 A\cos(\omega t + \phi)$

Simple Pendulum

- If a point mass is suspended with a massless, inextensible and perfectly flexible string from a rigid support, the arrangement is called simple pendulum.
- Restoring force acting on the bob, $F = -mg\sin\theta$
- If θ is very small, $F = -mg\frac{x}{L}$
- Acceleration of bob, $a = \frac{F}{m} = -\frac{gx}{L}$
- Time period, $T = 2\pi\sqrt{\frac{L}{g}}$

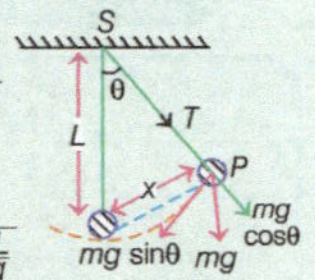

- **Effective length**
  Time period of pendulum depend on its effective length
  $T \propto \sqrt{L}$ or $T^2 \propto L$

Motion of a Body Attached to a Spring

- Let a particle of mass m is executing SHM with angular frequancy ω, then
- Acceleration of the body, $a = \frac{F}{m}$ or $a = -\omega^2 x$
- Time period, $T = 2\pi\sqrt{\frac{m}{k}}$

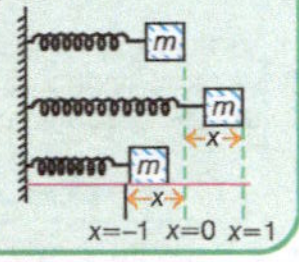

Energy In SHM

- A particle executing SHM posses both kinetic energy and potential energy.

Curves in S.H.M

- Suppose particle starts its simple harmonic motion from equilibrium position, therefore
- **Time-displacement equation**
  $y = A\sin\omega t$

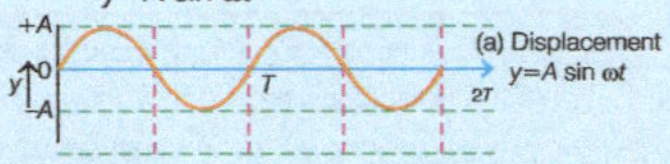

- **Time-velocity equation**
  $v = \frac{dy}{dt} = A\omega\cos\omega t$

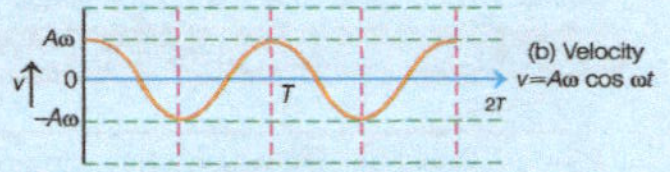

- **Time-acceleration equation**
  $a = \frac{dv}{dt} = -A\omega^2\sin\omega t$

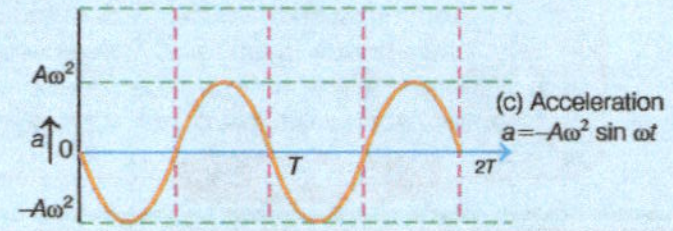

Conditions

- Time period of simple pendulum suspended from moving vehicle with horizontal acceleration,
  $T = 2\pi\sqrt{\frac{L}{g'}} = 2\pi\sqrt{\frac{L}{\sqrt{g^2 + a^2}}}$
- Simple pendulum suspended from the roof of a vehicle, which moves without friction down an inclined plane of inclination θ
  $T = 2\pi\sqrt{\frac{L}{g\cos\theta}}$
- If simple pendulum is brought inside a liquid, then effective acceleration,
  $g' = g\left[1 - \frac{\sigma}{\rho}\right]$

In vertical Plane

- Net force acting on the body at a distance x,
  $F = F_2 + mg = -k(l + x) + kl$
- Acceleraton of body,
  $a = \frac{F}{m} = -\frac{k}{m}x$
- Time period, $T = 2\pi\sqrt{\frac{m}{k}}$

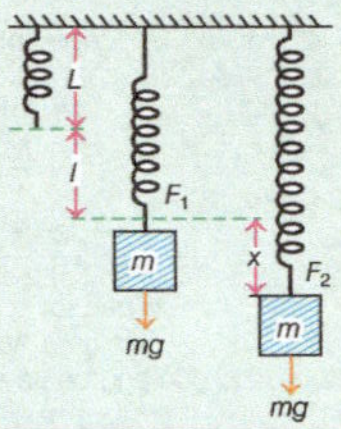

Kinetic Energy

A particle has kinetic energy due to its velocity in simple harmonic motion.
Kinetic energy, $K = \frac{1}{2}k(A^2 - x^2)$

Potential Energy

- When a particle displaces from its equilibrium position, then it does work against restoring force which store in the form of potential energy.
- Potential energy, $U = \frac{1}{2}M\omega^2 x^2$

Total Energy

- Total mechanical energy of a harmonic oscillation is independent of time or displacement, while depends on the maximum displacement.
  Total energy, $E = \frac{1}{2}kA^2$

Waves (Chapter at a Glance)

Matter Waves

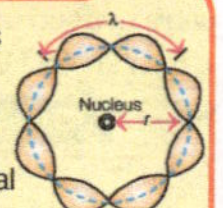

- These types of waves are associated with microscopic particles i.e., electron, proton and other fundamental particles.
- These waves represent the wave like nature of a moving particle.

Mechanical Waves

- The waves which require medium for their propagation are called mechanical or elastic waves.
Example : Sound waves, seismic waves, water waves, etc.

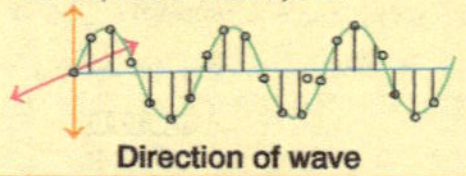

Electromagnetic Waves

Those waves which do not require any medium for their propagation are called electromagnetic or inelastic waves.
Example : Visible light, ultraviolet, heat waves etc.

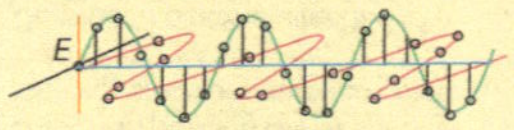

Frequency

Number of vibrations that a particle of medium completes in one second during the wave propagation.

$$f = \frac{1}{\text{Time period } (T)}$$

Phase

Physical quantity which refers to the position and direction of the motion of the particle at an instant during the propagation.

Wavelength

Distance travelled by a wave during one time period is called wavelength.

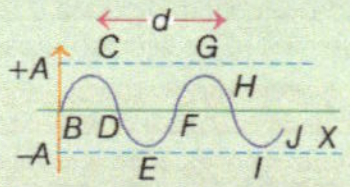

(Direction of propagation at instant t)

Transverse Waves

When particle of a medium vibrate perpendicular to the direction of propagation of wave, the wave is called transverse wave.
Examples : Waves produced in strings of musical instrument, visible light, etc.

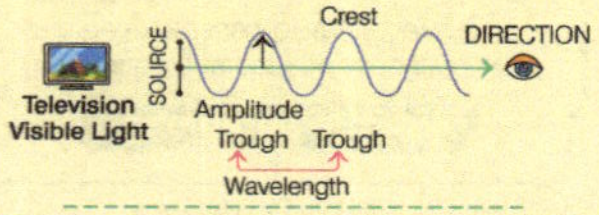

Longitudinal Waves

When particles of medium vibrate in the direction of propagation of wave, the wave is called longitudinal wave.
Examples : Spring waves, sound waves, etc.

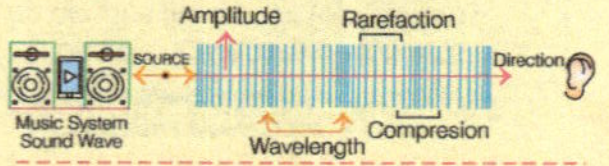

Definition of Waves

Wave is that disturbance produced in a medium (or vacuum) in which energy and momentum propagates without transport of the particles of medium.

Displacement in Progressive Waves

- Displacement, $y(x, t) = a \sin (kx - \omega t + \phi)$
$y(x, t) = A \sin (kx - \omega t) + B \cos (kx - \omega t)$
where, $a = \sqrt{A^2 + B^2}$ and $\phi = \tan^{-1}(B/A)$
- The wave travelling in the negative direction of X-axis, $y(x, t) = a \sin (kx + \omega t + \phi)$

Amplitude

Maximum displacement of a particle from their equilibrium position, as a wave pass through them is known as amplitude.

Time Period

Time taken by a particle of medium to complete its one vibration during the propagation.

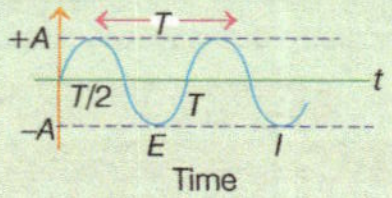

(At position X)

Media for Transverse Waves

- The particles motion is perpendicular to the direction of propagation of the wave. As the wave propagates, each element of the medium undergoes a shearing strain.
- Here, propagated only in those media which can sustain shearing stress, such as solids and surface of liquids but not gases and inside liquids.

Media for Longitudinal Waves

- A medium like a steel bar, both transverse and longitudinal waves can propagate while air can sustain only longitudinal waves.
- Waves may be one-dimensional, two dimensional or three dimensional. Mode of dimension will be according to the propagation of energy in one, two and three dimensions.

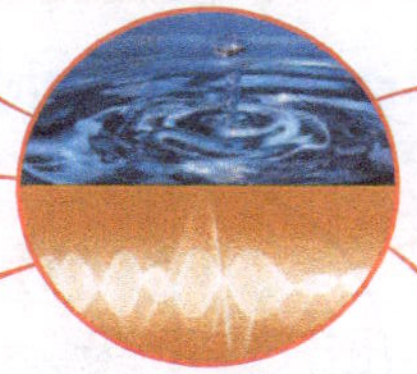

Speed of Wave

- Speed of travelling wave, $v = f\lambda = \frac{\lambda}{T}$

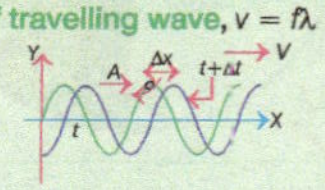

- Speed of a transverse wave, $v = \sqrt{\frac{T}{\mu}}$
Here, T = tension in string
μ = mass per unit length of the string
- Speed of a longitudinal wave (sound wave), $v = \sqrt{B/\rho} = \sqrt{\frac{Y}{\rho}}$
Here,
Y = Young's modulus of the material
B = Bulk modulus and
ρ = Density of the material

Newton's Formula

- According to Newton, propagation of sound wave through the gases in isothermal process $v = \sqrt{P/\rho}$

Laplace Correction

- According to Laplace, propagation of sound wave through the gas in an adiabatic process.
$v = \sqrt{\frac{\gamma P}{\rho}} = \sqrt{\frac{1.41 \times 1.101 \times 10^5}{1.3}} \simeq 331$ m/s

Beats

- When two sound waves of nearly same frequency are produced simultaneously, then the intensity of resultant sound wave increases and decreases with time.
- This change in the intensity of sound is called as the phenomenon of beats.
- Number of beats produced in one second called beat frequency. Beat frequency $= f_1 - f_2$

Principle of Superposition of Waves

- When two or more pulses overlap, the resultant displacement is the algebraic sum of the displacement due to each pulse.
- **Interference of wave**
Displacement, $y(x, t) = 2a \cos\frac{\phi}{2} \sin\left(kx - \omega t + \frac{\phi}{2}\right)$
- $\phi = 0$, then $y(x, t) = 2a \sin (kx - \omega t)$
- $\phi = \pi$, then $y(x, t) = 0$

Reflection of Waves

- A progressive wave travelling through a medium reached a rigid boundary, it gets reflected and the phenomena is called reflection of waves.
- If the reflecting end is rigid, there is a phase change of π between the incident and reflected waves.
- If the reflecting end is free to move, there is no phase difference between them.

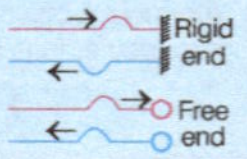

Standing Waves

- Standing waves arising from superposition of two travelling waves having same amplitude, time period, frequency and wavelength but moving in opposite directions.
- Net resultant standing wave, $y(t) = 2a \sin kx \cos \omega t$

Normal Mode

- Normal modes of oscillation is the set of natural frequencies at which a system vibrates.
- Point having zero amplitude are called **nodes** and the point having largest amplitude are known as **anti-nodes**.

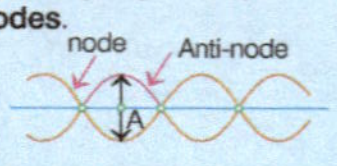

- For node, $x = \frac{n\pi}{k}$
$x = n\lambda/2$
- For anti-node, $x = (2n + 1)\frac{\lambda}{4}$

Vibration of String Fixed at Both Ends

- A stretched string having length L fixed at both ends, then boundary conditions.
$L = \frac{n\lambda}{2}$; $n = 1, 2, 3....$
- Possible wavelength,
$\lambda = \frac{2L}{n}$; $n = 1, 2, 3....$

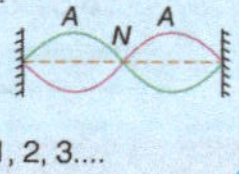

- Frequencies, $f = \frac{nv}{2L}$; $n = 1, 2, 3....$

Closed Organ Pipe

- Frequency, $f = (2n + 1)\frac{v}{4L}$
$n = 0, 1, 2, 3 ...$
- **Fundamental tone** If we blow at open mouth of organ pipe gently, then the lowest frequency is produced.
$L = \frac{\lambda}{4}$ or $\lambda = 4L$ or $f = \frac{v}{4L}$
- **First over tone**
$L = \frac{3\lambda}{4}$ or $\lambda = \frac{4L}{3}$
$\therefore$ Frequency of the node produced $f = \frac{3v}{4L}$
- It is also called **third harmonics**

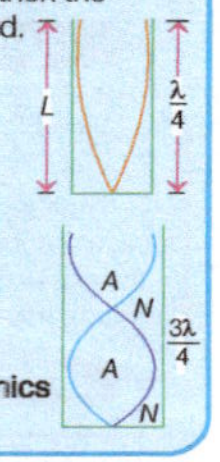

Open Organ Pipe

- For a pipe opened at both ends, each end is an anti-node.
- Frequency, $f = n.\frac{v}{2L}$
- **Fundamental tone**
If we blow air on one end of an organ pipe gently, then an anti-node is formed on both ends in between them.
$L = \frac{\lambda}{2}$ or $\lambda = 2L$
$f = \frac{v}{\lambda} = \frac{v}{2L}$
- **First overtone**
$L = 2\frac{\lambda}{2}$ or $\lambda = L$
$f = \frac{v}{\lambda} = \frac{v}{L}$

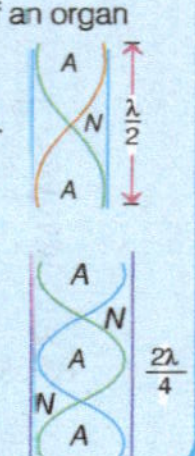

Vibration of Air Column

- An organ pipe is a cylindrical tube which may be closed at one end (closed organ pipe) or open at both ends (open organ pipe).

Modes of Vibration

The manner in which the string vibrates and give rise to a standing wave is known as mode of vibration of the string.

$L = \frac{n\lambda}{2}$, $f = \frac{nv}{2L}$

- **First mode of vibration** The mode of vibration in which string will vibrate in one segment or the lowest possible natural frequency (fundamental mode),
$L = \frac{\lambda}{2}$ and $f = \frac{v}{2L}$

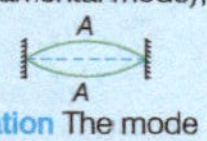

- **Second mode of vibration** The mode of vibration in which string will vibrate in two segments called second harmonic.
$L = \lambda$ and $f = \frac{v}{L}$

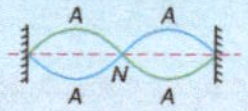